Richard Hunter
The Layers of the Text

Trends in Classics –
Supplementary Volumes

Edited by
Franco Montanari and Antonios Rengakos

Associate Editors
Stavros Frangoulidis · Fausto Montana · Lara Pagani
Serena Perrone · Evina Sistakou · Christos Tsagalis

Scientific Committee
Alberto Bernabé · Margarethe Billerbeck
Claude Calame · Jonas Grethlein · Philip R. Hardie
Stephen J. Harrison · Stephen Hinds · Richard Hunter
Christina Kraus · Giuseppe Mastromarco
Gregory Nagy · Theodore D. Papanghelis
Giusto Picone · Alessandro Schiesaro
Tim Whitmarsh · Bernhard Zimmermann

Volume 127

Richard Hunter

The Layers of the Text

Collected Papers on Classical Literature 2008–2021

Edited by
Antonios Rengakos and Evangelos Karakasis

DE GRUYTER

ISBN 978-3-11-127649-6
e-ISBN (PDF) 978-3-11-074757-7
e-ISBN (EPUB) 978-3-11-074776-8
ISSN 1868-4785

Library of Congress Control Number: 2021943323

Bibliographic information published by the Deutsche Nationalbibliothek
The Deutsche Nationalbibliothek lists this publication in the Deutsche Nationalbibliografie;
detailed bibliographic data are available on the Internet at http://dnb.dnb.de.

© 2022 Walter de Gruyter GmbH, Berlin/Boston
This volume is text- and page-identical with the hardback published in 2021.
Editorial Office: Alessia Ferreccio and Katerina Zianna
Logo: Christopher Schneider, Laufen
Printing and binding: CPI books GmbH, Leck

www.degruyter.com

Preface

The publication of a further volume of my 'Kleine Schriften', coinciding as it does with the end of my tenure of the Regius Professorship of Greek in Cambridge, should in principle be an opportunity to reflect on how my interests have shifted over the years and to seek significance in the pattern of those shifts. Staring at the list of titles in this volume, however, has not led me to detect more than the most obvious rebalancing of direction from the papers collected in *On Coming After*; as with the books I have published in the period covered by these papers, there is perhaps greater attention paid than before to the ancient critical tradition and to prose rather than poetry, but I think the central driving questions (and obsessions) remain the same. What has, however, come home very strongly to me (again) is just how lucky I have been to work in a Faculty of Classics with wonderful library resources and an institutional structure which has never imposed constraints or demands upon my research, but has just left me to get on with it, in my own way and to my own agenda. It helps, of course, often to have nothing much else to do anyway.

I am (once again) very grateful to Antonios Rengakos and Evangelos Karakasis for the time and effort they have devoted to make this volume possible. For some of the years covered here, Thessaloniki became my second home, and I am very happy to be again associated with the Aristotle University, an institution where I learned a great deal and to which I remain very attached.

Richard Hunter

Contents

Preface —— V
List of the Original Publication Venues —— XI
List of Papers not Included in the Present Collection —— XIII

Part I: Archaic and Classical Greek Literature

1 Alcibiades the Laughter-maker —— 3

2 The Songs of Demodocus: Compression and Extension in Greek Narrative Poetry —— 18

3 'Where do I begin?': An Odyssean Narrative Strategy and its Afterlife —— 46

Part II: Ancient Drama

4 The Garland of Hippolytus —— 67

5 Apollo and the *Ion* of Euripides: Nothing to do with Nietzsche? —— 84

6 Comedy and Reperformance —— 103

Part III: Hellenistic Poetry

7 Language and Interpretation in Greek Epigram —— 131

8 The Gods of Callimachus —— 156

9 Festivals, Cults and the Construction of Consensus in Hellenistic Poetry —— 175

10 Theocritus and the Style of Hellenistic Poetry —— 193

11 Sweet Stesichorus: Theocritus 18 and the Helen Revisited —— 214

12 A Philosophical Death? —— 235

13 Hellenistic Poetry and the Archaeology of Leisure —— 245

14 Death of a Child: Grief Beyond the Literary? —— 267

15 Reading and Citing the *Epigrams* of Callimachus —— 286

16 Enkelados: Callimachus fr. 1.36 (co-author Rebecca Laemmle) —— 307

17 Sappho and Hellenistic Poetry —— 314

18 Theocritus and the Bucolic Homer —— 328

Part IV: Latin Literature

19 Notes on the Ancient Reception of Sappho —— 349

20 One Verse of Mimnermus? Latin Elegy and Archaic Greek Elegy —— 364

21 Horace's other *Ars Poetica*: *Epistles* 1.2 and Ancient Homeric Criticism —— 376

22 Some Dramatic Terminology —— 399

23 *Regius urget*: Hellenising Thoughts on Latin Intratextuality —— 411

24 The Geographies of Plautus' *Menaechmi* —— 431

Part V: The Ancient Novel

25 Fictional Anxieties —— 449

26 Rythmical Language and Poetic Citation in Greek Narrative Texts —— 462

Part VI: Ancient Criticism and Scholarship

27 The *Trojan Oration* of Dio Chrysostom and Ancient Homeric Criticism —— 487

28 Plato's *Ion* and the Origins of Scholarship —— 506

29 Attic Comedy in the Rhetorical and Moralising Traditions —— 521

30 'Clever about Verses'?: Plato and the 'Scopas Ode' (*PMG* 542 = 260 Poltera) —— 537

31 Serpents in the Soul: The 'Libyan Myth' of Dio Chrysostom —— 560

32 'Palaephatus', Strabo and the Boundaries of Myth —— 578

33 The Rhetorical Criticism of Homer —— 598

34 The *Hippias Minor* and the Traditions of Homeric Criticism —— 633

35 Autobiography as Literary History: Dio Chrysostom, *On exile* —— 659

36 Eustathian Moments: Reading Eustathius' Commentaries —— 682

37 Dionysius of Halicarnassus and the Idea of the Critic —— 750

38 Dio Chrysostom and the Citation of Tragedy —— 770

39 Some Problems in the 'Deception of Zeus' —— 787

Part VII: Miscellaneous

40 The Letter of Aristeas —— 811

41 Pulling Apollo Apart (co-author Rebecca Laemmle) —— 824

42 The Poetics of Greek Inscriptions —— 850

43 John Malalas and the Story of the Cyclops —— 875

44 Homer in Origen, *Against Celsus* —— 883

General Index —— 909
Index of Passages Discussed —— 915

List of the Original Publication Venues

1. 'Alcibiades the Laughter-maker', in: M.L. Gatti/P. De Simone (eds.), *Interpretare Platone. Saggi sul pensiero antico* (Milan 2020) 83–99.
2. 'The Songs of Demodocus: Compression and Extension in Greek Narrative Poetry', in: S. Bär/M. Baumbach (eds.), *Brill's Companion to Greek and Latin 'Epyllion' and Its Reception* (Leiden 2012) 83–109.
3. '"Where do I begin?": An Odyssean Narrative Strategy and its Afterlife', in: D. Cairns/R. Scodel (eds.), *Defining Greek Narrative* (Edinburgh 2014) 137–155.
4. 'The Garland of Hippolytus', *Trends in Classics* 1 (2009) 18–35.
5. Apollo and the *Ion* of Euripides: Nothing to do with Nietzsche?', *Trends in Classics* 3 (2011) 18–37.
6. 'Comedy and Reperformance', in: R. Hunter/A. Uhlig (eds.), *Imagining Reperformance in Ancient Culture* (Cambridge 2017) 209–231.
7. 'Language and Interpretation in Greek Epigram', in: M. Baumbach/A. Petrovic/I. Petrovic (eds.), *Archaic and Classical Greek Epigram* (Cambridge 2010) 265–288.
8. 'The Gods of Callimachus', in: B. Acosta-Hughes/L. Lehnus/S. Stephens (eds.), *Brill's Companion to Callimachus* (Leiden 2011) 245–263.
9. 'Festivals, Cults, and the Construction of Consensus in Hellenistic Poetry', in: G. Urso (ed.), *Dicere Laudes. Elogio, comunicazione, creazione del consenso* (Cividale del Friuli 2011) 101–118.
10. 'Theocritus and the Style of Hellenistic Poetry', in: R. Hunter/A. Rengakos/E. Sistakou (eds.), *Hellenistic Studies at a Crossroads* (Berlin 2014) 55–74.
11. 'Sweet Stesichorus: Theocritus 18 and the *Helen* revisited', in: P.J. Finglass/A. Kelly (eds.), *Stesichorus in Context* (Cambridge 2015) 145–163.
12. 'A Philosophical Death?', in: E. Sistakou/A. Rengakos (eds.), *Dialect, Diction, and Style in Greek Literary and Inscribed Epigram* (Berlin 2016) 269–278.
13. 'Hellenistic Poetry and the Archaeology of Leisure', in: F. Fiorucci (ed.), *Muße, otium, σχολή in den Gattungen der antiken Literatur* (Freiburg 2017) 21–36.
14. 'Death of a Child: Grief Beyond the Literary?', in: M. Kanellou/I. Petrovic/C. Carey (eds.), *Greek Epigram from the Hellenistic to the Early Byzantine Era* (Oxford 2019) 137–153.
15. 'Reading and Citing the *Epigrams* of Callimachus', in: J. Klooster/M.A. Harder/R.F. Regtuit/G.C. Wakker (eds.), *Callimachus Revisited* (Leuven 2019) 171–191.
16. (with Rebecca Laemmle) 'Enkelados: Callimachus fr. 1.36', *Classical Philology* 114, 493–498.
17. 'Sappho and Hellenistic Poetry', in: P. Finglass/A. Kelly (eds.), *The Cambridge Companion to Sappho* (Cambridge 2021) 277–289.
18. 'Theocritus and the Bucolic Homer', in: P. Kyriakou/E. Sistakou/A. Rengakos (eds.), *Brill's Companion to Theocritus* (Leiden 2021) 223–241.
19. 'Notes on the Ancient Reception of Sappho', in: T.S. Thorsen/S. Harrison (eds.), *Roman Receptions of Sappho* (Oxford 2019) 45–59.
20. 'One Verse of Mimnermus? Latin Elegy and Archaic Greek Elegy', in: T. Papanghelis/S. Harrison/S. Frangoulidis (eds.), *Generic Interfaces in Latin Literature* (Berlin 2013) 337–349.
21. 'Horace's other *Ars Poetica*: Epistles 1.2 and Ancient Homeric Criticism', *Materiali e Discussioni* 72 (2014) 19–41.

22. 'Some dramatic terminology', in: S. Frangoulidis/S. Harrison/G. Manuwald (eds.), *Roman Drama and its Contexts* (Berlin 2016) 13–24.
23. '*regius urget*: Hellenising Thoughts on Latin Intratextuality', in: S. Harrison/S. Frangoulidis/T.D. Papanghelis (eds.), *Intratextuality and Latin Literature* (Berlin 2018) 451–469.
24. 'The geographies of Plautus' *Menaechmi*', *Classicum* 47 (2021).
25. 'Fictional anxieties', in: G. Karla (ed.), *Fiction on the Fringe* (Leiden 2009) 171–184.
26. 'Rhythmical Language and Poetic Citation in Greek Narrative Texts', in: G. Bastianini/A. Casanova (eds.), *I papiri del romanzo antico* (Florence 2010) 223–245.
27. 'The *Trojan Oration* of Dio Chrysostom and Ancient Homeric Criticism', in: J. Grethlein/A. Rengakos (eds.), *Narratology and Interpretation* (Berlin 2009) 43–61.
28. 'Plato's *Ion* and the origins of scholarship', in: S. Matthaios/F. Montanari/A. Rengakos (eds.), *Ancient Scholarship and Grammar* (Berlin 2011) 27–40.
29. 'Attic Comedy in the Rhetorical and Moralizing Traditions', in: M. Revermann (ed.), *The Cambridge Companion to Greek Comedy* (Cambridge 2014) 373–386.
30. '"Clever about verses"? Plato and the "Scopas-ode" (*PMG* 542 = 260 Poltera)', in: P. Agócs/L. Prauscello (eds.), *Simonides Lyricus* (Cambridge 2020) 197–216.
31. 'Serpents in the soul: the 'Libyan Myth' of Dio Chrysostom', in: G. Hawes (ed.), *Myths on the Map* (Oxford 2017) 281–298.
32. '"Palaephatus", Strabo and the boundaries of myth', *Classical Philology* 111 (2016) 245–261.
33. 'The Rhetorical Criticism of Homer', in: F. Montanari/S. Matthaios/A. Rengakos (eds.), *Brill's Companion to Ancient Greek Scholarship* (Leiden 2015) 673–705.
34. 'The *Hippias Minor* and the Traditions of Homeric Criticism', *Cambridge Classical Journal* 62 (2016) 85–107.
35. 'Autobiography as Literary History: Dio Chrysostom, *On exile*', in: J. Grethlein/A. Rengakos eds., *Griechische Literaturgeschichtsschreibung* (Berlin 2017) 248–270.
36. 'Eustathian moments', in: F. Pontani/V. Katsaros/V. Sarris (eds.), *Reading Eustathios of Thessalonike* (Berlin 2017) 9–75.
37. 'Dionysius of Halicarnassus and the idea of the critic', in: R. Hunter/C. de Jonge (eds.), *Dionysius of Halicarnassus and Augustan Rome: Rhetoric, Criticism and Historiography* (Cambridge 2019) 37–55.
38. 'Dio Chrysostom and the citation of tragedy', in: A. Lamari/F. Montanari/A. Novakhatko (eds.), *Fragmentation in Ancient Greek Drama* (Berlin 2020) 527–543.
39. 'Some problems in the "Deception of Zeus"', in: B. Beck/A. Kelly/T. Phillips (eds.), *The Ancient Scholia to Homer's Iliad: Exegesis and Interpretation*, *BICS* 64, 59–72.
40. 'The Letter of Aristeas', in: A. Erskine/L. Llewellyn-Jones (eds.), *Creating a Hellenistic World* (Swansea 2011) 47–60.
41. (with Rebecca Laemmle) 'Pulling Apollo apart', *Mnemosyne* 73 (2020) 377–404.
42. 'The poetics of Greek inscriptions', in: B. Kayachev (ed.), *Poems without Poets* (Cambridge 2021) 203–226.
43. 'John Malalas and the story of the Cyclops', in: G.B. D'Alessio et al. (eds.), *Il potere della parola. Studi di letteratura greca per Maria Cannatà Fera* (Alessandria 2020) 161–168.
44. 'Homer in Origen, *Against Celsus*', in: J. Carleton Paget/S. Gathercole (eds.), *Celsus in his World: Philosophy, Polemic and Religion in the Second Century* (Cambridge 2021) forthcoming

List of Papers not Included in the Present Collection

- 'Hesiod's style: towards an ancient analysis', in: F. Montanari/A. Rengakos/C. Tsagalis (eds.), *Brill's Companion to Hesiod* (Leiden 2009) 253–269.
- 'Greek elegy', in: T.S. Thorsen (ed.), *The Cambridge Companion to Latin Love Elegy* (Cambridge 2013) 23–38.
- 'Callimachus and Roman Elegy', in: B. Gold (ed.), *A Companion to Roman Love Elegy* (Malden MA 2012) 155–171.
- (with D. Koukouzika), 'Food in Greek literature', in: J. Wilkins/R. Nadeau (eds.), *A Companion to Food in the Ancient World* (Malden MA 2015) 19–29.
- 'Poetic Unity, Greek', in: S. Goldberg (ed.), *The Oxford Classical Dictionary Online* (New York).
- 'The idea of the classical in classical antiquity', *Proceedings of the Academy of Athens* 90 (2015) 51–68.
- 'Hesiodic studies: a cross-cultural endnote', *Seminari Romani di Cultura Greca* 5 (2016) 223–226.
- 'A striking parallel?', in: K. Coleman (ed.), *Albert's Anthology* (Cambridge MA 2017) 91–92.
- '*esse quam uideri*', in: N. Hatton/S. Hobe/V. Mastellari (eds.), *Hacks, Quacks and Impostors* (Freiburg 2019) 17–35.
- 'Afterword', in: A.-E. Beron/S. Weise (eds.), *Hyblaea avena. Theokrit in römischer Kaiserzeit und früher Neuzeit* (Stuttgart 2020) 197–200.
- 'Memory and its discontents in ancient literature', in: K. Mawford/E. Ntanou (eds.), *Ancient Memory. Remembrance and Commemoration in Graeco-Roman Literature* (Berlin 2021) 293–308.

Also omitted are Introductions to edited volumes, in all cases co-written with another editor.

Part I: Archaic and Classical Greek Literature

1 Alcibiades the Laughter-maker

In this paper I consider one aspect of the extraordinary text which is Alcibiades' speech in Plato's *Symposium*, namely how the mode of his speech is integrated into the sympotic atmosphere of the whole.[1] Plato has marked the text with a variety of pointers, and we must listen for these, if we are properly to appreciate this performance. I hope however that concentration on this one aspect will also allow something of the philosophical importance of Alcibiades' speech to emerge.

Alcibiades' riotous entry not only brings Dionysos back to the symposium from which he has been marginalised (176b1–e10),[2] but also — as many have pointed out — appears to echo the suddenness with which the philosophical lover at the climax of his ascent will catch sight of the Form of the Beautiful (210e4 ~ 212c6); Alcibiades is as physically present as the Form is metaphysically absent. Socrates' report of Diotima's speech has also — whatever one's view of the structuring of the work — functioned as a closural climax of sorts, just as Alcibiades represents, quite literally, a new entry into Agathon's house and the text of the *Symposium*. There is, however, another way also in which Plato has marked a break after Diotima's speech and prepared for Alcibiades' entry. After his direct report of Diotima's words, Socrates returns to his own voice:

> ταῦτα δή, ὦ Φαῖδρέ τε καὶ οἱ ἄλλοι, ἔφη μὲν Διοτίμα, πέπεισμαι δ' ἐγώ· πεπεισμένος δὲ πειρῶμαι καὶ τοὺς ἄλλους πείθειν ὅτι τούτου τοῦ κτήματος τῇ ἀνθρωπείᾳ φύσει συνεργὸν ἀμείνω Ἔρωτος οὐκ ἄν τις ῥᾳδίως λάβοι. διὸ δὴ ἔγωγέ φημι χρῆναι πάντα ἄνδρα τὸν Ἔρωτα τιμᾶν, καὶ αὐτὸς τιμῶ τὰ ἐρωτικὰ καὶ διαφερόντως ἀσκῶ, καὶ τοῖς ἄλλοις παρακελεύομαι, καὶ νῦν τε καὶ ἀεὶ ἐγκωμιάζω τὴν δύναμιν καὶ ἀνδρείαν τοῦ Ἔρωτος καθ' ὅσον οἷός τ' εἰμί.
>
> Plato, *Symposium* 212b1–8

This, Phaedrus and you others, is what Diotima said and I am persuaded by it. As I am persuaded, I attempt to persuade everyone else that one could not find a better co-worker than Eros for acquiring this possession. For this reason I say that every individual should show honour to Eros, and I myself honour erotic matters and practise them more than anything

---

I am grateful to audiences in Durham, Louvain-la-Neuve, Milan and Paris and to Christian Keime, Rebecca Laemmle and Frisbee Sheffeld for much helpful discussion.

---

1 The bibliography on Alcibiades' speech is of course very large; there is some helpful guidance in Destrée 2012, adding Hunter 2004, 98–112. There is an interesting, if speculative, account of Alcibiades' εἰκών of Socrates as a Silenus in Steiner 1996.
2 It is noteworthy that, in Xenophon's *Symposium* also, Dionysos only enters explicitly at the end (the Ariadne-mime) and there too is announced by the music of the *aulos* (9.3).

else, and I urge others to do the same, and both now and always I praise the power and courage of Eros to the very best of my ability.

Socrates professes his conviction that Diotima was correct in words that find, I think, striking parallels elsewhere in the corpus:

ἐγὼ μὲν οὖν, ὦ Καλλίκλεις, ὑπό τε τούτων τῶν λόγων πέπεισμαι, καὶ σκοπῶ ὅπως ἀποφανοῦμαι τῷ κριτῇ ὡς ὑγιεστάτην τὴν ψυχήν· χαίρειν οὖν ἐάσας τὰς τιμὰς τὰς τῶν πολλῶν ἀνθρώπων, τὴν ἀλήθειαν ἀσκῶν πειράσομαι τῷ ὄντι ὡς ἂν δύνωμαι βέλτιστος ὢν καὶ ζῆν καὶ ἐπειδὰν ἀποθνήσκω ἀποθνήσκειν.

Plato, *Gorgias* 526d3–8

Now for my part, Callicles, I am convinced by these accounts, and I consider how I may be able to show my judge that my soul is in the best of health. So giving the go-by to the honors that most men seek I shall try, by inquiry into the truth, to be really good in as high a degree as I am able, both in my life and, when I come to die, in my death.

(trans. Lamb)

καὶ οὕτως, ὦ Γλαύκων, μῦθος ἐσώθη καὶ οὐκ ἀπώλετο, καὶ ἡμᾶς ἂν σώσειεν, ἂν πειθώμεθα αὐτῷ, καὶ τὸν τῆς Λήθης ποταμὸν εὖ διαβησόμεθα καὶ τὴν ψυχὴν οὐ μιανθησόμεθα. ἀλλ' ἂν ἐμοὶ πειθώμεθα, νομίζοντες ἀθάνατον ψυχὴν καὶ δυνατὴν πάντα μὲν κακὰ ἀνέχεσθαι, πάντα δὲ ἀγαθά.

Plato, *Republic* 10.621c1–4

And so, Glaucon, the tale was saved, as the saying is, and was not lost. And it will save us if we believe it, and we shall safely cross the River of Lethe, and keep our soul unspotted from the world. But if we are guided by me we shall believe that the soul is immortal and capable of enduring all extremes of good and evil.

(trans. Shorey)

These passages come immediately after the Underworld 'myth' of the *Gorgias* (cf. Socrates' distinction between μῦθος and λόγος at 523a1–2) and the 'Myth of Er' in the *Republic*, and Socrates' language of 'belief' is usually put down to the fact that these accounts of the afterlife are not susceptible to 'proof' in any regular manner. What of the *Symposium*? Diotima may or may not be supposed to be 'real', but there is hardly any doubt that by conjuring up this mysterious γυνὴ Μαντινική, 'woman of Mantinea', (201d2), a phrase which certainly allows γυνὴ μαντική, 'prophetic woman', to resonate, Socrates offers his/her account as different in kind from the other speeches in the *Symposium*. Particularly close, perhaps, is the 'Myth of Er', as there too Socrates conjures another voice to offer an account of which Socrates can only be 'convinced'. Unlike in the *Gorgias* and the *Republic*, however, in the *Symposium* the closure marked by the 'mythic mode' (for want of a better term) is not final: a version of 'reality' returns in very physical shape.

As Alcibiades' komastic entry makes clear, that 'reality' is very firmly rooted in the practices (and *imaginaire*) of the elite symposium, as also — most famously — is Alcibiades' resort to an εἰκών to describe Socrates. In the first part of this paper, I want to look at another aspect of Alcibiades' speech and his role in the work which both evokes and reverses what seems to have been a feature of elite sympotic practice. This too will, I hope, be seen to have a significance beyond Plato's concern with 'effects of the real' in describing Agathon's party. My starting point is something not uncommon when people are drinking, namely laughter.

There is a sense in which Alcibiades' speech is framed by laughter. He begins by denying that his praise of Socrates δι' εἰκόνων will be aimed at τὸ γελοῖον: it will be aimed rather at τὸ ἀληθές (215a5–6);[3] the immediate response to the speech is 'laughter at his openness of speech' (παρρησία, 222c1–2). The comic poet Aristophanes had worried that his speech would be καταγέλαστα, 'laughable', rather than γελοῖα, 'funny' (189b6–7), but in the event it is greeted with no laughter at all — not perhaps the response a comic poet would want. If, then, there is a 'laughter-maker' in the *Symposium*, it is certainly Alcibiades.[4]

There is another sense too in which Alcibiades is the 'laughter-maker' in this text. In Xenophon's *Symposium*, Philip the self-confessed γελωτοποιός arrives uninvited, like Alcibiades, and his role is indeed to provide the guests with material for γέλως.[5] Philip arrives just as the symposium is getting going, Alcibiades at the end, but there are similarities too: both want the assembled guests to drink more than has been their wont (cf. Xen. *Symp*. 2.23–7), and Philip is said to be δεινὸς εἰκάζειν (6.8), 'good at making *eikones*', just as Alcibiades proves himself to be in Plato. There is indeed an implication (6.8–10) that τὸ εἰκάζειν is one of the skills in which γελωτοποιοί specialize. It is, however, the pointed differences between the two which stand out most strongly and with which I will be here concerned. To anticipate, the question — which Philip's arrival and his opening 'performance' seems almost to dramatise — namely what is the link between γέλως and the γελοῖον may be the frame for one of the most important differences

---

3 Capra 2016, 440–441 would see in Alcibiades' opening words an allusion to the comic and iconographic image of Socrates as a Silenus.
4 This, of course, is not to say that laughter in the *Symposium* is restricted to the final speech; at 202b10, Diotima laughs (indulgently?) at one of Socrates' misapprehensions.
5 On Philip and γελωτοποιοί cf., e.g., Halliwell 2008, 138–154 (a helpful account of aspects of the whole dialogue), Bremmer 1997, 11–16. I have in this essay deliberately not discussed the question of the relative chronology of Plato's *Symposium* and Xenophon's *Symposium*, although the comparison which I draw between Alcibiades and Philip may well be thought to bear upon the question. The scholarly *communis opinio* still gives, I think, the priority to Plato, but for a different view cf. Danzig 2005.

between the two 'laughter-makers'. Alcibiades' speech is met with γέλως, but not because what he has said is γελοῖον (cf. further below), whereas Philip's whole demeanour and performance is γελοῖον (and 'truth' hardly enters into it), but whether or not it is met with γέλως may well depend upon factors beyond his control, and the type of γέλως too which he eventually rouses is also rather different from that which greets Alcibiades. Philip 'tried to say something γελοῖον, so that he might carry out the reason why he was always invited to dinners, but stirred no γέλως' (1.14), a fruitless effort which he then repeats. The whole of the first passage of Xenophon's work which is concerned with Philip (1.11–6) may be seen in fact as a dramatisation of the complex relationship between γέλως and the γελοῖον. If we want to look ahead to the persistence of this distinction, consider Horace's chatty commentary in the first Satire of Book 1:

> praeterea, ne sic ut qui iocularia ridens
> percurram: quamquam ridentem dicere uerum
> quid uetat?
>
> Horace, Satires 1.1.23–5
>
> Anyway, so I don't skim laughing over this subject like someone laughing at a string of jokes — though what stands in the way of telling the truth with a laugh
>
> (trans. Gowers, adapted)

Horace will not deal with *iocularia*, like a *scurra* or (indeed) a γελωτοποιός, but like Alcibiades he will speak the truth. The γέλως that the free citizen wishes to raise is very different than that which may (or may not) greet the 'professional' γελωτοποιός (for the professionalism cf. 3.11).

From the point of view of ancient discussions of laughter, Philip is not the first γελωτοποιός in Greek literature. That honour belongs to two figures in the two opening books of the *Iliad*, Hephaestus at the banquet of the gods with which Book 1 concludes and Thersites at the Greek assembly in Book 2.[6] What is important, however, is that the γελωτοποιός has no problem with making himself or others γελοῖοι, and we should remember Alcibiades' opening denial — a denial, if you will, of being a 'laughter-maker' (a role to which we might otherwise assimilate him). There is also a suggestion in Xen. *Symp.* 6.8–10 that the sympotic activity of τὸ εἰκάζειν might easily tip into abuse (λοιδορία), as with Philocleon's drunken examples in Aristophanes' *Wasps*, and this too is part of Alcibiades' opening denial; in the contrast between ἐπαινεῖν and λοιδορεῖσθαι (6.9), Alcibiades certainly comes down on the former side. In Xenophon's *Symposium*,

---

6 Cf. Halliwell 2008, 58–63, 69–77, Thalmann 1988, Hunter forthcoming.

however, Philip's style of dancing (2.22, to which I shall return) deliberately makes his own body even more ridiculous than it is to begin with; there is nothing beautiful or graceful here, and here too he is an heir of Thersites. So too, Philip thinks that he has more right to be proud of his 'laughter-making' than Callippides the actor does for his skill in 'making large audiences weep' (3.11). Callippides was a very high profile actor, one who — according to the anecdotal tradition — rubbed shoulders with the great;[7] he was, in every way, the opposite of Philip 'the nobody'. Philip's gratuitous sideswipe, with its banal opposition between tears and laughter, is a paradigmatic case of the ὀνομαστὶ κωμῳδεῖν which there are good reasons for thinking were anathema to the *imaginaire* of the elite symposium and elite humour long before Aristotle's account in the *Nicomachean Ethics*.[8] There is no reason to think that Alcibiades' references to Brasidas and Pericles at 221c are anything but laudatory; Alcibiades is not motivated by φθόνος. So too, Alcibiades' accusation of ὕβρις against Socrates (215b7) is not merely clearly not motivated by malice, but reverses the standard later idea that the type of joke which the educated man must avoid at all costs is one which is itself ὑβριστικόν and causes pain.[9]

I have been suggesting that Alcibiades' performance both runs the risk of 'laughter-making' and goes out of its way to seek to establish difference from such *ridicula*. Alcibiades is, after all, the elite, educated Athenian citizen *par excellence*. We may even think that the παρρησία for which he wins (? admiring) laughter (222c2) does not merely express an ideal of the elite symposium at which openness — speaking ἐς μέσον in more than one sense — was indeed desiderated, in part because what was said in the symposium remained there ('I hate a drinking companion with a memory'), but also an ideal of Athenian democratic ideology. Be that as it may, far from making Socrates γελοῖος, his encomium has, if anything, revealed more about himself than about Socrates: 'he still seemed to be in love with Socrates' (222c2-3). Moreover it is elite *paideia* which is at the heart of the story which he proceeds to tell about his 'fleeing' (216b5-6) of Socrates.

One of the most famous anecdotes about Alcibiades is Plutarch's account of his youthful rebelliousness and high-mindedness:

---

7 Cf. O'Connor 1908, 107–109.
8 In his note on 3.11 Huss notes that several of the things which Philip is made to say recall Old Comedy.
9 Cf. already Aristophanes, *Wasps* 1319–1321 where Philokleon's drunken behaviour at an elite symposium is characterised by ὕβρις, ἀγροικία and ἀμαθία.

ἐπεὶ δ' εἰς τὸ μανθάνειν ἧκε, τοῖς μὲν ἄλλοις ὑπήκουε διδασκάλοις ἐπιεικῶς, τὸ δ' αὐλεῖν ἔφευγεν ὡς ἀγεννὲς καὶ ἀνελεύθερον· πλήκτρου μὲν γὰρ καὶ λύρας χρῆσιν οὐδὲν οὔτε σχήματος οὔτε μορφῆς ἐλευθέρῳ πρεπούσης διαφθείρειν, αὐλοὺς δὲ φυσῶντος ἀνθρώπου στόματι καὶ τοὺς συνήθεις ἂν πάνυ μόλις διαγνῶναι τὸ πρόσωπον. ἔτι δὲ τὴν μὲν λύραν τῷ χρωμένῳ συμφθέγγεσθαι καὶ συνᾴδειν, τὸν δ' αὐλὸν ἐπιστομίζειν καὶ ἀποφράττειν ἕκαστον, τήν τε φωνὴν καὶ τὸν λόγον ἀφαιρούμενον. 'αὐλείτωσαν οὖν' ἔφη 'Θηβαίων παῖδες· διαλέγεσθαι γὰρ οὐκ ἴσασιν· ἡμῖν δὲ τοῖς Ἀθηναίοις, ὡς οἱ πατέρες λέγουσιν, ἀρχηγέτις Ἀθηνᾶ καὶ πατρῷος Ἀπόλλων ἐστίν, ὧν ἡ μὲν ἔρριψε τὸν αὐλόν, ὁ δὲ καὶ τὸν αὐλητὴν ἐξέδειρε'. τοιαῦτα παίζων ἅμα καὶ σπουδάζων ὁ Ἀλκιβιάδης αὐτόν τε τοῦ μαθήματος ἀπέστησε καὶ τοὺς ἄλλους. ταχὺ γὰρ διῆλθε λόγος εἰς τοὺς παῖδας, ὡς εὖ ποιῶν ὁ Ἀλκιβιάδης βδελύττοιτο τὴν αὐλητικὴν καὶ χλευάζοι τοὺς μανθάνοντας. ὅθεν ἐξέπεσε κομιδῇ τῶν ἐλευθερίων διατριβῶν καὶ προεπηλακίσθη παντάπασιν ὁ αὐλός.

Plutarch, *Alcibiades* 2.4–6

At school, he usually paid due heed to his teachers, but he refused to play the flute, holding it to be an ignoble and illiberal thing. The use of the plectrum and the lyre, he argued, wrought no havoc with the bearing and appearance which were becoming to a gentleman; but let a man go to blowing on a flute, and even his own kinsmen could scarcely recognize his features. Moreover, the lyre blended its tones with the voice or song of its master; whereas the flute closed and barricaded the mouth, robbing its master both of voice and speech. 'Flutes, then,' said he, 'for the sons of Thebes; they know not how to converse. But we Athenians, as our fathers say, have Athena for foundress and Apollo for patron, one of whom cast the flute away in disgust, and the other flayed the presumptuous flute-player. Thus, half in jest and half in earnest, Alcibiades emancipated himself from this discipline, and the rest of the boys as well. For word soon made its way to them that Alcibiades loathed the art of flute-playing and scoffed at its disciples, and rightly, too. Wherefore the flute was dropped entirely from the programme of a liberal education and was altogether despised.

(trans. Perrin)

This story is occasionally mentioned in connection with Alcibiades' speech in Plato's *Symposium*,[10] but we shall see that the two can hardly be separated. First, however we need to consider how far back we may trace the Plutarchan story. There is in fact a fair chance that it arose early; Marsyas' contest with Apollo is first certainly attested at Herodotus 7.26, Aristotle is very familiar with Athena's rejection of the flute, and the iconographic tradition for both stories goes well back into the fifth century.[11] Plato (?), *Alc.* I 106e6–7 has Socrates tell Alcibiades that he knows that the latter learned 'letters and playing the lyre and wrestling;

---

10 Usher 2002, 215 writes of 'Plato's inversion of the motif' of Apollo's victory over Marsyas and mentions that 'Plutarch even lends an air of historicity to the comparison', but he does not go beyond that.

11 Cf. *LIMC* s.v. Marsyas I, Heinemann 2016, 303–17. *Trag. Adesp.* fr. 381 K-S are two verses in which a satyr tells Athena to abandon the *auloi* because οὗτοι πρέπει τὸ σχῆμα; it seems very likely that this derives from a fifth-century dramatization (? Euripides).

for you did not wish to play the *aulos*'. This evidence is, of course, not as powerful as we would like because of the modern uncertainty surrounding the authenticity and date of the *Alcibiades* I; nevertheless, we might with due caution use this text to argue that the story of the young Alcibiades rejecting *aulos*-playing arose relatively early. Whether this passage reflects the same story as we find in Plutarch or, indeed, gave rise to it we cannot say. Other than this, we have two pieces of evidence. One is a version of Plutarch's anecdote transmitted (with variations) at Aulus Gellius, *NA* 15.17; Gellius records that the story was told in the Neronian writer Pamphila, but, given the nature of her compendious writing, it is very unlikely to have originated with her. According to this version, the unfortunate *aulos*-teacher involved was Antigenidas of Thebes, a major musical figure of the late fifth-early fourth century, who had been brought in by Pericles to teach the young man.[12] On the other hand, Douris of Samos (late fourth-first half of third century BC) is recorded by Athenaeus to have reported, in a work 'On Euripides and Sophocles', that Alcibiades, from whom Douris elsewhere claimed descent, learned αὐλητική from no less a figure than Pronomos of Thebes (*FGrHist* 76 F29 = Ath. 4.184d).[13] It would, of course, be possible to reconcile the broad outline of these apparently discrepant accounts, if not the names of the teachers, but little purpose would be served by the attempt. What, I hope, is at least not tendentious is the claim that there is no strong reason to doubt that this story about the young Alcibiades might have pre-dated Plato.

Peter Wilson, noting the nature of Alcibiades' arrival at Agathon's house in Plato's *Symposium* and the fact that what else we know makes it entirely plausible that Alcibiades should have 'tried to co-opt the popularity and glamour of aulos music by ... association with its most radical practitioner', has suggested that the Plutarchan story of his youthful rejection of the *aulos* was in fact 'a direct rejoinder to the Pronomos tradition', one which restored Alcibiades to the (elite) side of those who saw in the *aulos* 'all that was wrong with democratic culture'. Wilson attractively suggests that 'in a range of literature, the fight for Alcibiades' soul was waged symbolically around the aulos'. This may well be true, but Alcibiades' account in the *Symposium* may suggest a different story, and one might in fact argue that the discrepancy between Alcibiades' *aulos*-accompanied entry and the story of his attempted rejection of 'Marsyas' is in fact perfectly consistent with the mass of contradictions which Alcibiades certainly was. Be that as it may,

---

12 It has been argued that Antigenidas' *floruit* was too late for him to have been Alcibiades' teacher, cf. Jan, *RE* 1. 2400.
13 On Pronomos see Wilson 2010, esp. 202–4, from which the following quotations come.

however, I suggest that there is much to be gained by reading Alcibiades' account against the Plutarchan narrative (in any version). The Platonic Alcibiades presents us with another rejection by Alcibiades of the *aulos*-music of Marsyas, a rejection which casts Alcibiades as an Athena, the guardian — as in Plutarch's anecdote — of the city's received values (including the role of public φιλοτιμία) and *paideia* (cf. Aristotle, *Politics* 8.1341b3–14); paradoxically, however, this *aulos*-music comes, without any musical instrument (215c6-7), from the mouth of Socrates, the only Athenian — to echo Plutarch's story again — who actually knew how to διαλέγεσθαι, and it is a music to which Alcibiades finds himself irresistibly drawn, time and again, however hard he tries to resist. What, of course, is particularly paradoxical here, as Alcibiades himself points out (215b8-c8), is indeed that this Marsyas only speaks, he does not play the flute, whereas in some later versions of the story of the contest of Apollo and Marsyas this difference was what was to prove crucial:

> ἐρίζοντος δὲ τοῦ Μαρσύου πρὸς τὸν Ἀπόλλω περὶ τῆς τέχνης, καὶ τῶν Νυσαίων ἀποδειχθέντων δικαστῶν, τὸν μὲν Ἀπόλλωνα πρῶτον κιθαρίσαι ψιλήν, τὸν δὲ Μαρσύαν ἐπιβαλόντα τοῖς αὐλοῖς καταπλῆξαι τὰς ἀκοὰς τῷ ξενίζοντι, καὶ διὰ τὴν εὐμέλειαν δόξαι πολὺ προέχειν τοῦ προηγωνισμένου. συντεθειμένων δ' αὐτῶν παρ' ἄλληλα τοῖς δικασταῖς ἐπιδείκνυσθαι τὴν τέχνην, τὸν μὲν Ἀπόλλωνά φασιν ἐπιβαλεῖν τὸ δεύτερον ἁρμόττουσαν τῷ μέλει τῆς κιθάρας ᾠδήν, καθ' ἣν ὑπερβαλέσθαι τὴν προϋπάρξασαν τῶν αὐλῶν ἀποδοχήν· τὸν δὲ πρότερον ἀγανακτήσαντα διδάσκειν τοὺς ἀκροατὰς ὅτι παρὰ πᾶν τὸ δίκαιον αὐτὸς ἐλαττοῦται· δεῖν γὰρ γίνεσθαι τέχνης σύγκρισιν, οὐ φωνῆς, καθ' ἣν προσήκει τὴν ἁρμονίαν καὶ τὸ μέλος ἐξετάζεσθαι τῆς κιθάρας καὶ τῶν αὐλῶν· καὶ πρὸς τούτοις ἄδικον εἶναι δύο τέχνας ἅμα πρὸς μίαν συγκρίνεσθαι.
>
> Diodorus Siculus 3.59.2-3

> When Marsyas strove with Apollo in a contest of skill and the Nysaeans had been appointed judges, the first time Apollo played upon the lyre without accompanying it with his voice, while Marsyas, striking up upon his *aulos*, amazed the ears of his hearers by their strange music and in their opinion far excelled, by reason of his melody, the first contestant. But since they had agreed to take turn about in displaying their skill to the judges, Apollo, they say, added, this second time, his voice in harmony with the music of the lyre, whereby he gained greater approval than that which had formerly been accorded to the *aulos*. Marsyas, however, was enraged and tried to prove to the hearers that he was losing the contest in defiance of every principle of justice; for, he argued, it should be a comparison of skill and not of voice, and only by such a test was it possible to judge between the harmony and music of the lyre and of the *aulos*; and furthermore, it was unjust that two skills should be compared in combination against but one.
>
> (trans. Oldfather)

When you play the *aulos* you cannot speak, as the Alcibiades of Plutarch's anecdote points out: the instrument takes away both φωνή and λόγος.[14] Socrates' mouth, on the other hand, was much the most active part of him. That Alcibiades' reference to Socrates' ἄνευ ὀργάνων ψιλοὶ λόγοι, 'plain words without instruments', at 215c7 wrily evokes the flourishing genre of Σωκρατικοὶ λόγοι and, in particular, Plato's dialogues themselves has often been observed.[15] The strangeness of Alcibiades' apparent claim that one might hear these words from 'a poor speaker' and that they might be listened to by 'a woman or a man or boy' (215d4–5) has, however, not always been appreciated. We could of course see here a list of the range of characters who do appear in Socratic dialogues; women are indeed found in both Platonic and Xenophontic dialogues, though when they are it is usually they who, like Diotima, are talking, rather than listening. The universality of the effect of Socrates' words is, however, obviously related to their 'corybantic' effect which Alcibiades describes at 215e:

> ἡμεῖς γοῦν ὅταν μέν του ἄλλου ἀκούωμεν λέγοντος καὶ πάνυ ἀγαθοῦ ῥήτορος ἄλλους λόγους, οὐδὲν μέλει ὡς ἔπος εἰπεῖν οὐδενί· ἐπειδὰν δὲ σοῦ τις ἀκούῃ ἢ τῶν σῶν λόγων ἄλλου λέγοντος, κἂν πάνυ φαῦλος ᾖ ὁ λέγων, ἐάντε γυνὴ ἀκούῃ ἐάντε ἀνὴρ ἐάντε μειράκιον, ἐκπεπληγμένοι ἐσμὲν καὶ κατεχόμεθα. ἐγὼ γοῦν, ὦ ἄνδρες, εἰ μὴ ἔμελλον κομιδῇ δόξειν μεθύειν, εἶπον ὀμόσας ἂν ὑμῖν οἷα δὴ πέπονθα αὐτὸς ὑπὸ τῶν τούτου λόγων καὶ πάσχω ἔτι καὶ νυνί. ὅταν γὰρ ἀκούω, πολύ μοι μᾶλλον ἢ τῶν κορυβαντιώντων ἥ τε καρδία πηδᾷ καὶ δάκρυα ἐκχεῖται ὑπὸ τῶν λόγων τῶν τούτου, ὁρῶ δὲ καὶ ἄλλους παμπόλλους τὰ αὐτὰ πάσχοντας· Περικλέους δὲ ἀκούων καὶ ἄλλων ἀγαθῶν ῥητόρων εὖ μὲν ἡγούμην λέγειν, τοιοῦτον δ' οὐδὲν ἔπασχον, οὐδ' ἐτεθορύβητό μου ἡ ψυχὴ οὐδ' ἠγανάκτει ὡς ἀνδραποδωδῶς διακειμένου, ἀλλ' ὑπὸ τουτουῒ τοῦ Μαρσύου πολλάκις δὴ οὕτω διετέθην ὥστε μοι δόξαι μὴ βιωτὸν εἶναι ἔχοντι ὡς ἔχω.
>
> Plato, *Symposium* 215d1–216a1

When we hear any other person — quite an excellent orator, perhaps — pronouncing one of the usual discourses, no one, I venture to say, cares a jot; but so soon as we hear you, or your discourses in the mouth of another, – though such person be ever so poor a speaker, and whether the hearer be a woman or a man or a youngster — we are all astounded and entranced. As for myself, gentlemen, were it not that I might appear to be completely drunk, I would have affirmed on oath all the strange effects I personally have felt from his words, and still feel even now. For when I hear him I am worse than anyone in a corybantic trance; I find my heart leaping and my tears gushing forth at this man's words, and I see great numbers of other people having the same experience. When I listened to Pericles and other skilled orators I thought them eloquent, but I never felt anything like this; my spirit was not left in a tumult and had not to complain of my being in the condition of a common slave:

---

14 According to Plutarch, *Mor.* 713d, Marsyas was justly punished for trying to compete with instrumental music (ψιλῷ μέλει) against 'song and lyre'.
15 Good discussion in Ford 2017.

whereas the influence of our Marsyas here has often thrown me into such a state that I thought my life not worth living on these terms.

(trans. Lamb, adapted)

Socrates' unaccompanied words, Socrates' 'music', have, according to Alcibiades, the same orgiastic effect as the *aulos* was traditionally thought to have (215e1–4), an effect which reached all genders and age-classes.[16] Those gripped by any kind of 'possession' may be perceived as forming an alternative society which, taken to extremes, imperils ordinary political structures and discourse; Euripides' *Bacchae* is one surviving exploration of this theme (though not of this theme alone).

Alcibiades is torn between two quite different lives, and he can see only one way out, escape from 'Siren Socrates' (216a6–8).[17] Socrates' words contain an irresistible and shaming force of compulsion urging one to a complete revolution of life. The universality of the Socratic effect — 'a woman or a man or boy' — is one further way in which the philosophical life is contrasted with the public life of engaged male citizens. The decision which Alcibiades must make is essentially the same, though rather differently expressed, as that which Callicles lays before Socrates in the *Gorgias*. What for Alcibiades was the prospect of 'growing old beside Socrates' (216a7–8) is for the scornful Callicles 'whispering in a corner with three or four lads (μειρακίων)' (*Gorgias* 485d7–8).

Alcibiades, moreover, famously and somewhat puzzlingly, repeatedly compares his enthrallment to Socrates to a kind of slavery (215e6, 216b5–6), and many have felt that this deserves more explanation than simply being a reprise of Pausanias' disquisition on the 'voluntary slavery' into which the *erastēs* who acts out of the best motives towards his *erōmenos* enters (184b–d).[18] In Alcibiades' case, the language of slavery reverses the proper relationship in a democracy between a politician/orator and his audience: whatever effect political speeches might have, they appeal to the audience's sense of belonging to a privileged community in which they, not the orators, are in charge and are thus truly 'free'. Both Plato elsewhere and, in his comedies, Aristophanes might well suggest a different view, but that at least was the shared ideology of a city in which, theoretically, anyone could 'speak', as the herald's famous τίς ἀγορεύειν βούλεται; question at meetings of the assembly seemed to suggest. In elite contexts, ἐλεύθερος of course conveys a message to a particular sub-group of citizens who imagine

---

[16] Porter 2016, 598–599 sees in Alcibiades' description a reworking of Sappho's account of her physical distress in fr. 31; Alcibiades 'is living through a Sapphic moment'.
[17] For Alcibiades' use of the image of the Sirens cf. Hunter 2018, 211–212.
[18] For the language of slavery in Socratic discussions of paederasty cf. also Xen. *Mem.* 1.3.11.

themselves as sharing ideals and education not shared by all 'free citizens', and Alcibiades would certainly have seen himself in this group. Callicles in the *Gorgias* repeatedly throws the term ἐλεύθερος in Socrates' face: it is ἐλευθέριον to philosophise when young (485b4, c5), whereas a grown man who philosophises will never say anything ἐλεύθερον (485e1). It is at least tempting to bring the repeated language of ἐλεύθερος/ἐλευθέριος of Plutarch's anecdote into connection with Alcibiades' language of slavery in Plato; both could simply be exploiting (one, admittedly, rather more subtly than the other) a shared public ideology, but we may also see here one more reversal, or rather paradoxical confirmation, in Plato of the attitudes espoused by Alcibiades in the Plutarchan anecdote. There Alcibiades insists on behaviour appropriate to the status of an ἐλεύθερος, and so he must, in the name of Apollo and Athena, reject Marsyas and the *aulos*. In Plato, that rejection, and the rejection of 'slavery', comes at a terrible personal price. We do not have to be very subtle readers of Plato to understand that that rejection also came at a terrible price for Athens. Alcibiades says that Socrates' words force him to admit that 'though I myself lack a great deal, I neglect myself and do the Athenians' business' (216a5–6). It is very hard, I think, here not to be reminded of a famous passage in Plato's *Apology* in which Socrates says that, for as long as he is alive in Athens, he will just keep on doing what he has always been doing:

εἰ οὖν με, ὅπερ εἶπον, ἐπὶ τούτοις ἀφίοιτε, εἴποιμ' ἂν ὑμῖν ὅτι 'Ἐγὼ ὑμᾶς, ὦ ἄνδρες Ἀθηναῖοι, ἀσπάζομαι μὲν καὶ φιλῶ, πείσομαι δὲ μᾶλλον τῷ θεῷ ἢ ὑμῖν, καὶ ἕωσπερ ἂν ἐμπνέω καὶ οἷός τε ὦ, οὐ μὴ παύσωμαι φιλοσοφῶν καὶ ὑμῖν παρακελευόμενός τε καὶ ἐνδεικνύμενος ὅτῳ ἂν ἀεὶ ἐντυγχάνω ὑμῶν, λέγων οἷάπερ εἴωθα, ὅτι 'Ὦ ἄριστε ἀνδρῶν, Ἀθηναῖος ὤν, πόλεως τῆς μεγίστης καὶ εὐδοκιμωτάτης εἰς σοφίαν καὶ ἰσχύν, χρημάτων μὲν οὐκ αἰσχύνῃ ἐπιμελούμενος ὅπως σοι ἔσται ὡς πλεῖστα, καὶ δόξης καὶ τιμῆς, φρονήσεως δὲ καὶ ἀληθείας καὶ τῆς ψυχῆς ὅπως ὡς βελτίστη ἔσται οὐκ ἐπιμελῇ οὐδὲ φροντίζεις; καὶ ἐάν τις ὑμῶν ἀμφισβητήσῃ καὶ φῇ ἐπιμελεῖσθαι, οὐκ εὐθὺς ἀφήσω αὐτὸν οὐδ' ἄπειμι, ἀλλ' ἐρήσομαι αὐτὸν καὶ ἐξετάσω καὶ ἐλέγξω, καὶ ἐάν μοι μὴ δοκῇ κεκτῆσθαι ἀρετήν, φάναι δέ, ὀνειδιῶ ὅτι τὰ πλείστου ἄξια περὶ ἐλαχίστου ποιεῖται, τὰ δὲ φαυλότερα περὶ πλείονος. ταῦτα καὶ νεωτέρῳ καὶ πρεσβυτέρῳ ὅτῳ ἂν ἐντυγχάνω ποιήσω, καὶ ξένῳ καὶ ἀστῷ, μᾶλλον δὲ τοῖς ἀστοῖς, ὅσῳ μου ἐγγυτέρω ἐστὲ γένει. ταῦτα γὰρ κελεύει ὁ θεός, εὖ ἴστε, καὶ ἐγὼ οἴομαι οὐδέν πω ὑμῖν μεῖζον ἀγαθὸν γενέσθαι ἐν τῇ πόλει ἢ τὴν ἐμὴν τῷ θεῷ ὑπηρεσίαν. οὐδὲν γὰρ ἄλλο πράττων ἐγὼ περιέρχομαι ἢ πείθων ὑμῶν καὶ νεωτέρους καὶ πρεσβυτέρους μήτε σωμάτων ἐπιμελεῖσθαι μήτε χρημάτων πρότερον μηδὲ οὕτω σφόδρα ὡς τῆς ψυχῆς ὅπως ὡς ἀρίστη ἔσται'.

Plato, *Apology* 29d1–30b2

If you should let me go on this condition which I have mentioned, I should say to you, 'Men of Athens, I respect and love you, but I shall obey the god rather than you, and while I live and am able to continue, I shall never give up philosophy or stop exhorting you and pointing out the truth to any one of you whom I may meet, saying in my accustomed way: 'Most excellent man, are you who are a citizen of Athens, the greatest of cities and the most famous for wisdom and power, not ashamed to care for the acquisition of wealth and for reputation and honor, when you neither care nor take thought for wisdom and truth and the perfection of your soul?' And if any of you argues the point, and says he does care, I shall not let him go at once, nor shall I go away, but I shall question and examine and cross-examine him, and if I find that he does not possess virtue, but says he does, I shall rebuke him for scorning the things that are of most importance and caring more for what is of less worth. This I shall do to whomever I meet, young and old, foreigner and citizen, but most to the citizens, inasmuch as you are more nearly related to me. For know that the god commands me to do this, and I believe that no greater good ever came to pass in the city than my service to the god. For I go about doing nothing else than urging you, young and old, not to care for your persons or your property more than for the perfection of your souls, or even so much'.

(trans. Fowler)

If Alcibiades is a special case of the random Athenian male citizen to whom Socrates addresses his protreptic in the *Apology*, then his desertion, his turn to the life of politics rather than the life of philosophy, also cost Socrates very dear indeed, or would to most people have appeared so to do. One exception of course is Socrates himself, for whom death is indeed a step into the unknown, but every indication is that it is step towards something better.

As a footnote, I should add that I am tempted by the idea that Douris' tale of Alcibiades' instruction by Pronomos (or indeed Antigenidas) — both in fact Thebans and, therefore, perhaps evoked by Alcibiades' scorn for 'the sons of Thebans'[19] in the anecdote — was in fact an attempt to restore the prestige of αὐλητική in the face of stories circulating about both Athena and Alcibiades. Alcibiades' youthful schoolroom revolt may indeed show him on the side of traditional, elite education, but more than that it shows him as (already) a rebel, a charismatic leader whom others followed, and one given to the mode of σπουδαιογέλοιον. Whoever first recorded or invented it may, of course, have been influenced by classical portrayals of Alcibiades, such as those of Thucydides and Plato, or may have been in touch with the same images of, and attitudes to, the politician as they refracted in their more famous texts.

To return to the other laughter-maker with whom we are concerned. The Plutarchan Alcibiades' concern with the facial distortion of flute-playing as unbefitting a free man picks up (or anticipates) and reverses two aspects of Philip's performance in Xenophon's *Symposium*. First, Plutarch describes Alcibiades' condemnation of the flute as a paradigmatic case of the mixture of the *spoudaion* and the *geloion*, as is also true — as has often been observed — of his speech in Plato's Symposium, which Alcibiades himself almost explicitly places under the sign of the *spoudaiogeloion*, as indeed he does the behaviour of the subject of the

---

[19] For the associations between Thebes and aulos-playing cf. also Euripides fr. 556 K, *CEG* 509.

speech, Socrates (216e); Philip, on the other hand, says that he could no more be *spoudaios* than he could be immortal (1.15). The real γελωτοποιός may have many different routines, but he is really a 'one-trick pony': he knows only γελοῖα and nothing else. As such, he could never be a fully integrated equal partner at the elite symposium; he will always be an outsider, there to perform a service, not entirely unlike the flute-girls (even if the service is somewhat different).[20] Secondly, Philip's dance at 2.22 is explicitly a parody of the dance of the girl and boy which the company had witnessed and in which the dance-σχήματα had made the boy seem καλλίων. Philip's parody, on the other hand, makes every part of his body γελοιότερον; he flings about his legs, arms and head in an uncontrolled way which is a denial of the very notion of σχήματα, let alone graceful ones. Even the satyric *sikinnis* must have been controlled by comparison. This is not how ἐλεύθεροι dance. As Aristotle observes: 'Those who jest with good taste are called witty or versatile (εὐτράπελοι) — that is to say, full of good turns; for such sallies seem to spring from the character, and we judge men's characters, like their bodies, by their movements' (*EN* 4.1128a9–12). Philip of course is a licensed clown, and so his self-conscious refusal to play by the elite rules recalls in both performance and effect, but is utterly different from, Hippocleides table-dancing his wedding away in Herodotus' famous story.

Alcibiades' final observation about Socrates returns to the theme I have been tracing:

καὶ γὰρ οὖν καὶ τοῦτο ἐν τοῖς πρώτοις παρέλιπον, ὅτι καὶ οἱ λόγοι αὐτοῦ ὁμοιότατοί εἰσι τοῖς σιληνοῖς τοῖς διοιγομένοις. εἰ γὰρ ἐθέλοι τις τῶν Σωκράτους ἀκούειν λόγων, φανεῖεν ἂν πάνυ γελοῖοι τὸ πρῶτον· τοιαῦτα καὶ ὀνόματα καὶ ῥήματα ἔξωθεν περιαμπέχονται, σατύρου δή τινα ὑβριστοῦ δοράν. ὄνους γὰρ κανθηλίους λέγει καὶ χαλκέας τινὰς καὶ σκυτοτόμους καὶ βυρσοδέψας, καὶ ἀεὶ διὰ τῶν αὐτῶν τὰ αὐτὰ φαίνεται λέγειν, ὥστε ἄπειρος καὶ ἀνόητος ἄνθρωπος πᾶς ἂν τῶν λόγων καταγελάσειεν. διοιγομένους δὲ ἰδὼν ἄν τις καὶ ἐντὸς αὐτῶν γιγνόμενος πρῶτον μὲν νοῦν ἔχοντας ἔνδον μόνους εὑρήσει τῶν λόγων, ἔπειτα θειοτάτους καὶ πλεῖστα ἀγάλματ' ἀρετῆς ἐν αὐτοῖς ἔχοντας καὶ ἐπὶ πλεῖστον τείνοντας, μᾶλλον δὲ ἐπὶ πᾶν ὅσον προσήκει σκοπεῖν τῷ μέλλοντι καλῷ κἀγαθῷ ἔσεσθαι.

Plato, *Symposium* 221d7–2a7

For there is a point I omitted when I began — how his talk most of all resembles the Silenuses that are made to open. If you chose to listen to Socrates' discourses you would feel them at first to be quite ridiculous; on the outside they are clothed with such absurd words and phrases, the skin of some mocking satyr. His talk is of pack-asses, smiths, cobblers, and

---

20 Thus, according to Plutarch (*Mor.* 629c), a γελωτοποιός such as Philip is not at all 'necessary' to the proper conduct of a symposium of educated men; Alcibiades' appearance at and performance in Plato's *Symposium* is, by contrast, the quintessence of grace and wit (*Mor.* 710c–d), which has set a standard which no subsequent symposium could hope to match.

tanners, and he seems always to be using the same terms for the same things; so that anyone inexpert and thoughtless might laugh his words to scorn. But when these are opened, and you obtain a fresh view of them by getting inside, first of all you will discover that they are the only words which have any sense in them; and secondly, that none are so divine, so rich in images of virtue, so largely — nay, so completely — intent on all things proper for the study of such as would attain both grace and worth.

(trans. Lamb, adapted)

Let me just make two points about how Alcibiades here picks up and realigns themes from the earlier part of the speech. Any fool, he says, who has no experience of Socrates would laugh at (καταγελάσειεν) Socrates' words. This is precisely the position of Callicles in the *Gorgias* for whom the idea of a grown man philosophising, rather than spending his life in public action, is καταγέλαστον (485a7). Secondly, it emerges that it is Socrates' words, the music of a Marsyas, which are appropriate to someone who wishes to be καλὸς κἀγαθός, that is, from one perspective, a full member of the Athenian elite.[21] Here lies the real paradox — and the radical challenge — which the Platonic Socrates posed to the received wisdom of Athenian public discourse.

Bibliography

Bremmer, J. 1997. 'Jokes, jokers and jokebooks in ancient Greek culture', in: J. Bremer/H. Roodenburg (eds.), *A Cultural History of Humour. – From Antiquity to the Present Day*, Cambridge, 11–128.
Capra, A. 2016. 'Transcoding the Silenus: Aristophanes, Plato and the invention of Socratic iconography', in: M. Tulli/M. Erler (eds.), *Plato in Symposium*, Sankt Augustin, 437–442.
Danzig, G. 2005. 'Intra-Socratic polemics: The *Symposia* of Plato and Xenophon', *Greek, Roman and Byzantine Studies* 45, 332–357.
Destrée, P. 2012. 'The speech of Alcibiades', in C. Horn (ed.), *Platon, Symposion*, Berlin, 191–205.
Ford, A. 2017. 'Alcibiades' *eikôn* of Socrates and the Platonic text: *Symp*. 215a–222d', in: P. Destrée/R.G. Edmonds (eds.), *Plato and the Power of Images*, Leiden, 11–28.
Halliwell, S. 2008. *Greek Laughter*, Cambridge.
Heinemann, A. 2016. *Der Gott des Gelages*, Berlin.
Hunter, R. 2004. *Plato's Symposium*, Oxford.
Hunter, R. 2018. *The Measure of Homer*, Cambridge.

---

[21] That Socrates' aim in his dealings with Athenians was to seek to make them καλοὶ κἀγαθοί and this too was the aim of his true 'followers' is a prominent motif in Xenophon's *Memorabilia*, cf., e.g., 1.2.48, 1.6.14.

Hunter, R. forthcoming. 'Humour in the ancient critical tradition', in: P. Destrée/A. Zucker/R. Rosen (eds.), *A Companion to Ancient Greek Humour*, Cambridge.
O'Connor, J.B. 1908. *Chapters in the History of Actors and Acting in Ancient Greece*, Chicago.
Porter, J. 2016. *The Sublime in Antiquity*, Cambridge.
Steiner, D. 1996. 'For love of a statue: a reading of Plato's *Symposium* 215a–b', *Ramus* 25, 89–111.
Steiner, D. 2001. *Images in Mind*, Princeton.
Thalmann, W.G. 1988. 'Thersites: comedy, scapegoats, and heroic ideology in the *Iliad*', *Transactions of the American Philological Association* 118, 1–28.
Usher, M.D. 2002. 'Satyr play in Plato's *Symposium*', *American Journal of Philology* 123, 205–228.
Wilson, P. 2010. 'The man and the music (and the choregos?)', in: O. Taplin/R. Wyles (eds.), *The Pronomos Vase and its Context*, Oxford, 181–212.

2 The Songs of Demodocus: Compression and Extension in Greek Narrative Poetry

Compression and extension I

Compression and extension are such universal characteristics of all poetic narratives, both long and short,[1] that they attract attention only when attention is called to them. Perhaps the most common way that our attention is drawn to these techniques is when comparable narratives are juxtaposed or meaningfully included in the same work or when a narrative openly asks to be read against another, whether or not the intended audience is familiar with 'the model'. The *Ilias Latina*, for example, offers a paradigm case of a summary narrative created through both compression and extension.[2] Attention can also be directed to these features by internal textual signals and/or our familiarity with 'roads not taken'. Consider, for example, the opening section of the fifty-nine verse *Homeric Hymn to Dionysus* (late sixth century?):

ἀμφὶ Διώνυσον Σεμέλης ἐρικυδέος υἱόν
μνήσομαι, ὡς ἐφάνη παρὰ θῖν' ἁλὸς ἀτρυγέτοιο
ἀκτῇ ἔπι προβλῆτι νεηνίῃ ἀνδρὶ ἐοικώς
πρωθήβῃ· καλαὶ δὲ περισσείοντο ἔθειραι
κυάνεαι, φᾶρος δὲ περὶ στιβαροῖς ἔχεν ὤμοις
πορφύρεον· τάχα δ' ἄνδρες ἐϋσσέλμου ἀπὸ νηὸς
ληϊσταὶ προγένοντο θοῶς ἐπὶ οἴνοπα πόντον
Τυρσηνοί· τοὺς δ' ἦγε κακὸς μόρος· οἱ δὲ ἰδόντες
νεῦσαν ἐς ἀλλήλους, τάχα δ' ἔκθορον, αἶψα δ' ἑλόντες

I am grateful to many seminar audiences for much instructive criticism of earlier versions of this essay. I am very conscious that, no doubt partly through ignorance, I have done nothing like justice to the bibliography on this subject, and it is not to be assumed that the absence of a bibliographical reference implies that I am claiming novelty for any particular idea.

---

1 The same is of course true for narratives not in verse form, but I restrict myself to what will concern me in this paper. I have also deliberately avoided extended (or indeed any) discussion of 'compression and extension' within the context of how oral compositional technique is currently understood; I am aware that this has led me to speak of 'poets making choices' etc., language which is not universally shared.
2 Thus, for example, in dealing with the early events of Book 1, Chryses' speech to the Greeks and Agamemnon's brutal reply are both covered in seven verses (19–26) of narrative, not direct speech, whereas Chryses' prayer to Apollo is expanded (32–43).

The Songs of Demodocus: Compression and Extension in Greek Narrative Poetry — 19

εἶσαν ἐπὶ σφετέρης νηὸς κεχαρημένοι ἦτορ.
υἱὸν γάρ μιν ἔφαντο διοτρεφέων βασιλήων
εἶναι, καὶ δεσμοῖς ἤθελον δεῖν ἀργαλέοισι.
τὸν δ' οὐκ ἴσχανε δεσμά, λύγοι δ' ἀπὸ τηλόσ' ἔπιπτον
χειρῶν ἠδὲ ποδῶν· ὁ δὲ μειδιάων ἐκάθητο
ὄμμασι κυανέοισι, κυβερνήτης δὲ νοήσας
αὐτίκα οἷς ἑτάροισιν ἐκέκλετο φώνησέν τε·

Homeric Hymn to Dionysus 1–16

Of Dionysus, the son of glorious Semele, I shall sing, how he appeared at the shore of the barren sea, on a jutting headland, looking like a young man in first manhood. His lovely dark hair waved, and around his strong shoulders was a crimson cloak. Suddenly men on a well-benched ship appeared, pirates from Tuscany racing over the wine-dark sea; an evil doom led them on. When they saw Dionysus, they nodded to each other and quickly jumped out; they immediately seized him and set him on their ship, rejoicing in their hearts, for they thought that he was the son of Zeus-nurtured kings. They wanted to bind him in harsh bonds, but the bonds did not hold him: the osiers fell far away from his hands and feet. He sat smiling with his dark eyes. The helmsman understood and at once cried out to his comrades...

This is very rapid narrative which does not stop to explain itself, and it is narrative which advertises its rapidity (τάχα, θοῶς, τάχα, αἶψα, αὐτίκα); on a different day, or with a different poet, this narrative could have been much extended (perhaps, for example, with an ekphrasis of the cloak Dionysus was wearing — such things are not unheard of — or with a speech from the wicked captain telling his men what to do and forecasting the profit they will make). After this initial 'scene-setting' (and I am aware that this is a tendentious description) the pace becomes, if not actually leisurely, rather slower as more details are spelled out;[3] we will find a not dissimilar shift in the 'Song of Ares and Aphrodite'.[4] The *Odyssey* is a work which, as is well known, revels in the display of narrative possibilities of all kinds, and compression and extension are no exception; Odysseus' summary of his adventures to Penelope in Book 23, with its opening insistence on the exhaustiveness of the account (ὅσα ... ὅσα ... πάντ' ... ἅπαντα) seems "programmatically" to call attention precisely to this poetic concern.[5] The three reported songs of Demodocus in Book 8, with which this paper will largely be concerned, are an obvious case where close juxtaposition draws attention to

---

3 I discuss this narrative further in Hunter 2011.
4 Cf. below, p. 40.
5 Cf. the song of the Sirens (12.189–191), presented by them in the briefest summary form (and which, of course, may not actually exist in any other form). On the summary in Book 23, which was athetised by Aristarchus, cf., e.g., Danek 1998, 460–461, de Jong 2001, 562–563.

differences of narrative scale and mode, but many other well-known examples are also available.

Menelaos' account of his encounters with Eidothea and Proteus and his seals (4.351–392) bears, as is well known, many similarities to Odysseus' *Apologoi*, in particular to Odysseus' encounter with and escape from the Cyclops. When we look back to Book 4 from Book 9, and indeed from Books 9–12 more generally, then the opportunities for expansion which were not taken become even clearer. Menelaos does not, for example, tell us how he reached Egypt and Pharos;[6] unlike Odysseus, before he reached the Cyclopes, Menelaos has no intermediary deeds of heroism to report, and this is clearly significant within the context of the poem's presentation of its principal figure. There is no description of what Eidothea looked like (vv. 364–366) — contrast, for example, Odysseus' description of Hermes, another god offering assistance, at 10.277–279 — and no account of any explanation or report of what she had said that Menelaos may have given to his comrades (vv. 428–434). In retrospect, one of the effects of this distinction between Menelaos and Odysseus as narrators is to advertise Odysseus' skill as narrator and quasi-bard; Menelaos' amusing seal-story, the whole second half of which is occupied by proteus' speech,[7] lacks the *poikilia* of Odysseus' narrative, as well as the cat-and-mouse dialogic interchange between the Cyclops and Mr. Nobody.[8] If the contrast between these narratives operates across a significant body of text, catalogue form, on the other hand, parades different narrative decisions within the very short space of a single speech. It is hardly accidental that the longest narrative in the 'Catalogue of Women' in Book 11 (if we exclude Odysseus' meeting with his mother) is also the first, namely the account of Tyro (vv. 235–259). The juxtaposition of this narrative, which includes the only direct speech of the Catalogue, to the extremely abbreviated story of Antiope (vv. 260–265) is a powerful advertisement of Odysseus' (and Homer's) ability to expand and compress at will.[9]

Odysseus' account of Tyro has a particular interest within the subject of the present volume, as a series of allusions in Moschus' *Europa* to this Homeric

---

6 Pharos, a place of hunger, is opposed to Odysseus' 'Goat Island', a place of plenty; the similarity of 4.354 to 9.116 might be thought to point the analogy very markedly. The 'auffallend knapp' (Danek 1998, 113) opening of Menelaos' speech was a puzzle even in antiquity.
7 If we take Menelaos' narrative as commencing in v. 351, then Proteus' speech (vv. 472–492) occupies precisely the second half.
8 For other aspects of Menelaos as narrator cf. de Jong 2001, 105–107.
9 Danek 1998, 231 rightly notes that the very short narratives of the Catalogue, which is itself but a selection (vv. 328–330), make clear 'die Macht ..., die der Erzähler über seine Stoffe ausübt'.

narrative construct it as one of Moschus' forerunners, not merely perhaps in terms of subject-matter (a god deceives and then sleeps with a young woman he desires), but also in terms of narrative form, of 'genre', if you like.[10] Moschus' poem 'is, as it were, a single episode from the Hesiodic *Catalogue* treated in the modern manner',[11] and this relationship between catalogue-poetry and what have traditionally been called "epyllia" has important ramifications for, say, the *Metamorphoses* of Ovid.

Tyro's story, a narrative of female desire, of deception and metamorphosis, of love-making (did Ποσειδάων ἐνοσίχθων — the name placed potently at the end of his speech — make the earth move for Tyro, or did she sleep through the whole thing [cf. v. 245]?),[12] and of children who carry their own stories with them, looks in fact like an 'epyllion' waiting to happen, or perhaps it has got there already. Be that as it may, the possibilities for extension and compression are obvious. It is possible that, in the Hesiodic version of her story, Tyro was simply ravished by Poseidon without the narrative motif of her love for Enipeus;[13] poets make choices at every turn — what does narrative *need*? Here perhaps it is Tyro's regular trips to the Enipeus which most provoke our imagination and memory. Apollodorus' gloss (1.9.8) on Homer and/or Hesiod seems to say that what Tyro used to do beside the waters of her beloved Enipeus was 'lament': this makes her sound like nothing so much as a poet — it is not difficult to imagine what, for example, an Ovid could do with this material[14] — but we can be more specific than that. We might think of Gallus in *Eclogue* 6, of Orpheus in *Georgic* 4, of — and here Tyro's name 'Miss Cheesy' does her no favours — the cheese-making Cyclops who cannot reach his sea-dwelling and 'milky' beloved in Theocritus 11, or Antimachus lamenting his love for Lyde beside the stream of the Paktolos (Hermesianax fr. 7.41–46 = Antimachus T 11

---

10 Cf. *Europa* 79 ~ *Odyssey* 11.245, *Europa* 153–161 ~ *Odyssey* 11.248–252, *Europa* 162–164 ~ *Odyssey* 11.245–246; Campbell 1991, 122–123.
11 Fantuzzi/Hunter 2004, 216.
12 It is worth noting that Hermogenes, in discussing this passage as an example of how a shameful deed can be indicated in a serious manner but not made explicit by saying what happened before and after, does not consider the place of sleep in the narrative (201.11–202.2 Rabe, cf. also [Plutarch], *De Homero* 22.8). For an attempt to give the sleep a function within the narrative cf. Doherty 1993, 5, 7. On the Tyro-narrative in general cf. also Dräger 1993, 77–82.
13 Unfortunately, Hesiod fr. 30 MW breaks off at just the wrong point. Hirschberger 2004, 236, 240 assumes that the Enipeus-motif was in Hesiod, whereas Osborne 2005, 16–17 and Irwin 2005, 49 take the other view. Much might hang on what one takes to be the source of Apollodorus 1.9.8.
14 The transmitted ἀπωδύρετο is regularly changed to ἐπωδύρετο or ἐπενήχετο (Hercher).

Matthews).[15] Given the apparent importance of Antimachus' poem and paradigm for later poetry, the epic narrative of Tyro suddenly assumes a potentially very interesting place in literary history.[16]

The Songs of Demodocus

The three reported songs of Demodocus in Book 8 would probably be on most people's list of the *Odyssey's* greatest hits, and not just, I think, because of the central concern in recent *Odyssey* scholarship with the (admittedly fascinating) subject of what we might call the "poetics and para-poetics" of the epic, a subject in which Demodocus must rightly take centre-stage. The three songs of Demodocus have of course a complex (and very much discussed) relationship to the epic in which they are embedded,[17] but this is not my principal concern here. They offer also an extraordinary *epideixis* of the possibilities open to the poet for extension and compression, and — as noted above — it is their close proximity to each other, as well as the fact that the first and third songs at least seem to embrace the beginning and the end of the trojan War, that precisely calls attention to this issue. Moreover, that the songs in various ways foreshadow (though this might not be the best way to describe the genetic relationship) certain features of Hellenistic narrative, including epyllion (as the term is currently used) is, or should be, generally familiar, but there is perhaps more to be said in this direction.[18]

If, for example, we look back at Demodocus' third song (the 'Fall of Troy') from the perspective of later narrative poetry, rather than worry about the (indeed important) question of its relation to the cyclic *Iliou Persis*, we may be

---

15 For discussion and bibliography cf. Matthews 1996, 26–39, 258–259.
16 A complementary possibility for what Tyro is doing is offered by Iphimedeia, another of Poseidon's conquests whom Odysseus saw in the underworld (*Odyssey* 11.305–320). Odysseus tells us merely that 'she said that she slept with Poseidon and bore him two sons...', but Apollodorus (1.7.4), presumably glossing the *Catalogue of Women* (cf. Hes. fr. 19 MW, and perhaps also fr. 10a.102–106 and fr. 117), describes her, in very similar terms to his description of Tyro (συνεχῶς φοιτῶσα in both descriptions presumably derives from a Hesiodic πωλέσκετο) 'falling in love with Poseidon and constantly going to the seashore, where she would draw up the waves with her hands and pour them into her lap (κόλποι)'.
17 Cf., e.g., Newton 1987; some recent guidance and bibliography in Rinon 2006, and cf. also Krummen 2008. As far as the 'Song of Ares and Aphrodite' is concerned, the relationship of the song to the wider context of the *Odyssey* was already discussed in antiquity, and in ways not far removed from some modern discussions, cf. Athenaeus 5.192c–e, Eustathius, *Hom*. 1597.46–47.
18 Cf. Fantuzzi/Hunter 2004, 194.

tempted to divide it into just two sections, which we might tendentiously call 'the Wooden Horse' (vv. 500–513) and 'The Sack of Troy' (vv. 514–520), rather than the four which seems to be a critical norm.[19] Triphiodorus, for example, announces his theme as 'the delayed end of the war which brought much suffering and the ambush, the equine handicraft of Argive Athena' (vv. 1–2),[20] and it is clear that it is indeed Demodocus' third song which is the principal Homeric, as opposed to cyclic, inspiration for Triphiodorus' poem. The final section of Triphiodorus' poem, describing the chaotic slaughter of the Trojans, though itself very brief (and self-consciously marked as such, vv. 664–667)[21] in comparison with the 'horse' section, might indeed be seen as an extended rhapsody on the theme briskly announced in v. 516 of *Odyssey* 8 ('[he sang how] all going in different directions, they plundered the lofty city'), and Triphiodorus of course does not neglect the confrontation of Odysseus and Menelaus with Deiphobus (vv. 613–629), which is singled out for particular mention in the report of Demodocus' song. A more extended comparison of Demodocus' third song with Triphiodorus would, I suspect, be an illuminating exercise in 'how epic (or should that be 'epyllion'?) is written'; in this case we have some sort of 'control' for how compression and extension may work. Thus, for example, the report of Demodocus' third song offers no direct speeches, but Triphiodorus and Virgil, among others, were to write them. In the case of Demodocus' first song, whatever its relation to 'our *Iliad*', our knowledge of *Iliad* 1 allows us very easily to imagine the ἔκπαγλα ἔπη (v. 77) with which Odysseus and Achilles might have argued; ἔκπαγλα ἔπη marks in fact a particular opportunity for the poet (taken, for example, by Homer in *Iliad* 1, but not taken in Demodocus' first and third songs). So too, similes are an obvious mode of expansion: in the abbreviated report of Demodocus' song, the Greeks pour out from the horse' (ἱππόθεν ἐκχύμενοι *Od.* 8.515), whereas Triphiodorus has them 'flow forth' (ἔρρεον ... ἀμφιχυθεῖσαι, v. 533) 'like bees from an oak...';[22] narratives grow by accretion, with poets making choices at every turn. Similes and speeches advertise themselves plainly; the selection of narrative material does not always do so. There is much, for example, that we would like to know about the relationship between Demodocus' third song and earlier Trojan traditions, such as those reflected in the cyclic *Ilias Parva* and the *Iliou Persis*, but one avenue at least may be open to us.

---

19 Cf., e.g., Goldhill 1991, 52–53, Danek 1998, 156–157.
20 On these verses cf. Paschalis 2005b, 107–109.
21 Cf. Hunter 2005b, 161–162.
22 Cf. also *Danai... effundunt uiros* in Eumolpus' 'Capture of Troy' (Petronius, *Sat.* 89, v. 57).

The Greeks have fired their camp and sailed away:

φαῖνε δ' ἀοιδήν,
ἔνθεν ἑλών, ὡς οἱ μὲν ἐϋσσέλμων ἐπὶ νηῶν   500
βάντες ἀπέπλειον, πῦρ ἐν κλισίῃσι βαλόντες,
Ἀργεῖοι, τοὶ δ' ἤδη ἀγακλυτὸν ἀμφ' Ὀδυσῆα
εἵατ' ἐνὶ Τρώων ἀγορῇ κεκαλυμμένοι ἵππῳ·
αὐτοὶ γάρ μιν Τρῶες ἐς ἀκρόπολιν ἐρύσαντο.
ὣς ὁ μὲν ἑστήκει, τοὶ δ' ἄκριτα πόλλ' ἀγόρευον   505
ἥμενοι ἀμφ' αὐτόν· τρίχα δέ σφισιν ἥνδανε βουλή,
ἠὲ διατμῆξαι κοῖλον δόρυ νηλέϊ χαλκῷ,
ἦ κατὰ πετράων βαλέειν ἐρύσαντας ἐπ' ἄκρης,
ἦ ἐάαν μέγ' ἄγαλμα θεῶν θελκτήριον εἶναι·

Homer, *Odyssey* 8.499-509

[Demodocus] set forth his song, taking it from the point where the Greeks had embarked on their well-benched ships, after setting fire to the huts; the others with glorious Odysseus sat in the Trojan gathering-place, concealed in the horse. The Trojans themselves had dragged it to the citadel. There the horse stood, and the Trojans sat around in endless argument. Their views divided three ways: either they should pierce the hollow structure with pitiless bronze, or drag it to a cliff and hurl it headlong from the rocks, or leave it as a great offering to appease the gods.

The Greeks leave their colleagues 'around the glorious Odysseus' concealed in the horse; the horse was in the place where the Trojans meet, 'for the Trojans had dragged the horse to their acropolis'. Demodocus' song, as it is reported to us, then fully responds to the disguised Odysseus' hint (v. 494) that Odysseus is to be given the principal role in the song; only one other Greek is mentioned — Menelaus, who accompanied Odysseus in pursuit of Deiphobus (v. 518) — and Odysseus is the subject of the only likeness or simile in the account of the song ('Odysseus, like Ares', v. 518). Odysseus' very request to Demodocus to tell of the horse 'which godlike Odysseus brought to the acropolis' is, as Garvie 1994, 33 put it, 'odd';[23] doubtless other explanations can be found, but we may wish to see Odysseus here directing the singer in none too subtle a way.[24] Homer then makes the blind singer fit the song to the person requesting it, even when that audience is in disguise; the self-absorbed Odysseus is not in the mood to share

---

23 *Pace* Dawe 1993, 342-343.
24 For a related, though rather different, suggestion cf. Harrison 1971 (accepted by Grandolini 1996, 141).

the limelight with anyone.[25] Vv. 503–504 (above), however, invite us to remember that there was an earlier history of the horse: the Greeks leave it on the plain and, in some versions (e.g. Virgil and Triphiodorus), the debate about what to do with it takes place there, not in the city.[26] What other traditional parts of the story are here 'summarised' and/or excluded? The quickest glance at Virgil and Triphiodorus will confirm that the most striking element of the familiar story not included in the report of Demodocus' song is the role of Sinon. Proclus tells us that in the *Iliou Persis* 'Sinon raised torches for the Greeks, having previously entered the city under a pretence (προσποίητος)'; this is not as helpful as we might have wanted, but it does at least confirm that, in that poem at least and presumably in other early traditions,[27] another Greek than Odysseus played a significant and guileful role, and it looks likely that he also was at least mentioned in the *Ilias Parva*.[28] Sinon, of course, is a kind of double of Odysseus;[29] one tradition made him Odysseus' cousin, through the disreputable Sisyphus (cf. Lycophron, *Alexandra* 345), and Triphiodorus calls him πολυμήχανος ἥρως (291) and ἀπατήλιος ἥρως (220). As we saw in relation to Tyro, Homer's 'summary' technique invites us to the imaginative reconstruction of fuller, wider songs and, just as importantly, forces us to think about choice and selectivity in narrative. So too do later 'epyllia', on any definition of this term.

A Hymn for Aphrodite?

The hymnic quality of the 'Song of Ares and Aphrodite' has often been noted, and Wilamowitz, for whom Demodocus' song was the model for the Homeric *Hymn to Aphrodite*, influentially connected it with a 'Hymn to Hephaestus'.[30] There are of course at least two (potentially) separate questions here. One concerns the poetic archaeology of the passage (Wilamowitz's question), and the other, upon which I will focus, is our sense of 'genre' as we (and the Phaea-

---

25 Cf., e.g., Garvie 1994, 331 on vv. 487–498. I hope that it will not need spelling out that I am not suggesting anything as simplistic as the idea once current that Demodocus has 'recognised' Odysseus.
26 Although it is not completely certain, it looks from Proclus' summary as if the *Iliou Persis* had the same sequence as *Odyssey* 8.27.
27 Cf. Apollodorus, *Epit.* 5.19.
28 Cf. Apollodorus, *Epit.* 5.15. For a summary of the evidence for Sinon and modern bibliography cf. Horsfall 2008, 93–94.
29 Cf., e.g., Jones 1965, though his interpretation of *Odyssey* 8.494 differs from mine.
30 Wilamowitz 1895.

cians) listen to the song. There are clearly significant differences between the report of Demodocus' song and the longer *Homeric Hymns*; in particular, the song does not concern, at least directly, the interaction of men and gods or indeed the distribution of spheres of influence among the Olympians, as do the *Hymns* to Demeter, Apollo, and Aphrodite. There can be no suggestion that we could just add a different beginning and end in order to create a 'Hymn to Hephaestus' or a 'Hymn to Aphrodite' which would fit perfectly within our corpus of hexameter hymns. Nevertheless, the narrative structures of the song do seem to have much in common with both archaic and later hymns, and I want here to explore how far the assumption of some hymnic resonance can help us to understand Demodocus' song.

The song is introduced as 'about the love-making of Ares and fair-crowned Aphrodite, how they first made love secretly in the house of Hephaestus' (vv. 267–269), and it is they — or more specifically Aphrodite (Ares' name is effaced, v. 361) — who dominate the end;[31] this would be a very odd way to begin a 'Hymn to Hephaestus', but far less odd if this were a 'Hymn to Ares and Aphrodite', or just — particularly given the ending — a 'Hymn to Aphrodite' the generic sense of 'a hymn' may be triggered by the initial 'how they first...', where the phrasing can certainly be paralleled in hymnic contexts,[32] but it is the end of the song which really is of the greatest interest in this connection. Different views about the tone and significance of the ending have been taken but, for what it is worth, it seems to me that Jasper Griffin was close to the mark when he claimed that in these verses Aphrodite '[re]assumes all the splendour of her divinity';[33] closer certainly — inasmuch as such things can be judged — than Douglas Olson who has us at the end 'ogling [Hephaestus'] wife at her toilet ... in disturbing parallel both to the suitors on Ithaca surrounding Penelope, and the giggling gods at Hephaestus' door'.[34] If this song has a hymnal feel, it is (or rather is closely analogous to) a 'Hymn to Aphrodite'; it is she, not Hephaestus, who is triumphant at the end. It would, I think, hardly surprise if after v. 366 the singer were to turn to address the goddess with a hymnic χαῖρε. When some (?) thousand years later Reposianus wrote his 'epyllion' *De concubitu Martis et Veneris*

---

31 We may perhaps compare Callimachus' 'Acontius and Cydippe' in which the couple are named together at the beginning (fr. 67.1–2 Pf.), but it is Acontius only (or rather 'Acontius and Calliope") who dominate the end. Some take παιδός in fr. 75.76 Pf. to be Cydippe (so Trypanis 1975, D'Alessio 1997 [very hesitantly], Massimilla 1996), but this is I think difficult in the face of fr. 67.2.
32 Cf. Mineur 1984, 77 on Callimachus, *Hymn to Delos* 30.
33 Griffin 1980, 200; cf. also, e.g., Halliwell 2008, 84.
34 Olson 1989, 145.

he ends with the guilty couple ensnared in their *locus amoenus*, but Venus is feeling anything but shame and, here taking a lead from Ovid (*Met.* 4.190–192, cf. further below), the poem ends with another foretaste of her power:

> Stat Mauors lumine toruo
> atque indignatur, quod sit deprensus adulter.
> At Paphie conuersa dolet non crimina facti;
> sed quae sit uindicta sibi tum singula uoluens
> cogitat et poenam sentit si Phoebus amaret.
> Iamque dolos properans decorabat cornua tauri,
> Pasiphaae crimen mixtique cupidinis iram.
>
> Reposianus, *Mars and Venus* 176–182

> Mars stands grim-faced and angry because he has been caught in adultery. But the Paphian does not grieve for the overturning of her guilty deed; rather, she ponders every detail of the revenge she may take and feels it a proper penalty if Phoebus were to fall in love. Now already she was hurrying on with her trick and beautifying the horns of the bull, to prepare Pasiphae's guilt and the anger of mixed desire.

The *Homeric Hymn to Aphrodite* shows that hymnic narratives in praise of that goddess can encompass material that might seem embarrassing to her; shame and embarrassment are perhaps an inevitable part of sexual love and desire, and hence have a place in 'Hymns to Aphrodite', the purpose of which is to explain and celebrate the goddess' nature.[35] Such material does not lessen the praise of the goddess.

The final words of the song apparently invite us to envision the goddess in her beauty, to experience divine epiphany in our minds, which is, as John García in particular has stressed, a feature (indeed the directing *telos*) of a common narrative pattern in the *Homeric Hymns*,[36] and one with a striking *Nachleben* in the *Hymns* of Callimachus. θαῦμα ἰδέσθαι in v. 366 is almost always used in early epic of a material object, and thus probably here refers primarily to the goddess' lovely clothes (cf. *Odyssey* 6.306, 13.108), as at *Hymn to Aphrodite* 90 it refers to the goddess' marvellous jewellery and at Hesiod, *Theogony* 575 to Pandora's veil.[37] Nevertheless, there may perhaps be more going on as well, and I offer a speculation about the 'poetic archaeology' of this passage. The scholia on v. 363 report that there is no cult statue (ἄγαλμα) of the goddess at Paphos and that the fact that Homer refers only to the goddess' 'precinct and altar'

---

[35] Cf. Faulkner 2008, 17–18. On the *Homeric Hymn to Aphrodite* and the 'Song of Ares and Aphrodite' cf. further Baumbach 2012.
[36] Cf. García 2002. cf. further Bergren 1989, 11.
[37] Cf. further Bergren 1989, 11.

shows that he knew this; in the parallel passage of the *Homeric Hymn to Aphrodite* the goddess has a 'fragrant temple' as well as a precinct and altar (vv. 58–59), and observation of this difference (or something like it) perhaps lies behind the scholiast's note.[38] Nevertheless, at least later in antiquity the cult image of the goddess at Paphos was (uniquely for Aphrodite) an aniconic conical stone,[39] and there are good reasons for believing that this goes back to a date before Homer; it is in fact generally accepted that one such cult stone has been found on site.[40] It is thus perhaps worth considering the possibility that behind Demodocus' θαῦμα ἰδέσθαι (and behind the scholiast's observation) lies the anointing and dressing (as a divine woman) of this stone block; this would indeed be a 'wonder', just as Philostratus (*VA* 3.58) reports that Apollonius of Tyana 'wondered' (θαυμάσαι) at the Paphian image. Be that as it may, these verses suggest (or, at the very least, could easily be taken to suggest) the *kosmêsis* of a cult image (of whatever kind),[41] and the linkage of that theme to a 'hymnic' narrative is at least very suggestive (*inter alia*) for the later hymns of Callimachus. This of course can only be one speculation among many. Paphos is also rich with female figurines wearing elaborate jewellery (see further below), and Jacqueline Karageorghis (in Maier/Karageorghis 1984, 365–366) suggests that the various epic descriptions of Aphrodite's 'toilet' in fact reflect rather an elaborate dressing of 'the priestess who represents the goddess' by 'young priestesses' who, in the epic vision, become 'the Hours and Graces'.

However this may be, there remain interesting links between the *Hymn* and Demodocus' song, and it might be thought that the end of the 'song' and the parallel passage of the goddess' preparations at *Homeric Hymn to Aphrodite* 58ff. was a good test case for 'intertextuality' in archaic 'oral' epic.[42] The matter is complicated (*inter alia*) by the fact that the passage in the *Hymn* also shares elements with *Iliad* 14.166 sqq., where, in a *thalamos* built by Hephaestus, Hera

---

38 As far as I can see, Faulkner 2008 does not comment upon this aspect of the relationship between the two passages.
39 For the evidence and bibliography cf. Karageorghis 2005, 29–31, *LIMC* ii.1 s.v. Aphrodite, 9.
40 Cf. Karageorghis 2005, 29–31. The fullest study of the sanctuary at Palaepaphos is Maier/Karageorghis 1984, 81 sqq. (where the stone is fig. 83).
41 For such anointing of statues cf., e.g., Callimachus *Hymn* 2.38, fr. 9.11–14 Massimilla (with Massimilla's note on v. 12), *Epigram* 51 Pf., I. Petrovic/A. Petrovic 2003, 182–184. The Callimachean *Hymn to Athena* of course precisely thematises the kind of unguents which Aphrodite and Athena 'use' (vv. 15–16). The stone which Kronos vomited up, θαῦμα θνητοῖσι βροτοῖσιν (Hesiod, *Theogony* 500, where see West's 1966, 303 note), and which was preserved at Delphi, was anointed every day and decorated on special occasions (Pausanias 10.24.6).
42 See especially Baumbach 2012.

prepares to seduce Zeus (we are clearly dealing with a type scene going back to Near Eastern poetry of 'goddess does her make-up before sex'), and by the probably relatively early date of the *Hymn to Aphrodite*, but the possibility of a direct relationship between the passages can hardly be ruled out. If the hymn writer was thinking of the *Odyssey*, did he simply echo one 'disgraceful' episode in another or did he take the end of Demodocus' song, which shows the goddess in her full power, and reverse it — she is trapped by the very power she embodies? In either case, perhaps, we should entertain the possibility that the poet of the *Homeric Hymn* 'read' Demodocus' song as a 'Hymn to Aphrodite', and it will be clear that I think he was on the right track; if the chronology of the two poems should be reversed, then the point would carry even more force.

One further epiphanic passage is perhaps worth citing in this context. after the parallel passage of *kosmêsis* in the *Homeric Hymn to Aphrodite*, the goddess presents herself in front of Anchises:

στῆ δ' αὐτοῦ προπάροιθε Διὸς θυγάτηρ Ἀφροδίτη
παρθένῳ ἀδμήτῃ μέγεθος καὶ εἶδος ὁμοίη,
μή μιν ταρβήσειεν ἐν ὀφθαλμοῖσι νοήσας.
Ἀγχίσης δ' ὁρόων ἐφράζετο θαύμαινέν τε
εἶδός τε μέγεθος καὶ εἵματα σιγαλόεντα.   85
πέπλον μὲν γὰρ ἕεστο φαεινότερον πυρὸς αὐγῆς,
εἶχε δ' ἐπιγναμπτὰς ἕλικας κάλυκάς τε φαεινάς,
ὅρμοι δ' ἀμφ' ἁπαλῇ δειρῇ περικαλλέες ἦσαν
καλοὶ χρύσειοι παμποίκιλοι· ὡς δὲ σελήνη
στήθεσιν ἀμφ' ἁπαλοῖσιν ἐλάμπετο, θαῦμα ἰδέσθαι.   90

Homeric Hymn to Aphrodite 81–90

Aphrodite, daughter of Zeus, stood in front of him, like in stature and form to an unmarried girl, so that he would not be afraid when he saw her with his eyes. Anchises looked at her and took note in amazement of her form and stature and her shining clothes. She wore a robe more brilliant than the gleam of fire, and twisted bracelets and shining ear-rings, and around her soft neck were necklaces of gold, exceedingly beautiful and elaborate; around her soft breasts it shone like the moon, a wonder to behold.

Here is another case where the goddess' 'accessories' are θαῦμα ἰδέσθαι, but where attempting to distinguish between wonder at her clothes and/ or accessories and wonder at the goddess herself seems wasted effort, as Anchises' 'wonder' (v. 84) makes clear. As θαῦμα ἰδέσθαι invites us to imagine the goddess' jewellery, it also invites us to imagine her soft breasts and to put ourselves in Anchises' position; the only 'real experience' which we can feed into our imagining at such a moment is perhaps our memory of images of the goddess decked out with brilliant jewellery. Once again, it is material images of the god which inform our own image-making; whatever links to Near Eastern epic there are here, we should perhaps remember the archaic female statues from the eastern Aegean and Cyprus, very probably of Aphrodite, wearing heavy and elaborate jewellery.[43]

If Demodocus' song is a celebration of Aphrodite, not of Hephaestus, what has mislead us? Partly, of course, it is the obvious Hephaestus ~ Odysseus analogy; as the *Odyssey* is very obviously *ad maiorem gloriam Ulixis*, the song should play the same role for Hephaestus — but manifestly frame and included narrative have very different outcomes. Hephaestus' finest hour comes in fact in vv. 326–332 in which the gods laugh (though *why* they laugh has been endless debated) and praise his cleverness and the fact that Ares will now have to pay recompense. It is true, of course, that Hephaestus' position, as he himself makes very clear, is not one of untrammelled happiness, though Ruth Scodel's 'Hephaestus appears ridiculous' perhaps goes too far.[44] Eustathius (in his note on v. 335, *Hom.* 1597.22–36), perhaps reflecting ancient theories which traced the origin of comedy to Homer,[45] notes how Homer has mingled σπουδαῖα καὶ γελοῖα καὶ πικρά, the last being exemplified by the position of the cuckolded Hephaestus. However that may be, the jests of Hermes and Apollo change things. From their perspective, Ares has not done so badly out of the affair, and in the event Hephaestus will need the protection of Poseidon as guarantor of Ares' payment; Hephaestus does not really end up on the winning side. The gnomic οὐκ ἀρετᾷ κακὰ ἔργα (v. 329) has regularly been taken in modern times as the moral of the tale,[46] and may well have been so taken in antiquity, for of course it had immediate didactic and educational attractions, and the scholia on v. 267 set out a clear moralising interpretation of the 'Song'.[47] One can certainly imagine that, in educational contexts, not only vv. 333–342, which — according to the scholia — were missing from some texts, would be passed over in silence, but everything after v. 332, whether or not we are to imagine actual texts without these verses; οὐκ ἀρετᾷ κακὰ ἔργα· κιχάνει τοι βραδὺς ὠκύν would then

---

[43] Cf. esp. Karageorghis 1977, *LIMC* ii.1., 18–19 'die kyprische Aphrodite', Faulkner 2008, 20–21, 161–162, 168–170.
[44] Scodel 2002, 86. Halliwell 2008, 77–86 offers a helpful and balanced account.
[45] Cf. [Hermogenes] 454.6–14 Rabe, citing the opening of the *Acharnians*, on the characteristic mixture of πικρὰ καὶ γελοῖα in comedy, Plutarch, *De Homero* 214; ancient inferences from *Frogs* 389–90 are unlikely to be far away. According to Hermogenes, what the πικρά do is σωφρονίζειν, which is the same verb as the *Odyssey* scholiast uses to explain why Demodocus sings such a racy song (scholium on v. 267).
[46] Cf., e.g., Hölscher 1988, 271: '[U]m diese Spruchweisheit herum ist die Geschichte erfunden'.
[47] Cf. also Athenaeus 1.14c and Plutarch, *Mor.* 19d (with Hunter 2009, 188–189).

indeed be the "closing moral" of the song. Vv. 326–332 form in fact a 'false ending': they are certainly gnomic enough to be closural, and they close down the story by telling us what to think. Just, however, when we know where we are — the episode offered a safe moralising interpretation by the anonymous τις among the immortals (thus giving the ancient scholiasts their cue) — up pop Hermes and Apollo to take the song and its interpretation in a new direction, and it is hard to think of two interpreters of poetry with whom one would less like to disagree.

In his seminal discussion of Demodocus' song, Walter Burkert observed that 'the whole song culminates in v. 326' ('unquenchable laughter arose among the blessed gods').[48] Manifestly it does not, but Burkert had excellent precedents for his view. Leuconoe's tale of the adultery itself ends in Book 4 of Ovid's *Metamorphoses* as follows:

> Lemnius extemplo ualuas patefecit eburnas   185
> immisitque deos. illi iacuere ligati
> turpiter, atque aliquis de dis non tristibus optat
> sic fieri turpis; superi risere, diuque
> haec fuit in toto notissima fabula caelo.
>
> Ovid, *Metamorphoses* 4.185–189

> Straightaway the Lemnian opened wide the ivory doors and let in the gods. The two lay there in bonds, a matter for shame, and one of the gods, who were in jolly mood, prayed to be shamed in just this way; the heavenly ones laughed, and for a long time this was the best known tale in all of heaven.

Ovid has to some extent anticipated Burkert.[49] Admittedly, Leuconoe then passes on to Venus' revenge upon the sun, and the story of Venus and Mars is actually told, not for its own sake, but within the context of the *solis amores* (*Met.* 4.170). Nevertheless, in fusing the anonymous τις speech of the Homeric original with the jests of Hermes and Apollo, both here in the *Metamorphoses* and in the version of the *Ars Amatoria* (2.585–586), and by concluding the narrative in the *Metamorphoses* with divine laughter, Ovid has had a formative influence, not just upon the modern conception of Homer's 'laughing gods', but also upon modern readings of Homer himself. Finally, it is worth noting that Eustathius

---

48 Burkert 1960 134–135. So too Bömer 1976, vol. 2, 68 puts the laughter of the gods 'am Schluss der Szene'.
49 In Ovid's other reworking of the 'Song' he adds a twist which takes the story beyond the Homeric ending (*Ars. am.* 2.589–592); on the Latin versions of the 'Song' cf. Bömer 1976, vol. 2, 67–69 and Janka 1997, 404–420 on Ovid, *Ars am.* 2.561–592.

(*Hom.* 1600.48) seems to link the 'smile-loving' of the goddess at the conclusion to the song (v. 362) with the 'unquenchable laughter' which has gone before, and Garvie 1994, 311 at least is prepared to admit some contextual resonance for this 'formulaic' epithet here.

Poetic lies?

Are we, as we listen to Homer, supposed to be familiar with the subject matter of the 'Song of Ares and Aphrodite'? There are good reasons for thinking that Demodocus' two other songs (or at least their subject matter), the songs of κλέα ἀνδρῶν, are to be understood as familiar to the audience (cf. vv. 75, 492–498), but with regard to the 'Song of Ares and Aphrodite' we may well wonder, and this is of course a different question from the poetic antecedents of this song.[50] Many would, I think, agree with Garvie that '[i]t is tempting to suppose that this [song] is H[omer]'s own invention, or at least that it is a recent entrant to his tradition',[51] but again that is not quite the same thing as wondering whether this is a song new to its audience.

The scholium on v. 267 famously claims that Demodocus himself is responsible for making Hephaestus and Aphrodite a married couple, because for Homer Hephaestus' wife was Charis. We of course will not want to distinguish between Homer and his character in quite that way (though Burkert has some interesting remarks along these lines), but this scholiastic note may suggest a wider ancient search for novelty here. It is perhaps also relevant that when Odysseus praises Demodocus and asks him to sing of the Wooden Horse (vv. 489ff.), he does not mention the 'Song of Ares and Aphrodite', only (apparently) the bard's first song; I say 'apparently' because in antiquity at least the question was asked how Odysseus could know that Demodocus sang 'the fate of the Achaeans, all that they did and suffered and laboured λίην κατὰ κόσμον', without (as far as we know) someone saying 'well, it's obviously a reference to Demodocus' first song'. This however is the modern consensus, both among those who see the Song of Ares and Aphrodite as well integrated into Book 8 and those who take their cue from the ancient scholars who athetised the whole Song.[52] However we wish to understand μετάβηθι in v. 492,[53] however, it is clear

---

50 Cf., e.g., Danek 1998, 153–154. On Demodocus' first song cf. Finkelberg 1998, 146–147, citing earlier bibliography.
51 Garvie 1994, 293. The idea recurs in many guises in modern writing, cf., e.g., Dalby 2006, 124.
52 Cf. scholium on Ar. *Pax* 778, Garvie 1994, 294. An exception to the consensus is Dawe 1993, 341 who realises that there is a problem here.

that one could ask a Demodocus to sing of (e.g.) a quarrel between two great heroes or the fate of the Achaeans at Troy, but one could not ask him to sing of Olympian events unknown to mortals (though known to bards through their particular gifts);[54] one could, I imagine, ask a bard to (e.g.) 'sing that song of the adultery of Ares and Aphrodite, which I heard you singing last week', but this does not seem to be how Homer envisages bardic performance (there is an interesting contrast here with the goatherd's urging of Thyrsis to sing of the ἄλγεα Δάφνιδος in Theocritus 1).

Odysseus' famous praise for Demodocus (vv. 487–491) seems to elide the 'Song of Ares and Aphrodite' because there are no criteria by which mortals (even Odysseus, who was not an eyewitness) can judge it, let alone determine that it is λίην κατὰ κόσμον.[55] That Odysseus and the Phaeacians took pleasure in the song (vv. 367–369)[56] does not help us here. More instructive, however, might be the fact that Odysseus notes that Demodocus' skill shows that he was taught either by the Muse or by Apollo, when this is placed alongside the fact that whereas Demodocus' two 'Iliadic' songs seem to derive from the inspiration of the Muse (vv. 73, 499), nothing is said of any role for the Muse in the 'Song of Ares and Aphrodite'; Demodocus sings 'off his own bat', no less than the Phaeacian dancers prove their superiority to other dancers (note vv. 250–251).[57] It could, of course, be objected that anything which Demodocus sings has the sanction and/or authority of the Muse:[58]

καλέσασθε δὲ θεῖον ἀοιδόν,
Δημόδοκον· τῷ γάρ ῥα θεὸς περὶ δῶκεν ἀοιδὴν
τέρπειν, ὅππῃ θυμὸς ἐποτρύνῃσιν ἀείδειν.

Homer, *Odyssey* 8.43–45

---

53 Cf., e.g., Grandolini 1996, 144, Ford 1992, 42–43.
54 Cf., e.g., Scodel 2002, ch. 3, Graziosi/Haubold 2005, 81–82, who in my view put too much stress on the bard's 'special relationship with the Muses', at least where the 'Song of Ares and Aphrodite' is concerned.
55 On this much discussed phrase cf., e.g., Walsh 1984, 8–9.
56 Cf. v. 45 with Garvie's note 1994, 245. Eustathius points out that one could save Odysseus' philosophical reputation by making him take pleasure, not in the subject-matter of the song, but rather in Demodocus' skillful rhythm and poetic grace, or — of course — one could understand that he interpreted the song allegorically whereas the hedonistic Phaeacians took it at face value, *Hom.* 1601.16.
57 Grandolini 1996, 123 presents alternative explanations for the absence of the Muse.
58 The bibliography on the subject is, of course, enormous. Helpful guidance to some of the issues can still be found in Murray 1981.

> Summon the divine bard, Demodocus; to him god gave the gift of song, to offer delight in whatever way his spirit urges him to sing.

Nevertheless, Homer's silence about the Muse before the 'Song of Ares and Aphrodite' remains potentially significant, at least from a later perspective.

It might be tempting to see in the presence or absence of the Muse a distinction between 'epic' and 'hymn', but the poets of the *Homeric Hymns* to Hermes, Aphrodite and Pan (at least) invoke the Muse, and there is clearly no simple generic demarcation here, which is not to say that there is no differentiation at all; the god being praised may him or herself be imagined as the source of the hymnic bard's inspiration. Callimachus' *Hymns* have virtually no place for inspiration by the Muses.[59] It is of course a very familiar idea of modern Homeric scholarship that the Muse is some kind of figure for 'received poetic tradition', and thus we may see here one further indication of the 'novelty' of Demodocus' second song; although everything falls within the purview of the Muses, they have a particular responsibility for the great deeds of the heroes of the past, who are of course completely absent from Demodocus' second song. For what it is worth, the very fact of the scope of the song, in comparison with the summary report of the two 'Iliadic' performances, would also seem to point to the 'Song' as a special site of Homeric *epideixis*. Looking forward, moreover, we may note that there is no role for the Muses in Callimachus' *Hecale*, Theocritus 24 and 25, Moschus' *Europa* or Catullus 64, whereas both Apollo and the Muses have (disputed) roles in the proem of the *Argonautica*,[60] the Muses or Muse in the proems of Ennius' *Annales* and the *Aeneid*, and 'gods' in the proem of Ovid's *Metamorphoses*. If there is anything to this,[61] we may at least wonder whether the small-scale hexameter narrative has no need of the apparatus of 'tradition'.[62] Finally,

---

59 The possible exception, *Hymn to Delos* 4–8, in fact makes clear that the poet himself is taking responsibility for his song.
60 The role assigned to the Muses at the opening of the *Batrachomyomachia* is perhaps analogous to that which Apollonius assigns them; on this proem cf. Wölke 1978, 84–90.
61 The poet does address the Muses *more Homerico* at the start of the 'Aristaeus epyllion' in Virgil, *Georgics* 4.315, but the generic issues which surround this text are well beyond the scope of the current paper, cf. Morgan 1999, 17–20. It may, however, be worth noting that vv. 315–316 to some extent stand apart from what follows, and familiarity with Hellenistic and Roman 'epyllion' would lead us to take the highly Graecising v. 317, *pastor Aristaeus fugiens Peneia Tempe*, as the first verse of the embedded 'epyllion'; with *ut fama* in v. 318 cf. the opening of Catullus 64.
62 Calliope reappears in the proem of Triphiodorus (v. 4), but vv. 664–667 show the poet distancing himself from the Muses, who are there associated rather with long, 'traditional' epic (presumably the Cycle), cf. Hunter 2005b, 161–162.

we may also wonder if, at least for the 'Song of Ares and Aphrodite', the absence of any reference to the Muse withholds a particular (Homeric) guarantee of 'truth' from the song, as Odysseus' silence about it also implies. The doings of the Olympians are in fact the first site of poetic fiction; the early onset of defensive 'allegorical interpretation' is perhaps in part a sign of the freedom that divine characters offered to the poets.

One final thought: except for a very slight hiccough up at the beginning (where we might feel that we are still hearing Homer's voice, rather than Demodocus'),[63] the 'song of Ares and Aphrodite' proceeds in a relatively straightforward, chronologically linear pattern, whereas what we are offered of the two 'Iliadic' songs suggests more complex (we might be tempted to say more 'Homeric') time arrangements. In part, this is of course a function of its very extension, but it is perhaps also one further small sign of a song which marks itself off from the dominant tradition; in doing so, it also points the way to later small-scale narratives.

Compression and extension II

The *Homeric Hymns* as a group would offer considerable scope for a study of compression and extension in hexameter narrative. The longer *Hymns* themselves thematise the question of where narrative should begin and end, as do Demodocus' third performance in *Odyssey* 8 and, to a certain extent also, the 'Song of Ares and Aphrodite'. Where then does Demodocus start the 'Song of Ares and Aphrodite'? Of course we do not know, and the question itself may be wrong-headed. I think many hearers/readers would be tempted to believe that they start to hear Demodocus' voice, rather than Homer's (a problematic distinction, of course),[64] when Hephaestus enters the scene (vv. 272ff.),[65] which is also the point from which the narrative proceeds in a broadly chronological order (but note vv. 300–302). This might be right, but one of the remarkable things about, particularly, the first part of this narrative is not just our uncertainty

---

[63] Calliope reappears in the proem of Triphiodorus (v. 4), but vv. 664–667 show the poet distancing himself from the Muses, who are there associated rather with long, 'traditional' epic (presumably the cycle), cf. Hunter 2005b, 161–162.
[64] Cf., e.g., de Jong 2009, 99–101.
[65] Bowie 1997b, 54 explicitly puts the beginning of Demodocus' song, as opposed to Homer's summary, at v. 270b; transition in mid-verse would be a very strong marker of the transition in voice.

about 'whose voice is this?',⁶⁶ but how the song seems to dramatise the ever-present possibilities of extending and compressing narrative in another display of the power the poet has over his audience.

The possibilities of narrative suppression and expansion are indeed paraded at the very beginning of the Song:

αὐτὰρ ὁ φορμίζων ἀνεβάλλετο καλὸν ἀείδειν
ἀμφ' Ἄρεος φιλότητος ἐϋστεφάνου τ' Ἀφροδίτης,
ὥς τὰ πρῶτ' ἐμίγησαν ἐν Ἡφαίστοιο δόμοισι
λάθρῃ· πολλὰ δὲ δῶκε, λέχος δ' ᾔσχυνε καὶ εὐνὴν
Ἡφαίστοιο ἄνακτος. ἄφαρ δέ οἱ ἄγγελος ἦλθεν
Ἥλιος, ὅ σφ' ἐνόησε μιγαζομένους φιλότητι.

Homer, *Odyssey* 8.266–271

Playing on his lyre he began a lovely song about the love-making of Ares and Aphrodite of the fair garland, how they first had sex secretly in the house of Hephaestus; he gave many things and shamed the marriage and couch of lord Hephaestus. But straightaway a messenger went to him, Helios, who had seen them making love.

About this first love-making and Ares' gifts we learn almost nothing: the song begins with an announcement of its subject 'the love-making of Ares and fair-garlanded Aphrodite' and then a very abbreviated summary of what we are to imagine as the early parts of the song (vv. 268–270a).⁶⁷ Hephaestus is then informed by Helios who had seen the couple making love (vv. 270–271). It is perhaps a pity that no report is given of the θυμαλγὴς μῦθος in which Helios broke the news to Hephaestus (Reposianus' version with its mocking sun-god, vv. 152ff., seems very modern in its flavour), but for how an 'extended' version of this narrative might work – on another occasion, by another bard, in a different context – we can look to the opening of the *Hymn to Demeter* in which Hecate and Helios are the only witnesses to Persephone's rape and Helios tells Demeter what has happened, after which the angry goddess withdraws to roam in sorrow; clearly the episode of Helios seeing the lovers could, in another telling, have been similarly (or indeed much further) drawn out. So too Hephaestus at

---

66 Eftychia Bathrellou (private communication) has observed that the very unusual (for the *Odyssey*) role played by Poseidon increases the sense of this as a 'Phaeacian' song and hence our uncertainty as to whether it is Homer's song or Demodocus'.
67 It has been suggested that this first 'love-making' is actually the act in which the gods are caught by Hephaestus and which forms the subject of the song, by a kind of Homeric *hysteron proteron*; it is then very difficult to reconstruct the 'time line' of events. The very fact, however, that some students of the song have received this impression is itself testimony to the very rapid and summary mode of the opening verses.

his forge (vv. 273–275): we have many descriptions from both narrative epic and later hymns (e.g. *Iliad* 18.372 ff. where the god is (again) making δεσμοί, Callimachus, *Hymn to Artemis* 46 sqq. etc.) of the blacksmith god at work, and in the *Odyssey* too the description — on another occasion, by another bard, in a different context — could have been much extended. The description of the invisible bonds is accompanied by a simile 'like fine spider-webs' (v. 280), but such a simile could also of course have been much extended, had the singer so wished.

Such an analysis of how the narrative parades possibilities for compression and expansion could itself be much extended, but not much would, I think, be gained; to the objection that this is true of every narrative, I think it can be answered that the 'Song of Ares and Aphrodite' advertises the possibilities open to the poet in very particular ways, which are, at one level, the result of the mixed diegetic and mimetic form, but — at another level — may with hindsight be seen to look forward to the strong interest in narrative pace which characterises small-scale Hellenistic and Roman hexameter narrative.

It seems hardly possible, however, to pass over the extraordinary narrative compression, if that is what it is, at vv. 295–298:

ὣς φάτο, τῇ δ' ἀσπαστὸν ἐείσατο κοιμηθῆναι.
τὼ δ' ἐς δέμνια βάντε κατέδραθον· ἀμφὶ δὲ δεσμοὶ
τεχνήεντες ἔχυντο πολύφρονος Ἡφαίστοιο,
οὐδέ τι κινῆσαι μελέων ἦν οὐδ' ἀναεῖραι.

Homer, *Odyssey* 8.295–298

So he spoke, and she welcomed the idea of going to bed. They lay on the bed and slept, and around them the artful bonds of cunning Hephaestus poured; they could not move or raise any limb

Most recent translators into English translate κατέδραθον as 'they lay down', or something very close to that (Fagles, Hammond, Rieu, Rouse, Shewring), and it is hard to deny that the verb could mean that,[68] particularly if we extended it to mean 'lay down to sleep (together)', with a suggestion of euphemism as in the English 'sleep together' (so Samuel Butler). This might be supported by the apparent gloss at vv. 313–314 (καθεύδειν ἐν φιλότητι) and by standard euphemistic usages such as we find in v. 337 ("sleep beside"). Nevertheless, we might think that the 'natural' meaning of this verb was 'slept/fell asleep' and both Lattimore and Dawe opt for this.[69] Edward McCrorie has it both ways: 'the two made love in

---

68 Cf. esp. *Odyssey* 5.471, with *LfgrE* s.v. δραθεῖν.
69 Note too Halliwell 2008, 79: 'the lovers are trapped, during their post-coital sleep …'.

the bed. They dozed'. It is of course true that Homer is elsewhere not very explicit about love-making, but we might think that he here raises and defeats his listeners' expectations rather naughtily (did Ovid, with his *cetera quis nescit?*, learn the trick from here?).[70] We might here also recall the observation of the learned scholiast on *Iliad* 14 who notes that, although Homer gave a full description of Hera washing and then dressing up, elaborate jewellery and all, in order to seduce Zeus, he omitted to represent (δεῖξαι) her taking her clothes off 'so as not to put dirty thoughts in the audience's mind' (Schol. bT on *Iliad* 14.187). Be that as it may, we might here see (again) a sign of the kind of compression which marks the in-between state of this narrative with its two simultaneous narrators (something which we perhaps have to look forward to Ovid to parallel).[71]

If, however, we ask 'What *could* an archaic hexameter poet have said here?', another passage from the *Homeric Hymn to Aphrodite* might be helpful. When Anchises gets the mysterious stranger into bed (so to speak), there follows a quite lengthy description:

οἱ δ' ἐπεὶ οὖν λεχέων εὐποιήτων ἐπέβησαν,
κόσμον μέν οἱ πρῶτον ἀπὸ χροὸς εἷλε φαεινόν,
πόρπας τε γναμπτάς θ' ἕλικας κάλυκάς τε καὶ ὅρμους.
λῦσε δέ οἱ ζώνην ἰδὲ εἵματα σιγαλόεντα
ἔκδυε καὶ κατέθηκεν ἐπὶ θρόνου ἀργυροήλου   165
Ἀγχίσης· ὁ δ' ἔπειτα θεῶν ἰότητι καὶ αἴσῃ
ἀθανάτῃ παρέλεκτο θεᾷ βροτός, οὐ σάφα εἰδώς.

Homeric *Hymn to Aphrodite* 161–167

---

[70] Commentators on this phrase should, however, pay more attention to Aristotle's discussion of the phrase 'Who does not know?' at *Rhetorica* 1408a 32–36.
[71] It is perhaps somewhere here that we should seek an explanation for what seems, to me at least, to be another narrative difficulty. Verses 300–58, particularly vv. 315–317, suggest that Ares and Aphrodite are actually asleep during the divine discussion; apparently (v. 299 and perhaps v. 298) they are not, but why do they say nothing? Perhaps because there is nothing they *could* say, or because this is still a summary of a song, or because they were, despite v. 299, asleep (perhaps the laughter woke them up?); if the last (or perhaps a mixture of the second and third explanations), then their escape at v. 360 will also be a site of narrative compression. it may be relevant that in his telling of the tale Lucian's Hermes clears up any narrative uncertainty: not only were the couple not asleep, they were 'on the job' (ἐν ἔργῳ) when the invisible chains closed around them, and Aphrodite had no way to preserve her modesty and Ares begged for release (*Dialogues of the Gods* 21, cf. *On the Dance* 63); Lucian has pictured the scene and come up with a neat little drama with all the fuzzy edges removed. So too, in the *Ars Amatoria* the trapped couple are very awake as the gods enjoy the sight (*Ars am.* 2.582–588). Dawe 1993, 330–331 seeks to identify other phenomena which might suggest that the current poem shows traces of 'two different ways of telling the story'.

> When they had got on to the well-made bed, he first took the shining jewellery from her body, the pins and twisted bracelets and ear-rings and necklaces; Anchises undid her girdle and took off her shining clothes and laid them on a silver-studded chair. Then, by the will of the gods and destiny, he, a mortal, lay with an immortal goddess, not knowing the truth.

The elaborate undressing, together with the phrase λῦσε δέ οἱ ζώνην, suggests a 'wedding night' in which the bride is an inexperienced virgin, as indeed Aphrodite has represented herself to Anchises (v. 133);[72] that in other respects too the meeting of Aphrodite and Anchises looks to aspects of wedding ritual and iconography has of course been noted before.[73] I wonder, then, whether the rapidity of the 'bed scene' in the 'Song of Ares and Aphrodite' marks the divine pair as experienced lovers who have done this before, just as Aphrodite's pleasure at the thought of sleeping with Ares (v. 295) marks her as anything other than a blushing bride.[74] The two great Iliadic scenes of 'seduction' — Paris and Helen in Book 3 and Zeus and Hera in Book 14 — are here, I think, the exceptions which prove the rule. Both of these scenes involve couples who have known each other intimately for many years; in both cases, however, reference is made to the male's desire on the first occasion they made love (3.442–446 in Paris' mouth, 14.295–296 in the mouth of the poet), in part, I would suggest, to excuse the exceptionality of the erotic description. For Ares and Aphrodite, however, this is just one more night in paradise.

If some of this analysis is along the right lines, then we should return to the very opening of the song. We have no good model, I think, for how an epic poet might have handled such an adulterous approach, any more than we know 'in detail' how Anteia sought to seduce Bellerophon (*Iliad* 6.160–161). The reference to Ares' 'many gifts' is, however, very interesting. The phrase occurs elsewhere of 'bride-price' (*Iliad* 11.243–245, and cf. the gifts brought by Helen's suitors in the Hesiodic *Catalogue of Women*), and if the phrase might evoke formal marriage, then its use in a context of adulterous seduction is very pointed (particularly, of course, if we are to remember that, in other traditions, Ares and Aphrodite were actually married).[75] We may perhaps compare Mimnermus' list of the things which really matter, κρυπταδίη φιλότης καὶ μείλιχα δῶρα καὶ εὐνή 'secret love-making and winning gifts and bed' (fr. 1.3), though it has been denied that

---

72 λῦσε ζώνην and similar phrases seem regularly (always?) used of the first sexual intercourse for the female partner. cf. further Bergren 1989, 24.
73 Bergren 1989 is perhaps the fullest discussion.
74 Sowa 1984, 91–92 has some remarks which move in a related direction.
75 cf. West 1966, 415 on Hesiod, *Theogony* 933.

this verse can actually refer to adulterous affairs (cf. Allen *ad loc.*). Alex Garvie would probably command general assent when he observes (1994,] 295, note on v. 269) 'Ares' giving of presents to Aphrodite must precede ἐμίγησαν', but there are no rules to this game, or else there were none until Ovid came along. Ovid advises the man not to tire of *promising* gifts (in return for sex), *hoc opus, hic labor est, primo sine munere iungi* (*Ars am.* 1.453), and he advises the woman only to grant sex when the gifts have actually been handed over (*Ars am.* 3.461–462). We might think that Aphrodite is not one to give her favours only for promises, but two points are worth making as we look ahead to Roman comedy and elegy: the motif of corrupting gifts is clearly in the erotic tradition from a very early date and, perhaps, the arrangement of vv. 268–270 left open to later interpreters the actual chronological relation between 'giving gifts' and 'getting sex'.

Whatever view we might take of individual cases, our sense, and it can probably be no more than that, that such compression is no longer such an issue once the speeches begin (vv. 305ff.) perhaps helps to confirm the preceding analysis; in this song the ἔκπαγλα ἔπη are indeed spelled out for us, and it is in the composition of speeches that we hear the 'true voice' of the poet. If it is Demodocus' skill which gives pleasure to Odysseus and the Phaeacians, then it is in the composition of speeches (something only implicitly present in his two 'Iliadic' songs) that that skill is most on show (cf. the very heavy concentration of speeches in the *Dios apatê* of *Iliad* 14), and here we might be tempted to see an implicit 'poetics' which foreshadows Aristotle's praise for the dramatic quality of Homeric poetry in which character-speech predominates (*Poetics* 1460a 5–11); here too may be where there might be some sense in saying that Demodocus is Homer's self-portrait.

Appendix: Ovid and the 'Song of Ares and Aphrodite'

In *Amores* 3.7 Ovid's impotence disappoints the 'summoned goddess' (cf. v. 2 *uotis saepe petita meis*) who, having finally despaired of the poet's member, 'leaps down' (*desiluit*, v. 81, cf. *Odyssey* 8.361) and seeks her own form of washing to deceive her *ministrae*, whereas Aphrodite's attendants play a full part in the 'Song' of Demodocus:

> Nec mora, desiluit tunica uelata soluta
>   (et decuit nudos proripuisse pedes),
> neue suae possent intactam scire ministrae,
>   dedecus hoc sumpta dissimulauit aqua.

Ovid, *Amores* 3.7.81–84

Without delay, her tunic in disarray, she leapt down (very becoming was the movement of her naked legs), and so that her maids should not know that she remained as before, she disguised this disgrace with the use of water.

The casting of Ovid as an impotent Ares gives particular point to (e.g.) *militia* in v. 68 and *deprensus* in v. 71, but also plays with the fear of impotence as the reward for anyone who slept with a goddess, a motif which we interestingly find in the *Homeric Hymn to Aphrodite*.[76] In the 'Song of Ares and Aphrodite' neither Aphrodite nor Ares finds themselves able 'to move or raise any limb' (v. 298, a verse used in the *Homeric Hymn to Aphrodite* [v. 234] of the aging Tithonus), but — so Ovid presumably saw, perhaps under the influence of the *Hymn to Aphrodite* — it might have been Ares who found this situation particularly embarrassing, whereas Aphrodite's principal emotion might have been disappointment. In vv. 27–35 and 79–80 Ovid also exploits the tradition of erotic 'binding spells' which may not merely make the loved one desire you, but may also cause impotence to one's enemy; in *Amores* 3.7, Ovid thus amusingly 'reads' the main plot of the song 'allegorically', i.e. the δεσμοί which Hephaestus cast upon the couple were actually magical "binding spells" which induced paralysis of all the relevant limbs.[77] In a related form of magic, we have in fact two examples from late antiquity in which wax figurines of a man and a woman in a tight embrace and wrapped in a papyrus on which was written a love-spell binding the woman 'with unbreakable shackles' (δεσμοῖς ἀλύτοις, cf. *Odyssey* 8.274–275) were buried in a pot.[78] Ovid is also perhaps a would-be Ares who is in fact really a Hephaestus. When the latter summons the gods he complains of both his wife and his parents:

Ζεῦ πάτερ ἠδ' ἄλλοι μάκαρες θεοὶ αἰὲν ἐόντες,
δεῦθ', ἵνα ἔργ' ἀγέλαστα καὶ οὐκ ἐπιεικτὰ ἴδησθε,
ὡς ἐμὲ χωλὸν ἐόντα Διὸς θυγάτηρ Ἀφροδίτη
αἰὲν ἀτιμάζει, φιλέει δ' ἀΐδηλον Ἄρηα,
οὕνεχ' ὁ μὲν καλός τε καὶ ἀρτίπος, αὐτὰρ ἐγώ γε   310
ἠπεδανὸς γενόμην· ἀτὰρ οὔ τί μοι αἴτιος ἄλλος,
ἀλλὰ τοκῆε δύω, τὼ μὴ γείνασθαι ὄφελλον.

Homer, *Odyssey* 8.306–312

---

[76] *Hymn. Hom. Ven.* 188–190, with Faulkner 2008, 248–251, Giacomelli 1980, 13–19.
[77] cf. Faraone 1999, 12–14. Verse 10 of Ovid's poem, *lasciuum femori supposuitque femur*, may ape the fevered wishes of the erotic magical papyri which are characterised by the juxtaposition (both verbally and in the imagination of the practitioner) of the body parts of the beloved with his or her matching parts; cf. also Theocritus 2.140 (spoken by someone practising love magic). Stephen Harrison points out that ἔχυντο in v. 297 is a verb that would 'naturally' be used of sleep.
[78] Cf. Brashear 1992, Faraone 1999, 62.

Father Zeus and all you other immortal gods, come here to see bitter and undeserved events, how Aphrodite, Zeus' daughter, ever dishonours me, because I am lame, whereas she loves terrible Ares, because he is handsome and sound of limb, not weak as I was born. there is no one to blame for this, but my two parents — I wish I had never been born!

Just as he has 'read' Aphrodite's final bath as a contraceptive douche,[79] so Ovid has 'read' the contrast between Ares 'sound of foot'[80] and 'weak' Hephaestus in terms of sexual performance. Whether χωλός and/or κυλλός (cf. κυλλοποδίων of Hephaestus) could be used of those suffering from impotence, I do not know, but just as ἀρτι-compounds may suggest 'straight, (?) upright', so χωλός implies 'bent', i.e. an inability to be 'straight'.

As something of a footnote, we might observe that the song of Ares and Aphrodite would have lent itself very well to dramatisation in, or influence upon, one of the many versions of later mime, particularly given the popularity in later times of 'the adultery mime';[81] the famous 'Dionysus and Ariadne' mime from the end of Xenophon's *Symposium* is an obvious *comparandum*, and Lucian preserves an account of how a pantomime in the age of Nero danced the whole story of Ares, Aphrodite and Hephaestus 'without musical accompaniment' (*On the dance* 63). Eustathius refers to the whole episode as τὸ κατὰ τὴν Ἀφροδίτην καὶ τὸν Ἄρην δρᾶμα (*Hom.* 1597.38). Whether or not one understands that Demodocus performs the song while the young man dance around him (vv. 262–264, cf. Athenaeus 1.15d), a matter on which modern scholars have been divided, the juxtaposition of dance and the 'Song of Ares and Aphrodite' in Homer might have been suggestive for later ages. Be that as it may, Jim McKeown has suggested that *Amores* 3.7 (cf. above) might have drawn on mime as one of its sources[82] and, if so, this would certainly sit happily with my account of that poem's debt to *Odyssey* 8.

If the ending of the 'Song of Ares and Aphrodite' evokes material representations of the goddess, then it is perhaps worth pointing out an Ovidian version of this idea, though not in *Amores* 3.7. In *Amores* 1.5 the poet describes a (real or imaginary) afternoon with Corinna. Not only, as is well understood, is her appearance very obviously a divine epiphany, but vv. 17–18

---

[79] Sowa 1984, 93–94 seems to have come closest of modern scholars to such a reading of the Homeric passage (without of course reference to Ovid): 'another possible reason [for the bath] is that Aphrodite has done something impure and must bathe it'.
[80] The evidence for the use of πούς to refer to the penis is much less strong than is often claimed, cf. Bain 1984, 210.
[81] Cf., e.g., Reynolds 1946, McKeown 1979.
[82] McKeown 1979, 79.

> ut stetit ante oculos posito uelamine nostros,
> in toto nusquam corpore menda fuit
>
> Ovid, *Amores* 1.5.17–18

As she stood revealed to my eyes, her robe laid aside, there was no fault anywhere on her body.

evoke the famous story of the young man who made love to the Cnidian Aphrodite (for whom *posito uelamine* has a particular resonance), thus leaving a stain (κηλίς, *menda*) in the marble; the story is told at greatest length in [Lucian's] *Amores*, but it may well be Hellenistic and is cited from a Περὶ Κνίδου of one Posidippus (*FGrHist* 447 = *SH* 706 = Posidippus fr. *147 Austin/Bastianini).[83]

Bibliography

Badino, C. (ed.) 2010. *Filostefano di Cirene. Testimonianze e frammenti*, Milan.
Bain, D. 1984. 'Review of R. Hunter, *Eubulus. The Fragments*, Cambridge, 1983', *JHS* 104, 209–210.
Baumbach, M. 2012. 'Borderline Experiences with Genre: The Homeric *Hymn to Aphrodite* between Epic, Hymn and Epyllic Poetry', in: M. Baumbach/S. Bär, *Brill's Companion to Greek and Latin Epyllion and Its Reception*, Leiden/Boston, 135–148.
Bergren, A.L.T, 1989. 'The Homeric *Hymn to Aphrodite*: Tradition and rhetoric, praise and Blame', *ClAnt* 8, 1–41.
Bömer, F. 1976. *P. Ovidius Naso. Metamorphosen. Kommentar*, 8 Vols., Heidelberg.
Bowie, E.I. 1997. 'The *Theognidea*: a step towards a collection of fragments?', in: G.W. Most (ed.), *Collecting Fragments. Fragmente sammeln*, Göttingen, 53–66.
Burkert, W. 1960. 'Das Lied von Ares und Aphrodite. Zum Verhältnis von *Odyssee* und *Ilias*', *RhM* 103, 130–144.
D' Alessio, G.B. 1997. *Callimaco*, Milan.
Danek, G. 1998. *Epos und Zitat. Studien zu den Quellen der Odyssee*, Vienna.
Dawe, R. 1993. *The Odyssey. Translation and Analysis*, Sussex.
de Jong, I. 2001. *A Narratological Commentary on the Odyssey*, Cambridge.
de Jong, I./Nünlist, R./Bowie, A. (eds.). 2004. *Narrators, Narratees, and Narratives in Ancient Greek Literature*, Leiden/Boston.
Doherty, L.I. 1993. 'Tyro in *Odyssey* 11: Closed and open readings', *Helios* 20, 3–15.
Dräger, P. 1993. *Argo Pasimelousa. Der Argonautenmythos in der griechischen und römischen Literatur*, Vol. 1: *Theos Aitios*, Stuttgart.
Fantuzzi, M./Hunter, R. 2004. *Tradition and Innovation in Hellenistic Poetry*, Cambridge.
Faulkner, A. 2008. *The Homeric Hymn to Aphrodite. Introduction, Text, and Commentary*, Oxford.

---

[83] Cf. Badino 2010, 77–87. Does *cetera quis nescit?* evoke the familiarity of the story?

Finkelberg, M. 1998. *The Birth of Literary Fiction in Ancient Greece*, Oxford.
García, J.F. 2002. 'Symbolic action in the *Homeric Hymns*: The Theme of recognition', *ClAnt* 21, 5–39.
Garvie, A.F. 1994. *Homer. Odyssey. Books VI–VIII*, Cambridge/New York/Melbourne.
Goldhill, S. 1991. *The Poet's Voice. Essays on Poetics and Greek Literature*, Cambridge.
Grandolini, S. 1996. *Canti e aedi nei poemi omerici*, Pisa/Rome.
Graziosi, B./Haubold, J. 2005. *Homer: The Resonance of Epic*, London.
Griffin, J. 1980. *Homer on Life and Death*, Oxford.
Halliwell, S. 2008. *Greek Laughter. A Study of Cultural Psychology from Homer to Early Christianity*, Cambridge.
Harrison, E.I. 1971. 'Odysseus and Demodocus: Homer, *Odyssey* θ 492f.', *Hermes* 99, 378–379.
Hirschberger, M. 2004. *Gynaikōn Katalogos und Megalai Ēhoiai. Ein Kommentar zu den Fragmenten zweier hesiodeischer Epen*, Munich/Leipzig.
Hölscher, U. 1988. *Die Odyssee. Epos zwischen Märchen und Roman*, Munich.
Horsfall, H. 2008. *Virgil, Aeneid 2. A Commentary*, Leiden/Boston.
Hunter, R. 2005. 'Generic Consciousness in the Orphic *Argonautica*?', in: M. Paschalis (ed.), *Roman and Greek Imperial Epic*, Heraklion, 149–168.
Hunter, R. 2008. *On Coming After. Studies in Post-Classical Greek Literature and its Reception*, 2 vols., Berlin/New York.
Hunter, R. 2009. *Critical Moments in Classical Literature. Studies in the Ancient View of Literature and its Uses*, Cambridge.
Hunter, R. 2011. 'The gods of Callimachus', in: B Acosta-Hughes/L. Lehnus/S. Stephens (eds.), *Brill's Companion to Callimachus*, Leiden/Boston, 245–263 [= this volume 157–175].
Irwin, E. 2005. 'Gods among men? The social and political dynamics of the Hesiodic *Catalogue of Women*', in: R. Hunter (ed.), *The Hesiodic Catalogue of Women. Constructions and Reconstructions*, Cambridge, 35–84.
Janka, M. 1977. *Ovid Ars Amatoria. Buch 2. Kommentar*, Heidelberg.
Jones, J.W. 1965. 'Trojan legend: Who is Sinon?', *CJ* 61, 122–128.
Karageorghis, J. 2005. *Kypris. The Aphrodite of Cyprus*, Nicosia.
Krummen, E. 2008. '«Jenen sang seine lieder der ruhmvolle Sänger …». Moderne Erzähltheorie und die Funktion der Sängerszenen in der *Odyssee*', *A&A* 54, 11–41.
Maier, F.G./Karageorghis, V. 1984. *Paphos. History and Archaeology*, Nicosia.
Massimilla, G. 1996. *Callimaco. Aitia. Libri primo e secondo*, Pisa.
Matthews, J. 1996. *Antimachus of Colophon. Text and Commentary*, Leiden/New York/Cologne.
McKeown, J.C. 1979. 'Augustan Elegy and Mime', *PCPhS* 25, 71–84.
Mineur, W.H. 1984. *Callimachus. Hymn to Delos. Introduction and Commentary*, Leiden.
Most, G.W. 1989. 'The Structure and Function of Odysseus' *Apologoi*', *TAPhA* 119, 15–30.
Newton, N. 1987. 'Odysseus and Hephaestus in the *Odyssey*', *CJ* 83, 12–20.
Olson, S.D. 1989. '*Odyssey* 8: Guile, Force, and The Subversive poetics of Desire', *Arethusa* 22, 135–145.
Osborne, R. 2005. 'Ordering women in Hesiod's *Catalogue*', in: R. Hunter (ed.), *The Hesiodic Catalogue of Women. Constructions and Reconstructions*, Cambridge, 5–24.
Paschalis, M. 2005. 'Pandora and the Wooden horse: a reading of Triphiodorus' "Ἅλωσις Ἰλίου', in: M. Paschalis (ed.), *Roman and Greek Imperial Epic*, Heraklion, 91–115.
Petrovic, I./Petrovic, A. 2003. 'Stop and Smell the Statues. Callimachus' Epigram 51 Pf. reconsidered (four times)', *MD* 51, 179–208.
Reynolds, R.W. 1946. 'The adultery Mime', *CQ* 40, 77–84.

Rinon, Y. 2006. 'Mise en abyme and Tragic Signification in the *Odyssey*: The Three Songs of Demodocus', *Mnemosyne* 59, 208–225.

Scodel, R. 2002. *Listening to Homer. Tradition, Narrative, and Audience*, Ann Arbor.

Sowa, C.A. 1984. *Traditional Themes and the Homeric Hymns*, Chicago.

Trypanis, C.A. 1975. *Callimachus Aetia, Iambi, Lyric Poems, Hecale, Minor Epic and Elegiac Fragments and Other Fragments*, London/Cambridge.

Wilamowitz-Moellendorff, U. von. 1895. 'Hephaistos', in: *Nachrichten von der Königlichen Gesellschaft der Wissenschaften zu Göttingen. Philologisch-historische Klasse*, Göttingen, 217–245.

Wölke, H. 1978. *Untersuchungen zur Batrachomyomachie*, Meisenheim am Glan.

3 'Where do I begin?': An Odyssean Narrative Strategy and its Afterlife

If modern narratology has a point of origin, or its own aetiology, then Odysseus' words to Alcinous at the start of Book 9 of the *Odyssey* have as good a claim as any to take pride of place:

σοὶ δ' ἐμὰ κήδεα θυμὸς ἐπετράπετο στονόεντα
εἴρεσθ', ὄφρ' ἔτι μᾶλλον ὀδυρόμενος στεναχίζω.
τί πρῶτόν τοι ἔπειτα, τί δ' ὑστάτιον καταλέξω;
κήδε' ἐπεί μοι πολλὰ δόσαν θεοὶ Οὐρανίωνες. 15
νῦν δ' ὄνομα πρῶτον μυθήσομαι, ὄφρα καὶ ὑμεῖς
εἴδετ', ἐγὼ δ' ἂν ἔπειτα φυγὼν ὕπο νηλεὲς ἦμαρ
ὑμῖν ξεῖνος ἔω καὶ ἀπόπροθι δώματα ναίων.

Od. 9.12–18

But your spirit has determined to ask about my grievous troubles, so that even more must I groan in lamentation. What then shall I recount first, what last? Many are the troubles which the gods of heaven have given me. First, I shall tell you my name, that you may know it, and that, if I escape the day of destruction, I may be your guest-friend, though I live far from here.

Throughout ancient literature, narrators and public speakers return time and again to Odysseus' proem, though very few perhaps with the pointed bitterness of one of the earliest imitators, Gorgias' Palamedes, who begins his *apologia* against Odysseus' accusations with an echo of Odysseus' own *apologos:*

περὶ τούτων δὲ λέγων πόθεν ἄρξωμαι; τί δὲ πρῶτον εἴπω; ποῖ δὲ τῆς ἀπολογίας τράπωμαι;

Gorgias, *Palamedes* 4[1]

In speaking about these things, from what point shall I begin? What am I to say first? To which part of my defence am I to turn?

This chapter will be concerned with a few more examples drawn from the afterlife of Odysseus' opening words, but there is an important point to be made at once.

---

[1] There is uncertainty about the text at the beginning, but it does not affect the point being made. It is a pity that we do not know more of the context of Cephisodorus fr. 13 K-A, cited by Athenaeus at the head of Book 11, ἄγε δή, τίς ἀρχὴ τῶν λόγων γενήσεται;

Although Odysseus' proem sees him behaving very much like a bard or rhapsode[2], his 'rhetorical' question at 9.14 seems at the first level simply to emphasise how much he has suffered, that is, how much material exists for a narration of suffering, rather than to express a quandary about narrative τάξις, 'ordering'; nevertheless, the two issues are here already mutually implicated. One of our most important ancient narratological texts, Aelius Theon's discussion of διήγημα, devotes considerable space to these issues, and when he notes right at the beginning that, under the heading of χρόνος (the fifth of the six elements of 'narrative', which seems as good a translation of διήγημα as any), falls 'what came first, what second and so forth' (78.32–33 Sp.), we should, I think, hear a faded scholastic echo of Odysseus' question. Odysseus' *apologoi* indeed set the ancient narratological agenda. When Theon later warns against saying the same things twice (80.28 Sp.), we should recall the final words of Odysseus' narration:

> τί τοι τάδε μυθολογεύω;   450
> ἤδη γάρ τοι χθιζὸς ἐμυθεόμην ἐνὶ οἴκῳ
> σοί τε καὶ ἰφθίμῃ ἀλόχῳ· ἐχθρὸν δέ μοί ἐστιν
> αὖτις ἀριζήλως εἰρημένα μυθολογεύειν.
>
> *Od.* 12.450–3

Why am I telling these tales? Already yesterday I told them in your house to you and your noble wife. It is hateful to me to tell again tales which have already been very clearly told.

These verses were in fact to embarrass the scholiasts, as 'repetitions' were one of the most familiar features of the Homeric texts, though explanations for Homeric practice were not hard to find (cf. the scholia on 12. 453)[3]. The reason why one did not want to repeat oneself was that such repetition was the enemy of clarity, σαφήνεια (cf. Theon *loc. cit.*, Anon. Seg. 82 Dilts-Kennedy), and it is probably not too rash a speculation that not merely the injunction against repetition, but also Odysseus' emphasis upon not repeating things already described 'very clearly', the standard ancient interpretation of ἀριζήλως,[4] had its effects in

---

[2] Cf., e.g., Kelly 2008a, 178. Odysseus' 'problem' of narrative choice is, of course, also Homer's (cf. below p. 63), one implied by his request to the Muse at 1.10 (where see Di Benedetto's note, 2010, *ad loc.*). For other relevant aspects of the 'Golden Verses' cf. Ford 1999.
[3] Cf. Nünlist 2009, 198 n. 15. Empedocles fr. 25 D-K, 'it is a fair thing to say twice what is necessary', may have looked directly to Odysseus' words; for those in the audience who remembered the Homeric Odysseus' words, Neoptolemus' question to him at Sophocles, *Philoctetes* 1238 (δὶς ταὐτὰ βούλῃ καὶ τρὶς ἀναπολεῖν μ' ἔπη;) will have carried a particular charge.
[4] Cf. *LfgrE* s.v.

the rhetorical schools. Eustathius observes that Odysseus' final words in Book 12 were 'useful (χρήσιμος) for everyone who does not wish to repeat what has already been clearly stated' (*Hom.* 1730.17). Odysseus' strategies thus survived in the way that narrative practice was taught at a very basic level.

It is not of course the opening verses of Book 9 alone which gave the impulse to the very rich ancient discussion of narrative τάξις, of 'natural' and 'anastrophic' narrative, and so forth,[5] but these verses must be set against Odysseus' similar address to Arete in Book 7:

ἀργαλέον, βασίλεια, διηνεκέως ἀγορεῦσαι,
κήδε᾽ ἐπεί μοι πολλὰ δόσαν θεοὶ Οὐρανίωνες·
τοῦτο δέ τοι ἐρέω, ὅ μ᾽ ἀνείρεαι ἠδὲ μεταλλᾷς.

Od. 7.241–243

It is difficult, Queen, to tell in full: many are the troubles which the gods of heaven have given me. But I shall tell you this, what it is you enquire and ask of me.

Odysseus proceeds (famously) to answer the queen's second and third questions, leaving the issue of his name to slip from sight, but as 7.242 is identical to 9.15, it is very hard not to see 7.241 and 9.14 as addressing the same issue, if not in fact pointed variations of each other, and also very hard not to think that that would have been a conclusion drawn in antiquity. Here is not the place for yet another discussion of διηνεκέως and related words in ancient theory and practice,[6] though these passages spoken by Odysseus clearly did play an important role in shaping ancient ideas of narrative. Dionysius of Halicarnassus was not alone in criticising Thucydides' loss of τὸ διηνεκές by choosing to narrate by summers and winters (*Thucydides* 9.4; cf. Theon 80.16–26 Sp.).[7] In Theon's classification, the *Odyssey* (or perhaps rather 'Odysseus' story') belongs, like Thucydides' *Histories*, to those texts which move 'middle–beginning–end' (86.10–19 Sp.), for the poem opens with Odysseus on Calypso's island, and then what

---

5 Cf. Hunter 2009, 52–55, citing earlier bibliography.
6 For some discussion and bibliography cf. Harder 2012, 2.20–21.
7 Cf. Hunter 2009, 55. It is worth noting that this chapter of Dionysius' *Thucydides* both uses τὸ διηνεκές and describes the historian in a way which, to us, seems very 'Callimachean': 'He wished to travel a road which was new and untrodden (ἀτριβής) by others' (9.4). In the extant works Dionysius never mentions Callimachus' poetry, only his scholarly views (cf. Hunter 2011, 233), but I wonder whether the 'Reply to the Telchines' does not lurk somewhere in the background of Dionysius' criticisms of the difficulties which Thucydides put in the way of his readers. It is certainly much easier to assume that Dionysius knew the prologue to the *Aitia* than that he did not.

we call Books 9–12 provide the antecedent events to that, and then the poem continues in orderly, chronological sequence to the end. Theon does not say so, but Odysseus' narrations to the Phaeacians thus both parallel and differ from Homer's own narrations. In Book 7 we get a retelling of Calypso, the storm, Nausicaa etc.,[8] so that we have had 'the present situation' long before the *apologoi* proper get under way in Book 9. As for the *apologoi* themselves, they do indeed proceed διηνεκέως, after Odysseus has implicitly answered Arete's first question and revealed his name and where he comes from; that he will 'begin at the beginning' is clearly advertised by the repetition of Τροίηθεν ~ Ἰλιόθεν across 9.38–39. Odysseus manages in fact both to 'begin at the beginning', a practice which for example the exegetical scholia on *Il.* 11.671–761 deprecate as dull 'in more extended narrations', *and* to begin ἐκ τῶν πρακτικῶν as the same scholia recommend as ἡδύ. We might also note, however, that whereas it might seem obvious to us that this beginning hooks the narration not just to the third song of Demodocus in the previous book, the song of 'Odysseus and the fall of Troy', but also to what we call the *Iliad*, so that this passage might have been very important in the familiar ancient notion of the *Odyssey* as an 'epilogue' to the *Iliad* ('Longinus', *On the Sublime* 9.12),[9] the point does not seem to have been made in antiquity.

The question of 'where to begin?' never left ancient narratives and narrative theory. And rightly so, for very much was and is at stake; Genette's 'unavoidable difficulty of beginning', the 'Where do I begin?' question, is not *just* a (very difficult) question of narrative sequence, though it is that too. Behind each 'beginning' always stands another explanatory narrative with the power to seep out and complicate, if not in fact undermine, the subsequent narrative. Ever since Homer, in other words for the western world 'always', the link between questions of 'origins' and issues of where literary accounts of 'origins', 'histories' in fact, begin has been almost indissoluble. Making choices about one almost always implies a choice about the other. It was of course Thucydides who famously thematised the issue of where something really begins, and who nudges us towards the realisation that 'cause' and 'beginning' are not (always) synonyms; this he does by his distinction (1.23.4–6) between when and how the war 'began', with — on the one hand — its *aitiai* and 'differences' between the sides which explain (ἐξ ὅτου) the war, and — on the other — the 'truest *prophasis*', which was growing Athenian power and the fear provoked by this in Spar-

---

[8] De Jong 2001, 184–186 offers a helpful account of Odysseus' narration in Book 7, though she does not comment on διηνεκέως.
[9] For the ancient testimonia cf. Bühler 1964, 46–47, Mazzucchi 1992 on 'Longinus' *ad loc.*

ta. If we return to Book 1 of the *Iliad*, we will see (because Homer makes us see) that whereas Achilles and Agamemnon quarrel over, and Achilles' wrath can be traced to, Briseis, the truest *prophasis* of the quarrel and the wrath lies far deeper, in the nature of the two men and the system of values in which they find themselves embedded. At the beginning of Greek literature there is a problem of beginnings and causation, or — perhaps more important — a recognition that this *is* a problem.

One ancient narrator who has learned much from Homer's Odysseus is Simaitha in Theocritus' *Second Idyll*.[10] Like Odysseus, she thematises the problem of 'where to begin':

νῦν δὴ μώνα ἐοῖσα πόθεν τὸν ἔρωτα δακρύσω;
ἐκ τίνος ἄρξωμαι; τίς μοι κακὸν ἄγαγε τοῦτο;   65
ἦνθ' ἁ τωὐβούλοιο καναφόρος ἄμμιν Ἀναξώ
ἄλσος ἐς Ἀρτέμιδος, τᾷ δὴ τόκα πολλὰ μὲν ἄλλα
θηρία πομπεύεσκε περισταδόν, ἐν δὲ λέαινα.
φράζεό μευ τὸν ἔρωθ' ὅθεν ἵκετο, πότνα Σελάνα.

Theocritus 2.64–69

Now that I am alone,[11] from what point shall I weep for my love? From what am I to begin? Who brought this evil upon me? Anaxo, Eubulus' daughter, went as a basket-carrier to the grove of Artemis; many wild beasts were paraded that day for the goddess, including a lioness. 'Observe, lady moon, from where my love came.'

For Simaitha, 'where to begin (my narration)?' and 'where did my love begin?' are horribly and mutually implicated, but we have seen that this is in fact a very old problem. It is normally assumed (I think) that τίνος in 2.65 is neuter, and this is probably correct, but it might (also) be masculine/feminine,[12] so that the two halves of 2.65 would then essentially be asking the same question; Simaitha is to prove very adept at shifting the blame to others, whether that be Anaxo, whose cultic role was the occasion of Simaitha's fateful encounter, the Thracian nurse who 'begged and pleaded' with Simaitha to go to see the show (2.70–72),[13]

---

10 Cf. esp. Andrews 1996.
11 That the lover needs solitude in order to pour out his or her woes is a familiar trope of ancient poetry; we think especially of Callimachus' Acontius (fr. 72 Pf. = 171 M) and his many Roman descendants, e.g., Propertius 1.18. The bT-scholium on Homer, *Il.* 1.349 (Achilles going to the seashore), notes that 'Homer perfectly depicts (χαρακτηρίζει) the lover, for they seek empty places so that they might indulge their passion undisturbed by anyone.'
12 Acosta-Hughes 2010, 18 makes a similar point.
13 ὡμάρτευν (2.73) continues the suggestion that it was the nurse, not Simaitha herself, who instigated the excursion.

or, as we shall see, the servant Thestylis herself. On the other hand, the question of 'where it began' is stressed through the refrain, which again allows us to see the implication of narrative order and 'cause': 2.64 'from where (πόθεν) shall I lament my love?' looks like a question about narrative order (which it is), but the refrain 'observe from where (ὅθεν) my love came' shows that more than narrative sequence is at stake here. Where it 'began' is in fact a complex question, as a protracted sequence, given particular emphasis by the refrain, is involved, and more than one answer apparently possible, depending in part on what sense one wants to give to ἔρως.

One answer to the question is indeed offered by the pattern of the refrain, which occurs every five verses, almost always after strong punctuation (even while Delphis is speaking), although there is a powerful exception at 2.105 where the refrain divides Delphis' entrance from Simaitha's physical reaction to it, and I shall return in a moment to this passage. This pattern of repetition leads us therefore to expect a refrain after 2.140, but instead there is at that point a strongly enjambed description of sexual foreplay:

> καὶ ταχὺ χρὼς ἐπὶ χρωτὶ πεπαίνετο, καὶ τὰ πρόσωπα
> θερμότερ' ἦς ἢ πρόσθε, καὶ ἐψιθυρίσδομες ἁδύ.
>
> Theocritus 2.140–141

> Soon body grew warm on body,[14] and our faces were hotter than before, and we whispered sweet things.

ἔρως ('making ἔρως' in fact) has now arrived, and there is no further need for the refrain. Whether we are to understand that Simaitha's memories of that afternoon are now so powerful that, all formal restraint abandoned, she quite forgets to put in the regular refrain is probably something upon which we can only speculate.

Other answers to Simaitha's question are also possible. Delphis, of course, is Simaitha's 'love', and Simaitha's first sight of him, and ours, might be thought to mark precisely 'the coming of love':

> ἤδη δ' εὖσα μέσαν κατ' ἀμαξιτόν, ᾇ τὰ Λύκωνος,
> εἶδον Δέλφιν ὁμοῦ τε καὶ Εὐδάμιππον ἰόντας·
> τοῖς δ' ἦς ξανθοτέρα μὲν ἐλιχρύσοιο γενειάς,
> στήθεα δὲ στίλβοντα πολὺ πλέον ἢ τύ, Σελάνα,
> ὡς ἀπὸ γυμνασίοιο καλὸν πόνον ἄρτι λιπόντων.   80

---

14 Lentini 2012, 188–190 suggests that the verb πεπαίνετο brings with it negative associations from related ideas in Archilochus.

φράζεό μευ τὸν ἔρωθ' ὅθεν ἵκετο, πότνα Σελάνα.
χὼς ἴδον, ὣς ἐμάνην, ὥς μοι πυρὶ θυμὸς ἰάφθη
δειλαίας, τὸ δὲ κάλλος ἐτάκετο.

Theocritus 2.76–83

When I was already halfway along the path, where is Lycon's, I saw Delphis, and with him Eudamippus, coming along. Their beards were more golden than helichryse, and their breasts gleamed far more brightly than you, Moon, as they had just left the fair work of the gymnasium.

'Observe, lady moon, from where my love came'.

I saw, I went mad, my poor heart was pierced by flame, and my beauty wasted away.

Both the reworking of Sappho fr. 31 V[15] and the echo of *Il.* 14.293–294 (the effect on Zeus of the arrival of Hera, in full possession of the powers of Aphrodite) show that the 'burning disease' of ἔρως has now arrived; we even know 'from where' ἔρως/Delphis has come, namely 'from the gymnasium'.

We have not yet, however, exhausted the potential answers to the question of the origin of Simaitha's love. The answer to the question 'Who brought this evil upon me?' (2.65) is, quite literally, Thestylis (cf. 2.102 ἄγαγε τὸν λιπαρόχρων),[16] and Delphis' arrival at Simaitha's house (2.103–110) might well be thought to be yet another ἀρχὴ ἔρωτος.

This second reworking of Sappho fr. 31 V puts Simaitha's two Sapphic moments in counterpoise and suggests that *both* are originary moments of ἔρως: Simaitha knows what this Sapphic poem designates, and uses it to punctuate her story.

It is not just τάξις, both as the order in which one tells things and the relation between that order and the order in which events actually occurred, which Odysseus' narration puts on the narratological agenda. He announces the subject of the narration which he begins in Book 9 as νόστον ἐμὸν πολυκηδέα (9.37), but it is the κήδεα and the κακά which have already been repeatedly stressed (7.212–14, 242, 9.12–13). First-person narration is almost necessarily a tale of woe, as Glenn Most argued in a well-known discussion of Achilles Tatius,[17] but there are (again) interesting survivals of relevant ancient discussion. The scholia on *Od.* 9.12 and 14 note that this stress on his 'troubles' creates 'an-

---

15 I discuss the Sapphic echoes in Theocritus 2, together with relevant bibliography, in Hunter 2019.
16 Cf. Segal 1985, 105.
17 Most 1989; for some qualifications to Most's discussion cf. Repath 2005.

ticipation' in the listeners, just as the exegetical scholia on the opening of the *Iliad* tell us that οἱ περὶ Ζηνόδοτον offered as one solution to the famous ζήτημα of why Homer began from such an ill-omened word as μῆνις that this would 'rouse the hearers' minds and make them more attentive' (bT-scholia on 1.1b);[18] this explanation also appears, though without the reference to Zenodotus, in the A and D scholia. It is, however, on another scholium on *Il.* 1.1 that I wish to dwell for a moment. Another answer to this ζήτημα which is shared by the A and D scholia connects this opening with our psychological well-being; I quote part of the relevant A-scholium:

διὰ δύο ταῦτα, πρῶτον μέν, ἵν' ἐκ τοῦ πάθους ἀποκαταρρεύσῃ τὸ τοιοῦτο μόριον τῆς ψυχῆς καὶ προσεκτικωτέρους τοὺς ἀκροατὰς ἐπὶ τοῦ μεγέθους ποιήσῃ καὶ προεθίσῃ φέρειν γενναίως ἡμᾶς τὰ πάθη, μέλλων πολέμους ἀπαγγέλλειν· δεύτερον δέ, ἵνα τὰ ἐγκώμια τῶν Ἑλλήνων πιθανώτερα ποιήσῃ... ἤρξατο μὲν ἀπὸ μήνιδος, ἐπείπερ αὕτη τοῖς πρακτικοῖς ὑπόθεσις γέγονεν· ἄλλως τε καὶ τραγῳδίαις τραγικὸν ἐξεῦρε προοίμιον· καὶ γὰρ προσεκτικοὺς ἡμᾶς ἡ τῶν ἀτυχημάτων διήγησις ἐργάζεται, καὶ ὡς ἄριστος ἰατρὸς πρῶτον ἀναστέλλων τὰ νοσήματα τῆς ψυχῆς ὕστερον τὴν ἴασιν ἐπάγει. Ἑλληνικὸν δὲ τὸ πρὸς τέλει τὰς ἡδονὰς ἐπάγειν.

A-scholium, *Il.* 1.1

[Homer begins with μῆνις] for two reasons, first so that the relevant part of the soul might flow clear (ἀποκαταρρεύσῃ) of this passion and so that he could make his listeners more attentive to the scale and accustom us to bear sufferings nobly. Secondly, to make the encomia of the Greeks more persuasive... He began from wrath, since this was the subject of the events to be narrated. Moreover, for tragedies he found a tragic *prooimion*. The narration of misfortunes makes us attentive, and like an excellent doctor Homer first stirs up the diseases of the soul and then applies the remedy;[19] bringing on pleasure at the end is characteristically Greek.

There is much here which resonates with ancient rhetorical teaching on the function of prooemia,[20] but two related aspects draw attention to themselves in the present context. The translation and interpretation of the first sentence pose difficulties, but one thing at least is clear, and becomes even clearer when we note that the D-scholia read ἀποκαθαρεύσῃ for ἀποκαταρρεύσῃ. We have in this scholium, as has been recognized,[21] an echo at an unknown number of removes

---

18 Cf. Nünlist 2009, 137–138.
19 For this image cf. Nünlist 2009, 143.
20 Cf., e.g., *Anon. Seg.* 5 Dilts/Kennedy: 'A prooemion is defined as a speech which stirs or calms (κινητικὸς ἢ θεραπευτικός) the hearer's passions.' Prooemia are, of course, also crucially concerned with making the hearers attentive.
21 Cf., e.g., N.J. Richardson 1980, 274.

of the Aristotelian theory of *katharsis*, understood as a medical process in which emotional disturbances are aroused in order to be cleansed away. The Homeric scholia are very fond of asserting what is 'Greek' and what 'barbarian', words which can sometimes seem little more than general terms of approbation and disapprobation, but the claim that a particular structuring of narrative is 'Greek' is of considerable interest. Of course, one could argue about just what kind of 'final pleasures' the *Iliad* itself actually brings (cf. especially bT-scholia on 24.776), but the scholia on 1.1 are presumably at one level assuring us that, however grim the consequences of Achilles' wrath may be, things will turn out well for the Greeks in the end;[22] more generally, however, we are not too far from ideas of 'the happy end', which Aristotle famously associated with the 'pleasure' appropriate to comedy (*Poetics* 1453a35–37). Glenn Most noted that 'a Greek erotic romance without a happy ending is not a Greek erotic romance',[23] and we ought to wonder how much emphasis should be given to the word 'Greek' in that sentence.

A sub-Aristotelian reading of the *Odyssey* would certainly be possible (we might even wish to associate the 'pleasures at the end' in the *Iliad* scholium cited above with the Alexandrian τέλος (or πέρας) of the *Odyssey* at 23.296), but it is another text to which I would like to draw attention in this connection. One of the most famous passages in the Greek novels is Chariton's declaration at the head of his last book:

> νομίζω δὲ καὶ τὸ τελευταῖον τοῦτο σύγγραμμα τοῖς ἀναγινώσκουσιν ἥδιστον γενήσεσθαι· καθάρσιον γάρ ἐστι τῶν ἐν τοῖς πρώτοις σκυθρωπῶν. οὐκέτι λῃστεία καὶ δουλεία καὶ δίκη καὶ μάχη καὶ ἀποκαρτέρησις καὶ πόλεμος καὶ ἅλωσις, ἀλλὰ ἔρωτες δίκαιοι ἐν τούτῳ <καὶ> νόμιμοι γάμοι.
>
> Chariton, *Callirhoe* 8.1.4
>
> And I think that this book will be the sweetest for my readers, for it cleans away the grim events of the earlier books. No longer will there be piracy and slavery and law-cases and battles and suicide and war and capturing, but honourable love and lawful marriage.

This passage and its relation to Aristotelian *katharsis* has been very much discussed, most recently and in greatest depth by Stefan Tilg,[24] though it has not,

---

22 I am grateful to Ruth Scodel for focusing my attention on this explanation. We might also consider whether the scholia imply that 'barbarians' are given over *entirely* to pleasure, whereas the pattern of light emerging from darkness is a 'Greek' one.
23 Most 1989, 118.
24 Cf. Tilg 2010, 130–137, Whitmarsh 2011, 182–183. Heath 2011, 107 is 'not convinced that καθάρσιον in [Chariton] 8.1.4 is an Aristotelian allusion'.

to my knowledge, been brought together with the scholarship on the opening of the *Iliad* which is visible in the scholium to 1.1 (above). It is hard to believe on general grounds, however, that Chariton was not familiar with the kind of learning on show in these Homeric scholia, and in any case he very obviously fashions his novel as a new 'Homer' (however we wish to define the relationship) and, moreover, he too is fond of asserting what is 'Greek' and what 'barbarian'. I suggest, then, that, however we understand this claim at the head of Book 8, Chariton has here adapted a scholastic observation about the emotional and narrative structure of the *Iliad*, one associated with the opening of the poem, and placed it rather at the head of his last book. It is Homeric literary virtues that he is (again) here claiming for his work; Chariton's creation of a 'prose epic' uses not just Homer, but also the Homeric critical tradition, even if less elaborately than Heliodorus was to do.

In narrative technique, as in so much else, it was of course the ancient novel which most self-consciously presented itself as the heir to the heritage of the *Odyssey*, and it is indeed Heliodorus' *Aethiopica* which takes pride of place. Heliodorus' most famous narrator is the wise Egyptian Calasiris, and he certainly has picked up the lesson of Odysseus and his commentators that promise of a narrative of woe will make the audience attentive and keen to listen. When Cnemon first meets him by the banks of the Nile and asks him why, though an Egyptian, he is wearing Greek dress, the first word of Calasiris' reply is enough to ensnare his listener: δυστυχήματα ... (2.21.4); we will not be surprised when Cnemon then immediately asks 'to learn' what Calasiris' συμφοραί have been, and Calasiris instantly launches into full Odyssean mode, Ἰλιόθεν με φέρεις κτλ, 'you are carrying me from Troy' (cf. *Od.* 9.39). Much has been written about Calasiris' mode of narration and its contrast with that of Cnemon,[25] but there is perhaps more to be teased out about Calasiris' self-construction as a 'Homeric' character (in more than one sense) and narrator, and this will be my final example of the afterlife of Odyssean narrative practice.

As is well understood, Calasiris' first meeting with Cnemon pointedly replays and varies Cnemon's earlier introduction of himself to Charicleia and Theagenes; for ease of reference I set the two passages out:

"εἰ δέ μοι μέλει τῶν ὑμετέρων οὐκ ἄξιον ὑμῖν θαυμάζειν, τύχης τε γάρ μοι τῆς αὐτῆς ἐοίκατε κοινωνεῖν καὶ ἅμα Ἕλληνας ὄντας οἰκτείρω καὶ αὐτὸς Ἕλλην γεγονώς." "'Ἕλλην; ὢ θεοί" ἐπεβόησαν ὑφ' ἡδονῆς ἅμα οἱ ξένοι. "'Ἕλλην ὡς ἀληθῶς τὸ γένος καὶ τὴν φωνήν· τάχα τις ἔσται τῶν κακῶν ἀνάπνευσις." "ἀλλὰ τίνα σε χρὴ καλεῖν;" ἔφη ὁ Θεαγένης. ὁ δὲ "Κνήμωνα." "πόθεν δὲ γνωρίζειν;" "Ἀθηναῖον." "τύχῃ τίνι κεχρημένον;" "Παῦε" ἔφη· "τί ταῦτα

---

25 Cf. esp. Winkler 1982 (a seminal article); Hunter 1998b (citing earlier bibliography).

κινεῖς κἀναμοχλεύεις; τοῦτο δὴ τὸ τῶν τραγῳδῶν. οὐκ ἐν καιρῷ γένοιτ' ἂν ἐπεισόδιον ὑμῖν τῶν ὑμετέρων τἀμὰ ἐπεισφέρειν κακά· καὶ ἅμα οὐδ' ἂν ἐπαρκέσειε τὸ λειπόμενον πρὸς τὸ διήγημα τῆς νυκτὸς ὕπνου καὶ ταῦτα δεομένοις ὑμῖν ἀπὸ πολλῶν τῶν πόνων καὶ ἀναπαύσεως."

Heliodorus, *Aethiopica* 1.8.6–7

'You should not be amazed at the fact that I am concerned for you, for you seem to share the same misfortune as myself and, since you are Greeks, I pity you as I myself was born a Greek.' 'A Greek! O gods!' shouted the strangers in joy. 'Truly a Greek in race and voice! Perhaps there will be some break from our troubles.' 'What is your name?' asked Theagenes. 'Cnemon' said the other. 'And where do you come from?' 'I am Athenian.' 'What is your story?' 'Stop!' he said, 'Why do you stir up and unbolt these things?, as the tragedians say [cf. Eur. *Med.* 1317]. This is not the time to bring on my misfortunes as a new scene for your own. Besides, what is left of the night would not be enough for this narration, particularly when you need sleep and rest after your many sufferings.'

ὁ Κνήμων... κατὰ πρόσωπον ὑπαντιάσας πρῶτα μὲν χαίρειν ἐκέλευε. τοῦ δὲ οὐ δύνασθαι φήσαντος, ἐπειδὴ μὴ οὕτω συμβαίνειν αὐτῷ παρὰ τῆς τύχης, θαυμάσας ὁ Κνήμων "Ἕλλην δὲ" εἶπεν "ὁ ξένος;" "οὐχ Ἕλλην" εἶπεν "ἀλλ' ἐντεῦθεν Αἰγύπτιος." "πόθεν οὖν ἑλληνίζεις τὴν στολήν;" "δυστυχήματα" ἔφη "τὸ λαμπρόν με τοῦτο σχῆμα μετημφίασε." τοῦ δὲ Κνήμωνος εἰ φαιδρύνεταί τις ἐπὶ συμφοραῖς θαυμάζοντος καὶ ταύτας μαθεῖν ἀξιοῦντος "Ἰλιόθεν με φέρεις" ἀπεκρίνατο ὁ πρεσβύτης "καὶ σμῆνος κακῶν καὶ τὸν ἐκ τούτων βόμβον ἄπειρον ἐπὶ σεαυτὸν κινεῖς. ἀλλὰ ποῖ δὴ πορεύῃ καὶ πόθεν, ὦ νεανία; πῶς δὲ τὴν φωνὴν Ἕλλην ἐν Αἰγύπτῳ;" "γελοῖον" ἔφη ὁ Κνήμων· "τῶν γὰρ κατὰ σεαυτὸν οὐδὲν ἐκδιδάξας, πρότερος καὶ ταῦτα ἐρωτηθείς, τῶν ἐμῶν γνῶσιν ἐπιζητεῖς."

Heliodorus, *Aethiopica* 2.21.3–5

Cnemon ... stood facing [the mysterious old man] and first of all bade him good day. When the other said that he could not have a good day, since this was not what fate had allotted him, Cnemon was amazed and said, 'The stranger is a Greek!' 'Not a Greek', he replied, 'but an Egyptian from hereabouts.' 'Why then is your dress Greek?' 'Misfortunes have given me this bright change of clothing' was the reply. Cnemon was amazed that anyone would dress brightly as a result of disasters and asked to learn about them. 'You are carrying me from Troy' answered the old man [cf. *Od.* 9.39], 'and you are stirring up for yourself a swarm of ills and an endless buzzing from them. But where are you heading and where do you come from, young man? Why is a Greek-speaker in Egypt?' 'This is absurd' replied Cnemon. 'You have given me no information about your own story, though I indeed asked you first, and you want information about mine!'

Alongside the obvious similarities, the most striking difference is that whereas Cnemon moves in the world of Attic drama (cf. also 2.23.5) and sees his story as a 'tragedy' — indeed he carries suitable citations around with him — Calasiris presents himself from the beginning as an epic character, namely Odysseus.[26] These are, of course, not by any means absolutely exclusive positions: thus, for example, Cnemon's subsequent attempt (real or half-hearted?) to defer his narration by pleading the need for sleep clearly evokes Odysseus' words to Alcinous at *Od.* 11.377–385. Moreover, what most holds these two passages together is the power of story. Cnemon claims that Charicleia and Theagenes need ἀπὸ πολλῶν τῶν πόνων... ἀνάπαυσις, whereas what they want is the virtually synonymous τῶν κακῶν ἀνάπνευσις; it is not sleep, but stories which hold out the hope for both kinds of relief, as is made immediately clear when the narrator tells us that Charicleia and Theagenes thought that 'listening to a story like their own would be the greatest consolation' (1.8.9).[27]

As for Calasiris, his opening Odyssean move is followed by a not untypical (as we come to learn) piece of one-upmanship: he picks up a verb, κινεῖς, from the verse of Euripides' *Medea* which Cnemon had cited in the earlier scene (although, of course, 'in reality' Calasiris did not hear Cnemon speak) and goes one better with his extended insect metaphor, σμῆνος... βόμβον ἄπειρον, which seems to amplify and 'exhaust' a metaphor already familiar in the narrative tradition (cf. Ach. Tat. 1.2.2). Calasiris, like Odysseus, is indeed a highly competitive narrator. These scenes in Book 2 have recently been enlighteningly discussed by Tim Whitmarsh,[28] so I will focus merely on what seems relevant to the present discussion.

With an elegant reworking of the *locus amoenus* of Plato's *Phaedrus*,[29] Calasiris leads Cnemon off to Nausicles' house, where their host's daughter plays the Nausicaa role to perfection (2.22.1–2). When Cnemon enquires about Nausicles, Calasiris describes him as a man resembling both himself and Odysseus:

"οὐκ εἰς Διός" ἔφη, "ἀλλ᾽ εἰς ἀνδρὸς Δία τὸν ξένιον καὶ ἱκέσιον ἀκριβοῦντος. βίος γάρ, ὦ παῖ, κἀκείνῳ πλάνος καὶ ἔμπορος καὶ πολλαὶ μὲν πόλεις πολλῶν δὲ ἀνθρώπων ἤθη τε καὶ νοῦς εἰς πεῖραν ἥκουσιν ὅθεν, ὡς τὸ εἰκός, ἄλλους τε κἀμὲ οὐ πρὸ πολλῶν τῶνδε ἡμερῶν ἀλύοντα καὶ πλανώμενον ὁμωρόφιον ἐποιήσατο."

Heliodorus, *Aethiopica* 2.22.3

'It is not to Zeus' house [that we are coming],' he said 'but to the house of a man who is very careful about Zeus, the protector of guests and suppliants. His life too, my child, is one of wandering and trade, and he has experience of many cities and the customs and

---

26 Cf., e.g., Paulsen 1992, 142–150; Elmer 2008, 414–418. Montiglio 2013, 148–152 sees the contrast rather as one between comedy (Cnemon) and epic-tragedy (Calasiris).
27 The hope is not, in fact, really fulfilled; cf. 5.33.4 with Hunter 1998b, 42.
28 Whitmarsh 2011, 232–238.
29 Cf. Hunter 2012, 13–14.

minds of many men; this is probably the reason why he has received others also into his house and not many days ago he took me in when I was wandering in despair.'

A very obvious reworking of the opening of the *Odyssey*[30] elegantly projects on to Nausicles what is, more importantly, Calasiris' self-image, but this passage may also introduce us to one of the most striking features of Calasiris' Odyssean persona. Not only is he himself fashioned after the epic hero, but he has also fully internalised Homeric lore and scholarship. Just as he is able later to expound Homer's Egyptian origin and the etymology of his name, along with sundry Homeric verses, here too it is tempting to think that his rewriting of the Odyssean verses allows both famous variant readings in *Od.* 1.3, νόον and the Zenodotean νόμον, to resonate alongside πόλεις, which appears in place of the Homeric ἄστεα; both the elegance and the scholarship were, however, probably lost on Cnemon. Something similar happens almost immediately after at 2.22.5. Calasiris defers his narration (again) by appealing to the needs of the stomach, 'which Homer wonderfully (θαυμασίως) called cursed (οὐλομένη)'. The Homeric passages in question are *Od.* 15.344 and 17.286–287, but the really important 'belly passage' is of course 7.215–221, where Odysseus defers telling of his κακά because he has to eat, but where the stomach is not in fact called οὐλομένη; like the good scholar, Calasiris groups parallel passages together and uses them to expound each other. Moreover, the adjective of approbation that he uses for Homer, θαυμασίως, is one very familiar from the scholia[31] and from Eustathius' commentaries; this is Calasiris in full scholarly mode.

In the scene which follows, Calasiris resumes his Odyssean character: weeping (2.23.1), deferring narration (2.23.6, 'I'll tell you, but… how I wish the excellent Nausicles were here: so often he has begged me to be initiated into my story but I have put him off with various excuses').[32] After Calasiris has explained something of Nausicles' current preoccupations, Cnemon will take no more and after another image drawn from the theatre (2.24.4) insists that Calasiris now tell his story:[33]

"εὕρηκα γάρ σε κατὰ τὸν Πρωτέα τὸν Φάριον, οὐ κατ' αὐτὸν τρεπόμενον εἰς ψευδομένην καὶ ῥέουσαν ὄψιν ἀλλά με παραφέρειν πειρώμενον." "μανθάνοις ἄν" ἔφη ὁ πρεσβύτης·

---

30 Noted by, e.g., Elmer 2008, 414.
31 Cf. e.g., the exegetical scholia on *Il.* 4.302, 7.128a, 8.385, 9.134b etc.; Nünlist 2009, 145.
32 Nausicles here is cast as an Alcinous, appropriately enough for a man whose daughter has just played the role of a 'Nausicaa'.
33 On the theatrical language of 2.24.4 cf. Telò 1999, 82–85.

"διηγήσομαι δέ σοι τἀμαυτοῦ πρότερον ἐπιτεμών, οὐ σοφιστεύων ὡς αὐτὸς οἴει τὴν ἀφήγησιν ἀλλ' εὔτακτόν σοι καὶ προσεχῆ τῶν ἑξῆς παρασκευάζων τὴν ἀκρόασιν."

Heliodorus, *Aethiopica* 2.24.4–5

'You [i.e. Calasiris] are like Proteus of Pharos, not that like him you turn into a deceptive and fluid vision, but because you try to lead me off the path.'
'You will learn the story', said the old man. 'First, however, I will give you a brief account of myself, not playing the sophist with the story, as you believe, but offering you an account which shows good order and is connected to what follows.'[34]

Cnemon's comparison of Calasiris to Proteus is, at one level, an acknowledgement that Cnemon is here playing the role of Menelaus in *Odyssey* 4, always an Odysseus-light. His claim that Calasiris seeks 'to lead him off the path' (παραφέρειν) must in fact, not merely be part of Calasiris' 'wandering' mode of speech, discussed by Tim Whitmarsh, but specifically be an echo of Menelaus' remonstrance to Proteus, when the old trickster has asked him who helped him and what he wants:

οἶσθα, γέρον· τί με ταῦτα παρατροπέων ἐρεείνεις;

Homer, *Odyssey* 4.465

You know this, old man. Why do you ask me this to turn me off the track?

παρατροπέων is a Homeric *hapax*; one of Eustathius' glosses on it, παραπλανῶν (*Hom.* 1505.31), is a clear synonym of Cnemon's παραφέρειν. Moreover, Cnemon's statement also suggests the link between the 'turnings' of *metamorphosis* and the turnings of speech which mark Calasiris (yet again) as an Odysseus: ψευδομένην and ῥέουσαν are of course pointed references to Calasiris' slipperiness, and to the fact that one of the sea-god's transformations in the *Odyssey* is into ὑγρὸν ὕδωρ (4.458), but they are also words which are readily applied to speech.

Cnemon's comparison of Calasiris to Proteus finds a striking parallel in Socrates' reproof to Ion at the end of Plato's work named after the rhapsode: there Socrates accuses Ion of 'turning this way and that, like the ever-changing (παντοδαπός) Proteus, until finally you escape me' (Plato, *Ion* 541e). The use of a Homeric character is very appropriate for Ion the rhapsode, but the Proteus analogy may have had quite wide currency in poetic and rhetorical discussion

---

[34] The final phrase has been variously understood, but the meaning seems to be as translated; it is, I think, misrepresented by Whitmarsh 2011, 235.

of the late fifth and early fourth century. In particular, it has been noted[35] that Cnemon's comparison may be connected to Socrates' description of the brother sophists in the *Euthydemus*:

"ἀλλ' οὐκ ἐθέλετον ἡμῖν ἐπιδείξασθαι σπουδάζοντε, ἀλλὰ τὸν Πρωτέα μιμεῖσθον τὸν Αἰγύπτιον σοφιστὴν γοητεύοντε ἡμᾶς. ἡμεῖς οὖν τὸν Μενέλαον μιμώμεθα, καὶ μὴ ἀφιώμεθα τοῖν ἀνδροῖν ἕως ἂν ἡμῖν ἐκφανῆτον ἐφ' ᾧ αὐτὼ σπουδάζετον·"

Plato, *Euthydemus* 288b7–c2

'They do not want to give us a demonstration of their seriousness, but they imitate the Egyptian sophist Proteus and seek to bamboozle us. Therefore let us imitate Menelaus and not let these men go until they reveal to us what it is that they are serious about.'

Some connection between the two passages is indeed likely, but it is important to try to be as specific as possible about this: would we in fact connect the two passages, rather than, say, Heliodorus 2.24.4–5 and *Ion* 541e, if it were not for Calasiris' σοφιστεύων? Perhaps. Cnemon means that Calasiris keeps slipping away and 'deviating' from the story he has been asked to tell, just as Plato's sophists, like Ion, will never properly confront Socrates' questions;[36] 'Proteus of Pharos' in Cnemon's accusation could be a variation of 'the Egyptian sophist Proteus', but it hardly demands to be read as such. If there is a Platonic background to Cnemon's question, we might well have been tempted to seek it rather in the discussion in *Republic* 2 of why stories of shape-changing gods such as Proteus are not to be admitted into the ideal city (380d–383c). Such a god, a nightmarish concept for a Plato, would be a γόης, who deceives and falsifies (ψεύδεσθαι, 382a–c); ὄψις in Cnemon's question might pick up φαντάζεσθαι (380d2) and φάντασμα (382a2) in the discussion in the *Republic*, and we can see from the scholia on *Od.* 4.456 that the view that Proteus did not really turn into animals, fire, water etc., but that these were φαντασίαι, became in fact standard grammatical lore.[37] It seems likely, then, that Calasiris, ever the competitive narrator, tops Cnemon's explicit allusion to the Homeric Proteus with a glance at another classical text which used this figure (the *Euthydemus*), but does nothing so vulgar as give the allusion away straightforwardly; 'as you believe' is (again) an elegant way of including the unknowing Cnemon in the sophistication of his banter.

---

35 Cf., e.g., Paulsen 1992, 149–150.
36 Cf. Hopkinson 1994, 10–11.
37 Cf. also Dionysius of Halicarnassus, *Demosthenes* 8.2 cited below.

There is here a further dimension also, of course. Cnemon's language of the 'turning' Proteus reminds us that the Odyssean epithet *par excellence* πολύτροπος is applied to Proteus himself in the proem of Nonnus' *Dionysiaca* (1.14); the scholia on *Od.* 4.456 which describe Proteus show how easy the connection is: τρέπεται εἰς πολλά... καὶ δι' ἄλλων ποικίλων τρόπων. Eustathius tells us that the name 'Proteus' is applied to πολύτροποι καὶ κακοήθεις πολυειδῶς ἄνθρωποι (*Hom.* 1503.36–7), and the connection between Proteus and linguistic facility and 'fluidity of speech' seems clear enough.[38] We would dearly like to know more of the 'On Proteus' of Antisthenes, whose famous discussion of πολύτροπος associates that word with the tropes of language.[39] So too, the contrast which Hippias draws in the Platonic *Hippias Minor* between the ἁπλοῦς Achilles and the πολύτροπος Odysseus comes very close to the language of the discussion of shape-changing gods in the *Republic*. Dionysius of Halicarnassus, moreover, compares Demosthenes' achievement in building his style from all the opposed possibilities of style to the shiftings of Proteus:

...οὐδὲν διαλλάττουσαν τοῦ μεμυθευμένου παρὰ τοῖς ἀρχαίοις ποιηταῖς Πρωτέως, ὃς ἅπασαν ἰδέαν μορφῆς ἀμογητὶ μετελάμβανεν, εἴτε θεὸς ἢ δαίμων τις ἐκεῖνος ἄρα ἦν παρακρουόμενος ὄψεις τὰς ἀνθρωπίνας εἴτε διαλέκτου ποικίλον τι χρῆμα ἐν ἀνδρὶ σοφῷ, πάσης ἀπατηλὸν ἀκοῆς, ὃ μᾶλλον ἄν τις εἰκάσειεν, ἐπειδὴ ταπεινὰς καὶ ἀσχήμονας ὄψεις οὔτε θεοῖς οὔτε δαίμοσι προσάπτειν ὅσιον.

Dionysius of Halicarnassus, *Demosthenes* 8.2

[Demosthenes'] style is no different from Proteus in the myths of the old poets, who easily assumed every kind of shape, whether he was a god or a *daimōn*, able to deceive men's vision, or some shifting marvel of language in a clever man, able to deceive every ear. This last is the most probable, as it is impious to attribute mean and ugly appearances to gods or *daimones*.

For much of Greek tradition διαλέκτου ποικίλον τι χρῆμα ἐν ἀνδρὶ σοφῷ would evoke Odysseus before it evoked anyone else. In calling Calasiris a Proteus, then, Cnemon reinforces (unknowingly) the presentation and self-presentation of the Egyptian wise man as an Odysseus figure.[40]

The association between Proteus and Odysseus is one fashioned after the *Odyssey* itself, for in that poem Proteus' nearest analogue is Teiresias, whom

---

38 Cf., e.g., Buffière 1956, 353.
39 N.J. Richardson 1975, 80 attractively suggests that Antisthenes had indeed compared Odysseus and Proteus.
40 At Max. Tyr. 1.1 Proteus is described as πολύμορφός τις καὶ παντοδαπὸς τὴν φύσιν (cf. Plato, *Ion* 541e above), and Odysseus is also there not far away, cf. Montiglio 2011, 117–119.

Odysseus consults in the underworld, with Menelaus playing the Odysseus role in Book 4. We have, however, already seen how Calasiris incorporates 'the Homeric interpretative tradition' as well as being a 'Homeric' character himself, and this exchange with Cnemon, whatever role Plato plays within it, fits this pattern. If the comparison to Proteus plays to Calasiris as Odysseus, his paraded concern to offer 'an account which shows good order (εὔτακτον) and is connected to what follows (προσεχῆ τῶν ἐξῆς)' is indeed, as Winkler calls it, a 'pose',[41] but it is the pose of the scholar, passing judgement on narrative structure. The concern of, say, Dionysius of Halicarnassus and the scholiasts with narrative τάξις is, as I have already noted, one of the most familiar themes of ancient criticism. Eustathius, for whom εὔτακτον is a favourite form of approbation, observes in his note on *Od.* 9.37, the start of Odysseus' narration: κατὰ φύσιν τάττει τὰ πράγματα· καὶ εὐτάκτως προιὼν φησὶν κτλ, 'he arranges the events in their natural order; proceeding in an orderly sequence, he says... '. Calasiris will, then tell his story, both as Homer's Odysseus and as the Odysseus of the critical tradition; or will he?

Finally, the temptation here to see the author of the *Aethiopica* gently reminding us of his constant presence is, I think, hard to resist; his character's concern with narrative order and persistent evocation of the *Odyssey*, itself the model for the ordering of the *Aethiopica*, must pick up the 'special relationship' which antiquity saw between Odysseus and his creator. It is not just that when, at the end of Book 12, Odysseus tells Alcinous that he does not like to repeat himself, Eustathius observes that this is really Homer speaking to the listener to remind him that 'what follows the events just narrated has already been told' (*Hom.* 1730.15). Ancient readers saw a very special relationship of closeness or identity between Homer and Odysseus as narrators; Strabo's account of Homer's 'untruths' almost makes the point explicitly (1.2.9) and very similar traditions lie behind Horace in the *Ars Poetica*:

> semper ad euentum festinat et in medias res
> non secus ac notas auditorem rapit, et quae
> desperat tractata nitescere posse relinquit,   150
> atque ita mentitur, sic ueris falsa remiscet,
> primo ne medium, medio ne discrepet imum.
>
> Horace, *Ars Poetica* 148–152

Always he hastens to the outcome and carries his listener into the midst of events, as though they were known to him; he leaves aside what he thinks will not stand out when

---

[41] Winkler 1982, 145.

treated, and he lies in such a way, mixing falsehood with truth, that the middle is not discordant with the beginning, nor the end with the middle.

Horace is describing Homer, but he might as well be describing Odysseus.[42] Odysseus' opening question, 'What shall I tell first, what last?', was of course Homer's question as well.

Bibliography

Acosta-Hughes, B. 2010. *Arion's Lyre: Archaic Lyric into Hellenistic Poetry*, Princeton.
Andrews, N. 1996. 'Narrative and allusion in Theocritus, *Idyll* 2', in: M.A. Harder/R.F. Regtuit/ G.C. Wakker (eds.), *Theocritus*, Groningen, 21–53.
Buffière, F. 1956. *Les mythes d'Homère et la pensée grecque*, Paris.
Bühler, W. 1964. *Beiträge zur Erklärung der Schrift vom Erhabenen*, Göttingen.
De Jong, I.J.F. 2001. *A Narratological Commentary on the Odyssey*, Cambridge.
Di Benedetto, V. 2010. *Omero, Odissea: Introduzione, Traduzione e Commento*, Milan.
Elmer, D.F. 2008. 'Heliodoros's "sources": Intertextuality, paternity, and the Nile River in the *Aithiopika*', *Transactions of the American Philological Association* 138, 411–450.
Ford, A. 1999. 'Odysseus after dinner: *Od.* 9.2–11 and the traditions of sympotic song', in: J.N. Kazazis/A. Rengakos (eds.), *Euphrosyne: Studies in Ancient Epic and its Legacy in Honor of Dimitris N. Maronitis*, Stuttgart, 109–123.
Harder, A. 2012. *Callimachus Aetia*, Oxford.
Heath, M.F. 2011. 'Greek literature', *Greece & Rome* 58, 104–112.
Hopkinson, N. 1994. 'Nonnus and Homer', in: N. Hopkinson (ed.), *Studies in the Dionysiaca of Nonnus*, Cambridge, 9–42.
Hunter, R. 1998. 'The *Aithiopika* of Heliodorus: Beyond interpretation?', in: R. Hunter (ed.), *Studies in Heliodorus*, Cambridge, 40–59.
Hunter, R. 2009. 'The Trojan Oration of Dio Chrysostom and ancient Homeric criticism', in: Grethlein, J./Rengakos, A. (eds.), *Narratology and Interpretation: The Content of Narrative Form in Ancient Literature*, Trends in Classics suppl. vol. 4, Berlin, 43–61 [= this volume 487–505].
Hunter, R. 2012. *Plato and the Traditions of Ancient Literature: The Silent Stream*, Cambridge.
Hunter, R. 2019. 'Notes on the ancient reception of Sappho', in: T.S. Thorsen/S. Harrison (eds.), *Roman Receptions of Sappho*, Oxford, 45–49 [= this volume 349–363].
Kelly, A. 2008. 'Performance and rivalry: Homer, Odysseus, Hesiod', in: M. Revermann/P. Wilson (eds.), *Performance, Iconography, Reception*, Oxford, 177–203.
Lentini, G. 2012. 'L'idillio 2 di Teocrito e il "genere" oaristys', *Materiali e discussioni per l'analisi dei testi classici* 68, 181–190.
Mazzucchi, C.M. 1992. *Dionisio Longino: Del Sublime*, Milan.

---

[42] V.151 indeed evokes the description of Odysseus at *Od.* 19.203 ἴσκε ψεύδεα πολλὰ λέγων ἐτύμοισιν ὁμοῖα; the point is curiously absent from Brink's commentary.

Montiglio, S. 2011. *From Villain to Hero: Odysseus in Ancient Thought*, Ann Arbor.
Montiglio, S. 2013. *Love and Providence: Recognition in the Ancient Novel*, New York.
Most, G.W. 1989. 'The stranger's stratagem: Self-disclosure and self-sufficiency in Greek culture', *Journal of Hellenic Studies* 109, 114–133.
Nünlist, R. 2009. *The Ancient Critic at Work: Terms and Concepts of Literary Criticism in Greek Scholia*, Cambridge.
Paulsen, T. 1992. *Inszenierung des Schicksals: Tragödie und Komödie im Roman des Heliodor*, Trier.
Richardson, N.J. 1975. 'Homeric professors in the age of the sophists', *Proceedings of the Cambridge Philological Society* 21, 65–81.
Richardson, N.J. 1980. 'Literary criticism in the exegetical scholia to the *Iliad*', *Classical Quarterly* 30, 265–287.
Segal, C.P. 1985. 'Space, time, and imagination in Theocritus' Second Idyll', *Classical Antiquity* 4, 103–119.
Telò, M. 1999, 'Eliodoro e la critica omerica antica', *Studi Italiani di Filologia Classica* 92, 71–87.
Tilg, S. 2010. *Chariton of Aphrodisias and the Invention of the Greek Love Novel*, Oxford.
Whitmarsh, T. 2011. *Narrative and Identity in the Ancient Greek Novel: Returning Romance*, Cambridge.
Winkler, J.J. 1982. 'The mendacity of Kalasiris and the narrative strategy of Heliodoros' *Aithiopika*', *Yale Classical Studies* 77, 93–158.

Part II: **Ancient Drama**

4 The Garland of Hippolytus

One of the most celebrated Euripidean passages is the dedicatory address and prayer which Hippolytus offers to Artemis as he places a garland at her statue, immediately after the hymn which he and his fellow-huntsmen have sung to her as they enter:

σοὶ τόνδε πλεκτὸν στέφανον ἐξ ἀκηράτου
λειμῶνος, ὦ δέσποινα, κοσμήσας φέρω,
ἔνθ' οὔτε ποιμὴν ἀξιοῖ φέρβειν βοτὰ   75
οὔτ' ἦλθέ πω σίδηρος, ἀλλ' ἀκήρατον
μέλισσα λειμῶν' ἠρινὴ διέρχεται,
αἰδὼς δὲ ποταμίαισι κηπεύει δρόσοις,
ὅσοις διδακτὸν μηδὲν ἀλλ' ἐν τῆι φύσει
τὸ σωφρονεῖν εἴληχεν ἐς τὰ πάντ' ἀεί,   80
τούτοις δρέπεσθαι, τοῖς κακοῖσι δ' οὐ θέμις.
ἀλλ', ὦ φίλη δέσποινα, χρυσέας κόμης
ἀνάδημα δέξαι χειρὸς εὐσεβοῦς ἄπο.
μόνωι γάρ ἐστι τοῦτ' ἐμοὶ γέρας βροτῶν·
σοὶ καὶ ξύνειμι καὶ λόγοις ἀμείβομαι,   85
κλύων μὲν αὐδῆς, ὄμμα δ' οὐχ ὁρῶν τὸ σόν.
τέλος δὲ κάμψαιμ' ὥσπερ ἠρξάμην βίου.

Euripides, *Hippolytus* 73–87

Mistress, I bring you this woven garland which I have fashioned from an unravaged meadow, where no herdsman chooses to graze his animals nor has iron ever passed there, but in the springtime the bee traverses the unravaged meadow and *Aidôs* nurtures it with river waters; those who have no share in the taught, but in their natures *sôphrosynê* has its place in all things for all time – these may pluck [from the meadow], but for the wicked it is not permitted. Mistress of mine receive from a pious hand a wreath to bind your golden hair. Alone of men do I enjoy this privilege, for I keep company with you and converse with you, hearing your voice, though I do not see your face. May I end my life as I have begun it.

The extant scholia on these famous verses offer a compilation of detailed and rather remarkable readings, extracts from which deserve to be quoted at length:[1]

I am grateful to Hans Bernsdorff and audiences in Cambridge, Frankfurt, Ioannina, Leiden, Sydney, Thessaloniki and Washington D.C. for helpful discussion of earlier versions

[1] I generally follow Schwartz's text, though more work clearly needs to be done on the text of the scholia.

Scholia on v. 73: This is a notorious problem (*zêtêma*). Some suppose that Hippolytus garlands Artemis with a garland of flowers, but others suppose that Hippolytus is saying this about himself, namely 'Goddess, I dedicate myself as a garland to you', that is as the most blooming ornament (*kosmos*), for it is an ornament to the virgin to pass time with the most *sôphrôn* of the young men. Others say that the poet is not riddling (αἰνίττεσθαι) or allegorising at all, but using words in their straightforward sense (κυρίως λέγειν) and Hippolytus is in fact carrying a garland which he derived from a meadow in which it is not holy (ὅσιον) for us to pluck flowers. 'Iron has never entered it' (v. 76) indicates that the meadow has never been cropped or worked by anyone. Others say that Euripides metaphorically (τροπικώτερον) calls the hymn to Artemis a garland, for it would be remarkably strange to imagine that there was a flowery meadow where flowers were picked and it was of such a kind that those who entered were examined as to whether their *sôphrosynê* was taught or naturally acquired and the meadow was irrigated by *aidôs*. Like a philosopher he says that he is bringing a woven garland to the statue, a hymn to the god. 'From an unravaged [meadow]' means 'from my mind (διάνοια) which lacks deceit and corruption'.

Alternatively: Poets quite reasonably liken their own natures to meadows or rivers or bees, and their poetry to garlands: the flowers indicate the variety and beauty of poetry, the rivers its mass and the impetus (ὁρμή) to creation, the bees its sweetness, and the garlands the honour (*kosmos*) of the subjects of song. The poet has combined all of these things and thus made the nature of his allegory more brilliant (ἐφαίδρυνε). 'From an unravaged meadow' indicates that someone who is to practice *mousikê* must have a soul which is pure and unravaged, unstained by any evil, and most of all partakes of *aidôs*. It is because of the importance of *aidôs* that they represent the Muses, who are most fertile (γονιμώταται), as virgins.

Alternatively: ...He calls the hymn a woven garland because they compose hymns by putting together words as in weaving. The unravaged meadow from where the flowers are woven into the garland and where not even a shepherd thinks it proper to graze his animals is an allegory for a virginal and undeceitful intention (ἔννοια). The flowers of this meadow are the results of wisdom and virtue. No iron has come to cut this meadow and crop its flowers; by 'iron' he means either evil meddlesomeness (φιλοπραγμονία) and wrong-doing or the corruption of shameful pleasures, and in this way he makes clear Hippolytus' virginal and guileless character. The bee, however, is an allegory of the soul itself, for the bee is the purest of creatures (whence poets call priestesses 'bees'). He calls it[2] 'of the springtime' either because bees rejoice in the spring because of the flowers or because pure souls are always blooming, and spring is when flowers are produced.

Scholia on v. 78: This cannot be understood if one wants to understand it literally (κυρίως) as being about gardens. Therefore there is an allegory here. Poets reasonably liken their own natures to bees and rivers and meadows, and poetry itself to garlands; the flowers indicate the variety and beauty of poetry, the rivers its mass and the impetus to creation, the

---

[2] The reference is either to the bee or the meadow, depending on which reading is adopted.

bees the labour (τὸ ἐπιμελές) and concentrated effort involved,³ as well as the sweetness of the poems, and the garlands indicate that those who are praised win glory through them. Euripides has combined all of these things and thus made more brilliant the allegory through which he wished to describe his hymn to Artemis; other poets use these devices (τρόποι) in a scattered fashion. Plucking from unravaged meadows indicates that a poetic soul must be pure and unravaged, and unstained by any evil. Those who are going to practice *poiêtikê* must most of all partake of *aidôs*. For this reason some call the Muses too virgins.

Scholia on v. 79: A quality which does not derive from nature, but is achieved by constant practice (μελέτη), is 'learned' (διδακτόν). Philosophers call bad things 'learned' and good things 'natural'...

Although the whole of Hippolytus' speech here eventually comes under the scholiastic microscope, the 'notorious problem' is introduced as that of the garland: is it a real or an allegorical garland? The scholars whose work lies behind the scholia presumably knew, and may even have been prompted to their interpretations by, the epithet Στεφανία or Στεφανηφόρος which was attached to this *Hippolytus* by at least the time of Aristophanes of Byzantium.⁴ Our scholia on Euripides go back ultimately to the work of Hellenistic scholars in Alexandria, most notably Aristophanes and Aristarchus,⁵ though we may find it hard to imagine either of these figures behind the metaphorical readings of the scholia. The very stark interpretative choice that the scholia offer between 'allegorical' or 'riddling' readings on the one hand and 'literal' (κυρίως) readings on the other is, of course, very familiar in ancient criticism, and these scholia are an excellent illustration of one turn of the scholiastic mind: interpretation begins from the question 'What do the verses say?', and if the answer is 'something which cannot be meant literally' (after all, *aidôs* is not 'literally' a gardener), then one must seek other explanations in 'troped' language and 'allegory'. This latter term covers a very wide range of phenomena,⁶ and in this instance we are dealing with a set of interpretations which largely appeal, not – as do many ancient 'allegorical' readings – to a scheme of the order of the cosmos, as for example does Porphyry in his famous discussion of Homer's 'Cave of the Nymphs',⁷ but rather more simply to a metaphorical system which ancient read-

---

3 Reading τὸ συντεταμένον for the transmitted τὸ συντεταγμένον, cf. *LSJ* s.v. συντείνω I 2.
4 Cf. Barrett 1964, 10 n. 1.
5 Cf., e.g., Pfeiffer 1968, 222–224, Dickey 2007, 32.
6 Struck 2004, Pontani 2005, 26–40 and the contributions to Boys-Stones 2003 offer an excellent introduction to this subject.
7 Nauck 1886, 56–81; translation and discussion in Lamberton 1983.

ers tended to think of as inherent in the art of poetry itself. Before turning to the question of how, if at all, these scholia can help us to understand the *Hippolytos*,[8] we should investigate the intellectual affiliations of the scholia in rather greater detail.

The principal individual elements of the 'troped', poetological interpretations (the poet as bee, the 'garland' of song, the meadow of the Muses etc.) are very familiar and familiar from poetry well before Euripides.[9] Behind these scholia lies a very long tradition of high poetic metaphors for song; Simonides is reported to have called Hesiod a gardener and Homer a garland-weaver because the former 'planted the mythologies of gods and heroes' and the latter 'wove from them the garland of the *Iliad* and the *Odyssey*' (Simonides T 47k Campbell).[10] Unsurprisingly, it is Pindar, whose victorious patrons receive both songs and (literal) garlands, who supplies our richest source of such figures (and this itself is a fact of some significance for the *Hippolytus*).[11] When Pindar asks the eponymous nymph of Akragas to 'receive this garland from Pytho' (*Pythian* 12.5), it is hard not to recall Hippolytus' prayer to Artemis. In *Nemean* 7 the song is a highly wrought and precious crown,[12]

> εἴρειν στεφάνους ἐλαφρόν, ἀναβάλεο· Μοῖσά τοι
> κολλᾶι χρυσὸν ἔν τε λευκὸν ἐλέφανθ' ἁμᾶ
> καὶ λείριον ἄνθεμον ποντίας ὑφελοῖσ' ἐέρσας.
>
> Pindar, *Nemean* 7.77–79

It is not difficult to weave garlands — strike up the prelude! The Muse binds together gold and white ivory together with the lily flower she has removed from the sea's dew.

and at *Nemean* 8.15 the song is a 'Lydian headband embroidered with resounding music',[13] where the scholia note that the poet is speaking 'allegorically'. *Nemean* 3 offers a particularly elaborate 'cocktail of song':

> ἐγὼ τόδε τοι
> πέμπω μεμιγμένον μέλι λευκῶι

---

8 Commentators on the play have (perhaps unsurprisingly) paid these scholia scant attention; unless I am mistaken, Barrett's only reference to them (n. on 76–77) is to label 'absurd' the 'allegorisation' of the bee as really referring to the soul.
9 Cf., e.g., Steiner 1986, 35–39, Nünlist 1998, 60–63, 206–223.
10 The story obviously implies the chronological priority of Hesiod, but to what extent it provides firm evidence for Simonides' view of the matter may be debated.
11 Cf. below p. 76.
12 Cf. further below pp. 76–77.
13 To the commentators add Kurke 1991, 190–191, Ford 2002, 117–118.

σὺν γάλακτι, κιρναμένα δ' ἔερσ' ἀμφέπει,
πόμ' ἀοίδιμον Αἰολίσσιν ἐν πνοαῖσιν αὐλῶν κτλ.

Pindar, *Nemean* 3.76–79

I send you this honey mingled with white milk, attended by the foam which has been stirred, a drink of song among the Aeolian breaths of pipes...

Here the scholia connect milk with the natural talent, the *phusis*, needed for poetry and the honey with the πόνος of bees, and this is precisely the realm of ideas in which the Euripidean scholia also move.

Poets freely used such images for their own work, but these were also the very stuff of how poetry was explained, and this intimate link with the imagery of poetry itself is fundamental for understanding the language of ancient poetic criticism; it is telling that two of Quintilian's three Latin examples of 'allegory through metaphor (*allegoria continuatis tralationibus*)' are poetological images from Lucretius and Virgil (Quintilian 8.6.45). In the present case, however, what stands out is the Platonic background of the Euripidean scholia. Like the scholia, many modern critics have stressed the analogy between the 'unravaged meadow' and Hippolytus' virginal soul, but crucial here is a famous passage of Plato's *Phaedrus* which was very important for later, particularly of course neo-Platonic, discussions of poetry:[14]

> τρίτη δὲ ἀπὸ Μουσῶν κατοκωχή τε καὶ μανία, λαβοῦσα ἁπαλὴν καὶ ἄβατον ψυχήν, ἐγείρουσα καὶ ἐκβακχεύουσα κατά τε ᾠδὰς καὶ κατὰ τὴν ἄλλην ποίησιν, μυρία τῶν παλαιῶν ἔργα κοσμοῦσα τοὺς ἐπιγιγνομένους παιδεύει· ὃς δ' ἂν ἄνευ μανίας Μουσῶν ἐπὶ ποιητικὰς θύρας ἀφίκηται, πεισθεὶς ὡς ἄρα ἐκ τέχνης ἱκανὸς ποιητὴς ἐσόμενος, ἀτελὴς αὐτός τε καὶ ἡ ποίησις ὑπὸ τῆς τῶν μαινομένων ἡ τοῦ σωφρονοῦντος ἠφανίσθη.
>
> Plato, *Phaedrus* 245a

There is a third sort of possession and madness which comes from the Muses. It takes hold of a tender and untrodden soul, and by rousing it and inducing a state of Bacchic possession in song and other forms of poetry, it educates future generations by celebrating the countless deeds of men of old. But whoever comes to the doors of poetry without madness from the Muses, in the belief that craft (*technê*) will make him a good poet, both he and his poetry, the poetry of a sane man, will be incomplete[15] and eclipsed by the poetry of the mad.

---

14 It is intriguing to find part at least of this passage cited already in Satyrus' *Life of Euripides* (F 6 fr. 16 col. I Schorn), perhaps in a contrast between Euripides and truly 'inspired' poetry (? Aeschylus), cf. Schorn 2004, 193–194.

15 Commentators rightly note that ἀτελής both means 'uncompleted' and also suggests 'uninitiated'.

In his commentary on the *Phaedrus*, Proclus explains that the soul which is to receive the divine inspiration of the Muses must be clear of all other distracting influences and ideas, including (we may assume) over-subtle intellectual calculations;[16] we are here not far from the scholiastic explanation that the rejected 'iron' of Hippolytus' speech stands for 'evil meddlesomeness (φιλοπραγμονία)'.[17] Be that as it may, the soul which, in Proclus' words, is ἀπαθὴς καὶ ἄδεκτος καὶ ἀμιγής to everything except the 'breath of the divine' (1.181.16–17 Kroll) is at least how Hippolytus sees himself, even if, of course, his Artemis is much more associated with *sôphrosynê* than with *mania*; the language of poetic inspiration and the language of mystical religious devotion are here, as so often, very close.

Plato's ἄβατος 'untrodden' for a young man's soul is a word, like Hippolytus' ἀκήρατος or, which can have sacral resonance — it is used for a holy place (such as a meadow) which may not be entered except under special circumstances; whereas, however, the sexual resonance of ἀκήρατος and related words is very well attested, ἄβατος in the sense '(sexually) unmounted' is only found in a humorous context in Lucian (*Lexiphanes* 19). Nevertheless, it is easy enough to see how any reader would feel this resonance in the Platonic passage, particularly when ἄβατος is put together with ἁπαλός (and particularly in the context of the ἐρωτικὸς λόγος of the *Phaedrus* as a whole), and here perhaps lies part of the origin of the scholiastic stress upon the purity of soul needed by those who wish to practice *mousikê* or *poiêtikê*. So too, although Hippolytus use κοσμήσας (v. 74) in the sense 'arranging, putting together [i.e. the garland]', it is clear that the scholia felt that the word contributed importantly to the 'metaphorical' sense of the passage, and the explanation that poets compare their poems to garlands to indicate 'the honour (*kosmos*) of the subjects of song' (p. 13. 23 Schwartz) picks up Plato's claim that possession from the Muses 'celebrates (κοσμοῦσα) the countless deeds of the ancients' (*Phaedrus* 245a4).

In choosing ἄβατος Plato was also, as often, imitating in language the subject of his discourse. 'Untrodden' to describe a soul is, to put it simply, the kind of 'metaphor' which one might expect to find in poetry;[18] in describing the possession which comes from the Muses, Socrates speaks like one possessed in just that way. The most significant analogy here, as for the passage of the *Phaedrus* itself, is Socrates' famous account in the *Ion* of poetic inspiration and of why poetry is precisely the result of ecstatic inspiration rather than *technê* (533c8–

---

16 Commentary on Plato's *Republic* 1.181.2–17 Kroll.
17 For scholarly and intellectual 'meddlesomeness' cf. Hunter 2009, Struck 2004, 72.
18 The discussion of Plato's style at Dion. Hal. *Dem.* 5–7 is obviously relevant here.

535a2). Here too poets are like bees and the language imitates their alleged 'flights':

> Poets tell us that, like bees (μέλιτται), they are bringing us songs (μέλη) which they have gathered (δρεπόμενοι) from springs flowing with honey (μελιρρύτων) in gardens and groves of the Muses, and they do this in flight. They speak the truth: for a poet is a light and winged and holy thing, and unable to compose before the god is inside him and he becomes out of his senses and his mind no longer resides in him.
>
> Plato, *Ion* 534a7–6

It is precisely poetic imagery and metaphor, of a kind very close to Hippolytus' imagery, which 'proves' the irrational nature of poetic composition.[19] Aristotle more than once stressed that 'metaphor' was the most important aspect of poetic language and that making metaphors was a natural gift:

> It is important to use each of the elements I have mentioned appropriately, including double nouns and glosses, but by far the most important aspect of diction is the metaphorical. This is the only aspect which cannot be acquired from another and it is a sign of natural gifts (εὐφυΐα), for to make good metaphors is to observe similarity.
>
> Aristotle, *Poetics* 1459a4–8[20]

Although this is not the same point as Plato's insistence that poetry is the result of inspiration, not *technê*, they could clearly be seen to stand in the same tradition, particularly as it is metaphorical language which Plato uses in the *Ion* to illustrate the irrational nature of poetic composition. From the perspective of this later tradition, Hippolytus' highly metaphorical address to Artemis would illustrate the very lesson he teaches, namely the primacy of *phusis* over 'taught qualities', for only someone with a very special εὐφυΐα, who does not in any sense rely on what he has 'learned', could 'make metaphor' like this. We will see that Euripides certainly had other reasons as well for making Hippolytus speak like this,[21] but it is perhaps not utterly idle to wonder whether the tradition of reflection upon the nature of poetic metaphor which we have found in Plato and Aristotle had roots already in fifth-century discussion of poetry and is reflected in Hippolytus' opening speech.

Before proceeding, it may be as well to cast a quick glance at the poetological ideas themselves which the scholia display. Many are, as we have noted,

---

19 We might compare the comparison of poetic inspiration to the workings of a magnet (*Ion* 533d–e) which some have seen as (pointedly) an adoption of the mode of epic simile.
20 Cf. *Rhetoric* 3.1405a8–10.
21 Cf. below p. 78.

very familiar and not to be traced to any particular intellectual tradition, but we may suspect that much can again be traced back to Plato's *Ion*. The notion that poets and poetry are likened to rivers because of 'mass (πληθύς) and the impetus (ὁρμή) to creation' might seem, on one hand, to pick up Socrates' claim that poets and rhapsodes only perform in that one 'genre' 'towards which the Muse impels (ὥρμησεν) them' (*Ion* 534c1–2).[22] On the other hand, however, the reference to 'mass', suggestive of epic grandeur or the raging and swollen mountain torrent which is Horace's vision of Pindar (*Odes* 4.2),[23] might seem untrue to the apparent exclusivity of the ποτάμιαι δρόσοι which water Hippolytus' garden of *Aidôs*, a source perhaps more Callimachean than epic.[24] The scholia are, of course, nothing if not eclectic. If rivers denote the rushing power of poetry, the bee indicates, as it does for Horace in the same poem, the *labor plurimus* involved in making *operosa ... carmina*;[25] in the scholiast's τὸ ἐπιμελὲς καὶ τὸ συντεταμένον we are not far from 'Callimachean' ideals, and Aratus's σύντονος ἀγρυπνίη (Callimachus, *Epigram* 27.4 Pfeiffer), if that is the right reading, may particularly come to mind.

As compilations, the scholia are of course less concerned with a consistent poetic 'program' than with the very overload of poetological imagery which they find in the Euripidean verses. For us that imagery looks both forward and back. Callimachus' famous image for his poem at the end of the *Hymn to Apollo* shares more than one element with Hippolytus' remarkable prayer:

Δηοῖ δ' οὐκ ἀπὸ παντὸς ὕδωρ φορέουσι μέλισσαι,
ἀλλ' ἥτις καθαρή τε καὶ ἀχράαντος ἐνέρπει
πίδακος ἐξ ἱερῆς ὀλίγη λιβὰς ἄκρον ἄωτον

Callimachus, *Hymn to Apollo* 110–112

To Deo the bees do not carry water from every source, but only from that which rises up pure and untainted, a tiny trickle from a holy spring, the height of perfection.

---

22 Murray 1996, 119 notes that Plato's expression here picks up the Homeric ὁρμηθεὶς θεοῦ (*Odyssey* 8.499 of Demodocus, where, though many modern editors take a different view, the scholia note the ὁρμή from the god); *pace* Murray, however, it is far from clear that Proclus, *Commentary on Plato's Republic* 1.184.27–28 Kroll, who notes Homeric influence on Plato here, is actually thinking of this passage of the *Odyssey*.
23 On this imagery cf., e.g., Hunter 2003, 220–223. Somewhere behind the scholiast's language is probably *Iliad* 2.488 πληθὺν δ' οὐκ ἄν ἐγὼ μυθήσομαι κτλ.
24 Cf. below.
25 The etymological play in the scholia on μέλισσα and ἐπιμελές is not, to my knowledge, found elsewhere, though it might be thought that the Horatian passage implies it.

The bee image (the Euripidean scholia note the usage of 'bee' as 'priestess' which must be part of Callimachus' image)[26] and the stress on a sacral purity and exclusivity strongly recall Hippolytus' attitudes, the metaphorical language in which he expresses them, and the explanations of the scholia.[27] Modern criticism has tended to write 'religion' out of Callimachus' poetry, with the result that his sacral language is seen as 'purely literary', but Hippolytus' prayer should make us pause. If the scholia offer as one interpretation that Hippolytus' garland is in fact the song in the goddess' honour, the Callimachean *Hymn to Apollo* is indeed an offering to the god, and one which we know that he accepts.[28] Callimachus draws the sacral boundaries in much the same terms as does Hippolytus:

ὡπόλλων οὐ παντὶ φαείνεται, ἀλλ' ὅτις ἐσθλός·
ὅς μιν ἴδηι, μέγας οὗτος, ὃς οὐκ ἴδε, λιτὸς ἐκεῖνος·
ὀψόμεθ', ὦ Ἑκάεργε, καὶ ἐσσόμεθ' οὔποτε λιτοί·

Callimachus, Hymn to Apollo 9–11

Apollo does not appear to everyone, but to he who is good; he who sees him, this man is great, he who does not see him, that man is of no value; we shall see [you], Far-Worker, and we shall never be of no value.

If Hippolytus knows that he will never actually 'see' his goddess (cf. vv. 85–86, 1391–1396), it is nevertheless the κακοί — those whom Callimachus would call the ἀλιτροί (v. 2), the οὐκ ἐσθλοί (cf. v. 9), and the λιτοί (vv. 10–11) — who may not enter the meadow.[29] If viewed through a Callimachean lens, the 'metaphorical' interpretation of Hippolytus' speech which we find in the scholia becomes, if not necessarily easier to accept, at least firmly contextualised. As we have seen, there are important differences between the various elements of the pattern. Whereas Hippolytus, like Pindar before him (cf., e.g., *Olympian* 9.100–104), rejects 'the taught' in favour of natural gifts,[30] the scholia seem to acknowledge both as important poetic ideas; if Callimachus does not explicitly

---

26 For discussion cf. Williams' note on v. 110; of particular importance is *Supplementum Hellenisticum* 990.2.
27 καθαρός is a particularly good example of the seepage between sacral and critical language, cf., e.g., 'Longinus', *On the Sublime* 33.2.
28 For these ideas in Hellenistic and Roman poetry cf. Hunter 2006, 14–15.
29 On a second century AD inscription from Attica members of a club are to be tested to see εἴ ἐστι ἁγνὸς καὶ εὐσεβὴς καὶ ἀγαθός (Sokolowski 1969, no. 53, line 33). There is a helpful discussion of the mystical aspect of Hippolytus' language in Asper 1997, 51–53.
30 Barrett calls the idea 'a commonplace of old aristocratic thought' (1964, 173).

(but cf. vv. 42–46) stress *technê* in the *Hymn to Apollo* and the image of the pure spring would seem to foreground the gifts of divine nature, nevertheless, his emphasis on this elsewhere is well known, and it can be argued that the 'Reply to the Telchines' precisely lays claim to both *technê* and the divine inspiration of the *Ion*.[31]

Hippolytus' mode of speech looks back also. As we have seen, some of the closest parallels are to be found in Pindar, and it is in Pindar too where the sharpest lines are drawn between those who can and cannot understand. A famous passage of Pindar's *Second Olympian* asserts the special nature of what Pindar has to say:

> πολλά μοι ὑπ'
> ἀγκῶνος ὠκέα βέλη
> ἔνδον ἐντὶ φαρέτρας
> φωνάεντα συνετοῖσιν· ἐς δὲ τὸ πᾶν ἑρμανέων
> χατίζει. σοφὸς ὁ πολλὰ εἰδὼς φυᾷ·
> μαθόντες δὲ λάβροι
> παγγλωσσίᾳ κόρακες ὣς ἄκραντα γαρυέτων
>
> Διὸς πρὸς ὄρνιχα θεῖον·
>
> Pindar, *Olympian* 2.82–89

> I have under my arm many swift arrows inside their quiver which speak to those who understand; in general, however, they require interpreters. Wise is the man who naturally knows many things. Those who have learned are unruly and their words spill out; they are like a pair of crows who caw in vain against the divine bird of Zeus.

Eustathius took this passage as programmatic of Pindar's poetry as a whole, and to ancient scholars (at least from Aristarchus on),[32] confronted — as in Euripides' *Hippolytus* — with a passage where a 'non-allegorical' reading was simply not possible (Pindar does not 'literally' have arrows and a quiver, any more than *Aidôs* is a market-gardener), where there is an explicit contrast between 'the wise man who knows much by nature' and 'those who have learned', and which followed directly on a passage of apparently mystical eschatology, it was clear that Pindar was asserting that his difficult poems required 'interpreters' (i.e. commentators) for ordinary people ('common folk', 'the non-specialists', 'the many'). It was then entirely 'natural' to see the crows and the eagle as 'riddling' references to (respectively) Simonides and Bacchylides and Pindar himself. The

---

31 Cf. Hunter 1989.
32 Aristarchus is cited by the scholia on v. 85 (Drachmann p. 98). For Eustathius cf. Drachmann III.287.1–8.

text itself seemed to direct the scholars to read 'riddlingly'. Such dichotomies in the potential audience either originally arose in or were confirmed by sacral or mystical contexts; Hippolytus' exclusivity suggests this, and indeed any claim to purity implies a group of the 'impure', as we can see, for example, on the gold leaves of the Underworld.[33] These dichotomies soon found their way, however, into the exegesis of texts, particularly, though not exclusively, what we might call 'allegorical' exegesis, for such interpretation inevitably constructs a dual readership — the 'few', the 'wise', the 'initiated' on the one hand, and 'the many', 'the vulgar', the 'uninitiated' on the other.[34] The process is now most familiar from the Derveni papyrus, where the commentator seems to distinguish (the text is unfortunately broken) between 'the many' and 'those pure (?) of hearing' (col. VII.10–11); given the nature of that text, the process of transition from 'religious' to 'literary' exegesis is here starkly exposed. 'Metaphorical' and 'riddling' language creates boundaries and displays them openly. On the elaborate 'crown of song' at *Nemean* 7.77–79, Andrew Ford comments that this image 'is a form of kenning ... but it is also a form of knowing, a mode of addressing the *sophoi*';[35] just the same could be said of Hippolytus' images.

Another, though closely related, distinction drawn within archaic poetry is also relevant here. The language of the ἀγαθός and the κακός, and indeed of σωφροσύνη, is of course most familiar from the socio-political world of sympotic elegy. Theognis describes a world turned upside down:

νῦν δὲ τὰ τῶν ἀγαθῶν κακὰ γίνεται ἐσθλὰ κακοῖσιν
ἀνδρῶν· ἡγέονται δ' ἐκτραπέλοισι νόμοις·
αἰδὼς μὲν γὰρ ὄλωλεν, ἀναιδείη δὲ καὶ ὕβρις
νικήσασα δίκην γῆν κατὰ πᾶσαν ἔχει.

Theognis 289–292

But now good men's evils have become virtues for the base; they rejoice in customs turned upside down. *Aidôs* has perished, and shamelessness and outrage have defeated justice and hold sway over the whole land.

αἰδώς is as much a catch-word for the self-appointed ἀγαθοί in Theognis' world of aristocratic power and values, as it is in Hippolytus' dominating sense of self; elsewhere the same point is made explicitly:

---

33 Cf., e.g., texts 5–7 and 9 in Graf/Johnston 2007.
34 Through Philodemus we can see traces of these dichotomies in Hellenistic literary criticism, cf. Fantuzzi/Hunter 2004, 452. [Plutarch], *De Homero* 92 also explicitly refers to the two classes of Homeric audience, the φιλομαθοῦντες and the ἀμαθεῖς, cf. Pontani 2005, 32–33.
35 Ford 2002, 123.

ἀνδράσι τοῖσ' ἀγαθοῖσ' ἕπεται γνώμη τε καὶ αἰδώς·
οἵ νῦν ἐν πολλοῖς ἀτρεκέως ὀλίγοι

Theognis 635–636

Judgement and *aidôs* attend the good; now they are really few among many.

In another well-known passage which concludes one of the fullest early examples of the 'ship of state' allegory, the now familiar language of the ἀγαθός (or the ἐσθλός) and the κακός is combined with an appeal to the 'decoding' of poetic imagery:[36]

φορτηγοὶ δ' ἄρχουσι, κακοὶ δ' ἀγαθῶν καθύπερθεν.
δειμαίνω, μή πως ναῦν κατὰ κῦμα πίηι.
ταῦτά μοι ἠινίχθω κεκρυμμένα τοῖσ' ἀγαθοῖσιν·
γιγνώσκοι δ' ἄν τις καὶ κακός, ἂν σοφὸς ἦι.

Theognis 679–682

The cargo-carriers are in charge, and the base are above the good; I am afraid that a wave will swallow up the ship. Let these be my veiled riddles for the good; even a base man, if he is wise, would know the meaning.

If we then ask about the resonances of Hippolytus' extraordinary imagery for an Athenian audience in the late fifth century, there will of course be more than one answer, but prominent among them will be not just the sacral, but also the world of the aristocratic, perhaps now 'old-fashioned', symposium and the poetry which accompanied it; this is one of the important truths to which the neglected scholia direct us. When at the start of the *Homeric Problems* 'Heraclitus' illustrates what *allêgoria* is, the three examples he chooses are now famous instances of archaic poetry — Archilochus (fr. 105 W) and Alcaeus (frr. 208,6V) describing storms, which are 'in fact' war and internal strife, and Anacreon (*PMG* 417) addressing a Thracian filly, who is really a lovely girl. The setting for all such poems was very probably a male gathering such as the symposium, i.e. a closed 'reception context', a gathering of 'those who know', and one in which, as we have seen, both 'coded' modes of speech, such as the riddle and the *eikôn*, and (at least during the later fifth century) what we now call 'poetic criticism' flourished. The gradual disappearance of this style of figured speech is a major issue of literary history; how archaic this style was already felt to be as Hippolytus spoke is a question to which the scholia direct us.

---

36 Cf. further Ford 2002, 75–76, Hunter 2010.

Hippolytus' prayer takes us, of course, in other (related) interpretative directions as well. We may wish (rightly) to set this speech within an epistemological pattern whereby the three central characters of the tragedy are each characterised by a different form of knowledge which orders (but eventually undermines) their world: Phaedra, particularly of course in her great speech to the chorus at 373ff., by moral reflectiveness leading to clear ethical principles, Theseus by a straightforward reliance upon perception and inherited values, and Hippolytus by a 'revealed' truth and certain sense of self; the very way he speaks shuts out 'the many'. So too, critics have long discussed the battle for control of language in this play, for example for control of the meaning of σωφροσύνη or Phaedra's struggle with the semantic range of αἰδώς;[37] Hippolytus' speech, with its claims to the control of ὀρθοέπεια while also revealing the traps language sets for us (the ambiguity of σεμνός etc.), introduces this theme.

The division of the world into 'those who understand' and 'those who do not' which is implied in Hippolytus' prayer and which, as we have seen, is a prominent feature not just of forms of religious worship but also of the world of archaic poetry and its exegesis, resurfaces, as do Hippolytus' claims to σωφροσύνη (vv. 995, 1007, 1013, 1034–1035) and αἰδώς (v. 998), in the speech of self-defence which he makes to his father. He begins with a very striking proemium:

ἐγὼ δ' ἄκομψος εἰς ὄχλον δοῦναι λόγον,
ἐς ἥλικας δὲ κὠλίγους σοφώτερος·
ἔχει δὲ μοῖραν καὶ τόδ'· οἱ γὰρ ἐν σοφοῖς
φαῦλοι παρ' ὄχλωι μουσικώτεροι λέγειν.
ὅμως δ' ἀνάγκη, ξυμφορᾶς ἀφιγμένης,   990
γλῶσσάν μ' ἀφεῖναι.

                                                                Euripides, *Hippolytus* 986–991

I am not clever at speaking to the rabble, but more skilled before my equals and a small audience. This is only reasonable. Those who fail before the wise have more success with speaking in front of the rabble. Nevertheless, in this present misfortune, I must let loose my tongue.

This 'tactless ... contempt for his audience' (Barrett) might seem a truly remarkable form of the 'unaccustomed as I am' *topos*, but much is at stake here. Barrett notes that Hippolytus' reference to the *ochlos* is 'especially tactless since although there is of course a crowd gathered round ... it is only to Theseus that his arguments are addressed', but we may wonder if this is not one of those places

---

37 Cf., e.g., Goldhill 1986, 132–137, Gill 1990.

in tragedy where the audience may well feel itself involved, if not specifically addressed; *ochlos* is (unsurprisingly) one of the terms for the audience used in the famous account of Athenian theatrical history offered by Plato, yet another élitist (*Laws* 3.700a–701b). It is the fact of public 'performance', as well as the ignorance of the broad audience, which Hippolytus rejects. Words matter to him, 'letting loose the tongue' (991) is not a mode which he favours; as we know from the violence of his reaction to the Nurse's attempt to win him over (653–655), even hearing words of a morally corrupt kind threatens to make him κακός stains his purity (ἁγνεύειν) so that he will need to wash out his ears with 'water from running streams'. Here it is now very hard not to remember (again) the distinction in the Derveni commentary between 'the many' and 'those pure (?) of hearing' (col. VII.10–11), in a chapter precisely about the exegesis of an 'allegorical' text; Tsantsanaglou's τὴ]ν ἀκοὴν [ἁγνεύ]οντας is there almost universally accepted.

As the rejected crows of Pindar's Second Olympian are indiscriminate in their choice of language (λάβροι παγγλωσσίαι), so the exercise of linguistic choice is the activity of the *sophos*. The Plutarchan treatise 'On the Education of Children' quotes *Hippolytus* 986–989 in support of the need to expose children only to the right kind of education, and the distinctions which Plutarch draws make the passage worth quoting at length:

> I say again that parents must cling to the uncorrupted and healthy education and must take their sons as far away as possible from the rubbish of public speeches (τῶν πανηγυρικῶν λήρων), for to give pleasure to the many (οἱ πολλοί) is to displease the wise (οἱ σοφοί). Euripides supports this ... *Hippolytus* 986–989 ... I see that those whose practice it is to speak in a manner which pleases and wins favour with the vulgar rabble (τοῖς συρφετώδεσιν ὄχλοις) turn out generally to be dissolute in their lifestyle and fond of pleasure. This is just what we would expect. If as they provide pleasure for others they neglect what is honourable (τοῦ καλοῦ), they would be slow in deed to place what is morally correct and healthy (τὸ ὀρθὸν καὶ ὑγιές) above the pursuit of their own luxurious pleasures or what is modest (τὸ σῶφρον) above the delightful (τοῦ τερπνοῦ).
> Plutarch, *On the education of children* 6a–c

The context here is quite different from that of the *Hippolytus*, but Plutarch too is the spokesman for a self-appointed élite, the σοφοί, whose authority depends upon a shared body of knowledge (*paideia*) which excludes the 'uninitiated'; like Hippolytus, Plutarch equates verbal excess and facility with a morally impure life and an absence of *sôphrosunê*.

From the outside such claims, whether those of a Hippolytus or of a Plutarch, are always open to charges of hypocrisy (as, for example, Lucian knew only too well). Thus Theseus famously throws in Hippolytus' face the charge of hypocritical allegiance to 'Orphic' behaviour:

ἤδη νυν αὔχει καὶ δι' ἀψύχου βορᾶς
σίτοις καπήλευ' Ὀρφέα τ' ἄνακτ' ἔχων
βάκχευε πολλῶν γραμμάτων τιμῶν καπνούς·
ἐπεί γ' ἐλήφθης.

Euripides, *Hippolytus* 952–955

> Now hold your high opinions and with your lifeless food make a show of your diet; with Orpheus as your leader revel on and honour writings, insubstantial as smoke. You have been found out!

What is important here is not whether or not Hippolytus was really an Orphic, but rather the familiar and much commented upon phenomenon of the association of 'Orphics' with 'books' (cf. Plato, *Rep.* 2.364e) ; here, if anywhere, were Greeks with 'sacred books' to be honoured (v. 954) and, as the Derveni papyrus has shown us, interpreted.[38] Such books offered a kind of knowledge not (to be) widely available and one which both seemed to invite, and may perhaps have exploited, *allêgoria*. Texts which are intended for and/or taken up as privileged by particular groups are always fertile ground for 'metaphorical' or 'allegorical' reading, for this is precisely one of the ways in which the specialness of the text is preserved. In principle, of course, this may also apply to oral 'texts', as we see not just in pre- or partially literate societies, but in, say, the 'secret knowledge' of closed societies (fraternities, Masons etc.) in highly literate contexts. Committing knowledge to writing risks its promulgation among the 'profane', and if this must be done, the knowledge must therefore be 'encoded' in such a way that it is of no use if it falls into the wrong hands; metaphor and 'allegory' are forms of literary code. In antiquity the idea of religious 'mysteries' is never far away in this context: the Platonic Socrates seems to link 'allegory' with eschatological rites (*Phaedo* 69c), the critic Demetrius tells us that 'the mysteries are conducted through allegory to increase their power to instil amazement and terror ... for allegorical language is like darkness and night' (*On Style* 101), and the Hippocratic 'Law' concludes by noting that the holy facts of medicine are to be revealed only to those who have been initiated through knowledge (*CMG* I.i.8).[39]

The metaphorical and mystical mode of Hippolytus' opening speech may thus be seen to prepare us for his terrible fate. Theseus' angry words — ironical-

---

38 Cf. Henrichs 2003 for a discussion of the general phenomenon.
39 On allegory and the Mysteries cf., e.g., Pontani 2005, 34–36.

ly placed in the mouth of a 'tyrant' — reflect the 'democratic' suspicion that those who hide things in books have something (perhaps risible) to hide; metaphorical language may, by its very nature, seem antithetical to the proclaimed transparency of democratic principles.[40] Hippolytus, who of course surrounded himself with ἄριστοι φίλοι (v. 1018), is thus damned both ways: on the one hand, his language and behaviour suggest the closed circle of the aristocratic symposium, predominantly of course an oral culture, and on the other he can be assimilated to suspect sects who claimed to find revealed truth in writings. Both frames testify to the very singularity of this character and the struggle to find the appropriate categories for him. That singularity was strikingly signalled by his opening dedicatory address to Artemis which invites 'interpretation', whether we call this 'allegorical' or prefer (with Barrett) to speak of 'transparent symbolism'.[41] It is this invitation to interpretation upon which the ancient scholiasts focused, and so should we.

The scholiasts sought to understand the intellectual structure which lay behind Hippolytus' words; we may not wish to follow the path they trod, but their curiosity is something we should ponder hard before going our own way. If there is a continuing tradition of criticism from antiquity to the present, then it is one of debate and struggle, and the authors of many of our scholia knew that the texts of the past mattered and were worth struggling over. Old trends are often the best.

Bibliography

Asper, M. 1997. *Onomata allotria. Zur Genese, Struktur und Funktion poetologischer Metaphern bei Kallimachos*, Stuttgart.
Barrett, W.S. 1964. *Euripides, Hippolytos*, Oxford.
Boys-Stones, G.R. (ed.) 2003. *Metaphor, Allegory and the Classical Tradition*, Oxford.
Dickey, E. 2007. *Ancient Greek Scholarship*, Oxford.
Fantuzzi, M./Hunter, R. 2004. *Tradition and Innovation in Hellenistic Poetry*, Cambridge.
Ford, A. 2002. *The Origins of Criticism*, Princeton.
Gill, C. 1990. 'The articulation of the self in Euripides' *Hippolytus*', in: A. Powell (ed.), *Euripides, Women, and Sexuality*, London/New York, 76–107.
Goldhill, S. 1986. *Reading Greek Tragedy*, Cambridge.
Graf, F./Johnston, S.I. 2007. *Ritual Texts for the Afterlife*, London.

---

40 Cf. the remarks of Ford 2002, 87.
41 Barrett 1964, 172.

Henrichs, A. 2003. 'Hieroi logoi and hierai bibloi: the (un)written margins of the sacred in ancient Greece', *Harvard Studies in Classical Philology* 101, 207-266.
Hunter, R. 1989. 'Winged Callimachus', *Zeitschrift für Papyrologie und Epigraphik* 76, 1-2 [= Hunter 2008, 1.86-88].
Hunter, R. 2003. 'Reflecting on writing and culture. Theocritus and the style of cultural change', in: H. Yunis (ed.), *Written Texts and the Rise of Literate Culture in Ancient Greece*, Cambridge, 213-234 [= Hunter 2008, 1.434-456].
Hunter, R. 2006. *The Shadow of Callimachus*, Cambridge.
Hunter, R. 2008. *On Coming After. Studies in Post-Classical Greek Literature and its Reception*, Berlin/New York.
Hunter, R. 2009. 'The curious incident ...: polypragmosyne and the ancient novel', in: S.J. Harrison et al. (eds.), *Readers and Writers in the Ancient Novel*, Groningen, 51-63 [= Hunter 2008, 2.884-896].
Hunter, R. 2010, 'Language and Interpretation in Greek Epigram', in: M. Baumbach/A. Petrovic/ I. Petrovic (eds.), *Archaic and Classical Greek Epigram*, Cambridge, 265-288 [= this volume 131-155].
Kurke, L. 1991. *The Traffic in Praise*, Ithaca/London.
Lamberton, R. 1983. *Porphyry. On the Cave of the Nymphs*, Barrytown NY.
Murray, P. 1996. *Plato on Poetry*, Cambridge.
Nauck, A. 1886. *Porphyrii Philosophi Platonici Opuscula Selecta*, Leipzig.
Nünlist, R. 1998. *Poetologische Bildersprache in der frühgriechischen Dichtung*, Stuttgart/Leipzig.
Pfeiffer, R. 1968. *History of Classical Scholarship*, Oxford.
Pontani, F. 2005. *Eraclito. Questioni omeriche sulle allegorie di Omero in merito agli dèi*, Pisa.
Schorn, S. 2004. *Satyrus aus Kallatis*, Basel.
Sokolowski, F. 1969. *Lois sacrées des cités grecques*, Paris.
Steiner, D. 1986. *The Crown of Song*, London.
Struck, P.T. 2004. *Birth of the Symbol*, Princeton.

5 Apollo and the *Ion* of Euripides: Nothing to do with Nietzsche?

To Nietzsche's *The Birth of Tragedy* — or, rather, to various ways in which that work has been read[1] — classical scholarship owes a number of very powerful ideas, not least (indeed first of all) a way of structuring our experience and our imagining of antiquity as a continuing struggle and/or compromise between the 'Apolline' and the 'Dionysiac'. My concern here is, to some extent, with this idea, but I am also concerned with Nietzsche's charge that Euripides, with his 'naturalism', which 'brought the spectator onto the stage', and his 'Socratic rationalism', which produced a drama of thoughts rather than emotions, killed tragedy, or at least that tragedy's death throes were played out in his dramas (*Birth*, chs. 11–14). When a new and dominant dramatic genre arose, it was these Euripidean dramas, not the real 'tragedies' of Aeschylus and Sophocles, that had fathered it and to which it declared its allegiance; this was of course the New Comedy of Menander and his contemporaries. The second of these ideas we do not, of course, literally 'owe' to Nietzsche; he himself acknowledges the presentation of Euripides in Aristophanes' *Frogs* as anticipating his argument (ch. 11), and indeed Nietzsche's closeness to (and borrowing from) Aristophanes' comically schematic opposition between Aeschylus and Euripides is one of the most striking things about these chapters of *The Birth of Tragedy*.[2] As for the

---

This is a revised version of a presentation to the 'Crisis on Stage' conference at Thessaloniki in December 2009; I am grateful to the audience on that occasion and to John Gibert for helpful criticism. I am very conscious that, not only have I no claims to expertise in Nietzsche, I have not attempted to read all that has been written about Euripides' *Ion* in recent years; this essay may, however, be seen as an attempt to acknowledge the influence of Nietzsche's view which I ought perhaps have done more to recognise in chapter 1 of Hunter 2009a. Translations from *The Birth of Tragedy* are taken from F. Nietzsche, *The Birth of Tragedy*, translated by Douglas Smith (Oxford 2000), sometimes adapted.

1 Given the limited scope of this essay, I have thought it not unreasonable to take a fairly simplistic, 'at face value' view of Nietzsche's rhetoric; for a more sophisticated approach based on the development of Nietzsche's thought cf., e.g., Porter 2000.
2 The details are well set out by Reibnitz 1992, 281–296. It is also worth remarking that, in the course of their illuminating exposition of Nietzsche's work, Silk-Stern too sometimes adopt (? provocatively) an Aristophanic posture, cf., e.g., Silk-Stern 1981, 261, 'Euripides is an uneven writer whose work has some indefensible characteristics. One thinks of the tediously insistent emotive-operatic repetitions of single words in his lyrics — or the self-sufficient rhetorical debates ...'. Criticism of Nietzsche's view of Euripides is easy enough (cf., e.g., Wright 2005, 243–246), but its importance does not lie in its correctness.

debt of New Comedy to Euripides, this was already a commonplace of literary history by the Hellenistic period. Nevertheless, the way in which these two ideas intertwine in some modern thought and writing is indeed, I think, owed to Nietzsche's powerful advocacy of his position, partly perhaps through a misunderstanding of how Nietzsche used the idea of Apollo; for Nietzsche, of course, Euripides was very far from the embodiment of the Apolline spirit (ch. 12).

Euripides' *Bacchae* is a fundamental text, perhaps *the* fundamental text, for the study of Dionysus, not just in Attic tragedy, but in the classical period as a whole. The influence of this play upon Nietzsche's presentation of the Dionysiac is, or should be, clear; for Nietzsche, the *Bacchae* was Euripides' acknowledgement that the Dionysiac was not to be driven out of tragedy (ch. 12), though in fact, for Nietzsche, that expulsion had already happened when the *Bacchae* was produced.[3] It does not need to be demonstrated that the same privileged position is not accorded to the *Ion* by those concerned with the study of Apollo, let alone 'the Apolline' in any sense (Nietzsche would have had very little time for the *Ion*), though a reasonable case can in fact be made that, in Anne Burnett's words, 'the revelation of the quality of Apollo's power is the true purpose of [the *Ion*]',[4] no less than Euripides' own Dionysus explains that the *Bacchae* will make him an ἐμφανὴς δαίμων to men (cf. v. 22 etc.). Set at *the* Apolline site *par excellence*, as the *Bacchae* is set at *the* Dionysiac site, the plot of the *Ion* dramatises many aspects of what we may call Apolline ideology before a truly Apolline reconciliation is reached at the end, and a comparison between the two plays may, as several scholars have seen,[5] be a helpful way to proceed, regardless of the weight to be given or denied to Nietzsche. If the conventional date of the *Ion* (c. 413) is correct, then towards the end of his career Euripides produced major dramatic reflections of both Apollo and Dionysus within a few years of each other; it may only be subsequent developments, including of course Nietzsche's essay, which seem to impose potential significance upon this fact, but those concerned with the ancient roots of Nietzsche's dichotomy should at least ponder the fact.[6]

---

3 Nietzsche was of course following a familiar nineteenth-century view of the *Bacchae* as a 'palinode', cf. Reibnitz 1992, 318, citing relevant bibliography.
4 Burnett 1962, 94.
5 Cf., e.g., Murnaghan 2006, 107–112.
6 I would have to express myself differently, though perhaps not radically so, if Froma Zeitlin were correct that 'Dionysos ... is more powerfully at work in the [*Ion*] than is the lord of Delphi' (Zeitlin 1989, 156). Zeitlin's discussions (1989, 1993) have illuminated very many aspects of the *Ion*, and she is right to call attention to the Dionysiac elements of the play (cf. also Zacharia 2003, 110–117), but the balance in the *Ion* seems to me clearly Apolline, rather than Dionysiac.

1

The clearest contrast between the *Bacchae* and the *Ion* is, of course, the fairly constant presence, though more unrecognised than acknowledged, of Dionysus in the *Bacchae*, set against the apparently complete absence of Apollo from the *Ion*. At one level we may wish to see here the dramatisation of a 'religious reality': cultic experience of Dionysus almost inevitably involved the very unusual nearness of the god, whereas 'far-working' Apollo acts, particularly of course at Delphi, through intermediaries (such as the Pythia), rather than directly. I say 'apparently complete absence of Apollo' because, at Delphi, the god is — except in the winter months — always 'present', and Ion's opening monody makes very plain that Apollo is 'there' — both in the bright sunlight which illumines the earth and in the ordered and regular rhythms of life at the shrine and of Ion's daily work. The established power of Apollo is, as at the opening of *Iliad* 1, a 'given', a 'starting-point', whereas Dionysus is always arriving, always a new- or late-comer, even when he is returning home. It is indeed Ion's opening monody, with its repeated stress on brightness and purity,[7] which seems to be the 'Apolline high point' of the play, after which — according to some modern critics — all goes downhill for the oracular god. In the *Bacchae*, it is the choral parodos which, correspondingly, most emphatically describes the pleasures of a Dionysiac world; the familiar parallels between the two songs[8] invite not just reflection upon religious commonplaces, but also a consideration of the differences to which the similarities point. It may not be too far-fetched to suggest that, however much we elsewhere associate Apollo with choral poetry, in the *Ion* the monodic form emphasises not just Ion's sense of specialness, his sense of self — itself, of course, an idea which Nietzsche associated very closely with Apollo —[9] but also the more general appeal of the god to individual experience; the absence of monody from the *Bacchae* is usually (and rightly) taken as one of the play's 'archaising features',[10] but monody would also not be true to the communal nature of Dionysiac worship upon which the play lays such emphasis and of which Nietzsche writes with such enthusiasm in chapter 1 of *The Birth of Tragedy*.

---

7 Cf., e.g., Burnett 1962, 95.
8 *Ion* 128–135 ~ *Ba.* 65–67. Both *Ion* and the Bacchic chorus also stress both the perpetuity and repetitiveness of their praise of and service to the god.
9 Cf. *The Birth of Tragedy* ch. 1 on Schopenhauer' s *principium individuationis* and its collapse under the pressure of the Dionysiac.
10 Cf. Dodds 1960, xxxvi–vii.

A text which has as good a claim as any to be antiquity's nearest anticipation of Nietzsche[11] is Plutarch's account of the differences between the Delphic god as Apollo and the Delphic god as Dionysus:

> ἀκούομεν οὖν τῶν θεολόγων τὰ μὲν ἐν ποιήμασι τὰ δ' ἄνευ λεγόντων καὶ ὑμνούντων, ὡς ἄφθαρτος ὁ θεὸς καὶ ἀίδιος πεφυκώς, ὑπὸ δὴ τινος εἱμαρμένης γνώμης καὶ λόγου μεταβολαῖς ἑαυτοῦ χρώμενος ἄλλοτε μὲν εἰς πῦρ ἀνῆψε τὴν φύσιν πάντα ὁμοιώσας πᾶσιν, ἄλλοτε δὲ παντοδαπὸς ἔν τε μορφαῖς καὶ ἐν πάθεσι καὶ δυνάμεσι διαφόροις γιγνόμενος... κρυπτόμενοι δὲ τοὺς πολλοὺς οἱ σοφώτεροι τὴν μὲν εἰς πῦρ μεταβολὴν Ἀπόλλωνά τε τῆι μονώσει Φοῖβόν τε τῶι καθαρῶι καὶ ἀμιάντωι καλοῦσι. τῆς δ' εἰς πνεύματα καὶ ὕδωρ καὶ γῆν καὶ ἄστρα καὶ φυτῶν ζώιων τε γενέσεις τροπῆς αὐτοῦ καὶ διακοσμήσεως τὸ μὲν πάθημα καὶ τὴν μεταβολὴν διασπασμόν τινα καὶ διαμελισμὸν αἰνίττονται, Διόνυσον δὲ καὶ Ζαγρέα καὶ Νυκτέλιον καὶ Ἰσοδαίτην αὐτὸν ὀνομάζουσι καὶ ᾄδουσι τῶι μὲν διθυραμβικὰ μέλη παθῶν μεστὰ καὶ μεταβολῆς πλάνην τινὰ καὶ διαφόρησιν ἐχούσης· 'μιξοβόαν' γὰρ Αἰσχύλος (fr. 355 R) φησὶ 'πρέπει διθύραμβον ὁμαρτεῖν σύγκωμον Διονύσωι', τῶι δὲ παιᾶνα, τεταγμένην καὶ σώφρονα μοῦσαν, ἀγήρων τε τοῦτον ἀεὶ καὶ νέον ἐκεῖνον δὲ πολυειδῆ καὶ πολύμορφον ἐν γραφαῖς καὶ πλάσμασι δημιουργοῦσι· καὶ ὅλως τῶι μὲν ὁμοιότητα καὶ τάξιν καὶ σπουδὴν ἄκρατον, τῶι δὲ μεμιγμένην τινὰ παιδιᾶι καὶ ὕβρει καὶ μανίαι προσφέροντες ἀνωμαλίαν, 'εὔιον ὀρσιγύναικα μαινομέναις Διόνυσον ἀνθέοντα τιμαῖς' (PMG 1003) ἀνακαλοῦσιν, οὐ φαύλως ἑκατέρας μεταβολῆς τὸ οἰκεῖον λαμβάνοντες.
>
> Plutarch, *The E at Delphi* 388f–389b

We hear the theologians affirming and celebrating, both in poetry and prose, that the god is indestructible and eternal by nature, but that because of some fated ordinance and reason he undergoes changes; at some times he kindles his nature into fire, making it in every way like all else, and at other times he becomes manifold in his forms and experiences and powers ... More sophisticated interpreters conceal from the many the metamorphosis into fire and call him Apollo from his solitariness and Phoebus from his purity and stainlessness. As for the transformation into winds and water and earth and stars and the generations of plants and animals and his realignment, they describe what he suffers and the transformation riddlingly as a tearing apart and a dismemberment; they call him Dionysus and Zagreus and Nuktelios and Isodaites ... To him they sing dithyrambic songs full of emotion and metamorphosis containing wandering and dispersal; as Aeschylus said,
It is fitting that the dithyramb with its mixed cry should attend Dionysus and revel with him. To the other [i.e. Apollo] they sing the paean, a well-ordered and chaste music. In paintings and artistic creations they fashion Apollo as ever ageless and young, but Dionysus as of many shapes and many forms; to the former they attribute uniformity and order and unmixed seriousness, to the latter inconsistency mixed with playfulness and outrageous behaviour and madness. They call upon him as, Euios, Rouser of women, Dionysus, ablaze with frenzied honours, properly understanding what is particular to each transformation.

---

11 Cf. Silk-Stern 1981, 184–185.

Much in this discussion is of course owed to theorising closer in time to Plutarch than to Euripides, but much is also already anticipated in classical literature. Thus, for example, it is not just Plutarch's reference to the standard association of the title *Phoibos* with 'purity and stainlessness' (388f) that may remind us of Ion's opening monody,[12] but we may also sense in Ion's words the importance to the Apolline ideal of changelessness and familiar order, which Plutarch makes explicit and which is clearly connected to Plutarch's repeated reference to the Pythagorean and Egyptian identification of Apollo (the *a-polu* 'not much') with unchanging unity and the number one (354f, 381f, 388f, 393c): the opening of the *Ion* shows us one more perfect, sacral day at Delphi, a day like every other day. By contrast, the *Bacchae* begins with the ordinary life of Thebes completely turned upside down.

This monumental changelessness is vividly caught in Nietzsche's vision of Apolline culture where 'we see first the magnificent figures of the Olympian pantheon which stand on the gables of the building and whose deeds adorn its friezes in brilliant reliefs visible from a great distance' (*Birth of Tragedy* ch. 3). Sculpture was, of course, for Nietzsche the Apolline art *par excellence* (ibid. ch. 1). Nietzsche does not specify which temple he has in mind — the standard commentary on *The Birth of Tragedy* assumes that it must be the Parthenon,[13] rather than, say, the temple of Zeus at Olympia — and it is most unlikely (to say no more) that he was thinking of the *parodos* of the *Ion*,[14] whatever we imagine is being described there.[15] Nevertheless, Euripides' decision to draw particular attention to 'still-lifes' depicting Olympian power as a crucial part of 'what Delphi is' gains something, I think, when viewed through a Nietzschean lens; it is not just that, as Kevin Lee expresses it in summary of much recent scholarship on the play, 'the scenes with the monsters and the gigantomachy impress on the audience the struggle between Olympian, civilizing powers and monstrous, earth-born figures which represent violence and uncultivated brutality',[16] but the fixing of that struggle in monumental art, thus conferring an unchanging, didactic presence upon it, is itself a crucial element of Apolline ideology.

---

12 For a collection of such explanations cf. *Etymologicum Magnum* 796.53–797.2 Gaisford.
13 Reibnitz 1992, 123 and *passim*.
14 Nietzsche's description of the reliefs continues 'If Apollo too stands among them as one deity among others without claiming a pre-eminent place ...'; this certainly does not suit the *Ion*, both because Apollo is not among the depicted scenes to which the women refer and because, in another sense, Apollo really is pre-eminent in the *Ion*.
15 For a helpful discussion and bibliography cf. Lee 1997, 177–179; particularly suggestive is Zeitlin 1994, 148–152.
16 Lee 1997, 178.

By way of something of a footnote, it is worth observing that, if Euripides' Apollo is (unsurprisingly) associated with monumental building and sculpture, then the Dionysus of the *Bacchae* is seen rather to destroy Pentheus' palace.[17] The 'palace miracle' scene of the *Bacchae* is a typically Dionysiac twist on a familiar motif of epiphany: the god's presence causes buildings and the earth to shake. Whereas, however, at the opening of Callimachus' *Hymn to Apollo* such shaking of the temple is integrated into a rite which serves in fact to confirm the continuing existence and power of the god's temple, a quasi-paradox pointed by the instruction to the chorus to sing and dance when Phoebus is present (i.e. when the temple is shaking) 'if the city-wall is to stand on its ancient foundations' (v. 15), Dionysiac 'shaking', which also marks the presence of the god, has rather the destructive effect of an earthquake. Monumental permanence is not part of the Dionysiac.[18]

Plutarch's musical contrast is not just obviously applicable in general terms to a contrast between Apollo and Dionysus, but specifically also to that between Ion's monody and the *parodos* of the *Bacchae*. Plutarch calls the *paian* to Apollo τεταγμένη καὶ σώφρων μοῦσα 'a music [or 'Muse'] which is well-ordered and chaste'; Ion's song in aeolics (vv. 112–143) is not perhaps in a formal sense a *paian*, but the refrain certainly gestures towards this Apolline form, and it is hard to imagine anything more 'well-ordered and chaste' than what Ion actually sings. As for the parodos of the *Bacchae*, which is predominantly in a mixture of ionics and aeolics, Dodds observes that 'the excited and swiftly changing rhythms seem to reflect ... the Dionysiac unrest';[19] Plutarch could hardly have put it better. The parodos of the *Bacchae* is indeed full of excited movement and change, as Plutarch describes the dithyramb, and Richard Seaford for one identifies it as a dithyramb.[20]

Ion's invocation of his laurel broom is one of the best known pieces of Euripidean poetry, though critical judgement has been anything but uniform; Bernard Knox claimed that it 'reminds us irresistibly of Aristophanes' merciless

---

17 Cf. Seaford 2006, 43: 'Dionysos ... [has] relatively few elaborate temples. He seems more inclined to destroy buildings than to construct them'.
18 Nietzsche alluded wonderfully to the 'palace miracles' of the *Bacchae* in lamenting the 'death of tragedy' at the hands of Euripides and Socrates: 'In spite of Euripides' efforts to console us with his retraction [i.e. the *Bacchae*], he fails: the most magnificent temple lies in ruins; of what use to us is the lament of the man who destroyed it and his admission that it had been the most beautiful of temples?, *The Birth of Tragedy*, ch. 12.
19 Dodds 1960, 73.
20 Seaford 1996, 156, referring to earlier discussions.

parody of Euripidean monody ...',[21] an observation which seems to me (for what it is worth) to miss the mark completely, but this is perhaps not something about which one can argue. What ought to be clear, however, is that Ion's description of the broom is a projection of his view of himself. Like him, it is 'a young shoot' (νεηθαλές) in service to the god; προπόλευμα (v. 113) is a *hapax* neuter form of πρόπολος, which, together with the corresponding verb, is standardly used of 'temple attendants', 'those who serve the god', and thus an image of Ion himself. Both Ion and the broom sweep the ground before the god's temple; the repetition of σαίρεις (115) ~ σαίρω (121) is anything but a repetition of the kind which compelled Aristophanic parody. The broom's pure origins in 'immortal[22] gardens watered by sacred and ever-flowing streams' owes perhaps more to Ion's idealism than to his own sense of himself, though the audience will know that Ion's origin is as Apolline as that of the broom. Ion's broom finds in fact a rather close analogue in the garland which Hippolytus dedicates to Artemis at the beginning of his play and on to which he projects the pure and sacral chastity which he ascribes to himself.[23] The comparison between Ion and Hippolytus themselves is (rightly) a commonplace of criticism, but the prominence given to sacral objects in both plays, one connected with Apollo and the other with his virginal sister, is also worth observing. Both characters are thus associated with a single, particular object, which offers an image of themselves, a clearly delineated whole without the blurred edges which Dionysiac communality inevitably brings.

The closing choral reflection of the *Ion*, set within a specifically Apolline context, divides the world into the ἐσθλοί and the κακοί:

ὦ Διὸς Λητοῦς τ' Ἄπολλον, χαῖρ'· ὅτωι δ' ἐλαύνεται
συμφοραῖς οἶκος, σέβοντα δαίμονας θαρσεῖν χρεών·   1620
ἐς τέλος γὰρ οἱ μὲν ἐσθλοὶ τυγχάνουσιν ἀξίων,
οἱ κακοὶ δ', ὥσπερ πεφύκασ', οὔποτ' εὖ πράξειαν ἄν.

Euripides, *Ion* 1619–1622

Apollo, son of Zeus and Leto, hail! He whose house is wracked by misfortunes, should feel confidence in honouring the gods. In the end the good receive their deserts, but the evil, such is their nature, would never fare well.

---

21 Knox 1979, 259.
22 No doubt part of the meaning is 'always green' (so Lee, echoing the translation of Wilamowitz), but the literal meaning gives an obviously important resonance.
23 I have discussed some of the details of Hippolytus' language and imagery in Hunter 2009b.

It may be true that the final two verses are 'so general that they might fit anywhere'[24] and this dichotomy is, of course, ubiquitous, but it is at least tempting to see here a 'religious', as well as a moral distinction, in which Hippolytus, who distinguishes between himself and the κακοί (cf. *Hippolytus* 81, 654), and Ion would represent extremes at one end; that the distinction is rooted in nature (ὥσπερ πεφύκασι cf. *Ion* 441 [spoken by Ion], *Hippolytus* 79) corresponds both to ordinary Greek ideas and to the very special contexts evoked by such as Ion and Hippolytus. In the religious sphere the distinction is certainly not exclusively Apolline, but it is hard not to think (again) of Callimachus' *Hymn to Apollo* with its distinction between the ἀλιτρός and the ἐσθλός (vv. 2, 9–11). The thrust of these final verses of the *Ion* is not in fact as straightforward as it might appear: in bad times we should continue in piety and remain confident, provided that we are inherently 'good'. Who, we might ask, are the κακοί of the *Ion*? If no immediate answer is forthcoming,[25] we might also note that there is an implied warning in these verses not to try to use the gods, and specifically Apollo and his oracle, to effect particular ends — Delphi cannot be used by the κακοί to seek justification before or after evil deeds, any more than the good should turn against the god because of present misfortunes. In such acceptance, many might be tempted to find something genuinely Apolline.

2

In tracing the origins of New Comedy to Euripides' naturalistic drama, Nietzsche was, as we have noted, following a path which ancient criticism had already marked out. For Nietzsche the principal debt of New Comedy lay in the ordinariness of the characters with whom Euripides filled his dramas and the ordinary language they used; many more recent scholars have followed Nietzsche's lead, though he is perhaps not cited as often as he might be. For the *Ion*, of course, arguments of this kind have enjoyed a particular vitality and have become important to discussion of the play, far beyond acknowledgement of the familiar plot elements of exposed children and recognition tokens which have been catalogued since antiquity.[26] Rather, thanks significantly to an essay of Bernard

---

24 Dunn 1996, 17; for this approach to the verses see also, e.g., Mastronarde 2010, 105 n. 35.
25 Cf. Lowe 2000, 178–179 on 'the villainless happy end of *Ion*' as 'a striking and isolated oddity in its genre'; this makes the final verses, on which Lowe does not comment, even more noteworthy.
26 I am inclined to think that Ion's observation at 1340, after the Pythia has mentioned for the first time the casket in which he was exposed, 'This is a new story', is in part a metatheatrical

Knox,[27] it is the whole shape of the plot to which attention is now usually directed: the characters all begin labouring under misapprehensions, but at the end 'normalcy' and the 'traditional values of society' are restored; Knox leant heavily upon Northrop Frye's typology of comedy, in which what happens at the end is 'an integration of society which usually takes the form of incorporating a central character into it'.[28] Put like this, it is easy enough to see where the *Ion* fits, but let us return first to the closing verses which I have just considered from a 'religious' perspective, but which clearly also invite a reading at the perhaps simpler level of plot.

For Aristotle, the characters of drama, indeed of any *mimesis*, are – because they are shown 'acting' (πράττοντες) – necessarily either 'good' (σπουδαῖος) or 'bad' (φαῦλος) and thus 'either better (than us) or on our level or worse…' (*Poetics* 1448a1–5); if this does not quite map neatly on to the final dichotomy of the *Ion*, another passage of the *Poetics* seems very close. After having described the 'most tragic' plot structure, Aristotle goes on to other possibilities:

> Second comes the plot structure to which some give first place, namely the one with a double structure like the *Odyssey* and which finishes (τελευτῶσα) differentially for the better and worse characters. This is thought to be the best because of the weakness of audiences, for poets compose in accordance with the wishes of the audience and follow them. This, however, is not the pleasure from tragedy but it is more appropriate to comedy.
>
> Aristotle, *Poetics* 1453a30–36[29]

The choral *telos* of the *Ion* about the *telos* of life (and of drama) might seem to be anticipating Aristotle here, and might well lend colour to the general gist of Knox's argument, though Knox himself found the closing verses an 'uninspired jingle'. Aristotle blames 'the weakness of audiences' and here too Nietzsche probably would not dissent. Be that as it may, we have in this passage of Aristotle the link, familiar from subsequent ancient criticism, between the *Odyssey* and comedy; Aristotle's observation about plot structure, when put beside the

---

reference of a kind not unusual in Euripides; recognition tokens for exposed children were probably not a 'new' dramatic motif, but the verse gains a particular resonance when viewed from the later perspective of New Comedy. We may compare the similar and different *Helen* 1056.

27 Knox 1979.

28 Knox 1979, 266. Lowe 2000, 182–184 draws attention to the *Ion* as 'the most striking pointer to future [plot] directions', though his concerns are rather different from mine; he offers, however, a number of remarks on how this play looks forward to New Comedy, see Index s.v. Euripides, *Ion*.

29 I omit the final and problematic sentence of this passage – about a comedy in which Orestes and Aegisthus end up as friends – because I do not think it affects the present argument.

closing reflection of the *Ion*, tantalises us, as we so often are (or should be), by the possibility that, in outline, some ancient dramatic criticism was foreshadowed, or rather early manifestations of it reflected, in late fifth century drama (particularly Euripides).

Let me add one further footnote. Nietzsche famously did not stop with the link between Euripides and New Comedy. In another of his grand gestures of literary history, he traces the origin of the novel back to Plato:

> The Platonic dialogue was the raft as it were on which the earlier poetry rescued itself and all its children from shipwreck: huddled together in a confined space and fearfully subservient to the single helmsman Socrates, they now sailed into a new world which never tired of the fantastic image passing before it. Plato really gave to all prosperity the model for a new art-form, the *novel*: which may be characterised as the infinitely intensified Aesopian fable, in which poetry lives in a hierarchical relation to dialectical philosophy similar to that in which for centuries this same philosophy lived with theology: namely as ancilla. This was the new position into which poetry was forced by Plato under the pressure of the daemonic Socrates.
>
> Friedrich Nietzsche, *The Birth of Tragedy* ch. 14

This is not the place for a full discussion of this fascinating passage, though it is only fair to observe that the links between the Platonic dialogues and the ancient novel have been a source of increasingly illuminating research in the last couple of decades, even if the directions of this scholarly effort have not really been Nietzschean.[30] Rather, Nietzsche's placement of the novel at the culmination of his account of serial literary decline, serves, in the context of the final verses of the *Ion*, to recall Miss Prism's famous *aperçu* about her own novel in Oscar Wilde's *The Importance of Being Earnest*:

> 'The good ended happily, the bad unhappily. That is what Fiction means'.

The end of the *Ion* thus looks forward not merely to a particular kind of plotting, which is certainly on show, if not universal, in the extant Greek 'ideal novels', but also to a way of viewing the construction of literary fiction, whose significance goes well beyond Wilde's witticism.

Whatever view one takes of Apollo's actions and his oracle in the *Ion*, a comparison with the *Bacchae* makes one thing at least very clear about the plot structure of the two plays: whereas the Dionysiac play has a powerful unidirectional teleology which brings events to the ending willed by the god, in the *Ion* the shape of the plot is importantly dictated by human ignorance and weakness

---

[30] For some guidance and bibliography cf. Hunter 2006, 295–296.

and therefore characterised by narrative 'surprises' in a way in which is not true for the *Bacchae*. We may, for example, consider this potentially 'comic' plotting in the *Ion* through the functioning of *tyche* in the play, and this has been helpfully done in a number of studies.[31] Of particular interest is the exchange between Ion, Creusa and the chorus immediately after the recognition and after Creusa has told Ion of her rape by Apollo:

Κρ. ἰώ <ἰώ> δειναὶ μὲν <αἱ> τότε τύχαι,
δεινὰ δὲ καὶ τάδ'· ἑλισσόμεσθ' ἐκεῖθεν
ἐνθάδε δυστυχίαισιν εὐτυχίαις τε πάλιν,   1505
μεθίσταται δὲ πνεύματα.
μενέτω· τὰ πάροιθεν ἅλις κακά· νῦν δὲ
γένοιτό τις οὖρος ἐκ κακῶν, ὦ παῖ.
Χο. μηδεὶς δοκείτω μηδὲν ἀνθρώπων ποτὲ
ἄελπτον εἶναι πρὸς τὰ τυγχάνοντα νῦν.   1510
Ἴων. ὦ μεταβαλοῦσα μυρίους ἤδη βροτῶν
καὶ δυστυχῆσαι καὖθις αὖ πρᾶξαι καλῶς,
τύχη, παρ' οἵαν ἤλθομεν στάθμην βίου
μητέρα φονεῦσαι καὶ παθεῖν ἀνάξια.

Euripides, *Ion* 1501–1515

Cr. Ah, ah! Terrible were my misfortunes then, this too is terrible. I am tossed here and there from misfortune to good fortune, as the winds shift. Let them stand still! My previous ills were enough! My son, I pray that a breeze to relieve these ills should come!
Chorus. In the light of these events, no one should ever regard anything as unexpected.
Ion. Fortune, which changes the lives of countless men from misfortune to renewed good fortune, how very close I came to killing my mother and suffering an undeserved fate.

The insistent stress upon *tyche* at this point of the play, a stress that bridges the transition from the emotional exchange of vv. 1439ff., in which Creusa expresses herself in lyrics, to the more sedate trimeters of 1510ff., raises a number of questions. First, the verses find an interesting parallel in the familiar formulaic verses with which a number of Euripidean plays end and where unexpected events are ascribed to god(s):

πολλαὶ μορφαὶ τῶν δαιμονίων,
πολλὰ δ' ἀέλπτως κραίνουσι θεοί·
καὶ τὰ δοκηθέντ' οὐκ ἐτελέσθη,
τῶν δ' ἀδοκήτων πόρον ηὗρε θεός.
τοιόνδ' ἀπέβη τόδε πρᾶγμα.

Euripides, *Andromache* 1284–1288

---

31 Cf. esp. Gauger 1977, 105–114, Giannopoulou 1999/2000.

> Many are the shapes of divine things, and many are the things which the gods bring about contrary to expectation. What was expected has not been brought to fulfilment, and god has found the way of the unexpected. What happened here is such a case.

Ion 1510–1515 function in fact like a false ending to the play; were this a New Comedy, this might indeed be the end, though in Menander at least there tends often to be a new impetus to the plot in the final act after the principal confusions have apparently been sorted out.[32] The corresponding role of *tyche* in New Comedy does not require lengthy discussion, though one aspect has particular significance in the present context.

There can in New Comedy be an ironic and knowing tension between the operation of 'chance' in the world of the characters and the controlling intention of the dramatist, always known in principle to the audience and sometimes partially revealed through the foreshadowings of a divine prologist.[33] Looking back from the perspective of New Comedy, therefore, we can see some of this narrative tension latent already in the formulaic verses of, e.g., *Andromache* 1284–8, and *Ion* 1501–15 may be seen as another version of this idea, but one in which the divine, if not specifically written out, is at least suppressed; this will be a particularly Euripidean irony, given that here, if anywhere, the divine has very much been at work. There is of course no necessary inconsistency between accepting divine intervention in the world and ascribing events to *tyche*; indeed it seems 'natural' that characters within a drama, with their necessarily limited perspective, will see the operations of chance where the audience may know that something higher is at work,[34] and Euripides is clearly interested in the relationship between these two patterns of explanation. Looking ahead, on the other hand, we can see that the question of whether 'divine action' is actually an explanatory pattern which we impose retrospectively upon events, often as a form of consolation, was to have very great significance in subsequent narrative literature, and it is perhaps here, as much as anywhere, that the *Ion* can be seen to foreshadow later developments; the workings of Apollo in the play mean, of course, that we could also turn the formulation around to ask whether 'chance' is actually an explanatory pattern which we impose retrospectively upon events.

As has long been recognised, the principal route by which the narrative pattern of plays such as the *Ion* reached New Comedy was most probably through

---

32 Cf., e.g., Hunter 1985, 40–42.
33 Cf. Hunter 1985, 141–144. There is a parallel, and perhaps even more marked, phenomenon in the ancient novel, which cannot be pursued at length here.
34 Cf., e.g., Giannopoulou 1999/2000, 262.

the mythological burlesque of Middle Comedy: comic versions of tragic plots with divine and heroic characters gradually transmuted into plays with bourgeois characters, above all through the presentation of those divine and heroic characters as precisely bourgeois and 'ordinary' in their behaviour. As we have seen, Aristophanes and Nietzsche both saw this development as having already happened in Euripidean drama itself. As Middle Comedy seems to have presented its divine and heroic characters in a world which mixed both 'mythical' and 'contemporary' features and institutions, the remaining distance to travel was perhaps not so great.[35] With hindsight, we can see that the *Ion* itself foreshadows these developments by its repeated reference to the possibility that Ion was the offspring of a purely human sexual encounter (vv. 545–554, 1521–1527); in the latter verses, Ion, rather like a Verrall *avant la lettre*, calls Creusa aside to invite what we might call a rationalising reading of the plot:

τὰ δ' ἄλλα πρός σὲ βούλομαι μόνην φράσαι. 1520
δεῦρ' ἔλθ'· ἐς οὖς γὰρ τοὺς λόγους εἰπεῖν θέλω
καὶ περικαλύψαι τοῖσι πράγμασι σκότον.
ὅρα σύ, μῆτερ· μὴ σφαλεῖσ' ἃ παρθένοις
ἐγγίγνεται νοσήματ' ἐς κρυπτοὺς γάμους,
ἔπειτα τῶι θεῶι προστίθης τὴν αἰτίαν, 1525
καὶ τοὐμὸν αἰσχρὸν ἀποφυγεῖν πειρωμένη,
Φοίβωι τεκεῖν με φῄς, τεκοῦσ' οὐκ ἐκ θεοῦ;

Euripides, *Ion* 1520–1527

As for the rest, I want to speak to you privately. Come here, for I want to speak into your ear and conceal what I say in darkness. Make sure, Mother, that you did not experience the sort of misfortune that young girls have with regard to illicit unions, and now you shift the blame to the god and, in seeking to avoid disgrace for me, claim that you bore me to Phoebus, when it was not the god who fathered your child.

A private 'whispered' conversation outlines a reading which always lurks just around the corner waiting to be discovered, as indeed it eventually was. As we look forward to New Comedy, the juxtaposition and interplay of analogous divine and human patterns within the *Ion* seem to foreshadow a literary history which is, on the basis of quite other textual evidence, very plausible.

Against this background, an earlier passage which has always attracted critical attention deserves comment. In vv. 436 ff Ion reacts with indignation to Creusa's story of her friend who had exposed the child she had borne to Apollo:

---

35 Cf., e.g., Hunter 1983, 24–30.

> νουθετητέος δέ μοι
> Φοῖβος, τί πάσχει· παρθένους βίᾳ γαμῶν
> προδίδωσι; παῖδας ἐκτεκνούμενος λάθρᾳ
> θνῄσκοντας ἀμελεῖ; μὴ σύ γ᾽ ἀλλ᾽, ἐπεὶ κρατεῖς,
> ἀρετὰς δίωκε. καὶ γὰρ ὅστις ἂν βροτῶν 440
> κακὸς πεφύκῃ, ζημιοῦσιν οἱ θεοί.
> πῶς οὖν δίκαιον τοὺς νόμους ὑμᾶς βροτοῖς
> γράψαντας, αὐτοὺς ἀνομίαν ὀφλισκάνειν;
> εἰ δ᾽ (οὐ γὰρ ἔσται, τῷ λόγῳ δὲ χρήσομαι)
> δίκας βιαίων δώσετ᾽ ἀνθρώποις γάμων, 445
> σὺ καὶ Ποσειδῶν Ζεύς θ᾽ ὃς οὐρανοῦ κρατεῖ,
> ναοὺς τίνοντες ἀδικίας κενώσετε.
> τὰς ἡδονὰς γὰρ τῆς προμηθίας πάρος
> σπεύδοντες ἀδικεῖτ᾽. οὐκέτ᾽ ἀνθρώπους κακοὺς
> λέγειν δίκαιον, εἰ τὰ τῶν θεῶν καλὰ 450
> μιμούμεθ᾽, ἀλλὰ τοὺς διδάσκοντας τάδε.
>
> Euripides, *Ion* 436–451

I must reprove Phoebus for his behaviour. Does he rape young girls and abandon them? Does he father children in secret and then leave them to die? Not you! Since you are powerful, follow virtue. After all, the gods punish any man whose nature is evil. How can it be just for you to write the laws for mankind and yourselves act lawlessly? If — as will not happen, but as a hypothesis — you and Poseidon and Zeus who rules the heaven pay the penalty to men for your rapes, then the payment for your crimes will empty the temples. By pursuing pleasures without forethought, you do wrong. We should no longer call men wicked, if we imitate what the gods consider good, but rather those who teach us these practices.

Ion's reflections have obvious connections to certain familiar strands of contemporary thought. The gods 'misbehave' precisely in stories and poems which we tell about them and which we indeed might invent (this is what we might call the Platonic point); it is we who *both* depict them as immoral *and* look to them for paradigmatic behaviour and the regulation of *nomoi*. We may think it a very Euripidean conceit that Apolline wisdom about sensible forethought (προμηθία) and the importance of *nomoi* should here be turned against the god himself, but more is at stake than just an amusing paradox. Ion's strictures against the god are, for the audience, predicated not just upon the single 'false' story which Creusa has told him, but — as Ion's broadening reference to Poseidon and Zeus makes clear — upon the myriad such stories of divine-mortal couplings with which the world of 'mythology' was filled. Ion's argument that the gods who 'wrote the laws for mortals' should not act 'lawlessly' demands of course a higher moral standard from the gods than traditional story-telling promulgated, but here again analogous divine and human actions (rape and the exposure of children) are set beside each other — in this case within a pattern of 'imitation'. It is precisely that pattern of 'imitation' which was to be realised in the plots, or at least the background to them, of New Comedy. In a quite different sphere, the question of whether or not gods do exercise any 'forethought' in their concern with their own pleasure was a problem which was before long to move to the centre of an important intellectual agenda.

3

The *Ion* is full of Apolline themes. Ion's famous speech at 585ff. in which he tries to explain to Xouthos why it would not be a good idea for him to go to Athens is, from one perspective, a transference into the political arena of the standard Apolline themes of 'self-knowledge' and 'contentment with one's lot', particularly as these manifest themselves in a refusal to hanker foolishly after τὰ ἀπέοντα, the theme of, for example, Pindar's *Pythian* 3. Of greatest interest of course is the oracle and its workings, and here perhaps the play's full investment in the Apolline has not been completely explored.

The scene with the Pythia seems almost to dramatise the problem of the nature of the relationship between her actions, of which the prophecies are of course the prime example, and Apolline knowledge, a problem that was to occupy many in antiquity and is a central theme of Plutarch's essay *The Oracles at Delphi*.[36] The Pythia claims to know and to have known what the god wanted (βούλεσθαι), vv. 1343, 1353, 1359, and in 1345 she simply says to Ion that Apollo 'is sending you from this land after having declared your father'.[37] The mechanism by which she knew the god's will is first explained in the exchange at 1346–7 after she has brought out the casket with Ion's tokens:

Ἴων   σὺ δ' ἐκ κελευσμῶν ἢ πόθεν σῴζεις τάδε;
Πρ.   ἐνθύμιόν μοι τότε τίθησι Λοξίας

                                                                    Euripides, *Ion* 1346–7

Ion Did you preserve this because you were ordered to, or why?
Pyth. Loxias at that time put the thought into me.

---

36 For a helpful introduction to some of the modern views which have been held cf. Graf 2009.
37 πατέρα κατειπών in 1345 does not necessarily imply, *pace*, e.g., Wilamowitz, that the Pythia believes that Xouthos is Ion's father. More important, however, than 'what does the Pythia believe?' is 'How will the audience understand these words?', and the phrase is at best ambiguous as to whether or not Xouthos actually is Ion's father.

As James Diggle observes, 'the words are most naturally taken to mean that Apollo's wish or command took the form of an ἐνθύμιον, a thought implanted by him in her mind',[38] rather than that the Pythia draws a distinction between a κελευσμός and an ἐνθύμιον, between, as Owen (on v. 1359 puts it), 'an inward prompting from the god' and 'an explicit command', presumably in which the priestess actually heard the god speaking to her. ἐνθύμιον is suitably vague for describing a process which must inevitably remain mysterious (cf. also vv. 97–98),[39] and if it is the case that for the Pythia also, not just for humans, Apollo 'neither speaks nor conceals but gives signs', as Heraclitus put it (fr. 93 D-K), then we might think that this is indeed a rather suitable way for this mystery to have been put. Five hundred years later, one of the characters in Plutarch's *The Oracles at Delphi* argues that the god's role in the Pythia's prophecies is limited to providing the ἀρχὴ τῆς κινήσεως, which acts on each priestess in accordance with her own nature; the words and style of the prophecies are entirely those of the priestess, whereas the god 'presents only *phantasiai* to her and makes a light in her soul with regard to the future' (397c). This theorising is of course owed to authors and thinkers later than Euripides,[40] and Euripides' Pythia is talking about an action she performed, not a prophecy, but it is hard not to see in her exchange with Ion reflection of contemporary speculation about the nature of prophecy, speculation which is one of the ancestors of the material gathered in Plutarch's essay. It is perhaps important that the Pythia's intervention is a μηχανή by the god (cf. 1565), which corrects the course of action set in train by the oracle to Xouthos; Apollo's two interventions through his priestess are thus structurally analogous.[41]

---

38 Diggle 1981, 114.
39 LSJ's 'make [the Pythia] have scruples about [keeping the chest]' (s.v. ἐνθύμιος) seems quite mistaken. Cf. Bond on Eur. *HF* 722.
40 For the theories of *enthousiasmos* in this essay cf. Schröder 1990, 25–59 and his commentary in the appropriate places.
41 The priestess' closing speech gives further cause for pause. It is difficult to understand what is meant by '[the god] wanted me unordered to preserve the casket' (v. 1358); as James Diggle (again) put it, 'even if she were sharply distinguishing in 1346–1347 between a direct order and an implanted thought, there is little point in her going out of her way to insist in 1359 that the god wished her to act without a direct order' (Diggle 1981, 11). It is the case that the Pythia sometimes prophesied αὐθωρί, 'off her own bat' (Plutarch, *Mor.* 512e), even before any question had been put to her (cf. Parke-Wormell 1956, 1.34 with n. 80), but such utterances had of course the same Apolline 'prompting' or 'ordering' as all other utterances. As for the unmetrical and (to date) unemended 1360, Diggle 1981, 115 points to 1352–1353 and observes that 'it is hardly true that she did not know the god's purpose'. The Pythia certainly knew what the babyclothes could be used for, but this does not mean that she understood the god's 'purposes' in

It is of course the oracular response delivered to Xouthos himself which has attracted reams of bibliography. Whether or not the oracle was simply false or just ambiguous and misleading has been endlessly debated; much might, for example, be thought to turn on whether πεφυκέναι (vv. 70, 536, 1533–1534) necessarily and always implies a blood relationship,[42] but the fact that Ion will in Athens be regarded as Xouthos' son (1601–1602) means that he will indeed forever be (believed to be) πεφυκέναι from Xouthos, and it would be a very unimaginative interpreter of oracles who could not, with hindsight, suggest that this is what the god's words 'really' meant. Similar cases of interpretation abound in the scholia to ancient texts, and grammatical interpretation has much in common, as is well known, with the interpretation of oracular texts. What is important may in fact be dealt with fairly briefly. The words of the god are never quoted *verbatim* but only reported by Hermes, Xouthos and then Ion and Creusa (on the evidence of Xouthos); this pattern dramatises the crucial fact that the god never speaks directly to mortals, but only ever through intermediaries such as the Pythia. Secondly, two scenes show mortals, Ion and Xouthos and then Ion and Creusa, trying to work out the 'meaning' of the oracle, on the assumption — normal for most mortals — that words have a single referent and that utterances therefore have a single meaning; this is manifestly untrue of preserved oracles (both 'real' and 'fictional') and may well be untrue of how 'the language of the gods' was conceived more broadly.[43]

Oracles are, from this point of view, neither 'true' nor 'false'; only particular interpretations of them fall into these categories. Xouthos may be making the very common mistake of interpreting an oracle in accordance with what he wants it to mean, but the problem is more generalised than that. The giving of signs is what divinity does, man's role is to interpret and reinterpret those signs. When Ion, who elsewhere knows about αἰνίγματα (v. 533), asks 'Is the god truthful or is the oracle false?' (1537), the matter is for him particularly painful be-

---

preserving them: she does what the god 'wants' her to do, without necessarily understanding the νόος behind it. Nevertheless, despite this perfectly comprehensible theology, I must confess to a sympathy with Diggle's serious suspicion of 1357–1362; if these verses were excised, 'the Priestess's part has become brisk and businesslike ... She came abruptly; abruptly she departs'. Such abruptness would help to preserve the mysteriousness of the Priestess' relationship to the god, and this is an important consideration.

42 For some bibliography cf. Neitzel 1988.
43 Good remarks (and bibliography) on this subject in Kindt 2007, 3–7; on the *Ion* cf. also Stehle 2009, 251.

cause of his up-bringing and closeness to the god,[44] but he is also thinking in mortal, rather than divine categories.

Events did not go in the way that Apollo, *qua* character in the drama, originally planned because oracles determine neither the future nor how mortals will react to them. Human beings make choices, acting usually in ignorance of divine purpose, as was certainly the case with Creusa's attempted killing of Ion and his murderous intention towards her. In the end the divine purpose, however, is brought to fulfilment. If Apollo feared 'reproof for what had happened in the past' (1558), this is hardly surprising; given the play's extraordinary presentation of what rape and the subsequent loss of a child has done to Creusa, he could expect no less. Of course there is 'satire' of various kinds in the *Ion*, but there is also a powerful exploration of how human beings seek to make sense of what happens to them, whether they think that 'sense' has divinity behind it, or it is all just a matter of random chance.

Bibliography

Burnett, A.P. 1962. 'Human resistance and divine persuasion in Euripides' *Ion*', *Classical Philology* 77, 89–103.
Diggle, J. 1981. *Studies on the Text of Euripides*, Oxford.
Dodds, E.R. 1960. *Euripides, Bacchae*, 2nd ed., Oxford.
Dunn, F.M. 1996. *Tragedy's End*, New York/Oxford.
Gauger, B. 1977. *Gott und Mensch im Ion des Euripides*, Bonn.
Giannopoulou, V. 1999/2000. 'Divine agency and *tyche* in Euripides' *Ion*: ambiguity and shifting perspectives', *Illinois Classical Studies* 24/5, 257–271.
Graf, F. 2009. 'Apollo, possession, and prophecy', in: L. Athanassaki et al. (eds.), *Apolline Politics and Poetics*, Athens, 587–605.
Hunter, R. 1983. *Eubulus, the Fragments*, Cambridge.
Hunter, R. 1985. *The New Comedy of Greece and Rome*, Cambridge.
Hunter, R. 2006. 'Plato's *Symposium* and the traditions of ancient fiction', in: J. Lesher et al. (eds.), *Plato's Symposium. Issues in Interpretation and Reception*, Washington DC, 295–312 [= Hunter 2008, 845–866].
Hunter, R. 2008. *On Coming After. Studies in Post-Classical Greek Literature and its Reception*, Berlin/New York.
Hunter, R. 2009a. *Critical Moments in Classical Literature*, Cambridge.
Hunter, R. 2009b. 'The garland of Hippolytus', *Trends in Classics* 1, 18–35 [= this volume 67–83].

---

[44] A rather similar dramatic moment, but in a quite different mode, is Aristophanes, *Wasps* 696–697, where Philocleon is slowly weaned off some of his most long-cherished views.

Kindt, J. 2007. 'Apollo's oracle in Euripides' *Ion*. Ambiguous identities in fifth century Athens', *Ancient Narrative* 6, 1–30.

Knox, B.M.W. 1979. 'Euripidean comedy', in: *Word and Action. Essays on the Ancient Theater*, Baltimore/London, 250–274.

Lee, K.H. 1997. *Euripides, Ion*, Warminster.

Lowe, N.J. 2000. *The Classical Plot and the Invention of Western Narrative*, Cambridge.

Mastronarde, D.J. 2010. *The Art of Euripides*, Cambridge.

Murnaghan, S. 2006. 'The daughters of Cadmus: chorus and characters in Euripides' *Bacchae* and *Ion*', in: J. Davidson/F. Muecke/P. Wilson (eds.), *Greek Drama III. Essays in honour of Kevin Lee*, London, 99–112.

Neitzel, H. 1988. 'Apollons Orakelspruch im 'Ion' des Euripides', *Hermes* 116, 272–279.

Parke, H.W./Wormell, D.E.W. 1956. *The Delphic Oracle*, Oxford.

Porter, J.I. 2000. *The Inventon of Dionysus*, Stanford.

Reibnitz, B. von. 1992. *Ein Kommentar zu Friedrich Nietzsche, "Die Geburt der Tragödie aus dem Geiste der Musik" (Kap. 1–12)*, Weimar.

Schröder, S. 1990. *Plutarchs Schrift De Pythiae oraculis*, Stuttgart.

Silk, M.S./Stern, J.P. 1981. *Nietzsche on Tragedy*, Cambridge.

Seaford, R. 1996. *Euripides, Bacchae*, Warminster.

Seaford, R. 2006. *Dionysos*, London/New York.

Stehle, E. 2009. 'Speech genres and reproductive roles in Euripides' *Ion*', in: L. Athanassaki et al. (eds.), *Apolline Politics and Poetics*, Athens, 249–262.

Wright, M. 2005. *Euripides' Escape-Tragedies*, Oxford.

Zacharia, K. 2003. *Converging Truths. Euripides' Ion and the Athenian Quest for Self Definition*, Leiden.

Zeitlin, F. 1989. 'Mysteries of identity and designs of the self in Euripides' *Ion*', *Proceedings of the Cambridge Philological Society* 215, 144–197.

Zeitlin, F. 1993. 'Staging Dionysus between Thebes and Athens', in: T.H. Carpenter/C.A. Faraone (eds.), *Masks of Dionysus*, Ithaca, 147–182.

Zeitlin, F. 1994. 'The artful eye: vision, ecphrasis and spectacle in Euripidean theatre', in: S. Goldhill/R. Osborne (eds.), *Art and Text in Ancient Greek Culture*, Cambridge, 138–196.

6 Comedy and Reperformance

Comedy and ancient discussion about it provide some of our most explicit evidence both for dramatic reperformance and for the textual revision which often accompanied such reperformance. As will, I hope, become clear, comedy also forces us to think hard about the different phenomena which are often grouped together under the umbrella title of reperformance, but which may profitably be separated from one another. In this chapter, I want to pick away at the links between comedy and both the practice and 'idea' of reperformance, and I begin with two texts which may illuminate these two sides of the idea of reperformance, namely, how comedy itself consciously exploits the idea of reperformance as constitutive of the very idea of comedy, and how comedy offered ancient scholars a rich body of material on actual reperformances and revisions.

My starting point is what is for us almost — barring the fragments of *Banqueters* and *Babylonians* — the earliest piece of Aristophanes we possess and certainly therefore (for us) an originary comic moment:

ὅσα δὴ δέδηγμαι τὴν ἐμαυτοῦ καρδίαν,
ἥσθην δὲ βαιά, πάνυ γε βαιά, τέτταρα·
ἃ δ' ὠδυνήθην, ψαμμακοσιογάργαρα.
φέρ' ἴδω, τί ἥσθην ἄξιον χαιρηδόνος;
ἐγᾦδ' ἐφ' ᾧ γε τὸ κέαρ ηὐφράνθην ἰδών·   5
τοῖς πέντε ταλάντοις οἷς Κλέων ἐξήμεσεν.
ταῦθ' ὡς ἐγανώθην, καὶ φιλῶ τοὺς ἱππέας
διὰ τοῦτο τοὔργον· ἄξιον γὰρ Ἑλλάδι.
ἀλλ' ὠδυνήθην ἕτερον αὖ τραγῳδικόν,
ὅτε δὴ 'κεχήνη προσδοκῶν τὸν Αἰσχύλον,   10
ὁ δ' ἀνεῖπεν, "εἴσαγ', ὦ Θέογνι, τὸν χορόν".
πῶς τοῦτ' ἔσεισέ μου δοκεῖς τὴν καρδίαν;
ἀλλ' ἕτερον ἥσθην, ἡνίκ' ἐπὶ Μόσχῳ ποτὲ
Δεξίθεος εἰσῆλθ' ᾀσόμενος Βοιώτιον.
τῆτες δ' ἀπέθανον καὶ διεστράφην ἰδών,   15
ὅτε δὴ παρέκυψε Χαῖρις ἐπὶ τὸν ὄρθιον.
ἀλλ' οὐδεπώποτ' ἐξ ὅτου' γὼ ῥύπτομαι
οὕτως ἐδήχθην ὑπὸ κονίας τὰς ὀφρῦς
ὡς νῦν, ὁπότ' οὔσης κυρίας ἐκκλησίας
ἑωθινῆς ἔρημος ἡ Πνὺξ αὑτηί,   20
οἱ δ' ἐν ἀγορᾷ λαλοῦσι κἄνω καὶ κάτω
τὸ σχοινίον φεύγουσι τὸ μεμιλτωμένον.
οὐδ' οἱ πρυτάνεις ἥκουσιν, ἀλλ' ἀωρίαν

I am grateful to Rebecca Lämmle and Anna Uhlig for helpful criticism of earlier versions.

ἥκοντες, εἶτα δ' ὠστιοῦνται πῶς δοκεῖς
ἐλθόντες ἀλλήλοισι περὶ πρώτου ξύλου,   25
ἀθρόοι καταρρέοντες· εἰρήνη δ' ὅπως
ἔσται προτιμῶσ' οὐδέν· ὦ πόλις πόλις.

Aristophanes, *Acharnians* 1–27

'How many are the things which have bitten my heart, and how few, very few, the things which have brought pleasure – four; the things which have pained me – sand-hundred-piles! Let me see – what brought me a pleasure worthy of delightment? I know a sight which cheered my heart! The five talents which Cleon vomited up! That I really enjoyed, and for that I love the knights: it was worthy of Greece! But on the other hand I had a truly tragic pain when I was sitting all agape waiting for Aeschylus, and he announced 'Bring on your chorμs, Theognis'; how do you think that shook my heart? There was another pleasure when after Moschos Dexitheos came in to sing the Boeotian tune. But this year a sight tortured me to death: Chaeris popped up to play the 'orthian'. Never, however, since I took my first wash have I been so bitten in my eyebrows with soap as now, when a full assembly is to meet first thing in the morning and the Pnyx here is empty – they're all in the agora chatting and going anywhere to avoid the red rope. Not even the officers have arrived – they will come late, and then there will be shoving and pushing – you can't imagine – as to who will get the front bench. They'll pour in in a flood! They don't give a damn about making peace! O city city!'

Dikaiopolis is waiting, and what he has to say at first suggests (erroneously) that he is waiting for a musical performance or (as we are) for a play to begin. Dikaiopolis is no 'first time viewer', but rather someone, like – despite the obvious differences – Dionysus in the *Frogs*, who embodies Athenian theatrical tradition and knowledge, a paradigmatic viewer as well as a protagonist.[1] This embodiment of shared theatrical experience is prominent again when Dikaiopolis subsequently asks Euripides to lend him 'some [costume] rag from the old play' (vv. 414–17); as is well known, in that scene our sense that Dikaiopolis somehow represents the comic playwright/ Aristophanes is important,[2] and these two aspects of his character clearly illuminate and reinforce each other. A first point to be made, then, is that comedy exploits the audience's shared knowledge of theatrical tradition, and its expectations based on that knowledge, in such a way as to suggest that the idea of 'reperformance' may have a particular role to play within the very construction of the comic; it is not irrelevant to be reminded, in this respect at least, of such 'formulaic' genres as

---

[1] This aspect of Dikaiopolis is foregrounded even if, as however seems unlikely, the reference to 'the five talents which Cleon disgorged' is to an actual political event and not rather to a comedy, perhaps even to Aristophanes' own *Babylonians*, cf. Olson on vv. 6–8.
[2] Cf. Hunter 2016, 13–14.

commedia dell'arte and modern pantomime. Under this capacious umbrella fit the broad scene-types and indeed specific scenes shared by comic poets,[3] as well as the openness with which characters refer to the parts of drama, both familiar to and waited for by the audience, whether it be, for example, 'the anapaests' (*Ach.* 627, *Knights* 504) or the explanation of 'the plot' (*Wasps* 54, 64, *Peace* 50). Of particular importance too is the prominence of tragic parody within the Aristophanic tradition: much of *Thesmophoriazousai* is reperformance of a kind, that is, the transference of already performed tragic material into a comic mode. The snatches of tragic language within Dikaiopolis' opening monologue are not, then, merely preparation for the wholesale use of Euripides' *Telephos* which is to follow and for Dikaiopolis' 'role-playing' as a tragic character, but also illustrate comedy's exploitation of 'used' tragic language to mark out its own space.[4] Comic audiences were trained in tragedy, comedy, and comic para-tragedy, and clearly wanted poets to acknowledge and exploit their shared experience.

When Dikaiopolis is granted his private peace treaty, the first thing he does, after too long a break, is to perform (or reperform) the processional phallic song of the Rural Dionysia (v. 202);[5] with the end of war (at least for thirty years), what is truly pleasurable in life can be re-instituted and celebrated, and there can be a fresh beginning. What Dikaiopolis' celebration stresses is indeed a simplicity freed of all the pretence that we have seen in the opening urban scenes, a simplicity and directness symbolized by the raising of the ritual phallus. Such a celebration might well make us think, as indeed many students of the *Acharnians* have, of Aristotle's famous claim that comedy developed 'from an improvisatory beginning ... from those who lead off (ἐξάρχειν) the phallic performances which even now are still practised in many of the cities' (*Poetics* 1449a10–12). It is perhaps more likely that the procession in the *Acharnians* has contributed to Aristotle's theorizing on the origins of comedy[6] than that Aristophanes was anticipating that theorizing or indeed knew that the connection had already been made, although the easy link between the phalluses of come-

---

[3] Sidwell 2009 is a prolonged argument for very specific 'metacomedy', notably between Aristophanes and Eupolis, rather than what he calls 'the default position', namely that 'all [comic poets] fish in a generic pool of material' (p. 24).
[4] Dover 1987, 224–236 remains the best account of the layers of language in Dikaiopolis' opening monologue, but cf. also Goldhill 1991, 186 on the 'self-awareness and self-projection' of comedy's discourse.
[5] On the evidence for these festivals cf. Caspo/Wilson 2015, 322–328.
[6] Cf., e.g., Pickard-Cambridge 1962, 147. On phallic processions connected with the City Dionysia and early comedy, cf. Csapo 2015 and 2016.

dy and the phalluses of Dionysiac processions may well have been made more than once and in more than one context. Nevertheless, it is tempting to think that this simple rural procession also in some way celebrates a new opportunity for the performance and enjoyment of comedy, a new beginning in fact, here linked to the rural Dionysia, just as the end of the play fuses the victory of Dikaiopolis at the drinking contests of the Anthesteria with the expected victory of Aristophanes in the comic contest. The play plots a movement through the overcoming of the grimly serious chorus and the obstacles of petty-minded Athenians to the full restoration of Dionysiac celebration. Our understanding and enjoyment of that pattern is built on our familiarity with it — comic 'reperformance' is in this instance (as so often) a reassuring comfort. More broadly, the pleasures of familiarity, both in anticipation and in activation, are not the least of the hold that theatrical reperformance has both in antiquity and today.[7]

It is, moreover, striking that what Dikaiopolis leaves behind had also been portrayed in theatrical terms. The farcical meeting of the assembly which he seeks to interrupt is a dramatization of the interchange of theatre and 'serious politics': peace can now only be achieved in the comic theatre, as the assembly has abandoned any pretence at serious engagement with saving Athens. The supposedly democratic assembly is in fact a theatre of collusion where everyone knows his roles and costumes and plays his well-rehearsed parts. Once again, we have all been here before: the assembly is indeed a 'reperformance', a drama of repetition and delusion. Dikaiopolis, and we in the audience, know the rules of the game; Dikaiopolis will take the first step in leaving all that behind.

My second passage may seem somewhat surprising in this context, as its most immediate reference is not to comedy, but to tragedy. In the *Poetics*, Aristotle concludes his brief and notoriously problematic remarks on the chorus with a reference to the practice of *embolima*, for which he fingers Agathon as the πρῶτος εὑρετής (I print the most commonly accepted text):

> καὶ τὸν χορὸν δὲ ἕνα δεῖ ὑπολαμβάνειν τῶν ὑποκριτῶν, καὶ μόριον εἶναι τοῦ ὅλου καὶ συναγωνίζεσθαι μὴ ὥσπερ Εὐριπίδῃ ἀλλ' ὥσπερ Σοφοκλεῖ. τοῖς δὲ λοιποῖς τὰ ἀδόμενα οὐδὲν μᾶλλον τοῦ μύθου ἢ ἄλλης τραγῳδίας ἐστίν· διὸ ἐμβόλιμα ἄδουσιν πρώτου ἄρξαντος Ἀγάθωνος τοῦ τοιούτου. καίτοι τί διαφέρει ἢ ἐμβόλιμα ᾄδειν ἢ εἰ ῥῆσιν ἐξ ἄλλου εἰς ἄλλο ἁρμόττοι ἢ ἐπεισόδιον ὅλον;
>
> Aristotle, *Poetics* 1456a25–31

> The chorus must function like one of the actors and be a part of the whole and act the drama with the others, not as happens with Euripides but rather in the manner of Sopho-

---

[7] This is obviously very relevant also to the appeal of satyr-play, cf. later in this chapter.

cles. With other poets the sung parts no more belong to the story than to another tragedy. For this reason they sing *embolima*, a practice first begun by Agathon. Yet what is the difference between singing *embolima* and fitting a speech or a whole episode from one [play] to another?

Like so much in the *Poetics*, these remarks have been interpreted in a variety of ways.[8] Is Aristotle simply, though with some sarcasm, producing another limit-case, which is unthinkable in reality: in other words, is he saying, 'If you use *embolima* you might as well go the whole hog and move speeches and whole episodes from one play to another,' which is such an inherently absurd idea that *embolima* (whatever they might be) are put firmly in their place? Other views have, however, been taken. For Gerald Else, for example, what is at issue here is actors' interpolations, i.e., nothing to do with the poets' deliberate intentions,[9] but the principal problem with such a reading is not so much that the evidence for such 'messing about' with classical plays is very thin on the ground (cf. further later in this chapter), but rather that Aristotle's focus here seems very much to be on how plays should be constructed by *poets*. This is not, of course, to say that actors and/or poets may not have 'interpolated' (in some sense) whole speeches from time to time, but rather that that does not seem to be what is on Aristotle's mind. It is notable that when Aristotle does refer to the effect of actors on plays, it concerns how poets write their plays to suit actors, not what the latter do off their own bat:

---

[8] On some of the problems in this passage, cf. Halliwell 1986, 242–252.
[9] Else 1957, 556–557. Else's view is echoed by, e.g., Janko 1987, 124, and Sidwell 2001 suggests the reference is to innovations in plays (such as the transmitted end of Aeschylus' *Septem*) and he associates Aristotle's remark with the Lycurgan legislation about the texts of the three great tragedians. Else cites Page 1934, 89 for the practice of 'actors lifting a speech from one play and incorporating it into another', but Page's one example is Antigone's 'I would only do it for a brother' speech (Soph. *Ant.* 904–920), and that seems a very fragile basis on which to build any general theory; for sceptical surveys of the whole question of 'actors' interpolations', cf. Hamilton 1974, Finglass 2015, and cf. also Garzya 1981. In a recent helpful review of the issues, Paolo Scattolin 2011, 200–209 has revived the idea that Aristotle is not talking about adapting 'a speech or a whole episode' from one *drama* to another, but rather from one part of a play to another; the argument depends on the primacy of Aristotle's sense of plot: if the parts of a *muthos* have to be constructed in such a way that 'if any part is displaced or removed, the whole is disturbed and jumbled' (1451a33–34), then it is this law which determines not only what is said or sung, but also the order of performance. A song is as much part of the ordered *muthos* as is a speech. Such a view seems, however, at least counterintuitive; it attempts to deal with the fact that there is very little evidence for the kinds of practice which the traditional view has assumed, but itself raises more problems than it solves.

λέγω δ' ἐπεισοδιώδη μῦθον ἐν ᾧ τὰ ἐπεισόδια μετ' ἄλληλα οὔτ' εἰκὸς οὔτ' ἀνάγκη εἶναι. τοιαῦται δὲ ποιοῦνται ὑπὸ μὲν τῶν φαύλων ποιητῶν δι' αὑτούς, ὑπὸ δὲ τῶν ἀγαθῶν διὰ τοὺς ὑποκριτάς· ἀγωνίσματα γὰρ ποιοῦντες καὶ παρὰ τὴν δύναμιν παρατείνοντες τὸν μῦθον πολλάκις διαστρέφειν ἀναγκάζονται τὸ ἐφεξῆς.

Aristotle, Poetics 1451b34–2a1

I call a plot episodic when there is no probability or necessity in the sequence of the episodes. Inferior poets compose such plots for their own reasons, whereas good poets do it because of the actors. They write showpieces for competition and thus stretch the plot beyond its natural parameters; as a result they are often compelled to distort sequentiality.

If, however, it is probable that at 1456a25–31 Aristotle was not thinking of actors' interpolations, it is as certain as such things can be that he was not thinking of Roman comedy,[10] although it is of course Roman comedy which gives us our best evidence for the practices ('fitting a speech or a whole episode from one [drama] to another') which Aristotle here apparently evokes, humorously or otherwise. Aristotle's sentence has indeed called to mind Roman practices for many scholars. I do not need to rehearse the very familiar evidence at any length, so here are two famous passages which can carry the weight:

Menander fecit Andriam et Perinthiam.
qui utramuis recte norit ambas nouerit:					10
non ita dissimili sunt argumento, [s]et tamen
dissimili oratione sunt factae ac stilo.
quae conuenere in Andriam ex Perinthia
fatetur transtulisse atque usum pro suis.
id isti uituperant factum atque in eo disputant			15
contaminari non decere fabulas.
faciuntne intellegendo ut nil intellegant?
qui quom hunc accusant, Naeuium Plautum Ennium
accusant quos hic noster auctores habet,
quorum aemulari exoptat neglegentiam					20
potius quam istorum obscuram diligentiam.

Terence, Andria 9–21

Menander composed an *Andria* and a *Perinthia*: if you know one of them properly, you know both. It is not that the plots are so different, but rather they are composed with different language and styles. [Terence] admits that he has transferred whatever suited him from the *Perinthia* to the *Andria* and used it for his own purposes. These people abuse him

---

10 In fact, however, Aristotle's observation has occasionally been thought to be a later interpolation by someone who was familiar with Roman *contaminatio*. Gudeman 1934, 329, however, deleted ἢ ἐπεισόδιον ὅλον as an interpolation going back to someone perhaps familiar with *contaminatio* in Greek comedies and tragedies of the Hellenistic era.

for this and argue that plays should not be contaminated. Do they use their understanding to show that they understand nothing? When they take the poet to task for this, they also take to task Naevius, Plautus, and Ennius, whose authority our poet is following. He prefers to imitate their 'negligence' rather than his opponents' obscure punctiliousness.

Colax Menandrist: in east parasitus κόλαξ   30
et miles gloriosus: eas se non negat
personas transtulisse in Eunuchum suam
ex Graeca; sed eas fabulas factas prius
Latinas scisse sese id uero pernegat.
quod si personis isdem huic uti non licet: 35
qui mage licet currentem seruom scribere,
bonas matronas facere, meretrices malas,
parasitum edacem, gloriosum militem,
puerum supponi, falli per seruom senem,
amare odisse suspicari? Denique   40
nullumst iam dictum quod non dictum sit prius.

Terence, *Eunuchus* 30–41

There is a *Kolax* of Menander: it contains a parasite or κόλαξ and a boastful soldier. The poet does not deny that he transferred these characters from the Greek play to his own *Eunuchus*, but he strongly denies that he knew that these plays had been turned into Latin before. Moreover, if he is not permitted to use the same characters – how is it more permissible to write of a running slave, or to compose good-hearted matrons, wicked prostitutes, a greedy parasite, a boastful soldier, children being swapped, an old man deceived by a slave, love-affairs, hatreds, suspicions? After all, nothing has ever been said which has not been said before.

quae conuenere (*Andria* 13), 'whatever suited [the poet]', is provocatively teasing, but many may be reminded by those verses of Aristotle's laconic comment from which I began. It is not perhaps irrelevant that the alleged didactic mode of Terence's opponents – *non decere*, etc. – is exactly that of an Aristotle laying down the law through the frequent use of χρή, δεῖ, etc.; part of Terence's rhetorical framework is indeed to construct an opposition between a living theatrical practice (*neglegentia*) and the dead hand of prescriptive criticism (*obscura diligentia*). The claim that Terence practised *furtum* (*Eun.* 23, 28. etc.) precisely belongs with the considerable Hellenistic scholastic literature on literary theft and plagiarism. How dramatic practice and dramatic theory diverged from each other (if they did) during the Hellenistic and Roman periods would make for an extremely interesting study (the dramatic scholia give us something at least to go on), but it seems not improbable that Aristotelian analysis had an effect in both areas. I cannot pursue here the history of critical discourse at Rome, but however much the Terentian prologues are a display of shadow-boxing with phantoms of Terence's own creation, there can be little doubt that there is some substance lurking behind the dramatist's posturing. The combination of material from more than one Greek play (*contaminatio*) must be accepted as a fact of life about Roman comedy, almost certainly for Plautus as well as for Terence.

It is indeed comedy, rather than tragedy, which provides the fullest circumstantial evidence for a whole range of 'reperformance practices' which seem at least close to this passage of Aristotle. Aristotle's 'a speech or a whole episode' may evoke for us what we might call 'generic monologues' often delivered by 'stock characters' such as cooks and parasites; these are speeches where, as far as we can tell, there is almost no obvious hook to a specific plot or dramatic moment. Our fragments of Greek Middle and New Comedy are full of such things, thanks largely of course to the interests of Athenaeus, but Roman comedy (again) offers splendid examples set in dramatic context. Consider Terence's *Eunuchus* again. The famous entrance monologue of Gnatho at 232–264 presumably belongs to the material which Terence took from the *Kolax* of Menander, rather than to the Greek *Eunouchos*, but it is obvious that this monologue could in fact fit into any play featuring a boastful parasite; there is not a single word which has been adapted so as to hook these verses specifically to the plot of the *Eunuchus*, and it is likely enough that the only connection it in fact had even with the plot of the *Kolax* was in foregrounding the character of the parasite who gave the play its title.[11] *Embolimon* would perhaps not be a bad word for such a speech.

Roman comedy, moreover, not only offers us plays in which material from more than one earlier Greek play has been combined, but it also offers, quite explicitly, texts of 'reperformances'. The prologue of Plautus' *Casina* was written for a production when (apparently) it was possible that some who saw the original production were in the audience:

> qui utuntur uino uetere sapientis puto
> et qui lubenter ueteres spectant fabulas.
> antiqua opera et uerba quom uobis placent,
> aequomst placere ante alias ueteres fabulas.
> nam nunc nouae quae prodeunt comoediae
> multo sunt nequiores quam nummi noui.   10
> nos postquam populi rumore intelleximus
> studiose expetere uos Plautinas fabulas,
> antiquam eius edimus comoediam,
> quam uos probastis qui estis in senioribus:
> nam iuniorum qui sunt, non norunt, scio,   15
> uerum ut cognoscant dabimus operam sedulo.

---

11 For various aspects of this speech, cf. Fontaine 2014.

haec quom primum actast, uicit omnis fabulas.
ea tempestate flos poetarum fuit,
qui nunc abierunt hinc in communem locum:
sed tamen absentes prosunt pro praesentibus.   20

Plautus, *Casina* 5–20

In my view the wise drink old wine and enjoy watching old plays. Since ancient works and words bring you pleasure, it's reasonable to like old plays rather than other ones. The new comedies which are appearing are much worse than new coins. When popular rumour led us to understand that you very much wanted plays of Plautus, we put on this old comedy, which won great favour with those of you who are older; the younger amongst you do not know it, I know, but we will do our very best to help them get to know it. When it was first acted, it defeated all plays. At that time there was a flowering of good poets who have now departed hence to where we all must go; but in absence they can benefit us as though they were present.

What does it tell us that someone thought fit, not just to compose these verses, but to have them written down so that they survive?[12] Where do these verses fit in what might be called a narrative of textualization? Were they in fact ever performed, or are they primarily a piece of literary history posing as a prologue?[13] We should also be inquisitive about the ending of the play which explicitly cuts out the recognition and subsequent marriage (vv. 1012–1018): does the surviving script reflect the Plautine 'original', or rather a reperformance in which the acting troupe gave the audience what it was believed to want? Very divergent views are, of course, held about what our texts of Plautus actually represent; the work of Otto Zwierlein put this whole subject back on the scholarly agenda, even for those who could not agree with either his detailed conclusions or the premise on which they were based, namely, that Plautus' adaptations were far closer to the Greek originals than our surviving texts would indicate.[14] If, however, there is any truth in the assertion that 'some scripts changed their verbal shape each time they were used in the theatre. Actors

---

12 On the possible date of the *Casina* prologue, cf. Deufert 2000, 30–31; the matter seems to me, however, rather more uncertain than Deufert suggests.
13 In their Cambridge commentary, MacCary and Willcock, following Abel 1955, 55–61, think that they can identify three layers in the prologue of the *Casina*: Plautine translation of Diphilus, Plautine 'free composition', and composition for the revival by a post-Plautine 'anon'. Such a belief is far too optimistic: for all we are able to tell, the whole prologue is the work of the unnamed post-Plautine poet. The prologue of the *Casina* is in fact an extremely interesting document of theatrical and critical history and deserves greater attention than it usually receives.
14 The best critical introduction to Zwierlein's work, particularly for Anglophone students, are Jocelyn's two lengthy reviews (1993, 1996).

seemed to be under little compulsion to reproduce in close details the paradosis' (Jocelyn 1993, 126), then we are bound to ask whether we can be sure that these Roman theatrical traditions had no close counterpart in Greece.

As usual, several issues are here wrapped up together. On one hand, there is no good indication that our Greek texts of either Old or New Comedy show anything like the state of 'conflation' that we find in Roman comedy, whether that refers to Terentian *contaminatio* or the running together of alternative scripts, as seems to have happened, for example, with the ending of Plautus' *Poenulus*. There are a few well-known possibilities in Aristophanes, such as the apparent conflation of verses from two versions of the final questioning of the two tragedians in Aristophanes' *Frogs* (vv. 1431–1466),[15] but a recent examination by Martin Revermann has given good grounds for thinking that, in essence, our surviving texts of Greek comedy are pretty close to the 'master script' which was used for the performance of a play at a major Athenian festival, despite the fact that in the late fifth and fourth centuries 'Greek performance culture [was] a reperformance culture'.[16] The plays of Aristophanes appear to suffer hardly at all from 'actors' interpolations', which has in fact become a (probably misleading) catch-all title for nearly all forms of post-authorial textual additions which derive from theatrical rather than from scholarly traditions. This will partly be the result of the difficulty of expanding the Aristophanic text — far easier to add gnomic sentiment to tragic speeches, and partly of the fact that Aristophanes was, as far as we can tell, rarely reperformed at Athens in the fourth century and very rarely indeed thereafter. Our texts of tragedy probably go back to the texts established as 'official' by Lycurgus,[17] which were then passed on, by whatever means, to Alexandrian scholarship, and it is likely that most, if not certainly all,[18] of the theatrical additions to those texts predate this institutionalization. The case of Menander is very different from this, but it seems likely enough that his plays were 'archived' from a very early date, perhaps from that of the origi-

---

15 On our text of Aristophanes' *Clouds*, cf. later in this chapter.
16 Revermann 2006, 72. On pp. 254–260 Revermann reviews the case for believing that the Spartan song at the end of the *Lysistrata* does not represent the ending of the original performance in Athens. It must be remarked that most of the arguments which Revermann 2006, 78–81 uses for Old Comedy will not work for a non-political drama like that of Menander. Nervegna 2007, 15–18 also usefully collects some of the evidence for comic reperformances in the fifth and fourth centuries.
17 For discussion and bibliography, cf. Hanink 2014, ch. 2.
18 Cf. Günther 1996. A case of particular interest, of course, is the transmitted end of Aeschylus' *Seven against Thebes*, which Hutchinson 1985, xliii and n. on 1005–1078 dates to 'the fourth or early third century'.

nal performance, and there is no good reason to suspect that the texts which chance has preserved for us are very far from what Menander wrote, barring of course the normal processes of textual corruption.

If we can have a certain confidence in the state of the texts which have reached us, we must nevertheless face up to set of phenomena regularly grouped under the catch-all heading of *diaskeuai*, 'makeovers', a set of practices with which Aristotle would have been only too familiar.[19] We are here confronted with essentially two types of revision and two types of evidence. We know that comic poets regularly 'reworked' their own plays and then put them on again under the same or different titles, although of course we normally have no idea just how different the second version might have been; second, playwrights 'reworked' the plays of earlier poets and presented them as their own, usually under different titles. Our natural concentration on the, in fact rather special, case of Aristophanes' *Clouds* often makes us forget just how 'normal' the practice of revision actually was. As for the two types of evidence, we have both statements to the effect that such-and-such a play was a *diaskeue* of another and occasional fragments which seem to reflect this situation (cf. later in this chapter), and also a couple of brief passages which seem to shed general light on the nature of *diaskeuai*. I begin with the latter.

At the opening of the work περὶ διαίτης ὀξέων, 'On regimen in acute diseases', the Hippocratic author criticizes deficiencies in the remedies offered by 'those who wrote the so-called Cnidian Sentences' and he notes that 'those who later revised them' (οἱ ὕστερον ἐπιδιασκευάσαντες) handled the subject with greater medical knowledge. In his commentary on this passage Galen explains the verb:

> A book (βιβλίον) which is written in succession (τὸ δεύτερον) to one written earlier is said to have been 'revised' (ἐπιδιεσκευάσθαι) when it has the same argument (ὑπόθεσις) and the majority of the speeches (ῥήσεις) are the same, but some things have been removed from the previous work (σύγγραμμα), some added and some changed. If you want an example for the sake of clarity, have the second *Autolykos* of Eupolis which was revised from the first. So the Cnidian doctors published second Cnidian Sentences in addition to the first; some things were entirely the same, some things added, some things removed, and indeed there were also changes.
>
> Galen, *Commentary on Regimen in Acute Diseases*, CMG V 9.1, p. 120 = XV, p. 424 Kühn

---

[19] For the evidence cf., e.g., Hunter 1983, 147; Nervegna 2013, 88–99. Despite Nervegna's excellent survey, I hope that something will emerge from a fresh collection of the evidence.

What is particularly striking here is that, in describing a 'revision', Galen's mind turns automatically to comedy, although the context is medical literature. Although σύγγραμμα perhaps suggests prose literature, ὑπόθεσις, ῥήσεις,[20] and the example of Eupolis all point to drama. Galen's interest in Old Comedy is well known, and here he does not miss an opportunity to display a piece of rare learning.[21] Galen's definition is perhaps unsensational in its generality, and the same may be said of another passage which is normally adduced in this context, namely, a gloss from Phrynichus' *Praeparatio sophistica* (p. 69 Borries), where two shoemakers' terms are glossed:

> 'To sole and heel' (ἐπικαττύειν καὶ πτερνίζειν): to revise what is old. The metaphor [is drawn] from those who fit new soles and heels on to old shoes. They say this of those who remake and restitch old plays.

As with many of Phrynichus' glosses, it is likely enough that this is drawn from fourth-century comedy, and perhaps the most interesting aspect of this gloss is the possibility that it derives from a parabasis (or whatever replaced a parabasis in the fourth century); whether the reference is to tragedy or comedy, and whether the reference is to overt refashioning in διασκευαί or to accusations of plagiarism (common enough in Old Comedy), we cannot say.[22] Be that as it may, neither Galen nor Phrynichus really helps us to know what kinds of changes would normally fit an audience's horizon of expectations about the διασκευή of one play from another.[23]

---

[20] Nervegna 2013, 88 translates 'expressions' and Csapo and Slater 1995, 6 'phraseology', but it is hard to resist 'speeches', given the context (so also Revermann 2006, 330 n. 17); Storey 2003, 83 too accepts the dramatic resonance, 'it has the same plot and most of the same text...'.

[21] Why Galen chose to refer to Eupolis' *Autolykos* we can only guess, though it is tempting to see a piece of scholastic one-upmanship. Although the *Suda* (= Eupolis T 14 K-A) seems to suggest that Eupolidean *diaskeuai* were not uncommon, this is in fact the only case of which we know.

[22] Why Günther 1996, 95 assumes the reference to be to actors' changes to tragedies I do not know; cf. also Sidwell 2001, 83.

[23] A couple of other occurrences of the noun διασκευή deserve notice. The *Suda* τ 620 ascribes διασκευαί to the lyric poet Timotheus, but we must admit that we have no idea to what that might refer, cf. Hordern 2002, 10. More interestingly, Dio Chrysostom 32.11 refers to διασκευαί alongside comedies in the context of what look like standard comic plots; the meaning is as obscure as the passage is tantalizing. Veyne 1989 understands this to refer to '"remaniements" pseudépigraphiques de comédies classiques', whereas Nervegna 2013, 97 sees rather a reference to 'contemporary comedies first presented as new plays and later revised to be performed again as new plays'; neither explanation is convincing, and neither explains why Dio goes out of his way to say this.

Terence's famous remark (cited previously) about the similarity of Menander's *Andria* and *Perinthia* is of course special pleading, but there may at least be some fire behind the smokescreen, and it is a plausible and now quite old suggestion that Terence is there tendentiously exploiting the framework of Greek criticism and the practice of *diaskeuai*, although Terence is not of course claiming that one of these Greek plays was a reworking of the other. It would be very much in Terence's mode to exploit a Greek critical background, allegedly unknown to his less sophisticated rivals. What this would mean is that Terentian *contaminatio* is claimed to be sanctioned by long Greek practice, as indeed it might have been, though we have no hard evidence for the idea that, for example, the insertion of Gnatho's monologue into the *Eunouchos* would have been a very familiar type of revision.

As for Roman comedy more generally, it is certainly tempting to set Roman practices of adaptation and translation from Greek plays within the general umbrella of διασκευαί, and Sebastiana Nervegna has recently claimed that the 'Romans' "spoiled" dramas look very similar to the "revamped" plays of the Greeks' (Nervegna 2013, 99). Unfortunately, we here suffer from a dearth of evidence about what Greek διασκευαί did actually look like, with the possible exception of Aristophanes' *Clouds* (later in this chapter). If our criteria, following Galen, are to be 'some things the same, some added, some omitted, some changed', then almost anything will pass muster, and Roman adaptations, notably our most famous case, that of Plautus' rewriting in the *Bacchides* of Menander's *Dis exapaton*, can certainly be made to fit the criteria, although that will not help us to understand how the ancient theatrical and critical tradition conceived of 'revisions'. What perhaps mattered in establishing a play as a διασκευή of an earlier play, rather than a 'new' play, was both what was preserved from one version to the next and, second, the extent of the changes and/or omissions. Clearly, Greek critics thought they knew a διασκευή when they saw one, though no doubt the term and its related verbs were used with varying degrees of 'technicality' — not every revision need be classified as a 'revision' — and one ancient notice (Aulus Gellius 3.3.13) even suggests that Latin critics, presumably following in the wake of Greek criticism, did indeed identify some Plautine plays as διασκευαί, though not of Greek plays, but rather of earlier Latin ones,[24] a notice that emphasizes the need for caution when applying the term to Roman comedy more generally.

Before passing to the case of Aristophanes' *Clouds*, we should note that although comedy and texts about comedy supply the bulk of the evidence, the

---

24 Cf. Jocelyn 1996, 404.

term διασκευή and related verbs are also found with reference to tragedy,²⁵ such as the famous claim in the *Hypothesis* to Euripides' *Medea*, which allegedly goes back at least to Aristotle (fr. 774 Gigon), that that play is a διασκευή of a play of Neophron. The case, however, that has attracted most attention is Quintilian's version of the notice which appears in various ancient sources concerning the reperformance of Aeschylean tragedy:

> tragoedias primus in lucem Aeschylus protulit, sublimis et grauis et grandilocus saepe usque ad uitium, sed rudis in plerisque et incompositus: propter quod correctas eius fabulas in certamen deferre posterioribus poetis Athenienses permisere: suntque eo modo multi coronati.
>
> Quintilian, IO 10.1.66
>
> Aeschylus was the first to bring tragedies into the light; his style is lofty and serious and grandiloquent, often in fact to a fault, but in many respects he is rough and unpolished. For this reason the Athenians allowed later poets to enter corrected versions of his plays in the competition; many won the prize in this fashion.

In general, scholars are increasingly sceptical of the ancient claim that, in the words of the Aeschylean *vita*, 'the Athenians so cherished Aeschylus that they voted after his death that someone who wished to stage (διδάσκειν) Aeschylean plays should receive a chorus' (Aeschylus, T1.12 Radt).²⁶ The claim of an official Athenian decree is clearly very different from the general 'culture of reperformance' in local theatres and elsewhere for which there is good evidence for the late fifth century. Quintilian seems to imply that what needs noting is not so much the fact that the Athenians granted this licence to 'later poets', but that later poets were allowed to 'correct' Aeschylus' plays, because of their stylistic

---

25 An interesting example is the spurious prologue transmitted in *Hypoth.* b of the *Rhesos* (= *Adesp. Trag.* 8l K-S); the author of those verses has introduced a divine conversation with which to start the play (itself, of course, a perfectly Euripidean prologue structure), and Hera's reference to 'past pains' seems almost metapoetic, rather like the apparent references to earlier plays in the prologues of Ar. *Ach.* and Eur. *Cycl.* The author of the *Hypothesis* tentatively suggests that the verses derive from actors. On this passage, cf. Fantuzzi 2015.

26 Cf. Biles 2006/7 and (less sceptical) Lamari 2015b. Biles argues that all ancient notices of the decree go back in essence to a single source, represented for us by the *Vita*; this may well be right. Quintilian's characterization of Aeschylean grandeur is very familiar, but *rudis in plerisque et incompositus* (for which cf. also Quint. *IO* 9.4.17 on Lysias) finds a striking parallel in the very interesting claim of the *Vita* that, by comparison with those who came after him, one might judge the simplicity of Aeschylus' dramas to be φαῦλον ... καὶ ἀπραγμάτευτον; LSJ offer no parallel for this sense of ἀπραγμάτευτος. The topos is put to a rather different use at Philostratus, *VA* 6.10, where ἀκατάσκευόν τε καὶ μήπω κεκοσμημένην describes tragedy as Aeschylus inherited it from his predecessors.

roughness.²⁷ The corresponding section of the surviving epitome of Book 2 of Dionysius of Halicarnassus, *On imitation*, which is known to be very closely connected to Quintilian's survey of Greek literature, shares some of the characterization of Aeschylus' style, but has nothing to say about reperformances. Quintilian's notice suggests not a decree permitting reperformances, but rather a decree permitting either διασκευαί by other poets, presented in competition under their own name, or versions of Aeschylus 'corrected' by contemporary poets to be entered under Aeschylus' name. Quintilian's claim, in the form we find it, stretches credulity, but his agenda is familiar enough: attention to stylistic polish, to *corrigere*, is crucial for the budding orator, and Aeschylus falls down badly in this regard, in comparison to Sophocles and, above all, Euripides (cf. also Dio Chrys. 18.7, 52.11). Such attention to style will bring the young orator success in his contests, just as 'corrected' plays of Aeschylus were successful.

The case that always puzzles and intrigues is of course Aristophanes' *Clouds*, where our evidence suggests that authorial revision could indeed be extensive:

τοῦτο ταὐτόν ἐστι τῷ προτέρῳ. διεσκεύασται δὲ ἐπὶ μέρους, ὡς ἂν δὴ ἀναδιδάξαι μὲν αὐτὸ τοῦ ποιητοῦ προθυμηθέντος, οὐκέτι δὲ τοῦτο δι' ἥν ποτε αἰτίαν ποιήσαντος. καθόλου μὲν οὖν σχεδὸν παρ' ἅπαν μέρος γεγενημένη <ἡ> διόρθωσις ... τὰ μὲν γὰρ περιῄρηται, τὰ δὲ παραπέπλεκται καὶ ἐν τῇ τάξει καὶ ἐν τῇ τῶν προσώπων διαλλαγῇ μετεσχημάτισται. ἃ δὲ ὁλοσχερῆ τῆς διασκευῆς τοιαῦτα ὄντα τετύχηκεν. αὐτίκα ἡ παράβασις τοῦ χοροῦ ἤμειπται, καὶ ὅπου ὁ δίκαιος λόγος πρὸς τὸν ἄδικον λαλεῖ, καὶ τελευταῖον ὅπου καίεται ἡ διατριβὴ Σωκράτους.

Hypoth. Ar. *Clouds* VI Wilson

γεγενημένη] γεγένηται Bücheler <ἡ> Bücheler lacunam statuit Dover ἃ δὲ] τὰ δὲ Dindorf ὁλοσχερῆ] -ρῆς VE: -ροῦς Dindorf τοιαῦτα ὄντα del. Bergk

This play is the same as the previous one. It has been revised in part, as if the poet was keen to re-stage it, but no longer did so for some reason. In general, the correction covered every part ... some things have been removed, some included in the play, and there have been changes in structure and in the exchange of characters. Some things as we find them belong entirely to the revision: for example, the chorus' parabasis has been exchanged, and where the just argument rants at the unjust, and finally where Socrates' school burns.

---

27 Some of the difficulties posed by Quintilian's wording are recognized by Garzya 1981, 57, who however suggests emending *correctas* to *corruptas*.

The text presents a number of thorny and unresolved problems of interpretation and translation,[28] but of particular interest in the present context is the fact that the language of the *Hypothesis* is strikingly reminiscent of Galen's 'formula' for a διασκευή cited earlier; it is as if the author of the *Hypothesis* is here applying that 'formula' to the case of the *Clouds*. The extent of the alleged changes is very notable, whether or not (as modern scholars dispute) the revision was in fact designed for actual reperformance, but we may also wonder whether 'it has been revised in part, as though the poet did want to re-stage it, but for some reason did not do so' can tell us something about the expectations of a διασκευή. The second *Clouds* seems to have been very different from the first, but the language of the *Hypothesis* seems to allow two different interpretations: either, partial revision suggests that Aristophanes did intend to restage it as a διασκευή, which by any definition must be only a partial revision, or the fact of only partial revision suggests that something happened which stopped work on the revision.[29] Whatever the truth, the case of the *Clouds*, and the very frequency of the practice of revision, perhaps indeed becoming ever more common as the fourth century wore on, suggests that in comedy there is what we may call a provisionality of structure, an exploited or latent expectation of revision and reperformance, built into the very fabric of drama. Ralph Rosen[30] has argued that the revision of Aristophanes' *Clouds*, with the poet's stress on the play's *phusis* (v. 537), implies 'that dramatic performances were not in fact considered ephemeral, teleologically complete events', and that this points towards a developing notion of a fixed text and a life for drama in written and read form. This is a suggestive and important argument, but from another, rather more theatrical perspective, comedies, like the *Clouds*, were not 'teleologically complete events' because there was *always* the potential of a future performed life, whether in an unchanged shape, or — and this perhaps is where theatrical tradi-

---

28 *Pace* Dover 1968, lxxxiv, it is hard to believe that the transmitted text, ἃ δὲ ὁλοσχερῆ τῆς διασκευῆς ... τετύχηκεν, could mean 'have been composed in their entirety for the new version'. I suspect rather that the genitive depends on ὄντα, with ὄντα τετύχηκεν amounting to 'are'. Bergk deleted τοιαῦτα ὄντα, but perhaps we should just remove τοιαῦτα, to give the required 'some things belong entirely to the revised version'. Many understand τοιαῦτα ὄντα as 'in their present form'.
29 The wording of the *Hypothesis* has been very much discussed, cf. Revermann 2006, 326–332 citing earlier bibliography.
30 Rosen 1997, arguing that a written text must have played a very significant role in the preparation of a διασκευή, no matter what role written texts played in rehearsals and preparations for an original performance; for reservations about Rosen's argument, cf. also Revermann 2006, 332.

tions and audience expectations were most powerful – in a lightly or radically revised form.

The second kind of *diaskeue* of which we hear is that in which one poet took over and reworked the play of another; here we are at the mercy of ancient gossip (and worse) about plagiarism, joint authorship, and so forth. Thus, for example, the Atticist Caecilius (fr. 164 Ofenloch) is reported as declaring that Menander's *Deisidaimon* (T iii K-A) is, 'from start to finish', a rewriting (μεταγράψαι is the term used) of Antiphanes' *Oionistes*, and there is similarly more than one case where the allegation seems to be that Alexis took over a play of Antiphanes and 'with very few changes' presented it as his own.[31] Perhaps in this category belongs the famous case of Straton fr. 1 K-A (a householder protesting about the absurd Homeric language used by the cook he has hired), where we have a papyrus version, a rather longer version cited by Athenaeus, and a further citation by Athenaeus of vv. 1–4 as being by Philemon (fr. 114 K-A). Do we have here Straton revised and expanded by an unknown poet for a reperformance, with the reference to Philemon being a simple mistake, or do we have Philemon reworked by Straton, or some other of the imaginable scenarios?[32] What I think is not in doubt is that these practices were widespread and at some level 'acceptable' (whatever that might mean) in dramatic competitions. Once again, there seems to be a sense of flexibility and provisionality built into the nature of comedy: the complaints about the cook obviously belong to a scene-type which could very easily be expanded or contracted.

The surviving alternative endings of Plautus' *Poenulus* show the kind of thing which we must assume was always possible, in Greek no less than in Latin; though there is no scholarly agreement on how to distinguish the different layers from one another, the various versions which have been combined into our text of that play seem to be alternative ways of contracting or expanding the ending. As the case of the *Casina* suggests (cf. earlier in this chapter), and also – though this is a very different case – the transmitted final scene of Aeschylus' *Septem*, endings of plays were particularly liable to intervention in performance;[33] it is perhaps here that we should group the doubts that arise as to whether the transmitted conclusion of Aristophanes' *Lysistrata* belongs to the original performance or to a subsequent restaging.[34] We are of course more used

---

31 Discussion in Arnott 1996, 813–814.
32 Cf. Kassel 1974, 125–126.
33 Roger Dawe has argued that the end of Sophocles' *Oedipus Tyrannus* has suffered a similar fate, cf. Dawe 2006, 193.
34 Cf. Revermann 2006, 254–260, note 17 of this chapter.

to phenomena such as 'alternative scripts' not so much in extant Greek comedy as in its relative mime, though how closely the two forms are related is a subject where new texts always threaten to shiftthe parameters. Famously, the papyrus of the *Charition*-mime (fr. mim. 6 Cunningham) contains on the *verso* a variant version, written in a different hand (but the same hand which wrote the *Moicheutria* mime also on the *verso*), of part of the *Charition*-mime preserved on the *recto*; the differences suggest that we are not just dealing with, for example, an abbreviation, but with the same scene played and conceived in two different ways (the *verso* version probably adds, for example, a new and not unimportant character). We can only guess at the circumstances which moved someone to include this variant version on the same papyrus, and very different views have been held as to whether this is an 'acting script', and — if so — what kind of script, but the phenomenon is not isolated. The mime-like performance scenario preserved on *POxy* 5189 seems to offer a repeated scene with variant characters, rather than alternate versions of the same performance, but clearly we are in the same 'reperformance' world: in Peter Parsons' words, 'similar texts have been seen as skeletons, to be fleshed out in performance, so that spoken words may be related to improvised action.'[35] We associate such phenomena with that whole world which passes under the titles 'sub-literate', 'letteratura di consumo', etc., where — so our textual evidence might suggest — fidelity to a particular written text carries relatively little weight, where there is in fact no 'fixed text' and, we might well say, no performance, *only* reperformance. Beyond 'mime', primary examples would be, in the traditional account of such things, narrative texts such as the *Life of Aesop* and the *Alexander Romance*.

It is, of course, unsurprising that comedy shares scene-types and motifs with that whole cluster of performance-types which we label 'mime'.[36] Thus, for example, a famous set of comic illustrations which feature a young man obviously the worse for wear from drink and being supported by a slave has been thought to go back to a comedy of the time of Menander, perhaps even to illustrate Menander's *Methe*.[37] Athenaeus informs us that one of the characters played by a μαγῳδός was 'a man who is drunk and on a *komos* to his girlfriend' (14.621c), and a preserved fragment of a mime (3 Cunningham) shows just this scenario, where the text plainly gives much room for improvisation and theatrical fun; Plautus has a very similar 'drunk scene' in the *Mostellaria*, where

---

35 Parsons 2014, 28.
36 For mime as a kind of 'para-comedy', cf. Hunter 1995.
37 Cf. Green 1985, Csapo 2014, 117–119.

Callidamatas, like the mime character, is affected by both love and drink and requires support (v. 324).[38]

It might be thought that the avoidance of verbal improvisation and the use of relatively fixed scripts were among the ways in which 'high' comedy, whether that of an Aristophanes or a Menander, differentiated itself from 'lower' mimic forms; Aristophanes' claims in the parabasis for the higher art of the *Clouds* are well known (vv. 537–543). Farcical violence, such as we see for example in the mime-script of *POxy* 5189, and rude dancing belong, so the parabasis of *Clouds* suggests, to the realm of 'the low';[39] ideologically, we might say, repetition more generally is a mark of a performance style from which high comedy seeks (at least rhetorically) to differentiate itself. The situation, however, is unsurprisingly more nuanced than that. Consider the scene of the *Acharnians* in which Lamachus and Dikaiopolis equip themselves for their respective 'expeditions' (vv. 1097–1142); every verse spoken by Dikaiopolis echoes and mocks the previous verse of Lamachus. Clearly, we have here a version of a very common type of popular song contest ('botta e risposta'),[40] and just as with the opening phallic song and with the very 'Megarian' humour of the Megarian 'pig'-seller, Dikaiopolis' triumph is here expressed through very familiar modes of 'popular entertainment'; such 'scripted improvisation' invites us to share in Dikaiopolis' victory, while also encouraging us to award the victory to Aristophanes. Rather different perhaps is the 'scripted improvisation' of the final scene of Menander's *Dyskolos* in which Sikon and Getas torment the injured Knemon; the links between this scene, with its farcical repetitiveness, obscenity and lewd dancing, and traditions of the mime are well established,[41] but it is worth noting that both the place of the scene within the dramatic structure – Getas wants to seize the *kairos* (v. 885), that is the unexpected opportunity for revenge which has been handed to him – and the scene itself as it develops emphasize the (allegedly) 'unplotted' nature of the scene, in keeping with the low status of the characters responsible for it. It may be worth noting that this scene could in fact be omitted

---

38 Cf. also *Pseudolus* 1296–1297. The Plautine scenes remind us of Bruno Gentili's work on the links between traditions of Hellenistic performance and Plautine comedy; Nervegna 2007 successfully shows that the textual evidence for theatrical performance of abbreviated and musicalized Greek plays is far less strong than Gentili argued (most of the papyri he adduced, which might suggest the performance of extracts, do not in fact seem connected with theatrical traditions), but some of the links between Plautus and Hellenistic lyric are not easily dismissed.
39 In vv. 549–550 Aristophanes suggests that the 'violence' of his plays is metaphorical.
40 Cf. Wallochy 1992, 16–21, Palumbo Stracca 1996.
41 Cf. Hunter 2002.

in any given performance of the play: we might think (rightly) that such a performance would be much the poorer for the omission, and consider that this would leave Knemon and his view of the world as uncomfortable loose ends, but the actual excision would be painless for any director to perform. As it stands, the separability of the scene serves its dramatic purpose: by being outside the tight narrative structure of the plot, its difference is marked and emphasized.

Even if, therefore, our surviving texts of Greek comedy seem relatively free of large-scale interventions, our notion of 'the text' of a play, as an artefact with discrete boundaries, which were occasionally invaded by 'actors' interpolations' and other foreign matter, but which remained essentially sovereign, at the very least needs caution, and the reasons for that caution are built into the very nature of comedy. We are here moving very much in the realm of the speculative, but this is inevitable in any attempt to plot the history of post-classical dramatic poetry. What does seem worth doing is the attempt to relate this phenomenon of comic practice, if indeed something along these lines is not a mere shadow, to what else we know of that history.

Whatever other changes we can trace in comic structures through the fourth century, the most significant seems to be that associated with the chorus. This is not the place to rehearse the evidence or the arguments again, so let me just assume for present purposes what I take to be the *communis opinio*, namely, that there was a gradual move towards a drama of five acts, which were separated by some sort of musical interlude by a 'chorus', but those interludes were not normally either specially composed by the poet or 'relevant' to the *muthos* being enacted by the actors. We see an early stage of this history in Aristophanes' last surviving play, the *Ploutos*, and its full flowering in our texts of Menander. How then, if at all, are these developments related to the phenomena I have been discussing?

The engaged presence and participation of a chorus with a particular dramatic identity as wasps, birds, or frogs is of course one of the most striking features of Old Comedy, but, as is well known, this chorus does not just embody its particular dramatic character, but its members are also (though the intensity of this might vary through the play) 'Athenian citizens' who speak and sing to fellow citizens in the audience. Chris Carey has recently discussed how the choral voice also links the dramatic past, present, and future by, to use my rather than his words, embodying the institution of comedy which is a stable and recurrent feature of Athenian life, though here-today-and-gone-tomorrow poets are allowed to make temporary use and offer temporary transformation of the institution each year.⁴² There is some analogy, and something of interest in the analogy, with the familiar fact that satyr-play is similarly very generically self-aware, in the sense that the chorus 'knows' that it is not just the chorus of one particular play, but — in an important sense — the chorus of every satyr-play, who have seen it all and done it all before. Every satyr-play evokes the spirit of satyr-plays of the past and looks forward to satyr-plays of the future, and this is of course bound up with the repetitive motifs and plot structures of satyr-drama.⁴³ In both comedy and satyr-play, then, it is the chorus who are the guardians of tradition.

What then happens when the extraordinary institution of the chorus loses its intimate connection with the plot being acted out in front of it? One consequence (though here there is the inevitable chicken-and-egg question) has been much discussed in recent years — namely, how the diminishing role of the chorus was one factor in the ease with which Attic drama spread to centres outside (and in some cases far outside) Attica. Much harder to document, but potentially as important, is a structural consideration. If it was the chorus which (to put it very banally) held the comedy together, by giving it, as it were, a centre of gravity, did the removal of that force also loosen the sinews which held the spoken parts together, so that, in Aristotle's words about *embolima* (see earlier in this chapter, though he principally has tragedy in mind), 'a speech or a whole episode' could be adapted from one play to another. Even Aristotle, with his notorious undervaluation (or so it would seem) of the tragic chorus, nevertheless saw in the use of choral ἐμβόλιμα a threat to the bodily integrity of a tragedy, so that (almost) one could no longer discern one play from another. The separation of the chorus from the 'action on stage' presumably gave greater emphasis to the chorus as indeed just that, 'the chorus'; in other words, that aspect of the chorus as an element of stability which we have already identified in Old Comedy became more prominent, as a special identity for the chorus which changed with every play gradually disappeared. It was perhaps the removal of the presence of a special chorus which led to a shift in the sense of the identity and unity of any performance. Chorusless Roman comedy could, on the other hand, take this more flexible unity, and hence the possibility of moving material from

---

42 Carey 2013, esp. 157–158.
43 Cf., e.g., Hunter 2009, 56–59, Lämmle 2013, ch. 7. Analogies between comedy and satyr-play, of course, go well beyond this choral pattern, cf. earlier in this chapter on the 'full restoration of Dionysiac celebration' at the end of Ar. *Ach*.

one play to another, as a starting point: it was not a position to which it had to move.

There is at least one obvious objection to this speculative comic history. We have a very significant amount of Menander and, although (unsurprisingly) there are apparent similarities of motif and character across the corpus, there is really no sign of the kind of authorial moving around or repetition of scenes or speeches such as I have conjured up, or indeed of any extensive intervention by actors in performance. One could plead that the nature of the Menandrean texts which survive probably preclude any sign of this, but any such speculation will have to admit that it is short of evidence. Nevertheless, it is, I think, worth asking to what extent Menander was a special case, perhaps even the exception which proves the rule. Certainly by the time of Terence and probably earlier,[44] Menander's renown had far eclipsed that of his rivals, and we may wonder whether part of that success was owed to the fact that his drama was actually rather more innovative and radical than our picture allows us to see. New Comedy still tends to make many people's eyes glaze over — everything seems to be so much the same — but Menander may have gradually worked towards a drama where parts and episodes were not in fact interchangeable, where cooks did not issue long monologues with little bearing on the plot of a particular play (and I say that in full knowledge of what I wrote previously about Gnatho's monologue in Terence's *Eunuchus*), where — to go back to Aristotle again — scene succeeded scene 'by probability or necessity'. To accept some, even watered-down, version of this view, is not (I think) to damn, e.g., Diphilus and Philemon when they cannot defend themselves; rather it is in part to wonder why antiquity found Menander to be so far ahead of his rivals. Whether this reputation for extraordinary plotting also protected Menander's text from major interference when being acted we cannot say, but it is perhaps not unlikely.

One apparent difference between Greek and Roman New Comedy is that, whereas Roman comedy is not only intensely self-reflexive, but also offers rich evidence, and not just in Terence's prologues, for the development of a Latin critical terminology, Greek New Comedy shows various (relatively gentle) metatheatrical techniques, but is otherwise largely free of critical and generic engagement. In this, it differs notoriously not just from Roman comedy, but also of course from Old Comedy. Why? Is some of the loss of critical engagement on the Greek side in part due, not just (again) to the disappearance of a 'special' chorus, but also to a growing sense of the repetitiveness of the genre, that sense in fact which allowed Terence, paradoxically, to make some of his most provoca-

---

[44] Cf., e.g., Nesselrath 2011.

tive critical claims? Aristophanes had made jokes about the repetitiveness of some comedy, had indeed himself repeated verses from play to play (the description of Cleon in *Wasps* and *Peace*), perhaps because he knew they had been well received and repetition would bring the success of familiarity, but at the same time he also made his choruses intensely proprietorial about his own work. These two tendencies — on one hand, a rich underbelly of repetition and copying and, on the other, the agonistic posturing of poets well aware that they were all as alike as they were different — had long lived in productive tension; in the Hellenistic theatre it was the repetition and copying which won out, whereas the agonistic posturing now became the stuff of anecdote and biography.

Bibliography

Arnott, W.G. 1996. *Alexis: The Fragments*, Cambridge.
Biles, Z.P. 2006–7. 'Aeschylus' afterlife: reperformance by decree in 5th-C. Athens?', *Illinois Classical Studies* 31–2, 206–242.
Csapo, E. 2014. 'The Iconography of Comedy', in: M. Revermann (ed.), *The Cambridge Companion to Greek Comedy*, Cambridge, 95–127.
Csapo, E. 2015. 'The Earliest Phase of "Comic" Choral Entertainments in Athens. The Dionysian Pompe and the "Birth" of Comedy', in: S. Chronopoulos/C. Orth (eds.), *Fragmente einer Geschichte griechischen Komödie, Fragmentary History of Greek Comedy*, Heidelberg, 66–108.
Csapo, E. 2016. 'The "Theology" of the Dionysia and Old Comedy', in: E. Eidinow/J. Kindt/R. Osborne (eds.), *Theologies of Ancient Greek Religion*, Cambridge, 117–152.
Csapo, E./Slater, W.J. 1995. *The Context of Ancient Drama*, Ann Arbor.
Csapo, E./Wilson, P. 2015. 'Drama outside Athens in the fifth and fourth Centuries BC', in: A. Lamari, *Reperformance of Drama in the Fifth and Fourth Centuries BC (Trends in Classics 7)*, Berlin, 316–95.
Dawe, R.D. 2006. *Sophocles, Oedipus Rex*, 2nd ed., Cambridge.
Dover, K.J. 1968. *Aristophanes' Clouds*, Oxford.
Dover, K.J. 1987. *Greek and the Greeks*, Vol. I, Oxford.
Else, G.F. 1957. *Aristotle's Poetics: The Argument*, Cambridge.
Fantuzzi, M. 2015. 'Performing and Informing: on the prologues of the [Euripidean] *Rhesus*', in: A. Lamari, *Reperformance of Drama in the Fifth and Fourth Centuries BC (Trends in Classics 7)*, Berlin, 224–236.
Finglass, P.J. 2015. 'Ancient reperformances of Sophocles', in: A. Lamari, *Reperformance of Drama in the Fifth and Fourth Centuries BC (Trends in Classics 7)*, Berlin, 207–223.
Fontaine, M. 2014. 'Dynamics of appropriation in Roman comedy: Menander's *Kolax* in three Roman receptions (Naevius, Plautus and Terence's *Eunuchus*)', in: S.D. Olson (ed.), *Ancient Comedy and Reception*, Berlin, 180–202.

Garzya, A. 1981. 'Sulla questione delle interpolazioni degli attori nei testi tragici', in: I. Gallo (ed.), *Studi Salernitani in memoria di Raffaele Cantarella*, Salerno, 53–75.
Goldhill, S. 1991. *The Poet's Voice*, Cambridge.
Green, J.R. 1985. 'Drunk again: a study in the iconography of the comic theater', *American Journal of Archaeology* 89, 465–472.
Gudeman, A. 1934. *Aristoteles περὶ ποιητικῆς*, Berlin/Leipzig.
Günther, H.-C. 1996. *Exercitationes Sophocleae*, Göttingen.
Halliwell, S. 1986. *Aristotle's* Poetics, London.
Hamilton, R. 1974. 'Objective evidence for actors' interpolations in Greek tragedy', *Greek, Roman and Byzantine Studies* 15, 387–402.
Hanink, J. 2014. *Lycurgan Athens and the Making of Classical Tragedy*, Cambridge.
Hordern, J.H. 2002. *The Fragments of Timotheus of Miletus*, Oxford.
Hunter, R. 1983. *Eubulus: The Fragments*, Cambridge.
Hunter, R. 1995. 'Plautus and Herodas', in: L. Benz/E. Stärk/G. Vogt-Spira (eds.), *Plautus und die Tradition des Stegreifspiels*, Tübingen, 155–169 [= Hunter 2008, 212–228].
Hunter, R. 2002. '"Acting down": the ideology of Hellenistic performance', in: P. Easterling/ E. Hall (eds.), *Greek and Roman Actors*, Cambridge, 189–205 [= Hunter 2008, 643–662].
Hunter, R. 2009. *Critical Moments in Classical Literature*, Cambridge.
Hunter, R. 2016. 'Some Dramatic Terminology', in: S. Frangoulidis/S. Harrison/G. Manuwald (eds.), *Roman Drama and its Contexts*, Berlin, 13–24 [= this volume 399–410].
Hutchinson, G.O. 1985. *Aeschylus, Septem contra Thebas*, Oxford.
Janko, R. 1987. *Aristotle, Poetics I*, Indianapolis.
Jocelyn, H.D. 1993. Review of O. Zwierlein, *Zur Kritik und Exegese des Plautus. I: Poenulus und Curculio* (Stuttgart, 1990), *Gnomon* 65, 122–137.
Jocelyn, H.D. 1996. Review of O. Zwierlein, *Zur Kritik und Exegese des Plautus. II: Miles Gloriosus* (Stuttgart 1991), *Gnomon* 68, 402–420.
Kassel, R. 1974. 'Ärger mit dem Koch (Com. Gr. Fr. 219 Austin)', *Zeitschrift für Papyrologie und Epigraphik* 14, 121–127.
Lamari, A. 2015. 'Aeschylus and the beginning of tragic reperformances', in: A. Lamari, *Reperformance of Drama in the Fifth and Fourth Centuries BC (Trends in Classics 7)*, Berlin, 189–206.
Lämmle, R. 2013. *Poetik des Satyrspiels*, Heidelberg.
Nervegna, S. 2007. 'Staging scenes or plays? Theatrical revivals of "old" Greek drama in antiquity', *Zeitschrift für Papyrologie und Epigraphik* 162, 14–42.
Nervegna, S. 2013. *Menander in Antiquity: The Contexts of Reception*, Cambridge.
Nesselrath, H.-G. 2011. 'Menander and his rivals: new light from the Comic Adespota?', in: D. Obbink/R. Rutherford (eds.), *Culture in Pieces*, Oxford, 119–137.
Olson, S.D. 2002. *Aristophanes: Acharnians*, Oxford.
Page, D.L. 1934. *Actors' Interpolations in Greek Tragedy*, Oxford.
Palumbo Stracca, B.M. 1993. 'Corinna e il suo pubblico', in: R. Pretagostini (ed.), *Tradizione e innovazione nella cultura greca da Omero all'età ellenistica. Scritti in onore di Bruno Gentili*, Rome, 3.403–412.
Parsons, P.J. 2014. '5187–5189. "Mimes"', in: *The Oxyrhynchus Papyri* Vol. LXXIX, London, 13–41.
Pickard-Cambridge, A. 1962. *Dithyramb Tragedy and Comedy*, 2nd ed. rev. by T.B.L. Webster, Oxford.

Revermann, M. 2006. *Comic Business: Theatricality, Dramatic Technique, and Performance Contexts of Aristophanic Comedy*, Oxford.
Rosen, R.M. 1997. 'Performance and textuality in Aristophanes' *Clouds*', *Yale Journal of Criticism* 10, 397–421.
Scattolin, P. 2011. 'Aristotele e il coro tragico (*Poetica* 12, 18)', in: A. Rodighiero/P. Scattolin (eds.), '*...un enorme individuo, dotato di polmoni soprannaturali'. Funzioni, interpretazioni e rinascite del coro drammatico Greco*, Verona, 161–215.
Sidwell, K. 2001. 'Aristotle, *Poetics* 1456a25–32', in: K. McGroatry (ed.), *Eklogai. Studies in Honour of Thomas Finan and Gerard Watson*, Maynooth, 78–84.
Sidwell, K. 2009. *Aristophanes the Democrat: The Politics of Satirical Comedy during the Peloponnesian War*, Cambridge.
Storey, I. 2003. *Eupolis. Poet of Old Comedy*, Oxford.
Veyne, P. 1989. 'ΔΙΑΣΚΕΥΑΙ: le théâtre grec sous l'empire (Dion de Pruse, XXXII, 94)', *Revue des Études Grecques* 102, 339–345.
Wallochy, B. 1992. *Streitszenen in der griechischen Komödie*, Tübingen.

Part III: **Hellenistic Poetry**

7 Language and Interpretation in Greek Epigram

The study of the relationship between Hellenistic epigram and the archaic and classical poetry which nourished it has largely been conducted in terms of motifs and structures.[1] Language and imagery have received less attention, in part perhaps because it is not easy to find the critical language in which such matters, particularly the thorny issue of change over time, may profitably be discussed. I offer here four brief soundings into different, but related, aspects of the issue of whether differences between archaic and classical poetry, on the one hand, and Hellenistic poetry, on the other, can usefully be generalised; even if the answer will prove largely negative, we may hope to learn things along the way about the poetry of different periods. In Sections 1 and 2 I focus particularly upon the way in which poets explain (or do not) the language and images of their poems; Section 3 considers the treatment of a particular idea in poems of (probably) different periods, and Section 4 confronts a Hellenistic epigram directly with its archaic model.

1

I begin from Meleager, *AP* 5.190 (= LXIV *HE*)

> κῦμα τὸ πικρὸν Ἔρωτος ἀκοίμητοί τε πνέοντες
> ζῆλοι καὶ κώμων χειμέριον πέλαγος,
> ποῖ φέρομαι; πάντηι δὲ φρενῶν οἴακες ἀφεῖνται·
> ἦ πάλι τὴν τρυφερὴν Σκύλλαν ἐποψόμεθα.

> Bitter wave of Love and unceasing blasts of jealousy and stormy
> the sea of the *kômos:* where am I drifting? The rudder of my mind
> is loosed out of control; shall I see the sexy Scylla again?

The introductory note in Gow/Page is more sober than the speaker of the epigram: 'Two common motifs are combined, (a) the Jealous Lover, inebriated, walking through bad weather...to his mistress; and (b) the comparison of Love to a storm at sea...'. This is certainly true, but what is most striking, beyond the obvious reworkings of the *Odyssey* is what might be called (with some awkwardness) the interpretative closedness of the poem. Readers do not have to

---

[1] For the former Giangrande 1968 remains a bibliographically rich survey; for the latter see ch. 7 of Fantuzzi/Hunter 2004.

guess what the wave' (desire), the 'winds' (jealousy), the wintry sea' (a *kômos*), and the 'rudder' (the reasoning mind) represent, as the poem itself quite explicitly tells us. We may be rather more uncertain about the identity of 'sexy Scylla', but the speaker apparently would like to (survive to?) see her again, though 'seeing Scylla' is the very last thing a sailor would normally wish to do (cf. *Odyssey* 12.88, 258).[2] I will return to the subject of 'consistency' in poetic imagery in Section 2 below, but we may note here that πικρὸν has been thought to be an odd epithet for a wave and thus explicable only with regard to the poet's ἔρως;[3] opinions may differ as to whether we should in fact understand it as 'bitter, pungent, salty' of the wave (as when the literally shipwrecked Odysseus spits out ἅλμην πικρήν from his mouth, *Odyssey* 5.322–323) and as 'bitter' of the poet's desire, as ἀκοίμητοι 'unceasing, unsleeping' clearly points both to the blasts of jealousy and to the lover's sleeplessness. If the more complex reading is correct, however, we can see in the first distich a clear (and, presumably, deliberately overt) set of constructed analogies; we are supposed to see the poet, not just on his passionate *kômos*, but also at work on his poem.[4] This is literary art as *epideixis*.

The elements of Meleager's storm are, of course, very familiar: the 'wave of desire' is a common *topos* with archaic roots,[5] and the mind as the governing rudder takes us back to Plato's extended analogy between the 'governance' of the individual soul and the governance of the state. It is indeed the 'ship of state' of which we are here most closely reminded: in the epigram, however, it is not the whole state, but rather a single individual sailor (like Odysseus in *Odyssey* 5) who is drifting at the mercy of the storm. The 'ship of state' (not necessarily a very helpful label) is one of the most common images of archaic and classical poetry,[6] and it would be neither possible nor helpful to try to draw up an exhaustive list of the categories in which it appears. The most famous instance, of course, is Alcaeus 208 Voigt, quoted by 'Heraclitus' as an example of 'allego-

---

[2] It is not clear to me that we have to see here a reference to a girl called Tryphera (cf. Meleager, *AP* 5.154 = LXIII HE).

[3] So, e.g., Tarán 1979, III.

[4] There may be felt to be more doubt about χειμέριον, but we should not exclude the possibility that Meleager could use the word to mean both 'wintry' of the sea and 'stormy' of the lover's emotions, cf. Meleager, *AP* 12.167 = CIX *HE*. For the situation in general cf. particularly the 'wintry' opening of Menander's *Misoumenos*.

[5] Cf. further below on Pindar fr. 123: Ap. Rhod. *Arg.* 4.445–449 is of particular interest in this regard (cf. Hunter 1993, 116–117).

[6] Some earlier bibliography in Nisbet and Hubbard's introduction to Horace, *Odes* 1.14; particularly relevant here is Gentili 1988, 197–215. See also Cucchiarelli 2004/5.

ry'; here the ship seems to represent the parlous state of Alcaeus' faction after the coming to power of the tyrant Myrsilus:

ἀσυννέτημμι τὼν ἀνέμων στάσιν,
τὸ μὲν γὰρ ἔνθεν κῦμα κυλίνδεται,
τὸ δ' ἔνθεν, ἄμμες δ' ὂν τὸ μέσσον
 νᾶϊ φορήμεθα σὺν μελαίναι

χείμωνι μόχθεντες μεγάλωι μάλα·
πὲρ μὲν γὰρ ἄντλος ἰστοπέδα ἔχει,
λαῖφος δὲ πᾶν ζάδηλον ἤδη,
 καὶ λάκιδες μέγαλαι κὰτ' αὖτο,

χάλαισι δ' ἄγκυραι, <τὰ δ' ὀήϊα>
[   ]
[   ]
 τοι πόδες ἀμφότεροι μενο[

ἐν βιμβλίδεσσι· τοῦτό με καῖ σ[άοι
μόνον κτλ.

Alcaeus, 208.1–14 Voigt[7]

I do not grasp the position of the winds; one wave rolls in from one side, another from another, and we in the middle are carried along with our black ship, labouring in a very mighty storm. The bilge rises above the mighty storm, all the sail lets light through, and there are huge rents in it. The anchors sway slack...the feet stay...in the sheets. This alone might save me...

We do not know how Alcaeus' poem ended; the 'interpretation' of the poem may have been made explicit within the poem itself, as seems to have happened in the case of another Alcaean 'ship of state' poem (6 Voigt);[8] appeal to the still disputed case of Horace, *Odes* 1.14 *o nauis, referent in mare te noui/fluctus*) is

---

7 There are some famous textual problems in this poem (cf., e.g., Bonanno 1990, 207–232), but they do not, I think, affect the present discussion.
8 This is indicated both by what seems to be the general tenor of stanzas 4–7 and, particularly, by μοναρχίαν in v. 27. After quoting the opening of Alcaeus 208, 'Heraclitus' (cf. below p. 134) observes: 'Who would not immediately think from the preceding (προτρεχούσης) image of the sea that this was a description of the terror felt by sailors on the sea? But this is not so' (5.7). Russell/Konstan *ad loc.* understand this to mean that 'the image precedes the explanation rather than following it' (cf. Quintilian 8.3.77); if so, this would seem to settle the matter. We might, however, wonder how much of the poem 'Heraclitus' actually knew (see. n. 13 below), though he certainly knew that this was the opening of the poem. LSJ s.v. III understand 'the foregoing likeness', but it is hard to see why 'Heraclitus' would have bothered to say this.

unlikely to settle the matter. It may well be that the manner of the opening stanzas themselves made clear, though not apparently to 'Heraclitus',[9] that this is not a 'real' storm at sea which is being described,[10] but that is a rather different aspect of the relationship between poet and audience. Anacreon, *PMG* 417, which is quoted in the same chapter by 'Heraclitus' and which may be a complete poem, may shed some light on the general problem:

> πῶλε Θρηικίη, τί δή με
>   λοξὸν ὄμμασι βλέπουσα
> νηλέως φεύγεις, δοκεῖς δὲ
>   μ' οὐδὲν εἰδέναι σοφόν;
> ἴσθι τοι, καλῶς μὲν ἄν τοι
>   τὸν χαλινὸν ἐμβάλοιμι,
> ἡνίας δ' ἔχων στρέφοιμί
>   σ' ἀμφὶ τέρματα δρόμου·
> νῦν δὲ λειμῶνας τε βόσκεαι
>   κοῦφά τε σκιρτῶσα παίζεις,
> δεξιὸν γὰρ ἱπποπείρην
>   οὐκ ἔχεις ἐπεμβάτην.

Anacreon, PMG 417

Thracian filly, why with sideways glances do you flee from me relentlessly and think that I know no clever schemes? Be assured, I would put the bit properly on you, and holding the reins I would steer you around the end-points of the course. Now you are grazing in the meadows, skipping lightly about as you play; you do not have a skilled rider who has experience with horses.

Here, quite unlike Meleager's poem, it is the very indeterminacy of the language which is crucial; the language gestures towards very particular, in some cases very physical, meanings, but leaves open the gap of uncertainty, which is central to all erotic experience (as also to much language-use).[11] We may wish to invoke the sympotic traditions of riddling and role-playing, which of course remain as powerful influences also on Hellenistic epigram, but the difference in mode between Meleager and the archaic poems is clear enough.

Despite its provocative opening appeal to '(failure of) understanding', an appeal which challenges the audience to interpret as it also directs them towards a particular model of reception, Alcaeus 208 is not generally held by

---

9 See previous note.
10 Cf. Rösler 1980, 134–148, esp. 137 citing Kassel 1973, 102–104.
11 Cf., e.g., Goldhill 1987, 14–15. On the language of the poems cited by 'Heraclitus' see also Silk 1974, 122–124.

scholars to be a 'detailed allegory'. If Anacreon 417 playfully exploits our drive towards and past experience of interpretation, Alcaeus' audiences (including ourselves) are not invited to make each detail (the waves, the bilge, the torn sails etc.) correspond to something in 'the state / the position of the group etc.'; what is important is rather the very vivid description of 'trouble at sea', corresponding to trouble on land.[12] Our principal source for Alcaeus 208, 'Heraclitus' (*Quaest. Hom.* 5.5–7A) explains the poem as an allegory about 'Myrsilus and the tyrannical conspiracy against the Mytileneans'[13] and notes that, as an islander, Alcaeus naturally likens the ills caused by the tyrants to storms at sea. So too, in interpreting Horace, *Odes* 1.14, Quintilian notes *nauem pro re publica, fluctus et tempestates pro bellis ciuilibus, portum pro pace atque concordia dicit* (8.6.44), without trying to 'interpret' the broken mast, torn sails and so forth;[14] it is indeed of some interest for the history of interpretation that 'detailed' allegorical readings of the Horatian poem seem to enter the tradition rather later, as can be seen from the commentaries of ps.-Acro and Porphyrio. Bruno Gentili's claims that 'if allegory is an extended metaphor...it is obvious that every element must convey a piece of information' and that 'if the image is an allegory, every element in it should have a precise reference'[15] seem false both to the archaic poems which survive and to the history of the ancient tradition of 'allegorical interpretation'. In particular, Hellenistic epigram seems very far from the mode of both Alcaeus and Horace.

Another very common erotic topos is 'the hunt of love'. Consider first Rhianus, *AP* 12.146:

ἀγρεύσας τὸν νεβρὸν ἀπώλεσα, χὦ μὲν ἀνατλὰς
μυρία, καὶ στήσας δίκτυα καὶ στάλικας,

---

12 I am aware, of course, that many different positions might be, and are, held on this question, particularly if 're-performance' is brought into the equation. Burnett 1983, 155 observes 'There is no way of knowing how far to press the allegory...' and Gentili 1988, 199–201 precisely offers a 'detailed' decoding (which seems to me, for what it is worth, quite misguided). For some general considerations cf. Rosier 1980, 119–120, 140–144, and cf. further Bonanno 1990, 207–232.
13 'Heraclitus' probably drew this knowledge as much from the critical tradition (cf. the apparent occurrence of 'Myrsilus' in Alcaeus 305b Voigt, which seems to be a commentary on Alcaeus 208) as from personal knowledge of the latter half of Alcaeus' poem. Our other witness for Alcaeus 208, Cocondrius 3.234–235 Spengel, merely observes that the true subject of the poem is 'political disturbance'.
14 For an example of 'detailed allegory' (or rather its interpretation) involving the rigging of a ship cf. Achilles Tatius 5.16.4–6.
15 Gentili 1988, 199, 215.

> σὺν κενεαῖς χείρεσσιν ἀπέρχομαι· οἱ δ' ἀμογητὶ
> τἀμὰ φέρουσιν, Ἔρως· οἷς σὺ γένοιο βαρύς.

I caught the fawn and lost it; I who had suffered endless trouble, who had set up nets and stakes, come away with empty hands. Others have done nothing and carry off my prize; Eros, be cruel to them.

Rhianus, AP 12.146 = v HE

Rhianus may or may not have in mind Theognis 949–54 (which in origin may or may not be paederastic),[16] but these verses do shed light upon Rhianus' strategy:

> νεβρὸν ὑπὲξ ἐλάφοιο λέων ὣς ἀλκὶ πεποιθὼς
> ποσσὶ καταμάρψας αἵματος οὐκ ἔπιον·
> τειχέων δ' ὑψηλῶν ἐπιβὰς πόλιν οὐκ ἀλάπαξα·
> ζευξάμενος δ' ἵππους ἅρματος οὐκ ἐπέβην·
> πρήξας δ' οὐκ ἔπρηξα, καὶ οὐκ ἐτέλεσσα τελέσσας,
> δρήσας δ' οὐκ ἔδρησ', ἤνυσα δ' οὐκ ἀνύσας.

Theognis, 949–954

Like a lion trusting in its strength, I snatched a fawn from a deer with my claws, and did not drink its blood; I scaled the high walls of a city and did not sack it; I yoked horses and did not mount on the chariot; having acted, I did not act, and having completed, I did not complete; having performed, I did not perform, and having accomplished, I did not accomplish.

As transmitted to us, the riddling Theognidean verses speak to and challenge 'those who understand' (cf. further below); we must, however, never forget that we do not know whether anything originally (or in Rhianus' text, if indeed he had these verses in mind) preceded or followed them, and so we must be cautious about drawing conclusions. Nevertheless, as things stand there is a clear contrast with Rhianus' poem, in which the appeal to Eros in the last verse makes sure that we do not miss the point: the 'allegory' is decoded for us. Secondly, consider Callimachus, *AP* 12.102:

> ὡγρευτής, Ἐπίκυδες, ἐν οὔρεσι πάντα λαγωὸν
> διφᾶι, καὶ πάσης ἴχνια δορκαλίδος,
> στίβηι καὶ νιφετῶι κεχρημένος· ἢν δέ τις εἴπηι,
> "τῆ, τόδε βέβληται θηρίον", οὐκ ἔλαβεν.
> χοὑμὸς ἔρως τοιόσδε· τὰ μὲν φεύγοντα διώκειν
> οἶδε, τὰ δ' ἐν μέσσωι κείμενα παρπέταται.

Callimachus, AP 12.102 (= Epigram 31 Pf. = I HE)

---

[16] Vv. 948–949 are repeated in the paederastic Book 2 of Theognis (= 1278c–d). It seems unlikely that 949–954 are a complete poem.

On the mountains, Epicydes, the hunter pursues every hare and the tracks of each deer, enduring frost and snow; but if someone says 'Look! This animal's been hit', he does not take it. This is how my love is: it knows how to pursue what flees, but it flies past anything which lies ready and waiting.

This very influential poem (translated by Horace, cited by Ovid, perhaps resonating in Virgil's simile of Dido as a wounded deer) sets us and Epicydes a riddle (presumably in the context of a symposium), but it also gives us in the final couplet the answer to that riddle, something which the Theognidean verses, as transmitted to us, do not explicitly do.[17]

Much has been written in the last couple of decades about the reception community for archaic lyric and elegy and about how different forms of 'coded' language – the riddle, the *ainos*, the fable etc. – both create group-cohesiveness and also act as a boundary which excludes 'outsiders'.[18] This is perhaps best displayed in a famous example of the 'ship of state' from the Theognidean corpus:

εἰ μὲν χρήματ' ἔχοιμι Σιμωνίδη, οἷα περ ἤδη,
οὐκ ἄν ἀνιώμην τοῖς ἀγαθοῖσο συνών.
νῦν δέ με γιγνώσκοντα παρέρχεται, εἰμὶ δ' ἄφωνος
χρημοσύνηι, πολλῶν γνοὺς ἄν ἄμεινον ἔτι,   670
οὕνεκα νῦν φερόμεσθα καθ' ἱστία λευκὰ βαλόντες
Μηλίου ἐκ πόντου νύκτα διὰ δνοφερήν,
ἀντλεῖν δ' οὐκ ἐθέλουσιν, ὑπερβάλλει δὲ θάλασσα
ἀμφοτέρων τοίχων. ἦ μάλα τις χαλεπῶς
σώιζεται, οἷ ἔρδουσι· κυβερνήτην μὲν ἔπαυσαν   675
ἐσθλόν, ὅτις φυλακὴν εἶχεν ἐπισταμένως·
χρήματα δ' ἁρπάζουσι βίηι, κόσμος δ' ἀπόλωλεν,
δασμὸς δ οὐκέτ' ἴσος γίνεται ἐς τὸ μέσον·
φορτηγοὶ δ' ἄρχουσι, κακοὶ δ' ἀγαθῶν καθύπερθεν.
δειμαίνω, μή πως ναῦν κατὰ κῦμα πίηι.   680
ταῦτά μοι ἠινίχθω κεκρυμμένα τοῖς ἀγαθοῖσιν·
γιγνώσκοι δ' ἄν τις κακός, ἄν σοφὸς ἦι.

Theognis, 667–682

---

17 Further important aspects of 'the Hellenistic' in this poem are discussed by Walsh 1990, 12–13. Richard Rawles points out to me that the brief comparison in Theognis 949 and the (at first) uncertain boundaries of that comparison may be a signal to us of the need for a 'figurative reading'.
18 Helpful guidance and bibliography in Ford 2002, 74–77; the remarks of Gentili 1988, 42–44 are particularly stimulating.

> If I had money, Simonides, as once I had, I would not be distressed in the company of good men. But I know that it passes me by, and need deprives me of a voice, though I would realise better than many that, with white sails lowered, we are being carried beyond the Melian sea through the gloomy night, and that they do not want to bail the ship out, though the sea washes over both sides. Indeed, with the things they are doing, salvation is not easy for anyone. They have got rid of the good steersman who kept a skillful watch; they plunder possessions, all good order is lost, and there is no longer a fair distribution for all. The cargo-carriers are in charge, and the base are above the good; I am afraid that a wave will swallow up the ship. Let these be my veiled riddles for the good; even a base man, if he is wise, would know the meaning.

Here one can presumably argue about how 'detailed' the allegory is (vv. 675–680 make things easier for us by focusing on the sailors rather than damage to individual parts of the ship), but what is not in doubt is that the opening and closing verses make it plain that the central allegory is precisely that, an allegory (though one hardly requiring much 'interpretation'). The speaker claims that he is deprived of a voice because poverty excludes him from full equality with the *agathoi*, but — to be very dogmatic about it — his ability to speak as a master of the coded language of the *agathoi*, an ability which he then advertises in vv. 681–682 (cf. Pindar's similar self-advertisement at *Olympian* 2.84–86), lays a powerful claim to group membership and to 'a voice'.[19] Alcaeus and Anacreon, by contrast, can use the figured speech of 'the group' without apology or advertisement. It would be normal to associate this latter (unexplained) mode with the (real or implied) sympotic setting of both elegy and lyric: such poets address the group in ways which the group will understand, and the mode of the poem is grounded in a performative context where 'explanation' would be superfluous. When, moreover, the poem is re-performed or read away from that context, it is nevertheless that assumed context which 'travels with' the poem.[20] It is therefore both obvious and tempting to trace some of the changes between this mode and that of Hellenistic poetry to changes in reception context.

Of course, this is far from a complete answer. Hellenistic epigrammatists and their audiences used the poetry of the past and a now lengthy tradition of its interpretation as shared points of reference: 'hunting' was thus inevitably erotic, and the focus of poems on such a theme was no longer on revealing that

---

19 Cf. Nagy 1985, 22–26, though his nuance is rather different. *Pace* Nagy, I also prefer Brunck's κακός in v. 682 to the transmitted κακόν.

20 On issues of re-performance and the 'pseudo-intimacy' which attends it cf. Scodel 1996; the apparent absence from Hellenistic epigram of many of the features to which she points is worth further investigation. There is a helpful introduction to the differences in setting between archaic elegy and Hellenistic epigram in Gutzwiller 1998, 115–122.

fact from behind the veils of language, but rather on exploring the consequences of the analogy. The growth of 'literary criticism' and interpretative practice (what Plato makes Socrates call 'examining/ decoding (ἐξετάζεσθαι) the *eikôn*, *Rep.* 6.48934) has thus affected how poetry is written.[21] It is well known that Hellenistic epigram is fond of dramatising the process of interpretation – whether that be of works of art, of tombstones or of literary allusion; Posidippus' famous poem on Lysippus' statue of Kairos serves as an emblem of this interest (*APlan.* 275 = XIX *HE* = 142).[22] This interest in process, what might be thought of as a second-, or 'meta-', level phenomenon, goes hand-in-hand with the way in which poetic imagery is actually used.

2

A poem of the sixth century AD, Macedonius, *AP* 5.235, takes us into familiar Meleagrean waters:

ἦλθες ἐμοὶ ποθέοντι παρ' ἐλπίδα· τὴν δ' ἐνὶ θυμῶι
 ἐξεσάλαξας ὅλην θάμβεϊ φαντασίην,
καὶ τρομέω, κραδίη τε βυθῶι πελεμίζεται οἴστρου,
 ψυχῆς πνιγομένης κύματι Κυπριδίωι.
ἀλλ' ἐμὲ τὸν ναυηγὸν ἐπ' ἠπείροιο φανέντα
 σῶε, τεῶν λιμένων ἔνδοθι δεξαμένη.

Macedonius, *AP* 5.235 (= 8 Madden)

Your coming to me in my longing was beyond my hopes. In my amazement, you blasted all my mind's power of imagination, and I am trembling. In the depths of desire my heart flutters, as my soul drowns in Kypris' wave. I am a shipwrecked sailor who has appeared near land: save me and welcome me inside your harbour.

The 'safe harbour' which the poet imagines is probably very different than that which Alcaeus (fr. 6.8 ἐς δὲ ἔχυρον λίμενα δρό[μωμεν) and Horace (*Odes* 1.14.2-3) imagine for their imperilled craft, but the transference from 'ship of state allegory' to the emotions of the lover is now very familiar. With poets as late as Macedonius it is often very difficult – and often probably misguided – to seek to identify explicit models, but there must here be a fair chance that we are to think specifically of the opening of Theocritus 12:

---

21 Trends in Hellenistic simile-technique offer an obvious parallel to the developments traced here, cf. Hunter 1993, 129–138.
22 For the process of interpretation with works of art cf., e.g., Goldhill 1994, Gutzwiller 2002; for literary allusion cf. Fantuzzi/Hunter 2004, 339–340.

ἤλυθες, ὦ φίλε κοῦρε· τρίτηι σὺν νύκτι καὶ ἠοῖ
ἤλυθες· οἱ δὲ ποθεῦντες ἐν ἤματι γηράσκουσιν.

You have come, dear lad; after two nights and days
you have come. Those who feel longing grow old in a day.

Macedonius does not, however, follow Theocritus in his depiction of erotic self-delusion, but rather combines the 'welcome to the beloved'[23] with the obviously closely related poetic scenario of the effect upon the lover of the sight of the beloved. The most famous and influential example of this latter motif is, of course, Sappho 31 (which may have been influential on Macedonius' trembling and his quivering heart), but we think also of passages such as Pindar fr. 123, where it is completely understandable that, in quoting the passage, Athenaeus (13.601d) should have regarded Theoxenus as an *erômenos* of the poet himself:

χρῆν μὲν κατὰ καιρὸν ἐρώ-
    των δρέπεσθαι, θυμέ, σὺν ἁλικίαι·
τὰς δὲ Θεοξένου ἀκτῖνας πρὸς ὄσσων
μαρμαρυζοίσας δρακείς
ὃς μὴ πόθωι κυμαίνεται, ἐξ ἀδάμαντος
ἢ σιδάρου κεχάλκευται μέλαιναν καρδίαν
ψυχραι φλογί, πρὸς δ' Ἀφροδί-
    τας ἀτιμασθεὶς ἑλικογλεφάρου
ἢ περὶ χρήμασι μοχθίζει βιαίως
ἢ γυναικείωι θράσει
ψυχρὰν † φορεῖται πᾶσαν ὁδὸν θεραπεύων.
ἀλλ' ἐγὼ τᾶς ἕκατι κηρὸς ὣς δαχθεὶς ἕλαι
ἱρᾶν μελισσᾶν τάκομαι, εὖτ' ἂν ἴδω
παίδων νεόγυιον ἐς ἥβαν·
ἐν δ' ἄρα καὶ †Τενέδωι
Πειθώ τ' ἔναιεν καὶ Χάρις
υἱὸν Ἀγησίλα.

Pindar, fr. 123 Maehler

When the time is right, my heart, you should pluck the flower of love in youth, but whoever has seen the rays flashing from the eyes of Theoxenus and is not flooded with desire has a black heart forged from adamant or steel with a cold flame, is dishonoured by bright-eyed Aphrodite, and either is forced to toil for money or with a womanly bravado...[24] But Aphrodite makes me melt like the wax of holy bees which has been attacked by the warmth of the sun, whenever I look upon the beautiful young limbs of boys. So then in Tenedos Persuasion and Grace dwell in the son of Hagesilas.

---

23 Cf., e.g., Cairns 1972, 18–31.
24 Text and meaning uncertain.

Like the speaker of Sappho 31, Macedonius loses all power of rational thought,[25] but whereas Sappho's poem derives much of its power from the tension between the repeated experience described and the taut language and structure within which that experience is described, Macedonius' 'loss of control' is belied, not by structure, but by the imagery of the poem. In v. 2 Macedonius seems to play with the language of literary criticism — θάμβος, φαντασία and ἐξεσάλαξας, suggesting the ἔκπληξις which φαντασία in poetry can properly produce (cf. 'Longinus' 15.2)[26] — but the dominant imagery of the poem is again nautical. This is obvious for vv. 3–6, but those verses (as Madden notes) provoke us to reconnect ἐκσαλάσσειν with the σάλος of the sea and to see in παρ' ἐλπίδα (v. 1) an echo of Aeschylus, *Agamemnon* 900 (from another speech of welcome) γῆν φανεῖσαν ναυτίλος παρ' ἐλπίδα. What Macedonius offers, in other words, is a linking thread of imagery, the coherence of which will presumably be judged differently by different readers, but it is a coherence demanding, as does Meleager in the poem from which we began, interpretative effort (involving rereading) by his readers and one which draws attention to itself, in part by self-consciously exploiting the language of poetic criticism (v. 2). We might perhaps compare its blending of 'viewing of the beloved' with the contemplation of poetic models (Aeschylus, Theocritus etc.) to Catullus' translation of and meditation upon Sappho 31 Voigt, where emotional arousal is also combined with, and indeed arises from, the demands of a mimetic poetics.[27] Be that as it may, Macedonius' nautical imagery seems, as we read, to evolve out of, and constitute a set of variations upon, the allusion to Aeschylus, rather than to follow 'naturally' from the opening statement of the situation; the beloved is, after all, both the storm at sea and the potentially saving harbour. In Pindar fr. 123, by contrast, we find patterns of light vs. dark (vv. 2–5), of soft vs. hard, and of the 'wave of desire' picked up by the liquefaction of the speaker like heated wax, but what we do not find is the 'thought-through' and hence overt image-making of Macedonius. None of this is very surprising, but it is only by focusing on such details that we can hope to capture what is actually characteristic of (rather, of course, than limited to) the Hellenistic and/or late antique mode.

The fact that the attempt to distinguish 'the Hellenistic' from 'the archaic' on stylistic grounds is littered with (sometimes heroic) failures[28] does not mean

---

25 This seems the most obvious way to understand v. 2, cf. further below; Madden *ad loc.* canvasses other possibilities.
26 On ἔκπληξις see Russell's note *ad loc.*
27 Cf. Fantuzzi/Hunter 2004, 472–474.
28 Dover 1971, lxvii–lxviii remain amusing pages.

that the game may not be instructive. Consider the following verses transmitted in Theognis 'Book 2', which use a version of the 'welcome to the beloved' motif of Theocritus 12 and Macedonius, *AP* 5.235:

παῖ, σὺ μὲν αὕτως ἵππος, ἐπεὶ κριθῶν ἀκορέσθης
αὖθις ἐπὶ σταθμοὺς ἤλυθες ἡμετέρους
ἡνίοχόν τε ποθῶν ἀγαθὸν λειμῶνά τε καλόν
κρήνην τε ψυχρὴν ἄλσεά τε σκιερά.

Theognis 1249–52

Just like a horse, lad, when you have had your fill of barley, you have come back again to my stables, longing for your good charioteer, a lovely meadow, cool spring, and shady groves.

Here again we are in the world of sympotic 'likenesses' (cf. esp. Theognis 1267–1270),[29] but is the mode of the imagery that of Anacreon 417 (cf. above), that of Macedonius (and later epigram), or something else again? We are explicitly told that the address is to a boy (who is likened to a horse), not merely to a 'filly' whom we can then choose, if we wish, to understand as a human female. Some critics have wanted to see a not very well disguised *double entendre* in ἐπεὶ κριθῶν ἐκορέσθης and the idea of the erotic 'charioteer' is of course familiar (if by no means monovalent),[30] but, to my knowledge, no one has suggested that 'the meadow, the spring, and the groves' of the *locus amoenus* are to be 'decoded' into, for example, parts of the *erastês*' body. The real issue, of course, as with Anacreon 417, is not whether we 'decode' it or not (anything is, after all, possible, particularly in re-performance situations), but whether or not the poem exploits our drive to 'decode' by inviting detailed interpretation, but then keeping us uncertain about whether there is in fact something there to decode. In his commentary on these verses, Massimo Vetta does not consider the matter worth discussing — for him the *locus amoenus* as a whole seems to be an image of the φιλία which the *erastês* offers, perhaps (though this is not said explicitly) in contrast to the purely sexual desires of other *erastai*. One way of putting one part of the issue would be to ask how much interpretative pressure we should apply to ἀγαθόν in v. 1251 — are we to translate 'skilled' (cf. Anacreon's δεξιόν...ἱπποπείρην), or perhaps rather 'good' (in a socio-political sense)? Another way would be by comparing *Anacreontea* 18 (West's text):

---

29 Cf. Vetta *ad loc.*
30 Cf. Dover 1978, 58–59; my discussion of these verses in Hunter 1996, 188–189 was inadequate.

τὸ δὲ καῦμα τῶν ἐρώτων,
κραδίη, τίνι σκεπάζω;
παρὰ τὴν σκιὴν Βαθύλλου
καθίσω· καλὸν τὸ δένδρον,
ἁπαλὰς δ' ἔσεισε χαίτας
μαλακωτάτωι κλαδίσκωι·
παρὰ δ' αὐτὸ νέρθε ῥοιζεῖ
πηγὴ ῥέουσα Πειθοῦς.
τίς ἂν οὖν ὁρῶν παρέλθοι
καταγώγιον τοιοῦτο;

Anacreontea 18.8–17

How, my heart, shall I keep off the heat of desires? I will sit down in the shade of Bathyllus. The tree is a lovely one, it shakes its soft foliage on a very delicate little branch; right underneath it a flowing spring of Persuasion bubbles up. Who could see such a resting-place and pass by?

How 'worked out' is the comparison of Bathyllus ('Mr Thickwood' in Patricia Rosenmeyer's translation)[31] to a tree? Modern criticism suggests that, as with the archaic poems we have been considering, it is possible to disagree about this.[32] The conceit of the poem may in fact derive much of its inspiration from the same models as Macedonius' poem, cf. Aeschylus, *Agamemnon* 899 [Agamemnon is] ὁδοιπόρωι διψῶντι πηγαῖον ῥέος, 966–7 (by his arrival Agamemnon has spread protective shade over the house), and Theocritus 12.8–9:

τόσσον ἔμ' εὔφρηνας σὺ φανείς, σκιερὴν δ' ὑπὸ φηγὸν
ἠελίου φρύγοντος ὁδοιπόρος ἔδραμον ὥς τις.

Such was the delight your appearance brought me, and I ran to you as a traveller runs into the shade of an oak when the sun is burning.

Certainly, the idea of Bathyllus as a καταγώγιον looks like a variation on the more familiar idea, used by Macedonius in the poem which we have considered, of the beloved (or a part of his/her body) as a λιμήν into which one hopes to sail. The combination of the boy's Πειθώ and his universal appeal (vv. 15–17) also recalls Pindar fr. 123, but the difference between how the two poems work out these ideas might be thought very telling. The fact that the poet of *Anacreontea* 18 is deliberately writing in (a constructed version of) the manner of Anacreon (and perhaps specifically of Anacreon 417) is obviously important; the poem

---

31 Cf. Rosenmeyer 1992, 199.
32 Cf. West 1984, 210, noting that v. 13 refers to Bathyllus' penis, rather than his neck; I do not know whether West was the first to suggest this in print.

challenges us to consider whether contemporary modes of reading Anacreon — for which the evidence of pseudo-Heraclitus is crucial — are appropriate here also. 'Boy as (part of a) *locus amoenus*' has replaced 'girl as free-roaming young horse'; are, however, the ecphrastic wit of the former and the allusive play of the latter at all similar? Important too, of course, is the combination of such imaginative *mimêsis* of both a poetic mode and the ways in which it was interpreted with a clear allusion to the *locus amoenus* at which Plato's most famous discussion of paederastic love, the *Phaedrus*, is set.[33] The Anacreontic poem uses such consciousness of tradition to advertise its literariness; Anacreon 417 floats more freely, as indeterminate as its subject is anonymous.

3

If Anacreon's authorship of *PMG* 417 has never been doubted, the same cannot be said for *AP* 7.226 (= Anacreon, *Epigram* 1 Page = fr. 191 Gentili):

Ἀβδήρων προθανόντα τὸν αἰνοβίην Ἀγάθωνα
πᾶσ' ἐπὶ πυρκαιῆς ἥδ' ἐβόησε πόλις.
οὔ τινα γὰρ τοιόνδε νέων ὁ φιλαίματος Ἄρης
ἠνάρισε στυγερῆς ἐν στροφάλιγγι μάχης.

Anacreon (?), AP 7.226

The whole city cried in lamentation at the pyre for the terrible Agathon who died for Abdera. No other young man like him was killed by bloodthirsty Ares in the whirlwind of hateful battle.

If this is an archaic poem, then it is an early example[34] of the explicit expression of the motif of 'the whole city mourned', which is familiar in inscribed epitaphs for private citizens from die fourth century on (cf. *CEG* 643, 644, 667, *GG* 149, 193, 315). That the whole city is affected by deaths is, of course, also fundamental to the public inscriptions on collective 'polyandria', as on the memorial to the Athenian dead at Potideia:

---

33 Cf. Rosenmeyer 1992, 200–201.
34 For Tyrtaeus 12.27–28 cf. below p. 147; on 'Simonides' *AP* 7.302 = 77 Page cf. below p. 146. *CEG* 143 (perhaps late seventh century from Corcyra, cf. further below) is often supplemented to contain the motif, but the matter remains uncertain; see Hansen's commentary.

ἄνδρας μὲν πόλις ἥδε ποθεῖ καὶ δῆ[μος Ἐρεχθέως],
πρόσθε Ποτειδαίας οἵ θάνον ἐν προμάχοις
παῖδες Ἀθηναίων·

CEG 10.9–11

This city and the people of Erechtheus long for these men, sons of the Athenians, who died in the front ranks at Potideia...

The mode of Anacreon 1 is, however, that of a public honorific poem for a single named individual; at the heart of the poem are the identity of the dead man, the city for which he died, and his prowess in battle. Certain examples of such epigrams from public memorials are not common from earlier than 400 BC; *CEG* 143 (Corcyra, sixth century) and 11 (Athens, fifth century) honour *proxenoi* and *CEG* 12 (Athens, fifth century) honours an ally from Rhegium, but these seem a long way from Anacreon 1 which honours exceptional service in battle.[35] Closest in some ways to Anacreon 1 is the honorific epitaph in Gela for another foreigner, Aeschylus of Athens, which is quoted in the *Life of Aeschylus* (T 1.11, 162 Radt = *GVI* 43):

Αἰσχύλον Εὐφορίωνος Ἀθηναῖον τόδε κεύθει
μνῆμα καταφθίμενον πυροφόροιο Γέλας·
ἀλκὴν δ' εὐδόκιμον Μαραθώνιον ἄλσος ἄν εἴποι
καὶ βαθυχαιτήεις Μῆδος ἐπιστάμενος.

This memorial conceals Aeschylus, son of Euphorion, an Athenian, who died in wheat-bearing Gela;[36] the grove of Marathon and the long-haired Mede could tell with knowledge of his glorious prowess.

Whatever the provenance and date of this poem, however,[37] it makes almost explicit that Aeschylus, unlike Agathon, did not die in battle, and there is no mention, within the poem itself, of the grief which his death caused or of the fact (which we must take on trust from the texts which quote the poem) that it was inscribed as a public act. How important it is for the effect of the poem that it is completely silent about what Aeschylus was really famous for is perhaps a subject where disagreement is possible; at the very least, however, the rhetoric of this epitaph is quite different from that of Anacreon 1.

A second notable feature of Anacreon 1 is its recall of the public and universal grief displayed at Agathon's funeral. The grief of those left behind is, of

---

35 *GVI* 45, for Chaerippus, is very likely to be Hellenistic.
36 For the syntax cf. Sommerstein 1995/96, 113.
37 Cf. Page 1981, 131–132, Radt's commentary on Aeschylus, T 161, and Sommerstein 1995/96.

course, the most common of all epitaphic motifs, but the closest parallels for Anacreon's vivid narrative are memorials which may be read as referring to the grieving of private individuals, rather than of whole populations, as they actually buried someone close to them. Thus a sixth century Attic distich:

Χαιρεδέμο τόδε σέμα πατὲρ ἔστε[σε θ]ανόντος
Ἀνφιχάρ<ε>ς ἀγαθὸν παῖδα ὀλοφυρόμενος

CEG 14

His father Amphichares set up this tomb of the dead Chaeredemus, mourning for his splendid son.

Similarly, on *CEG* 139 (Troezen, c. 500 BC) we read that Praxiteles' friends set up a *sâma* for him βαρέα στενάχοντες. Anacreon's picture of universal grief is clearly related to such language, but it seems also to draw on other traditions.

The combination of universal grief and its expression at the moment of burial takes us, inevitably, to Homer. The death of Hector causes grief both to his family and to all the Trojans, because 'it was as though the whole of lofty Troy was smouldering with fire' (*Iliad* 22.405–411); when Priam returns with his son's body, 'there was not a single man or woman left in the city, for unbearable grief had come to all of them' (*Iliad* 24.707–708), and after his body has burned 'the people gathered around the pyre of famous Hector' (*Iliad* 24.789). In Homer, the grief of family members, the most common of all topoi of private funerary inscriptions (cf., e.g., *CEG* 104, the death of Herseis caused γνωτοῖσι πᾶσι...πόθον), is set off against the public grief of the whole city for a great fighter killed in battle; the combination is in fact thematised in a distich ascribed to Simonides:

τῶν αὐτοῦ τις ἕκαστος ἀπολλυμένων ἀνιᾶται,
 Νικοδίκου δὲ φίλοι καὶ πόλις ἥδε † πόλη.

'Simonides', *AP* 7.302 = *Epigram* 77 Page[38]

Everyone feels pain when one of his own dies, but when Nicodicus died, those dear to him and this city...[felt pain].

The influence of the mourning for and burial of Hector in *Iliad* 24 upon Greek funerary epigram would require a long study in itself, but if it is correct to sense that scene behind the opening distich of Anacreon 1, then we should also note

---

38 Page adopts Fettes' γ' ὅλη at verse-end, which would make explicit the combination I have been pursuing.

that that poem's use of Homer is generally allusive and subtle.³⁹ ὁ φιλαίματος Ἄρης/ ἠνάρισε seems to derive from τὸν μὲν Ἄρης ἐνάριζε μιαιφόνος at *Iliad* 5.844, but in Homer 'Ares' is the god himself, in 'Anacreon' the name is used metonymically of 'war', as commonly in Homer⁴⁰ and inscribed epigram. So too, ἐν στροφάλιγγι is a Homeric phrase, but Anacreon has used it in a pentameter in a position impossible in Homer, and it is never used metaphorically in Homer; the Homeric 'whirlwind of dust' caused by battle and in which slain warriors lie (*Iliad* 24.39–40) has become in Anacreon the 'whirlwind of hateful battle' itself. The rare epithets αἰνοβίης and φιλαίματος are also not Homeric. Moreover, it may also be worth suggesting that Anacreon wants us to reflect upon the meaning of the name of the dead, 'Mr Agathos'. The suggestion is reinforced by another very early example of the ideas we have been examining, namely Tyrtaeus' account of the universal grief for the man who has in battle proved himself ἀγαθός:

> τὸν δ' ὀλοφύρονται μὲν ὁμῶς νέοι ἠδὲ γέροντες,
> ἀργαλέωι δὲ πόθωι πᾶσα κέκηδε πόλις,
> καὶ τύμβος καὶ παῖδες ἐν ἀνθρώποις ἀρίσημοι
> καὶ παίδων παῖδες καὶ γένος ἐξοπίσω.
>
> Tyrtaeus, 12.27–30 W

> The young and the old alike mourn him, the whole city grieves with its painful loss, and his tomb and his children and his children's children and his family are ever after notable among men.

That 'the *agathoi* die young' is of course a familiar motif of both literary and inscribed epigram (cf. *CEG* 489.1 τὸς ἀγαθὸς ἔστερξεν Ἄρης κτλ., Athens, fourth century), and the sentiment is in fact made explicit in another *epitymbion* ascribed to Anacreon:

> κάρτερος ἐν πολέμοις Τιμόκριτος, οὗ τόδε σᾶμα·
> Ἄρης δ' οὐκ ἀγαθῶν φείδεται, ἀλλὰ κακῶν.
>
> Anacreon, *AP* 7.160 = *Epigram* 2 Page

> This is the tomb of Timocritus, mighty in war; Ares spares not the good, but the base.

Whether the use of the Homeric tradition in the style of Anacreon 1 differs in any significant way from that which is standard in early inscribed epigram is pre-

---

39 Most modern commentary on the poem derives from Weber 1895, 36–37.
40 Cf. Reichenberger 1891, 11–17.

sumably another matter where difference of opinion is inevitable,[41] but a poem such as the well-known *CEG* 145 (Corcyra, c. 600) in hexameters shows how the epic inheritance was used in a creative manner from a relatively early date:[42]

σᾶμα τόδε Ἀρνιάδα· χαροπὸς τόνδ' ὄλεσεν Ἄρες,
βαρνάμενον παρὰ ναυσὶν ἐπ' Ἀράθθοιο ῥοϝαῖσι.
πολλὸν ἀριστεύ<ϝ>οντα κατὰ στονόϝεσαν ἀϝυτάν.

CEG 145

This is the tomb of Arniadas. Fierce (?) Ares killed him as he fought by the ships at the streams of the Arachthus; he was by far the best in the midst of grievous war.

Anacreon 1 uses both the epitaphic tradition and Homer in innovative ways, but it is at least worth asking whether anything in the poem's style helps us to date it to the time of Anacreon, rather than, for example, to the fourth century. How do we recognise the emergence of 'the literary'?

The motifs of Anacreon 1 were to have a long afterlife in Hellenistic epigram, but it may be instructive to look at two particular examples:

ἠῷοι Μελάνιππον ἐθάπτομεν, ἠελίου δὲ
δυομένου Βασιλὼ κάτθανε παρθενικὴ
αὐτοχερί· ζώειν γάρ, ἀδελφεὸν ἐν πυρὶ θεῖσα,
οὐκ ἔτλη. δίδυμον δ' οἶκος ἐσεῖδε κακὸν
πατρὸς Ἀριστίπποιο· κατήφησεν δὲ Κυρήνη
πᾶσα, τὸν εὔτεκνον χῆρον ἰδοῦσα δόμον.

Callimachus, *AP* 7.517 = *Epigram* 20 Pf.

At dawn we were burying Melanippus, and as the sun set the maiden Basilo died by her own hand, for she could not endure to live after placing her brother on the fire. The house of their father Aristippus beheld a double disaster, and the whole of Cyrene cast down its eyes after seeing the house which had been blessed with children left bereft.

κυάνεον νέφος ἦλθε δι' ἄστεος, ἡνίκα κούρην
τοῦθ' ὑπὸ σῆμα τιθεὶς ἔστενεν Ἠετίων,
ἀγκαλέων Ἡδεῖαν ἑὸν τέκος, ἧς Ὑμέναιος
ἠρίον οὐ θαλάμου χερσὶν ἔκοψε πύλην·
συμπαθὲς ἄλγ[   ]πόλει, ἀλλὰ τὰ κεινῶν
ἀστῶν ἀρκε[ίτω δάκρυ]α καὶ στοναχαί.

Posidippus 50 A-B[43]

---

41 Cf. further Bing 2009, ch. 8.
42 Cf., e.g., Lumpp 1963, Skiadas 1972, 75–79. Lumpp's discussion is particularly valuable.

A black cloud came over the city when Eetion grieved as he placed his daughter under this tomb, calling upon Hedeia, his own child; Hymenaeus knocked not at the door of her chamber, but at her tomb. The [? whole] city felt grief, but may the tears and laments of the bereft citizens suffice.

When we move from Anacreon 1 to the two certainly Hellenistic epigrams, what is most striking is the shift from the public nature of Agathon's service 'on behalf of Abdera' to the private disaster represented by the deaths of Melanippus, Basilo, and Hedeia. Even if, as is not improbable, Callimachus' poem honours one of Cyrene's leading families, the whole city is now caught up in the grief of a particular family; here again we may be reminded of *Iliad* 24. The shadow, or rather 'black cloud', of Homer hangs over Posidippus also, but his shift of focus from the identity of the dead to the grief of the city and father of the dead girl marks a change that we might think emblematic of the directions in which 'literary' epigram moved. Here again, of course, distinctions are nuanced, rather than clearcut. The point is well seen by comparing Posidippus 50 A-B with *CEG* 587 (Athens, fourth century BC):

οὔ σε γάμων πρόπολος, Πλαγγών, Ὑμέναιος ἐν οἴκοις
ὤλβισεν, ἀλλ' ἐδάκρυσε ἐκτὸς ἀποφθιμένην·
σῶι δὲ πάθει μήτηρ καταλείβεται, οὐδέ ποτ' αὐτὴν
λείπουσι θρήνων πενθίδιοι στεναχαί.

Hymenaeus who attends marriages did not, Plangon, bless you in your house, but wept for you outside after your death. Your fate causes your mother to melt away in tears, and the grieving cries of lamentation never leave her.

So too, Posidippus, like Anacreon 1, combines a memory of the funeral with the deictic present of inscription ('under this stone', v. 2) but, by not naming the city in which the tomb stands, assumes (or imitates the situation of) a community which knows those involved; such a situation is, of course, very common in inscribed epitaphs. Posidippus' voice is not far removed from that of archaic epigram or that of Anacreon 1 — a reporter who may or may not have shared in the communal grief; greater certainty about the text and interpretation of the final distich would no doubt shed further light upon the positioning of the poetic voice.[44]

---

[43] In v. 5 Austin's πάσηι] πόλει seems very likely; Lloyd-Jones' κείνων or Gronewald's κεινά both seem improvements at the end of the verse; see further below.

[44] ἀρκείτω in the final verse seems certain, but its interpretation is not (the translations of Bastianini/Austin notably try to soften the blow of 'enough of tears'). It could be a variation on

As for Callimachus, the extraordinary narrative of his poem is clearly far removed from that of early epigram; the death that the poem should be commemorating is disturbingly displaced by another, and the memory of that terrible day is powerfully evoked through the vivid imperfect ἐθάπτομεν which stands in contrast to the shocking suddenness of the aorist κάτθανε. Nevertheless, such a cumulation of death does not stand alone in Hellenistic epigram[45] — Theocritus, *Epigram* 16 Gow tells of a seven-year-old girl who died 'longing for her twenty-month old baby brother who had tasted the savagery of death' — and we might recall poems such as *CEG* 561 (Attica, fourth century BC):

> τῶν μὲν δοὺς βάσα[νον
>   Καλλιμέδων, ἀρετῆς πλεῖστον ἔπαινον ἔχεις.
> σοὶ δὲ πατὴρ φθιμένωι συνεπέσπετο τὴν πολύκλαυτον
>   Καλλιτέλης παιδὸς μοῖραν ἰδὼν θανάτου.

> Callimedon, giving proof of some things…you have the highest praise for virtue. When you died, your father Calliteles followed you, having lived to see the miserable fate of the death of his son.

Other aspects also of Callimachus' poem, such as the 'emptying' of the house,[46] can, of course, be paralleled from inscribed epigram, but what is striking is how Callimachus has transformed the whole through a shift in perspective. The poet was personally involved in the grief (ἐθάπτομεν) and can thus speak for the community with the special authority of an insider; Annemarie Ambühl well compares the voice to that of a tragic messenger.[47]

Finally, if we are uncertain whether the names of the dead in Anacreon ('Mr Agathos') and Posidippus ('Miss Sweet') resonate meaningfully, there is hardly a doubt in Callimachus. The shocking nature of the events of the poem are anticipated by the opening paradox ἠῶιοι Μελάνιππον, not just because the 'black horses' cast a shadow over the brightness of dawn, but specifically because 'dawn' should have white horses (as she does at Bacchylides fr. 20C.22 Maehler); it is Night whose horses are black (cf. Aeschylus fr. 69 Radt).

---

the instruction to the passer-by not to weep — 'there were enough tears in the past'; the echo of ἔστεχεν in στοναχαί would support this interpretation.
45 Cf. Ambühl 2002, 7–8.
46 Cf., e.g., *CEG* 154, *SGO* 01/20/38.
47 Ambühl 2002, 11. Ambühl, however, then considers whether the voice is not rather that of a 'chorus member'; this is to underplay the extent to which 'messengers' are themselves affected by, and involved in, what they report.

4

If we are in search of 'the Hellenistic', we can presumably hardly do better than to turn to Hellenistic poems which direct our attention to specific archaic models. One famous such example is Asclepiades, *AP* 12.50 (= xvi *HE*):

> πῖν', Ἀσκληπιάδη· τί τὰ δάκρυα ταῦτα; τί πάσχεις;
> οὐ σὲ μόνον χαλεπὴ Κύπρις ἐληίσατο,
> οὐδ' ἐπὶ σοὶ μούνωι κατεθήξατο τόξα καὶ ἰοὺς
> πικρὸς Ἔρως· τί ζῶν ἐν σποδιῆι τίθεσαι;
> πίνωμεν Βάκχου ζωρὸν πόμα· δάκτυλος ἀώς·
> ἦ πάλι κοιμιστὰν λύχνον ἰδεῖν μένομεν;
> † πίνωμεν, δύσερως † μετά τοι χρόνον οὐκέτι πουλύν,
> σχέτλιε, τὴν μακρὰν νύκτ' ἀναπαυσόμεθα.

> Drink, Asclepiades. Why these tears? What's wrong? You're not the only one cruel Cypris has captured, nor are you the only one against whom bitter Love has directed his bow and arrows — why become ash while you're alive? Let us drink the strong draught of Bacchus. There's only a finger breadth left till dawn; or shall we wait to see again the lamps which escort us home to bed?.... In not much longer, poor fool, we shall rest through the long night.

The archaic poem at issue is of course Alcaeus 346 (which I give in Voigt's text):

> πώνωμεν· τί τὰ λύχν' ὀμμένομεν; δάκτυλος ἀμέρα·
> κὰδ δ' ἄερρε κυλίχναις μεγάλαις, ἄιτα, ποικίλαις·
> οἶνον γὰρ Σεμέλας καὶ Δίος υἶος λαθικάδεα
> ἀνθρώποισιν ἔδωκ'. ἔγχεε κέρναις ἕνα καὶ δύο
> πλήαις κὰκ κεφάλας, ἀ δ' ἀτέρα τὰν ἀτέραν κύλιξ
> ὠθήτω

> Let's drink! Why are we waiting for the lamps? There's only a finger breadth left of the day. Take down the large decorated cups, lad! The son of Semele and Zeus gave wine to men to make them forget their cares; mix them one-to-two and fill them to the brim, let one cup push against another...

Asclepiades exploits the fact that Alcaeus' rhythm, the 'greater Asclepiad' (glyconic extended by two choriambs), is in its effect not unlike dactylic rhythm[48] — there is clearly an element of metrical *ludus* here; perhaps Asclepiades had in mind that Alcaeus himself had turned a passage of Hesiod's *Works and Days* into a drinking-song in this same metre (fr. 347 Voigt). Moreover, Asclepiades'

---

[48] δάκτυλος in v. 5 immediately follows the first dactyl of that verse, which begins with three spondees.

poem falls into two quatrains, both of which begin with echoes of Alcaeus' opening verse, though it is perhaps only after we have reached the much fuller 'quotation' in v. 5 that the faint echo we heard in v. i (πῖν'...τί τά) is confirmed as indeed from Alcaeus; the poem thus dramatises the always developing process of reading an allusive text. We may perhaps compare the way in which the second half of Macedonius' poem (*AP* 5.235 = 8 Madden, p. 139 above) forces us to re-read the imagery of the opening verses. So too both quatrains conclude with allusions to the topic of coming death, though it is the final verse again which does so more obviously;[49] we do not know whether Alcaeus too had the 'tomorrow we die' motif, but another Alcaean exhortation to drink, beginning πῶνε, certainly does (38 Voigt), and Asclepiades may well have thought of the motif as at least at home in an Alcaean context.[50] So too, we do not know whether λαθικάδεα in Alcaeus' poem was later given a specific weight and, if it was, whether those κήδεα were political or erotic;[51] Asclepiades' reading may of course have been a creative misreading. If the second half of the epigram picks up the faint Alcaean allusion of v. 1 and 'runs with it', the second half of the poem also represents a switch from the private to the public, from the 'anti-social' self-absorption of the injured lover to the solidarity of the drinking-group, marked by the switch to the first-person plural; the second half of the poem thus recreates the Alcaean situation in more than just language. These considerations cannot, of course, be divorced from the vexed question of 'Who speaks?'.[52]

Whether, however, we imagine the poem spoken by Asclepiades to himself or by others to him or some third alternative (e.g. vv. 1–4 by Asclepiades to himself, vv. 5–8 by Asclepiades to the group), or if we regard the very indeterminacy as crucial to the epigrammatic voice (would such doubt about self-address be possible in archaic poetry?), the quotation of Alcaeus in v. 5 is a call to proper

---

49 This parallelism suggests that, whatever has happened to the text in v. 7, the idea of eros should not be removed from it.
50 Cf., e.g., Hutchinson 1988, 276 n. 106 and cf. further below. In view of the Alcaean model, it must be at least doubtful whether πίνωμεν at the head of Hedylus V G-P is 'clearly an echo' of Asclepiades (so Gutzwiller 1998, 179), though the two poems do share other motifs.
51 Page 1955, 307 classes the poem among 'the non-political poems', but that whole category may be misleading, as Page himself (p. 300) recognises; cf. Rösler 1980, 140–141. The source of Asclepiades' erotic pain is not specified, but the poem survives in Book 12 of the *Anthology* between two poems by Meleager and Callimachus which are similar calls to drinking and which are explicitly paederastic.
52 To the commentaries add Gutzwiller (next note) and E.W. Handley, 'Two epigrams by Asclepiades (XXV, XVI G.-P.)', *MH* 53 (1996) 140–147, 145–7. I am grateful to Alex Sens for showing me a draft of his forthcoming commentary on this poem.

sympotic behaviour, authorised by a 'classical' sympotic model, and a reminder that 'in a densely textual poetics, the poet is *never* alone'.[53] Everything has always happened before, and it is that past baggage which epigrams carry with them, more intensely perhaps than any other ancient poetic form; sometimes, as here or with Callimachus' ironically deluded claims to exclusivity, which actually rework Theognis (*AP* 12.43 = *Epigram* 28 Pf),'[54] that baggage may be paraded — the 'wornness' of epigrammatic language openly worn — but it is never entirely absent. Moreover, as is becoming increasingly clear, in a physical sense too no single epigram was ever 'alone': all contributed, like stones in a mosaic, to a whole greater than its individual parts, whether that whole was a particular collection of poems or the more general and ever-expanding flourishing of the epigram form. We need, of course, to know more than we do about Hellenistic editions of, say, Alcaeus, but even in the absence of that knowledge we can catch some of the flavour of Hellenistic epigrams which were both discrete, self-contained poems and also intensely dependent upon an intertextual relationship with earlier and contemporary poems for their effect.

Alcaeus' poem is clearly addressed both to himself and to his fellow-drinkers, who are reminded that it is their pious duty as mortals to drink the gift of 'the son of Semele and Zeus'. Asclepiades picks up this point in a rather lower key in v. 5,[55] but replaces Alcaeus' explicit and 'uncommonly strong mixture'[56] by the more straightforward, though apparently even stronger, ζωρὸν πῶμα; in juxtaposition to Βάκχου, both elements stress that it is time to get seriously wild — soon everyone will be going home to bed, so we should get in some hard drinking.[57] It is, however, also tempting to see in this difference from the model a marker of a different composition reception context; ζωρόν, which may resonate etymologically with ζῶν in the previous verse,[58] probably in fact means 'strong' rather than literally 'unmixed, pure',[59] and the lack of concern with the

---

53 Taken from my *BMCR* review of Gutzwiller 1998.
54 I have briefly discussed this epigram in Hunter 2003, 480. For the use of Theognis cf. esp. Henrichs 1979.
55 Alcaeus would probably not have called the god Βάκχος (first found in classical and Hellenistic poetry), cf. M.L. West, *ZPE* 18 (1975), 234–235, S.G. Cole, *GRBS* 11 (1980), 226–231; did Asclepiades know this and use the name as a marker of difference?
56 Page 1955, 308. Anacreon *PMG* 356 seems to specify this same mixture in similar circumstances.
57 Cf. Giangrande 1968, 132–135.
58 Cf. Schol. *Iliad* 9.203, *Etym. Mag.* s.v. ζωρότερον.
59 Cf. the passages collected by Massimilla 1996, 408, and see also Diggle on Theophrastus, *Char.*, iv 6.

details of the mixture — a lack of concern highlighted by the existence of the Alcaean model — suggests that the recreation of the fiction of a sympotic present is not foremost among Asclepiades' literary aims.⁶⁰ There are doubtless further stylistic features of Asclepiades' poem that we would be tempted to put down to the alleged 'mannerism' of Hellenistic epigram — the grammatical and prosodic (μόνον, μούνωι) variation between v. 2 and v. 3, Κύπρις matched against πικρὸς Ἔρως, the almost oxymoronic ζῶν ἐν σποδιῆι etc. — but however hard we wish to press individual details, a general sense of 'the literary' seems hard to deny. If it is true that the 'call to drink, as a call to the symposium, urges the solace of song, so that Asclepiades' collection (or, we might prefer to say, 'poem') is offered as both a statement of the lover's condition and a source of escape from it',⁶¹ then the closing idea is not merely one more variation on 'gather ye rosebuds...' (cf. esp. Catullus 5), but is an assertion of the immortal *kleos* which song can confer; as Theocritus echoed Homer and Simonides in offering his patrons a glory equivalent to that which these archaic poets had conferred upon their patrons and characters, so Asclepiades rewrites the still 'living' Alcaeus as proof of how poetry defeats 'the long night'.⁶²

Bibliography

Ambühl, A. 2002. 'Zwischen Tragödie und Roman. Kallimachos' Epigramm auf den Selbstmord der Basilo (20 PF. = 32 Gow-Page = AP 7.517)', in: M.A. Harder/R.F. Regtuit/G.C. Wakker (eds.), *Hellenistic Epigrams*, Leuven, 1–26.

Bing, P. 2009. *The Scroll and the Marble: Studies in Reading and Reception in Hellenistic Poetry*, Ann Arbor.

Bonanno, M.G. 1990. *L'allusione necessaria*, Rome.

Burnett, A.P. 1983. *Three Archaic Poets*, London.

Cairns, F. 1972. *Generic Composition in Greek and Roman Poetry*, Edinburgh.

Cucchiarelli, A. 2004/5. 'La nave e lo spettatore. Forme dell'allegoria da Alceo ad Orazio', *Studi Italiani di Filologia Chassica* 97–98, 188–206, 30–72.

Dover, K.J. 1971. *Theocritus. Select Poems*, London.

Dover, K.J. 1978. *Greek Homosexuality*, Oxford.

---

60 Cf. Rufinus, *AP* 5.12 (= 11 Page) for this set of motifs.
61 Gutzwiller 1998, 149; Gutzwiller's whole discussion of Asclepiades XVI as a closural poem in which the internal auditor responds to the collection should be consulted.
62 I am grateful to Marco Fantuzzi and Richard Rawles and to audiences in Cambridge and Giessen for their provocative criticism; the editors have been models of persistent encouragement.

Fantuzzi, M./Hunter, R.L. (eds.) 2004. *Tradition and Innovation in Hellenistic Poetry*, Cambridge.
Ford. A. 2002. *The Origins of Criticism. Literary Culture and Poetic Theory in Ancient Greece*, Princeton.
Gentili, B. 1988. *Poetry and its Public in Ancient Greece. From Homer to the Fifth Century*, Baltimore/London.
Giangrande, G. 1968. 'Sympotic literature and epigram', in: A.E. Raubitschek, *L'epigramme grecque* (= Fondation Hardt, Entretiens sur l'antiquité classique 14), Geneva, 93–177.
Goldhill, S. 1987. 'The dance of the veils. Reading five fragments of Anacreon', *Eranos* 85, 9–18.
Goldhill, S. 1994. 'The naïve and knowing eye. Ecphrasis and the culture of viewing in the Hellenistic world', in: S. Goldhill/R. Osborne (eds.), *Art and Text in Ancient Greek Culture*. Cambridge, 197–223.
Gutzwiller, K. 1998. *Poetic Garlands. Hellenistic Epigrams in Context*, Berkeley/Los Angeles/London.
Gutzwiller, K. 2002. 'Art's echo. The tradition of Hellenistic ecphrastic epigram', in: M.A. Harder/ R.F. Regtuit/G.C. Wakker (eds.), *Hellenistic Epigrams*, Leuven, 85–112.
Hunter, R.L. 1993. *The Argonautica of Apollonius. Literary Studies*, Cambridge.
Hunter, R.L. 1996. *Theocritus and the Archaeology of Greek Poetry*, Cambridge.
Hutchinson, G. 1988. *Hellenistic Poetry*, Oxford.
Kassel, R. 1973. 'Kritische und Exegetische Kleinigkeiten II (Vgl. Band 106, 1963, S. 298)', *RhM* 116, 97–112 (= *Kleine Schriften*, ed. H.-G. Nesselrath, Berlin 1991, 376–91).
Lumpp, I.L.M. 1963. 'Die Arniadas-Inschrift aus Korkyra', *Forschungen and Fortschritte* 37, 212–215.
Nagy, G. 1985. 'Theognis and Megara. A poet's vision of his city', in: T.J. Figueira/G. Nagy (eds.), *Theognis of Megara. Poetry and the Polis*, Baltimore/London, 21–81.
Page, D.L. 1955. *Sappho and Alcaeus*, Oxford.
Page, D.L. 1981. *Further Greek Epigrams. Epigrams before AD 50 from the Greek Anthology and other Sources not included in 'Hellenistic Epigrams' or 'The Garland of Philip'*, Cambridge.
Reichenberger, S. 1891. *Die Entwicklung des metonymischen Gebrauchs von Gotternamen in der griechischen Poesie bis zum Ende des Alexandrinischen Zeitalters*, Karlsruhe.
Rosenmeyer, P.A. 1992. *The Poetics of Imitation*, Cambridge.
Rösler, W. 1980. *Dichter und Gruppe: Eine Untersuchung zu den Bedingungen und zur historischen Funktion früher griechischer Lyrik am Beispiel Alkaios*, Munich.
Scodel, R. 1996. 'Self-correction, spontaneity, and orality in archaic poetry', in: I. Worthington (ed.), *Voice into Text. Orality and Literacy in Ancient Greece*, Leiden, 59–79.
Silk, M.S. 1974. *Interaction in Poetic Imagery*, Cambridge.
Skiadas, A.D. 1972. 'Ἐπὶ τύμβῳ. Ein Beitrag zur Interpretation der griechischen metrischen Grabinschriften', in: G. Pfohl, *Inschriften der Griechen. Grab-, Weih-, und Ehreninschriften*, Darmstadt, 59–84.
Sommerstein, A.H. 1995/96. 'Aeschylus' Epitaph', *MCr* 30/31, 111–117.
Spengel, L. 1853–1856. *Rhetores Graeci*, 3 vols. Leipzig.
Taran, S.L. 1979. *The Art of Variation in the Hellenistic Epigram*, Leiden.
Vetta, M. 1980. *Theognis. Elegiarum liber secundus*, Rome.
Walsh, G.B. 1990. 'Surprised by self. Audible thought in Hellenistic poetry', *CPh* 85, 1–21.
Weber, L. 1895. *Anacreontea*, Diss. Göttingen.
West, M.L. 1984. 'Problems in the Anacreontea', *CQ* 34, 206–221.

8 The Gods of Callimachus

Creating Gods

In a famous passage of his second book Herodotus describes the development of the Greek conception of the gods and its debt to Egypt.¹ The Greeks inherited the names of most of their gods from the ancient Pelasgians, who had by their own account taken them from the barbarians (i.e., according to Herodotus, from the Egyptians); but the elaborations beyond the names were largely the work of Hesiod and Homer:

> From where each of the gods came into being [ἐγένοντο], whether they had all existed for all time [αἰεί], and what they looked like in appearance, the Greeks were unaware until, so to speak, the day before yesterday; for I think that Hesiod and Homer lived four hundred years and not more before me. It is they who created divine genealogies [ποιήσαντες θεογονίην] for the Greeks, gave the gods their special names [ἐπωνυμίας],² distributed honors and crafts among them, and told us of their appearance.³ The poets who are said to have preceded these men in fact came after them, in my opinion. The source for the first part of this account [i.e., the taking over of foreign names] is the priestesses at Dodona, but I myself am responsible for the part about Hesiod and Homer.
>
> Herodotus 2.53

The influence of early hexameter poetry on Greek thinking about the gods and on actual religious practice can indeed hardly be exaggerated,⁴ but it is the terms in which Herodotus expresses himself that are first of interest. It was, says Herodotus, the two great poets who taught the Greeks where the gods came from; the verb ἐγένοντο is studiedly ambiguous, but with θεογονίη immediately following – and Herodotus can hardly not be thinking of Hesiod's *Theogony* (cf. vv. 46, 108, εἴπατε δ' ὡς τὰ πρῶτα θεοὶ καὶ γαῖα γένοντο. 'tell how first the gods and earth were born') – we most naturally think of parentage and birth. The disjunctive question that the poets solved for the Greeks is in fact the same quasi-paradox that Callimachus places at the head of the *Hymn to Zeus*:

---

1 For helpful introductions to the passage and its links to contemporary speculation, cf. Burkert 1985b; Thomas 2000, 274–282; Graziosi 2002, 180–184.
2 This is usually understood either of cult names, such as Σμινθεύς for Apollo in the opening scene of the *Iliad* (cf. further below), or of formulaic epithets, such as "far-shooting" of Apollo in the same scene.
3 Here Herodotus is probably thinking of epic anthropomorphism in general, as well as the special physical features of each god (Zeus's dark locks, Hera βοῶπις, etc.).
4 Burkert 1985a, 119–125 are familiar and influential pages.

https://doi.org/10.1515/9783110747577-008

πῶς καί νιν, Δικταῖον ἀείσομεν ἠὲ Λυκαῖον;
ἐν δοιῇ μάλα θυμός, ἐπεὶ γένος ἀμφήριστον.
Ζεῦ, σὲ μὲν Ἰδαίοισιν ἐν οὔρεσί φασι γενέσθαι,
Ζεῦ, σὲ δ' ἐν Ἀρκαδίῃ· πότεροι, πάτερ, ἐψεύσαντο;
'Κρῆτες ἀεὶ ψεῦσται'· καὶ γὰρ τάφον, ὦ ἄνα, σεῖο
Κρῆτες ἐτεκτήναντο· σὺ δ' οὐ θάνες, ἐσσὶ γὰρ αἰεί.

Callimachus, *Hymn to Zeus* 4–9

How shall we hymn him, as Dictaean or Lycaean? My heart is very much in doubt, as his origin [*genos*] is disputed. Zeus, some say that you came into existence on the Idaean mountains; some, Zeus, say in Arcadia: Which group, father, are lying? 'Cretans are always liars'; for the Cretans even devised a tomb for you, Lord, but you did not die, for you are for all time.

Zeus was indeed born but is (also) forever.[5] Callimachus is thus taking upon himself the role that Herodotus ascribed to his great predecessors; the *Hymn to Zeus* is in fact Callimachus' *Theogony* (as the *Theogony* is also Hesiod's *Hymn to Zeus*),[6] and Callimachus, like Hesiod and Homer before him, is fashioning the gods before our eyes.

In the *Theogony* it is Zeus who distributes honors and functions to the Olympians (vv. 73–74, 111–112, 885, etc.), though there is in fact no consistent program of distribution carried out through the poem;[7] in the *Iliad*, by contrast, Poseidon famously reports how Zeus, Hades, and he himself divided the cosmos among themselves by lot (15.187–193). The distribution that established the current order may in fact be seen as the central subject of all cosmogonic and theogonic poetry: Hermes' first song for Apollo tells of 'the immortal gods and the dark earth, how they first came into being [γένοντο] and how each received his share [λάχε μοῖραν]' (*Homeric Hymn to Hermes* 427–428). Herodotus' description of how Hesiod and Homer 'distributed honors and crafts [among the gods]' thus ascribes a Zeus-like function to the poets; this is not merely an example of the trope, particularly familiar from later poetry, whereby poets are said to have done what their characters in fact did, but it is rather a powerful dramatization of the central role that Herodotus ascribes to the poets. Whether or not Herodotus also had what we call the *Homeric Hymns* in mind cannot be known, but it is certainly the case that the major hymns are centrally concerned with the birth,

---

5 On the significance of γένος in v. 5, cf. Cuypers 2004, 97. Cuypers also discusses (pp. 104–105) the relationship of this paradox to contemporary views (e.g., those of Euhemerus) in which Zeus really did die; cf. also Stephens 2003, 90–91.
6 Cf. Hunter/Fuhrer 2002, 167–168.
7 Cf. West 1966 on lines 112–113.

honors, and spheres of activity of the deities. In the *Hymns* of Callimachus, and particularly in those to Zeus, Apollo, and Artemis, the division of honors and spheres of activity is also a persistent and explicit theme. In the *Hymn to Zeus*, after having rejected the Iliadic story of the division of the cosmos (vv. 60–67), the poet recounts how Zeus 'chose' the particular group of mortals (city-governing kings) under his special control, leaving other groups to 'lesser gods,' and how the actions of those kings mirror the actions of Zeus himself (as, of course, the actions of mortal poets mirror those of Apollo); in the *Hymn to Apollo* a central section is devoted to the manifold τέχναι that the god has as his portion (ἔλαχε), and Artemis' initial encounter with Zeus in the hymn in her honor is precisely to do with her τιμαί and τέχναι. The explicitness of these hymns on this subject and the repeated concern with how myriad individual parts form a single Olympian whole presumably reflects not merely the systematization of the archaic system, but also reflection upon that systematization.

Homer and Hesiod did not just create the genealogies of the gods; they also created ways of talking about divine action and about the interactions between men and gods. For later Greeks it will hardly have been an accident that the very first such interaction in the *Iliad* is Chryses' prayer to Apollo (whose genealogy is also repeatedly stressed: *Il.* 1.9, 36); G.S. Kirk (in his commentary *ad loc.* 1.37–42) notes that this is a prayer that 'follows the regular religious pattern,' but what is actually interesting is that we here see that 'regular' pattern being created before our eyes. The fact that Chryses' *da quia dedi* prayer sounds familiar becomes part of the passage's didactic force,[8] just as it also teaches us who Apollo's parents were. The poets literally taught later Greeks how to worship the gods by such paradigmatic scenes of prayer, sacrifice (e.g., *Od.* 3.1–66), and cultic song, no less than they gave to (educated) Greeks a way of thinking about divine action. In the first divine intervention in the human action, Apollo comes down 'like night,' the arrows clanking in the quiver on his back (vv. 46–47); it is not merely ancient scholars who have wondered how literally all this is to be taken: the verses, like the account of Apollo's shooting the mules and dogs that immediately follows, precisely problematize the ways of speaking about divine action. Are these verses metaphorical, or does divine action always lend itself to more than one mode of description (which is also, of course, interpretation)? Is such ambiguity of characterization fundamental to the very conception of supernatural action? So much later Homeric criticism, like so much later religious

---

8 Pulleyn 1997, 16–38 considers whether prayers of this form were indeed a Homeric construct or had purchase in real life. For very many Greeks, however, these verses may well have been the first introduction to how to pray.

history, takes its cue from interpretive directions to which Homer himself gave the impetus.

In the *Homeric Hymns* the links between paradigmatic scenes of a divine past and the human present are often visible. It is, for example, clear that the scene of Olympian festivity in the *Homeric Hymn to Apollo* (vv. 187–206) provides a pattern for human celebration of the god, just as the pattern of the original Delphic paean and procession of which the hymnist tells was repeated every year. (Cf., e.g., Furley/Bremer 2001, 1.14–15; Fantuzzi/Hunter 2004, 365–366.) So too in Callimachus' *Hymns*, which are rooted both in the poetry of the past and also in contemporary cultic practice, the past breaks through and embraces us at every point. The Cyrenean rites for Apollo that 'we' are now performing, for example, were witnessed immemorially long ago by Apollo himself (*Hymn to Apollo* 90–95). At the end of the *Hymn to Delos* the poet tells of a tree-biting rite in the god's honor:

Ἀστερίη πολύβωμε πολύλλιτε, τίς δέ σε ναύτης
ἔμπορος Αἰγαίοιο παρήλυθε νηὶ θεούσῃ;
οὐχ οὕτω μεγάλοι μιν ἐπιπνείουσιν ἀῆται,
χρειὼ δ' ὅττι τάχιστον ἄγει πλόον, ἀλλὰ τὰ λαίφη
ὠκέες ἐστείλαντο καὶ οὐ πάλιν αὖτις ἔβησαν,
πρὶν μέγαν ἢ σέο βωμὸν ὑπὸ πληγῇσιν ἑλίξαι
ῥησσόμενον καὶ πρέμνον ὀδακτάσαι ἁγνὸν ἐλαίης
χεῖρας ἀποστρέψαντας· ἃ Δηλιὰς εὕρετο νύμφη
παίγνια κουρίζοντι καὶ Ἀπόλλωνι γελαστύν.

Callimachus, *Hymn to Delos* 316–324

Asterie of many altars and many prayers, what merchant sailor on the Aegean passes you by in his speeding ship? Such strong winds never urge him on; never must he make so swift a voyage! Quickly they furl the sails and do not go on board again before they have gone around your great altar while being beaten with blows and have bitten the sacred trunk of the olive, their hands held behind their backs. The nymph of Delos devised this as a game and source of laughter for the young Apollo.

The rite has been practiced since the god was a baby, and it is something that every passing sailor does, however urgent his business. Moreover, there are here two presents, that of cultic practice and that of the hymn we are hearing or reading. As the poet is about to take his leave of the island, a parallelism is suggested between the passing sailors and the poet on his own journey: as the sailors never pass by without paying their respects, so the poet has not forgotten Delos. (Cf. v. 8.) The sailors will then continue on, but will do so having pleased the god; so too will the poet, who thus solves in yet another new way (cf. the end of the *Hymn to Apollo*) the eternal problem of when to stop hymning the god.

The relationship of past and present is again central to, but configured differently in, the reverent silence with which songs in praise of Apollo must be heard, a silence authorized by figures from the distant past, Thetis and Niobe, who nevertheless bring their potentially disruptive mourning into the present (*Hymn to Apollo* 20–24). Behind this latter passage may lie the famous opening of Pindar's *Pythian* 1, in which both Zeus's eagle and 'violent Ares', two creatures unlikely to lower their guard, respond with quiet calm to the music of the Apolline lyre, whereas 'those whom Zeus does not love', including the Giant beneath Etna, are panicked by the sound; when Callimachus draws the moral from the case of Niobe that 'it is a bad thing to compete with the blessed ones' and establishes a clear parallelism between such opposition to Apollo and opposition to 'my king' (vv. 25–27), he may be contracting and sharpening the clear parallelism that *Pythian* 1 draws between Zeus and Apollo and Hieron of Syracuse. (For another Callimachean use of this passage of Pindar, cf. Hunter 2006a, 95.)

The interaction between past and present is in fact probably nowhere as dynamic as in poems in honor of the gods; epic poetry tells of heroes whose deeds still have a powerful meaning for their cities as well as a general didactic force, but it is gods whose favor and attention are always urgently sought in the present. Stories about the past are therefore told because of their relation to, and power to work in, the present. Callimachus' revelation of what poetic myths are for is particularly on show in celebrating the new gods of the Ptolemaic house. Philadelphus' newly deceased sister-wife, Arsinoe, and her sister Philotera play the roles of Persephone and Demeter in *The Apotheosis of Arsinoe* (fr. 228 Pf.; cf. Hunter 2003c, 50–53), and the running together of Apollo and Ptolemy and the mingling of the past history of Delos with the contemporary history of the Delian and Cycladic league in the *Hymn to Delos* are a sharply explicit use of this traditional power of song. Somewhat similar is the association between Zeus and 'our ruler' (v. 86) in the *Hymn to Zeus*. Whether or not Callimachus understood the βασιλῆες, who are praised in Hesiod's *Theogony* (vv. 80–103) and who have a special relationship with the Muses and with poets, to have been Hesiod's patrons (cf. M.L. West 1966, 44–45), it is not a very big step from there to the encomium of the poet's king in the *Hymn to Zeus*. Hellenistic ruler cult has an obvious importance also for the related subjects of the two remaining sections of this chapter, the centrality of statues and of ideas of epiphany to Callimachean poetry and Hellenistic religious life.

Seeing Gods

Some five hundred years after Herodotus, Dio Chrysostom expanded on Herodotus' insight in his *Olympic Oration* (*Or.* 12), in which he discourses upon the sources of human conceptions of the divine. These are said to be, first, an innate sense of divinity that is common to all human, rational beings and without which all other sources have no validity and, second, the ideas we acquire from the poets, lawgivers, artists, and philosophers. In the second part of the speech Dio puts into the mouth of Phidias, the sculptor of the colossal image of Zeus at Olympia, a defense of his representation of the god and a contrast between the resources and limitations of the plastic arts and the freedom enjoyed by poets, a contrast taking its start not just from the familiarity, by Dio's time, of the analogy between the verbal and plastic arts but also (chapters 25–26) from the commonly cited anecdote in which Phidias admitted that the inspiration for his Zeus had come from Homer's description of Zeus nodding assent to Thetis' request at *Iliad* 1.528–530.[9] Both the setting and the role of Phidias are entirely appropriate to the subject of the discourse, as the Zeus at Olympia was by common consent, with the only possible rival being Phidias' own Athena Parthenos on the Athenian Acropolis, the closest man had come to the representation of divinity, and it was a statue that itself, just like the poetry of Homer from which it was derived, was argued to have influenced human notions of the divine; as Quintilian (12.10.9) puts it, 'the beauty of the statue seems to have added something more to the inherited sense of the divine [*recepta religio*], so exactly did the majesty of the work equal the god.' So too, Cicero traces the pattern for Phidias' two great masterpieces not to any human likeness, but rather to a mental image of perfect beauty that he compares to Platonic Forms (*Orator* 2.8–10). The sight of Phidias' Zeus produces a religious awe even in dumb animals (Dio 12.51); it can provoke us to contemplation of the divine, just as do the Homeric verses on which it is based (Strabo 8.3.30).

Phidias' Zeus is therefore a very special case of the complex and ambiguous relationship throughout Greek antiquity between, on the one hand, gods and our conceptions of them and, on the other, the images and representations of them that men create.[10] Callimachus' best-known exploration of this productive tension is the *Hymn to Athena* (cf. Hunter 1992b), but this is also the background

---

9 Cf. Strabo 8.3.30 (on which see further below). Most of the ancient sources on Phidias' Zeus are collected in Overbeck 1868, 125–136; and cf. Lapatin 2001, 79–86.
10 There is a large bibliography; guidance can be found throughout Tanner 2006; and with particular regard to poetic exploitations of the relationship, cf. also Kassel 1983.

against which we must view the poem devoted precisely to Phidias' Zeus, namely *Iambus* 6.[11] According to the *diegesis*, the poem, addressed to an acquaintance who was sailing off to see the statue,[12] consisted of a detailed description of it, an account of how much it cost, and the fact that the artist was Phidias the Athenian, son of Charmides. The only verse that remains from the first part of the poem is in fact the opening verse, but it has much to tell us:

Ἀλεῖος ὁ Ζεύς, ἁ τέχνα δὲ Φειδία.

Callimachus, fr. 196.1 Pf.

The Zeus is Elean; the artwork Phidias.

In our sources the people of Elis are always very closely associated with the building and protection of the statue — after all, they commissioned it — but 'Elean' is nowhere else used of Zeus.[13] The form suggests a cult title, and it obviously evokes the very cult title of the statue itself, Ὀλύμπιος, meaning both 'Olympian' (i.e., dwelling on Mt. Olympus) and (unusually) 'of Olympia'; the local epithet both prefigures the pedantic *akribeia* that is to be a hallmark of the poem and humorously downgrades the majesty of the Panhellenic Olympian god to that of a local divinity.

The chiastic arrangement of the opening verse opposes Zeus to 'the artwork': that is, principally, the statue (cf. Kerkhecker 1999, 150), though the word choice also suggests the skill of the craftsman. That opposition, however, evokes a central element in the Greek sense of the divine, and Callimachus will have expected his readers to wonder what such an opposition might actually mean: In what sense can 'the Zeus' be 'Elean' but the statue be 'Phidias'? If we obviously have 'the playful identification of god and statue,'[14] issues of divine identity are also in play. Diogenes Laertius reports a story concerning Stilpo of Megara (late fourth and early third century BC):

> They say that he argued concerning the Athena of Phidias in the following way: 'Is Athena [daughter] of Zeus a god?'; when the interlocutor agreed, he said, 'This one at any rate is

---

11 Recent discussion in Manakidou 1993, 238–242; Acosta-Hughes 2002, 288–294; Kerkhecker 1999, 147–181; Prioux 2007, 114–121.
12 This fact cannot be confirmed from the remains of the poem itself (cf. Kerkhecker 1999, 174), though the existence of an addressee is confirmed by vv. 45–46 and 62.
13 At fr. 76.2 Pf. (= 175.2 M.) Zeus is apparently given the epithet Πισαῖος, "of Pisa" (cf. Pfeiffer 1949–1953 *ad loc.*); for Zeus and Elis, cf. fr. 77 Pf. (= 179 M.).
14 Kerkhecker 1999, 150. For the Stilpo anecdote that follows, cf. Stewart 1998, 271–273; Lapatin 2010, 126–127.

not of Zeus but of Phidias,' and when this too was agreed, he said, 'Then she is not a god.' When he was summoned before the Areopagus, he did not deny that he had said this, but claimed that he had argued correctly, for she was not a god, but a goddess, and it was the males who were gods. Nevertheless, the Areopagites ordered him to leave the city immediately.

Diogenes Laertius 2.116 (= Stilpo fr. 12 Giannantoni)

Stilpo is playing here with a number of linguistic issues, but one of them is the force of a genitive when it is attached to the name of a god; this is not just a play with the apparent polyvalency of the genitive case, but it also draws attention to the problematic relationship of god and statue. So does the opening verse of *Iambus* 6 by evoking the possibility of, while avoiding, saying 'Zeus of Phidias,' with all the theological complications that that would bring. There is perhaps some further indication that these implications of Callimachus' verse were appreciated in antiquity.

The earliest account of, though not reference to, the Seven Wonders of the World that survives from antiquity is an essay ascribed in the principal manuscript to Philo of Byzantium, though there is general consent that this cannot be the writer on mechanical subjects of the late third-early second century BC; the essay on the Seven Wonders is now generally dated to late antiquity.[15] In the account of Phidias' Zeus, Philo too plays with both questions of paternity and the relation between god and statue:

> In heaven Cronus is Zeus's father; in Elis it is Phidias: the one was engendered by immortal nature; the other by the hands of Phidias, which alone are able to give birth to gods. Blessed is he who alone beheld the ruler of the cosmos and was able to show the Wielder of the Thunder to others. If Zeus is ashamed to be called [the son] of Phidias,[16] art [τέχνη] was the mother of the image of him. Therefore we only wonder at the other of the Seven Wonders, but this one we also worship: as a work of art it is remarkable [παράδοξον]; as a representation [μίμημα] of Zeus it is holy.[17] The labor that went into it wins praise, but its immortality wins our honor.
>
> Philo of Byzantium, *Seven Wonders* 3.1.3

---

15 The most recent edition is Brodersen 1992; cf. also Hercher 1858. Kroll's short notice in *RE* 20.54–55 remains the most helpful account.

16 Brodersen softens the force of this ("Man mag sich scheuen, von Zeus als Sohn des Pheidias zu sprechen"), but I do not see any grammatical or thematic justification for that.

17 Accepting the conjecture ὅσιον for the transmitted ὅμοιον.

Callimachus' poem seems to have been well known in antiquity,[18] and we should not rule out faint echoes of it here. Philo will, of course, have had access to other sources as well. His praise of Phidias ('Blessed is he...') is picked up at the end of the section on the Zeus of Olympia, as he apostrophizes the lucky period to which Phidias belonged:

> You could show to men visions [ὄψεις] of the gods; a man who had seen them would not be able to look at images from other times (3.4).[19]

Both observations seem very close to a *bon mot* about Homer that Strabo (8.3.30) quotes in the same connection, 'the only man to see or to show the images [εἰκόνες] of the gods,' a *bon mot* that could easily within Strabo's text be understood to refer to Phidias rather than Homer and has indeed been so understood in modern times.[20]

If a direct debt to Callimachus cannot be established with certainty, Philo's essay does have one very striking link to *Iambus* 6. The wit of Philo's description of the Zeus at Olympia is that it tells us absolutely nothing about what the statue looked like; Philo's sketches of the other Wonders may be vague and given to cliché, 'nicht... eine Beschreibung, sondern... eine rhetorische Plauderei' as Kroll (*RE* 20. 54) puts it, but there is in each of them some attempt at detailed description, usually involving quantitative numerical description. Philo, however, offers no help whatsoever with the Zeus, and as such this case might seem the furthest removed from the stated purpose of his essay. He begins by observing the extraordinary labor involved in actually visiting the Seven Wonders, a task that would take a whole lifetime, whereas:

> Education [παιδεία] is an amazing possession and wonderful gift, because it releases a man from traveling and shows him beautiful things in his own home, by giving eyes to the soul. What is most amazing is that the man who has gone to the places and seen things once goes away and forgets, for he does not take in the details [τὸ ἀκριβές] of the works, and his memory of each part fades; whereas the man who has studied the marvel and the craftsmanship of its construction through writing [ὁ δὲ λόγῳ τὸ θαυμαζόμενον ἱστορήσας καὶ τὰς ἐξεργασίας τῆς ἐνεργείας] has observed the whole of art's creation as in a mirror and preserves impressions of each image that cannot be wiped out, for he has seen amazing things with his soul. My account will be convincing if my speech vividly [ἐναργῶς] ex-

---

18 It is cited at Strabo 8.3.30: "Certain writers have given an account of the measurements of the statue, and Callimachus recorded them in an iambic poem." Cf. Pausanias 5.11.9; Kerkhecker 1999, 166–167.
19 The sense and the text are not absolutely clear.
20 Radt's assertion *ad loc.*, "εἰκόνας δείξας könnte nicht von einem bildenden Künstler gesagt sein," seems improbable at best, and is almost disproved by Philo.

plores each of the Seven Wonders and persuades the hearer to assent to the fact that it has brought him the impression of personal observation [θεωρία].

Philo of Byzantium, *Proem.* 2–3

There is much here that could be said about the philosophical and rhetorical background of Philo's observations, but two points will suffice in the current context. The stated purpose of Philo's essay is to remove the necessity of seeing the Wonders in person; some have argued that the wit of *Iambus* 6 too lies precisely in the fact that it offers an alternative to autopsy, one ironically addressed to someone just setting off to see the statue. Philo does not explicitly say that he has not seen the Wonders, but that would seem to be the natural inference to draw from the prologue: he too is a beneficiary of the same παιδεία that he offers his readers. As for Callimachus, it may well be that we are to understand that the speaking voice in *Iambus* 6 belongs to someone who himself has never been to Olympia; this would fit not merely with the stay-at-home persona familiar from elsewhere in Callimachus' works but, more important, with the whole conception of the poem. The statue is reduced to a series of measurements, and those measurements could be acquired from a book more easily than by autopsy or by reliance on local guides; the apparently dismissive ἀπέρχευ, 'go forth', with which the poem ends suggests that the proposed trip will be a waste of time, because the addressee now knows all that there is to be known about the statue. Callimachus is here Herodotean in his concern with exactness of description, down to the cost of the statue,[21] but anti-Herodotean in his rejection of autopsy.

If Callimachus and Philo both offer an alternative to autopsy, their strategies for so doing seem utterly different. Philo ends his essay with what might seem a paradoxical appeal to the significance of vision:

> And Phidias has so far surpassed Olympus as vividness [ἐνάργεια] is better than guesswork [ὑπόνοια], knowledge [γνῶσις] than investigation [ἱστορία][22] and autopsy [ὄψις] than report [ἀκοή].

Philo's appeal to autopsy may seem to undermine his own project of making a visit to the Wonder unnecessary, but there may be more at stake here than just rhetorical incompetence. It was a familiar observation that no description of the

---

21 Cf. Holford-Strevens *apud* Kerkhecker 1999, 161 n. 78. The broken v. 47 with its οὐ λογιστὸν οὐδ' ... may have contained a Herodotean expression of doubt.
22 I am unsure of the exact meaning here, and this may be thought to sit oddly with τὸ θαυμαζόμενον ἱστορήσας in the proem.

statue could do it justice; it was a work that called forth thoughts of the divine, and it is to this metaphysical level that Philo's rhetorical sleight of hand appeals. This is a work that can be 'seen with the soul' only, through a particularly potent form of *phantasia*: in refusing to describe it in any banal, physical way, Philo is in fact making clear the most important fact about Phidias' Zeus.[23] Just as Cicero's Phidias took his pattern for the statue from a mental image (*Orator* 2.8–10), so the statue itself can be grasped only as a mental image; we still need autopsy, but it is not autopsy as normally understood.[24] Callimachus' strategy in this regard is utterly different. If Philo is right that the onetime visitor to one of the Wonders will be unable to grasp τὸ ἀκριβές, 'the details,' then Callimachus has averted this danger by an excess of accurate detail; whereas, however, Philo's silence seems to point to the overwhelming impact of the statue, Callimachus' detail shuts the metaphysical out: 'The statue's visual impact is ignored. The standard elements of ἔκφρασις are avoided. The measurements do not convey the viewer's experience. The poem frustrates all such expectations.'[25]

Nothing in what survives of *Iambus* 6 appears to evoke the famous verses of *Iliad* 1 that were widely believed to have been Phidias' inspiration. Nevertheless, the familiarity of the anecdote allows the suspicion that Callimachus wants us to recall these verses, and the contrast between the epic and the iambic representation then carries a potent generic charge. The Homeric verses are characterized by a richness of poetic epithets (κυανέῃσιν, ἀμβρόσιαι, ἀθανάτοιο) and vocabulary (ἐπερρώσαντο, ἐλέλιξεν), whereas the *Iambus* offers a prosaic vocabulary in its description of the parts of the statue, homely touches such as the hare and the tortoise (v. 22, whatever the reference might be), and – so far as the remains allow us to see – a very limited descriptive range (χρύσιον, 25; ἄγιον, 29; etc.); in Homer the god acts in a moment of sublime movement; in Callimachus the god remains very unsublimely stationary. Homer's Zeus could not possibly be a statue, whatever inspiration it provided for Phidias, whereas Callimachus challenges us to (be able to) remember that his Zeus really is a

---

[23] Whether or not Philo did in fact know anything serious about the statue (cf., e.g., Brodersen 1996, 69) is therefore a secondary question.
[24] The discussion of *phantasia* at Philostratus *VA* 6.19.2 is particularly relevant here.
[25] Kerkhecker 1999, 168. It is worth noting that, in his discussion of the sophist Acacius, Eunapius (497 = XVII Giangrande) draws a contrast, apparently descending from Libanius himself, between, on the one side, the sublimely inspired (and hard to explain) skill of Homer and Phidias and, on the other, the careful learning and *akribeia* of Libanius. Here perhaps is a later echo (or at least analogy) for the humorous contrast that lies at the heart of *Iambus* 6; for the use of Callimachean ideas in such later texts, cf. Hunter 2008b, 536–558).

δαίμων (v. 37). Homer in fact has very little reference to images of gods, but the most famous such passage is instructive in the present context.

In *Iliad* 6 the Trojan women offer a robe to the image of Athena, together with a prayer that she should save them from the rampaging Diomedes. The god, however, does not grant the prayer: ἀνένευε δὲ Παλλὰς Ἀθήνη (v. 311).[26] This passage may well have been in Callimachus' mind when he reworked Zeus's proud assertion to Thetis, which immediately precedes the nod that inspired Phidias, at the end of the *Hymn to Athena*:

> οὐ γὰρ ἐμὸν παλινάγρετον οὐδ' ἀπατηλόν
> οὐδ' ἀτελεύτητον, ὅ τι κεν κεφαλῇ κατανεύσω.
>
> Homer, *Iliad* 1.526–527

Whatever I confirm with a nod of my head cannot be withdrawn and neither deceives nor lacks fulfillment.

> ὣς φαμένα κατένευσε· τὸ δ' ἐντελές, ᾧ κ' ἐπινεύσῃ
> Παλλάς, ἐπεὶ μώνᾳ Ζεὺς τόγε θυγατέρων
> δῶκεν Ἀθαναίᾳ πατρώια πάντα φέρεσθαι.
> λωτροχόοι, μάτηρ δ' οὔτις ἔτικτε θεάν,
> ἀλλὰ Διὸς κορυφά. κορυφὰ Διὸς οὐκ ἐπινεύει
> ψεύδεα   ἁ θυγάτηρ.
> ἔρχετ' Ἀθαναία νῦν ἀτρεκές κτλ.
>
> Callimachus, *Hymn to Athena* 131–137

So saying she nodded in confirmation. Whatever Pallas confirms with a nod will be fulfilled, since Zeus gave to her alone of his daughters that she should have all her father's privileges, and it was no mother who gave birth to the goddess, but the head of Zeus. Zeus's head does not nod untruths '...' daughter. Athena is really coming out now.

If Homer's Zeus could not be a statue, Callimachus' nodding Athena is both a statue and a goddess who speaks and bathes in mountain streams.

Juxtaposed to *Iambus* 6 is (in the same meter) *Iambus* 7, in which an image of Hermes, a minor work (πάρεργον) of Epeius, the creator of the Trojan Horse, tells of its many vicissitudes before ending up in the Thracian city of Aenus. The pointed contrast with the Panhellenic grandeur of Phidias' Zeus is obvious, but the pairing, together with *Iambus* 9, which is a conversation with an ithyphallic

---

[26] Aristarchus athetized this verse, and one of the reasons (not necessarily Aristarchan) that the A scholia offer is "the idea of Athena nodding refusal is ridiculous [γελοία]." If this refers, as it seems to, to the statue, then the question of the relationship between god and statue was, for later interpreters, directly thematized: Athena herself, like Zeus in *Iliad* 1, certainly could nod, but the idea of the statue doing so is absurd.

statue of Hermes, points to the importance of the materiality of Callimachus' gods, and in this Callimachus offers us a glimpse of the Hellenistic religious world, which is far from being simply a poetic fiction. This was indeed a world full of gods, and the most visible sign of those gods was their images and the festivals that celebrated them, both of which take center stage in the poetry of the high Alexandrian period. The Graces whom Callimachus asks to bestow immortality upon his elegies are both gods with birth narratives and stories to tell (Schol. Flor. p. 13 Pf., p. 76 M.) and statues of beautiful women, sometimes nude and sometimes wearing fine, delicate clothes (fr. 7.9–11 Pf. = 9.9–11 M.). Probably in Book 3 of the *Aetia* Callimachus presented a conversation with the cult statue of Apollo on Delos in which the god-statue explained the symbolic significance of why he was represented carrying the Graces in his right hand and his bow in the left (fr. 114 Pf.= 64 M.).[27] The papyrus that preserves the first part of this conversation seems to conclude with the end of the preceding *aition*, in which πολυγώνιε χαῖρε, 'Hail, you of many corners' (fr. 114.2 Pf.), suggests that this was a conversation with, or an account of, an aniconic image of a god, and Pfeiffer made the very attractive suggestion that this was in fact one of the blocks of stone that represented Apollo in a Milesian cult of the god; if so, πολυγώνιε presumably plays with the frequent, and Callimachean (cf. *Hymn to Apollo* 68–70), association of the god's name with πολύς.[28] Be that as it may, such a juxtaposition of a rude stone to the elaborate image of the Delian god bearing 'the lovely Graces' both recalls the juxtaposition of *Iambi* 6 and 7 and reminds us that Callimachus' gods tend to be local rather than Panhellenic, or rather, as in the *Hymn to Artemis*, to be the sum of myriad local parts (cf. Hunter/Fuhrer 2002, 148); if Callimachus was here influenced by prose handbooks about local cults, he himself may well have influenced subsequent scholarly tradition, as witness, for example, the Ἐπιφάνειαι Ἀπόλλωνος (*Appearances of Apollo*) of his follower Istrus (*FGrHist* 334 F 50–52).[29] Moreover, both the emphasis on materiality and the multiplicity of divine images, both anthropomorphic and aniconic, may from a literary point of view be seen as in part a reaction to Herodotus' stress, from which I began, on the role of Hesiod and

---

[27] In addition to the standard commentaries, cf. Pfeiffer 1952; Manakidou 1993, 225–235; Borgonovo/Cappelletto 1994; D'Alessio 1995a.
[28] Cf. Hunter/Fuhrer 2002, 163. For πολυγώνιε, cf. also Cameron 1995, 168, with further bibliography.
[29] Cf. Dillery 2005, 511–512. The whole of Dillery's discussion is important for setting Hellenistic poetry against the wider background of the interest in and recording of cultic history.

Homer in shaping the Greek divinities; those grand epic figures have been replaced by real divinities made of tangible substances such as marble and wood.

Examples could be multiplied from across the Callimachean corpus. In Book 4 of the *Aetia* poems devoted to two images of Hera on Samos were juxtaposed (frr. 100, 101 Pf. = 203, 204 M.). The first *aition* involved the oldest aniconic wooden representation of Hera on the island:

> οὔπω Σκέλμιον ἔργον ἐύξοον, ἀλλ' ἐπὶ τεθμόν
> δηναιὸν γλυφάνων ἄξοος ἦσθα σανίς·
> ὧδε γὰρ ἱδρύοντο θεοὺς τότε· καὶ γὰρ Ἀθήνης
> ἐν Λίνδῳ Δαναὸς λιτὸν ἔθηκεν ἕδος.
>
> Callimachus fr. 100 Pf.

Not yet was the finely carved work of Scelmis, but in the old manner you were a plank that had not been carved with chisels. This is how they set up gods in those days: at Lindus Danaus had set up a simple image of Athena.

If the representation of Hera changed over time from an aniconic plank to anthropomorphic form, can she be said to be 'forever,' αἰεί, like Callimachus' Zeus? The historical interest in change over time ('That's how they represented gods at that time') is, moreover, both typical of Callimachus' age and speaks to the concern with particularity that is everywhere the hallmark of his treatment of the divine. That said, there clearly are differences of nuance between, on the one hand, the divine statues of the *Aetia* and the *Iambi* and, on the other, the gods of the hexameter *Hymns* that may appear as statues but that remain recognizably also the gods of poetic tradition.

Experiencing Gods

Statues are to be seen, though usually in circumstances and times determined by the god and his or her attendants; and central too to the presentation of the divine in the *Hymns* of Callimachus is the concept and imagining of divine epiphany, as indeed we know it to have been to the practice of Hellenistic religion. Albert Henrichs has noted that the sense of anticipation that (in particular) the hymns to Apollo and Athena create represents with some accuracy the experience of cultic participants.[30] Here too Callimachus is building not just upon archaic lyric but also upon the foundation of the *Homeric Hymns*, which

---

[30] Henrichs 1993, 142–145; the subject has been much discussed, but cf. also Petrovic 2007, 142–181.

narrate and explore epiphany in various ways, not all of which have always been fully appreciated.[31] In this final section, I want to consider some of the archaic roots of a poetic form that has always seemed quintessentially Callimachean.

The *Homeric Hymn to Dionysus* (no. 7) seems to look forward to Callimachus in various ways;[32] the date of this poem is uncertain, however suggestive a link with Exekias' famous depiction of Dionysus and the dolphins (ca. 530 bc) may be, but there is no good reason not to consider it archaic. The poem begins with an epiphany:

ἀμφὶ Διώνυσον Σεμέλης ἐρικυδέος υἱόν
μνήσομαι, ὡς ἐφάνη παρὰ θῖν' ἁλὸς ἀτρυγέτοιο
ἀκτῇ ἔπι προβλῆτι, νεηνίῃ ἀνδρὶ ἐοικώς
πρωθήβῃ·

Homeric Hymn to Dionysus 1–4

> I will celebrate Dionysus, the son of glorious Semele, how he appeared by the shore of the unharvested sea, on a steep headland, looking like a young man in the prime of youth.

Here is a very familiar narrative pattern: Dionysus 'appears' to those who do not know or recognize him and demonstrates his divinity; in the *Bacchae* of Euripides his purpose is to become ἐμφανὴς δαίμων to mortals. Both Ovid (*Met*. 3.572–700) and Nonnus (*Dion*. 45.103–169) acknowledged this affinity to later narratives by embedding their versions of the pirate story into the story of the destruction of Pentheus.[33] Games of recognition are here, as they always are with Dionysus, fundamental. We recognize the god both because of what the hymn's singer tells us and because of our familiarity with narrative patterns, but the Tyrrhenian pirates do not. Knowledge of the Lycurgus-Pentheus pattern, together with the unsettling lack of geographical specificity as the narrative of this *Hymn* begins — Where is the 'steep headland'? — and the god's announcement of his name, genealogy, and nature (ἐρίβρομος) at the conclusion of the narrative (vv. 55–57) makes us wonder in fact whether we are to understand that this

---

[31] Cf., e.g., Fantuzzi/Hunter 2004, 364–366 on the *Homeric Hymn to Apollo*; the discussion of the hymns of Isidorus there also contains much of relevance to the present chapter.
[32] On the narrative pattern shared between this hymn and Callimachus' tale of Erysichthon, cf. Bulloch 1977, 99–101.
[33] Ovid introduces the character of Acoetes, who may or may not be the god, so that even we readers, let alone Pentheus, do not recognize the god, or are not sure whether we do; Bömer's rather sad survey of modern discussion of the question reveals nothing so clearly as how successfully Ovid has achieved this effect.

is Dionysus' first appearance or that every appearance of Dionysus is in some senses the first. As in the *Bacchae*, Dionysus is both a new god and immemorially old.³⁴ (The sea is already οἶνοψ, v. 7.) Do we know the god, or can you only understand this poem if you put yourself in the position of an audience that has never heard the name Dionysus, let alone Semele?

Whereas the terrified sailors (ἐκπληγέντες, v. 50) leap overboard, where they are transformed into dolphins, the god restrained the σαόφρων (v. 49) steersman who realized (νοήσας, v. 15) that they had captured no ordinary young man,³⁵ made him 'all blessed' (πανόλβιος, v. 54), and revealed his identity to him. This pattern, including the urging of the worshipper θαρσεῖν (v. 55), is strikingly reminiscent of what (little) we know of initiation into Mystery cults;³⁶ the steersman is now in the happy position of the initiate into Demeter's cult at Eleusis:³⁷

ὄλβιος ὃς τάδ' ὄπωπεν ἐπιχθονίων ἀνθρώπων,
ὃς δ' ἀτελὴς ἱερῶν ὅς τ' ἄμμορος, οὔ ποθ' ὁμοίων
αἶσαν ἔχει φθίμενός περ ὑπὸ ζόφῳ εὐρώεντι.

Homeric Hymn to Demeter 480–482

> Blessed is he of men upon the earth who has witnessed these things; he who is uninitiated or who has no share in the holy things enjoys no similar fate after death in the moldy dark.

The epiphanic revelation toward which the *Homeric Hymn to Dionysus*, like so many hymns (including some of Callimachus'; on this pattern, see esp. García 2002), has been moving represents also the revelatory sight offered to the blessed. The god's θάρσει (v. 55) finds parallels in texts that there are reasonable grounds for thinking reflect encouragement to those undergoing initiation,³⁸ and the god's revelation of himself in pity (v. 53) for a mortal may make us think of Isis appearing to Lucius: 'adsum tuos miserata casus, adsum fauens et propitia' (Apuleius *Met.* 11.5).

This pattern will also make us ask who speaks the closing verses:

---

34 I am in fact tempted to take πρώτιστα in v. 35 as "for the first time," but I doubt that many will follow me.
35 The participle may of course mean no more than "when he saw this" (M.L. West), but the choice of the verb remains suggestive; García 2002, 17–20 has the steersman having "an insight" and discusses other examples of this verb in the context of hymnic recognition.
36 Cf., e.g., Lada-Richards 1999, 236–237, 319. I hope it will not need stressing that I am not suggesting that this text is actually a mystical or initiatory one.
37 Cf. also Homeric Hymn to Demeter 486–489.
38 Cf. Seaford on Eur. *Ba.* 607; Joly 1955; Lada-Richards 1999, 86–87, 93 n. 188.

χαῖρε, τέκος Σεμέλης εὐώπιδος· οὐδέ πῃ ἔστιν
σεῖό γε ληθόμενον γλυκερὴν κοσμῆσαι ἀοιδήν.

Homeric Hymn to Dionysus 58–59

Hail, child of fair Semele! It is not possible for him who forgets you to adorn sweet song.

At one level, these verses are obviously spoken by the hymn's singer as he greets and bids farewell to the god, but after what has preceded we may also sense the voice of the steersman acknowledging the ἐμφανὴς δαίμων in front of him and the divine favor he has been shown. (Note the ironically laden δαίμων of v. 31.) The steersman and the poet are in fact in the same position in having received the god's χάρις. (Cf. v. 55.) The narrative of an epiphany of the god in the timeless past, the mingling of voice, the interaction between the divinity praised and the hymnist doing the praising, however appropriate to the nature of Dionysus,[39] and the evocation of cultic practices all look forward to the so-called mimetic *Hymns* of Callimachus.

In Callimachus' *Hymn to Apollo* the worshippers are waiting for the god to appear — their situation is thus very different from that of the pirates who capture Dionysus — but here too the epiphanic revelation will be limited to a blessed group:[40]

ὠπόλλων οὐ παντὶ φαείνεται, ἀλλ' ὅτις ἐσθλός·
ὅς μιν ἴδῃ, μέγας οὗτος, ὃς οὐκ ἴδε, λιτὸς ἐκεῖνος.
ὀψόμεθ', ὦ Ἑκάεργε, καὶ ἐσσόμεθ' οὔποτε λιτοί.

Callimachus, *Hymn to Apollo* 9–11

Apollo does not appear to everyone, but only to the good. He who sees him, that man is great; he who does not see him, that man is of no account. We shall see, Far-Worker, and we shall never be of no account.

That this is not just a pious hope is made clear by the end of the poem, in which Apollo does actually appear (with startling suddenness) to Callimachus' readers to confirm their poetic principles. The exchange between Phthonos and Apollo took place somewhere in an unspecified past, but just as the final address of the hymnist in the *Homeric Hymn to Dionysus* picks up the immediately preceding words of the god, in part perhaps in a kind of cultic repetition and in part to link the present experience of the hymnist (and his audience) to the story that has

---

39 There are analogous phenomena in the *Homeric Hymns to Apollo* and *Demeter*, but in neither case is the closeness of the hymnic voice to that of the figure in the narrative who has received the god's favor as marked as in the *Hymn to Dionysus*.
40 On such language in the *Hymn to Apollo*, cf. now Petrovic 2012.

just been narrated, so the closing verse of the Callimachean hymn both salutes the appearance of the god (χαῖρε) and (on the most probable interpretation) links the alleged present experience of the poet — μῶμος, 'criticism,' 'blame' — to the past just narrated; if Apollo speaks like Callimachus, then Callimachus' dismissal of Blame is in its turn a very Apolline act.

Bibliography

Acosta-Hughes, B. 2002. *Polyeideia: The Iambi of Callimachus and the Archaic Iambic Tradition*, Berkeley/Los Angeles.
Borgonovo, P./Cappelletto, P. 1994. 'Callimaco frr. 114 e 115 Pf.: Apollo 'poligonale' e Apollo delio', *Zeitschrift für Papyrologie und Epigraphik* 103, 13–17.
Brodersen, K. 1992. *Reiseführer zu den sieben Weltwundern: Philon von Byzanz und andere antike Texte*, Frankfurt.
Brodersen, K. 1996. *Die sieben Weltwunder*, Munich.
Bulloch, A.W. 1977. 'Callimachus' Erysichthon, Homer and Apollonius Rhodius', *American Journal of Philology* 98, 97–123.
Burkert, W. 1985. 'Herodot über die Namen der Götter: Polytheismus als historisches Problem', *Museum Helveticum* 42, 121–132.
Burkert, W. 1985. *Greek Religion*, Oxford.
Cuypers, M.P. 2004. 'Prince and Principle: The Philosophy of Callimachus' Hymn to Zeus', in: M.A. Harder/R.F. Regtuit/G.C. Wakker (eds.), *Callimachus II*, Louvain, 95–115.
D'Alessio, G.B. 1995. 'Apollo delio, i Cabiri milesii e le cavalle di Tracia: Osservazioni su Callimaco frr. 114–115 Pf.', *Zeitschrift für Papyrologie und Epigraphik* 106, 5–21.
Dillery, J. 2005. 'Greek Sacred History', *American Journal of Philology* 126, 505–526.
Fantuzzi, M./Hunter, R. 2004. *Tradition and Innovation in Hellenistic Poetry*, Cambridge.
García, J.F. 2002. 'Symbolic Action in the Homeric Hymns: The Theme of Recognition', *Classical Antiquity* 21, 5–39.
Graziosi, B. 2002. *Inventing Homer*, Cambridge.
Henrichs, A. 1993. 'Gods in Action: The Poetics of Divine Performance in the Hymns of Callimachus', in: M.A. Harder/R.F. Regtuit/G.C. Wakker (eds.), *Callimachus*, Groningen, 127–147.
Hercher, R. 1858. *Claudii Aeliani De natura animalium, Varia historia, Epistolae et fragmenta; Porphyrii philosophi De abstinentia et De antro nympharum; Philonis Byzantii De septem orbis spectaculis*, Paris.
Hunter, R./Fuhrer, T. 2002. 'Imaginary Gods? Poetic Theology in the Hymns of Callimachus', in: F. Montanari/L. Lehnus (eds.), *Callimaque*, Vandœuvres, 143–187.
Joly, R. 1955. 'L'exhortation au courage (θαρρεῖν) dans les Mystères', *Revue des Études Grecques* 68, 164–170.
Kerkhecker, A. 1988. 'Ein Musenanruf am Anfang der *Aitia* des Kallimachos', *Zeitschrift für Papyrologie und Epigraphik* 71, 16–24.
Lada-Richards, I. 1999. *Initiating Dionysus*, Oxford.
Lapatin, K.D.S. 2001. *Chryselephantine Statuary in the ancient Mediterranean World*, Oxford.

Lapatin, K.D.S. 2010. 'New Statues for Old', in: J.N. Bremmer/A. Erskine (eds.), *The Gods of Ancient Greece*, Edinburgh, 126–151.

Manakidou, F. 1993. *Beschreibung von Kunstwerken in der hellenistischen Dichtung*, Stuttgart.

Overbeck, J. 1868. *Die antiken Schriftquellen zur Geschichte der bildenden Künste bei den Griechen*, Leipzig.

Petrovic, I. 2007. *Von den Toren des Hades zu den Hallen des Olymp: Artemiskult bei Theokrit und Kallimachos*, Leiden.

Petrovic, I. 2012. 'Callimachus' Hymn to Apollo and Greek Metrical Sacred Regulations', in: M.A. Harder/R.F. Regtuit/G.C. Wakker (eds.), *Gods and Religion: Proceedings of the Ninth Groningen Workshop on Hellenistic Poetry*, Louvain, 264–285.

Pfeiffer, R. 1952. 'The Image of the Delian Apollo and Apolline Ethics', *Journal of the Warburg and Courtauld Institutes* 25, 20–32. [Reprinted as pp. 55–71 in *Ausgewählte Schriften* (Munich, 1960).]

Prioux, É. 2007. *Regards alexandrins: Histoire et théorie des arts dans l'épigramme hellénistique*, Louvain.

Pulleyn, S. 1997. *Prayer in Greek Religion*, Oxford.

Rosalind, T. 2000. *Herodotus in Context: Ethnography, Science, and the Art of Persuasion*, Cambridge.

Seaford, R. 1996. *Euripides: Bacchae, with an Introduction, Translation and Commentary*, Warminster.

Stephens, S.A. 2003. *Seeing Double: Intercultural Poetics in Ptolemaic Alexandria*, Berkeley/Los Angeles.

Tanner, J. 2006. *The Invention of Art History in Ancient Greece*, Cambridge.

West, M.L. 1966. *Hesiod: Theogony*, Oxford.

9 Festivals, Cults and the Construction of Consensus in Hellenistic Poetry

The importance of festivals and public cult in the construction and re-enforcement of social cohesion and political power in the Hellenistic age is a familiar fact of the history of the period. Very few Ptolemaic events, for example, have been as much studied from these perspectives as the 'Grand Procession' of Ptolemy II.[1] It is a similarly familiar fact about Hellenistic poetry that narratives and representations of song, of cult, and of festivals are (perhaps surprisingly) common. This is often (and rightly) associated with the fact of the greater spread of, and assumption of, reception through reading — to put it banally, the further poetry gets away from live enactment in performance, the more it scripts versions of such performances, as some kind of 'compensation' — and with changes in the nature of poetry itself (the separation of the music from the words, the fact that elite poets now wrote predominantly, though not of course exclusively, in hexameters and elegiacs etc.). Other factors are, however, clearly involved also. Both representational art and the lyric texts themselves which had survived from the archaic and classical periods were suggestive of a past culture which was both very different from the conditions — social, political and literary — prevailing in the Hellenistic period, but also suggestive of striking continuities. As the rich epigraphic record attests, festivals and cultic performance of all kinds blossomed all over the Hellenistic world, and the support for festivals, and the buildings and temples associated with them, by rulers both great and small was a fact of life which, from the point of view of the great poets of the third century, must have seemed a vital part of the archaic and classical heritage which they sought to reconstruct. In this paper I cast a brief glance at two themes in Hellenistic poetry which are both related to this interest in festival and cult and also related to each other. One is how this interest manifests itself in the representation of a participating audience in the act of observing and being drawn into cult and song, and the other is cultic aetiologies, which are, of course, ubiquitous in Hellenistic poetry, but whose function and resonance are not always as straightforward as is sometimes made out.

In one of Theocritus' best known poems, *Idyll* 15, two women of relatively humble means have a day out to the Alexandrian palace to take part in the Adonis-festival staged by Queen Arsinoe and to listen to the singing of the

---

1 Bibliography in Hunter 2003, 2 n. 5.

'Adonis song' by a solo performer.² The women are what we might call participant observers, not really so far removed in fact from the voices of Callimachus' so-called mimetic hymns to Apollo, Athena and Demeter, and this is, as I have already observed, a position repeatedly dramatised and narrativised in Hellenistic poetry. Of course, this is hardly new. The famous description of the Delian festival in the *Homeric Hymn to Apollo* places both the poet and his audience in the position of spectators and admirers of the performers and also scripts the appropriate reaction: 'anyone who was there when the Ionians gathered together would say that they were immortal and ageless' (151–152), 'everyone would say that he himself was speaking [when the Deliades imitate voices]' (163–164). It is just such a reaction – an admiration for 'lifelikeness' – that the women of Theocritus 15 give us, but this time in mimetic form: 'Look first at the tapestries, how fine and graceful they are! You will say that they are the garments of the gods' (15, 78–79).³ The poet of the *Homeric Hymn* almost makes the god too an observer – 'they delight you with boxing and dancing and song' (149) – as indeed performers of any cultic enterprise would expect the relevant god to watch them doing honour to him or her. Callimachus goes one step further, and in more than one poem. In his *Hymn to Apollo*, the Cyrenean rites and dances for Apollo which 'we' are now performing were witnessed immemorially long ago by Apollo himself, who 'was very delighted' (85) at what he saw, as in the *Homeric Hymn*. What might be thought a 'typically Hellenistic' touch is that the god was not just a passive observer/member of the audience, but he pointed things out to his new bride (90–91), just like the excited women of Theocritus 15. In Hellenistic poetry the gods still look on, but can be more animated about it. We may compare the scene in the fourth book of the *Argonautica* (922–964) in which Thetis and the Nereids, as like a maiden-chorus as Nausicaa and her friends on the beach, escort the *Argo* through the Planktai, while Hephaestus takes a break to watch (like the Syracusan women?) and Hera throws her arms around Athena in excited fear, just like two teenagers watching a scary movie. Visualisation, *our* visualisation, is at the core of such scenes. Apollonius has perhaps gone some of the way towards breaking down the sharp Homeric distinction between the divine audience and

---

2 The description of women visiting a shrine of Asclepius in Herodas 4 is standardly and rightly compared, and if that shrine is indeed supposed to be the great Coan site, then the Ptolemaic dimension of that poem is unavoidable, cf., e.g., Zanker 2006.
3 Some might think it indicative of the shift from the archaic to the Hellenistic period that in the *Homeric Hymn* what is being described is real cultic performance, whereas in Theocritus it is a work of art, but 1 cannot pursue that subject here.

the contemporary one, composed of 'men of now' who fail to measure up to the great figures of the past, but it was always a distinction which implied a complex and suggestive similarity. We may perhaps compare the multi-faceted relationship between the watching chorus and the watching spectators of Attic tragedy.

In his *Hymn to Delos* Callimachus produces yet another take on this. With an extraordinary geographical perspective (or the perspective of one who has been looking at a map), he imagines the islands performing circular dances around Delos (as may well have been in fact re-enacted in historical times), and it is again observer status which is emphasised; 'Hesperos looks down upon (καταβλέπει) you neither silent nor without sound, but always ringing with noise' (vv. 302–303). Examples of this interest in the observer could be multiplied many times. When in a similar passage of Callimachus' *Hymn to Artemis* the nymphs honour Artemis with circular dances — obviously the divine avatar of a very common form of human performance — Helios stops his chariot to watch and the days become long: the sense of festival, of carnival time (cf, again, Ptolemy's 'Grand Procession'), affects the whole cosmic order. So too, when Apollo is praised, even Thetis and Niobe cease from their lamentation:

εὐφημεῖ καὶ πόντος, ὅτε κλείουσιν ἀοιδοί
ἢ κίθαριν ἢ τόξα, Λυκωρέος ἔντεα Φοίβου.
οὐδὲ Θέτις Ἀχιλῆα κινύρεται αἴλινα μήτηρ,   20
ὁππόθ' ἰὴ παιῆον ἰὴ παιῆον ἀκούσῃ.
καὶ μὲν ὁ δακρυόεις ἀναβάλλεται ἄλγεα πέτρος,
ὅστις ἐνὶ Φρυγίηι διερὸς λίθος ἐστήρικται,
μάρμαρον ἀντὶ γυναικὸς ὀϊζυρόν τι χανούσης.

Callimachus, *Hymn to Apollo* 17–24

The sea too keeps reverent silence, when bards celebrate the lyre or the bow, the implements of Lycorean Phoibos. Not even Thetis, his mother, mourns wretchedly for Achilles, whenever she hears 'Hie Paieon, Hie Paieon'. And the tearful rock postpones its woes, the moist cliff standing in Phrygia, a marble block taking the place of a woman crying piteously.

Here too we have a sense of festival/lyric time defying the laws of nature — not because Helios is not moving, but because even the sea is silent, in a familiar motif of divine epiphany. We move from the sea, to Thetis who dwells in the sea and may even be a metonymy for it (so that in some senses v. 20 expresses the same thought as v. 18, but expresses it in a different mode),[4] to the watery rock which is Niobe. The 'pun' (though that is an unhelpful term) in ἀναβάλλεται, 'postpones' but allowing the sense 'strike up' (musically) (cf. Pindar, *Pythian* 1.4) to resonate also, encapsulates precisely this configuration of lyric time — the time of music and dancing — as a time of postponement, of watching and listening.

The evocation of cultic experience and the perspective of the viewer/participant is thus one way in which Hellenistic poetry both draws its audience in and also offers (usually oblique) encomium of those responsible for these public events. Less obvious perhaps is to what extent the concern with cultic aetiology and history, which we find everywhere in Callimachus and Apollonius of Rhodes, serves similar ends. At least two, not mutually exclusive, approaches to this material seem possible. On the one hand, we can plot the areas of local cult against known areas of influence or interest to rulers, so that such poetic material may be seen to have an inherently 'political' dimension, even if any such explicit concern seems very far from the text. Very often of course we will have to leave matters at the level of suggestion. Delian cults under Ptolemy II are a special case, and certain other examples are hard to resist. Ptolemaic interest in the Samothracian mysteries has long been connected with the fact that Apollonius' Argonauts stop on the island on the voyage out in order to be initiated.[5] So too, H.W. Parke and Alan Cameron have rightly drawn attention to Callimachus' persistent interest in the oracular cult of Apollo at Didyma, where the temple was rebuilt on a massive scale and the cult reorganized, both to reflect the Delphic pattern, at the end of the fourth century and the early part of the third;[6] from 279–259, in the reign of Ptolemy II, Miletus was in the sphere of influence of Alexandria, and it is thus hard not to see, as Wilamowitz already did, poetic concerns here moving in step with major events of interest to the patron.[7] Callimachus celebrated (and perhaps helped forge, at least for later ages) the 'new' foundation legend in his poem 'Branchos' (fr, 229 Pf.), which seems to have told of Apollo's epiphany to a lovely shepherd boy of Delphian descent and his foretelling of the cult that Branchos would found on the site.[8]

---

4 Williams's helpful note *ad loc.* makes a similar, though differently directed, point. I discuss this passage also in Hunter 2011.
5 Bibliography and discussion in Hunter 1995, 20.
6 Cf. Parke 1986, 129–130, Cameron 1995, 167–169.
7 A helpful survey of the arguments in Ehrhardt 2003.
8 Texts relevant to the myths concerning Branchos are gathered by Lelli 2005, 71–73. Both Asper 2004, 271 and Lelli 2005, 79 rightly raise the possibility (it can be no more) that ἀνάκτων

Callimachus is here celebrating local traditions (of however recent reinvention) and local families, much as generations of 'wandering poets' had done, and would continue to do, in the hope of rewards and honours from the communities they had celebrated.[9] It is, however, unlikely that many such poets used stichic 'catalectic choriambic pentameters' for their songs of praise and commemoration,[10] and we must admit that it is very difficult to be sure how this combination of rewritten cultic tradition and metrical experimentation actually 'felt' to its original audiences. Too often, the fact that a poem of Philicus, which looks like a hymn to Demeter in choriambic hexameters, another metrical 'sport' which Hephaestion cites alongside Callimachus' choriambic pentameters, is explicitly offered to the γραμματικοί as an 'innovative composition' (*SH* 677) is taken as a sign that all such poems are just that; literary games with no purchase at all in the realities or imagination of cult or religious ideas (broadly understood). We must rather learn to be sensitive to difference as well as to similarity. The tension between generic and linguistic form, a tension found elsewhere in Callimachus (cf., e.g., the elegiac epinicians for Berenice and Sosibios), seems almost to reflect an acknowledgement of the complex cultural signals which the public creation of tradition brings with it.

Typical of the issues which arise in this area, though untypical in other ways, is Callimachus' account of the aetiology of the cult of Dictynna on Crete:

ἔξοχα δ' ἀλλάων Γορτυνίδα φίλαο νύμφην,
ἐλλοφόνον Βριτόμαρτιν ἐύσκοπον· ἧς ποτε Μίνως   190
πτοιηθεὶς ὑπ' ἔρωτι κατέδραμεν οὔρεα Κρήτης.
ἡ δ' ὁτὲ μὲν λασίῃσιν ὑπὸ δρυσὶ κρύπτετο νύμφη,
ἄλλοτε δ' εἰαμενῇσιν· ὁ δ' ἐννέα μῆνας ἐφοίτα
παίπαλά τε κρημνούς τε καὶ οὐκ ἀνέπαυσε διωκτύν,
μέσφ' ὅτε μαρπτομένη καὶ δὴ σχεδὸν ἥλατο πόντον   195
πρηνόος ἐξ ὑπάτοιο καὶ ἔνθορεν εἰς ἁλιήων
δίκτυα, τά σφ' ἐσάωσαν· ὅθεν μετέπειτα Κύδωνες
νύμφην μὲν Δίκτυναν, ὄρος δ' ὅθεν ἥλατο νύμφη
Δικταῖον καλέουσιν, ἀνεστήσαντο δὲ βωμοὺς
ἱερά τε ῥέζουσι· τὸ δὲ στέφος ἤματι κείνῳ   200

ἱερὴν γενεθλίην at v. 17, near the end of the poem, refers not to, e.g., the Branchidai, but rather to the Ptolemaic house. Lelli compares Σωτήρων ὕπατον γένος at *Hymn to Delos* 166, but a more suggestive 'parallel', particularly given the possibility that 'Branchos' was the closing poem of a collection, is the prayer to Zeus to preserve οἶκον ἀνάκτων in the 'epilogue' to the *Aitia* (fr. 112,8 Pf. = 215,8 Massimilla).
9 Cf., e.g., Hunter 2003, 26–27, Hunter/Rutherford 2009.
10 This is the ancient analysis; modern scholars describe the length rather as an aristophanean (-uu-u- -) expanded by the insertion of three choriambs.

ἢ πίτυς ἢ σχῖνος, μύρτοιο δὲ χεῖρες ἄθικτοι·
δὴ τότε γὰρ πέπλοισιν ἐνέσχετο μύρσινος ὄζος
τῆς κούρης, ὅτ' ἔφευγεν· ὅθεν μέγα χώσατο μύρτωι.

Callimachus, *Hymn to Artemis* 189–204

Particularly above others you loved the nymph of Gortyn, deer-slaying Britomartis, whose aim does not miss. Once Minos, crazed with love for her, roamed the mountains of Crete. The nymph hid, now under the leafy oaks, now in the low meadows, but for nine months he wandered over the crags and cliffs and he did not cease from his pursuit; when she was all but caught, she jumped into the sea from a lofty headland and fell into fishermen's nets (δίκτυα) which saved her. As a result of this, the Kydonians afterwards call the nymph Dictynna, and the mountain from which she jumped Diktaion, and they set up altars to her and conduct sacrifice. On that day garlands are made of pine or mastich, and hands do not touch myrtle; while she was fleeing, a myrtle-branch became entangled in the girl's robes, and for this reason she conceived a great anger against myrtle.

A number of features make this passage particularly worthy of attention in the current context. It is, for Callimachus, a relatively extended narrative, and one which has a fair chance of being innovative;[11] there are clear indications, moreover, that the value of Callimachus' account was discussed in antiquity (cf. below). Secondly, there are indications elsewhere that Callimachus was well informed about Cretan cult, whether through personal observation, informants, written sources or a combination of all three;[12] this does not, of course, of itself tell us anything about the nature of this particular narrative, but it is a salutary reminder (if we needed one) that such cultic tales *may* not be simply the result of an overheated scholarly imagination and thirst for witty combinations. Third — and a cause for both particular interest and particular frustration — is the fact that, although we know that several Cretan cities had political ties to Ptolemaic Alexandria and that there was important mercantile and intellectual exchange between Crete and Alexandria, the state of the evidence makes it very difficult to track the relationship in any detail;[13] the best evidence, beyond the presence of Cretans in Egypt and of Ptolemaic officials in Crete, is for the development of Itanos in the far north-east of the island as a Ptolemaic naval base, but Ptolemaic interest stretched much further west than that also. Chance survivals show us what we are missing. A treaty between Polyrrhenia and Phalasarna, recorded on a stone originally placed in the tem-

---

11 It is at least a peculiar misreading when Chaniotis 2001, 213 includes this passage among Cretan stories which were 'so well known to every educated Greek that Callimachus could content himself with vague allusions to them'.
12 Cf. Chaniotis 2001.
13 Cf., e.g., Spyridakis 1970, Bagnall 1976, 117–123, Kreuter 1992, 17–45.

ple of Dictynna near Kydonia (cf. below), shows the Spartan interest in west Crete;[14] other powers were no doubt sniffing around also. The treaty between Magas of Cyrene, whose shifting relationship with Ptolemy II was an important fact in Alexandrian politics (and may well have been so also for a Cyrenean poet resident in Alexandria), and a κοινόν of west-Cretan states, dating probably from the latter part of the first half of the third century, suggests a search for influence of a kind at which Ptolemy and his agents were also past masters;[15] the treaty was mediated by Gortyn, which seems to have been already allied with Magas, and the principal deity overseeing the treaty and in whose temple at Lisos the treaty was recorded was indeed Dictynna. It is not, of course, that this treaty has (necessarily) anything to do with Callimachus' *Hymn to Artemis*, where, in any case, we are hampered by our ignorance of the date of the hymn,[16] but rather it starkly reveals both our ignorance and the kind of question we ought at least to be asking. Britomartis also had a cult on Delos,[17] and how important that island was to the evocation of a specifically Ptolemaic world we have already seen.

The interrelations between the west-Cretan goddess Dictynna, the predominantly east- and central Cretan goddess Britomartis (or Britomarpis)[18] and Artemis are fraught with problems, not all the result of the (lack of) evidence, and cannot be pursued here in any detail.[19] Even if, moreover, we were able to sort out the cultic history with some kind of clarity, we know that, not only were ancient writers known to disagree widely about Cretan history and culture (cf. esp. Diodorus Siculus 5.80.4), but for ancient poets and chroniclers Crete was also very much a land of the imagination where invention and creative fantasy were as much at home as hard ethnographic fact.[20] There is indeed a broad consensus among historians of Cretan religion that Dictynna, Britomartis and Artemis remained discrete deities on Crete through the Hellenistic period, and that Callimachus' conflation of Britomartis and Dictynna as a beloved nymph of Artemis and 'Dictynna' as subsequently a name for Artemis

---

14 *ICret.* II xi, 1 = Chaniotis 1996, 179–181.
15 *ICret.* II xvii, 1 = Schmitt 1969, n. 468; cf. Keeuter 1992, 35–36.
16 Cf. Bornmann 1968, vii–xi.
17 Cf. e.g., Guarducci 1935, 198–199, 202.
18 That μαρπτομένη in v. 195 alludes to this Cretan form (so, e.g., tentatively Bornmann 1968, *ad loc.*) is an attractive suggestion; the nymph's leap marks the moment of transition from one name to another.
19 For some guidance cf. Guarducci 1935; 1939, 128–140, Willetts 1962, 179–193, Sporn 2001; 2002, 323–325, Flinterman 2009, 240–246.
20 There is much relevant information and bibliography in ch. 4 of Tzifopoulos 2010.

(vv. 204–5) — a syncretism indeed attested outside Crete — is, to put it simply, a literary fiction which plays to familiar types of scholarly construction and to Callimachus' particular interest in name-changes over the course of history.[21] So it might well be (see further below), but that does not exhaust what we need to ask.

A striking feature of Callimachus' narrative is what we might call its pan-Cretanism. Britomartis is 'correctly' placed in the centre-east of Crete by her identification as a 'nymph of Gortyn', whereas Dictynna is also properly associated with Kydonia (modern Chania) in the west, near where there was the most famous shrine of the goddess, on the eastern side of the headland of Tityros or Psakon (the most northerly point of Crete); the temple is already mentioned by Herodotus (III 3.59.2).[22] We know almost nothing of the history of the temple in Callimachus' day, though it would not be an unreasonable inference, if not strictly a necessary one, that the temple was under the control of Kydonia; in Strabo's day, on the other hand, it seems to have been under the control of Polyrrhenia (10.4.13).[23] How politically charged Callimachus' references are, we cannot say. Be that as it may, the narrative is in part framed by references to Crete (vv. 191, 205), and the nymph's wanderings take her over 'the mountains of Crete', i.e. — or so we are to understand — over the whole island. Geographical puzzles are, of course, a familiar feature of Callimachus' poetry, but here the bringing together of Britomartis and Dictynna, of Gortyn and Kydonia, and (perhaps) of Mt Dikte and the Kydonian Diktynnaion (cf. below) draws the traditions of the island together, in an overt, because at first puzzling, manner, and fashions a specifically Cretan pool of narrative traditions. Callimachus is by no means alone in this period in treating Crete as a 'single unit', but we would dearly like to know more of his motives.

Callimachus' narrative appealed to, and gained authority from, his audience's knowledge of or beliefs about Cretan practice. To what extent Callimachus' identification of Britomartis — Dictynna (whose name very likely really means 'Lady of Dikte') as a nymph-companion of Artemis, and his explanation

---

21 In the geographical poem of Dionysius, son of Calliphon (cf. further below), it is stated that 'men say' that there is a temple of Artemis at Phalasarna where the goddess is called Dictynna (vv. 118–122); Phalasarna lies in the far north-west of Crete, not very far from Kydonia and the temple of Dictynna. Dionysius' source is unknown; I would be tempted to guess it to be this very passage of Callimachus, but the specificity of the reference to Phalasarna gives pause.
22 Both, e.g., Guarducci 1939, 130 and Bornmann 1968, *ad loc.* understand Κύδωνες in v. 197 as simply a learned way of saying 'Cretans' (cf. *Hymn to Zeus* 45), but this seems most improbable in view of what we know of the shrine of Dictynna. Cf. further Sistakou 2005, 253–254.
23 On this temple and the problem of its control cf. Sporn 2002, 277–280.

both of the change of name and of the cultic practice of avoiding myrtle garlands were innovative, it is no longer really possible to say, though this relatively full narrative does seem to have found wide resonance.[24] Two critiques of versions of the story survive from writers quite close in time to each other, and one of them (Strabo 10.4.12) is explicitly a criticism of Callimachus;[25] this too suggests that Callimachus himself was treated as the principal authority for (and perhaps author of) the story. Strabo's objection is, he tells us, not his own but derived from unnamed others: Callimachus' story, according to these anonymous critics, cannot be correct, because Kydonia is nowhere near Mt Dikte, and the mountain shrine of the goddess near Kydonia is not Δικταῖον but Δικτυνναῖον; clearly, then, it was the ὄρος ... Δικταῖον which had most roused Callimachus' critics. Modern scholars see here rather a 'typically Callimachean' geographical conflation, based on similarity of names, between Mt Dicte and the Δικτυνναῖον, to match the conflation of Britomartis and Dictynna into a single character, or understand that Callimachus' Δικταῖον actually stands for Δικτυνναῖον,[26] or (D'Alessio *ad loc.*) see a humorous linguistic compromise between Δίκτη and Δικτυνναῖον; certainly, πρηόνος ἐξ ὑπάτοιο suggests the headland rather than a mountain. Diodorus Siculus 5.76.3–4 also criticises the story as we find it in Callimachus (who is, however, not named)[27] but on the grounds that it is not πιθανόν, not because it would take a pretty extraordinary leap to reach the coast from Mt Dicte, but because a goddess who was the daughter of 'the greatest of the gods' should not have got into such a helpless state as to need help from men,[28] nor was it δίκαιον to ascribe such an act of

---

24 Nicander, *Alex.* Δίκτυννα ... ἐχθήρατο κλῶνας (of myrtle) looks like an echo of v. 203 of Callimachus' hymn (note στέφος in v. 619); this passage of Nicander may be a late interpolation, but that does not affect the point at issue. Cf. further below on echoes in Roman poetry.
25 Callimachus is also named as the source for the story, though not necessarily the only one, by the scholiast on Eur. *Hipp.* 146. The scholiast on Ar. *Frogs* 1356 tells what might be a 'cleaned up' version: Britomartis was out hunting and fell 'by chance' into nets from where she was saved by Artemis; she then established a shrine of Artemis Dictynna. On Strabo's criticism cf. further F. Jacoby, *FGrHtst*, III A, 221–222.
26 Cf. Bornmann 1968, on vv. 199–200.
27 That Diodorus is here talking of Britomartis–Dictynna rather than Artemis–Dictynna seems probable because he is taking issue with the aetiology of the name, having just given an alternative aetiology which is explicitly attached to Britomartis–Dictynna. Moreover, although both Artemis and Britomartis are daughters of Zeus, it seems unlikely that Diodorus would adduce the paternity of the Olympian as one of the reasons for not believing the story.
28 Callimachus himself famously used this criterion to reject unwanted myths (*Hymn to Zeus* 65).

impiety to a man as renowned for his probity as Minos. It seems not improbable that Callimachus is at least one of Diodorus' targets here.

What was involved, and what at stake, in the criticisms of a poetic narrative? The criticisms of Callimachus are of a very familiar kind, and we might think that such activities, like other forms of philology, were one of the ways in which a particular elite group marked out its own territory,[29] and there must indeed be something in that. Nevertheless, the great interest in the story, and in Callimachus' version of it, attested by Strabo and probably Diodorus Siculus, suggests that such aetiological legend was not merely a poetic game, but one in which the identity and ideology of cultic sites and narratives was very much involved; 'getting it right' was something that actually mattered, however fast and loose a Callimachus could be with traditional tales. We perhaps tend to lose sight of the authority that an Alexandrian text, and particularly one bearing the name of Callimachus, might carry; the *Nachleben* of this passage in Latin poetry in fact says much of the central role that Alexandria now played in the preservation and dissemination of cultural knowledge. Callimachus' mini-narrative may have been taken up and expanded in Roman neoteric poetry (Valerius Cato's *Diana/Dictynna*),[30] if it had not already been so used in later Hellenistic poetry,[31] and it may have contributed something to Ovid's narrative of Apollo and Daphne, a narrative full of allusions to the *Hymns* of Callimachus (including the *Hymn to Artemis*). Here then, quite unusually, we can identify a Callimachean aetiological narrative which attracted the attention not just of fellow-scholars and poets, but also of mythographers and students of cult; poet and audience share knowledge of a type of narrative and of a mode of explanation, and (as importantly) of what such explanations are worth.

The aetiological mode itself appeals at more than one level.[32] Callimachus' audience share not just in the myriad local cults of the Greek world, but also in

---

29 Cf. Asper 2001, 109–110.
30 Cf. Lyne 1978, 223–224, 229.
31 It is often thought that the version of the story in Antonius Liberalis 40 goes back to Nicander. In this version, which links Britomartis to a number of Artemis cults in the Mediterranean, the nymph is hidden by Cretan fishermen in their nets, rather than falling into them, and is then conveyed by a fisherman (Andromedes, presumably one of her Cretan rescuers) to Aegina, where he tries to rape her; she escapes and disappears ('becomes ἀφανής') at the place where is now the cult of Aphaia. The argument of Maass 1923 that an epodic poem, partially preserved on *POxy* 661 (= *CA* 194–5), was on the subject of Dictynna has not won much favour.
32 Cf. Fantuzzi/Hunter 2004, 49–51; Asper 2001 is an important discussion to which I am indebted.

the stories that lie behind them; if it is true, as widely held, that Homeric epic was a potent force in forging a pan-Hellenic identity, the sense of a shared 'Greekness', then the return to the local which we see everywhere in, particularly, Callimachus performs a similar function with very different tools. The cult of the grand, rather remote Olympians gives way to very particular, sometimes embarrassingly so, deities and near-deities; Homer is, as has often been noted, notably short on the particularities of cultic detail, particularly as expressed in aetiology[33] — such 'local' detail would work against the kind of poetic world which he created and which was, in its own way, so influential on Greek culture. Explanation is a striking instance of this. Homeric characters wonder (in both senses) at and about the gods, but they devote almost as little time to their histories and particularities as they do to their statues.[34] The Hellenistic aetiological project is thus not merely the heir to Hesiod's *Theogony*, in moving from the gods themselves and the establishment of the Olympian order to their cults on earth,[35] but it also seizes territory (deliberately) abandoned by Homeric epic. As is well known, Hellenistic poets often adduce — or gesture towards (as Callimachus' geographical epithets in the Britomartis narrative perhaps do) — alternative aetiologies for particular practices, and even when they do not, the sense of competition, of histories which may compete with each other and hence ask audiences to make choices, to exercise *krisis* (which may of course range from the serious to the utterly frivolous), is always lurking. Audiences give or withhold 'consent' to aetiological poetry in a quite different way than 'consent' is offered to epic poetry, and this is not merely, I think, a question of emotional 'distance' from what is being narrated. In the present case, Callimachus' reason for why myrtle is avoided in the cult of Dictynna invites an alternative explanation: myrtle is the plant of Aphrodite, associated with sex and weddings, and hence utterly out of place in the cult and the event it commemorates.[36] The two explanations may of course be to some extent combined. Was Aphrodite actually behind the impediment caused by the myrtle as Britomartis fled? Minos' sexual designs on the nymph were, after all, honouring her. How loudly does silence speak? Are we in fact encouraged, or — perhaps better — do we encourage ourselves, to see the gods at work in

---

[33] Cf. recently Lane Fox 2008, 372–373.
[34] Cf. Hunter 2011.
[35] Cf. Fantuzzi/Hunter 2004, 51–60.
[36] Cf. Bornmann 1968, on v. 201, who however writes as though there were (real) reasons why myrtle was avoided, although we do not know what they were; rather, of course, there were explanations, all 'real' though in different senses. Andrew Ford has suggested that διωκτύν in v. 194 suggests yet another possible etymology of Dictynna.

narrative when other, more contingent, explanations may in fact be appropriate. Aetiology, no less than more traditional modes of epic narrative, raises questions about how and why gods act, and leaves silences waiting to be filled; in both cultic narrative and cultic performance there is an unexplained excess, and we might think that it is that excess, as much as anything else, which builds 'consensus'. Does what we believe about the history of ritual actually matter as we perform it?[37] Another kind of question which we might ask is: Was there such a thing as a clear answer, or indeed any kind of answer, to the question of whether in Callimachus' day Artemis was ever called Dictynna on Crete? What for Callimachus and his audience would constitute evidence?

One poem of Callimachus which addresses some of these same issues, and with much the same divine personnel, seems to have been *Iambus* 10. The *diegesis* gives us the opening verse (fr. 200a. 1 Pf.) and informs us as follows:

> 'The Aphrodites – for the goddess is not single' (τὰς Ἀφροδίτας – ἡ θεὸς γὰρ οὐ μία). In Aspendos in Pamphylia pigs are sacrificed to Aphrodite Kastnietis for the following reason: Mopsus, leader of the Pamphylians, when going out hunting vowed to [the goddess] that if the hunt was successful he would sacrifice to her whatever he first caught; when he caught a wild boar he fulfilled his vow. For this reason the Pamphylians too do this to this day, for if the goddess was not pleased, Mopsus would not have caught this animal. [The poet] also praises the Artemis of the Eretrians because she rejects nothing that is sacrificed to her.

This account is partially confirmed by a passage of Strabo:

> Καλλίμαχος μὲν οὖν φησιν ἐν τοῖς ἰάμβοις[38] τὰς Ἀφροδίτας (ἡ θεὸς γὰρ οὐ μία) τὴν Καστνιῆτιν ὑπερβάλλεσθαι πάσας τῶι φρονεῖν, ὅτι μόνη παραδέχεται τὴν τῶν ὑῶν θυσίαν (καὶ μὴν πολυΐστωρ, εἴ τις ἄλλος κτλ.)
>
> Strabo 9.5.17

> In the *Iambi* Callimachus says that the goddess of Kastnie surpasses all Aphrodites (for the goddess is not one) in good sense, because she alone accepts the sacrifice of pigs (and Callimachus is a very learned man, if anyone is...).

---

37 Important work in this area has been done on Roman literary representations of ritual and its explanation; for a helpful orientation cf. Feeney 1998, ch. 4.
38 Kerkhecker 1999, 208 proposed ἰάμβωι but Radt *ad loc.* objects that we might then also have expected the standard οὗ ἡ ἀρχή: Kerkhecker's point, however, that the parenthesis reads very oddly remains true, and I am not confident that Strabo's text was indeed as transmitted. Presumably through a slip, Kerkhecker also implies that the text of Strabo does not transmit τὰς Ἀφροδίτας. Kerkhecker's discussion (207–213) is the principal contribution since Pfeiffer's edition and I am much indebted to it; in particular, Kerkhecker rightly stresses the importance of the fact that there were indeed two Aphrodites at Aspendos.

How closely Strabo follows Callimachus' text is a difficult question, and editors vary in the extent to which they are prepared to make further iambic trimeters out of Strabo's prose; fortunately, progress in understanding is not entirely dependent upon certainty of reconstruction.

As the *Diegesis* says that this same poem referred also to the cult of Artemis at Eretria, it is universally accepted that a scholium on Aristophanes *Birds* 872 should also be referred to *Iambus* 10; the scholiast is discussing the cult of Artemis Κολαινίς:

> ...Euphronios says that Κολαινίς occurs at Amarynthos [in Euboea] because Agamemnon sacrificed a hornless (κόλος) animal because of the difficult situation (ἐκ τοῦ καιροῦ).[39]

Callimachus says about her:

> τὴν ὠγαμέμνων, ὡς ὁ μῦθος εἴσατο
> τῆι καὶ λίπουρα καὶ μονῶπα θύεται
>
> Callimachus fr. 200b Pf.
>
> ...whom Agamemnon established, so the story goes, to whom tailless and one-eyed animals are sacrificed...
>
> This may, however, be an improvisation, for the people of Myrrhinous [in Attica] call Artemis Κολαινίς...

Sorting out the various accounts and explanations of this cult title, which is known certainly to have existed at Myrrhinous, is beyond the scope of this paper,[40] but we must note that the standard title of Artemis at Amarynthos, her major shrine not far from Eretria, was Amarousia and that there is no confirmation in either the Callimachean couplet which the scholiast quotes or in the *Diegesis*, which refers merely to the omnivorousness of the 'Artemis of the Eretrians', that Callimachus actually mentioned the title Κολαινίς. Moreover, for what it is worth, the account given by the *Diegesis* would sit well with Pausanias' account of a cult of Artemis at Aulis, just across the Euripos strait:

> Here there is a temple of Artemis and images of white marble, one holding torches and the other like a woman shooting a bow. They say that when the Greeks were about to sacrifice Iphigenia on the altar in obedience to the soothsaying of Calchas, the goddess made the victim a deer rather than her ... It is also said that at Aulis the Greeks did not receive a favouring breeze, but when a favourable wind suddenly got up, they sacrificed to Artemis

---

39 Cf. below.
40 Cf. esp. Jacoby on *FGrHist* 323a F 13; 325 F 3.

> whatever each had, alike female and male victims; from that time it has remained the case that at Aulis all victims are acceptable.
>
> Pausanias 9.19.6–7

There is some unclarity surrounding the chronology of the various strands of Pausanias' narrative here, but certain points may be drawn out. Although Pausanias is talking about Aulis, not Amarynthos or Eretria, it is very hard to believe that both he and Callimachus are not referring to essentially the same cultic practice of the acceptance of 'imperfect' sacrificial victims; Pausanias says nothing of any cult title for Artemis. The practice for which Pausanias gives an *aition* and that for which the *Diegesis* says that Callimachus praises the Eretrian Artemis are the same: 'all victims are acceptable' ~ 'no victim is rejected'. The clear impression of Pausanias' narrative is that the Greeks at Aulis sacrificed 'whatever each man had' when the wind got up, not as the result of a seer's instruction (contrast the sacrifice of Iphigenia), but rather because they were caught unawares by the sudden turn of events and (perhaps) so that they could catch the favourable wind before it died. Whether or not Callimachus did call the Eretrian goddess Κολαινίς, it is easy enough to imagine a similar kind of narrative there: Agamemnon's offering was one usually disallowed, but he had no choice ἐκ τοῦ καιροῦ, 'given the (difficult) circumstances'. This phrase in the Aristophanic scholia is not necessarily to be emended away, as it almost always is.[41] Despite the fact that we cannot be sure that Callimachus gave an aetiology for the Eretrian cult of Artemis, it is at least worth considering the possibility that behind Pausanias' account of the cult at Aulis stands, precisely, Callimachus; it is curious, but perhaps no more, that the verses dedicated to this cult in the geographical poem of 'Dionysius, son of Calliphon' might (though, of course, need not) echo Callimachus:

> Αὐλίς τε Βοιωτῶν πόλις, πρὸς ἧι λιμήν
> κἀρτέμιδος ἱερὸν ἅγιον, ὅ λέγεται κτίσαι
> Ἀγαμέμνον, εἶτ' κτλ.
>
> Dionysius Calliphontis 88–90
>
> ...and Aulis, city of the Boeotians, where there is a harbour and a holy shrine of Artemis, which Agamemnon is said to have founded...

Why is Aphrodite Kastnie surpassing in φρονεῖν? Speculation about this cannot be divorced from the question of the goddess' role in Mopsus' successful hunt.

---

41 Holwerda proposed ἐκ τοῦ κλήρου 'as a result of a prophetic lot' (in other words, Agamemnon was instructed to do this by, e.g., a seer); this is adopted by Kerkhecker 1999, 211 n. 79.

Ever since the *Diegesis* was published it has been suspected that 'for if the goddess was not pleased, Mopsus would not have caught this animal' is a paraphrase of something in the poem itself, rather than a piece of reasoning by the author of the *Diegesis* or his predecessors. This is very likely right, and Arnd Kerkhecker thus suspects that her φρονεῖν consists in 'getting what she wants.'[42] He must be right to look for an explanation which would suit the iambic mood, but perhaps we can narrow down a little the range of possibilities. If Artemis is praiseworthy because she did not reject offerings which, though imperfect and unusual, were nevertheless a mark of piety and all that the Greeks had, might not Aphrodite reveal her common sense by taking a similarly broad view, even though she normally finds pig offerings anathema? 'If the goddess was not pleased, Mopsus would not have caught this animal' is a very 'human' piece of *post factum* reasoning, perhaps attributed in the poem to the Pamphylians. We, however, do not have to assume that Aphrodite actually sent the boar Mopsus' way or even that 'Aphrodite seems to be rather keen on pork';[43] for her common sense may rather have manifested itself in not turning away an offering which showed piety and brought her honour, even if it was very unusual. In broad outline, the aetiology for this very unusual sacrifice which Callimachus offers is almost certainly one offered by the people of Aspendos themselves long before Callimachus; it adapts to a Greek mode of explanation a practice which appears thoroughly un-Greek.[44] Nevertheless, it would be typical of Callimachus to drive a poetic wedge between aetiological explanation and ritual practice itself, or at least to make it clear that they do not necessarily stand or fall together. Callimachus indeed seems constantly to nudge us towards 'myth and ritual' questions which seem surprisingly modern; does the nature of the explanation adopted (and we may well have to make a choice between aetiologies) actually have any effect in the world of the ritual? Do we live in a world where things happen by divine design, or is 'design' one of the patterns we impose upon events in order to persuade ourselves that they make sense? How 'self-serving' is the reasoning of Mopsus and/or the Pamphylians once confronted with the apparent requirement of making what was usually an abhorrent offering? Is this indeed how we use the gods to justify ourselves across a much broader field of activity? Moreover, how does the ascription of such (very human) reasoning to the distant mists of aetiological time not just make us smile with self-recognition, but also bind

---

42 Kerkhecker 1999, 213.
43 Kerkhecker 1999, 212.
44 Cf. esp. Robert 1960, 177–178 for the evidence from Aspendian coinage as early as the fifth century, Lane Fox 2008, 232.

us in the same web of time as this Pamphylian of long ago, in other words build a social consensus based on shared identity?

In the state of our evidence it is of course impossible to say how the transition within Callimachus' poem from one cult to the other was made; we have already seen several motifs which they have in common. Further connections can be imagined. Mopsus' pig-sacrifice was the result of a vow while hunting, Agamemnon's problems at Aulis seem to have been the result of an intemperate boast while hunting. More rewarding might be to pause for a moment on the combination of a cult of Aphrodite in inland Pamphylia with a Boeotian cult of Artemis, a goddess traditionally opposed to Aphrodite; the former cult seems outlandish and 'marginal' (at best), the latter takes us into the heart of traditional Greece and the heart of perhaps the best known 'sacrifice story' of all Greek mythology: it is probably not fanciful to see a manifold contrast between the 'old world' and the 'new', a contrast which however is also a confirmation of continuity. Shared Greek identity stretches from Boeotia to Pamphylia (and presumably beyond); even the gods of epic and tragedy who are most opposed to each other (Aphrodite and Artemis) share fundamentally similar, and very Greek, values (φρονεῖν and φρόνησις).

What, if anything, did these cults mean to an Alexandrian audience? Pamphylia was a place of considerable interest to the Ptolemies,[45] and Aspendos was believed to be a foundation of Argos, a city central to much Ptolemaic self-fashioning; an Argive decree of probably the late fourth century offers privileges to Aspendos, which not long before had been harshly dealt with by Alexander.[46] For what it is worth, we know that there was an 'Iseon' at Eretria visited by Egyptians (or Egyptian Greeks) at least from the beginning of the third century.[47] This is, of course, not to suggest anything as definable as a 'Ptolemaic context' for *Iambus* 10, but it is worth stressing that we must not assume that what we are dealing with is simply learned and antiquarian *Spielerei* with no purchase in the actual experience or imagination of the audience. We do not know why Callimachus chose to tell and link these two aetiologies for an Alexandrian audience at a specific date in the third century, and it would be rash to assume that his audience would have given a univocal answer to the question of how and why (or indeed whether) they were linked with each other. Enough perhaps that we can make a good guess at the questions to be asked, and assure ourselves that they are worth asking.

---

45 Cf. Hunter 2003, 165 with earlier bibliography.
46 Cf. Stroud 1984, Lane Fox 2008, 237–238.
47 Cf. Bruneau 1975.

Bibliography

Asper, M. 2001. 'Gruppen und Dichter: Zu Programmatik und Adressatenbezug bei Kallimachos', *A&A* 47, 84–116.
Asper, M. 2004. *Kallimachos. Werke*, Darmstadt.
Bagnall, R. 1976. *The Administration of the Ptolemaic Possessions outside Egypt*, Leiden.
Bornmann, E. 1968. *Callimachi Hymnus in Dianam*, Firenze.
Bruneau, P. 1975. *Le sanctuaire et le culte des divinités égyptiennes à Erétrie*, Leiden.
Cameron, A. 1995. *Callimachus and his Critics*, Princeton.
Chaniotis, A. 1996. *Die Verträge zwischen kretischen Poleis in der hellenistischen Zeit*, Stuttgart.
Chaniotis, A. 2001. 'Ein alexandrinischer Dichter und Kreta. Mythische Vergangenheit und gegenwärtige Kultpraxis bei Kallimachos', in: S. Böhm/K.-V. von Eickstedt (eds.), *IΘAKH. Festschrift für Jörg Schäfer zum 75. Geburtstag am 25. April 2001*, Würzburg, 213–217.
Ehrhardt, N. 2003. 'Poliskulte bei Theokrit und Kallimachos: das Beispiel Milet', *Hermes* 131, 269–289.
Fantuzzi, M./Hunter, R. 2004. *Tradition and Innovation in Hellenistic Poetry*, Cambridge/New York.
Feeney, D. 1998. *Literature and Religion at Rome*, Cambridge.
Flinterman, J.-J. 2009. 'Apollonius' Ascension', in: K. Demoen/D. Praet (eds.), *Theios Sophistes. Essays on Flavius Philostratus' Vita Apollonii*, Leiden/Boston, 225–248.
Guarducci, M. 1935. 'Diktynna', *SMSR* 11, 187–203.
Guarducci, M. 1939. *Inscriptiones Creticae*, II, Roma.
Hunter, R. 1995. 'The Divine and Human Map of the *Argonautica*', *Syllecta Classica* 6, 13–27 [= Hunter 2008, 257–277].
Hunter, R. 2003. *Theocritus. Encomium of Ptolemy Philadelphus*, Berkeley.
Hunter, R. 2008. *On Coming After. Studies in Post-Classical Greek Literature and its Reception*, Berlin/New York.
Hunter, R. 2011. 'The Gods of Callimachus', in: B. Acosta-Hughes/S. Stephens (eds.), *Brill's Companion to Callimachus*, Leiden [= this volume 156-174].
Hunter, R./Rutherford, I. (eds.) 2009, *Wandering Poets in Ancient Greek Culture*, Cambridge.
Kerkhecker, A. 1999. *Callimachus' Book of Iambi*, Oxford.
Kreuter, S. 1992. *Aussenbeziehungen kretischer Gemeinden zu den hellenistischen Staaten im 3. Und 2. Jh. v. Chr.*, München.
Lane Fox, R. 2008. *Travelling Heroes: Greeks and their Myths in the epic age of Homer*, London.
Lelli, E. 2005. *Callimachi Iambi XIV–XVII*, Roma.
Lyne, R.O.A.M. 1978. *Ciris. A Poem attributed to Vergil*, Cambridge.
Maass, E. 1923. 'Diktynna', *Hermes* 58, 175–186.
Parke, H.W. 1986. 'The Temple of Apollo at Didyma: the Building and its Function', *JHS* 106, 121–131.
Robert, L. 1960. 'Monnaies et divinités d'Aspendos', *Hellenica* 11–12, 177–188.
Schmitt, H. 1969. *Die Staatsverträge des Altertums*, III, München.
Sistakou, E. 2005. *Η γεωγραφία του Καλλιμάχου και η νεωτερική ποίηση των ελληνιστικών χρόνων*, Athens.

Sporn, K. 2001. 'Auf den Spuren der kretischen Diktynna', in: S. Böhm/K.-V. von Eickstedt (eds.), *ΙΘΑΚΗ. Festschrift für Jörg Schäfer zum 75. Geburtstag am 25. April 2001*, Würzburg, 225–233.

Sporn, K. 2002. *Heiligtümer und Kulte Kretas in klassischer und hellenistischer Zeit*, Heidelberg.

Spyridakis, S. 1970. *Ptolemaic Itanos and Hellenistic Crete*, Berkeley.

Stroud, R.S. 1984. 'An Argive Decree from Nemea Concerning Aspendos', *Hesperia* 53, 193–216.

Tzifopoulos, Y. 2010. *'Paradise' Earned. The Bacchic-Orphic Gold Lamellae of Crete*, Washington DC.

Willetts, R.F. 1962. *Cretan Cults and Festivals*, London.

Zanker, G. 2006. 'Poetry and Art in Herodas, *Mimiamb* 4', in: M.A. Harder/R.F. Regtuit/G.C. Wakker (eds.), *Beyond the Canon*, Leuven, 357–377.

10 Theocritus and the Style of Hellenistic Poetry

Of the major poets of the third century it is perhaps Theocritus who most invites us to reflect upon what we think we know about Hellenistic poetry and upon the usefulness, or otherwise, of the label itself. Theocritus was not — as far as we know — a scholar-poet, that figure identified by Rudolf Pfeiffer 1955, 69 as 'the feature of the Hellenistic age';[1] there is, moreover, no reason to associate many of his poems with any particular situation of patronage, however clearly the Ptolemaic world looms in the background of several of them. On the other hand, it is his poetry which has given particular impetus to some of the ideas about Hellenistic poetry which have been most influential in modern scholarship — the appeal to the ordinary and the everyday, 'Kreuzung der Gattungen', the dominance of the miniature over the grand structures of epic, the interest in poetic and reconstructive dialect, and so forth. In this essay I want to use one poem in particular, *Idyll* 16, to explore some of the phenomena that we think of as most characteristic of the poetry of the third century.

I choose to revisit *Idyll* 16, the Charites, for a number of reasons. First, because there is every reason to suppose that it has nothing to do with Alexandria, and is therefore not an example of 'Alexandrian poetry', as that phrase is most commonly used. Secondly, of course, because it is one of the most intriguing and puzzling of the poems which survive to us from the earlier part of the century. It has recently been argued (Willi 2004) that we can see here poetry in transition: Theocritus has written in a new form but preserved poetry's traditional social function of protreptic advice; it was to be left to Callimachus to change both form and function, the latter in the direction of a purely aesthetic function, 'art for art's sake'.[2] It matters less for present purposes that I cannot share this view of Callimachus' poetry, than that *Idyll* 16 continues to attract attention as marking a new stage in the Greek poetic tradition. From another perspective, *Idyll* 16 has recently been the subject of interesting work which seeks to link it very closely to a historical context — something which, I think, scholars of Hel-

---

An earlier version of this essay formed part of the opening lecture to the 2012 Thessaloniki conference; I have not sought to remove all marks of its origin in an oral presentation for a specific occasion.

---

1 Much might be thought to hang on whether the writing of prose treatises, as well as poetry, was thought to be a necessary criterion for classification as a 'scholar-poet'.
2 For this as a view of *Idyll* 16, however, cf., e.g., Fabiano 1971, 519 n. 7. Sistakou 2008a, 42–44 offers a clear account of the poetics of *Idyll* 16.

lenistic poetry still try to do less often than they should, perhaps because they know in their hearts that, where the burden of proof is so heavy, such arguments have traditionally failed to carry conviction. Thus, José González (González 2010) has seen a traditional social function in *Idyll* 16 — Theocritus revives the poetic voice of Theognis, a poet associated in some traditions with Sicily, to lecture and cajole his Syracusan fellow-citizens about the terrible state into which their city has fallen. For Malcolm Bell, on the other hand (Bell 2011), Theocritus joins his bucolic voice to the hopes of the young Hieron to rescue Syracuse from the agrarian crisis which besets it; we have nothing less than 'a political and economic program for the new leader'.[3] Much here would demand discussion on another occasion, but for the present I will focus on some very traditional critical criteria, to see if we can pick out features that we might wish to label 'Hellenistic', and whether that label helps or hinders understanding.

First, structure. It is clear, and generally recognized,[4] that the poem falls into two halves, with something of a fresh start at v. 58:

ἐκ Μοισᾶν ἀγαθὸν κλέος ἔρχεται ἀνθρώποισι,
χρήματα δὲ ζώοντες ἀμαλδύνουσι θανόντων.

Theocritus 16.58–59

From the Muses comes excellent renown to men, but the living waste away the possessions of the dead.

ἐκ Μοισᾶν with which this second part of the poem begins — starting 'from the Muses' is a good move for any poet in any section of his song — takes us back to the opening quatrain:

αἰεὶ τοῦτο Διὸς κούραις μέλει, αἰὲν ἀοιδοῖς,
ὑμνεῖν ἀθανάτους, ὑμνεῖν ἀγαθῶν κλέα ἀνδρῶν.
Μοῖσαι μὲν θεαὶ ἐντί, θεοὺς θεαὶ ἀείδοντι·
ἄμμες δὲ βροτοὶ οἵδε, βροτοὺς βροτοὶ ἀείδωμεν.

Theocritus 16.1–4

It is always the task of the daughters of Zeus, always of singers, to hymn the immortals, to hymn the glorious deeds of excellent men. The Muses are goddesses, goddesses sing of gods; we here are mortals, let us mortals sing of mortals.

---

3 Bell also draws suggestive connections between Theocritus' bucolic poems and the 'pastoral' art of third-century Sicily.
4 An exception here is Meincke 1965, 34–35 who appears to place the major break in the poem after v. 70; this cannot, I think, be correct. On the sequence of thought in vv. 68ff cf. below 211–212.

Both halves of the poem thus begin with the Muses, just as ἀγαθὸν κλέος in v. 58 picks up ἀγαθῶν κλέα ἀνδρῶν in v. 2. This second part of the poem itself is bounded in ring composition:

> τί γὰρ Χαρίτων ἀγαπητόν
> ἀνθρώποις ἀπάνευθεν; ἀεὶ Χαρίτεσσιν ἅμ' εἴην.
>
> Theocritus 16.108–109
>
> What is desirable for men apart from the Graces? May I always be together with the Graces.

ἐκ Μοισᾶν... ἀνθρώποισι (v. 58) is picked up by ἀνθρώποις... Χαρίτεσσιν (v. 109), with variation between the two sets of goddesses with whom the poem has been concerned. There is of course no 'clean break' between the two sections of the poem: the transitional verse, 'From the Muses comes excellent renown to men' (v. 58), also summarises the immediately preceding section on the 'benefits' conferred by Simonides and Homer on the characters (real and fictional) about whom they wrote; moreover, the 'formal' break after v. 57 is by no means the only important structural moment within the poem. Nevertheless, it is not always appreciated just how neat is the formal division between the two 'halves' of the poem. If we include the opening quatrain in the first part, then the division is into 57 and 52 verses, or if we separate off the opening quatrain, as there seems every reason to do — among which will be both the very distinctive style of vv. 1–4 and the fact that we then have one part beginning with the Charites and the second with the Muses — we have 53 and 52 verses respectively, all but a complete equality. Are these figures simply the kind of accident which happens? Perhaps, but along with the 'materiality' of poetry — poems figured as unloved papyrus rolls etc. — which is so central to *Idyll* 16, we ought perhaps also consider whether the stichometric habit has here encouraged an attention to neat divisions, as part of an *epideixis* of what poetry is or can be, and this is one manifestation of a set of such phenomena which become important in the Hellenistic period; we think, for example, of pattern poems ('*technopaignia*'), acrostics, the organization of poetry books and so forth.[5] We will want to associate these phenomena with the writing habit, though their roots in archaic and classical verse require careful attention;[6] it would, above all, be very nice to know just how such formally marked structures were 'felt'. Be that as it may, if this structural analysis is on the right lines, then the neat division of *Idyll* 16 is a

---

[5] Bing 1988 remains a valuable guide in these areas; on pattern-poems, acrostics etc. cf. Luz 2010.
[6] Relevant here is Faraone 2008.

special case within a general tendency of Theocritean poetry. *Idyll* 17 falls into verse paragraphs of roughly (though certainly not exactly) equal lengths;[7] a case has recently been made for a very neat triptych structure of 72–28–72 for *Idyll* 24;[8] the main body of *Idyll* 18 falls into ten-verse paragraphs, and similar structures may be found in the *Hymns* of Callimachus[9].

What is true of the second part of the poem is also true of the poem as a whole. ἀνθρώποις in the final verse does not just take us back to v. 58, but also picks up the repeated βροτοί of v. 4. More is going on here than just the formal device of ring-composition. As is well known, the closing prayer to the Graces of Orchomenos in vv. 104–109 reworks the opening of Pindar's *Olympian* 14 for a victor from Orchomenos:

Καφισίων ὑδάτων
λαχοῖσαι αἴτε ναίετε καλλίπωλον ἕδραν,
ὦ λιπαρᾶς ἀοίδιμοι βασίλειαι
Χάριτες Ἐρχομενοῦ, παλαιγόνων Μινυᾶν ἐπίσκοποι,
κλῦτ', ἐπεὶ εὔχομαι· σὺν γὰρ ὑμῖν τά <τε> τερπνὰ καί
τὰ γλυκέ' ἄνεται πάντα βροτοῖς,
εἰ σοφός, εἰ καλός, εἴ τις ἀγλαὸς ἀνήρ.
οὐδὲ γὰρ θεοὶ σεμνᾶν Χαρίτων ἄτερ
κοιρανέοντι χοροὺς
οὔτε δαῖτας·

Pindar, *Olympian* 14.1–9

Controllers of the waters of Kephisos, dwellers in a place of fine horses, O Graces, queens, celebrated in song, of shining Orchomenos, guardians of the ancient Minyans, hear when I pray. With you come all things pleasant and sweet for mortals, whether a man be wise, or handsome, or of glittering fame. Not even the gods organize dances or feasts without the holy Graces.

Theocritus' opening distinction between gods and men is in fact, as we now see, repeated at the end of the poem, but implicitly, through evocation of that same distinction within a model text. This is sophisticated, allusive poetry which makes demands upon us: ἀνθρώποις in v. 109 is anything but a mere line-filler.

---

[7] One division would be 1–12 (proem), 12–33 (Soter, 21 verses), 34–57 (Berenice, 24), 58–76 (Cos), 77–94 (Ptolemy's power, 18), 95–120 (wealth, 26), 121–134 (piety, 14), 135–137 (envoi, 3); various subdivisions within this structure are readily identifiable.
[8] Cf. Bernsdorff 2011. A perhaps more obvious division is into 1–63 (Heracles and the snakes), 64–102 (Teiresias), 103 to the end (Heracles subsequent education and career), i.e. 63-39-70 verses, or (more likely?) 1–63, 64–102, 103–(??)166 (Heracles' education and early career), 167–172 (hymnic envoi and prayer for victory).
[9] Cf. Hunter 1996b, 155–156.

As for the initial quatrain itself, this falls — as do the three quatrains of the proem to *Idyll* 17[10] — into paired couplets; the couplets in this instance are held together by rhythmical identity and difference from each other (vv. 3-4 are *spondeiazontes* and share an identical pattern of syllables per word throughout the verse), and by the mannered verbal repetitions and parallelisms which they display.[11] In running through the three classes of gods, (epic) heroes (ἀγαθοὶ ἄνδρες), and ordinary mortals (βροτοί), as also does the proem of *Idyll* 17 (though to somewhat different effect), the proem to *Idyll* 16 repeats with variation the same priamel-like function as the opening of Pindar's *Second Olympian*, and the following τίς question in v. 5 perhaps makes it not impossible that Theocritus was here actually reworking that grand opening for a Sicilian patron:[12]

ἀναξιφόρμιγγες ὕμνοι,
τίνα θεόν, τίν' ἥρωα, τίνα δ' ἄνδρα κελαδήσομεν;

Pindar, *Olympian* 2.1-2

Hymns, masters of the lyre, which god, which hero, which man shall we celebrate?

Theocritus' choice of βροτοί for emphasis in v. 4 will have been influenced by, and evoke, the Homeric tendency to use this form to refer purely generally to (ordinary) 'mortals' of any time; 'mortals' also introduces the central theme of the poem — the power of the poet to offer immortal κλέος, such as that already achieved by the ἀγαθοὶ ἄνδρες. Hanging over the opening fifteen verses of the poem are Homer's deprecatory οἷοι νῦν βροτοί εἰσι (*Iliad* 5.304, 12.383, 449, 20.287) and οἳ νῦν βροτοί εἰσιν ἐπιχθόνιοι (*Iliad* 1.272), a memory with particular bite in v. 15, τίς τῶν νῦν τοιόσδε;, which picks up the question of vv. 5-7 after the parenthesis of vv. 8-12.[13] Theocritus' complaints about 'men of the present day' turn out to have Homeric precedent: both look back to a lost time of heroic

---

10 Cf. Hunter 2003, 93-94.
11 These parallelisms would be increased were we to emend ἀείδοντι in v. 3 to the subjunctive ἀείδωντι. I am not aware that this has ever been suggested; Austin 1967, 3 paraphrases the verse as 'Let gods hymn gods ...', but does not suggest the emendation. In favour of the transmitted text, it may be argued that the poet is describing what the Muses *do* (habitually), as in the opening of Hesiod's *Theogony*, whereas the subjunctive is appropriate for the human poet at the start of a new song.
12 For other aspects of the opening quatrain cf., e.g., Gutzwiller 1983, 217-219, Fantuzzi 2000, 142-145.
13 The first half of v. 15 is more usually associated with Simonides fr. 10 Poltera (= *PMG* 506), cf. Gutzwiller 1983, 222-223, Vox 2002, 199-200 (adducing the contextual appropriateness of the Simonidean poem); I see no difficulty in the Theocritean question evoking both Homer and Simonides.

deeds (ὡς πάρος, v. 14), but — unlike his epic model — Theocritus will be able to express the hope that such days may yet return.

There is, of course, particular point in creating a neat stichometric division within *Idyll* 16, as one of the differences between the two parts is that whereas the first one illustrates the power of poetry from the great figures of the past (Simonides, Homer), the second focuses on the present and future and on what Theocritus himself could do for a worthy patron; present and future possibilities are indeed to be equal to those of the past. Both halves also move from the allegedly current distorted relations between poet and patron (vv. 5–21, 60–65) to an imagined ideal. Theocritus offers Hieron the same or even more in fact than the patrons of the past. A particular effect here is the replay of vv. 36–39 in the poet's wishes for peace in Sicily in the second half of the poem:

πολλοὶ δὲ Σκοπάδαισιν ἐλαυνόμενοι ποτὶ σακοὺς
μόσχοι σὺν κεραῆισιν ἐμυκήσαντο βόεσσι·
μυρία δ' ἂμ πεδίον Κραννώνιον ἐνδιάασκον
ποιμένες ἔκκριτα μῆλα φιλοξείνοισι Κρεωνδαις·

Theocritus 16.36–39

Many were the calves which lowed as they were driven to the stalls of the Scopadae, together with the horned cattle; countless the splendid sheep which shepherds pastured for the hospitable Creondae over the plain of Crannon.

    αἱ δ' ἀνάριθμοι
μήλων χιλιάδες βοτάναι διαπιανθεῖσαι
ἂμ πεδίον βληχῶιντο, βόες δ' ἀγεληδὸν ἐς αὖλιν
ἐρχόμεναι σκνιφαῖον ἐπισπεύδοιεν ὁδίταν·
νειοὶ δ' ἐκπονέοιντο ποτὶ σπόρον, ἁνίκα τέττιξ
ποιμένας ἐνδίους πεφυλαγμένος ὑψόθι δένδρων   95
ἀχεῖ ἐν ἀκρεμόνεσσιν· ἀράχνια δ' εἰς ὅπλ' ἀράχναι
λεπτὰ διαστήσαιντο, βοᾶς δ' ἔτι μηδ' ὄνομ' εἴη.

Theocritus 16.90–97

May numberless thousands of sheep, fattened by pasturing, bleat over the plain, and cattle moving in herds towards their home stalls speed the evening traveller on his way. May the fallow fields be worked for sowing, while high up in the trees the cicada watches the shepherds in the sun, and trills in the branches. May spiders weave delicate webs over weapons, and not even the name of the war-cry remain.

Some of the correspondences may be simply set out in schematic form: πολλοί ... μυρία ~ ἀνάριθμοι ... χιλιάδες, ἐλαυνόμενοι ποτὶ σακούς ~ ἀγεληδὸν ἐς αὖλιν | ἐρχόμεναι, ἂμ πεδίον ~ ἂμ πεδίον, ἐμυκήσαντο (cattle) ~ βληχῶιντο (sheep), ἐνδιάασκον | ποιμένες ~ ποιμένας ἐνδίους;[14] σκνιφαῖον in v. 93 spells out what is implied in the action of vv. 36–37. The replay, and indeed *auxêsis*, of the first passage in the second is reinforced by a reworking of part of Bacchylides' famous encomium of peace from a paean to Apollo Pythaieus at Asine:

ἐν δὲ σιδαροδέτοις πόρπαξιν αἰθᾶν
ἀραχνᾶν ἱστοὶ πέλονται,

ἔγχεα τε λογχωτὰ ξίφεα
τ' ἀμφάκεα δάμναται εὐρώς.
<–⏑ – – ⏑ – – ⏑ –
– ⏑⏑ – ⏑⏑ – –>
χαλκεᾶν δ' οὐκ ἔστι σαλπίγγων κτύπος κτλ.

Bacchylides fr. 4, vv. 69 –75 Maehler

Over the iron shield-grips lie the webs of reddish spiders, and rust eats away at the sharp spears and double-edged swords... no sound is heard from the bronze trumpets...

Bacchylides was another encomiast of the first Hieron, but — more significantly in the present context — he was Simonides' nephew, and in setting himself to write 'Simonidean' verse as a 'Bacchylides' for Hieron II, Theocritus here tropes literary affiliation and imitation in genealogical terms; the trope was to become much more familiar in Roman poetry.[15]

After structure, style. A case can be made, I think, that, for all our proper interest in Callimachean programmatics, the slender Muse and the tiny drop of pure water, and the very welcome recent concern with possible links between Hellenistic poetry and the kind of euphonist criticism about which we are constantly learning more from the papyri of Philodemus,[16] there still remains much to be done in determining how the styles of Hellenistic poetry differed from what went before.[17] The history of style is, of course, very difficult to trace, not

---

14 This last case calls particular attention to itself as (cf. Gow *ad loc.*) v. 38 seems to offer the only example of ἐνδιάω used transitively. In vv. 94–96 a reminiscence of Plato, *Phaedrus* 259a, with its repeated reference to the middle of the day, is possible; ἐνδιάω and related words are standardly associated in ancient lexica with midday, cf. the scholia on vv. 94–97b, Gow on v. 38, and the scholia on *Odyssey* 4.450. There may be a memory of one or both of these passages at [Theocritus] 25.85–99.
15 Cf., e.g., Hardie 1993, ch. 4.
16 Helpful orientation in Gutzwiller 2010, 346–354.
17 Any full account would, of course, have to give due acknowledgement to the important work which has been done, such as that of Marco Fantuzzi on the style of Apollonius' *Argonautica*.

least because 'style' is hardly separable from form and meaning, but there is no area of Greek, and specifically Hellenistic, poetics which remains as underexamined and as important. The remarks which follow will, of course, hardly make a dent in the surface.

That *Idyll* 16 contains almost a potpourri of stylistic levels is familiar critical territory,[18] and it might be thought that a poem probably (though not certainly) entitled Χάριτες by its author would have style as a central concern, for χάρις and χάριτες are important terms in the ancient stylistic vocabulary. It is noteworthy that the discussion of χάριτες in Demetrius, *On style* gives a prominent place to both Sophron, the Syracusan mime-poet, and to the use of proverbs (156), and this will remind us that the marvellously inventive description of the poet's Χάριτες in vv. 5–21 is itself full of χάρις. Stylistic levels are, however, a crucial vehicle of poetic meaning throughout the poem. Consider Theocritus' demonstration of the power of Homeric poetry:

οὐδ' Ὀδυσεὺς ἑκατόν τε καὶ εἴκοσι μῆνας ἀλαθείς
πάντας ἐπ' ἀνθρώπους, Ἀίδαν τ' εἰς ἔσχατον ἐλθών
ζωός, καὶ σπήλυγγα φυγὼν ὀλοοῖο Κύκλωπος,
δηναιὸν κλέος ἔσχεν, ἐσιγάθη δ' ἂν ὑφορβός
Εὔμαιος καὶ βουσὶ Φιλοίτιος ἀμφ' ἀγελαίαις   55
ἔργον ἔχων αὐτός τε περίσπλαγχνος Λαέρτης,
εἰ μή σφεας ὤνασαν Ἰάονος ἀνδρὸς ἀοιδαί.

Theocritus 16.51–57

Not even Odysseus, who wandered through all men for one hundred and twenty months and went alive to furthest Hades and escaped from the cave of the murderous Cyclops, would have secured long-lasting renown, and the swineherd Eumaeus and Philoitios whose task was the herds of cattle and great-hearted Laertes himself would have been covered in silence, had not they benefited from the songs of a man of Ionia.

Odysseus 'wandered through all men for one hundred and twenty months'; here we have, I think, a rewriting, or perhaps explanatory gloss, on the opening of the *Odyssey* (ὃς μάλα πολλὰ | πλάγχθη... πολλῶν δ' ἀνθρώπων κτλ.). It is perhaps not accidental that the opening of the *Odyssey* may also be evoked in Pindar's *Seventh Nemean*, a poem which is very important to *Idyll* 16:[19]

σοφοὶ δὲ μέλλοντα τριταῖον ἄνεμον
ἔμαθον, οὐδ' ὑπὸ κέρδει βλάβεν·

---

[18] Cf., e.g., Fabiano 1971, 519–520.
[19] V. 63 φιλοκερδείηι βεβλαμμένον ἄνδρα seems to pick up οὐδ' ὑπὸ κέρδει βλάβεν in *Nemean* 7.18; on various aspects of the use of *Nemean* 7 in *Idyll* 16 cf. Sbardella 2004.

ἀφνεὸς πενιχρός τε θανάτου παρά
σᾶμα νέονται. ἐγὼ δὲ πλέον' ἔλπομαι   20
λόγον Ὀδυσσέος ἢ πάθαν
  διὰ τὸν ἁδυεπῆ γενέσθ' Ὅμηρον·

ἐπεὶ ψεύδεσί οἱ ποτανᾶι <τε> μαχανᾶι
σεμνὸν ἔπεστί τι· σοφία
  δὲ κλέπτει παράγοισα μύθοις. τυφλὸν δ' ἔχει
ἦτορ ὅμιλος ἀνδρῶν ὁ πλεῖστος.

Pindar, Nemean 7.17–24

> The wise understand the wind which will come on the third day, and they are not damaged by pursuit of profit, for rich and poor alike go to the tomb of death. I think that Odysseus' story has become greater than his suffering, as a result of sweet-voiced Homer; upon his lies and winged art there is something magnificent, and his skill deceives and leads men astray with stories. The vast majority of men have a blind heart.

Although the power of poetry is a ubiquitous theme in Pindar, the scholia (III 120–121 Drachmann) on this famous passage give a clear idea as to why it is particularly important for *Idyll* 16:

> Intelligent men should not be deluded by their present wealth, but should take thought for what comes after and do something worthy, so that, afterwards also, they may be hymned and have immortal renown (εὐδοξία). Both the rich and the poor die, and therefore it is necessary to give thought to one's future renown... Men must not be mean (φιλοκερδεῖς), but offer pay (μισθός) to poets, so that they may have an eternal memorial of their virtue.

Scholium, Pindar, Nemean 7.17

> Poets are able to magnify and increase ordinary deeds; therefore you too should give thought to being hymned.

Scholium, Pindar, Nemean 7.20

This gloss on Pindar's argument could well stand also as a gloss on much of *Idyll* 16. Should we therefore leap to the conclusion, as we tend to do in such situations, that Theocritus' reworking of Pindar (or indeed of any archaic poet) is influenced by contemporary or near-contemporary scholarship (of various intellectual levels)? What are the rules for determining when this approach is correct and when it is misleading? All reading and creative imitation is after all, to a greater or less extent, and with greater or lesser degrees of self-consciousness, a product of the educational and cultural context of the later reader and/or writer. In this case, some may think it significant for Theocritus' difference from, say, Callimachus that we are here not dealing with the intrusion of rare (scholarly) glosses in the Theocritean text, but rather with broad structures of meaning in an earlier text.

This Pindaric passage has been the subject of much debate and bibliography in modern times, and this is not the place to add to that[20]. There is, however, no good reason to doubt that Theocritus would have understood Pindar to be saying that the power of Homer's poetry, its σεμνότης, had given the story of Odysseus a greater circulation and renown than would be commensurate with what he actually 'suffered'; πλέον'... λόγον Ὀδυσσέος ἢ πάθαν in v. 21 alludes to and trumps πολλά... πάθεν ἄλγεα in *Odyssey* 1.4.[21] Theocritus then chooses the two most extended, but also most 'fabulous', episodes of that λόγος, the Underworld and the Cyclops' cave, to make the related point that no one would ever have heard even of Odysseus, had it not been for Homer; whether or not the memory of *Nemean* 7 also encourages us to entertain a doubt about the reality of those adventures — look what a poet can do for you! — may be debated. What is clear, however, is that the style of Theocritus' rewriting of the opening of the *Odyssey*, 'Odysseus wandered through all men for one hundred and twenty months', also contributes to the point that Theocritus is making. One ancient explanation of Pindar's description of Homer's (and Odysseus') ποτανὰ μαχανά (*Nemean* 7.22) is that the Homeric poems 'exalt and raise up (ὑψοῖ καὶ μετεωρίζει) the virtuous deeds of those who are hymned' (III 121.9–10 Drachmann). The language of ὕψος is suggestive here, because the *akribeia* of 'wandered for one hundred and twenty months' is very far from any ancient notions of stylistic grandeur or sublimity; Theocritus' phrase is, in fact, as prosaic a gloss on the opening of the *Odyssey* as one could imagine, and that perhaps is the point. The σεμνότης of Homeric verse can turn the bald facts and numbers of 'what happened' into something memorable. Theocritus here takes Odysseus' own echo of the opening of the poem,

ἀλλ' ὅδ' ἐγὼ τοιόσδε, παθὼν κακά, πολλὰ δ' ἀληθείς,
ἤλυθον εἰκοστῶι ἔτεϊ ἐς πατρίδα γαῖαν

Homer, *Odyssey* 16.205–206

I am that man as you see him, having suffered misfortunes and wandered much, and I have returned to my fatherland in the twentieth year,

---

20 Fränkel 1960b, 360–361 is an important contribution, cf. Most 1985, 149.
21 Although associating πάθα with *Odyssey* 1.4, Fränkel (previous note) thought the most important passage for Pindar here was *Odyssey* 11.363–376 (Alcinous' intervention).

and surpasses it. Mortals count up and reckon, because our time is painfully finite and ever-diminishing; Muses operate across much larger and much more impressionistic vistas of time and space. The tedious detail of τὸ ἀκριβές matters to us in ways in which it cannot matter to higher powers. So too, Philoitios' 'job' (the very prosaic ἔργον ἔχων) was looking after the cattle (vvv. 55–56); Homer could make something wonderful even of so banal a phrase and of such unpromising material. Whether we can move from these examples to speculations about the critical discussions of Homeric, and more generally poetic, style which were available to Theocritus is (again) a matter for further discussion.

As for περίσπλαγχνος Λαέρτης, commentators rightly look to *Odyssey* 24.365 where the poet calls Laertes μεγαλήτωρ; the *hapax* περίσπλαγχνος, a formation of a relatively common type found, e.g., in medical texts as well as in poetry, is here used, as with the previous examples, to illustrate what a poet can do for you. It is, however, not just the epithet μεγαλήτωρ which is at issue here.[22] In Homer the epithet introduces the passage in which Laertes is bathed and given a splendid cloak, and Athena – acting, so Theocritus might observe, like Homer or another encomiastic poet – restores his physical beauty so that he looks like the immortal gods and becomes an object of θαῦμα to those around him (*Odyssey* 24.365–374); Laertes then proceeds to recall a glorious deed of his youth. The transformation of Odysseus' father from the pitiful sight he presented when Odysseus first saw him at 24.226–231 (and cf. 11.187–196) becomes a paradigm case of what a poet, and poetic style, can do for you. The power of style at which Theocritus hints finds a later resonance in Dionysius of Halicarnassus' famous comparison (*De compositione verborum* 4.12) of the power of verbal arrangement (σύνθεσις) to Homer's Athena who could give Odysseus different appearances, from the lowly to the magnificent, at different times; word arrangement too, claims Dionysius, can make ideas (νοήματα) expressed in the selfsame words either 'ugly and low and beggarly' or 'lofty (ὑψηλά) and rich and beautiful'. Though Dionysius is extolling verbal arrangement rather than style and lexical choice, it is (again) at least worth wondering whether there is any shared background for poet and critic here, or whether (as so often) we have a foreshadowing of a critical notion within poetry itself.[23]

---

[22] Gow on v. 55 tentatively suggested that Theocritus in this passage was thinking of the scene in which 'Odysseus and Telemachus, attended by Eumaeus and Philoetius, go to visit Laertes'; this is surely correct.

[23] Behind Dionysius here lies, of course, a rich tradition, cf. Isocrates, *Panegyricus* 8 (criticized at 'Longinus', *On the sublime* 38.2–3). For a not dissimilar phenomenon cf. Strabo 1.2.9 where Homer's alleged practice of adding myth to 'historical fact' is illustrated by three Homeric descriptions of beautification or the creation of brilliant artefacts.

An earlier passage of *Idyll* 16 operates through a related stylistic effect. Like Pindar in *Nemean* 7 (cf. above), Theocritus uses the universality of death as a reason to employ poets:

Μοισάων δὲ μάλιστα τίειν ἱεροὺς ὑποφήτας,
ὄφρα καὶ εἰν Ἀίδαο κεκρυμμένος ἐσθλὸς ἀκούσῃς,   30
μηδ' ἀκλεὴς μύρηαι ἐπὶ ψυχροῦ Ἀχέροντος,
ὡσεί τις μακέλαι τετυλωμένος ἔνδοθι χεῖρας
ἀχὴν ἐκ πατέρων πενίην ἀκτήμονα κλαίων.

Theocritus 16.29–33

[The best use of wealth is] most of all to honour the holy prophets of the Muses, so that even when you are hidden in Hades your reputation will be an excellent one, and you will not mourn, fameless, beside chilly Acheron, like a poor man from a poor family, the palms of his hands hardened by use of the mattock, who bewails his empty poverty.

Some recent criticism, picking up a hint from Gow, has wanted to see Sappho 55 Voigt behind Theocritus' reference to the unknown peasant languishing in Hades:[24]

κατθάνοισα δὲ κείσῃ οὐδέ ποτα μναμοσύνα σέθεν
ἔσσετ' οὐδὲ +ποκ'+ ὕστερον· οὐ γὰρ πεδέχῃς βρόδων
τῶν ἐκ Πιερίας· ἀλλ' ἀφάνης κἀν Ἀίδα δόμωι
φοιτάσῃς πεδ' ἀμαύρων νεκύων ἐκπεποταμένα.

Sappho fr. 55 Voigt

When you are dead, you will lie there, and in future time there will be no memory of you, for you have no share in the roses of Pieria. Unnoticed in the house of Hades when you have flitted away, you will go here and there amidst the insubstantial dead.

The theme is, however, a common one, and, however close in thrust the two passages may be, there seems no particular reason to think of Sappho here. Given what immediately follows in *Idyll* 16, we might rather think of Simonides' θρῆνοι,[25] and that at least would be in keeping with the principal intertexts of the poem. Horstmann, however, tentatively suggested that behind this passage lay Achilles' famous exchange with Odysseus in the Underworld:[26]

---

24 Cf., e.g., Griffiths 1979, 29 n. 55, Sbardella 1997, 137–139.
25 Acosta-Hughes 2010a, 183 associates vv. 40–43 with the θρῆνοι.
26 Horstmann 1976, 126 n. 55.

'σεῖο δ', Ἀχιλλεῦ,
οὔ τις ἀνὴρ προπάροιθε μακάρτερος οὔτ' ἄρ' ὀπίσσω·
πρὶν μὲν γάρ σε ζωὸν ἐτίομεν ἶσα θεοῖσιν
Ἀργεῖοι, νῦν αὖτε μέγα κρατέεις νεκύεσσιν   485
ἐνθάδ' ἐών· τῶ μή τι θανὼν ἀκαχίζευ, Ἀχιλλεῦ.'
ὣς ἐφάμην, ὁ δέ μ' αὐτίκ' ἀμειβόμενος προσέειπε·
'μὴ δή μοι θάνατόν γε παραύδα, φαίδιμ' Ὀδυσσεῦ.
βουλοίμην κ' ἐπάρουρος ἐὼν θητευέμεν ἄλλωι,
ἀνδρὶ παρ' ἀκλήρωι, ὧι μὴ βίοτος πολὺς εἴη,   490
ἢ πᾶσιν νεκύεσσι καταφθιμένοισιν ἀνάσσειν.'

Homer, *Odyssey* 11.482–491

'No man, Achilles, is more fortunate than you, either from times past or in the future. Before, when you were alive, we Argives honoured you equally to the gods, and now again you hold mastery over the dead down here. Therefore, Achilles, do not grieve at death.' So I spoke, and he replied: 'Do not try to console me for death, glorious Achilles. I would rather be a bonded workman to another man, an impoverished peasant without much livelihood, than rule over all the lifeless dead.'

Theocritus' point is of course, as Kathryn Gutzwiller points out[27], different from Achilles', but we may at least be encouraged to speculate further in this direction by the fact that v. 30 begins with a verbal repetition of another verse from *Odyssey* 11 (v. 211); the *Nekuia* does seem to have been in Theocritus' mind here. The poor man, 'the palms of his hands hardened by use of the mattock', will then be an expansive gloss, with characteristic Theocritean earthiness, upon Achilles' ἐπάρουρος, which is glossed in the scholia either as γεωργός or as ἐπίγειος καὶ ζῶν. So too, it will be Achilles' ἀνὴρ ἄκληρος, glossed in the scholia as πένης, κλῆρον καὶ οὐσίαν μὴ ἔχων, which is the starting-point for Theocritus' ἀχὴν ἐκ πατέρων.

There are two other reasons for seeing Achilles' words behind this passage, and both may be classed as stylistic. The closest verbal model for these verses in Homer is not in *Odyssey* 11, but rather in the famous simile of *Iliad* 23, in which Achilles' attempts to escape the river-god are compared to a man clearing an irrigation channel:

ὡς δ' ὅτ' ἀνὴρ ὀχετηγὸς ἀπὸ κρήνης μελανύδρου
ἂμ φυτὰ καὶ κήπους ὕδατι ῥόον ἡγεμονεύηι
χερσὶ μάκελλαν ἔχων, ἀμάρης ἐξ ἔχματα βάλλων·
τοῦ μέν τε προρέοντος ὑπὸ ψηφῖδες ἅπασαι   260
ὀχλεῦνται· τὸ δέ τ' ὦκα κατειβόμενον κελαρύζει
χώρωι ἔνι προαλεῖ, φθάνει δέ τε καὶ τὸν ἄγοντα·

---

27 Gutzwiller 1983, 226 n. 55; cf. also Kyriakou 2004, 238 n. 32.

ὡς αἰεὶ Ἀχιλῆα κιχήσατο κῦμα ῥόοιο
καὶ λαιψηρὸν ἐόντα· θεοὶ δέ τε φέρτεροι ἀνδρῶν.

Homer, *Iliad* 21.257–264

As when a man working on irrigation directs water from a dark spring through his plants and fruit, by working with a mattock and throwing muck out of the channel. As the stream flows forward, all the pebbles roll down and the swift-flowing water gurgles as it runs down the slope and catches up with the gardener. Just so did the river's wave ever catch up with Achilles, swift as he was: gods are more powerful than men.

The style of this famous simile, which contains the only occurrence of μάκελλα in Homer, is discussed in the scholia in terms of a move by Homer from his grand style to a much plainer manner (τὸ ἰσχνόν);[28] Theocritus, in running together two scenes involving Achilles, has made the language as plain as possible, including the only instance of τυλόω in poetry, to reinforce the warning about what happens to those who do not give thought to how poets can benefit them. The second reason for thinking of Achilles in this passage of *Idyll* 16 derives from another aspect of style. Odysseus' attempted consolation to the hero, μή τι θανὼν ἀκαχίζευ, Ἀχιλλεῦ, will certainly have evoked the familiar connection between Achilles' name and ἄχος (cf., e.g., AT-scholia on *Iliad* 1.1 h Erbse), and these sounds seem strangely persistent in this Theocritean passage: ἀκλεής, Ἀχέροντος, ἀχήν, ἀκτήμονα. ἀχήν, which does not otherwise appear in literature (cf. Gow *ad loc.*), may in fact have been chosen to activate or reinforce a connection with Achilles and ἄχος.

The very variety of Theocritus' engagement with, and reproduction of, the poetry of the past, even within a single poem, and the lesson for the study of Hellenistic poetry more generally that this carries, does not need to be laboured at length, but another example, where it is again Achilles who carries the weight of the past, may suggest something of the range of phenomena which the Theocritean text has to offer.

As is well known, in his account in *Idyll* 14 of the disastrous party which revealed to him that his girlfriend's mind was on someone else, Aischinas uses two Achillean similes in very quick succession:

ἁ δὲ Κυνίσκα
ἔκλαεν ἐξαπίνας θαλερώτερον ἢ παρὰ ματρί
παρθένος ἑξαετὴς κόλπῳ ἐπιθυμήσασα.
τᾶμος ἐγώ, τὸν ἴσαις τύ, Θυώνιχε, πὺξ ἐπὶ κόρρας

---

28 Cf. Hunter 2009a, 158–160.

ἤλασα, κἄλλαν αὖθις. ἀνειρύσασα δὲ πέπλως   35
ἔξω ἀποίχετο θᾶσσον. 'ἐμὸν κακόν, οὔ τοι ἀρέσκω;
ἄλλος τοι γλυκίων ὑποκόλπιος; ἄλλον ἰοῖσα
θάλπε φίλον. τήνωι τεὰ δάκρυα; μᾶλα ῥεόντω.'
μάστακα δοῖσα τέκνοισιν ὑπωροφίοισι χελιδών
ἄψορρον ταχινὰ πέτεται βίον ἄλλον ἀγείρειν·   40
ὠκυτέρα μαλακᾶς ἀπὸ δίφρακος ἔπτετο τήνα
ἰθὺ δι' ἀμφιθύρω καὶ δικλίδος, ᾇ πόδες ἆγον.

Theocritus 14.31-42

Kyniska suddenly burst into tears, more violently than a six year-old girl crying for her mother's lap. Then I — you know what I'm like, Thyonichus — punched her on the temple with my fist, and then gave her another one. Gathering up her dress, she took off as fast as she could. 'Wretch, don't you like me? You prefer some other lover? Be off and keep your new friend warm! Are your tears for him? Let them flow down big as apples!'. The swallow gives her young under the roof a morsel to eat and swiftly flies back off to gather more nourishment; more quickly than that did Kyniska fly off her soft seat, straight through the porch and the door, wherever her feet took her.

The first of these similes goes back of course to Achilles' address to Patroclus at the opening of *Iliad* 16:

τίπτε δεδάκρυσαι Πατρόκλεις, ἠΰτε κούρη
νηπίη, ἥ θ' ἅμα μητρὶ θέουσ' ἀνελέσθαι ἀνώγει
εἰανοῦ ἁπτομένη, καί τ' ἐσσυμένην κατερύκει,
δακρυόεσσα δέ μιν ποτιδέρκεται, ὄφρ' ἀνέληται;
τῇ ἴκελος Πάτροκλε τέρεν κατὰ δάκρυον εἴβεις.

Homer, *Iliad* 16.7-11

Why are you crying, Patroclus, like a young girl who runs to her mother and begs to be picked up, tugging at her dress and holding her back as she tries to hurry off, and as she cries she looks at her until she is picked up? Like her, Patroclus, you are shedding womanly tears.

In his note on v. 33 Gow observes 'There is some force in the criticism that ἑξαετής is old for such behaviour'. If we ask why Theocritus introduced this change in his model, a number of answers might come to mind, but — as often — we could do worse than begin with the Homeric scholia. The bT-scholia on the simile of *Iliad* 16 note how the poet uses similes to enable him to include all ages of females in his poem and how he here 'takes a banal (εὐτελές) event and represents it with grandeur and envisionment (μεγαλοπρεπῶς καὶ μετ' ἐναργείας)'. At one level this is merely a specific instance of the standard ancient view that similes aid *enargeia*,²⁹ but I am sure that many modern readers of Homer will gladly concur with the particularly memorable power of this 'realistic' image. Why did Theocritus replace the unspecific Homeric κούρη νηπίη by the more specific παρθένος... ἑξαετής? For Dover, to some extent echoing (I do not know whether deliberately) the Homeric scholia, Theocritus' image is 'a much less vivid picture of everyday life', though he says nothing as to whether he thinks this was simply Theocritus' lack of competence or whether it served some artistic purpose.³⁰ There would of course be much more to say about why Aischinas is made to appropriate an Achillean voice, but I want to ask a simpler question: can we be sure that Theocritus did not make his character use the specific (or, in Greek, ἀκριβές) epithet ἑξαετής precisely to increase the image's vividness, to out-Achilles Achilles, if you like? How secure are our judgements about ancient stylistic effects? Theocritus poses, as is well known, some of the thorniest problems in this area: to move from the micro- to the macro-level, how many modern readers are sure they understand the stylistic level of the Adonis-hymn in *Idyll* 15 and the purpose of that level.

We may well think that, leaving everything else aside, the image of the crying girl is much more powerful when used, as in Homer, of a man than, as in Theocritus, to describe an older female, but the narrative situation hardly allowed that in the case of Theocritus. There is, in any case, obvious humour in the Iliadic echoes: a lovers' spat at a party is improbably made as portentous as the story of the *Iliad* and, particularly, as tragic as the story of Achilles and Patroclus. The following verses in which Aeschinas twice hits Kyniska have been compared to the violence sometimes exercised against women in New Comedy, but what seems more likely is that we have here a version of Achilles' anger when faced with the prospect of losing *his* girl in *Iliad* 1, an anger that puts him on the point of running Agamemnon through. 'You know what I'm like' (v. 34) functions (*inter alia*) as a kind of reference back to that scene: yes, we all do know the model text here — and Achilles' emotional character was probably the most notorious of any literary figure. Not for Aischinas, however, the indecision of the Homeric scene — he just let Kyniska have it ... Not for nothing, too, has Theocritus placed *antilabe* in each of the first three verses of *Idyll* 14³¹ — it is

---

29 Cf., e. g., Nünlist 2009, 291.
30 Griffiths 1979, 114–115 argues that this 'literary posturing' by Aischinas cuts a very poor figure, as indeed do other Theocritean lovers: 'He has only the dimmest grasp of what his [Achillean] images mean...'; for a very different approach cf. Burton 1995, 49–52.
31 There is a similar phenomenon at the head of *Idyll* 15.

these verses which mark how the hexameter of epic poetry has been brought down to the level of mime.

The source of Aischinas' second Achillean image is Achilles' account of his own labours in *Iliad* 9:

> οὐδέ τί μοι περίκειται, ἐπεὶ πάθον ἄλγεα θυμῶι,
> αἰεὶ ἐμὴν ψυχὴν παραβαλλόμενος πολεμίζειν.
> ὡς δ' ὄρνις ἀπτῆσι νεοσσοῖσι προφέρηισι
> μάστακ' ἐπεί κε λάβηισι, κακῶς δ' ἄρα οἱ πέλει αὐτῆι,
> ὣς καὶ ἐγὼ πολλὰς μὲν ἀΰπνους νύκτας ἴαυον,   325
> ἤματα δ' αἱματόεντα διέπρησσον πολεμίζων,
> ἀνδράσι μαρνάμενος ὀάρων ἕνεκα σφετεράων.
>
> Homer, *Iliad* 9.321–327

> Nor do I gain any advantage from the fact that I have suffered grievously in my spirit, always putting my life at risk in war. Like a bird which brings its flightless chicks whatever morsel it finds, but itself goes without, so I have passed through many nights without sleep and endured blood-filled days of warfare, fighting with men over their women.

Again, there would be much to say about Theocritus' turning of this image into a paratactic simile: when we remember the surrounding context in Homer we note (with a smile) that Aischinas' subsequent counting of the days suggests an eroticization of Achilles' 'I have passed through many sleepless nights' (v. 325) – no doubt Aischinas really had, whereas Achilles' 'I have spent (many) blood-filled days in warfare' (v. 326) is probably somewhat remote from Aischinas' experience. Achilles may fight with men 'over' women, but we have just witnessed Aischinas fighting 'with' women. Here, however, I want merely to draw attention to one stylistic feature of Theocritus' reworking. V. 39 begins with the same Homeric gloss as stands in necessary enjambment at the head of *Iliad* 9.324, μάστακα.[32]

Nevertheless, the Theocritean reworking precisely inverts every element of the corresponding Homeric utterance; the matter may be set out in a table, with the elements numbered as they appear in their respective texts:

---

[32] Three interpretations of Homeric μάστακ' at *Iliad* 9.324 seem to have had ancient currency, cf. the scholia *ad loc.*, Gow on Theocr. 14.39: 'a mouthful, morsel', 'a locust' (both understanding μάστακα), and 'with the mouth' (understanding μάστακι, accepted by, e. g., Hainsworth *ad loc.*). Theocritus' μάστακα allows only the first two interpretations, and the first is, as far as I know, universally accepted by modern editors and translators; I am not convinced that Theocritus' usage here is a strong case of overt interpretation within a poem of a disputed Homeric word, but this is an area where differences of opinion are certainly possible.

Tab. 1: Word-order in Theocritus 14.39.

Theocritus		Homer	
μάστακα	1	μάστακα	5
δοῖσα	2	προφέρῃσιν	4
τέκνοισιν	3	νεοσσοῖσι	3
ὑπωροφίοισι	4	ἀπτῆσι	2
χελιδών	5	ὄρνις	1

Is this an accident (we can hardly doubt that such accidents do happen)? Would such *uariatio* (deliberate or not) surprise us at an earlier date? Is a dichotomy in such matters between 'accident' and 'design' a misleading one — are things rather more complicated than that? Are such things only possible in a poetry which relies upon writing and expects reception through reading? The Theocritean text, of course, abounds in patterns and echoing repetitions of all kinds, and not just in the bucolic poems (as usually understood).

Another poem of Pindar which has long been seen to have a special importance for *Idyll* 16 is the *Second Isthmian*, also for a Sicilian victor. It is, after all, in this poem that Pindar complains that the Muse of old was 'neither φιλοκερδής nor ἐργάτις', whereas today the watchword is χρήματα χρήματ' ἀνήρ. The scholia spin a story about how this poem was prompted by the μικρολογία of a patron, but also — more interestingly — interpret Pindar's reference to the avaricious Muse as a reference to Simonides and cite iambics of Callimachus (fr. 222 Pf.) which echo this Pindaric passage in an explicit reference to the Cean poet; if nothing else, the Callimachus fragment suggests the familiarity of the Pindaric passage and its probable link to Simonides in the third century. Reference to *Isthmian* 2 may in fact be able to help with a difficult passage of *Idyll* 16, in a way which is perhaps exemplary for the poetry of the third century.

Not far into the second part of the poem Theocritus dismisses the potential patron who does not want to part with his money:

χαιρέτω ὅστις τοῖος, ἀνήριθμος δέ οἱ εἴη
ἄργυρος, αἰεὶ δὲ πλεόνων ἔχοι ἵμερος αὐτόν· 65
αὐτὰρ ἐγὼ τιμήν τε καὶ ἀνθρώπων φιλότητα
πολλῶν ἡμιόνων τε καὶ ἵππων πρόσθεν ἑλοίμαν.

Theocritus 16.64–67

Farewell to such a man—let him have measureless silver and ever be possessed by desire for more. For myself, I would choose honour and the friendship of men in front of many mules and horses.

Here Theocritus puts the old hymnic/rhapsodic structure χαῖρε ... αὐτὰρ ἐγώ to brilliant (and ?? very Hellenistic) new use.[33] Whereas χαῖρε is used to 'hail' the deity who has just been the object of song, with a sense that he or she 'appears' in response to the power of the rhapsode's hymn,[34] χαιρέτω dismisses the mean patron out of hand, as the poet moves on to a worthy subject of song; this is clearly an important structural moment in the poem, and one that cuts across the formal division I was considering earlier. Moreover, the wish (or curse) that such a patron should suffer from unquenchable desire for money (like Erysichthon for food) is a corresponding inversion of the closing hymnic request to the god who has been praised for ἀρετή and/or ὄλβος, a request that Theocritus also reworks at the end of *Idyll* 17, as Callimachus does at the end of the *Hymn to Zeus*.[35] This poet has now risen above such considerations. Theocritus is here, *inter alia*, exploring the relation between 'modern' encomiastic poetry and traditional hymnic poetry. What follows has been described as a 'baffling' transition:[36]

δίζημαι δ' ὅτινι θνατῶν κεχαρισμένος ἔλθω
σὺν Μοίσαις· χαλεπαὶ γὰρ ὁδοὶ τελέθουσιν ἀοιδοῖς
κουράων ἀπάνευθε Διὸς μέγα βουλεύοντος.   70
οὔπω μῆνας ἄγων ἔκαμ' οὐρανὸς οὐδ' ἐνιαυτούς·
πολλοὶ κινήσουσιν ἔτι τροχὸν ἅματος ἵπποι·
ἔσσεται οὗτος ἀνὴρ ὃς ἐμεῦ κεχρήσετ' ἀοιδοῦ κτλ.

Theocritus 16.68–73

I am looking for the mortal to whose house I may come as a welcome guest (κεχαρισμένος) in company with the Muses, for the ways are difficult for singers without the daughters of great-counselling Zeus. Not yet have the heavens wearied of leading round the months and years; often still shall the horses set the wheel of the day in motion. There will come the man who will need me to be his singer...

Gow glosses the reference to the Muses as 'in plain prose it appears to mean no more than that it is useless for a poet to travel unless he carries his inspiration with him' (n. on 69 f.), a rather lame explanation which, however, is in its essence taken over by Dover. The image of the ὁδοί of poetry is of course ubiquitous, but it is important that Theocritus is looking for a worthy patron, someone who — as he will go on to say — has the deeds of an Achilles or an Ajax to his

---

33 Cf., e.g., González 2010, 100. Acosta-Hughes 2010a, 185 wants Simonides fr.eleg. 11.19–20 W to be the specific model here, but there seems nothing to activate such specific reference. On the transitional formula αὐτὰρ ἐγώ cf. further Hunter 2003, 103 with earlier bibliography.
34 Cf. García 2002.
35 Cf. Hunter 2003, 197–198.
36 Griffiths 1979, 35. For other aspects of this transition cf. Hunter 1996, 105.

credit; it is to such a man that one makes journeys 'with the Muses'. In the *Second Isthmian* Pindar uses the 'journey' metaphor in a similar manner:

οὐ γὰρ πάγος οὐδὲ προσάντης
ἁ κέλευθος γίνεται,
εἴ τις εὐδόξων ἐς ἀν-
δρῶν ἄγοι τιμὰς Ἑλικωνιάδων.

Pindar, Isthmian 2.33–34

> There is no hill, nor is the path steep, if one brings the honours of the maidens of Helicon to the homes of famous men.

The interpretation of these verses is (inevitably) disputed, but it is not hard to believe that Theocritus understood them as does the scholiast: 'For those who are praising glorious men the road (ὁδός) is not rough (τραχεῖα), but the opposite — easy and gentle, for they themselves (i.e. the subjects of song) provide the starting-points (ἀφορμαί) for praise' (scholium on v. 33, p. 219 Drachmann). If Theocritus has found *his* ἀφορμή in this passage,[37] then his 'Muses' will be songs in praise of great deeds (a meaning which also suits the reprise in v. 107): if there are no great deeds to praise, then poets really do find the going tough, but Theocritus is confident enough that there is still time for a worthy patron to arise. Behind both Pindar and Theocritus may of course lurk Hesiod's steep path towards virtue (*WD* 286–292): the patron will have to work very hard for the successes which manifest his ἀρετή, but it is those successes which make the way easy for poets.

The language of Hellenistic poetry thus leaves us with much to do, and much that leads to frustration. If only we could more often be sure of our stylistic sense: when in v. 75 of *Idyll* 16 Theocritus describes the plain of Troy as 'the plain of Simois, where is the tomb of Phrygian Ilos', is it important that Homer never says 'the plain of Simois' and never uses the singular Φρύξ, that in Homer the Phrygians are, in any case, quite distinct from the Trojans (a fact commented upon by the Homeric scholia),[38] and that to make the eponymous hero of Ilion a 'Phrygian' might in some circumstances be highly loaded (cf. Callimachus, *Hymn to Athena* 18 of Paris),[39] and that ἠρίον occurs only once in Homer (of the mound which Achilles 'devised' for himself and Patroclus, *Iliad* 23.126)

---

37 Perrotta 1925, 21 illustrates this Theocritean passage from *Olympian* 1.109–111, where there seems indeed to be a similar thought: Olympian success by the victor will offer the poet an ἐπίκουρον ... ὁδὸν λόγων.
38 Cf. bT- scholia on *Iliad* 10.415.
39 Cf. Bulloch's note *ad loc.*

and only here in our corpus of Theocritus? Was Theocritus thinking of the opening of *Iliad* 6 in which the plain of Troy, the Simois (in the genitive in the same *sedes*), and a heroic exploit of Ajax all come together? So many questions...

Bibliography

Acosta-Hughes, B. 2010. *Arion's Lyre: Archaic Lyric into Hellenistic Poetry*, Princeton.
Bell, M. 2011. 'Agrarian policy, bucolic poetry, and figurative art in early Hellenistic Sicily', in: R. Neudecker (ed.), *Krise und Wandel: Süditalien im 4. und 3. Jahrhundert v. Chr.*, Wiesbaden, 193–211.
Bernsdorff, H. 2011. 'Der Schluss von Theokrits "Herakliskos" und Vergils vierte Ekloge', *Archiv für Papyrusforschung* 57, 187–194.
Bing, P. 1988. *The Well-Read Muse. Present and Past in Callimachus and the Hellenistic Poets*, Göttingen.
Bulloch, A.W. 1985. *Callimachus. The Fifth Hymn*, Cambridge.
Fabiano, G. 1971. 'Fluctuation in Theocritus' Style', *GRBS* 12, 517–537.
Fantuzzi, M. 2000. 'Theocritus and the "Demythologizing" of Poetry', in: M. Depew/D. Obbink (eds.), *Matrices of Genre: Authors, Canons, and Society*, Cambridge, 135–151.
Fränkel, H. 1960. *Wege und Formen frühgriechischen Denkens*, 2nd ed., Munich.
García, J.F. 2002. 'Symbolic Action in the Homeric Hymns: the Theme of Recognition', *CA* 21, 5–39.
González, J.M. 2010. 'Theokritos' Idyll 16. The Χάριτες and Civic Poetry', *HSCPh* 105, 65–116.
Griffiths, F.T. 1979. *Theocritus at Court*, Leiden.
Gutzwiller, K. 1983. 'Charites or Hiero: Theocritus' *Idyll* 16', *RhM* 126, 212–238.
Hardie, P. 1993. *The Epic Successors of Virgil*, Cambridge.
Horstmann, A.E.-A. 1976. *Ironie und Humor bei Theokrit*, Meisenheim am Glan.
Hunter, R. 1996. *Theocritus and the Archaeology of Greek Poetry*, Cambridge.
Hunter, R. 2003. *Theocritus. Encomium of Ptolemy Philadelphus, Text and Translation, Introduction and Commentary*, Berkeley.
Hunter, R. 2009. *Critical Moments in Classical Literature*, Cambridge.
Kyriakou, P. 2004. 'κλέος and Poetry in Simonides fr. 11 W and Theocritus, *Idyll* 16', *RhM* 147, 221–246.
Meincke, W. 1965. *Untersuchungen zu den enkomiastischen Gedichten Theokrits*, Diss. Kiel.
Most, G.W. 1985. *The Measures of Praise*, Göttingen.
Nünlist, R. 2009. *The Ancient Critic at Work*, Cambridge.
Perrotta, G. 1925. 'Studi di poesia ellenistica', *SIFC* 4, 5–68.
Sbardella, L. 1997. 'Il poeta e il bifolco', *MD* 38, 127–141.
Sbardella, L. 2004. 'Teocrito pindarico. Il κέρδος, la fama e la poesia omerica in Nemea 7.17–31 e nell'Idillio XVI', *Seminari Romani* 7, 65–83.
Sistakou, E. 2008. *Reconstructing the Epic: Cross-Readings of the Trojan Myth in Hellenistic Poetry*, Leuven/Paris/Dudley.
Vox, O. 2002. 'ἀγαθὸν κλέος: poeta e committente nelle Cariti (Theocr. 16)', *Kleos* 7, 193–209.
Willi, A. 2004. 'Poétique au seuil de de l'Alexandrisme : idylle 16 de Théocrite', *AC* 73, 31–46.

11 Sweet Stesichorus: Theocritus 18 and the Helen Revisited

I begin with one of the few ancient testimonia about Stesichorus' style which does not (apparently) focus on his closeness to Homer. This is from Hermogenes' discussion of stylistic γλυκύτης, 'sweetness', part of which is Stesichorus Tb28 Ercoles:

> ἀλλ' ἐπανιτέον πάλιν ἐπὶ τὸν περὶ λέξεως γλυκείας λόγον. γλυκεῖα γὰρ λέξις καὶ ἡ διὰ τῶν ἐπιθέτων ὀνομάτων, οἷον "ἄγετε δή, ὦ Μοῦσαι λίγειαι". καὶ κατ' αὐτὴν δὲ τὴν ποίησιν φύσει οὖσαν γλυκεῖαν παρὰ τὸν ἄλλον λόγον ἐκφαίνεται τὰ ἐπίθετα καὶ γλυκύτερά πως ὄντα καὶ πλείονα ποιοῦντα τὴν ἡδονήν. ταῦτά τοι καὶ ὁ Στησίχορος σφόδρα ἡδὺς εἶναι δοκεῖ διὰ τὸ πολλοῖς χρῆσθαι τοῖς ἐπιθέτοις.
>
> Hermogenes, Περὶ Ἰδεῶν pp. 338.19–339.1 Rabe

> But we must return again to the discussion of sweet style. Sweet style is also the style which employs epithets, such as 'Come then, clear-voiced Muses'. Poetry is by nature sweet, but epithets stand out from the rest of the style and are in some way sweeter and productive of greater pleasure. For this reason Stesichorus seems to be very sweet because he uses many epithets.

Why is Stesichorus singled out here? If it is simply — as indeed has been suggested[1] — that, like Homer, he does indeed have a lot of epithets, then we might both complain that Hermogenes is not playing fair — scholars do not like things being quite that simple — and also ask why Hermogenes did not name Homer here. An obvious answer to the latter question is that Stesichorus was a lyric poet, and ἡδονή makes much more sense as a central characteristic of the diction of a lyric poet than of Homer.[2] At one level, this just rephrases our question: why was Stesichorus' use of epithets thought notable among *lyric poets*? I do not think that it will be enough to note that late sources report that a nightingale sat on the lips of the baby Stesichorus and sang its sweet song from that position, as, for example, bees sat on the lips of the baby Hesi-

---

I am grateful to audiences at Cambridge, Harvard, New York University, and Oxford for helpful discussion and stimulating scepticism.

---

1 Cf. Willi 2008, 71, Ercoles 2013, 583; also Lerza 1982, 25.
2 In ancient criticism Homer's diction does have 'sweet' and 'pleasant' elements, just as it has examples of every positive quality, though it is Hesiod who stands out in this regard among hexameter poets; cf. Hunter 2014, 282–315.

od.[3] As with all ancient rhetorical theory, we must ask first to what extent Hermogenes' observation was largely theory-driven, or the result of empirical observation, or simply based on one notorious case, and then to what extent it agrees with what *we* might feel tempted to say. When we alight almost at random on a passage such as fr. 10.1–4 F., do we feel that we are here unusually well supplied with epithets?

⏑⏑]κ[ύ]μαθ' ἁλὸς βαθ[έ]ας ἀφικον-
το θ]εῶν περικαλλέ[α ν]ᾶσον
τ]όθι Ἑσπερίδες π[αγχρ]ύσεα δώ-
μα]τ' ἔχοντι·

...waves of the deep sea, they reached the very lovely island of the gods, where the Hesperides have their houses all of gold.

Certainly, no one will need to be reminded that Stesichorus does indeed make liberal use of standard Homeric epithets;[4] that is a different point from the one that Hermogenes is making, though it might have made a significant contribution to the ancient tradition of the poet as Ὁμηρικώτατος. In the first part of this chapter I want to pick away behind Hermogenes' observation to see whether we may be able to refine our understanding a little. It is in the nature of the subject that much that will be said must remain in the realm of speculation.

The first example of a 'sweet' epithet in Hermogenes' discussion, which descends at an unknown number of removes from Aristotle's discussion of epithets in the third book of the *Rhetoric*, is taken from Socrates' invocation to the Muses at Plato *Phaedrus* 237ab:

ἄγετε δή, ὦ Μοῦσαι, εἴτε δι' ᾠδῆς εἶδος λίγειαι, εἴτε διὰ γένος μουσικὸν τὸ Λιγύων ταύτην ἔσχετ' ἐπωνυμίαν, "ξύμ μοι λάβεσθε" τοῦ μύθου, ὅν με ἀναγκάζει ὁ βέλτιστος οὑτοσὶ λέγειν, ἵν' ὁ ἑταῖρος αὐτοῦ, καὶ πρότερον δοκῶν τούτωι σοφὸς εἶναι, νῦν ἔτι μᾶλλον δόξηι.

Come then, Muses, 'clear-voiced', whether from the form of your song you acquired this appellation or because of the musical race of the Ligurians, 'join with me' in the story which this splendid fellow here compels me to tell, so that his friend, who previously too seemed to him wise, may now seem even more so.

---

3 Cf. Pliny *HN* 10.82, Christodorus *A.P.* 2.125–130 = Ta22, Ta23 Ercoles; the former text foregrounds *suauitas*, the latter links Στησίχορον... λιγύθροον to the λιγυρὴ μολπή of the nightingale. Hesiod: T26 Most.

4 For a list of examples see Curtis 2011, 48–49.

Hermogenes has compressed Socrates' words to produce an opening lyric invocation of a very familiar type, just as Socrates has broken up such an invocation with his own witty prose. This passage of the *Phaedrus* was famous in antiquity — it was at this point of the Platonic work that Dionysius of Halicarnassus placed the switch from a graceful and pure style to one of poetic tastelessness[5] — but Hermogenes' example puts us on notice that some epithets were more 'sweet' than others. Although the passage of Hermogenes from which I began does not make the point explicitly, it is not enough just to count epithets; the quality and meaning of those epithets are crucial contributors to the quality of 'sweetness'. It is not irrelevant that Socrates' invocation is the opening to an ἐρωτικὸς λόγος.

A glance at some of the lyric examples of the type of invocation which Socrates imitates may confirm some of this analysis. Alcman fr. 14(a) *PMGF* is clearly the beginning of a maiden-song, which may well have shared the emphasis on beauty and ornamentation which are so important to the Louvre *partheneion*:

Μῶσ' ἄγε Μῶσα λίγηα πολυμμελές
    αἰὲν ἀοιδὲ μέλος
νεοχμὸν ἄρχε παρσένοις ἀείδην

Muse come, singer Muse clear-voiced, ever rich in song, begin a new song for maidens to sing.

In Alcman fr. 27 *PMGF*, there is an almost overwhelming emphasis on beauty, desire, and grace:

Μῶσ' ἄγε Καλλιόπα, θύγατερ Διός,
ἄρχ' ἐρατῶν ἐπέων, ἐπὶ δ' ἵμερον
ὕμνωι καὶ χαρίεντα τίθη χορόν.

Muse come, Calliope, daughter of Zeus, begin the lovely verses; place desire on the song and make the chorus full of grace.

When we move back to Stesichorus, we find that in the snatch of song preserved as fr. 277a F., δεῦρ' ἄγε Καλλιόπεια λίγεια, 'come hither clear-voiced Calliope', the same epithet which Hermogenes had singled out is placed next to 'Calliope', thus allowing the etymology of her name, 'beautiful voice', to resonate. Here again, the 'sweetness' of the later critic is not just confined to the existence of an

---

5 Dion. Hal. *Dem.* 7.3–4; cf. Hunter 2012, 169–170.

epithet. So too, in fr. 327 F., the emphasis on 'loveliness' shines through textual corruption:

ἄγε Μοῦσα λίγει' ἄρξον ἀοιδᾶς †ἐρατῶν ὕμνους†
Σαμίων περὶ παίδων ἐρατᾶι φθεγγομένα λύραι

Come, clear-voiced Muse, begin the song... concerning Samian children, singing to your lovely lyre

These verses are the opening of the *Rhadine*, a poem whose authorship was doubted even in antiquity and which is now standardly denied to Stesichorus, but it is worth noting that the story of the poem preserved for us by Strabo may well have contained a prominent (heterosexual) erotic element, and this would certainly have been classed by Hermogenes as 'sweet'.[6] Beginnings of poems, and their consequences, often survive in the critical tradition long after knowledge of the body of the poem has faded. Alongside the *Rhadine* we should put the stories of Calyce (fr. 326 F.) and Daphnis (fr. 323), which were at least believed to have been treated by Stesichorus.

Of considerable interest in this connection are the verses which were echoed by the chorus of Aristophanes' *Peace* and probably all derive from the opening of Stesichorus' *Oresteia* (frr. 172–174 F.)[7]

Μοῖσα σὺ μὲν πολέμους ἀπωσαμένα πεδ' ἐμοῦ
κλείοισα θεῶν τε γάμους ἀνδρῶν τε δαῖτας
καὶ θαλίας μακάρων

Muse, thrusting aside wars and with me celebrating marriages of gods and banquets of men and feasts of the blessed...

τοιάδε χρὴ Χαρίτων δαμώματα καλλικόμων
ὑμνεῖν Φρύγιον μέλος ἐξευρόντα‹ς› ἁβρῶς
ἦρος ἐπερχομένου.

Such are the public songs of the lovely-haired Graces which we must sing, delicately bringing forth a Phrygian melody at the approach of spring.

ὄκα ἦρος
ὧραι κελαδῆι χελιδών.

when in the springtime the swallow calls out its song.

---

6 For this poem and the others mentioned in this paragraph, see Rutherford 2015.
7 For the attribution to this poem, see Bowie 2015.

In the case of fr. 172 Stesichorus' actual words must to some extent remain conjectural, but three aspects of this group of fragments are to be noted in the present context. First, if these fragments do indeed come from the beginning of the poem, then they were probably well known to, and perhaps influential upon, the critical tradition long after Aristophanes incorporated them in his play and perhaps expected some at least of his audience to recognise them; there were obvious reasons why scholars would have been interested in the *Oresteia*, given the prominence of the story elsewhere, notably in Aeschylus. Secondly, the themes of the fragments are 'sweet', as a critic such as Hermogenes would have perceived the matter: the rejection of war in favour of weddings, celebrations, springtime, 'lovely-haired Graces'; here too, diction and subject-matter blend. Finally, the scholia describe Aristophanes' *Peace* 775–780 and, by implication, the Stesichorean passage upon which it is based as σφόδρα γλαφυρόν. The adjective has a wide range of nuance in critical discussion — 'smooth', 'harmonious', 'polished', and so on – but in the present context we may naturally think of Demetrius' discussion in *On Style* of the χάριτες attaching to the style which he calls the γλαφυρὸς χαρακτήρ: among the subjects marked by χάριτες are 'gardens of the nymphs, wedding-songs, loves, all the poetry of Sappho' (132). When Demetrius turns to χάριτες of diction, it is the interlocking of subject and diction to which he immediately turns (133):

> ὥστε ἡ μέν τις ἐν πράγματι χάρις ἐστί, τὰ δὲ καὶ ἡ λέξις ποιεῖ
> ἐπιχαριτώτερα, οἷον
>   ὡς δ' ὅτε Πανδαρέου κούρη, χλωρηῒς ἀηδών,
>   καλὸν ἀείδηισιν, ἔαρος νέον ἱσταμένοιο·
> ἐνταῦθα γὰρ καὶ ἡ ἀηδὼν χάριεν ὀρνίθιον, καὶ τὸ ἔαρ φύσει
> χάριεν, πολὺ δὲ ἐπικεκόσμηται τῆι ἑρμηνείαι, καὶ ἔστι χαριέστερα τῶι
> τε "χλωρηῒς" καὶ τῶι "Πανδαρέου κούρη" εἰπεῖν ἐπὶ ὄρνιθος, ἅπερ τοῦ
> ποιητοῦ ἴδιά ἐστι.

> There is charm in the subject-matter itself, but diction also can increase the charm, as in
>   As when the daughter of Pandareos, the pale nightingale, sings beautifully at the
>   very beginning of spring. (Hom. *Od.* 19.518–519)
> Here the nightingale is a charming little bird, and spring is naturally charming, but the passage has been greatly ornamented by the style, and it is more charming both because of 'pale' and through calling the bird 'daughter of Pandareos'; these things are contributions of the poet.

Here too we may well be reminded of Stesichorus fr. 173–174. The other principal ancient theorist of τὸ γλαφυρόν is Dionysius of Halicarnassus, who classes Stesichorus (along with Homer) in the 'mixed style', that is, a style which blends the 'austere' and the γλαφυρόν (*De comp. verb.* 24.5). Nevertheless, some of what Dionysius says of his γλαφυρόν style may seem to fit, for example, fr. 172–174 rather well. Thus the words used in such a style are to be 'euphonious and smooth and soft and maidenly of face' (*De comp.* verb. 23.4, cf. *Demosthenes* 40.1, 3), or 'as in musical performances (μουσικαὶ συμφωνίαι), pleasant and clear (ἡδεῖα καὶ λιγυρά)' (*Demosthenes* 40.6).

The upshot of this discussion would seem to be that an ancient critic looking for 'sweetness' in Stesichorus would not have been too hard pressed to find it. On the other hand, it may be that Hermogenes' choice of Socrates' invocation in the *Phaedrus* has much to tell us. The *Phaedrus* is very important to Hermogenean γλυκύτης, and is cited no fewer than five times in his discussion: it is used to illustrate γλυκύτης arising from mythic subject-matter (p. 330.6–8 Rabe), from descriptions of natural beauty (331.22–24, where the Phaedran *locus amoenus* is set beside Sappho fr. 2 Voigt), from the ascription of rationality to irrational things (333.16–334.4, an interesting discussion of 'the trees do not wish to teach me anything'), from the interweaving of poetry (337.8–21), and finally from the use of epithets (above). As Hermogenes also directs our attention to Stesichorus, it is inevitable to ask whether it is a coincidence that it is in the *Phaedrus* that we are told of Stesichorus' *Palinode*, that Socrates there seems to play on a supposed connection between Himera, the home city of Stesichorus son of Euphemos ('He who speaks well')[8] and ἵμερος (244a), itself a very 'sweet' thought, and that Socrates puts his great speech on *erōs*, his 'palinode', under the aegis of Stesichorus, thus at least associating the archaic poet with erotic knowledge. Earlier in the dialogue Socrates had claimed that any knowledge he had about *erōs* had come from 'the beautiful Sappho or the wise Anacreon or even from certain writers of prose' (δῆλον δὲ ὅτι τινῶν ἀκήκοα, ἢ που Σαπφοῦς τῆς καλῆς ἢ Ἀνακρέοντος τοῦ σοφοῦ ἢ καὶ συγγραφέων τινῶν, 235c), and the dialogue's generous use of archaic lyric is well known. It is therefore worth suggesting that the critical reception of the *Phaedrus* has here seeped into the reception of Stesichorus, making him a partner with such as Sappho and Anacreon in the 'sweet and pleasant' lyric project. More specifically, if the ancient critical view of Stesichorus' 'sweet' epithets did have something to do with Plato's *Phaedrus* and Stesichorus' own *Helen/Palinode*, to which I shall return presently, then this would suit the fact that Hermogenes identifies 'erotic' sub-

---

8 The name presumably evokes εὐφημεῖν, which is, as Stesichorus came to realise, what one should always do in matters concerning the gods; the significance of 'Euphemos' and 'Himera' in this passage of the *Phaedrus* was noted at least as early as Hermias' commentary (p. 81.17 Couvreur). On the ancient lists of the poet's father's name cf. Curtis 2011, 3–5, Finglass 2014a, 16–17.

ject-matter as notably 'sweet' (p. 333.4–5 Rabe) and that, as we have seen, Demetrius notes that 'gardens of the nymphs, wedding-songs, loves, and all the poetry of Sappho' are examples of 'charm (χάριτες) consisting in subject-matter' (*On Style* 132).

There are perhaps two further indications that, behind Hermogenes, lies (at an unknown number of removes) Stesichorus' place in Plato's *Phaedrus*. First, at 237a, Socrates covers his head so that he can 'run through the speech as quickly as possible and not be at a loss out of shame as he looks at [Phaedrus]' (ἐγκαλυψάμενος ἐρῶ, ἵν' ὅτι τάχιστα διαδράμω τὸν λόγον καὶ μὴ βλέπων πρὸς σὲ ὑπ' αἰσχύνης διαπορῶμαι). He is in effect making himself blind. Even if many readers will only get the point at 243b, when Socrates declares that he will deliver his palinode 'with his head bare, and not covered out of shame, like before' (γυμνῆι τῆι κεφαλῆι καὶ οὐχ ὥσπερ τότε ὑπ' αἰσχύνης ἐγκεκαλυμμένος), that is, fully sighted, we are still entitled to ask whether — even only in retrospect — we are to realise that his invocation to the Muse at 237a was not just generally 'lyric', but specifically Stesichorean. About the opening of the *Helen* we have no specific information, but the possibility that it began rather like Socrates' invocation is, I hope, not an absurdly wild speculation. Socrates' muffling and uncovering of his head is in fact a playing-out of the Stesichorean story (μὴ βλέπων 237a ~ ἀνέβλεψεν 243b), but with the blinding and restoration of sight enacted before, rather than after, the offending and compensatory performances.[9] Secondly, as so often, later critical theory may have picked up (or followed up) a hint in the model text itself. When Socrates tells Phaedrus that he will go one better than both Stesichorus and Homer by delivering *his* palinode before he has suffered at Eros' hands, Phaedrus responds that Socrates 'could not have told him anything sweeter (ἡδίω) than this' (243b); is Phaedrus, a man who 'lives' rhetorical theory and practice, here commenting on the inevitable stylistic quality of anything inspired by Stesichorus' *Palinode*, as well as expressing his pleasure that he will get the chance to listen to another Socratic speech?

A notice in Athenaeus (13.601a = Stes. Tb°7 Ercoles) tells us that Stesichorus was οὐ μετρίως ἐρωτικός and wrote erotic poems which, in ancient times (τὸ παλαιόν), were called παίδεια καὶ παιδικά; if correct, this notice would be one more 'sweet' feather in Stesichorus' cap. Wilamowitz may have been correct that these poems did not survive into the libraries of post-classical antiquity,[10]

---

[9] Nelson 2000, 39 rather associates Socrates' covering of his head with the Mysteries, and Adrian Kelly suggests to me that Euripides' *Hippolytus Kalyptomenos* should be added to the mix.
[10] Wilamowitz 1913, 239–240.

but this whole passage of Athenaeus presents problems of more than one kind, and it has been suggested that the reference to Stesichorus is an *ad hoc* invention of Athenaeus himself.[11] However that may be, it seems safest to draw very few conclusions from it. Rather, the indications that link the tradition of 'sweet Stesichorus' to the *Helen* seem a more profitable subject to pursue, and in the second part of this chapter I want to revisit the possible links between Stesichorus' *Helen* and Theocritus 18, the epithalamian for Helen and Menelaus.[12] This case is, however, distinctly unpromising, because the *hypothesis* in the Theocritean scholia merely report that 'some things (τινα) in this poem are taken from the first book of the *Helen* of Stesichorus' (= fr. 84 F.). Such remnants of ancient scholarship in the scholia on Theocritus are not uniform in kind. On *Idyll* 2 we are told that 'with a lack of sophistication Theocritus took over the character of Thestylis from the *Mimes* of Sophron',[13] and that 'the plot concerning drugs (τὴν τῶν φαρμάκων ὑπόθεσιν) he took over from the *Mimes* of Sophron';[14] this last notice seems to have originally been followed by a quotation from Sophron (cf. frr. 6–7 *PCG*). On *Idyll* 15 the report runs: 'He modelled (παρέπλασε) this poem on *'Those observing the Isthmian festival* of Sophron' and it is removed from the poetic character' (κεχωρισμένον ἐστὶ τοῦ ποιητικοῦ προσώπου, Σ init. p. 305.7–10 Wendel), an observation which, if here interpreted correctly, is in line with modern analysis of, for example, the versification and style of at least the first parts of that poem.[15] Whatever credence we give to these assertions, their specificity is different from that of the notice concerning *Idyll* 18 and Stesichorus' *Helen*. We are here at the mercy of the tradition. The *hypotheseis* to *Idylls* 2 and 15, together with relatively full scholia, are preserved in both the Ambrosian (much the best) and the Vatican recensions, whereas *Idyll* 18 and its sparse

---

11 Cingano 1990, 204–208, and (more cautiously) Ercoles 2013, 528–530.
12 Cf. Hunter 1996, 139–166; as far as possible, I shall avoid subjects handled in that earlier discussion, knowledge of which will be assumed here.
13 Σ init. a (pp. 269.18–270.1 Wendel). Text and interpretation are uncertain, cf. the notes in Wendel's edition, p. 270. The basis of the ancient criticism of Theocritus is unclear; cf. Wendel 1920, 70. Hordern 2004a, 47 translates ἀπειροκάλως as 'inappropriately', but his discussion on p. 143 concludes that the adverb 'may mean no more than that Sophron's character was portrayed as somehow obscene or indecent'.
14 Cf. Σ 11–12b = p. 272.4–5 Wendel.
15 The phrase is thus to be associated with ancient discussion of whether or not Sophron's mimes were 'poetry', however defined, cf. test. 1, 2, 13, 19 *PCG*, etc.; the meaning would be much the same if manuscript K's τρόπου was read for the προσώπου of the other manuscripts. Hordern 2004a, 145 understands this to be a remark about the difference in poetic character between Sophron's mime and *Idyll* 15; this cannot, I think, be correct.

scholia survive only in the poorer Vatican recension.[16] What lay behind the surviving observation we can only guess: did the hypothesis originally identify some of the alleged borrowings from Stesichorus, or was Stesichorus merely mentioned as having treated this subject, an observation that, in the course of transmission, has been rewritten as an assertion about literary borrowing? It is hard to say. Hordern suggested that the notice about *Idyll* 2 probably went back to the work on Sophron of Apollodorus of Athens, who also wrote on Epicharmus, in the second century BC.[17] If so, this would be extremely interesting, though my instinct rather is that we should be looking somewhat later — it seems to have been the first century BC which saw the great leap forward in the scholarly appreciation of Theocritus — and despite the fact that Apollodorus' Περὶ Θεῶν is explicitly cited in the scholia on 2.35/36a (p. 279.3–5 Wendel), Wendel is likely to have been closer to the mark in tracing the literary history in the *hypotheseis* to Idylls 2, 15, and 18 to Theon in the late first century BC.[18] Be that as it may, one fragment of Stesichorus' *Helen* at least has traditionally been taken as indicating that that poem did indeed describe the marriage of Helen and Menelaus,[19] and we are also informed by the A and D scholia on *Il.* 2.339 that Stesichorus (fr. 87, in what poem is not stated) told the story of the oath extracted by Tyndareus from all of Helen's suitors (cf. Theocr. 18.16–17), after which he gave Helen to Menelaus, and then of how Paris' abduction of Helen led to war; if all of this was in Stesichorus, then so certainly was the wedding. There is no good reason, then, to doubt that something of substance — whatever, and however little, that may be — lies behind the notice in the *hypothesis* to *Idyll* 18, whether or not χορὸν ἐστάσαντο in line 3 alludes to Stesichorus' name.[20]

It would hardly surprise if Theocritus reworked Stesichorean poetry, as he may have done — or believed he was doing — with the story of Daphnis in *Idyll*

---

16 Cf. the survey in Gow 1952, I lxxxi–lxxxii.
17 Hordern 2004a, 142.
18 Wendel 1920, 89–90.
19 Stes. fr. 88 F. West 2013, 93 seems to suggest that the fragment may rather have described the wedding of Paris and Helen.
20 Cf. further Hunter 1996, 150–151. That Eur. *Hel.* 722–725 (at least) contains a reminiscence of the Stesichorean wedding-scene is an attractive speculation. In the following discussion of the possibly Stesichorean origin of 'parallels' between Gorgias, Isocrates, and Theocritus, we have also to bear in mind the episode of the 'suitors of Helen' from the final book of Hesiod's *Catalogue*, which all four may have known (in some form). We know, for example, that the crucial oath which Tyndareus extracted from the suitors appeared already in the *Catalogue of Women* ([Hes.] fr. 204.78–87 M-W).

1; it is very hard not to believe that the mention of the river Himeras in connection with the death of Daphnis at Theocritus 7.75 evokes Stesichorus of Himera.[21] Sophron and Epicharmus (cf. Theocr. *A.P.* 9.600 = 3454–3463 *HE*) were, like Theocritus himself, from Syracuse, and the likely debt of *Idylls* 6 and 11 to Philoxenus' *Cyclops* also shows Theocritus using a poem and a myth with strong Syracusan connections, but the greatest lyric poet of Doric Sicily surely belonged within Theocritus' immediate poetic heritage, even if Himera was not Syracuse.[22] Moreover, Stesichorus' place in Plato's *Phaedrus*, a work certainly known and used by Theocritus (cf. above all *Idyll* 7), may have given that poet a notable place within Theocritus' heritage. There is, however, a problem, about which we can reach no firm conclusion, but on which a moment's reflection may not be wasted. The connection between Stesichorus' *Helen* and the *Palinode* (singular or plural) is one of the great unknowns, but if it is not unreasonable to assume that the *Helen* contained what the Platonic Socrates calls the Ἑλένης κακηγορία (*Phaedrus* 243a) and the *Suda* ψόγος Ἑλένης, then how could any poet, particularly a Sicilian poet, evoke that poem without also stirring up memories of the baggage that that poem carried with it, to say nothing of the danger to which Stesichorus himself was exposed? To anticipate somewhat, if we take seriously the possibility that we are to hear in Theocritus echoes of Stesichorus' *Helen/Palinode*, then the modern debate about how 'ironic' *Idyll* 18 is, that is, how much of the future of Menelaus and Helen we are to recall, can be seen to have been anticipated and met head on by Theocritus, and not just by depicting Helen as, in Griffiths's words, 'a model schoolgirl, who is much devoted to Athena and Artemis and... clearly... did not spend her youth being raped by Theseus and his successors;[23] no, she was running laps around Sparta'.[24] Theocritus has also used the literary heritage to mark out the meaning of his poem.

It is normally assumed that in lines 16–18 the Spartan choir rework (*inter alia*) Proteus' prophecy to Menelaus in the fourth book of the *Odyssey* that the gods will send him to the Elysian plain because he 'has Helen and is Zeus's son-in-law':

---

21 Cf. Hunter 1999, *ad loc*. For the ancient traditions linking Stesichorus, Sicily, and bucolic poetry, see also Ornaghi 2013.
22 Cf. further Willi 2012, 284–288.
23 For these traditions cf. Stesichorus fr. 86 F. Massimilla 1990b (and cf. 1995, 49–50) argues that it was Theseus' rape and, particularly, Stesichorus' introduction of the fact that Iphigenia was Helen's daughter by Theseus, that made the *Helen* stand in particular need of a palinode.
24 Griffiths 1979, 89–90. A helpful guide to 'ironic' readings is Stern 1978; cf. Hunter 1996, 164–165.

ἀλλά σ' ἐς Ἠλύσιον πεδίον καὶ πείρατα γαίης
ἀθάνατοι πέμψουσιν, ὅθι ξανθὸς Ῥαδάμανθυς,
τῆι περ ῥηΐστη βιοτὴ πέλει ἀνθρώποισιν·   565
οὐ νιφετός, οὔτ' ἄρ χειμὼν πολὺς οὔτε ποτ' ὄμβρος,
ἀλλ' αἰεὶ Ζεφύροιο λιγὺ πνείοντος ἀήτας
Ὠκεανὸς ἀνίησιν ἀναψύχειν ἀνθρώπους,
οὕνεκ' ἔχεις Ἑλένην καί σφιν γαμβρὸς Διός ἐσσι.

Hom. *Od.* 4.563–569

The immortals will send you to the Elysian plain and the ends of the world, where is fair Rhadamanthys and life is easiest for men; there is no snow, no great tempest, no rainstorm, but Ocean ever sends forth the breezes of the clear-blowing west wind to cool men. This they will do because you have Helen and are Zeus's son-in-law.

ὄλβιε γάμβρ', ἀγαθός τις ἐπέπταρεν ἐρχομένωι τοι
ἐς Σπάρταν ἅπερ ὧλλοι ἀριστέες, ὡς ἀνύσαιο·
μῶνος ἐν ἡμιθέοις Κρονίδαν Δία πενθερὸν ἑξεῖς.

Theocr. 18.16–18

Lucky bridegroom, some good man sneezed for your success when you came to Sparta with the other princes; you alone of the demigods shall have Zeus, son of Cronus, as father-in-law.

Odyssey 4.569 is a famously problematic verse[25], but if it does lie behind Theocritus 18.16–18, then we can see a way in which those verses need not in fact be 'ironic', or at least not straightforwardly so: we do not, then, *need* the Palinode version (or indeed Stesichorus at all) to make sense of them. I wonder, however, whether the *Odyssey* verse really is the model (or the only one) for line 18, attractive as it is to see Theocritus inverting the shape of the verse so that πενθερός replaces the Homeric γαμβρός, with γαμβρός being used immediately before in a different sense (line 16). Long before Theocritus, Isocrates, who followed the traditional version of Helen's abduction, notes that 'although Zeus fathered very many ἡμίθεοι, of [Helen] alone he consented to be called father' (*Helen* 16); he is there making the same point as does Theocritus in line 18, and he helps to explain what some commentators have felt as an awkwardness in that verse. Does Stesichorus, who would in turn be picking up the Homeric verses, lie behind Isocrates? So, too, in what is, in the present context, a suggestive passage (*Helen* 62–64), Isocrates notes Menelaus' divine reward:

After this, [Helen] so rewarded Menelaus for his labours and risks on her behalf that, when the whole race of the Pelopidai had been destroyed and fallen into irremediable dis-

---

25 Cf. S. West *ap.* Heubeck et al. 1988, *ad loc.*

aster, not only did she release him from these catastrophes but she even made him a god rather than a mortal and established him in her house (σύνοικον) and as her partner (πάρεδρον) for all time. As witness for these things, I can provide the city of the Spartans which more than any other preserves ancient traditions: even to the present day there are at Therapnai in Laconia holy and traditional sacrifices to them both, not as heroes but as gods. And she also displayed her power to the poet Stesichorus. When, as he was beginning his song, he made a blasphemous remark about her, he stood up deprived of his sight, but when he realised the cause of the disaster and composed the so-called 'palinode', she restored him to his ordinary condition.

Menelaus' blessedness, Spartan preservations of ancient traditions and cult for Helen, and Stesichorus' *Palinode*, all following on praise of Helen's more than mortal beauty (61 and *passim*) — the Isocratean nest of themes recalls nothing so much, I think, as Theocritus 18, and must make us at least wonder whether both go back to Stesichorus. At the very least, it seems hard to believe that, as has often been suggested, Isocrates' knowledge of Stesichorus' poem was limited to having read Plato's *Phaedrus*.[26] However that may be, *Idyll* 18, which would certainly fit the description ἐγκώμιον Ἑλένης which the *Suda* gives to the *Palinode*, emerges as a remarkable experiment in the use of the literary and mythological heritage in general.

Speculation does not have to end there, because there is yet another 'Encomium of Helen' which must be brought into the picture. It is a curious fact that, although Gorgias came from Leontini, and may therefore be thought to have a particular reason for interest in Stesichorus and, in turn, may have been of special interest to Theocritus of Syracuse, the three are only very rarely brought into connection with each other by modern scholars. Gorgias can hardly not have known the *Helen/Palinode*, and the plot thickens if we take into account the well-known links between his 'Encomium' and Helen's speech of self-defence in Euripides' *Trojan Women*, given that very shortly afterwards Euripides was to dramatise the *Palinode* version in his *Helen*. If it is unsurprising that Gorgias' 'Encomium' and Theocritus 18 share certain motifs, there is at least one

---

26 So rightly, e.g., Sider 1989, 427. Incidentally, by mentioning the *Palinode* Isocrates evokes a version of the Helen story which would be in part ruinous to his own praise of Helen; it is presumably for this reason that he does not tell us explicitly what happened in the *Palinode*, but this is a good case of how one version of Helen's story can be invoked actually to reinforce the other. Is Theocritus 18 another such case? Whatever the relationship of Stesichorus' *Helen* and the *Palinode*, in this poem or poems the two versions did indeed co-exist.

shared pattern which attracts attention.[27] The opening sentence of Gorgias' 'Encomium' runs as follows:

κόσμος πόλει μὲν εὐανδρία, σώματι δὲ κάλλος, ψυχῆι δὲ σοφία, πράγματι δὲ ἀρετή, λόγωι δὲ ἀλήθεια· τὰ δὲ ἐναντία τούτων ἀκοσμία.

Gorg. Hel. 1

The ornament/proper order of a city is excellent men, of a body beauty, of a soul wisdom, of an action virtue, of words truth; the opposite of these is disorder.

There is a particular sting in the tail of the sentence here. The most natural association between κόσμος and λόγος is in the realm of verbal 'ornamentation': Aristotle uses κόσμος in this sense (e.g., *Rhet.* 3.1408a14), and we may recall, in particular, the distinction which the Platonic Socrates draws at the head of the *Apology* between ἀλήθεια and κόσμος in language (17b); at the head of the *Helen*, however, Gorgias (of all people) claims that ἀλήθεια is the κόσμος of λόγος. We do not, therefore, have to look beyond Gorgias himself to find any motivation for the opening, but, if we imagined for one moment coming to Gorgias' 'Encomium' with Stesichorus' *Palinode* fresh in our minds, it would be very hard (I think) not to see κόσμος ... λόγωι δὲ ἀλήθεια as an allusion to the most famous verses of Stesichorus' poem, οὐκ ἔστ' ἔτυμος λόγος οὗτος κτλ. (fr. 91a F.), unless Wright is correct in his suggestion that Plato in fact wrote those verses.[28] The real paradox and challenge of Gorgias' 'Encomium' is in fact that it accepts the traditional story of Helen and Paris and turns that to encomium and, as Isocrates pointed out, defence of her: no need for Stesichorean innovations, then, the (simple?) 'truth' will suffice. It is Stesichorus, as much as anyone, who is both evoked by and the target of κόσμος... λόγωι δὲ ἀλήθεια. When at the end of the prologue Gorgias says that he will set out the reasons why 'it was *eikos* that Helen set off for Troy' (τὰς αἰτίας, δι' ἃς εἰκὸς ἦν γενέσθαι τὸν τῆς Ἑλένης εἰς τὴν Τροίαν στόλον, ch. 5), this is normally — and rightly — taken to refer to the reasons, which Gorgias is about to expound, why Helen might well have gone;[29] are we, however, also to hear 'the reasons why it is *eikos* that Helen's departure

---

27 Also worthy of note is line 37 of Theocritus' poem, ὡς Ἑλένα, τᾶς πάντες ἐπ' ὄμμασιν ἵμεροι ἐντί, alongside Gorgias *Helen* 4 πλείστας δὲ πλείστοις ἐπιθυμίας ἔρωτος ἐνειργάσατο. I wonder if there is a Stesichorean common model here?

28 Wright 2005, 105; Wright's whole discussion of what little we can positively say about Stesichorus' poem(s) should be consulted (pp. 87–110), and cf. also Kelly 2007c.

29 Cf. MacDowell's translation, 'the causes which made it reasonable for Helen's departure to Troy to occur' (MacDowell 1982, 23); Buchheim's 'die Gründe ... durch die es wahrscheinlich zu Helenas Fahrt nach Troia kam' (1989, 7) is at least ambiguous.

for Troy happened', and again we will then sense Gorgias evoking and contradicting his Sicilian forerunner? If elsewhere Gorgias does seem (pointedly?) to ignore Stesichorus (cf. 2 ὁμόφωνος καὶ ὁμόψυχος of traditions about Helen), then this will not be the most provocative of his claims.³⁰

If we return to Gorgias' opening sentence and move forwards rather than back, it is at least remarkable that Theocritus 18 also has an example of this κόσμος-priamel:

πιείραι μεγάλα ἅτ' ἀνέδραμε κόσμος ἀρούραι
ἢ κάπωι κυπάρισσος, ἢ ἅρματι Θεσσαλὸς ἵππος,
ὧδε καὶ ἁ ῥοδόχρως Ἑλένα Λακεδαίμονι κόσμος.

Theocr. 18.29–31³¹

As a tall cypress rises as an ornament to a rich field or a garden, as a Thessalian horse adorns a chariot, so too is rosy-skinned Helen an ornament to Lacedaemon.

It might be argued (with some justification) that κόσμος bears a rather different nuance in Gorgias and Theocritus,³² but that is hardly going to explain away the coincidence (if that is what it is), and it is obviously tempting, and the temptation has not been resisted, to see both Gorgias and Theocritus as here going back to Stesichorus.³³ The Theocritean passage comes in a passage of praise for Helen which has reminded many modern readers of both Alcman's *partheneia* and Sappho, and we ought at least to entertain the possibility that the κόσμος-priamel (or something like it) goes back to Stesichorus; if so, Gorgias' opening will be a very pointed look indeed at the poet of Himera.

Probably the most familiar fact about the style of *Idyll* 18 is the richness of its Sapphic colour, in both specific allusion and overall texture,³⁴ a texture so

---

30 For a different reading of this claim, and one that gives full weight to Stesichorus' presence in Gorgias, cf. Porter 1993, 277–280.
31 The text of line 29 is uncertain (cf. Gow 1952, *ad loc.*), but that uncertainty is not crucial to the point being made here.
32 Cf. the notes of MacDowell 1982 and Buchheim 1989 on Gorgias *ad loc.*, with the reservations of Wardy 1996, 29–30, 156 n. 8. Halliwell 2011, 267 with n. 4 also rightly insists on giving κόσμος its full weight in Gorgias, but the paradox that Gorgias' claim poses, through the evocation of the sense of 'adornment', cannot be ignored; the very double sense of κόσμος already introduces the game with truth which Gorgias is to play. It does not, I hope, need to be spelled out that I offer here nothing like a 'complete' account even of the couple of sentences of Gorgias' *Helen* with which I am concerned.
33 Cf. Luccioni 1997. With regard to Gorgias, however, Luccioni merely considers the priamel form, not the relationship between both writers' claims of 'truth'.
34 Cf. Gow 1952, II 348–349, Dagnini 1986, Hunter 1996, 151–152, Acosta-Hughes 2010, 29–38.

rich that we might perhaps compare the way in which Theocritus himself is used in Virgil's *Eclogues*. Sappho was not just the poet of wedding-songs, but was also a poet who seems to have taken — at least in some poems — a sympathetic view of Helen (frr. 16, 23 Voigt), particularly when set against the much harsher view on show in certain poems of her Lesbian colleague Alcaeus (frr. 42, 283), to whom I shall return. Secondly, the evocation throughout *Idyll* 18 of the world of Alcman and archaic Spartan maiden-song is also (rightly) a critical commonplace;[35] Helen did indeed have a cult at Sparta, and no Greek city took her as seriously (cf. the songs of Euripides' *Helen*, Aristophanes' *Lysistrata*, etc.). It is normally assumed that Stesichorus' *Helen/Palinode* had a context either in Sparta itself or in a pro-Spartan colony in the west, such as Tarentum,[36] and if so, Stesichorus himself might have made much, as does Theocritus, of the Spartan setting and of Spartan cult, might even — who knows? — have echoed or evoked Alcman's poetry, while doing so; ancient tradition made Stesichorus later than Alcman and a contemporary of Alcaeus (cf. *Suda* c 1095 = Stes. Ta10 Ercoles). Theocritus' re-creation of the world of Alcman might in fact turn out to be part of the poem's imaginative debt to Stesichorus.[37] Trying to identify such evocative references across three poets is not easy, or perhaps even sensible, but for what it is worth I have to confess that Aristophanes' *Lysistrata* 1303–10 have often made me wonder about the beating feet of lines 7–8 of Theocritus' poem.

The metrical form itself of *Idyll* 18 may be over-determined. We might think first of Theocritus' habitual metre and of Sappho's dactylic wedding-songs. As for Stesichorus, two kinds of information are relevant. One is that the metre of both fr. 88 F. of the *Helen* (the 'wedding fragment') and fr. 91a from the *Palinode* are predominantly dactylic, just as is true for Stesichorus' poetry generally.[38] Secondly, in an extract from Heraclides Ponticus discussing early lyric (fr. 157 Wehrli = Stes. Tb22 Ercoles), 'Stesichorus and the old lyric poets' are said to have 'composed verses (ἔπη) and clothed them in songs (μέλη περιετίθεσαν)'. It is reasonable to believe, particularly given the full context in Heraclides, that he

---

35 To Hunter 1996, 152–155 add now Calame 2012, 256–257.
36 One of the rare dissenting voices is Bowie 1993, 25–26, and see also now Hutchinson 2001, 114 n. 1, Morgan 2012, 45–46, Finglass 2012c, 43–4; 2014a, 27–29.
37 Wilamowitz 1900, 92 saw the Theocritean choir's representation of Helen as a chorus-leader, 'ganz wie Hagesichora bei Alkman', as probably indebted to Stesichorus. Relevant here may be Ibyc. fr. S166 *PMGF* which Martin West has argued is in fact Stesichorean, even just possibly the *Helen*; cf. West 1969, 142–149 = (2011–13) II 98–105 (with supplementary note on p. 106), and West 2015.
38 Cf. the surveys in West 1982, 48–51, Haslam 1974; 1978, Finglass 2014a, 47–52.

was thinking of dactylic verse, if not actually hexameters.[39] Theocritus will have known such lore, and other views like it, such as the report in Athenaeus that, in his work *On Stesichorus*, Chamaeleon (late fourth–early third century BC) reported that 'not only the works of Homer, but also those of Hesiod and Archilochus and Mimnermus and Phocylides were set to music'.[40] When Theocritus leaves us in no doubt (lines 7–8) of the musical nature of the song of the Spartan choir, we should perhaps see a specific piece of musical archaeology written into the poem, particularly as those verses seem to evoke the dancing and singing of the Muses of the proem of Hesiod's (hexameter) *Theogony* (lines 3–4, 7–8, 70). It is tempting also to see some of the stylistic effects of the poem as seeking to recreate the effects of song, whether or not my earlier argument for some kind of imitative strophic structure is accepted;[41] I think particularly of the remarkable patterning (and epithets) of lines 43–6, of which more in a moment, but not just of those verses. What are we to say, for example, of lines 50–53, verses which Gow found 'singularly frigid'?[42]

Λατὼ μὲν δοίη, Λατὼ κουροτρόφος, ὕμμιν
εὐτεκνίαν, Κύπρις δέ, θεὰ Κύπρις, ἶσον ἔρασθαι
ἀλλάλων, Ζεὺς δέ, Κρονίδας Ζεύς, ἄφθιτον ὄλβον,
ὡς ἐξ εὐπατριδᾶν εἰς εὐπατρίδας πάλιν ἔνθηι.

May Leto grant you, Leto nurse of children, good offspring, and may Cypris, divine Cypris, grant you to love each other equally, and may Zeus, Zeus son of Cronus, grant you prosperity unbounded, so that it may pass again from nobles to nobles.

It seems clear enough that these verses seek to capture an effect of lyric κάλλος: ancient stylistic theory noted various forms of repetition as productive of beauty in poetry (cf. Hermogenes pp. 302.9–303.5 Rabe, Demetrius, *On Style* 140–141, taking examples from Sappho), and this is the effect which Theocritus' mimetic technique is here seeking.

---

[39] Cf. West 1971, 307–309 = 2011–2013, II 86–90; on this testimonium cf. also D'Alfonso 1994a, 64–71.
[40] Cham. fr. 27 Giordano = Tb21 Ercoles. Whatever the exact nuance of μελωιδηθῆναι, Olson's translation in the Loeb 'were recited' (2006–2012, VII 135) looks misleading; in the older Loeb, Gulick 1927–1941, VI 341 tried 'were chanted'. Ercoles's 'messi in musica' (Ercoles 2013, 205, with discussion on pp. 552–524) seems much closer to the mark.
[41] Cf. Hunter 1996, 155–157.
[42] Gow 1952, on Theocr. 18.50ff.

Of particular interest here are lines 38–48, the aetiology of the Spartan tree-cult for Helen.⁴³ Despite the silence of the commentators, line 45 is a very Theocritean reworking of a Homeric verse which occurs twice in the Nausicaa episode of the Odyssey:

πρᾶται δ' ἀργυρέας ἐξ ὄλπιδος ὑγρὸν ἄλειφαρ
λαζύμεναι σταξεῦμες ὑπὸ σκιερὰν πλατάνιστον.

Theocr. 18.45–46

We shall be the first to take running unguent from a silver flask and let it drip beneath the shady plane-tree.

δῶκεν δὲ χρυσέηι ἐν ληκύθωι ὑγρὸν ἔλαιον

Hom. Od. 6.79 (= 215)

She gave her running oil in a golden bottle

The mannered stylistic reworking, with variation of every word, including the preposition, except ὑγρόν, which is preserved to call attention to the reworking, would in another context itself be of great interest, but I want to concentrate here on what the memory of *Odyssey* 6 does in the poem. Our thoughts might already have turned to Nausicaa in lines 28–29, which seem somehow reminiscent of the famous comparison of Nausicaa with her playmates to Artemis with hers (*Od.* 6.102–109), and Homer had already compared Helen too to Artemis, in the context of her marriage to Menelaus (4.121–122). In Theocritus, however, the echo assimilates the Spartan girls' trip to the Dromos and 'the meadows' to the trip of Nausicaa and her attendants to the seashore, and thus fashions that trip as a pre-nuptial washing ritual, as indeed in some sense it was, given its Homeric motivation; in the context of Theocritus 18, we note, not just the oil of line 45, but also the stress on Nausicaa's suitors (*Od.* 6.34–35, with the same word ἀριστῆες as Theocritus uses, line 17 ἀριστέες) and on the dawn hour at which the expedition takes place.⁴⁴ Theocritus thus finds his Homeric model in Nausicaa's expedition, and this also strongly suggests, as for example Calame argued along quite other lines,⁴⁵ that the rite in Helen's honour which the Spartan girls foreshadow was conceived of as a pre-nuptial rite for Spartan παρθένοι, whatever the nature of Helen's cult at Sparta 'actually' was historically. So Theocritus'

---

43 Cf. Wide 1893, 342–346, Brillante 2003, West 1975 = 2011–2013, I 80–96.
44 Hom. *Od.* 6.31, 36, Theocr. 18.39; for ἦρι cf. Hunter 1996, 160 n. 83.
45 Calame 1977, I 333–350 = 2001, 191–202; I reached this conclusion at Hunter 1996, 161, but had missed Theocritus' evocation of Nausicaa.

Helen is in some sense a Nausicaa.⁴⁶ Did Theocritus have a forerunner in Stesichorus here? We cannot say,⁴⁷ but the possibility that we have found Stesichorus Ὁμηρικώτατος lurking in a rather unexpected place has a certain attraction.

If we take seriously the possibility that *Idyll* 18 makes evocative use of Stesichorus' *Helen*, then the rich Sapphic and Alcmanic texture is yet one more way in which the poet covers his tracks, but it is not just that. I started from an unusual ancient testimonium which stresses the ἡδονή of Stesichorus' poetry, a quality which precisely draws him towards his fellow lyric poets. It is also important that, in describing the *Palinode*, the Platonic Socrates notes that Stesichorus recognised the cause of his blindness, unlike Homer (who died blind),⁴⁸ and Socrates suggests that he did this because he was μουσικός (unlike Homer, presumably). How hard we wish to push this passage may be disputed: at one level, Stesichorus is given this laudatory label because Socrates too, *qua* φιλόσοφος, is μουσικός, and Stesichorus is thus adopted into the Socratic project,⁴⁹ but there is probably also a more local resonance. Is Socrates distinguishing epic from musically accompanied lyric to the advantage of the latter, as the myth of the cicadas is going to praise singing (*Phaedr.* 259b6–d7)? Given, moreover, that the close association of Homer and Stesichorus, which is the principal thrust of the ancient critical tradition about the poet of Himera, goes back (for us) at least to Simonides (cf. fr. 273 Poltera), then Plato's separation of the two is perhaps not merely another recognition of that tradition, but (again) gave the impulse to a rather different strand of Stesichorean reception, the faint traces of which I have been following.

Let me finish by returning to the question of the control of myth. In Alcaeus fr. 42 Voigt there is a pointed contrast between Helen, who brought ruin on Troy and the Trojans, and Thetis, as model a bride as is the Helen of *Idyll* 18; this

---

46 Various modern interpretations of Alcman's Louvre *partheneion* come to mind here – and Nausicaa and her colleagues offer a heroic model for maiden-song (μολπή, 6.101). Cf. Calame 1977, I 90–92 = 2001, 42–43.
47 Cf. Kaibel 1892, 258–259.
48 Despite the report of the unknown author of P.Oxy. 2506 (= Stes. fr. 90.1–4 F.) that Stesichorus 'blames' (μέμφεται) Homer for having Helen rather than her phantom go to Troy, it would be dangerous to assume a strongly anti-Homeric *Tendenz* in Stesichorus' *Palinode*, as for example does Graziosi 2002, 147–150, 215–216 (and cf. Beecroft 2006); the contrast between Homer and Stesichorus may be Plato's as much as Stesichorus' (it is absent, for example, from Isocrates' very similar notice, *Helen* 64), and it is at least an overstatement to claim that 'Plato... reads the [Palinode] as a polemic against Homer' (Graziosi 2002, 147).
49 Cf. D'Alfonso 1994b.

remains true even if ἐκ σέθεν in line 3 of that poem refers to Paris, rather than Helen.[50] Scholars have naturally worried about whether in Alcaeus fr. 42 we are to remember the future which awaited Peleus and Thetis (there is a similar debate about Catullus 64). In a helpful look at the problem, Davies noted that the principle, enunciated by Fraenkel (though only, I would stress, for the interpretation of Aeschylus), that "'the poet does not want us to take into account any feature of a tradition which he does not mention" has been applied far too widely in the past, but it does seem particularly at home in the context of paradigmatic myth. And paradigmatic myth is also very receptive to the careful reworking and revision of traditional versions.'[51] Davies's observation has an immediate relevance to how Hellenistic poets revised traditional representations, particularly that of Helen and particularly in the context of the Ptolemaic court, but it is the allusive nature of much of this poetry which makes the issue particularly pressing. How, in fact, should we understand 'mention' in Fraenkel's pronouncement? To take a very simple example, commentators assume (surely rightly) that line 20 of Theocritus' poem, οἵα Ἀχαιιάδων γαῖαν πατεῖ οὐδεμί' ἄλλα, is modelled on *Odyssey* 21.107, οἵη νῦν οὐκ ἔστι γυνὴ κατ' Ἀχαιίδα γαῖαν (Telemachus about his mother). This Helen is, then, a Penelope, with all the possible layering that such an identification brings. We would love to be able to say what 'evocation' (however explicit, or not) of Stesichorus' *Helen* (and the *Palinode*(s)?) does for (or to) our reading of *Idyll* 18, but the evidence on which we can base ourselves with confidence is simply not there. On the other hand, we can be confident that Stesichorus was important for this poem and how it is to be read, and that is some comfort at least.

Bibliography

Acosta-Hughes, B. 2010. *Arion's Lyre. Archaic Lyric into Hellenistic Poetry*, Princeton/Oxford.
Bernsdorff, H. 2014. 'Notes on P. Mch.inv. 3498 + 3250b recto, 3250a and 3250c recto (list of lyric and tragic incipits)', *APF* 60, 3–11.

---

50 For the arguments and bibliography, cf. Pallantza 2005, 22–34. Page 1955, 280–281 raised the possibility that Alcaeus fr. 42 Voigt may have been influenced by Stesichorus' harsh treatment of Helen, or whatever the Platonic Socrates means by Ἑλένης κακηγορία. There is no other evidence we may bring to bear on the question, but the initial ὡς λόγος of fr. 42 might just have something to do with the Stesichorean οὐκ ἔστ' ἔτυμος λόγος, though – if so – this might be thought to argue for Alcaean priority. Ἑ]λένην ποτὲ λόγος is found as the *incipit* of a lyric poem on P.Mich. 3250c; cf. Bernsdorff 2014, 6–7.
51 Davies 1986, 258, citing Fraenkel 1950, II 97.

Bowie, E.L. 1993. 'Lies, fiction and slander in early Greek poetry', in: C. Gill/T.P. Wiseman (eds.), *Lies and Fiction in the Ancient World*, Exeter, 1–37.
Bowie, E.L. 2015. 'Stesichorus at Athens', in: P. Finglass/A. Kelly (eds.), *Stesichorus in Context*, Cambridge, 111–124.
Brillante, C. 2003. 'Sull'idillio XVIII di Teocrito', in: F. Benedetti/S. Grandolini (eds.), *Studi di filologia e tradizione greca in memoria di Aristide Colonna*, 2 vols., Naples, 179–192.
Buchheim, T. 1989. *Gorgias von Leontinoi. Reden, Fragmente und Testimonien*, Philosophische Bibliothek 404, Hamburg.
Calame, C. 1977. *Les choeurs de jeunes filles en Grèce archaique*, 2 vols., Rome.
Calame, C. 2012. 'Les figures d'Hélène et de Ménélas dans le poème XVIII de Théocrite: entre fiction poétique, pratique rituelle et éloge du pouvoir royal', in: C. Cusset/N. Le Meur-Weissman/F. Levin (eds.), *Mythe et pouvoir à l'époque Hellénistique*, Hellenistica Groningana 18, Leuven/Paris/Walpole, 253–271.
Cingano, E. 1990. 'L'opera di Ibico e di Stesicoro nella classificazione degli antichi e dei moderni', *Annali dell'Istituto Universitario Orientale di Napoli Sezione Filologico-Letteraria* 12, 189–224.
Curtis, P. 2011. *Stesichoros's Geryoneis*, Mnem. Suppl. 333, Leiden/Boston.
D'Alfonso, F. 1994. *Stesicoro e la Performance. Studio sulle modalità esecutive dei carmi stesicorei*, Filologia e Critica 74, Rome.
Dagnini, I. 1986. 'Elementi saffici e motivi tradizionali in Teocrito, Idillio xviii', *QUCC* ns 24, 39–46.
Davies, M. 1986. 'Alcaeus, Thetis and Helen', *Hermes* 114, 257–262.
Ercoles, M. 2013. *Stesicoro. Le testimonianze antiche*, Eikasmos Studi 24, Bologna.
Finglass, P.J. 2012. 'Ethnic identity in Stesichorus', *ZPE* 182, 39–44.
Finglass, P.J. 2014. 'Introduction', in: M. Davies/P.J. Finglass (eds.), *Stesichorus. The Poems*, Cambridge Classical Texts and Commentaries 54, Cambridge, 1–91.
Fraenkel, E. 1950. *Aeschylus. Agamemnon*, 3 vols., Oxford.
Gow, A.S.F. 1952. *Theocritus*, 2 vols., Cambridge.
Graziosi, B. 2002. *Inventing Homer. The Early Reception of Epic*, Cambridge.
Griffiths, F.T. 1979. *Theocritus at Court*, Mnem. Suppl. 55, Leiden.
Halliwell, S. 2011. *Between Ecstasy and Truth. Interpretations of Greek Poetics from Homer to Longinus*, Oxford.
Haslam, M. 1974. 'Stesichorean metre', *QUCC* 17, 7–57.
Haslam, M. 1978. 'The versification of the new Stesichorus (P.Lille 76abc)', *GRBS* 19, 29–57.
Heubeck, A./West, S.R./Hainsworth, J.B. 1988. *A Commentary on Homer's Odyssey. Volume I. Introduction and Books I–VIII*, Oxford.
Hordern, J.H. 2004. *Sophron's Mimes*, Oxford.
Hunter, R. 1996. *Theocritus and the Archaeology of Greek Poetry*, Cambridge.
Hunter, R. 1999. *Theocritus. A Selection. Idylls 1, 3, 4, 6, 7, 10, 11 and 13*, Cambridge.
Hunter, R. 2012. *Plato and the Traditions of Ancient Literature. The Silent Stream*, Cambridge.
Kaibel, G. 1892. 'Theokrits ΕΛΕΝΗΣ ΕΠΙΘΑΛΑΜΙΟΝ', *Hermes* 27, 249–259.
Kelly, E. 2007. 'Stesikhoros and Helen', *MH* 64, 1–21.
Lerza, P. 1982. *Stesicoro*, Genoa.
Luccioni, P. 1997. 'Un éloge d'Hélène? (Théocrite, Id. XVIII, V. 29-31, Gorgias et Stésichore)', *RÉG* 110, 622–626.
MacDowell, D.M. 1982. *Gorgias. Encomium of Helen*, Bristol.
Massimilla, G. 1990. 'Un sogno di Giocasta in Stesicoro?', *PdelP* 45, 191–199.

Massimilla, G. 1995. 'L'influsso di Stesicoro sulla poesia ellenistica', in: L. Dubois (ed.), *Poésie et lyrique antiques. Actes du colloque organisé par Claude Meillier à l'Université Charles-de-Gaulle – Lille III du 2 au 4 Juin 1993*, Villeneuve d'Ascq, 41–54.
Morgan, K.A. 2012. 'A prolegomenon to performance in the West', in: K. Bosher (ed.), *Theater outside Athens. Drama in Greek Sicily and South Italy*, Cambridge, 35–55.
Nelson, M. 2000. 'The lesser mysteries in Plato's Phaedrus', *Echos du Monde Classique/Classical Views* NS 19, 25–43.
Ornaghi, M. 2013, 'Stesicoro, Teocrito, Epicarmo e i padri della poesia bucolica', *SIFC* 4th ser. 11, 42–81.
Page, D.L. 1955. *Sappho and Alcaeus. An Introduction to the Study of Ancient Lesbian Poetry*, Oxford.
Pallantza, E. 2005. *Der Troische Krieg in der nachhomerischen Literatur bis zum 5. Jahrhundert v. Chr.*, Hermes Einzelschrift 94, Stuttgart.
Porter, J.I. 1993. 'The seductions of Gorgias', *CA* 12, 267–299.
Rutherford, I. 2015. 'Stesichorus the romantic', in: P. Finglass/A. Kelly (eds.), *Stesichorus in Context*, Cambridge, 98–108.
Sider, D. 1989. 'The blinding of Stesichorus', *Hermes* 117, 423–431.
Stern, J. 1978. 'Theocritus' Epithalamium for Helen', *Revue belge de philologie et d'histoire* 56, 29–37.
Wardy, R. 1996. *The Birth of Rhetoric. Gorgias, Plato and Their Successors*, London/New York.
Wendel, C. 1920. *Überlieferung und Entstehung der Theokrit-Scholien*, Berlin.
West, M.L. 1969. 'Stesichorus redivivus', *ZPE* 4, 135–49.
West, M.L. 1971. 'Stesichorus', *CQ* NS 21, 302–14.
West, M.L. 1975. *Immortal Helen*, London.
West, M.L. 1982. *Greek Metre*, Oxford.
West, M.L. 2015. 'Epic, lyric, and lyric epic', in: P. Finglass/A. Kelly (eds.), *Stesichorus in Context*, Cambridge, 63–80.
Wide, S. 1893. *Lakonische Kulte*, Leipzig.
Wilamowitz, U. von, 1900. *Die Textgeschichte der griechischen Lyriker*, Abhandlungen der Königlichen Gesellschaft der Wissenschaften zu Göttingen, *philologisch-historische Klasse* NF Bd. 4 Nr. 3, Berlin.
Wilamowitz, U. von 1913. *Sappho und Simonides. Untersuchungen über griechische Lyriker*, Berlin.
Willi, A. 2008. *Sikelismos. Sprache, Literatur und Gesellschaft im griechischen Sizilien (8.–5. Jh. v. Chr.)*, Bibliotheca Helvetica Romana 29, Basel.
Willi, A. 2012. '"We speak Peloponnesian": tradition and linguistic identity in post-classical Sicilian literature', in: O. Tribulato (ed.), *Language and Linguistic Contact in Ancient Sicily*, Cambridge, 265–288.
Wright, M.E. 2005. *Euripides' Escape-Tragedies. A Study of Helen, Andromeda, and Iphigenia among the Taurians*, Oxford.

12 A Philosophical Death?

The history of Greek poetic style has never properly been written, but when that does happen, epigram will have an honoured place, because our very large corpus of inscribed poems allows us to ask questions about what might be important and/or distinctive about the style and diction of so-called 'literary' epigrams.[1] With epigram we are able to take a view of the history of a poetic form (or perhaps 'forms') which is both synoptic, embracing the earliest inscribed examples, and also properly respectful of diachronic change over time; for no other poetic genre is the comparative material nearly so rich. The current paper has, however, a very modest aim. I wish merely to draw attention to certain features of two closely related funerary epigrams which, as all such poems do, both reflect the general issues which confront us in dealing with this rich textual resource and also raise very specific issues of interpretation and context. These small poems demand that we do not lose sight of the bigger picture.

SGO 01/20/25 from Miletos falls into three parts:[2]

Ἀντήνωρ Εὐανδρίδου
Ἀντιφάνης Μοσχίωνος
Χίονις Χιόνιδος

τὸν Ἑστιαίου τῆς τραγωιδίας γραφῆ
Εὐανδρίδαν κέκρυφ' ὁ τυμβίτας πέτρος
ζήσαντα πρὸς πάντ' εὐσεβῶς ἀνὰ πτόλιν
ἔτων ἀριθμὸν ὀγδοήκοντ' ἀρτίων
                                                    5

οὐχὶ κεναῖς δόξαις ἐζηκότα τόνδε δέδεκται
    τύμβος ὅδ' ἐκ προγόνων, ταῖς δ' ἀπὸ τᾶς σοφίας
ταῖς ἀπὸ Σωκράτεω πινυταῖς μάλα τοῦ τε Πλάτωνος
    κοὐκ Ἐπικουρήοις ἡδονικαῖς ἀθέοις

An earlier version of this brief paper formed part of the 'opening remarks' at the Thessaloniki conference. I am grateful to David Sedley and James Warren for their advice on certain points.

---

[1] Hunter 2010 pursues some related questions but from a rather different perspective than the present paper; I return to the question of the style of 'literary' and 'non-literary' epigrams in Hunter 2019.

[2] I have, as conventionally, indented the pentameters; all three parts of the inscription are in fact aligned to the left. The *editio princeps* of the inscription is Rayet 1874, 113–114 and before *SGO* it is printed as *GVI* 2018 and Peek 1960, 280–283.

Ἑστιαῖον τὸν φύντα πατρὸς κλεινοῖο Μενάνδ[ρου?]
ἐσθλοτάταν βιοτᾶς ἐξανύσαντος ὁδόν.
κούφη γαῖα χυθεῖσ' ὁσίως κρύπτοις σὺ τὸν ἄν[δρα?]
βαίνοντ' εὐσε[βέ]ων τοὺς ἱεροὺς θαλάμου[ς.]

Antenor son of Euandrides
Antiphanes son of Moschion
Chionis son of Chionis

This funerary stone conceals Euandrides, son of Hestiaios, the writer of tragedy, who lived in the city piously in every way, for the full count of eighty years.

This tomb, established by his ancestors, received a man who lived not by empty doctrines, but by very intelligent ones derived from the wisdom of Socrates and Plato, not by Epicurean, hedonist, godless ones, Hestiaios, offspring of a glorious father Menander who brought to completion a most excellent course of life. Earth scattered piously may you lightly conceal the man as he passes to the holy chambers of the blessed.

After the names of three family members, perhaps the earliest deaths to be commemorated on the stone, there follow an epitaph in (appropriately enough) iambic trimeters for Euandridas, a 'writer of tragedy', and an elegiac epitaph for Hestiaios, apparently a man with philosophical pretensions. The trimeters are most plausibly dated to the middle of the second century BC, whereas the script of the elegiacs shows them, in the judgement of the experts, to be notably later than the trimeters, and thus probably first century BC; the elegiacs have been fitted in to the space available, using smaller letters than those of the trimeters. Both position on the stone and letter-size suggest that we, the 'passers-by', are very likely to read the trimeters before the elegiacs, and the poet of the elegiacs seems to refer to the position of the poem through τύμβος ὅδ' ἐκ προγόνων in v. 6 (2), which picks up the two inscribed texts 'above' it; one poem 'follows' the other, both in its message and in physical position, just as pious living (εὐσέβεια) runs through the generations.³ Whether allusivity and intertextuality function differently when we can see the poems physically juxtaposed in front of us, whether on a stone or in a book of poems, is a question to which students of epigrams need to pay close attention.

Questions of linguistic level and register are probably nowhere as difficult as in the field of epigram, and inscribed poems often also demand that we make choices about 'correctness' in language, that feature which, together with met-

---

3 The criticism of the 'atheistic' views of the Epicureans in v. 8 can be very amply paralleled from antiquity; it is indeed a reasonable conclusion from *Letter to Menoeceus* 123–124 that Epicurus was the object of such criticisms in his own lifetime.

rical practice, is often responsible for the label 'sub-literary'.[4] In the present case, for example, we need to decide what, if any, conclusions are to be drawn about the poet of the iambics from the irregular long second syllable of κέκρυφ' in v. 2; is this the kind of *ad hoc* expedient which characterizes a 'non-literary' poet, or — perhaps rather — is the avoidance of such *ad hoc* linguistic expedients one of the features by which 'literary poets' marked themselves off.[5] One area where both 'literary' and inscribed epigram present very knotty problems is dialect; it is well known that in many cases we must honestly admit ignorance that we do not know why an epigram, or some words within it, are given a particular dialectal colouring.[6] The current poems are not untypical in this feature also. The accusative γραφῆ in v. 1 may simply be a current *koine* form, rather than a choice poeticism (even for a tragic poet) or perhaps even a Doricism, as the grammatical tradition would have it,[7] but what are we to make of ὁ τυμβίτας πέτρος? The adjective is found in only one other place in the texts known to *TLG*, namely in an epitaph for a grasshopper by Leonidas (*AP* 7.198.2 = *HE* 2085), where we have the expression λᾶας ὁ τυμβίτης, with the expected Ionic ending. In Leonidas, we might suspect a choice poeticism in keeping both with the paradoxical idea of a stone memorial for a grasshopper or cricket and with the (humorously) high style of the remainder of the poem, but what about the inscription? Was perhaps the adjective more common than our texts suggest, or is it here marked as a choice word in a style appropriate to a tragic poet? Is it, moreover, relevant that -ίτης and related forms were productive suffixes for the naming of kinds of stones and gems (e. g. αἱματίτης, πυρίτης etc).[8] Why, moreover, the Doric long alpha ending? I have already noted the familiar problem of dialect mixture within epigram, and here we might wonder whether this is another touch of 'the other' to gesture, however inappropriately within iambics, towards the diction of a tragic poet, or a homage to the dead Euandridas, whose name also appears in the Doric form which the honorand himself presumably used, or simply one of those inexplicable (to us) dialect shifts with which our corpus of epigrams is littered, and which may perhaps also be illustrated by ἐσθλοτάταν βιοτᾶς in v. 6 of the elegiac poem; whether this should make us

---

4 It is a pity that Rayet did not explain what he meant by calling the language of these poems 'aussi incorrecte' and their sense 'aussi obscur' (Rayet 1874, 114).
5 For such self-fashioning in metrical terms cf. Hunter 2019, with the bibliography cited there.
6 On this subject cf., e.g., Sens 2004 and the contribution (and bibliography) of Dowie 2016.
7 Cf. K-B I 449, 451; cf. further below.
8 Cf. Buck-Petersen 1944, 545.

reconsider the implications of γραφῇ in v. 1 is a further question which must be left open.

Issues of register of a different kind are raised by ἡδονικαῖς in v. 8 (4 of the elegiacs). The adjective can (particularly in later and Byzantine texts) just mean 'given to/addicted to pleasure' or 'causing pleasure', but next to 'Epicurean' it can hardly fail to evoke a 'technical' usage to refer, first, to Aristippus and the Cyrenean 'hedonist' school and, secondly, to the Epicureans themselves, as it standardly does in the late commentators. We should translate it here as something like 'hedonist', precisely to catch this quasi-technical flavour. Whoever composed the poem for Hestiaios knew something about rival philosophies, admittedly at a very general level, or was working to fairly close instructions, and the question of who wrote this poem is another of those nagging questions which we cannot answer but which will not go away. It is of some interest to find literary and high-brow interests, of rather different kinds, running in what seems to have been a prominent Miletan family, and we can hardly rule out the possibility that Hestiaios himself composed his own epitaph. The standard answer to 'who composed inscribed funerary poems?' is usually 'local poets who worked to commission', but we must recognise that this easy response almost certainly smooths over a much more complex set of variables.

Louis Robert suggested that κεναῖς δόξαις in the first hexameter of the elegiacs may be a sharp allusion to Epicurus' Κύριαι Δόξαι, but we can perhaps go a little further.[9] Whether or not Robert is correct, the most important κυρία δόξα in this context must, of course, be the second, 'Death is nothing to us', for this poem (and this stone) proclaim a view of the afterlife which is radically different to the Epicurean. Epicurus and his followers were in fact loud in their attacks on the κεναὶ δόξαι or κενοδοξία (or, as Diogenes of Oinoanda put it (fr. 3.IV.7 Smith) ψευδοδοξία), with which our lives are too full and which disturb our serenity with 'false imaginings'. An epigram (of quite uncertain date, except that it is earlier than Diogenes Laertius) about Epicurus by one Athenaeus also highlights this aspect of Epicurean thought:

ἄνθρωποι, μοχθεῖτε τὰ χείρονα, καὶ διὰ κέρδος
ἄπληστοι[10] νεικέων ἄρχετε καὶ πολέμων·

---

9 Cf. Robert 1960, 485 n. 1. The earliest certain reference to the title Κύριαι Δόξαι seems to be in Demetrius Lacon (*PHerc*, col. LII), i. e. mid-second century, and then a generation (or more) later in Philodemus and in Cicero, cf. Usener 1887, 68–70; whether in fact the collection and the title go back to Epicurus himself remains disputed, cf., e.g., Usener 1887 xliii-li, *RE* 6.140–141, Bailey 1926, 344–344.
10 This is Usener's correction of the transmitted ἄπληστον.

τᾶς φύσιος δ' ὁ πλοῦτος ὅρον τινὰ βαιὸν ἐπίσχει,
αἱ δὲ κεναὶ κρίσιες τὰν ἀπέραντον ὁδόν.
τοῦτο Νεοκλῆος πινυτὸν τέκος ἢ παρὰ Μουσέων   5
ἔκλυεν ἢ Πυθοῦς ἐξ ἱερῶν τριπόδων.

Athenaeus, *SH* 225 = *FGE* 444–449

Mortals, you labour at what is harmful, and in greedy pursuit of gain you start quarrels and wars, but the wealth of nature offers a narrow limit, while empty judgements [enjoy] a boundless path. This is what the clever son of Neocles heard either from the Muses or from the holy tripods of Pytho.

Mortals devote their energies in harmful and indeed destructive directions, as they indulge what Epicurus called κεναὶ ἐπιθυμίαι, 'empty desires';[11] the lesson they should learn is contained in vv. 3–4, which offer a poetic version of one of the Κυρίαι Δόξαι:

ὁ τῆς φύσεως πλοῦτος καὶ ὥρισται καὶ εὐπόριστός ἐστιν· ὁ δὲ τῶν κενῶν δοξῶν εἰς ἄπειρον ἐκπίπτει.

Epicurus, *Kyriai Doxai* 15

The wealth required by nature is both bounded and easily acquired; that required by empty imaginings reaches into the boundless.[12]

Athenaeus' epigram illustrates how κεναὶ δόξαι, here varied poetically as κεναὶ κρίσιες, was an instantly recognisable Epicurean idea, put in the epitaph for Hestiaios to a novel use. If Robert was correct to see an evocation of the Κυρίαι Δόξαι in the opening verse of the poem for Hestiaios, then the point will be that Epicurus' κυρίαι δόξαι are the ultimate example of the κεναὶ δόξαι against which the Epicureans themselves were thought to campaign; the point would be a sharp one, and would once again raise the question of who wrote this poem. If,

---

11 Cf., e.g., *Letter to Menoeceus* 127; Lucian, *Alexander* 47 says that the Κύριαι Δόξαι free us from ἐλπίδων ματαίων καὶ περιττῶν ἐπιθυμιῶν. Athenaeus' other extant epigram (*SH* 225 = *FGE* 438–443) is in praise of the πανάριστα δόγματα of the Stoics, notably their unique stress on ἀρετή; that poem refers to σαρκὸς ἡδυπάθημα, 'pleasure of the flesh', as the *telos* of 'other men', i.e. Epicureans.
12 For other testimonia to this central Epicurean idea cf. *Vatican Sayings* 69, Usener 1887, 301–2, Bailey 1926, 357–8. The expression in vv. 3–4 of Athenaeus' epigram is somewhat awkward: Page explains ἐπίσχει as 'presents, offers' (his reference should be corrected to *LSJ* s.v. ἐπέχω II 1), so that there is a slight zeugma: '…presents some narrow limit… [presents] the boundless road'. The image of the road picks up both the 'literal' sense of ὅρος and explains how Athenaeus understood εἰς ἄπειρον ἐκπίπτει.

however, we reject Robert's suggestion as 'unnecessary', we still have a clear evocation of a familiar Epicurean tag in κεναί δόξαι.

A small corpus of inscribed funerary epigrams alluding to the Hellenistic philosophical schools provide a wider context of (as in Hestiaios' case, sometimes polemical) self-display into which the poem for Hestiaios must be set.

This is not the place for any extended treatment, but we may briefly consider *IG* VII.3226 (= 491 Kaibel = *GVI* 1516) from second or first-century Orchomenos:

> Φιλοκράτης Φιλοκράτους Σιδώνιος.
>
> οὐ νόθον ἐκ προτέροιο, Φιλόκρατες, ἤνεσας ἔργον
> σεῖο βίου, πινυταῖς θηγόμενος πραπίσιν·
> ἦ γὰρ ἀπὸ πράτας μεμελημένος ἧς Ἐπικούρου
> δόγμασιν εὐξυνέτοις, ὡς θέμις, ἁλικίας.
> αὖθι τύχης δ' οἴακι παλιμπλανέος βιότοιο
> εἴκων ἐν Μινύαις φῶτας ἐπαθλοκόμεις.
> κεῖσαι δ' ἀγχόθι παιδὸς ἑοῦ, ψαύων μελέεσσιν,
> ἄσμενος ἐκ ζωᾶς εἰς προθανόντα μολών.
>
> *IG* VII.3226 (= 491 Kaibel = *GVI* 1516)[13]

Philocrates of Sidon, son of Philocrates

Not false, Philocrates, to your earlier life did you bring your task to completion, as you were sharpened in your intelligent mind; from earliest youth you gave thought, as was right, to the sensible doctrines of Epicurus. Then, yielding to the steering-oar of fortune in your wandering life, you trained men for contests among the Minyai. You lie near your son, touching his limbs, having passed gladly out of life to join him who died before you.

Philocrates' wandering life, which seems to have brought him (at least) from Sidon to Orchomenos, gestures towards the stories of Odysseus and Jason, leader of the Minyans on their travels, and perhaps even also to Achilles, if he is reunited with his son in death, ψαύων μελέεσσιν, as Achilles was with Patroclus (cf. *Iliad* 23.83–92). Be that as it may, however, δόγμασιν εὐξυνέτοις in v. 4 looks like another allusion to the κυρίαι δόξαι; the δόξαι are εὐξύνετοι and hence appropriate to a boy setting out at the beginning of his serious education, a

---

13 This poem is also Peek 1960, no. 201. The reading at the end of v. 1 is somewhat uncertain. The transcript of the stone given in *IG* VII reads ΕΒΓ followed by an erasure at the end of the verse; it is, however, hard to think of anything other than ἔργον.

point reinforced by ὡς θέμις.¹⁴ Perhaps, indeed, we are to understand that, not only were the Κυρίαι Δόξαι the most easily obtainable and familiar (believed) work of Epicurus,¹⁵ but the aphoristic nature of at least the first handful of κυρίαι δόξαι made them particularly suited to the education of the young, at which stage rote learning played an important role. We do not, of course, need to see here a simple reflection of how the Κυρίαι Δόξαι were in fact used in introducing young men to Epicurus' teachings, for it is the image of a life of sequential stages which the epigram promotes. Nevertheless, it is at least worth noting that Epicurus begins *the Letter to Menoeceus* with the statement that one is never too young or too old for philosophy, and ὡς θέμις may perhaps pick up this statement (or something like it) to suggest that Philocrates acted properly in beginning philosophical training at a young age. We are more familiar with the idea that the young began with poetry as a propaedeutic to philosophy; this is the central thesis, for example, of Plutarch's *How the young man should study poetry*. Epicurus notes (*Men*. 122) that the value of philosophy to a young man is that it makes him 'fearless about the future', and perhaps Philocrates' Epicurean training then helped him with equanimity to 'yield' to the steering oar of τύχη.¹⁶ The pleasure that he is said to have found in meeting his son again in death suggests, of course, that Philocrates was not entirely 'hard core' in his Epicureanism, but a mixture of gestures towards a particular set of philosophical attitudes and rather more conventional consolation would be anything but unexpected in such a funerary epigram.

Hestiaios too is happy in death in 'the sacred chambers of the pious'. The language of the final couplet of the poem in his honour is entirely standard — the isles or chambers of the pious or blessed are a common destination in epitaphic epigram.¹⁷ One of the questions, however, which epigrams (both literary

---

14 I have considered the possibility of emending to εὐξυνέτως, cf. 493 Kaibel where the dead Philon is described: ὃς ἐμμούσοις γράμμασιν εὐξυνέτως | παιδείαν ἤσκησεν. In 491 Kaibel, however, the adverb would create a very awkward expression.
15 Demetrius Lacon (above n. 9) calls this τὸ προχειρότατον βυβλίδιον, and cf. Cicero, *De fin*. 2.20 where Epicureans are teased for having 'learned by heart' (*ediscere*) the Κύριαι Δόξαι.
16 An Epicurean recognized the instability of Fortune and sought to prepare himself through λογισμός to be as little affected by its vicissitudes as possible, cf. *Letter to Menoeceus* 131–136, KD 16, Long 1977, 68–70. It is perhaps of some interest in the context of *IG* VII. 3226 that *Vatican Sayings* 17 uses the image of life as a sea-voyage (a young man 'wanders' (πλάζεται) because of the vicissitudes of Tyche, whereas an old man who has lived well has 'anchored' in a harbour), but such imagery, like Tyche's rudder, is very common.
17 Cf., e.g., Lattimore 1962, 33–36. On 'the chamber(s) of Persephone' cf. Tsagalis 2008, 86–134. *SH* 980 is a particularly familiar example.

and inscribed) constantly raise is how and when such standard, formulaic if you like, language can be given a specific, contextual charge. In the present case the obvious question to ask is where we would expect a follower of Socrates and Plato to go after death. Almost no issue could, of course, so separate a Platonist, for whom, as indeed for the popular religion of Greek epitaphs more generally, 'all soul is immortal' (*Phaedrus* 245c2), from an Epicurean. More than one answer is possible for the late Hellenistic period, but an obvious place to start would be with the two texts with which Hestiaios himself probably started.

In Plato's *Apology*, Socrates offers two possibilities for what might happen to us after death. One, the absence of any perception whatsoever (40c6–7), might be thought to be in some ways one of the intellectual ancestors of the later Epicurean view (though of course very different from it), the other being the soul's removal to 'another place' (40c7–9), Hades, where the soul will find real judges, such as Minos and Rhadamanthys; a stay (ἀποδημία) there offers the chance to converse with such as Orpheus and Homer, or Palamedes and Ajax, or Odysseus and Sisyphus, and indeed to question them to discover who is wise and who only thinks he is (41a1–c7). Socrates does not actually call this afterworld 'the Land of the Blessed' or any such thing, but he does say that those there are εὐδαιμονέστεροι than people 'here' (41c5), and also that one will find there 'all of the ἡμίθεοι who were just during their own lives' (41a4–5), a description which might well be thought to conjure up Hesiod's description of the fate of his ἡμίθεοι, a 'juster and better race' (*WD* 158), who after death live happy 'on the Islands of the Blessed beside deep-eddying Ocean'. My guess is that Socrates' account in the *Apology* was influential upon later images of the afterlife, and if you asked someone who claimed allegiance to Platonic teaching where Socrates (or Socrates' soul) went after death, then the answer would be to a kind of Islands, or indeed Chambers (θάλαμοι), of the Blessed/Pious/Good. Some support for this is, I think, to be found in Lucian's 'Island of the Blessed' in the *True Histories*, where indeed Rhadamanthys holds sway, Socrates chats with Palamedes, just as the *Apology* forecast (*VH* 2.17), and Homer and Odysseus are also prominent inhabitants. Lucian of course never borrows straight from a 'classical' text, and this is no exception: Plato is absent because he lives in his own fictional city (2.17), as are the Stoics, still stuck somewhere up the mountain of Virtue, whereas both Aristippos and Epicurus are in residence because they are both party-animals and contribute to the general jollity. Presumably, this is not quite what a Histiaios had in mind, but we may be sure that he did have a clear idea what 'the chambers of the pious' looked like; for him, and for his poet, this was not an empty epitaphic formula. Socrates' final words in the *Apology* must indeed have offered comfort to many a Socratic:

ἀλλὰ γὰρ ἤδη ὥρα ἀπιέναι, ἐμοὶ μὲν ἀποθανουμένωι, ὑμῖν δὲ βιωσομένοις·
ὁπότεροι δὲ ἡμῶν ἔρχονται ἐπὶ ἄμεινον πρᾶγμα, ἄδηλον παντὶ πλὴν ἢ τῶι θεῶι.

Plato, *Apology* 42a2–5

Now the time has come to depart, me to death and you to life. Which of us goes to a better state, is known to no one except the god.

The second particularly important Platonic text is the *Phaedo*, where Socrates describes the fates which await different people, depending on how they have lived their lives (cf. *Gorgias, Republic* etc). Unsurprisingly perhaps, the most blessed fate awaits those 'who have been purified by philosophy' (114c3) and those who have, like Histiaios we might feel tempted to say, rejected bodily pleasures (114e1), pursued learning and adorned their souls with the cardinal virtues (114e5–115a1); it is they who can look forward to the journey after death with confidence. Socrates, for one, is confident that he is about to depart 'for the happinesses of the blessed' (115d4), εἰς μακάρων δή τινας εὐδαιμονίας, which evokes, without specifying, the Islands (Chambers) of the Blessed. Once again, we may feel sure that Histiaios took comfort from Socrates and Plato as to what lay ahead of him. An epitaph for Plato ascribed to Speusippus places the philosopher's soul precisely among the blessed (*AP* 16.31, Diog. Laert. 3.44).

Abbreviations

AP *Anthologica Palatina.*
FGE Page, D.L. (ed.) 1981. *Further Greek Epigrams*, Cambridge.
GVI Peek, W. (ed.) 1955. *Griechische Vers-Inschriften I: Grab-Epigramme*, Berlin.
HE Gow, A.S.F./Page, D.L. (eds.) 1965. *The Greek Anthology: Hellenistic Epigrams*, 2 vols., Cambridge.
IG *Inscriptiones Graecae*, Berlin 1860ff.
LSJ Liddell, H.G./Scott, R. 1968. *A Greek-English Lexicon*, rev. and augm. throughout by H. Stuart Jones with the assist. of R. McKenzie and with the cooperation of many scholars, Oxford 1940 + *A Supplement*, ed. by E.A. Barber with the assist. of P. Maas/ M. Scheller/M.L. West, Oxford + *Revised Supplement*, ed. by P.G.W. Glare with the assist. of A.A. Thompson, Oxford 1996.
SGO Merkelbach, R./Stauber, J. (eds.) (1998 – 2004), *Steinepigramme aus dem griechischen Osten*, 5 vols., Stuttgart/Munich/Leipzig.
SH Lloyd-Jones, H./Parsons, P. (eds.) 1983. *Supplementum Hellenisticum*, Berlin.

Bibliography

Bailey, C. 1926. *Epicurus*, Oxford.
Bowie, E. 2016. 'Doing Doric', in: E. Sistakou/A. Rengakos (eds.), *Dialect, Diction, and Style in Greek Literary and Inscribed Epigram*, Trends in Classics Supplementary Volumes 43, Berlin/Boston, 3–22.
Buck, C.W./Petersen, W. 1944. *A Reverse Index of Greek Names and Adjectives*, Chicago.
Hunter, R. 2010. 'Language and interpretation in Greek epigram', in: M. Baumbach/A. Petrovic/I. Petrovic, *Archaic and Classical Greek Epigram*, Cambridge, 265–88 [= this volume 131–155].
Hunter, R. 2019. 'Death of a child: grief beyond the literary?', in: M. Kanellou/I. Petrovic/C. Carey (eds.), *Greek Epigram from the Hellenistic to the early Byzantine Era*, Oxford, 137–153 [= this volume 267–285].
Lattimore, R. 1962. *Themes in Greek and Latin Epitaphs*, Urbana IL.
Long, A.A. 1977. 'Chance and natural law in Epicureanism', *Phronesis* 22, 63–88.
Peek, W. 1960. *Griechische Grabgedichte*, Berlin.
Rayet, O. 1874. 'Inscriptions inédites trouvées à Milet, Didymes et Héraclée du Latmos', *Revue Archéologique* 28, 103–14.
Robert, L. 1960. *Hellenica*, Vol. XI-XII, Paris.
Sens, A. 2004. 'Doricisms in the new and old Posidippus', in: B. Acosta-Hughes/E. Kosmetatou/M. Baumbach (eds.), *Labored in Papyrus Leaves*, Washington DC, 65–83.
Tsagalis, C. 2008. *Inscribing Sorrow: Fourth-Century Attic Funerary Epigrams*, Trends in Classics Supplementary Volumes 1, Berlin/New York.
Usener, H. 1887. *Epicurea*, Leipzig.

13 Hellenistic Poetry and the Archaeology of Leisure

The association of song and poetry with 'leisure' — left for the moment quite undefined — and/or the absence of pressing obligations is as old as Homer. Achilles sings of 'the glorious deeds of men' precisely when he has withdrawn himself from that activity (*Il.* 9.186–9), and the two keenest audiences for song in the *Odyssey*, the suitors on Ithaca and the Phaeacians, are both (in very different ways) at 'leisure', the suitors so far from being productive as to be utterly wasteful of the property of others. In the famous 'Golden Verses' at the start of his narrative to the Phaeacians, Odysseus links song to the pleasure of peaceful feasting:

> Ἀλκίνοε κρεῖον, πάντων ἀριδείκετε λαῶν,
> ἦ τοι μὲν τόδε καλὸν ἀκουέμεν ἐστὶν ἀοιδοῦ
> τοιοῦδ', οἷος ὅδ' ἐστί, θεοῖσ' ἐναλίγκιος αὐδήν.
> οὐ γὰρ ἐγώ γέ τί φημι τέλος χαριέστερον εἶναι   5
> ἢ ὅτ' ἐϋφροσύνη μὲν ἔχηι κάτα δῆμον ἅπαντα,
> δαιτυμόνες δ' ἀνὰ δώματ' ἀκουάζωνται ἀοιδοῦ
> ἥμενοι ἑξείης, παρὰ δὲ πλήθωσι τράπεζαι
> σίτου καὶ κρειῶν, μέθυ δ' ἐκ κρητῆρος ἀφύσσων
> οἰνοχόος φορέηισι καὶ ἐγχείηι δεπάεσσι·   10
> τοῦτό τί μοι κάλλιστον ἐνὶ φρεσὶν εἴδεται εἶναι.
>
> Homer, *Odyssey* 9.2–11

'Noble Alcinous, illustrious among all the people, this is indeed a fine thing, to listen to a bard such as this man here, a bard with a voice like the gods. I say that there is no situation more full of charm than when delight reigns through the whole people, and through the hall banqueters sit in order listening to a bard, and beside them are tables full of bread and meat, and the wine-pourer draws wine from the mixing-bowl and carries it round, pouring it into their cups. In my heart I think that this is the finest thing.'

Later echoes of this passage fashion the listening Phaeacians as πεπαιδευμένοι *avant la lettre*, the ancestors of the educated Greek élite of the Roman empire.[1]

This is a revised version of a lecture delivered in Freiburg in June 2015; I am grateful to the organisers of the series on 'Muße' for their invitation to think about this subject and to audiences in Alexandria, Freiburg and Venice for much helpful discussion. I have kept as close as appropriate to the oral form, in part because anything like a full treatment of the some of the subjects touched on here would fill more than one book.

1 Cf. Hunter 2018, ch. 3.

Aristotle adduces this passage as an illustration of the fact that μουσική has become part of 'liberal education', not because it is 'useful' or 'necessary' in any direct sense, unlike, say, learning to write, but because it is a proper pastime for free men enjoying σχολή (*Pol.* 8. 1338a13–30);[2] Alcinous' fellow-Phaeacians were certainly 'free' in one sense, if not quite as democratic Athenians were.[3] I will return to Aristotle, but we may note immediately that his use of Homer suggests that, when considering 'leisure' in Hellenistic and imperial culture, particularly poetry, it would be a mistake to seek to draw too firm a distinction between ideas of 'leisure' in poetry and other creative writing and the theorising of leisure by philosophers and moralists. The two had long since intertwined and both streams flowed into the world of Hellenistic literature and scholarship. One way of laying out the space of any full investigation of this subject would be to see an attempt to trace a path, which is however only intermittently visible, from Odysseus' 'Golden Verses' to the Solon of Plutarch, who is made to argue that the need to eat makes one a slave to food (*Symposium of the Seven Sages* 159d–e); true freedom consists in the absence of any such bodily want, allowing a genuine σχολή which can be devoted to conversation (λόγοι).[4]

Various approaches to the subject of leisure in Greek literature are possible. One might, for example, look at genres and characters associated, or not associated, with such ideas. Early epic song may have been listened to by men (and women) 'at leisure', but the subjects of such song were usually drawn from areas far removed from the sphere of leisure — war and conflict, adventure, travel and so forth. The embodiment of such activity is perhaps Heracles, the hero of πόνος and labour; though images of the (?deified) Heracles at feasts and symposia are very familiar at all periods, and in the Hellenistic period are often connected with representations of royal power,[5] it would, I think, be not unfair to suggest that the enjoyment of leisure, and in particular the enjoyment of intellectual and aesthetic pursuits which went with leisure, was never an important element in the traditional representation of the great civilizing hero, Ἡρακλῆς ὁ καλλίνικος as he declares himself in Euripides' tragedy named after him (vv. 581–582), when he realizes that, although he has just returned from the Underworld, yet more πόνοι await. The need to strangle snakes in his cradle was

---

2 Cf. Ford 1999, 121–122.
3 For the constitutional position on Scherie cf. *Od.* 8.390–391, with A. Bowie's note on *Od.* 13.7.
4 Cf. Romeri 2002, 119–125; the account of the philosophical life in Plato's *Theaetetus* (cf. below 254–255) is clearly one of the Platonic models which Plutarch has in mind here.
5 Cf., e.g., Theocr. 17.20–33, Kosmin 2014, 162–164. For Heracles as a symposiast in the archaic and classical periods cf. esp. Wolf 1993.

not itself a mark of lack of leisure (babies do not, I think, have 'leisure' as such), but it did symbolize the life of labour which awaited him. So too in Apollonius' *Argonautica* we have a Heracles whose 'hands were unused to being at rest' (1.1171). When, in that same poem, Jason and his colleagues while away their time enjoying the delights offered by the Lemnian women, it is Heracles whose patience eventually wears thin and who gets the expedition back under way (1.861–874).[6] Apollonius there uses the language of 'delay', ἀμβολίη (1.861), rather than of leisure and/or inactivity, but when Virgil came to use this episode in the context of Aeneas' 'delay' at Carthage with Dido, he did indeed translate it into the language of *otium* (*Aen.* 4.271). Just as the Apollonian Heracles had appealed to the Argonauts' sense of κλέος, to be achieved by heroic exploit such as the securing of the Golden Fleece (*Arg.* 1.869–871), so the Virgilian Jupiter speaks of *tantarum gloria rerum* and of *laus* achieved by *labor* (*Aen.* 4.231–232, cf. v. 272).[7] Virgil's adaptation of the Apollonian scene required in fact very little refocusing to fit his new purposes. Heracles' eventual loss to the Argonautic expedition at the end of Book 1 comes about in part because, while his comrades prepare dinner and then dine, he goes off to prepare a new oar for himself: for Heracles there is always the next thing to be done, and even the appetite of the comic Heracles is not satisfied 'at leisure' — he grabs whatever he can to eat, whenever he can.

Hellenistic poetry in fact offers rich material for anyone interested in leisure in literature. Theocritus' poetry established 'leisure' as central to the whole tradition of Western pastoral, particularly because of the close link between leisure and/or inactivity and erotic desire. The goatherd of Theocritus 3 who serenades the cave-dwelling Amaryllis while Tityrus looks after his goats, and the Cyclops of Theocritus 11 who leaves his flocks to make their own way home while he gazes out to sea towards his beloved Galatea, embody one aspect of the familiar, many-sided relationship between σχολή and *eros*. We may, however, leave more potentially complex cases, such as the narrator's *persona* in Callimachus' *Aitia*, until the scope of this whole subject has become clearer. For this we will have to turn to pre-Hellenistic texts which address issues of σχολή more directly than does poetry itself, for it will, I hope, emerge that σχολή in Hellenistic poetry and culture, together with the link between σχολή and scholarship, particularly as practised at Alexandria, can only be understood within a broader account of the history of this and related ideas. First, however, we need to try to determine what we are talking about.

---

[6] For various aspects of this scene cf. Hunter 1993, 33–36.
[7] Cf. Nelis 2001, 155–158 for other important intertexts for the Virgilian scene.

Definitions of 'leisure' are notoriously difficult, even without paying proper attention to how culturally specific such definitions need to be, whether with reference to past cultures or to the contemporary world. In his study of 'leisure' in ancient Rome, Jeremy Toner proposes working definitions of 'leisure' and 'work' modelled on Clifford Geertz's well known definition of religion:

> Leisure is a system of symbols which acts to establish a feeling of freedom and pleasure by formulating a sense of choice and desire.

> Work is a system of symbols which acts to establish a feeling of restraint and effort by formulating a sense of obligation and necessity.

Without placing too much weight upon the wording of these, essentially heuristic, definitions,[8] we will see that the most important Greek texts do in fact emphasise some of these same ideas of freedom and pleasure, on one side, and restraint and obligation on the other. Moreover, just as *otium* became a central plank in the self-constructed identity of the Roman elite, so in discussions of σχολή notions of social 'class' and hierarchy are never far away. I begin from two well known passages of Euripides. In the *Ion*, the eponymous young man explains to his putative father, Xouthos, the advantages which his life in Delphi offers and which he would be loath to abandon:

> ἃ δ' ἐνθάδ' εἶχον ἀγάθ' ἄκουσόν μου, πάτερ·
> τὴν φιλτάτην μὲν πρῶτον ἀνθρώποις σχολὴν
> ὄχλον τε μέτριον, οὐδέ μ' ἐξέπληξ' ὁδοῦ   635
> πονηρὸς οὐδείς· κεῖνο δ' οὐκ ἀνασχετόν,
> εἴκειν ὁδοῦ χαλῶντα τοῖς κακίοσιν.

> Euripides, *Ion* 633–637

> Father, listen to the good things I enjoyed here. First of all, I had what is sweetest for men — leisure and little disturbance. No wretch shoved me aside in the street; it is unbearable when someone has to yield the road to the worthless.

The elitist turn of Ion's language here (πονηρός,[9] κακίονες) is unmistakable, and we may be reminded of the amazement expressed by the 'Old Oligarch' that in

---

8 Toner 1995, 17, 19.
9 Cf., e.g., [Xen.], *Ath. Pol.* 1.4 (the Athenians) 'in all matters give the advantage to the worthless and the poor and the common people rather than to good men' (τοῖς πονηροῖς καὶ πένησι καὶ δημοτικοῖς ἢ τοῖς χρηστοῖς); the 'Old Oligarch' standardly uses οἱ πονηροί for the mass of citizens. The idea that πόνος damages human nature and is therefore appropriate for slaves, but not free men, is not uncommon in ancient political theory; for a rather extreme version, but

Athens slaves do not step aside for one in the street (Xen. *Ath. Pol.* 1.10). The link between σχολή (or *otium*) and a sense of social hierarchy was to persist throughout antiquity.[10] This may, of course, be one of those several places in Euripides where we feel that a character speaks a language which is not really their own or does not, as we would say, speak 'in character', but that will not detract from the value of the passage for understanding one kind of context in which an appeal to σχολή seems to have been appropriate. The current instance, which seems to be the earliest extant praise of σχολή,[11] may surprise somewhat, given that Ion's life seems in fact to be one of (manual) 'work', as witness his sweeping of the ground in the opening monody; if we recall Jeremy Toner's definition, however, we will see that Ion is actually talking about the 'freedom' he has at Delphi to organize the life he loves as he chooses, and 'freedom' was to become an important element in later conceptions of σχολή.

The second Euripidean passage on which I wish briefly to dwell is (almost inevitably) Phaedra's famous analysis of why we fail to do what we know to be right:

> τὰ χρήστ' ἐπιστάμεσθα καὶ γιγνώσκομεν,
> οὐκ ἐκπονοῦμεν δ', οἱ μὲν ἀργίας ὕπο,
> οἱ δ' ἡδονὴν προθέντες ἀντὶ τοῦ καλοῦ
> ἄλλην τιν'· εἰσὶ δ' ἡδοναὶ πολλαὶ βίου,
> μακραί τε λέσχαι καὶ σχολή, τερπνὸν κακόν,
> αἰδώς τε· δισσαὶ δ' εἰσίν, ἡ μὲν οὐ κακή,
> ἡ δ' ἄχθος οἴκων· εἰ δ' ὁ καιρὸς ἦν σαφής,
> οὐκ ἂν δύ' ἤστην ταῦτ' ἔχοντε γράμματα.

Euripides, *Hippolytus* 380–387

We understand and know what is good, but we do not carry it through, some because of laziness, whereas others put some other pleasure in front of honorable behavior. There are many pleasures in life, long chats and leisure, a sweet delusion, and shame. There are two kinds of shame: one is not harmful, but the other is a burden on houses. If the difference was clear, there would not be two kinds with the same name.

This passage presents, as is very well known, more than one difficult problem of text and interpretation, but two points may be drawn out here. First, the distinction between ἀργία, 'laziness, lack of drive, fecklessness' and σχολή, 'leisure, free time', is important and should not be blurred; Barrett's translation of σχολή

---

one in which τρυφή is brought uncomfortably close to σχολή, cf. Heraclides Ponticus fr. 55 W = 39 Schütrumpf, with the discussion of Schütrumpf 2009.
10 Cf., e.g., Nightingale 2004, 209–210 on Aristotle, *EN* 10.
11 Cf. Carter 1986, 160.

as 'idleness', therefore, might be thought to do less than full justice to the attraction of what Phaedra is saying and, more importantly, to the cultural values she is actually describing.[12] Secondly, Phaedra counts σχολή among life's pleasures, even if it is a 'sweet evil', and we may here be reminded (again) of the role which Toner gave to pleasure in his attempt at a definition of leisure (above). To what extent Phaedra is describing, or perhaps rather elliptically alluding to, her own 'leisured' palace-life is disputed among critics of the play, but the mere fact of counting 'long conversations and leisure' among life's pleasures may be thought to betoken, at the very least, an aristocratic or élitist outlook.[13] Be that as it may, the pairing of 'long conversations and leisure', which some critics take to be essentially a hendiadys, whether or not it is to be understood specifically to evoke the 'long gossiping conversations' of women,[14] seems to look forward to later ideas of leisure which will concern us again. 'Talking' is indeed a fundamental activity of leisure, whether that be in the philosophical tradition (to which I shall return) or in the later poetic tradition, though neither are likely to have regarded leisure as a κακόν. We may recall Callimachus' famous poem for Heraclitus,

εἶπέ τις, Ἡράκλειτε, τεὸν μόρον, ἐς δέ με δάκρυ
ἤγαγεν· ἐμνήσθην δ' ὁσσάκις ἀμφότεροι
ἥλιον ἐν λέσχηι κατεδύσαμεν. ἀλλὰ σὺ μέν που,
ξεῖν' Ἁλικαρνησεῦ, τετράπαλαι σποδιή,
αἱ δὲ τεαὶ ζώουσιν ἀηδόνες, ἧισιν ὁ πάντων
ἁρπακτὴς Ἀΐδης οὐκ ἐπὶ χεῖρα βαλεῖ.

Callimachus, *Epigr.* 2 Pfeiffer

Heraclitus, someone spoke of your death, and it brought me to tears. I remembered how often the two of us sank the sun with our talking. You, friend from Halicarnasus, have been ashes for long years, but your nightingales live on: Hades, which snatches everything away, will not cast his hands on these.

or the narrator's observation to his Ikian neighbor at the symposium of the Athenian Pollis described in Callimachus' *Aitia*:

---

[12] Barrett 1964, 229.
[13] Professor Ettore Cingano suggests to me that there is a kind of wordplay here (and elsewhere?) between λέσχη and σχολή.
[14] So Mastronarde 2010, 177.

ἦ μάλ' ἔπος τόδ' ἀληθές, ὅ τ' οὐ μόνον ὕδατος αἶσαν,
ἀλλ' ἔτι καὶ λέσχης οἶνος ἔχειν ἐθέλει.

Callimachus fr. 178.15–16 Pf.

Indeed the saying is a true one, that wine must have its share not only of water, but also of conversation.

σχολή will, moreover, turn out to be central to the self-representation which Callimachus creates here for himself and his interlocutors.

The social implications of σχολή, which we have found in, for example, Euripides' *Ion*, are very clear in one of our best sources for social attitudes in one Greek city on the verge of the Hellenistic age, though it might of course not have known that, namely the plays of Menander of Athens. The central characters of most of these plays belong to a monied élite, though how monied and how élite are matters for debate. In one contextless fragment a slave observes that a poor man should not live in the city where the constant sight of someone τρυφῶντα καὶ σχολὴν ἄγειν / δυνάμενον, 'well off and able to afford leisure', merely drives home the wretchedness of his own existence (fr. 299 K-A), and in the *Dyskolos* the hard-working farmer Gorgias tells just such a rich man, a τρυφῶν, from the city, whom he thinks has come to the countryside with evil designs on his half-sister:

> οὐ δίκαιόν ἐστι γοῦν
> τὴν σὴν σχολὴν τοῖς ἀσχολουμένοις κακὸν
> ἡμῖν γενέσθαι.

Menander, *Dyskolos* 293–295

It is not right that your leisure should harm those who have no leisure.

Of particular interest is Moschion's opening monologue in the *Samia*, in which he relates how Demeas brought him up wanting nothing (ἐτρύφησα, v. 7), and as he grew up he enjoyed all the privileges and roles of the wealthy Athenian élite:

> τῶι χορηγεῖν διέφερον
> καὶ τῆι] φιλοτιμίαι· κύνας παρέτρεφέ μοι,
> ἵππο]υς· ἐφυλάρχησα λαμπρῶς· τῶν φίλων   15
> τοῖς δεομένοις τὰ μέτρι' ἐπαρκεῖν ἐδυνάμην.
> δι' ἐκεῖνον ἦν ἄνθρωπος. ἀστείαν δ' ὅμως
> τούτων χάριν τιν' ἀπεδίδουν· ἦν κόσμιος.
> μετὰ τοῦτο συνέβη — καὶ γὰρ ἅμα τὰ πράγματα
> ἡμῶν δίειμι πάντ'· ἄγω γάρ πως σχολήν —   20

Σαμίας ἑταίρας εἰς ἐπιθυμίαν τινὰ
ἐλθεῖν ἐκεῖνον, πρᾶγμ' ἴσως ἀνθρώπινον ...

Menander, *Samia* 13–22

I excelled in equipping choruses and public service. He reared dogs and horses for me; I served as phylarch with distinction; I was able to offer those of my friends who were in need some moderate support; he made me a man. A very nice return I gave him for this: I was well behaved. Subsequently it happened (I have some leisure, so I will tell you my whole story) that he fell in love with a hetaira from Samos, something which perhaps is only human ...

By 'I have some leisure (now)' Moschion is referring to his very immediate situation, but, particularly after his account of his young life, we will also understand that σχολή precisely characterizes this life — as we might say, he has no job to go to. As it unfolds, the play might be thought to suggest that he in fact always has too much time on his hands.

To return to the *Hippolytus*. Critics have often wondered about a possible connection between what Phaedra has to say and philosophical, particularly Socratic, reflection on the sources of wrong-doing, although no philosophical tradition is likely to have made σχολή an impediment to τὸ καλόν. It was principally the philosophical tradition that both theorised the place of σχολή in human life and activity[15] and also gave σχολή an important place in creative literature. This is unsurprising in view of the concern of the philosophical tradition with the question of what constituted the philosophical life (for which μακραὶ λέσχαι is not in fact a bad description).[16] It is Plato who is for us the key figure here, although Xenophon too places his *Symposium* explicitly under the sign of the σπουδή — παιδιά dichotomy (*Symp.* 1.1), and that pairing is clearly related to ἀσχολία — σχολή, although Aristotle at least distinguished sharply between σχολή, 'leisure', and παιδιά, 'play', the latter being necessary 'relaxation' and therefore belonging to the sphere of work rather than of σχολή properly understood (*Pol.* 8.1337b35–43, *EN* 10.1176b32–7a1); modern theorists also distinguish 'leisure' from 'play', though not necessarily along Aristotelian lines.[17] To antici-

---

15 Cf. Stocks 1936.
16 As early as Epicrates fr. 10.31 K-A Plato's philosophical teaching is described as λέσχαι.
17 Cf. Toner 1995, 20–21. There would be much to be said about Greek ideas of 'learning through παιδιά', as for example children do (cf., e.g., Pl. *Laws* 1.643b-d), but this is a very different from the learning normally associated with σχολή. The Thucydidean Pericles' praise for Athenian festivals and sacrifices as ἀναπαῦλαι τῶν πόνων (2.38) in some ways looks forward to Aristotelian views on 'relaxation'.

pate somewhat, however, we will come to see that σπουδή and σχολή are by no means incompatible in intellectual contexts.

In Plato's *Gorgias*, Callicles grants philosophy a place in παιδεία, 'education', and therefore sees it as a fit activity for μειράκια, though it is ridiculous to pursue it into later life, for such a pursuit makes someone ignorant of what makes a man καλὸς κἀγαθός and εὔδοκιμος (484c–485d, cf. 499b–c); the proper activities for a grown man, according to Callicles, are public affairs, including political and forensic oratory. Behind Callicles' scorn one may sense the idea of philosophy, not just as παιδεία, but also as παιδιά. However that may be, the *Gorgias*, which is in part precisely a manifesto for the philosophical and intellectual life, is an important witness to the idea of σχολή in philosophical discussion. Thus Chaerephon expresses horror at 458c at the very idea that any ἀσχολία should take precedence over the λόγοι to which he is currently listening; these are discussions which, as far as the participants are concerned, could go on without end (458c–d), and we see here both how Plato sets philosophical discussion against epic recitation, and particularly the recitation of an Odysseus, to which Alcinous famously declared himself able to listen all night long (*Od.* 11.375–376), and also how the *Gorgias* anticipates the account of the philosophical life in the *Theaetetus* (cf. below p. 254–5). We may, moreover, sense the dichotomies of the *Gorgias* recalibrated in Aristotle's discussions of whether 'the political and practical life' or the life of θεωρία and philosophy is preferable (*Pol.* 7.1324a25–29, 1325a16–24, *EN* 10.1177b1–12). For Aristotle, however, both lives, the philosophical and the political, require σχολή (*Pol.* 7.1329a1–2), and here we may sense how the Aristotelian view foreshadows the development of Roman ideas about *otium*.

The *Gorgias* is also of course very important in this context for its use of the debate from Euripides' *Antiope* between Zethos and Amphion, in which Amphion's devotion to lyre-playing and 'culture' (broadly understood) is replaced in the Platonic dialogue by the pursuit of philosophy.[18] In the tragedy Zethos had represented Amphion's lyre-playing as an unhealthy pursuit of pleasure which, being ἀργόν, makes no contribution to his city or his *philoi*;[19] only the proper pursuit of πόνοι can do that, not the σοφίσματα with which Amphion wastes his time (frr. 183, 187 K). Amphion for his part privileges intelligence and good judgement as the greatest good for society (frr. 199, 200 K). We would like to know much more about the Euripidean debate than we actually do, but it is

---

[18] On the debate in the *Antiope* and how it is used in the *Gorgias* cf. esp. Carter 1986, 163–178, Nightingale 1995, 69–92, Wilson 2000, Tarrant 2008.
[19] Cf. further below.

clear that, both for itself and through its re-use in the *Gorgias*, this became a central text which brought poetry and philosophy together on the same side, as it were, of a debate about the proper place and use of σχολή. We will sense the presence of this debate again, as also of Aristotle's views on μουσική (cf. above), when we turn to consider how Hellenistic poets and scholars represent the practice of σχολή, but we may note immediately that one of our best witnesses to a line of argument which developed precisely to confront the charges of a Callicles or a Zethos is Cicero's defence of the Greek poet Archias. According to Cicero, the poet himself, like Socrates, knows nothing of the law courts because of his *otium ac studium* (*Pro Arch*. 3), and therefore much of the defence of poetry must rest not on him but on the example of Cicero himself. No one could accuse Cicero, as Zethos accused Amphion, of not helping his city and his friends, of putting *otium* or pleasure before public service, but one of the most important things which allows Cicero to be such a public, and public-spirited, figure is precisely his devotion to *doctrina*, including poetry. Literary study is how Cicero relaxes and refreshes himself — this is his *otium* — so he has the strength and the learning to carry on the daily struggle of *negotia* (*Pro Arch*. 12–13). Those who deserve censure are those 'who hide themselves away in literary studies and therefore do not use them for the common good or bring them forth into the open light of day' (*Pro Arch*. 12); Callicles' charge against someone who shuns public life and 'spends his life skulking in a corner, whispering with three or four young men, and never says anything worthy of a free man or important or effective' (Plato, *Gorgias* 485d5–e2) here resounds very loudly in the background.

In the famous digression in the *Theaetetus* on the philosophical life (172c–177c), Socrates lays stress upon the fact that philosophers always have time (σχολή) to follow the arguments wherever they lead;[20] peace, σχολή and true freedom (ἐλευθερία) are in fact the hallmarks of the philosophical life, as philosophers do not live under compulsion or the restraints of time, but are themselves raised 'in freedom and leisure' and are the 'masters' of the arguments they discuss, not the other way around; there is thus nothing slavish about the philosophical life, whereas the person who busies themself in the lawcourts is the servant both of the water-clock and the necessary rules of the lawcourt: such a person has no freedom to talk about what they want to talk about or to

---

[20] The idea is of course very familiar in Platonic texts other than the *Theaetetus*, cf., e.g., *Rep*. 3.394d7–8. For the later influence of the *Theaetetus*-passage cf., e.g., Dio Chrys. 12.38.

follow an argument wherever it leads.²¹ This principle of the pursuit of 'free research', of following an argument wherever it leads, is still very powerful in 'scholarship' today, particularly, it might be argued, in the biological and social sciences, where the pursuit of knowledge can lead in potentially very dark (and very unfashionable) directions. The illusion of freedom and σχολή as depicted in the *Theaetetus* continues to exercise a powerful hold on how modern scholars often imagine themselves.

The dramatic frame of the *Theaetetus* in part dramatises how σχολή may in fact also characterize those 'on the margins' of philosophy, as it were; in a startling foretaste of literary scholarship to come,²² Eucleides made corrections to his ὑπομνήματα of Socrates' account of his conversation with Theaetetus κατὰ σχολήν (143a1–4), and the book is read to Eucleides and Terpsion as they rest (ἀναπαύεσθαι). This last is, as we have seen, not synonymous with σχολή, but it is clear that, like the true philosopher, they are in absolute charge of how they spend their time. In one sense, this idealisation of σχολή is a developed, positive spin on the comic (and popular?) charge of 'idleness' or 'laziness' (ἀργία) which was always easy to throw at philosophers. ἀργία carries resonances not just of idleness but, as in Euripides' *Antiope* (above), also of making no contribution to the good of one's community. Thus the chorus of Aristophanes' *Frogs* celebrates Aeschylus' victory over Euripides with a brief song which contrasts the public benefit which Aeschylus' return will bring to the city at large and to his *philoi* with the pointlessness of sitting around for private chats with Socrates:

μακάριός γ' ἀνὴρ ἔχων
ξύνεσιν ἠκριβωμένην.
πάρα δὲ πολλοῖσιν μαθεῖν.
ὅδε γὰρ εὖ φρονεῖν δοκήσας
πάλιν ἄπεισιν οἴκαδ' αὖ,
ἐπ' ἀγαθῶι μὲν τοῖς πολίταις,
ἐπ' ἀγαθῶι δὲ τοῖς ἑαυτοῦ
ξυγγενέσι τε καὶ φίλοισ‹ι›,
διὰ τὸ συνετὸς εἶναι.

χαρίεν οὖν μὴ Σωκράτει
παρακαθήμενον λαλεῖν,
ἀποβαλόντα μουσικὴν

---

21 Distant echoes of the claims of the *Theaetetus* may be heard in Cicero's discussion of the life of political activity and the life of scholarly *otium* in *De officiis* 1.69–92; on this Ciceronian passage cf., e.g., Roman 2014, 15–16, 63–64, citing earlier bibliography.
22 Cf. below 259–260.

> τά τε μέγιστα παραλιπόντα
> τῆς τραγωιδικῆς τέχνης.
> τὸ δ' ἐπὶ σεμνοῖσιν λόγοισι
> καὶ σκαριφησμοῖσι λήρων
> διατριβὴν ἀργὸν ποιεῖσθαι,
> παραφρονοῦντος ἀνδρός.
>
> Aristophanes, *Frogs* 1482-1499

> Blessed is the man of sharpened intelligence; this you can learn from abundant evidence. This man, whose good sense has been proved, will go back home again, to benefit his fellow-citizens and to benefit his family and friends, because he is a man of intelligence.
> It's a thing of wit not to sit down to chatter with Socrates, rejecting *mousike* and ignoring what is finest in the art of tragedy. To indulge in pointless and time-wasting twaddle over pompous phrases and hair-splitting nonsense is the mark of a lunatic.

The principal target of the second verse is of course Euripides, whose supposed fondness for Socrates and abstract thought has ruined his tragedies.[23] διατριβὴ ἀργός might well be thought a comically prescient foreshadowing of philosophical σχολή, but — be that as it may — knowledge of what was to follow in the fourth century allows the thought that, from this later perspective, we may see here a comic defence of the value, not just of Aeschylean tragedy, but of drama as a whole, particularly when it is set against a new form of *logoi*, namely philosophy, which was to lay claim to be the highest form of μουσική.[24]

If it is the *Theaetetus* which most explicitly theorises the role of σχολή in the philosophical life, it is the *Phaedrus* which most fully dramatises that role. Socrates and Phaedrus have all the time they need to enjoy the pleasures of the banks of the Ilissos (cf., e.g., 227d2-5, 242a3-6) and, as with the *Gorgias*, the whole dialogue is placed under the sign of σχολή (227b7-11). So too, just as Lysias is said to have composed his speech κατὰ σχολήν (228a1), Phaedrus' repeated listenings and practisings of that speech suggest the man of leisure; 'work' in Phaedrus' world is a leisurely but health-giving walk and the activity of μελετᾶν (228b6, e2).[25] The bulk of the conversation between Socrates and Phaedrus is conducted as they 'recline in peace' (229a2), and as the subject changes to the nature of writing 'well and not well', a subject introduced by Socrates' telling of the myth of the cicada-men, the theme of σχολή explicitly

---

23 Cf., e.g., Nightingale 1995, 61–63. For other aspects of this song cf. Halliwell 2011, 150–153.
24 Nightingale 1995, 64 is, however, certainly correct to note that this passage 'falls far short of the notion that poetry as a whole is battling some distinct intellectualist movement'.
25 For such περίπατοι as themselves marking out a member of the Greek educated élite cf. O'Sullivan 2011, 1–2 and *passim*. Dio similarly marks himself out within an imitation of the *Phaedrus* at the opening of the 'Borysthenitikos', *Oration* 36.

returns (258e6). Like Euripides' Phaedra, only more so, the Platonic Phaedrus is addicted to the pleasure (ἡδονή) of μακραὶ λέσχαι. There is, however, a right and a wrong way to use σχολή. In his famous remarks on the story of Boreas and Oreithyia, Socrates observes that the rationaliser of myths, the person who explains this story as a mythicisation of a historical event, will need a great deal of σχολή, simply because there are so many stories and creatures requiring his attention; Socrates, however, has no σχολή for such activities (πρὸς αὐτά, 229e3–4), because he has much bigger intellectual fish to fry. σχολή in this account is not merely the time to choose one's activity, but it is the freedom to pursue intellectual and philosophical questions to a valuable and purposeful end, and this is also one of the lessons of the myth of the cicadas: the slavish many may be lulled to sluggish torpor, to intellectual ἀργία in fact (259a3), by the cicadas' song in the mid-day heat, but the philosopher will avoid the lure of their Siren-song by engaging in serious discussion (διαλέγεσθαι) even in the heat of the day.[26]

The *Phaedrus*, then, perhaps even more than the *Theaetetus*, establishes an ideal of intellectual activity, characterised as σχολή.[27] Like many of Plato's dialogues, we sense that the *Phaedrus* is, among many other things, a charter-narrative for the practice of philosophy by Plato and his pupils.[28] Like many charter-narratives, it is an idealised and partly ironised picture, but its programmatic force seems hard to deny. It is even tempting to think that we have here some kind of imaginative aetiology for the Academy, which Plato established near a gymnasium in a 'shady' rural area outside the city-walls to the north-west (rather than the south-east where the Ilissos runs).[29] It is at least

---

26 Cf. Ferrari 1987, 26–28, on the difference between Socrates and Phaedrus in this regard.
27 Cf. Ferrari 1987, 15. For some later uses of the σχολή-motif from the *Phaedrus* cf. Hunter 2012, 12–14.
28 After delivering this lecture in Freiburg, I discovered that Capra 2014, 17–19, 143–146 has also explored, from a rather different perspective and in much greater detail, the links between the *Phaedrus* and Plato's Academy. Those interested should consult his discussion and the further bibliography which he cites.
29 'Shady' comes from Eupolis fr. 36 K-A, where see the notes of Kassel-Austin for further attestations for the trees of the Academy; cf. Cic. *De consulatu suo* fr. 10.72–73 Courtney, the wisdom of those *otia qui studiis laeti tenuere decoris, / inque Academia umbrifera nitidoque Lyceo*. For the ancient testimony for the Academy more generally cf. *RE* 1.1132–1137, Herter 1952, Riginos 1976: ch. 10, Baltes 1993, Berti 2010. There is a tradition attested in late sources that Plato deliberately chose an 'unhealthy' spot for the Academy (*RE* 1.1135, Riginos 1976, 121–123). If there is anything to this, then the beauties of the *locus amoenus* of the *Phaedrus* would be doubly amusing, but there is no good reason to think that the tradition goes back to the classical period, cf. Ar. *Clouds* 1005–1009 (above). Plutarch reports that Cimon turned the

noteworthy that Aristophanes could set a picturesque *locus amoenus* at the Academy (*Clouds* 1005–1009); that idyllic picture includes a plane-tree, as notoriously does the *Phaedrus*, and centuries later Pliny reports that the plane-trees of the Academy were famous (*HN* 12.9). None of this is of course to be pushed very far, but the sense of the *Phaedrus* as a charter-narrative remains, particularly when we take into account the dialogue's closing concern with the philosophical status of written texts and thus, by implication, with the status of Platonic texts. Even Socrates' professed reluctance to leave the city because he is φιλομαθής and the trees do not wish to teach him anything (230d3–4) would presumably have brought a smile to those reading (or writing) these words in the parks of the Academy. A century or so after the *Phaedrus*, Timon of Phlius satirically compared Plato to the cicadas 'which sit on the tree of Hekademos [i.e. the Academy] and pour out their lovely voice' (fr. 30 Di Marco);[30] it may be worth suggesting that Timon is not merely alluding to the *Phaedrus*, but is also conscious of a tradition which acknowledged some connection between the Academy and the *locus amoenus* of the *Phaedrus*. Later, of course, any philosophical or rhetorical discussion might evoke or allude to the *Phaedrus* as the classic setting to 'do philosophy' or, indeed, just to pass the day in discussion. Thus, for example, Cicero's *Brutus*, which also is placed under the sign of *otium* (chap. 10), evokes both the *Phaedrus* and also the Academy, or perhaps rather runs them together, as Cicero and Brutus 'sit on the grass by a statue of Plato' to hold their discussion (chap. 24, cf. *De oratore* 1.28). This can, of course, only be suggestive for how the *Phaedrus* may have evoked, or been read in, the Academy itself. Nevertheless, there are two further reasons why, at least from the perspective of Hellenistic poetry and scholarship, the presentation of σχολή in the *Phaedrus* is important.

The *Phaedrus* is one of the Platonic dialogues in which (for us) the term φιλόλογος makes its first appearances. Socrates declares himself both φιλομαθής, 'a lover of learning [new things]' (230d3), and φιλόλογος, 'a lover of *logoi*' (236e5), which is essentially the meaning of the term elsewhere in Plato also (e.g. *Tht.* 161a7). Socrates' apparently ironical use of the term is cashed out in full at the end of the dialogue when, in the context of the condemnation of writing as mere play, we come to see that φιλόλογος and φιλόσοφος should in fact be synonymous, if full weight is given to the Socratic emphasis on non-written λόγοι (cf. 278b–d). Subsequently, of course, φιλόλογος required a different set

---

Academy from a 'waterless and arid place' to a 'well-watered grove which he fitted out with clear tracks and shaded walks' (*Cimon* 13.8).
30 On this fragment cf. further Hunter 2012, 161–162.

of associations:³¹ Eratosthenes is reported to have been the first to adopt the term φιλόλογος as a self-description, and Strabo describes those who 'have a share in the [Alexandrian] Museum' as φιλόλογοι ἄνδρες (17.1.8), although to what extent this should actually be considered a 'formal title' is debated.³² The *diegesis* to Callimachus' *Iambus* 1 tells us that in that poem Hipponax summoned the Alexandrian φιλόλογοι or φιλόσοφοι – the papyrus seems to attest both readings – to listen to him, although there is no reason to think that Callimachus himself used either (rhythmically awkward) term in the poem.³³ One question which therefore arises is the nature of the trajectory from Platonic to Alexandrian φιλολογία; the semantic history of the word, based on what evidence survives to us, is not too difficult to trace, but it may be that the concept of σχολή provides one at least of the crucial links as the notion of φιλολογία evolves between Plato and Hellenistic scholarship.

It has long been recognized that the Alexandrian Μουσεῖον owed more than a little – though exactly how much is very disputed – to the Athenian philosophical schools.³⁴ Strabo describes the Museum as 'part of the palace quarters with a walk and a seating area (ἐξέδρα) and a large house, in which is the common dining area of those men of learning (φιλόλογοι ἄνδρες) who share in the Museum' (17.1.8). How early a similarly communal life, and one associated with dedication to the Muses, was established in the Athenian schools is disputed,³⁵ but both the schools and the Alexandrian Museum (with associated Library) may be seen as institutionalisations of elevated conceptions of σχολή, whatever differences there may have been at the level of detail. We can hardly put much weight on the fact that our evidence for the Academy similarly refers to a gymnasium, a garden, a μουσεῖον established by Plato and an ἐξέδρα,³⁶ for similarities were all but inevitable; rather, it is less important, at least for present purposes, to establish the Museum as a 'copy' of the Athenian philosophical centres than to recognise a shared way of embodying conceptions of σχολή which were indeed closely related. Theophrastus' will concerning arrangements at the Lyceum and his own estate at Stagira is also very suggestive for Alexandrian practice and, looking back, for the possible significance of the *Phaedrus*. Theophrastus stresses the need for the beautification of the μουσεῖον (Diog.

---

31 On the history of the term cf. Kuch 1965 and the further bibliography in Pfeiffer 1968, 156 n. 3.
32 Cf., e.g., Fraser 1972, I 318, II 471–472.
33 Cf., e.g., Pfeiffer 1968, 159.
34 For discussion and bibliography cf., e.g., Montana 2015, 77–79.
35 Cf., e.g., Fraser 1972, I 314–315.
36 Cf. Epicrates fr. 10.11 K-A, Cic. *De finibus* 5.1.1–2, Diog. Laert. 3.7, 20, 4.1, 19.

Laert. 5.51), and he refers to a garden and a walk and houses near the garden which he leaves to a list of friends who may use them when they wish 'to study and philosophise together' (συσχολάζειν καὶ συμφιλοσοφεῖν, Diog. Laert. 5.52–53). This is probably the earliest extant occurrence of συσχολάζειν, and it here clearly denotes a sense of shared intellectual enterprise; σχολή is something held and used in common with the like-minded. Alongside this development in the meaning of the verb, it is clear that the senses of 'lecture, learned disquisition' and 'gathering for intellectual discussion' for σχολή were already current in the fourth century,[37] and it is to this period that crucial steps in both the semantics of this set of words and the ideals they designated must be traced. Plato's determination of philosophy as the true or highest form of μουσική may have given his Muses a rather different nuance than the goddesses who presided over the scholarship and learning (and the poetry) of the Museum,[38] but this difference may seem more significant to us than it will have done in antiquity.

If intellectual activity, whether philosophical or philological, is σχολή, it is (or can be) also very hard 'work'; the paradox becomes less striking, however, the greater the emphasis is given to the 'freedom of choice' implied by σχολή. In philosophical texts, particular emphasis may indeed be laid upon the πόνοι necessary in preparation for the philosophical life. The author of the *Seventh Letter* ascribed to Plato refers repeatedly to the fact that a willingness to go through these 'labours' is the best way to test whether someone really does have a desire for philosophy (cf. 340c1, 340d8, 341a5), and it is a similarly rigorous and prolonged training that the *Republic* lays down for the Guardians (cf., e.g., 8.539d–e); this is a σχολή which is not for the faint-hearted. As for other areas of non-physical activity, the language of craft (cf., e.g., Ar. *Thesm.* 52–8) and 'labour', and indeed *labor*, became standard in some descriptions of poetic activity, and was particularly common in the Hellenistic and Roman periods;[39] it is of course central to the essence of Roman 'neoteric' poetics, where it sits happily alongside a significant place given to 'play', παίζειν, *ludere* (cf. Catullus 51 etc). The language of πόνος also attaches itself very readily to scholarship. We think, on the one hand, of the jokes and anecdotes about Philitas whose researches

---

[37] Cf. LSJ s.v. II, Newman on Arist. *Pol.* 5.1313b3, Arnott on Alexis fr. 163.3, where σχολὴ Πλάτωνος suggests that the noun is felt as carrying a slightly uncolloquial, philosophical flavour; whether we may also infer that this usage was particularly associated (in the comic or popular mind) with Plato is uncertain, but the thought is tempting.

[38] Cf., e.g., Murray 2004, 386–387.

[39] Cf., e.g., Hunter on Theocritus 7.51. On craft metaphors in the lyric and comic poets cf. also Wright 2012, 116–120.

caused him to waste away (like a cicada??),⁴⁰ and on the other of the 'chalcentericity' of a Didymus.

A case such as Didymus is of course at one end of a spectrum. Aristotle had warned that, just as 'banausic' activities 'take away the intellect's σχολή [lit. 'make the intellect ἄσχολος'] and make it lowly (ταπεινή)', so a similar danger attends too great an attention to 'liberal arts' (αἱ ἐλευθερίαι ἐπιστῆμαι), *Pol.* 8.1337b10–17;⁴¹ one must not be unnecessarily concerned to achieve full *akribeia*, and such a warning, coming from a philosophical perspective, suggests interesting questions about the world of Alexandrian (and indeed modern) scholarship which lay ahead. Modern scholars lay great stress on nailing down the last detail with the greatest *akribeia*, but perhaps there is, after all, something to be said for the broad generalisation, even within the context of scholarly discourse. The interplay of πόνος and σχολή, of *labor* and *otium*, becomes in fact a hallmark of philological and poetic activity, including the activity of reading and studying, and how they are represented in the Hellenistic and Roman periods. In *Oration* 18, for example, Dio offers advice on reading to a man of some substance, perhaps a Roman, who seeks to increase his 'public engagement', to become a proper πολιτικὸς ἀνήρ, and his rhetorical preparedness for that; Dio flatters his addressee that the latter does not shrink from the *ponos* of education (18.1), but also hastens to assure him that there is no need (in his case) of πόνος καὶ ταλαιπωρία, for such hard work is only a benefit to those who are already far advanced in rhetorical training (18.6). Moreover, whereas some poetry, notably of course Homer, is 'first, last and in the middle' of compulsory reading for the would-be public figure, only someone with σχολή will have time for 'lyric poetry and elegy and iambics and dithyrambs' (18.8); similarly, Quintilian notes that only someone who is fully mature in his rhetorical education 'will have time for' (*uacabit*) elegy (10.1.58). What you read speaks volumes about yourself and your seriousness; leisure is a valued ideal, but it too needs direction and purpose — we are back with the always fragile boundary between παιδεία and παιδιά.

'Longinus' shows us one literary and rhetorical turn on Aristotle's warning against excessive ἀκρίβεια when he praises 'godlike' writers such as Plato and Demosthenes 'who aimed at what is greatest in writing and scorned *akribeia* in everything' (*De subl.* 35.1–2, cf. 36.3); this argument transfers to prose the com-

---

40 Cf. Spanoudakis 2002, 54–55.
41 Newman ad loc. adduces similar observations elsewhere; Xen. *Mem.* 4.7 ascribes to Socrates the view that there are clear limits to the study which ὁ ὀρθῶς πεπαιδευμένος should devote to geometry, astronomy and arithmetic.

parisons between poets made in *De subl.* 33.4–5, where the contrast is between 'polished flawlessness' and explosive sublimity, a quality shown by great poets, even though their writing may sometimes fall flat.[42] Poets such as Homer, Pindar and Sophocles who exemplify this sublimity reveal their μεγαλοφροσύνη, 'greatness of mind'. The social implications of this term are not to be overlooked. Writers capable of the sublime, the μεγαλοφυεῖς, also appeal to the values of an educated élite, for whom a concern with the niceties of τέχνη, rather than the proper φύσις of man (cf. *De subl.* 36.3–4), might seem demeaning; the social assumptions which inform 'Longinian' sublimity descend at an unknown number of removes from some of the same assumptions which are embodied in the classical conception of σχολή. Rather similar conclusions may be drawn from the mode of self-presentation chosen by Aulus Gellius in the Preface to *Attic Nights*.[43] Gellius admits to having tired himself out with searching through books in every hour of *otium* which he could 'steal' from his *negotia* (*Praef.* 12, cf. 14 *lucubratiunculas istas*, 23); he is, however, keen to assure us (almost as if he is conscious of the passage of Aristotle which I have just cited) that, even on difficult and obscure subjects, he has not gone too deeply into such obscurities, but rather offers us 'the first fruits, as it were, and a sampling of the liberal arts (*ingenuae artes*)', *Praef.* 13, 17. Gellius' imagined audience will themselves enjoy his work *in otio atque in ludo* (*Praef.* 17), though these will be people used to both the pleasure and the *labor* (and the sleeplessness) of reading and research (*Praef.* 19). Those whom Gellius specifically bans from his audience, those who, as a Callimachus might have said, are 'no friends of the Muse' (cf. *Praef.* 19–21, citing Ar. *Frogs* 356), are those too occupied with 'disturbances and business' (*intemperiae negotiaque*) ever to have enjoyed such intellectual pursuits. The contrast is, in various guises, very familiar; the enthusiastic Apollodorus at the start of Plato's *Symposium* similarly contrasts the pleasure and benefit he gets from philosophical discussion with the distaste and uselessness of the conversation of 'the wealthy and those engaged in business' (173c6). The pursuit of money and power is a relentless task-master.

When we turn back to Hellenistic poetry, it is natural to think first of the 'Reply to the Telchines' at the head of Callimachus' *Aetia*. Callimachus' famous association of himself there with the cicada ('the light, the winged one') has

---

42 These passages of 'Longinus' may, from one perspective, be seen as a transference to literary and rhetorical criticism of Aristotle's ethical views, cf. *EN* 4.1123b6–7, 'greatness of soul exists in size, as also does beauty in a tall body; the short are witty and well-proportioned, but not beautiful'.

43 On other aspects of this passage cf. Holford-Strevens 2003, 36–38.

been read as a way of reading his poetics into the myth of the *Phaedrus*,⁴⁴ and allusion to Plato's most famous aetiological myth would obviously not be out of place at the head of the *Aetia* and also clearly suits a poem in which the poet appears to chat freely with the Muses. Whereas the cicada is free to sing as it chooses — it reports to no master other than the Muses — the braying ass which Callimachus rejects (or would like to) is not merely proverbially unmusical, but is also the quintessential beast of burden, of slavish labour;⁴⁵ the ass has no freedom and no autonomous σχολή, that prize which the Callimachean *persona* feels is threatened by the burden of old age which weighs upon him.⁴⁶ The uncertainty about how the 'Reply' was linked to the main body of the *Aetia* means that some questions will always remain unanswered, but the poetic *persona* of the narrator of Books 1–2, at least, might seem (*inter alia*) to embody an ideal of σχολή appropriate to a 'free man'.⁴⁷ Callimachus can pursue his enquiries wherever curiosity and/or wonder takes him; he is, as Socrates would have said in the *Theaetetus*, not pressed by time. Fr. 178 on the antiquities of Ikos, a fragment to which I have already referred, dramatizes the freedom and 'leisure' of free men, not just to reject any compulsion, including the compulsion to drink a lot, but also to pursue any subject they wish, even if it concerns a girl carrying a spring-onion. Whether, on the other hand, the researches of, say, a Callimachus or an Eratosthenes were pursued 'for their own sake' and not for the sake of others, as Aristotle repeatedly claims to be uniquely true for philosophy (e.g. *Met.* 1.982b24–27, *EN* 10.1177b1–4), may be debated.

The ideal of intellectual σχολή that I have been tracing arose in a particular political and social environment, that of democratic Athens; as we have seen, it reflects the pattern of social hierarchy and the basic slave-free distinction of that society. As this ideal is taken over and incorporated into societies which are arranged rather differently, then it will naturally adapt to new conditions; as an ideal it is an aspirational model, not a tool of sociological analysis. For poets and scholars of the Hellenistic period a particular restraint on 'freedom' might seem to be the system of patronage under which many operated for at least some of the time.⁴⁸ I have argued that the Museum represented an 'institutionalisation' of σχολή, but it might be argued that it rather stood as a physical em-

---

44 Cf. Acosta-Hughes/Stephens 2002, 252–253; 2012, 36–40, Fantuzzi/Hunter 2004, 72. On the allusion in this passage to Plato's *Ion* cf. Hunter 1989.
45 Cf. Griffith 2006, 224–9, 318–19.
46 Cf. Fantuzzi/Hunter 2004, 74–76.
47 Cf. Fantuzzi/Hunter 2004, 59–60.
48 On poetic patronage in the Hellenistic period cf. Hunter 2003, 24–45.

bodiment of the dependence of its members upon the support and generosity of the king. Both perspectives of course are true.[49]

In Books 1–2 of the *Aitia*, at least, Callimachus conversed with the Muses in a dream, but whether that dream was nocturnal or the result of a mid-day snooze (as, in a brief moment of σχολή, I once suggested)[50] we cannot say; either way, we may think of this more as 'rest' than 'leisure', but it certainly severs any overt link between the process of poetic composition and *ponos*. Ovid may have picked this up, as he picked up much else from Callimachus. In *Amores* 1.5 the poet is having his siesta when he receives a very welcome visitor:

> aestus erat, mediamque dies exegerat horam;
>   adposui medio membra leuanda toro.
> pars adaperta fuit, pars altera clausa fenestrae;
>   quale fere siluae lumen habere solent,
> qualia sublucent fugiente crepuscula Phoebo,   5
>   aut ubi nox abiit, nec tamen orta dies.
> illa uerecundis lux est praebenda puellis,
>   qua timidus latebras speret habere pudor.
> ecce, Corinna uenit, tunica uelata recincta,
>   candida diuidua colla tegente coma—   10
> qualiter in thalamos famosa Semiramis isse
>   dicitur, et multis Lais amata uiris.
>
> Ovid, *Amores* 1.5.1–12

It was sweltering, and the day had passed the middle hour; I had laid my limb in the middle of the couch for a rest. One of the window-shutters was open, the other closed; the light was like that in woods, or when the even in shadows still have a glow as Phoebus takes his leave, or when night has passed but day has not yet arisen. This is the light proper for shy girls whose frightened modesty hopes to find somewhere to hide. Behold! Corinna appears, dressed in a tunic bound around her, her parted hair falling over her gleaming neck, just as famed Semiramis is said to have gone to her bedchamber, and Lais who was loved by many men.

It has long been recognised that Corinna's appearance resembles the epiphany of a god appearing in the heat of the day, but we may also see Corinna here as the coming of poetry (or a poetry book called *Corinna*?) to the poet as he dozes in the heat and the half-light. Ovid clearly suggests that her coming was a dream of his imagination, occasioned by the conditions and the interplay of light and shade, and he teases us to decide just how 'real' the subsequent love-

---

[49] An analogy might be sought in the mixture of continuity and innovation which the Hellenistic courts brought to the traditional language of φιλία, cf., e.g., Herman 1980/1.
[50] Hunter 1989, 2.

making actually was. Corinna is, of course, Ovid's 'Muse' and her appearance brings with it the creativity of the poet: without 'rest' (or 'leisure') there is no creative (or, in the case of the elegiac poet, sexual) impulse. Whereas Callimachus exchanged thousands of verses of learned discourse with the Muses, Ovid wastes not a second on conversation: *deripui tunicam* (v. 13) probably does not correspond to anything in the *Aitia*, and it is unlikely (to say the least) that the young Callimachus felt himself physically, as well as intellectually, aroused by the presence of the Muses. For Ovid, however, the two are inseparable and, as he lies fantasising on his bed, he feels an elegy coming on.

Ovid's spirit (and that of *otium*) lives on, and where better than beneath the dreaming (or should that be 'snoozing') spires of Oxford. Here is Robin Nisbet's account of 'How textual conjecture are made' (Nisbet 1995, 361):

> Conjectures are not made in the Bodleian Library: the spectacle of so much earnest activity is inhibiting ... Conjectures can be made on uncrowded trains, if one is operating from a plain text without any aids of scholarship. They can be made on holiday, when one feels no obligation to be busy, and the relaxed mind summons up and integrates things long forgotten. The period after Christmas is particularly productive, when everything is shut and one is slouched in an armchair half-asleep. The Muse of Textual Conjecture (let us call her Eustochia) only visits those who have worked, but she does not visit us when we are actually working.

I do not know whether Nisbet was deliberately evoking *Amores* 1.5, though I would not put it past him; I am, however, pretty certain that his plans for Eustochia differed somewhat from Ovid's for Corinna. Be that as it may, it is again in the relation between work and relaxation, between ἀσχολία and σχολή, that the moment (or in Ovid's case, window) of creative generation opens and demands to be seized. σχολή can be very hard work indeed.

Bibliography

Acosta-Hughes, B./Stephens, S. 2002. 'Rereading Callimachus' *Aetia* Fragment 1', *Classical Philology* 97, 238–253.
Acosta-Hughes, B./Stephens, S. 2012. *Callimachus in Context*, Cambridge.
Baltes, M. 1993. 'Plato's School, the Academy', *Hermathena* 155, 5–26.
Barrett, W.S. 1964. *Euripides, Hippolytus*, Oxford.
Berti, E. 2010. *Sumphilosophein. La vita nell'Accademia di Platone*, Rome/Bari.
Capra, A. 2014. *Plato's Four Muses*, Washington DC.
Carter, L.B. 1986. *The Quiet Athenian*, Oxford.
Fantuzzi, M./Hunter, R. 2004. *Tradition and Innovation in Hellenistic Poetry*, Cambridge.
Ferrari, G.R.F. 1987. *Listening to the Cicadas*, Cambridge.

Ford, A. 1999. 'Odysseus after dinner: *Od.* 9.2–11 and the traditions of sympotic song', in: J.N. Kazazis/A. Rengakos (eds.), *Euphrosyne. Studies in Ancient Epic and its Legacy in honor of Dimitris N. Maronitis*, Stuttgart, 109–123.
Fraser, P.M. 1972. *Ptolemaic Alexandria*, Oxford.
Griffith, M. 2006. 'Horsepower and donkeywork: equids and the ancient Greek imagination', *Classical Philology* 101, 185–246, 307–358.
Halliwell, S. 2011. *Between Ecstasy and Truth*, Oxford.
Herman, G. 1980/1. 'The "friends" of the early Hellenistic rulers: servants or officials?', *Talanta* 12/13, 103–149.
Herter, H. 1952. *Platons Akademie*, 2nd ed., Bonn.
Holford-Strevens, L. 2003. *Aulus Gellius. An Antonine Scholar and his Achievement*, 2nd ed., Oxford.
Hunter, R. 1989. 'Winged Callimachus', *Zeitschrift für Papyrologie und Epigraphik* 76, 1–2 [= Hunter 2008, 86–88].
Hunter, R. 1993. *The Argonautica of Apollonius: Literary Studies*, Cambridge.
Hunter, R. 2003. *Theocritus. Encomium of Ptolemy Philadelphus*, Berkeley/Los Angeles.
Hunter, R. 2008. *On Coming After. Studies in Post-Classical Greek Literature and its Reception*, Berlin/New York.
Hunter, R. 2012. *Plato and the Traditions of Ancient Literature. The Silent Stream*, Cambridge.
Hunter, R. 2018. *The Measure of Homer*, Cambridge.
Kosmin, P.J. 2014. *The Land of the Elephant Kings*, Cambridge MA.
Kuch, H. 1965. ΦΙΛΟΛΟΓΟΣ. *Untersuchung eines Wortes von seinem ersten Auftreten in der Tradition bis zur ersten überlieferten lexikalischen Festlegung*, Berlin.
Mastronarde, D.J. 2010. *The Art of Euripides*, Cambridge.
Montana, F. 2015. 'Hellenistic scholarship', in: F. Montanari/S. Matthaios/A. Rengakos (eds.), *Brill's Companion to Ancient Greek Scholarship*, Leiden, 160–183.
Murray, P. 2004. 'The Muses and their arts', in: P. Murray/P. Wilson (eds.), *Music and the Muses*, Oxford, 365–389.
Nelis, D. 2001. *Vergil's Aeneid and the Argonautica of Apollonius Rhodius*, Leeds.
Nightingale, A.W. 1995. *Genres in Dialogue*, Cambridge.
Nightingale, A.W. 2004. *Spectacles of Truth in Classical Greek Philosophy*, Cambridge.
Nisbet, R.G.M. 1995. *Collected Papers in Latin Literature*, Oxford.
O'Sullivan, T.M. 2011. *Walking in Roman Culture*, Cambridge.
Pfeiffer, R. 1968. *History of Classical Scholarship*, Oxford.
Riginos, A.S. 1976. *Platonica: the Anecdotes concerning the Life and Writings of Plato*, Leiden.
Roman, L. 2014. *Poetic Autonomy in Ancient Rome*, Oxford.
Romeri, L. 2002. *Philosophes entre mots et mets*, Grenoble.
Schütrumpf, E. 2009. 'Heraclides, *On Pleasure*', in: W.W. Fortenbaugh/E. Pender (eds.), *Heraclides of Pontus. Discussion*, New Brunswick NJ, 69–91.
Spanoudakis, K. 2002. *Philitas of Cos*, Leiden.
Stocks, J.L. 1936. 'ΣΧΟΛΗ', *Classical Quarterly* 30, 177–187.
Tarrant, H. 2008. 'The dramatic background of the arguments with Callicles, Euripides' *Antiope*, and an Athenian anti-intellectual argument', *Antichthon* 42, 20–39
Toner, J.P. 1995. *Leisure and Ancient Rome*, Cambridge.
Wilson, P. 2000. 'Euripides' tragic Muse', *Illinois Classical Studies* 24/25, 427–449.
Wolf, S.R. 1993. *Herakles beim Gelage*, Cologne.
Wright, M. 2012. *The Comedian as Critic*, London.

14 Death of a Child: Grief Beyond the Literary?

From Notion, the port of Colophon, there survives a well-known poem of imperial date on a three-year-old boy who drowned in a well:[1]

ἡνίκα δ' ἥλιος μὲν ἔδυ πρὸς δώματα [.........]
δειπνήσας, ἦλθον μετὰ τοῦ μήτρω λο[έασ]θαι,
καὐθύς με Μοῖραι προκαθίζανον εἰς φ[ρέ]αρ αὐτοῦ·
ἔγδυνον γὰρ ἐγὼ καὶ ἀπῆγέ με Μοῖρα κακίστη.
χὼς εἶδεν δαίμων με κάτω, παρέδωκε Χ[άρ]ωνει·   5
αὐτὰρ ὁ μήτρως μου ψόφον ἤκουσεν φρεατισμοῦ,
κεὐθύς μ' ἐζήτει γ' ἄρ'· ἐγὼ δὲ οὐκ ἐλπίδαν εἶχον
ζωῆς τῆς κατ' ἐμαυτὸν ἐν ἀνθρώποισι μιγῆναι.
ἔτρεχεν ἡ νάννη καὶ σχείζει τόν γε χιτῶνα·
ἔτρεχε κὴ μήτηρ καὶ ἵστατο ἤγε τυπητόν.   10
κεὐθὺς Ἀλεξάνδρῳ πρὸς γούνατα πρόσπεσε νάννη,
κοὐκ ἔτ' ἔμελλεν ἰδών, ἐνπήδα δ' εἰς φρέαρ εὐθύς.
ὡς εὑρέν με κάτω βεβυθισμένον ἐξήνεν[κ]εν ἐ<ν> κοφίνῳ·
κεὐθὺς δὴ νάννη με διάβροχον ἥρπασε θᾶσ<σ>ον,
σκεπτομένη ζωῆς ἤτιν' ἔχω μερίδα·
ὦ δ' ἐμὲ τὸν [δύσ]τηνον τὸν οὐκ ἐφιδόντα παλαίσ[τρα]ν,   15
ἀλλ' ἤδη τριετῇ Μοῖρα [κάλ]υψε κακή.

GV 1159 = SGO 03/05/04

When the sun had gone down to the halls [...],
I came after dinner with my uncle to wash.
At once the Fates sat me there on the well,
for I fell in and a most hateful Fate took me away.
When the *daimon* saw me below, he handed me over to Charon.
But my uncle heard the sound of my falling into the well,
and straightaway he went looking for me, but I no longer had any hope
of mixing with men in my lifetime.
My aunt ran up and tore her gown;
my mother ran up and started beating her breast.

I am grateful to audiences in Cambridge, Chicago, Dublin, London, and Venice for much stimulating discussion and to the editors of this volume for their help. All translations are my own, unless otherwise stated.

1 I reproduce essentially the text of *SGO* and pass over in silence several textual and interpretative problems; I hope (and believe) that none of these problems has a significant bearing on the argument of this chapter.

> Straightaway my aunt fell to embrace Alexander's knees,
> and when he saw this, he did not hesitate, but straightaway jumped into the well.
> When he found me down there drowned, he brought me out in a basket.
> Straightaway my aunt snatched my dripping body
>   to see whether I had any share of life left.
> Alas for my wretched fate! I did not live to see the *palaistra*,
>   but an evil Fate concealed me when I was just three years old.

This remarkably vivid poem offers serious problems of text and interpretation — the meaning of προκαθίζανον in verse 3,[2] the related problem of γάρ in verse 4, the hypermetric verse 13,[3] and so on — but the plainness of the colloquial language, the evocation of the voice and thought processes of a young child, and such stylistic effects as the anaphora of ἔτρεχεν (vv. 9–10) contained within a detailed narrative, which is both relatively lengthy and breathlessly swift, make this a text fully deserving of attention; it is virtually without close parallel in our corpus of sepulchral poetry.[4]

The language and versification of the Notion poem, as well as its remarkable narrative technique, offer the opportunity to consider the implications of the term 'literary', as it is applied to Hellenistic and later epigram and regularly denied to poetry that survives only on inscriptions. One feature of the Notion poem will strike any modern reader at once: the introduction of two pentameters at the end of the poem, which results in an elegiac rather than hexameter conclusion to the poem. The irregular mixing of hexameters and pentameters is a familiar feature of inscribed, particularly sepulchral, poetry, though 'irregularity' may not be the best way to describe the phenomenon. It appears early in

---

2 LSJ s.v. προκαθίζω understands 'cause to sit down in', which makes some sense in the context and is essentially accepted by Merkelbach and Stauber (SGO); Vérilhac 1978, 155 (cf. 1982, 113), however, translates *me firent tomber* ('made me fall'), which is harder to get from the ordinary usage of related verbs. Giambattista D'Alessio has suggested correcting με to μοι, but the author was presumably familiar with initial μ- lengthening the preceding syllable in Homer.

3 Peek (GV) suggested that ἐ<ν> κοφίνῳ, as read by Louis Robert, was in fact the start of a new verse, the rest of which has fallen out; Enrico Magnelli has noted the possibility that this lost verse was a pentameter, thus giving an ending to the poem (three distichs) that is even closer to that of Posidipp. AP 7.170 (see p. 272 here) than the text we possess.

4 Vérilhac 1982, 113 describes this text as 'completely exceptional' (*tout à fait exceptionnel*). The closest parallel she can find is GV 1988 = GG 459, which mourns a family killed (apparently) when their house collapsed; the second part of that poem (or diptych) is spoken by the young boy who was killed, and he notes that the family went to sleep 'after the evening meal' (μεταδόρπιον). This poem is, however, very far from the Notion poem in terms of both style and narrative technique.

the tradition,[5] and from later epitaphs for children one may cite *GV* 684 (hex – pent – 2 hex – pent), 734 (hex – pent – 4 hex – pent), 745 (2 hex – pent – hex – pent – 3 hex – pent – hex), 874 (= *SGO* 05/01/36), a poem for an eleven-year old boy who was killed in a fall from a tree (hex – pent – 3 hex – pent – hex – pent – 3 hex), 969 (= *SGO* 04/08/02, 2 hex – pent – hex – pent – 2 hex – pent – 2 hex), 1038 (3 hex – pent – 2 hex), and 1270 (hex – pent – 3 hex – pent – hex – pent). Two general points may be made here. In any given case, there may be a particular reason for a pattern of hexameters and pentameters, although this is an area where difference of opinion is almost inevitable. Thus, for example, *GV* 1331 = *SGO* 04/21/03 is a sepulchral epigram of the second century CE from Lydia:

ζητεῖς, ὦ παροδεῖτα, τίς ἡ στήλλη, τίς ὁ τύμβος.
τίς δ' ἐν τῇ στήλλῃ εἰκὼν νεότευκτος ὑπάρχει·
 υἱὸς Τρύφωνος τοὔνομα τάτὸν ἔχων·
τεσσαρακαιδεκέτη δόλιχον βιότου σταδιεύσας
τοῦθ' ὅ ποτε ὢν γέγονα· στήλλη, τύμβος, λίθος, εἰκών.   5

GV 1331 = *SGO* 04/21/03

You wonder, passer-by, what is this stele, what is this tomb,
whose is the newly crafted image on the stele?
 The son of Tryphon, which is my name also.
I ran the race of life for fourteen years,
and this is what I, who once existed, have become: a stele, a tomb, a stone,
an image.

Here, I think, it is easy to believe that the central pentameter carries the essential message of this extraordinarily powerful poem — the deceased's and his father's name — whereas the surrounding pairs of hexameters respond to each other through the pathetic repetition of nouns between verses 1–2 and 4–5 and the fact that, though the passer-by will move on, Tryphon's race is over: all movement, and indeed existence itself, has come to an end, and all that is left is 'an image'.[6] This case is a relatively simple one, but it also serves to remind us that, in the inscribed funerary poetry of the empire (and indeed before), it is the pentameter that is the 'marked' length, the hexameter being the default verse form. Hexameters may readily be multiplied, pentameters not; the process may be thought of as a kind of 'extension', which disturbs or expands the elegiac

---

5 Cf. e.g. *CEG* 108, 171, 518, 524, etc.; Allen 1885–1886, 52–5, Clairmont 1970, 51. Single pentameters regularly close a sequence of hexameters; cf. e.g. *CEG* 509, 543, 585, 704.
6 Comparable in some respects is a much earlier poem from Euboea, *CEG* 108, of the mid-fifth century BCE. In it two hexameters call the attention of passers-by to the key information — the deceased's name and origin — contained in a following pentameter.

pattern but does not fundamentally destroy it. The rarity of pairs of pentameters, let alone longer runs of stichic pentameters,[7] at all periods of Greek verse makes the relation between hexameter and pentameter very clear; as the 'marked' length, the pentameter may also have a tendency to carry significant meaning. There is a further, related issue raised by the poem for Tryphon that cannot be pursued at any length here. The poem is inscribed on a stele that depicts Tryphon with his dog; the first two hexameters stand in the frame above the relief, but the pentameter and the start of the next hexameter encircle the top of the relief. The pentameter is thus prominently positioned near the representation (to aid with the identification of the deceased?), but is not otherwise marked out. The spatial relation between a poem and any image that accompanies it can never be left out of account in considering the pattern of the verses.[8] I will return briefly to this question with regard to the Notion poem.

The pattern of hexameters and pentameters in inscribed poetry also raises the question of the relationship between such poetry and the 'literary' funerary epigrams composed by famous and not-so-famous poets from the high Hellenistic period onwards, which are very largely preserved for us in the manuscripts of the anthology tradition. Such 'literary' epigrams do not show irregularities in this matter: elegiac distichs follow each other with perfect regularity, as they also in fact do in the majority of inscribed epitaphs. The elimination of irregularities, if that indeed is what we are dealing with, may readily be understood as one further way in which an Asclepiades or a Meleager marked off their funerary epigrams from the poems actually inscribed on tombs. With regard to the metrical technique of 'literary' epigrammatists, Marco Fantuzzi and Alex Sens have written that they

> adopt[ed] a style of versification that in and of itself distinguished their compositions from the poetry that was actually inscribed on tombs during their lifetimes ... their verse-technique ... seems to serve as a crucial 'sphragis' marking not only their literariness but

---

7 Cf. *GV* 1805, Heliod. *Aeth.* 3.2.3–3.1. Reports of 'literary' poems ἐν πενταμέτρῳ (e.g. *Suda* π 248 on Panyassis) are usually (and surely rightly) understood as references to elegiac distichs, cf. Matthews 1974, 26–27. Single pentameters do appear as early epitaphs, cf. *GV* 928, *CEG* 176, 678 (with Hansen's note) and, for pairs of pentameters, cf. *CEG* 667, 689, 841; for pairs of pentameters sandwiched between hexameters, cf. *CEG* 171, 177 (ii), 518, 524, and for three pentameters after a hexameter, cf. *CEG* 82, 662, 715. *SGO* 01/12/17 (Halicarnassus, late Hellenistic) shows the pattern hex – pent – hex – 2 × pent, the final pentameters carrying the central thrust of the message.

8 For the archaic and classical periods, see especially Clairmont 1970.

also the difference between their compositions and the minor poetry, largely anonymous, of professional authors who composed for a diverse market.⁹

The inevitable regularity of the verse pattern may be one further marker of difference and of a sense, not just of specialness, but also of 'literary tradition': a Mimnermus or a Theognis, too, surely never strayed from the regularity of the distich pattern.

When we return to the Notion poem, we note that the two pentameters come at the end and are closely bound to the hexameters that precede them; in other words, we may say that the poem concludes with two distichs. This may simply mark, as Valentina Garulli put it, *il recupero di uno stile più tradizionalmente epigrammatico*¹⁰ as the poem draws to a close, and there are certainly parallels for such a shift of versification at the end of a poem.¹¹ We might regard the Notion poem as effecting a kind of 'gliding transition' from narrative to 'epitaph proper', with verse 15, the first pentameter, bearing most of the weight of the transition. What is, however, most striking is how our recognition, halfway through verse 15, that we are suddenly reading a pentameter, not a hexameter, coincides with the aunt's recognition that the child is dead: ζωῆς is the hinge around which the poem turns, 'life' really on the edge. Nor is this the only poetic effect that points in this direction. If we exempt the final distich, the poem falls into two sections: the speaker's fate dominates the first (vv. 1–8), the reaction of those left behind the second (vv. 9–15); ζωῆς, or rather its negation, closes the first section and that closing, which is an ending in more ways than one, is poetically marked by the only example of enjambment between verses in the poem. The closing of the second section is then marked by another stylistic effect, namely the intrusion of pentameters, the rhythmical hallmark of an epitaph. Epitaphs are acknowledgements of death, of a finality from which there is no turning back, and they are, specifically, acknowledgements ('recognition', we might say) made by those who are left behind, even when the epitaph is made to speak, as the Notion poem does, in the deceased's voice. The child knew of, had 'recognized', his death (vv. 5, 7–8) long before those to whom he was dear did so; the dawning of the horrible truth upon those left behind is marked by the familiar consolation (or absence of it) offered by elegiac distichs, the epitaphic rhythm par excellence. 'Recognition' is a term also appropriate to the dramatic,

---

9 Fantuzzi/Sens 2006, 118.
10 Garulli 2012, 180 ('the recovery of a more traditionally epigrammatic style').
11 In *SGO* 01/02/01 (third century BCE, Tymnos), a poem in five distichs explains the image of a snake on the tomb, and then two hexameters tell the passer-by where to look to see the deceased's name.

theatrical quality of this narrative: the dead child is the audience of his own tragedy, for tragedy (for the living) may consist not in what happens but — as we and Oedipus know only too well — in discovering what has happened.

The feature of the Notion poem that has been most discussed is the fact that verse 15, the first pentameter, is a very lightly varied version of a verse from another poem, variously ascribed in the *Greek Anthology* to Posidippus and Callimachus, on the death of a three-year-old in a well, and verse 14 also seems to borrow directly from this same poem:

> τὸν τριετῆ παίζοντα περὶ φρέαρ Ἀρχιάνακτα
> εἴδωλον μορφᾶς κωφὸν ἐπεσπάσατο,
> ἐκ δ' ὕδατος τὸν παῖδα διάβροχον ἅρπασε μάτηρ
> σκεπτομένα ζωᾶς εἴ τινα μοῖραν ἔχει.
> Νύμφας δ' οὐκ ἐμίηνεν ὁ νήπιος, ἀλλ' ἐπὶ γούνοις   5
> ματρὸς κοιμαθεὶς τὸν βαθὺν ὕπνον ἔχει.
>
> Posidipp. *AP* 7.170 = *HE* 21 = 131 A–B[12]

> As the three-year old Archianax was playing around a well,
>   the dumb image of his form drew him in.
> His mother snatched her dripping son from the water,
>   wondering whether he still had any part of life.
> The child did not defile the Nymphs, but lying
>   on his mother's knees he rests in deep sleep.

No doubt, many young children were in fact drowned in wells,[13] and the citation of a verse (and more) from a (famous?) poem, or at least one believed to have been written by a famous poet, inscribes the death of our nameless child within a tradition in which that death may be somehow ennobled and memorialized. With the Notion poem, however, we are confronted on the stone with the shock of a death that is not something to be read about at a safe distance, in a book of poetry, but is rather a thing of vivid horror: not for this child and his parents the consolation and almost blessed relief of euphemism, 'deep sleep on his mother's knees' (which perhaps evokes, as has often been suggested, a sculptural image on a real or imagined stele),[14] and piety, 'he did not defile the nymphs',[15]

---

[12] I accept the now standard attribution, though I do not think that much hangs on it for my argument. I print the text of Austin/Bastianini 2002.
[13] *SGO* 08/06/10 is an imperial epitaph from Hadrianouthera for a three-year-old who was apparently drowned at a bath (Νυμφῶν παρὰ λουτροῖς).
[14] Cf. Gow and Page 1965, 2: 501 (= *HE* 3179); Vérilhac 1978, 154. Callimachus all but explicitly acknowledges this euphemism in *AP* 7.451 = *HE* 1231–1232: 'Here Saon from Acanthus, the son

but rather the inconsolable reality of a wet and wretched Fate, which did not allow him even to reach the age for the *palaistra*.¹⁶ Students of literary *uariatio* will note not only that the Notion poet has moved Posidippus' τριετῆ from the first verse to a perhaps more significant and pathetic position in the last one, but that the rewriting in verse 15, which uses the form μερίς, allows the poet to keep the form μοῖρα for a more significant role in his poem (vv. 3–4, 17).

Not everyone will interpret these phenomena as I just have. Anne-Marie Vérilhac, for example, sees the pentameters as simply a result of the poet's incompetent *imitatio*: 'The author, a mediocre versifier, could neither write a narrative in distichs nor disentangle himself sufficiently from his models to abandon the metre they had used.'¹⁷ More helpful, however, than such judgements may be to use the Notion poet's imitation of Posidippus to tease out distinctive features of both poems. Let me start with a striking feature of the Notion poem: we nowhere learn the dead child's name, and a glance through any collection of poems on this subject, such as that of Vérilhac 1978, will show how rare it is for such an epitaphic poem not to contain the deceased's name, even when the poem is cast as a first-person address by the dead. It is possible (just) that the name is concealed by corruption or textual loss, but it is much more likely that the name was either displayed separately on the tomb, physically separated from the poem (cf. e.g. *GV* 632, 1270, 1595, etc.),¹⁸ or even occurred in another poem (cf. *GV* 1988). The former possibility could be seen as an elaboration of a very early and common type of epitaph (e.g. *GV* 928–30, *CEG* 722), in which the deceased's name was displayed on one line, followed or preceded by a brief

---

of Dicon, rests in holy sleep: say not that the good die'. *GV* 647 (imperial Rome) makes the same point and need not be a memory of Callimachus.

15 Piacenza 1998 offers an interesting discussion of the final couplet of Posidipp. *AP* 7.170, but it seems very improbable that the stress is on the fact that the mother's action in 'snatching' her child from the water deprived it of the immortality bestowed upon those taken by the nymphs. The principal point rather must be that the child did not 'defile' the nymphs by death in the well (cf. E. *Hipp.* 1437–1438 with Barrett's note).
16 On this motif, see further, p. 284.
17 Vérilhac 1978, 156 (my translation).
18 *GV* 1595 is cited at p. 277. *GV* 1765 = *SGO* 05/01/64 (Smyrna, perhaps third century CE) is a first-person account, by a young boy, of how, after death from illness, he was carried to Olympus like Ganymedes; the poem does not record the boy's name or that of his parents, but the sixteen hexameters may not form the whole poem, and the names perhaps appeared either in the missing part or elsewhere on the tomb. See further Hunter 2018, 49–55.

metrical epitaph.[19] It is clear from the stone that we have the whole of the Notion poem,[20] but what accompanied it we cannot tell; we certainly cannot rule out the possibility that there was, for example, a representation of a child, and even a well. Nevertheless, the namelessness in the poem remains and tells its own story. We may see this as part of the surprisingly consistent *ethopoiia* of the dead child's voice[21] — 'this narrative concerns 'me', and I do not use my own name when talking about myself' — but the namelessness is also of a piece with the inwardness of this bleak narrative: no passer-by is addressed, there is no protreptic 'cease your lamentations' addressed to the parents, and no overt suggestion that this poem is to offer the recompense of *kleos* away from the scene of death. The child's concentration on his own fate blots everything else out; the poem is anchored to a perpetual rerunning of terrible events where everyone who matters knows who everyone else is. Posidippus' poem, by contrast, is very different. As has already been noted, the final verses of that poem in particular have often also been seen as ecphrastic, that is, as associated with a representation of the dead child, but in this case the poem gives us the deceased's name, and the story is not freighted with the specificity and detail of the Notion poem; Posidippus' poem can be read anywhere, away from any particular monument, and the effect will be the same. The repeated 'mother' of verses 3 and 6 lends the poem a generalizing pathos, enhanced by the obvious allusion to the myth of Narcissus, and perhaps also to that of Hylas;[22] Narcissus, at least, takes his place among images of the lost and untimely dead. Archianax's death thus follows a poetic and mythic pattern that, like the use of euphemism, removes some of the harsh reality of death by assimilating the dead to figures of story. No such consolations for the three-year-old, or his family, in the Notion poem.

Tradition, and specifically literary tradition, is, however, also central to the effect of the Notion poem. Whether we wish to look at the idea of 'death by water' quite generally or focus more narrowly on 'falling into a well', the sense of tradition in this poem is very strong. 'Falling into a well' can have its funny side, as the title *Into the Well* for a comedy of Alexis testifies.[23] A long sequence of

---

19 Tsagalis 2008, 243–244, records that in some 78 per cent of fourth-century Attic funerary epitaphs the deceased's name occurs within the funerary poem itself; cf. also Clairmont 1970, 46–49.
20 For a photograph of the stone, see Demangel/Laumonier 1923, 379.
21 See p. 284 in this chapter.
22 See Piacenza 1998, 348–349; p. 277 in this chapter.
23 For other comic scenes involving wells, see Arnott 1996, 229; and note Lucill. *AP* 11.137 = 46 Fl[b].

Menander's *Dyskolos*, in which Cnemon has to be rescued from a well, shows a striking number of motifs shared with the Notion poem: the tough Gorgias plays the uncle's rescuing role (*Dys.* 670, 683–5) — they both act 'immediately', with no thought for personal safety — while Cnemon's daughter tears her hair and beats her breast, as do the women in the Notion poem.[24] The Notion poet and his audience will have met the motif in several places, in their readings in school, and (probably) also in the theatre. Closer in tone, however, to the child's story is Elpenor's narrative, in the *Odyssey*, of how, his wits befuddled with wine, he fell off Circe's roof:[25]

ἆσέ με δαίμονος αἶσα κακὴ καὶ ἀθέσφατος οἶνος·
Κίρκης δ' ἐν μεγάρῳ καταλέγμενος οὐκ ἐνόησα
ἄψορρον καταβῆναι ἰὼν ἐς κλίμακα μακρήν,
ἀλλὰ καταντικρὺ τέγεος πέσον· ἐκ δέ μοι αὐχὴν
ἀστραγάλων ἐάγη, ψυχὴ δ' Ἄϊδόσδε κατῆλθε.

Hom. *Od.* 11.61–65

The wretched fate of a *daimon* and too much wine brought ruin on me.
I was lying on Circe's roof and did not realize
that I should use the long ladder to come back down again.
I fell headlong from the roof; the bones of my neck
were broken and my spirit went down to Hades.

The δαίμονος αἶσα κακή that settled the young Elpenor's fate looks forward to the Notion child's tale of Μοῖρα κακίστη and a δαίμων,[26] and Elpenor's arrival in the Underworld seems just as swift as the child's. The Notion poet certainly knew Homer,[27] and the poem evokes literary scenes of high pathos.

Two passages of early epic had particular importance for subsequent epitaphic poetry, and both seem evoked by the Notion poem. A noise and a search are followed by the tearing of clothes and other signs of mourning, and we should be reminded of the opening of the *Homeric Hymn to Demeter* (cf. vv. 20, 39, 41, 44, 57, 67, 81, etc.); even the child's almost instantaneous abandonment of hope in the Notion poem (v. 7) finds its counterpart in the *Hymn*, where Persephone still 'hopes', as long as she sees the familiar world around her (vv. 33–37). Persephone herself tells the story of how she was carried to the Underworld

---

24 It is noteworthy that the cook sees the nymphs as responsible for Cnemon's fate (v. 643): these are the nymphs of the well, exactly as in Posidipp. *AP* 7.170.
25 I owe this parallel to Ivana Petrovic.
26 On Elpenor's age, cf. *Od.* 10.552, νεώτατος.
27 See p. 282.

later in the poem, when she is reunited with her mother (vv. 406–433), and it is not unreasonable to see in that telling marks of an attempt to produce a subjective, perhaps even 'girlish', narrative that distinguishes itself from the narrator's initial narrative.[28] Here again, however, we note how bleak is the picture that the Notion poem paints: the child has no time even to cry out, and the sound that he leaves behind is simply the inarticulate noise (ψόφος) of falling into the well (v. 6). Death is always the 'snatcher': ἥρπαξεν in verse 3 of the *Homeric Hymn to Demeter* (cf. v. 19) was to have a very long afterlife,[29] but we may note here how Posidippus and the Notion poet pathetically vary the motif by using the verb of an inevitably vain attempt to snatch a child from Death.

The importance of the *Homeric Hymn to Demeter* and of the figure of Persephone in the epitaphic tradition is well known.[30] Persephone is the paradigmatic 'bride of Hades' whose rape, like the plucking of flowers in which she was engaged when Death snatched her, signifies the taking away of life before its due time; Demeter, in her turn, is the archetype of all grieving parents who are left behind, inconsolably bereft.[31] The blending of event and image is already there in the archaic poem, as καλυκώπιδι, used of Persephone in verse 8, identifies the girl with the beautiful flowers that she picks, however exactly we wish to understand the epithet ('with buds in her eyes', perhaps); Hades' snatching of Persephone is the violent, male version of Persephone's celebration of the beauty of flowers. Persephone is, moreover, still very young, still — in Nicholas Richardson's words — 'something of a child',[32] and as such she is the model for all the untimely dead who follow her. A poem from Rome, perhaps roughly contemporary with the Notion poem, on a five-year-old girl who may also have drowned (note the Naiads in v. 10),[33] well illustrates this simple and powerful idea:

---

28 See e.g. Foley 1993, 60. The catalogue of Persephone's playmates in vv. 418–423, for example, may carry such a personal tone.
29 Forms of ἁρπάζειν with Fate, Death, etc. as the subject are ubiquitous in sepulchral epigram; see e.g. Vérilhac 1982, 174–180.
30 See e.g. Tsagalis 2008, 100–110.
31 It is presumably just a coincidence that in the *Hymn* the goddess disguises herself as an old nurse and sits in grief beside a well, vv. 98–104.
32 Richardson 1974, note on v. 16.
33 This is not certain, as the motif of being snatched by nymphs, or by a particular kind of nymph, is a common consolatory motif in epitaphs, cf. Moretti's commentary on *IGUR* III 1344, Cumont 1949, 325–326, Nock 1972, 924–925. *GV* 952 is the epitaph of a very young girl ('not yet two') who was snatched by Νύμφαι κρηναῖαι (did she drown?) but consoles herself with the thought that this was intended 'perhaps to honour her', τάχα που τιμῆς εἵνεκα.

οὐχ ὁσίως ἥρπαξες ὑπὸ [χθόνα], κοίρανε Πλουτεῦ,
πενταέτη νύμφην πᾶσιν ἀγαλλομένην·
οἷα γὰρ ἀρχόμενον ῥόδον εὔπνοον εἴαρος ὥρῃ
ἐξέτεμες ῥείζης, πρὶν χρόνον ἐκτελέσῃ.
ἀλλ' ἄγ' Ἀλεξάνδρα καὶ Φίλτατε, μηκέτ' ὀδυρμοῖς   5
εἱμερτῇ κούρῃ σπένδετε μυρόμενοι·
εἶχεν γὰρ χάριν, εἶχεν ἐφ' ἡδυχρόοισι προσώποις,
αἰθέρος ὥστε μένειν ἀθανάτοισι δόμοις.
τοῖς πάρος οὖν μύθοις πιστεύσατε· παῖδα γὰρ ἐσθλὴν
ἥρπασαν ὡς τερπνὴν Ναΐδες, οὐ Θάνατος.   10

GV 1595 = *IGUR* III 1344

It was not right, lord Plouteus, to snatch away under [the earth]
  your five-year old bride, in whom all took delight.
Like a young, sweet-smelling rose in springtime,
  you cut her off from the root, before her time had come.
But come, Alexandra and Philtatos, no longer pour
  the libation of your tears in lamenting for your lovely daughter.
She had grace, she had it in the sweet skin of her face,
  and so will dwell in the immortal houses in the sky.
Believe too in the old myths. It was the Naiads, not Death,
  which snatched away the noble child to enjoy her.

Death's νύμφη is five years old; brides (or at least betrothed girls) of that age were anything but unknown in antiquity, but here there is a particular pathos, as the comparison to a budding rose in verses 3–4 very clearly continues the opening evocation of the *Homeric Hymn to Demeter*. It is, however, probably not that poem but rather the story of Hylas — compare the Naiads of verse 10 — that is evoked by the reference to 'stories of former times' in verse 9.[34] The connections between the *Homeric Hymn to Demeter* and the Hylas narratives of Theocritus and Apollonius, paradigmatic 'deaths by water', are both strong and direct,[35] and the story of Hylas was clearly part of the allusive repertoire of epitaphic poets.[36] One other motif, however, that calls attention to itself in this

---

[34] So e.g. Nock 1972, 924.
[35] See Hunter 1993, 40–41, citing earlier bibliography. It is relevant that, according to some versions, Hades and Persephone disappeared at a spring, or the god caused a spring to rise up at the point where he took his bride below the earth.
[36] Wypustek 2013, 165, claims that the Notion poem 'refers to the tale of Hylas'; even if 'evokes' rather than 'refers to' is what is meant, it does not seem to me that there is enough there that explicitly calls Hylas to mind, even were we to see the uncle playing the role of Polyphemus in Apollonius' narrative. Piacenza 1998, 348–349 sees a direct link between Theoc. *Id.* 13.53 and Posidipp. *AP* 7.170.5. *GV* 1732 = *SGO* 14/13/05 (from imperial Isaura in central Anatolia) compares the young Zenobius to 'Hylas, the most outstanding of all heroes, who died in a

context is the idea that the Naiads took the child ὡς τερπνήν, 'as a source of pleasure' (v. 10); the expression is awkward, and various emendations have been attempted (we might think rather of a noun, such as τέρψιν or τέρπος), but there is a consolatory rhetoric at work: the child who was a source of pleasure on earth is now performing that role elsewhere.

How this idea might play out can be seen on an imperial epitaph for a young boy from Syros:[37]

[οὐ φατὸ]ν οὐδ' ἐπίελπτον ἔην κάλλος τε νόος τε
  [ἔμπεδ]ος ἠνορέη τ' ἐξαέτους βρέφεος
[   ]ράτευς, ὃν τίκτε γυνὴ καλή τε καὶ ἐσθλὴ
  [...ιο]ν, αἰδοίη Νικοκράτευς ἄλοχος,
[...το]ῦ κλέος εὐρὺ Πανέλλησίν τε καὶ αὐτοῖς   5
  [Αἰνεά]δαις σοφίης εἵνεκεν ἠδ' ἀρετῆς.
[πάτρη] δ' Ἀντιόχεια κλυτῆς ἀλόχοιο παρ' ὄχθαις
  [Μαιάνδ]ρου ποταμοῦ καλλινάου χθαμαλαῖς.
[τοὔνε]κεν ἁρπάξας Ἐριούνιος Εὐβουλῆι
  [   ]ἄθυρμα φέρεν Φερσεφόνηι τ' ἀλόχωι,   10
[   ]ἄχος λείπων πάππωι μεγακυδέϊ φωτὶ
  [...]ωι πάτραις τ' ἠδὲ γονεῦσι φίλοις.

GV 2030 = IG XII.5.677

[Not to be expressed] and beyond expectation was the beauty and
  intelligence and [steadfast] the courage of the six-year-old...
whom a beautiful and noble woman bore...
  the reverend wife of Nicocrates....
[The father's] fame spread abroad to all the Greeks and to the very descendants
  of [Aeneas] because of his wisdom and virtue.
The [home city] of his glorious wife was Antioch, beside the low-lying banks
  of the [Maeander] with its fair streams.
[For this reason] Eriunius snatched him up
  and brought ... toy for Eubuleus and his wife Persephone,
leaving ... grief for his grandfather..., a man of great renown,
  and his homeland and his dear parents

Here the dead child is offered to Hades and Persephone as an ἄθυρμα, something that will perhaps appeal more to the girlish Persephone than to her husband. In the *Homeric Hymn to Demeter*, Persephone reaches for the deceitful

---

spring, a wonder to the immortals'; there is, however, no necessary implication in that poem that Zenobius too was drowned. In v. 10 of GV 1595 = IGUR III 1344, Kamp 1875, 86 proposed ὥσπερ Ὕλαν for ὡς τερπνήν.

37 I adopt the standard restorations where nothing hangs on them for my argument.

narcissus as a καλὸν ἄθυρμα (v. 16), and perhaps in verse 10 of the Syros poem we should restore καλόν or τερπνόν, rather than Kaibel's almost universally accepted τέκνον;[38] this would leave ἁρπάξας (v. 9) without an object but would restore a familiar phrase and perhaps also a charged echo of the *Homeric Hymn to Demeter*.

One further motif of which the Notion poem reminds us is that of the messenger who brings the report of death, or possible death, to those close to the victim. In the *Homeric Hymn to Demeter*, we have the double role of Hecate and Helios, who slowly reveal the truth to the goddess, and we might also think of Apollonius' Hylas narrative, where Polyphemus brings the terrible news to Heracles (*Arg.* 1.1253–1260). In the Notion poem, however, as in Theocritus' *Idyll* 13, there is no human being with any 'knowledge' who can mediate the tragic event to those left behind; the absence of a messenger, the sudden inexplicable disappearance of, or threat to, all that is dearest to one, is, as Theocritus realized in writing his Hylas narrative, a doubling of loss. In sepulchral epigram, of course, both 'literary' and 'non-literary', the messenger motif is widened beyond internal communication and made to play a dominant role in the dissemination of the message: the epigram now proclaims its message, or asks a passer-by to do so, to all the world. The motif runs all the way from 'Go tell the Spartans' ('Simon.' 22b *FGE*) to two of Callimachus' finest funerary epigrams, which ring very Callimachean changes upon the motif: 'Someone, Heraclitus, mentioned your death and it/he brought me to tears' (*AP* 7.80 = *HE* 1203–1208) and 'If you go to Cyzicus ... you will tell [Hippacus and Didyme] a painful report' (*AP* 7.521 = *HE* 1237–1240).[39] Through the use of this motif, epigrams transcend the fixity of monumental inscription to encompass vast distances,[40] but — as I have already noted — such spatial consolation is denied to the drowned child of the Notion poem. In its place the whole poem has become a kind of messenger speech, beginning with an indication of time, as messenger speeches in tragedy often do, and bringing news of a sad death, again as tragic messenger speeches so often do. The abrupt, if stylistically elaborate,[41] beginning of the narrative, with its refusal of all the normal epitaphic conventions, forces our attention upon its generic form. What gives this messenger speech such power is, of course, that

---

38 Peek (*GV*) restored [αὐτόν].
39 For other aspects of Call. *AP* 7.521, cf. Walsh 1991, 91–92, Hunter 2003, 478. Tarán 1979, 132–149 discusses the messenger motif in several 'literary' Hellenistic epigrams; cf. also Bing 2009, 131–132.
40 There is here clearly a contrast to be drawn with 'literary' epigrams, which did indeed circulate freely in book form; cf. Bing 2009, 141–142.
41 See p. 282 in this chapter.

the messenger is reporting his own death, whereas the messengers of tragedy, though often moved to tears by what they have to report, are essentially separated from the events of their narrative: it is the suffering of others that takes centre stage.

A link has often been drawn between the narrative of the first part of the *Homeric Hymn to Demeter* and the sequence in *Iliad* 22 in which Andromache comes to learn of Hector's death:[42]

> ἄλοχος δ' οὔπώ τι πέπυστο
> Ἕκτορος· οὐ γάρ οἵ τις ἐτήτυμος ἄγγελος ἐλθὼν
> ἤγγειλ', ὅττί ῥά οἱ πόσις ἔκτοθι μίμνε πυλάων,
> ἀλλ' ἥγ' ἱστὸν ὕφαινε μυχῷ δόμου ὑψηλοῖο   440
> δίπλακα πορφυρέην, ἐν δὲ θρόνα ποικίλ' ἔπασσεν.
> κέκλετο δ' ἀμφιπόλοισιν ἐϋπλοκάμοις κατὰ δῶμα
> ἀμφὶ πυρὶ στῆσαι τρίποδα μέγαν, ὄφρα πέλοιτο
> Ἕκτορι θερμὰ λοετρὰ μάχης ἐκ νοστήσαντι·
> νηπίη, οὐδ' ἐνόησεν, ὅ μιν μάλα τῆλε λοετρῶν   445
> χερσ' ὑπ' Ἀχιλλῆος δάμασε γλαυκῶπις Ἀθήνη.
> κωκυτοῦ δ' ἤκουσε καὶ οἰμωγῆς ἀπὸ πύργου·
> τῆς δ' ἐλελίχθη γυῖα, χαμαὶ δέ οἱ ἔκπεσε κερκίς.
> ἡδ' αὖτις δμῳῇσιν ἐϋπλοκάμοισι μετηύδα·
> 'δεῦτε, δύω μοι ἕπεσθον· ἴδωμ' ὅτιν' ἔργα τέτυκται. 450
> αἰδοίης ἑκυρῆς ὀπὸς ἔκλυον, ἐν δέ μοι αὐτῇ
> στήθεσι πάλλεται ἦτορ ἀνὰ στόμα, νέρθε δὲ γοῦνα
> πήγνυται· ἐγγὺς δή τι κακὸν Πριάμοιο τέκεσσιν.
> αἲ γὰρ ἀπ' οὔατος εἴη ἐμεῦ ἔπος, ἀλλὰ μάλ' αἰνῶς
> δείδω, μὴ δή μοι θρασὺν Ἕκτορα δῖος Ἀχιλλεὺς   455
> μοῦνον ἀποτμήξας πόλιος πεδίονδε δίηται,
> καὶ δή μιν καταπαύσῃ ἀγηνορίης ἀλεγεινῆς
> ἥ μιν ἔχεσκ', ἐπεὶ οὔποτ' ἐνὶ πληθυῖ μένεν ἀνδρῶν,
> ἀλλὰ πολὺ προθέεσκε, τὸ ὃν μένος οὐδενὶ εἴκων.'
> ὣς φαμένη μεγάροιο διέσσυτο μαινάδι ἴση,   460
> παλλομένη κραδίην· ἅμα δ' ἀμφίπολοι κίον αὐτῇ.

Hom. *Il.* 22.437–461

Hector's wife had not yet learned anything,
for no truthful messenger had come to report to her
that her husband had remained outside the gates.
In the recesses of the lofty dwelling she was weaving
a purple double-cloak, inset with colourful flowers,
and she had told her lovely tressed maidservants in the house
to set a great tripod on the fire so that there would be

---

42 See Richardson 1974, 161.

hot water for Hector's bath when he returned from the fighting.
Poor woman: she did not know that, far from his bath,
bright-eyed Athena had killed him through the hands of Achilles.
She heard the wailing and lamentation from the tower;
her limbs quaked, and her shuttle fell to the ground.
Again she called to her lovely tressed maids:
'Come, two of you follow me. I must see what has happened.
I heard the voice of my reverend mother-in-law, and my heart inside
my chest leaps to my mouth and below my limbs
are frozen. Some evil hangs over the children of Priam!
May such a thing as I say never reach my ears, but I am very much
afraid lest godlike Achilles may have cut off bold Hector
away from the city and be pursuing him over the plain.
Achilles would put an end to that grievous impetuousness
of Hector's, for he never remained with the mass of soldiers
but always ran out in front. His spirit took second place to no one.'
With these words she rushed through the hall like a maenad,
her heart pounding; her maids went with her.

Andromache is in apparently blissful ignorance, 'for no truth-telling messenger had come to her' (cf. Hom. Hymn Dem.44–46). Verses 438–439 seem to reflect what would have been a familiar epic-type scene,[43] and the poet thus draws our attention to what is striking and powerful in this moment of emotional contrast: Andromache had been spared the anguish of knowing that Hector was to face Achilles, only to find that this ignorance was to exact a terrible price. The Homeric narrative technique by which Andromache's hearing of the lamentation on the tower and her rushing off 'like a maenad'[44] are separated by a ten-verse speech of foreboding to her maidservants is a remarkable manifestation of the stylization of high epic narrative; such a form, which to some extent represents in speech Andromache's unarticulated, internal fears, has of course no counterpart in the narrative of the Notion poem, though — were this a more extended narrative form — it would be easy enough to imagine one placed in the uncle's mouth after verse 6. As with Andromache, it is a noise that draws the attention of those nearest to the deceased; for Homer's concern with narrative tension and the revelation of character through speech, the Notion poem has substituted a breathlessly fast narrative, which wonderfully catches the panic of the moment. It is in details such as

---

[43] See further de Jong 2012, on vv. 438–439.
[44] At Ov. Fast. 4.457–458 Ceres is compared to a maenad, as she takes off in search of her daughter; Ovid has excellent Roman models here (see the commentators ad loc.), but the possibility that he is connecting Andromache in Iliad 22 with the distraught goddess should at least be raised.

this one that we understand the compression and extension of different narrative forms, or rather perhaps we catch one of the essences of Homer's art.

The death narrative that the Notion poet has created for the three-year-old victim resonates, then, not just with the high art of a Posidippus (or Callimachus), but with the two narratives that had the greatest influence on all Greek epitaphic poetry, namely the death of Hector and the rape of Persephone. The general stylistic level of the poem's diction is, however, (in conventional terms) low, unadorned, and 'prosaic': terms such as φρεατισμός and τυπητός[45] will probably not turn up again in inscribed epitaphs (and may also be thought to be somewhat unlikely in the mouth of a three-year-old).[46] Homeric touches, on the other hand, frame the narrative in such a way as to suggest poetic design.[47] The opening verse is fashioned after the Homeric sequence ἦμος δ' ἠέλιος κατέδυ καὶ ἐπὶ κνέφας ἦλθεν ('when the sun went down and darkness came', used once in the *Iliad*, six times in the *Odyssey*),[48] and the child's exclamation in the final hexameter picks up the Homeric phrase ἐμὲ τὸν δύστηνον (cf. *Od.* 7.223, 248, *Il.* 22.59). The poet might indeed have in mind this final instance, from Priam's doomed appeal to Hector:

> πρὸς δ' ἐμὲ τὸν δύστηνον ἔτι φρονέοντ' ἐλέησον,
> δύσμορον, ὅν ῥα πατὴρ Κρονίδης ἐπὶ γήραος οὐδῷ   60
> αἴσῃ ἐν ἀργαλέῃ φθείσει, κακὰ πόλλ' ἐπιδόντα,
> υἷάς τ' ὀλλυμένους ἑλκηθείσας τε θύγατρας
> καὶ θαλάμους κεραϊζομένους, καὶ νήπια τέκνα
> βαλλόμενα προτὶ γαίῃ ἐν αἰνῇ δηϊοτῆτι,
> ἑλκομένας τε νυοὺς ὀλοῆς ὑπὸ χερσὶν Ἀχαιῶν.   65
>
> Hom. *Il.* 22.59–65

---

45 The form is presumably *metri gratia*; τυπετός is found once in Dionysius of Halicarnassus.

46 Peek 1932, 240 offers a very harsh judgement of the poem's style ('beyond repair', *ganz hilflos*).

47 On reminiscences of Homer in inscribed epigram, Thonemann 2014 is an instructive essay; cf. also Bing 2009, ch. 8, Hunter 2018, ch. 1. Marked differences of levels of diction within a poem are also a familiar feature of inscribed epigram. Among the more striking examples, and of some interest in the context of *SGO* 03/05/04, is *GV* 874 = *SGO* 05/01/36, a late Hellenistic or early imperial funerary epigram for an eleven-year-old boy who fell out of a tree and broke his neck: as he died 'he drenched his father's lap with the wetness of the blood of his piteous death' (πατρὸς κόλπους ἐνιδεύσας| αἵματος οἰκτροφόνου ψυχολιπῆς νοτίσιν), an image that inevitably recalls passages such as A. *Ag.* 1389–1390 and S. *Ant.* 1238–1239; οἰκτροφόνου is an absolute *hapax legomenon* in extant Greek.

48 Peek 1932, 239, claims that the initial δέ (with μέν following) shows that the verse is actually copied from an epic poem, but such weight should not be attached to what may be a simple fusion of two Homeric snippets.

> Moreover, pity me in my wretchedness while I still have my senses,
> an ill-fated man whom father Zeus will destroy with a grim
> fate on the threshold which is old age. I have lived to see many horrors,
> my sons killed, my daughters dragged off,
> my chambers looted, helpless children
> thrown to the ground in the terror of war,
> and my daughters-in-law dragged off by the cruel hands of the Achaeans.

An echo of this early moment in the story of the death of Hector in any poem about the death of a child, even a very young child, would be obviously appropriate, and it may be the memory of this scene that suggested the choice of ἐφιδόντα in verse 16 (compare *Iliad* 22.61), where we might have expected the future tense.[49] Some might think that the contrast between the aged Priam's lament and the child's regret at 'not having seen the *palaistra*' verges on the bathetic, but Homeric memory is here used, as so often, to lend depth and resonance to a moment of pathos; the 'helpless child' of the Notion inscription has fallen 'to the earth' in the most terrible way. The poeticism of the opening verse announces the drama and horror of what is to follow.

The grief of those left behind is immortalized time and again on countless Greek epitaphs, but we will not find many three-year-old children delivering relatively extensive narratives.[50] Posidippus *AP* 7.170, for example, is in the third person, and the dead child, literally νήπιος, 'without a voice', plays, dies, and sleeps with no more sound than the 'dumb image' that led him on to his

---

[49] For the meaning 'live to see', cf. *LSJ* s.v. ἐπεῖδον 3. Unsurprisingly, the exegetical scholia on these Homeric verses see here not just a foreshadowing of the sack of Troy but, specifically, the origin of the tragic treatments of Cassandra and Astyanax; the latter was thrown by the Greeks off the battlements of Troy. Giacomo Fedeli suggests to me that the story of Astyanax, who had a (paternal) uncle called Alexander, is relevant to the Notion poem; at E. *Tr.* 1188–1191, Hecuba bitterly imagines what might be written on his epitaph.

[50] The closest analogue is perhaps *IGUR* IV 1702, a third-century CE account by a four-year old boy of how a succession of medical conditions finally brought about his death. *GV* 1155 = *GG* 167, a Hellenistic poem from Amorgos, tells of the death of a sixteen-year-old from a javelin in the gymnasium; it becomes clear in the final four distichs that the poem is spoken by the deceased, though the first twelve verses give no hint of that. *AP* 7.334 = *SGO* 08/01/41 is a poem in nine distichs in which a boy who died before shaving his first beard laments the grief his death caused to his mother; he does not explain how he died, though there is a narrative element in the fact that his father 'abandoned me as an orphan in their house when [I] was very small' (vv. 7–8). *GV* 1350 = *SGO* 07/06/05, an imperial-age poem from Ilion, is a first-person address by a boy who died old enough to have learned the trade of a barber; most of the poem concerns his parents' grief, but there is also a very mysterious narrative element: 'From behind a hand cast wretched me into Hades and within two weeks I departed from life'. On *GV* 1765 = *SGO* 05/01/64, see n. 18 in this chapter.

death. Noiselessness is a constitutive feature of the art of the epigram: even Archianax's mother pulls him from the water without lamentation, and now he sleeps deeply, forever embalmed in stone. The Notion poet, however, has given his child a voice — and one characterized, for the most part, by the kind of language and concerns we associate with children: dinner, family (ὁ μήτρως μου, ἡ νάννη, ἡ μήτηρ),[51] the emphatic superlative κακίστη in verse 4,[52] the regret for the *palaistra*, that earthly nirvana on which any young boy set his heart from a very early age.[53] So, too, the unelaborated nature of the narrative, its breathless verbal pace, the syntactic completeness of most hexameters that eschew enjambment,[54] and the presentation of the child as a passive object of forces beyond his control are clearly also part of a persistent, though perhaps variably successful, attempt in the main body of the narrative to characterize the voice that the poet has created. This three-year-old's narrative, however, is also characterized by poetic reminiscence and the construction of a 'literary' narrative of events of which the dead child cannot possibly have known. We may, if we wish, say that this is a sequence of events that the child will have wished to have happened, one constructed for him by the poet out of familiar scenes, and one that absolves his uncle of any blame for the death; this familiarity and literariness carries its own (cold?) consolation in memorialization and assimilation to famous forebears. The Notion poem fills in the terrible silences of Posidippus *AP* 7.170, thus drawing both poems into the web of tradition.

Bibliography

Allen, F.D. 1885–6. 'On Greek Versification in Inscriptions', in: *Papers of the American School of Classical Studies at Athens*, vol. 4, Boston, 35–204.

Arnott, W.G. (ed.) 1996. *Alexis: The Fragments*, Cambridge Classical Texts and Commentaries 31, Cambridge.

---

[51] We do not have to be told explicitly who Alexander (v. 11) is: the child knows, and that is sufficient. The use of the proper name in that verse is perhaps intended to mimic the women shouting his name. The prominence given to the uncle, if indeed 'Alexander' is the uncle, is in fact one of the puzzling features of the poem; was the child's father already dead? Others have suggested that 'Alexander' is in fact the child's father or a family slave.

[52] In *IGUR* IV 1702 (see n. 50 here) one of the child's conditions is a νόσος κακίστη (v. 20).

[53] Entry to the *palaistra* or gymnasium might be almost as much of a landmark as marriage was for girls, see *GV* 119; Vérilhac 1982, 51–52.

[54] Cf. p. 141 on vv. 7–8.

Austin, C./Bastianini, G. (eds.) 2002. *Posidippi Pellaei quae supersunt omnia*, Biblioteca classica 3, Milan.
Bing, P. 2009. *The Scroll and the Marble: Studies in Reading and Reception in Hellenistic Poetry*, Ann Arbor.
Clairmont, C.W. 1970. *Gravestone and Epigram: Greek Memorials from the Archaic and Classical Period*, Mainz.
Cumont, F.V.M. 1949. *Lux perpetua*, Paris.
De Jong, I.J.F. (ed.) 2012. *Homer: Iliad Book XXII*. Cambridge Greek and Latin Classics, Cambridge.
Demangel, R./Laumonier, A. 1923. 'Fouilles de Notion (1921) (Pl. X–XIII)', *BCH* 47, 353–386.
Fantuzzi, M./Sens, A. 2006. 'The Hexameter of Inscribed Hellenistic Epigram', in: M.A. Harder/R.F. Regtuit/G.C. Wakker (eds.), *Beyond the Canon* (Hellenistica Groningana 11), Leuven, 105–122.
Fedeli, P. (ed.) 1981. 'Attis e il leone: Dall'epigramma ellenistico al c. 63 di Catullo', in: *Letterature comparate: Problemi e metodo: Studi in onore di Ettore Paratore*, 4 vols., Bologna, vol. 1, 247–256.
Foley, H.P. (ed.) 1993. *The Homeric Hymn to Demeter: Translation, Commentary, and Interpretive Essays*, Princeton.
Garulli, V. 2012. *Byblos lainee: Epigrafia, letteratura, epitafio* (Eikasmos 20), Bologna.
Gow, A.S.F./Page, D.L. (eds.) 1965. *The Greek Anthology: Hellenistic Epigrams*, 2 vols., Cambridge.
Hunter, R. 1993. *The Argonautica of Apollonius: Literary Studies*, Cambridge.
Hunter, R. 2003. 'Literature and its Contexts', in: A. Erskine (ed.), *A Companion to the Hellenistic World*, Blackwell Companions to the Ancient World, Oxford, 477–493.
Hunter, R. 2018. *The Measure of Homer: The Ancient Reception of the Iliad and the Odyssey*, Cambridge.
Matthews, V.J. (ed.) 1974. *Panyassis of Halikarnassos: Text and Commentary*, Mnemosyne Suppl. 33, Leiden.
Nock, A.D. 1972. *Essays on Religion and the Ancient World*, 2 vols., Oxford.
Peek, W. 1932. 'Zu griechischen Epigrammen', *Philologus* 87, 229–241.
Piacenza, N. 1998. 'L'immortalità negata: Osservazioni sull' epigramma VII 170 dell'*Antologia Palatina*', *AevumAnt* 11, 345–350.
Richardson, N.J. (ed.) 1974. *The Homeric Hymn to Demeter*, Oxford.
Tarán, S.L. 1979. *The Art of Variation in the Hellenistic Epigram*, Columbia Studies in the Classical Tradition 9, Leiden.
Thonemann, P. 2014. 'Poets of the Axylon', *Chiron* 44, 191–232.
Tsagalls, C.C. 2008. *Inscribing Sorrow: Fourth-Century Attic Funerary Epigrams*, Trends in Classics Supplementary Volumes 1, Berlin/New York.
Vérilhac, A.-M. 1978. Παῖδες ἄωροι: *Poésie funéraire*, vol. 1, Πραγματεῖαι τῆς Ἀκαδημίας Ἀθηνῶν 41, Athens.
Vérilhac, A.-M. 1982. Παῖδες ἄωροι: *Poésie funéraire*, vol. 2, Πραγματεῖαι τῆς Ἀκαδημίας Ἀθηνῶν 41, Athens.
Walsh, G.B. 1991. 'Callimachean Passages: The Rhetoric of Epitaph in Epigram', *Arethusa* 24, 77–105.
Wypustek, A. 2013. *Images of Eternal Beauty in Funerary Verse Inscriptions of the Hellenistic and Greco-Roman Periods*, Mnemosyne Suppl. 352, Leiden.

15 Reading and Citing the *Epigrams* of Callimachus

Introduction

Our picture of the Greek reception of Callimachus' poetry in the three or four centuries which followed him is desperately thin. This is not (principally) because far more scholarly energy has been devoted to the Roman reception of the poems; rather, it is because far too little of the Greek literature where we might expect to look for that reception has survived. A certain amount can be (and has been) done with imitations of Callimachus in what survives of later Hellenistic poetry, notably in Euphorion and in Greek epigram (from both before and after Augustus), but Callimachus is to us (and was in antiquity) such an important figure that we need to know far more than we do about his reception in literary culture beyond poetic mimesis. We know rather more, if still very little, about the position in later antiquity and Byzantium.[1] The excellent survey 'Callimachus cited' by Filippomaria Pontani 2011 offers the chance (not yet, I think, really taken up) to consider what more the indirect tradition might be able to tell us about how Callimachus' poetry was read and used in the high Hellenistic and early imperial period, although one lesson which emerges from Pontani's survey is (again) how very scarce are the traces of Callimachus' poetry, particularly if we discount the grammatical tradition (but on this see below). In this paper I want to follow up a few leads offered by the indirect tradition of (in particular) the *Epigrams* to see if any more colour can be added to our almost disappearingly faint picture.

The *Epigrams* offer both a particular challenge and an opportunity, as we know that the poems which we have (or indeed that we know about) are only a selection of what was known in antiquity; speculation about how high (or low) a percentage has survived is just that, speculation, though not necessarily idle.[2] It can still come as something of a shock to recall that one of the epigrams which seems to have been most important in Callimachus' Roman poetic reception and/or reputation, the poem on Antimachus' *Lyde* (the subject of an important discussion by Nita Krevans in the very first *Hellenistica Groningana* volume), did not survive the cuts which eventually resulted in our Anthology and that we only have part of (almost certainly) the first verse (fr. 398 Pf.),

---

[1] For some soundings here cf. Hunter 2011a.
[2] Cf. Parsons 2002, 100–101, 137–138.

thanks to the scholarly tradition on Dionysius Periegetes. We also know a little (far too little, of course) about the reception and imitation of the *Epigrams* before the high period of Roman and Greek imperial poetry.³

Callimachus and the grammatical tradition

More attention is now paid to the extent to which the Alexandrian grammatical and interpretative tradition, here represented not by chance papyrus finds (such as the famous 'Oyster', *SH* 983–4) but by the information largely offered by the extant Homeric scholia, concerned itself with Hellenistic poetry, whether for the purposes of settling issues in the text of Homer or 'for its own sake', though the dichotomy is very far from a neat one.⁴ Unsurprisingly perhaps, Callimachus seems to have been the Hellenistic poet most exploited by the grammatical tradition,⁵ but whether it was *qua* poet that he most appealed must remain a moot point. An interesting case is offered by the citation of two epigrams in Sextus Empiricus, *Adversus Grammaticos*; both epigrams have multiple citations in the indirect tradition but only one of them made it to the Anthology.

Sextus is discussing the etymology of the term γραμματική, which, so he explains, is standardly derived from γράμμα in the sense of 'letter of the alphabet' (στοιχεῖον). There is, however, an alternative etymology:

τάχα δέ, ὥς φασιν οἱ περὶ τὸν Ἀσκληπιάδην, καὶ αὐτὴ ἀπὸ μὲν γραμμάτων ὠνόμασται, οὐκ ἀπὸ τούτων δὲ ἀφ' ὧν καὶ ἡ γραμματιστική, ἀλλ' ἐκείνη μέν, ὡς ἔφην, ἀπὸ τῶν στοιχείων, αὕτη δὲ ἀπὸ τῶν συγγραμμάτων περὶ οἷς πονεῖται. γράμματα γὰρ καὶ ταῦτα προσηγορεύετο, καθὰ καὶ δημόσια καλοῦμεν γράμματα, καὶ πολλῶν τινὰ γραμμάτων ἔμπειρον ὑπάρχειν φαμέν, τουτέστιν οὐ τῶν στοιχείων ἀλλὰ τῶν συγγραμμάτων. καὶ Καλλίμαχος δέ, ποτὲ μὲν τὸ ποίημα καλῶν γράμμα ποτὲ δὲ τὸ καταλογάδην σύγγραμμα, φησί·

Κρεωφύλου⁶ πόνος εἰμί, δόμῳ ποτὲ θεῖον ἀοιδόν
δεξαμένου, κλείω δ' Εὔρυτον ὅσσ' ἔπαθεν

---

3 Cf. Parsons 2002, 102–103. Parsons' claim, however, that 'within a generation, *Epigr.* 19 inspired an inflated imitation at Kios [i.e. *SGO* 09/01/03 = *GVI* 661] ...' is very far from secure, both chronologically and poetically; it seems to me far from certain that the inscribed epitaph (in iambic trimeters) imitates Callimachus. So too, the alleged echo of *Epigr.* 16 in (?) Agatharcides seems anything but certain.
4 Cf., e.g., Montanari 1995; 2002, Rengakos 2000.
5 The survey by Pfeiffer 1949, II xxix–xxxiii remains the fundamental starting-point; the earliest attestations seem to be in the work of Aristophanes of Byantium (frr. 224, 543 Pf.).
6 The alternative reading, τοῦ Σαμίου, is almost universally accepted by editors into Callimachus' text.

καὶ ξανθὴν Ἰόλειαν, Ὁμήρειον δὲ καλεῦμαι
γράμμα· Κρεωφύλῳ, Ζεῦ φίλε, τοῦτο μέγα.

Epigr. 6 Pf. = *HE* 1293–1296

καὶ πάλιν (*Epigr.* 23 Pf. = *HE* 1273–1276)

εἴπας "Ἥλιε χαῖρε' Κλεόμβροτος Ἀμπρακιώτης[7]
ἥλατ' ἀφ' ὑψηλοῦ τείχεος εἰς Ἀΐδην,
ἄξιον οὐδὲν ἰδὼν θανάτου τέλος,[8] ἀλλὰ Πλάτωνος
ἓν τὸ περὶ ψυχῆς γράμμ' ἀναλεξάμενος.

Sextus Empiricus, *Adversus Grammaticos* 1.47–48

Perhaps, as the school of Asclepiades says, this art too was named from letters, but not those letters from which *grammatistike* was named; that art, as I said, was named from the elements, whereas the former [i.e. *grammatike*] was named from the compositions with which it is concerned. For these also were called letters, just as we refer to public letters and say that someone is skilled in many letters, meaning not the elements but compositions. Callimachus also on one occasion calls a poem a letter and on another a prose composition:

I am the labour of Kreophylos who once received the divine bard into his home; I sing of all that Eurytos suffered and of blonde-haired Iole. I am called a composition of Homer: for Kreophylos, dear Zeus, that is really something.

And in another poem:
After saying 'Sun farewell', Cleombrotus of Ambracia jumped from a high wall into Hades. He had not seen any event worth dying for, but had read one work of Plato, the *On the Soul*.

It is standardly assumed that οἱ περὶ τὸν Ἀσκληπιάδην refers to Asclepiades of Myrlea (second half of 2nd cent. – 1st half of first BC),[9] presumably from the work περὶ γραμματικῆς to which Sextus elsewhere makes explicit reference.[10] We cannot of course be certain that the citation of the two epigrams also goes back to Asclepiades, but the circumstantial case is in fact a strong one.

In the first place, it seems quite likely, as Rudolf Pfeiffer and others have argued,[11] that a good part of our information, largely to be found in Sextus and the scholia to Dionysius Thrax, about the history of the term γραμματική does in fact derive from Asclepiades, who seems to have written not just '*On grammar*'

---

[7] Editors generally accept ὠμβρακιώτης as the true reading.
[8] The correct reading is θανάτου κακόν.
[9] On the (disputed) chronology cf., e.g., Pagani 2007, 12–13.
[10] Cf. Blank 1998, 118, Pagani, 2007, 31–34.
[11] Cf. Pfeiffer 1968, 158, 162.

but also 'On the grammarians', which was presumably biographical in orientation (cf. further below). The definition of grammar which Sextus ascribes to Asclepiades stands in a clear relation to other important stages in that history: Eratosthenes defined γραμματική as a ἕξις παντελής ἐν γράμμασι, using, as the ancient sources explain, γράμματα in the same sense in which Callimachus does,[12] and the τέχνη of Dionysius Thrax, a work which (in some form) Asclepiades may well have known, begins:

> γραμματική ἐστιν ἐμπειρία τῶν παρὰ ποιηταῖς τε καὶ συγγραφεῦσιν ὡς ἐπὶ τὸ πολὺ λεγομένων.
>
> Dionysius Thrax, Techne 1
>
> Grammar is the empirical knowledge of what is for the most part being said by poets and prose writers (trans. R. Pfeiffer).[13]

The equal status given to prose-writers alongside poets is shared with the 'Asclepiadean' definition; Rudolf Pfeiffer suggested that Dionysius put prose-writers second 'because they had not been treated by any scholar before [Dionysius' teacher] Aristarchus',[14] noting that ἐμπειρία τῶν ποιητῶν is still a definition of μεγάλη γραμματική found in the scholia to Dionysius (cf. Cicero, De oratore 1.187).[15] There is, of course, a complex history concerning the inclusion of prose-writers within the legitimate area of philological attention (the Platonic Protagoras' claims (Pl. Prt. 338e7–8) about being δεινὸς περὶ ἐπῶν are one famous stage before the journey has really begun), but Pfeiffer's view cannot, I think, be correct, even if Aristarchus was in fact the first Alexandrian scholar to write a commentary on a prose work. Παντελής in the definition of Eratosthenes might well be thought implicitly to include prose-works, and if we needed an example of a scholar whose activities embraced both poetry and prose, then we need of course look no further than Callimachus; for what it is worth (admittedly not much), the Suda-life labels Callimachus a γραμματικός and the pupil of a γραμματικός before anything else,[16] and, after dealing with his family, notes that he was ἐπιμελέστατος ('sehr fleissig' is perhaps the best translation) and that he 'composed poems in every metre and wrote very many works in prose'. I suspect, in fact, that Asclepiades (and perhaps others before him) had given

---

12 Gr. Gr. I iii. 160.10–12, cf. Pfeiffer 1968, 162.
13 Cf. Pfeiffer 1968, 268.
14 Pfeiffer 1968, 268.
15 Cf. the definition of μεγάλη γραμματική at Gr. Gr. I iii. 114.27–34 Hilgard and also Gr. Gr. I iii. 164.3–4 Hilgard, the γραμματικός is πολλῶν ποιημάτων ἐπιστήμων.
16 Cf. below on Hermocrates of Iasos.

Callimachus a prominent place in the history of γραμματική and/or in a catalogue of the leading γραμματικοί; we know in any case that the term was applied to Alexandrian scholars and poets at a date contemporary with Callimachus.[17] The choice of two epigrams of Callimachus to illustrate the use of γράμμα to refer to a work of 'literature', whether in poetry or prose, will not have been fortuitous. Strabo, who elsewhere refers to Asclepiades of Myrlea (3.4.3, 12.4.9), included both Callimachus and Eratosthenes in his list of famous Cyreneans, describing the former as ποιητὴς ἅμα καὶ περὶ γραμματικὴν ἐσπουδακώς (17.3.22), and however much the famous epigrams of Philip and Antiphanes (T69, 71 Pf.) attacking both Callimachus and the γραμματικοί owe to a later period, they may be added to the cumulative (and, of course, unsurprising) case for believing that Callimachus was afforded a prominent place in the history of γραμματική from a relatively early date. In Cicero's *De oratore*, Lucius Crassus names Callimachus and Aristophanes of Byzantium as pre-eminent in the discipline (3.132), just as the *Suda* seems to reflect a roll-call of the greatest γραμματικοί of each generation – Zenodotus, Callimachus, Aristophanes (T17 Pf.). Dionysius of Halicarnassus names 'Callimachus and the γραμματικοί from Pergamum' in such a way as to suggest that they represent his principal forerunners in 'bio-bibliography' (*Deinarchos* 1). If anyone, then, offered a 'killer quotation' in an argument about the meaning of γραμματική, that was Callimachus.

Asclepiades' interest in what we call Hellenistic poetry is well attested, though the scope and nature of that work remains inevitably uncertain: Aratus, Theocritus and Apollonius of Rhodes all fell within his scholarly purview,[18] and the long extract from his work '*On the Cup of Nestor*', cited and paraphrased by Athenaeus (11.489a–492a = Asclepiades fr. 4 Pagani), includes citations from (*inter al.*) Aratus, Simmias and Posidippus. Asclepiades is in fact found once elsewhere in connection with Callimachus, and specifically with the epigrams. This is a passage from the beginning of the ancient Vita of Aratus (*Vita* I Martin):

---

17 Philicus, *SH* 677, cf. Pfeiffer 1968, 157.
18 Cf., e.g., D'Alessio 2000, Pagani 2007, 27–31.

Ἄρατος ὁ ποιητὴς πατρὸς μὲν ἦν Ἀθηνοδώρου, μητρὸς δὲ Λητοφίλας. ἀδελφοὺς δὲ ἔσχε τρεῖς, Μύριν καὶ Καλιόνδαν καὶ Ἀθηνόδωρον ὁμώνυμον τῷ πατρί. μέμνηται δὲ αὐτοῦ τῶν ἀδελφῶν ἐν ταῖς εἰς αὐτὸν ἀναφερομέναις ἐπιστολαῖς. Ἀσκληπιάδης δὲ ὁ Μυρλεανὸς ἐν τῷ ἑνδεκάτῳ περὶ γραμματικῶν Ταρσέα φησὶν αὐτὸν γεγονέναι, ἀλλ' οὐ Σολέα, Καλλιμάχου πολυΐστορος ἀνδρὸς καὶ ἀξιοπίστου Σολέα λέγοντος αὐτὸν γεγονέναι διὰ τούτων· (Epigr. 27.2–3 Pf. = HE 1298–1299)

ἀλλ' ὀκνέω μὴ τὸ μελιχρότατον
τῶν ἐπέων ὁ Σολεὺς ἀπεμάξατο,

καὶ τῶν ἄλλων σχεδὸν πάντων.

Vita Arati I, p.6.6–13 Martin = 1.2 Di Maria

The poet Aratus' father was Athenodorus and his mother was Letophila. He had three brothers, Muris, Kaliondas and Athenodoros, who had the same name as his father. He mentions his brothers in the letters which are ascribed to him. In Book 11 of the 'On Grammarians' Asclepiades of Myrlea says that [Aratus] was a Tarsian, not a citizen of Soloi, although Callimachus, a man of great learning and deserving trust, says in the following verses that he was from Soloi:
'It may be that the man from Soloi has caught the sweetest of verses',[19] and virtually everyone else agrees with this.

Pontani, noting that Strabo (9.5.17) also calls Callimachus πολυΐστωρ (in the context of citing the poet for the cult celebrated in *Iambus* 10),[20] assigned the judgement about Callimachus in the Aratean *Life* to Asclepiades.[21] On the face of it, this seems improbable. Callimachus' verses, together with the judgement about his creditworthiness, are cited in order to illustrate a view of Aratus' origin other than that promoted by Asclepiades and one which the author of the *Life* (? Achilles)[22] appears to accept, namely that Aratus came from Soloi in Cilicia; it might therefore seem doubtful whether Asclepiades would have praised Callimachus' creditworthiness at this point in his discussion of Aratus (presumably in one of his grammatical works).[23] It is not, however, out of the question. Asclepiades may have cited and praised Callimachus as an exponent of the standard view, in order to give greater weight to his own (unique) knowledge of the true position; in view

---

19 On the meaning of these very disputed verses cf. Hunter 2014, 292–294.
20 On this citation and its implications cf. Hunter 2011b, 111–112.
21 Pontani 2011, 100 n. 28.
22 Cf. Di Maria 1996, vii–xii
23 For Aratus as γραμματικός cf., e.g., *Vita* I, p. 8.18–24 Martin. Martin 1998, I xxi suggests that Asclepiades' view of Aratus' hometown is less aberrant than it appears; he notes that Chrysippus too is assigned to both Tarsus and Soloi, because his father originally came from the former.

of his likely attitude to Callimachus' evidence with regard to the origin of γραμματική, it may be thought unlikely that he was harshly critical of Callimachus anywhere. There are, of course, the inevitable problems of the text and structure of the Aratean *Life*, a subject which cannot be pursued in any detail here; in such texts, which are ultimately put together by processes of selection, paraphrase and epitomisation, processes very visible in the fact that all of *Epigram 27* Pf. is cited later in the *Life* to illustrate Aratus' debt to Hesiod, gaps in the argument very often do not imply lacunae in the text which has survived, but rather point to that process of selection. In the present case, however, it may be worth suggesting that there is indeed a lacuna, whether of text or argument or both, before the reference to Asclepiades' view, as it seems odd to introduce Asclepiades' 'aberrant' view, 'he was from Tarsus, not Soloi', before a statement of what was to become the standard view; the δέ in Ἀσκληπιάδης δὲ ὁ Μυρλεανός would then be adversative rather than continuative.

What does seem very likely, regardless of the history and state of the text of the *Life*, is that, in his discussion of Aratus (probably in the biographical work 'On Grammarians'), Asclepiades will have cited Callimachus' epigram, even if in rather different terms than those found in the Aratean *Life*. It is clear from the preserved extract of 'On Nestor's Cup' that Asclepiades peppered his writing with poetic quotations, and Callimachus' epigram was, in any case, a near contemporary witness to Aratus' place of origin and poetic affiliations. Whoever first described Callimachus as 'a man of great learning and deserving trust' cited him as an authority, as someone (not improbably Asclepiades) had done on the meaning of γράμμα, and as Strabo was soon enough to do. Callimachus was, as Strabo puts it, 'both a poet and a very serious γραμματικός' (17.3.22, cf. above), and it was the second half of that pairing which gave citations from his poetry particular force and particular authority. Callimachus was a *doctus poeta*, long before the idea was current, and that idea did not merely derive from the character of his poetry or from the declaration of the primacy of τέχνη in the 'Reply to the Telchines'. Critical and rhetorical arguments about the relative roles of φύσις and τέχνη, of *ars* and *natura*,[24] normally apply to the relative contributions which each make to a particular literary form or one example of it, but the two parts of Callimachus' activity which Strabo identifies were formative in the reception of his work long before the programmatic utterances of the Roman 'Callimacheans'. Modern students of Callimachus are (perhaps understandably) a bit vague about what the poet means by τέχνη in v. 17 of the 'Reply to the

---

24 Cf. Brink 1971, 394–395 for a helpful survey. Ovid, *Am.* 1.15.13–14 applies the dichotomy to Callimachus himself (*qua* poet).

Telchines': to what qualities of poetry is he there referring, except that, whatever they are, his own poetry is the prime exhibit? There is, of course, a very long backstory here, in which Socrates' denial of τέχνη to the rhapsode Ion plays an important role,²⁵ but if Housman's κρίνετε at the head of v. 18 is correct (and it is very hard indeed — at least for me — to think of a plausible alternative), then we are firmly in the world of κριτικοί and the τέχνη γραμματική, whether or not that phrase was in current use.²⁶ Commentators on the 'Reply' naturally (and rightly) turn to Pindar and Aristophanes' *Frogs* at this point,²⁷ but the combination of τέχνη and κρίνειν points in a decidedly more contemporary direction. Callimachus here all but invites 'commentary' on his own poetry.

There is a further aspect of Asclepiades' citation of *Epigrams* 6 and 23 which deserves a moment's attention. As is well known, Epigram 23, on Cleombrotus' suicide, has a very rich ancient tradition, largely though not exclusively in philosophical texts,²⁸ and it will almost certainly have been cited in philosophical contexts long before Asclepiades (or someone else) paired it with *Epigr.* 6 for a completely different reason. Our earliest witness to its ancient tradition is Cicero, who uses the story as an exemplum in *Pro Scauro* 4 and in *TD* 1.84 does so again, explicitly ascribing it to an epigram of Callimachus:²⁹

> a malis igitur mors abducit, non a bonis, uerum si quaerimus. et quidem hoc a Cyrenaico Hegesia sic copiose disputatur, ut is a rege Ptolomaeo prohibitus esse dicatur illa in scholis dicere, quod multi is auditis mortem sibi ipsi consciscerent. Callimachi quidem epigramma in Ambraciotam Cleombrotum est, quem ait, cum ei nihil accidisset aduersi, e muro se in mare abiecisse, lecto Platonis libro. eius autem, quem dixi, Hegesiae liber est Ἀποκαρτερῶν, in quo a uita quidem per inediam discedens reuocatur ab amicis, quibus respondens uitae humanae enumerat incommoda.
>
> Cicero, *Tusculan Disputations* 1.83–84

---

25 Cf. Hunter 1989.
26 I do not, of course, refer to the euphonist κριτικοί now made famous by the remains of Philodemus, *On Poems*, but Kathryn Gutzwiller's attempt to place Callimachus, and Hellenistic poetry more generally, within the principal strands of Hellenistic criticism (including euphonist criticism) is an important and suggestive contribution, Gutzwiller 2010, 342–354. Cf. further Steiner 2015.
27 Cf. also Pfeiffer 1968, 137.
28 Cf. White 1994, Williams 1995.
29 The difference in technique of citation is in keeping with Cicero's standard practices for formal, public speeches and the philosophical dialogues, cf. Jocelyn 1973. Beyond these references, Cicero's only citation of Callimachus is at *TD* 1.93, where the proverbial fr. 491 Pf. appears in Latin translation and is explicitly ascribed to Callimachus.

Death therefore removes us from bad things, not good, if it is the truth we pursue. This matter is discussed at such length by the Cyrenaic Hegesias that it is said that King Ptolemy stopped him from lecturing on the subject, because many who heard the lectures then killed themselves. There is an epigram of Callimachus on Cleombrotus of Ambracia who, according to Callimachus, threw himself from the wall into the sea after he had read Plato's book, though nothing bad happened to him. There is a book by this Hegesias, called Ἀποκαρτερῶν, in which someone who is trying to kill himself by fasting is called back by his friends, and in answer to them he catalogues the miseries of human life.

Cicero links Callimachus' epigram to Hegesias, a 'Cyrenaic' if not actually, like Callimachus, from Cyrene, in such a way that we might be tempted to think that he found the epigram cited in Hegesias' book; as, however, the Ptolemy of the anecdote is probably Soter, rather than Philadelphus, chronology seems against the idea that Hegesias might have cited a Callimachean epigram.[30] The reverse, i.e., the possibility that Callimachus found the story of Cleombrotus in Hegesias, cannot however be ruled out, though any number of other possible sources can of course be imagined.[31] Stephen White raises the possibility of a borrowing from the biographical works of Hermippos of Smyrna, ὁ Καλλιμάχειος, a younger contemporary and presumably 'pupil' of our poet, but it seems equally likely that Hermippos in fact cited the epigram and that it passed from there into philosophical literature.[32] However that may be, it seems very likely that the epigram on Cleombrotus was cited in biographical/ philosophical texts very near in time to Callimachus' own lifetime.[33] One at least of Asclepiades' chosen epigrams was thus very well known.

Callimachus and the philosophical tradition

As the case of Asclepiades of Myrlea and *Epigram* 27 demonstrates, epigrams were a particularly valuable resource for scholars of all kinds, in part because they very often concerned (or mentioned) important historical and literary figures. The same is true for iambic poetry. One of the most remarkable citations of Callimachus occurs in the chapter (1.7) τίς ὁ θεός;, contained in the Pseudo-Plutarchan 'Opinions of the Philosophers' (880d–f), an essay which — ever since the work of Hermann Diels — has been taken to be a principal source for

---

30 Cf., e.g., White 1994, 142.
31 Cf. White 1994, 151–152.
32 Hermippos frr. 40–41 Wehrli concern Plato's life.
33 Cf. Cameron 1995, 223–224; Cairns 2016, 67–68 sees the epigram as a product of Callimachus 'the court poet'.

the doxography ascribed to Aëtius, which Diels and those who have followed him trace back to ultimate origins in Theophrastus.³⁴ Two extracts from this chapter, coming very close to each other in the text, are relevant here:

ἔνιοι τῶν φιλοσόφων, καθάπερ Διαγόρας ὁ Μήλιος καὶ Θεόδωρος ὁ Κυρηναῖος καὶ Εὐήμερος ὁ Τεγεάτης, καθόλου φασὶ μὴ εἶναι θεούς· τὸν δ' Εὐήμερον καὶ Καλλίμαχος ὁ Κυρηναῖος αἰνίττεται ἐν τοῖς Ἰάμβοις γράφων· (fr. 191.9–11 Pf.)

εἰς τὸ πρὸ τείχευς ἱερὸν ἀλέες δεῦτε,
οὗ τὸν πάλαι Παγχαῖον ὁ πλάσας Ζᾶνα
γέρων ἀλαζὼν ἄδικα βιβλία ψήχει.

[Plutarch], *Opinions of the Philosophers* 880d–e

Some philosophers, such as Diagoras of Melos and Theodoros of Cyrene and Euhemeros of Tegea, deny absolutely the existence of gods. Callimachus of Cyrene alludes to Euhemeros in the *Iambi*:

'Come all of you to the sanctuary before the wall, where the deceitful old man who fashioned the ancient Zeus Panchaios scribbles his impious books'.

ἀναιρείσθω γάρ, φησίν, ὁ ποιητικὸς λῆρος σὺν Καλλιμάχῳ τῷι λέγοντι· (fr. 586 Pf.)

εἰ θεὸν οἶσθα,
ἴσθ' ὅτι καὶ ῥέξαι δαίμονι πᾶν δυνατόν'.

οὐδὲ γὰρ ὁ θεὸς δύναται πᾶν ποιεῖν· ἐπεί τοί γε, εἰ θεὸς ἔστι, ποιείτω τὴν χιόνα μέλαιναν τὸ δὲ πῦρ ψυχρὸν τὸν δὲ καθήμενον ὀρθὸν καὶ τὸ ἐναντίον.

[Plutarch], *Opinions of the Philosophers* 880f

Away, he says, with the poetic nonsense of such as Callimachus who says:

'If you acknowledge a god, acknowledge also that a divinity can do anything'.

For god is not able to do everything: if a god does exist, let him turn snow black and fire cold and upright the man who is seated and vice versa.'

V. 11 of *Iambus* 1 also occurs in an identical context in two other texts (Schol. Clem. Alex. *Protrep.* 2.24.2, Sext. Emp. *Adv. Math.* 9.51), and it seems very likely that all three share a common source;³⁵ the earliest extant witness to this tradition of an 'Atheistenkatalog', Cicero, *De natura deorum* 1.117–119 (spoken by the

---

34 Cf. Mansfeld-Runia 1997–2000.
35 Diels 1879, 58 took Aetius to be responsible for the citation of vv. 9–11, not just v. 11.

Academic Cotta), does not cite Callimachus in association with Euhemeros, but is nevertheless still of considerable interest in this connection:

> quid, qui aut fortis aut claros aut potentis uiros tradunt post mortem ad deos peruenisse eosque esse ipsos, quos nos colere, precari uenerarique soleamus, nonne expertes sunt religionum omnium? quae ratio maxime tractata ab Euhemero est, quem noster et interpretatus est et secutus praeter ceteros Ennius; ab Euhemero autem et mortes et sepulturae demonstrantur deorum; utrum igitur hic confirmasse uidetur religionem an penitus totam sustulisse?
>
> <div align="right">Cicero, <i>De natura deorum</i> 1.119</div>

> Those who claim that men who are brave or famous or powerful join the gods after death and that it is these very ones whom we are accustomed to worship and pray to and venerate — are they not devoid of all religious sense? This argument was principally developed by Euhemerus, whose main translator and imitator was our Ennius. Euhemerus, however, describes the deaths and burials of gods: does he, then, seem to have upheld religion or to have utterly destroyed it?

There may be several reasons for Cicero's omission (if that is what it is) of a quotation from Callimachus: Cicero never cites Greek verse in the original in his philosophical dialogues, only in Latin translation,[36] and perhaps the Callimachean verse (even in Latin translation) was ruder about *Euhemerus* than Cicero thought appropriate. It is, however, also possible that the evocation of Ennius' *Euhemerus* replaces a reference to a Greek poet in Cicero's source with a Latin work (note *noster ... praeter ceteros*) suitable for the style of the *De natura deorum*. If there is anything to this speculation, then (paradoxically perhaps) even Cicero's silence may be suggestive of Callimachus' presence in the tradition. At the very least, the absence of Callimachus from Cicero's discussion of atheists is no argument against a relatively early date for his inclusion in such discussions.

The ultimate source of this chapter of Pseudo-Plutarch and of the other related 'catalogues' cannot be established with any certainty, and it is in any case very unlikely that only one 'common source' is involved, but a not implausible case can be made out for the importance of the work of Clitomachus, an Academic philosopher of the late second century BC; some of our extant texts may derive from him directly, and some will (also) have used intermediary sources.[37] It is, for example, clear that, in the relevant chapter of Pseudo-Plutarch, there is an Epicurean text (and epitome) lying between 'Aëtius' and the 'common

---

36 Cf. Jocelyn 1973, esp. 73.
37 Cf. Diels 1879, 58–59, Winiarczyk 1976, Whitmarsh 2016, 165, 213.

source', perhaps Clitomachus. If indeed Clitomachus is the key figure here, then it is at least to be noted that his teacher and promoter, Carneades, came from Cyrene, and it may thus have been he who introduced Clitomachus to Callimachus' poetry, which he could of course have done in conversation (Carneades was believed to have written nothing down, Diog. Laert. 4.65).[38] The citation of Callimachus certainly stands out markedly in the Pseudo-Plutarchan essay; the other poets cited in our extant text are Aratus (twice), Euripides (five times), Hesiod (once),[39] and Homer (four times).

As for the citation of fr. 586 Pf., this need not of course go back ultimately to the same source as the quotation of *Iambus* 1, but I cannot suppress the admission that, if asked 'blind' to identify the poet of this verse and a bit, Callimachus would have been very low on my list of guesses, despite the elegiac metre. Nothing in the pentameter seems to suggest Callimachean refinement of diction, word order or wit. Such speculation is of course not to be pushed very far: we lack any context, we do not know who is speaking or to whom, and Callimachus certainly has more than one style in elegiacs. I have (inevitably) toyed with the notion that Καλλιμάχωι is an error for another name, the error arising from the preceding quotation of the Cyrenean poet.

The doxographical and biographical turn of Hellenistic philosophy means that collections of epigrams focusing on individuals might well have been fertile ground for historians of the subject. Let me illustrate this from the fragments of one of Callimachus' epigrams which did not make the cuts through to the *Anthology*. Two citations about Diodorus Cronus, the logician who was an older contemporary of Callimachus, are preserved, one by Diogenes Laertius and the Vatican scholia to Dionysius Thrax and one by Sextus Empiricus:

αὐτὸς ὁ Μῶμος
ἔγραφεν ἐν τοίχοις 'ὁ Κρόνος ἐστὶ σοφός'.

ἠνίδε κοί[40] κόρακες τεγέων ἔπι 'κοῖα συνῆπται'
κρώζουσιν καὶ 'κῶς αὖθι γενησόμεθα;'.

Callimachus fr. 393 Pf. = HE 1333–1336

Momos himself used to write on the walls 'Kronos is wise'.
Look! The ravens on the roofs croak 'of what kind are the joinings?' and 'How shall we be in the future?'

---

38 For Carneades' 'atheism' cf. Sedley 2013, 147–150.
39 On this citation cf. Hunter forthcoming.
40 κοί Wilamowitz: κου codd. Gow-Page prefer Fabricius' καί.

There is virtually universal critical agreement that these two citations come from the same epigram, but considerable disagreement about the order in which they are to be read and whether or not they are consecutive. Here again, I think, there are good grounds for guessing that this hypothesized epigram was taken into a doxographical work at a relatively early date (perhaps second century BC) and is thus another example of an early use to which Callimachus' poetry was put. Be that as it may, it is of some interest to see Callimachus in an epigram using (even semi-seriously) serious logical puzzles, even if we remain very unclear as to the interpretation and point of the second of the ravens' questions.[41]

Diodorus' teacher Apollonios Kronos came, as did Callimachus, from Cyrene, and Strabo (17.3.32) includes them both in his list of notable Cyreneans; moreover, Diodorus himself came from Iasos, the hometown, for what it is worth, of Hermocrates ὁ γραμματικός whom the *Suda* states was Callimachus' teacher. There is, then, at least a circumstantial case for thinking that Callimachus may have had personal, as well as intellectual, reasons for his interest in Diodorus. Be that as it may, one anecdote about Diodorus which gained notoriety at least later and which Diogenes Laertius puts alongside his quotation from Callimachus' epigram, and which was even used to explain how he came to inherit his teacher's nickname,[42] concerned his embarrassment at a symposium of Ptolemy I:

> When he was at the court of (διατρίβων παρά...) Ptolemy Soter,[43] he was questioned on certain dialectical arguments by Stilpo. As he was not able to solve them on the spot, he was criticised by the king and in particular was given the mocking name Kronos; he left the symposium, wrote a *logos* on the problem, and ended his life in despondency.
>
> Diogenes Laertius 2.111–112

A version of the anecdote occurs already at Pliny, *HN* 7.180 (= Diodorus fr. 100 Döring), where Diodorus is one of only three Greeks, alongside very many Romans, in a catalogue of those who died a sudden and quick death. How far back the epigram goes we can hardly say, but David Sedley at least is prepared to ac-

---

41 Cf., e.g., Sedley 1977, 108 n. 35, White 1986, Blank 1998, 342–345, Kurzová 2009. Cairns 2016, 66 endorses (without argument) Gow-Page's observation (*HE* II 216) that 'we need not suppose that C[allimachus] fully understood what he merely ridicules as a catch-phrase', but, leaving aside the question of 'ridicule', I see no reason to suppose (and good reason for the opposite view) that Callimachus did not know what he was doing.
42 Sedley 1977, 78 n. 27 enjoins caution about simply accepting this explanation.
43 For such language in connection with presence at Hellenistic courts cf. Herman 1980/1, 105–106.

cept the chronology that such an anecdote implies, even if the detail of what happened at the symposium may have been embroidered and fictionalised.⁴⁴ If the anecdote seems in part to breathe some of the spirit of Machon's Χρεῖαι or any number of pages of the reminiscences preserved in Athenaeus' *Deipnosophistai*, rather than that of Timon's *Silloi*,⁴⁵ the setting at a symposium, where so many epigrams are set, is at least suggestive for the context of Callimachus' epigram.

The survival of nearly four verses of an epigram inevitably invites speculation about the original poem, and I am certainly not going to refuse. The verses are usually thought to be mocking, i.e. this is a *Spottepigramm*,⁴⁶ but the point of the reference to Momos might rather be that even Momos, who normally did not have an undiluted good word for anyone, had had (in the past) to acknowledge Diodorus' wisdom;⁴⁷ instead of scratching καλός and the name of a beautiful young boy on walls, his graffito praises the wisdom of someone whose name proclaims him to be a Methuselah. Momos' action took place in the past, whereas the ravens croak Diodoran logical puzzles in the present tense. That the ravens are familiar with Diodorus' teaching (and dialect) is particularly appropriate if Diodorus, like Socrates, wrote nothing and all his teaching was oral, but the difference of tense perhaps suggests that this poem celebrates Diodorus' enduring fame after death⁴⁸ — his *kleos* lives on, preserved by his puzzles, just as Herakleitos' 'nightingales' (i.e. his poems) live on after his death (*Epigr.* 2 Pf.). If it is correct that this epigram was epitaphic (though whether or not it had anything to do with Diogenes' anecdote about his death we cannot say), then the couplet about the ravens is likely to have been the final couplet, i.e. Pfeiffer's ordering of the verses will be correct, though the preserved couplets may not have been contiguous.⁴⁹ Beyond the 'Herakleitos' epigram, we may also compare *Epigram* 23 (cited above) on the suicide of Cleombrotus after

---

44 Cf. Sedley 1977, 80, 109 n. 37. 45.
45 Diodorus appears in Timon, *SH* 805, 806.
46 Cf. Wilamowitz 1906, 172 n. 1, Clayman 2007, 504–505, Cairns 2016, 66.
47 So Sedley 1977, 108 n. 35, White 1994, 144.
48 Sedley 1977, 109 n. 36 rightly raises the possibility that Diodorus was dead at the time of the epigram.
49 The strongest case for the other ordering is that of Diehl 1937, 365. He points out (*inter alia*) that Sextus' introduction to the couplet he cites, 'the epigram written by Callimachus on Diodorus Cronus', most naturally suggests that Sextus then proceeds to cite the opening of the poem, in accordance with normal ancient habits of citation. As, however, this is indeed the couplet concerned with logical puzzles which Sextus alleges to be beyond grammarians, i.e. this is the couplet that is germane to the point that Sextus is making, Diehl's point cannot be thought probative.

reading Plato's *Phaedo* and (just possibly) fr. 396 (= Menander T 23 K-A), which offers some very fragile evidence suggesting that Callimachus may have written an epigram on the death of Menander. The fragility is such that nothing can hang on this, but Pfeiffer is surely correct that it is *'veri non omnino dissimile'* that Callimachus should have written an epigram on the death of the famous dramatist.

Finally, it is perhaps worth noting that Sextus does not apparently see the irony of attacking the ignorance and inadequacy of the γραμματικοί through a 'philosophical' epigram of Callimachus, who — as we have seen — deserved the title ὁ γραμματικός, if anyone did. It is very clear why this example appealed to Sextus — when he describes it as τὸ τυχὸν ἐπιγραμμάτιον, 'a random epigram' (ch. 309), he is being disingenuous at best — but when he writes that a γραμματικός, confronted with the ravens' second question, 'will fall silent, being unable to explain the reference' (ch. 311, cf. 309 'they are unable to understand'), we may at least wonder whether he (or his sources) in fact knew of any such silences in the grammatical tradition. The identity of the Hedylos who is credited in part of the etymological tradition with a commentary on the *Epigrams* (T 45 Pf. = SH 458) is a familiar problem of Callimachean scholarship,[50] but there is no good reason to doubt that such a work (whatever its date and authorship) had once existed, any more than we need doubt the reality of the commentary (ἐξήγησις) ascribed in the *Suda* to 'Archibios, son of Apollonios, γραμματικός' (T 44 Pf.). It is certainly not necessary to suppose that Sextus had any particular commentary or commentaries in mind, but the possibility that we have here a witness to the Callimachean commentary tradition cannot, I think, be dismissed out of hand.

Callimachus and the ethical tradition

My final example is the famous epigram to Archinos:

εἰ μὲν ἑκών, Ἀρχῖν', ἐπεκώμασα, μυρία μέμφου,
εἰ δ' ἄκων ἥκω, τὴν προπέτειαν ἔα.
ἄκρητος καὶ Ἔρως μ' ἠνάγκασαν, ὧν ὁ μὲν αὐτῶν
εἷλκεν, ὁ δ' οὐκ εἴα τὴν προπέτειαν ἐᾶν.
ἐλθὼν δ' οὐκ ἐβόησα, τίς ἢ τίνος, ἀλλ' ἐφίλησα   5
τὴν φλιήν· εἰ τοῦτ' ἔστ' ἀδίκημ', ἀδικέω.

Callimachus, *Epigram* 42 Pf. = HE 1075–1080

---

50 Cf., e.g., Gutzwiller 1998, 183–184.

If willingly I came on the revel, heap endless reproach upon me, but if I came unwillingly, forget my rashness. Unmixed wine and Love compelled me: one of them dragged me forward and the other would not allow me to drop my rashness. When I came, I did not call out your name or that of your father, but I kissed the doorpost; if this a crime, I am a criminal.

The rich modern discussion of this poem has focused upon its relation to Asclepiades, *AP* 5.167 (= *HE* 870–5), the text of vv. 3–4, in the light of the striking difference between the text of the *Anthology* and that of the inscription of this poem on a Roman wall of late Republican – early imperial date (see further below), the remarkable sound effects of the verses, and the background to the ideas and language of the poem and in particular whether these are to be sought in what we might call a poetic and popular tradition or rather in something more explicitly philosophical and 'technical'. This last issue and that of the text of v. 4 are, of course, intimately related, and it is on the possible philosophical affiliations of the poem that I wish to focus, both because, particularly when placed alongside the epigram for Diodorus Cronus, this may shed light upon an aspect of Callimachus' poetry which does not always receive its proper due, and also because it too might lead us towards Callimachus' early reception.

Georg Kaibel pointed to the Stoic affiliations of προπέτεια, 'hastiness, over-rashness, lack of judgement in assenting' and its opposite ἀπροπτωσία (cf. *SVF* II 130, 131, III 281), as well as to 'technical' uses of ἕλκειν found in the same Stoic contexts, and he argued that Callimachus was to some extent teasing Archinos with a Stoic education.[51] Kaibel's identification of Stoic terminology has often been accepted, even if the interpretation of the poem which he drew from it has not.[52] προπέτεια is, however, not solely a Stoic term (in the *Nicomachean Ethics* Aristotle makes it one form of *akrasia*, *EN* 7.1150bff.),[53] and some have looked rather to the Aristotelian account of types of fault to understand the rhetoric of the poem.[54] However familiar in poetic and popular morality ideas of the 'unwilling fault' may be (cf., e.g., Eur. fr. 272b K), it is indeed hard to think away the Peripatetic tradition when reading Callimachus' epigram. In 1135a–b of Book 5 of the *Nicomachean Ethics*, Aristotle distinguishes between types of fault on the basis of whether or not they were committed willingly; ἀδικεῖν (and indeed δικαιοπραγεῖν) are not applicable to actions done ἄκων, and

---

51 Kaibel 1896, 266–268. 52.
52 Helpful account in Gutzwiller 1998, 217–218. Gow-Page dismiss Kaibel's discussion ('seems very far-fetched'), without engaging seriously with it.
53 I have (very) idly wondered whether ἄκρητος in v. 3 might suggest ἀκρασία.
54 Cf., e.g., Barigazzi 1984.

any action done under compulsion (or because of the exercise of βία) is an 'unwilling' action performed κατὰ συμβεβηκός. It is only true ἀδικήματα which should be the subject of censure (ψέγεται, cf. μυρία μέμφου in v. 1 of Callimachus' epigram). In these chapters Aristotle produces a threefold division of βλαβαί into μετ' ἀγνοίας ἁμαρτήματα, ἀτυχήματα and ἀδικήματα. In a closely related discussion in Book 1 of the *Rhetoric* (1374b), Aristotle considers which types of human action it is 'reasonable/equitable (ἐπιεικές) to pardon'; ἁμαρτήματα will clearly fall under this category, whereas ἀδικήματα will not, because they arise from 'viciousness', πονηρία. If it is impossible to disregard the Aristotelian discussions in considering Callimachus' epigram, then we will accept that Callimachus here alludes to more than one ethical tradition in making his case to Archinos. The clinching argument of the final words obviously draws on the very rich poetic tradition of erotic ἀδικεῖν (Sappho fr. 1 etc.), but Callimachus' point seems to be that his silent kiss upon the doorpost would not have attracted any attention (unlike calling out his name) and so he avoided bringing any notoriety upon the beloved boy.

Unfortunately, we can only guess why someone painted this epigram (in careful and elegant lettering)[55] on an outside wall of the so-called 'Auditorium of Maecenas'.[56] The walls of Pompeii also offer many familiar passages of high Latin poetry painted or scratched by people of (apparently) very varying educational levels, and there are also two Greek epigrams of Leonidas (or one of Leonidas and one of Euenus).[57] My concern here is rather with a citation of the final couplet which we find in Plutarch's work, 'On the restraint of anger':

ἔστι γάρ τις, ὦ ἑταῖρε, πρώτη καθάπερ τυράννου κατάλυσις τοῦ θυμοῦ, μὴ πείθεσθαι μηδ' ὑπακούειν προστάττοντος αὐτοῦ μέγα βοᾶν καὶ δεινὸν βλέπειν καὶ κόπτειν ἑαυτόν, ἀλλ' ἡσυχάζειν καὶ μὴ συνεπιτείνειν ὥσπερ νόσημα ῥιπτασμῷ καὶ διαβοήσει τὸ πάθος. αἱ μὲν γὰρ ἐρωτικαὶ πράξεις, οἷον ἐπικωμάσαι καὶ ᾆσαι καὶ στεφανῶσαι θύραν, ἔχουσιν ἀμωσγέπως κουφισμὸν οὐκ ἄχαριν οὐδ' ἄμουσον·

ἐλθὼν δ' οὐκ ἐβόησα τίς ἢ τίνος, ἀλλ' ἐφίλησα
τὴν φλιήν. εἰ τοῦτ' ἔστ' ἀδίκημ', ἀδικῶ.

---

55 Cf. Kaibel 1876, 3.
56 It is now normally assumed that the graffito shows that the 'auditorium' had something to do with dining and sympotic practice, cf., e.g., Steinby 1996, 74, but the argument is not a strong one. Murray 1985, 43 misrepresents the substance of the epigram, but suggests that the scribe 'recreates the original function of the literary genre by actually writing the poem on a wall (leaving it as a 'kiss on the doorstep')'. I am grateful to Emily Gowers for allowing me to read a draft of her forthcoming discussion of the 'auditorium'.
57 Cf. *Epigr.* 1103, 1104 Kaibel, Gow–Page, *Hellenistic Epigrams* II 342.

αἵ τε τοῖς πενθοῦσιν ἐφέσεις τοῦ ἀποκλαῦσαι καὶ ἀποδύρασθαι πολύ τι τῆς λύπης ἅμα τῷ δακρύῳ συνεξάγουσιν· ὁ δὲ θυμὸς ἐκριπίζεται μᾶλλον οἷς πράττουσι καὶ λέγουσιν οἱ ἐν αὑτῷ καθεστῶτες. ἀτρεμεῖν οὖν κράτιστον ἢ φεύγειν καὶ ἀποκρύπτειν καὶ καθορμίζειν ἑαυτὸν εἰς ἡσυχίαν, ὥσπερ ἐπιληψίας ἀρχομένης συναισθανομένους κτλ.

Plutarch, *On the restraint of anger* 455b–c

The first way, my friend, to overthrow anger, as you would a tyrant, is not to obey or listen to it when it bids you shout out loud and look fierce and beat your breast, but to keep quiet and not to aggravate the emotion, as if a disease, by tossing around and calling out. Lovers' actions, such as komoi and singing and garlanding doors, do in some way offer an alleviation which is neither charmless nor remote from the Muses:

When I came, I did not call out your name or that of your father, but
I kissed the doorpost; if this a crime, I am a criminal.

So too, weeping and lamentation carry away from those who are grieving much of the pain, together with the tears. Anger, however, is rather fanned by the deeds and actions of those in that state. The best course, therefore, is to remain calm or to flee and hide and seek anchor in tranquillity, as though we had realised that an epileptic fit was imminent...

Whereas, so Plutarch argues, the indulgence of *eros* or grief leads to some not unpleasant alleviation of suffering,[58] anger is merely increased and made wilder by its indulgence. Plutarch's citation of the Callimachean couplet, coming as it does from a poem recalling a κῶμος, is entirely appropriate to the point he is making, and may be thought to be pointedly introduced by οὐδ' ἄμουσον, and yet there is something remarkable about the fit between poem and context. On the one hand, although it is not unreasonable to sense κουφισμός in the poet's kissing of the beloved's doorpost, this is not made explicit either in the cited couplet or elsewhere in the poem. We might argue that, whereas most komasts seek the κουφισμός which admission to the beloved's bedroom would bring, for Callimachus the simple and silent kiss of the doorpost was (unusually) an end in itself which he could fulfill without restraint; unlike most komasts, he achieved what he wanted and so felt a lightening of the pain. If so, then Plutarch has, with fine judgement, chosen a κῶμος-epigram which does indeed illustrate the point he is making. On the other hand, anger, according to Plutarch, wants the sufferer (*inter alia*) to 'shout loudly' (μέγα βοᾶν, διαβόησις), which is precisely what, in the epigram, Callimachus asserts to Archinos that he did not do. Callimachus' epigram recalls a very unusual κῶμος, which itself in fact staged a display of control (though not, or at least not primarily and/or

---

[58] With regard to *eros*, this is a version of the familiar doctrine of, e.g., Theocritus 11.1–3 (with my note on v. 3).

explicitly, over anger), a refusal to 'shout out' and a model of ἡσυχάζειν, which makes the citation's relationship to the surrounding Plutarchan context much richer and multi-layered than is often the case in Plutarch's quotations of poetry.[59] Two (unanswerable) questions arise. At some earlier stage of the tradition on this subject (i.e. in one of Plutarch's sources) was the whole epigram, not just the final couplet, quoted? Does Plutarch (and/or whoever first embedded just the final couplet in this discussion) expect readers to remember the rest of the poem from which it comes?[60]

The sources of 'On the restraint of anger' have been much discussed, and this is certainly not the place to add to that bibliography. The possibility, however, that the final couplet of the poem (or perhaps even the whole poem) was embedded in a discussion of restraint, perhaps even the 'control of anger', well before Plutarch cannot, I think, be discounted. Here too is where the philosophical texture of the poem again becomes relevant, a texture which might well have attracted attention in Hellenistic ethical treatises. My guess – and it is of course nothing more than a guess – is that the citation of Callimachus' epigram came to Plutarch through an earlier tradition in which this poem was indeed cited in an ethical or moralizing tradition. Whoever painted it on a Roman wall may well have known that tradition also.

This of course is just (one more) speculation. As far as quotation of Callimachus is concerned, Plutarch to some extent stands out from other writers of the imperial age; Pontani went so far as to suggest that Plutarch is 'perhaps the only ancient Greek writer who not only betrays direct familiarity with Callimachus but also refers to his poetry not merely in order to display his erudition'.[61] Of certain citations, however, it is the *Aitia* which takes the lion's share; no other epigram is certainly cited,[62] though Plutarch presumably knew the epigrams well.

This paper has been built on a quicksand of speculation and fragile inference, but these are one's inevitable companions in any investigation of this

---

59 'Control' is also central to Propertius' rewriting of Callimachus' epigram at 1.3.9–14; commentators on Propertius do not seem to discuss whether v. 11 of that poem implies a particular text in v. 4 of the Greek epigram, but the matter is at least worth pondering.
60 ἐπικωμάσαι in Plutarch's introduction to the citation from Callimachus is a verb he uses elsewhere also, but it may also prepare for the citation, as it appears in v. 1 of the epigram. If this is correct, we would have a 'glide' into the citation of a kind familiar both from Plutarch and from other prose texts, cf. Hunter 2010.
61 Pontani 2011, 101.
62 *Moralia* 13f need have nothing directly to do with *Epigr*. 1, just as the reference to the 'cup of Bathycles' at *Moralia* 155e (cf. *Solon* 80e) need not derive from *Iambus* 1.

kind. What I hope has nevertheless emerged is that the indirect tradition still has things to teach us about how Callimachus was received, used and cited in the centuries which succeeded him, even though we have lost all but the tiniest fraction of the literature where we might most naturally look for him. It is neither surprising nor regrettable that the search for Callimachus' *Nachleben* in Greek and Latin poetry takes the lion's share of scholarly attention, but Callimachus' importance for other traditions deserves our attention also. Callimachus is for us so central a figure that we tend in fact to take that centrality for granted; seeking to know as much as we can of what antiquity made of him is the very least we can do to acknowledge his importance.

Bibliography

Barigazzi, A. 1984. 'Callimaco, *Ep.* 42 (*A.P.* 12.118): Non sono colpevole', in: *Lirica greca da Archiloco a Elitis. Studi in onore di Filippo Maria Pontani*, Padua, 197–204.

Blank, D.L. 1998. *Sextus Empiricus. Against the Grammarians*, Oxford.

Brink, C.O. 1971. *Horace on Poetry, the 'Ars Poetica'*, Cambridge.

Cairns, F. 2016. *Hellenistic Epigram. Contexts of Exploration*, Cambridge.

Cameron, A. 1995. *Callimachus and his Critics*, Princeton.

Clayman, D.L. 2007. 'Philosophers and philosophy in Greek epigram', in: P. Bing/J.S. Bruss (eds.), *Brill's Companion to Hellenistic Epigram*, Leiden, 497–517.

D'Alessio, G.B. 2000. 'Le *Argonautiche* di Cleone Curiense', in: R. Pretagostini (ed.), *La letteratura ellenistica. Problemi e prospettive di ricerca*, Rome, 91–112.

Diehl, E. 1937. 'Hypomnema. De Callimachi librorum fatis capita selecta', *Acta Universitatis Latviensis, Philologorum et Philosophorum ordinis series IV.2.*, Riga, 305–476.

Diels, H. 1879. *Doxographi Graeci*, Berlin.

Di Maria, G. 1996. *Achillis quae feruntur Astronomica et in Aratum Opuscula*, Palermo.

Gutzwiller, K.J. 1998. *Poetic Garlands. Hellenistic Epigrams in Context*, Berkeley.

Gutzwiller, K.J. 2010. 'Literary criticism', in: J.J. Clauss/M. Cuypers (eds.), *A Companion to Hellenistic Literature*, Malden MA, 337–365.

Herman, G. 1980/81. 'The "friends" of the early Hellenistic rulers: servants or officials?', *Talanta* 12/13, 103–149.

Hunter, R. 1989. 'Winged Callimachus', *Zeitschrift für Papyrologie und Epigraphik* 76, 1–2 [= Hunter 2008, 86–88].

Hunter, R. 2008. *On Coming After*, Berlin.

Hunter, R. 2010. 'Rhythmical language and poetic citation in Greek narrative texts', in: G. Bastianini/A. Casanova (eds.), *I papiri del romanzo antico*, Florence, 223–245 [= this volume 462–484].

Hunter, R. 2011a. 'The reputation of Callimachus', in: D. Obbink/R. Rutherford (eds.), *Culture in Pieces*, Oxford, 220–238 [= Hunter 2008, 537–558].

Hunter, R. 2011b. 'Festivals, cults, and the construction of consensus in Hellenistic poetry', in: G. Urso (ed.), *Dicere Laudes. Elogio, comunicazione, creazione del consenso*, Cividale del Friuli, 101–118 [= this volume 175–192].

Hunter, R. 2014. *Hesiodic Voices*, Cambridge.
Hunter, R. forthcoming. 'Hesiod and the Presocratics: a Hellenistic perspective', in: H. Koning/ L. Iribarren Baralt (eds.), *Hesiod and the Beginnings of Greek Philosophy*, Leiden.
Jocelyn, H.D. 1973. 'Greek poetry in Cicero's prose writing', *Yale Classical Studies* 23, 61–111.
Kaibel, G. 1876. 'De Callimachi epigrammate XLIII ed. Schneid.', *Hermes* 10, 1–6.
Kaibel, G. 1896. 'Zu den Epigrammen des Kallimachos', *Hermes* 31, 264–270.
Krevans, N. 1993. 'Fighting against Antimachus: the *Lyde* and the *Aetia* reconsidered', in: M.A. Harder/R.F. Regtuit/G.C. Wakker (eds.), *Callimachus*, Groningen, 149–160.
Kurzová, H. 2009. 'What worried the crows in Callimachus' epigram?', *Graeco-Latina Brunensia* 14, 125–129.
Mansfeld, J./Runia, D.T. 1997–2000. *Aëtiana. The Method and Intellectual Context of a Doxographer*, Leiden.
Martin, J. 1998. *Aratos, Phénomènes*, Paris.
Montanari, F. 1995. 'Filologi alessandrini e poeti alessandrini: la filologia sui "contemporanei"', *Aevum Antiquum* 8, 47–63.
Montanari, F. 2002. 'Callimaco e la filologia', in: *Callimaque (Entretiens sur l'antiquité Classique XLVII)*, Vandoeuvres/Geneva, 59–97.
Murray, O. 1985. 'Symposium and genre in the poetry of Horace', *Journal of Roman Studies* 75, 39–50.
Pagani, L. 2007. *Asclepiade di Mirlea. I frammenti degli scritti omerici*, Rome.
Parsons, P.J. 2002. 'Callimachus and the Hellenistic epigram', in: *Callimaque (Entretiens sur l'antiquité Classique XLVII)*, Vandoeuvres/Geneva, 99–141.
Pfeiffer, R. 1949. *Callimachus*, Oxford.
Pfeiffer, R. 1968. *History of Classical Scholarship*, Oxford.
Pontani, F. 2011. 'Callimachus cited', in: B. Acosta-Hughes/L. Lehnus/S. Stephens (eds.), *Brill's Companion to Callimachus*, Leiden, 93–117.
Rengakos, A. 2000. 'Aristarchus and the Hellenistic poets', *Seminari Romani* 3, 325–335.
Sedley, D. 1977. 'Diodorus Cronus and Hellenistic philosophy', *Proceedings of the Cambridge Philological Society* 23, 74–120.
Sedley, D. 2013. 'From the Pre-Socratics to the Hellenistic age', in: S. Bullivant/M. Ruse (eds.), *The Oxford Handbook of Atheism*, Oxford, 139–151.
Steinby, E.M. 1996. *Lexicon topographicum Urbis Romae III*, Rome.
Steiner, D. 2015. 'The Poetics of Sound: Callimachus' rereading of Pindar fragment 70B S.-M.', *Classical Philology* 110, 99–123.
White, M.J. 1986. 'What worried the crows?', *Classical Quarterly* 36, 534–537.
White, S.A. 1994. 'Callimachus on Plato and Cleombrotus', *Transactions of the American Philological Association* 124, 135–161.
Whitmarsh, T. 2016. *Battling the Gods. Atheism in the Ancient World*, London.
Wilamowitz, U. von 1906. *Die Textgeschichte der griechischen Bukoliker*, Berlin.
Williams, G.D. 1995. 'Cleombrotus of Ambracia: interpretations of a suicide from Callimachus to Agathias', *Classical Quarterly* 45, 154–169.
Winiarczyk, M. 1976. 'Der erste Atheistenkatalog des Kleitomachos', *Philologus* 120, 32–46.

16 Enkelados: Callimachus fr. 1.36

(co-author Rebecca Laemmle)

τῶι πιθόμη]ν· ἐνὶ τοῖς γὰρ ἀείδομεν οἳ λιγὺν ἦχον
τέττιγος, θ]όρυβον δ' οὐκ ἐφίλησαν ὄνων.
θηρὶ μὲν οὐατόεντι πανείκελον ὀγκήσαιτο
ἄλλος, ἐγ]ὼ δ' εἴην οὐλαχύς, ὁ πτερόεις,
ἃ πάντως, ἵνα γῆρας ἵνα δρόσον ἣν μὲν ἀείδω
προίκιον ἐκ δίης ἠέρος εἶδαρ ἔδων,
αὖθι τὸ δ' ἐκδύοιμι, τό μοι βάρος ὅσσον ἔπεστι
τριγλώχιν ὀλοῶι νῆσος ἐπ' Ἐγκελάδωι.
.... Μοῦσαι γὰρ ὅσους ἴδον ὄθματι παῖδας
μὴ λοξῶι, πολιοὺς οὐκ ἀπέθεντο φίλους.
............]σε [..] πτερὸν οὐκέτι κινεῖν
............]η τῆμος ἐνεργότατος.

Callimachus fr. 1.29–40[1]

[I obeyed him]; for we sing among those who have at heart the clear tone [of the cicada], but not the noise of asses. Let [someone else] bray just like the long-eared beast, but may I be the small one, the winged one, ah in all respects, so that as to old age and dew, I may sing the latter, eating the free food from the divine air, but the former may I cast off; its weight on me is like the three-cornered island on destructive Enkelados. ... For on all those on whom the Muses look when they are children with no sideways eye, these they do not set aside when they are grey. .... no longer to move the wing ... then busiest[2]

That Callimachus' prayer to rid himself of old age reworks a famous choral song from Euripides' *Heracles* and that that song is important not just for these verses but for the whole 'Reply to the Telchines' was recognised already by Rudolf Pfeiffer shortly after the new Callimachean text was published:[3]

ἁ νεότας μοι φίλον· ἄ-
χθος δὲ γῆρας αἰεὶ
βαρύτερον Αἴτνας σκοπέλων

---

[1] The text is that of Harder 2012; many papyrological marks have been omitted where they do not affect the argument of this paper.
[2] All translations, unless otherwise noted, are our own.
[3] Cf. Pfeiffer 1928, 329; for a recent discussion of Callimachus and this Euripidean ode cf. Prauscello 2011.

ἐπὶ κρατὶ κεῖται, βλεφάρων
σκοτεινὸν φάος ἐπικαλύψαν.⁴

                                                   Euripides, *HF* 637–641

Youth is dear to me, but old age, a burden ever heavier than the boulders of Etna, lies over my head, covering the light of my eyes so that they are dark.

Later in the same ode, the chorus describe themselves once as γέρων ἀοιδός (678), 'an aged singer', and once as κύκνος ὣς γέρων ἀοιδός, 'an aged singer like a swan', singing songs in honour of Apollo πολιᾶν ἐκ γενύων, 'from greying cheeks' (692–3); both the motif of the swan (almost certainly) and the grey hair and the singing for Apollo (certainly) find powerful resonance at the end of the 'Reply'.⁵ More broadly, the assertion of the Euripidean chorus that they will never 'cease from blending the Graces with the Muses, the sweetest of unions' (673–5), is precisely dramatised in the opening sequence (as we have it) of the *Aitia*, in which the 'Reply' is followed by the poet's dream of meeting the Muses on Helicon and, then, the *aition* of the cult of the Parian Graces.⁶

One aspect of these Callimachean verses which has attracted less attention than might have been expected is the fact that the poet identifies Enkelados, rather than Typhos/Typhoeus, as the Giant buried beneath Sicily; this might be thought particularly surprising in view of the fact that Pindar, *Pythian* 1 is one of the important earlier intertexts for the 'Reply',⁷ and in that famous poem it is indeed Typhos who lies beneath the volcano. Callimachus fr. 1 seems in fact to be the earliest explicit reference to Enkelados as the Giant beneath Sicily. In earlier texts Enkelados is standardly reported as killed by Athena during the Gigantomachy, but the story that, as he fled from the battle, Athena threw Sicily on top of him is first explicitly found in 'Apollodorus' *Bibl.* 1.6.2. Whether or not it was Callimachus who first identified the Giant beneath Sicily as Enkelados we cannot say.⁸ Some have indeed wanted to find an evocation of this identification

---

4 The text and colometry is that of Diggle's 1981 Oxford Classical Texts.
5 For a recent consideration of the likely image of the swan in the last preserved verses of the 'Reply' cf. Sberna 2015.
6 Cf. further Harder 2012, 2.120–121. It may even be that the chorus' prayer αἰεὶ δ' ἐν στεφάνοισιν εἴην (677) is picked up and reversed by the Parian *aition*, which explains why the cult does not use garlands and flute-music, cf. Prauscello 2011, 307–308.
7 Cf. Harder 2012, 2.58, and below p. 309.
8 A Pindaric scholium (I 132 Drachmann), in quoting Callim. fr. 1.36, notes the difference between Pindar and Callimachus concerning the identity of the Giant beneath Etna; this does not necessarily mean that the scholiast believed Callimachus to have been the first to name the

in Euripides' *Heracles*, a play that, as we have seen, was very important to the Reply':[9]

ἢ ἤ· τί δρᾶις, ὦ Διὸς παῖ, μελάθρωι;
τάραγμα ταρτάρειον, ὡς ἐπ' Ἐγκελάδωι ποτέ, Παλλάς,
ἐς δόμους πέμπεις.[10]

Euripides *HF* 907–910

Ah ah! What, child of Zeus, are you doing in the house? You send, Pallas, a confusion from hell, as once against Enkelados.

Whether or not this is the correct interpretation of those verses, it is to be noted that, in this same ode (679, 694), the chorus which has implicitly compared themselves to the Giant beneath Etna (vv. 637–40, cited above) twice uses κελαδεῖν to describe its aged singing, a repetition which strengthens the case for identifying the giant beneath Sicily in Euripides with Enkelados. In any case, Callimachus' identification of the Giant certainly grows out of the *Heracles*.

However innovative Callimachus was in naming the Giant beneath Etna as Enkelados, the importance of this figure for the prologue of the *Aitia* does indeed lie in his name. To the λιγὺς ἦχος of the tiny cicada is opposed the unmusical braying of donkeys,[11] and 'the man of κέλαδος'[12] certainly belongs with the latter. Callimachus is forced to admit that, despite his poetical principles, he is as oppressed as a prime representative of 'unmusical noise', even if old age is a less visible burden than 'the three-cornered island'.[13] Just as in Pindar's *Pythian* 1 enchanting Apolline music is set against the noisy πάταγος of Etna erupting over Typhos (v. 24),[14] so in the 'Reply', poetry sanctioned by Apollo is opposed to the inarticulate θόρυβος of donkeys and Giants. This passage will have been

---

Giant as Enkelados, but he may have done; at any rate, this scholium points to ancient discussion of the matter.
9 Cf. Bond's 1981, note on v. 907, Vian 1952, 201–202.
10 Both Bond 1981 and Diggle 1981 follow Wilamowitz in giving these verses to Amphitryon.
11 Cf., e.g., Acosta-Hughes/Stephens 2012, 84, Steiner 2015, 110.
12 For 'Bahuvrîhi' compounds of this type cf. Strömberg 1946, 115–136. The scholia on Ar. *Clouds* 158 state that ἐγκέλαδοι (presumably 'bumblebees', in the more recent scholia also glossed as βομβύκια) are so called 'because they have *kelados* inside them'; these scholia, which seem to reflect post-Aristotelian zoology, link ἐγκέλαδοι with ὁ μουσικὸς τέττιξ, and this, as an anonymous referee rightly observes, is hardly without interest in the context of Callimachus fr. 1. Callimachus' use of zoological lore in his poetry is familiar from several passages, most notably perhaps in the puzzling *envoi* of the *Hymn to Apollo*.
13 Cf. Fantuzzi-Hunter 2004, 72–73.
14 Cf. further below on Callim. *Hymn* 4.137–147.

central to the Roman Callimacheans' shaping of Gigantomachy as a prime example of the kind of poetry to be avoided.[15] The 'noise' of the Gigantomachy was also commemorated in the name of another Giant-victim of Athena on the frieze of the Siphnian Treasury, Ἐρίκτυπος.[16]

The noise of Enkelados' name had been crucial to the exploitation of this figure long before Callimachus, particularly in Dionysiac and satyric contexts.[17] It is, moreover, a curious fact that braying donkeys played a role in a version of Dionysus' participation in the Gigantomachy found in later texts. Eratosthenes, *Katasterismoi* 11 (cf. Hyginus *Poet. astr.* 2.23.3)[18] tells how the braying of the asses on which Dionysus, Hephaestus and the satyrs rode to the battle put the Giants to flight and this was the origin of the star group of Asses; there is no secure attestation for the story before Eratosthenes, but it is at least tempting to think that it is one more ingredient in Callimachus' Aesopic menagerie.

Knowledge of the nature of Callimachean poetry means that we would, in any case, have assumed that Callimachus chose the name of his giant with care. That assumption is confirmed by the other extant passage in which Callimachus refers to the Giant beneath Etna. In the *Hymn to Delos*, Ares beats upon his shield to terrify the river Peneios into refusing help to Leto:

> ἔτρεμε δ' Ὄσσης
> οὔρεα καὶ πεδίον Κραννώνιον αἵ τε δυσαεῖς
> ἐσχατιαὶ Πίνδοιο, φόβωι δ' ὠρχήσατο πᾶσα
> Θεσσαλίη· τοῖος γὰρ ἀπ' ἀσπίδος ἔβραμεν ἦχος.   140
> ὡς δ', ὁπότ' Αἰτναίου ὄρεος πυρὶ τυφομένοιο
> σείονται μυχὰ πάντα, κατουδαίοιο γίγαντος
> εἰς ἑτέρην Βριαρῆος ἐπωμίδα κινυμένοιο,
> θερμάστραι τε βρέμουσιν ὑφ' Ἡφαίστοιο πυράγρης
> ἔργα θ' ὁμοῦ, δεινὸν δὲ πυρίκμητοί τε λέβητες   145
> καὶ τρίποδες πίπτοντες ἐπ' ἀλλήλοις ἰαχεῦσιν,
> τῆμος ἔγεντ' ἄραβος σάκεος τόσος εὐκύκλοιο.

Callimachus, *Hymn to Delos* 137–147

The mountains of Ossa trembled and the plain of Krannon and the windy reaches of Pindos, and all of Thessaly danced in fear. Such a thundering rang from his shield. As when all the deepest recesses of Mt Etna smouldering with fire shake, when the Giant Briareus beneath the earth turns over to his other shoulder, and the furnaces roar at Hephaestus'

---

15 Cf. Hunter 2006, 37.
16 Cf. *LIMC* s.v.
17 Cf. Eur. *Cyc.* 7–8, Laemmle 2013, 178–191.
18 Cf. Pàmias i Massana-Zucker 2013, 35, 183, Robert 1878, 92–93, Laemmle 2013, 184–185.

tongs, as also his works, the fire-wrought cauldrons and tripods clatter terribly as they fall upon one another, so then was the sounding of his well-rounded shield.

As has long been recognised, Callimachus not only here names the Giant as the hundred-hander Briareus (or Braireos), but also alludes in v. 141 (τυφομένοιο) to the identification of the giant as Typhos or Typhoeus. Such play with mythic variants is very familiar in Callimachus and Hellenistic poetry more generally. It is less important that Callimachus, therefore, knew at least three names for the Giant beneath Etna, than that in the *Hymn to Delos* we have, as in the prologue to the *Aitia*, the pattern of opposition between Apolline order (in this case, Apollo's birth) and crashing cosmic noise. In the opening of *Pythian* 1, 'even violent Ares' sets aside his spears and is lulled to sleep by Apolline music (v. 11–12); in the *Hymn to Delos*, he has taken them up again and volcanic eruption is replaced by threatened earthquake, here indeed compared to the eruption of Etna. In the prologue to the *Aitia*, this pattern has affected also the naming of the Giant.

Finally, there is another famous classical text which seems to have served as a precedent for Callimachus, namely Pratinas' famous *hyporchema*:

τίς ὁ θόρυβος ὅδε; τί τάδε τὰ χορεύματα;
τίς ὕβρις ἔμολεν ἐπὶ Διονυσιάδα πολυπάταγα θυμέλαν;
ἐμὸς ἐμὸς ὁ Βρόμιος, ἐμὲ δεῖ κελαδεῖν, ἐμὲ δεῖ παταγεῖν
ἀν' ὄρεα σύμενον μετὰ Ναϊάδων
οἷά τε κύκνον ἄγοντα ποικιλόπτερον μέλος.   5
τὰν ἀοιδὰν κατέστασε Πιερὶς βασίλειαν· ὁ δ' αὐλὸς
ὕστερον χορευέτω· καὶ γάρ ἐσθ' ὑπηρέτας.
κώμωι μόνον θυραμάχοις τε πυγμαχίαισι νέων θέλοι παροίνων
ἔμμεναι στρατηλάτας.
παῖε τὸν φρυνεοῦ ποικίλου πνοὰν ἔχοντα,   10
φλέγε τὸν ὀλεσισιαλοκάλαμον
λαλοβαρύοπα παραμελορυθμοβάταν
ὑπαὶ τρυπάνωι δέμας πεπλασμένον.
ἢν ἰδού· ἄδε σοι δεξιᾶς καὶ ποδὸς διαρριφά·
θρίαμβε διθύραμβε κισσόχαιτ' ἄναξ,   15
<ἄκου'> ἄκουε τὰν ἐμὰν Δώριον χορείαν.

Pratinas, *PMG* 708

What uproar is this? What dances are these? What outrageous behaviour has come to Dionysus' tumuluous altar? Bromios is mine, mine! It is I who must shout, I who must create a clatter as I rush over the mountains with the naiads, producing a song that flits this way and that, like a swan. Pieris gave the throne to song; let the pipe take second position when it dances, since it is a servant! Let it aspire to serve as general only for drunken wanderings and for the fist-fights in which intoxicated young men engage in front of others' doors. Punch the man with the spotted breath of a toad! Set fire to the chatteringlydeep-voiced, out-of-time-with-the-music-marching, spit-wasting-made-of-reed (pipe), whose form was moulded by an auger! Look at this! Here is a tossing of my right hand and my foot for you! *Thriambos, Dithyrambos*, ivy-crowned lord – listen, listen to my Doric dance-song!

trans. S.D. Olson

What matters here is not the much-debated issue of the performance context of this song, but rather the motifs which this passage shares with Callimachus fr. 1. The speaker, who compares himself to a swan (v. 5),[19] rejects the θόρυβος of the *aulos* because ἐμὲ δεῖ κελαδεῖν, ἐμὲ δεῖ παταγεῖν.[20] What in Pratinas is a territorial claim – the speaker protests that κελαδεῖν and παταγεῖν belong to him not to the *aulos* – has become in Callimachus a distinction between two types of poetry which involves a rejection of 'loud resounding song' and thundering noise:

μηδ' ἀπ' ἐμεῦ διφᾶτε μέγα ψοφέουσαν ἀοιδήν
τίκτεσθαι· βροντᾶν οὐκ ἐμόν, ἀλλὰ Διός.

Callimachus fr. 1.19–20

Do not seek from me the birth of a loudly resounding song: it is not mine to thunder, that is Zeus's task.

Callimachus thus inverts Pratinas in order to reject loud noise, but at the same time he imitates Pratinas' paradoxical gesture of replacing one kind of noise with another: for not only does Callimachus have to admit that he is, in one way at least, like 'the man of κέλαδος', but the very act of rejection involves imitation of the inarticulate braying of the donkey (ὀγκήσαιτο, v. 31). The knowing self-irony might well be thought very Callimachean.[21]

The *hyporchema* is introduced in Athenaeus as an expression both of Pratinas' and of more general anger 'at the fact that the *aulos*-players did not offer musical accompaniment to the choruses, as was traditional, but the choruses sang an accompaniment to the *aulos*-players' (ἐπὶ τῶι τοὺς αὐλητὰς μὴ συναυλεῖν τοῖς χοροῖς, καθάπερ ἦν πάτριον, ἀλλὰ τοὺς χοροὺς συνάιδειν τοῖς αὐληταῖς, Ath. 14.617b–c). The territorial claim is indeed a claim about hierarchy and primacy, and it is one where Callimachus may well have sympathized

---

19 Cf. Sberna 2015, 219.
20 Cf. Steiner 2015, 108–109; Steiner 2015 is an important study of the poetics of sound in Callim. fr. 1 more generally, and cf. also Männlein-Robert 2007, 220–226. For the soundscape of the Typhoeus-episode in Hesiod's *Theogony* cf. Goslin 2010.
21 The ending of *Epigram* 28 Pfeiffer would be an obvious *comparandum*.

with Pratinas. ἀοιδά should take pride of place, particularly in relation to the music of the *aulos*, the traditional instrument which accompanied elegy. In Callimachean elegy there is no doubt that it is the words which matter.

Bibliography

Acosta-Hughes, B./Stephens, S. 2012. *Callimachus in Context*, Cambridge.
Bond, G.W. (ed.) 1981. *Euripides: Heracles*, Oxford.
Diggle, J. (ed.) 1981. *Euripides: Fabulae*, Vol. 2, Oxford.
Fantuzzi, M./Hunter, R. 2004. *Tradition and Innovation in Hellenistic Poetry*, Cambridge.
Goslin, O. 2010, 'Hesiod's Typhonomachy and the Ordering of Sound', *TAPA* 140, 361–373.
Harder, A. 2012. *Callimachus 'Aetia'*, Oxford.
Hunter, R. 2006. *The Shadow of Callimachus*, Cambridge.
Laemmle, R. 2013. *Poetik des Satyrspiels*, Heidelberg.
Männlein-Robert, I. 2007. *Stimme, Schrift und Bild. Zum Verhältnis der Künste in der hellenistischen Dichtung*, Heidelberg.
Olson, S.D. 2006–2012. *Athenaeus. The Learned Banqueters*, Cambridge MA.
Pàmias i Massana, J./Zucker, A. (eds.) 2013. *Eratosthène de Cyrène, Catasterismi*, Paris.
Pfeiffer, R. 1928. 'Ein neues Altersgedicht des Kallimachos', *Hermes* 63, 302–341 [= *Ausgewählte Schriften*, Munich 1960, 98–132].
Prauscello, L. 2011. 'Digging up the musical past: Callimachus and the New Music', in: B. Acosta-Hughes/L. Lehnus/S. Stephens (eds.), *Brill's Companion to Callimachus*, Leiden/Boston, 289–308.
Sberna, D. 2015. 'λιγύς swan and intratextual unity in Callimachus's *Aitia* prologue', *MD* 74, 207–223.
Steiner, D. 2015. 'The Poetics of Sound: Callimachus' rereading of Pindar fragment 70B S.-M.', *CP* 110, 99–123.
Strömberg, R. 1946. *Greek Prefix Studies on the use of Adjective Particles*, Göteborg.
Vian, F. 1952. *La guerre des Géants. Le mythe avant l'époque héllenistique*, Paris.

17 Sappho and Hellenistic Poetry

Remembering Sappho

I begin from three Hellenistic testimonia to Sappho's life and poetry:

(1) ἀφ' οὗ Σαπφὼ ἐγ Μιτυλήνης εἰς Σικελίαν ἔπλευσε φυγοῦσα [ἄρχο]ντος Ἀθήνησιν μὲν Κριτίου τοῦ προτέρου, ἐν Συρακούσσαις δὲ τῶν γαμόρων κατεχόντων τὴν ἀρχήν

From the time when Sappho sailed in exile [or 'in flight'] from Mytilene to Sicily [... years], when the earlier Kritias was archon at Athens,[1] and at Syracuse the Gamoroi held office.

Parian Marble A36 Rotstein (test. 5)

(2) Naucratis too produced famous *hetairai* ('courtesans') who were exceptionally beautiful, including Doricha, who became a lover of Sappho's brother Charaxus when he sailed to Naucratis for trade;[2] in her poems the lovely Sappho abuses (διαβάλλει) Doricha for having taken a great deal from Charaxus. Herodotus, however, calls her Rhodopis (2.134–135 = test. 9, fr. 202), being unaware that this is a different person from Doricha ... Posidippus composed the following epigram on Doricha ...

Δωρίχα, ὀστέα μὲν σὰ πάλαι κόνις ἦν ὅ τε δεσμὸς
  χαίτης ἥ τε μύρων ἔκπνοος ἀμπεχόνη,
ἧι ποτε τὸν χαρίεντα περιστέλλουσα Χάραξον
  σύγχρους ὀρθρινῶν ἥψαο κισσυβίων.
Σαπφῶιαι δὲ μένουσι φίλης ἔτι καὶ μενέουσιν
  ὠιδῆς αἱ λευκαὶ φθεγγόμεναι σελίδες
οὔνομα σὸν μακαριστόν, ὃ Ναύκρατις ὧδε φυλάξει
  ἔστ' ἂν ἴηι Νείλου ναῦς ἐφ' ἁλὸς πελάγη.

Doricha, your bones have long been dust, and the band for your hair and the shawl which breathes out perfume with which you once enfolded the lovely Charaxus, skin on skin, and took hold of the wine-cups at dawn. Sappho's white columns of her dear song, however, still remain and will remain; they speak your name and make it celebrated. Naucratis here will keep it safe as long as a ship sails out from the Nile over the stretches of the sea.

Athenaeus, Scholars at Dinner 13.596b-d (= Posidippus 122 A-B)[3]

---

1 The date is a few years either side of 600 BC.
2 Strabo 17.1.33 (fr. 202), a passage which seems to share a source with Athenaeus, *Scholars at Dinner* 13.596bc (test. 15, if it is not a source itself), reports that Charaxus traded Lesbian wine in Naucratis.
3 There are serious problems of text and interpretation in this poem, but I hope that they do not impede the relatively simple use to which it is put here. For a recent interpretation, see Bing 2018, 157–163.

(3) Contemporary with [Alcaeus and Pittacus] was Sappho, an extraordinary person (θαυμαστόν τι χρῆμα): in all of recorded history, I know of no woman who could rival Sappho, in even the slightest degree as far as poetry goes.

Strabo 13.2.3

For literate Greeks of the Hellenistic age, as for the Romans who followed, the very idea of Sappho creates θαῦμα 'wonder';[4] she is almost a τέρας, a phenomenon defying the normal parameters in which we understand the world. Pseudo-Longinus, author of *On the Sublime*, another critic apparently poised, like Strabo, between Greece and Rome, also identifies θαῦμα as the appropriate reaction to Sappho's art in what was perhaps her most frequently echoed poem in antiquity, φαίνεταί μοι κῆνος.[5] The sources of our wonder, in this ancient view, are several. First, and most obviously, Sappho was a woman; there is a significant corpus of Hellenistic and later epigrams which celebrates her poetry, but the fact she was a woman, perhaps indeed the 'female Homer', is almost always foregrounded.[6] She was, however, not just a female poet, but one whose poetry had survived in considerable quantity, far greater than it is easy for us to imagine today;[7] that sense of wondrous survival and of Sappho's presence 'still among us' is another leitmotif of the poems about her.[8] In part, this is presumably a transference to poems about Sappho of what was very likely a repeated motif of her poetry, namely the survival of poetry after death, a survival which grants κλέος ἄφθιτον, 'immortal renown', to the poet no less than to the subjects of his or her song, whether that be an Achilles or even a Doricha, as in Posidippus' epigram. Aelius Aristides (second century AD) claimed to know a poem or poems in which Sappho said that 'the Muses had made her fortunate and blessed, and that there would be no forgetting of her even after death',[9] and we can sense this confidence in four lines which survive in more than one ancient quotation:

κατθάνοισα δὲ κείσηι οὐδέ ποτα μναμοσύνα σέθεν
ἔσσετ' οὐδὲ †ποκ'† ὕστερον· οὐ γὰρ πεδέχηις βρόδων

---

4 Strabo's θαυμαστόν τι χρῆμα is usually underplayed as being, as indeed it is, an example of a not uncommon colloquial periphrasis in Hellenistic prose (so Bergson 1967, 105, followed by Radt on Strabo *ad loc.*, vii 525); here, however, the sense of 'wonder' is important.
5 Fr. 31, Pseudo-Longinus, *On the Sublime* 10.3; cf. below, pp. 284-288.
6 Rosenmeyer 1997, 133-136.
7 For the extent of Sappho's poetry and the form of the Alexandrian edition, see Prauscello.
8 Cf. 'Sappho's white columns of her dear song, however, still remain and will remain' in Posidippus above, Dioscorides, *Greek Anthology* 7.407.9-10 (test. 58), etc.
9 *Oration* 28.51 = fr. 193; Bowie, 308.

τὼν ἐκ Πιερίας, ἀλλ' ἀφάνης κἀν Ἀίδα δόμωι
φοιτάσηις πεδ' ἀμαύρων νεκύων ἐκπεποταμένα.

Sappho fr. 55

In death you will lie and there will never be any memory of you in future time, for you have no share in the roses from Pieria. Unseen in the house of Hades once you have flown away, you will flitter about with the shadowy dead.

Whether or not the object of Sappho's scorn was indeed unnamed in the poem from which this fragment comes, the nature of the survival of these verses has certainly ensured the truth of Sappho's prophecy; if it is true (cf. Athenaeus cited above) that Sappho 'abused Doricha' in her poems, then she has also, perhaps ironically, as Posidippus realised, made the *hetaira's* name 'celebrated'.[10]

The motif of the eternal survival of poetry is not, of course, restricted to Sappho and her *Nachleben*. It is, for example, central to Callimachus' funerary poem for Heraclitus (*Epigr*. 2 Pfeiffer = *HE* 1203–1208), which shares more than one motif with Posidippus' poem on Doricha,[11] allowing the suspicion that Callimachus' poem too may be indebted to Sapphic motifs. Nevertheless, the motif of the survival to the present day of poetic 'immortal daughters' may have particular force in Sappho's case.[12] Her poetry produces an overwhelming sense of the poet's almost physical presence through her voice, that sense that Pseudo-Longinus describes as evoked by fr. 31 and that Catullus too captures in his translation of that same poem, addressed to the 'Lesbian woman' (poem 51); this sense of presence cannot be divorced, in antiquity any more than now, from the fact that Sappho was a woman. For readers of poetry after the classical period it was, above all, the style of a famous poet, that is the audience's knowledge of, and familiarity with, a 'classical' voice, still existing and repeatedly ventriloquised, which brought the writers of the past 'close' to that audience; in antiquity there was no more distinctive or individual poetic voice than that of Sappho, even within the markedly personal world of archaic lyric. Whoever originally chose to place first in the 'Alexandrian edition' the poem which we call Sappho fr. 1, the prayer to 'elaborately throned immortal Aphrodite', in which Sappho

---

10 Christian 2015, 63–64, who sees a direct allusion in Posidippus' poem to fr. 55, an allusion pointed by the naming of Doricha with the first word of Posidippus' epigram. These Sapphic verses seem also to resonate (along with Asclepiades, *Greek Anthology* 7.11 = 942–945 *HE* and Callimachus fr. 1 Harder) in Antipater of Sidon, *Greek Anthology* 7.713 (560–567 *HE*) about Erinna (often associated with or compared to Sappho).
11 The Callimachean parallel is cited by Austin/Bastianini in their edition.
12 Dioscorides, *Greek Anthology*, 7.407.10 (test. 58).

recalls a previous epiphany of the goddess to her, certainly recognised the power of that signature voice.[13]

Sappho's powerful presence is partly acknowledged and partly deflected by the echoes and reworkings of her poetry with which Hellenistic poetry is filled and which this chapter will briefly survey.[14] Virtually every new papyrus of her poetry reveals Sapphic echoes lurking unnoticed in the high poetry of the third century BC and beyond, and this too is an area where there seems room for unprovable speculation. It is, for example, hardly rash to suspect that there are evocations of Sappho's poetry in Posidippus' epigram quoted above; the quatrain concerning the lovemaking of Doricha and Charaxus is one obvious candidate,[15] and the suspicion is not lessened by the similarity of these verses to the lovemaking of Dionysus and Ariadne in Apollonius of Rhodes' *Argonautica*, recalled through the marvellous cloak on which they lay:

> τοῦ δὲ καὶ ἀμβροσίη ὀδμὴ ἄεν ἐξέτι κείνου
> ἐξ οὗ ἄναξ αὐτὸς Νυσήιος ἐγκατέλεκτο
> ἀκροχάλιξ οἴνωι καὶ νέκταρι, καλὰ μεμαρπὼς
> στήθεα παρθενικῆς Μινωίδος, ἥν ποτε Θησεὺς
> Κνωσσόθεν ἑσπομένην Δίηι ἔνι κάλλιπε νήσωι.
>
> Apollonius of Rhodes, *Argonautica* 4.430–444

> An ambrosial scent hovered over it ever since the time when the Nysaean lord himself, tipsy with wine and nectar, lay upon it as he pressed against himself the lovely breasts of the maiden daughter of Minos, whom Theseus once abandoned on the island of Dia after she had followed him from Knossos.

Posidippus' poem illustrates a further way in which Sappho's particularity was felt: much of the surviving Hellenistic and later discussion of her has a biographical slant, whether that be focused on the girls addressed in her poems or on her relations with her brothers, a subject already highlighted by Herodotus and forcefully brought home to us by the recent publication of the Brothers Poem. Biographical criticism in antiquity is (again) far from limited to Sappho, but her femaleness gave the details of her life an enduring fascination, and almost inevitably led to the assumption that the voice of her poems was indeed a strongly autobiographical one. Sappho, moreover, names herself with a marked frequency, and real events and people seem to fill her poetry; Sappho's

---

13 For other consequences of the placing of fr. 1, cf. Hunter 2007, 219–221 – Thorsen/Harrison 2019, 158–160, Prodi 2017, 572–582, and below p. 321.
14 The fullest recent account is Acosta-Hughes 2010.
15 Obbink 2016, 221.

presence was also the presence of a whole world of intrigue, erotic suffering, and cultic observance. Moreover, Charaxus' dalliance with the lovely Doricha at Naucratis and its immortalisation first in Sappho's own poetry and then in Herodotus gave Sappho a direct presence in the Greek culture of North Africa, and Posidippus' poem incorporates her within that culture in its confident Ptolemaic manifestation.[16]

No ancient notice about Sappho is more surprising than the entry in the Parian Marble (erected 264/3 BC) that records her exile (or perhaps 'flight') from Mytilene to Sicily at the end of the seventh century or the beginning of the sixth. This event is not recorded anywhere else in the biographical or historical record,[17] but Cicero claims that Verres stole a statue of the poet by Silanion (late fourth century) which had stood in the town hall of Syracuse, and it is an easy guess that this was commissioned by the city to celebrate its belief that Sappho had visited or lived in the city.[18] Cicero says that the loss of the statue deeply affected the Syracusans:

atque haec Sappho sublata quantum desiderium sui reliquerit dici vix potest.
Cicero, *Against Verres* 2.4.127 (test. 24)

The depth of the longing which the removal of the statue of Sappho caused can hardly be expressed.

It is tempting to see Cicero here employing a Sapphic motif: we may be reminded of her poems (frr. 94, 96) for female friends no longer present. However that may be, there are good reasons to believe that in the late fourth and early third century there was a tradition that Sappho had visited Sicily, and that the Syracusan Theocritus may well have known of this tradition, may indeed have seen Sappho's statue on display in his home city. Sappho, then, would have been an

---

[16] Barbantani ap. Acosta-Hughes and Barbantani 2007, 439 suggests that Posidippus' poem 'subtly celebrates the edition of Sappho's poems, now in the process of being produced in the Alexandrian Library'.

[17] Parian Marble A36 Rotstein (test. 5), with p. 111; the source was perhaps Phaenias of Eresus (second half of the fourth century; thus Mosshammer 1979, 253).

[18] Cicero, *Against Verres* 2.4.125–127 (test. 24). This is the standard assumption, though other scenarios are possible; Rosenmeyer 2007, 295, 280 assumes (probably rightly) that 'the statue was meant to remind the citizens that their city had once offered asylum to this famous poet' and thus Sappho is 'a famous adopted daughter of the city'. Cicero's report about Silanion's statue, a work which would fit with what else we know of his bronzes, is supported (or at least not undermined) by Tatian, *Oration to the Greeks* 33; cf. Coarelli 1972, A. Stewart 1990, I 296–297, 1998, 278–281.

'honorary Syracusan'; she too, like the Cyclops, was 'one of us' (Theocritus 11.7). For Theocritus, Sappho took her place alongside the great figures of the Sicilian poetic heritage — Stesichorus, Epicharmus, Sophron — all of whom are echoed in his poetry.[19] When, therefore, the opening verses of the Sicilian Cyclops' address to Galateia (11.19–24) are replete with echoes of Sappho,[20] the Sicilian, or indeed Syracusan, lover is made to echo *the* (honorary) Sicilian love poet, and we might guess that more Sapphic echoes lie behind the close of his speech; ὦ Κύκλωψ Κύκλωψ (11.72) may imitate Sappho's habit of using her own name, particularly as the Cyclops' break-off has reminded more than one modern reader of the final (*otium*, 'leisure') stanza of Catullus 51, which probably imitates, rather than translates, a Sapphic pattern.[21]

For Theocritus, then, Sappho was not just one more poet of the past to be echoed and incorporated, but rather part of a closely felt local poetic heritage. The situation has something in common with the epigrams of Nossis from Locri (in the toe of Italy) which seem to recreate a female Sapphic world in the west in conscious mimesis of Sappho's eastern Lesbian world.[22] In *Idyll* 15, two women proud of their Syracusaness listen at the royal palace in Alexandria to a hymn in honour of Aphrodite and Adonis performed by a female singer of (in the judgement of the Syracusan women) amazing skill (τὸ χρῆμα σοφώτατον ἁ θήλεια, 145). The Adonis cult makes its first appearance in a few Sapphic fragments,[23] but Dioscorides' epigram for Sappho suggests that the theme was felt to have some prominence in her poetry, alongside the wedding songs for which she was so renowned;[24] the epithalamia are richly echoed and evoked in *Idyll* 18, the wedding song for Helen and Menelaus,[25] and it is a reasonable suspicion that echoes of Sappho's poetry on Adonis lurk in the Adonis hymn of *Idyll* 15, perhaps, particularly, in the opening lines 100–105.[26] About *Idyll* 28, 'The Distaff', however, there can be no doubt. This poem is in Sapphic language and metre and debts of motif and specific verbal echoes have long been identified.[27] The

---

19 Willi 2012, 285–288.
20 Hunter 1999, 229–231.
21 D. Fowler 1994, 245–249 = 2000, 22–27, Hunter 2019, 54–55.
22 Nossis, *Greek Anthology* 7.201 (2831–2834 *HE*); Skinner 1989, Gutzwiller 1998, 85–88, Bowman 1998.
23 Fr. 117Bb Voigt = Sappho or Alcaeus fr. 24(b) Campbell, frr. 140, 168 C., test. 211c V.
24 Dioscorides, *Greek Anthology* 7.407.58 (test. 58).
25 Hunter 1996, 151–152, 2015, 158–160.
26 For other possible Sapphic resonances in *Idyll* 15, cf. Acosta-Hughes 2010, 16, 72–73.
27 Spelman 2017, with new arguments for Sapphic echoes; Papadopoulou 2016, 224–237 argues for an essentially political and Ptolemaic motive for the form of this poem.

distaff is to travel with the poet to Miletus as a gift to the wife of his ξέννος ('guest-friend') Nicias (lines 5–9), and the distaff and the 'Distaff' poem are thus essentially identified: both are gifts for, and celebrate the virtues of, Theugenis. Both come from Syracuse, 'from', as the poet puts it, 'my land' (16–8); this is Theocritus of Syracuse speaking as Sappho of Syracuse. In celebrating a woman and female virtues, Theocritus chooses to ventriloquise not just any female poet, but the one who can most obviously speak for him, namely one with a (real or believed) claim to belong to Syracuse.

Theocritus is likely also to have been conscious of an earlier imitation of Sappho, though one very different from his own. The 'Distaff' of Erinna (? late fourth century BC), though it is not certain that the title is original, was a poem of three hundred hexameters, in which Erinna, a female poet from the eastern Aegean, seems to have lamented the death of her childhood friend Baucis, who died shortly after marrying. Some fifty-four badly damaged verses of this poem, which was much admired in the Hellenistic period, survive on a papyrus.[28] This was a poem of memory and loss, suffused with Sapphic echoes and an evocation of a now shattered world of female friendship and closeness.[29] It is a great pity that we cannot trace in detail how Erinna presented the relationship between Baucis' marriage and her death; were they fused so as to become all but synonymous? Erinna's themes of separation and regret were an inheritance from Sappho, and we see them again in the marked Sapphic colouring of the lament by the lock of hair which Berenice II dedicated for her husband's safe return but which is now forever sundered from the royal head, a poem which brought Callimachus' four-book *Aitia* to an extraordinary conclusion (fr. 110 Harder). The lock is grammatically masculine (contrast the *coma* of Catullus' translation, poem 66), but its experience is very female,[30] and as such it borrows the voice of the female poet to protest at its fate.

Erotic Suffering

Dioscorides opens his epigram on Sappho (p. 319 above) by calling her 'the sweetest support for the desires of young men in love',[31] thus foregrounding that

---

28 Erinna fr. 401 *SH* = fr. 4 Neri.
29 We may be reminded particularly of Sappho fr. 94; cf. Rauk 1989, Rayor 2005.
30 Fantuzzi and Hunter 2004, 87–88, Acosta-Hughes 2010, 68.
31 Dioscorides, *Greek Anthology* 7.407.1 (test. 58), ἥδιστον φιλέουσι νέοις προσανάκλιμ' ἐρώτων. Cf. Demetrius, *On Style* 132 (test. 45) on *charis* arising from subject matter: 'gardens of the nymphs, wedding songs, loves, all of Sappho's poetry'.

theme of her poetry which was always given the greatest prominence in the Hellenistic period. Desire and the repeated sufferings that it brings were advertised by the placement of fr. 1 at the head of the Alexandrian edition.[32] At issue was not just subject matter, but also style, as the author of *On Style*, ascribed to Demetrius (Hellenistic or early Roman period), makes clear:

> When Sappho sings of beauty (κάλλος), her words are beautiful and sweet, and when she sings of loves and springtime and the halcyon. Every beautiful word is woven into her poetry, and some she herself has created (εἰργάσατο).
>
> Demetrius, *On Style* 166 = fr. 195

Sappho was, then, the 'natural' poet to whom to turn when later poets sought to depict erotic suffering, particularly female suffering. Fr. 31, the famous poem whose survival we owe to Pseudo-Longinus (*On the Sublime* 10.1–3) and which was translated by Catullus (poem 51), seems to have been singled out from a relatively early date as a particularly memorable description of erotic suffering. Echoes of this poem are very frequent in Greek and Latin literature.[33] It was, for example, to this poem (though not to this Sapphic poem alone) that Apollonius in the *Argonautica* turned to chart crucial moments in the progress of the Colchian princess Medea's desire for the handsome Greek stranger, Jason, who had arrived in her land.[34] When Eros first shoots Medea with his arrow, the effect is described with an evocation of Sapphic motifs:

> ἧκ' ἐπὶ Μηδείηι· τὴν δ' ἀμφασίη λάβε θυμόν.
> αὐτὸς δ' ὑψορόφοιο παλιμπετὲς ἐκ μεγάροιο
> καγχαλόων ἤιξε, βέλος δ' ἐνεδαίετο κούρηι
> νέρθεν ὑπὸ κραδίηι φλογὶ εἴκελον. ἀντία δ' αἰεὶ
> βάλλεν ἐπ' Αἰσονίδην ἀμαρύγματα, καί οἱ ἄηντο
> στηθέων ἐκ πυκιναὶ καμάτωι φρένες· οὐδέ τιν' ἄλλην
> μνῆστιν ἔχεν, γλυκερῆι δὲ κατείβετο θυμὸν ἀνίηι·
>
> Apollonius of Rhodes, *Argonautica* 3.284–290

---

32 Above, p. 316. It is, however, always worth remembering that we owe the preservation of this poem to Dionysius of Halicarnassus (*On the Arrangement of Words* 23.10–15), who does not cite it for its erotic subject matter.
33 Costanza 1950, Acosta-Hughes 2010, Index locorum s.v. Sappho. Plutarch, perhaps roughly contemporary with Pseudo-Longinus, is an important witness to the fame of this poem: Bowie, 305–306.
34 For what follows cf. Acosta-Hughes 2010, 49–57 and the relevant sections of Hunter 1989, 2015.

He shot at Medea, and her spirit was seized by speechless stupor. Eros darted back out of the high-roofed palace with a mocking laugh, but his arrow burned deep in the girl's heart like a flame. Full at Jason her glance shot, and the wearying pain scattered all prudent thoughts from her chest; she could think of nothing else, and her spirit was flooded with a sweet aching.

When Jason and Medea meet at the temple of Hecate, it is again echoes of Sappho which describe the sickness of desire:

ἐκ δ' ἄρα οἱ κραδίη στηθέων πέσεν, ὄμματα δ' αὔτως
ἤχλυσαν, θερμὸν δὲ παρηίδας εἷλεν ἔρευθος·
γούνατα δ' οὔτ' ὀπίσω οὔτε προπάροιθεν ἀεῖραι
ἔσθενεν, ἀλλ' ὑπένερθε πάγη πόδας.

Apollonius of Rhodes, Argonautica 3.962–965

Her heart within her breast dropped, her eyes grew misty, and a hot flush seized her cheeks; she had no strength at all to move her legs, but her feet were held fast beneath her.

For Medea, however, there is no turning back once she has betrayed her father. At the beginning of Book 4 Apollonius describes her panic as she assumes that her father knows about her assistance to the Argonauts:

ἐν δέ οἱ ὄσσε
πλῆτο πυρός, δεινὸν δὲ περιβρομέεσκον ἀκουαί·
πυκνὰ δὲ λαυκανίης ἐπεμάσσετο, πυκνὰ δὲ κουρὶξ
ἑλκομένη πλοκάμους γοερῆι βρυχήσατ' ἀνίηι.

Apollonius of Rhodes, Argonautica 4.16–19

Fire filled her eyes, and in her ears was a terrible roaring; often she felt her throat, often she screamed in pain and lamentation, pulling her hair out by the roots.

The causal link between her love and her panic is thus marked through different reworkings of Sappho fr. 31.

A strikingly similar pattern occurs in Simaetha's narrative of her love affair with Delphis in Theocritus 2.[35] Simaetha's first sighting of Delphis on his return from the gymnasium led to a 'Sappho fr. 31 experience':

καί μευ χρὼς μὲν ὁμοῖος ἐγίνετο πολλάκι θάψωι,[36]
ἔρρευν δ' ἐκ κεφαλᾶς πᾶσαι τρίχες,[37] αὐτὰ δὲ λοιπὰ

---

35 Acosta-Hughes 2010, 17–29, Hunter 2014, 142–144.
36 There is no firm evidence (pace Acosta-Hughes 2010, 27) that Sappho used the word θάψος (cf. fr. 210), though there may well be a thicker literary texture than we can now recover.

ὀστί᾽ ἔτ᾽ ἦς καὶ δέρμα. καὶ ἐς τίνος οὐκ ἐπέρασα,
ἢ ποίας ἔλιπον γραίας δόμον ἅτις ἐπᾷδεν;

Theocritus 2.88–91

Often my skin became pale like fustic, all the hair was falling from my head, and all that was left of me was bones and skin. To whose house did I not go, or what dwelling of an old woman who knows incantations?

When Delphis enters her house, Simaetha describes her reactions with a further reworking of Sappho fr. 31:

πᾶσα μὲν ἐψύχθην χιόνος πλέον, ἐκ δὲ μετώπω
ἱδρώς μευ κοχύδεσκεν ἴσον νοτίαισιν ἐέρσαις,
οὐδέ τι φωνῆσαι δυνάμαν, οὐδ᾽ ὅσσον ἐν ὕπνωι
κνυζεῦνται φωνεῦντα φίλαν ποτὶ ματέρα τέκνα·
ἀλλ᾽ ἐπάγην δαγῦδι καλὸν χρόα πάντοθεν ἴσα.

Theocritus 2.106–110

My whole body was colder than snow, and from my forehead sweat flowed like the damp dews, and I could say nothing, not even as much as children mumble in the sleep as they call to their dear mothers. My fair body was stiff all over like a doll.

Roberto Pretagostini argued that whereas the first reworking of fr. 31 marked the onset of love, the second marked 'the fear of love' (and love-making),[38] though he did not go on to suggest that this reflected two different ways in which fr. 31 had been understood in ancient tradition, as indeed it has in modern discussion.[39] The study of ancient interpretations of fr. 31 offers rich material, but here I would like rather to explore a link between these passages which may shed light on how the poetry of Sappho might be seen within the wider context of the literary heritage.

When she can bear her passion for Delphis no more and can find no remedy for it (we are perhaps reminded of Euripides' Phaedra), Simaetha sends her slave Thestylis to fetch him:

κἤπεί κά νιν ἐόντα μάθηις μόνον, ἄσυχα νεῦσον,
κεἴφ᾽ ὅτι "Σιμαίθα τυ καλεῖ", καὶ ὑφαγέο τεῖδε.
ὣς ἐφάμαν· ἁ δ᾽ ἦνθε καὶ ἄγαγε τὸν λιπαρόχρων
εἰς ἐμὰ δώματα Δέλφιν·

Theocritus 2.100–103

---

37 Simaetha is here perhaps made (comically) to evoke Hesiod's lustful Proetides: Hunter 2019, 56.
38 Pretagostini 1984, 114 (see also 114–116).
39 F. Ferrari 2010, 171–192.

'And when you see that he is alone, sign secretly to him, and say "Simaetha calls you" and bring him here.' So I spoke. She went and brought Delphis of the gleaming skin to my house.

Nancy Andrews attractively suggested that Simaetha here recalls (with appropriate reversal — Delphis is a kind of Paris) Aphrodite's opening words to Helen in the famous scene which concludes *Iliad* 3:[40]

δεῦρ' ἴθ', Ἀλέξανδρός σε καλεῖ οἰκόνδε νέεσθαι.

Homer, *Iliad* 3.390

'Come hither: Paris calls you to come to your home.'

The servant Thestylis then brings Delphis to Simaetha, as Aphrodite disguises herself as one of Helen's aged retainers to bring the couple together. This same Homeric scene is also recalled when, on sitting down next to Simaetha, Delphis 'fixes his eyes upon the ground', as Helen 'turns her eyes aside' when faced with Paris,[41] and perhaps also when Delphis notes that 'thanks are first owed to Cypris' (line 130). The reworking of Sappho fr. 31 as Delphis enters the house thus follows on from an evocation of Aphrodite's summoning of Helen, in such a way as to suggest that fr. 31 may (at least in part) be read as an exploration of that Homeric scene.[42] This is, in other words, how such a scene may be reimagined in lyric mode, and we may even speculate that the object of desire in such a reading of fr. 31 would be Helen, who, as is well known, figures prominently and unusually in Sapphic poetry; in another critical mode we would say that *Iliad* 3 is 'read through' fr. 31. Some support for such a reading is perhaps found in the fact that Aphrodite places a chair so that Helen sits 'opposite Paris' (*Iliad* 3.424–426), just as fr. 31 initially focuses on 'that man...whoever sits opposite you'.

---

40 Andrews 1996, 33.
41 *Iliad* 3.426–427; cf. Lentini 2012, 185–186. Delphis' gesture is more usually associated with Odysseus as described in *Iliad* 3.217; cf. Andrews 1996, 36–41. What Theocritus has done, and this technique is familiar elsewhere in Hellenistic and Roman poetry, is to substitute one phrase from elsewhere in the poetic model for a similar one found in the scene which is being imitated; in this case, Theocritus has not only taken a phrase from the same book of the *Iliad*, but also one which suggests a character (Odysseus) who is also very appropriate in the new context.
42 Winkler 1990, 178–180 reads fr. 31 in the light of the meeting of Odysseus and Nausicaa in *Odyssey* 6 (cf. especially lines 242–245), but there seem fewer signals of such a model text than in the reading proposed above for Theocritus. See further Rosenmeyer 1997, 137–140.

As for Simaetha's 'Sapphic symptoms' at lines 88–91, they result from an experience partly modelled on Zeus's reaction to the sight of Hera in *Iliad* 14:

χὼς ἴδον, ὣς ἐμάνην, ὥς μοι πυρὶ θυμὸς ἰάφθη

Theocritus 2.82

I saw, I went mad, my heart burst into flame.

ὡς δ' ἴδεν, ὥς μιν ἔρος πυκινὰς φρένας ἀμφεκάλυψεν

Homer, *Iliad* 14.294

He saw, desire enveloped his wise mind...

Theocritus' Simaetha thus associates both her reworkings of fr. 31 with the two most prominent scenes of desire in the *Iliad*, whose close verbal and thematic similarity to each other was often noted in the later critical tradition. Theocritus thus becomes an early witness to this tradition, and this serves to remind us of how poets helped to fashion that tradition, as much as they also reflected it. The two greatest moments of male desire in the *Iliad* are reshaped as female desire through reworkings of the most famous poetic description of such an emotion, but so as to intimate that the Sapphic poem itself is a response to the Iliadic scenes. This is not a matter of finding the 'source' of Sappho's poetry in the epic poet from whom all culture was thought to derive, but rather of exploiting what was most distinctive about the Sapphic voice when set against the Homeric, even those erotic scenes of Homer which might be thought closest in spirit to her.

Further Reading

The principal echoes of Sappho in Hellenistic poetry, at least before the recent additions to the corpus, are recorded in the major commentaries to the poets. Acosta-Hughes 2010 is the fullest survey covering third-century poetry as a whole. For Sapphic influence on particular poets, cf. Rauk 1989 (Erinna), Skinner 1989 (Nossis).

Bibliography

Acosta-Hughes, B. 2010. *Arion's Lyre. Archaic Lyric into Hellenistic Poetry*, Princeton/Oxford.

Acosta-Hughes, B./Barbantani, S. 2007. 'Inscribing lyric', in: P. Bing/J.S. Bruss (eds.), *Brill's Companion to Hellenistic Epigram*, Leiden/Boston, 429–457.

Andrews, N.E. 1996. 'Narrative and allusion in Theocritus, *Idyll* 2', in: M.A. Harder/R.F. Regtuit/ G.C. Wakker (eds.), *Theocritus*, Hellenistica Groningana 2, Groningen, 21–53.

Bergson, L. 1967. 'Zum periphrastischen χρῆμα', *Eranos* 65, 79–117.

Bing, P. 2018. 'Tombs of poets' minor characters', in: N. Goldschmidt/B. Graziosi (eds.), *Tombs of the Ancient Poets. Between Literary Reception and Material Culture*, Oxford, 147–170.

Bowie, A.M. 1981. *The Poetic Dialect of Sappho and Alcaeus*, Salem NH.

Bowman, L. 1998. 'Nossis, Sappho and Hellenistic poetry', *Ramus* 27, 39–59.

Christian, T. 2015. *Gebildete Steine. Zur Rezeption literarischer Techniken in den Versinschriften seit dem Hellenismus*, Hypomnemata 197, Göttingen.

Coarelli, F. 1972. 'Il complesso pompeiano del Campo Marzio e la sua decorazione scultorea', *Atti della Pontificia Accademia Romana di Archeologia (Rendiconti)* 3rd ser. 44, 99–122.

Costanza, S. 1950. *Risonanze dell'ode di Saffo Fainetai moi kēnos da Pindaro a Catullo e Orazio*, Messina/Florence.

Fantuzzi, M./Hunter, R. 2004. *Tradition and Innovation in Hellenistic Poetry*, Cambridge.

Ferrari, F. 2010. *Sappho's Gift. The Poet and Her Community*, transl. B. Acosta-Hughes/L. Prauscello, Ann Arbor.

Fowler, D. 1994. 'Postmodernism, romanticism, and classical closure', in: I.J.F. De Jong/J.P. Sullivan (eds.), *Modern Critical Theory and Classical Literature*, Mnemosyne Supplement 130, Leiden/New York/Cologne, 231–256.

Gutzwiller, K.J. 1998. *Poetic Garlands. Hellenistic Epigrams in Context*, Berkeley/Los Angeles/London.

Hunter, R.L. 1989. *Apollonius of Rhodes. Argonautica Book III*, Cambridge.

Hunter, R.L. 1996. *Theocritus and the Archaeology of Greek Poetry*, Cambridge.

Hunter, R.L. 1999. *Theocritus. A Selection. Idylls 1, 3, 4, 6, 7, 10, 11 and 13*, Cambridge.

Hunter, R.L. 2007. 'Sappho and Latin poetry', in: G. Bastianini/A. Casanova (eds.), *I papiri di Saffo e di Alceo. Atti del convegno internazionale di studi, Firenze, 8–9 giugno 2006*, Studi e Testi di Papirologia 9, Florence, 213–225 [= Thorsen/Harrison 2019 (eds.), 151–163].

Hunter, R.L. 2014. '"Where do I begin?": An Odyssean narrative strategy and its afterlife', in: D. Cairns/R. Scodel (eds.), *Defining Greek Narrative*, Edinburgh Leventis Studies 7, Edinburgh, 137–155 [= this volume 46–64].

Hunter, R.L. 2015. 'Sweet Stesichorus: Theocritus 18 and the Helen revisited', in: P.J. Finglass/ A. Kelly (eds.), *Stesichorus in Context*, Cambridge, 145–163 [= this volume 214–234].

Hunter, R.L. 2015. *Apollonius of Rhodes. Argonautica Book IV*, Cambridge.

Hunter, R.L. 2019. 'Notes on the ancient reception of Sappho', in: T.S. Thorsen/S. Harrison (eds.), *Roman Receptions of Sappho*, Oxford, 45–59 [= this volume 349–363].

Lentini, G. 2012. 'L'idillio 2 di Teocrito e il "genere" oaristys', *Materiali e Discussioni per l'Analisi dei Testi Classici* 68, 181–190.

Mosshammer, A.A. 1979. *The Chronicle of Eusebius and Greek Chronographic Tradition*, Lewisburg PA/London.

Obbink, D. 2016. 'Goodbye family gloom! The coming of Charaxos in the Brothers Song', in: A. Bierl/A. Lardinois (eds.), *The Newest Sappho. P. Sapph. Obbink and P. GC inv. 105, frs. 1–4*, Mnemosyne Supplement 392, Studies in Archaic and Classical Greek Song 2, Leiden/Boston.

Papadopoulou, M. 2016. 'Textile and textual poetics in context: Callimachus' 4th *Iamb* and Theocritus' *Idyll* 28', in: G. Fanfani/M. Harlow/M. Nosch (eds.), *Spinning Fates and the Song of the Loom. The Use of Textiles, Clothing and Cloth Production as Metaphor, Symbol and Narrative Device in Greek and Latin Literature*, Ancient Textiles Series 24, Oxford/Philadelphia, 217–239.

Prauscello, L. 2007. 'Le "orecchie" di Saffo: qualche osservazione in margine a Sapph. 31, 11–12 V. e alla sua ricezione antica', in: G. Bastianini/A. Casanova (eds.), *I papiri di Saffo e di Alceo. Atti del convegno internazionale di studi, Firenze, 8–9 giugno 2006*, Studi e Testi di Papirologia 9, Florence, 191–212.

Pretagostini, R. 1984. *Ricerche sulla poesia alessandrina. Teocrito, Callimaco, Sotade*, Filologia e Critica 48, Rome.

Prodi, E.E. 2017. 'Text as paratext: Pindar, Sappho, and Alexandrian editions', *Greek, Roman, and Byzantine Studies* 57, 547–582.

Rauk, J. 1989. 'Erinna's Distaff and Sappho fr. 94', *Greek, Roman, and Byzantine Studies* 30, 101–116.

Rayor, D.J. 2005. 'The power of memory in Erinna and Sappho', in: E. Greene (ed.), *Women Poets in Ancient Greece and Rome*, Norman OK, 59–71.

Rosenmeyer, P.A. 1997. 'Her master's voice: Sappho's dialogue with Homer', *Materiali e Discussioni per l'Analisi dei Testi Classici* 39, 123–149.

Rosenmeyer, P.A. 2007. 'From Syracuse to Rome: the travails of Silanion's Sappho', *Transactions of the American Philological Association* 137, 277–303.

Skinner, M.B. 1989. 'Sapphic Nossis', *Arethusa* 22, 5–18.

Spelman, H. 2017. 'Borrowing Sappho's napkins: Sappho 101, Catullus 12, Theocritus 28', *Harvard Studies in Classical Philology* 109, 237–260.

Stewart, A. 1990. *Greek Sculpture. An Exploration*, vol. I, New Haven/London.

Stewart, A. 1998. 'Nuggets: mining the texts again', *American Journal of Archaeology* 102, 271–282.

Thorsen, T.S./Harrison, S. (eds.) 2019, *Roman Receptions of Sappho*, Oxford.

Willi, A. 2012. '"We speak Peloponnesian": tradition and linguistic identity in postclassical Sicilian literature', in: O. Tribulato (ed.), *Language and Linguistic Contact in Ancient Sicily*, Cambridge, 265–288.

Winkler, J.J. 1990. *The Constraints of Desire. The Anthropology of Sex and Gender in Ancient Greece*, New York/London.

18 Theocritus and the Bucolic Homer

Theocritus is rightly regarded as the 'first inventor' of bucolic poetry and the *Idylls* as an originary moment in European literature; if it was Theocritus' successors who gave bucolic poetry the recognisability of a generic form, it was Theocritus himself and his native Sicily to which the subsequent tradition always looked back. When the *Eclogues* then became a kind of second beginning for poetry of this kind, there was a creative tension available to be exploited between two founding poets, one Greek and one Latin, a tension which could also be expressed as that between the old and the new. This tension, which is still sometimes described as one between 'bucolic' and 'pastoral', should not surprise, for that tension is already there at the moments of origin themselves. As is well known, Theocritus creates a sense both of the timelessness of the rural performances he describes – the ἄλγεα Δάφνιδος has always been sung before – and the newness of his poetic undertaking, the 'beginning of bucolic song', as the refrain of *Idyll* 1 has it. The continuing fame of that poetry, its constant repetition and survival as *Nachleben*, was already there at the very beginning.

Theocritus' own acknowledged moments of origin are both multiple and well known. There are not only the apparently timeless song traditions of rural Sicily and southern Italy, but there are the great figures of Sicilian poetry, Stesichorus, Epicharmus, Sophron,[1] and the figures of Sicilian story, above all Daphnis and the Cyclops, though a Cyclops who is both before and later than the Homeric depiction, one who has not yet met Odysseus, but also one whose depiction owes a great deal to post-Homeric poetic forms. One non-Sicilian poet who is part of Theocritus' own set of originary moments is (inevitably) Homer, whose importance, as both model and anti-model, is suffused over all of Theocritus' bucolic poetry,[2] in both macro-structures (the κισσύβιον in *Idyll* 1, for example) and everywhere in the micro-structures of language. David Halperin's *Before Pastoral* of 1983 was the book which taught many modern students of Theocritus to give proper thought to the Sicilian poet's Homeric, particularly Odyssean, heritage, and the influence of that book deserves proper acknowledgement. Ten years later Jasper Griffin gathered together many apparently

---

[1] Hunter 2021 argues that Theocritus also exploited Sappho as an 'honorary Syracusan'.
[2] This essay is concerned exclusively with the Theocritean poems which are standardly acknowledged as 'bucolic'; there are obvious dangers in dividing up the Theocritean corpus in this way, but I hope that these do not vitiate the limited aims of the essay. The debt of the 'non-bucolic' poems to Homer is of course well established and much discussed.

'bucolic' moments scattered through the *Iliad*, particularly in similes and the brief biographies which accompany many less significant figures, and he sought in them echoes of a non-martial world of poetry which Theocritus may have inherited, directly or indirectly, from the Near East (Griffin [1992]). In this paper, I will turn back to two very familiar Homeric passages, with which Theocritus marked the epic heritage of his bucolic poetry. This is, of course, in no sense an attempt to survey all of those passages in Homer which Theocritus was able to construct as part of his bucolic heritage, indeed as significant 'originary moments' in that heritage, but there is little doubt of their significance for the bucolic and pastoral traditions which Theocritus himself inaugurated.

The silence of the ram

Few moments of the *Odyssey* are as famous as the Cyclops' address to his favourite ram, as it struggles with the weight of Odysseus clinging to its underside:

κριὲ πέπον, τί μοι ὧδε διὰ σπέος ἔσσυο μήλων
ὕστατος; οὔ τι πάρος γε λελειμμένος ἔρχεαι οἰῶν,
ἀλλὰ πολὺ πρῶτος νέμεαι τέρεν' ἄνθεα ποίης
μακρὰ βιβάς, πρῶτος δὲ ῥοὰς ποταμῶν ἀφικάνεις,   450
πρῶτος δὲ σταθμόνδε λιλαίεαι ἀπονέεσθαι
ἑσπέριος, νῦν αὖτε πανύστατος. ἦ σύ γ' ἄνακτος
ὀφθαλμὸν ποθέεις; τὸν ἀνὴρ κακὸς ἐξαλάωσε
σὺν λυγροῖσ' ἑτάροισι, δαμασσάμενος φρένας οἴνῳ,
Οὖτις, ὃν οὔ πώ φημι πεφυγμένον ἔμμεν ὄλεθρον.   455
εἰ δὴ ὁμοφρονέοις ποτιφωνήεις τε γένοιο
εἰπεῖν, ὅππῃ κεῖνος ἐμὸν μένος ἠλασκάζει·
τῶ κέ οἱ ἐγκέφαλός γε διὰ σπέος ἄλλυδις ἄλλῃ
θεινομένου ῥαίοιτο πρὸς οὔδεϊ, κὰδ δέ τ' ἐμὸν κῆρ
λωφήσειε κακῶν, τά μοι οὐτιδανὸς πόρεν Οὖτις.

Homer, *Odyssey* 9.447–460

Good ram, why please do you come out thus through the cave the last of the flock? Previously you did not lag behind the sheep, but you were far the first to feed on the tender flowers of the grass, moving proudly with long strides, and you were the first to reach the streams of the river, and the first to long to return to the stall at evening. Now you come last of all. Surely you are sorrowing for the eye of your master; an evil man, along with his terrible comrades, blinded me, when he had overmastered my wits with wine, Noman, who, I tell you, has not yet escaped destruction. If only you and I were like-minded and you could be empowered with speech to tell me where he skulks away from my strength, then could I strike him and his brains would be smashed on the ground all over the cave; my heart would be relieved of the sorrows which nobody Noman has brought me.

The wishful pathetic fallacy (cruelly ironic in view of the real reason why the ram is last out),[3] the idea that the ram feels πόθος and a sympathy for its master, would seem to mark the first part of this passage as truly βουκολικόν before its time. So, at any rate, the grammarians whose work has filtered into the scholia thought:

> δοκεῖ δὲ βουκολικὸν εἶναι τοῖς νεωτέροις τὸ πρὸς κριὸν διαλέγεσθαι. δαιμονίως δὲ ὑπὸ Ὁμήρου πρώτου κατώρθωται τὸ αὑτοῖς τοῖς ζῴοις ὡς φρονοῦσι διαλέγεσθαι, ὡς Ἕκτωρ, "Ξάνθε τε καὶ σὺ Πόδαργε".
>
> Scholium, Homer, *Odyssey* 9.456
>
> Later (i.e. post-Homeric) poets think that talking to the ram is bucolic. With marvellous skill, Homer was the first to succeed in representing men talking to animals as though they had intelligence, as Hector (*Iliad* 8.185) 'Xanthos and you Podargos'.

The scholium reflects the standard view of late Hellenistic and Byzantine scholarship that Homer was the source of all literary forms, in this case the interaction between man and animal typical of bucolic and pastoral literature. Nevertheless, one of the most striking things about this passage of *Odyssey* 9 is that, despite its obvious importance in subsequent bucolic literature, its own explicit *Nachleben* is, to say the least, meagre. For his Teubner edition of the *Odyssey* Martin West could not find a single ancient quotation of vv. 447–456 to list in his apparatus of the indirect tradition, and, with the exception of the scholium I have cited, the scholia on the passage are threadbare, even by the standards of the *Odyssey* scholia. Moreover, if we look at ancient critical and rhetorical traditions, we will not find this passage where we might have expected to find it. Thus, for example, Hermogenes shows that, in the second century AD (and presumably before), ἀφέλεια, 'simplicity', was known to be a stylistic trait appropriate to bucolic (he cites the opening of *Idylls* 1 and 3),[4] but the Cyclops is nowhere to be found in his discussion (perhaps because the Homeric Cyclops *qua* character is anything but ἀφελής, and the last part of the speech to the ram veers back to the grim splattering of human brains). That silence is compensated (as so often) by Eustathius, who notes that to call the ram πέπων is the action of a character which is 'uncomplicated and simple and a bit childlike' (ἁπλοῦ ... ἤθους καὶ ἀφελοῦς καὶ ὑπό τι νηπίου, *Hom.* 1638.59). Eustathius is here very clearly echoing the passage of Hermogenes about bucolic ἀφέλεια

---

[3] Cf., e.g., Halperin 1983, 233. On the projection of human motives to the ram in this speech cf. the note of Di Benedetto *ad loc.* 2010, 532–533.
[4] Hermogenes 322.19–20, 323.20 Rabe.

which introduces a citation of the opening of *Idyll* 3;[5] Eustathius, who was of course very familiar with the grammatical traditions on view in the extant scholia, has fully appreciated the 'bucolic' nature of the Cyclops' address and replaced Hermogenes' Theocritean example with one of its Homeric forebears.

Even more striking perhaps is that Hermogenes has nothing to say about the Cyclops and his ram when he comes to discuss the γλυκύτης, 'sweetness', which arises from giving animals human characteristics and motives (335 Rabe), and it is unlikely that the reason for this silence is that it is the Cyclops, not the poet, who is speaking the relevant verses; all Hermogenes' examples come in fact from Xenophon *On Hunting*. This ancient silence, broken only by a single scholium, does not of course mean that the Homeric scene went 'underground' until the Hellenistic age. If we only had a play-title and brief plot-summary, we would never guess that Aristophanes' *Wasps* contains a relatively extended reworking of the escape of Odysseus and his men from the cave.[6] Philocleon, desperate to escape from the house, hides under a donkey which he claims should be sold; Bdelycleon's concerned query to the donkey, κάνθων, τί κλάεις; (179–181), clearly picks up the Cyclops' address to his ram with which we are concerned. Aristophanes' audience knew the Homeric scene well; for whatever reason the grammatical tradition was less interested.

The Cyclops' apparent affection for his ram is not just a remarkable poetic effect in its context, but also — as we have seen — almost preternaturally prescient in its foreshadowing of the bucolic tradition. At least as early as the fifth century, Sicily had been identified as the land of the Cyclopes, and it is very likely indeed that the Syracusan Epicharmus set his comic *Cyclops* (first half of the century?) in the region of Mt Etna, as Euripides was to set his *Cyclops*. The parodos of Euripides' play, which very clearly picks up and varies the Homeric Cyclops' address to his ram, is also another remarkable foreshadowing of Theocritean motifs and very likely it does not merely 'exploit the audience's belief' in Sicilian song traditions,[7] but actually mimics (real or believed) features of such traditions;[8] this is something different from the long acknowledged debt of pastoral to the real traditions of rustic song-exchange which Reinhold Merkelbach famously found in Theocritus.[9] How much, if any, 'bucolic song' (of any

---

5 At 322.12–21 Rabe Hermogenes notes that 'simple thoughts' are those ἁπλάστων ἠθῶν καὶ ὑπό τι νηπίων; on the opening of *Idyll* 3 cf. further below.
6 To the standard commentaries add Davies 1990.
7 Hunter 1999, 9.
8 Cf. esp. Serrao 1969, Hunter – Laemmle 2020, 103–104.
9 Merkelbach 1956.

form) lies behind the Cyclops' address to his ram, or is what is said too specific to the Cyclops' own desperate situation to allow us to think of a wider context? Does Homer want us to think of bucolic song traditions when we hear these verses, just as elsewhere (particularly in the *Odyssey*) he appropriates many different poetic traditions into his all-encompassing epic? If so, were these traditions for Homer and his audience at all localised? It may be worth considering, if only for a moment, the possibility that the poet of the *Odyssey*, whoever and whenever he was, also associated such song with Sicily, and that the localisation of the land of the Cyclopes as Sicily is already there somehow in the *Odyssey*, though necessarily submerged beneath the 'unreal' geography which governs Odysseus' account of his adventures. Might Sicilian poetic traditions already surface in the Cyclops' address to his ram?

One very important aspect of these verses of the *Odyssey* is that the Cyclops' speech is presumably intended to work very much to the greater *kleos* of Odysseus who lies beneath the ram (in two senses); the Cyclops' speech is given to him by Odysseus as part of his *apologoi* to the Phaeacians, and so it is really Odysseus' speech as much as the Cyclops'. Odysseus thus makes the Cyclops confirm the hero's narrative out of his own mouth; it is, after all, Odysseus who has already identified this ram as a 'hero' among the sheep, μήλων ὄχ' ἄριστος ἁπάντων (432), just as Odysseus himself stands out from his crew. It is obviously important that the misguided 'pathetic fallacy' and the emotional empathy with the ram's normal behaviour are all placed in the Cyclops' mouth by Odysseus himself, but what then is the tone of these verses? Is it just a way of mocking the Cyclops' stupidity and exalting Odysseus' cleverness? It has long been acknowledged by most commentators that μακρὰ βιβάς in v. 450 assimilates the movement of the ram to that of an Iliadic hero striding towards the battle,[10] though not all are prepared to see humour in the phrase.[11] Is Odysseus inviting us to smile at a victim who is so deluded that (in his solitariness) he creates a daily epic drama in which his sheep are the principal characters? If so, 'bucolic' Homeric poetry would then itself evoke a very different, Homeric world, just as Theocritus was constantly to do, and I shall return to this possibility. Tone here is indeed hard to catch. Immediately before the Cyclops' speech, Odysseus describes how the ram was the last to leave the cave:

---

[10] In the *Iliad* the phrase is most associated with Ajax; the only other example in the *Odyssey* is μακρὰ βιβᾶσα of Achilles' ghost at 11.539.
[11] Stanford *ad loc.* (strangely) denies the possibility of 'intentional humour' because of the nature of formulaic language.

ὕστατος ἀρνειὸς μήλων ἔστειχε θύραζε,
λάχνῳ στεινόμενος καὶ ἐμοὶ πυκινὰ φρονέοντι.

Homer, *Odyssey* 9.444–445

The ram came last of the sheep to the entrance, weighed down by its fleece and by me with my close-set thoughts.

Eustathius (*Hom.* 1638.56–57) found something witty (ἔχει τι ἀστεισμοῦ) in v. 445, as Odysseus describes himself as πυκινὰ φρονέοντι while clinging to the fleece of the ram which itself was πυκινόν.[12] Eustathius' instincts are surely correct here: Odysseus celebrates his own guile with what amounts to a wry twisting of formulaic language. We are left in no doubt as to who is in charge both of the action and of the narration, but we might also ask whether, in giving the 'bucolic' speech to the Cyclops, Odysseus creates the kind of ironic and distanced *de haut en bas* empathy with which we are familiar from later pastoral and in which pity for the herdsman's lot is always the result of a sense of readerly superiority.

Any consideration of this scene in *Odyssey* 9 must take into account Priam's description of Odysseus on the plain in front of Troy in *Iliad* 3:

δεύτερον αὖτ' Ὀδυσῆα ἰδὼν ἐρέειν' ὁ γεραιός·
'εἴπ' ἄγε μοι καὶ τόνδε, φίλον τέκος, ὅς τις ὅδ' ἐστίν·
μείων μὲν κεφαλῇ Ἀγαμέμνονος Ἀτρεΐδαο,
εὐρύτερος δ' ὤμοισιν ἰδὲ στέρνοισιν ἰδέσθαι.
τεύχεα μέν οἱ κεῖται ἐπὶ χθονὶ πουλυβοτείρῃ,   195
αὐτὸς δὲ κτίλος ὣς ἐπιπωλεῖται στίχας ἀνδρῶν·
ἀρνειῷ μιν ἔγωγε ἐΐσκω πηγεσιμάλλῳ
ὅς τ' οἰῶν μέγα πῶϋ διέρχεται ἀργεννάων.'
τὸν δ' ἠμείβετ' ἔπειθ' Ἑλένη Διὸς ἐκγεγαυῖα·
'οὗτος δ' αὖ Λαερτιάδης πολύμητις Ὀδυσσεύς,   200
ὃς τράφη ἐν δήμῳ Ἰθάκης κραναῆς περ ἐούσης
εἰδὼς παντοίους τε δόλους καὶ μήδεα πυκνά.'

Homer, *Iliad* 3.191–202

Odysseus was the second whom the old man saw and enquired about: 'Come, tell me also, dear child, who this man here is. He is shorter than Agamemnon the son of Atreus, but to look upon he is broader in the shoulders and the chest. His arms lie on the richly fertile earth, but he patrols the ranks of men like the leading ram; I liken him to a thick-fleeced

---

12 Stanford *ad loc.* notes (without reference to Eustathius): 'the zeugma (or metalepsis) is almost comic'; Dawe 1993, 382 describes the verse as 'the strangest thing of all' in its passage. It is (inevitably) tempting to recall Helen's praise of Odysseus' μήδεα πυκνά, immediately after Priam's comparison of him to a ram (*Iliad* 3.202, below).

ram which roams among a large flock of snowy sheep'. Then Helen, the daughter of Zeus, answered: 'This is the son of Laertes, Odysseus of the many wiles; he was brought up on Ithaca, a rocky land, and he is the master of all sorts of trickery and cunning plans'.

Odysseus is like a thick-fleeced ram, the leading ram of the flock in fact, the κτίλος (cf. further below); although we have seen Odysseus in action already in Books 1 and 2, the *teikhoskopia* is in some senses his 'presentation' to the audience of the *Iliad*, as Helen's lapidary verses about him make clear (200–202).[13] It is tempting to think that the *Odyssey*-poet knew these Iliadic verses and that some early audiences at least will have appreciated how the particular version of the folktale motif of escape from the giant's cave which Homer gave to Odysseus in Book 9 resonated against the presentation of the hero in the Iliadic *teikhoskopia*. If any scene illustrated Odysseus' παντοίους δόλους καὶ μήδεα πυκνά, it was the blinding of and escape from the Cyclops. Moreover, the relation between the two scenes suggests again that the interplay between bucolic foreground and Homeric background which shimmers everywhere through Theocritus' bucolic poetry is in fact repeating a poetic gesture which was there already in Homer, as I suggested above in noting the 'heroic' descriptions of Odysseus' ram. What was a 'bucolic' simile in the *Iliad* becomes a bucolic song in the *Odyssey*, and one in which the language gestures to a larger and martial world of heroic poetry. Theocritus has borrowed and adapted a Homeric technique for the display of the Homeric heritage.

In his discussion of the Cyclops' ram, Eustathius noted that the anaphora of πρῶτος in the Cyclops' address made it clear that the ram was a κτίλος, that is the sheep (or goat) which led the flock (cf. Hesychius κ 4319); it was indeed a κτίλος ram to which Priam had compared Odysseus in the *Iliad*. Aristotle (*HA* 6.573b25–27) reports that herdsmen would choose one male sheep to be trained from a young age to do this task of leading, whenever 'he was called by name'. The Cyclops' ram as the flock-leader takes us immediately to a famous Theocritean opening:

κωμάσδω ποτὶ τὰν Ἀμαρυλλίδα, ταὶ δέ μοι αἶγες
βόσκονται κατ' ὄρος, καὶ ὁ Τίτυρος αὐτὰς ἐλαύνει.
Τίτυρ', ἐμὶν τὸ καλὸν πεφιλημένε, βόσκε τὰς αἶγας,
καὶ ποτὶ τὰν κράναν ἄγε, Τίτυρε· καὶ τὸν ἐνόρχαν,
τὸν Λιβυκὸν κνάκωνα, φυλάσσεο μή τυ κορύψῃ.

Theocritus 3.1–5

---

[13] Cf. the observation of the scholia *ad loc.* which rightly identify the epigrammatic quality of the verses: 'the epigram gives everything in a short space'; cf. further Nünlist 2009, 249 n. 39.

I go to serenade Amaryllis; my goats are grazing on the mountain, and Tityrus drives them. Tityrus, my very dear friend, graze my goats and lead them to the spring, Tityrus; and watch out for the billy-goat, the tawny Libyan one, in case he butts you.

This is one of the passages which Hermogenes uses to illustrate bucolic ἀφέλεια, 'when someone explains things and narrates them, though there is no need to do so and no one has enquired' (322.14–16 Rabe). There is of course a longstanding debate as to whether we are to understand Tityrus here as a herdsman or as a goat, i.e. the leading goat of the flock, as Odysseus' ram led the Cyclops' flock; there is ancient lexical support for such a view.[14] If Tityrus is understood as a goat, then the situation will be rather like that of the Cyclops in *Idyll* 11: the flocks go home alone (11.12–13), while the lovesick shepherd busies himself with his girl.

The opening of *Idyll* 3 is the subject of a very interesting passage of pastoral *Nachleben*, namely Aulus Gellius' discussion of Virgil's adaptation of these Theocritean verses. The context is Virgil's skill in knowing what to translate and what to leave alone:

sicuti nuperrime, apud mensam cum legerentur utraque simul *Bucolica* Theocriti et Vergilii, animaduertimus reliquisse Vergilium quod Graecum quidem mire quam suaue est, uerti autem neque debuit neque potuit. sed enim quod substituit pro eo, quod omiserat, non abest quin iucundius lepidiusque sit:

βάλλει καὶ μάλοισι τὸν αἰπόλον ἁ Κλεαρίστα
τὰς αἶγας παρελᾶντα καὶ ἁδύ τι ποππυλιάζει.

Theocr. 5.88–89

malo me Galatea petit, lasciua puella,
et fugit ad salices et se cupit ante uideri.

Virgil, *Ecl.* 3.64–65

illud quoque alio in loco animaduertimus caute omissum, quod est in Graeco uersu dulcissimum:

Τίτυρ', ἐμὶν τὸ καλὸν πεφιλημένε, βόσκε τὰς αἶγας
καὶ ποτὶ τὰν κράναν ἄγε, Τίτυρε· καὶ τὸν ἐνόρχαν
τὸν Λιβυκὸν κνάκωνα φυλάσσεο, μή τυ κορύξῃ.

Theocr. 3.3–5

quo enim pacto diceret: τὸ καλὸν πεφιλημένε, uerba hercle non translaticia, sed cuiusdam natiuae dulcedinis? hoc igitur reliquit et cetera uertit non infestiuiter, nisi quod caprum

---

14 Cf. Gow's note *ad loc.*

dixit, quem Theocritus ἐνόρχαν appellauit. auctore enim M. Varrone is demum Latine caper dicitur, qui excastratus est:

Tityre, dum redeo (brevis est uia) pasce capellas
et potum pastas age, Tityre, et inter agendum
occursare capro (cornu ferit ille) caueto.

Virgil, Ecl. 9.23–5

Aulus Gellius, NA 9.9.4–11

For example, when very recently the *Bucolics* of Theocritus and Virgil were being read together at table, we perceived that Virgil had omitted something that in the Greek is, to be sure, wonderfully pleasing, but neither could nor ought to have been translated. But what he has substituted for that omission is almost more charming and graceful:

Cleärista pelts the goatherd with apples as he drives his goats past her and she whistles sweetly to him. (Theocr. 5.88–89)

Galatea throws an apple at me, the playful girl, and flees to the willow-trees, but wants to be glimpsed first. (Virgil, *Ecl.* 3.64–65)

Also in another place we noticed that what was very sweet in the Greek was prudently omitted:

Tityrus, my very dear friend, graze my goats and lead them to the spring, Tityrus; and watch out for the billy-goat, the tawny Libyan one, in case he butts you. (Theocr. 3.3–5)

But how could Virgil reproduce τὸ καλὸν πεφιλημένε, words that, by Heaven!, defy translation, but have a certain native charm? He therefore omitted that expression and translated the rest very cleverly, except in using *caper* for Theocritus' ἐνόρχας; for, according to Marcus Varro, a goat is called *caper* in Latin only after he has been castrated:

Tityrus, until I return (it is a short trip), graze my goats and, Tityrus, lead them to drink once they are full, and while leading them make sure not to come up against the he-goat—he butts with his horn. (Virgil, *Ecl.* 9.23–25)

trans. Rolfe, adapted

For Gellius, bucolic/pastoral is, above all, the realm of the *suaue* and the *dulce*, but in identifying τὸ καλὸν πεφιλημένε as *dulcissimum*, he draws our attention to a perhaps colloquial adverbial use of the neuter adjective (and one which certainly puzzled the scholiasts) and a phrase which certainly does not lessen the case for seeing Tityrus in *Idyll* 3 as a goat; we will here recall again not just the Cyclops' address to his ram, presumably the model for this opening to *Idyll* 3, but also Hermogenes' account of the stylistic sweetness which results when animals are described in human terms. Gellius' observation about Virgil's unfortunate use of *caper* for an uncastrated he-goat, contrary to Varro's lexical distinctions (Varro was presumably distinguishing between *caper* and *hircus*), is normally simply an excuse for modern scholars to grumble about Gellius' pedantry; Virgil in fact has most of Latin literature on his side. Nevertheless, that alleged pedantry should direct our attention to the interesting questions which arise and perhaps underlie Gellius' discussion.

Ancient lexicographers, as well as Eustathius (cf. *Hom.* 403.31, 404.13, 943.31), were clear that κτίλος as an adjective meant 'tame, gentle';[15] the scholia on *Iliad* 3.197, the comparison of Odysseus to a κτίλος (cf. above), note that Odysseus is there compared to the 'most gentle' (πραΰτατος) animal,[16] and D'Arcy Thompson recalled that *il manso* (i.e. *mansueto*) to designate the leading sheep in Italian exemplified the same synonymy (Thompson [1932]). One reason why the leading ram might be 'tame, gentle' is of course that it has been castrated (cf. *il castrone, castrù* in Italian/Sicilian, 'bell-wether' in English). If we are to imagine such a situation in *Idyll* 3, then we suddenly find a real point in τὸν ἐνόρχαν in v. 4: Tityrus, perhaps himself a goat, needs to be careful of a he-goat which, unlike Tityrus, is still in full possession of its goathood. There are of course other issues about these verses which would require discussion in any full treatment (e.g. the resonances of ἐλαύνει in 2), but the present case is an excellent example of the constant need to balance up what we can learn from the grammatical tradition and what we think the poetic tradition teaches us. We might guess, incidentally, that Virgil, who will certainly have known Varro's pronouncement, used *caper* in his adaptation of these verses in order, as far as possible, to remove ambiguity about the identity of Tityrus, an ambiguity of which he would have known *inter alia* from the Theocritean scholia;[17] had he used *hircus* he would have left open the possibility that Tityrus was himself a (castrated) goat.

Polyphemus and his ram are also at the centre of what is one of the most extraordinary moments of Theocritean *Nachleben*, Aeneas' description of the blinded Cyclops in the third book of Virgil's *Aeneid*:

uix ea fatus erat summo cum monte uidemus
ipsum inter pecudes uasta se mole mouentem

---

[15] Modern scholarship connects the word with κτι- (as in κτίζω): 'près de l'habitation' (Chantraine), 'belonging to the dwelling place' (Beekes). Cf. further Morpurgo 1960.
[16] Cf. also Eustathius, *Hom.* 403.31–37, 404.6–8.
[17] For the relationship between the *Eclogues* and the Theocritean scholia cf. Keeline 2017. The relevant part of *Eclogue* 9 is itself something of a meditation on translation from Greek to Latin, and Virgil will certainly have expected his audiences to reflect upon his lexical choices.

> pastorem Polyphemum et litora nota petentem,
> monstrum horrendum, informe, ingens, cui lumen ademptum.
> trunca manum pinus regit et uestigia firmat;
> lanigerae comitantur oues; ea sola uoluptas   660
> solamenque mali. [de collo fistula pendet].
> postquam altos tetigit fluctus et ad aequora uenit,
> luminis effossi fluidum lauit inde cruorem
> dentibus infrendens gemitu, graditurque per aequor
> iam medium, necdum fluctus latera ardua tinxit.
>
> Virgil, *Aeneid* 3.655–665

Scarcely had he spoken when we saw him on the top of the mountain, the shepherd Polyphemus moving with his huge bulk among his flocks and seeking the shores he knew well—a monster awful to behold, hideous, huge, his eye removed. In his hand a cut pine leads and steadies his steps. The fleeced sheep accompany him; this is his only pleasure and consolation for his distress; [from his neck his pipe hangs down]. When he reached the deep waves of the sea, he washed the bloody gore which flowed from where his eye had been removed; he gnashed his teeth and groaned, and as he walked through the open sea, the wave did not touch his lofty flanks.

Behind Aeneas' description lies the same passage of the *Odyssey* we have been considering. Virgil seeks to create a 'mixed' emotional and generic effect, to match the two very different parts of the Cyclops' address to the ram; it might be thought typical of Virgilian *mimesis* that there is not the apparently clean distinction between the parts which we find in Homer. In most modern editions of the *Aeneid*, the second half of v. 661 *de collo fistula pendet*, which has an uncomfortably fragile status in the manuscript tradition, is treated as a late antique attempt to complete a verse which Virgil had left as half a verse. A decision on that matter is in fact separate from a recognition that Virgil here takes us back, not just to Homer, but also to the bucolic Cyclops of Theocritus (and perhaps also to the *Eclogues*).[18] Virgil's *solamen* not merely recalls the Cyclops' 'shepherding of his love' in *Idyll* 11 but also brings out very finely something important about the Homeric scene of *Odyssey* 9: the wishful pathetic fallacy *is* a consolation for the Cyclops in the loss of his eye, which is like a kind of death (*lumen ademptum*). *comitantur* in v. 660 both evokes the ὁμοφροσύνη between man and beast for which the Homeric Cyclops longs and reverses the situation of *Idyll* 11 in which the flocks return to the steading without their shepherd; *comitantur* also reminds us, as does *uoluptas*, that that shepherd has no human, particularly female, company to soothe the pain and the loneliness, marked out

---

18 Cf. esp. Glenn 1972, 55–59, Thomas 1999, 260–263.

by the echoing *sola ... solamen*. Whoever added *de collo fistula pendet* to Virgil's half-verse recognised something very important about it.

Finally, the Homeric scene of the Cyclops and his ram can illustrate an important aspect of the modern reaction to ancient bucolic and pastoral. In the parodos of Euripides' *Cyclops* (52), which has already been identified as both a descendant of *Odyssey* 9 and a prescient foreshadowing of Theocritean motifs (cf. above), a ram (clearly the Homeric ram *rediuiuus*) is addressed as ὦ κεράστα (or perhaps Κεράστα, if this is actually the animal's name). In 1932 D'Arcy Thompson suggested that a Sicilian dialect word for the sheep that leads the flock, *crastù* 'can surely be no other than Greek κεράστης ... it is highly interesting, it is very beautiful, to find Euripides putting into the mouths of his Sicilian chorus a shepherds' word, which shepherds on the slopes of Etna have in use today'.[19] Thompson was all but certainly wrong about the etymology (the word is, very likely, simply dialect for *castrone*), but what really *is* 'interesting and beautiful' here is Thompson's desire to get in touch with 'the real', to find in ancient bucolic poetry timeless practices and language which one can still see today by going to the wild places. However artificial and mannered pastoral poetry might be, we have a yearning, by no means limited to D'Arcy Thompson and a world before the Second World War, to find in it something 'real', and the more complicated and sophisticated our own lives, the stronger the πόθος for a lost innocence, for, to use Hermogenes' terms, an ἀφέλεια to which we can no longer lay claim. Even if the desire, perhaps most famously enshrined in Thomas Rosenmeyer's *The Green Cabinet* of 1969, to associate the rise of bucolic with a quasi-Epicurean desire to escape the complications of life in the large Hellenistic cities such as Alexandria is now seen as at best overstated, we nevertheless should acknowledge the powerful hold that such nostalgia for life before the Fall holds over us. The characters of pastoral can seem to represent our own prelapsarian selves; the wistful longing of the satyrs in the parodos of Euripides' *Cyclops* is our longing also. What is so powerful, then, about Virgil's dispossessed herdsmen, Meliboeus in *Eclogue* 1 and Moeris in *Eclogue* 9, is that they are both before and after the Fall; they have a share both in pastoral simplicity and in the ruthlessness of modernity. To this extent, they re-embody the violent failure of another of Homer's bucolic intimations, the innocent and doomed syrinx-players on the Shield of Achilles (*Iliad* 18.525–526).

---

19 Thompson 1932, 54.

The bucolic journey

In *Odyssey* 17 Eumaeus escorts the disguised Odysseus into town; this is the hero's first approach to his own palace for twenty years:

> ἦ ῥα, καὶ ἀμφ' ὤμοισιν ἀεικέα βάλλετο πήρην,
> πυκνὰ ῥωγαλέην, ἐν δὲ στρόφος ἦεν ἀορτήρ·
> Εὔμαιος δ' ἄρα οἱ σκῆπτρον θυμαρὲς ἔδωκε.
> τὼ βήτην, σταθμὸν δὲ κύνες καὶ βώτορες ἄνδρες   200
> ῥύατ' ὄπισθε μένοντες. ὁ δ' ἐς πόλιν ἦγεν ἄνακτα
> πτωχῷ λευγαλέῳ ἐναλίγκιον ἠδὲ γέροντι,
> σκηπτόμενον· τὰ δὲ λυγρὰ περὶ χροῒ εἵματα ἕστο.
> ἀλλ' ὅτε δὴ στείχοντες ὁδὸν κάτα παιπαλόεσσαν
> ἄστεος ἐγγὺς ἔσαν καὶ ἐπὶ κρήνην ἀφίκοντο   205
> τυκτὴν καλλίροον, ὅθεν ὑδρεύοντο πολῖται,
> τὴν ποίησ' Ἴθακος καὶ Νήριτος ἠδὲ Πολύκτωρ·
> ἀμφὶ δ' ἄρ' αἰγείρων ὑδατοτρεφέων ἦν ἄλσος,
> πάντοσε κυκλοτερές, κατὰ δὲ ψυχρὸν ῥέεν ὕδωρ
> ὑψόθεν ἐκ πέτρης· βωμὸς δ' ἐφύπερθε τέτυκτο   210
> Νυμφάων, ὅθι πάντες ἐπιρρέζεσκον ὁδῖται·
> ἔνθα σφέας ἐκίχανεν υἱὸς Δολίοιο Μελανθεὺς
> αἶγας ἄγων, αἳ πᾶσι μετέπρεπον αἰπολίοισι,
> δεῖπνον μνηστήρεσσι· δύω δ' ἅμ' ἕποντο νομῆες.
>
> Homer, *Odyssey* 17.197–214

With these words he threw the shabby, very tattered bag over his shoulders — there was a strap on which it hung — and Eumaeus gave him a staff which suited him. The two of them headed off, while the dogs and the herdsmen stayed behind to protect the steading. So he led to the town his master, looking like a wretched beggar and an old man, leaning on a staff; the clothes on his body were tatters. When along the steep path they were close to the town, they reached a fountain, manmade, fair-flowing, where the townspeople drew water; it had been made by Ithakos, together with Neritos and Polyktor. Around it was a grove of water-nurtured poplar trees, a spreading circle, and cold water flowed down from the rock high up. Above, an altar to the Nymphs had been built, where all travellers performed sacrifice. There they were met by Melantheus, the son of Dolios, who was bringing the very finest goats of the flock to serve as dinner for the suitors; two shepherds accompanied him.

In 1972 Ulrich Ott pointed out that this scene was an important model for Theocritus, *Idyll* 7,[20] in which Simichidas and his friends travel 'from the *polis*' into the countryside. That poem celebrates a fountain and *locus amoenus* (cf. esp. 7–9,

---

[20] Ott 1972, 146–149, cf. Halperin 1983, 226–227, Griffin 1992, 194–195, Hunter 1999, 147–148.

135–137) created by early founders of Cos (Klytia and Chalkon),[21] and the travellers meet a goatherd (at least someone who 'looked very much like a goatherd', 14); the suggestion that this goatherd is not quite what he seems to be reflects the Homeric motif of Odysseus disguised as a beggar ('like a wretched beggar and an old man', 202): Odysseus is certainly more than he seems to be.[22] Theocritus' reworking thus fashions the subsequent quarrel between Eumaeus and Melantheus into an originary 'bucolic' exchange (cf. Komatas and Lakon in *Idyll* 5).

Odysseus' approach to his palace repeats two of the significant geographical names from his self-presentation to the Phaeacians:

εἴμ' Ὀδυσεὺς Λαερτιάδης, ὅς πᾶσι δόλοισιν
ἀνθρώποισι μέλω, καί μευ κλέος οὐρανὸν ἵκει.   20
ναιετάω δ' Ἰθάκην εὐδείελον· ἐν δ' ὄρος αὐτῆι,
Νήριτον εἰνοσίφυλλον, ἀριπρεπές· ἀμφὶ δὲ νῆσοι
πολλαὶ ναιετάουσι μάλα σχεδὸν ἀλλήλῃσι,
Δουλίχιόν τε Σάμη τε καὶ ὑλήεσσα Ζάκυνθος.
                                            Homer, *Odyssey* 9.19–24

I am Odysseus, son of Laertes; all men know of my trickery, and my fame has reached heaven. I dwell in Ithaca seen from afar. There is a mountain, leafy Neriton, which clearly stands out, and round about there are many inhabited islands, all set close together, Doulichion and Same and wooded Zacynthos.

The repetition supports De Jong's view that the description of the fountain is '(implicitly) focalised' by Odysseus and Eumaeus: they, and particularly Odysseus, have the appropriate knowledge of Ithacan history; Odysseus' knowledge and recognition of the landmark is in fact part of his reclaiming of his homeland.[23] The eponymous Ithakos and Neritos make no other appearance anywhere in literature, except in the lore preserved in the scholia and Eustathius on 207 (cf. below). The same is true of Polyktor, if — as seems entirely probable — he is to be understood as a figure from the island's legendary past; the name is, however, also given to the father of one of Penelope's suitors (18.299, 22.243), who, so perhaps we are to understand, traces his family back to that 'founder', just as Simichidas' hosts in *Idyll* 7 trace their ancestry back to significant names in the history of the island.[24] That Homer offers no further explanation of these

---

[21] We are here reliant on the scholia on 5–9, cf. Hunter 1999, 153.
[22] The description of Lycidas in 15–19 picks up Odysseus' preparations at *Od.* 17.197–199.
[23] De Jong 2001, 406; for an attempt to identify the location of the *locus amoenus* cf. Bittlestone 2005, 458–462.
[24] This seems much more probable than the suggestion of Di Benedetto 2010, 901–902 that we are to understand the three names as those of contemporaries or near contemporaries of Odys-

three names is both a striking technique (is the significance of the names too obvious to require explanation?),[25] and also one which helps to reinforce the sense that Odysseus is reaching a familiar landmark. Not only is his self-introduction to the Phaeacians recalled, but also his first 'unclouded' vision of Ithaca, as Athena points out the significant landmarks to him:

ἀλλ' ἄγε τοι δείξω Ἰθάκης ἕδος, ὄφρα πεποίθῃς·	
Φόρκυνος μὲν ὅδ' ἐστὶ λιμήν, ἁλίοιο γέροντος,	345
ἥδε δ' ἐπὶ κρατὸς λιμένος τανύφυλλος ἐλαίη·	346
τοῦτο δέ τοι σπέος εὐρὺ κατηρεφές, ἔνθα σὺ πολλὰς	349
ἔρδεσκες Νύμφῃσι τεληέσσας ἑκατόμβας·	350[26]
τοῦτο δὲ Νήριτόν ἐστιν ὄρος καταειμένον ὕλῃ.	
ὣς εἰποῦσα θεὰ σκέδασ' ἠέρα, εἴσατο δὲ χθών·	
γήθησέν τ' ἄρ' ἔπειτα πολύτλας δῖος Ὀδυσσεὺς	
χαίρων ᾗ γαίῃ, κύσε δὲ ζείδωρον ἄρουραν.	
αὐτίκα δὲ Νύμφῃσ' ἠρήσατο χεῖρας ἀνασχών·	355
'Νύμφαι Νηϊάδες, κοῦραι Διός, οὔ ποτ' ἐγώ γε	
ὄψεσθ' ὔμμ' ἐφάμην· νῦν δ' εὐχωλῇσ' ἀγανῇσι	
χαίρετ'· ἀτὰρ καὶ δῶρα διδώσομεν, ὡς τὸ πάρος περ,	
αἴ κεν ἐᾷ πρόφρων με Διὸς θυγάτηρ ἀγελείη	
αὐτόν τε ζώειν καί μοι φίλον υἱὸν ἀέξῃ.'	

Homer, *Odyssey* 13.344–346, 349–360

But come, I will show you the layout of Ithaca, so that you will believe. This is the harbour of Phorkys, old man of the sea; here at the head of the harbour is an olive-tree with its slender leaves; here is the broad, vaulted cave where you often offered perfect sacrifices to the Nymphs. Here is Mt Neriton, covered in forest. With these words, the goddess scattered the mist, and the land became clear. Long-suffering noble Odysseus rejoiced with pleasure in his homeland and he kissed the fertile soil. At once he raised his arms and prayed to the Nymphs: 'Naiad Nymphs, daughters of Zeus, I thought that I would never

---

seus (i.e. the two Polyktors are identical). Di Benedetto offers, however, a valuable discussion of the scene of *Odyssey* 17; he also notes how the construction of v. 207 gives precedence to Ithakos over the other two builders of the shrine of the Nymphs. 'Polyktor' is also the name which Hermes chooses for his alleged father when he meets Priam at *Iliad* 24.397: 'suitable for a rich man' (Richardson *ad loc.*).

25 The D scholia explain that Ithakos and Neritos, sons of Pterelaos, settled Ithaca from Cephallonia, and they adduce Akousilaos of Argos (late sixth century) as their authority (fr. 43 Jacoby – Fowler); the BQ scholia (and cf. Eustathius, *Hom.* 1815.48–50) claim that the third brother, Polyktor, gave his name to a place on Ithaca (not otherwise attested), cf. Fowler 2013, 556. It seems very unlikely that the poet of the *Odyssey* knew or expected his audience to know such lore; it is, rather, very probable that this is a (very interesting) post-Homeric construction of local history.

26 Along with most recent editors, I omit what are transmitted as 347–348 (= 13.103–104).

see you again; now take pleasure in my loving prayers. I shall also offer you gifts, as I did before, if the daughter of Zeus, the plunderer, graciously allows me to live and brings my dear son to manhood'.

Ithaca, Mt Neriton and the Nymphs all reappear (the first two through reference to their eponymous heroes), as Odysseus finally approaches his own palace; so too the piety to the Nymphs which Odysseus shows in *Odyssey* 13 (vv. 355–360) is evoked again in *Odyssey* 17 (vv. 210–211, 240–246), as it will be picked up in the festive ending of *Idyll* 7 (vv. 135–137, 148).

The Homeric spring and grove of the Nymphs was built 'close to the *astu*', presumably as a benefaction to the inhabitants, as it was there that 'the people of the *polis* drew water' (v. 206). The only other occurrence of πολῖται in the *Odyssey* is in exactly the same half-verse at 7.131 describing the springs in front of Alcinous' palace, also — like the grove of *Odyssey* 17 — as seen by Odysseus (cf. 7.133–5). The Ithacan spring to some extent marks a boundary where *polis*- or *astu*- life begins and the countryside recedes;[27] there are, of course, no very sharp divisions between the two, whether in Homer or Theocritus (cf. 16.87–97), but the importance in the *Odyssey* of a distinction between the two realms is very clear: in one the suitors lay siege to Penelope and waste to Odysseus' house, in the other Eumaeus and Laertes ('whom they say no longer comes to the *polis*, but leads a hard life far away in the countryside (ἐπ' ἀγροῦ)', *Od.* 1.189–190) embody an older virtue. That this Homeric scene is reworked in *Idyll* 7 is of particular significance, as this is the poem which, perhaps more than any other of Theocritus' poems, defines the nature of bucolic song in terms of the boundaries between *polis* and country. Simichidas is a '*polis*-dweller', for whom 'bucolic song' is a poetic mode to be adopted, not — as it is for Lykidas — a mode of life.

The city, in all its forms, plays very little part in Theocritus' bucolics. Other than 7.2, the term πόλις appears in the 'bucolics' only at 4.32, a snatch of song καλὰ πόλις ἅ τε Ζάκυνθος, and at 5.78, where Lakon tells Komatas not to delay Morson, the judge of their contest, too long, but 'let him get back to the *polis*'; Morson may be going there to sell the heath he has cut (cf. vv. 64–65), but Lakon is also trying to flatter the judge to get him on his side: Morson is a sophisticated man who knows the *polis* and will (no doubt) judge Lakon's song to be superior. As for ἄστυ, this occurs in the bucolic poems only at 7.24 in Lykidas' teasing of Simichidas, a teasing which makes clear that Simichidas belongs in the town and only comes into the countryside for celebratory pleas-

---

27 Cf. Scully 1990, 13–14.

ure.[28] There is of course nothing in the bucolic poems to match the place of Rome in Virgil's *First Eclogue*, and Virgil perhaps draws attention to this move away from tradition:

> Vrbem quam dicunt Romam, Meliboee, putaui
> stultus ego huic nostrae similem, cui saepe solemus   20
> pastores ouium teneros depellere fetus.
> sic canibus catulos similes, sic matribus haedos
> noram, sic paruis componere magna solebam.
> uerum haec tantum alias inter caput extulit urbes
> quantum lenta solent inter uiburna cupressi.
>
> Virgil, Eclogues 1.19–25

The city which they call Rome, Meliboeus, in my foolishness I thought was like ours here, where we shepherds regularly take[29] the tender offspring of the sheep. Thus I knew that puppies were like dogs and kids like she-goats, thus I used to compare great things with small. But this city raises its head among all others as cypresses do amidst bending climbers.

The contrast between Rome and 'this *urbs* of ours' is not just a contrast between (perhaps) Rome and Mantua, but also between Rome and the towns which hide 'off-stage' in Theocritus' bucolics, such as in *Idyll* 5 (above). The *urbs*, which Rome has really surpassed, namely Ptolemaic Alexandria, has of course a major place in Theocritus' poems, above all *Idylls* 15 and 17, but the difference is telling: when we do catch a possible glimpse of Ptolemy and his capital in the bucolic poems, it should not surprise that it is in the mouth of the town-dweller Simichidas, the fame of whose songs may have reached 'the throne of Zeus' (7.93).[30]

---

28 The two occurrences of ἀστικά at *Idyll* 20.4, 31 perhaps suggest that post-Theocritean bucolic made more of the city-country distinction than did Theocritus; this would not surprise. There is a distinction in *Idyll* 25 between the *astu* and Augeas' 'country estate' which Heracles visits, cf. vv. 45–46.
29 The meaning of *depellere* is disputed.
30 The praise of Ptolemy at Theocritus 14.58–68 is in the mouth of a character who is plainly not a 'bucolic herdsman'.

Bibliography

Bittlestone, R. 2005. *Odysseus Unbound*, Cambridge.
Davies, M.I. 1990. 'Asses and rams: Dionysiac release in Aristophanes' *Wasps* and Attic vase-painting', *Metis* 5, 169–181.
Dawe, R.D. 1993. *The Odyssey. Translation and Analysis*, Lewes.
De Jong, I. 2001. *A Narratological Commentary on the Odyssey*, Cambridge.
Di Benedetto, V. 2010. *Omero, Odissea*, Milan.
Fowler, R.L. 2013. *Early Greek Mythography, Vol. II Commentary*, Oxford.
Glenn, J. 1972. 'Virgil's Polyphemus', *G&R* 19, 47–59.
Griffin, J. 1992. 'Theocritus, the *Iliad*, and the east', *AJPh* 113, 189–211.
Halperin, D.M. 1983. *Before Pastoral: Theocritus and the ancient tradition of bucolic poetry*, New Haven/London.
Hunter, R. 1999. *Theocritus, A Selection*, Cambridge.
Hunter, R. 2021. 'Sappho and Hellenistic Poetry', in: P. Finglass/A. Kelly (eds.), *The Cambridge Companion to Sappho*, Cambridge, 277–289 [= in this volume 314–327].
Hunter, R./Laemmle, R. 2020. *Euripides, Cyclops*, Cambridge.
Keeline, T. 2017. 'A poet on the margins: Vergil and the Theocritean scholia', *CPh* 112, 456–478.
Merkelbach, R. 1956. 'ΒΟΥΚΟΛΙΑΣΤΑΙ (Der Wettgesang der Hirten)', *RhM* 99, 97–133.
Morpurgo, A. 1960. 'ΚΤΙΛΟΣ (Pind. *Pyth.* II 17)' *Rivista di Cultura Classica e Medioevale* 2, 30–40.
Nünlist, R. 2009. *The Ancient Critic at Work*, Cambridge.
Ott, U. 1972. 'Theokrits "Thalysien" und ihre literarischen Vorbilder', *RhM* 115, 134–149.
Scully, S. 1990. *Homer and the Sacred City*, Ithaca NY.
Serrao, G. 1969. 'La parodo del 'Ciclope' euripideo', *Museum Criticum* 4, 50–62.
Thomas, R. 1999. *Reading Virgil and his Texts*, Ann Arbor.
Thompson, D.W. 1932. 'Κτίλος', *CR* 46, 53–54.

Part IV: **Latin Literature**

19 Notes on the Ancient Reception of Sappho

There is, of course, more than one Roman mode of engagement with Sappho, though the trickle never seems to have become a flood.[1] One of the most striking moments in this history is Quintilian's account of Greek lyric:

> Alcaeus in parte operis aureo plectro merito donatur, qua tyrannos insectatus multum etiam moribus confert, in eloquendo quoque breuis et magnificus et diligens et plerumque oratori similis, sed et lusit et in amores descendit, maioribus tamen aptior.
> Quint. *Inst.* 10.1.63

> Alcaeus is deservedly awarded a 'golden plectrum' for that part of his work in which he attacks tyrants and upholds proper morals; his style is concise and grand and accurate and largely like that of an orator. Nevertheless, he also wrote frivolously and stooped to love poetry, though he was more suited to higher themes.

Quintilian names and gives brief notices to four of the canon of Greek lyric poets (Pindar, Stesichorus, Alcaeus, Simonides, cf. *Inst.* 10.1.61–64), but notes that there were nine of them, thus passing by the other five in a way which calls attention to the omitted names. For Sappho, however, a very special silence is reserved.[2] Quintilian's notice of Alcaeus evokes Horace's famous Underworld scene of *Odes* 2.13, where he describes the pleasure he so nearly experienced in the afterlife:

> quam paene furuae regna Proserpinae
> et iudicantem uidimus Aeacum
>   sedesque discretas piorum et
>   Aeoliis fidibus querentem
>
> Sappho puellis de popularibus,
> et te sonantem plenius aureo,
>   Alcaee, plectro dura nauis,
>   dura fugae mala, dura belli.

---

1 The full pursuit of some of the very familiar and very complex issues touched on here would have led to a very different essay, and, particularly in the light of how rapidly the ground is moving in Sapphic studies, I have decided to leave this essay largely as it was drafted some years ago for the conference in Oxford. My thanks to Thea S. Thorsen for her invitation to the colloquium and her subsequent encouragement, and to Lucia Prauscello for her comments on an earlier draft. All translations are my own, unless I have indicated otherwise.
2 The remaining four are Alcman, Ibycus, Anacreon, and Bacchylides.

> utrumque sacro digna silentio
> mirantur umbrae dicere, sed magis
>   pugnas et exactos tyrannos
>   densum umeris bibit aure uolgus.
>
> Hor. *Carm.* 2.13.21–32

> How nearly did I see the kingdom of dusky Proserpina and Aeacus passing judgement and the seats set aside for the pious and Sappho complaining on her Aeolian lyre about the girls of Lesbos, and you, Alcaeus, singing in grander mode with your golden plectrum of the hardships at sea, the hardships of exile, and the hardships of war. The ghosts marvel at both of them as they sing songs worthy of reverend silence, but the dense mob, standing shoulder to shoulder, pay more attention to the fights and stories of tyrants banished.

The shades listen to the songs of both Sappho and Alcaeus, which are *sacro digna silentio*, but Quintilian both passes Sappho by in (very loud) silence, and also, through the allusion to Horace's poem, draws our attention to that *praeteritio*. For Quintilian her poetry was presumably nothing other than *lusus et amores*, whereas at least a part of Alcaeus' oeuvre was concerned with serious things (cf. also Hor. *Carm.* 1.32).

Quintilian's assessment of Alcaeus shares certain features with that in the extant epitome of Book 2 of Dionysius of Halicarnassus' *On Imitation*, a work (also written in Rome) which has long been seen as either one of Quintilian's sources or as sharing common sources itself with Quintilian:

> Ἀλκαίου δὲ σκόπει τὸ μεγαλοφυὲς καὶ βραχὺ καὶ ἡδὺ μετὰ δεινότητος, ἔτι δὲ καὶ τοὺς σχηματισμοὺς καὶ τὴν σαφήνειαν, ὅσον αὐτῆς μὴ τῆι διαλέκτωι τι κεκάκωται· καὶ πρὸ ἁπάντων τὸ τῶν πολιτικῶν πραγμάτων³ ἦθος· πολλαχοῦ γοῦν τὸ μέτρον τις εἰ περιέλοι, ῥητορείαν ἂν εὕροι πολιτικήν.⁴
>
> Dion. Hal. *De imit.* 2.8 (*Epitome*) = II 205.16–21 U-R

> Observe Alcaeus' grandeur and concision and mixture of pleasantness with vehemence; observe too his figures and his clarity, inasmuch as it is not damaged by his dialect.⁵

---

3 ποιημάτων Usener. There is presumably some link between Quintilian's *moribus* and the ἦθος in the Epitome of Dionysius' work.

4 Sic Usener: ῥητορικὴν ... πολιτείαν P: ῥητορικὴν ... πολι with lacuna HW. Lucia Prauscello points out how close this observation is to Pl. *Gorgias* 502c5–7 (Socrates is speaking), 'Tell me, if one were to strip all poetry of melody and rhythm and metre, what would be left except speeches (λόγοι)'; Socrates proceeds to conclude that poetry, though he is principally thinking of tragedy, is ῥητορικὴ δημηγορία ('deliberative rhetoric'). Dionysius of course knew the *Gorgias* very well.

5 Dionysius' observation about the difficulty of Alcaeus' Lesbian dialect should make us wonder what Roman poets made of it, and to what — if any — extent they sought to compensate for or evoke this dialect in their own poetry which was indebted to Sappho or Alcaeus.

> Above all, there is his political character: in many cases, if you took his metre away, you would find political rhetoric.

The *Epitome* preserves notices of the same four lyric poets as Quintilian, though the order in the two texts differs. The coincidence of the names suggests that the *Epitome* has not omitted any names, though it may have abbreviated the entries for those which it does preserve. Both Dionysius and Quintilian are concerned with the training of an orator or writer of πολιτικοὶ λόγοι ('political speeches'), and so it is perhaps unsurprising that Sappho does not get a look in. Nevertheless, this is not the only time in the Roman reception of Sappho when she will prove an awkward presence or absence.

When we consider the Roman reception of Sappho, we realize how many important frames of understanding we are lacking. Most importantly, of course, we still have very little of Sappho's poetry. Secondly, we have far too little of the Greek scholarship (of various levels of 'seriousness') on Sappho which presumably influenced, and may be reflected in, her Roman reception. I have suggested that in *Odes* 4.1 and 4.2 Horace reflects either Dionysius' discussion of Sapphic style in *De compositione uerborum* or something very like it;[6] we can certainly see how the probable placing of Sappho 1 at the head of the Alexandrian edition of Sappho has been used by Horace (*Carm.* 4.1), and we can ourselves use that placing to conclude that when, in *Heroides* 15,[7] Sappho recalls how she imagined that Venus might carry Phaon *in caelum curru ... eburno* (Ov. *Her.* 15.91, 'to heaven in an ivory chariot'), this is more likely than not to be an evocation (and reversal) of Aphrodite's descent in the same Sapphic poem. That fr. 1 contains the name of Sappho was, presumably, one factor in its positioning in the Alexandrian edition, and this may be reflected in the opening motif of *Heroides* 15:

> ecquid, ut aspecta est studiosae littera dextrae,
>   protinus est oculis cognita nostra tuis?
> an, nisi legisses auctoris nomina Sapphus,
>   hoc breue nescires unde ueniret opus?
>
> Ov. Her. 15.1–4

> When you glimpsed the letter formed by my eager hand, did your eyes know at once that they were mine? Or, had you not read Sappho as the author's name, would you not know the source of this brief work?

---

6 See Hunter 2007.
7 For the debate regarding the authenticity of *Heroides* 15, see Thorsen 2014a, 96–122.

Sappho asks Phaon if he recognizes her handwriting and alludes (presumably) to a superscription such as *Sappho Phaoni sal.* or something similar; in asking the question, however, she both names herself (a very familiar hallmark of Sapphic poetry),[8] and replicates the onomastic 'seal' of the beginning of Sappho's collected edition. As for the tradition of biographical commentary, the very closeness of part of the preserved fragment of Chamaeleon's *On Sappho* (T 252 Voigt) to verses 31–36 of *Heroides* 15 suggests some of what we are missing:[9]

> κ[α]τηγόρηται δ' ὑπ' ἐν[ί]ω[ν] ὡς ἄτακτος οὖ[σα] τὸν τρόπον καὶ γυναικε[ράσ]τρια. τὴν δὲ μορφὴν [εὐ]καταφρόνητος δοκεῖ γε[γον]ένα[ι κα]ὶ δυσειδεστάτη[[ν]], [τ]ὴν μὲν γὰρ ὄψιν φαιώδης [ὑ]πῆρχεν, τὸ δὲ μέγεθος μικρὰ παντελῶς.
>
> Chamaeleon fr. 27 Wehrli = Sappho T 252 Voigt (*P.Oxy.* 1800 fr. 1)[10]

[Sappho] is accused by some of having been disorderly in her character and a woman who loved women. She seems to have been of very mean appearance and very ugly; her complexion was dark, and she was very short...

> si mihi difficilis formam natura negauit,
>   ingenio formae damna repende[11] meae.
> sum breuis, at nomen, quod terras impleat omnes,
>   est mihi; mensuram nominis ipsa fero.
> candida si non sum, placuit Cepheia Perseo
>   Andromede, patriae fusca colore suae.
>
> Ov. *Her.* 15.31–36

If grudging nature has denied me beauty, compensate by my talent for the loss of beauty. I am short, but I have a name which fills every land: my measure is that of my name. If I am not gleaming white, Perseus fell in love with Cepheian Andromeda, whose darkness was that of her homeland.

Somewhat later in *Heroides* 15 Sappho becomes coy about having sex and an orgasm in her sleep: *ulteriora pudet narrare, sed omnia fiunt: | et iuuat et siccae non licet esse mihi* (Ov. *Her.* 15.133–134, 'Shame prevents me telling more, but

---

8 For possible traces of a tradition of such a superscription recorded by the bibliophile Guido de Grana in thirteenth-century Paris, see Stagni 2006, 274, n. 113. See also Ingleheart 2019, 221 n. 64.
9 See also Elisei 2019, 230–233. On the Hellenistic reception of Sappho, see also Hunter, forthcoming.
10 Cf. Thorsen 2019, 33 n. 30 regarding Chamaleon, and *P.Oxy.* 1800 fr. 1 and Thorsen/Berge 2019, 369–371.
11 This is Bentley's emendation of the transmitted *rependo*, cf. Elisei 2019, 230 n. 8 and Thorsen 2014a, 106.

the whole thing happens: I feel pleasure and cannot stay dry').[12] Here it is presumably important not just that this seems to echo a preserved snatch of Sappho,[13] θέλω τί τ' εἴπην, ἀλλά με κωλύει | αἴδως (Sappho fr. 137 Voigt, 'I want to say something to you, but shame prevents me'), but also that the fragment was believed, by a tradition at least as early as Aristotle, to be part of a dialogue between Sappho and Alcaeus, i.e. between Sappho and an admiring man.[14] Without that knowledge, we cannot properly appreciate the wit of the poet of *Heroides* 15. As for the orgasm itself, it might be worth wondering whether *sed omnia fiunt* evokes ἀλλὰ πᾶν τόλματον (Sappho fr. 31.17 Voigt, 'but all can be endured'), just as *siccae non licet esse mihi* may or may not be an interpretative rewriting of χλωροτέρα δὲ ποίας ἔμμι (Sappho fr. 31.14–16 Voigt, 'I am greener than grass');[15] if any of this is on the right lines, then the poet of *Heroides* 15 would (once again) foreshadow those modern interpreters of Sappho 31 who have 'read' that poem as depicting the poet's orgasm.[16]

In *Heroides* 15 the critical (in both senses) tradition is retrojected back to Sappho's own day when she tells Phaon that she loved her many girls *non sine crimine* (*Her.* 15.19, 'not without reproach'). The voice of *Heroides* 15 is of course a Sappho constructed both from her poetry and also from the commentary tradition, in the forefront of which stood the question of the exact nature of Sappho's relationship to the girls who fill her poems; it is this tradition which lies behind Horace's *temperat Archilochi musam pede mascula Sappho* (Hor. *Epist.* 1.19.28, 'manlike Sappho moulds her Muse by the rhythm of Archilochus'), however that verse is to be understood.[17] Chamaeleon, as we have seen (above p. 352), reports that Sappho 'had been accused by some people of being disorderly (ἄτακτος) in her character and a woman who loved women', and the *Suda* says much the same (Σ 107 = Sappho T 253 Voigt). Seneca famously mocks Didymus of Alexandria, who was working at the same time as the poets of the late Republic and early Empire, for an interest in this and other similarly fruitless subjects:

---

12 See also Ingleheart 2019, 216.
13 The very vexed issues surrounding the interpretation and even authorship of this fragment do not affect this point. It may also be worth suggesting that Penelope's remarkable account of dreaming that Odysseus 'slept beside her' (*Od.* 20.88–90), a dream that 'made her heart rejoice' (cf. *iuuat*), lies somewhere behind the Ovidian Sappho's much more explicit account.
14 See Nagy 2007 and Thévenaz 2019, 132–136.
15 For the various modern interpretations of Sappho's phrase cf. Zellner 2006.
16 For further echoes of Sappho in *Heroides* 15, see Thorsen 2014a, 49–68, Elisei 2019, 233 n. 18 and Thorsen 2019b.
17 For ancient interpretations of this verse, see Gram 2019, 106.

> quattuor milia librorum Didymus grammaticus scripsit: misererer si tam multa superuacua legisset. in his libris de patria Homeri quaeritur, in his de Aeneae matre uera, in his libidinosior Anacreon an ebriosior uixerit, in his an Sappho publica fuerit, et alia quae erant dediscenda si scires. i nunc et longam esse uitam nega.
>
> Seneca Epist. 88.37
>
> Didymus the grammarian wrote four thousand books; I would feel sorry for him if he had read so many unnecessary works. In the course of his writings he enquires into Homer's native city, the true identity of Aeneas' mother, whether Anacreon was more given to lust or drunkenness, whether Sappho was a common prostitute, and other matters which you would want to unlearn, should you know them. Off with you, and deny that life is long![18]

If it is unsurprising that some at least of Didymus' researches were 'biographical', this may nevertheless serve to remind us that no ancient poet posed more sharply the 'literature and life' question than did Sappho. In Latin literature we associate that question primarily with Catullus, and it is presumably no accident that it is Catullus who is as close to a 'Roman Sappho' as we have; one of the commentators on Horace *Epist.* 1.19.28 (= T 260c Voigt) defends Sappho as *non mollis, nec fracta uoluptatibus nec impudica*, 'no voluptuary, not broken by pleasures and not unchaste', and these are just the charges against which Catullus amusingly defends himself in Poem 16. That poem should indeed be considered (*inter alia*) as part of the Catullan self-positioning as a Sapphic voice, with Aurelius and Furius cast in the role of the critical tradition.

Beyond what survives of the critical tradition we would very much like to know more about how Sappho was 'conceived'. Did Catullus think of Sappho and Callimachus, the two Greek poets we know he translated, as belonging to different worlds and chronologies, or just as two Greek poets who could serve his needs in different ways?[19] He seems to have thought of them as connected in some way, and of course the Cologne Sappho,[20] which seems to be echoed by Callimachus in the 'Reply to the Telchines', has now deepened that particular plot. Tony Woodman has argued attractively that Sappho is echoed in Poem 65, the 'Callimachean' introduction to a translation from Callimachus,[21] and Poem 66 itself, with its female speaker, interest in female adornment and a wedding rite, is not very far from concerns of Sapphic poetry; not merely does 'the pathos

---

18 Cf. Thorsen/Berge 2019.
19 Cf. Hunter 2006, 142 and Thorsen 2019.
20 *P.Köln* 429, giving a new text of Sappho fr. 58 Voigt, cf. Gronewald/Daniel 2007.
21 Woodman 2002, 59; cf. further Acosta-Hughes 2010, 77.

[of Catull. 66] recall that of Sapphic poems of separation',[22] but *inuita, o regina, tuo de uertice cessi* (Catull. 66.39, 'unwillingly, O queen, did I leave your head'), an all but certainly Callimachean verse which Apollonius may have echoed in the mouth of the virgin Medea,[23] may go back to something such as Ψάπφ', ἦ μάν σ' ἀέκοισ' ἀπυλιμπάνω (Sappho 94.5 Voigt, 'Sappho, truly I leave you behind unwillingly').[24] Thus Horace's (Callimachean) construction of Sappho as not a poet for the *uolgus* probably has earlier roots already in the Latin tradition.

In the second part of this paper I want to pick away at these two questions, namely the relationship between ancient scholarship and the Latin reception and, secondly, the question of Sappho's 'archaicness', through yet another look at Catullus 51:

> ille mi par esse deo uidetur,
> ille, si fas est, superare diuos,
> qui sedens aduersus identidem te
>   spectat et audit
> dulce ridentem, misero quod omnis
> eripit sensus mihi: nam simul te,
> Lesbia aspexi, nihil est super mi
> ...
> lingua sed torpet, tenuis sub artus
> flamma demanat, sonitu suopte
> tintinant aures, gemina teguntur
>   lumina nocte.
> otium, Catulle, tibi molestum est:
> otio exsultas nimiumque gestis:
> otium et reges prius et beatas
>   perdidit urbes.

He seems to me to be equal to a god, he, if it may be, seems to surpass the very gods, who sitting opposite you again and again gazes at you and hears you sweetly laughing. Such a thing takes away all my senses, alas! for whenever I see you, Lesbia, at once no sound of voice remains within my mouth, but my tongue falters, a subtle flame steals down through my limbs, my ears ring with inward humming, my eyes are shrouded in twofold night. Idleness, Catullus, does you harm, you riot in your idleness and wantonness too much. Idleness before now has ruined both kings and wealthy cities.

---

22 Fantuzzi/Hunter 2004, 87. On the Sapphic flavour of the 'Lock of Berenice' cf. further Vox 2000, Acosta-Hughes 2010, 63–81; cf. Thorsen 2019b, 81, 84, 89.
23 Ap. Rhod. 4.1019–1022, cf. Hunter 1995, 24–25.
24 Cf. Vox 2000, 178, see also Elisei 2019, 243–244.

It would, on one hand, be remarkable if Catullus' translation of Sappho 31 did *not* reflect ancient discussion of that poem; the fact that not much of that discussion survives gives us license to push hard at it. Our principal witness is, of course, later in time than Catullus, namely [Longinus] *On the Sublime* 10.1-3, our primary source for Sappho's poem. [Longinus] introduces his citation of Sappho 31 by drawing our attention to Sappho's choice and combination of different παθήματα ('sufferings'), and after the citation he continues:[25]

> οὐ θαυμάζεις ὡς ὑπ<ὸ τὸ> αὐτὸ τὴν ψυχὴν τὸ σῶμα, τὰς ἀκοὰς τὴν γλῶσσαν, τὰς ὄψεις τὴν χρόαν, πάνθ' ὡς ἀλλότρια διοιχόμενα ἐπιζητεῖ, καὶ καθ' ὑπεναντιώσεις ἅμα ψύχεται καίεται, ἀλογιστεῖ φρονεῖ †ἢ γὰρ φοβεῖται ἢ παρ' ὀλίγον τέθνηκεν†[26] ἵνα μὴ ἕν τι περὶ αὐτὴν πάθος φαίνηται, παθῶν δὲ σύνοδος; πάντα μὲν τοιαῦτα γίνεται περὶ τοὺς ἐρῶντας, ἡ λῆψις δ' ὡς ἔφην τῶν ἄκρων καὶ ἡ εἰς ταὐτὸ συναίρεσις ἀπειργάσατο τὴν ἐξοχήν.
>
> [Longinus] *Subl.* 10.3

> Are you not amazed how at the same moment she seeks out soul, body, hearing, tongue, eyes, skin, all as though they belonged to someone else and had left her? With contradictory feelings she is cold and burning at the same time, out of her mind and in control ... so that she reveals herself feeling not a single emotion, but a gathering of emotions. Lovers experience all of these things, but as I said, what makes this description superlative is how she takes up the fiercest of these and combines them into a unit.

Catullus' *omnis ... sensus* may reflect an observation such as [Longinus'] reference to Sappho's παθῶν σύνοδος ('gathering of emotions'), whatever else has determined Catullus' severe reduction of Sappho's list of how her body is affected,[27] but of greater interest perhaps is the claim that Sappho πάνθ' ὡς ἀλλότρια διοιχόμενα ἐπιζητεῖ ('seeks out all as though they belonged to someone else'). This is the origin of so much that used to be written about Sappho's 'objective' description, but the resonances of [Longinus]' language have perhaps not yet been fully explored. The language of literary 'searching and finding', of *inuentio* (cf. e.g. Catull. 116.1), resonates here,[28] but if πάνθ' ὡς ἀλλότρια διοιχόμενα ἐπιζητεῖ could be said of anyone, it could be said of Catullus, for 'translation' is precisely the finding of the οἰκεῖον, 'what is one's own', in the ἀλλότριον, 'what belongs to someone else', *aliena* as Quintilian puts it in a discussion of paraphrase (Quint. *Inst.* 10.5.9). So too διοιχόμενα might suggest the poetry of the past, which is (again) where Catullus searches for 'his own emotions as though

---

25 For the passage to which this quotation belongs, see Thorsen/Berge 2019, 342–344.
26 Text uncertain; Mazzucchi and Russell, in the Loeb edition, accept Weiske's deletion of ἢ γὰρ φοβεῖται ἢ παρ' ὀλίγον τέθνηκεν.
27 For discussion and a survey of the views which have been held cf. e.g. Clark 2008.
28 Cf. Hunter 2006, 31.

they were someone else's'; at the very least [Longinus]' account of Sappho's extraordinary poem may be suggestively applied to the process of translation.[29] There is indeed at least some reason for thinking that Catullus associated the idea of 'translation' with the adoption of a female voice, a voice in other words which really is ἀλλότριον, but which Catullus makes οἰκεῖον, whether through the address in 51 to the ambiguous Lesbia and (perhaps) the final *otium* stanza, or by juxtaposing 66 to a poem about separation from another beloved brother.

As for the *otium* stanza itself, there are two stylistic features, which call for notice in the present context. First, Demetrius, *De elocutione* 140–141 notes that 'charm' (χάριτες) arising from the use of forms of repetition, namely anadiplosis and anaphora, is particularly characteristic of Sappho, and he illustrates this feature with two examples, probably both drawn from wedding-songs (frr. 104a and 114 Voigt).[30] Catullus' familiarity with this Sapphic feature, if not also with the relevant critical tradition (whatever the date of the *De elocutione*), might be thought sufficiently established by the extensive use of repetition and anaphora in the 'Sapphic' wedding-song, Catull. 62 (cf. ll. 1, 3–4, 8–9, 12–13, etc.).[31] It is tempting, then, to take the triple anaphora of *otium* in the final stanza of Poem 51 as a markedly 'Sapphic' feature (and cf. *ille ... ille* and *deo ... diuos*). Secondly, it may be that such changes of direction as that of the *otium* stanza were also seen as distinctively Sapphic,[32] though here the evidence is more fragile. A few chapters after his discussion of repetition in Sappho, Demetrius (*De eloc.*, 148) notes a different, but perhaps related, form of μεταβολή ('change') as indeed Sapphic:

ἔστι δέ τις ἰδίως χάρις Σαπφικὴ ἐκ μεταβολῆς, ὅταν τι εἰποῦσα μεταβάλληται καὶ ὥσπερ μετανοήσηι, οἷον ὕψου δή, φησί, τὸ μέλαθρον ἀέρατε τέκτονες· γαμβρὸς εἰσέρχεται ἶσος Ἄρηϊ, ἀνδρὸς μεγάλου πολλῶι μείζων (fr. 111 V), ὥσπερ ἐπιλαμβανομένη ἑαυτῆς, ὅτι ἀδυνάτωι ἐχρήσατο ὑπερβολῆι, καὶ ὅτι οὐδεὶς τῶι Ἄρηϊ ἶσός ἐστίν.

Demetr. *De eloc.* 148[33]

---

[29] For Poem 51 as a study of the process of translation and imitation cf., e.g., Fantuzzi/Hunter 2004, 472–474.
[30] Marini 1995 surveys quotations of Sappho in Demetrius *De eloc.* See also Thorsen/Berge 2019, 320–323.
[31] See also Harrison 2019, 138.
[32] On the 'turn' in the final stanza of (probably) both Sappho and Catullus cf. e.g. Knox 1984, D'Angour 2006.
[33] I give the text of the quotation from Sappho in Demetrius' version (but with ὕψου for the transmitted νίψω), without seeking to restore the Sapphic text. Cf. Thorsen/Berge 2019, 322.

Charm also arises from a kind of change which is peculiarly characteristic of Sappho. She says something, but then changes direction, as though changing her mind, such as 'Raise high the roof of the hall, builders! The bridegroom, the equal of Ares, is approaching, much taller than a tall man' (fr. 111 Voigt). It is as though she checks herself, because she has used an impossible hyperbole and no one is the equal of Ares.

It is of course a critical commonplace that, in marking a break in the poet's description of physical symptoms and a change of direction, the *otium* stanza may well have been imitative of the end of Sappho's poem (ἀλλὰ πᾶν τόλματον ...), but we should at least consider the possibility that such 'self-correction' had been theorized in Hellenistic criticism as a 'Sapphic' feature.[34] At the very least, there seem to be strong circumstantial reasons to believe that Catullus has completed his translation with a stanza which was not 'Sapphic', but was in the best Sapphic manner, as identified by part at least of the critical tradition, and this would be brilliantly in keeping with the best ancient practice and theory of imitation.[35]

Poetic reworkings of Sappho 31 may also be evidence for ancient discussion of that poem.[36] As is well known, for example, Sappho 31 is reworked in two separate passages of Simaetha's account of her sufferings in Theocritus 2 (Theoc. *Id.* 2.82–90, 106–110), and Roberto Pretagostini argued that whereas the first marked the onset of love, the second marked 'the fear of love (and lovemaking)',[37] though he did not go on to suggest that this reflected two different ways in which Sappho 31 had been understood in ancient tradition, as indeed it has in modern discussion.[38] Nevertheless, creative *mimesis* always involves interpretation as well, and the current example may be no exception. When Simaetha says that she was reduced to 'skin and bones' (Theoc. *Id.* 2.90), this may be no more than a very direct way of saying what Sappho had said, 'I seem

---

34 For a medical interpretation of Catullus' *otium*, see Woodman 2006.
35 Relevant here is the observation of D'Angour 2006, 300 that the self-address *Catulle* in the opening verses of the final stanza may be intended as a 'Sapphic' feature; see also Ingleheart 2019, for a similar point in Ovid, p. 216.
36 Cf., e.g., Wills 1967 and Marcovich 1972.
37 Pretagostini 1984, 105–117; on the use of Sappho 31 in Theocritus 2 cf. also Timpanaro 1978, 233–238 and Acosta-Hughes 2010, 17–29, citing earlier bibliography.
38 Ap. Rhod. 4.16–17 is an evocation of Sappho 31 in a context of panic, rather than erotic desire; given that Sappho 31 had been used in Book 3 to describe Medea's desire for Jason (Ap. Rhod. 3.284–290, 962–965), the repeated echo does not merely chart the consequences of Medea's desire (cf. Hunter 1987, 137, Acosta-Hughes 2010, 42–45), but perhaps also reflects two different ancient understandings of the Sapphic poem. Apollonius' echoing phrases κάματος δυσίμερος (Ap. Rhod. 3.961) and πῆμα δυσίμερον (Ap. Rhod. 4.4) might almost be seen as glossing descriptions of or 'titles for' Sappho 31.

little short of death', but nothing quite seems to correspond in Sappho to Theoc. *Id.* 2.89, ἔρρευν δ' ἐκ κεφαλᾶς πᾶσαι τρίχες, 'all my hair was falling from my head'. Women who do suffer from hair-loss in Greek poetry are, however, the daughters of Proetus, afflicted with μαχλοσύνη ('lewdness, lust') and madness for an offence against Hera (or, just possibly, Dionysus):

καὶ γάρ σφιν κεφαλῇσι κατὰ κνύος αἰνὸν ἔχευεν·
ἀλφὸς γὰρ χρόα πάντα κατέσχεθεν, αἱ δέ νυ χαῖται
ἔρρεον ἐκ κεφαλέων, ψίλωτο δὲ καλὰ κάρηνα.
                            Hesiod fr. 133.3–5 MW = 82 Most = 49 Hirschberger

> On to their heads she poured a terrible scratching, and scabs seized all their skin, and their hair fell from their heads, and their beautiful crowns became bald.

Another verse, surely to be placed very close to this, identifies the cause of the problem: εἵνεκα μαχλοσύνης στυγερῆς τέρεν ὤλεσεν ἄνθος (Hesiod fr. 132 MW = 81 Most = 47 Hirschberger, 'Because of their hateful lewdness she destroyed their delicate flower'). This is just what happens to Simaetha (cf. Theoc. *Id.* 2.83 τὸ δὲ κάλλος ἐτάκετο). Simaetha, then, is made to evoke the lustful daughters of Proetus within a reworking of Sappho 31; this may reflect a moralistic reading of Sappho 31, which Simaetha 'unknowingly' evokes, and/or in trying to make her symptoms as graphic as possible, Simaetha goes beyond Sappho and, again 'unknowingly', condemns herself and her condition from her own mouth by the symptom which she adds to the Sapphic description. The evocation of the Proetides allows us to see how Theocritus then gives full weight to ὡς ἐμάνην (Theoc. *Id.* 2.82, 'I was seized with madness'), as the daughters of Proetus really did go mad. If this suggestion is correct, it may help with the appearance in *Eclogue* 6 (Verg. *Ecl.* 6.48–51) of the Proetides (daughters of Proetus); whatever their place in Calvus[39] or any other Latin poetry to which Vergil there alludes, we now have a place for them in Vergil's main model, Theocritus.[40]

A second passage which falls broadly into the same category is Lucretius' reworking of Sappho 31:[41]

---

[39] Calvus' *Io*, cf. frr. 20–25 Hollis.
[40] Any full discussion of this passage would have to factor in other 'bad' women from Greek poetry: we might think particularly of Neoboule, another μαινόλις γυνή ('raving woman') who has had too much sex, in Archilochus' Cologne epode (a passage well known to Theocritus, cf. Theoc. *Id.* 7.121).
[41] See also Fulkerson 2019, 68.

uerum ubi uementi magis est commota metu mens,
consentire animam totam per membra uidemus
sudoresque ita palloremque exsistere toto
corpore et infringi linguam uocemque aboriri,
caligare oculos, sonere auris, succidere artus,
denique concidere ex animi terrore uidemus
saepe homines: facile ut quiuis hinc noscere possit
esse animam cum animo coniunctam, quae cum animi ui
percussast, exim corpus propellit et icit.

Lucr. 3.152–160

When the mind is moved by a more powerful fear, we see the whole soul through the body share this feeling, with sweating and pallor over the whole body, the tongue broken, the voice fading away, the eyes covered in darkness, the ears ringing, the limbs failing; in short we often see men collapsing because of the mind's terror. From this anyone could easily recognize that the soul is linked to the mind, for when the soul is struck by the strength of the mind, it drives the body forward and propels it.

Lucretius is discussing the relation between the *animus* ('mind') and the *anima* ('soul'), and here he explains how, when the governing *animus* or *mens* ('mind') receives a very powerful emotional stimulant, in this case fear, then there is a bodily reaction as well, i.e. the pattern is *animus* upon *anima* upon *corpus*. We can use this passage, as for example Franco Ferrari has done,[42] to seek to understand the nature of what is happening to Sappho in fr. 31 (panic attack or erotic desire?), but other, more limited conclusions may also be drawn. One thing Lucretius wants to teach us here is not merely that effects upon the *animus* can produce bodily reactions, but that the governing *animus* is located, not in the head, but in the middle of the chest (cf. Lucr. 3.140). Echoes of Sappho 31 were appropriate for making both of these points, with καρδίαν ἐν στήθεσιν (fr. 31.6 Voigt, 'heart ... in the breast') particularly suited to Lucretius' argument. The argument, and its nature, would be related to one made on more than one occasion by Plutarch (cf. *Mor.* 442d–e) in discussing not the body's emotional collapse, but rather the controlling power of reason over the reactions of the body. Odysseus' reason was so strong, we are told, that, though his wife was weeping beside him and he felt pity for her, θυμῶι μὲν γοόωσαν ἐὴν ἐλέαιρε γυναῖκα, | ὀφθαλμοὶ δ' ὡς εἰ κέρα ἕστασαν ἠὲ σίδηρος | ἀτρέμας ἐν βλεφάροισι· δόλωι δ' ὅ γε δάκρυα κεῦθεν (*Od.* 19.210–212, 'his eyes were fixed motionless in their lids, like horn or iron, and with guile did he conceal his tears'); Odysseus is thus a

---

[42] Cf. Ferrari 2010, 175–176.

kind of inversion of Sappho in fr. 31, or vice versa.[43] The use of archaic poetry to illustrate a very 'modern' psychological account would, of course, have been regular in Plutarch's Hellenistic sources, and once again we can get some sense of the ancient discussion we are missing. When [Longinus] notes how Sappho brings 'soul and body' together, he need not of course be reflecting any such discussion, but he might be.

In turning to the question of Sappho's 'archaicness', we could begin, for example, from Syndikus's helpful survey, which notes how in Poem 51 Catullus has transformed Sappho's 'archaic style' (e.g. simple, paratactic listing of symptoms) into one marked by Hellenistic sensibility.[44] There may well be something in this, but I want rather to approach this question (again) by considering Catullus 50 and 51 as a diptych.[45] Much in Poem 50 does indeed seem to look forward to 51 (e.g. Catull. 50.13 foreshadows the impossibility of speech), and the speaker of Catullus 51 or indeed Sappho 31 could easily have uttered 50.16–17, 'I wrote you this poem so that you could realize my pain'. The best modern discussion of the poems as a diptych is that of David Wray[46], but when he observes that the description of 'erotic distress' in the two poems is 'strikingly similar' (p. 98) we should, I think, pause. The symptoms of desire in 50 are largely behavioural – no appetite, inability to sleep, tossing and turning leading (admittedly) to desperate weariness, whereas in Sappho 31 and Catullus 51 they are largely internal and physical. There is, of course, no firm distinction to be drawn, but when we put the poems together, what should strike us is in fact the difference between them. In Sappho and in Catullus 51 we have a 'fine fire', whereas in 50 the poet is *tuo lepore / incensus... facetiisque* (Catull. 50.7–8, 'fired by your wit ... and fun'), and seem to have crossed the line into metaphor; Sappho sees nothing, and in 51 the poet's eyes are 'hidden in night' (*gemina teguntur / lumina nocte*), whereas in 50 'sleep will not cover the eyes in rest', *nec somnus tegeret quiete ocellos* (Catull. 50.10, 'nor sleep spread rest over my eyes'), where the similarity of vocabulary between the poems merely calls attention to the differ-

---

[43] It is worth noting in this context that when Sappho hears the news of Phaon's departure in *Heroides* 15 and we have an evocation of fr. 31, one of her symptoms is *lacrimae deerant oculis* (l. 111), for which there is no parallel in Sappho or Catullus, cf. Thorsen 2014a, 64–65. One of the most striking uses of Sappho 31 in subsequent literature is Plut. *Mor.* 81d–e, where Sappho's 'broken tongue' and 'fire under the skin' are signs not of erotic desire, but of a previously self-confident young man who has started to make real progress in philosophy, see Thorsen/Berge 2019, 350–351.
[44] Syndikus 1984, 255–256.
[45] Cf. Hunter 2007, 221, and 2019, 160.
[46] Wray 2001, 95–109.

ence. Is this difference perhaps a marker of what we might call the 'modernity' of Poem 50, i.e. the evolution of a metaphorical language of desire, itself owing much to Sappho, but distinguished in various ways from her poetic mode? When at the opening of *Amores* 1.2 Ovid describes his symptoms, they are precisely the symptoms of Catullus 50, not 51; this is how love is for the 'modern' poet. The suggestion then is that Poems 50 and 51 may at least allow us to approach the question of Catullus' placing of Sappho within literary history, even if most of the answer remains shrouded in darkness.

Bibliography

Acosta-Hughes, B. 2010. *Arion's Lyre: Archaic Lyric into Hellenistic Poetry*, Princeton.
Clark, C.A. 2008. 'The poetics of manhood? Nonverbal behaviour in Catullus 51', *CPh* 103, 257–281.
D'Angour, A. 2006. 'Conquering love: Sappho 31 and Catullus 51', *CQ* 56.1, 297–300.
Elisei, C. 2019. 'Sappho as a Pupil of the praeceptor amoris and Sappho as magistra amoris: Some Lessons of the *Ars amatoria* Anticipated in *Heroides* 15', in: Th.S. Thorsen/S. Harrison (eds.), *Roman Receptions of Sappho*, Oxford, 227–248.
Elisei, C. forthcoming. *P. Ovidii Nasonis Heroidum Epistula 15: Sappho Phaoni, edited with introduction and commentary*, Berlin.
Fantuzzi, M./Hunter, R. 2004. *Tradition and Innovation in Hellenistic Poetry*, Cambridge.
Ferrari, F. 2010. *Sappho's Gift*, Ann Arbor.
Fulkerson, R. 2019. 'Lucretius and Sapphic Voluptas', in: T.S. Thorsen/S.J. Harrison (eds.), *Roman Receptions of Sappho*, Classical Presences, Oxford, 61–76.
Gram, L.M. 2019. '*Odi et amo*: on Lesbia's name in Catullus', in: T.S. Thorsen/S.J. Harrison (eds.), *Roman Receptions of Sappho*, Classical Presences, Oxford, 95–118.
Harrison, S.J. 2019. 'Shades of Sappho in Vergil', in: T.S. Thorsen/S.J. Harrison (eds.), *Roman Receptions of Sappho*, Classical Presences, Oxford, 137–150.
Hunter, R. 1987. 'Medea's flight: the fourth book of the *Argonautica*', *CQ* 37.1, 129–39 [= Hunter 2008, 42–58].
Hunter, R. 1995. 'The divine and human map of the *Argonautica*', *SyllClass* 6.1, 13–27 [= Hunter 2008, 257–277].
Hunter, R. 2006. *The Shadow of Callimachus: Studies in the Reception of Hellenistic Poetry at Rome*, Cambridge.
Hunter, R. 2007. 'Sappho and Latin poetry', in: G. Bastianini/A. Casanova (eds.), *I papiri di Saffo e di Alceo*, Florence, 213–225.
Ingleheart, J. 2019. '*Vates Lesbia*: Images of Sappho in the Poetry of Ovid', in: T.S. Thorsen/S.J. Harrison (eds.), *Roman Receptions of Sappho*, Classical Presences, Oxford, 205–226.
Knox, P.E. 1984. 'Sappho, fr. 31 LP and Catullus 51: a suggestion', *QUCC* 17.2, 97–102.
Marcovich, M. 1972. 'Sappho fr. 31: anxiety attack or love declaration?', *CQ* 22.1, 19–32.
Marini, N. 1995. 'Saffo nel *De Elocutione* di Demetrio', in: L. Dubois (ed.), *Poésie et lyrique antiques*, Lille, 73–95.

Nagy, G. 2007. 'Did Sappho and Alcaeus ever meet? Symmetries of myth and ritual in performing the songs of ancient Lesbos', in: A. Bierl/R. Lämmle/K. Wesselmann (eds.), *Literatur und Religion I, Wege zu einer mythisch-rituellen Poetik bei den Griechen, Basiliensia – Mythos Eikon Poiesis*, vol. 1.1, Berlin, 211–269.

Prauscello, L. 2005. 'Note di commento a testi poetici', *Communicazioni dell'Istituto Papirologico G. Vitelli* 6, 51–67.

Pretagostini, R. 1984. *Ricerche sulla poesia alessandrina*, Rome.

Stagni, E. 2006. 'Testi latini e biblioteche tra Parigi e la valle della Loira (secoli XII–XIII): i manoscritti di Guido de Grana', in: S.M. Peruzzi (ed.), *Boccaccio e le letterature romanze tra Medioevo e Rinascimento: Atti del Convegno internazionale 'Boccaccio e la Francia', Firenze-Certaldo 19–20 Maggio 2003—19–20 Maggio 2004*, Florence, 221–287.

Syndikus, H.P. 1984. *Catull, Eine Interpretation*, vol. 1, Darmstadt.

Thorsen, T.S. 2014. *Ovid's Early Poetry: From his Single Heroides to his Remedia amoris*, Cambridge.

Thorsen, T.S. 2019. 'Introduction: Ecce Sappho', in: T.S. Thorsen/S.J. Harrison (eds.), *Roman Receptions of Sappho, Classical Presences*, Oxford, 1–26.

Thorsen, T.S. 2019b. 'Sappho: Transparency and Obstruction', in: T.S. Thorsen/S.J. Harrison (eds.), *Roman Receptions of Sappho, Classical Presences*, Oxford, 27–244.

Thorsen, T.S. 2019c. 'As Important as Callimachus? An Essay on Sappho in Catullus and Beyond', in: T.S. Thorsen/S.J. Harrison (eds.), *Roman Receptions of Sappho, Classical Presences*, Oxford, 77–94.

Thorsen, T.S. 2019d. 'Sappho, Alcaeus, and the Literary Timing of Horace', in: T.S. Thorsen/S.J. Harrison (eds.), *Roman Receptions of Sappho, Classical Presences*, Oxford, 165–184.

Thorsen, T.S. 2019e. 'The Newest Sappho (2016) and Ovid's Heroides 15', in: T.S. Thorsen/S.J. Harrison (eds.), *Roman Receptions of Sappho, Classical Presences*, Oxford, 249–264.

Thorsen, T.S./Berge, R.E. 2019. 'Receiving receptions received: A new collection of testimonia sapphica c. 600 BCE-1000 CE', in: T.S. Thorsen/S.J. Harrison (eds.), *Roman Receptions of Sappho, Classical Presences*, Oxford, 289–402.

Timpanaro, S. 1978. *Contributi di filologia e di storia della lingua Latina*, Rome.

Vox, O. 2000. 'Sul genere grammaticale della Chioma di Berenice', *MD* 44, 175–181.

Wills, G. 1967, 'Sappho 31 and Catullus 51', *GRBS* 8.3, 167–197.

Woodman, T. 2002. '*Biformis vates*: the *Odes*, Catullus and Greek lyric', in: D. Feeney/T. Woodman (eds.), *Traditions and Contexts in the Poetry of Horace*, Cambridge, 53–64.

Woodman, T. 2006. 'Catullus 51: a suitable case for treatment?', *CQ* 56.2, 610–611.

Wray, D. 2001. *Catullus and the Poetics of Roman Manhood*, Cambridge.

Zellner, H. 2006. 'Sappho's supra-superlatives', *CQ* 56, 292–297.

20 One Verse of Mimnermus? Latin Elegy and Archaic Greek Elegy

What archaic Greek elegy might have meant for Roman poets, and indeed how much of it they knew, have usually been discussed in the context of 'the origins of Latin love-elegy';[1] at least as instructive (as so often) is the literary history which Roman poets and scholars themselves constructed.

In the *Ars Poetica* Horace offers more than one brief history of poetic genres. When he is setting out the historical functions of poetry within society, an account which does not rely upon a strict regard for metre as the defining criterion of 'genre' (vv. 391–407),[2] Horace speaks of poetry of an early (i.e. in our terms 'archaic') date as 'showing men how to live' (*uitae monstrata uia est*), and he is no doubt there thinking of elegiac ὑποθῆκαι and gnomic verse, as well presumably of Hesiod's hexameter *Works and Days* and (perhaps) the Hesiodic *Precepts of Cheiron*; Isocrates too observes that Hesiod, Theognis and Phocylides are praised as 'the best advisers for men's lives', although their ὑποθῆκαι are on the whole ignored (*To Nicocles* 5 = Theognis T 5 Gerber), and it was certainly possible to view the poetry of Theognis as γνωμολογίαι (Plutarch, *How to study poetry* 16c),[3] or as simply 'about virtue and vice' and as 'an essay about people' ('Xenophon', Theognis T 6 Gerber).[4] More specific, however, is a much discussed history of poetic genres from earlier in the poem:

> res gestae regumque ducumque et tristia bella
> quo scribi possent numero, monstrauit Homerus;
> uersibus impariter iunctis querimonia primum,   75
> post etiam inclusa est uoti sententia compos;
> quis tamen exiguos elegos emiserit auctor,
> grammatici certant et adhuc sub iudice lis est.
> Archilochum proprio rabies armauit iambo;
> hunc socci cepere pedem grandesque coturni,   80
> alternis aptum sermonibus et popularis
> uincentem strepitus et natum rebus agendis.

Horace, *Ars Poetica* 73–82

---

1 Cf. ch. 9 of Cairns 1979, which also usefully reviews earlier contributions.
2 On this passage add to the commentators Hunter 2009, 48–52.
3 Cf. Hunter/Russell 2011, 88.
4 On this very interesting passage of uncertain authorship cf. H.R. Breitenbach, *RE* 9 A.1927–1928, West 1974, 56. For other references to the poetry of Theognis as 'precepts' cf. West 1992, I 172.

With an interestingly refined and almost 'modern' historical perspective, Horace seems here to come very close to a distinction between 'anonymous' oral and inscribed poetry, on one side, and written poems of identifiable authors, on the other. The dichotomy may hold, as in fact it does historically, for hexameter poetry as much as for elegy – Aristotle was unable to name any poet before Homer, 'but it is likely that there were many' (*Poetics* 1448b28–30) – but Horace apparently draws a distinction between the treatment of 'authored' elegy (*quis... auctor*) and that of the immediately surrounding genres. Homer's genius set the pattern for the writing of historical and martial epic in hexameter, but it is not said that Homer 'invented' the hexameter, any more than Archilochus 'invented' *iambi* – he merely brought out their true nature and set the pattern for drama and subsequent iambic poets to follow; Horace's literary history here has good Greek precedent.[5] Ancient writers may indeed use the idea of 'the first inventor' for a great originary figure, such as Homer for epic poetry,[6] and it may be thought that the explicit raising of the question of the 'first inventor' of elegy suggests an analogous role for Homer and Archilochus (i. e. these are genres on which the *grammatici* have in fact reached a conclusion), but there is, I think, something at stake and something to be gained by pushing hard here at the idea of 'invention' in the strict sense.[7]

A very late text tells us that Democritus (B 16 D-K) ascribed the invention (in whatever meaning) of the hexameter to Musaeus and that the late fifth-century Athenian politician and poet Critias ascribed it to Orpheus (B 2 D-K),[8] but Horace, both here and in the poetic history at vv. 391–407, in which Orpheus actually occurs, keeps quiet about any such 'invention'. In the beginning, then, was the hexameter (as also the iambus), almost existing by nature.[9] Horace has an important forerunner here in the Hellenistic elegist Hermesianax who, in his account of the love-life of famous poets (fr. 7 Powell), follows a partly chronological, partly generic order: Orpheus, Musaeus, Hesiod, Homer, followed by

---

5 Cf., e.g., Brink on v. 74.
6 Rostagni's notes on this passage of the *Ars Poetica* focus these issues more clearly than do Brink's.
7 Whether or not Horace's verses have anything to do with Roman love-elegy has been much debated (cf., e.g., Fries 1993), but v. 78 makes it clear that the reference of v. 77 is primarily to archaic Greek elegy; it is not a question of a difference between *exigui elegi* and other *elegi*.
8 Mallius Theodorus, *Grammatici Latini* VI.589 Keil.
9 This is a slightly different point from, though obviously related to, Aristotle's view that nature herself 'found' (εὗρε) the iambic trimeter as the appropriate metre for the spoken parts of drama (*Poetics* 1449a24) and 'teaches' that the hexameter is the appropriate metre for a lengthy narrative (1460a4).

Mimnermus and Antimachus (*qua* elegiac poet), but of all the genres which Hermesianax includes — hexameters, elegiacs, lyric and tragedy — only elegiacs are given an 'invention', by Mimnermus:[10]

> Μίμνερμος δέ, τὸν ἡδὺν ὃς εὕρετο πολλὸν ἀνατλὰς
> ἦχον καὶ μαλακοῦ πνεῦμα τὸ πενταμέτρου,
> καίετο μὲν Ναννοῦς, πολιῶι δ' ἐπὶ πολλάκι λωτῶι
> κημωθεὶς κώμους εἶχε σὺν Ἐξαμύηι.
>
> Hermesianax fr. 7. 35–38 Powell[11]

> Mimnermus, who after long endurance discovered the sweet sound and the breath of the soft pentameter, burned for Nanno, and –bound with his ancient flute– often went revelling with Examyes.

Mimnermus' invention was, strictly speaking, the pentameter, which he then linked to the hexameter to create the elegiac couplet. Horace too raises the issue of elegy's invention, though he is unable to name an inventor, because the matter remained one of scholarly dispute (in the theory most familiar to us the three contenders were Archilochus, Callinus and Mimnermus).[12] Why this matters is because the rhetoric of 'invention' comes to mark the elegiac couplet, whether or not it does so in this passage of Horace, as a secondary development from stichic hexameters, and elegy as a 'deviation' from an approved, we might almost say 'normal', rhythm of both poetry and life was then an idea which was extremely important to the Roman elegists. The idea of elegy as deviation, as the removal of something from every second hexameter, is probably most starkly expressed by Ovid at the head of his *Amores*:

> arma graui numero uiolentaque bella parabam
>   edere, materia conueniente modis.
> par erat inferior uersus; risisse Cupido
>   dicitur atque unum surripuisse pedem.
>
> Ovid, *Amores* 1.1.1–4

---

10 On other aspects of this passage cf. Hunter 2006b, 120–122.
11 In v. 36 πνεῦμα τό is Dalecamp's emendation for the transmitted πνεῦμ' ἀπό.
12 Didymus p. 387 Schmidt, cf. further Hunter 2006b, 120–121. For a suggestion as to how 'rivalry' between Archilochus and Mimnermus may have played out in Hellenistic poetry cf. Hunter 2011, 235–236 [= 2008, 555–556].

Hermesianax's description of Mimnermus[13] allows us to see that, although the elegiac couplet is, historically speaking, not a secondary derivation from the hexameter, this idea was not very far away in the literary theorizing of the Hellenistic period, and Roman elegists did not have to push very hard to reach what was for them an ideologically satisfactory version of literary history.

Few conclusions about individual poets can be drawn from Horace's refusal to name a specific Greek elegist in *Ars Poetica* 75–78; it is in fact the case that there was, by common consent, no towering archaic elegist to match Homer in epic, and there is no clear evidence for an Alexandrian 'canon' of elegiac poets, to sit alongside, for example, the nine lyric poets.[14] Tyrtaeus is sometimes cited alongside Homer, as indeed he is at *Ars Poetica* 401–402 (cf., e.g., Dio Chrysostom 2.29, 36.10 = Tyrtaeus T 34, 10 G-P),[15] but in the specific context of the power of verses to inspire soldiers. Archilochus, whose stature in the critical tradition as a whole was second only to Homer, was primarily conceived of as an iambic poet, though his achievements in elegy were very far from neglected,[16] and the Alexandrian edition of his elegies was presumably available for any Roman poet who wished to find it.[17] Nevertheless, the complete absence of explicit reference to archaic elegists, not just in Quintilian (if we ignore a curious passage (10.1.56) which seems to treat Tyrtaeus as a hexameter poet), but also in a poet as conscious of literary history as Ovid is worth pondering, even if you believe — as I

---

13 Spanoudakis 2001, 428–429 suggests that Hermesianax may here be indebted to Philitan praise of Mimnermus. He also interprets πολλὸν ἀνατλάς in Hermesianax's notice of Mimnermus as a reference to the Hellenistic and Roman ideal of scholarly toil, cf. πολλὰ μογήσας in Philitas fr. 10 Powell; others have seen this rather as a reference to something in Mimnermus' alleged biography and associated it with a (curious) note of Porphyrio on Horace, *Epistles* 1.6.65 'Mimnermus ... shows that love affairs bring more trouble than pleasure' (T 11 Gerber). I have wondered whether we should not (also?) recall *Milanion nullos fugiendo ... labores* (Propertius 1.1.9) and Ovid, *Amores* 1.9 (*militat omnis amans...*), and see in the contrast between 'soft' elegiac poetry and the alleged rigours of the elegiac life another occasional theme of Roman elegy building upon something already in the Greek tradition. It may or may not be worth suggesting that the repeated *turpe* in *Amores* 1.9.4 would in Greek be αἰσχρόν (both words have both moral and physical senses), and this is a word which is prominent in, for example, Mimnermus fr. 1 (v. 6) and cf. also Tyrtaeus 10.21–27 (the sight of a fallen 'old soldier' is αἰσχρόν in both senses).
14 Cf. Lightfoot 1999, 90–91, Hunter 2011, 233 [= 2008, 552–553].
15 Russell accepts Emperius' deletion of the reference to Tyrtaeus at Dio 36.10, but even if it is an interpolation, it illustrates how the interpolator, rather in this case than Dio himself, put the two poets together.
16 Cf. Hunter 2011, 234–235 [= 2008, 554–555].
17 There was probably a single book of elegies in the Alexandrian edition of Archilochus, cf. Obbink 2006, 1–2.

do — that, for example, the 'sphragis' poem, *Amores* 1.15, evokes Theognis' *sphragis* (vv. 237–252), in part to create 'a sense of elegiac tradition, a chain of great poets, Theognis, Callimachus, Ovid himself, through whom that tradition is constantly refreshed';[18] when Ovid looks explicitly to archaic Greek forebears in love poetry, it is always to Sappho and Anacreon that he turns,[19] with Callimachus and Philitas heading the elegiac list (cf. *AA* 3.329–331, *RA* 757–762). In *Tristia* 2 Ovid virtually argues that *all* past poetry (including Homer) was about love, but again there is no mention of archaic Greek elegy (vv. 361ff.).

Nevertheless, despite this general Roman silence about archaic Greek elegy, a silence for which there is all but certainly more than one reason, including the relative unfamiliarity of texts, Mimnermus clearly held something of a special place for some Roman poets. At *Epistles* 1.6.65–66 Horace cites him for the view 'that there is no pleasure without love and jests', in a context in which this sentiment could be used to justify an entirely hedonistic lifestyle. The reference of course is to verses of Mimnermus, perhaps a complete poem,[20] which are preserved for us by Stobaeus:

τίς δὲ βίος, τί δὲ τερπνὸν ἄτερ χρυσῆς Ἀφροδίτης;
τεθναίην, ὅτε μοι μηκέτι ταῦτα μέλοι,
κρυπταδίη φιλότης καὶ μείλιχα δῶρα καὶ εὐνή,
οἷ' ἥβης ἄνθεα γίνεται ἁρπαλέα
ἀνδράσιν ἠδὲ γυναιξίν· ἐπεὶ δ' ὀδυνηρὸν ἐπέλθῃ   5
γῆρας, ὅ τ' αἰσχρὸν ὁμῶς καὶ κακὸν ἄνδρα τιθεῖ,
αἰεί μιν φρένας ἀμφὶ κακαὶ τείρουσι μέριμναι,
οὐδ' αὐγὰς προσορῶν τέρπεται ἠελίου,
ἀλλ' ἐχθρὸς μὲν παισίν, ἀτίμαστος δὲ γυναιξίν·
οὕτως ἀργαλέον γῆρας ἔθηκε θεός.

Mimnermus fr. 1 West[21]

What life is there, what is sweet without golden Aphrodite? May I die, when these things are no longer what I care about — secret love-making and winning gifts and bed, the flowers of youth which men and women must snatch. When grievous old age comes, which makes a man both ugly and wretched, then destructive cares wear his mind away and he finds no pleasure in looking upon the rays of the sun, but he is hateful to young boys and held in no honour by women. So terrible a thing has god made old age.

---

18 Hunter 2012b, 165, where the case for Ovid's evocation of Theognis is argued.
19 Joined as erotic experts as early as Plato, *Phaedrus* 235c3.
20 Cf., e.g., Faraone 2008, 19–20, citing earlier bibliography.
21 κακόν in v. 6 is Hermann's emendation for καλόν.

That Horace should refer to verses preserved for us also in a late anthology is perhaps not an accident. How much of Mimnermus' poetry was readily available at Rome is not easy to guess, though Strabo at least, whether at Rome or elsewhere, seems to have had access to texts of some substance.[22] For elegiac poets who felt a particular closeness to Callimachus, however, Mimnermus' name had of course a particular significance, because of the place of honour which, in the 'Reply to the Telchines', Callimachus gives that archaic poet as one of his forebears in 'sweet elegy'. At *Epistles* 2.2.99–101 Horace notes that the designation 'an Alcaeus' is the highest (empty) compliment which can be paid to a lyric poet, whereas for an elegist it is 'a Callimachus', but one could go even further to 'a Mimnermus':

> discedo Alcaeus puncto illius; ille meo quis?
> quis nisi Callimachus? si plus adposcere uisus,
> fit Mimnermus et optiuo cognomine crescit.
>
> Horace, *Epistles* 2.2.99–101

No extensive knowledge of Mimnermus' poetry is necessarily assumed in this passage. He is a great (and perhaps shadowy) figure, made well known by (a single passage of) Callimachus, and of whom (perhaps) a few famous passages were familiar; it would indeed suit Horace's satirical tone if 'Mimnermus' was indeed little more than a name to be adopted or evoked by a pretentious poet. It has in the past often been thought that Horace here has Propertius in mind; that does not seem strictly necessary, but it is indeed Propertius who famously gives Mimnermus an explicit place in his poetry:

> quid tibi nunc misero prodest graue dicere carmen
>   aut Amphioniae moenia flere lyrae?
> plus in amore ualet Mimnermi uersus Homero:
>   carmina mansuetus lenia quaerit Amor.
>
> Propertius 1.9.9–12

Propertius is here addressing an epic poet who has fallen in love, and who therefore needs verses to win over his beloved; Mimnermus is chosen as both a 'love poet' and as an elegist.[23] *Mimnermi uersus* is, from one perspective, virtual-

---

[22] Cf. the summary in Bowie 1997, 60.
[23] Note the familiar contrast with *graue carmen* (cf., e. g., Ovid, *Amores* 1.1.1, cited above) and the elegiac resonance of *tibi ... misero*, pointing to the *miserum me* of the opening verse of the book (and cf. Hinds 1998, 29–34); *flere* in v.10 makes the point that what Ponticus needs is *flebilis elegia*, not grim epics.

ly synonymous with *mollem... uersum* at 1.7.19, in the poem which forms a pair with, and is recalled by, 1.9. 'Soft verse' is elegiac poetry on love, and in 1.9 Propertius may have chosen Mimnermus as simply a founding father of elegy and/or as one made famous by Callimachus,[24] and he may be thinking particularly of the *Nanno*, or even just what we call Mimnermus fr. 1 West (cited above, famous verses perhaps reworked as early as Simonides, *PMG* 584 = 298 Poltera). Propertius' expression, however, allows us also to feel the meaning 'in love a [i.e. one] verse of Mimnermus is more effective than Homer',[25] and this is indeed how many earlier critics have understood Propertius' line.[26] If we ask which Mimnerman verse fits the bill, then — as Horace, *Epistles* 1.6.65–66 suggest — we can hardly go past what we call fr. 1.1.[27] Ponticus needs verses which will help him win his girlfriend (*prodest*, v.9), and to remind the object of desire that there is no pleasure in life without the joys of Aphrodite cannot at least do any harm in such a situation. To put the case in extreme form: what better example to prove that 'one verse of elegy' is worth more than (all of) Homer than a poet of whom 'one verse' was indeed far better known than all the rest?

However Propertius' reference to Mimnermus is to be interpreted, there are good grounds for believing that Mimnermus fr. 1 was indeed important more generally for establishing the 'elegiac lifestyle'.[28] The two themes of the pleasures of Aphrodite and the hatefulness of old age have of course a general significance here, but v. 3 'secret lovemaking and winning gifts and bed' seems also

---

[24] There is in fact a parallel sequence at Propertius 2.34.25–32 with Callimachus and Philetas taking the place of Mimnermus. It is not, I think, necessary to see Propertius here taking a position on the identity of the πρῶτος εὑρετής of elegy (so, e.g., Rothstein and Fedeli *ad loc.*), a view I adopted too hastily in Hunter 2006b, 125; so too, the interpretation of *Mimnermi uersus* as 'the pentameter' offers too narrow a focus for Propertius' point.

[25] It is hard to doubt that the implication is 'than all of Homer', whether or not (cf. Fedeli *ad loc.*) we see here a *comparatio compendiaria*. Commentators rightly adduce *Anth. Pal.* 9.190.3 [= Anon. xxxviii *FGE* = Erinna T 7 Neri], where Erinna's three lines are claimed to be 'equal to Homer'.

[26] Cf., e.g., the commentaries of Butler and Barber, Enk, and Richardson *ad loc.*, and the translation of Guy Lee, 'a line of Mimnermus is more help than Homer'.

[27] It is, of course, tempting to extend that to the whole couplet, fr. 1.1–2, so that the elegiac form is clear; *uersus*, however, more obviously suggests a single verse than a single couplet. The 'verse (ἔπος) of Mimnermus' referred to at Alexander Aetolus fr. 5.4–5 Powell-Magnelli [= fr. 8 Lightfoot] may indeed also have been our fr. 1.1, as almost suggested by Bach 1837, 344; for ἔπος of a single verse cf. LSJ s.v. IVa. Lightfoot's translation, 'borrowing Mimnermus' axiom', suggests that interpretation. Wilamowitz 1913, 285 rightly notes that the Mimnerman verse(s) referred to by Alexander need not have specified paederastic love, and in the state of the text of v.5 we need not assume that it necessarily contained a reference to drinking.

[28] Cf. further Hunter 2006a, 39–40.

to prescribe an Ovidian programme for a happy life. The meaning of v. 3 has in fact been much debated, but even if 'Mimnermus can hardly be talking here of adulterous love' (Allen *ad loc.*), it is not difficult to see what an Ovid would make of this verse. The μείλιχα δῶρα, however they are to be interpreted in Mimnermus himself,[29] make obvious sense within the context of the erotic/elegiac lifestyle; it is at least worth noting that Ares seems to have 'given much' to Aphrodite to persuade her to 'commit adultery' with him (*Odyssey* 8.269), and this song of Demodocus is another passage of early verse which looks forward in various ways to Roman elegy.[30]

The opening couplet of Mimnermus fr. 1, with χάρις replacing βίος, is cited by Plutarch within the context of a discussion, heavily indebted to Aristotle, about the difference between *akrasia*, 'incontinence' in which the passions get the better of the reason which urges good conduct and which 'unwillingly betrays τὸ καλόν', and *akolasia*, 'intemperance, abandon', in which reason happily yields to the immoral urgings of the desires and 'willingly is swept away into τὸ αἰσχρόν' (*On moral virtue* 445d-6c). Mimnermus fr. 1.1–2, together with Alexis fr. 273.4–5 K-A ('eating, drinking, success with Aphrodite: everything else are added extras'), is there cited as the kind of thing which the *akolastoi* say. In the opening passage of the opening poem of Book 1 Propertius portrays himself as the defeated victim of *improbus Amor*, compelled *nullo uiuere consilio*, perhaps 'to live without the guidance of reason',[31] and held under the sway of *furor*.[32] Plutarch might well class such a man as *akolastos*,[33] and Mimnermus fr. 1.1–2

---

29 Allen sees δῶρα καὶ εὐνή as a hendiadys, a view which I do not really understand. On 'the gifts of the gods' cf. further below. ἁρπαλέα is another word which may have taken on new resonances in the light of the developing poetic tradition: 'alluring, attractive', but then also 'to be seized', with reference to the 'gather ye rosebuds while ye may' idea.
30 Cf. Hunter 2012a.
31 Cf. Fedeli *ad loc.* At Aristotle, *EN* 7.1150b22, the impetuous (προπετεῖς) among the *akrateis* 'are led by passion because they do not deliberate (βουλεύσασθαι)'; at Terence, *Eunuchus* 57–58 Parmeno says of *amor, quae res in se neque consilium neque modum / habet ullum*. Heyworth 2007, 4–5 understands *nullo uiuere consilio* in the narrower sense 'live to no purpose', i.e. not write poetry.
32 Cf. Cairns 1974, 102–107.
33 Relevant here, as Roy Gibson reminded me, is the closeness of depictions of the hedonistic life of Mark Antony to that of the elegiac, notably Propertian, *persona*, cf. esp. Griffin 1985, ch. 2, though Griffin does not consider how Greek ethical terminology would have described either Antony or the Propertian *persona*. In his *Life of Antony*, Plutarch uses both *akolasia* (2.3, 36.1 (the 'bad horse of Plato's *Phaedrus*') and *akrasia* (*Comparatio* 4) of Antony, but presumably without precisely distinguishing between them as he does in *On moral virtue*; cf. further Duff 1999, 279–280.

stands for Plutarch as a motto for such a dissolute lifestyle. It might be worth noting in this context that some ancient scholars appear to have associated elegy with madness (τὸ παραφρονεῖν) and unrestrained sexual behaviour (τὸ ἀκολασταίνειν), cf. *Etymologicum Magnum* 326.6–10; not very much can, of course, be made of this tenuous evidence,[34] but if Propertius was aware of the connection, then this becomes another way (of many) in which the opening poem of the *Monobiblos* is a 'display' of what elegy is.[35] So too, for what it is worth, in *On moral virtue* Plutarch describes the lover who tries to use his reason against his passion as using the healthy part of his soul against the part which is swollen and unhealthy (448b), and this may remind us of the pleas of Propertius in 1.1 for *non sani pectoris auxilia*.

On occasion Roman elegists, most notably Propertius and Ovid, do indeed seem to open themselves to criticism of this kind, to be — if you like — Mimnermuses, as Plutarch sees it, though it is of course part of the strategy of Propertius 1.1, and perhaps of Roman love-elegy more generally, that the poetic voice hovers between someone who enjoys the situation in which he finds himself (an *akolastos*) and someone who knows that there is a better way and wishes he had the strength to take it (an *akratês*). We might also construct the elegiac position of *akolasia* from another famous fragment of early elegy, Callinus fr. 1, which might have been known to Roman poets, though there is in fact no evidence that it, or indeed the poet himself,[36] actually was; the fragment reaches us only through preservation in Stobaeus' collection of extracts 'in praise of boldness':

μέχρις τέο κατάκεισθε; κότ' ἄλκιμον ἕξετε θυμόν,
 ὦ νέοι; οὐδ' αἰδεῖσθ' ἀμφιπερικτίονας
ὧδε λίην μεθιέντες; ἐν εἰρήνῃ δὲ δοκεῖτε
 ἧσθαι, ἀτὰρ πόλεμος γαῖαν ἅπασαν ἔχει ...

Callinus fr. 1.1–4 West

---

34 Cf. West 1974, 8.
35 The Milanion-exemplum is clearly programmatic for the book as a whole: Propertius will seek to get his girl, *nullos fugiendo labores*. I do not rule out the possibility that this exemplum owes something to Theognis 1283–1294, tormented verses which nevertheless put Atalante in the elegiac mainstream.
36 Strabo clearly knew more Callinus than we do, though I think we should be more cautious than, e.g., Aloni/Iannucci 2007, 117 (and cf. Aloni 2009, 171) in using the few testimonia as evidence for an extensive familiarity with his poetry; later Roman metricians knew him as a name, but probably no more than that that. Christensen 2000 argues that Achilles Tatius 2.5.1 alludes to Callinus fr. 1.1; if this is correct, it is important that it is indeed fr. 1.1 to which Achilles' readers are referred.

> How long will you recline? When, young men, will you have a bold spirit? Have you no shame before those who live around, when you are so very slack like this? You think that you are sitting around in peace, but warfare grips the whole land...

The poetic voice seeks to rouse the young men's fighting spirit. Scholars debate as to whether they are in fact preparing to fight, so that the 'abuse' designed to make them feel αἰδώς is a kind of martial tactic, or whether (as seems to me more likely) they are reclining at a symposium,[37] but looking back from later ages the answer must have seemed clear. The Propertian *persona* can sometimes sound as if it is Callinus' 'young men' answering back, 'How long will you lie there? Well, actually, we like it where we are ...'; one thinks of Propertius' claims for his 'lifestyle',

> qualem si cuncti cuperent decurrere uitam
>   et pressi multo membra iacere mero,
> non ferrum crudele neque esset bellica nauis,
>   nec nostra Actiacum uerteret ossa mare,
> nec totiens propriis circum oppugnata triumphis
>   lassa foret crinis soluere Roma suos.
> me certe merito poterunt laudare minores:
>   laeserunt nullos pocula nostra deos
>
> Propertius 2.15.41–48

or Tibullus' rejection of military campaigning in favour of staying in his beloved's arms:

> me retinent uinctum formosae uincla puellae,
>   et sedeo duras ianitor ante fores.
> non ego laudari curo, mea Delia; tecum
>   dum modo sim, quaeso segnis inersque uocer.
>
> Tibullus 1.1.55–58

Tibullus will endure the charge of being *segnis inersque*, i.e. of 'sitting around' ὧδε λίην μεθιέντες (Callinus fr. 1.3), and he welcomes a 'death at home' (dismissed by Callinus in vv. 14–16 of the same poem), provided that he dies in his woman's arms — then he will be truly ποθεινός (Callinus fr. 1.16).

Callinus fr. 1 inscribes at the very beginnings of the elegiac tradition a contrast between, on the one hand, sympotic and erotic pleasures and, on the other, the public service of military campaigning, or so it may have seemed looking back. This was one element from the broad palette of Greek elegy that Roman

---

37 Cf., e.g., Bowie 1990, 223, Aloni 2009, 185–186.

elegists took up and made central to their much narrower focus.³⁸ Closely connected to this is another feature of early elegy, and very notably of Mimnermus, which was to prove very important to its Roman reception. The language of early elegy shows unsurprising affiliations to that of the epic tradition; for the earliest period of elegy, whether in certain cases there is a specific intertextual relation and in which direction influence flows, are almost always matters for scholarly debate,³⁹ but it is again helpful here to try to see things as they might have looked in the Hellenistic and Roman periods. In the case of Mimnermus fr. 1, it has been noted that there are similarities of phrasing to the story of Anteia's illicit passion for Bellerophon which Glaucus tells in *Iliad* 6; these similarities would probably not give cause to pause, were it not for the fact that Mimnermus fr. 2, 'we, like the leaves which the flowered season of spring brings forth...', reminds us of the famous opening of the same speech of Glaucus, 'as are the generations of leaves, so of men also...' (*Iliad* 6.146). Whether or not in fr. 2 Mimnermus has his eye specifically on *Iliad* 6 has been much debated,⁴⁰ though it would be easy to understand how later readers might interpret this passage as taking the Homeric original, which is spoken on the battlefield where death is never far away, and changing its point so that it becomes an(other) exhortation to the pursuit of pleasure while we have the chance ('we take pleasure in the flowers of youth for a cubit's length of time'). Where Glaucus speaks of vast periods of time and the 'generations of men' as a single, universalizing (and third person) concept, a truly 'epic' perspective in other words, Mimnermus is concerned rather with what life is like for each and every one of *us* (ἡμεῖς... τέρπομεθα), caught in a moment; from the former (epic) perspective, individuals fade in significance, but those of us living now know, as does Mimnermus, that our 'window' for pleasure is very small indeed. As for Mimnermus fr. 1, at the very least we may say that, from the perspective of the *Iliad*, this passage privileges a life which later ages associated above all with the Trojan lover Paris, and which clearly offers a different set of priorities to those of the epic. For the Roman elegists, that perhaps was enough.⁴¹

---

38 This is not the place for a survey of all uses of early elegy, for example Theognis, in Roman poetry, and my concentration here on Mimnermus and Callinus is not to be taken as a dismissal of possible reflections of other poets; in an unpublished paper Hans Bernsdorff has argued for the importance for Propertius 4.6 of Simonides' 'Plataea' elegy.
39 Cf. now West 2011, 226–232.
40 Cf. Allen 1993, 41; the most important study of the poem, and of the positive case for intertextual reference, is Griffith 1975.
41 I am grateful to Hans Bernsdorff and to the audience of the Thessaloniki conference for instructive criticism.

Bibliography

Allen, A. 1993. *The Fragments of Mimnermus*, Stuttgart.
Aloni, A. 2009. 'Elegy', in: Budelmann 2009, 168–188.
Aloni, A./Iannucci, A. 2007. *L'elegia greca e l'epigramma dalle origini al V secolo*, Florence.
Bach, N. 1837. 'Epiphyllides elegiacae', *Zeitschrift für das Alterthumswissenschaft* 4, 337–346.
Bowie, E. 1990. '*Miles ludens?* The Problem of Martial Exhortation in Early Greek Elegy', in: O. Murray (ed.), *Sympotica*, Oxford, 221–229.
Bowie, E. 1997. 'The Theognidea: A Step Towards a Collection of Fragments?', in: G. Most (ed.), *Collecting Fragments – Fragmente sammeln*, Göttingen, 53–66.
Budelmann, F. (ed.) 2009. *The Cambridge Companion to Greek Lyric*, Cambridge.
Cairns, F. 1974. 'Some Observations on Propertius 1.1', *Classical Quarterly* 24, 94–110.
Cairns, F. 1979. *Tibullus: a Hellenistic Poet at Rome*, Cambridge.
Christensen, D. 2000. 'Callinus and *militia amoris* in Achilles Tatius' *Leucippe and Cleitophon*', *Classical Quarterly* 50, 631–632.
Duff, T. 1999. *Plutarch's Lives: Exploring Virtue and Vice*, Oxford.
Faraone, C.A. 2008. *The Stanzaic Architecture of Early Greek Elegy*, Oxford.
Freis, R. 1993. '*Exiguos elegos*: Are *Ars Poetica* 75–78 Critical of Love Elegy?', *Latomus* 52, 364–371.
Griffin, J. 1985. *Latin Poets and Roman Life*, London.
Griffith, M. 1975. 'Man and the Leaves: A Study of Mimnermos fr. 2', *California Studies in Classical Antiquity* 8, 73–88.
Heyworth, S. 2007. *Cynthia*, Oxford.
Hinds, S. 1998. *Allusion and Intertext*, Cambridge.
Hunter, R. 2006. *The Shadow of Callimachus*, Cambridge.
Hunter, R. 2006b. 'Sweet Nothings – Callimachus fr. 1.9–12 Revisited', in: G. Bastianini/A. Casanova (eds.), *Callimaco: cent'anni di papiri*, Florence, 119–131 [= Hunter 2008, 523–536].
Hunter, R. 2008. *On Coming After. Studies in Post-Classical Greek Literature and its Reception*, Berlin/New York.
Hunter, R. 2009. *Critical Moments in Classical Literature*, Cambridge.
Hunter, R. 2011. 'The Reputation of Callimachus', in: D. Obbink/R. Rutherford (eds.), *Culture in Pieces*, Oxford, 220–238 [= Hunter 2008, 537–558].
Hunter, R. 2012a. 'The Songs of Demodocus: Compression and Extension in Greek Narrative Poetry', in: S. Bär/M. Baumbach (eds.), *Brill's Companion to Greek and Latin 'Epyllion' and Its Reception*, Leiden, 83–109 [= this volume 18–45].
Hunter, R. 2012b. 'Callimachus and Roman Elegy', in: B. Gold (ed.), *Blackwell's Companion to Roman Love Elegy*, Malden MA, 155–171.
Hunter, R./Russell, D. 2011. *Plutarch, How to Study Poetry (De poetis audiendis)*, Cambridge.
Lightfoot, J. 1999. *Parthenius of Nicaea*, Oxford.
Obbink, D. 2006. 'A New Archilochus Poem', *Zeitschrift für Papyrologie und Epigraphik* 156, 1–9.
Spanoudakis, K. 2001. 'Poets and Telchines in Callimachus' *Aetia*-prologue', *Mnemosyne* 54, 425–441.
West, M.L. 1974. *Studies in Greek Elegy and Iambus*, Berlin/New York.
West, M.L. 1992. *Iambi et elegi Graeci ante Alexandrum cantati*, 2nd ed., Oxford.
West, M.L. 2011. *Hellenica I: Epic*, Oxford.
Wilamowitz-Moellendorff, U. von 1913. *Sappho und Simonides*, Berlin.

21 Horace's other *Ars Poetica*: *Epistles* 1.2 and Ancient Homeric Criticism

Much surviving ancient 'literary criticism' is of a moralising and didactic kind, in which what is looked for in texts are lessons which we can apply to our lives; the Homeric scholia repeatedly tell us what Homer 'teaches', and this can be matters of fact, skills such as military tactics (cf. already Ar. *Frogs* 1034–1036, Plato, *Ion* 537a–541c), or moral lessons about proper behaviour. Already the Platonic Socrates can readily get the young Alcibiades' assent to the proposition that the *Iliad* and the *Odyssey* are "poems about the difference between the just and the unjust" (Plato, *Alcibiades* 112b4–5), and a late source reports that in the fifth century BC Anaxagoras had demonstrated, with what detailed arguments we do not know, that the poetry of Homer was 'about virtue and justice' (Diog. Laert. 2.11 = Anaxagoras, 59 A 1.11 D-K). It was, above all, Homer's rich cast of characters who carried the moral force of his poetry:

> The books [of 'classical literature'] are full of characters who are just or unjust, temperate or lewd, brave or cowardly, wise or stupid, gentle or irritable. It is possible to omit the names but pick out the characters and so draw philosophical lessons for the events of life, by imitating some characters and shunning others.
>
> [Dionysius of Halicarnassus] 2.375.20–25 U-R

After illustrating this from examples of good (Nestor, Hector) and bad (Paris, Pandaros) characters in Homer, the author of this treatise cites Socrates' claim in Plato's *Phaedrus* that 'poetry[1] educates those who come after by celebrating countless deeds of the ancients' (245a4–5) and adds that 'education is exposure (ἔντευξις) to characters'.[2] So too, in noting the practical value of 'classical literature' for our own productions, the grammarian Aelius Theon observes that "excellent examples will mould our soul and lead to splendid imitation" (61.32–33 Sp.),[3] but that Homeric mimesis involved both good and bad characters, both ἀρεταί and κακίαι ψυχῆς, and characters who sometimes behaved well and sometimes ill was standard lore (cf., e.g., [Plutarch], *On Homer* 2.5; Plutarch,

---

1 Socrates in fact refers of course not to 'poetry' but to 'possession and madness from the Muses...in lyric and other kinds of poetry' (245a4), but such extravagance is certainly not suited to [Dionysius's] purposes.
2 On this passage cf. Russell 1979, 120–121.
3 Theon is here very close to Dionysius of Halicarnassus, *On Imitation*: cf. Hunter 2009, ch. 4.

How to study poetry 25b–c).[4] This search for the moral lessons of literature may glide into what we would be tempted to call full-scale allegorising, but as often we find a milder, philosophically inflected, moralism to guide our reading; only rarely does it make sense in considering ancient criticism to seek to draw very firm distinctions between different types of 'hard' or 'soft' allegorising.

One of the most familiar texts illustrating this is Horace, *Epistles* 1.2, and in this paper I will try to fill out some of the background in ancient criticism which both gives the context for Horace's poem and also allows us to judge what is most important about the attitude to this material which Horace adopts. In *Epistles* 1.2 Horace sets out some of the lessons to be learned from the *Iliad* and the *Odyssey* and the turns to offer direct moral advice for life to his young addressee and his readers:[5]

> Troiani belli scriptorem, Maxime Lolli,
> dum tu declamas Romae, Praeneste relegi;
> qui, quid sit pulchrum, quid turpe, quid utile, quid non,
> planius ac melius Chrysippo et Crantore dicit.
> cur ita crediderim, nisi quid te detinet, audi.   5
> fabula qua Paridis propter narratur amorem
> Graecia barbariae lento conlisa duello,
> stultorum regum et populorum continet aestus.
> Antenor censet belli praecidere causam:
> quid Paris? ut saluus regnet uiuatque beatus,   10
> cogi posse negat. Nestor componere litis
> inter Peliden festinat et inter Atriden:
> hunc amor, ira quidem communiter urit utrumque.
> quidquid delirant reges, plectuntur Achiui.
> seditione, dolis, scelere atque libidine et ira   15
> Iliacos intra muros peccatur et extra.
>
> Horace, *Epistles* 1,2.1–16

While you are declaiming at Rome, Maximus Lollius, at Praeneste I have been re-reading the writer of the Trojan War; what is honourable, what shameful, what expedient, and what not, he sets out more clearly and better than Chrysippus and Crantor. Unless something else keeps your attention, listen to why I have come to this view.

The story which tells of how Greece clashed in a long-drawn war with a barbarian land because of Paris' love contains the passions of foolish kings and peoples. Antenor

---

4 For this latter passage cf. below, p. 392–393.
5 There is much valuable illustrative material in the commentary of Kiessling-Heinze which will not be repeated here; Keane 2011, a helpful account, reached me after my account of the poem had been drafted. Any full consideration of the poem would also have much more to say about the various contrasts to which the opening two verses gesture; cf. Laird 2003, 168–169.

proposes cutting away the cause of the war; and Paris? He says that he cannot be compelled to reign in safety and to live in happiness. Nestor hurries to settle the strife between the son of Peleus and the son of Atreus: one is burned by love, but anger burns both of them in common. Whatever madness the kings commit, it is the Achaeans who are punished. Within the walls of Troy and without, it is faction, deceit, wickedness and lust and anger which fuel the mistakes.

The relationship between poetry, notably that of Homer, and philosophy, with which Horace begins, is variously figured throughout antiquity, and many of the constructions of the Hellenistic and later periods may ultimately be seen as attempts to rescue for poetry a useful place in educated society, after the destructive attack of Plato's *Republic*. Poetry, particularly if taught in the 'correct' way, was often seen as preparatory to the study of philosophy, or — at a rather higher level — poets could be seen to be in harmony with philosophers, whether in the weak sense that what is found in the poets is 'not in opposition to', or travels in the same direction as, what the philosophers say, or in the strong sense — often, though certainly not necessarily, associated with the allegorical tradition — that what both parties say is the same, it is merely the mode which varies (for a statement of the general position, cf., e.g., Maximus of Tyre, *Oration* 4); in extreme versions, the strong position may amount to saying, as more than one critic of Plato in fact did, that Plato took most of his most important doctrines from Homer.[6] Horace here offers a lightly ironised version of familiar patterns of argument.[7]

Homer's lessons — what is *pulcrum* 'right', becoming', *honestum*, καλόν, and what is not (*turpe*), what is utile, 'expedient', 'advantageous', συμφέρον, and what is not — are here couched in the language of the Stoic analysis of actions (cf., e.g., Cicero, *De officiis* 1.9), in order to make the point that Homer teaches the same lessons as the philosophers; echoes of these words in the actual account of the Homeric poems (w. 25, 30) reinforce the message. A passage of Dio's essay *On Homer and Socrates* is very close to Horace here:

πρὸς δὲ τούτοις ὑπέρ τῶν αὐτῶν ἐσπουδαζέτην καὶ ἐλεγέτην, ὁ μὲν διὰ τῆς ποιήσεως, ὁ δὲ καταλογάδην· περὶ ἀρετῆς ἀνθρώπων καὶ κακίας καὶ περὶ ἁμαρτημάτων καὶ κατορθωμάτων καὶ περὶ ἀληθείας καὶ ἀπάτης καὶ ὅπως δοξάζουσι οἱ πολλοὶ καὶ ὅπως ἐπίστανται οἱ φρόνιμοι.

Dio Chrysostom, 55.9

---

6 On this tradition cf. Hunter 2012, ch. 2.
7 Another Latin example with interesting points of contact and contrast with Horace is Seneca, *Epistles* 88.5–8; cf. below.

> [Socrates and Homer] were concerned and spoke about the same matters, one in poetry, the other in prose: human virtue and vice, wrong actions and right ones, truth and deceit, the fact that the many have opinions whereas the wise have knowledge.

Here too Stoic vocabulary is used, however anachronistically as far as Homer is concerned, to make the point about communality of subject-matter.[8] Horace and Dio no doubt have common sources — no ancient philosophical school took poetry and its potential value as seriously as did the Stoics,[9] but comparison of the two passages points up how Horace goes out of his way to 'demystify' the language of philosophy by sticking to very simple ethics and avoiding both epistemology and any language which too insistently suggests the 'technical' language of philosophy (such as κατωρθώματα), or indeed adherence to any particular philosophical school.[10] Horace himself, like Homer, speaks *planius ac melius*. The principal terms of Stoic ethics belonged in any case to the general Roman language of approbation and disapproval, and so their use never threatens to turn Horace's poem into an ethical treatise. The point seems reinforced by an echo of a passage of Lucilius, Horace's Roman forerunner in moralising verse:[11]

> uirtus, Albine, est pretium persoluere uerum
> quis in uersamur quis uiuimus rebus potesse;
> uirtus est homini scire id quod quaeque habeat res;
> uirtus scire homini rectum utile quid sit honestum,
> quae bona quae mala item, quid inutile turpe inhonestum;
> uirtus quaerendae finem re scire modumque...
>
> Lucilius, 1196–1201 Warmington

> Virtue, Albinus, consists in paying a true price in all the affairs in which life involves us; virtue consists in knowing what each affair contains for a man; virtue consists in knowing what is right and advantageous, what is honourable, what things are good and likewise what are bad, what is disadvantageous, shameful, dishonourable; virtue consists in knowing the end and limit of seeking after something...

---

8 Cf. SVF, IV, Index, s.vv. ἁμάρτημα, κατόρθωμα; these are the actions corresponding, respectively, to κακία and ἀρετή.
9 Cf., e.g., De Lacy 1948, Long 1992, Nussbaum 1993, Hunter/Russell 2011, 11–15.
10 Cf. further below. The issue of the philosophical flavour of *Epistles* 1.2 is very disputed and radically differing views have been held. That Horace's principal stance in this poem is Epicurean has been argued by, e.g., Gigante 1995, 75–78, and Armstrong 2004, 276–281 ('the Epicureans appear to have the whole show to themselves from beginning to end'), both of whom lay particular weight upon Philodemus' *On the Good King according to Homer* (cf. n. 29 below), and cf. also Grilli 1983, 281–291. For a quite different approach cf. Moles 1985, 34–39.
11 Cf. Edwards 1992, 87.

Here too is the familiar language of Roman Stoicism, but the echo reinforces the two related points of Horace's opening: poetry is a more helpful guide (for someone like Lollius) in getting one's moral bearings for life than is technical (Greek) philosophy, and (paradoxically) it is a Greek poet telling a Greek story who is the best guide to a very Roman ethics. Horace will, moreover, not make the mistake that Seneca claims is all too common:

> Perhaps [scholars] persuade you that Homer was a philosopher, although they prove this false by the very arguments they use to support it. For at one time they make him a Stoic, who approves only of virtue, avoids pleasures, and does not abandon what is right [*honestum*] even for the reward of immortality; at another an Epicurean, praising the condition of a state at peace which passes its time in feasting and song; at another a Peripatetic...
>
> Seneca, *Epistles* 88.5

To make his point, Seneca's first two illustrations both evoke the same Homeric character, Odysseus; first, as the Horatian and allegedly Stoic exemplar of virtue and wisdom, who refused Calypso's offer of immortality, and then the alleged Epicurean whose famous praise for peaceful feasting (*Odyssey* 9.2–11) had ancient apologists working overtime. Horace himself, however, is philosophically eclectic (*Epistles* 1.1.13–19), and the Homer of *Epistles* 1.2 is shaped in his image.

Horace presumably chooses Chrysippus and Crantor, *inter alia*, because of the serious interest that both took in poetry. Chrysippus,[12] the most famous and prolific Stoic of all, wrote about Homer and, perhaps more than any other philosopher, used citations of classical poets to illustrate what he was saying; as Stoicism was the philosophy with the greatest resonance at Rome, the choice of Chrysippus was almost ready made for Horace. As for the Academic Crantor (late fourth-early third century),[13] he too is reported as an admirer of, above all, Homer and Euripides, as well as being a poet in his own right (Diog. Laert. 4.25–26),[14] and Sextus Empiricus reports how in one of his ethical writings he imagined a contest "in a theatre belonging to all the Greeks" between the various Goods, with Virtue coming out as the winner ahead of health, pleasure and wealth;[15] he too, then, was a philosopher to whom one might be tempted to look for what was more readily available and accessible in Homer. By his choice of philosophers, Horace suggests that Homer will serve you better, not just than

---

12 Mette 1984, 16 emends *Chrysippo* to *Speusippo*, thus giving two philosophers from the Academy, but there seems no good reason to adopt this proposal and several against it.
13 On Crantor cf. Dillon 2003, 216–231.
14 An (all but certainly) Hellenistic funerary epigram for him describes him as 'pleasing to men, but more pleasing to the Muses' (Theaetetus, 11 Gow – Page, from Diog. Laert. 4.25).
15 Cf. *Against the Ethicists* 51–58 = Crantor fr. 7 Mette.

thorny philosophical prose which, by its very nature, is addressed to a limited audience of specialists, but also than what philosophers say about Homer; why go to an interpreter, when you can get the same message much more clearly from the poetic source itself? The crabbed difficulty and lack of polish of Chrysippus' style was, moreover, a critical commonplace (cf. *SFV*, 2, 24–26, 28–29) — how could Homer *not* write *planius*?, and the very number and nature of his writings might recall Horace's account elsewhere of Lucilius or, worse, the 'boor' of *Satires* 1.9; Diogenes Laertius reports Carneades commenting in unflattering terms on how Chrysippus insisted on writing on any subject on which Epicurus had written, 'as a result of which he wrote the same thing many times over, or the first thing which occurred to him, and in his haste he left things uncorrected' (Diog. Laert. 10.26–27; cf. Hor. *Sat*. 1.4.8–13, 9–2.3–25).[16] Crantor too was known for the voluminousness of his writings (30,000 lines was the traditional reckoning)[17] and such a φιλόπονος, offered a ready contrast to the apparently effortless grace of Homer.[18] There is perhaps a further barb. In all critical traditions, including the Aristotelian with its stress upon σαφήνεια. for poetry no less than for prose (cf. *Poetics* 1458a17–18, etc.), it is poetry which is 'less clear' than prose; Maximus of Tyre makes the point that Homer says the same as the philosophers but it is the latter who are 'more accessible' because of the αἰνίγματα of poetry (4.7). Horace reverses such lore — Homer's moral lessons are very plain for anyone who reads with their eyes open.

If Horace pointedly reverses some standard lore about the relationship between poetry and philosophy, the whole thrust of the first part of the epistle is in keeping with a familiar ancient theme. Philosophers, particularly those who trace their descent ultimately from Socrates, discuss moral states and passions such as 'cowardice', 'friendship' and 'love'; they may use illustrations from the poets or indeed — as Socrates famously did — from life around them, but they operate basically at the level of the general and abstract. Poets, on the other hand, operate with specific examples drawn from mythical or historical traditions, but these are very easily seen as having wider, 'general' application.[19] Dio, 55.12–13 (cf. above) offers an interesting variant of this argument — Socrates (we would here tend rather to say 'Plato') has named (often well known) interlocutors who are suffering from ethical faults and passions, because this allows the nature (ὁποῖα ἐστίν) of those faults and passions to be laid bare 'more clearly'

---

16 Cf. also Diog. Laert. 7.180.
17 Diog. Laert. 4.24, Philodemus, *PHerc*. 1021, col. xvi.12 Dorandi.
18 For Crantor as φιλόπονος cf. Philodemus, *PHerc*. 1021, col. xvi.10 Dorandi.
19 For this distinction cf., e.g., Plutarch, *How to study poetry* 19b.

(σαφέστερον) than if the matters were discussed in the abstract; when, for example, Socrates is talking to an angry man, then really it is 'anger' which is the subject, and so forth. Whatever we may think of the accuracy of Dio's account, Dio's point here is that there is no difference in this between Homer and Plato's ethical dialogues.[20] Homer's characters too (55.14–21) are specific exemplifications of moral weaknesses; when Homer tells us about the actions of Dolon, he is discoursing περὶ δειλίας καὶ φιλοδοξίας (55.14), the narrative of Pandarus is περὶ δωροδοκίας καὶ ἀσεβείας καὶ τὸ ξύμπαν ἀφροσύνης (55.16), and so forth. So too for Maximus of Tyre, Homer's characters are εἰκόνες of moral states (26.5–6).

Horace turns first, as was also traditional, to the *Iliad*. The generally negative picture of the *Iliad* which he paints is in part due to a wish to highlight a contrast with the *Odyssey*,[21] but it is also in keeping with an important direction of ancient criticism which saw the *Iliad* as, above all, a poem of 'passions' (πάθη; cf. *aestus* in v. 8 and the list of v. 15) – of particular importance for Horace will be *amor*, which works its destructiveness on both sides (v. 6 ~ v. 13; cf. *libidine*, v. 15). The *Odyssey*, by contrast, is 'ethical' (Aristotle, *Poetics* 1459b13–16; 'Heraclitus', *Homeric Problems* 60.2, etc.), and – as we shall see – Horace does not dissent from this view. The *Iliad* is also a poem of suffering (πάθος in another sense), a tragedy in fact; the scholia on the opening word, μῆνιν, bear the most eloquent witness to this, and Plato's repeated insistence in *Republic* 10 on Homer as 'first of the tragedians' (595c2, 605c10, etc.) looks, above all, to the *Iliad*. Dio tells us that Homer's particular skill lay in his knowledge of human πάθη (61.1). Horace's apparently harsh and simplistic account of the *Iliad* has puzzled modern readers (it has been called 'perhaps the most tendentious sketch of the *Iliad* ever written'),[22] but it must be set in the context both of the simple ethical oppositions of the opening verses and of the preliminary stages of ethical education reached by both Lollius and the book of *Epistles* itself. Horace has proclaimed that he is now entirely occupied with issues of ethics (*quid uerum atque decens curo et rogo et omnis in hoc sum* 1.1.11), and the reading which he offers of both Homeric poems reflects this; it is a fair conclusion from the opening of the poem, particularly as it follows on from the end of *Epistles* 1.1, that not only is it ethical guidelines which Horace has found in Homer, but that was his purpose in picking up the text again in the calm seclusion of Praeneste (*relegi*, v. 2). That such a reading is (as we would say) partial, not the

---

20 Cf. Valgimigli 1911, 6–7.
21 cf. Aristotle, *Poetics* 1459b13–6; Pontani 2005, 222–223, Cairns 1989, 85–87.
22 Edwards 1992, 85. Keane 2011 argues that it is a deliberately tendentious and 'smug' reading, as Lollius is supposed to realise.

only thing to be said about Homer, and certainly not the last word, is a truism that Horace will have seen no need to spell out. In his negative view of the plot of the *Iliad*, Horace is again close to Plutarch, who shows how we should absolve Zeus from criticism for the sufferings at Troy and who takes a similarly dim view of (at least) Greek behaviour in the opening books of the *Iliad*:

> Homer is correctly pointing out the necessity of things, namely that even cities and armies and leaders are destined to prosper and prevail over their enemies if they behave wisely, but if – like the Greeks – they fall into passions [πάθη] and errors [ἁμαρτίαι] and dispute and quarrel with one another [διαφέρωνται πρὸς ἀλλήλους καὶ στασιάζωσιν, cf. Horace's *seditione*],[23] they are destined to disorder and confusion and a bad end.
> Plutarch, *How to study poetry* 23d–e

One noteworthy feature, however, of Horace's treatment is that he puts no pro-Greek spin on his presentation of the *Iliad* here — there is folly, vice and disastrous dissension on both sides.

Antenor and Nestor are found elsewhere paired as the wise and elderly (cf. *Iliad* 3.145–152) orator and adviser on, respectively, the Trojan and Greek sides,[24] and the exegetical scholia on the episode to which Horace refers (bT-schol. on *Iliad* 7.345) make precisely this point about their corresponding roles; moreover, Antenor's speech in *Iliad* 7 is immediately preceded in the text by one from Nestor. In the episode of the *Iliad* to which Horace here refers (7.345–364), an episode which seems to have been picked out by the grammatical tradition as a paradigm case of Trojan folly and dissension,[25] Antenor advises an assembly of the Trojans to give back to the Greeks Helen and all the possessions with her. Homer introduces him here as Ἀντήνωρ πεπνυμένος and — apart from heralds — the only other Trojans so described are Antenor's once-mentioned colleague Oukalegon (3.148, where he is paired with Antenor) and Polydamas (18.249), before a speech of good advice which Hector and the Trojans foolishly reject, as the poet makes explicit (18.311–313).[26] In book 7 Antenor expresses his proposal briskly and straightforwardly:

---

23 Plutarch's expression is a prose version of *Iliad* 1.6 διαστήτην ἐρίσαντε.
24 Cf. Schol.bT Hom. *Iliad* 3.396, Eur. fr. 899 K, Plato, *Symp.* 221d1.
25 In their introduction to the Shield of Achilles, the T-scholia on *Iliad* 18.483–606 offer a very interesting view of the city of peace and the city of war: 'The city at peace is intended to make the Trojans reflect how many good things they would have enjoyed, if they were at peace, and the city at war reflects their dissension [διχόνοια]; for in Troy some supported Paris and some Antenor'.
26 On Polydamas see esp. Schofield 1986, 18–22.

δεῦτ' ἄγετ', Ἀργείην Ἑλένην καὶ κτήματ' ἅμ' αὐτῆι
δώομεν Ἀτρεΐδηισιν ἄγειν. νῦν δ' ὅρκια πιστὰ
ψευσάμενοι μαχόμεσθα· τῶ οὔ νύ τι κέρδιον ἥμιν
ἔλπομαι ἐκτελέεσθαι, ἵνα μὴ ῥέξομεν ὧδε.

Homer, *Iliad* 7.350–353

Come now, let us hand over Argive Helen and the possessions she brought with her to the sons of Atreus to take away. We are now engaged in a war in which we have broken solemn oaths, and I do not think that things can turn out well for us, unless we act in this way.

The final verse of his speech is certainly odd in its expression (cf. Kirk, *ad loc.*) and was athetised by Aristarchus; the A-scholia explain that the verse was added by someone who did not know that οὔ νύ τι κέρδιον ἥμιν was syntactically complete in itself, as ἔσται could be supplied. Dio 55.15 quotes vv. 351–352 with οὔ νύ τι κάλλιον ἐστι closing v. 352. Horace may have been thinking of either text: with κέρδιον Antenor looks to what is *utile* for the Trojans, with κάλλιον what is *pulchrum*. As for Paris, he simply replies that he will give back the possessions, but not Helen, and accuses Antenor of having lost his wits, if indeed his proposal was intended as a serious one. Horace's basic point is that Paris is an example of someone who will not listen to good advice – he does not know what is good for him: he could live free from *curae*, in an almost philosophic calm, and enjoy untroubled power (v. 10), but he refuses to do so. The scholia on these Homeric verses help to bring out some of the fuller discussion which lies behind Horace's brief account: Paris is not interested in 'what is advantageous for the group' (τὰ κοινῆι συμφέροντα), but rather only in his own private interest, and he does this because it is he, not Antenor, who has lost his wits (cf. *stultorum*, v. 8): for the scholiasts Paris here is 'sunk deep [καταβυθισθεὶς] in desire for Helen',[27] 'mastered by his madness for women' and suffering from the highest degree of 'derangement' (φρενοβλάβεια). Whereas Antenor's proposal is eminently right, *pulchrum* in Horace's terms (τὶ βέλτιον; ask the scholiasts, 'what could be *more* right?'),[28] Paris' refusal to surrender Helen is the action of 'someone who has lost all shame' (Horace's *turpe*).

Similar folly and stasis are not hard to find on the Greek side. Horace singles out Nestor's famous intervention between the quarrelling Agamemnon and

---

[27] I have wondered whether this watery image has something to do with Horace's *aestus*.
[28] Eustathius uses rather the language of 'justice' in describing Antenor and his proposal (*Hom.* 684.48, 685.10–11), and a modern analysis too might well emphasise this aspect, given that Antenor has stressed that the Trojans have broken oaths; cf. Schofield 1986, 28 on the balance between prudential arguments and arguments from justice in Nestor's speech.

Achilles, which is also our introduction to the aged counsellor; Horace's *Nestor...Peliden...Atriden* gestures towards *Iliad* 1.245–247, Πηλείδης...Ἀτρείδης... Νέστωρ, as a kind of shortcut signal to the Homeric text.[29] In his speech (1.254–284), Nestor appeals first to the pleasure which a quarrel between the greatest of the Greeks 'in both counsel and military prowess' would give the Trojans (w. 254–248),[30] with the clear implication that his hearers should cease from such behaviour. After he has established that better men than Agamemnon and Achilles paid heed to his advice, he appeals to the Greeks to do as he suggests, for this would be ἄμεινον (v. 274), an idea which probably carries with it a mixture of the *utile* and the *pulchrum*.[31] Nestor's intervention was much discussed in antiquity. Dio Chrysostom considers in Oration 56 why Agamemnon did not follow Nestor's advice with regard to Briseis and how Nestor deals with that subsequently in book 9, and *Oration* 57 is almost completely devoted to the question of why Nestor spoke as he did in book 1; at issue in *Oration* 57 is whether Homer simply presented Nestor as a braggart (ἀλαζών), or whether this mode of speech had a prudential and rhetorical purpose. Unsurprisingly perhaps, in view of the fact that he will present himself as a 'latter-day' Nestor, Dio comes down for the positive interpretation of Nestor's speech (note 57.6

---

[29] Horace's description of Nestor, *componere litis / inter Peliden festinat et inter Atriden*, finds a striking parallel (cf. Sudhaus 1909) at Philodemus, *On the Good King according to Homer*, col. xxviii Dorandi τὸν Νέστορα παρεισάγων σπεύδοντα λύειν τὴν στάσιν...πρὸς Ἀγαμέμνονα, whether we read στάσιν κά[ν τ]οῖς πρὸς Ἀγαμέμνονα with Fish 2002, 200 or στάσιν [Ἀχιλλέω]ς with earlier editors; Philodemus seems to be discussing how Homer makes plain his hatred for war and fighting, Horace will, of course, have known Philodemus' treatise (cf., e.g., Asmis 1991, 21 n. 95, and Gigante and Armstrong cited in p. 379 n. 10 above), and there is much in *Epistles* 1.2 which recalls the spirit, if not the wording, of Philodemus' work. Cf., however, also [Plutarch], *On Homer* 165 [Nestor] μετάγνωσιν ἐμποιεῖν πειρᾶται τοῖς διαφερομένοις ἀριστεῦσιν...τοῦτον τὸν τρόπον πραΰνειν αὐτοὺς ἐπιχειρεῖ. That Nestor's interventions, here and elsewhere, were not terribly successful is often forgotten in ancient encomiastic accounts of his oratory – nice examples at Max. Tyr. 26.5; Apuleius, *De deo Socratis* 158. Cf. further below, p. 388; Schofield 1986, 15–16 interestingly discusses why lack of immediate success does not necessarily affect the esteem arising from such interventions, and on Nestor's interventions and reputation in general cf. Roisman 2005. Nestor s intervention in Book 1 was also of course an admired rhetorical model.

[30] Eustathius observes that Homer is here teaching us that the good man may lie when the occasion demands it, for it is plain that Agamemnon is no match for Achilles in warfare nor a match for Nestor in counsel (*Hom.* 99.29–34); Schofield 1986, 29 takes almost exactly the same view as Eustathius, expressed in almost the same language ('tactful insincerity, designed to coax...'), though apparently without knowing of Eustathius' discussion.

[31] Cf. Schofield 1986, 28 (citing earlier bibliography), who does not, however, refer to Horace's poem.

ὄφελος). For both Dio and Dio's Nestor, Agamemnon and Achilles are showing themselves ἀνόητοι, (57.3, 9), they are displaying ἀφροσύνην καὶ ἀναισθησίαν (57.3), their errors are the result of ὕβρις and μεγαλαυχία, of τῦφος and μανία (57.6, 8); Horace's *delirant* seems mild by comparison.

For Horace it is again 'passions' which are the stumbling block, just as, some two centuries later, Maximus of Tyre described Achilles and Agamemnon as 'images [εἰκόνες] of the emotions, of youth and power' (26.5). For Horace there is a fateful mixture of *amor* and *ira* at work here, though of course much more was involved in the Iliadic dispute than just those two driving forces.[32] All modern commentators agree that the *hunc* of v. 13 is Achilles, and it is indeed his affection for Briseis which occurs time and again in ancient poetic allusions to the story.[33] That said, *amor* or ἔρως is not in fact an explicit motive in the quarrel of *Iliad* 1 – Achilles feels ἄχος at Agamemnon's plan to take Briseis in recompense for the loss of Chryseis (1.188) – although it was not hard to find for anyone looking for it. Horace's account here both owes something to post-Homeric analysis of the scene and is also shaped to fit well with the Antenor parallel (Paris and Achilles playing paradoxically analogous roles), thus illustrating the folly on both sides. The scholia on 1.348–349 ('in tears Achilles went away from his companions and sat on the shore of the grey sea, looking out over the dark sea') well illustrate one version of an exegetical tradition which Horace will have known well:

> Homer perfectly depicts (χαρακτηρίζειν) the lover, for they seek empty places so that they might indulge their passion undisturbed by anyone.
>
> bT-scholium, *Iliad* 1.349

It is perhaps hard for us to imagine Achilles as the model for, e.g., Callimachus' Acontius, but it was not so hard for Horace.[34] The opening quarrel of the *Iliad* was both a rich enough text and the subject of such a rich critical tradition that a wide range of 'readings' was possible. Thus, Maximus of Tyre (again) can

---

32 With Horace we may compare Apuleius' brief summary of the scene at *De deo Socratis* 158: there it is Agamemnon's *superbia* and Achilles' *ferocia* which must be held in check by Nestor. Within Greek tradition a distinction was often made between Achilles' μῆνις and Agamemnon's ὀργή, the former being etymologised from μένειν and hence thought of as long-lasting (e.g., Max. Tyr. 26.5, AbT-scholia on *Iliad* 1.1c with Erbse's note); Horace's *ira* covers both (cf Dio, 55.9, ὀργή).
33 Cf. in general Fantuzzi 2012.
34 Cf. also *Odes* 2.4.1–4. This passage of *Iliad* 1 is also the starting point for Ovid, *Heroides* 3.

portray the quarrel as a wonderfully vivid (and modern) contrast between two rivals in love:

> In the first book two lovers compete for a prisoner-of-war: one is bold and crazed [ἐπιμανής], the other gentle and emotional [ἐμπαθής]; one's eyes blaze and he abuses and threatens everyone; the other withdraws into inactivity and lies weeping and distraught and says that he will leave and does not leave.
>
> Maximus of Tyre 18.8[35]

The eroticisation of the opening quarrel of the *Iliad*, with a new emphasis on Agamemnon's 'love' or 'desire' for Chryseis, an emphasis which, admittedly, the Homeric Agamemnon's professed attraction to Chryseis (*Iliad* 1.111–115) made very easy, was a particular feature of the reception of the scene in Latin poetry;[36] in a relatively extended rewriting of the quarrel, Ovid makes Agamemnon an example of a sensible man who simply replaced one girlfriend with another (*Remedia Amoris* 467–486).[37] Horace could thus pick and choose what kind of a paradigm *Iliad* 1 might provide. What was most important, however, is what we would call the sobering moral: *quidquid delirant reges, plectuntur Achiui*. In their commentary on Horace, Kiessling-Heinze see this as a pointed reformulation of the second verse of the *Iliad*, 'the destructive [wrath], which brought countless sufferings upon the Achaeans', but we might rather see a semi-proverbial expression of a central (formulaic) idea of the *Iliad*, namely the folly of leaders (notably Agamemnon) who 'destroy/ruin the people';[38] Horace's aphorism points in fact to one of the most tragic aspects of the *Iliad*.

Finally, we should note that the interventions of Antenor and Nestor are chosen precisely because they were utterly unsuccessful; on both sides of the war, passion and folly refused to listen to reasoned argument and good advice. None of Nestor's proposals to either of the squabbling commanders (vv. 275–284) yields any fruit.[39] With typical discretion, Homer had pointed us towards noticing Nestor's failure by the elaborate (and famous) introduction describing his honeyed speech (vv. 248–249), and then by Agamemnon's first words in reply: 'Old man, you have said all of these things very properly (κατὰ μοῖραν) indeed, but...'; Agamemnon s agreement with what Nestor has said turns out to

---

[35] Theocritus, 1.32–38, which principally evokes the Shield of Achilles, perhaps also suggests that this construction of the quarrel of *Iliad* 1 goes a long way back.
[36] Cf. however, also Dio, 61.2, 14, 18. For a Priapic version of Agamemnon's and Achilles' desires cf. *Carmina Priapea* 68.11–18.
[37] Cf. further Scaffai 1982, 63–64.
[38] Cf, e.g., 1.10, 2.115; Haubold 2000, 28–32, 48–60, 198.
[39] Cf. Roisman 2005 and p. 385 n. 29 above.

refer solely to Nestor's advice to Achilles, and Agamemnon, apparently angrier than ever, wastes not a word on how Nestor had urged the king himself to act. If Nestor spoke very properly, 'why then does Agamemnon not follow the advice?' asks the T-scholium on v. 286, reasonably enough, and in explaining to us why Nestor recalled his success as a counsellor in the past Dio also explains his present failure:

> Do you think that it was just at random that Homer gave these words to Nestor, who he says is the most eloquent speaker among men and the power of whose words he likens to the properties of honey, which is the most pleasant and sweetest thing of all to men who are healthy, but is said to be the most unpleasant to men who are sick and feverish and which can cleanse and irritate parts which have sores and are in pain. Nestor's speech, which appeared sweet to others, seemed bitter to Achilles and Agamemnon, as they were sick and corrupted by anger, so that in their folly they did not follow his advice.
>
> Dio Chrysostom 2.8–9

Even the healing power of rhetoric has its limits.[40] Horace's *Iliad* is, then, a poem without progress, whereas the *Odyssey* will show us just what can in fact be achieved (*quid uirtus et quid sapientia possit*).

Odysseus indeed offers a lesson of a quite different kind:

> rursus, quid uirtus et quid sapientia possit,
> utile proposuit nobis exemplar Ulixen,
> qui domitor Troiae multorum prouidus urbes
> et mores hominum inspexit latumque per aequor,
> dum sibi, dum sociis reditum parat, aspera multa
> pertulit, aduersis rerum inmersabilis undis.
>
> Horace, *Epistles* 1.2.17–22

> Again, as to what virtue and wisdom can accomplish, [Homer] has set out for us a helpful (*utile*) model in Odysseus. He conquered Troy and with discernment (*prouidus*) looked upon the cities and customs of many men; while he sought to win safe return for himself and his comrades, he endured many hardships on the expansive ocean, but could not be drowned in the hostile waves of events.

Odysseus as a paradigm of virtue is very familiar in the ancient tradition — perhaps a century after Horace, 'Heraclitus' called Odysseus 'an instrument [ὄργα-

---

40 In *Oration* 56 Dio returns to Agamemnon's failure to follow Nestor's advice to give Briseis back to Achilles, noting that he paid a very heavy penalty; in book 9 Nestor upbraided his folly before the other leaders and Agamemnon was forced to plead with Achilles, to offer him vast wealth, and also one of his daughters in marriage. This part of *Oration* 56 turns the Greek camp into a kind of proto-democratic Athens in which leaders are called to account.

νου] of all of virtue' (*Hom. Probl.* 70.2) and for Pseudo-Plutarch Odysseus owes his glorious renown to his ἀρετὴ ψυχῆς (*On Homer* 2.136) — and the moralising/allegorical account of his wanderings which Horace offers may be paralleled many times over.[41] Here, for example, is Maximus' summation of the same tradition as that upon which Horace draws;

> Do you not see how virtue and the courage which arises from it preserve Odysseus as he struggles with every kind of disaster [παντοίαις συμφοραῖς ἀντιτεχνώμενον]?[42] ... It is this which rescues the man [τὸν ἄνδρα] from Polyphemus' grasp, this which brings him up from Hades, this which constructs the raft, this which persuades Alcinous, this which endures being pelted by the suitors, wrestling with Iros and being insulted by Melanthios. This frees his hearth, this avenges his marriage, this makes him [ἄνδρα] 'godly' and 'like the immortals', as Plato claims the happy [εὐδαίμων] man is.
>
> Maximus of Tyre 26.9

Dio too offers an account of the dangers of pleasure which is very close to Horace:

> It is impossible to live with Pleasure or to have constant contact with her without being completely caught. When she takes control and masters the soul with her drugs, the rest of the story of Circe is inevitable: pleasure strikes with her wand and drives a man into a pigsty, where she shuts him up, and from that time he lives as a pig or a wolf.
>
> Dio Chrysostom 8.24

The version of the opening verses of the *Odyssey* which Horace offers is part translation, part paraphrase, and part interpretative gloss; Horace has also gone out of his way to provide a stylistic variation on the Homeric word-order, with Homeric pairs broken up or separated by verse-end, and vv. 20–22 representing a rearrangement of *Odyssey* 1.4–5, in part perhaps to 'defamiliarise' this overfamiliar text and therefore make us focus afresh on its meaning, rather than just taking it as read.[43] *providus* offers a positive and semi-philosophical[44] choice

---

41 How familiar this view was can be seen in the extended and Christianising version of it by St. Basil in his essay on the value of pagan literature (5.25–46 Wilson): echoing a motif that Plato applied to the wives of the Guardians (*Rep.* 5.457a 6–7), Basil notes that it was appropriate for Odysseus to be naked when he met Nausicaa because Homer 'represented him adorned with virtue rather than garments', etc. For recent discussion and bibliography on 'the philosophical Odysseus' cf. Montiglio 2011.
42 Cf Horace's *aduersis rerum inmersabilis undis* (v. 22), and cf. further below.
43 This effect is particularly noticeable if set alongside Horace's other version of the opening of the *Odyssey* at *Ars poetica* [from now onwards simply *Ars*] 141–142; there Horace is concerned with the right kind of epic prologue, and hence his version of Homer's verses is much 'straighter'.

from the many ancient interpretations of Homer's πολύτροπος;[45] among the standard glosses for this term are συνετός and ἐπὶ πολλὰ τρέπων τὴν διάνοιαν, and Maximus glosses πολύτροπος as σώφρων (26.9), in an essay which, as we have seen, has much in common with *Epistles* 1.2. *prouidus* also of course fits the lesson which the Horatian Homer teaches, namely *quid uirtus et quid sapientia possit* (v. 17); *prouidus* suggests *prudentia* and *sapientia* (φρόνησις and σοφία), which are the hallmark of Odysseus,[46] and at the close of the *De deo Socratis* Apuleius offers a moralising version which is both quite close to Horace and may serve to illustrate a very rich ancient tradition:

> This is precisely the lesson which Homer teaches you in the character of Odysseus, whose constant companion he made wisdom [*prudentia*], which he called Minerva, as poets do. With her as companion he endured all his terrible adventures and overcame all adversity. With her help he entered the cave of the Cyclops, and got out; he saw the cattle of the sun, and did not eat them; he went down to the shades of the dead, and came back up again; with this same wisdom [*sapientia*] for his companion he sailed past Scylla and was not snatched away; he was enclosed by Charybdis, but he got out; he drank Circe's potion and was not metamorphosed; he visited the Lotus-eaters and did not remain; he listened to the Sirens but did not approach them.
>
> Apuleius, *De deo Socratis* 177–178

Horace's final phrase in his description of Odysseus, *adversis rerum inmersabilis undis* (v. 22), draws out an implication of Homer s proem (Odysseus' colleagues

---

44 Cf, e.g., Moles 1985, 35. Moles also calls attention to *inspexit* as a 'loaded' translation of Homer's ἴδεν (contrast, again, *Ars* 142). There is, however, a close parallel at Max. Tyr. 26.1, where Maximus rewrites the opening verses of the *Odyssey* to describe Homer himself who travelled everywhere 'with his soul' and πάντα ἐπεσκόπει; here again we would like to know more of Hellenistic discussion (cf. the gloss ἴδεν· ἔμαθεν in at least one scholium on v. 3 (Pontani 2007, 11).
45 For discussion and bibliography cf. Luzzatto 1996.
46 Strabo, 1.2.4–5 offers an interesting version of Odysseus' 'virtue'. Homer 'adorns Odysseus with every virtue' — he is, *inter alia*, expert in generalship and rhetoric (which is (φρόνησις περὶ λόγους), which, for Strabo (in an argument that descends at least from Plato's *Ion*), shows that Homer himself was the master of those arts. Strabo begins, as does Horace, from *Odyssey* 1.3, but moves from Odysseus' 'virtue' to that of Homer himself; this is, however, not a technical 'virtue' like that of a blacksmith, but rather moral virtue itself, for 'it is not possible to be a good poet, if one was not first a good man'. It is noteworthy also that, earlier in the proem, Strabo had cited *Odyssey* 1.3 in support of the contention that 'the poets declare that the wisest [φρονιμώτατοι] of the heroes are those who have travelled to many places and been wanderers' (1.1.16); one of the other pieces of evidence that Strabo adduces is precisely Nestor's pride that the Lapiths summoned him (*Iliad* 1.270), taken from the speech to which Horace alludes in *Epistles* 1.2.

perished at sea, but he did not), and also interprets Homer's prominent reference to Odysseus' θυμός; Odysseus survived importantly through his all-enduring θυμός which he famously exhorts to patience in the course of the poem, an action we should imitate. The phrase thus forms a transition to the more obviously moralising-allegorising reading which follows — the Sirens and Circe as the temptations of the flesh, etc. Odysseus' journey over the sea becomes a journey over 'seas of adversity'; it may be correct that *aduersis* should be taken with *rerum* 'by enallage' (so Mayer, *ad loc.*), but this grammatical trope not only suggests, as does the grand coinage *inmersabilis*, a high style appropriate to epic,[47] but also helps to blur the boundary between the literal and the metaphorical, a technique which is in fact characteristic of much of Horace's reading of Homer. More importantly, perhaps, this also points (again) to why Homer should be so important for us. We may not literally sail over oceans and encounter storms as Odysseus did, but we will certainly encounter 'life's storms', and that is where the paradigm of Odysseus can help;[48] Seneca puts the point with great force in comparing the pursuit of (in his view, trivial) 'Homeric problems', of a kind which we know the Alexandrians and their descendants actually pursued,[49] with the real study of philosophy;

> Do you investigate the path of Odysseus' wanderings [*errauerit*], rather than seeking to prevent us from constant wandering [*erremus*]. There is no time to listen to whether he was storm-tossed between Italy and Sicily or beyond the world known to us...every day we are tossed around by storms of the spirit and wickedness pushes us into all the troubles Odysseus faced. There is never a lack of beauty to provoke our eyes, or of hostile forces; on one side are savage monsters which take pleasure in human blood, and on another treacherous allurements for the ears, and on another shipwreck and countless forms of disaster. Teach me rather how I am to love my fatherland, my wife, my father, how I am to sail to these honourable ends, even after shipwreck. Why do you investigate whether Penelope was chaste or whether she fooled her contemporaries? Or whether she suspected that the man she saw was Odysseus before she knew for certain? Teach me what moral purity [*pudicitia*] is and what great advantage it brings, and whether it is located in the body or the soul.
>
> Seneca, *Epistles* 88.7–8

---

47 Cf. Conte 2007, 70–73.
48 Cf. further Fowler 2000, 216–217.
49 The attitude is familiar in satirical texts, cf., e.g., Bion fr. 5 Kindstrand: 'Bion said that the grammarians who investigated Odysseus' wanderings did not enquire into their own, nor did they perceive that it was in this very matter that they wandered, as they laboured on matters which were of no value'.

What, then, is the relationship between the moralising account of the Homeric poems and the remaining two-thirds of *Epistles* 1.2 which offer Lollius (and ourselves) advice not necessarily tied to specific texts? The transition is effected through the emphatic *nos* at the head of v. 27, which introduces the comparison between most of mankind and Penelope's suitors and the idle young men of Alcinous' court. Some of the advice, of course, has a mildly philosophical flavour and some of it directly picks up lessons learned from Homer (e.g. the dangers of *amor*, v. 38, the control of anger, vv. 59–63); in telling Lollius *sapere aude*, 'have the strength to be wise/be a *sapiens*' (v. 40), Horace is telling him (and us) to imitate Odysseus, both wise and audacious. Thus, in introducing the paradigm of Odysseus at the end of the *De deo Socratis* (cf. above), Apuleius too explicitly makes the hero (along with Socrates) a model for his addressee; 'Why then do you too not turn yourself in all haste to the study of philosophy [*sapientia*], so that all the praise you receive will really be yours [as opposed, e.g., to praise for your father] ... as Accius praised Ulysses...' (176). We may well be reminded here of vv. 34–38 of Horace's protreptic.

Some of the approach which ancient moralisers took to Homer also seeps into the advice to Lollius. Thus, for example, medical images such as those of vv. 33-4 and 48-9 are ubiquitous in Hellenistic moralising, but it is striking that they play a prominent role also in Dio's account of *Iliad* 1. For Dio, Achilles and Agamemnon are both 'sick and corrupted by ὀργή' (55.9), their souls are 'swollen' and in need of pricking back to size (57.7); there is in fact no clean break between Homer and our approach to his poetry and our own lives. Here is where the real difference between Homer and philosophy lies. We carry the lessons learned from Homer — and the language of the classroom is very appropriate here (cf. vv. 34–38, 64–70) — throughout our lives; there is nothing 'theoretical' about them. The proverbial character and rustic imagery of much the second part of the poem, on one hand, reduce the moral message of both Homer and philosophy to gnomic nuggets which speak as simply and *plane* as could be imagined, although the structure of the poem allows a light irony to play over Horace's schoolmasterly didacticism, but they also reinforce the message that what matters is not theory, but how we live our lives. Here *Epistles* 1.2 has (again) much in common with Plutarch's essay, *How the young man should study poetry*, even though the latter treats the study of poetry as explicitly preparatory for philosophy. Like Horace (cf. v. 3, etc.), Plutarch stresses that Homer (and poetry generally) conveys both positive and negative models, images of both virtue and vice; Plutarch allows us to see another nuance of the contrast with 'technical philosophy' with which Horace opens his poem:

Time and again we must remind young men that poetry is a mimetic mode...but it does not abandon likeness to the truth, as the attractiveness of imitation lies in the credible. Therefore imitation, not being altogether neglectful of reality, mixes indications both of vice and of virtue in the actions which it represents. So Homer bids a very firm farewell to the Stoics, who claim that nothing bad attaches to virtue and nothing good to vice, but that the ignorant man is always mistaken in everything and the good man, on the other hand, universally successful. This is what we hear in the schools, but in real life [good and bad are always mixed together]...

Plutarch, *How to study poetry* 25b–c

It is not just that philosophy may obfuscate, it may misrepresent; Homer, or rather a reading of Homer informed by generations of tradition, really does say things both *planius* and *melius*.

Various aspects of the passage of Plutarch just quoted — the link between poetry as mimesis and its representation of 'truth', and the relationship of similarity and difference between poetry and philosophy — bring it close to a passage of Horace's *Ars* which itself is related in several ways to *Epistles* 1.2:

> ergo fungar uice cotis, acutum
> reddere quae ferrum ualet exsors ipsa secandi;   305
> munus et officium, nil scribens ipse, docebo,
> unde parentur opes, quid alat formetque poetam,
> quid deceat, quid non, quo uirtus, quo ferat error.
> scribendi recte sapere est et principium et fons.
> rem tibi Socraticae poterunt ostendere chartae,   310
> uerbaque prouisam rem non inuita sequentur.
> qui didicit, patriae quid debeat et quid amicis,
> quo sit amore parens, quo frater amandus et hospes,
> quod sit conscripti, quod iudicis officium, quae
> partes in bellum missi ducis, ille profecto   315
> reddere personae scit conuenientia cuique.
> respicere exemplar uitae morumque iubebo
> doctum imitatorem et uiuas hinc ducere uoces.

Horace, *Ars* 304–318

Therefore, I shall perform the function of a whetstone, which can make steel sharp, but cannot itself cut. Without writing anything myself, I shall teach the role and duty, from where resources are drawn, what nurtures and fashions the poet, what is fitting for him and what not, where virtue leads, and where error. The beginning and fount of writing properly is knowledge. Socratic pages will be able to show you subject-matter, and once you have seen to that, the words will willingly follow. The man who has learned what is owed to his country and his friends, what kind of love is appropriate for a parent, a brother, a guest, what is the duty of a senator or a judge, what is the role of a general sent off to war, that man certainly knows how to give each character what is fitting for it. I would bid the learned imitator to look at the pattern of life and manners and to draw thence living voices.

Before proclaiming that knowledge (*sapere*), and specifically moral knowledge, is the most important element of good writing, Horace effects a transition through language that may be applied to both literary and moral qualities: *munus et officium, deceat, uirtus, error*.[50] What then surprises, however, is that 'Socratic texts', whatever precise nuance one wishes to give to this phrase,[51] are apparently to provide the raw material for poetry; here Horace has taken the conventional moralising approach to how poetry should be read, as witnessed for example in *Epistles* 1.2, and focused this same perspective upon how a poet should learn this trade. It is not that the poet has to be a professional philosopher to write well, but — given that the characters of literature will reveal their moral choices (in Aristotelian terms, their προαιρέσεις) and moral characters through what they say — it is only reasonable that the poet should understand such demands in order to give the appropriate words to each character (v. 316).

Commentators on this passage of the *Ars* have stressed that there is an important element here of searching for the best patterns, of finding — again to use Aristotelian terminology — the general rather than the particular, indeed an *exemplar* such as Odysseus who incorporates the universal at which we should be aiming (cf. *Epistles* 1.2.17–19). What is most important, however, is that the knowledge possessed by the *doctus imitator* is not (or not only) at the level of abstract theory, and this is where there is a particularly close link to *Epistles* 1.2. The kind of ethical understanding required of the poet is rooted in real situations and real (types of) people (*Ars* 312–315), and here 'life' is indeed the best teacher; in order to render 'true voices' to his characters the poet is first to have himself looked to the truth of life. As always, however, with rhetorically inflected poetry, an appeal to 'life' does not necessarily imply an unmediated opening of oneself to the everyday; Rostagni and others have rightly felt the familiar Hellenistic idea of poetry as 'an imitation of life' resonate behind Horace here, but in fact we may be able to be more specific than that. Horace is here strongly prescriptive:

---

50 The shape of v. 308 irresistibly recalls *Epistles* 1.2.3: Horace will now teach what Homer was there said to do.

51 On this phrase and on the interpretation of the whole passage cf. Sedley 2014. Cf. further the notes of Rostagni and Brink, *ad loc.* and cf. also Brink 1963, 130–131.

> respicere exemplar uitae morumque iubebo
> doctum imitatorem et uiuas hinc ducere uoces.
>
> Horace, *Ars* 317–318

I shall bid the imitator who has been trained look to the pattern of life and habits and from there draw living voices.

From any perspective, the language and ideas here are not (to us) pellucid, but Horace may have a particular model text in mind. In a famous passage of Terence's *Adelphoe*, Demeas, deluded as to his son's virtuous behaviour, boasts to the mocking slave Syrus of how he has trained the young man;

> *Dem.* fit sedulo:
> nil praetermitto; consuefacio; denique
> inspicere, tamquam in speculum, in uitas omnium
> iubeo atque ex aliis sumere exemplum sibi:
> 'hoc facito'. *Sy.* recte sane. *Dem.* 'hoc fugito'. *Sy.* callide.
> *Dem.* 'hoc laudist'. *Sy.* istaec res est. *Dem.* 'hoc uitio datur'.
>
> Terence, *Adelphoe* 413–418

Demeas I work hard at it: I overlook nothing; I train his habits; I bid him look into the lives of all men, as into a mirror, and take from others a model for himself: 'do this'. *Syrus* Very proper. *Demeas* 'Avoid this'. *Syrus* Clever! *Demeas* 'This deserves praise'. *Syrus* The very thing! *Demeas* 'This is accounted an error'.

Horace knew this passage well, for he had earlier used it to describe, with a suitable irony, how his father inculcated moral standards in him by pointing to specific examples of vice and error (*Satires* 1.4.105–126).[52] This too was a matter of 'habituation' (cf. ibidem 1.4.105 *insueuit*), and here too his father draws a distinction between the kind of education he is providing and that which 'technical philosophy' will subsequently provide (*sapiens, uitatu quidque petitu / sit melius, causas reddet tibi*, ibidem 1.4.115–116). The pompous banality of Demeas' words[53] might seem an odd text for Horace to allow to resonate at this point of the *Ars*, but not merely does Horace take an amused stance as *praeceptor* throughout the poem, but the echo anchors Horace's advice in the world of practical ethics and literature. Where one learns 'true' moral lessons is not just from the 'real life' around one, but also — or even especially — from literature, and comedy, with its familiar character types, held a prominent place here, but

---

52 Cf. esp. Citroni Marchetti 2004.
53 To the commentators add Fantham 1972, 68–69; a passage which is rightly always adduced in connection with these Latin texts is Plato, *Protagoras* 323d.

comedy was not alone. As *Epistles* 1.2 has made very clear, the great literature of the past has a prime educational role to play. In the *Ars* Horace has sent us off to *Socraticae chartae* to learn, but there are other relevant forms of literature also. In the fourth century BC the rhetorician Alcidamas had called the *Odyssey* 'a fair mirror of human life' (Aristotle, *Rhet.* 3 3.1406b12–13), and the analogy with Demeas' words in Terence's *Adelphoe* shows how both 'life' and 'literature' could contribute to ethical habituation. In this passage of the *Ars*, Horace treads a fine line between the two; in *Epistles* 1.2 the first half of the poem had been dominated by the former, and in the second half our own lives take over. What *Satires* 1.4, *Epistles* 1.2 and this passage of the *Ars* all share is a productive distinction between 'technical philosophy' and other sources of knowledge, notably poetry and the observation of experience. In *Epistles* 1.2 Horace had brought Homer dangerously close to philosophy, and so it is that the final part of the poem veers away from Homer to a homespun, proverbial wisdom that carries its own persuasive force, quite independent of both technical philosophy and the Homeric poems.[54]

sperne uoluptates, Horace tells us (v. 55), and these are, in particular, the bodily pleasures of excess and luxury; the language of greed which immediately follows (v. 56) takes us back to Odysseus' encounter with Circe: what saved the hero was that he did not 'drink greedily' (*cupidusque bibisset*, v. 24). Book 1 of Athenaeus' *Deipnosophistai* preserves extracts from one or more works on Homeric culture, and a passage such as the following gives a good sense of the kind of discussion which lies behind Horace here:

> Homer saw that moderation [σωφροσύνη] is the most fitting and leading virtue for young men ... and wishing to implant it again from the beginning and for the future, so that they would spend their leisure and energy on noble deeds and help each other in partnership, he made the lives of all his characters simple and without excess [εὐτελῆ...καὶ αὐταρκῆ]; he reckoned that desires and pleasures [ἐπιθυμίαι καὶ ἡδοναί] are very powerful, above all the engrained pleasures of food and drink, and that those who have always preserved a simple lifestyle are well-ordered and controlled in the rest of their lives as well.
>
> Athenaeus 1.8e–f

Weaknesses of the flesh always lead to and/or are symptoms of moral and psychological failings, and this is Horace's point: the habituation of pleasure is corruptingly addictive (vv. 51–61), *semper auarus eget*.

---

[54] Keane 2011, 448 argues for a rather different relationship: '[A]s the epic summaries distill both Homer's texts and the teachings of moral philosophy, the nuggets of wisdom in the epistle's second half represent "philosophizing" on a miniature and particularly mundane scale'.

Bibliography

Armstrong, D. 2004. 'Horace's *Epistles* 1 and Philodemus', in: D. Armstrong/J. Fish/P.A. Johnston/M.B. Skinner (eds.), *Vergil, Philodemus, and the Augustans*, Austin, 267-298.
Asmis, E. 1991. 'Philodemus' poetic theory and *On the Good King According to Homer*', *ClAnt* 10, 1-45.
Brink, C.O. 1963. *Horace on Poetry: Prolegomena to the Literary Epistles*, Cambridge.
Brink, C.O. 1971. *Horace on Poetry. The Ars Poetica*, vols. 2, Cambridge.
Cairns, F. 1989. *Virgil's Augustan Epic*, Cambridge.
Citroni Marchetti, S. 2004. 'I precetti e le lezioni dei filosofi; Demea, il padre di Orazio ed altri padre e figli', *MD* 53, 9-63.
Conte, G.B. 2007. *The Poetry of Pathos. Studies in Virgilian Epic*, Oxford.
De Lacy, P. 1948. 'Stoic views of poetry', *AJP* 69, 241-271.
Dillon, J. 2003. *The Heirs of Plato*, Oxford.
Edwards, M.J. 1992. 'Horace, Homer and Rome: *Epistles* 1.2', *Mnemosyne* 45, 83-87.
Fantham, E.A. 1972. *Comparative Studies in Republican Latin Imagery*, Toronto.
Fantuzzi, M. 2012. *Achilles in Love. Intertextual Studies*, Oxford.
Fowler, D. 2000. 'The didactic plot', in: M. Depew/D. Obbink (eds.), *Matrices of Genre: Authors, Canons, and Society*, Cambridge, 205-219.
Gigante, M. 1995. *Philodemus in Italy*, Ann Arbor.
Grilli, A. 1983. 'Oratio e l'epicureismo', in: *Corollas Philologicas in honorem Josephi Guillen Cabanero*, Salamanca, 267-292.
Haubold, J. 2000. *Homer's People*, Cambridge.
Heinze, R. 1914. *Q. Horatius Flaccus Briefe*, erklärt von A. Kiessling bearbeitet von R. Heinze, 4. Aufl., Berlin.
Hunter, R. 2009. *Critical Moments in Classical Literature*, Cambridge.
Hunter, R. 2012. *Plato and the Traditions of Ancient Literature*, Cambridge.
Keane, C. 2011. 'Lessons in reading: Horace on Homer at *Epistles* 1.2.1-31', *CW* 104, 427-450.
Laird, A. 2007. 'Figures of allegory from Homer to Latin epic', in: G.R. Boys-Stones (ed.), *Metaphor, Allegory, and the Classical Tradition*, Oxford, 151-175.
Long, A. 1992. 'Stoic readings of Homer', in: R. Lamberton/J.J. Keaney (eds.), *Homer's Ancient Readers*, Princeton, 41-66.
Luzzatto, M.T. 1996. 'Dialettica o retorica? La polytropia di Odisseo da Antistene a Porfirio', *Elenchos* 17, 275-357.
Mette, H.J. 1984. 'Zwei Akademiker heute: Krantor von Soloi und Arkesilaos von Pitane', *Lustrum* 26, 7-94.
Moles, J. 1985. 'Cynicism in Horace *Epistles* 1', *Papers of the Liverpool Latin Seminar* 5, 33-60.
Montiglio, S. 2011. *From Villain to Hero. Odysseus in Ancient Thought*, Ann Arbor.
Nussbaum, M.C. 1993. 'Poetry and the passions: two Stoic views', in: J. Brunschwig/M.C. Nussbaum (eds.), *Passions and perceptions*, Cambridge, 97-149.
Pontani, F. 2005. *Eraclito. Questioni omeriche sulle allegorie di Omero in merito agli dèi*, Pisa.
Pontani, F. 2007. *Scholia graeca in Odysseam; 1, scholia ad libros α-β*, Rome.
Roisman, H.M. 2005. 'Nestor the good counsellor', *CQ* 55, 17-38.
Rostagni, A. 1930. *Arte poetica di Orazio. Introduzione e commento*, Torino.

Russell, D.A. 1979. 'Classicizing rhetoric and criticism: the pseudo-Dionysian *Exetasis* and *Mistakes in Declamation*', in: H. Flashar (ed.), *Le classicisme à Rome aux I^{ers} siècles avant et après J.-C.*, Geneva, 113–130.

Scaffai, M. 1982. *Baebii Italici Ilias Latina*, Bologna.

Schofield, M. 1986. '*Euboulia* in the *Iliad*', *CQ* 36, 6–31.

Sedley, D. 2014. 'Horace's *Socraticae chartae* (*Ars Poetica* 295–322)', *MD* 72, 97–120.

Valgimigli, M. 1911. *La critica letteraria di Dione Crisostomo*, Bologna.

22 Some Dramatic Terminology

The history of the word δρᾶμα has been written many times,[1] but in this short paper I want to pick away at some of the implications of the usage of it and related terms in Greek and, then, to consider how Roman dramatists adapted Greek terminology in their plays. This study should be seen as a contribution to the history of the development of the language of criticism in Rome.

The origin of the word δρᾶμα is for these purposes less important than its 'flavour'. The earliest extant occurrences are probably Herodotus' two references to Phrynichus' famous play on 'The capture of Miletus' as a δρᾶμα (6.21.2), perhaps (and I offer this speculation hesitantly) because δρᾶμα was a more 'pan-Hellenic', less parochially Attic, term than τραγωιδία, which is what Phrynichus' play of 493 BC presumably was; δρᾶμα thus came more 'naturally' to Herodotus of Halicarnassus than did τραγωιδία, and would have seemed more natural also to a pan-Hellenic audience.[2] Herodotus in fact never uses τραγωιδία or κωμωιδία. As for Aristophanes, who uses the word frequently, it is well known that δρᾶμα in the extant comedies seems always to refer to tragedy, but of equal interest at least is the identity of those who use the word. In the *Frogs*, which seems the natural place to start, it will not surprise that the word is only found in the mouth of Aeschylus (1021) and Euripides (920, 923, 946–947), and in *Thesmophoriazousai* we similarly find it used by Agathon's servant (52), Agathon himself (149, 151, 166), and once by Euripides' old relation as he ponders which 'drama' (of Euripides) he will use to get Euripides to come to his aid (849); this scene shows the old man as not just an expert in Euripides' plays, but also as well versed in the 'new-fangled' language of criticism. In the *Acharnians*, Euripides himself uses the word (470), but most instructive of all perhaps is Dicaiopolis' plea to him:

ἀτὰρ τί τὰ ῥάκι'; εἰς τραγωιδίας ἔχεις
ἐσθῆτ' ἐλεινήν; οὐκ ἐτὸς πτωχοὺς ποιεῖς.
ἀλλ' ἀντιβολῶ πρός τῶν γονάτων σ', Εὐριπίδη,
δός μοι ῥάκιόν τι τοῦ παλαιοῦ δράματος.   415
δεῖ γάρ με λέξαι τῶι χορῶι ῥῆσιν μακράν·
αὕτη δὲ θάνατον, ἢν κακῶς λέξω, φέρει.

Aristophanes, *Acharnians* 412–417

---

[1] Cf. Richards 1900, and further bibliography in Austin/Olson on Ar. Thesm. 52.
[2] Strabo 14.1.7 cites the Alexander-historian, Callisthenes, as also recording (FGrHist 124 F30) that Phrynichus ὁ τραγικός staged (δρᾶμα ἐποίησε) the capture of Miletus; it is unclear whether Callisthenes is following Herodotus.

> But why these rags? The wretched clothes are for your tragedies? No wonder you create beggars! But please, Euripides, by your knees, give me some rag of the old drama. I have to deliver a long speech to the chorus, and if I speak badly, the reward will be death.

The 'tragic' nature of τραγωιδία determines its use here alongside 'piteous clothing',[3] but when Dicaiopolis tells Euripides that he needs 'some rag from/of an old drama', because he has to deliver 'a long *rhesis* to the chorus' it is clear that he appeals to Euripides with the kind of 'theatrical' language that will precisely carry weight with the tragedian. Whether or not we should see here a comic poet, 'Aristophanes-Dicaiopolis', appealing to the solidarity of a tragic fellow-craftsman may be debated, but what should, I think, be clear is that the language, while not 'technical' in the sense of language not understood by anyone except a practitioner, carries nevertheless a kind of professional flavour. δρᾶμα is a word that playwrights use. I am reminded somewhat of the way pilots tell you over the intercom about the 'aircraft', rather than 'the aeroplane' or even 'the plane', or about 'the airfield' rather than 'the airport'; these are ordinary words which everyone understands, but they are only (or mainly) used by those in the profession.[4]

Little can be added from the fragments of the rest of Greek comedy, but it is worth noting that δρᾶμα appears in the famous fragment of Antiphanes' *Poiesis* (fr. 189), perhaps spoken by 'Poiesis' herself or by 'Komoidia', pouring scorn on the habits of tragic poets ἐν τοῖς δράμασιν, and in Ecphantides fr. 3 K-A (probably the earliest fragment to contain the word), in which a character (a poet?) claims that he is ashamed 'to make τὸ δρᾶμα Megarian'. Elsewhere, we find the word (again) in connection with Euripides (Strattis fr. 1, Telecleides fr. 41, Diphilus fr. 74), and at Euphron fr. 1.35 a pretentious cook draws a distinction between δρᾶμα and παίγνιον; the distinction may there too characterise a professional interest. Fragments never, of course, give everything away, and it can hardly be claimed that δρᾶμα was never used in comedy (or indeed at Athens) entirely 'neutrally', perhaps even in the Aristophanic play or plays entitled Δράματα.[5] So too, the conclusions to be drawn from the fact that δρᾶμα seems

---

[3] Cf. also τραγωιδία at *Peace* 148.
[4] For a rather more sophisticated analysis of the range of such language in comedy cf. Willi 2003, ch. 3; on p. 60 Willi discusses the very relevant class of words which are understood, but not normally used by, non-specialists.
[5] At Ephippus fr. 16.1 Διονυσίου δράματα are the object of scorn, and there seems no reason why τραγωιδίας could not have been substituted (cf. esp. Ar. *Knights* 401). An interesting case is Adesp. Com. 51 K-A ἤδη δὲ λέξω τὸν λόγον τοῦ δράματος, which Wilamowitz (*Kleine Schrift-*

never to appear in what survives of Menander are certainly debatable; it might be thought unsurprising that it is indeed explicitly τραγωιδία against which κωμωιδία continues to measure itself (cf., e.g., *Aspis* 329, *Epitr.* 325, 1125, *Samia* 590),[6] as in Dicaiopolis' famous claim that 'τρυγωιδία also knows what is just' (Ar. *Ach.* 500). δρᾶμα was subsequently to have a full life as a word of grammarians, writers of dramatic *hypotheseis* and so on, but it seems never to have been fully adopted on to the dramatic stage itself.

When we move forward to Roman comedy, where *fabula* might be thought the nearest equivalent for δρᾶμα, it may be sensible to work backwards from Terence to Plautus, and to begin not in fact with *fabula*, but rather with *comoedia*. The latter term occurs only once in Terence outside the prologues, at *Hecyra* 866:

> placet non fieri hoc itidem ut in comoediis
> omnia omnes ubi resciscunt. hic quos par fuerat resciscere
> sciunt; quos non autem aequomst scire neque resciscent neque scient.
> Terence, *Hecyra* 866–868

> I don't want it to be like in comedies where everyone learns everything. In this case those who should find out know; those who have no need to know will neither learn nor know.

Although *fabula* in the sense of 'play' never, I believe, occurs in Terence outside the prologues, there seems no reason to doubt that here *fabulae* could have taken the place of *comoediae*; we may, however, ask what the choice of the Greek word, which may of course have appeared in Apollodorus' Greek play, lends to this very 'metatheatrical' passage[7]. What is *not* at stake here, I think, is Greek κωμωιδία vs Roman *fabula*, a contrast which — to anticipate — we shall see in Terence's prologues; the Roman audience are likely to see themselves, not Greek audiences and institutions, as the subject of the joke here. Rather, I suggest, *comoediae* is here used as the unmistakably theatrical, and hence distancing, 'formal' term: *this* action, so Pamphilus insists, is not going to be like an artificial performance on the stage, as far removed from 'real life' as *comoediae* is (in origin) from the Latin language. In 'real life' some people do remain in the dark and it is not the case that, as happens in comic drama, 'everybody gets to know everything'; it is almost as though 'everybody gets to know every-

---

en IV (Berlin 1962) 157–158) argued to come from a Menandrean metrical hypothesis, rather than from a play itself; the matter must, however, be considered quite uncertain.
6 Cf., e.g., Hunter 1985, 118–121, 134–135.
7 The matter is not really discussed in Goldberg's recent commentary.

thing at the end' is one of the generic criteria for comedy, and this term here thus points to a rather sophisticated play with the dramatic illusion,[8] or whatever we want to call such effects. The fact that Terence nowhere uses *comicus*, *tragicus*, or *tragoedia* reinforces the suspicion that *comoediae* at *Hecyra* 866 carries a very distinctive charge.

If we move to the prologues, we find that *comoedia* can reinforce the 'Greekness' of a Greek title (*Phormio* 26, *HT* 4–5), and can indeed stand in contrast to a Latin adaptation designated as fabula (*Ad.* 6–7), a distinction we do not, I think, find in Plautus[9]. On the other hand, the *fabulae* which Terence's alleged opponents claim should not be 'contaminated' (*Andria* 16) seem to be Greek plays, rather than Roman adaptations (cf. *HT* 16–17), and in the same prologue it is *comoediae* which Terence looks forward to composing in the future (*Andria* 26, contrast *quas fecisset fabulas*, v. 39). This last seems in fact to be something of an exception to general practice, as *fabula* is essentially the default term for 'play' (including Terence's plays) in the prologues (cf. *Eun.* 23–25, 33–34, *Hecyra* 1, *Phormio* 4, *Ad.* 11 (with reference to Diphilus' play)). The terminology is clearly fluid enough for the case of *Andria* 26 to carry little or no significance, but given that Terence is apparently so sparing with the term *comoedia*, we should at least keep an open mind here. I wonder in fact whether Terence is not making something of a statement about the nature of his drama: he will continue to write in both Greek and Roman (vv. 18–21) traditions, and the use of the borrowed Greek term thus carries a charge. Everything we think we know about Terence and the context in which he wrote at Rome makes that 'Hellenising' claim a very pointed one.

When we move to Plautus, who is much less sparing with the term *comoedia*, no very clear distribution emerges, but it may again be possible to discern some interesting patterns. Unlike in Terence, of course, Plautine characters freely use both *fabula* and *comoedia*, thus giving, as is well known, a much more 'metatheatrical' flavour to Plautine plays; it is not difficult to show that the two terms can be virtually interchangeable, but also that the Greekness of *comoedia* can be activated when Plautus (or the prologue-speakers) desire it, as for example at *Menaechmi* 7:

> atque hoc poetae faciunt in comoediis:
> omnis res gestas esse Athenis autumant,

---

[8] Cf. Bain 1977, 212 n. 3.
[9] Note a case such as *MG* 84–87, where *comoedia* might be thought to reinforce the Greek title Ἀλαζών, but seems also to be used of the Latin play being acted; *Casina* 31–33 presents a similar case.

quo illud uobis graecum uideatur magis;
ego nusquam dicam nisi ubi factum dicitur. 10
atque adeo hoc argumentum graecissat, tamen
non atticissat, uerum sicilicissitat.

Plautus, Menaechmi 7–12

This is what poets do in comedies: they declare that everything takes place in Athens, just so you will think it more Greek; as for me, I won't say it took place anywhere except where it is said to have happened. Therefore, this plot Grecises, but does not Atticise so much as Sicilise.

comoediis here introduces the 'Greek theme' of the following verses. *fabula* is by contrast, as it is in Terence, the neutral, unmarked term. This is particularly clear from the several instances where *fabula* is used when a character (or the whole troupe) declares at or near the end that 'the play is over', or words to that effect, cf. *Cas.* 1006, *Merc.* 1007, *Most.* 1181, *Poen.* 1370, *Pseud.* 1335, *Rud.* 1421, *Truc.* 967. Only once does *comoedia* appear in such a position, and this case seems telling:

nunc, quod postremum est condimentum fabulae,
si placuit, plausum postulat comoedia.

Plautus, Poenulus 1370–1371

Now, as the last seasoning for the play, if you liked it, the comedy asks for your applause.

The *uariatio* of terms (*fabula* ~ *comoedia*) might be thought to suggest that the two terms are here strictly synonymous, but it might be suggested that *fabula* here refers to standard theatrical practice (applause at the end), whereas *comoedia* reminds the audience of the jolly time they have had, a pleasure which they can return by their applause.

The case of the Plautine prologues is notoriously problematic, and notoriously fascinating, for more than one reason. Whatever view we take of the history of the Plautine text, we all but certainly have, particularly in the prologues, the work of a number of different poets/troupe-managers, whatever you want to call them; in these circumstances, any search for consistency in semantic usage must be a very cautious one, and any proper consideration of the matter would have to take this into account. Here I will limit myself to brief remarks on a couple of passages, before turning to the plays themselves.

When the difference between tragedy and comedy is at stake, then of course *comoedia* and related terms are inevitably chosen. The prologist of the *Captiui* refers to the play about to be acted as a *fabula* (52, 54), but then turns to the *virtues* of what the audience are about to see:

> profecto expediet fabulae huic operam dare.
> non pertractate facta est neque item ut ceterae: 55
> neque spurcidici insunt uersus, immemorabiles;
> hic neque periurus leno est nec meretrix mala
> neque miles gloriosus; ne uereamini,
> quia bellum Aetolis esse dixi cum Aleis:
> foris illic extra scaenam fient proelia.   60
> nam hoc paene iniquomst, comico choragio
> conari desubito agere nos tragoediam.
>
> Plautus, Captiui 54–62

It will certainly be to your advantage to pay attention to this play. It is not composed in a very familiar style nor is it like other plays. It contains no dirty verses which are not for repetition. Here there is no perjured pimp nor wicked courtesan nor boastful soldier. Don't be afraid because I said that the Aetolians and the Eleans are at war; the battles will take place over there off-stage. It would almost be an outrage for us with our comic gear suddenly to try to put on a tragedy.

Warfare belongs with tragedy, not comedy.[10] The theme of 'decent comedy' returns at the very end of the play (1029–34):

> spectatores, ad pudicos mores facta haec fabula est,
> neque in hac subigitationes sunt neque ulla amatio   1030
> nec pueri suppositio nec argenti circumductio,
> neque ubi amans adulescens scortum liberet clam suom patrem.
> huius modi paucas poetae reperiunt comoedias,
> ubi boni meliores fiant.

Spectators, this play was composed with chaste morals: it contained no illicit sex, no love-story, no supposititious child, no fraudulent extraction of money, no young man in love setting free a prostitute without his father knowing. Poets find few comedies of this kind, in which the good become better.

Here, at first glance, *fabula* and *comoedia* might be thought exactly interchangeable, particularly as 1030–1032 describe the typical plot elements of a comedy. Nevertheless, it may be worth suggesting that *ubi boni meliores fiant* at least gestures towards rather different ideas of what kind of a representation comedy is; this is not, of course, to suggest that Plautus (or a Greek poet) has in mind, for example, Aristotle's ideas of comedy normally being an imitation of 'the worse' (*Poetics* 1448a11–17, cf. 1453a30–38), but a sense of generic defini-

---

10 The argument is a very old one, cf., e.g., Isocrates, *To Nicocles* 48–49.

tion does seem to resonate here in the marked term *comoediae*. In the case of the famous prologue of the *Amphitruo*, the matter seems clear:

> nunc quam rem oratum huc ueni primum proloquar,   50
> post argumentum huius eloquar tragoediae.
> quid? contraxistis frontem, quia tragoediam
> dixi futuram hanc? deus sum, commutauero.
> eandem hanc, si uoltis, faciam iam ex tragoedia
> comoedia ut sit omnibus isdem uorsibus.   55
> utrum sit an non uoltis? sed ego stultior,
> quasi nesciam uos uelle, qui diuos siem.
> teneo quid animi uostri super hac re siet:
> faciam ut commixta sit: <sit> tragicomoedia.
> nam me perpetuo facere ut sit comoedia,   60
> reges quo ueniant et di, non par arbitror.
> quid igitur? quoniam hic seruos quoque partes habet,
> faciam sit, proinde ut dixi, tragicomoedia.
>
>   Plautus, *Amphitruo* 50–63

First I'll tell you the request I have come here to make and then I will explain the plot of this tragedy. What? You're frowning because I said that this would be a tragedy? I'm a god, I'll change it. If you like, I'll make this same play not a tragedy but a comedy, with the very same verses. Do you want that or not? Silly me! Of course I know what you want, as I'm a god. I understand your desires in this matter. I'll make it a mixture: let it be a tragicomedy. I don't think it would be right for me to make it a comedy outright when kings and gods will appear. What then? As a slave has a role here, I'll make it, just as I said, a tragicomedy.

Here 'generic definition' is clearly at issue, and this will, I think, shed light on a passage later in the same prologue:

> ipse hanc acturust Iuppiter comoediam.
> quid? admirati estis? quasi uero nouom
> nunc proferatur, Iouem facere histrioniam;   90
> etiam, histriones anno cum in proscaenio hic
> Iouem inuocarunt, uenit, auxilio is fuit.
> praeterea certo prodit in tragoedia.[11]
> hanc fabulam, inquam, hic Iuppiter hodie ipse aget,
> et ego una cum illo. nunc <uos> animum aduortite,   95
> dum huius argumentum eloquar comoediae.
>
>   Plautus, *Amphitruo* 88–96

---

11 Leo's deletion of this verse is very attractive.

Jupiter himself will have a role in this comedy. What? You're surprised? As if we were now doing something new, making Jupiter an actor. Last year, right here on this stage, the actors called on Jupiter and he came and helped them. Moreover, he certainly appears in tragedy. To repeat: Jupiter himself will have a role in this play, and myself alongside him. Now pay attention while I tell you the plot of this comedy.

Here we might well think that vv. 88 and 94 are a very clear case of the interchangeability of *comoedia* and *fabula*, but I would suggest that the formal term in v. 88 triggers the generic joke which follows, so that *fabula* in v. 93 shows that the whole matter is closed: this is now just 'a play' and the issues of its genre settled, or perhaps rather no longer important (the 'generic' joke has now been played out). On his second run through the idea of Jupiter appearing as a character, Mercury avoids having to deal with a surprised audience reaction by using the neutral term *fabula*; one can imagine that considerable emphasis was in fact given to *fabulam* by the actor playing Mercury. Far, in this instance, from being interchangeable, *comoedia* and *fabula* are in fact potently different.

In turning to the plays themselves, I begin with a famous piece of mockery by the slave Stasimus in *Trinummus*:

> non enim possum quin exclamem: eugae, eugae, Lysiteles, πάλιν.
> facile palmam habes: hic uictust, uicit tua comoedia.
> hic agit magis ex argumento et uorsus meliores facit.
>
> Plautus, Trinummus 705–707

> I can only exclaim: well done, well done, Lysiteles! Encore! You easily carry off the prize; he's beaten, your comedy has won! This chap follows the script more closely and makes better verses.

The mocking use of Greek, and the theatrical terms with which Stasimus expresses himself, here make *comoedia* (or should we print κωμωιδία?) much more pointed than *fabula* would have been; the slave is comparing alternative 'performances', and suggesting that both are 'posed' and artificial (cf., e.g., *Pseudolus* 1080–1083, 1239–1241). Here again, then, *comoedia* functions as the marked term which emphasizes the distance between a 'performance' and 'real life'. Over one hundred and thirty years ago, in a famous discussion of such phenomena, Friedrich Leo drew a distinction within Roman comedy between references to plays and matters theatrical of the kind which people do make 'in real life', and which do not (as we, glossing Leo, might say) 'break the dramatic illusion', and those which make it clear and explicit that the spectators are watching a play; Leo classed *Trinummus* 705–707 in the former category.[12] We would not, I think, today make such a straightforward distinction, or at least not in those terms and/or without considerable nuancing, but Leo's other claim that *Trinummus* 705–707 is very likely to be a 'faithful' adaptation from the Greek original does deserve a moment's attention. Leo claimed that the verses referred to Greek, not Roman, practices. Again, it is a measure of the change that has come over the study of Roman comedy that, even were this true, it would no longer be thought to be a convincing demonstration of 'Greekness'. In fact, however, that claim is at best uncertain. This passage represents one of three references in Roman comedy to contests between actors, and the other two occur in Plautine prologues (*Amph.* 69, *Poen.* 37); there is also a reference in a Terentian prologue to the *palma* available for anyone involved in *ars musica* (*Phormio* 17). The onus of proof would in fact seem to be on those who see Greek practice here.[13]

Stasimus' justification of his award of the palm to Lysiteles is itself not without interest. He claims that Lysiteles' acting 'follows the script' more closely (I think that this is what *ex argumento* means — or is it 'contributes to the plot'?), and that he produces 'better verses'. We seem to have here a pairing somewhat analogous to Terence's famous claim in the prologue of the *Andria* about Menander's *Andria* and *Perinthia*:

> Menander fecit Andriam et Perinthiam.
> qui utramuis recte norit ambas nouerit: 10
> non ita dissimili sunt argumento, [s]et tamen
> dissimili oratione sunt factae ac stilo.
>
> Terence, *Andria* 9–12

> Menander composed an *Andria* and a *Perinthia*. Anyone who knows one of them, knows them both; it's not the plots which are different, but rather they are composed with different verbal manner and style.

However tendentious that assertion, and however familiar in Greek criticism and rhetoric the distinction between 'plot' and 'verbal elaboration' might be,[14] we might at least wonder whether we catch here echoes of a developing Roman critical discourse, and one which was fostered precisely by the fact that early Latin literature (and, of course, most notably drama) was precisely a literature of translation and adaptation. It is such a literature which puts pressure on

---

12 Leo 1883, 561–562.
13 Cf. Brown 2002, 234, Jory 1988, Maurach on *Poen.* 37 (non-committal).
14 Cf., e.g., Jocelyn 1967, 24.

inuentio, and which draws particular attention to the various elements which may be the object of imitation and elaboration; the quality of *oratio* or *stilus* moves 'centre stage' (so to speak) when one is moving from one language to another (think, to go no further, of Catullus' translations of Sappho and Callimachus). If there is anything to this, then this critical discourse comes to Rome not (or not principally) from the Greek critical heritage, but rather from the very practice of Roman writing.

The *Trinummus* passage has suggested that Plautus could (at need) use *comoedia* to stress 'comedy' as something set apart as an artificial performance, with its own motifs and rules. It seems natural to move from there to the famous instance[15] of *Mostellaria* 1149–1151:

> *Theopropides.* quid ego nunc faciam?
> *Tranio.* si amicus Diphilo aut Philemoni es,
> dicito eis, quo pacto tuos te seruos ludificauerit:
> optumas frustrationes dederis in comoedias.
>
> Plautus, *Mostellaria* 1149–1151
>
> comoedias Kassel: comoediis
>
> *Theopropides.* What am I to do now? *Tranio.* If you're a friend of Diphilus or Philemon, tell them how your slave fooled you. You'll give them marvellous bamboozlements for their comedies.

Almost every possible permutation of answer has been given to the question of whether these verses of the *Mostellaria* come from Plautus' Greek model or not,[16] but — if I was a betting man — I would have a small wager on the fact that, whatever the Greek text had at this point, there was no reference to 'comedy'. This is there in the Roman text not just to remind Plautus' audience of who Diphilus and Philemon are, but also precisely to reinforce the 'theatricality' of what Tranio is saying: his deception was so brilliant it deserves to be commemorated in art. The only other occurrence of *frustratio* in our extant corpus of Plautus is in Jupiter's second prologue to the *Amphitruo* and this may be thought to support the suggestion made here:

> nunc Amphitruonem memet, ut occepi semel,
> esse adsimulabo, atque in horum familiam
> frustrationem hodie iniciam maxumam; 875

---

15 Cf., e.g., Bain 1977, 211–212.
16 Cf. Bain *loc. cit.*, Williams 1983, 215 (resurrecting the idea that Plautus found only Diphilus in the original).

post igitur demum faciam res fiat palam
atque Alcumenae in tempore auxilium feram
faciamque ut uno fetu et quod grauida est uiro
et me quod grauidast pariat sine doloribus.

Plautus, *Amphitruo* 873–879

Now, as I once started, I'll pretend myself to be Amphitruo, and today I'll throw the highest degree of bamboozlement into this family. After that, I will finally make everything plain and I'll help Alcmena just when it's needed: I'll bring it about that, in one painless birth, she has both her husband's child and mine.

Almost immediately before this, Jupiter has explained the reason for his appearance:

ego sum ille Amphitruo, cui est seruos Sosia,
idem Mercurius qui fit, quando commodumst,
in superiore qui habito cenaculo,
qui interdum fio Iuppiter, quando lubet;
huc autem quom extemplo aduentum adporto, ilico   865
Amphitruo fio et uestitum immuto meum.
nunc huc honoris uostri uenio gratia,
ne hanc incohatam transigam comoediam.

Plautus, *Amphitruo* 861–868[17]

I am that Amphitruo, whose slave is Sosia, but who is also Mercury when it suits. I live in the upper storey, and when I take the fancy, I sometimes become Jupiter. Whenever however I have occasion to come here, I immediately become Amphitruo and I change my clothes. I've come here now out of respect for you, so as not to bring this comedy to a premature end.

That this second prologue is a highly 'metatheatrical' moment within the comedy hardly requires discussion (Jupiter also makes a joke about changing his costume (866) and addresses the audience directly (867); my guess would be that *frustratio* itself had some kind of theatrical resonance,[18] as though *frustratio* and *faciam res fiat palam* (*Amph.* 876) represented the Roman comic equivalent of Aristotelian δέσις and λύσις. Tranio's advice to Theopropides in the *Mostellaria* comes, then, pointedly at the time when the *frustrationes* are set aside and the typical comic ending of reconciliation and revelation take over. Greek

---

17 The sense of v. 868 must be something like De Melo's 'so as not to bring this comedy to a premature end', but the expression is at least awkward (which presumably led to Havet's *ut* for *ne*), cf. Christensen *ad loc.*, making the nice suggestion that Jupiter is also suggesting that he has not arrived as a closing *deus ex machina*.
18 Cf. Christensen *ad loc.* Very similar are Mercury's words to the audience at vv. 470–478.

equivalents for the language of *frustratio* are, of course, not hard to find,[19] but it is less important here to wonder about 'Plautinisches im Plautus' than to feel a developing Roman language in which the literariness of comedy, and no doubt tragedy also, could be discussed.

I have in these brief remarks taken two different, but I hope complementary, approaches to teasing out the development of a Roman critical discourse, centred on the adaptation of Greek comedies to the Roman stage. The picture is inevitably a very partial one, and our sight is blocked as often as it is allowed glimpses of searchable terrain. What matters, I think, is that there is indeed searchable terrain, and progress seems possible as long as we ask the right questions.

Bibliography

Bain, D. 1977. *Actors and Audience*, Oxford.
Brown, P. 2002. 'Actors and Actor-Managers at Rome in the Time of Plautus and Terence', in: P. Easterling/E. Hall (eds.), *Greek and Roman Actors*, Cambridge, 225–237.
Hunter, R. 1985. *The New Comedy of Greece and Rome*, Cambridge.
Jocelyn, H.D. 1967. *The Tragedies of Ennius*, Cambridge.
Jory, E.J. 1988. 'Publilius Syrus and the Element of Competition in the Theatre of the Republic', in: N. Horsfall (ed.), *Vir Bonus Discendi Peritus. Studies in Celebration of Otto Skutsch's Eightieth Birthday*, London, 73–81.
Leo, F. 1883. '*Lectiones Plautinae*', *Hermes* 18, 558–587 [= *Ausgewählte kleine Schriften*, Rome 1960, 13–33].
Richards, H. 1900. 'On the Word Δρᾶμα', *CR* 14, 388–393.
Willi, A. 2003. *The Languages of Aristophanes*, Oxford.
Williams, G. 1983. 'Roman Poets as Literary Historians. Some Aspects of *imitatio*', *ICS* 8, 211–227.

---

19 Cf. ταραχὴ in Tyche's prologue at Men. *Aspis* 137.

23 *Regius urget*: Hellenising Thoughts on Latin Intratextuality

This paper briefly considers three aspects of the Greek background reflected both in the 'intratextuality' of Latin literature and in some modern discussions of what that term might mean. The three case-studies are overlapping in their concerns, as is, I hope, appropriate for the subject of this volume.

Empedocles and Horace

Any discussion of 'intratextuality' in ancient literature must, sooner or later, turn to the opening and closing of Horace's *Ars Poetica*:

> humano capiti ceruicem pictor equinam
> iungere si uelit et uarias inducere plumas
> undique collatis membris, ut turpiter atrum
> desinat in piscem mulier formosa superne,
> spectatum admissi risum teneatis amici?   5
> credite, Pisones, isti tabulae fore librum
> persimilem, cuius, uelut aegri somnia, uanae
> fingentur species, ut nec pes nec caput uni
> reddatur formae. 'pictoribus atque poetis
> quidlibet audendi semper fuit aequa potestas.'   10
> scimus, et hanc ueniam petimusque damusque uicissim,
> sed non ut placidis coeant immitia, non ut
> serpentes auibus geminentur, tigribus agni.
>
> Horace, *Ars Poetica* 1–13

Imagine a painter who wanted to combine a horse's neck with a human head, and then clothe a miscellaneous collection of limbs with various kinds of feathers, so that what started out at the top as a beautiful woman ended in a hideously ugly fish. If you, friends, were invited to the private view, could you help laughing? Let me tell you, Pisones, a book whose different features are made up at random like a sick man's dreams, with no unified form to have a head or a tail, is exactly like that picture. 'Painters and poets have always enjoyed recognised rights to venture on what they will'. Yes we know; indeed, we ask and

---

An earlier version of this essay was delivered as the closing lecture at the 'Intratextuality' conference in Thessaloniki in May 2017. In accordance with tradition, I have not sought to remove all traces of its origin in an oral performance.

grant this permission turn and turn about. But it doesn't mean that fierce and gentle can be united, snakes paired with birds or lambs with tigers.

trans. D.A. Russell, adapted

ut mala quem scabies aut morbus regius urget
aut fanaticus error et iracunda Diana,
uesanum tetigisse timent fugiuntque poetam,
qui sapiunt; agitant pueri incautique sequuntur.
hic dum sublimis uersus ructatur et errat,
si ueluti merulis intentus decidit auceps
in puteum foueamue, licet 'succurrite' longum
clamet 'io ciues', non sit qui tollere curet.   460
si curet quis opem ferre et demittere funem,
'qui scis an prudens huc se deiecerit atque
seruari nolit?' dicam, Siculique poetae
narrabo interitum. deus inmortalis haberi
dum cupit Empedocles, ardentem frigidus Aetnam
insiluit. sit ius liceatque perire poetis;
inuitum qui seruat, idem facit occidenti.
nec semel hoc fecit nec, si retractus erit, iam
fiet homo et ponet famosae mortis amorem.
nec satis apparet cur uersus factitet, utrum   470
minxerit in patrios cineres, an triste bidental
mouerit incestus; certe furit, ac uelut ursus,
obiectos caueae ualuit si frangere clatros,
indoctum doctumque fugat recitator acerbus;
quem uero arripuit, tenet occiditque legendo,
non missura cutem nisi plena cruoris hirudo.

Horace, *Ars Poetica* 453–476

Men of sense are afraid to touch a mad poet and give him a wide berth. He's like a man suffering from a nasty itch, or the jaundice, or fanaticism, or Diana's wrath. Boys chase him and follow him round incautiously. And if, while he's belching out his lofty lines and wandering round, he happens to fall into a well or a pit, like a fowler intent on his birds, then, however long he shouts 'Help! Help! Fellow citizens, help!' there'll be no one to bother to pick him up. And if anyone should trouble to help and let down a rope, my question will be, 'How do you know that he didn't throw himself down deliberately? Are you sure he wants to be saved?' And I shall tell the tale of the Sicilian poet. Empedocles wanted to be regarded as an immortal god, and so he jumped, cool as you like, into burning Etna. Let poets have the right and privilege of death. To save a man against his will is the same as killing him. This isn't the only time he's done it. If he's pulled out now, he won't become human or lay aside his love of a notorious end. It's far from clear why he keeps writing poetry. Has the villain pissed on his father's ashes? Or disturbed the grim site of a lightning-strike? Anyway, he's raving, and his harsh readings put learned and unlearned alike to flight, like a bear that's broken the bars of his cage. If he catches anyone, he holds on and kills him with reading. He's a real leech that won't let go of the skin till it's full of blood.

trans. D.A. Russell

The relationships between the way in which literary works or corpora begin and end is one of the big intratextual questions: as T.S. Eliot ought to have said, do our ends *ever* know our beginnings? Let me begin, however, at the beginning. It might be asked more often than it is *why* the *amici* of v.5 will inevitably laugh at what Charles Brink has christened 'a grotesque';[1] which of the traditional causes of laughter is appropriate here?[2] The usual answer, and one which must at least in part be important to Horace, is that this is a bonding form of laughter for *amici* (including ourselves) who recognise the lack of πρέπον when they see it and also the linkage in critical theory between unity and beauty.[3] Nevertheless there is a real discontinuity here. This painter, so often labelled 'inept' etc. in modern criticism,[4] apparently *wants* to paint a grotesque (*uelit* v. 2). Who then, we should ask, is focalising *turpiter* in v. 3?: the standard view, of course, is that this is 'Horace's judgement',[5] but can we be sure that *turpiter* does not describe the effect at which the painter is actually aiming? So too, can we be absolutely sure that *ut* in v. 3 does not (or could not) introduce a purpose clause rather than a result clause or even (so Brink, citing Wickham) a clause of 'added qualification'; if so, this painter might in fact be delighted when his work is received with laughter (even the laughter of Horace's *amici*, perhaps provoked by thoughts of which the painter would not approve). The clear implication which follows that *poets* produce such 'grotesque' effects unwittingly and would not welcome audience laughter must be set against this opening ambiguity. Horace's painter may be operating within an entirely different critical structure than the one Horace will adopt (however loosely) in the rest of the poem, and this needs to be borne in mind in any assessment of the intratextual relation between the opening and the rest; moreover, as the ending will make clear, it is not just painters who can operate *extra leges*. Far from pointing unambiguously to a similarity between painters and poets (v. 9), the opening passage at least seems to draw from and contribute to that other ancient discourse about the difference in potential between poetry (or literature more broadly) and the plastic and representational arts. Horace sets himself up as critic and judge (v. 11), but some people just could not care less — and that irony might itself be thought very Horatian.

---

[1] But see, e.g., Schwindt 2014.
[2] Cf. (briefly) Beard 2014, 37–39; Beard does not discuss the opening of the *AP* in her book.
[3] For a more nuanced answer cf., e.g., Oliensis 1998, 201.
[4] Not untypical is Citroni 2009, 19, 'a glaring example of an artistic failure, clearly recognizable as such, immediately and intuitively ...'.
[5] Oliensis 1998, 201.

The opening 'grotesque' gives way at the end to a blood-sucking leech, no longer the stuff of a sick man's dreams (v. 7) or Plato's worst nightmares, but instead a small singularity, utterly focused, utterly *simplex et unum*, almost utterly self-reliant (leeches are hermaphroditic), a creation designed by nature to have (at least to the naked eye) no head, neck or tail (never mind feathers), but to have a very clear purpose, and to leave no room for *risus*, a creature which — like poetry — claims to have medicinal properties, but ends up killing you. The long recognised ring-composition and variation which frames the *Ars Poetica* is richly meaningful.[6] The friends let in to view the painting at the beginning suggest also the audience for a *recitatio* of poetry, and that implied audience becomes real at the end, as the mad poet latches (or rather 'leeches') on to someone — rather like the 'boor' in *Sat.* 1.9[7] or Eumolpus in the *Satyrica* — and recites him to death, as at this moment we are listening to the *AP* and just wishing it would end... Poetry needs audiences — just as a leech needs a blood-filled host; but the audience for poetry, unlike the leech's host, needs to make critical choices, needs to engage more than passively with the give and take of poetic creation.

The mad poet-*recitator*-leech, who operates *extra leges artis* like the opening painter (who may or may not be 'mad'), had already been exemplified by Empedocles, who, paradoxically or not, had prayed to the gods to avoid μανίη in what he sang (fr. 3 = D44 L-M).[8] Empedocles threw himself into Etna, but he does not disappear from Horace's poem. The image of the (medicinal) leech has something to do with the famous opening passage of the *Katharmoi*, in which Empedocles claims healing powers:

ὦ φίλοι, οἳ μέγα ἄστυ κατὰ ξανθοῦ Ἀκράγαντος
ναίετ' ἀν' ἄκρα πόλεος, ἀγαθῶν μελεδήμονες ἔργων,
ξείνων αἰδοῖοι λιμένες, κακότητος ἄπειροι,
χαίρετ'· ἐγὼ δ' ὑμῖν θεὸς ἄμβροτος, οὐκέτι θνητός
πωλεῦμαι μετὰ πᾶσι τετιμένος, ὥσπερ ἔοικα,
ταινίαις τε περίστεπτος στέφεσίν τε θαλείοις.
<πᾶσι δὲ> τοῖς ἂν ἵκωμαι ἄστεα τηλεθάοντα,
ἀνδράσιν ἠδὲ γυναιξί, σεβίζομαι· οἱ δ' ἅμ' ἕπονται
μυρίοι ἐξερέοντες, ὅπηι πρὸς κέρδος ἀταρπός,
οἱ μὲν μαντοσυνέων κεχρημένοι, οἱ δ' ἐπὶ νούσων

---

6 On the ring-composition of the *Ars* cf., e.g., Russell 2006, 339, Oliensis 1998, 215–218, Laird 2007, 137.
7 Cf., e.g., Oliensis 1998, 218–219.
8 For the abbreviation L-M cf. the bibliography, under Laks/Most.

παντοίων ἐπύθοντο κλυεῖν εὐηκέα βάξιν,
δηρὸν δὴ χαλεπῇσι πεπαρμένοι <ἀμφ' ὀδύνῃσιν>.

Empedocles fr. 112 D-K = D4 L-M

Friends, who live in the great city of the yellow Acragas, up on the heights of the citadel, caring for good deeds, I give you greetings. An immortal god, mortal no more, I go about honoured by all, as is fitting, crowned with ribbons and fresh garlands; <and by all> whom I come upon as I enter their prospering towns, by men and women, I am revered. They follow me in their thousands, asking where lies the road to profit, some desiring prophecies, while others ask to hear the word of healing for every kind of illness, long transfixed by harsh <pains>. (trans. KRS 1983, 313[9])

In introducing this fragment, Diogenes Laertius (8.61) reports that Heraclides Ponticus called Empedocles 'a doctor and a prophet' (P16 L-M), just as Satyrus described him as 'a doctor and excellent orator' (P24 L-M); Empedocles was credited in antiquity with medical treatises in both verse and prose (P25b, 26 L-M), and Hippocratic writers treat him as a rival (cf., e.g., *Ancient Medicine* 20, *Nature of Man* 1). The ancients were as familiar as we are with jokes about how doctors ('leeches', in an archaic English usage) kill as many as they cure, and this lies behind *occidit* in v. 475; the Romans certainly knew that the use of medicinal leeches for blood-letting was potentially fatal (Pliny, *HN* 32.123). Empedocles himself, however, had claimed to be able to teach how to 'bring the strength of a dead man out of Hades' (fr. 111 D-K = D43 L-M), and the sudden Horatian transformation from a bear to a leech was a mere bagatelle for a poet who had been 'a boy, a girl, a bush, a bird and a fish' (fr. 117 D-K = D13 L-M) and who claimed magical powers which could turn nature upside down (fr 111 D-K = D43 L-M).

If Empedocles brings up the rear, he is also there at the beginning, for both the opening description and vv. 7–9 can, as Philip Hardie has pointed out,[10] hardly fail to recall Empedocles' zoogony:

Ἐμπεδοκλῆς τὰς πρώτας γενέσεις τῶν ζῴων καὶ φυτῶν μηδαμῶς ὁλοκλήρους γενέσθαι, ἀσυμφυέσι δὲ τοῖς μορίοις διεζευγμένας, τὰς δὲ δευτέρας συμφυομένων τῶν μερῶν εἰδωλοφανεῖς, τὰς δὲ τρίτας τῶν ἀλληλοφυῶν κτλ.

Empedocles A 72 D-K = D151 L-M

Empedocles: the first generations of animals and plants were not at all born as complete entities, but were disconnected, with parts that had not grown together; the second ones,

---

9 For the abbreviation KRS cf. the bibliography.
10 Hardie 2018 (originally a conference paper from some years earlier). Hardie's argument is picked up by Tamás 2014, 188–190.

when the parts had grown together, had the appearance of phantasms; the third ones, when the parts had grown in conformity with one another...

trans. L-M

ἧι πολλαὶ μὲν κόρσαι ἀναύχενες ἐβλάστησαν,
γυμνοὶ δ' ἐπλάζοντο βραχίονες εὔνιδες ὤμων,
ὄμματά τ' οἶ' ἐπλανᾶτο πενητεύοντα μετώπων.

Empedocles B 57 D-K = D154 L-M

Here sprang up many faces without necks, arms wandered without shoulders, unattached, and eyes strayed alone, in need of foreheads.

trans. KRS 1983, 303

πολλὰ μὲν ἀμφιπρόσωπα καὶ ἀμφίστερνα φύεσθαι,
βουγενῆ ἀνδρόπρωιρα, τὰ δ' ἔμπαλιν ἐξανατέλλειν
ἀνδροφυῆ βούκρανα, μεμειγμένα τῆι μὲν ἀπ' ἀνδρῶν
τῆι δὲ γυναικοφυῆ σκιεροῖς ἠσκημένα γυίοις.

Empedocles B 61 D-K = D156 L-M

Many creatures were born with faces and breasts on both sides, man-faced ox-progeny, while others again sprang forth as ox-headed offspring of man, creatures compounded partly of male, partly of female, and fitted with shadowy parts.

trans. KRS 1983, 304

The Empedoclean texture is in fact very thick in Horace's opening verses. Horace's 'dreams of a sick man' reflect the same original as Aetius' εἰδωλοφανεῖς (31 A 72 D-K), a word which could have appeared in a hexameter, or it may even be more to the Horatian point to recall Circe's Empedoclean pets in the fourth book of Apollonius' *Argonautica*:

θῆρες δ', οὐ θήρεσσιν ἐοικότες ὠμηστῆισιν
οὐδὲ μὲν οὐδ' ἄνδρεσσιν ὅλον δέμας, ἄλλο δ' ἀπ' ἄλλων
συμμιγέες μελέων, κίον ἀθρόοι, ἠύτε μῆλα
ἐκ σταθμῶν ἅλις εἶσιν ὀπηδεύοντα νομῆι.
τοίους καὶ προτέρους ἐξ ἰλύος ἐβλάστησε
χθὼν αὐτὴ μικτοῖσιν ἀρηρεμένους μελέεσσιν,
οὔπω διψαλέωι μάλ' ὑπ' ἠέρι πιληθεῖσα
οὐδέ πω ἀζαλέοιο βολαῖς τόσον ἠελίοιο
ἰκμάδας αἰνυμένη· τὰ δ' ἐπὶ στίχας ἤγαγεν αἰών   680
συγκρίνας. τὼς οἵ γε φυὴν ἀίδηλοι ἔποντο,
ἥρωας δ' ἕλε θάμβος ἀπείριτον.

Apollonius Rhodius, *Argonautica* 4.672–682

Her beasts — which were not entirely like flesh-devouring beasts, nor like men, but rather a jumble of different limbs — all came with her, like a large flock of sheep which follow the shepherd out of the stalls. Similar to these were the creatures which in earlier times the earth itself had created out of the mud, pieced together from a jumble of limbs, before it had been properly solidified by the thirsty air or the rays of the parching sun had eliminated sufficient moisture. Time then sorted these out by grouping them into proper categories. Similarly unidentifiable were the forms which followed after Circe and caused the heroes amazed astonishment.

Horace's *undique conlatis membris* is, however Lucretian, virtually a translation of ἄλλο δ' ἀπ' ἄλλων / συμμιγέες μελέων.[11] Moreover, when the Argonauts come upon Circe she is just purifying herself from a nightmare such as a (really) sick man might have had. I also wonder whether *amici* in *AP* 5 picks up ὦ φίλοι, the opening word of the *Purifications* (see above), which also perhaps became a recurrent mode of address in the poem (cf. fr. 114 D-K = D6 L-M); the echo helps to confirm that, whatever the syntax of *amici*, we are to feel ourselves, not just the Pisones, addressed here. Even Horace, after all, has — as many critics have recognised — more than a little of the Empedoclean leech within. The whole opening description of a painter reverses, as Philip Hardie also noted, a famous Empedoclean simile (fr. 23 D-K = D60 L-M) of skilled painters who can 'fashion shapes similar to all things, creating trees and men and women, wild animals and birds and fish nourished in the water and long-lived gods', but not apparently all jumbled together.[12] Horace's *Ars Poetica* (though that, of course, might not have been the original title) thus begins with a description of the apparent abandonment of all *ars* in a passage which unsurprisingly exhibits, through a remarkable 'window allusion' (and many other things), *ars poetica* to the highest degree.[13]

As a 'didactic poet', and one given such a prominent place by Lucretius, Empedocles was a very important part of Horace's heritage in the *Ars*, functioning to some extent both like and unlike the figure of Lucilius in *Satires* 1. Moreover, Empedocles hovers on the edges of the ancient and modern critical traditions, which can never really make up their minds whether he is a poet or a philosopher; Aristotle is of course the key figure here.[14] Empedocles poses Hora-

---

[11] Hardie 2009, 140–141 suggests that Ovid drew on this passage of *Arg.* 4 in the Pythagorean discourse in *Met.* 15.
[12] This catalogue appears to be formulaic in Empedocles, cf. D73.270–272 L-M. It is perhaps worthy of note that the author of the Hippocratic *On Ancient Medicine* 20 claims that what has been written about the origins of man by Empedocles and others has less to do with medicine than with γραφική, which seems most naturally understood as 'painting'. Bad painting and bad medicine frame the *Ars Poetica*. On Empedocles fr. 23 D-K cf. Iribarren 2013.
[13] On the opening verses see, in addition to the commentaries and the works I have cited elsewhere, Schwindt 2014, Gantar 1964, Frischer 1991, 68–74, Geue 2014, 152–153.
[14] Cf. Hunter forthcoming.

tian questions, or rather poses challenges to Horatian positions; v. 470, *nec satis adparet cur uersus factitet*, is a Horatian spin precisely on Aristotelian and other debates about 'philosophical poetry'. Empedocles serves Horace in more than one way, just as he can also help us to read 'intratextually'. When, for example, our suspicions about the Empedoclean colour of the opening of the poem appear to be confirmed by the end, we re-read and the two passages become somehow re-inforcing. Details always come in and out of focus, at both macro- and micro- levels. So it is, for example, that once we get explicitly to the story of Empedocles we realise that *ructatur* in v. 457 is preparing us for Mt Etna, whereas *errat* in the same verse (and cf. *error* in v. 454) becomes (*inter alia*) a specific reference to the central place of 'wandering' in Empedocles' account of souls:

τῶν καὶ ἐγὼ νῦν εἰμι, φυγὰς θεόθεν καὶ ἀλήτης,
Νείκεϊ μαινομένωι πίσυνος.

Empedocles fr. 115.13–14 D-K = D10.13–14 L-M

I too am now one of them, an exile from the divine and a wanderer, who trusted in crazed Strife.

Empedocles was a 'wandering poet' in a very particular way.

Intratextual unities

A leitmotif of all discussion of 'intratextuality' is how the term self-consciously plays with its relationship with its older sister, 'intertextuality' (the original IT girl); Horace's use of Empedocles in the opening of the *Ars Poetica* well illustrates how this issue, if not the modern terms, were well understood in antiquity. Consider one of the earliest surviving explicitly intratextual observations. In 1.97.2 Thucydides explains his 'digression' on Athenian power as follows:

ἔγραψα δὲ αὐτὰ καὶ τὴν ἐκβολὴν τοῦ λόγου ἐποιησάμην διὰ τόδε, ὅτι τοῖς πρὸ ἐμοῦ ἅπασιν ἐκλιπὲς τοῦτο ἦν τὸ χωρίον καὶ ἢ τὰ πρὸ τῶν Μηδικῶν Ἑλληνικὰ ξυνετίθεσαν ἢ αὐτὰ τὰ Μηδικά· τούτων δὲ ὅσπερ καὶ ἥψατο ἐν τῆι Ἀττικῆι ξυγγραφῆι Ἑλλάνικος, βραχέως τε καὶ τοῖς χρόνοις οὐκ ἀκριβῶς ἐπεμνήσθη. ἅμα δὲ καὶ τῆς ἀρχῆς ἀπόδειξιν ἔχει τῆς τῶν Ἀθηναίων ἐν οἵωι τρόπωι κατέστη.

Thucydides 1.97.2

I have recorded these things and have made this digression from my narrative for the following reason: this theme was neglected by everyone before me, who composed their work either about Greek affairs before the Persian Wars or about the Persian Wars themselves. The man who did touch on these matters in his *Atthis* was Hellanicus, but he dealt with it only briefly and was inaccurate in his chronology. At the same time my account serves as an exposition of how the Athenian empire was established.

trans. Mynott

The intratextual dynamic, the relationship, as Alison Sharrock put it in her Introduction to Sharrock/Morales 2000, between parts and (w)holes, is here governed by a very clear intertextual imperative, the need to make good a gap (ἐκλιπές is almost a perfect translation for 'gap'), not in Thucydides' own work, but in that of his predecessors. The part is indeed related to the (w)hole, but it is someone else's (w)hole. That relationship between inter- and intra-textuality may also be (in part) why the modern pursuit of intratextual questions has always seemed to matter more to Latinists than to their Hellenist colleagues. If there is any reality behind this impression, it may be that that big sister again, intertextuality, hangs from the very beginning over Latin literature and its study much more importantly (and threateningly) than she does over Greek literature. There is a real question here about the different kinds of problems posed by the two literatures and about what role 'intratextuality' can play in helping us to make discussion of those differences as sharp as possible. It is not, of course, that Greek literature is any less 'intertextual' (or indeed 'intratextual'), it is just differently so. Antiquity's most quintessentially 'intratextual' readers were in fact probably the scholars whose work lies behind the epitomized notes which make up our corpus of Homeric scholia. They always read for part and (w)hole, and they read with extraordinarily sensitive eyes and noses for what was unusual and seemed to disturb the perfection of the surface. To that perfect surface I will return.

Thucydides' term for his 'digression', ἐκβολή, is one of a familiar cluster of terms which suggest that a *logos* is a path or a journey, one with twists and turns, with stopping and starting, as well as a hoped-for destination. Other examples include ἐκτροπή and, above all, πλάνη, 'wandering', a term which may or may not have something to do with the structure and story of the *Odyssey*. At the opening of the *Laws*, for example, Plato's Athenian Stranger proposes entertainment for the journey ahead:

προσδοκῶ οὐκ ἂν ἀηδῶς περί τε πολιτείας τὰ νῦν καὶ νόμων τὴν διατριβήν, λέγοντάς τε καὶ ἀκούοντας ἅμα κατὰ τὴν πορείαν, ποιήσασθαι. πάντως δ' ἥ γε ἐκ Κνωσοῦ ὁδὸς εἰς τὸ τοῦ Διὸς ἄντρον καὶ ἱερόν, ὡς ἀκούομεν, ἱκανή, καὶ ἀνάπαυλαι κατὰ τὴν ὁδόν, ὡς εἰκός, πνίγους ὄντος τὰ νῦν, ἐν τοῖς ὑψηλοῖς δένδρεσίν εἰσι σκιαραί, καὶ ταῖς ἡλικίαις πρέπον ἂν ἡμῶν εἴη τὸ διαναπαύεσθαι πυκνὰ ἐν αὐταῖς, λόγοις τε ἀλλήλους παραμυθουμένους τὴν ὁδὸν ἅπασαν οὕτω μετὰ ῥᾳστώνης διαπερᾶναι.

ΚΛ. Καὶ μὴν ἔστιν γε, ὦ ξένε, προϊόντι κυπαρίττων τε ἐν τοῖς ἄλσεσιν ὕψη καὶ κάλλη θαυμάσια, καὶ λειμῶνες ἐν οἷσιν ἀναπαυόμενοι διατρίβοιμεν ἄν.

ΑΘ. Ὀρθῶς λέγεις.

ΚΛ. Πάνυ μὲν οὖν· ἰδόντες δὲ μᾶλλον φήσομεν. ἀλλ' ἴωμεν ἀγαθῆι τύχηι.
ΑΘ. Ταῦτ' εἴη. καί μοι λέγε· κατὰ τί τὰ συσσίτιά τε ὑμῖν συντέταχεν ὁ νόμος καὶ τὰ γυμνάσια καὶ τὴν τῶν ὅπλων ἕξιν;

Plato, *Laws* 1.625a6-c7

Athenian: ... I suspect that you would not be unwilling for us to proceed on our way by contributing and listening to discussion on constitutions and laws. Certainly, the road from Knossos to the cave and shrine of Zeus is, so we are told, not short, and in this heat there will doubtless be shaded resting-places provided by the tall trees; there we can often rest, as men of our age should do, and by cheering ourselves with discourse we can thus complete the journey in some ease.
Cleinias: Indeed, stranger, as you proceed you find in the groves tall and wonderfully beautiful cypress-trees, and meadows where we can rest and discuss.
Ath.: Excellent idea!
Cleinias: Indeed, and when we have seen them we shall agree all the more. Well, let's be off!
Ath.: Fine! Now tell me: why does the law ordain your common messes and the gymnasia and the nature of your arms?

Reading the *Laws* will be a long journey, one requiring resting-places. A few years ago I suggested that Plato is here also alluding playfully to the *locus amoenus* of the *Phaedrus*, already famous by the time of the *Laws*, as a passage which had already come to be seen as quintessentially intratextual, that is as marking structures within the *Phaedrus*.[15] Be that as it may, allusions from one part of a writer's corpus to another is today how 'intratextuality' is largely understood (when it is) in several countries (notably Germany), and here of course writers such as Cicero, Ovid and Horace offer very rich pickings indeed.[16]

One passage to be placed alongside Thucydides 1.97.2 is the famous Herodotus 4.30:

θωμάζω δέ (προσθήκας γὰρ δή μοι ὁ λόγος ἐξ ἀρχῆς ἐδίζητο) ὅ τι ἐν τῆι Ἠλείηι πάσηι χώρηι οὐ δύναται γίνεσθαι ἡμίονοι, οὔτε ψυχροῦ τοῦ χώρου ἐόντος οὔτε ἄλλου φανεροῦ αἰτίου οὐδενός·

Herodotus 4.30.1

But I wonder at the fact (for it was the way of my *logos* from the beginning to seek out additions) that in the whole of Elis no mules can be conceived although the country is not cold, nor is there any evident cause...

trans. Godley, adapted

---

15 Hunter 2012, 193–194.
16 Cf. Scheidegger Lämmle 2016.

The *logos*, whether that be the whole work, in whatever shape it was when Herodotus wrote this chapter, or just 'the Scythian *logos*', 'has from the beginning been seeking προσθῆκαι'. We can debate what is meant by the Greek term and by what form of critical orthopedics we are to distinguish 'prosthetic' from 'natural' limbs, but what is clear is that Herodotus' intratextual consciousness is on open display here: the habits of the mules of Elis might be digressive to the habits of Scythian mules and hornless oxen, but what is the real *logos*, the 'path' if you like, of the Scythian *logos*? Herodotus is clearly already playing with audience expectations about the nature of extended narrative journeys and, in particular, with expectations about what we might as well call 'unity'. Moreover, the verb ἐδίζητο suggests that the *logos* has a life of its own, it is not content with any simple, pre-ordered narrative path.

In the context of unity, τὸ ἕν, the language of searching almost inevitably suggests Parmenides, who set before us two ὁδοὶ διζήσιος, though one is not really a followable path at all (B2 = D6 L-M, B6.3 = D7.3 L-M, B7.2 = D8.2 L-M); those who foolishly follow the imaginary path of 'what is not' are characterized by 'wandering minds' (πλαγκτὸς νόος, B6.6 = D7.7 L-M, B8.53 = D8.59 L-M), whereas the true perfect reality of 'what is' exists by necessity (ἀνάγκη, B8.16, 30 = D8.21, 35 L-M), lacks nothing (B8.33 = D8.38) and may be compared to a perfectly-rounded ball:

αὐτὰρ ἐπεὶ πεῖρας πύματον, τετελεσμένον ἐστί
πάντοθεν, εὐκύκλου σφαίρης ἐναλίγκιον ὄγκωι,
μεσσόθεν ἰσοπαλὲς πάντηι· τὸ γὰρ οὔτε τι μεῖζον
οὔτε τι βαιότερον πελέναι χρεόν ἐστι τῆι ἢ τῆι.   45
οὔτε γὰρ οὐκ ἐὸν ἔστι, τό κεν παύοι μιν ἱκνεῖσθαι
εἰς ὁμόν, οὔτ' ἐὸν ἔστιν ὅπως εἴη κεν ἐόντος
τῆι μᾶλλον τῆι δ' ἧσσον, ἐπεὶ πᾶν ἐστιν ἄσυλον·
οἷ γὰρ πάντοθεν ἶσον, ὁμῶς ἐν πείρασι κύρει.

Parmenides B8.42–49 D-K = D8.47–53 L-M

But since there is a furthest limit, it is perfected, like the bulk of a ball well-rounded on every side, equally balanced in every direction from the centre. For it needs must not be somewhat more or somewhat less here or there. For neither is it non-existent, which would stop it from reaching its like, nor is it existent in such a way that there would be more being here, less there, since it is all inviolate: for being equal to itself on every side, it lies uniformly within its limits.

trans. KRS 1983, 252–253

We do not (necessarily) have to believe that Parmenides' poem is the origin of the intratextual turn, but a concern with whether everything in a text is in fact μεσσόθεν ἰσοπαλὲς πάντηι, 'equally balanced in every direction from the centre', was presumably not far away when intratextuality was conceived. Parmenides shows us, moreover, that any temptation we might have had to think of intratextuality as only a 'textual' phenomenon is misplaced; Parmenides can serve to remind us that textual structures may be understood as imitations of metaphysical structures which govern what is intelligible. If that sounds a bit too much like 'popularised Plato' for comfort, then I can only plead that we can hardly keep Plato out of this discussion, whether it be readers or writers with whom we are concerned. In the context of the former, we may think that the tripartition of the soul has a particular significance in considering *how* we read; the soul-chariot of the *Phaedrus*, in which the two horses pull in opposite directions, is in fact by no means the worst image for the reading experience. As for the creation of texts, perhaps the most famous intratextual discussion of them all, one that Horace certainly picks up, along with Empedocles, at the head of the *AP*, is indeed Platonic:

> οὐ χύδην δοκεῖ βεβλῆσθαι τὰ τοῦ λόγου; ἢ φαίνεται τὸ δεύτερον εἰρημένον ἔκ τινος ἀνάγκης δεύτερον δεῖν τεθῆναι, ἤ τι ἄλλο τῶν ῥηθέντων; ἐμοὶ μὲν γὰρ ἔδοξεν, ὡς μηδὲν εἰδότι, οὐκ ἀγεννῶς τὸ ἐπιὸν εἰρῆσθαι τῶι γράφοντι· σὺ δ' ἔχεις τινὰ ἀνάγκην λογογραφικὴν ἧι ταῦτα ἐκεῖνος οὕτως ἐφεξῆς παρ' ἄλληλα ἔθηκεν;... ἀλλὰ τόδε γε οἶμαί σε φάναι ἄν, δεῖν πάντα λόγον ὥσπερ ζῶιον συνεστάναι σῶμά τι ἔχοντα αὐτὸν αὑτοῦ, ὥστε μήτε ἀκέφαλον εἶναι μήτε ἄπουν, ἀλλὰ μέσα τε ἔχειν καὶ ἄκρα, πρέποντα ἀλλήλοις καὶ τῶι ὅλωι γεγραμμένα.
>
> Plato, *Phaedrus* 264b4–c3

> Don't you think the parts of the discourse are thrown out helter-skelter? Or does it seem to you that the second topic had to be put second for any cogent reason, or that any of the other things he says are so placed? It seemed to me, who am wholly ignorant, that the writer uttered boldly whatever occurred to him. Do you know any logographic necessity why he arranged his topics in this order?... But I do think you will agree to this, that every discourse must be organized, like a living being, with a body of its own, as it were, so as not to be headless or footless, but to have a middle and extremities, composed in fitting relation to each other and to the whole.
>
> trans. Fowler, adapted

No lengthy discussion of this famous passage is necessary, however difficult it is to catch its tone. For Neoplatonists, Socrates' observations were quite literally a godsend. In his commentary on the *Phaedrus* Hermeias (p. 231 Couvreur) notes that 'beauty and the good' are the result of unity, and associates this with the fact that beauty (κάλλος) is not really beautiful if there is no 'unification' (ἕνωσις) of the parts. We will think of the opening of the *Ars Poetica* again. So too, this passage of the *Phaedrus*, like Parmenides' denial of change, reminds us that the unity which intratextual studies interrogate is also fundamental to classicism and ideas of the classical, best illustrated by Plato's account of perfect beauty in the *Symposium*:[17]

πρῶτον μὲν ἀεὶ ὂν καὶ οὔτε γιγνόμενον οὔτε ἀπολλύμενον, οὔτε αὐξανόμενον οὔτε φθίνον, ἔπειτα οὐ τῆι μὲν καλόν, τῆι δ' αἰσχρόν, οὐδὲ τοτὲ μέν, τοτὲ δὲ οὔ, οὐδὲ πρὸς μὲν τὸ καλόν, πρὸς δὲ τὸ αἰσχρόν, οὐδ' ἔνθα μὲν καλόν, ἔνθα δὲ αἰσχρόν, ὡς τισὶ μὲν ὂν καλόν, τισὶ δὲ αἰσχρόν· οὐδ' αὖ φαντασθήσεται αὐτῶι τὸ καλὸν οἷον πρόσωπόν τι οὐδὲ χεῖρες οὐδὲ ἄλλο οὐδὲν ὧν σῶμα μετέχει, οὐδέ τις λόγος οὐδέ τις ἐπιστήμη, οὐδέ που ὂν ἐν ἑτέρωι τινι, οἷον ἐν ζώωι ἢ ἐν γῆι ἢ ἐν οὐρανῶι ἢ ἔν τωι ἄλλωι, ἀλλ' αὐτὸ καθ' αὑτὸ μεθ' αὑτοῦ μονοειδὲς ἀεὶ ὄν, τὰ δὲ ἄλλα πάντα καλὰ ἐκείνου μετέχοντα τρόπον τινὰ τοιοῦτον, οἷον γιγνομένων τε τῶν ἄλλων καὶ ἀπολλυμένων μηδὲν ἐκεῖνο μήτε τι πλέον μήτε ἔλαττον γίγνεσθαι μηδὲ πάσχειν μηδέν.

Plato, *Symposium* 210e5–211b5

It is eternal; it does not come to be or cease to be, and it does not increase or diminish. It is not beautiful in one respect and ugly in another, or beautiful at one time but not at another, or beautiful in one setting but ugly in another, or beautiful here and ugly elsewhere, depending on how people find it. The lover will not perceive beauty as a face or hands or any other physical feature, or as a piece of reasoning or knowledge, and he will not perceive it as being anywhere else either — in something like a creature or the earth or the heavens. No, he will perceive it in itself and by itself, constant in form and eternal, and he will see that every beautiful object somehow partakes of it, but in such a way that their coming to be and ceasing to be do not increase or diminish it at all, and it remains entirely unaffected.

Unsurprisingly perhaps, intratextual studies point us to a far larger set of questions than the agenda they set for themselves.

Plotting necessity

Socrates' insistence, perhaps an inheritance from Parmenides, that there should be a λογογραφικὴ ἀνάγκη (Plato, *Phaedrus* 264b8), which is to determine the proper order of things in a speech, as it does in a living creature, is of particular importance in this context. The laughter which greets the composite animal at the start of Horace's *AP* is in part — by a familiar theory of the laughable — a recognition precisely that 'the necessary' has been breached. As far as poetry is concerned, we are very familiar with the idea that necessity, like fate, can function as a way of expressing authorial decisions about otherwise surprising features of narrative:

---

17 Cf. further Hunter 2015.

ἀλλά, θεαί, πῶς τῆσδε παρὲξ ἁλὸς ἀμφί τε γαῖαν
Αὐσονίην νήσους τε Λιγυστίδας, αἳ καλέονται
Στοιχάδες, Ἀργώιης περιώσια σήματα νηός
νημερτὲς πέφαται; τίς ἀπόπροθι τόσσον ἀνάγκη
καὶ χρειὼ σφ' ἐκόμισσε; τίνες σφέας ἤγαγον αὖραι;

Apollonius Rhodius, Argonautica 4.552–556

> How is it, goddesses, that beyond this sea, in the Ausonian land and the Ligurian islands called Stoichades, many clear traces of the *Argo's* voyage appear? What necessity and need took them so far away? What winds directed them?

As so often, the later developments familiar from Hellenistic and Roman epic are developments from Homer. Let me illustrate this with two examples from Odysseus' narration in *Odyssey* 10. After the terrified Eurylochus has reported to him about the disappearance of their comrades who went to Circe's house and has urged flight, Odysseus allows him to stay by the ship, whereas he himself 'must' take the same path that they did, κρατερὴ δέ μοι ἔπλετ' ἀνάγκη (*Od.* 10.273). Odysseus, of course, is presenting himself to the Phaeacians as a caring leader, just as he had earlier in the book with the description of how he killed a large deer in order to allow his men to eat. Moreover, Odysseus is driven by that mixture of inquisitiveness and desire for honour which leads him constantly to seek out, rather than to avoid, dangerous situations.[18] From Homer's point of view, however, there is another 'necessity' driving Odysseus' decision, namely the 'necessity' that Odysseus meets Circe; as often, then, poetic 'necessity' is not simple, and the movement of the plot, the relationship and ordering of the parts, is multiply determined.[19] After Odysseus and his men have spent a year with Circe, it is time to go, and Circe knows it:

ὣς ἐφάμην, ἡ δ' αὐτίκ' ἀμείβετο δῖα θεάων·
'διογενὲς Λαερτιάδη, πολυμήχαν' Ὀδυσσεῦ,
μηκέτι νῦν ἀέκοντες ἐμῶι ἐνὶ μίμνετε οἴκωι.
ἀλλ' ἄλλην χρὴ πρῶτον ὁδὸν τελέσαι καὶ ἱκέσθαι   490
εἰς Ἀΐδαο δόμους καὶ ἐπαινῆς Περσεφονείης
ψυχῆι χρησομένους Θηβαίου Τειρεσίαο,
μάντιος ἀλαοῦ, τοῦ τε φρένες ἔμπεδοί εἰσι·'

Homer, Odyssey 10.487–493

---

18 According to Dio Chrysostom (52.11–12), Odysseus was made to reflect upon this φιλοτιμία in the prologue of Euripides' *Philoctetes*.
19 Another aspect of this nest of issues which deserves fuller treatment is the grammarians' use, amply attested in the scholia, of 'necessity' as an argument in discussions of the *athetesis* of Homeric verses.

So I spoke, and the splendid goddess straightway made answer: 'Son of Laertes, Zeus-born, Odysseus of many devices, stay no longer in my house against your will; but you must first complete another journey, and come to the house of Hades and dread Persephone, to consult the spirit of Theban Teiresias, the blind seer, whose mind is firm as before'.

Generations of students have been asked to discuss 'Why does Odysseus have to go to the Underworld?' (particularly in view of what actually happens there), and very few teachers will accept 'Because Circe tells him he has to' as a full and proper answer. Nevertheless, this is, in summary, what the Homeric narrative pattern offers us. Heubeck's observation in the Oxford commentary, 'The divine authority of Circe... provides convincing motivation for the journey to Hades, which could not be omitted from the series of adventures...', acknowledges, but utterly mistakes, the nature of the ποιητικὴ ἀνάγκη operative here. Part of that λογογραφική or indeed ποιητικὴ ἀνάγκη is what we might call μυθικὴ ἀνάγκη, and some of the implications of this will form the final case-study of this paper.

One of the most famous structural (or indeed 'intratextual') problems in Greek drama is posed by Euripides' *Heracles Furens*. After Heracles has taken his revenge on the tyrannical usurper Lykos, Iris and Lyssa ('Madness') enter and Iris, speaking for Hera, reports that Heracles must now suffer and she rides roughshod over Lyssa's protests; Lyssa acknowledges that she must follow Hera's instructions — ἀναγκαίως ἔχει are her words (v. 859). Many critics believe that Euripides here innovates in placing Heracles' madness after the labours, but — be that as it may — it is (again) poetic and mythic 'necessity' which is strongly advertised. Euripides is not just being 'clever' in making his Lyssa seek to offer 'rational' *parainesis* and *nouthetesis* to apparently 'irrational' powers, but he is setting us to wonder just what sort of 'necessity' is driving this μῦθος, particularly as Iris has already explained (vv. 827–829) that, before the labours had been completed, Heracles had been saved by 'necessity (τὸ χρή) and the intervention of Zeus'. In the *Poetics* Aristotle privileged μῦθοι in which what was done and said unfolded in a pattern driven by 'probability or necessity', which is why poetry, which concerns itself with τὰ καθόλου, is 'more philosophical and more serious (σπουδαιότερον) than history' (1451b5–9); Aristotle's 'necessity' is not (necessarily) the 'necessity' of any tragic plot which has survived,[20] but this is by no means the only case where we find the impetus for an important critical idea of the *Poetics* already foreshadowed in fifth-century drama itself. The voluminous modern debate about the 'unitary' or 'broken' status of the *muthos* in the *Heracles* (cf. the survey in Bond's introduction to his edition) are

---

20 There is a huge bibliography: Halliwell 1986, 98–106 is a good place to start.

the aftershocks of Aristotle's systematisations, although they are not always acknowledged as such.

Heracles is indeed a figure around whom questions of μυθική ἀνάγκη readily cluster. Aristotle also famously criticises the 'errors' of poets 'who have written *Heracleids*, *Theseids*, and such poems, who think that since Heracles was one individual (εἷς), the *muthos* must also be (εἶναι προσήκειν) unitary (εἷς)' (1451a19– 22). The action of Euripides' play is set against the background of the series of Heracles' labours, which are twice catalogued in the play in very different modes and at very different length, vv. 359–435, 1270–1280; from the perspective of later criticism, the juxtaposition might be seen as that between an expansive epic 'telling', or indeed cataloguing, of Heracles and a dramatic one. Aristotle wanted epic to be as close to his ideal of tragedy as he could make it, and he found his wish fulfilled in (as well as created by) Homer, but here again the seeds of the idea of two different ways of telling can already be sensed in drama itself. If Aeschylus thought of his tragedies as 'slices' (τεμάχη) from Homer's 'great feasts' (T 112 Radt), then Euripides' drama is a 'slice' from the 'great feast' of Heraclean myth; the relation between narrative epic and drama, more generally, is probably characterized as well in this fashion as in any other.

The *Heracles* has not exhausted its surprises for, after the killing of the children, Heracles responds to Theseus' attempted consolation in yet more famous verses:

οἴμοι· πάρεργα < > τάδ' ἔστ' ἐμῶν κακῶν·   1340
ἐγὼ δὲ τοὺς θεοὺς οὔτε λέκτρ' ἃ μὴ θέμις
στέργειν νομίζω δεσμά τ' ἐξάπτειν χεροῖν
οὔτ' ἠξίωσα πώποτ' οὔτε πείσομαι
οὐδ' ἄλλον ἄλλου δεσπότην πεφυκέναι.
δεῖται γὰρ ὁ θεός, εἴπερ ἔστ' ὀρθῶς θεός,   1345
οὐδενός· ἀοιδῶν οἵδε δύστηνοι λόγοι.

Euripides, *Heracles* 1340–1346

Alas! this is quite beside the question of my troubles. For my part, I do not believe that the gods indulge in sexual unions which are not right; and as for putting bonds on hands, I have never thought that worthy of belief, nor will I now be so persuaded, nor again that one god is naturally lord and master of another. For the deity, if he be really such, has no wants; these are miserable tales of the poets.

trans. Coleridge, adapted

These verses seem to deny the very foundations of the play we have been watching, let alone Heracles' own bitter view expressed immediately before (vv. 1303–

1310); a rehearsal of modern critical approaches to this problem would itself make for a slender volume on 'intratextuality'.[21] Godfrey Bond's rightly standard commentary is, however, a good place to start: 'These lines... must be taken firmly in their context as a direct and detailed answer to the argument of Theseus... Heracles' arguments must not be removed from their context... In particular [1341-1342] should not be taken from the context of incest between gods and used to deny Zeus' intercourse with Alcmena and his fathering of Heracles ... These lines must not be taken as Heracles' considered views: that way lie delusions like Verrall's rationalistic explanation of the play. Heracles is not an academic philosopher who has thought out the implications of everything he says ... 1341-1346 may well represent Euripides' own considered view; but that is another matter ...' (Bond then continues with a helpful note about the possible influence of Xenophanes). 'Incest' in fact is not at issue here, but let us not quibble.[22] It is, however, worth insisting[23] that Theseus' own arguments do not really fit the case he needs to make:

οὐδεὶς δὲ θνητῶν ταῖς τύχαις ἀκήρατος,
οὐ θεῶν, ἀοιδῶν εἴπερ οὐ ψευδεῖς λόγοι.   1315
οὐ λέκτρ' ἐν ἀλλήλοισιν, ὧν οὐδεὶς νόμος,
συνῆψαν; οὐ δεσμοῖσι διὰ τυραννίδα
πατέρας ἐκηλίδωσαν; ἀλλ' οἰκοῦσ' ὅμως
Ὄλυμπον ἠνέσχοντό θ' ἡμαρτηκότες.
καίτοι τί φήσεις, εἰ σὺ μὲν θνητὸς γεγὼς   1320
φέρεις ὑπέρφευ τὰς τύχας, θεοὶ δὲ μή;

Euripides, *Heracles* 1314-1321

---

21 There is a helpful survey in Brown 1978.
22 Bond apparently derives his notion that 'incest' is involved from Theseus' claim at 1315-1317, to which Heracles is responding, that 'if the tales of bards are not false', the gods λέκτρ' ἐν ἀλλήλοισιν, ὧν οὐδεὶς νόμος, / συνῆψαν; in his note on that passage Bond observes that the reference is 'to incestuous intercourse like that of Zeus and his young sister Hera or Ares and Aphrodite'. It is, however, at least doubtful that Zeus and Hera are in fact evoked here; in the first instance it is probably Ares and Aphrodite from *Odyssey* 8 of whom we first think, and although by some genealogies they are half-brother and half-sister (through their common father Zeus), there is, I think, no suggestion in the song of Demodocus that we are to think of their relationship as incestuous, as well as adulterous, despite some shared diction between *Il.* 14.295-296 and *Od.* 8.268-270. However closely Heracles' declaration in 1341-1342 rewrites Theseus' assertion of 1316-1317, it is (I think) not easy to erase all reference to Heracles' own parentage from 1341-1342; many of the audience may remember Amphitryon's harsh charge against Zeus at 344-345.
23 Cf. Brown 1978, 24.

There is no mortal who is unravaged by misfortune, nor any god either, if what poets sing is true. Have not those whom the law forbids slept with one another? Have they not defiled their own fathers with chains to gain sovereign power? Still they inhabit Olympus and brave the issue of their crimes. And yet what shall you say in your defence, if you, a mortal, take your fate excessively hard, while they, as gods, do not?

trans. Coleridge, adapted

Theseus apparently needs Olympian 'parallels' for Heracles' killings or, at the very least, for violent outrages against φίλοι, which have not had serious consequences; although putting chains on your father is not a course of action to be recommended, it is hardly on a par with what has happened to Heracles. Moreover, gods cannot die, and that is the course of action on which Heracles seems set. To put the killing of the children down to τύχη or to consider it as just a 'misfortune' (1314, 1321) also hardly seems to fit the case; when Heracles echoes Theseus' language at 1357, τῆι τύχηι δουλευτέον, the bitterness is hard to ignore.[24] When Heracles apparently dismisses Theseus' arguments from the Olympians as πάρεργα... ἐμῶν κακῶν, it is hard not to sympathise.

The exchange between Theseus and Heracles, then, is characterized by a dramatization of rhetorical practice, in which the relationship between argument and exemplum (Theseus) and argument and generalization (Heracles) was always subject to the contingencies of the moment. To insist, as Godfrey Bond does (above), on 'context' simply means that we ought always to be asking 'which context?'. In this case, too narrow a focus on 'the immediate (dramatic) context' and upon Heracles' character conceals what is really at stake here. In rejecting the consolation which 'the wretched tales of poets' were so often used to provide, in many different rhetorical contexts, Heracles rejects a literary and cultural practice which for us begins with Homer. Achilles urges Priam to eat and wait until morning before seeing Hector's corpse, and he tells him how Niobe ate, though she had lost twelve children to Apollo and Artemis. To this story Priam makes no response; the silence is deafening. Heracles is different, and Theseus is a less frightening proposition than the still very fragile Achilles (we cannot, I think, imagine Priam telling Achilles that he finds no comfort whatsoever in the story of Niobe), but time too has moved on. This Heracles inhabits a world which, for many decades, had given serious thought to how poetry and myth work in the world and to the nature of the gods; the intratextual fractures in the surface of the text which are the product of that reflection

---

24 Cf. the similar bitterness of the earlier 1263, Ζεὺς δ', ὅστις ὁ Ζεύς κτλ.

point us towards the very complex relationship between literature and the culture out of which it grew.[25]

Bibliography

Beard, M. 2014. *Laughter in Ancient Rome*, Berkeley.
Bond, G.W. 1981. *Euripides, Heracles. With Introduction and Commentary*, Oxford.
Brink, C.O. 1971. *Horace on Poetry. The "Ars Poetica"*, Cambridge.
Brown, A.L. 1978. 'Wretched Tales of Poets: Euripides, Heracles 1340–6', *Proceedings of the Cambridge Philological Society* 24, 22–30.
Citroni, M. 2009. 'Horace's Ars Poetica and the Marvellous', in: P. Hardie (ed.), *Paradox and the Marvellous in Augustan Literature and Culture*, Oxford, 19–40.
Frischer, B.D. 1991. *Shifting Paradigms: New Approaches to Horace's* Ars Poetica, Atlanta.
Gantar, K. 1964. 'Die Anfangsverse und die Komposition der horazischen Epistel über die Dichtkunst', *Symbolae Osloenses* 39, 89–98.
Geue, T. 2014. 'Editing the Opposition: Horace's Ars Politica', *Materiali e Discussioni* 72, 143–172.
Halliwell, S. 1986. *Aristotle's* Poetics, London.
Hardie, P. 2009. *Lucretian Receptions: History, The Sublime, Knowledge*, Cambridge.
Hardie, P. 2018. 'Horace et le sublime empédocléen', in: S. Franchet d'Esperey/C. Lévy (eds.), *Les Présocratiques et la literature latine*, Paris, 263–282.
Heubeck, A./Hoekstra, A. 1990. *A Commentary on Homer's Odyssey. Volume II. Books IX–XVI*, Oxford.
Hunter, R. 2012. *Plato and the Traditions of Ancient Literature. The Silent Stream*, Cambridge.
Hunter, R. 2015. 'The Idea of the Classical in Classical Antiquity', *Proceedings of the Academy of Athens* 90, 51–68.
Hunter, R. (forthcoming), 'Hesiod and the Presocratics: A Hellenistic Perspective?', in: H. Köning/L. Iribarren (eds.), *Hesiod and the Beginnings of Greek Philosophy*, Leiden.
Iribarren, L. 2013. 'Les peintres d'Empédocle (DK 31 B23): enjeux et portée d'une analogie préplatonicienne', *Philosophie antique* 13, 83–115.
KRS=Kirk, G.S./Raven, J.E./Schofield, M. (eds.) 1983. *The Presocratic Philosophers*, 2nd ed., Cambridge.
Laird, A. 2007. 'The *Ars* Poetica', in: S. Harrison (ed.), *The Cambridge Companion to Horace*, Cambridge, 132–143.
Laks, A./Most, G.W. (eds.) 2016. *Early Greek Philosophy*, Cambridge MA.
Oliensis, E. 1998. *Horace and the Rhetoric of Authority*, Cambridge.
Russell, D.A. 2006. '*Ars Poetica*', in: A. Laird (ed.), *Oxford Readings in Ancient Literary Criticism*, Oxford, 325–345.

---

[25] Another development which would have to be taken into account in any proper survey of 'intratextual dynamics' in the late fifth and fourth centuries would be the rise of the anthological habit and the practice of poetic citation. Parts of wholes could now have a life of their own, and that expectation may even have coloured composition.

Scheidegger Lämmle, C. 2016. *Werkpolitik in der Antike: Studien zu Cicero, Vergil, Horaz und Ovid*, Munich.

Schwindt, J.P. 2014. 'Ordo and Insanity: On the Pathogenesis of Horace's *Ars poetica*', *Materiali e Discussioni* 72, 55–70.

Sharrock, A./Morales, H. (eds.) 2000. *Intratextuality: Greek and Roman Textual Relations*, Oxford.

Tamás, A. 2014. 'Reading Ovid Reading Horace. The Empedoclean Drive in the *Ars poetica*', *Materiali e Discussioni* 72, 173–192.

24 The Geographies of Plautus' *Menaechmi*

The setting

The *Menaechmi* is set in Epidamnus, which had been founded in the late seventh century as a joint colony from Corcyra and Corinth and had for centuries been a flourishing Greek port and commercial centre. A recent critical consensus, however, seems to be that Plautus' play might as well be set in any Greek city or none in particular. Thus, for example, for Adrian Gratwick in his Cambridge commentary, Epidamnus is just another example of 'Plautopolis', and Gratwick indeed argues that the geographical catalogue of 235–237 (to which I shall return) implies 'that "Epidamnus" was *not* where it really was at all';[1] so too, Timothy Moore claims that the Plautine Epidamnus is 'not the real Greek city across the Adriatic Sea, but a creation of the physical stage ... an arbitrary creation of the playwright and the theatrical company';[2] the epithet 'arbitrary' turns up again in Kathleen McCarthy's discussion of the prologue of the *Menaechmi*: 'this prologue develops more thoroughly than any other prologue the idea that the stage is and isn't a space in Rome, while it also both is and isn't a city in the Greek world which the playwright has arbitrarily designated as the location of these events';[3] Matthew Leigh, on the other hand, narrows this generality down somewhat by claiming that Plautus' Epidamnus and its dangers represent any maritime city focused on a port, i.e. all ports are full of shady individuals wishing to separate new arrivals from their money and their virtue.[4] There is certainly some important truth in these claims. One of the central conceits of the prologue is, not that the setting in Epidamnos does not matter for the *Menaechmi*, but rather that the unchanging stage-setting can represent any city for any play:

One of the many things that Frances Muecke taught me as an undergraduate was that Plautus deserves to be taken seriously; this paper is a small token of thanks for her teaching and her friendship. I am grateful to audiences in Cambridge, Geneva and Ioannina and to Rebecca Laemmle and Cédric Scheidegger Laemmle for much stimulating discussion; I have also benefitted from the suggestions of *Classicum*'s anonymous reader.

1 Gratwick 1993, 165.
2 Moore 1998, 56–58.
3 McCarthy 2016, 207, Sharrock 2009, 41–45 is along similar lines.
4 Leigh 2004, 121–122.

> atque hoc poetae faciunt in comoediis:
> omnis res gestas esse Athenis autumant,
> quo illud uobis graecum uideatur magis;
> ego nusquam dicam nisi ubi factum dicitur.   10
> haec urbs Epidamnus est, dum haec agitur fabula: 72
> quando alia agetur, aliud fiet oppidum;
> sicut familiae quoque solent mutarier:
> modo hic habitat leno, modo adulescens, modo senex,   75
> pauper, mendicus, rex, parasitus, hariolus.   76
> atque adeo hoc argumentum graecissat, tamen   11
> non atticissat, uerum sicilicissitat.
> †huic argumento antelogium hoc fuit;†
> nunc argumentum uobis demensum dabo,
> non modio, neque trimodio, uerum ipso horreo: 15
> tantum ad narrandum argumentum adest benignitas.
>
> Plautus, *Menaechmi* 7–10, 72–76, 11–16[5]

> This is what writers do in comedies: they claim that everything took place in Athens, intending that it should seem more Greek to you. I shall say what happened nowhere except where it is said to have happened. This city is Epidamnus as long as this play is being staged. When another is staged it'll become another town, just as households too always change. At one time a pimp lives here, at another a young man, at yet another an old one, a pauper, a beggar, a king, a hanger-on, a soothsayer. And besides, this plot summary has a Greek air; nevertheless, it doesn't have an Attic air, but a Sicilian one. †This was the preamble to this plot summary.† Now I'll give you your ration of the plot, not by the peck or the triple peck, but by the granary itself; so benevolent am I when it comes to telling you the summary.[6]

Behind this approach to the city in which the *Menaechmi* is set lies a long and very significant tradition of Plautine scholarship, most of which can trace its intellectual roots back to Eduard Fraenkel's *Plautinisches im Plautus*,[7] which (*inter alia*) emphasised how much more overtly 'theatrical' and 'metatheatrical' Plautus is than Greek New Comedy, both as Fraenkel knew it and, thanks to the publication of so many new papyri, as we do today. Plautus never lets us forget that we are watching a play, whereas the experience of watching Menander (at

---

5 I print Gratwick's transposition of vv. 72–76, although it cannot be regarded as entirely certain; the verses cannot, at any rate, stay where they are transmitted. An alternative to the solution adopted here is to regard them as a fragment of an alternative prologue. On vv. 75–76 cf. Richlin 2016, 2017, 434–451.

6 Unless otherwise indicated, all translations in this paper are my own, except for offset translations from Plautus, which are taken from W. de Melo's Loeb edition.

7 Frances Muecke's role in the translation of Fraenkel's book into English is not the least of her services to our subject. Muecke 1987 is a helpful and accessible introduction to the *Menaechmi*.

least) is, in this respect as in so many others, very different. Nor could one claim that the *Menaechmi* is an outlier in the Plautine *oeuvre* in this regard. Very far from it, in fact. A play which centres on the theme of identical twins and how one is constantly mistaken for the other is inevitably a play which has theatricality, role-playing, costume and illusion at its heart; moreover, a play on the doubling theme also raises fascinating theatrical questions, particularly of course about the portrayal of identical twins.[8] How do the poet and the director exploit our willingness to enter fully into the spirit of drama? How does a masked theatre differ from an unmasked one in this matter?

Against this background, it would indeed be easy enough to move from the acknowledgement in *Menaechmi* 72–76 of 'play' to the idea that everything, including geography, is an illusion to be swept away in a moment: there is no meaningful and specific geography of culture and location here, just a playwright's whimsy in which Epidamnus is a fantasy-place full of *mira*. And yet ... the prologue *is* insistently 'geographical', and with respect to places which we know mattered at least to some Romans in the later third century: we are, for example, very explicitly *not* in Athens, which vv. 8–9 imply is as Greek as you can get — that is the centre of the Greek world.[9] Plautine prologues offer, of course, particular, often acute, problems of authenticity and coherence, and we must always bear in mind that this part of the prologue of the *Menaechmi* may date from some decades after Plautus' lifetime (and at this period decades make a difference), but at the very least there are, I think, no particular reasons for excessive scepticism in this case. What I want to do in this paper, if only as a thought experiment, is to take seriously the geography, real and imaginary, of the *Menaechmi*.

One city, two names

The plot of the *Menaechmi* 'puts on the Greek' (*graecissat*, v. 11), of which 'to put on the Sicilian' (*sicilicissitare*, v. 12) is a subset;[10] *graecissare* may cover all three of the cities which feature in the narrative of the *Menaechmi*: Syracuse, Tarentum and Epidamnus. Be that as it may, by the late third century, Syracuse and Tarentum were very much in the Roman orbit and at the centre of the Roman-

---

8 Cf. Marshall 2006, 105–106, who argues that the two brothers would have been played by the same (masked) actor, until the final scene when the two brothers meet.
9 For other 'Graecising' aspects of these verses cf. Hunter 2016, 16–17.
10 For some speculations about this verb cf. Fontaine 2006. Richlin 2017, 374–375 notes that Sicily tends to be represented unfavourably in Plautus.

Greek interface: what of Epidamnus? Epidamnus, along with most of Illyria, in fact passed into Roman protection in 229 as a result of what is called the 'First Illyrian War'. Polybius (2.9-12) tells the story and concludes his account as follows:

ἡ μὲν οὖν πρώτη διάβασις Ῥωμαίων μετὰ δυνάμεως εἰς τὴν Ἰλλυρίδα καὶ ταῦτα τὰ μέρη τῆς Εὐρώπης, ἔτι δ' ἐπιπλοκὴ μετὰ πρεσβείας εἰς τοὺς κατὰ τὴν Ἑλλάδα τόπους, τοιάδε καὶ διὰ ταύτας ἐγένετο τὰς αἰτίας. ἀπὸ δὲ ταύτης τῆς καταρχῆς Ῥωμαῖοι μὲν εὐθέως ἄλλους πρεσβευτὰς ἐξαπέστειλαν πρὸς Κορινθίους καὶ πρὸς Ἀθηναίους, ὅτε δὴ καὶ Κορίνθιοι πρῶτον ἀπεδέξαντο μετέχειν Ῥωμαίους τοῦ τῶν Ἰσθμίων ἀγῶνος.

Polybius 2.12.7-8

Such were the circumstances and causes of the Romans crossing for the first time with an army to Illyria and those parts of Europe, and of their first coming into relations through an embassy with Greece. But having thus begun, the Romans immediately afterward sent other envoys to Athens and Corinth, on which occasion the Corinthians first admitted them to participation in the Isthmian games.

trans. Paton/Walbank/Habicht

So Polybius at least was able to represent this as a defining moment in the relations between Rome and what we would call 'mainland Greece'. Epidamnus was, at least later, famous as the landfall on the shortest standard sea-crossing from Italy to Greece, namely Brundisium to Epidamnus; it is very likely that some at least of Plautus' early audiences had themselves made that trip. When the Syracusan Menaechmus and Messenio enter, Menaechmus exclaims on the pleasures of catching sight of land *ex alto procul* (vv. 227-228); this must have been the very experience of those making that precise open-sea crossing. We do not know where the pair are coming from (I shall return to vv. 235-237), but the verses do not at least suggest that they have arrived by following the eastern coast of the Adriatic, whether from the north or the south. Their experience is a Roman experience, even if not Roman alone.

One fact about Epidamnus might seem almost too good to be true in the context of the *Menaechmi*: it changed its name. Probably by the time of Augustus the standard name of the city was Dyrrachion, the origin of modern Durrës, the city's name in Albanian, and of Italian Durazzo; already for Catullus the city was *Durrachium Hadriae tabernam* (36.15). The reasons, process and chronology of this name change are anything but certain; ancient testimonies also disagree as to whether we are dealing with (originally) one city which changed its name to that of the headland on which it stood or two originally separate foundations, each with its own name, which eventually coalesced into one.¹¹ Both names are Greek and/or local, but the standard Greek name in the classical and Hellenistic period was certainly Ἐπίδαμνος, with Δυρράχιον attested solely on coins and occasional inscriptions from the fifth century on. What for our purposes is more interesting than 'what really happened' is what was believed to have happened. There are stories of rival eponymous founders (e.g. Appian, *Civil Wars* 2.39), but one version, attested first in the first century AD, has it that the Romans changed the name to Dyrrachium to avoid the ill-omen of a name involving *damnum*. Pomponius Mela 2.56 asserts that the 'Romans changed the name, because [Epidamnos] seemed to be an omen of those going to suffer loss (*uelut in damnum ituris omen id uisum est*)'.¹² The Latin etymology demands that Romans be made responsible for the name 'change' (which in reality was, of course, the adoption or privileging of one pre-existing name in place of another), so that one name (Dyrrachium) 'becomes' Roman, while the other (Ἐπίδαμνος) stays Greek. What, then, of Messenio's joke at *Menaechmi* 263–264 (a joke perhaps already anticipated by the possibly post-Plautine *prologus* at 51–55)?¹³

> propterea huic urbi nomen Epidamno inditumst,
> quia nemo ferme huc sine damno deuortitur.
>
> Plautus, *Menaechmi* 263–264
>
> This city is called Epidamnus because practically nobody puts up here without being damnified.

Is this simply a strange but fortuitous foreshadowing of what was, at least later, held to be the 'serious' reason for the change, or has Plautus in fact influenced the later geographers and annalists?

More significant perhaps in the current context is the question of how stale Messenio's joke is. In other words, is he making a Latin pun on the city-name which was already familiar to some at least of the Roman audience? Was in fact the contestation for the name of the city — is it to be the Greek Ἐπίδαμνος or what came to be adopted as the Roman/Latin Dyrrachium — already well under way when the *Menaechmi* was first performed, which might of course have been

---

11 Cf. Strabo 7.5.8, Pausanias 6.10.8, Beaumont 1936, 166–167, Wilkes/Fischer-Hansen 2004, 330–331. Livy 43.21 reports that in the mid-second century BC Ἐπίδαμνος was the standard Greek name.
12 Cf. also Pliny, *HN* 3.145, Cassius Dio 41.49.3.
13 Cf. Gratwick's note on vv. 51–52.

three or four decades after Epidamnos passed into Roman protection?[14] If we were instead to consider re-performances of the play later in the second century (as we should), then the question becomes perhaps rather easier to answer, as we know something about the history of the city and its name in the second century. As all periods of ancient and modern history teach us, changes of place-names can be strongly marked signs of cultural and indeed political appropriation; whereas 'going to Epidamnos' was for Romans the equivalent of 'crossing to Greece', 'going to Dyrrachium' was like never leaving Roman territory. Where in this story of Roman expansion into Greece does *Menaechmi* fit?

There are various 'literary' directions in which we might take forward the ideas I have been tracing. One is by pursuing the possible connections between the change of name of the city and the change of name and identity which are central to the plot of the play; in other words, how does the city of two names encompass and reflect the dramatic plot — two characters, one name — which is played out in its streets? The second is the question of how far the city's change of name might serve as an analogy to Plautine appropriation of Greek texts: both may be seen as imperialist gestures which make Greek territory, geographical and cultural, 'safe' for Latin-speakers by the imposition of the Latin language, Roman cultural norms and gestures. The move from Ἐπίδαμνος to *Dyrrachium* is much more than just a change of name. I am tempted to compare the various metaphors and images by which Virgil describes the transposition of Greek pastoral to Latin in the *Eclogues*.[15]

Messenio's map

I turn now to Messenio's presentation of the five years of travelling undertaken by his master and himself in vv. 234–238:

> hic annus sextust postquam ei rei operam damus.
> Histros, Hispanos, Massiliensis, Hilurios,   235
> mare superum omne Graeciamque exoticam
> orasque Italicas omnis, qua adgreditur mare,
> sumus circumuecti.
>
> Plautus, *Menaechmi* 234–238

---

14 The date of the original performance of *Menaechmi* is unfortunately quite uncertain, cf. Jocelyn 1984, 12–16.
15 Cf. Hunter 2006, ch. 4.

This is the sixth year that we've been doing this. We have travelled round the Istri, the Spaniards, the people of Marseille, the Illyrians, the entire upper sea, *Graecia exotica*, and all the Italian shores, wherever the sea reaches. [my translation]

Messenio's catalogue is clearly not arranged in sequential order: Histria (the very north-east corner of the Adriatic), Spain (presumably the south-east coast and the islands), Marseille, Illyria, *mare superum omne*, *Graecia exotica* and 'all the Italian shores'. Although Italy would seem to be at the centre of the to-and-fro travelling, the catalogue is in part driven by Messenio's exasperation and tiredness; the apparent incoherence and the alliteration stress that, in his view, there is no place they have not visited. As Amy Richlin has stressed, moreover, the geographical non-sequiturs (as it were) offer plenty of opportunity for stage business by a skilled actor.[16] On the other hand, despite the apparent geographical chaos, there are marked signs of order. The verbs *circumimus* (231) and *sumus circumuecti* (238) point very clearly to the Greek tradition of περίπλους or περιήγησις writing, just as the witticism in 231, *an quasi mare omnis circumimus insulas?*, 'are we to go around all the islands as the sea does?', seems to play on the Greek adjective περίρρυτος and thus to reinforce the point. Messenio himself seems almost explicitly to acknowledge the resonances of his language in v. 248:

> quin nos hinc domum
> redimus, nisi si historiam scripturi sumus?
>
> Plautus, *Menaechmi* 247–248

Why don't we go back home unless we're going to write a travel book?

The author of one of our earliest examples of such Greek geographical writing, the περίοδος γῆς in iambic trimeters now conventionally ascribed to 'Pseudo-Scymnus' (late second century BC), describes his work as a ἱστορικὸς λόγος (v. 111, cf. *historiam*, *Men.* 248) and vv. 128–136 of the prologue of that work give something of the flavour of Messenio's catalogue:

ἃ δ' αὐτὸς ἰδίᾳ φιλοπόνως ἐξητακὼς
αὐτοπτικὴν πίστιν τε προσενηνεγμένος,
ὡς ἂν θεατὴς οὐ μόνον τῆς Ἑλλάδος   130
ἢ τῶν κατ' Ἀσίαν κειμένων πολισμάτων,
ἵστωρ δὲ γεγονὼς τῶν τε περὶ τὸν Ἀδρίαν
καὶ τῶν κατὰ τὸν Ἰόνιον ἑξῆς κειμένων,
ἐπεληλυθὼς δὲ τούς τε τῆς Τυρρηνίας

---

16 Richlin 2017, 383–385; Richlin reaches very different conclusions about these verses, but rightly seeks to think through the implications of Messenio's itinerary.

καὶ τοὺς Σικελικοὺς καὶ πρὸς ἑσπέραν ὅρους   135
καὶ τῆς Λιβύης τὰ πλεῖστα καὶ Καρχηδόνος.

                                          Pseudo-Scymnus, *Periodos* 128–136

[And I will set forth] that which I myself investigated with great energy and relying on the confidence which autopsy brings, as an observer not merely of Greece and the cities lying on the boundary to Asia; I also investigated [lit. 'became *histōr* of'] the settlements around the Adriatic and those lying successively along the Ionian Sea, and I visited the areas of Tyrrhenia and Sicily and those to the west and most of Libya and Carthage.

Even Messenio's 'hellfire' warnings about the inhabitants of Epidamnus in vv. 258–262, which explain where the *damnum* in Epidamnus comes from, may ape the brief 'anthropological' notices of this mode of geographical writing:[17]

nam ita est haec hominum natio: in Epidamnieis
uoluptarii atque potatores maxumi;
tum sycophantae et palpatores plurumi   260
in urbe hac habitant; tum meretrices mulieres
nusquam perhibentur blandiores gentium.

                                            Plautus, *Menaechmi* 258–262

This nation of people is like this: among the Epidamnians there are the greatest hedonists and drinkers. Then lots of impostors and cajolers live in this city. And then the prostitutes are said to be the most coaxing anywhere.

Pseudo-Scymnus has very different things to say about the tribes of Illyria, but the 'ethnographic' mode of his verses is not unrelated to Messenio's account of the people of Epidamnus:

        θεοσεβεῖς δ' αὐτοὺς ἄγαν
καὶ σφόδρα δικαίους φασὶ καὶ φιλοξένους,
κοινωνικὴν διάθεσιν ἠγαπηκότας
εἶναι, βίον ζηλοῦν τε κοσμιώτατον.

                                          Pseudo-Scymnus, *Periodos* 422–425

They say that [the Illyrian tribes] are very pious and exceedingly just and hospitable, that they are devoted to very communal arrangements and that they esteem a very decent lifestyle.

---

17 The author of the *RE* article on Dyrrachium takes Messenio's account as serious evidence for the contemporary reputation of the people of Epidamnus (*RE* 5.1887); this seems unlikely, but for all we know perhaps correct, and it would of course suggest that *damnum* ~ *Epidamnus* was indeed not just a one-off Plautine joke; cf., in general, Jocelyn 1984.

All of the peoples mentioned by Messenio in v. 235 occur in Pseudo-Scymnus and, at least as interestingly, in the probably early Hellenistic περίπλους of Pseudo-Scylax; *Hispanos Massilienses* is in fact a περίπλους ordering (cf. Pseudo-Scylax 2, 4), as is *Histros ... Hilurios* (cf. Pseudo-Scylax 20, 22). Moreover, Pseudo-Scymnus shows that Epidamnos can in fact be treated separately from Illyria (vv. 415–43), as being a πόλις Ἑλληνίς, as Messenio in fact does treat it. Messenio's geography, it emerges, deserves to be taken seriously.

In vv. 236–237 Messenio's itinerary becomes (apparently) less detailed, or at least less simply catalogic; fixed names and geographical labels of individual peoples give way to brief descriptions of whole areas which, by implication, were home to very many different cities and peoples. What did these descriptions mean for Plautus' audience? *mare superum* was, at least later, to become a standard way of referring to the Adriatic, but the *TLL* and *OLD* offer no other example of this use before Cicero, and no example at all of *mare inferum* for the Tuscan sea on the other side of Italy before Cicero. How did *mare superum* in the mouth of a Syracusan sound, and what did it mean, to Plautus' audience? Not probably as exotic as *Graecia exotica*, but our familiarity with the later usage of *mare superum* has perhaps prevented us from asking necessary questions. It may of course be that the absence of attestations between Plautus and Cicero is simply the result of our limited evidence — after all, *Hadria, Hadriaticus* etc first appear in the time of Catullus and Cicero; we just do not have that much Latin literature from the second and early first centuries BC. Nevertheless, the phrase in the *Menaechmi* remains an *unicum* and therefore piques curiosity — or should do.

There are several current explanations of how *mare superum* came to mean 'the Adriatic', but the two which seem to hold the field are either that *superum/inferum* means (basically) 'north-south', and may be connected to the ancient view that Italy ran much more east-west than it actually does, so that the Adriatic is indeed, from a Roman perspective, 'upper' or (virtually) 'northern', or that the Adriatic, which Greeks at least until the Hellenistic period called the 'Ionian Sea' or the 'Ionian Gulf', as well as Ἀδρίας (perhaps originally a native Italian name),[18] is 'up' because Romans had to climb mountains, notably the Appenines, to get there, whereas the Tuscan Sea lay literally at their feet, 'down there'.[19] What is (apparently) universally agreed in modern scholarship is that the usage is entirely Latin, that the isolated instance in Plautus is no different

---

18 Cf. Beaumont 1936, 203–204.
19 For the various modern views and the ancient evidence cf. *TLL* s.v. *inferus* IC, Partsch, *RE* 1.417, Philipp, *RE* 14.1673, Burr 1932, 68–70.

from any of the later usages, and that the isolation is just a matter of chance. Nevertheless, it remains the case that what looks like a Roman usage in *Menaechmi* is embedded within Graecising geography and spoken by a Greek/Sicilian character. It may therefore be worth suggesting that we have here in the *Menaechmi*, not a purely Roman usage slipped into Messenio's language, but rather a calque on a Greek geographical use of ἄνω and κάτω, not to mean 'inland — by the coast', but rather 'upper' and/or 'to the north' and 'lower' and/or 'to the south'.[20] What is clear, however, even if we are unable to pinpoint precisely the resonance of Messenio's use of *mare superum* — might it even mean, not the Adriatic, but the 'sea above (Sicily)'? — there can be no doubt that the world which the Romans were fashioning in their image was in fact a Greek world already named *à la grecque*.

As for *Graecia exotica*, I would guess that this again evokes the language of Greek geographical writing, in which ἔξω and ἐντός are familiar ways of denoting spatial position (e.g. τὰ ἔξω τῆς θαλάττης, etc). Nevertheless, I know of absolutely no parallel for this Latin expression. Messenio's phrase has been variously understood, when scholars have bothered to ask what it might actually mean, and again we will not want to ignore the fact that Messenio is a Syracusan, or at least a Sicilian. *TLL* and many modern scholars take it as a way of saying Magna Graecia, though without adducing any arguments,[21] whereas de Melo in the recent Loeb edition translates it as 'Sicily'. In Latin, the loan word *exoticus* is indeed a rarity: it occurs three times in Plautus (in *Epid*. 232 and *Most*. 42 it is suggestive of Greek luxury), and not again until imperial prose (including, most famously, the prologue of Apuleius, *Metamorphoses*); one might wonder how *Graecia* in Plautus could be anything other than *exotica*, but — if so — with what other *Graecia* is it contrasted? *LSJ* offer no Greek example of the term in literature (broadly defined) before Epictetus. So what, then, might *Graecia exotica* mean? If it is supposed to mean 'Greece outside mainland Greece', then *exoticus* / ἐξωτικός does not seem the right word with which to express that idea.

The most common interpretation of *Graecia exotica* is indeed that it means Magna Graecia, but why *exotica* should take the place of *magna* remains unex-

---

20 Cf. Hdt. 1.72.2, 1.142.2, 7.20.2, Pl. *Rep.* 4.435e5, LSJ s.v. ἄνω (B) A IIe; it is not always easy to choose between 'inland' and 'to the north' in many attestations for the usage.
21 Thoresby Jones' commentary on the *Menaechmi* asserts that mainland Greeks called Magna Graecia ἡ ἔξω Ἑλλάς, but he does not offer any supporting evidence for the assertion. So too Maurice 2005, 48–49 claims that '*Graecia exotica* is an accepted term for Magna Graecia', but no evidence is offered. Richlin 2017, 383 translates as 'Greece abroad', but then assumes that the reference is to Magna Graecia.

plained. This is clearly not the place for a discussion of the origins of the term Magna Graecia, which first certainly appears in Polybius 2.39.1 and Pseudo-Scymnus 303–304, though earlier use can hardly be doubted (its absence from Pseudo-Scylax *may* be worthy of note). Later on, some writers included Sicily in the term and some did not, but the evidence points pretty clearly to a limitation in the third and second centuries to the Greek colonies of southern Italy, or even just to those in the toe and sole of Italy. What is of particular interest is that Pseudo-Scymnus appears to make 'Great Greece in the west' co-extensive with Ἰταλία (vv. 300–304), by which terms he designates the coast of southern Italy from Terina in the west round to Tarentum. There is much other evidence that Ἰταλία (also missing from Pseudo-Scylax) was also at first a Greek term for what we call southern Italy or indeed Magna Graecia, though extension beyond that seems already visible in Thucydides;[22] that had certainly changed by the time of, say, Polybius. Again, more questions than answers, but it is clear that we cannot consider the meaning of *Graecia exotica* in isolation from that of v. 237, *orasque Italicas omnis, qua adgreditur mare*. It is not difficult to guess that this also evokes the language of geographical writing, but of particular note is that this is the only instance of either *Italia* or *Italicus* in Plautus; according to *OLD*, we have to wait (again) until Cicero to find another instance of *Italicus* in literature. This is, of course, not the whole story: from inscriptions we know, for example, of the traders from southern and central Italy who called themselves *Italici*/Ἰταλικοί on Delos and elsewhere in the second century,[23] but there is little doubt that *orae Italicae* is a Greek term. To what does it refer? Might it, particularly in the mouth of a character from Syracuse, refer to the southern Italian shores (i.e. Magna Graecia), in which case *Graecia exotica* will have to be something else? Might the latter even refer, particularly in Messenio's mouth, to 'mainland' Greece?

The Roman confrontation with Greece is, then, a confrontation with Greek geography, both 'technical' and mythic, and with Greek science. We are familiar with the very close links between mapping, geography and political power in the Augustan period, but the subject deserves thought also for the earlier period of Roman expansion. As Rome pushed outwards it encountered not just Greeks and others, but also a world mapped (however imperfectly) by Greeks, and therefore a world and a map which needed changing; the name of Epidamnus is just one small example of this.

---

22 Cf. Marcotte 2000, 57–61.
23 Cf. Rauh 1993, Index s.v. *Italikoi/Italici* , Wallace-Hadrill 2008, 84–85.

Maps of culture

There is another Greek map which needs to be brought into the picture. I have suggested that the perspective of the Syracusan Menaechmus and Messenio when they enter might, even momentarily, evoke that of Romans arriving after the crossing from Brundisium; if so, we will have to add it to those places in the play where a Roman perspective is very clearly suggested, as of course it regularly is in Plautus — for the *Menaechmi* we will think particularly of Peniculus' complaints about how a *contio* kept him from lunch (446–465) and of the Epidamnian Menaechmus' complaints about how legal business is conducted in the city (571–599).[24] The Syracusan Menaechmus' view of arrival may, however, also suggest the perspective of an Odysseus, though this searching Odysseus has something of the Telemachus also about him, whereas Messenio, who enters with Menaechmus, just wants his νόστος.[25] It is hard (at least for me) not to think of aspects of the patterns of Odysseus and Telemachus when we hear, not just of how the Sicilian Menaechmus and Messenio have circumnavigated the Mediterranean, but how Menaechmus wants, if he cannot find his brother alive, to find someone who can give him clear information as to his death — this *mutatis mutandis* is why Telemachus travels to Pylos and Sparta in *Odyssey* 3 and 4. We could go further and turn Erotium, for example, into a kind of Circe/Calypso, but that might perhaps be self-indulgent fantasy. Much has, however, recently been written about the role of the *Odyssey* in the Roman confrontation with 'the other', notably with the Greek cities of southern Italy and Sicily;[26] the *Odyssey* was in fact one of the maps which the Romans used to make sense of their experiences in 'Magna Graecia' and Sicily.

The geographical imperative, if that is not too grand a phrase, of the opening verses of the *Odyssey* offers both a narrative of the past and a programme for future action. This is not the place for a discussion of why Livius Andronicus chose the *Odyssey* to translate into Latin in what, with hindsight, we may see as a foundational cultural act, but at the very least the *Menaechmi* deserves a place, however small, within a much larger picture. One surviving verse of Ennius' *Annales*,

> quom ueter occubuit Priamus sub Marte Pelasgo
>
> Ennius, *Annales* 14 Skutsch

---

24 Cf., e.g., Jocelyn 1984, 9.
25 Cf., Stärk 1989, 13.
26 Cf., e.g., Leigh 2010.

is often thought to have occurred right at the start of the 'story of Rome', and the apparent imitation of that verse at Virgil, *Aen.* 3.1–3 does nothing to dampen the suspicion; we cannot of course know for sure, though it is tempting to see here a kind of re-positioning of v. 2 of Book 1 of the *Odyssey*. Just as Odysseus' journey westwards, i.e. the *Odyssey*, positions itself as 'after' the fall of Troy, so both Aeneas and Ennius' account of the Trojan exiles move westwards. The *Odyssey* is a foundational text for Roman, as well as for Greek culture, including of course the Greek colonies of Magna Graecia,[27] and echoes of Odyssean patterns in the *Menaechmi* will increase the sense that this play is not just about the Roman engagement with Greece, as all plays of Plautus are at some level, but rather is so in a particular way and that we must be sensitive to this.

Let me return to the possible connections between the change of name of the city and the change of name and identity which are central to the plot of the *Menaechmi* and to the question of how far the city's change of name might analogise to Plautine appropriation of Greek texts. One thing which is clear, I think, is that we cannot make any neat schematic distinctions such as 'Menaechmus I ~ Roman culture, Menaechmus II ~ Greek culture etc ...'; the facts of the play will simply not bear this out. Moreover, we should hardly expect this in a Roman adaptation of a Greek play, though Plautus elsewhere precisely plays with our willingness (if not in fact our desire) to see sharp distinctions within the plays in Roman-Greek terms. A striking and familiar example is the clash between the country-slave Grumio and the town-slave Tranio in the opening scene of the *Mostellaria*. It is not just Grumio's repeated use of the verb *pergraecari* which suggests that he embodies what was already for Plautus' audience a comic stereotype of the Roman — an uncultured bumpkin smelling of garlic and more at home among pigs than pretty women. Both characters, however, are Attic slaves, and the distinction between them may be related to that between the young men in Menander's *Dyskolos*: Sostratos is a well-to-do young member of the urban elite, whereas Gorgias is a hard-working farmer in the tough Attic countryside. In a Plautine version of the *Dyskolos*, we might expect to find play with intercultural, not just intracultural, differences between the two young men, not dissimilar to that of the *Mostellaria* between the two slaves. With Plautus, we know that we are watching a Greek play in Latin and we have expectations that the meeting of those cultures will matter: intracultural difference within Greek plays is sometimes transformed in Plautus into intercultural difference.

---

[27] Malkin 1998 has rightly been very influential here.

The scene of the *Menaechmi* which has been the principal focus of this paper will have felt both more 'Greek' to some of the Roman audience than a comparable scene in Greek would have done to a Greek audience, because — so I have suggested — some of the geographical terminology is marked (for Romans) precisely as Greek, but I have also suggested that aspects of that scene also evoke Roman experience of travel; moreover, the setting of the play in Epidamnus would have had specific cultural and historical meaning for a Roman audience, however difficult it may be for us properly to grasp that significance. Such mixed effects are in fact typical of Plautus, and they are one of the reasons that the nature of these plays can be so hard to describe. The translation and assimilation of culture, whether verbal (as in the case of Plautine scripts) or in the way people actually experience others, is always likely to be messy.

Bibliography

Beaumont, R.L. 1936. 'Greek influence in the Adriatic Sea before the fifth century B.C.', *Journal of Hellenic Studies* 56, 159–204.

Burr, V. 1932. *Nostrum mare. Ursprung und Geschichte der Namen des Mittelmeeres und seiner Teilmeere im Altertum*, Stuttgart.

Frangoulidis, S./Harrison, S./Manuwald, G. (eds.) 2016. *Roman Drama and its Contexts*, Trends in Classics Supplementary Volumes 34, Berlin/Boston.

Fontaine, M. 2006. '*Sicilicissitat* (Plautus, *Menaechmi* 12) and early geminate writing in Latin (with an appendix on *Men.* 13)', *Mnemosyne* 59, 95–110.

Gratwick, A.S. 1993. *Plautus, Menaechmi*, Cambridge.

Hunter, R. 2006. *The Shadow of Callimachus*, Cambridge.

Hunter, R. 2016. 'Some Dramatic Terminology', in: Frangoulidis/Harrison/Manuwald 2016, 13–24 [= this volume 399–410].

Jocelyn, H.D. 1984. 'Anti-Greek elements in Plautus' *Menaechmi*', *Papers of the Liverpool Latin Seminar* 4, 1–25.

Leigh, M. 2004. *Comedy and the Rise of Rome*, Oxford.

Leigh, M. 2010. 'Early Roman epic and the maritime moment', *Classical Philology* 105, 265–280.

Malkin, I. 1998. *The Returns of Odysseus*, Berkeley.

Marcotte, D. 2000. *Géographes grecs, Tome I: Ps.-Scymnos: Circuit de la Terre*, Paris.

Marshall, C.W. 2006. *The Stagecraft and Performance of Roman Comedy*, Cambridge.

Maurice, L. 2005. 'A calculated comedy of errors: the structure of Plautus' *Menaechmi*', *Syllecta Classica* 16, 31–59.

McCarthy, K. 2016. 'Prologues between performance and fiction', in: Frangoulidis/Harrison/Manuwald 2016, 203–213.

Moore, T.J. 1998. *The Theater of Plautus*, Austin.

Muecke, F. 1987. *Plautus, Menaechmi*, Bristol.

Rauh, N.K. 1993. *The Sacred Bonds of Commerce*, Amsterdam.

Richlin, A. 2016. 'The kings of comedy', in: Frangoulidis/Harrison/Manuwald 2016, 67–95.
Richlin, A. 2017. *Slave Theater in the Roman Republic. Plautus and Popular Comedy*, Cambridge.
Sharrock, A. 2009. *Reading Roman Comedy*, Cambridge.
Stärk, E. 1989. *Die Menaechmi des Plautus und kein griechisches Original*, Tübingen.
Wallace-Hadrill, A. 2008. *Rome's Cultural Revolution*, Cambridge.
Wilkes, J./Fischer-Hansen, T. 2004. 'Epidamnos', in: M.H. Hansen/T.H. Nielsen (eds.), *An Inventory of Archaic and Classical Poleis*, Oxford, 330–331.

Part V: **The Ancient Novel**

25 Fictional Anxieties

1

'The genre: novels proper and the fringe' is the title of Niklas Holzberg's helpful survey in a standard handbook.[1] 'Proper' may denote not just 'the real thing', i.e. genuine examples of whatever we take a 'novel' to be (the risk of circularity here is obviously real, though it need not be paralysing), but also 'clean, conventional, decent, approved'; the word itself implies a boundary of exclusion. As is well known, all novels (and 'novel-like' works) in antiquity were 'fringe' performances in one or more senses; sometimes this was a status which they constructed for themselves and in which they revelled, sometimes it is a status conferred upon them, for better or ill, by modern scholarship, sometimes a bit of both. For ancient novels of all types the 'centre' was the inherited pattern of literary genres and their conventions; if modern scholars of the ancient novel have now created a 'central/proper' and 'fringe' distinction, we may be tempted to think that this is a way of taking revenge for all those decades of being patronised as a sad and/or lunatic fringe interest.

That 'centres' and 'fringes' are mutually implicating does not require much demonstration; you cannot have one without the other. The Edinburgh Festival Fringe is a helpful illustration. Although the Fringe is now nearly as 'organised' as the Festival itself, the title conveys notions of openness and accessibility, where anyone can stand up and ply his or her (comic) trade, a home for amateurs and experiments rather than for polished professionals. In such a structure, apparently separate forms of musical and dramatic entertainment blend freely, so that 'generic form' is less obviously static than in the performances at the Festival proper; the analogy with so-called 'fringe novels' should be obvious. Nevertheless, it is also important that the Fringe grew out of the Festival 'proper' and remains parasitic upon it; the sense of 'fringeness' remains important to its sense of self-identity, however conventional and accepted it itself has now become. 'Difference', deviation from an accepted model, and the vague aroma of the illicit are important to fringes.

This essay combines parts of two lectures given at various times in Athens, Dublin, Melbourne and Sydney; I have tried to preserve the flavour of the oral presentation as far as possible. I am grateful to those four audiences for the spirit in which they listened and to Grammatiki Karla for her hospitality.

---

1 Holzberg 1996.

Some of the texts which have been consigned to 'the fringe' might of course claim that they have nothing to do with 'the novel' and hence with 'deviation' from some supposed centre; the link between them is, rather, a construction of modern scholarship and the exigencies of academic organisation and careers. *The Life of Aesop*, a text which is (deservedly) attracting more and more attention, might be thought to be one such misused narrative. 'Mit dem antiken Roman hat [der *Aisoposroman*] nichts gemein' pronounced Paul Maas,[2] and Maas is not someone to be disagreed with lightly. Nevertheless, recent scholarship has not found it difficult to find motifs and ideas shared between the *Life* and the ancient novels, particularly the *Metamorphoses* of Apuleius;[3] Jack Winkler's comparison of the satirical moral outlook of the *Life* and that of the *Metamorphoses* has been very influential.[4] It is of course easy enough to think of further lines of enquiry one could pursue. Thus, for example, the celebrated (and almost impossible to translate) description of Aesop's mind-boggling ugliness with which the *Life* opens[5] could be taken as a parodic reversal of the impossible beauty of novel heroes and heroines which is usually described at the opening of the works (cf., e.g., Xen. *Eph*. 1.1–2). The point would perhaps be that, though Aesop is not a supernaturally handsome member of the elite, but rather an incredibly ugly slave whose parents are apparently not even worth mentioning (a more striking phenomenon in an ancient text than it would be in a modern one), this narrative, like Aesop himself, will be βιωφελέστατος.

However that may be, there is probably not much to be gained from prolonged agonising over whether there is an 'essential' centre and fringe among ancient fictional narrative texts; there have, of course, been many attempts to interrogate the related idea of a distinct 'genre' of 'ideal novel', and I need not repeat those here. Rather, what is important are the questions that such labels make us ask. It is obviously important that the grouping together of the five Greek novels which survive in a manuscript tradition forces us to ask questions about sameness and difference, though there is, as Helen Morales points out in her contribution to the present volume, a serious danger that such grouping tends to privilege sameness over difference. It is that grouping, as much as anything else, which has led to advances in our understanding of, for example, the chronology

---

[2] *Byzantinische Zeitschrift* 37 1937, 377.
[3] Cf., e.g., Anderson 1984, 211–212, Finkelpearl 2003, Jouanno 2006, 55, 215 n. 133, Hunter 2007, 42–43, Zimmerman 2007.
[4] Winkler 1985, 276–291.
[5] The description of this ugliness and its affiliations are interestingly discussed in Papademetriou 1997, 10–42.

and geographical focus of the 'ideal novels'. So too, the idea of 'fringeness' can be a helpful way of focusing upon some aspects of many different kinds of narrative text which may have become stale through over-familiarity. If 'fringeness' is importantly inherent in ancient novels, it is also very obviously a central creative force in modern literature and film (to go no further): art often moves towards the edge. In this brief essay I want to pursue some of the implications of this, and some of the continuities over time, through a glance at two modern Australian novels. The choice is obviously not a random one (and may be thought overdetermined), but Australian fiction is perhaps not without interest for students of the ancient novel. To paint it with the broadest brush, for much of its white existence Australia was a 'fringe' country in almost every respect, one overly conscious of, and anxious about, the fact that it derived from a powerful and normative 'centre' (which was also a long way away); however self-assured Australian writers and artists were, the consumers of Australian 'culture' were far from clear that this product was 'the real thing'. Even today, when Australia finds itself on the 'Pacific Rim' rather than the fringe and the sense of 'properly' belonging has finally (perhaps) taken root, there is no getting away from the unimaginable dangers which lurk in the 'nothingness' at the heart of the country, and it is hardly surprising that novelists and film-makers return to this theme time and time again.

In Patrick White's novel, *A Fringe of Leaves* (1976), which concerns an English woman shipwrecked in northern Australia and captured by Aboriginals in the early nineteenth century, the fringe marks the boundary between conventional society and its morality and that which such conventionality seeks to shut out; whether as a metaphorical border or as an improvised skirt whose value as a symbol is far greater than as a method of concealment, the very tenuousness of the fringe is a marker of just how important that boundary is, but also how easily it can be obliterated. There are very few societies as convention-bound as the social elite of fictionalised nineteenth-century Australia, and few societies where the abandonment of convention was so provocatively close a temptation (as it still is). The geography of that Australia — a thin coastal strip of green land and inhabitation, a 'fringe of leaves', behind which broods an unimaginably large 'other' into which White's most memorable characters are ineluctably drawn — dramatises how precarious our hold on convention is. One might compare (perhaps) the movement in Chariton's novel away from the Greek world and into the vast 'barbarian' spaces; White's Aboriginals are a cannibalistic 'anti- society' fashioned of white man's worst dreamings (cf. the *boukoloi* of Lollianus and others).

White's novel throws a number of issues into relief. Its heroine is herself not a member of the gentry but has married into it, and her upward social mobility is a constant source of anxiety to her and potential attack to others. It is often remarked that the central characters of the Greek 'ideal' novel come from the higher socio-political echelons of their respective states — we 'look up to' not only their physical attractiveness but also their 'success'. Even the characters who stand closest to the bucolic upbringing of White's heroine, namely Longus' Daphnis and Chloe, turn out to come from the highest social class. The 'ideal novel' regularly dramatises the threats to that class and its ideology, but at the end it is that class which closes around 'its own' in a re-establishment of good order, often marked by the end of dislocating travel and a return to roots. In White's novel, too, 'society', which once took Mrs Roxburgh in when she married 'above' herself, closes around her again at the end (whatever its worries about what might or might not have happened to her in the bush), and her return to the local centre, Sydney, is underway and that (her real *nostos*) to the 'proper' centre (England) is foreshadowed. For its part, the ancient 'fringe' (as commonly understood) often dramatises the lives and doings of those whose grip on 'society' is rather fragile; the question of the relation between the rise of the novel and 'social mobility' is of course a very big one in modern literary studies, and there have been important tentative steps in this direction for the ancient novel, but the constant struggle of the central characters of the 'ideal novel' to maintain that barrier, the 'fringe of leaves', which separates them from descent into the lower reaches of society and its practices is itself of interest. Unsurprisingly, perhaps, sex and the constant temptations of sensuality are at the heart of that struggle, one dramatised many times over, for example, in the works of such as Chariton and Xenophon of Ephesus. This struggle also lies at the heart of the distinction between types in White's vision:

> Just as she was to learn that death was for Mr Roxburgh a 'literary conceit', so she found that his approach to passion had its formal limits. For her part, she longed to, but had never dared, storm those limits and carry him off instead of submitting to his hesitant though loving rectitude. 'Tup' was a word she remembered out of a past she had all but forgotten, in which her own passive ewes submitted, while bees flitted wilfully from thyme to furze, the curlew whistled at dusk, and night was filled with the badger's chattered messages. She herself had only once responded with a natural ardour, but discovered on her husband's face an expression of having tasted something bitter, or of looking too deep. So she replaced the mask which evidently she was expected to wear, and because he was an honourable as well as a pitiable man, she would refrain in future from tearing it off.
>
> Patrick White, *A Fringe of Leaves* pp. 67–68[6]

---

6 I cite from the Penguin edition of 1977.

The heroine's desire for experience which is less generically constrained than 'ideal marriage' is in fact met in one brief act of adultery with her brother-in-law and then in an extended series of real and or dreamed nights with the escaped convict (more 'fringe'/'rough trade' material) who rescues her from the Aboriginals. If the 'ideal' novel works towards the inculcation of the dominant ideology, it of necessity also contains elements of interrogation, because without that interrogation there would be no narrative: the narrative always holds out the possibility that 'things will go wrong', and showing us how they could go wrong (e.g. our heroine enters into a passionate and adulterous affair with one of her admirers) entails the display of other modes of behaviour.

Convention, then, is very important to both centres and fringes. Thus, for example, whatever relationship we wish to posit between the *Satyrica* and the *Metamorphoses* on the one hand and the Greek 'ideal' novel on the other, it would, I think, be hard to deny that both Latin novels exploit a sense of difference from conventionally authorised texts; they — and their characters — operate *extra legem*, as Alessandro Barchiesi emphasised for the *Satyrica*.[7] They also, of course, are — from another point of view — fully licensed to be different; they are 'carnival' texts which are nourished and draw support from the very society which they overturn in their narratives.[8] To what extent the same is true for Greek 'fringe' texts may be debated, and it is likely that a wide spectrum of answers will fit the texts which survive in whole or part. To return to the *Life of Aesop*, for example, there are very interesting questions to be asked about the extent to which this alleged 'Volksbuch' is actually subversive of received, elite wisdom (which elite is likely to have taken Xanthos the philosopher seriously?).

2

The second topic on which I wish to touch briefly is that of 'truth' and historicity, an anxiety which is reflected in literary story-telling at all levels, central and fringe, throughout antiquity. It is famously thematised in, for example, the proems of both Chariton and Achilles Tatius and the opening chapters of Apuleius' *Metamorphoses*, but nowhere so obviously and explicitly (unsurprisingly) as in the prologue to Lucian's *True Histories* (a 'fringe' text?), and here I will be principally concerned with one of that work's descendants.

---

7 Barchiesi 1996. For the idea of the literal 'outlaw' in the novel cf. further below p. 457.
8 There is of course a huge post-Bakhtin bibliography on the general subject; both general and specific guidance in Branham 2005.

In order to illustrate the importance both of the theme and of the literary descent of the theme, however, I wish to begin with a small section of Porphyry's work *On Abstinence from Killing (and Eating) Animals* (late third century AD). In the early part of the third book Porphyry deals with the *logos*, 'speech and rationality', of animals:

> Yet, if we are to believe the ancients and those who lived in our own time and our fathers' time, there are those who are said to have heard and understood the speech of animals... A friend of mine used to relate how he was lucky enough to have a slave-boy who understood all the speech of birds, and everything they said was a prophecy announcing what would shortly happen; but he lost his understanding because his mother feared that he would be sent as a gift to the emperor, and urinated in his ears as he slept.
> Let us pass over these stories because of our natural trait of incredulity (*apistia*)...
> Porphyry, *On Abstinence* 3.3.6–4.1 (trans. G. Clark)

In moving on to information which will (apparently) not strain our sense of incredulity, Porphyry adduces the behaviour of the Indian hyena:

> The Indian hyena, which the natives call 'corocotta', speaks in so human a way, even without a teacher, that it prowls around houses and calls whoever looks like an easy prey, imitating their nearest and dearest and the speech to which the person called would respond in all circumstances. So the Indians, even though they know this, are deceived by the resemblance, go out in response to the call and get eaten.
> Porphyry, *On Abstinence* 3.4.5 (trans. G. Clark)

We may not wish to spend long on trying to decide whether these stories are true (the logistics of the urination story do not bear thinking about and the hyena story is at least unflattering to the intelligence of Indians), but the truth status of even such stories as this was clearly a matter of anxiety for the ancients, and this can, I think, shed light on this recurrent theme both within and beyond the fringe of story-telling. Moreover, the hyena's behaviour is clearly modelled upon that ascribed to Helen at Troy in Menelaos' narration in the fourth book of the *Odyssey*:

> τρὶς δὲ περίστειξας κοῖλον λόχον ἀμφαφόωσα,
> ἐκ δ' ὀνομακλήδην Δαναῶν ὀνόμαζες ἀρίστους,
> πάντων Ἀργείων φωνὴν ἴσκουσ' ἀλόχοισιν·
> Homer, *Odyssey* 4.277–279

> Three times you circled our hollow place of ambush [i.e. the wooden horse], running your hand over it, and you called out to the Danaan heroes by name, likening your voice to the wives of each of the Argives.

It is clear from the scholia that v. 279 enjoyed a mixed reputation at best in antiquity ('This imitation of the voices is utterly ridiculous and impossible! Why would the Greeks have believed that their wives were there?'), and Porphyry's hyena's imitation of it is unlikely to raise its standing. The Greeks are spared the fate of the Indians, however, by the fast actions of Odysseus whose intelligence, and perhaps his particular empathy with his own wife, understood what was going on. By whatever route, however, this reached Porphyry, the lesson to be drawn is not just the pervasive influence of Homer all over Greek culture, but rather the important truth that the shaping of stories to fit patterns inherited from Homer is not, of itself, an important criterion of truth status. Homeric poetry has come to provide a set of archetypes which confirm, rather than undermine, narrative credibility. If less starkly (and perhaps less amusingly) than Porphyry's hyena, the ancient novel shows a persistent debt to, particularly, the *Odyssey*, and the differences in the way in which the 'centre' and the 'fringe' handle that debt is a subject which would deserve further reflection in another place.

The effect of story-telling within novels (whether ancient or modern) always depends upon the social and generic conventions which operate within a particular literary tradition. The novels of such as Garcia Marquez (*100 Years of Solitude* etc.), Peter Carey and Salman Rushdie, for example, are filled with 'stories', told both by the 'fictional characters' of the works and in the voice of the narrator, whose 'truth status' is problematic, and indeed problematised, within the whole fictional structure which constitutes the work. Crucial to this process is the fact that the 'truth status' of the novel as a whole, in which the stories are set, may be itself actively made an issue for the reader in various ways. This is particularly foregrounded, of course, when the work in question is a version of 'the historical novel', but such anxieties are by no means limited to this extreme case. Rushdie's *The Satanic Verses* begins with two characters surviving a fall from a hijacked aircraft which is blown-up in mid-air, as if to say 'this story is not true', but the book was, as Hesiod's Muses might have said, sufficiently 'like truth' to have very unpleasant consequences for the author in the real world. So too, Rushdie's *Midnight's Children* and *Shame* are full of real characters and incidents in the history of India and Pakistan, but where 'truth' and 'fiction' begin and end is often neither easy (nor perhaps important) to identify, which is itself a truth about the Indian sub-continent which Rushdie is at pains to suggest, or perhaps rather to suggest that 'western' notions of what constitutes 'historical truth' are not necessarily appropriate for understanding the cultures of which he writes. The truth of social memory far transcends the 'what really happened' question. I like to think that Australia too is such a country.

For the classicist there are here major issues about *mythos* and *logos* and about how ancient cultures used 'history' (understood in the broadest sense from social memory to Thucydidean research) to define themselves; Herodotus, the almost unimaginably broad sweep of whose narrative defies modern categorization, is perhaps the author most central to any such investigation, at least on the Greek side. To stay, however, with traditions of the novel — we are perhaps so familiar with the genre that we have lost some of the *frisson* of the illicit which goes with reading a prose narrative which floats in the realm of the imaginary; in antiquity, however, the association between prose and 'truth', like its correlative of poetry and 'falsehood', was remarkably persistent. Mythographic handbooks, such as the early imperial *Library* of Apollodorus, are a very good place to start thinking about ancient attitudes to this matter. To some extent it is this over-familiarity with fictional convention which has bred the post-modern reaction which stresses the role of the author and thus allows us to watch fiction in the making. Ian McEwan's *Atonement* is a familiar example: the second half of the novel seems to offer us access to a 'true account' of the retreat towards Dunkirk (one based as we are subsequently reminded on original documents) and thus to the 'true' ending of the novel, only for the author to turn around and bite us at the end by admitting that we have been given the ending we wanted. The link between what we want to believe and what we do believe is, of course, crucial to the psychology of literature and film (to go no further).

The proem of Lucian's *True Histories*, which may or may not belong to 'the fringe', plays with our nagging sense (which itself we owe in large part to the *Odyssey*) that such first-person narratives should be true, or at least 'trueish'. Lucian declares, no doubt with as much truth as anything else in the work, that his 'plausible and credible' lies are all hits at the impossible fictions of earlier 'travel' writers, a couple of whom he names, and that the person responsible for such charlatanry is Homer's Odysseus, who showed the way with his tall tales to the Phaeacians:

> On reading all these authors, I did not find much fault with them for their lying... but I did wonder that they thought that they could write untruths without anyone noticing. Therefore, as I myself, thanks to my vanity, was eager to hand something down to posterity, that I might not be the only one excluded from the licence to make up stories (τῆς ἐν τῶι μυθολογεῖν ἐλευθερίας), and because I had nothing true to relate (ἀληθὲς ἱστορεῖν) — for nothing worthy of note had ever happened to me — I took to lying. But my lying is far more honest than theirs, for though I tell the truth in nothing else, I shall at least be truthful in declaring that I am lying. I think I can escape the censure of the world by my own admission that I am not telling a word of truth. Be it understood, then, that I am writing

about things which I have neither seen nor experienced nor heard about from others — which, in fact, do not exist at all and, in the nature of things, cannot exist. Therefore my readers should on no account believe in them.

Lucian, *VH* 1.4 (trans. Harmon, adapted)

Lucian's double bluff has, of course, something about it, not only of Socrates' famous explanation of the assertion of the Delphic oracle that no one was wiser than Socrates (if true it must refer to the fact that Socrates at least knew that he knew nothing), but also of the Cretan paradox — 'all Cretans are liars', said the Cretan. Its importance in the history of ideas about fiction is however often overlooked, in part because it is dismissed as one more Lucianic joke, and in part because 'science fiction' and the creation of 'possible worlds' and other imaginative forms have blunted our sense of wonder. Lucian's declaration of 'free composition' represents in fact a major step forward, regardless of whether it too is one big lie. Of course, we can trace ancestors for Lucian — Aristophanic plots, for example, are important here — but they do not, I think, alter the picture substantially. It is, of course, part of Lucian's bluff that what subsequently happens in that work never really tempts us to doubt the author's lack of veracity.

One modern work which evokes Lucian's and which may be of particular interest in this regard for the student of the ancient novel is Peter Carey's *True History of the Kelly Gang* (2000), which presents itself as the first-person memoirs, written for a daughter he never met, of the famous outlaw (a man really *extra legem*) of Irish extraction who has passed into Australian mythology as the hero of the oppressed who stood up against corrupt 'English' authority. The title of the novel evokes Lucian, but the careful reconstruction of 'historical' incident, clearly based upon documentary and first-hand research (to which I shall return), and of a 'historical' voice is utterly different from Lucian's jaunty taleteller. Nevertheless, our willingness to believe (and the fact, I suggest, that we *want to* believe a tale of injustice and social corruption) is here knowingly called into question by the very title of the work. At one level, of course, Carey's work presents itself as the 'true history', because it competes with all the other accounts and 'legends' (and indeed films) which have grown up around Ned Kelly, but (paradoxically) the very label of truth challenges and unsettles us: one does not have to know Lucian to wonder just how much 'truth' we are in fact being offered. Moreover, no history is probably as 'contested' as that of Ned Kelly, and any claim to 'truth' will be received by any audience for what it is, precisely a claim and a partial one.

Here is the opening of Peter Carey's Ned Kelly's autobiography:

> I lost my own father at 12 yr. of age and know what it is to be raised on lies and silences my dear daughter you are presently too young to understand a word I write but this history is for you and will contain no single lie may I burn in Hell if I speak false.
>
> God willing I shall live to see you read these words to witness your astonishment and see your dark eyes widen and your jaw drop when you finally comprehend the injustice we poor Irish suffered in this present age. How queer and foreign it must seem to you and all the coarse words and cruelty which I now relate are far away in ancient time.
>
> Your grandfather were a quiet and secret man he had been ripped from his home in Tipperary and transported to the prisons of Van Diemen's Land I do not know what was done to him he never spoke of it.

Carey/Kelly urges us to believe in the 'truth' of what we are going to read in a number of ways. Kelly's opening declaration of 'no single lie' (contrast Lucian!), confirmed with the powerful sanction of burning in Hell, is the most obvious. So too, 'I know... what it is to be raised on lies and silences' promises the end of 'lies' as the silence too is broken and the book begins. Secondly, there is the anticipation of his daughter's (and hence all readers') reaction to the tale: Kelly knows that it is going to be hard to believe what he writes, but it is that very anticipation and foreshadowing which cuts off our disbelief. (A tale of 'astonishment' and 'suffering' takes us back in fact to standard ancient ideas about the effects of literature and indeed to the ancient novel). Moreover, the fact that these events happened 'far away in ancient time' (in the novel Kelly's daughter was born, and may be presumed to have lived, in America), something which would normally increase our doubts as to their veracity, is here made confirmation of their truth. For Carey's readers, of course, the events related are indeed 'far away in ancient time', and his daughter who, like so many 'modern' Australians and Australian readers of the novel, lives in geographical exile from the land of their birth, comes to represent all readers; her *ekplêxis* will be theirs. In this way, the tale of a specific outlaw, though one with whom many 'identify', gains general force: this is also the imagined story of a whole nation. The familiar historical context of the tale, namely the nineteenth-century injustices inflicted upon the Irish and Irish-Australians by the English (a clear case of 'fringe' and 'centre'), is one which will clearly appeal to the implied readership of the novel, and hence confirm its truth.

Connected to the historical context of the novel is, of course, the fact that this is a first-person narration. As is well known, the 'truth status' of such narrations is problematised in various ways in the ancient novel (Achilles Tatius, Petronius, Apuleius' *Metamorphoses*): is there such a thing as 'pure and unmediated recollection'? With Ned Kelly, it is always likely that there will be more than one story to tell, but Carey establishes his narrator's *bona fides* from the very beginning. Kelly is unable to relate things for which he has no evidence — such as what happened to his father on Van Diemen's Land; Kelly is thus not an 'omniscient narrator', with a god-like command of narrative time, space, and event, though the narrative posture in fact breaks down from time to time in the course of the book. Such issues of narrative authority go back, of course, a very long way in antiquity: Homer famously makes Odysseus explain how he knows what went on in heaven (*Odyssey* 12.389–390). There are two further matters which are relevant to the fictional frames I have been considering: both may be considered as answers to the vital 'How do *you* know' question? One lies both inside and outside the written text.

Carey makes sure (through the Acknowledgements page, which follows the main text) that we know that he has carried out first-hand, on the spot research in northern Victoria (he even has a 'Research Assistant'), that he has read many books on the subject which have reminded him of 'the facts', and that he had a wonderful editor who helped him produce a 'tighter, truer (*sic*), better book'; most tellingly, of all, perhaps, he thanks several people who 'all led me towards information that had previously eluded me'. In other words, we are to understand not only that he writes with genuine authority, but that the 'real truth' was out there lurking (like Ned Kelly on the run), trying (unsuccessfully) to avoid capture. As far as the novel tradition is concerned, there is no real parallel for this rhetoric in antiquity, but there is a close analogy in fiction's nearest brother, or perhaps uncle would be more accurate, the historiographical tradition, where, at least in the post-classical, i.e. post-Thucydidean period, the question of whether one should do one's own 'battlefield' research was a very potent one: should one become oneself an Odysseus, travelling the world with an unlimited supply of curiosity, or should one let others do that, study their answers (both written and oral), and use Odysseus as a model for what one wrote, not for how one lived one's life? Polybius' savage attack upon Timaeus is perhaps the best known example of this debate[9]. That Peter Carey is able to use the whole array of what modern critics of the novel have come to call 'effects of the real', that incidental but persuasive (because well-researched) background of times, places, distances, and customs, in the pursuit of *fiction*, is an irony that would probably have been lost on Thucydides and Polybius, but it is one that we perhaps ought to relish.

The second part of the 'How do *you* know?' question is answered by the fact that Carey also builds into his work an account of how Kelly's memoirs came to

---

[9] I have discussed some aspects of this in Hunter 2001.

be written, to survive and be found. Here too ancient tradition shows the way, for the ancient novels often account for their existence (the so-called *Beglaubigungsapparat*) in ways which may or may not suggest an anxiety about 'fiction'; texts were allegedly found secreted in libraries, washed up in caskets, or were preserved in local memory. It is worth noting that one of the third-person narrative texts which uses this device, Xenophon of Ephesus' *Ephesiaka* (at least in the state in which it survives to us), also spurns, as do (at one end of the spectrum) Homer and (at the other) the author of the *History of Apollonius, King of Tyre*, the introductory or closural *sphragis* of authorial authority, together with the awkward questions of historicity which such explicit naming brings. There is no 'author' to get in the way of our access to 'what happened'; naming oneself, as do, for example, Chariton and Heliodorus, is a responsibility which can act as guarantee: no one holds a pistol to the head of a nameless storyteller.[10] The dichotomy of 'centre' and 'fringe' is thus (in more than one way) 'good to think with'; in particular, it focuses attention upon issues of personal and group identity, which may be seen as just as important in ancient novels as they are in their modern descendants. What kind of fiction we read (and enjoy) says, after all, a great deal about who we think we are and (what is almost the same thing) what we count as 'centre' and 'fringe'.

Bibliography

Anderson, G. 1984. *Ancient Fiction. The Novel in the Graeco-Roman World*, London.
Barchiesi, A. 1996. '*Extra legem:* consumo di letteratura in Petronio, Arbitro', in: O. Pecere/A. Stramaglia (eds.), *La letteratura di consumo nel mondo greco-latino*, Cassino, 189–206.
Branham, R. Bracht (ed.) 2005. *The Bakhtin Circle and Ancient Narrative*, Groningen.
Finkelpearl, E.D. 2003. 'Lucius and Aesop Gain a Voice: Apuleius *Met.* 11.1–2 and *Vita Aesopi* 7', in: S. Panayotakis/M. Zimmerman/W. Keulen (eds.), *The Ancient Novel and Beyond*, Mnemosyne Supplementum 241, Leiden/Boston, 37–51.
Holzberg, N. 1996. 'The Genre: Novels Proper and the Fringe', in: G. Schmeling (ed.), *The Novel in the Ancient World*, Mnemosyne Supplementum 159, Leiden/New York/Cologne, 11–28 [rev. ed. 2003].
Hunter, R. 2001. 'On Coming After', (Inaugural Lecture, Cambridge), available online at http://www.classics.cam.ac.uk/files/rlh_inaugural.pdf [= Hunter 2008, 8–26].

---

10 I have, however, occasionally wondered whether Xenophon's conclusion picks up the final sentence of Thucydides' (unfinished) history — 'so Tissaphernes came first to Ephesus and sacrificed to Artemis'— thus claiming a particular kind of historical authenticity, while also signing-off as author with an intertextual grace-note of the kind which precisely calls attention to the activity of an author.

Hunter, R. 2007. 'Isis and the Language of Aesop', in: M. Paschalis (ed.), *Pastoral Palimpsests. Essays in the Reception of Theocritus and Virgil*, Rethymnon Classical Studies 3, Rethymnon, 39–58 [= Hunter 2008, 867–883].
Hunter, R. 2008. *On Coming After. Studies in Post-Classical Greek Literature and its Reception*, Berlin/New York.
Jouanno, C. 2006. *Vie d'Ésope*, Paris.
Papademetriou, J.-Th.A. 1997. *Aesop as an Archetypal Hero*, Athens.
Winkler, J.J. 1985. *Auctor & Actor*, Berkeley.
Zimmerman, M. 2007. 'Aesop, the 'Onos', *The Golden Ass*, and a Hidden Treasure', in: M. Paschalis et al. (eds.), *The Greek and Roman Novel. Parallel Readings. Ancient Narrative Supplementum* 8, Groningen, 277–292.

26 Rythmical Language and Poetic Citation in Greek Narrative Texts

Introduction

Perhaps the two most important lessons — I will not say 'surprises' — which papyri have brought to the study of the ancient novel and novel-like texts are that the range of fictional forms was wider in antiquity than we might have imagined and that there is absolutely no room for over-confidence in the reliability of the transmission of our canonical Greek novels. In this paper I want to touch on both of these matters, but it is worth noting from the outset that they are of course not unrelated to each other. The very fluidity of narrative form and the fact that these forms do not, on the whole, tend to be subject to the increasingly rigid formal constraints of the inherited genres of *élite* literature mean that transmission in antiquity could show far wider variation than in those more formal genres. That such texts are less protected against wild textual variation is a familiar fact, perhaps to be ascribed to a diminished sense of an 'authorised' text associated with the authority of a famous name. There is of course a spectrum in these matters. Some of the texts I shall be concerned with in this paper, in particular the *Life of Aesop* (henceforth *VA*), which is a particular kind of anonymous composition with 'no fixed constitution',[1] and a reasonably explicit fragment about onophilia, are clearly situated at the 'low' end of the spectrum, but even texts which might be thought far ahead of these in sophistication and narrative coherence still pose puzzles which carry their own methodological warnings. Thus, for example, for a variety of reasons, not least P.Oxy. X 1250, the textual order of events at the end of Book 1 and early parts of Book 2 of Achilles Tatius is quite uncertain; such things have a tendency to slip off the scholarly radar, which only makes it more important to recall them.

I begin with a similarity of narrative structuring between a sequence in the *Life of Aesop* and the 'ass romance' of P.Oxy. LXX 4762 as the background to a consideration of the use of verse in both of these texts; I then move to a wider consideration of verse and poetic citation, notably in Chariton, before returning at the end to some general issues about verse in the *Life of Aesop* and texts like it.

---

[1] Haslam 1980, 54. Perry 1936, 1–70, remains a fundamental account of the nature of the text and the differences between the two principal traditions.

Two days in the life of Aesop

P.Oxy. XLVII 3331 of the III century, published by Michael Haslam, preserves (fr. 1) a tiny scrap of VA 18[2] and, more interestingly, a more significant fragment (fr. 2) of VA 75–6, the episode in which Aesop's master's wife takes a fancy to Aesop after seeing the size of his member (τὸ μῆκος καὶ τὸ πάχος) when she had come upon him (probably) masturbating,[3] and offers him a cloak if he can make love to her ten times in a row; Aesop manages nine, but on the tenth occasion ejaculates on her body rather than inside her and she refuses to pay up. Aesop then (once again) displays his cleverness by getting his master Xanthos to adjudicate the dispute in his favour and indeed to encourage Aesop to give his wife 'the tenth' which she is owed.[4] This episode survives in only one manuscript of the W recension of the Life, O (Cod. Barrocianus 194, XV cent.), and in a Latin translation preserved in Cod. Lollinianus 26 of the XIV century, the so-called Vita Lolliniana.[5] In G, which by common consent preserves the oldest version of the Life which we have, the entire episode is missing, though traces of it remain in the surrounding context, and it would appear that a whole sheet was missing from the exemplar which the scribe was copying; the reason why it was missing may only be conjectured.[6] P.Oxy. XLVII 3331 provides welcome confirmation of the ancient status of this episode[7] though the form of the text which it presents

---

2 Cf. Ferrari 1995.
3 This is the standard interpretation of the opening of chapter 75: 'clapping and shaking his hands, he began to perform the pastoral and disorderly figure'. Perry 1952, 175, was of the view that this rather extravagant description, together with Aesop's curious response to his mistress' question ('I derive benefit from this [?] and it helps my stomach'), was owed to the scribe of the sole manuscript which transmits this chapter rather than to the tradition he inherited. In the Latin version, Aesop is (straightforwardly) masturbating and tells the mistress that it helps him to keep warm. It is presumably relevant that χειρουργεῖν could mean 'to masturbate' (cf. Diog. Laert. 6, 46, 69 of Diogenes the Cynic). Degani 1997, 396, however, interpreted W's text as a reference to χειρονομία, a kind of gymnastic dancing recommended on health grounds (Xen. Symp. 2, 16–19, Oribasius 6, 29–30, etc.). Degani ignores the Vita Lolliniana and does not explain W's actual words, but his suggestion is nevertheless of some interest, particularly in view of the other connections between Socrates and Aesop; it is adopted by Merkle/Stramaglia in Stramaglia 2000, 314.
4 On such stories in other literatures cf. Perry 1936, 10 n. 9, Daube 1977.
5 Cf. Puche-López 2005.
6 Cf. Perry 1936, 7–8.
7 Andreassi 2001 argues for links (of various degrees of persuasiveness) between VA and the moicheutria mime of P.Oxy. III 413 (= 7 Cunningham), in which the slave who is the object of his mistress' lust is called Aesop; cf. also Andreassi 2001b, 33–34. He rightly calls attention to σκάπτειν in line 13 of the mime as possibly bearing a second, sexual level of meaning (cf. VA

is, perhaps unsurprisingly, so far from *O* 'as to prevent restoration of the papyrus text', as Haslam puts it; the apparent differences from *O* include elements of both compression and expansion.

The (not very) erotic encounter of Aesop with Xanthos' wife stands in a clear structural relationship to the account in chapters 31-33 of Aesop's first meeting with her. Xanthos' wife is repelled by the slave's ugliness, particularly as she has just had a dream in which Aphrodite presented her with a very handsome slave; Aesop repays her 'rudeness' with a true account of her motives:

> [You wanted a handsome slave] so that the handsome slave (ὁ καλὸc δοῦλος) could follow you to the baths, then the handsome slave could take your clothes from you, then as you came out from the baths the handsome slave could put your shawl on you and sit beside you and put your sandals on, then joke with you and look at you as though you were a pretty girl he had hired, then you would smile back and look at him afresh and get excited, and you would call him into the bedroom to rub your feet, then tingling with desire (κατανυγεῖσα) you would draw him towards you and kiss him passionately (καταφιλήσῃς) and do the kind of outrageous things one would expect of you, and the philosopher would be disgraced and mocked.
>
> *VA* 32, G version[8]

Aesop mocks his mistress by painting her very 'romantic' fantasy of the 'handsome slave'; the repetition of the phrase mocks the lady's obsession, and the relative decency of the language suits the fantasy. Aesop then strips the mask away, however, by recasting the mistress' desire in frankly brutal terms:

> I think you want to get laid (κινητιᾶν) and therefore you don't do what you should; take care that I don't show you the spirit (θυμός) of a new-bought man, you raging whore (ἱπποπόρνη).
>
> *VA* 32, G version

It is in chapters 75-76 that the mistress will indeed be shown to deserve the label ἱπποπόρνη (there she is καπριῶσα, no longer just, in Aesop's word, κατανυγεῖσα)[9]

---

75), but does not explain how the text would work and, oddly, also fails to call attention to ἀροτριᾶν, which, can easily bear the same double sense, in the same passage. The mistress in the mime might merely be being sarcastic — 'you would obviously find hard labour in the fields more fun than fucking me' — but, in view of *VA* 75, it might just be worth suggesting that the sarcasm is: 'Obviously I asked you too straightforwardly to fuck me; I should have used some euphemisms (as in the *VA* story)...'.

8 I have ignored the inevitable difficulties of the text, as they do not (I think) affect the point I am making.

9 On these words cf. further below. καπριῶσα is the description in part of the W tradition of the slave-girl who goes out to look at the new-bought Aesop in chapter 30. The feminine ἱπποπόρνη

and Aesop will certainly show her his *thymos*, in both senses if one meaning of that word (though with different accentuation) is correctly posited as 'penis'.[10] This answering structural relationship between the two episodes is of particular interest, given the mutilation of the later chapters in the G recension and the fact that the first meeting between Aesop and his mistress is drastically abbreviated in W; we may thus trace structural patterns across the divide which separates our two recensions, and the implications of this are in keeping with what we think we know about the original nature of the *Life*.

Aesop's grossly phallic endowment and his sexual prowess are part of the presentation of him, not just as a slave but as something less than human, and Jack Winkler and others have discussed similarities between Aesop and the heroes of the Lucianic *Onos* and of Apuleius' *Metamorphoses*, both in their roles as observers of and commentators upon the world and in the size of their members. Aesop literally plays the part of a pack-animal such as an ass in *VA* 18. Against this background, some similarities of language and incident between the chapters of the *Life* I have been considering and the fragment of 'narrative romance' published by Dirk Obbink as P.Oxy. LXX 4762 deserve a moment's attention. I reproduce here Obbink's text, though in his words 'it should be stressed that the text is quite uncertain in places...and that problems remain...'; the tentative translation is mine, though obviously based upon Obbink:

δεινῶς φλέγομαι· [
ρευμα μ' ἥκει δι[ὰ σε, ?
ἴδητε, κνωμένη[ν·
τί ποτέ με νύσ<σ>εις;" τὸ[ν

ὄνον φιλοῦσα ἀλ-   5
γ[ο]ῦντα, ὥς ποτε συν-
εισέ]πεσ' αὐτῶι· καὶ
αἰ[το]υμένη λέγει
"οὐώ, παχε<ῖ>α καὶ μεγά-
λη 'στιν, ὡς δοκός· / με-   10
νε, κατὰ μεικρόν· μὴ
ὅλην ἔσω βάλῃς. τί ποτ(ε);

οὔκ ἐστι τοῦτο; ἀλλὰ
τί; οὐ δὲ πᾶν τοῦτο.
ἀλλὰ ἄλλοτε; ἀναι-   15

---

is otherwise unattested; it has perhaps a more colloquial flavour than ἡ ἱπποπόρνος which occurs three times in Alciphron (2.31.2; 3.14.1; 4.11.8 Schepers).
10 Cf. Adrados 1993, 663, Schmidt 1860, 22. Whether or not that sense is accepted here, the sexual implication of Aesop's threat to his mistress is very clear.

'I am on fire terribly; a stream (?) comes over me...itching. Why on earth do you prick me?', as she kisses the ass which is (?) pained/worried, since at length she had (?) rushed in on him; and...she says 'Wow! It is fat and large, like a roof-beam! Wait, little by little! Don't put it all in! What on earth? Isn't this the case? But what? This isn't all! But another time...'

Some of the problems of interpretation are obvious, and w. 4–7 offer particular difficulties of both reading and comprehension; nevertheless certain important things are clear.[11]

We have here a version of the 'ass and woman have sex' scene most familiar to us from *Onos* 51 and Apuleius *Met.* 10.21–22; what of course we do not know is whether this ass was a metamorphosed man, or simply an ass, and the difficult state of the text requires us, I think, to withhold judgement on this matter. Nevertheless, between the two speeches of the enamoured woman there is a similar tonal contrast — that between 'romance' and brute (if nervous) lust — which Aesop and the narrator exploit in the *Life*. With the profession of desire in 1–4 Peter Parsons well compared 'the *Fragmentum Grenfellianum* with its asyndetic passion', but we may also think of the 'love duet' of Aristophanes' *Ekklesiazousai* 954–957, in which the young girl expresses her desire in rather similar terms, πάνυ γὰρ <δεινός> τις ἔρως με δονεῖ/τῶνδε τῶν σῶν βοστρύχων./ἄτοπος δ' ἔγκειταί μοί τις πόθος,/ὅς με διακναίσας ἔχει,, and the young man answers with a despairing question to the goddess, Κύπρι, τί μ' ἐκμαίνεις ἐπὶ ταύτηι; (v. 967), which may remind us of the lady's address (apparently) to the ass, τί ποτέ με νύσσεις; The Aristophanic young man's repeated διά τοι σὲ πόνους ἔχω (vv. 972, 975) has also perhaps some interest for the restoration of the end of line 2 of the 'ass papyrus'. As for the verb itself, νύσσεις, 'prick (with desire)', is, in the strengthened compound κατανύσσειν, used by Aesop in his mocking fantasy of the master's wife and her 'handsome slave' (quoted above).[12] The closest parallel for this term is probably Apuleius' Lucius' description of the *matrona* about

---

11 See Stramaglia 2010 and Zanetto 2010; in addition to Obbink's publication, the text is briefly described and discussed by Luppe 2006 and Barchiesi in Graverini/Keulen/Barchiesi 2006, 206–209. Obbink translates the suggested aorist συνεισέπεσ' as the verb of a ὥς clause, while also noting that 'it is tempting to take ὥς ποτε as parenthetic and elliptical'. There is, I think, some temptation to take ὥς ποτε with what precedes, 'kissing the ass which was [...] as once, she fell upon him and...said', unless we are to entertain the possibility of συνεισπε<σοῦ>σ' αὐτῶι. Obbink also takes the participle φιλοῦσα as dependent upon a verb of saying preceding the point at which our text begins, but we should perhaps consider the possibility that it goes with what follows; with either pattern, however, ὥς ποτε might well look back rather than forward.

12 This parallel has also been observed by Professor Zanetto.

to receive the ass' member as *ex unguiculis perpruriscens* (*Met.* 10.22), a phrase which Apuleius seems to have borrowed from Plautus (*Stichus* 760–761).

Aesop's mockery of his mistress in the *Life* allows us also to see some of the humour of the description of the love-making in the *Onos* 51: 'Then she kissed me passionately (καταφίληce) and said the kind of things she would say to her human lover and, grasping my halter, drew (εἷλκεν) me to the bed'. The humour here lies, as the *Life* shows, in just how close such a description is to one of purely human love-making; the comically unromantic detail of 'grasping my halter' brings us up with a start by calling attention to both similarity and difference. Just how different is 'woman with ass' from any moment of 'woman with man' love-making? This is not just a matter of the fact that, from the misogynistic perspective of low and comic literature, whether it be Aristophanes, the *Life of Aesop* (cf. *VA* 75) or the ass-narrative of P.Oxy. LXX 4762, what women really want is a male member (human or asinine) which is 'fat and large'. That both the *Onos* and the *Metamorphoses* ask us to think about 'What difference would it make if I were an animal or an animal-like slave?' is well known; are all men little better than asses?

Ass metrics

Peter Parsons observed that the lady's exclamation in 9–12 formed two comic trimeters:

οὐαί, παχεῖα καὶ μεγάλη 'στιν, ὡς δοκός.
μένε, κατὰ μικρόν· μηδ' ὅλην ἔσω βάλῃς.

One lesson which the publication of 'mime' and related papyri has taught us is that, in such texts, the boundaries between prose and verse may be more flexible than our usual categories allow, and we must also always be aware in such fragmentary texts of how readily snatches of language can appear metrical. Not every iambic trimeter is, in other words, an iambic trimeter, for what makes formal verse is not just the repetitiveness of rhythmical patterns but how an audience receives the utterance: is it felt as verse or not? The "ass romance" is clearly not straightforwardly a dramatic 'mime' (cf. further below), but the practices of such texts may still throw light upon a text which clearly moves in a not dissimilar *milieu*.

This is not the place for anything like a full treatment of the subject, but a few examples will illustrate the range of possibilities with which we are confronted. On the one hand, 'verse' and 'quasi-verse' may rub shoulders, as appears to be the case in the (?) 'Heracles and Omphale' mime of P.Oxy. LIII 3700 where, as the editor Michael Haslam put it, 'it is metrical in part: some of the lines, so far as can be seen, are impeccable iambic trimeters (unless trochaic tetrameters...), others apparently prose, but with a discernible tendency to iambic rhythm'. Alternatively, verse and 'prose' may sit happily beside each, as in the now conventional analysis of lines 96-106 of the 'Chariton' mime (= Cunningham 6).[13] Here iambic trimeters and trochaic tetrameters are apparently interspersed with utterances lacking rhythm, but the text offers problems of an exemplary kind. Consider 'Chariton', P.Oxy. III 413, 100-103 as transmitted:

Γ. σοί [λέ]γω, πρωρεῦ, παράβαλε δεῦρ' ἄγων τη[
Δ. ἐὰν π[ρ]ῶτος ἐγὼ ὁ κυβερνήτης κελεύσω.
Β. πάλι λαλεῖς, καταστροφεῦ;
ἀπο[λ]ίπωμεν αὐτὸν ἔξω καταφιλεῖν πύνδ[ακα.

Line 103, like line 98, looks like a tetrameter lacking one syllable, so editors must choose between very simple corrections (<τὸν> πύνδακα Grenfell - Hunt) or accept that 'faulty metre' is not impossible in such a text.[14] Line 102, πάλι λαλεῖς, καταστροφεῦ; is classified by the modern editors as prose, but it is plainly a catalectic trochaic dimeter.[15] Is this chance, is it 'felt' as verse — if indeed prose and verse are 'felt' differently in such a text — or does the 'prose' take on the colour of its surroundings? Such questions will recur. Finally, on the 'Tinouphis papyrus'[16] a passage of catalectic iambic tetrameters is set off in *ekthesis*, but whereas the narrative which follows is plainly prose, for what it is worth the preceding lines, as set out on the papyrus, look at least rhythmical (cretics and iambics?); it may be significant that part at least of this passage is an excited speech, whereas the passage after the tetrameters ('the prose') is 'straight' narrative. The association of verse with heightened emotion is a familiar fact of such texts.[17]

---

13 Cf. also Santelia 1991, Andreassi 2001.
14 Cunningham apparently chooses the second option by leaving Grenfell/Hunt's supplements in the apparatus; it is at least odd that both Santelia and Andreassi classify lines 98 and 103 as tetrameters, but neither mentions the fact that the metre is faulty or reports the suggested supplements. If I were editing this text, I would print the supplements.
15 Crusius (*apud* Grenfell/Hunt) suggested a major rearrangement of 101 so that 101-102 together would form a single tetrameter, divided between two speakers; nothing can be ruled out in such a text, but there seems no good reason for such serious intervention.
16 Haslam 1981, Stephens/Winkler 1995, 400-408.
17 Cf., e.g., Wiemken 1972, 67.

In returning to the 'ass papyrus', we can, I think, be reasonably confident that we are intended to feel the exclamation of 9–12 as rhythmical, though I would regard it as very improbable that we have an echo (or 'citation') of Aristophanes, *Peace* 927.[18] Among other reasons for confidence is the fact that the lady's earlier speech in 1–4, also marked off by a *paragraphos* (though of course we do not know if the speech began where the papyrus text does), seems clearly to fall into iambics (of a kind); for what it is worth, 3–4 (in Obbink's text) together form a catalectic trimeter (a length also found in the 'Charition' mime, line 96):

◡–◡ –◡– ◡ ◡◡ ◡ ––

ἴδητε κνωμένην. τί ποτέ με νύσσεις;

It may just be worth suggesting that the catalexis marks the strong emotion at the end of the speech and the move to 'action'; when the lady speaks again, the tone will be quite different. Be that as it may, the rhythmical possibilities of 1–2 are also very clear (δεινῶς φλέγομαι would serve as either an anapaestic or an iambic metron).[19] If this, together with the broken phrases of lines 12–15 which seem to point to dramatic action of some kind, all point towards, as Obbink put it, 'mime or farce (perhaps the narrative to a pantomime?)', we also apparently have narration, whether by a 'third-person narrator' outside the story or as recollection by a 'first-person narrator' (as, most famously, in Petronius' *Satyrica*),[20] and this mixed form offers us one more variation on what we are coming to recognise as the rich smorgasbord of forms of ancient narrative.

The practice of citation

This is clearly not the place for a proper discussion of so-called *prosimetrum* and the Greek background of Petronius' *Satyrica*,[21] but I want to consider briefly the question of verse and poetic citation in the ancient novel. We must first be clear, of course, that poetic citation is one specially marked form of the use of verse; it

---

18 The adjectives παχύς and μέγας standardly travel together in such contexts, cf. Obbink's note on line 9 of the papyrus.
19 Professor Zanetto kindly drew my attention to πρὸς τοῦ ἔρωτος φλεγομένη δεινῶς (a self-description by a young girl) at Aristaenetus 1.6.10–11 Mazal.
20 Recent helpful discussion in Jensson 2004, particularly Parts 1 and 3.
21 Barchiesi in: Graverini/Keulen/Barchiesi 2006, 193–209, is as good a place as any to start, though he does, I think, less than justice to the variety of Chariton's citational practice (see below); see also Conte 1996, ch. 5, Jensson 2004.

obviously has much in common with verse composed by the author of the surrounding prose, but there are also important differences in how the two may be felt, particularly as we might think that citation was both a more 'realistic' technique (people do actually cite familiar snatches of 'classical' verse) and also one that created a stronger link between the citing text and a tradition sanctioned by time and educational practice. Thus, one of the biggest surprises of the 'Iolaos papyrus' was the 'unmediated' quotation of (a version of) Euripides *Orestes* 1155–1157, gnomic verses on the value of friendship, as (apparently) a comment, ironical or otherwise, by the narrator on the action just described; the quotation is preceded by a small blank space on the papyrus, but begins and almost certainly ends in mid-column and is otherwise aligned as prose, in contrast to the sotadeans. The closest parallel, as Peter Parsons pointed out in the original publication,[22] is Petronius' *Satyrica*. Chariton's *Callirhoe* offers no real parallel for the closely juxtaposed 'in-character' verse of the 'Iolaos' sotadeans, but one thing which we should also have learned by now is that there is little sense in grouping loosely together texts which contain both prose and verse, even texts of narrative fiction, just for that reason.

It is, nevertheless, of course *Callirhoe* which offers the richest material for studying citational practice within the Greek novel. Before considering this material, however, we should cast a glance at ancient rhetorical theory about citation, for Chariton, being — or so he claims — ὑπογραφεύς to a rhetorician, will have been familiar with theory as well as practice. The use of poetic citation within prose is discussed both by Hermogenes and by the author of 'On forceful speaking' which is transmitted with the Hermogenean corpus'.[23] The whole subject must be set within the context of the extreme sensitivity of rhetorical practice and criticism to the need to differentiate oratory (and prose more generally) from poetry while remaining rhythmical, but that subject is, of course, well beyond the scope of the present essay.[24] In his discussion of 'sweetness' (336, 15–338, 18 Rabe), Hermogenes notes that the 'interweaving of poems' (παραπολοκαὶ τῶν ποιημάτων) brings pleasure, whether that be quotations of others (very often, of course, Homer) or of one's own poetry, as in the case of Agathon in Plato's *Symposium*; he also notes with approval the fact that both Agathon in the *Symposium* (197c) and Socrates in the *Phaedrus* (241d) explicitly call attention to their quotation of verse. What is most important, however, from

---

22 Cf. also Parsons 1971.
23 Cf. Spina 1992.
24 Important discussions include Aristotle, *Rhetoric* 3,1408b21–1409a23, Demetrius, *On Style* 118.179–186, Quintilian 9.4.56.72–78.

the point of view of 'sweetness' is that snatches of poetry should be 'interwoven' in such a way that 'they and the prose seem to form a single body' (338.2–3); the alternative form of παραπλοκή is to cite pieces of poetry 'with separation' (ἐκ διαστάσεως), so that they become like the laws and decrees which speakers have read out in the courts. The fact that in all of the Platonic instances which Hermogenes cites the prose and the verse form a single syntactical unit (sometimes rather mechanically) is presumably important for understanding the distinction which he is making; a later scholiast on Hermogenes describes the distinction as one between citation κατὰ σύνθεσιν and citation κατὰ παράθεσιν (RG 7, 1069 Walz). In a discussion 'On the use of verses in prose discourse' (447.5–448.2 Rabe), pseudo-Hermogenes distinguishes two forms of citation, κόλλησις and παρῳδία. The former, which again looks to the imperative of stylistic unity, is when 'a whole verse [or verses] is gracefully inserted into the prose, so that they seem to speak in harmony (συμφωνεῖν)', and the examples he gives are drawn from the poetic quotations in chapters 141–154 of Aeschines' speech *Against Timarchus*, which were for later rhetorical critics, and are for us, a veritable storehouse of examples of paraphrase, *paraploke* and direct quotation; the appearance of the ghost of Patroclus to Achilles in *Iliad* XXIII from which Aeschines cites and paraphrases is cited twice in Chariton's novel (2, 9, 6; 4, 1, 3), and its importance for Chariton may have lain not just in its Homeric origin, but also in its importance for the educational and rhetorical tradition. The author's second class of citation in this discussion, παρῳδία, is when an author 'says part of a passage of verse and then gives the sense of (ἑρμηνεύσῃι) the rest in his own words in prose, and then, having quoted further from the verses, he adds another which he himself has created, so that there is a unitary form';[25] this kind of παρῳδία is then illustrated from Demosthenes' mockery of Aeschines in *On the false embassy* 245.

These passages of Demosthenes and Aeschines are of interest for the citational and allusive practice of later literature, including the novel, though we must always bear in mind that the use of verse is here an explicit subject of the forensic analysis, not simply a stylistic tool to which no attention is called (as is common in narrative texts). Demosthenes cites three verses from a passage of Euripides (*Phoenix* fr. 812, 7–9 Kannicht) which Aeschines himself had used to his own advantage in *Against Timarchus* and then, in Hermogenes' terminology,

---

[25] On the interpretation of this difficult sentence cf. Pontani 2009, 407.

'parodies' them, as Demosthenes, *On the false embassy* (19) 245, puts it, 'correctly and appropriately' with verse of his own composition.[26]

ἔτι τοίνυν ἰαμβεῖα δήπου συλλέξας ἐπέραινεν, οἷον
ὅστις δ' ὁμιλῶν ἥδεται κακοῖς ἀνήρ,
οὐ πώποτ' ἠρώτησα, γιγνώσκων ὅτι
τοιοῦτός ἐσθ' οἵοισπερ ἥδεται ξυνών.
εἶτα "τὸν εἰς τοὺς ὄρνεις εἰσιόντα καὶ μετὰ Πιτταλάκου περιιόντα" καὶ τοιαῦτ' εἰπὼν "ἀγνοεῖτ'," ἔφη, "ποῖον τιν' ἡγεῖσθαι δεῖ;" οὐκοῦν, Αἰσχίνη, καὶ κατὰ σοῦ τὰ ἰαμβεῖα ταῦθ' ἁρμόσει νῦν ἐμοί, κἄν ἐγὼ λέγω πρὸς τούτους, ὀρθῶς καὶ προσηκόντως ἐρῶ·
ὅστις δ' ὁμιλῶν ἥδεται — καὶ ταῦτα πρεσβεύων — Φιλοκράτει,
οὐ πώποτ' ἠρώτησα, γιγνώσκων ὅτι
ἀργύριον εἴληφ' οὗτος, ὥσπερ Φιλοκράτης
ὁ ὁμολογῶν.

It may be debated whether or not ὁ ὁμολογῶν is intended to be part of Demosthenes' poetry,[27] but it certainly catches the iambic flavour of its surroundings, as also does καὶ ταῦτα πρεσβεύων, which disturbs the 'first trimeter', ὅστις δ' ὁμιλῶν ἥδεται Φιλοκράτει;[28] iambic 'verse' and iambic 'prose' very readily blend into each other. The words which introduce the 'parody', ὀρθῶς καὶ προσηκόντως ἐρῶ, take the form of a long syllable followed by two iambic metra: accident or design?[29] In view of the familiar closeness of 'ordinary speech' and iambic rhythm (Aristotle, *Rhetoric* 3.1408b 33–35 etc.), we cannot be sure, but the possibility here of a kind of 'glide' into iambic rhythm is not, I think, to be excluded, and we will see that it has later analogies.

As for Aeschines, his extended paraphrase of the words of Achilles and Patroclus deserves a much fuller analysis than is possible here, and so I will merely pick out one brief passage of particular interest, as it is the only place where Aeschines offers direct speech from a Homeric character within his prose para-

---

26 This passage of Demosthenes has recently been discussed by Pontani 2009, which became known to me after this essay was substantially completed; Pontani's discussion should be consulted for a wider consideration of some of the issues involved. It is very odd that, in his commentary, MacDowell does not even mention that Demosthenes' additions are metrical; for further bibliography on the views which have been held about Demosthenes' verses cf. Pontani 2009, 408.
27 The layout in Kannicht's quotation of the passage suggests that he would exclude it from the verses; he also gives Herwerden's deletion of the phrase a place in his apparatus.
28 Demosthenes presumably pronounced the "verse" in such a way as to bring out the double *entendre* in ὁμιλῶν (cf. *LSJ*, s.v. IV).
29 In his commentary (Cambridge 1844), Shilleto identified these words as part of a trimeter.

phrase. In Aeschines, *Against Timarchus* 147, he recalls *Iliad* XXIII 77–8, which he will go on to have read out verbatim a few lines later:

ὀδυρόμενος δὲ καὶ τὰς διατριβὰς διεξιὼν ἃς μετ' ἀλλήλων ζῶντες διέτριβον, λέγει ὅτι οὐκέτι περὶ τῶν μεγίστων, ὥσπερ τὸ πρότερον, καθεζόμενοι μετ' ἀλλήλων μόνοι ἄπωθεν τῶν ἄλλων φίλων βουλευσόμεθα...ἵνα δὲ καὶ διὰ τοῦ μέτρου τὰς γνώμας ἀκούσητε τοῦ ποιητοῦ, ἀναγνώσεται ὑμῖν ὁ γραμματεὺς τὰ ἔπη τὰ περὶ τούτων ἃ Ὅμηρος πεποίηκε...
οὐ γὰρ ἔτι ζωοί γε φίλων ἀπάνευθεν ἑταίρων
βουλὰς ἑζόμενοι βουλεύσομεν·

Of importance here is the absence, indeed perhaps deliberate avoidance, of any suggestion of dactylic rhythm in the prose paraphrase, a difference to which the introductory 'so that you may also hear the observations of the poet in metre' calls attention, together with a language which insists upon its difference from Homer. The prosaic (but also emotive) περὶ τῶν μεγίστων and ὥσπερ τὸ πρότερον gloss the Homeric scene,[30] καθεζόμενοι μετ' ἀλλήλων replaces the poetic ἑζόμενοι,[31] ἄπωθεν τῶν ἄλλων φίλων replaces the poetic vocabulary and order of φίλων ἀπάνευθεν ἑταίρων and βουλευσόμεθα provides the middle normal in prose. Aeschines' technique here foreshadows school exercises of paraphrase familiar from the papyri, and is a clear marker of how 'different' the dactylic verse of Homer was felt to be; for later writers, Euripides (like Menander) offered opportunities of a different kind.

When we move from the world of the rhetoricians to the poetic citations in Chariton's novel, some things remain familiar.[32] Chariton's poetic citations are virtually all 'integrated' syntactically with their prose context, even if some are not strictly necessary, in the sense that their removal would still leave a complete syntactic unit.[33] Quotations are rarely introduced as such: Homeric quotations are twice explicitly introduced (2.3.7; 5.6.9 – the latter ascribed to 'the divine poet') and on two other occasions prose allusions to the Homeric text name the poet (1.5.2; 4.1.8); ἀληθῶς twice marks a coming quotation as indeed just that (6.4.6; 7.4.3).

---

30 It is at least noteworthy that Aeschines' explanatory περὶ τῶν μεγίστων finds an echo in the bT *scholium* on *Iliad* XXIII 78, ... περὶ τῶν συμφερόντων ἐβουλεύοντο.
31 *LSJ* s.v. ἕζομαι note that 'in Attic prose καθέζομαι was always used'.
32 The best studies of Chariton's poetic citations are Müller 1976, 126–132, and Fusillo 1990, 34–42; Fusillo's concern is, however, with how the quotations work in the meaning of the text, rather than in Chariton's citational practice.
33 Cf. 2.9.6 (though the text is there problematic); 4.1.5; 4.7.5; 4.7.7; 5.10.9; 5.1.8; 6.2.4; 7.2.4; 7.3.5.

More of Chariton's verbatim quotations of poetry are in the speech of characters than is often acknowledged (2.3.7; 3.5.6; 4.1.3; 4.1.5; 4.4.5; 5.10.9; 6.4.6; 7.2.4; 1.3.5). At 5.10.9 Chaereas finishes off his pre-suicide appeal to the absent Callirhoe with a version of Achilles' promise to the dead Patroclus at *Iliad* XXII 389-90:

εἰπὲ δὲ προσκύψασα τῆι στήληι, κἂν ἀνὴρ καὶ βρέφος ὁρῶσιν, "οἴχηι, Χαιρέα, νῦν ἀληθῶς. νῦν ἀπέθανες· ἐγὼ γὰρ ἔμελλον ἐπὶ βασιλέως αἱρεῖσθαι σέ". ἀκούσομαί σου, γύναι· τάχα καὶ πιστεύσω. ἐνδοξότερόν με ποιήσεις τοῖς κάτω δαίμοσιν.
    εἰ δὲ θανόντων περ καταλήθοντ' εἰν Ἀΐδαο,
    αὐτὰρ ἐγὼ καὶ κεῖθι φίλης μεμνήσομαί σου.

The verses are not syntactically necessary and Chaereas does not mark his switch from prose to verse in any way (a fact of some interest in regard to Petronius). It would be very nice to know how Chariton understood the distinctly problematical v. 389, but more certain is the fact that his replacement in v. 390 of the Homeric...ἑταίρου by φίλης...σου destroys the dactylic rhythm of the verse.[34] The change happily prevents any suggestion that Callirhoe is a *hetaira*, but the faulty scansion is presumably a strong marker of emotion, which here breaks through even the educated principles of a young aristocrat like Chaereas. It is of some interest that in fact both of Chaereas' verbatim quotations of Homer offend metrically. At 7.3.5 his declaration to the Egyptian king adapts *Iliad* IX 48-49 (νῶι δ' ἐγὼ Σθένελός τε μαχησόμεθ' εἰς ὅ κε τέκμωρ/Ἰλίου εὕρωμεν· σὺν γὰρ θεῷ εἰλήλουθμεν):

ἂν δὲ καὶ πάντως θέλης, ὀλίγους ἐμοὶ κατάλιπε τοὺς ἑκουσίως μενοῦντας·
    νῶι δ', ἐγὼ Πολύχαρμός τε μαχησόμεθα·
    ...σὺν γὰρ θεῷ εἰλήλουθμεν.

Here the introductory ὀλίγους...ἑκουσίως clearly evokes (as we can see with hindsight) the context in *Iliad* IX, and the unmetrical name substitution suggests bravery (if not bravado) rather than high emotion. At 6.4.6 Eros, which has entered the Great King's heart, also finishes a speech with a Homeric quotation:

...ἐξέκαυσε τὴν ψυχὴν, ἔνδον παρὼν καὶ λέγων "οἷον ἦν ἐνθάδε Καλλιρόην ἰδεῖν, κνήμας ἀνεζωσμένην καὶ βραχίονας γεγυμνωμένην, πρόσωπον ἐρυθήματος πλῆρες, στῆθος ἀστάθμητον. ἀληθῶς
    οἵη δ' Ἄρτεμις εἶσι κατ' οὔρεος ἰοχέαιρα,
    ἢ κατὰ Τηΰγετον περιμήκετον ἢ Ἐρύμανθον,

---

34 The suggestion of Müller 1976, 129, n. 65, that Chariton might have treated the penultimate syllable of μεμνήσομαι as lengthened by μ seems very implausible.

τερπομένη κάπροισι καὶ ὠκείης ἐλάφοισι.
ταῦτα ἀναζωγραφῶν καὶ ἀναπλάττων ἐξεκαίετο σφόδρα...

Eros' speech, which amounts to an internal monologue by the desiderative part of the King's soul, suggests the cross-cultural power of Homer; ἀληθῶς marks not only the relationship of the imagined picture of the beloved to that of Homer's Artemis-Nausicaa but also the 'truth' of Homer's verses (*Od.* VI 102–104): in moments of crisis and longing it is the 'truth' of Homer which always comes back to us.[35] To conjure up a picture of the beloved as the virgin huntress Artemis does not, however, bode well for the satisfaction of one's desires.

Another character who caps the power of an appeal with a Homeric quotation is Chaereas' mother at 3.5.6:

ταῦτα λέγουσα περιερρήξατο τὴν ἐσθῆτα καὶ προτείνουσα τὰς θηλὰς "τέκνον", φησί,
"τάδ' αἴδεο καὶ μ' ἐλέησον
αὐτήν, εἴ ποτέ τοι λαθικηδέα μαζὸν ἐπέσχον".

The Homeric intertext here is of course Hecuba's plea to Hector in *Iliad* XXII 79–83[36] not to fight Achilles:

μήτηρ δ' αὖθ' ἑτέρωθεν ὀδύρετο δάκρυ χέουσα
κόλπον ἀνιεμένη, ἑτέρηφι δὲ μαζὸν ἀνέσχε·   80
καί μιν δάκρυ χέουσ' ἔπεα πτερόεντα προσηύδα·
"Ἕκτορ τέκνον ἐμὸν τάδε τ' αἴδεο καί μ' ἐλέησον
αὐτήν, εἴ ποτέ τοι λαθικηδέα μαζὸν ἐπέσχον·

Chariton's paraphrase both shows some of the features we have already noticed in Aeschines and also makes more dramatic the understated power of the Homeric scene. The mother now 'tears down' her dress and holds out her θηλαί to her son; the prosaic word, which also makes very explicit why the breast is used here, replaces the poetic μαζός and the plural 'doubles' the strength of the appeal. Of equal interest in the present context is the mode of transition to the quotation. Chariton's φησί seems (with hindsight) to break into the quotation, and such a parenthetic use of φησί within verse quotations is of course very common, and yet the dactylic rhythm of the words immediately before the 'quotation' are unmistakable; 'τέκνον' φησί, if read together with what follows,

---

35 ταῦτα ἀναζωγραφῶν καὶ ἀναπλάττων refers primarily to the King, but also hints at the vivid *enargeia* of the Homeric text.
36 Whether or not v. 81 is to be excised is not strictly relevant here, though it is clear that Chariton's paraphrase does not support its retention.

would in fact leave the first 'verse' missing only the first metron.[37] Here then we seem to have another example of a 'glide' into poetic quotation, and it is here too perhaps that we should seek an explanation of why Chariton omits the Homeric ἐμόν and changes τάδε τ' αἴδεο to τάδ' αἴδεο; both changes help the rhythmic integration of 'quotation' and 'introduction'. Chariton's technique here moreover takes us quite some way in the direction of a much discussed passage of the *Satyrica* (108.13):[38]

> protendit [sc. Tryphaena] ramum oleae a Tutela nauigii raptum atque in colloquium uenire ausa,
> 'quis furor' exclamat 'pacem conuertit in arma?
> quid nostrae meruere manus?

There are of course differences: *quis furor exclamat* completes a whole hexameter with what follows, unlike the still partial verse in Chariton, and — also unlike Chariton — the words are syntactically necessary for the understanding of what follows. Moreover, *quis furor* may well be felt as a poetic citation (cf. Virgil, *Aeneid* V 670, Lucan I 8), and this would clearly affect how they were received on first reading. Nevertheless, Petronius' technique may be seen to be a further step along a road already taken.[39] Perhaps editors of Petronius should in future rather present the text as

> protendit [sc. Tryphaena] ramum oleae a Tutela nauigii raptum atque in colloquium uenire ausa, 'quis furor' exclamat
> 'pacem conuertit in arma?
> quid nostrae meruere manus?

Chariton has of course other poetic reminiscences which are not direct 'quotations', and our knowledge both of rhetorical theory and of Chariton's usual citational practice can help us to judge some doubtful cases. At 3.2.2 Dionysius assures Callirhoe of his good intentions and mildly rebukes her for doubting him: σὺ γὰρ ἠπίστησας ὅτι ἔξω σε γαμετὴν παίδων ἐπ' ἀρότῳ κατὰ νόμους Ἑλληνικούς. Cobet[40] first observed that παίδων ἐπ' ἀρότῳ κατὰ νόμους Ἑλληνικούς form a comic trimeter and wondered whether this was accident or design; the 'verse' is now *Adesp.* *127 K-A. There can hardly be any doubt that παίδων

---

37 One could, of course, 'complete' the hexameter with θηλάς but syntax and natural pause militate against that.
38 Cf. Slater 1990, 170–173, Jensson 2004, 34–36.
39 The relative chronology of Petronius and Chariton is not of course literally at stake here.
40 Cobet 1859, 266.

ἐπ' ἀρότῳ is indeed an allusion to the formal tag very familiar from New Comedy[41] where παίδων is always qualified by γνησίων, though the two words are not always in the same verse (cf. Men. *Perik.* 1013–1014). A reminiscence of Menander, one of the central figures of Greek *paideia*, together with an allusion to 'Greek' laws, reinforces the characterisation of Dionysius which is consistent throughout the novel.[42] Such an allusion to Greek laws does, however, seem improbable in a comedy of Menander[43] and so it seems best, as Goold in the Loeb does, to treat only παίδων ἐπ' ἀρότῳ as an allusion to the formula; the omission of γνησίων reinforces the sense that we do not here have a direct 'verse quotation'. The iambic rhythm supports the characterizing import of the verses; here again we see that what is sometimes important is how rhythmical passages are 'felt', rather than whether they are specific 'quotations' or not.[44]

Verse in the Life of Aesop

One text which we might in fact have expected to contain more verse than it does is the *Life of Aesop*, which otherwise shares both material and thematic concerns, not just with 'low' Greek texts of various kinds, but also with the *Satyrica*.[45] In fact, however, with the exception of the *monostichoi* embedded in some versions of the 'Instructions of Aesop' which form part of the 'Ahiqar' section of the work (chapters 109–110),[46] there are only two certain passages of verse in the *Life*, and Aesop's very sparing use of poetry differentiates him markedly from, for example, the Diogenes of Diogenes Laertius' *Life*, with whom he otherwise shares some notable characteristics.

---

41 See Kassel/Austin on Menander fr. 453.
42 The only certain direct quotation of Menander in the novel, 4.7.7 from the famous opening scene of the *Misounenos*, is applied by the narrator to Dionysius, but as the narrator is describing Dionysius' state of mind, we may understand that Dionysius here casts himself 'in the role of' the nervous and unhappy soldier of that scene.
43 The text discussed by Geiger 1992 does not alter that.
44 Analysis of a somewhat similar kind could be applied to the gnomic 1.3.7 where Browne 1981 suggests that we should restore a trochaic tetrameter; an iambic analysis (so Goold) of the rhythm seems in fact more plausible.
45 Cf. Hunter 2009.
46 Cf. Luzzatto 2003 (I am grateful to Prof. Luzzatto for drawing my attention to this article). On p. 51 she notes a place in chapter 109 where a gnomic couplet of trimeters may be integrated syntactically with what precedes; the iambic rhythm is unmistakable and trimeters are indeed 'facilmente ricostruibili', but they are in fact not transmitted in any witness in this form and so caution is here (again) required.

In chapter 32, as part of his attack on Xanthos' wife (cf. above), Aesop quotes iambic trimeters against women which he explicitly ascribes to Euripides; the verses, also known from Stobaeus who also ascribes them to Euripides, appear as follows in Kannicht's edition (fr. 1059, 1–4 Kannicht):

δεινὴ μὲν ἀλκὴ κυμάτων θαλασσίων,
δειναὶ δὲ †ποταμοῦ† καὶ πυρὸς θερμοῦ πνοαί,
δεινὸν δὲ πενία, δεινὰ δ' ἄλλα μυρία,
ἀλλ' οὐδὲν οὕτω δεινὸς ὡς γυνὴ κακόν·

These verses are transmitted in interesting ways in the *Life*. The G text offers two of the four verses in an unmetrical, though still recognisably iambic, form; it is worth noting that the first verse of the quotation, which establishes the citation, has been preserved metrically complete in G. It is also of some interest for the matters I have been discussing in this paper that G transmits v. 4 in a form which is metrical, though it differs from the form offered by Stobaeus and preferred by modern editors:

VA (G)   πλὴν οὐδὲν οὕτως ὡς γυνὴ δεινὸν κακὸν

Stobaeus   ἀλλ' οὐδὲν οὕτω δεινὸν ὡς γυνὴ κακόν·

Of itself, of course, such variations in transmission are entirely commonplace, but in a text such as the *Life of Aesop* we must at least ask whether the editorial practice, evidenced in all modem editions of G, of printing (more or less) the text of Stobaeus (partially supported by the W text — see below), as being the likeliest text of Euripides, is in fact likely to misrepresent the probabilities as far as the text of the *Life of Aesop* is concerned. As for the unmetrical vv. 2–3, opinions may well differ as to what the 'original' form of the quotation was (if indeed that concept has any meaning in this context), but it is worth noting that the G text of these verses is also plainly corrupt on grounds of meaning as well as metre.[47] As for the W text, here there is plain sailing until the final verse, where manuscripts offer various unmetrical riffs on the wickedness of women;[48] one principal tradition seems to be the (appropriately) hyperbolic and unmetrical πλὴν οὐδὲν οὕτως ὡς γυνὴ ἐν ὑπερβολῆι κακῶν, whereas the other offers the equally approximately metrical πλὴν οὐδὲν οὕτως ὡς γυνὴ πονηρά.

---

47 δεινὴ δὴ παιδεία for δεινὸν δὲ πενία is a particularly nice 'corruption'.
48 Cf. Perry 1952, 152.

We may here have conflations of different versions, but there is little point in seeking to explain such variation in a text of this type. Whatever view one takes, in a text such as this — or indeed in a 'low mime' text — our attitude to the nature of poetic citations should at least be flexible.

Another question worth asking about this passage is why, almost uniquely in our texts,[49] does Aesop cite verse here. That Aesop should not regularly rely on the testimony of classical poets to enforce his wisdom makes perfect sense; his is a 'common wisdom' which sets itself apart from the *paideia* (or would-be *paideia*), not just of Xanthos, but of the whole *élite* tradition. In chapter 32, however, he aligns himself with the tradition of a misogynistic Euripides, or rather of a Euripides who uttered harsh truths about women, not just because such a tradition had itself long since become 'popular', but also because poetic quotation here suits the raised tone of the fantasy of desire which Aesop has painted (cf. above); he is here operating at a higher stylistic level, only — as we have seen — immediately to shatter it by 'calling a spade a spade'. *Mutatis mutandis*, we may compare the meaningfully heightened style of the bucolic *locus amoenus* in which Isis and the Muses granted him the gift of speech.[50]

If Aesop and the *Life* are certainly sparing with the use of verse, it is nevertheless unsurprising, given that – as the ancients well knew — ordinary speech often 'comes out iambic', that there are doubtful cases; in particular, sententious utterances in the *Life* may seem like, or in fact be, citations of popular wisdom expressed in verse. Here too Chariton and the *Life* may not be quite as far apart as they seem. When in chapter 26 Aesop (in the G version) urges his master, μὴ μου βλέπε τὸ εἶδος ἀλλὰ μᾶλλον ἐξέταζε τὴν ψυχήν, the iambic rhythm of the second half is plain enough, but there seems no good reason to start fashioning "verse" here. More interesting perhaps is chapter 28 where, in the G version, Aesop's violent reaction to his master urinating while walking leads Xanthos to assume that he has been slandered; G offers (roughly)[51] the following sequence from Xanthos' remonstration; μὴ πρόσεχε διαβολαῖς· μάτην ὀξύνηι διαβολὴ τερπνόν ἀκοῦσαι. Modern editors punctuate after διαβολαῖς and

---

[49] The exception is chapter 124 where Aesop appears to cite the famous *Iliad* VI 146 as a joke at the pale Delphians (the same anecdote is told about Stratonikos and the Caunians by Strabo 14 2, 3). In G this seems to have become badly corrupted and W omits the Homeric joke entirely, but some form of the verse was in the Golenischeff papyrus.
[50] Cf. Hunter 2007.
[51] διαβολαῖς is Perry's correction of the transmitted διαβολές. Perry read τερπνάν rather than τερπνόν in the text, but διαβολῇ (sic) τερπνόν does appear to be what stands in G, though Perry's 'mistake' is understandable, given that the final o unusually joins the v.

ὀξύνηι, but Papademetriou⁵² pointed out that ὦ Φανία, μὴ πρόσεχε διαβολαῖς μά[την is found on a first-century AD list of 'monostichs' (P.Vindob. G 19999A = *Menandri Sententiae* p. 7, 11 Jaekel = *1026 Pernigotti), and he suggested that this verse came from Menander's *Kitharistes*, in which we know that there was a character called Phanias;⁵³ it now stands as Men. *Kitharistes* fr. 10 Sandbach/ Arnott. It would not surprise to find that the pretentious Xanthos knew some standard 'school *gnomai*' about slander, but — regardless of the punctuation we wish to adopt — it must still be an open question whether these words are even felt as 'verse', let alone as a 'quotation' of some classical author. The context, as well as their very generality, works against that.

The final case I wish to consider here is the Hesiodic 'moral' which closes the opening episode of the *Life*, before Aesop has been granted a voice.⁵⁴ The slaves who plotted to have Aesop punished for their own greed learned from their subsequent flogging (*VA* 3, according to the G version), ὅτι ὁ κατὰ ἄλλου μηχανευόμενος κακὸν αὐτὸς καθ' ἑαυτοῦ τοῦτο λανθάνει ποιῶν. The iambic rhythm of at least the second half is clear enough and therefore it comes as no great surprise that the W tradition appears to offer two iambic trimeters:

ὅστις καθ' ἑτέρου δόλια μηχανεύεται
αὐτὸς καθ' ἑαυτοῦ τοῦτο λανθάνει ποιῶν.

Papathomopoulos rewrote the G version to produce two iambic trimeters, whereas in his text of the verses in W Perry adopted Eberhard's transposition ποιῶν λανθάνει which avoids a breach of Porson's Law; both may seem dangerous methodologies.⁵⁵ Both print Westermann's correction αὐτοῦ for ἑαυτοῦ in v. 2 of the W version, which certainly produces a 'cleaner' trimeter, but what is the standard of correctness here? In what we may call (not without risk) v. 1,

---

52 Papademetriou 1969, 257–259 (repr. with additions in Papademetriou 1989, 54–57).
53 The same suggestion was made by Borgogno 1971, without reference to the *Life of Aesop* and without knowledge of Papademetriou's article. On Menander's monostichs and the *Life* cf. also Luzzatto 2003.
54 On this 'moral' cf. further Hunter 2007, 45–46, and Hunter 2008. There is of course a great deal that could be said about how Aesopic and Hesiodic traditions overlap in antiquity; the *ainos* of the 'hawk and the nightingale' (*Works and Days* 202–212) was of course a prime reason for linking the two traditions.
55 Holzberg 1992, 44, n. 53, is sympathetic to Papathomopoulos' versification because he sees the opening of the *Life* shaped like the first act of a comedy of Menander, and *gnomai* are particularly common in the first act; this seems to me to have very little substance, but others may disagree.

μηχανεύεται, the reading of manuscript W[56] competes with the better attested μηχανᾶται, which would leave the verse a syllable short, but is otherwise unimpeachable; which, if either, is to be preferred, or is that not a question to be asked in a text such as this? As for the G text, it does indeed take very little rewriting (less indeed than Papathomopoulos imposed) to produce two trimeters (of a kind), but we need to be clear about what we are doing. What is at stake in such versification, beyond making decisions about printing conventions? Are we not rather in such texts — both narrative and dramatic or 'mimic' — sometimes at the boundaries of what we call 'verse' and 'prose', where what is important is a sense of heightened regularity and pattern in the rhythm (as sometimes, in a completely different kind of prose, in Plato),[57] rather than strictly correct 'classical' versification, or even of the familiar metrical 'mistakes' of inscribed epitaphic poetry. Such questions lead, of course, in a number of directions; we may think, on the one hand, of issues of Petronian versification, or rather of that of some of his characters,[58] and on the other of the way in which very sophisticated authors such as Longus and Achilles can weave phrases from classical poetry into their prose, which may be a generic signal of a kind which we have not yet fully appreciated.

Moralising comment by the narrator of the kind which we find at the end of the fig episode is extremely rare.[59] This is a text where virtually all of the authority is carried and expressed by Aesop himself, but — as the G version makes clear again at the start of chapter 4 — the wicked slaves paid the penalty for wronging someone who could not (yet) speak; hence, I think, the unusual 'moral' from the narrator at the start of the work. Such a moralising narrative voice only really reappears at the very end of the narrative, after Aesop's death, when we are told that the Delphians paid the penalty for their killing of him; we may wish to call this 'ring composition', but what is, I think, plain is that the moral at the end of the 'fig episode' is intended to evoke the style of the *epimythia* attached to Aesopic fables from (probably) a fairly early date.[60] The 'fig episode'

---

56 *Laurentianus Conv. Soppr.* 627, cf. Perry 1933, 203–204.
57 On the whole subject cf. Dover 1997, Chapter 8. The classic instances are the conclusion of Agathon's speech in the *Symposium* and *Phaedrus* 241d1; *Ion* 238c 2–3 (quoting what 'the poets' say) also deserves attention in this regard.
58 Recent discussion and bibliography in Jensson 2004, 10–11.
59 Holzberg 1992, 44, links this example with the narrator's observations about piety and its rewards in the G version of chs. 5 and 11; ch. 11, however, comments specifically about Aesop and is not a generalising 'moral', and chapter 5, though generalising — 'an utterance concerning an act of piety quickly reaches the ears of the gods' — is not really of the 'Aesopic' kind.
60 Cf. Perry 1936, 172. For an *epimythion* to a 'real fable' in the *Life* cf. ch. 97.

is thus shaped as an exemplary (almost allegorical) tale which stands at the head of the *Life* and stresses the importance of what we are about to read by evoking the whole tradition of Aesopic wisdom. Whether it also exploits a sense (at some level) that the *epimythia* are somehow separable from the voice of Aesop himself, i.e. are a commentary rather than the text itself, may be debated.

As to the question of form, it could be argued that this cuts both ways, as there are not only prose *epimythia* but also ones in verse attached to some Aesopic fables, as well as the verse *epimythia* to Babrius' fables. Nevertheless, it looks pretty clear that the style of the moral evokes that of the familiar prose *epimythia* attached to the vast majority of our fables; the λανθάνειν motif, i.e. people who do silly things do not realise the consequences, occurs more than twenty times in our extant collection, and the idea that "plotting harm against another damages yourself" (with its many variants) also occurs commonly. It would be an easy enough task to turn some of these morals into iambic trimeters (of a sort). Of particular interest, perhaps, is 258 Perry (= 269 Hausrath/Hunger), the lion, the wolf and the fox, another story in which those who slander a "colleague" to the powerful get their come-uppance; the wolf slanders the fox to a sick lion, but the cunning fox turns the tables by claiming that the cure for the lion's illness is to flay (ἐκδείρας) a wolf alive and dress in the still-warm skin. The moral attached to this tale is: ὁ μῦθος δηλοῖ ὅτι ὁ καθ' ἑτέρου μηχανώμενος καθ' ἑαυτοῦ τὴν μηχανὴν περιτρέπει, 'The fable shows that the person who plots against another turns the plot against himself'. The triumphant fox of the fable is, of course, like the ugly but clever Aesop, and it is at least worth observing that the punishment meted out in the 'fig episode' is also a 'skinning' (δείρεσθαι) which the wicked slaves had envisaged for Aesop. The closeness of this fable to the 'fig episode' need have no particular significance, though it certainly confirms the shaping as a fable which is imposed on the opening episode of the *Life*. As for the *epimythion* of 258 Perry, if this had been the moral of the 'fig episode' in the *Life*, no doubt modern attempts to produce iambic trimeters (not a difficult task) would have been undertaken. Fortunately, however, formal questions such as 'prose or verse?' must always be tools to aid interpretation, not the end to which interpretation moves.[61]

---

61 I am grateful to Filippomaria Pontani and to audiences in Florence and Komotini for helpful discussion of earlier versions of this paper.

Bibliography

Andreassi, M. 2001. 'Esopo sulla scena: il mimo della Moicheutria e la Vita Aesopi', *RhM* 144, 203–225.
Andreassi, M. 2001b. *Mimi greci in Egitto. Charition e Moicheutria*, Bari.
Borgono, A. 1971. 'Due nuovi frammenti del *Citharistes* di Menandro?', *Hermes* 99, 374–375.
Browne, G.B. 1981. 'Ad Charitonem', *AJPh* 102, 321.
Cobet, G.G. 1859. 'Annotiationes criticae ad Charitonem', *Mnemosyne* 8, 229–305.
Conte, G.B. 1996. *The Hidden Author*, Berkeley.
Daube, D. 1977. 'Counting', *Mnemosyne* 30, 176–178.
Degani, E. 1997. 'Review of Ferrari 1997', *Eikasmos* 8, 395–402.
Dover, K.J. 1997. *The Evolution of Greek Prose Style*, Oxford.
Ferrari, F. 1995. 'P.Oxy 3331 e *Vita Aesopi* 18', *ZPE* 107, 296.
Ferrari, F. 1997. *Romanzo di Esopo*, Milano.
Fusillo, M. 1990. 'Il testo nel testo: la citazione nel romanzo Greco', *Materiali e Discussioni* 25, 27–48.
Geiger, J. 1992. 'A note on Pyadin 18', *ZPE* 93, 67–68.
Graverini, L./Keulen, W./Barchiesi, A. (eds.) 2006. *Il romanzo antico. Forme, testi, problemi*, Rome.
Haslam, M.W. 1980. '3331. *Life of Aesop*', *The Oxyrhynchus Papyri* Vol. XLVII, London, 53–56.
Haslam, M.W. 1981. '8 Narrative about Tinouphis in prosimetrum', *Papyri Greek and Egyptian (P. Turner)*, London, 35–45.
Holzberg, N. (ed.) 1992. *Der Äsop-Roman. Motivgeschichte und Erzählstruktur*, Tübingen.
Hunter, R. 2007. 'Isis and the language of Aesop', in: M. Paschalis (ed.), *Pastoral Palimpsests. Essays in the Reception of Theocritus and Virgil*, Rethymnon, 39–58.
Hunter, R. 2008a. *On Coming After. Studies in Post-Classical Greek Literature and its Reception*, Berlin/New York.
Hunter, R. 2008b. 'Hesiod, Callimachus, and the invention of morality', in: G. Bastianini/A. Casanova (eds.), *Esiodo: Cent'anni di papiri*, Firenze, 153–164 [= Hunter 2008a, 559–571].
Hunter, R. 2009. 'The curious incident ... *polypragmosyne* and the ancient novel', in: M. Paschalis/S. Panayotakis/G. Schmeling (eds.), *Readers and Writers in the Ancient Novel*, Groningen, 51–63 [= Hunter 2008a, 884–896].
Jensson, G. 2004. *The Recollections of Encolpius*, Groningen.
Luppe, W. 2006. 'Sex mit einem Esel (P. Oxy. LXX 4762)', *ZPE* 158, 93–94.
Luzzatto, M.J. 2003. 'Sentenze di Menandro e «Vita Aesopi»', in: M.S. Funghi (ed.), *Aspetti di letteratura gnomica nel mondo antico*, Firenze, 35–52.
Müller, C.W. 1976. 'Chariton von Aphrodisias und die Theorie des Romans in der Antike', *A&A* 22, 115–136.
Papademetriou, J.-Th. 1969. Κριτικά, γλωσσικά καὶ ἑρμηνευτικὰ εἰς τὴν περὶ Αἰσώπου μυθιστορίαν, *Platon* 21, 251–267.
Papademetriou, J.-Th. 1989. Αἰσώπεια καὶ Αἰσιωπικά, Athens.
Papathomopoulos, M. 1989. *Aesopus Revisitatus. Recherches sur le texte des Vies Ésopiques*, Ioannina.
Papathomopoulos, M. 1990. Ὁ βίος τοῦ Αἰσώπου. Ἡ παραλλαγή G, Ioannina.
Papathomopoulos, M. 1999. Ὁ βίος τοῦ Αἰσώπου. Ἡ παραλλαγή W, Ioannina.
Parsons, P. 1971. 'A Greek *Satyricon*?', *BICS* 18, 53–68.

Perry, B.E. 1933. 'The text tradition of the Greek Life of Aesop', *TAPhA* 64, 198–244.
Perry, B.E. 1936. *Studies in the Text History of the Life and Fables of Aesop*, Haverford.
Perry, B.E. 1952. *Aesopica I*, Urbana.
Pontani, F. 2009. 'Demosthenes, parody and the *Frogs*', *Mnemosyne* 62, 401–416.
Puche-López, C. 2005. 'Aproximación a la Vita Aesopi Lolliniana' in: P. Conde-Parrado/I. Valazquez (eds.), *La filología Latina, mil anos más*, Madrid, 881–899.
Santelia, S. 1991. *Charition liberata (P. Oxy. 413)*, Bari.
Slater, N.W. 1990. *Reading Petronius*, Baltimore/London.
Spina, L. 1992. 'Ermogene e la citazione poetica', in: A. De Vivo/L. Spina (eds.), *Come dice il poeta. Percorsi greci e latini di parole poetiche*, Napoli, 7–20.
Stephens, S.A./Winkler, J.J. (eds.) 1995. *Ancient Greek Novels. The Fragments*, Princeton.
Stramaglia, A. (ed.) 2000. *Ἔρως. Antiche trame greche d'amore*, Bari.
Stramaglia, A. 2010. 'Le Metamorfosi di Apuleio tra iconografia e papiri', in: G. Bastianini/A. Casanova (eds.), *I papiri del romanzo antico*, Florence, 165–192.
Wiemken, H. 1972. *Der griechische Mimus*, Bremen.
Zanetto, G. 2010. 'P. Oxy. LXX 4762 e il Romanzo dell'asino', in: G. Bastianini/A. Casanova (eds.), *I papiri del romanzo antico*, Florence, 51–63.

Part VI: **Ancient Criticism and Scholarship**

27 The *Trojan Oration* of Dio Chrysostom and Ancient Homeric Criticism

In the *Trojan Oration* Dio argues, allegedly before a Trojan audience, that the Homeric Trojan narrative is a complete misrepresentation of 'what really happened': Helen was in fact properly given in marriage by Tyndareus to Paris (i. e. he, not Menelaos, was the successful suitor), Hector killed Achilles not vice versa, Troy was not captured by the Greeks, and so on. Critical discussion[1] of the *Trojan Oration* has largely centred on the decidedly problematic state of the text, which certainly contains both interpolations and alternative versions of various passages (even if not to the extent argued for by von Arnim (1898)),[2] on the reflections of ancient Homeric criticism in Dio's strictures on the poet,[3] and on the generic affiliations and purpose of the speech. Much remains, however, to be done on these and other aspects of the speech (as, for example, its historical context). I hope that, despite the limited nature of my concerns in this paper, some sense of Dio's overall strategy will also emerge.

If the whole project of the *Trojan Oration* is in one sense a distortion of a recurrent theme of ancient Homeric criticism — the skilfulness and quality of Homer's 'lies' (cf., e.g., Aristotle, *Poetics* 1460a18–19, Horace, *AP* 151–152) — it is often noted that some of Dio's criticisms have a distinctly modern ring to them: Dio as a neo-analyst *avant la lettre*.[4] Thus attention is often directed to claims in the essay such as that 'Patroclus is all but a substitute (ὑπόβλητος) whom Homer has put in the place of Achilles' (102), a view with a significant hold on many modern scholars. Other critical strategies almost look like parodies of

---

I am grateful to Jessica Wissmann, the audience at the Thessaloniki conference and the Editors for helpful criticism and to Michael Trapp for allowing me to see an unpublished paper on the *Trojan Oration*.

---

1 The best modern introductions to the *Trojan Oration* are Kindstrand 1973, 141–162 and Saïd 2000, 176–186, both with guides to earlier bibliography; I am indebted to both of these discussions. See also Lemarchand 1926, 35–56, Desideri 1978, 431–434, 496–503, and Szarmach 1978. For a brief account of the lively place that this oration has held in scholarly debate over the centuries cf. Swain 2000, 18–19; Kim 2008 is a helpful account of closely related issues in *Oration* 61.
2 My approach to Dio 11 in this paper will be a cautious unitarianism.
3 Cf. Vagnone 2003, 17–18. Montgomery 1902 remains a useful collection and Vagnone's commentary gathers a certain amount of material; there is much more to be done. I have not seen Jouan's 1966 Paris thesis on *Oration* 11.
4 Cf. esp. Seeck 1990.

modern concerns. The observation (21) that Homer could tell of what happened between Zeus and Hera on Mt Ida in *Iliad* 14, despite the enveloping cloud in which Zeus hid them, is not just a joke about omniscient narration, but turns Zeus' words ('no one will see us...') at 14.342–345 into a witty authorial excuse by Homer himself for the decent 'veil' which is drawn over what follows, a kind of epic *cetera quis nescit?*[5] In 108 Dio's Homer has lost control of his false narrative and so describes Achilles' pursuit of Hector and the latter's death 'as in a dream'; the narrative 'most closely resembles strange dreams (τοῖς ἀτόποις ἐνυπνίοις)'. Dio may be picking up the similarity of Athena's deceptive appearance to Hector (22.226–247) to a dream, though it is more likely that his likeness (προσέοικε) echoes one of Homer's, namely the famous dream simile of 22.199–201 describing the pursuit, which was athetised by Aristarchus and said by a scholiast to be 'without value in expression and thought' and to devalue Achilles' swiftness, and which is certainly by any standards ἄτοπον. If so, Dio has taken a simile describing action in the text and applied it to an understanding of the surrounding narrative context as a whole; modern critics who privilege metaliterary self-reference in the understanding of (particularly) Hellenistic and Roman epics will here recognise a kindred spirit. We have perhaps a similar phenomenon in the following chapter when Dio describes Homer's narrative of the funeral games in Book 23 as πάνυ γελοίως; this is most probably explained as, once again, a re-direction of a feature of the narrative itself, namely the rôle of laughter (cf. 23.784, 840).

What may be more interesting than these individual examples is that the *Trojan Oration* as a whole questions the limits and purposes of poetic myth. Is there such a thing as the 'irreducible core' of a myth, however many details may be changed; Dio 11 may make us think of Aristotle's note that, in a comedy, 'Orestes and Aegisthus can become friends and go off at the end, and no one is killed by anyone' (Poetics 1453a37–9).

The *Trojan Oration* is normally connected with the 'Homeric games' which imperial authors love to play (Diktys of Crete etc),[6] or with Dio's concern elsewhere for the revision of myth in accordance with the εἰκός and the πιθανόν,[7] but the antecedents of Dio's revisionist tale have deep roots. Dio is concerned not just with Homer's untruths, but also with the process by which poetic myth

---

[5] Dio's διηγεῖται ... τὴν συνουσίαν is suitably ambiguous; the narration of the συνουσία is anything but detailed. On the *Nachleben* of this passage of the *Iliad* cf. Hunter 2006, 311 and 2009, 893–894.
[6] Cf., e.g., Cameron 2004, 136–137.
[7] Cf., e.g., Ritoók 1995.

arises, and much of *Oration* 11 is best understood against the background of ancient critical discussions, such as that in Book 1 of Strabo, which are concerned not just with whether or not Homer 'got his facts right', but with how elaborated poetic versions of 'history' arise, whether through misunderstanding, rationalisation, 'mythologisation' (e.g. 1.2.36), the creation of symbolic genealogies (e.g. 1.2.10) or any other of the many representational modes open to a poet. As for Homer's veracity, for Strabo poetry contains material drawn from all of ἱστορία, διάθεσις ('rhetorical presentation') and μῦθος (1.2.17); there is much in Homer which is indeed 'as it happened/is', but there is also much which elaborates with poetic licence upon 'starting-points', ἀρχαί (1.2.9) or ἀφορμαί, (1.2.40), drawn from history, and which we can use as 'traces (ἴχνη) of historical people and events' (1.2.14). 'To invent everything (πάντα πλάττειν) is neither plausible nor in the Homeric manner', proclaims Strabo (1.2.17, cf. 1.2.9, 13), and, moreover, 'a man would tell more plausible lies if he mixed in a bit of truth as well' (1.2.9). There is very little here with which the Dio of *Oration* 11 would disagree; it needed but a small tilt of the balance to subvert,[8] not just Homer, but the whole tradition of criticism in praise of Homer. It is in that small tilt that the apparent modernity of some of Dio's observations most strikes home. Poetic myth is a recollection of 'real events' but told for particular purposes and with a particular spin aimed at particular contemporary audiences; it is thus not created *ex nihilo*, but neither is it a trustworthy record. Moreover, Homer stood in a particular relationship to his material:

> ...There were no other poets or prose writers who had recorded the truth, but Homer himself was the first who had undertaken to write of these events; he was composing many generations after the events, when both those with knowledge of them and their descendants had disappeared and all that was left was a faint and weak tradition (ἀμαυρᾶς...καὶ ἀσθενοῦς ἔτι φήμης ἀπολειπομένης), as is to be expected in the matter of events which are very ancient...
>
> Dio Chrysostom 11.92

Here then is a Homer not very far from how some modern scholarship imagines him; that the Trojan story had, at least at first, been preserved within the élite families who claimed personal connection with the Trojan expedition is also an idea which the modern study of oral narrative would certainly recognize.[9]

---

8 Cf. below p. 495–496.
9 Cf. further below p. 492 on chs. 145–6.

Dio does not explain the misrepresentation of history merely by Homer's desire to gratify a Greek audience,[10] but also suggests ways in which widely-held distortions of the truth may arise. Of particular interest is the account of Paris' successful wooing of Helen, where Dio may have drawn *inter alia* on the *Catalogue of Women* ascribed to Hesiod;[11] thus, for example, Agamemnon works to secure Helen for Menelaos (46), just as he does in the *Catalogue* (fr. 197.4–5 M-W = fr. 105.4–5 Hirschberger). Be that as it may, Dio sets the whole episode within the context of Mycenean *Realpolitik* with a vividness which may well also owe not a little to Dio's experience of such negotiations in the contemporary world. Agamemnon marries Clytemnestra in order to negate the potential threat to his kingdom from Clytemnestra's powerful brothers (46), and Tyndareus awards Helen to Paris in order to become allied to the strongest power in Asia (51), a decision which in turn increases Agamemnon's disquiet about possible Asian interference in Greek affairs (62). The report of the speech which Paris made to persuade Tyndareus and the Dioscuri (49–50) is a masterful parody of the kinds of arguments which we know were in fact employed in interstate relations; I will comment briefly on just two related details. Paris adduces in his favour the fact that he is the heir to Priam's power and wealth; to any ordinary reader of Homer, such as Herodotus (cf. 2.120.4), this would be plain nonsense – Hector was very obviously to be Priam's successor.[12] We can therefore see Paris' claim as one more indication of how erroneous was Homer's story, or – in my view, more probably – we can treat it as a simple untruth, and one not easy to unmask, told by Paris to bolster his case. This example may then form the background to a consideration of Paris' further claim that 'he was dear to the gods and that Aphrodite had promised him the finest of all marriages'. It is possible to see here either a motif borrowed from *Oration* 20 in which the Judgement is a daydream of Paris as he herds his flocks (20.19–23) or a motif designed to produce a narrative which combines the Judgement with the story of the wooing which Dio tells, but as Dio also casts scorn on the whole idea of the Judgement, such scholarly ingenuity would probably be wasted; there are, of course, inconsistencies and apparent contradictions elsewhere in the speech, and the proper strategy with which to deal with them is in fact an important

---

10 Cf. further below p. 493–494.
11 Cf. Cingano 2005, 133–134.
12 Cf. the bT-scholium on *Il.* 22.229b 'one may suspect that Hector is the oldest of the sons of Priam'.

interpretative issue,[13] but the present case at least admits of a fairly straightforward answer. It seems likely that what we have here is another rhetorical improvisation by Paris, designed to impress a family which already prided itself on its divine connections. In this case, however, we are dealing with a rhetorical improvisation which was to have a very long *Nachleben*, for it was to be taken up and become part of the canonical Judgement story. This is one way, so Dio teaches us, that 'myths' arise. That Dio does not spell this out for us, but rather forces us to reason it out for ourselves, is of a piece with his account of what followed Paris' winning of Helen.

After the departure of Paris and Helen, Agamemnon, who had his own political and military reasons for fearing an over-powerful Asia with a direct connection to Greece (62), gathers the unsuccessful suitors together; naturally enough, like all (good) politicians, he does not openly express fears for his own grip on power, but rather goes for the moral high ground: 'all the other suitors have been treated outrageously (ὑβρισθῆναι) and Greece with contempt (καταφρονηθῆναι)', he declares (62); it is Paris and Priam who are αἴτιοι, not Tyndareus (63), and Agamemnon succeeds in making each suitor feel 'that his own *gamos* had been taken away' (64). In Agamemnon's moral language, allied to his promise of lucrative plunder from a city of unimaginable wealth whose people were 'corrupted by τρυφή' (63), lies in fact the origin of the story of Paris as the seducing adulterer, not as a successful suitor. Few things distort the memory of 'what really happened' (38) more quickly than moral indignation, particularly where the self-esteem of nations is involved. Be that as it may, Dio's account of why the suitors in fact agreed to the foreign military adventure (64) has an alarmingly familiar ring to it: the disastrous decision to 'invade' Troy was an explosive cocktail of patriotism, wounded male pride and commercial calculation:

> Some [of the suitors] were angry when they heard what Agamemnon had to say and they thought that what had happened was in fact a disgrace to Greece, but others thought that the campaign would yield benefits, for it was widely believed that Asia was a land of great things and surpassing wealth.
>
> Dio Chrysostom 11.64

Whatever modern parallels might strike us, it is in these chapters hard not to recall Thucydides' account of why the Athenians decided in favour of the ulti-

---

[13] Cf. further below, Vagnone 2003, 136. Whether or not Homer knew the story of the Judgement was of course debated in antiquity (cf., e.g., the scholia to *Il.* 24.23), but Dio does not obviously make use of this debate.

mately disastrous expedition to Sicily (6.24); if Dio is indeed recalling that pattern, then the textual memory reinforces the accuracy of the revolutionary account he offers: in this particular also, the Sicilian expedition (which we know happened as Thucydides describes it) echoed the Trojan expedition (the truth of which we are now learning for the first time).[14]

In setting himself to correct Homeric narrative, Dio stands of course in a very long tradition, but it is Herodotus who occupies the principal position in that tradition. Just as Dio's alleged source is 'a very old Egyptian priest at [with a very probable emendation] Onouphi' (37) and the ultimate source is Menelaos himself (38, 135), so too Herodotus' source for his revision of the Homeric story is explicitly 'the priests' whose own source is (again) Menelaos (2.118.1); Herodotus' question to the priests, 'whether the Greek story about Troy was nonsense or not' (ibid.), is essentially the subject of Dio's speech. Dio and Herodotus, of course, part company on what the true story behind Homer's fiction actually was, but Dio's imitation of Herodotus is in fact quite close.[15] Just as Herodotus finds evidence in the Homeric text that Homer himself knew of the alternative (and truer) version but rejected it on poetic grounds (2.116), this too is a strategy which Dio borrows for his Homer (136); both authors of course draw on arguments from probability to make their case. The adoption of a Herodotean voice, though not one as explicit as in some imperial Greek texts, marks Dio's speech in particular ways. It is not a simple matter of the ambiguous reputation which Herodotus enjoyed as both historian and purveyor of untruths, for elsewhere Dio rehearses a Thucydidean declaration of his own concern for truth and most men's lack of concern, even where contemporary matters are involved (145–146, cf. Thuc. 1.20). Most men, says Dio, echoing his earlier account of Homer, 'listen only to φήμη' and subsequent generations accept whatever they have been told (146, cf. Thuc. 1.20.1). In these chapters Thucydides contrasts his own narrative with the work of both poets, who exaggerate the importance of their subjects, and *logographoi* (including Herodotus?), whose concern is with providing an attractive tale for their hearers (1.21.1);[16] Dio's account of how poetic myth is created is thus much indebted for its intellectual framework to these chapters, but it is also a radical critique of them.

---

[14] Modern scholarship too is, of course, interested in the relation between the Greek expedition to Troy and Thucydides' account of the Sicilian expedition, cf., e.g., Kallet 2001, 97–112.
[15] The device of an 'aged Egyptian priest' as informant is not, of course, limited to Herodotus; students of Dio 11 regularly refer to Plato, *Timaeus* 21e–2b.
[16] Cf. further below p. 494. In *Oration* 18 Dio echoes this chapter of Thucydides in praising the enjoyment to be gained from reading Herodotus: 'you will think that the work has a mythic rather than a historical character' (18.10).

In chapter 38 Dio ascribes the Egyptian preservation of a true account not just to the quality of their informant (Menelaos) but also to the fact that the Egyptians preserve written records; this is a familiar fact of the Greek ethnography of Egypt, but in the *Trojan Oration* it is made to do special work:

> The priest said that they had written down all of previous history, some on the temples,[17] and some on pillars. Some things were remembered only by a few, as the pillars had been destroyed, and much that was written on the pillars was disbelieved on account of the ignorance and lack of interest of subsequent generations. The material concerning Troy was among the most recent written accounts, because Menelaos had come to Egypt and recounted everything as it had happened (ἅπαντα ὡς ἐγένετο).
>
> Dio Chrysostom 11.38

The basic distinction between oral memory and the written record goes back (at least) to the same programmatic chapters of Thucydides, but whereas Thucydides projects the distinction forward (his history will be 'useful' both because of the pains he has taken to establish the truth and because his history has been composed primarily for written reception rather than for recitations), Dio projects it backwards. The Egyptian written records make up for the fact that Homer had only φήμη to go on (cf. above). What, however, our memory of these Thucydidean chapters does is humorously to undermine Dio's (and Herodotus') reliance upon the autopsy of Menelaos, for Thucydides makes explicit that the reports which an eyewitness offers are determined by each witness' 'prejudice or memory' (1.22.3). How reliable a witness do we imagine Menelaos was, when judged by these Thucydidean criteria? According to Herodotus, Menelaos told the Egyptians ἀληθείην τῶν πραγμάτων (2.119.1), just as Dio says that he told them ἅπαντα ὡς ἐγένετο (38) and 'concealed nothing' (135); who, however, is to say? Written records are only as good as the information on which they are based; if the Egyptians can laugh because the foolish Greeks have been deceived by one man (Homer), then how much wiser are the Egyptians who also put their faith in a single witness, albeit an eyewitness (37–8). The *Trojan Oration* is thus a reflection not just upon the creation of poetic myth, but also upon the creation of the 'history' which lies behind the myth.

Herodotus was of course 'the prose Homer',[18] and in adopting a Herodotean voice and in retelling the story of Troy Dio is setting himself up precisely as an alternative Homer; he can even imagine a scenario in which the Argives would drive him out for being an 'anti-Homer' (5, cf. 9), just as the ideal poetic imitator

---

17 This seems more likely than 'in the temples'.
18 So first in the 'Pride of Halicarnassus', *SGO* 0/12/02 (v. 43).

(such as Homer) was to be escorted out of Plato's republic (*Rep.* 3.398a). The *Trojan Oration* is to be delivered at more than one location around the Greek world (6), just as the standard view of Homer (15–16) is that poverty forced him to hawk his poems around the Greek world, and common sense, as well as the familiar *Lives* of Homer, suggests that he will have recited καθ' ἡδονήν for the audiences from which he hoped to gain support (15). As an anti-Homer, Dio protests (too much) that he will not seek to gratify (χαρίζεσθαι) his audience (11) and even claims that the *Trojan Oration* will not be 'to the liking' (πρὸς ἡδονήν) of his Trojan audience (6); well, perhaps... Here, as so often, we hear distorted echoes of ancient Homeric criticism. An aspect of the question of where Homer's sympathies lay is a repeated concern in the scholia with the fact that the poet does not want openly to favour (χαρίζεσθαι) the Greek side;[19] Dio overtly twists this scholarly idea in ch. 82 in which Homer 'shows an empty favouritism for Menelaos' (κενὰς αὐτῶι χαρίζεται χάριτας) by giving him a 'laughable victory' over Paris when his sword broke (*Il.* 3.361–368). Here too Dio can combine the traditions of Homeric criticism and historiography. For Dio, Homer was able to distort 'history', not just because of the faintness of the surviving traditions, but because his mass audiences were largely uneducated (τοὺς πολλοὺς καὶ ἰδιώτας) and he gave them what they wanted to hear, namely exaggerated Greek success and heroism; in this state of affairs, even those who knew the truth kept quiet and did not refute (ἐξελέγχειν) his claims (92), and it is (again) not hard to think of modern parallels for such a situation. Be that as it may, behind Dio's argument lies (again) Thucydides 1.21.1 where the historian contrasts himself with the poets who also exaggerated their subjects (ἐπὶ τὸ μεῖζον κοσμοῦντες, cf. Dio's description of Homer βελτίω ποιῶν τὰ τῶν Ἑλλήνων, 92) and the 'logographers' whose compositions aimed at being pleasing to their audiences rather than true; Thucydides also notes that what these performers reported about the distant past was in any case 'beyond verification' (ἀνεξέλεγκτα). Dio's argument picks up and lightly recasts Thucydides' criticism of 'the many' who are simply not interested in taking pains to discover the truth (1.20.3).

One aspect of Dio as a new (and anti-) Homer, and of Dio's appropriation of the tradition of epic criticism, to which there is space here merely to allude, is the possibility that Dio has composed the *Trojan Oration* in such a way as to make it open to some of the same modes of criticism as the Homeric poems themselves. Critics have rightly found it easy enough to discover inconsistencies

---

[19] Cf. bT-scholia to *Il.* 4.13, 11.116–117, 364; for the issue in general cf. Richardson 1980, 273–274, with earlier bibliography.

in the revisionist history which Dio offers, and the normal explanations of textual doublets, often arising from the conflation of alternative versions of the same passage (presumably originally from different versions of the speech), and of Dio's typical habits of composition must both contain elements of truth, however much, in extreme form, they may resemble some modern approaches to the text of Homer himself.[20] Nevertheless, Paris' reference to a promise made to him by Aphrodite, for example, which I have interpreted above as a rhetorical improvisation by Paris, could be seen as a sign that even the 'true story' of what happened contained within itself indications of rival versions, just as — as we have seen — both Herodotus and Dio later in the *Trojan Oration* find indications in the Homeric text of the rival (and truer) versions. For both Herodotus and Dio, Homer knows what he is doing in such cases; with regard to Aphrodite's promise to Paris in Dio, however, Seeck suggests that what we have is a 'Relikt des Mythos' which survives in Dio's version 'eher versehentlich';[21] perhaps, however, we should give Dio the same benefit of the doubt which he himself gave Homer. As the Platonic Socrates in very 'sophistic' mode claims to expose inconsistencies in Homer (Plato, *Hippias Minor* 369e–71e) and as Isocrates depicts 'worthless sophists' sitting around swapping what they thought were smart ideas about Homer and the other poets (*Panathenaicus* 18), so Dio, who actually envisages that 'the wretched sophists' will get to work on his speech to refute it (ἐξελέγχειν 6, cf. 14),[22] has played an amusing game by giving these critics material to work with.

Dio and Homer are alike in another way also. If Homer turned the truth completely upside down (36 ἀναστρέφειν ἄπαντα, 92 πάντα τὰ πράγματα ἁπλῶς ἀνέτρεψε), Dio does the same to received tradition, which many would take as the same thing as 'truth'. Here too Dio picks up and distorts an aspect of Homeric criticism. An important idea in the ancient admiration for Homeric narrative technique is ἀναστροφή, a concept which is used in two related ways. It may refer to the way in which the *Iliad* tells the story of a short and climactic period of the war, but through prolepeses and analepses and other modes of expansion, Homer manages to include the whole story of the war; important statements of this idea occur, for example, in the b-scholia to 1.8–9 and to 2.494–

---

20 Cf., e.g., Kindstrand 1973, 142–143.
21 Seeck 1990, 99.
22 Von Arnim excised the reference to 'sophists' in 6 (cf. von Arnim 1898, 168–169), and it must be admitted that the construction is not well paralleled. Nevertheless, it can hardly be without significance that Dio's overturning of the established Trojan story, i.e. an argument for the ἥττων λόγος, is itself a very 'sophistic' undertaking (cf. Plutarch, *De malignitate* 5,855e). Dio is certainly having it both ways.

877.²³ ἀναστροφή may also refer to the way in which the outcome of a single narrative may be adumbrated first, and then the speaker will go back to explain the causes and course of the narrative.²⁴ More generally, and with particular reference of course to the model of the *Odyssey*, ἀναστροφή denoted any mode of narration in which the order (τάξις) of events and the order of the telling were not coincident (the issue, in other words, from which all modern narratology takes off). The technique was clearly practised at a relatively early stage of ancient rhetorical education; in his account of the preliminary exercise of διήγημα, Aelius Theon identifies five possible narrative orderings (middle-beginning-end, as in the *Odyssey*, end-middle-beginning, middle-end-beginning, end-beginning-middle, beginning-end-middle).²⁵ What Dio has done is to take a much praised feature of Homeric narrative and, so to say, confused two senses of ἀναστροφή, so that Homer's ἀναστροφή now becomes a total 'subversion' of events, rather than a particular way of ordering them in the telling. For Dio, Homer's motive for behaving in such a way was his desire to please his audience and, sitting perhaps only apparently paradoxically alongside this, his contempt for them (35, 92); for criticism sympathetic to Homer, of course, ἀναστροφή was also a result of the poet's relationship with his audience, but in this case a cause and symptom of Homer's unique power to engage them and to hold their attention.

'Anastrophic' narrative (of all forms) calls attention to itself because it differs from the 'natural' order imposed by chronology. The bT-scholia on *Il.* 2.494–877 note that κατὰ τάξιν narrative, i.e. where the order of events and the order of the telling are coincident and which is elsewhere called κατὰ φύσιν narrative,²⁶ is characteristic of post-Homeric poetry (νεωτερικόν) and prose-writing and that it is not appropriate for poetic dignity (σεμνότης). Such narrative which starts ἀπὸ τῶν πρώτων and proceeds ἐπὶ τὰ ἐφεξῆς (Eustathius, *Hom.* 7.42–44) was, as is well known, believed to be characteristic of 'cyclic', rather than Homeric, epic, a judgement much influenced by Aristotle's views on the preferred structures for epic and tragic plotting and of Homer's superiority to other epic poets.²⁷ Nowhere, of course, is this subject more prominent than in discussions of how Homer's poems begin; Horace's view of the matter in the *Ars*

---

23 Cf., e.g., Richardson 1980, 267; Rengakos 2004, 291–292. Meijering 1987, 138–148 collects much ancient material on narrative τάξις. See also Nünlist 2009.
24 Cf., e.g., bT-scholia to *Il.* 11.671–761, 13.665b, Porphyry on *Il.* 12.127–154 (= I 176–178 Schrader).
25 Theon, *Progymnasmata* 86.9–87.12 Spengel (= pp. 48–49 Patillon-Bolognesi).
26 Cf., e.g., Theon, *Progymnasmata* 86.32 Spengel (= p. 49 Patillon-Bolognesi), Eustathius, *Hom.* 7.9–10, 42–44.
27 Cf., e.g., Hunter 2001, 105–119; Vagnone 2003, 120–121; Rengakos 2004.

Poetica is too well known to require discussion *(AP* 136-147). Unsurprisingly, this critical rhetoric is also very familiar to Dio:

> Though he set himself to tell of the war (ἐπιχειρήσας τὸν πόλεμον εἰπεῖν) between the Achaeans and the Trojans, [Homer] did not straightaway begin at the beginning, but at some random point (ὅθεν ἔτυχεν). This is what virtually all liars do: they entangle and twist (ἐμπλέκοντες καὶ περιπλέκοντες) and do not want to tell their story in sequence (ἐφεξῆς).
>
> Dio Chrysostom 11.24

We may here be reminded of the answer given in the Underworld by the Lucianic Homer, when asked — a notorious critical question — why he began the *Iliad* with μῆνις, that this opening just occurred to him without any planning (Lucian, *VH* 2.20). Be that as it may, Aristotle famously praises Homer because he did not 'set himself to compose a poem about the war in its entirety (μηδὲ τὸν πόλεμον... ἐπιχειρῆσαι ποιεῖν ὅλον), though it had a beginning and an end' (*Poetics* 1459a31-33); if the similarity of Dio's phrasing to that of Aristotle is coincidental, there is no doubt from where Dio's critical apparatus ultimately derives. Homer should have been a cyclic poet, like Horace's *scriptor cyclicus* who announced his subject as *fortunam Priami ... et nobile bellum* (*AP* 136), or a historian, like Thucydides who 'wrote the history of the war between the Peloponnesians and the Athenians' (1.1.1). This 'natural narrative' (κατὰ φύσιν, 25) is characteristic of those who 'wish to set forth the events as each thing happened (ὡς ξυνέβη ἕκαστον) and who report the first thing first, the second thing second, and then all successive events (τἄλλα ἐφεξῆς) likewise' (25); those who want to tell the truth, in other words.

Dio's mode of attack on Homer here is indebted to more than one overlapping intellectual tradition. We are, for example, constantly reminded of the tactics of a forensic orator in denigrating his opponent, subjecting his account to *elenchos* and exposing flaws in his argument.[28] More specifically, however, it was recognised as long ago as Eustathius[29] that Dio's procedure owes much to the rhetorical exercise of ἀνασκευή, in which mythical narratives and other stories were proved to be obvious falsehoods. Theon identifies the arguments to be employed in such an attack as 'unclarity (ἀσαφές), improbability (ἀπίθανον), inappropriateness (ἀπρεπές), defectiveness (ἐλλιπές), excessiveness (πλεονάζον), unusualness (ἀσύνηθες), inconsistency (μαχόμενον), ordering (τάξις), inoppor-

---
28 Cf. Classen 1994, 322-324.
29 Cf. Eustathius, *Hom.* 460.10-12; there is a fuller (and more recent) treatment in Mesk 1920-1921.

tuneness (ἀσύμφορον), unevenness (ἀνόμοιον), falsehood (ψευδές)',[30] and he gives an example of how one would go about disproving the story of Medea's killing of her children;[31] examples of these arguments are easy enough to find in *Oration* 11, and there can be no doubt that Dio was indebted, and wished to be seen to be indebted, to this tradition.

Finally, we may note another tradition in which the great writers of the past were exposed to serious criticism. Dio 11 has been compared to Plutarch's attack upon Herodotus,[32] but we may rather think of a more scholastic model, such as Dionysius of Halicarnassus' sharp criticism of Thucydides in his essay devoted to the historian. Dionysius certainly is not as harsh with his subject as Dio is with Homer – he goes out of his way in fact to emphasise the historian's virtues and the truth of what he reported is not at issue – but there are nevertheless interesting analogies. No full treatment is possible here, but we may note that Thucydides' arrangement of his narrative by summers and winters leads to a loss of continuity (τὸ διηνεκές) and imposes unreasonable demands upon his readers (*Thuc.* 9);[33] historical narrative should be 'straightforward and free from interruptions' (εἰρομένη καὶ ἀπερίσπαστος). Related to this is another aspect of τάξις and οἰκονομία: Thucydides made wrong choices about where to begin and end. The proper beginning, the κατὰ φύσιν ἀρχή (*Thuc.* 12.1), is from the point where 'there would be nothing (relevant) preceding', but Thucydides did not begin from 'the cause which was true and which seemed to him true' (*Thuc.* 10); it is indeed a question of nature:

> At the beginning of his enquiry into the causes of the war he should first have reported the true cause in which he himself believed; for nature demanded that prior events should have precedence over (ἄρχειν) later ones and true things be stated before false ones, and the introduction to his narrative would have been far more powerful if it had been arranged in this manner.
>
> Dionysius of Halicarnassus, *Thucydides* 11.1

Dionysius' essay gives us a glimpse into a world of narratological discussion which Dio knew well and which has made a significant contribution to *Oration*

---

[30] Theon, *Progymnasmata* 76.20–25 Spengel (= p. 36 Patillon/Bolognesi); cf. also 93.5–94.11 Spengel (= pp. 57–59 Patillon/Bolognesi).
[31] 94.12–95.2 Spengel (= pp. 59–60 Patillon/Bolognesi).
[32] Both works start from (different versions of) the topos of how literature deceives, and both authors claim (as did Plato, *Rep.* 10.595b-c) simply to be standing up for truth (Dio 11.11, Plutarch, *De malignitate* 1, 854f).
[33] Cf. also *Letter to Pompeius* 3; this was obviously a standard scholastic charge against Thucydides, cf. Theon, *Progymnasmata* 80.16–20 Spengel (= p. 41 Patillon/Bolognesi).

11; from one perspective we may say that Dio has replicated some of these arguments, while adding a consideration of why his author chose to proceed in this way. For Dio, of course, Homer's motives were not respectable.

There is, then, a lot of evidence to show us that Genette's 'unavoidable *difficulty of beginning*' was an ancient anxiety as well,[34] but let us return to Dio's argument. Where should Homer have begun the *Iliad*? Dio has a straightforward answer:

> From where would it have been more appropriate (μᾶλλον... ἔπρεπεν) to begin than from the outrageous wrong committed by Paris, which resulted in the war, since all readers of the poem would have been angry and been keen to see it accomplished and no one would have pitied the sufferings of the Trojans? In this way Homer would have had a more sympathetic and a more engaged (εὐνούστερον καὶ προθυμότερον) audience.
>
> Dio Chrysostom 11.28

We may object to Dio that Homer's announced subject was not in fact 'the war', but that will cut little ice. Dio's point is that, as an encomiast of the Greek war, Homer would have done his job far better, if he had begun from the beginning. Again Dio appeals to familiar critical arguments, and in fact is able to launch his attack without straying too far from the pattern of ancient praise for Homer. Among the reasons adduced already by the D-scholia on *Iliad* 1.1 as to why the *Iliad* began ἀπὸ τῆς μήνιδος are precisely to heighten the pathos, to make the audience 'more attentive',[35] and 'to make his encomia of the Greeks more convincing' by, apparently,[36] highlighting their sufferings and losses at the beginning. As Dio uses Homer to subvert Homer, so he uses Homeric criticism to subvert such criticism. More generally, of course, the quest for the audience's *eunoia* is a fundamental task of any poet, Homer included (cf., e.g., scholia to *Il.* 2.485–486); it is important to rouse the audience's indignation (cf., e.g., the T-scholium to *Il.* 17.205a). Dio's argument is in fact very reminiscent of a well known bT-scholium to *Il.* 6.58–59; Agamemnon urges Menelaos not to spare any Trojan, including unborn children, and the scholiast notes that audiences are revolted by such unfitting savagery, which is why, for example, tragedians do not put such murderous acts on the stage. There are, however, defences against such criticism, and it is within this tradition that Dio takes his stand:[37]

---

[34] Genette (1972) 1980, 46 (his italics), cf. Hunter 1993, 122–123.
[35] Cf. further below p. 503.
[36] There are uncertainties about the text here.
[37] I have discussed certain other aspects of this scholium in Hunter 2005b, 179–183.

> If these verses had been spoken before the breaking of the oath, they would be rightly criticised. Since, however, they come after the oaths and their transgression, Agamemnon is not hateful. The listener almost wants the whole race of oath-breakers to be wiped out; he is almost angry on behalf of the gods.
>
> bT-scholium to *Il.* 6.58–59

'Pity' is, of course, a prominent motif in ancient discussion of the *Iliad* (as, of course, in the *Iliad* itself): 'Homer ends the *Iliad* in the highest degree of pity' observes the bT-scholium on *Il.* 24.776, adding that this was the origin of the forensic practice of placing the appeal to the audience's pity last in one's speech.[38]

It is no surprise — Dio can have it both ways — that the defective end of the *Iliad* also tells its own story; Homer missed his poetic chance by not describing the sack of the city (which did not, of course, actually happen):

> If he had wanted to tell of the greatest and most fearful things, all forms of suffering and catastrophe, and moreover what everyone most of all was longing to hear (ἐπόθει ἀκοῦσαι), what greater or more powerful subject did he have than the capture of the city?
>
> Dio Chrysostom 11.29

Behind this question lies less the language of 'pity and fear' from Aristotle's *Poetics* than Gorgias' famous description of the effect of poetry (principally tragedy?) in the *Helen*:

> Those who hear poetry feel the shudders of fear, the tears of pity, the longings (πόθος) of grief. Through the words, the soul experiences its own reaction to successes and misfortunes in the affairs and persons of others.
>
> Gorgias, *Helen* 9 (trans. D.A. Russell)

Dio's point in chapter 29 is not that what a Greek audience would indeed have most 'longed' to hear was the deserved sufferings inflicted upon oath-breaking Trojans, but that descriptions of terrible suffering, such as accompanies the sack of cities, bring their own form of 'pleasure', an idea most famously expressed in this passage of Gorgias. The audience's 'desires' are another critical motif familiar in the Homeric scholia,[39] but here the idea is used to show that, even *qua* poet (let alone truth-teller), Homer did not do much of a job.

Dio's extended description of the sack of the city in chapters 29–30 is explicitly a prose version of Priam's piteous appeal to Hector at *Il.* 22.60–71, a version in which the rhetorical αὔξησις of the theme is another illustration of

---

[38] Cf. also the scholia to *Il.* 22.337, 370, 24.161–162, 309, 504, 776, Richardson 1980, 274–275.
[39] Cf. the scholia to *Il.* 2.6c, 20.443, 24.85.

what an opportunity Homer passed up;⁴⁰ the Homeric scholia, of course, take a different view and praise the *enargeia* and spare power of the verses. The links between this Homeric passage and other early epic poetry are rightly a subject of great interest,⁴¹ and one which takes its cue from the scholia ('though Homer did not write of the sack of Troy, he nevertheless described its sufferings [παθή-ματα]... he foreshadows the capture of Troy'), but it is clear that Dio is (once again) expressing the view that Homer should have been a 'cyclic poet', for behind the description of the sack in *Aeneid* 2, as behind Euripides' *Trojan Women*, lie (at least) the *Iliou Persis* and the *Little Iliad* of Lesches; unsurprisingly, these chapters of Dio share many motifs, not just with *Aeneid* 2,⁴² but also with Pausanias' famous description of Polygnotus' painting of the sack of Troy, a painting for which Pausanias sees Lesches' poem as an important source (Paus. 10.25–27). It is of some interest that these chapters of Dio are strongly reminiscent also of Polybius' famous strictures against Phylarchus' description of the sufferings of the Mantineans in chapters which gave rise to a very lively modern debate about 'tragic history':

> [Phylarchus] says that, after they had surrendered, the Mantineans endured such misfortunes... as to cause all Greeks to reflect and weep. In his eagerness to move his readers to pity and rouse their emotions, he brings on clinging women, their hair dishellevcd and their breasts exposed, and men and women weeping and lamenting along with their children and aged parents as they are led away.
>
> Polybius 2.56.6–7 = *FGrHist* 81 F5

As is well known, Polybius' objection is (basically) that such writing, which aims at the *ekplêxis* of the audience (Polybius 2.56.10, cf. Dio 11.30), is appropriate to poetry, particularly tragedy, not to historiography; the apparent similarity in these descriptions between some Hellenistic historiography and the narratives of cyclic epic is a piece of literary history not without interest,⁴³ but what is important here is that Polybius' view of the proper functions of poetry chimes

---

40 Verses 60–68 have in fact been interpolated into the text of chapter 32, perhaps from a misplaced marginal note. Vagnone 2003, *ad loc.* notes that Dio will also have had Euripides, *Troades* 1260–1332 in mind; Dio presumably knew that passage, but there are no obvious verbal echoes; cf. further below.
41 Cf., e.g., Anderson 1997, 29–38.
42 *Aeneid* 2.313 *exoritur clamorque uirum clangorque tubarum* is very like Dio 11.30 (the sounds of the sack) βοήν ἤ κτύπον χαλκοῦ, but very little should (presumably) be hung on this.
43 Cf. esp. Walbank 1960. Such set-piece descriptions (ἐκφράσεις) were a standard school exercise, cf. Theon, *Progymnasmata* 119.23 Spengel (= p. 68 Patillon/Bolognesi) for ἅλωσις.

with Dio's criticism of Homer: in failing properly to describe the sack of Troy he was failing properly to perform his rôle as a poet.

The choice of where to begin and end is, of course, a matter of planning. How much 'forward planning' went into the *Iliad* and the *Odyssey* which we possess is a matter which students of the poems still rightly discuss, for it is connected (*inter alia*) with the issue of how the poems were actually composed. The ancient scholarship which is reflected in the scholia, however, was in little doubt; the scholia 'assume that the poet has a clear idea from the beginning of the direction in which his narrative is moving'.[44] The idea of Homeric οἰκονομία and of narrative preparation are fundamental to the scholiastic view of Homer; already in the *Iliad* the poet is preparing for the *Odyssey*,[45] just as in *Iliad* 3 he is laying the groundwork for details of *Iliad* 24.[46] Unsurprisingly, Dio takes a different view, and once again it is one with a strikingly modern resonance. For Dio, Homer did not know where his poem was going to go when he set out, and important narrative decisions were made 'as the poem proceeded' (35); one merely has to look at the opening verses to see that (36). Later we learn that the major shift was (roughly) with what we call Book 16, when things start to go the Greek way again and Patroclus emerges as a principal character (92). What should be stressed here, however, is that Dio's subversion of a tenet of ancient Homeric criticism raises (still) important general questions about the assumptions of that criticism.

'Homer gave thought not just to what he should say, but also to what he should not' (bT-scholium to *Il.* 1.44a, cf. Horace, *AP* 149–150). The selection of what features and episodes to highlight is a crucial part of the good poet's art.[47] Like Horace, Dio too links Homeric selectivity with poetic licence, or 'lying' to give it its more straightforward name (*atque ita mentitur, sic ueris falsa remiscet*); for Dio, however, Homeric selectivity in fact proves Homeric untruthfulness:

> Those who tell lies usually behave like this. They tell some parts of the story and linger over them, but what they most want to conceal they do not offer freely nor when the listener is paying attention, nor do they put it in the place belonging to it, but where it may most escape notice.
>
> Dio Chrysostom 11.26

---

44 Richardson 1980, 268; pp. 267–269 of Richardson's discussion are all relevant here.
45 Cf. the scholia to *Il.* 2.260a, 10.252–253a, 260.
46 Cf. scholium to *Il.* 3.261–262b.
47 Brink's (1960) note on *AP* 148 collects much relevant material.

Liars not only leave things out, they also try to slip things past their audience when they are not paying full attention. Here Dio not only makes use of the very familiar idea of 'poetic licence', but he also (once again) picks up and 'spins' ideas from the critical tradition. The scholia frequently note how Homer or his characters do or say things λεληθότως;[48] in some of these cases the meaning of this adverb is really no more than 'implicitly', but the language of τὸ λανθάνειν is a powerful and polyvalent one in ancient Homeric criticism. Thus, for example, Duris of Samos criticised the famous simile of *Il.* 21.257–262, in which Achilles' pursuit by the river is compared to a man clearing an irrigation channel for a stream, because (in modern terms) the vehicle hardly corresponded 'in noise and threat' to the tenor;[49] readers, however, 'do not notice' this because they are distracted by the picture of horticultural irrigation. So too, when Dione uses a low (ταπεινόν) word (παππάζουσιν) as she consoles her daughter at *Il.* 5.408, this λανθάνει because the speaker is not a male god or hero, but a mother talking to her daughter (bT-scholia *ad loc.*). Examples could be multiplied,[50] but what is important is that this common language of secrecy and deceit opened the way to a potent charge. Of particular interest here are the few cases where the poet λανθάνει 'slips things by' the audience whose attention is focused elsewhere (cf. bT-scholia to *Il.* 16.395–398, 22.375b). Dio's mode of argument was almost ready-made here, for the idea of variations in the audience's attention is also important in the scholia;[51] Homer, for example, began the *Iliad* in the way he did in order to ensure the audience's attention (AT and bT-scholia on 1.1). In the scholia the idea of the poet's control over the audience's attention is part of a proper critical concern with the architecture of a long and complex poem; in Dio it is a sign of a much more dubious phenomenon.

Dio's *Trojan Oration* thus opens a window upon nearly every important issue in ancient narratology. If the speech has not recently attracted the attention it deserves, that may be in part the result of the obvious and obviously knowing humour which plays over the speech at every level; to borrow a famous phrase, Dio 'cannot be serious' (can he?). Modern narratology, by contrast, has generally been characterised by a proper scholarly seriousness and intellectual commitment to the patterns it has done so much to reveal. If, however, Dio's claim is

---

48 Cf. the scholia to *Il.* 1.242, 2.106b, 5.39, 6.358, 11.116–117, 251, 506, 13.365b, 712–721, 24.3, 249–251. The idea of doing things without being noticed appears, of course, in a number of critical contexts (cf., e.g., Aristotle, *Rhetoric* 3.1404b18).
49 Ge-scholium on *Il.* 21.257–262 = *FGrHist* 76 F89.
50 The language and ideas of τὸ λανθάνειν have in fact a wide spread in ancient literary and stylistic criticism, cf., e.g., 'Longinus', *On the Sublime* 17.
51 Cf. the scholia to *Il.* 11.218, 604c, 711b, 13.665b, 15.556–558, 610–614b, 16.112–113.

that Homer shows us how easy it is to make people believe the opposite of the truth, he also shows us that narratology can have exactly the same bewitching power.

Bibliography

Anderson, M.J. 1997. *The Fall of Troy in Early Greek Poetry and Art*, Oxford.
Arnim, H. von. 1898. *Leben und Werke des Dio von Prusa*, Berlin.
Brink, C.O. 1960. 'Tragic History and Aristotle's School', *PCPhS* 186, 6, 14–19.
Cameron, A. 2004. *Greek Mythography in the Roman World*, Oxford.
Cingano, E. 2005. 'A catalogue within a catalogue: Helen's suitors in the Hesiodic *Catalogue of Women* (frr. 196–204)', in: R. Hunter, *The Hesiodic Catalogue of Women. Constructions and Reconstructions*, Cambridge, 118–152.
Classen, C.J. 1994. 'Rhetorik und Literarkritik', in: F. Montanari (ed.), *La Philologie grecque à l'époque hellénistique et romaine*, (*Entretiens Fondation Hardt* vol. XL), Vandoeuvres-Geneva, 307–360.
Desideri, P. 1978. *Dione di Prusa. Un intellettuale greco nell'imperio romano*, Messina/Florence.
Genette, G. (1972) 1980. *Narrative Discourse: An Essay in Method*, Ithaca NY (Original Title: "Discours du récit", in: *Figures III*, Paris, 67–267).
Hunter, R. 2001. 'The Poetics of narrative in the *Argonautica*', in: T.D. Papanghelis/A. Rengakos (eds.), *A Companion to Apollonius Rhodius*, Leiden, 93–125 (= Hunter 2008a, 343–377).
Hunter, R. 2005b. 'Showing and telling: notes from the boundary', *Eikasmos* 16, 179–91 (= Hunter 2008a, 663–677).
Hunter, R. 2006. 'Plato's *Symposium* and the traditions of ancient fiction', in: J.H. Lesher/D. Nails/F.C.C. Sheffield (eds.), *Plato's Symposium. Issues in Interpretation and Reception*, Washington, 295–312 (= Hunter 2008a, 845–866).
Hunter, R. 2008a. *On Coming After. Studies in Post-Classical Greek Literature and its Reception*, Trends in Classics Supplementary Volumes 3, Berlin.
Hunter, R. 2009. 'The curious incident ... *polypragmosyne* and the ancient novel', in: M. Paschalis/S. Panayotakis/G. Schmeling (eds.), *Readers and Writers in the Ancient Novel*, Groningen, 51–63 [= Hunter 2008a, 884–896].
Jouan, F. 1966. *Euripide et les légendes des Chants Chypriens. Des origines de la guerre de Troie à l'Iliade*, Paris.
Kallet, L. 2001. *Money and the Corrosion of Power in Thucydides. The Sicilian Expedition and its Aftermath*, Berkeley etc.
Kim, L. 2008. 'Dio of Prusa, *Or.* 61, *Chryseis*, or reading Homeric Silence', *CQ* 58, 601–621.
Kindstrand, J.F. 1973. *Homer in der Zweiten Sophistik*, Uppsala.
Nünlist, R. 2009. 'Narratological concepts in Greek Scholia', in: J. Grethlein/A. Rengakos (eds.), *Narratology and Interpretation*, Berlin, 63–83.
Lemarchand, L. 1926. *Dion de Pruse. Les oeuvres d'avant l'exil*, Paris.
Saïd, S. 2000. 'Dio's use of mythology', in: S. Swain, *Dio Chrysostom. Politics, Letters, and Philosophy*, Oxford, 161–186.
Meijering, R. 1987. *Literary and Rhetorical Theories in Greek Scholia*, Groningen.
Mesk, J. 1920–1921. 'Zur elften Rede des Dio von Prusa', *WS* 42, 115–124.

Montgomery, W.A. 1902. 'Oration XI of Dio Chrysostomus. A study in sources', in: *Studies in Honor of Basil L. Gildersleeve*, Baltimore, 405–412.
Rengakos, A. 2004. 'Die *Argonautika* und das 'kyklische Gedicht'. Bemerkungen zur Erzähltechnik des griechischen Epos', in: A. Bierl/A. Schmitt/A. Willi (eds.), *Antike Literatur in neuer Deutung. Festschrift J. Latacz*, Munich/Leipzig, 277–304.
Richardson, N.J. 1980. 'Literary criticism in the exegetical scholia to the *Iliad*: a sketch', *CQ* 30, 265–287.
Ritoók, Z. 1995. 'Some aesthetic views of Dio Chrysostom and their sources', in: J.G.J. Abbenes/S.R. Slings/I. Sluiter (eds.), *Greek Literary Theory after Aristotle*, Amsterdam, 125–134.
Seeck, G.A. 1990. 'Dion Chrysostomos als Homerkritiker (Or. 11)', *RhM* 133, 97–107.
Swain, S. (ed.) 2000. *Dio Chrysostom. Politics, Letters, and Philosophy*, Oxford.
Szarmach, M. 1978. 'Le 'Discours Troyen' de Dion de Pruse', *Eos* 66, 195–202.
Vagnone, G. 2003. *Dione di Prusa. Troiano, Or. XI*, Rome.
Walbank, F.W. 1960. 'History and tragedy', *Historia* 9, 216–234.

28 Plato's *Ion* and the Origins of Scholarship

The *Ion* has always been regarded as a very important source for Plato's views on poetry and for the history of rhapsodic performance, but it hardly figures — unless I am mistaken — in modern accounts of the development of ancient scholarship,[1] although we might have expected a fourth-century work in which Socrates cross-examines an expert in the presentation and interpretation (understood very broadly) of Homer to be a precious stone in the lacunose mosaic which is our knowledge of the history of the discipline. This neglect is perhaps particularly surprising given the fact that at the heart of Socrates' discussion with the rhapsode lies the issue of how to judge (κρίνειν) poetry; whereas, for example, the famous discussions of *Republic* 2, 3 and 10 are largely concerned with the nature and effect of poetry, the *Ion* also focuses on the role and qualification of 'the critic', and *krisis* is, in the now canonical account, what lies at the heart of scholarship. When Socrates (no doubt ironically) counts rhapsodes lucky because they come thoroughly to learn/understand (ἐκμανθάνειν) Homer's *dianoia* and can then transmit this *dianoia* to the audience (530b–c),[2] he places them at the head of the whole scholarly tradition, as it was summed up some four and a half centuries later by Dio Chrysostom in his Περὶ Ὁμήρου:

> Many others [i.e. as well as Democritus] have written about Homer, some straightforwardly praising (ἐγκωμιάζοντες) the poet and illuminating (δηλοῦντες) some of the things he has said, and others precisely expounding (ἐξηγούμενοι) his *dianoia*; this latter group includes Aristarchus and Crates and a number of the others of those who were later called *grammatikoi*, but earlier *kritikoi*.
>
> Dio Chrysostom 53.1

Ion would see himself at the head of both camps.[3]

There are, I think, a number of reasons why historians of ancient scholarship have paid the *Ion* less attention than they might have done. One is both chronological and ideological. The prevailing narrative, enshrined in and to an important extent descending from Rudolf Pfeiffer's extraordinary *synthesis*, is that 'scholarship', defined as 'the art of understanding, explaining, and restoring the literary tradition', is a creation of the third century, whatever significant debt it owed to the intellectual activities of the previous three centuries, most

---

1 There are merely a couple of incidental references to the *Ion* in Pfeiffer 1968.
2 On the meaning of Socrates' statement cf. below p. 509–512 and Rijksbaron 2007, 120.
3 On 'praise' of Homer cf. below p. 515–516.

notably of course to Aristotle;[4] from this perspective, the *Ion*, if it has any importance at all, must belong to the 'background noise'. Even the alternative view, which we know from the same chapter of Dio quoted above to have been current in antiquity, namely that Aristotle provided the ἀρχή for κριτική and γραμματική offers little comfort to the reputation of the Platonic work.[5] Secondly, the emphasis throughout the *Ion* is on Ion as an oral performer, both as reciter and expounder of Homer;[6] if at the heart of scholarship lies the repeated examination of written texts in an atmosphere of dispassionate enquiry, then both Ion's histrionics and his effect on his audiences seem light years away from that. It has been interestingly suggested that 'Plato depicts a performer who is struggling to maintain a privileged position as a Homeric interpreter in the face of experts [i.e. Metrodorus etc.] who focus on Homer's compositions independently of their performance'.[7] If so, the *Ion* might be showing us the deaththroes of the old, rather than the birth of the new, but in fact it is more likely that both are involved.[8] Be that as it may, it ought at least to be worth asking whether Ion's business of λέγειν περὶ Ὁμήρου (530c9 etc.) was an utterly different activity, not just from Democritus' written περὶ Ὁμήρου (T 33, fr. 20a–25 D.-K.), but from the many like-named works from the Hellenistic and imperial periods of which we know, such as Dio *Or.* 53 (quoted above). It is, moreover, perhaps not flippant to observe that, as soon as Socrates provokes him to reveal his self-satisfaction, Ion puts his achievements in a competitive frame:

> I think that I speak best of all men about Homer. Neither Metrodorus of Lampsacus nor Stesimbrotus of Thasos nor Glaucon nor anyone who has ever lived has been able to utter as many splendid *dianoiai* about Homer as myself.
>
> Plato, *Ion* 530c8–d3[9]

There is no need here to describe at length the agonistic nature of all public activities in classical Athens, but it is worth stressing that Ion's pride here also looks forward to the very agonistic nature of Hellenistic scholarship; it is hard not to be reminded of Callimachus' *Iambos* 1. Strabo's refutation of Eratosthenes

---

4 Pfeiffer 1968, 3.
5 Pfeiffer of course takes pains to refute this view (cf. Pfeiffer 1968, 67).
6 Cf., e.g., Ferrari 2003, 92–99 (a helpful account) and the remarks of Yunis 2003, 190–192.
7 Graziosi 2002, 45.
8 I am tempted to add that the fact that *Ion* is apparently in the business for reward and prizes, including financial gain (530a–b, 535e), will not have encouraged modern scholars to take him very seriously; real scholars, as some believe, have no interest in salaries or glittering prizes – what matters is 'devotion to pure learning' (Pfeiffer 1968, 3).
9 On this passage cf. also below p. 512–515.

in 1.2 of the *Geography* is perhaps our clearest surviving example of how, at least in antiquity if not more recently, scholarly space is normally found by encroaching on the territory of others.

More important perhaps in the current context than the 'performative' nature of Ion's wisdom is the simple fact that we apparently do not see Ion perform in the dialogue named after him. On both occasions when he is about to give Socrates a display (*epideixis*) περὶ Ὁμήρου, Socrates sidetracks him into a question-and-answer session of Socrates' own devising (530d–1a, 536d–e). If anyone gives an *epideixis* περὶ Ὁμήρου in the *Ion*, it is Socrates, not Ion; Socrates' bravura central speech on magnetism and poetic inspiration deserves such a title as much as any other. As for Ion, we are clearly to understand that the kind of 'performance' he gives in the dialogue is not how he (or any rhapsode) usually 'speaks about Homer'. Although attention has been given to what can be gleaned from the dialogue about the bi-partite nature of Ion's performances, which seem to have consisted of both recitation of passages and some form of 'commentary' or discussion,[10] scholars have, unsurprisingly, on the whole looked elsewhere, to the *Protagoras* (to which I shall return) and the *Hippias Minor*, for example, for rather more informative accounts of poetic interpretative practice at the end of the fifth century, at least as that is presented by Plato. These works have, however, also figured in a long debate as to how, if at all, Ion's performances on Homer are to be understood within a 'sophistic' context and, more broadly, on the relation between rhapsodic practice as portrayed in the *Ion* and other contemporary practices of Homeric interpretation, including those of Metrodorus, Stesimbrotus, and the others against whom Ion measures himself.[11] On one hand, it is in fact easy enough to imagine Ion in a situation such as that described by Isocrates in a well-known passage of the *Panathenaicus*:[12]

> Some friends met me and told me how three or four of the common herd of sophists, the kind who claim to know everything and who appear anywhere at the drop of a hat, were sitting together in the Lyceum and discussing (διαλέγοιντο) the poets, particularly the poetry of Hesiod and Homer; they had nothing of their own to say, but they were reciting (ῥαψωιδοῦντες) these poets' verses and repeating the cleverest bits from what others had said about them in the past.
>
> Isocrates, *Panathenaicus* 18

---

10 Cf. below p. 513 n. 27, Velardi 1989, 21–36.
11 Cf. esp. Richardson 1975; Murray 1996, 98 offers a useful overview.
12 Cf. e.g., Méridier 1931, 9–10, Murray 1996, 97–98, Ford 2002, 71.

Isocrates' barbs are, of course, another paradigmatic instance of the agonistic nature of 'scholarship'. Ion would have denied the charge of crudely tralatician scholarship, but otherwise it might be just such a situation to which Ion is referring at 532b–c:[13]

> What is the reason, Socrates, that whenever someone discusses (διαλέγηται) another poet, I cannot concentrate and can make no worth while contribution — in fact I just nod off — but when someone brings up the subject of Homer (περὶ Ὁμήρου μνησθῆι),[14] I am immediately awake and focused and have a great deal to say?
>
> Plato, *Ion* 532b8–c3

A work such as Dio *Or.* 53 (cf. above), the first part of which almost amounts to an anthology of classical praise of Homer, may well stand in a direct line of descent from the kind of 'sophistic' discussion which Isocrates conjures up, though Isocrates presumably implies that his despised sophists do not, unlike Dio, take the trouble of acknowledging their sources.

The 'sophists' with whom Isocrates is concerned were probably rather different from the great fifth-century figures who fill the pages of Plato. Unlike a Protagoras or a Hippias or a Prodicus, Ion has no 'intellectual' activity beyond the recitation and discussion of Homer; he does not teach rhetoric or virtue or even write his own poetry, he is through and through a 'Homerist'. This makes him no less, say, an anti-Eratosthenes than he is an anti-Hippias, but Plato's stress on his self-proclaimed narrowness, however truly (or otherwise) it may reflect contemporary rhapsodic practice, does not merely serve an argument about the nature and unity of *technai*, but emphasises Ion as an expert in the poetry of the past and as a professional performer in public of his own *sophia* (this is 'what he does'), and as such he is actually much closer in some respects to the modern conception of 'the scholar' than are the great sophists of the later fifth century.

Perhaps no single passage of the *Ion* has provoked as much discussion as Socrates' initial provocation of the rhapsode:

> I have often, Ion, envied you rhapsodes for your craft (τέχνης). For not only does it befit your art to adorn yourselves (τὸ σῶμα κεκοσμῆσαι) and to appear at your splendid best, but you must also spend time with (διατρίβειν) many excellent poets, and above all with Homer, the greatest and most divine of poets; thoroughly to learn his meaning (διάνοια),

---

13 Ion might, of course, also have occasions such as symposia in mind, cf. Velardi 1989, 19.
14 Cf. 536c7. The sense of περὶ Ὁμήρου μνησθῆι seems to be as I have translated it, rather than the more specific 'makes commentaries about Homer' as a piece of 'rhapsodes' language', as Nagy 2002, 31 takes it.

not just his verses, is certainly to be envied. For no one could be a good rhapsode unless he understood (συνείη) what the poet said. The rhapsode must transmit (lit. 'be ἑρμηνεύς of) the poet's meaning (διάνοια) for those listening, and it is impossible to do this well without knowing (γιγνώσκοντα) what the poet says/means (λέγει).

Plato, Ion 530b5–c5

All of the key terms in this passage have been subjected to lengthy analysis: for some, Socrates is representing Ion as an interpretative 'commentator' who has to explain the poet's meaning to the less qualified, for others there is reference here to nothing other than standard rhapsodic recitation of Homeric poetry. In seeking to tease out Socrates' own διάνοια here, we might be tempted to start with a presumption that Socrates' statement is likely to be both ambiguous for the unwary and designed to steer Ion's response in a certain direction.

Socrates' ironic admiration is very close to a passage which Plato elsewhere puts in the mouth of Protagoras[15] and it clearly introduces the important question of whether rhapsodes (and poets) have 'knowledge'[16] but — taken by itself — it might indeed be thought to suggest a serious form of poetic 'interpretation'. συνίημι is, for example, used by Pindar in suggestive contexts: at Nemean 4.31 λόγον ὁ μὴ συνιείς is the person who cannot draw out a moral from the tale Pindar tells; at fr. 105.1 Maehler σύνες ὅ τοι λέγω (addressed to Hieron) is likely to have meant 'get my meaning (which I am not going to spell out)', though probably not with the threatening overtones of the absurd poet who uses the tag in Aristophanes' Birds (v. 945). Most striking of all is the use of συνετός at Bacchylides 3.85, φρονέοντι συνετὰ γαρύω, and in a notorious passage from Olympian 2:

> πολλά μοι ὑπ'
> ἀγκῶνος ὠκέα βέλη
> ἔνδον ἐντὶ φαρέτρας
> φωνάεντα συνετοῖσιν, ἐς δὲ τὸ πᾶν ἑρμανέων
> χατίζει. σοφὸς ὁ πολλὰ εἰδὼς φυᾷ·
> μαθόντες δὲ λάβροι
> παγγλωσσίαι κόρακες ὣς ἄκραντα γαρυέτων
> Διὸς πρὸς ὄρνιχα θεῖον·

Pindar, Olympian 2.83–88

---

15 Cf. below p. 514–515.
16 Cf. esp. Republic 10.598e3–4 for very similar language applied to poets. The irony of Socrates' provocation to Ion was of course of no importance for parts of the later tradition; thus Proclus cites 530b8–c1 for Platonic endorsement of the need to study Homer and to benefit from the poet's 'intellectual and scientific guidance' (Commentary on the Republic 158.3–11 Kroll). Proclus discusses the Ion itself at 182.21–185.7 Kroll.

> I have under my arm many swift arrows inside their quiver which speak to those who understand; in general, however, they require interpreters. Wise is the man who naturally knows many things. Those who have learned are unruly and their words spill out; they are like a pair of crows who caw in vain against the divine bird of Zeus.

Whatever the tortuous vagaries of modern interpretation of this passage, it was clear enough in later antiquity, at least, that Pindar 'is talking about his own poems' which need ἑρμηνεῖς 'interpreters' (*Sch. Pi. O. 2 ad loc.*);[17] such a passage was, of course, a godsend to interpreting scholars, who could simply ignore the irony of adopting as a motto and justification for their own activity a passage which rejected 'learning'. Be that as it may, the juxtaposition of these two ideas in both Pindar and Plato might encourage us to believe that Socrates is indeed teasing Ion in a language which suggests the 'decoding' of poetic meaning, an interpretative practice which may, but need not, be what we would call 'allegorical'.

The extant classical usages of ἑρμηνεύς are, however, at least not in favour of such an interpretation of the *Ion* passage,[18] and, as Albert Rijksbaron has perhaps most fully demonstrated,[19] there need in fact be no reference here to anything other than rhapsodic performance of Homer: 'To ensure a successful performance the rhapsode had first and foremost to make basic but important decisions about word division and accentuation, about the construal of the sentences, their declarative, interrogative or exclamative character, and about punctuation, i.e. pausing in a meaningful way while reciting the text, etc.'.[20] Rijksbaron well illustrates the continuity between such necessary decisions and much of the interpretative material which we find in the later scholia.[21] How the rhapsode performed indicated how he understood Homer's *dianoia*, and a 'good' rhapsode would precisely catch that authorial meaning and 'transmit' it to the audience;[22] a less good rhapsode might know the verses off by heart, but the performance of them would leave the audience short of the full Homeric experience.

This passage of Pindar's *Second Olympian* allows us also to catch some of the resonance of Ion's statement that understanding the poet's meaning is the part of his craft which has 'caused [him] most trouble (πλεῖστον ἔργον παρέ-

---

17 Cf. Eustathius at II 289 Drachmann. This is the only extant Pindaric use of ἑρμηνεύς.
18 Cf. Capuccino 2005, 124–137, citing Most 1986.
19 Cf. Rijksbaron 2007, 123–128.
20 Rijksbaron 2007, 125.
21 For some classical examples of just such problem cf. Arist. *S.E.* 166b1–9.
22 The discussion of *dianoia* in Nagy 2002, 29 goes in a rather different direction.

σχεν)' (530c7–8). Whereas the rhetoric of the *Ion* is heavily dependent upon a running-together of the activities of poet and rhapsode, the serious investment of 'effort/labour' distinguishes Ion in his rhapsodic activity from the idea of the soaring poet, promulgated by both Pindar and Socrates in his 'light and winged and holy' speech; Ion is much more like one of Pindar's cawing crows. Ion's assertion, however, also looks forward to the ideals of poetic and scholarly 'labour' which we know to be a hallmark of the Hellenistic and later periods, but which, as for example Aristophanes' *Frogs* shows only too clearly, were already important to conceptions of poetic composition at the end of the fifth century.[23] Horace, for example, likens himself to a bee (*Odes* 4.27–32) as Socrates claims all lyric poets do (534b1), but adds a repeated emphasis on the labour involved in composition (*per laborem/plurimum, operosa...carmina*). As for the ἔργα of scholarship, the fatal effect of Philitas' laborious researches stands as a humorous emblem for the world of Alexandrian scholarship.[24] Ion's self-description foreshadows a new world in more ways than one.

As for the 'many, fine *dianoiai* about Homer' on which Ion prides himself (530d2, cf. further below), a persistent strand in modern discussion of the *Ion* has sought to associate these with the ὑπόνοιαι ('under-meanings') of the Homeric text about which we hear in more than one other text of this period (Xenophon, *Smp.* 3.6, Plato, *R.* 2.378d6).[25] No doubt a rhapsode's or sophist's *dianoia* about Homer could take the form of elucidating an alleged *huponoia*, but there seems little reason to make the connection here. Whether or not it is likely that Ion's *dianoiai* are to be imagined as reaching any great level of intellectual sophistication or ingenuity may be debated; much might hang on how seriously we are to take Ion's claims to outdo such sophisticated interpreters as Metrodorus and Stesimbrotus (530c8–9). In Xenophon's *Symposium*, which seems to have some intertextual relation to the *Ion*,[26] Socrates explicitly associates rhapsodes and their stupidity with ignorance of the ὑπόνοιαι (3.6), and — with every allowance for the joking spirit of these exchanges — this at least does not en-

---

[23] Ion's words about the labour involved in being an interpreter of poetry find an instructive analogy, from the point of view of the poet, in Aristophanes' description of the first version of *Clouds* as the comedy which παρέσχε μοι/ἔργον πλεῖστον (*Clouds* 523–524). I have discussed some relevant material for the later period in Hunter 2003a.
[24] *Suid.* φ 332 = Philitas, T1 Dettori, Sbardella; Ath. 9.401e = T5 Dettori = T7 Sbardella.
[25] For such a connection cf., e.g., Diller 1955, 175 n. 3, Flashar 1958, 25; the use made of this alleged connection by Struck 2004, 43, 67 seems to me particularly misleading.
[26] Cf., e.g., Méridier 1931, 25–26, Huss 1999, 215.

courage us to associate Ion with this type of criticism (whatever it was).[27] More importantly, however, the dialogue itself gives no reason either to think of Ion as an 'allegorist' or to regard the matter as important for the understanding of the text. We must, I think, content ourselves with the reflection that, although the poet's *dianoia* was almost universally held to be a single authorial 'meaning' or 'intention', regardless of the extent to which critics might disagree as to what that was, the *dianoiai* of critics and performers about the poet very likely covered a very wide range of both mode and sophistication.

Nevertheless, there is more to be said about Ion's claim at 530d2. The claim to speak 'many, fine *dianoiai* about Homer' is strikingly expressed and its oddity (which is often, I think, underrated) is clearly designed to call attention to itself. As, however, some scholars have seen, *dianoiai* is chosen to play off against Socrates' repeated (530b10, c4) stress upon the rhapsode's knowledge of the poet's *dianoia*; both the poet and his performers and critics have *dianoiai*. At one level, of course, Ion's smugness merely condemns itself: there is a clear implication that Ion is more interested in his own *dianoiai* than in Homer's.[28] Secondly, the plurality of Ion's *dianoiai*, when set against the singularity of the poet's *dianoia*, is something which will always set alarm-bells ringing in a Platonic context.[29] Thirdly, and most importantly, the use of the same word points to a fundamental methodological problem: when someone speaks a *dianoia* about Homer's *dianoia*, how are we to able to distinguish the two? Elsewhere,

---

27 Ford 2002, 70–71 suggests that Ion's 'stock of observations [...] consisted in improving observations on the wisdom to be found in Homer's poetry' (cf. already Verdenius 1943, 246–253), and Méridier 1931, 11 notes that 'son commentaire doit être une paraphrase élogieuse'. Velardi 1989, 31–36 makes the interesting suggestion that Lycurgus, *Against Leocrates* 102–104 is an example of the kind of ἔπαινος which a rhapsode might offer. Given the persistence of encomiastic themes over the centuries, I would be looking not just to Dio *Or*. 53 (cf. above p. 506), but also to Dio *Or*. 2, which, when set beside, e.g., the *Hippias Minor*, is an excellent illustration of that consistency. The young Alexander's fixation with Homer in fact mirrors Ion's: 'Why on earth, my son,' Philip asks him, 'are you so besotted with (ἐκπέπληξαι) Homer that you concern yourself (διατρίβεις, cf. *Ion* 530b8) with him alone of the poets?' (D. Chr. *Or*. 2.3). It is likely also that the dialogue itself contains some hints as to the sort of extra-textual commentary which is envisaged. One example may be 535c, where Ion's response to Socrates may be evidence that the language of poetic *enargeia*, and its link to the emotional effect of poetry (cf. esp. 'Longinus', *On the Sublime* 15.1–2), goes a very long way back.
28 Cf. Flashar 1958, 34.
29 Aristophanes uses the plural to mean 'witty conceit' (*Clouds* 944, *Peace* 750, *Wasps* 1044, *Ecl.* 581) or 'thoughts/ideas' (*Frogs* 1059). Ion's pride in the amount of what he can say perhaps looks forward to the misplaced pride of the Horatian 'boor' (*quis me scribere pluris /aut citius possit versus?*, *Satires* 1.9.23–24).

Plato's Socrates seems to abandon the whole business of poetic 'criticism' because the poem cannot speak for itself and the poet is not present to be questioned;[30] here the point is similar, but the complex use of *dianoia* allows us to see how Plato has anticipated the debate which racked much of twentieth-century scholarship on classical literature and still occasionally surfaces in apologetic footnotes: is there in fact such a thing as 'authorial meaning', or is meaning 'created at the point of reception/interpretation'? *hinc illae lacrimae* ... The basic distinction in Socrates' opening gambit between the 'words' and the 'thought' introduces, though hardly for the first time,[31] the principal distinction upon which all subsequent rhetorical and stylistic criticism is built: the Homeric scholia repeatedly distinguish between, on the one hand, σύνθεσις or κατασκευή and, on the other, διάνοια or νοήματα, and Aristotle (no doubt like Ion) thought that the *Iliad* and the *Odyssey* 'surpassed all epics in lexis and *dianoia*' (*Poetics* 1459b16).

The discussion of Simonides' poem for Scopas in the *Protagoras* offers helpful confirmation of some of this analysis. Socrates introduces his long *epideixis* with the statement that he wishes to say 'what I think Simonides intends (διανοεῖσθαι) in this poem, if you want to test out how I stand, as you put it, in regard to verses (περὶ ἐπῶν)' (341e7–2a2). Socrates is here picking up Protagoras' opening gambit:

> I think, Socrates, that the greatest part of a man's *paideia* is to be clever in the matter of verses (περὶ ἐπῶν δεινὸν εἶναι). This means to be able to understand (συνιέναι) what the poets say and what has been composed well (ὀρθῶς) and what not, and to know how to make distinctions and, when questioned, to give an account.
>
> Plato, *Protagoras* 338e6–339a3

Here it is indeed the poet's 'meaning/intention' which is at stake, but when Socrates begins his exposition, the language slides: 'I shall attempt to explain to you what I think about this poem' (342a6–7). This may be no more than shorthand for '...what I think about Simonides' intention in this poem', for the fact that it is indeed Simonides' *dianoia* which is the object of the exposition is subsequently repeated (343c) and rounds off Socrates' speech (347a4–5) in a kind of simple ring-composition. Nevertheless, this speech, which in the terms of the *Ion* we could describe as a '*dianoia* concerning Simonides' or perhaps 'an *epideixis* containing many fine *dianoiai* concerning Simonides', is an example of

---

30 Cf. *Protagoras* 347e, *Hippias Minor* 365c8–d1.
31 Cf., e.g., *Phaedrus* 228d1–5. On this distinction in pre-Hellenistic texts cf., e.g., Halliwell 2000, 102.

the potential split between the *dianoia* of a poet and the *dianoia* of the critic; when Socrates has Simonides arguing for ideas which we recognise as quintessentially Socratic, such as that no one does wrong willingly (345d–e), the opportunities and dangers which still litter the path of literary scholarship lie plainly before our eyes.

The second description which Ion gives of his own activity points to a similar potential for confusion between poet and interpreter:

> It's certainly worth hearing, Socrates, how brilliantly I have embellished (κεκόσμηκα) Homer; I think that the Homeridai should crown me with a gold wreath.
> Plato, *Ion* 530d6–8

Whatever reference there may be here to the actual conduct of rhapsodic contests,[32] κοσμεῖν is another case where Ion's language picks up and re-directs that of Socrates (cf. 530b6). Ion's use of the verb has been variously interpreted,[33] but one thing that is clear is that κοσμεῖν, 'embellish, praise', is – like ἐπαινεῖν – a principal activity of poets, whether it be Pindar (cf. *Nemean* 6.46) or Homer himself, the ἀνδρῶν ἡρώων κοσμήτωρ, as the epitaph cited at the end of the *Certamen* calls him.[34] Ion's language here (for the first time in the dialogue) blurs the boundary between poet and rhapsode, thus suggesting again that the closely related boundary between poetry and exposition is not an easy one to draw. Between the poet and ourselves falls the shadow of the interpreter (ἑρμηνεύς). Is there in fact a way to the poet except through previous interpretation? We are all too familiar with the fact that literary interpretation (particularly of a text as 'central' as Homer) is, almost inevitably, interpretation of the body of interpretative material which has built up around a text over the centuries; there is, for example, a lot of modern writing about (ostensibly) Aeschylus' *Agamemnon* where one might justly wonder whether the subject is in fact the *Agamemnon* or rather Fraenkel or indeed Fraenkel's *Agamemnon*, and similar cases might easily be multiplied. Did Fraenkel 'embellish' Aeschylus? Ion

---

32 Victorious rhapsodes were no doubt crowned, but the image here may rather be of Homer as a victor in the games, or – perhaps rather – as a city which has been the subject of Ion's praises; the Homeridai thus play the role of the city's inhabitants who reward the encomiast. On the Homeridai cf. West 1999, Graziosi 2002, 208–217.

33 Cf. esp. Velardi 1989, 20–26. Boyd 1994, 115–121 offers an interesting account, partly based on the practices of Slavic bards, but his account seem to me to sit uncomfortably with the actual context in the *Ion*, where the act of *kosmein* is closely connected to 'uttering *dianoiai*'.

34 For various expressions of this idea cf., e.g., Plato, *Phaedrus* 245a4–5, Isocrates, *Panegyricus* 159, Dio 33.11, 55.9 (Homer 'embellished' his poetry with similes), [Plutarch] *De Homero* 2.216. Cf. further Graziosi 2002, 36.

claims to offer us a richer 'Homeric' experience than we would get by listening to another reciter or interpreter or simply picking up the text and reading it for ourselves; again, the whole history of literary scholarship lies before us.

One of the things which sets the *Ion* apart from other Platonic discussions of poetry and its performance is the focus on the person of the interpreter and his relation with the poet, to the exclusion of more 'communal' concerns. Thus, for example, in *Republic* 10 Socrates proscribes the Homeric poems from the ideal city in terms which may well make us think of Ion:

> Thus, Glaucon, when you come across admirers (ἐπαινέται) of Homer who say that this poet educated Greece and that for the management and education of human affairs one should take up and learn (μανθάνειν) his poems and lead the whole of one's life in accordance with this poet, you would be friendly and welcoming to these people as they are as virtuous as possible, and you would agree that Homer is the best poet of all and first among the tragedians; you would, however, know that the only poetry which is to be received into the city are hymns to the gods and encomia to good men.
>
> Plato, *Republic* 10.606e–607a

No doubt Ion would agree with these ἐπαινέται, a word which Socrates also uses of Ion himself (536d2, 542b3),[35] and Ion might well have said such things in his imagined *epideixeis*, but, for what it is worth, the *Ion* has almost nothing to say about the importance of Homeric poetry and its interpretation for the health of society or the education of individuals, and certainly nothing to say, either in seriousness or jest, about Homer's beneficial and/or educational effects on his fellow men. What is principally at stake in the *Ion*, at least from Ion's perspective is, if you like, what Ion can do for Homer (and *vice versa*), not what Ion can do for those around him. Moreover, when Ion's effect on his audience is at issue, it is the non-rational, emotional effect of his performances, their ψυχαγωγία, which is cited (535d8–e9), not any educational effect they might have (their ὠφέλεια); it was, of course, for the subsequent tradition (and perhaps already for Gorgias) precisely to find a beneficial educational effect within this emotional response. For Ion himself, however, Homer fills the rôle of the beautiful in the *Symposium*; when Ion is in the presence of (discussion about) Homer he 'floods and gives birth and procreates' (*Symposium* 206d4–5), whereas when any other poet is at issue 'he curls up and turns away' and has nothing to say. The persistent language of εὐπορεῖν and ἀπορεῖν throughout the *Ion* (536c7 etc.) encourages this analogy.

---

35 On this term cf. Velardi 1989, 31–36.

There is a great deal in the *Ion*, as also, for example, in the *Hippias Minor*, which with hindsight can be seen to foreshadow aspects of later literary scholarship, but I will conclude with what is perhaps the most important of all. The second half of the dialogue explores the 'technical' qualifications of the rhapsode/interpreter; Socrates is concerned with who is the correct judge of whether material in the poems has been 'well' (ὀρθῶς or καλῶς) made. From the point of view of later scholarship, there are two important (and related) aspects to this. First, Ion is made to admit that 'experts' in particular crafts are better judges of 'technical' material in Homer than are rhapsodes; the *technai* from which Socrates draws his Homeric material are prophecy and seercraft, arithmetic, medicine, charioteering, fishing, and generalship. The parallel and partly overlapping list of arts imparted by a knowledge of Homer in a jokingly sympotic passage at Xenophon, *Symposium* 4.6–7 (economics, public speaking, generalship, kingship, charioteering and medicine) suggests that claims for such Homeric omniscience were nothing new. Be that as it may, the arts listed in the *Ion*, however unsurprising, recur time and again in scholiastic and other discussions of Homeric knowledge in the subsequent scholarly and educational traditions. In one speech, for example, Dio singles out Homer's guidance in matters of 'prudence and generalship and seercraft' (5.5.19) and [Plutarch], *De Homero* ticks off (*inter alia*) Homeric arithmetic (2.1.45–46), generalship (2.1.92–97), medicine (2.200–211) and seercraft (2.212).[36] When Socrates asks 'whether it belongs to the halieutic or the rhapsodic art to judge whether [the fishing simile at *Iliad* 24.80–82] is well (καλῶς) said or not' (538d4–5), the answer seems, as Ion admits, to be obvious. Nevertheless, the question of the 'rightness' of these verses was indeed soon to fall within the scholarly realm and attracted the attention of Aristarchus, who did not (as far as we know) feel the need to ask a fisherman about the problem.[37] The work on Homeric culture on which Athenaeus draws extensively in Book 1 claims that Homer's knowledge of the *technê* of fishing was more exact than that of the many authors of poems and treatises on the subject (1.13b). Here again, the *Ion* obliquely points the path which later scholarship was to follow.

Secondly, we must consider one of Ion's fall-back positions:

> *Socrates*: I have selected for you from both the *Odyssey* and the *Iliad* parts which belong to the prophet and the doctor and the fisherman; since you are more experienced in the Ho-

---

[36] For generalship also, e.g., Philodemus, *On the Good King According to Homer* col. xxv Dorandi.
[37] Cf. Plutarch, *Moralia* 976f. and the texts gathered by Erbse under the Homeric scholia to *Il.* 24.81.

meric poems than I am, you, Ion, must select what belongs to the rhapsode and the rhapsodic craft, i.e. what it is fitting for the rhapsode to examine and judge in front of all other men. *Ion*: Well, Socrates, the answer is 'everything'.

Plato, *Ion* 539d5–e6

Ion's answer should make most modern commentators on ancient texts squirm with embarrassment, but more important in the present context is the fact that Socrates' challenge was the defining one for the history of literary scholarship: the answer to the 'just what is it you are expert in?' question developed slowly, but develop it did, and the answer is perhaps most clearly on view in the Homeric scholia. The expertise was basically linguistic, but it also depended on a sense, owed importantly to Aristotle, that the ὀρθότης of poetry needed to be understood on its own terms: when a poem was ὀρθῶς πεποιημένον, this did not necessarily mean that it was 'technically accurate' in every detail, as Socrates' cross-examination of *Ion* might lead one to believe necessary. When Protagoras gets Socrates to admit that a poem with internal inconsistency cannot be 'well (καλῶς) made' (*Protagoras* 339b10–12), we glimpse the possibility of a path forward to a mode of interpretation in which 'truth' and consistency may not be the highest criteria; so too, when in *Republic* 10 Socrates tells Glaucon that, until they have been offered a valid defence of the value of poetry, they will not 'concern themselves seriously (σπουδαστέον) with such poetry as though it had a share of truth and was a serious matter' (608a6–7), we can with hindsight see how the challenge to find the appropriately σπουδαῖον in poetry was ultimately met. The discussion of 'technical knowledge' in the *Ion* is one further Platonic challenge where the terms of the argument were re-framed and the status of poetry thus re-affirmed. If it is, again, Strabo's discussion of Homer and his critics in Book 1 which offers perhaps our best compendium of this new sense of poetic ὀρθότης, then the view found in Philodemus that the διάνοια of poetry lies between that of the σοφοί and that of the χυδαῖοι (*On Poems* 5, col. xxvi Mangoni) seems not very far in the future, when viewed from the perspective of the *Ion*. As critics have noted, Ion's desperate recourse at 540b to the notion of τὸ πρέπον in fact points to a central theme of later literary scholarship, and this paragraph alone should have been sufficient to guarantee the *Ion* a place in the history of scholarship,[38] but the Socrates of this dialogue chooses not to pursue the rhapsode's lead.

---

[38] Of particular interest here is the later view, attacked by Philodemus, that diction appropriate to each character is a distinguishing characteristic of good poetry, cf. Philodemus, *On Poems* 5, col. xxxv Mangoni, Asmis 1992, 410–412.

Despite its apparent inconsequentiality, the *Ion* remains a foundational text for the history of scholarship, for it maps the terrain where men such as Ion walked, directs attention to the uncharted territory which ancient literary scholarship eventually colonised, and poses what should still be awkward questions for the commentator who takes his or her job seriously.[39]

Bibliography

Asmis, E. 1992. 'An Epicurean Survey of Poetic Thories (Philodemus, *On Poems* 5, cols. 26–36)', *CQ* 42, 395–415.
Boyd, T. 1994. 'Where Ion stood, what Ion sang', *HSCPh* 96, 109–121.
Capuccino, C. 2005. *Filosofi e rapsodi*, Bologna.
Diller, H. 1955. 'Probleme des platonischen *Ion*', *Hermes* 83, 171–187.
Ferrari, G. 2003. 'Plato and poetry', in: G.A. Kennedy (ed.), *The Cambridge History of Literary Criticism*, vol. I: *Classical Criticism*, Cambridge, 92–148.
Flashar, H. 1958. *Der Dialog Ion als Zeugnis platonischer Philosophie*, Berlin.
Ford, A. 2002. *The Origins of Criticism*, Princeton.
Graziosi, B. 2002. *Inventing Homer*, Cambridge.
Halliwell, S. 2000. 'The Subjection of Muthos to Logos: Plato's Citations of the Poets', *CQ* 50, 94–112.
Hunter, R. 2003. 'Reflecting on Writing and Culture. Theocritus and the Style of Cultural Change', in: H. Yunis (ed.), *Written Texts and the Rise of Literate Culture in Ancient Greece*, Cambridge, 213–234 (= Hunter, R. 2008, *On Coming After. Studies in Post-Classical Greek Literature and its Reception*, Berlin/New York, 434–456).
Huss, B. 1999. *Xenophons Symposion. Ein Kommentar*, Stuttgart/Leipzig.
Méridier, L. 1931. *Platon. Oeuvres completes V.1*, Paris.
Most, G.W. 1986. 'Pindar, *O.* 2.83–90', *CQ* 36, 304–316.
Murray, P. 1996. *Plato, On Poetry*, Cambridge.
Nagy, G. 2002. *Plato's Rhapsody and Homer's Music*, Washington.
Pfeiffer, R. 1968. *History of Classical Scholarship. From the Beginnings to the End of the Hellenistic Age*, Oxford.
Richardson, N. 1975. 'Homeric Professors in the Age of the Sophists', *PCPhS* 21, 65–81.
Rijksbaron, A. 2007. *Plato, Ion or: On the Iliad*, Leiden.
Struck, P. 2004. *Birth of the Symbol: Ancient Readers at the Limits of their Texts*, Princeton.
Velardi, R. 1989. *Enthousiasmòs. Possessione rituale e teoria della communicazione poetica in Platone*, Rome.
Verdenius, W.J. 1943. 'L '*Ion* de Platon', *Mnemosyne* 11, 233–262.
West, M.L. 1999. 'The invention of Homer', *CQ* 49, 364–382.

---

[39] I am grateful to Nicholas Denyer for his comments on an earlier version of this essay.

Yunis, H. 2003. 'Writing for Reading: Thucydides, Plato, and the Emergence of the Critical Reader', in: H. Yunis (ed.), *Written Texts and the Rise of Literate Culture in Ancient Greece*, Cambridge, 189–212.

29 Attic Comedy in the Rhetorical and Moralising Traditions

For later writers Attic comedy was very 'good to think with'. Not only was it a poetic form where striking change over time could be traced and variously explained, but it could also be used to explore issues of continuing and always contemporary significance, such as the limits of free speech, the role of public criticism, and the relationship between individual and society, a theme as prominent in Aristophanes' *Acharnians* as in Menander's *Dyscolus*. This chapter offers three brief, but I hope exemplary, soundings into these later traditions. All concern how comedy and its history were understood and used in the public and private relations of the educated classes of the Hellenistic and Roman worlds. The depiction of character and the relationship between dramatic representations and real or idealized life, the extent to which New Comedy was constructed as reinforcing the humane ideals of an educated elite, and the actual effect of Old Comedy satire upon those who were satirized are themes which were far from having merely historical interest for men who were very conscious of the varying roles each of them played every day; 'life' itself was staged in public, and the dangers of unconvincing performance were very real.

'O Menander and life ...'

One of the most familiar (and most misused) ancient judgements about Menander is transmitted to us by the fifth century CE rhetorician and philosopher Syrianus, in his commentary on the treatise *On Issues* (Περὶ τῶν στάσεων) of Hermogenes of Tarsus, one of the greatest rhetoricians of the imperial period (late second/early third century).[1] Hermogenes begins his discussion by listing the different ways in which people may be designated and how those designations provide a basis for rhetorical argument from them; the fourth category is τὰ ἠθικά ('terms denoting character'), 'such as farmers, gluttons and such like' (29.18–19 Rabe). Syrianus' comment on this is as follows:

> Fourthly, terms denoting character such as farmers, gluttons and such like. The avaricious (φιλάργυροι), the difficult (δύσκολοι). He calls terms denoting character all those which offer the speaker material for confirmation or attack from character alone: thus farmers

---

[1] The best collections of ancient views on comedy are the *Prolegomena* in Koster 1975 and the *testimonia* for individual poets in *PCG*; Quadlbauer 1960 remains a useful, if superficial, survey.

are generally solitary and hard-working and prefer the anti-social life, and the avaricious are penny-pinching and have their eye constantly only on profit, and the gluttonous are ready to do anything at all for pleasure. Menander (T 83) imitated life best of all and all his plots are filled with such characters; for this reason the grammarian Aristophanes (T 7 Slater) hit the mark exactly with the well-known verse he composed about him:

ὦ Μένανδρε καὶ βίε,
πότερος ἄρ' ὑμῶν πότερον ἀπεμιμήσατο;

'O Menander and life, which of you imitated the other?'
   Syrianus, *Commentary on Hermogenes* 22.24–23.11 Rabe

Aristophanes of Byzantium (late third-early second century BCE) versified and varied a contemporary theory which saw comedy as an 'imitation of life',[2] and pressed home the point by making the trimeter about imitation almost as rhythmically 'unpoetic' as possible (with three resolutions in the first two metra). What is, however, too often forgotten about this testimonium is that, whatever Aristophanes meant by his praise, Syrianus sees Menander's supreme imitation of life as rooted in the representation of 'characters', and they are characters who conform, according to Syrianus, to familiar, generalizable patterns; if they are not quite 'stock characters', they are certainly representatives of 'types'. Syrianus' pattern of argument is in fact the heir of both dramatic and rhetorical traditions, which fed off, and nourished, each other from at least the fourth century BCE on.

Aristotle bequeathed to the ancient rhetorical tradition a pattern of generalizing about the 'character traits' of men of different ages and fortunes (*Rhetoric* 2.1388b–1391b); orators and declaimers found such patterns very useful, for the more closely one's account of someone's behaviour fitted the expected pattern, the more convincing the account. Moreover, thoughts of 'character' immediately evoked the idea of comedy and *vice versa*. That comedy was the dramatic genre of 'character' (*êthos*), as tragedy was that of *pathos*, became a commonplace of criticism (cf., e.g., Quintilian 6.2.20); the corresponding distinction in epic was between the 'characterful' *Odyssey* and the 'pathetic' *Iliad* (Aristotle *Poetics* 1459b14, 'Longinus' *On the Sublime* 9.15 etc.).[3] Menander himself was

---

2 Cf. Cicero quoted by *Prolegomena* XXVI 1–3 Koster; Pfeiffer (1968) 190–192. On Aristophanes' praise of Menander see also Halliwell 2002, 286f.
3 Cf. further Russell 1964, 99. 'Longinus' is probably referring principally, not to the 'events' on Ithaca, but to the cast of characters which, when viewed in a particular light, have a distinctly 'comic' feel: the rustic (Eumaeus), the young son (Telemachus), the wife (Penelope), the

heir to this way of thinking and, in turn, encouraged it. The titles of very many plays of both Middle and New Comedy suggest comedies about 'characters', and at least for New Comedy we may guess that it was the probably universal pattern of comic prologues, most notably divine prologues, which encouraged a view of comic characters as 'types'; prologues give direction to a play and to the way in which an audience views it. In Menander's *Aspis* the prologizing god Tyche describes Smicrines as follows:

> He surpasses absolutely everyone in villainy. He recognizes no one as friend or relation, and doesn't give a damn whether anything is disgraceful, but he wants to have everything; that's all he cares about. He lives alone, with one old serving-woman.
>
> Menander, *Aspis* 116–121

Here precisely is Syrianus' 'avaricious man' (cf. *Aspis* 123, 149) with his single focus in life (*Aspis* 120 ~ Syrianus 23.4 Rabe). So too, Pan's prologue in the *Dyscolus* introduces us to Cnemon, one of those 'who can farm the rocks at Phyle' (*Dyscolus* 3f.), where life is 'toilsome (ἐπίπονος, cf. Syrianus 23.2 Rabe) and tough' (*Dyscolus* 21); Cnemon is both 'quarrelsome' (δύσκολος) and a farmer who is 'solitary and hard-working and prefer[s] the anti-social life'.[4]

It is the Euripides of Aristophanes who first intimates a 'cast list' for plays in terms of social status and family relationship:

> From the very first verses I would leave no one idle, but the wife and the slave spoke like everyone else, and so did the master and the young maiden and the old woman.
>
> Aristophanes, *Frogs* 948–950

The comic Euripides' point is that his plays allowed everyone, not just 'heroic males', to speak, for this was 'democratic' (*Frogs* 952), but — particularly as we look back from the perspective of subsequent developments — his assertion goes closely together with his immediately following claim that he introduced into tragedy 'everyday matters (οἰκεῖα πράγματα), the kind of things we are familiar with and which are parts of our lives' (*Frogs* 959),[5] the βιολογούμενα which 'Longinus' (9.15) was subsequently to find in the *Odyssey*.

Such 'everyday matters' are not things 'which happened' but which 'might have happened', they are 'imitative of life' (rather than being 'life itself'), and as

---

master (Odysseus), even the old woman (Eurycleia), and of course what binds them together is a 'recognition'.

4 Alciphron's *Letters of Farmers* is one of the best pieces of evidence for the influence of comedy on such rhetorical literature in this regard.

5 I have discussed various aspects of this comic claim in Hunter 2009, 18–25.

such they both foreshadow the historical development of comedy and the later scholarly account which saw in comedy 'fictions of events drawn from life' (πλάσματα βιωτικῶν πραγμάτων: *Prolegomena* XVIIIb 1.9–10, 2.10 Koster). As for the Euripidean cast of characters itself, this looks forward to how later comedy was to be described and evoked, particularly, though not exclusively (cf. Satyrus cited below), in Roman literature:[6] 'the wife' looks forward to the *matronae* (cf. Terence *Eunuchus* 37); 'the slave' to perhaps the hallmark character of comedy (cf., e.g., Terence *Eunuchus* 36 and 39, *Heauton Timoroumenos* 37, Ovid *Amores* 1.15.17); 'the master' to the *senes* and *duri patres* (cf., e.g., Terence *Eunuchus* 39, *Heauton Timoroumenos* 37, Ovid *Amores* 1.15.17); and although 'virgins' are not common speaking characters in comedy (cf. Menander *Dyscolus* 189–213), they were central of course to the way in which comic plots were imagined (cf., e.g., Manilius *Astronomica* 5.472 *raptasque in amore puellas*).[7]

It is, of course, no surprise to find the (comic) Euripides as an influential figure in the shaping of traditions about comedy, for the link between Euripides and New Comedy is a commonplace of both ancient and modern discussion, one given particular notoriety by Nietzsche in *The Birth of Tragedy*. In the dialogic *Life of Euripides* by Satyrus (late third/early second century BCE) a speaker traces a clear line of descent from Euripides to comedy:

[? quarrels between husband] and wife, and father and son, and slave and master, or as far as concerns crucial events (*peripeteiai*), the rape of virgins, suppositious children, recognitions by means of rings and necklaces; these are the very stuff of more recent Comedy (τὴν νεωτέραν κωμῳδίαν), and it was Euripides who brought them to fullness, though they began with Homer[8]

Satyrus, *Life of Euripides* fr. 39 col. VII Schorn = Euripides T 137 Kannicht

This theory of the genesis of important elements of later comedy very likely goes back to the heyday of Alexandrian scholarship,[9] but as we have seen we may

---

[6] It may be argued that Roman representations of Menander assimilate him somewhat to the nature of Roman comedy and thus, from a modern perspective, rather misrepresent (cf., e.g., Fantham 1984, 302f.), but that 'misrepresentation' is itself very instructive. Apuleius' description of the comedy of Philemon (*Florida* 16 = Philemon T 7) is a very good example of how the virtues of New Comedy were conceived within a very standard pattern.

[7] At *Frogs* 957f. the comic Euripides claims to have taught the Athenians, *inter alia*, 'loving (ἐρᾶν), scheming, to suspect trouble'; most editors (for good reasons) consider ἐρᾶν corrupt, but it is at least worth noting the apparent parallel at Terence *Eunuchus* 39f. describing the 'typical' plots of comedy: *falli per seruom senem / amare odisse suspicari*.

[8] I follow most editors, though not Schorn, in assuming a lacuna after the reference to Homer.

[9] Cf., e.g., Nesselrath 1993. For 'recognitions' as the *telos* of comedy cf. *Prolegomena* XVIIIb 2.8–9, 3.9 Koster.

trace its origins further back than that, and indeed to comedy itself. Later criticism too came very close to tracing this genetic argument to comedy itself. In one of the best-known ancient assessments of Menander, Quintilian notes that Menander himself acknowledged his admiration for Euripides and imitated him:

> As he often testifies, Menander admired Euripides greatly and imitated him, though in a different genre. In my judgement at least, a careful reading of Menander would suffice to produce all the virtues I am recommending: he fashioned so complete an image of life, there is in him such fullness of invention and fluency of expression, so completely is he adapted to every circumstance, character and emotion.
> Quintilian 10.1.69 = Menander T 101

Menander's 'testimony' (*testatur*) to his admiration for Euripides is presumably a reference to places in the comedies where characters explicitly quote from Euripides (cf., e.g., *Aspis* 424–8),[10] but what is important in the present context is that here too we find the very close link between the 'imitation of life' and the presentation of 'characters'. Moreover, Quintilian's concern is literature which will be of benefit to the orator and here too he is able to draw on a very long critical tradition about Euripides and Menander. What was in the *Frogs* the endless 'chattering' of Euripidean tragedy became for subsequent ages, particularly for the educated elite, an enviable rhetorical skill from which the aspiring orator could learn much;[11] one of Satyrus' speakers noted that 'in his speeches Euripides regularly spoke in accordance with the rules of rhetoric' (fr.1 Schorn = T 184 Kannicht) and, as Quintilian notes (10.1.70), Menander not infrequently included judicial debates or speeches in his plays. Of the scenes which Quintilian cites, the one which is best known to us, the arbitration scene from *Men at Arbitration*, in fact evokes a Euripidean model within a play which everywhere reveals a very sophisticated and knowing sense of theatrical history and theatrical convention.[12] Here too ancient dramatic criticism is seen to be the heir of the 'criticism' internal to drama itself.

There was another way too in which Euripides and Menander could be drawn together. In his recommendation of the two dramatists to those who wished to train themselves in political oratory, Dio Chrysostom (18.6–7 = Me-

---

10 Cf. Satyrus, *Life of Euripides loc. cit.* (= Philemon fr. 153) where verses in praise of Euripides, spoken (presumably) by a character in one of Philemon's plays, are introduced as 'Philemon too bears witness (μαρτυρεῖ) to this.'
11 Cf. Hunter 2009, 39–48 on Dio 52.
12 Cf., e.g., Hunter 1985, 134–6.

nander T 102) adduces now familiar praise of Menander's powers of character portrayal, but he also anticipates criticism from the σοφώτεροι that he has preferred Menander to 'Old Comedy' and Euripides to 'the old tragedians'. It might surprise us to see the history of tragedy and comedy placed on this structurally equal footing, as though the close critical linkage between Euripides and Menander had worked back into the past to fashion an 'Old Tragedy' and a 'New Tragedy' on the pattern of 'Old Comedy' and 'New Comedy', but both poets could indeed be seen to stand at the end of a long development and to be the high point of that development; after both of them, on this model, the respective genres declined. That they seemed so close in other ways would merely confirm the structural parallel.

Dio defends his choice of 'the new' over 'the old' by an analogy: 'doctors do not prescribe the richest (πολυτελεστάτας) dietary regimes to those in need of treatment, but the ones which are beneficial'. The adjective refers not simply to price, for these are diets which are 'rich', with the implication of 'elaborate', 'varied', 'luxurious', and hence – by a familiar principle of ancient (and modern) dietetics – unhealthy.[13] A play of Menander is structurally and rhythmically much 'simpler' than a play of Aristophanes; the most obvious difference of course lies in the predominance in Menander of the iambic trimeter and the absence of the chorus – it is this which makes Menander a 'plain diet'. So too, the language of Menander is uniform in a way in which the extraordinary linguistic range of an Aristophanes is not. Dio is not really attacking Old Comedy, but is merely concerned with what will be the most beneficial reading for the budding *pepaideumenos*. The differences, however, between the 'forcefulness' (δεινότης) of Old Comedy and the realism and grace of Menander to which Dio points could, of course, be expressed much more negatively, and this is precisely what we do find in a number of places in Plutarch, most notably in the extant epitome of the *Comparison of Aristophanes and Menander* and in the *Sympotic Questions*; for Plutarch, Aristophanic comedy poses a threat to the political and social values of the educated elite which he (Plutarch) represents.[14] What for Dio is the 'rich diet' of Aristophanes is for Plutarch the disturbing 'unevenness' (ἀνωμαλία) of Old Comedy; the point is made particularly explicit with regard to language:

---

13 The point is rather misunderstood by Garzya 1959, 245f.
14 Cf. Hunter 2009, 78–89; the existence of that discussion precludes detailed treatment of the *Comparison* here.

Aristophanes' diction contains the tragic, the comic, the pretentious, the prosaic, unclarity, ambiguity, grandeur and elevation, idle chatter and sickening nonsense. Despite all these differences and unevennesses, his style does not even assign what is appropriate and fitting to each kind.
>
> Plutarch, *Comparison of Aristophanes and Menander* 853c–d

Menander's language, by contrast, is 'mingled' into a perfect unity (853d–e).[15]

Comedy for an elite

Plutarch's concern in *Sympotic Questions* 7.8 is with entertainment suitable for symposia, though there is of course a wider critical agenda in play as well (as the *Comparison* makes very clear).[16] The lack of decency and order (*kosmos*) which Plutarch sees everywhere in Old Comedy offers particular dangers for men enjoying their wine, and it is the elite symposium which has, for Plutarch, replaced the theatre as the proper arena for the enjoyment of 'literature'. Such social occasions always contain within themselves the danger that they will degenerate into drunken brawling (or worse). The danger is very clear in Plutarch's description of Old Comedy:

> There is in the so-called parabases a quite untempered (ἄκρατος) and intense seriousness and outspokenness, and in its tolerance of jokes and buffoonery it is appallingly surfeited (κατάκορος) and openly shameless and stuffed full (γέμουσα) of phrases which lack decency (κόσμος) and of outrageous (ἀκολάστων) words.
>
> Plutarch, *Sympotic Questions* 711f–712a[17]

For Plutarch the parabases present a particular danger because there the non-elite citizen body is directly addressed and invited to laugh at 'the great and the good'.[18] Moreover, Plutarch's language precisely evokes the 'unmixed' wine and

---

15 At 712d of *Sympotic Questions* 7.8 Plutarch refers to the 'enjoyable and smooth' style (τὸ τερπνὸν καὶ γλαφυρόν) of Menander's plays, and a comparison of what he has to say about Menandrean style both there and in the *Comparison* with Dionysius of Halicarnassus' account of the γλαφυρὰ σύνθεσις (*De comp. verb.* 23) is instructive; the latter too is characterized by words which blend and fit together so that no part stands out from any other.
16 *Sympotic Questions* 7.8 has been much discussed, cf., e.g., Gilula 1987, Aguilar 1997, Imperio 2004b, and my account inevitably overlaps to some extent with earlier accounts.
17 Very similar language is used at *Sympotic Questions* 712e of 'mimes called *paignia*, which should not be seen even by the slave boys who fetch our shoes'; the parallel is very telling for Plutarch's attitudes.
18 Cf. 'Platonius' I 39–41 Koster, who explicitly associates the parabases with radical democracy.

excess which would indeed lead to brawling and which is a symbol of the very antithesis of the elite symposium; the point is reinforced by an echo of a passage of Plato's *Phaedrus* in which Socrates retails the disgust of the *erōmenos* at the way his lover talks about him:

> the lover's reproaches are intolerable when he [the lover] is sober, but when he gets drunk (εἰς μέθην ἰόντος) and speaks with excessive and unrestrained freedom (παρρησίαι κατακορεῖ καὶ ἀναπεπταμένηι χρωμένου) they bring disgrace as well as being intolerable.
>
> Plato, *Phaedrus* 240e4–7

The echo evokes an image not only of disgusting drunkenness, which ruins the fellowship of a symposium,[19] but also of paederasty in its least attractive form, and the absence of paederasty from Menander (in contrast, we must suppose, to Old Comedy) is to be noted by Plutarch in the immediately following section of the 'question' (712c).

According to a well-known set of linguistic and iconographic images, the symposium was a 'sea voyage', with the symposiasts as sailors.[20] Plutarch alludes to the idea as he turns from the excesses of Old Comedy to Menander's appropriateness for the symposium:

> What objection could anyone make to New Comedy [as sympotic entertainment]? It is so blended (ἐγκέκραται) into symposia, that we could steer (διακυβερνῆσαι) the drinking-party more easily without wine than without Menander.
>
> Plutarch, *Sympotic Questions* 712b

Drinkers, like sailors, need to reach the calmness of harbour without the potentially destructive storms which Old Comedy threatens to stir up; a symposium, like a sea-voyage, can turn out well or ill. Menander's comedy brings its characters and its audience back safely to familiar calm waters; the thrust of this comedy is restorative, not radical.[21] The pattern of this movement is (again) picked up from the plays themselves. In the *Aspis*, the prologizing Tyche describes the state of the characters at the beginning of the play as 'wandering in a state of ignorance' (99); it is precisely from such a 'wandering' state, like sailors adrift on the sea, that the goddess will intervene to save them and restore them to

---

19 Somewhere behind these images may lie the proposal in Aristotle's *Politics* 'that younger men should not be in the audience for iambic verses or comedy until they have reached an age to share in common meals and serious drinking (μέθη) and they will be protected by their education (*paideia*) from the harmful effects of such things' (7.1336b20–23).
20 Slater 1976 remains the fundamental starting point.
21 Cf. the remarks of Knox 1979, 266f. on comedy and the inheritance from Euripides' *Ion*.

knowledge and a state of social acceptability. In Old Comedy as we know it, however, it is as often radical change, not restoration, which is established by the end of the play, or at least restoration may operate on a large and communal scale (*Acharnians*, *Frogs*, perhaps *Knights*).

Often, of course, in Menander restoration takes the form of the familiar calmness of marriage. Plutarch calls attention to marriage as a common ending for the plays, in which social norms are restored: 'rapes of virgins regularly end in marriage' (712c). He also establishes 'marriage' as the proper end for the audience, and one which the plays themselves promote:

> Love affairs in Menander are appropriate for men who have drunk and will shortly be going off to sleep with their wives; for there is no paederasty in these plays and rapes of virgins regularly end in marriage.
>
> Plutarch, *Sympotic Questions* 712c

The plays thus confirm the institution of marriage and the mutual fidelity of man and wife; the point is made by an obvious allusion to the end of Xenophon's *Symposium* in which the arousing and (relatively) sexually explicit pantomime of Dionysus and Ariadne makes 'the symposiasts who were not married swear that they would marry, and those who were married mount their horses and ride off to enjoy their wives' (Xenophon, *Symposium* 9.7). Xenophon here may also seem to be promoting marital love – the pantomime after all showed Dionysus and Ariadne on their 'wedding night' – but the allusion points a contrast between a mime which arouses the symposiasts physically and a play of Menander, which contains no scenes remotely like the kissing and embracing of Dionysus and Ariadne, and which privileges marriage as a social institution for the procreation of legitimate citizens (cf. *Dyscolus* 842f., *Misoumenos* 444f., *Samia* 726f.), not as an opportunity for pleasurable sex.[22]

Another reason why Plutarch considers Aristophanes unsuitable as entertainment at symposia is the arcane nature of much of his subject matter:

> Moreover, just as at official dinners a wine-steward stands beside each guest, so it would be necessary for each guest to have a grammarian to explain each allusion who is Laispodias in Eupolis (fr. 107) and Kinesias in Plato (fr. 200) and Lampon in Cratinus (fr. 62) and everyone mocked in comedy (τῶν κωμῳδουμένων ἕκαστος), so that our symposium would become a schoolroom or the jokes would be senseless and without meaning.
>
> Plutarch, *Sympotic Questions* 712a

---

22 For other aspects of this passage, cf. Brown 1990 with earlier bibliography.

Plutarch conjures up the world, not just of the schoolroom,[23] but also of the scholarly and scholiastic industry which had flourished since Alexandrian times, but — at least as far as Old Comedy is concerned — enjoyed a particular flowering in Plutarch's time and subsequently; of the examples he cites, our knowledge of Laispodias does indeed derive primarily from an Aristophanic scholium, and Plutarch's allusion to the scholarly activity of drawing up explanatory lists of 'those mocked in comedy' finds its echo in Athenaeus 8.344e, our source for Cratinus fr. 62, which clearly draws upon such lists.[24] The educated elite naturally loved to display their learning and *paideia* at symposia, but the kind of 'professional', curiously — in their view — banal, detailed[25] learning necessary to explain an arcane name in Old Comedy is not what they prided themselves upon; here is one measure of the difference between the symposia which Plutarch envisages and the discussions which Athenaeus dramatizes. Such scholarship was much less needed, and much less practised, in the case of Menander and New Comedy in general, in which allusions to real contemporary figures are very rare,[26] and in which the 'pleasant and prosaic' style (712b) was readily accessible to all and needed no constant glossing. To what extent this openness of Menandrian comedy, the fact that it did not need the attentive protection of scholars, contributed to the disappearance of texts we can only surmise.

What Menander did offer was plays based around ethical issues, and the enjoyment of Menander was therefore truly connected to the study of philosophy

---

23 The fourth-century CE rhetorician Libanius tells us that, when a young man, he was stunned by lightning one day as '[he] was standing beside my seated teacher (γραμματιστής) and reading the *Acharnians* of Aristophanes' (*Or.* 1.9). Plutarch reverses the hierarchy of teacher and pupil.

24 For such lists cf. Steinhausen 1910. Aristophanes is not included in Plutarch's examples, although he is almost an inevitable fixture on lists of the chief poets of Old Comedy. Perhaps he is excluded as being the best known and most familiar of the Old Comedy poets: as Plutarch wishes to stress the obscurity of Old Comedy, he chooses poets who really do belong to scholars. The vast majority of fragments of Cratinus do indeed come from scholia, lexica and Athenaeus.

25 The distaste in the repetition ἑκάστωι τὸ καθ' ἕκαστον ἐξηγεῖσθαι at 712a is almost audible. One thinks of Aristotle's distinction between generalizing poetry, on the one hand, and history, on the other, which deals in the details (τὰ καθ' ἕκαστον) of individual historical figures ('what Alcibiades [or Laispodias or Kinesias or Lampon, we might add] did or suffered'); it is the former which is 'more philosophical and more serious' (*Poetics* 1451b4–11). So too, Old Comedy, like 'iambic', may be characterized by 'real' names for its characters, whereas later comedy uses typical, generic names (*Poetics* 1451b11–15, Antiphanes fr. 189).

26 Cf. Hunter 1985, 13 with n. 31.

and the cultivation of 'human sympathy' (τὸ φιλάνθρωπον), which was what really mattered to men like Plutarch:[27]

> Valuable and simple (ἀφελεῖς) maxims[28] penetrate the mind and, with wine acting like fire, they soften even the hardest characters and work them into more reasonable shape (πρὸς τὸ ἐπιεικέστερον).
>
> Plutarch, *Sympotic Questions* 712c

Such maxims require no 'commentary'; they penetrate us imperceptibly (ὑπορρέουσαι), unlike Old Comedy with its insistent obscurities which call attention to themselves and demand interpretation. In his account of 'simplicity' (ἀφέλεια), Hermogenes notes that 'simple thoughts' are thoughts 'which are common to all men and occur to everyone, or seem to, and contain nothing deep or intricate' (322.6–8 Rabe), and although Hermogenes has in mind the speech of such as rustics, women and children (for which he says one could find myriad examples in Menander, 323.23–324.2 Rabe), his discussion can shed light on what Plutarch wants to highlight in Menander.

If the humour of Aristophanes was, in Plutarch's view, vulgar and crude, his grace and wit (χάριτες) are in fact a prominent motif of the ancient critical tradition; an epigram, very improbably ascribed to Plato, records that the Graces established a shrine to themselves in his soul (Ar. T 130).[29] One element of this 'grace' was a quality of his language and that of Old Comedy generally; Quintilian (10.1.65) asserts that Old Comedy was almost alone in retaining the 'pure grace of the Attic language' (*sinceram illam sermonis Attici gratiam*). The two elements are mutually reinforcing because 'Attica' itself was renowned, particularly by the Romans, as the home of graceful wit.[30] Praise of the 'Attic' quality of a writer carries of course a particular charge in the period of the Second Sophistic, both because of the general stress in education at all levels upon 'the Attic classics', and because of the purifying 'Atticist' linguistic movement. Rather later, Eunapius virtually describes the fourth-century orator Libanius of Antioch as a reincarnation of Aristophanes:

---

27 Cf. also *Comparison* 854b–c.
28 Here too Euripides and Menander stood together in the critical tradition, cf. Quintilian 10.1.68 on Euripides *sententiis densus*, though Plutarch's point is rather different from Quintilian's. On Menander's *gnômai* see also Aelius Theon, *Progymnasmata* 91.13–25 (citing fr. 255) and 92.15–22 (citing fr. 129).
29 Cf. Ussher 1977, 74f.
30 Cf. Otto 1890, 44.

> His writings are full of wit (χάρις) and comic ribaldry (κωμική βωμολοχία) and elegance (κομψότης) runs over the whole... [He has] what the people of Attica call a sharp nose (μυκτήρ) and urbane wit (ἀστεισμός); he cultivated this as the peak of culture (παιδεία), drawing entirely for his style upon the ancient comedy.
>
> Eunapius, *Lives of the Philosophers* 496 = XVI.2 Giangrande

Quintilian's praise of the language of Old Comedy is also very close to a report of the *Praeparatio sophistica* of the Atticist lexicographer Phrynichus (late second century CE); the Byzantine patriarch Photius (Ar. T 69)[31] reports that Phrynichus included Aristophanes among those writers who were 'models and rules of the genuine and pure and Attic language' (εἰλικρινοῦς καὶ καθαροῦ καὶ Ἀττικοῦ λόγου). For Menander's language, on the other hand, Phrynichus had nothing but contempt (Menander T 119), and here again we may wonder whether Atticist scruples counted against the survival of the greatest figure of New Comedy.

Old Comedy transformed

If the frankness and 'vulgarity' of Old Comedy could, when necessary, be dismissed as unworthy of the attention of an educated man, allusions to the works of Aristophanes and his fellow poets abound in the Greek prose texts of the Roman empire; the 'idea' of Old Comedy was in fact a potent and attractive one. Lucian, for example, repeatedly drew inspiration for his satire from Old Comedy, and moralists found appeal to the critical nature of Old Comedy a helpfully authorizing analogy for their own activity. Thus, for example, in criticizing the frivolity and addiction to low entertainment of the people of Alexandria, Dio Chrysostom urges them to imitate the Athenians 'who allowed their poets to reprove not just individuals, but the city as a whole, if they behaved in any way inappropriately' (32.6); so too, in the rather similar *First Tarsian Oration* (cf. below), Dio (33.44) claims that some of his audience will say that he is insulting (ὑβρίζειν) their city, just as in the parabasis of the *Acharnians* Aristophanes claims that Cleon falsely accused him of 'mocking (κωμῳδεῖν) our city and insulting (καθυβρίζειν) the people' (*Acharnians* 631). On the contrary, Dio's speeches will make men 'stronger and more sensible and better able to administer their cities' (32.7); here indeed is the claim of the Aristophanic parabasis (cf., e.g., *Acharnians* 650) and the only thing that Aeschylus and Euripides can agree on in the *Frogs*:

---

31 Cf. also T 88–89.

Aeschylus. Tell me, for what should a poet be admired?
Euripides. For cleverness and the advice he gives, because we make men in their cities better.

Aristophanes, Frogs 1008–1010

Dio makes a rather more complex use of the model of Old Comedy in *Oration* 33 in which he takes to task the people of Tarsus for the mysterious, and presumably immoral, practice of 'snorting' (ῥέγχειν).[32] The speech is characterized throughout by a witty and allusive tone which sets it squarely within more than one tradition of satirical writing, but Old Comedy is never far away. Dio begins by contrasting himself with the ordinary, run-of-the mill speakers who deceive the audience with empty and commonplace encomium of the city, its surrounding countryside and people (cf. also chapter 23); the strategy is itself commonplace, but we may recall again the parabasis of *Acharnians* in which the chorus claim that the poet has worked much benefit in stopping the citizens from being deceived and taking pleasure in empty flattery, such as when ambassadors from the allied cities proclaim Athens 'violet-crowned' or 'shining' (both standard poetic epithets) (*Acharnians* 633–642). In chapter 9, Dio then introduces the standard paradigm of Athenian willingness to put up with the criticism of Old Comedy, though this criticism is now significantly called 'abuse' (λοιδορία); this paradigm is, moreover, no longer straightforwardly positive, as it is contrasted with the Athenian unwillingness to put up with the criticisms of Socrates, though the philosopher was carrying out 'the god's instruction' and also not performing any vulgar dance such as the *kordax*. The criticism of Old Comedy is now presented as anything but an unmixed blessing:

> The comic poets viewed the *dêmos* with suspicion and feared it, so they flattered it like a master (δεσπότης), only biting gently and with a smile; it was like wetnurses who smear honey around the edge of the cup when their young charges have to drink something unpleasant.[33] So it was that the comic poets did as much harm as good, for they filled the city with arrogant pride and jests and vulgar knockabout (βωμολοχία).

Dio Chrysostom 33.10

---

[32] On this speech see especially Bost Pouderon 2006; brief accounts in Desideri 1978, 122–129, Jones 1978, 73–75; and Swain 1996, 214–216; cf. also Bonner 1942.

[33] The closeness to Lucretius 1.936–938 is, of course, noteworthy, but of particular interest in the present context is Horace, *Satires* 1.1.23–26, where Horace seems, as in *Satires* 1.4, to reject the charge of *bômolochia*, and to compare one satirical technique ('telling the truth with a laugh') to teachers who reward children with cakes so that they will learn the alphabet. Given Horace's later claims in 1.4 for the genetic relationship of Old Comedy and Roman satire, the closeness to Dio 33.10 deserves more attention than it has received.

Old Comedy did have a serious purpose, but it was so hedged around with comic byplay to make the *dêmos* laugh that the effect was at best mixed. Dio's view of Old Comedy here overturns its own claims by drawing material from it. The picture of the poets 'flattering' the *dêmos* clearly looks to Aristophanes' *Knights*, the whole of which might be described as a contest in flattery of Demos. Like Dio's audiences (or so Dio claims), the Aristophanic Demos 'enjoys being flattered' and 'all men fear [him] like a tyrant' (*Knights* 1111–1120).[34]

Dio has a second alternative to Old Comedy, alongside Socrates, to brandish as his model in this speech. This is Archilochus, all of whose poetry is (according to Dio) devoted to attacking men's faults and who was very greatly honoured by Apollo. Archilochus thus becomes the spiritual ancestor of the 'Cynic preacher' such as Dio, not least in the fact that he censured himself; such a man will offer no 'flattery or deceit' (chapter 14). By implication, both Archilochus and the Cynic (lit. 'dog-like') Dio carry a real 'bite' (cf. 16, 44), not the 'gentle biting' of Old Comedy (10, above).[35] Dio's preaching is thus one descendant of Archilochus' abusive poetry, as in some ancient theory was Old Comedy also. Aristotle sees in Old Comedy the inheritance of iambic (*Poetics* 1449a4, 1449b8), and later theory made the abuse (λοιδορία) of Cratinus, in particular, heir to the Parian poet (*Proleg.* II 1–2 Koster = Cratinus T 17).[36] This may simply be a result of the fact that Cratinus wrote an Ἀρχίλοχοι ('Archilochus and his colleagues'), but it is quite likely that that play did indeed create some kind of analogy between Cratinus' comedy and Archilochus' abusive poetry, and it was that analogy which in part lies behind the later critical tradition. As is very clear from, for example, Horace's treatment of the links between comedy and Roman satire in *Satires* 1.4,[37] the constructions of ancient literary history were flexible tools to be adapted to the rhetorical demands of different situations; no one will challenge the 'historicity' of Dio's account. Dio is, moreover, in part disingenuous: laughter, such as greeted Old Comedy, is one response which he seeks, and satirical denunciation may, in antiquity no less than now, 'flatter' the object of the attack and actually strengthen the hold of the practices denounced. It may indeed be that Dio's attack upon Tarsian 'snorting' is more aligned with the 'innuendo' (ὑπόνοια) which Aristotle saw as a feature of 'new comedies' and of the 'educated man' (*pepaideumenos*), which Dio certainly claims to be, than with the 'blunt

---

34 Cf. also *Wasps* 620–630.
35 Callimachus fr. 380 Pf. paints a probably negative picture of Archilochus' angry bite.
36 Cf. Perusino 1989, 64–66 and Bakola 2010, 4f., 17f. and 70–79.
37 Cf. Hunter 2009, 99–106.

abuse' (αἰσχρολογία) of 'old comedies' and, we might add, of Archilochus as he was traditionally represented (*Nicomachean Ethics* 4.1128a20–24).[38]

Bibliography

Aguilar, R.M. 1997. 'Plutarco y la comedia ateniense', in: C. Schrader/V. Ramón/J. Vela (eds.), *Plutarco y la historia*, Zaragoza, 3–28.
Bakola, E. 2010. *Cratinus and the Art of Comedy*, Oxford.
Bonner, C. 1942. 'A Tarsian peculiarity (Dio Prus. *Or.* 33) with an unnoticed fragment of Porphyry', *Harvard Theological Review* 35, 1–11.
Bost Pouderon, C. 2006, *Dion Chrysostome. Trois discours aux villes (Orr. 33–35)*, Salerno.
Brown, M. 1990. 'Plots and prostitutes in Greek New Comedy', *Papers of the Leeds Latin Seminar* 6, 241–266.
Desideri, P. 1978. *Dione di Prusa*, Messina/Florence.
Fantham. E. 1984. 'Roman experience of Menander in the late republic and early empire', *Transactions of the American Philological Association* 114, 299–309.
Garzya, A. 1959. 'Menandro nel giudizo di tre retori del primo impero', *Rivista di Filologia Classica* 37, 237–252.
Gilula, D. 1987. 'Menander's comedies best with dessert and wine (Plut. *Mor.* 712e)', *Athenaeum* 55, 511–516.
Halliwell, S. 2002. *The Aesthetics of Mimesis: Ancient Texts and Modern Problems*, Princeton.
Hunter, R. 1985. *The New Comedy of Greece and Rome*, Cambridge.
Hunter, R. 2009. *Critical Moments in Classical Literature: Studies in the Ancient View of Literature and its Uses*, Cambridge.
Imperio, O. 2004. 'I comici a simposio. Le *Quaestiones convivales* e la *Aristophanis et Menandri Comparatio* di Plutarcho', in: Gallo, I. (ed.), *La biblioteca di Plutarcho*, Naples, 185–196.
Jones, C.P. 1978. *The Roman World of Dio Chrysostom*, Cambridge.
Knox, B.M.W. 1979. *Word and Action. Essays on the Ancient Theater*, Baltimore/London.
Koster, W.J.W. 1975. *Scholia in Aristophanem Pars I*, Fasc. 1A: *Prolegomena de Comoedia*, Groningen.
Nervegna, S. 2013. *Menander in Antiquity: The Contexts of Reception*, Cambridge.
Nesselrath, H.-G. 1993. 'Parody and later Greek comedy', *Harvard Studies in Classical Philology* 95, 181–195.
Otto, A. 1890. *Die Sprichwörter und sprichwörtlichen Redensarten der Römer*, Leipzig.
Perusino, F. 1989. *Platonio: la commedia greca*, Urbino.
Pfeiffer, R. 1968. *History of Classical Scholarship from the Beginnings to the End of the Hellenistic Age*, Oxford.
Quadlbauer, F. 1960. 'Die Dichter der griechischen Komödie im literarischen Urteil der Antike', *Wiener Studien* 73, 40–82.

---

[38] Cf. 33.32, 'If I am unable clearly to explain what this fault is, you should try to work it out (ὑπονοεῖν)'; contrast the proclaimed clarity (34.5) of the *Second Tarsian Oration*, perhaps in deliberate contrast with the manner of the *First*.

Russell, D.A. 1964. *'Longinus': On the Sublime*, Oxford.
Slater, W.J. 1976. 'Symposium at sea', *Harvard Studies in Classical Philology* 80, 161–170.
Steinhausen, J. 1910. *Kômôidoumenoi*, Diss. Bonn.
Swain, S. 1996. *Hellenism and Empire*, Oxford.
Ussher, R.G. 1977. 'Old Comedy and "character": some comments', *Greece and Rome* 24, 71–79.
Van Steen, G.A.H. 2000. *Venom in Verse: Aristophanes in Modern Greece*, Princeton.

30 'Clever about Verses'?: Plato and the 'Scopas Ode' (*PMG* 542 = 260 Poltera)

In 1978 Matthew Dickie declared that 'there is... little that is new left to say about [the ode to Scopas]', but that does not seem to have stopped people from trying.[1] One reason for that, apart from the importance of the subject and the intellectual pleasure that difficult puzzles bring with them, is that the Scopas Ode and the Platonic discussion of it serve as interesting examples of, and offer rich material for, certain critical tendencies in the modern Academy. In his still seminal treatment of the poem, Wilamowitz noted 'we [i.e. modern scholars] take it as self-evident that a poem has a single correct interpretation and one that can be demonstrated to be so. But Plato did not believe that...'.[2] We may smile knowingly at what seemed self-evident a century ago, but so much of the more recent discussion of Simonides' poem has been precisely as Wilamowitz said — an attempt to pin down a single meaning for it. This, of course, is in one sense what Socrates in the *Protagoras* is doing also, namely finding a meaning for the poem which makes sense to him; modern scholars on the whole differ from Socrates (in this matter) principally in that the 'message' of the poem for which they search and which they reconstruct is not (necessarily) one to which they themselves subscribe — enough to believe that Simonides subscribed to it. Plato may, however, have chosen a poem which was already known to be open to interpretative disagreement, as one reading of Socrates' rejection of the whole business of poetic interpretation at 347c–e might indeed suggest. Be that as it may, the fact that Hippias observes, as soon as Socrates has finished his account of the poem, that he (Hippias) too has a 'splendid *logos* about this poem' (347b1) does not, at the very least, inspire confidence that *we* will find it easy to reach agreement. Fortunately, however, despite such uncertainty, there is very much to discuss.

The brief exploration of Socrates' 'discussion of Simonides' poem falls into three parts. Section 1 considers the overall shape of the discussion and the rela-

---

I am grateful to the participants at the Cambridge conference for helpful discussion, to Richard Rawles for his comments on a subsequent version, and to Andrew Ford for allowing me to see an unpublished paper, now published as Ford 2014, on the Scopas ode.

[1] Dickie 1978, 21. The large bibliography on the poem can be most easily accessed through Poltera's edition, Giuliano 1991, and Ledbetter 2003, 100 n. 2. Brittain 2017 is a close analysis of Socrates' argument.
[2] Wilamowitz 1913, 167.

tionship between the practices of the Seven Sages which Socrates conjures up and his own debate with Protagoras; the various critical techniques which Socrates employs and which strikingly foreshadow the critical and grammatical practices of later ages will be briefly reviewed. Section 2 looks in greater detail at Socrates' account of the opening of the poem, in the light of Adam Beresford's radical suggestion concerning the poem's structure. It is in the discussion of how the poem begins that Socrates moves beyond critical techniques to wrestle with how poetry 'refers' both to other texts and to the world beyond the text. Finally, I raise the question of why, when Plato devotes so much attention to this poem on an ethical subject, he gives so little space elsewhere to the archaic elegy to which Simonides' poem seems so closely related. It is likely that the answer will be connected to how Plato saw his own position with regard to earlier 'wise men', such as both Simonides and Protagoras.

1

It is a *Leitmotif* of recent discussion of the 'Scopas ode' that Plato is responsible for an earlier modern misunderstanding, namely that the poem is περὶ ἀρετῆς, 'about virtue', whereas really the poem appears to be about praise and blame and the position of the poet in conferring these. In fact, of course, the matter is much more nuanced than that.[3] Certainly, Socrates does repeatedly insist that the whole poem is directed against Pittacus' γνώμη that it is 'difficult to be good' (343c3–5, 344b4–5, 345c–d, 347a2–3), and this might well be thought to put ἀρετή at the centre of the poem; in introducing the ability to discuss poetry as the most important mark of education, however, Protagoras says that his question to Socrates will be on that subject, namely ἀρετή, which they have just been discussing, 'transferred to poetry' (339a4–5). In fact what they have been discussing is what Protagoras can offer his pupils and indeed 'whether virtue is teachable' (320c1, 328c3–4); Simonides' poem, at least as Plato allows us to reconstruct it, turns out to fit that bill as much as any other. Protagoras' earlier reference to Hesiod as one of the 'early sophists' (316d7) and Socrates' later allusion to the Hesiodic path to ἀρετή (340c–d) to some extent construct the *Works and Days* also as a poem which demonstrates what ἀρετή is and that it is teachable. Plato perhaps wants us to understand that the test which Protagoras sets Socrates was a standard one in his lectures (or at least of a standard kind), designed to demonstrate both his own δεινότης περὶ ἐπῶν (338e7–8) and the

---

3 Helpful remarks in Rawles 2018, 65–66.

fact that by attending to those lectures his pupils will indeed learn things about ἀρετή. That it is 'hard to be good' (or is it?) would certainly have been of interest to anyone considering the nature of what Protagoras had to offer.

One of our problems in interpreting this scene of the *Protagoras* is, in fact, our natural desire to know how 'realistic' Plato's scene is. This is not just wanting to learn about the literary criticism of the second half of the fifth century (though it is that too) — would we be able to recognize deliberate archaizing in the discussion, if Plato had indeed inserted such phenomena? — but it is also an important textual effect in Plato's marvellously vivid writing. We would of course dearly love to know whether the real Protagoras ever discussed the 'Scopas-ode', and — if he had — what Plato's first audience knew of that discussion; but we are, of course, unlikely ever to know either of those things.[4] Still it is Plato who makes us want to know and who exploits our hunger for 'the real' in his writing. It has been argued that the applause which greets Protagoras' demonstration of inconsistency in Simonides' poem (339d10) suggests that this idea had never occurred to anyone before,[5] but 'fans' are known (even today) to applaud performances which they have heard many times over, and Socrates' description of his dazed reaction to Protagoras, 'I felt as though I had been hit by a skilled boxer, my eyes clouded over and my head spun' (339e1–2), has as good a claim as almost anything in Plato not just to be ironic, but to be marked as such. It might of course be that we are to understand that Socrates really was discomposed to be confronted with a problem which had never occurred to him in a poem which he had just claimed to know well (339b5–6), but it also might not... What we can say is that vv. 1–3 and 11–13 are all we get from Protagoras. The rest of the poem is cited and paraphrased by Socrates, and we might be intended to understand that the Platonic Protagoras at least is actually surprised to have the rest of the poem thrown back at him. When at 339b4 Protagoras asks Socrates 'Do you know this poem, or shall I go through the whole thing for you?', he is surely expecting 'yes' to the first half of his question (Plato thus suggests that the poem was, at some level, a well known one)[6] and 'no' to the second half: who, after all, however little they knew of poetry, would be foolhardy enough to admit to ignorance of a poem of Simonides when confronted face-to-face by the great Protagoras, particularly when he has just announced

---

4 Giuliano 1991, 126–130 argues that what Protagoras does to the poem of Simonides was in fact quite close to the kinds of critical performance staged by the real Protagoras.
5 Cf. Babut 1975, 31–32.
6 Just how well known, either in the second half of the fifth century or the time of Plato, may be debated; for some general considerations, cf. Ford 2020.

that knowledge about poetry is a supreme mark of education? Protagoras' opening question can thus be seen as a (practised?) move to wrongfoot any interlocutor; he will have been as surprised as we are by Socrates' subsequent willingness to offer an account of the whole poem: this is not at all what he had in mind when he began by noting that the educated man will be able 'when questioned [about well and ill made poems] to give an account (*logos*)' (339a3), but a *logos* is precisely what he gets from Socrates. In an important discussion, Glenn Most has identified Socrates' detailed contextualization of the poem as an important hermeneutic step forward, one utterly opposed to Protagoras' mode of finding inconsistencies between what we might wish to call fragments,[7] but we must acknowledge that that critical novelty is indeed scripted into Plato's drama.

Whereas we are hard pressed to find anything comparable in classical literature to Socrates' *logos* (cf. further below), Protagoras' demonstration of contradiction in Simonides is indeed a standard kind of 'problem' or ζήτημα, and would be instantly recognizable if transposed, say, to the Homeric scholia. It is, however, also another protreptic *epideixis* to set alongside his great speech from the earlier part of the dialogue, and we may thus compare both performances to Prodicus' 'Fable of Heracles', which is similarly protreptic, and presumably also similarly an advertisement for what the speaker can offer.[8] Prodicus' *epideixis* draws on Hesiod's famous verses on ἀρετή,[9] which Socrates brings together with Simonides' verses (340d). At *Rep.* 2.364e–d these Hesiodic verses are cited as the sort of things people use to avoid the hard path of virtue, with the upshot that it is in part the Hesiodic tradition against which Socrates is there made to argue, in defending the thesis that justice and virtue are to be pursued for their own sakes, regardless of what material and other benefits arise from them.[10] These Hesiodic verses are also reworked by Simonides in *PMG* 579 = fr. 257 Poltera, and it is at least worth asking whether Plato was the first to link them to *PMG* 542 (260 Poltera); I suspect not – but there is so much about the literary critical discussion of the late fifth century which we would like to know, and do not.[11]

---

[7] Most 1994. For foreshadowings of Most's argument cf., e.g., Babut 1975, 43–44, Giuliano 199, 149–150.
[8] Cf., e.g., Ford 2010, 150–151.
[9] On Prodicus' debt to Hesiod in general cf. Wolfsdorf 2008.
[10] Cf. Hunter 2008b.
[11] Mayhew 2011, 202 speculates that, in addition to his debt to Hesiod, Prodicus drew on the reworking (*PMG* 579 = fr. 257 Poltera) of those verses by his fellow Cean, Simonides, for his fable of Heracles.

We have already noted that Socrates' 'reading' of a whole poem (344b3–5) is a great rarity in antiquity; its closest relative may be the discussion of the Lysianic speech in the *Phaedrus*.[12] As for his individual critical techniques, these strikingly foreshadow the techniques of Alexandrian scholarship, but also presumably reflect techniques familiar both in Plato's day and earlier.[13] These include concern with inconsistency (339b–d),[14] dialect glosses as explanation of 'oddities' (341b–c), reference to what is in the typical manner of the poet (343e), grammatical tropes such as hyperbaton (343e),[15] arguments from punctuation and sense-breaks (346e, where Socrates uses διαλαμβάνειν for what is usually διαστέλλειν in later scholia) etc. It is of some interest that, in a well-known passage (*Mem.* 1.2.56), Xenophon claims that Socrates' accuser (Polycrates?) said that 'Socrates chose the most disgraceful passages from the best-known poets' and used them to teach immorality. The first example which Xenophon adduces, Hes. *Op.* 311 ἔργον δ' οὐδὲν ὄνειδος, ἀεργίη δέ τ' ὄνειδος, again involves taking together two words, ἔργον and οὐδέν, which plainly (we might have thought) do not belong together, and this construal is assumed both in the charge against Socrates and in Xenophon's defence of Socrates.[16] Neither here nor in the Hesiodic scholia, which follow the similar discussion of the verse in Plato's *Charmides*, is there any sense that ἔργον and οὐδέν belong together.[17] We seem here really quite close to the *Protagoras*.

One final possible example of Socrates' critical technique brings us again close to modern critical practices.[18] At 344d8 Socrates rather insouciantly cites a hexameter by 'another poet' to show that the ἐσθλός man may become κακός,

---

12 Note *Phdr.* 264e4 ~ *Prot.* 347c. Richard Rawles rightly reminds me that we must not forget the possibility that Socrates in fact only focuses on part of the poem, while claiming that his analysis of its structure and intention covers 'the whole'. Most scholars accept that we are missing a small section (cf. Section 2 below), but can we be utterly confident that there was not significantly more than Socrates quotes or alludes to?
13 Cf. Hunter 2012, 99 n. 194. For Socrates' analysis as a foreshadowing of philosophical exegesis, cf. Baltussen 2004.
14 Cf. Nünlist 2009, 11, 176 'Aristarchus repeatedly argues that one must not scrutinise poets like Homer too rigorously', and Index s.v. inconsistency.
15 Hyperbaton is one of the phenomena adduced by the author of the Derveni-commentary to support his interpretations, cf. col. VIII 6–11, Scodel 1986, 31–33.
16 Cf. Wolfsdorf 2008, 1–3, Graziosi 2010, 120–121, Hunter 2014, 208–215.
17 The words are, however, construed as moderns do by the T-scholium on *Iliad* 24.370.
18 The suggestion which follows has already appeared in Hunter 2017.

αὐτὰρ ἀνὴρ ἀγαθὸς τοτὲ μὲν κακός, ἄλλοτε δ' ἐσθλός

and a good man can be now bad, now noble

We might be tempted to think that this verse is simply too good to be true in the context of the *Protagoras* argument, were it not for the fact that Xenophon also cites this verse at *Mem.* 1.2.20, though he identifies the author merely as 'the poet who said...'; Xenophon there joins the citation of this verse to what we call Theognis 35–36, which are cited with equal anonymity.[19] Xenophon's argument at *Mem.* 1.2.20 is that bad company can breed bad character even in those who were good before, as witness Critias and Alcibiades. Whereas, however, the verses of Theognis (and their larger context which might have been in Xenophon's mind) fit his argument perfectly, the anonymous hexameter does not suit so well (admittedly, we do not know its original context, if it had one), though it is not utterly out of place. The context in Xenophon is not very far from that of the discussion of Simonides' poem in the *Protagoras* – the virtuous can lose their virtue, just as the good man can be subverted by ἀμήχανος συμφορά (to which I shall return) – and it might just be worth floating the idea that Xenophon has borrowed the verse from the *Protagoras* (there is at least nothing in what little we can say with confidence about the relative chronology to rule out the possibility), and – even worse, perhaps – that we are to understand that (the Platonic) Socrates composed the hexameter himself and inserted it into his *epideixis*, thus claiming a specious authority in 'poetic tradition'. Plato may or may not have fooled Xenophon. Be that as it may, there certainly is light parody here of the use of poetic authority in exposition and criticism, and we would do well to reflect upon what this instance might teach us about our own practice of citing 'parallels'.[20] The verse would in fact look like nothing so much as a verse of Hesiod, were it not for the fact that, although ἄλλοτε ... ἄλλοτε is extremely common in Hesiod, there appears to be not a single example of τοτὲ ... ἄλλοτε; for what it is worth, the majority of examples of this latter correlative pair in LSJ come from Plato himself.[21] However that may be, questions of

---

19 Xenophon cites these verses again and ascribes them to Theognis at *Symp.* 2.4; it may be relevant that there Socrates is speaking in a sympotic context, where citation and naming of Theognis, a sympotic poet *par excellence*, was very appropriate, whereas at *Mem.* 1.2.20 Xenophon is speaking in his own voice. On the citation at *Mem.* 1.2.20 cf. now Kurke 2011, 216–217.
20 For a helpful survey of some of the issues cf. Gibson 2002.
21 At *Mem.* 1.2.20 Hude adopts ὁτὲ μὲν ... ἄλλοτε in the anonymous hexameter from manuscript A; this, a Homeric pairing (though always strung across two verses, rather than within a

wisdom and authority are clearly at stake here, and this brings us to how the debate between Protagoras and Socrates is framed.

The general structuring of the debate between Protagoras and Socrates as a replay of, and challenge to, the exchanges of the Seven Sages is reasonably clear and has been very well discussed by Kathryn Morgan.[22] The wisest Greeks of the present day gather 'at the very *prytaneion* of wisdom' (337d4–6), just as – according to Socrates – (343b) the Seven Sages gathered at Delphi; 'the very *prytaneion* of wisdom' is readily explained as a description of Athens (cf., e.g., Denyer *ad loc.*), but it is hard not also to think of Delphi. The 'long speeches v βραχυλογία' debate (334c–8a) ends in a decision in favour of a middling third way, but it clearly aligns Socrates with the Sages who, he is to claim, favoured Laconian brevity, whereas Protagoras has presented himself as in the line of earlier sophists such as Homer, Hesiod and indeed Simonides (316d7), and he has very clearly placed himself on the side of lengthy speeches. Protagoras casts himself as in competition with the sophists of the past – a competition he will win, both because he openly declares his status as sophist and has nothing to hide, and because he is able to demonstrate incoherence in a well known work of one of them (Simonides' poem). His agonistic attitude to the poetry of the past stands in nice contrast with, for example, Parmenides' affectionate paraphrase of an ἐρωτικόν of Ibycus (*Parmenides* 137a = PMG 287), as one marker of Plato's two very different characterizations of great figures from the previous century. So too, Socrates accounts for Simonides' poem as a result of his φιλοτιμία (343c1), that quality which Protagoras has shown in abundance: according to Socrates, Simonides wanted to join the club of the σοφοί and the best way of doing this would be to 'overturn [Pittacus'] saying' (343c1), thus (presumably) taking Pittacus' place. We are perhaps almost encouraged to believe that each of the Sages had one saying and this was Pittacus' (cf. 343b6); perhaps each saying had to pass the test of all the Sages before it could win the ultimate acceptance of inscription at Delphi, like the pre-eminent pair of γνῶθι σαυτόν and μηδὲν ἄγαν.[23] The parallelism may be reinforced by the fact – which may or may not mean something and which may or not have been pointed out before – that there are in fact just seven contributors to the discussion at Callias' house: Cal-

---

single verse as here), would certainly be *lectio difficilior* as it involves lengthening the final syllable of ἀγαθός *in arsi*.

22 Morgan 2009; cf. also Trapp 1987, 47–48. Both of these discussions became known to me only after the first draft of this paper was complete.

23 Morgan 2009, 553 is perhaps misleading when she says that the ἀπαρχή of the Sages at Delphi 'included' γνῶθι σαυτόν and μηδὲν ἄγαν; rather, they were the ἀπαρχή (343b1–3).

lias, Alcibiades, Critias, Prodicus, Hippias, Socrates and Protagoras. There are, of course, many others present, including Hippocrates who got Socrates to go along (but does not speak once there), but at 336d5 Alcibiades says that 'each person' should express a view as to how the debate between Socrates and Protagoras should proceed, and it is indeed the five other named individuals who express their view. The charmed circle, then, numbers just seven. If there is anything to this, and perhaps even if there is not, it will bring us back to the old question of how innovative Socrates' account of the Seven Sages at 343a–b actually is. As is well known, Detlev Fehling argued that the list of seven here enters Greek culture for the first time, along with their association with gnomic wisdom, and that other early references to the seven, including *Ti.* 20d8, go back to the *Protagoras*.[24]

2

The actual reconstruction of Simonides fr. 260 Poltera (=*PMG* 542) has remained largely agreed, in all but smaller linguistic details, since Wilamowitz's discussion; here is Poltera's text and colometry:

ἄνδρ' ἀγαθὸν μὲν ἀλαθέως γενέσθαι
   χαλεπὸν χερσίν τε καὶ ποσὶ καὶ νόωι
τετράγωνον ἄνευ ψόγου τετυγμένον·
[
[
[
[
[
[
[

οὐδέ μοι ἐμμελέως τὸ Πιττάκειον   11
νέμεται, καίτοι σοφοῦ παρὰ φωτὸς εἰ-
   ρημένον· χαλεπὸν φάτ' ἐσθλὸν ἔμμεναι.
θεὸς ἂν μόνος τοῦτ' ἔχοι γέρας, ἄνδρα δ' οὐκ
   ἔστι μὴ οὐ κακὸν ἔμμεναι,   15
ὃν ἀμήχανος συμφορὰ καθέληι·
πράξας γὰρ εὖ πᾶς ἀνὴρ ἀγαθός,
κακὸς δ' εἰ κακῶς < - >

---

24 Fehling 1985, 13–15. Fehling's argument is rejected by Busine 2002, 33–34, though not for particularly good reasons.

ἐπὶ πλεῖστον δὲ καὶ] ἄριστοι
τούς κε οἱ θεοὶ φιλέωσιν. 20

τοὔνεκεν οὔ ποτ' ἐγὼ τὸ μὴ γενέσθαι
δυνατὸν διζήμενος κενεὰν ἐς ἄ-
πρακτον ἐλπίδα μοῖραν αἰῶνος βαλέω·
πανάμωμον ἄνθρωπον, εὐρυεδέος ὅσοι
    καρπὸν αἰνύμεθα χθονός· 25
ἐπὶ δή μιν εὑρὼν ἀπαγγελέω.
πάντας δ' ἐπαίνημι καὶ φιλέω,
ἑκὼν ὅστις ἔρδηι
μηδὲν αἰσχρόν· ἀνάγκαι δ'
οὐδὲ θεοὶ μάχονται. 30

[
[
[οὐ γὰρ εἰμὶ φιλόψογος ἐπεὶ ἔμοιγ' ἐξαρκεῖ]
ὃς ἂν ἦι κακὸς μηδ' ἄγαν ἀπάλαμνος εἰ-
    δώς γ' ὀνησίπολιν δίκαν, 35
ὑγιὴς ἀνήρ· οὐ < u - > ἐγὼ
μωμήσομαι· τῶν γὰρ ἀλιθίων
ἀπείρων γενέθλα.
πάντα τοι καλά, τοῖσί τ'
αἰσχρὰ μὴ μέμεικται.[25] 40

                              Simonides fr. 260 Poltera = *PMG* 542

As Poltera, however, rightly observed, Blass's idea that the fourth strophe should actually be the second is still worth pondering;[26] vv. 29–30 would cer-

---

25 Here is Poltera's text translated; I use D. A. Campbell's rendering as a basis and modify it where necessary: 'It is difficult for a man to be truly good, four-square in hands, in feet and in mind, fashioned without flaw... [*7 verses are missing*] || Nor does that saying of Pittacus ring true to me, although it was spoken by a wise man: he said that it was difficult to be good. Only a god could have that privilege: a man cannot avoid being bad, when he is the grip of irresistible misfortune. When his luck is good, any man is good; when it is bad he is bad [..., and for the most part even] the good are those whom the gods love || And so I shall never throw away my span of life on an empty, vain hope in quest of the impossible, the completely blameless man among all of us who win the fruit of the wide earth. When I find him I will report back to you. No, I commend and love any man who of his own will does nothing shameful: against necessity not even the gods fight || [*2 verses missing*] [I am not a fault-finder: I am satisfied with the man who is not bad] nor too shiftless, one who understands the justice that helps the city, a sound man. I shall not find fault with him; for the generation of fools is numberless. All things are fair in which the base is not mingled'.
26 Poltera 2008, 454–455. The metre of the poem has recently been reconsidered by Lidov 2010.

tainly make an effective ending for a poem, which is of course not to say that
this was in fact how the poem ended. Beyond that, the only radical alternative
since Wilamowitz to the now received text is that proposed by Adam Beresford.[27]
Beresford argued that we have, in fact, the whole poem and it was just three
stanzas long, rather than four, with — as in Blass' reconstruction — the poem
ending with our vv. 27–30:

ἄνδρ' ἀγαθὸν μὲν ἀλαθέως γενέσθαι
χαλεπὸν χερσίν τε καὶ ποσὶ καὶ νόωι
   τετράγωνον ἄνευ ψόγου τετυγμένον·
θεὸς ἂν μόνος τοῦτ' ἔχοι γέρας· ἄνδρα δ' οὐκ
   ἔστι μὴ οὐ κακὸν ἔμμεναι,   5
ὃν ἀμήχανος συμφορὰ καθέληι·
πράξας γὰρ εὖ πᾶς ἀνὴρ ἀγαθός,
κακὸς δ' εἰ κακῶς < οὓς
δ' οἱ θεοὶ φιλέωσιν
πλεῖστον, εἰσ' ἄριστοι. >   10

οὐδέ μοι ἐμμελέως τὸ Πιττάκειον
νέμεται, καίτοι σοφοῦ παρὰ φωτὸς εἰ-
   ρημένον· χαλεπὸν φάτ' ἐσθλὸν ἔμμεναι.
< ἐμοὶ ἀρκεῖ > μήτ' ἄγαν ἀπάλαμνος εἰ-
   δώς τ' ὀνησίπολιν δίκαν   15
ὑγιὴς ἀνήρ· οὐ μὴν ἐγὼ
μωμήσομαι· τῶν γὰρ ἠλιθίων
ἀπείρων γενέθλα.
πάντα τοι καλά, τοῖσιν
τ'αἰσχρὰ μὴ μέμεικται.   20

τοὔνεκεν οὔ ποτ' ἐγὼ τὸ μὴ γενέσθαι
δυνατὸν διζήμενος κενεὰν ἐς ἄ-
   πρακτον ἐλπίδα μοῖραν αἰῶνος βαλέω,
πανάμωμον ἄνθρωπον, εὐρυεδέος ὅσοι
   καρπὸν αἰνύμεθα χθονός·   25
ἐπὶ δ' ὕμμιν εὑρὼν ἀπαγγελέω.
πάντας δ' ἐπαίνημι καὶ φιλέω,
ἑκὼν ὅστις ἔρδηι
μηδὲν αἰσχρόν· ἀνάγκαι δ'
οὐδὲ θεοὶ μάχονται.[28]   30

---

27 Cf. Beresford 2008, 2009.
28 Here is the fragment in Beresford's translation (as it appears in his article), with his transpositions: 'For a man it's certainly hard to be truly good — perfect in hands, feet, and mind,

Bernd Manuwald replied at length to Beresford in 2010, and little would be served by a full review here of the very knotty arguments. I will, rather, be very selective, but there is a very important point with which to begin.

Beresford argues that we have no grounds for assuming any 'good faith' in Socrates in the order in which he cites the poem, even where there seem to be explicit references to the ordering ('moving on a little' etc, 339d3–4, 341e1, 344b6). Manuwald, however, countered that such snippets of information 'are not of themselves to be called into question, as many contemporary readers will have known the text, and Plato would have destroyed his credibility by giving false indications of the ordering of the bits of text he cites and he would have distracted attention from Socrates' interpretation'[29]. There are large and very interesting issues here, not just about Plato, but (again) about the reception of Simonides (and archaic lyric more generally) in the fourth century. How 'well known' the Scopas-ode actually was is, of course, an important issue for understanding the Platonic scene; moreover, the interest of the Platonic Socrates in the ordering of parts within a literary work, and whether that ordering matters, is very familiar from, above all, the *Phaedrus*. In considering the scene in the *Protagoras*, there is a 'How far can you go?' issue. Thus, for example, I am not aware that it has been suggested (or certainly not often suggested) that the 'missing verses' (if there were any) of the first stanza revealed that vv. 1–3 are in fact a citation of someone else's view or of popular belief and the poet does not agree with them, i.e. 'It's hard to be truly good, four-square etc … well, people say this, but they are wide of the mark… it's actually impossible'; there would, on such a scenario, be absolutely no contradiction with what the poet then says about Pittacus' saying, but the Platonic Protagoras would have played very fast and loose: how far *can* you go?

---

built without a single flaw; only a god can have that prize; but a man, there's no way he can help being bad when some crisis that he cannot deal with takes him down. Any man's good when he's doing well in life, bad when he's doing badly, and the best of us are those the gods love most. || But for me that saying of Pittacus doesn't quite ring true (even though he was a smart man): he says "being good is hard"; for me, a man's good enough as long as he's not too lawless, and has the sense of right that does cities good; a solid guy. I won't find fault with a man like that. After all, isn't there a limitless supply of fools? The way I see it, if there's no great shame in it, all's fair. || So I'm not going to throw away my dole of life on a vain, empty hope, searching for something there cannot be, a completely blameless man — at least not among us mortals who win our bread from the broad earth. (If I do find one, mind you, I'll be sure to let you know). So long as he does nothing shameful wilfully, I give my praise and love to any man. Not even the gods can fight necessity'.

29 Manuwald 2010, 12.

Secondly, Manuwald makes much of the fact that Beresford's reconstruction offers no place in the poem for naming the addressee, whereas in the traditional reconstruction that could easily have happened in the missing verses of the first strophe.³⁰ There is, again, more than one issue here. Plato makes Protagoras claim that 'Simonides somewhere says to Scopas the son of Kreon the Thessalian...', which is normally — and perfectly naturally — understood to imply that he goes on to quote from a poem explicitly addressed to Scopas. Manuwald claims that there is no reason to doubt Protagoras' claim, but the matter seems to me at least to deserve thought. Poltera, for example, follows those who believe that there was in fact no necessity for such a song to have had a named addressee, and — if this were in fact the case — it would be a nice touch if Protagoras, very conscious of his own status with the great and the good, wanted to make clear that Simonides, an earlier 'sophist', dealt merely with Thessalian princes, whereas he himself of course consorted with Athenians ... If Scopas was not named in the poem or it was not addressed to anyone in particular, then either the poem had somehow become associated with Scopas at an early date,³¹ or Protagoras himself will have chosen one of Simonides' Thessalian patrons, known from elsewhere, as a suitable recipient. The tone of 'to Scopas, the son of Kreon the Thessalian' (339a7) is in fact hard to catch. Plutarch reports an anecdote in which Simonides mocks Thessalians (presumably his Thessalian patrons) for being ἀμαθεῖς (*How to study poetry* 15c, where see Hunter-Russell *ad loc.*), and there is perhaps a suggestion in Theocritus 16 that the Skopadai were such nobodies that no one would ever have heard of them but for Simonides; Protagoras' recital of name, patronym, and geographical affiliation *may* drip with sarcasm, whether or not the details were in fact taken from the poem he goes on to cite. If Scopas was in fact named somewhere in the poem, it was perhaps indeed with a patronymic 'son of Kreon' rather than with his own name; we may compare the information given by the scholiast on Theocritus 16.36–7 (= *PMG* 529 = fr. 247 Poltera, and cf. Ath. 10.438c).

As to Beresford's reconstruction itself, let us first consider the opening verses. In the traditional version, τοῦτο γέρας in v. 14 is presumably 'being (considered) ἐσθλός' (v. 13). In Beresford's version we need not insist that it must be 'being a foursquare truly good *man* ... fashioned without reproach', because no god would want that *geras* ('prize, mark of honour'), so it must then be 'being foursquare truly good... fashioned without reproach'. Such a *geras* almost inevitably suggests Simonides' interest in statues and the relation between poetry

---

30 Manuwald 2010, 6–7.
31 This seems to be the scenario favoured by Poltera 2008, 455.

and art,[32] but I wonder whether Beresford's version does not necessitate separating to some extent ἄνδρα from ἀγαθόν in v. 1, as indeed in Beresford's own translation 'For a man it's certainly hard to be truly good ...', and this is (I think) the case whether we understand v. 1 as Protagoras and Socrates do, or as Ben Henry suggested (followed by Poltera), 'it is hard for a truly good man to come to be ...'.[33] It is very difficult to avoid taking ἄνδρ' ἀγαθόν together as a unit, and this of course is a common syntagm in, e.g., sympotic elegy. So too, it is at least open to question whether any archaic Greek poet would say what amounts to 'it is easy to be good' (provided that goodness is defined with suitably lax criteria), as Beresford must have Simonides saying (Beresford 2008, 244–245), although to ask for 'parallels' for such a thought risks missing the point of what may have in fact been a truly innovative sequence of thought. There is, however, a detailed point about the beginning which is worth pursuing at a little length.

In 343d–e Socrates discusses the initial μέν, with a marvellously eye-opening account of how a Greek might 'feel' such linguistic detail, even such an untypical Greek as the Platonic Socrates. Socrates' explanation might, incidentally, suggest one very good reason why Plato did not make him cite or allude to the rest of the first stanza, if indeed there was a rest of the first stanza; these verses would be missing, not because – as standardly asserted – they contained nothing relevant to Plato's discussion, but precisely because they did, namely a δέ (or some other responding particle) to answer the μέν, and that we could never have, because it would ruin the explanation which Socrates gives.[34] Behind that explanation we can also sense more than one contemporary strand of critical and rhetorical discussion. It was apparently standard rhetorical teaching, reflected in the fragments of Isocrates' τέχνη (fr. 22 Radermacher),[35] in the *Rhetoric to Alexander* (1435a38–35b5), and in Aristotle's *Rhetoric* (3.1407a20–30), that if one used an introductory particle, the corresponding particle should be also used and used within a very short space; both the *Rhetoric to Alexander* and Aristotle illustrate the matter by the need to follow μέν at a short distance by δέ. Why this is important, of course, is that this aids clarity (σαφήνεια) and comprehensibility; for this rhetorical tradition, in other words, a clear and 'correct' use of particles is a mark of good prose, and its opposite – obscurity in this, as in any aspect of writing – is a mark rather of poetry and

---

[32] Cf., e.g., Steiner 2001, 273–278. The reference to hands and feet certainly encourages such an association.
[33] Henry 1999; cf., however, Hutchinson 2001, 294–295.
[34] Cf. Poltera 2008, 460.
[35] Cf. Radermacher 1951, 157.

bad prose. The *Rhetoric to Alexander* interestingly places this rule alongside the need to avoid hyperbata and 'confused' word order, and in the *Rhetoric* Aristotle too places it in the same section as strictures against ambiguous word order, which makes sentences hard to punctuate, as in Heraclitus (*Rh* 3.1407b11–25).[36] It is not just that here (again) we may sense the importance of the *Protagoras* for later criticism, but we can also see how Plato makes Socrates home in on linguistic features (or alleged features) which, in contemporary discourse (contemporary to Plato, that is), characterize poetry and make discussion of it unhelpful for those engaged in serious matters; its obscurity resists intellectual progress (and, of course, you cannot question it to get the right answer).

Nevertheless, Socrates' discussion of the opening of the poem has its own interest, which goes in fact far beyond the narrow confines of contemporary rhetorical teaching (Pl. *Prot*.343c7–344a4):

εὐθὺς γὰρ τὸ πρῶτον τοῦ ἄισματος μανικὸν ἂν φανείη, εἰ βουλόμενος λέγειν ὅτι ἄνδρα ἀγαθὸν γενέσθαι χαλεπόν, ἔπειτα ἐνέβαλε τὸ 'μέν'. τοῦτο γὰρ οὐδὲ πρὸς ἕνα λόγον φαίνεται ἐμβεβλῆσθαι, ἐὰν μή τις ὑπολάβηι πρὸς τὸ τοῦ Πιττακοῦ ῥῆμα ὥσπερ ἐρίζοντα λέγειν τὸν Σιμωνίδην· λέγοντος τοῦ Πιττακοῦ ὅτι 'χαλεπὸν ἐσθλὸν ἔμμεναι', ἀμφισβητοῦντα εἰπεῖν ὅτι "οὔκ, ἀλλὰ γενέσθαι μὲν χαλεπὸν ἄνδρα ἀγαθόν ἐστιν, ὦ Πιττακέ, ὡς ἀληθῶς" – οὐκ ἀληθείαι ἀγαθόν, οὐκ ἐπὶ τούτωι λέγει τὴν ἀλήθειαν, ὡς ἄρα ὄντων τινῶν τῶν μὲν ὡς ἀληθῶς ἀγαθῶν, τῶν δὲ ἀγαθῶν μέν, οὐ μέντοι ἀληθῶς (εὔηθες γὰρ τοῦτό γε φανείη ἂν καὶ οὐ Σιμωνίδου), ἀλλ' ὑπερβατὸν δεῖ θεῖναι ἐν τῶι ἄισματι τὸ 'ἀλαθέως', οὑτωσί πως ὑπειπόντα τὸ τοῦ Πιττακοῦ, ὥσπερ ἂν εἰ θεῖμεν αὐτὸν λέγοντα τὸν Πιττακὸν καὶ Σιμωνίδην ἀποκρινόμενον εἰπόντα· "ὦ ἄνθρωποι, χαλεπὸν ἐσθλὸν ἔμμεναι", τὸν δὲ ἀποκρινόμενον ὅτι "ὦ Πιττακέ, οὐκ ἀληθῆ λέγεις· οὐ γὰρ εἶναι ἀλλὰ γενέσθαι μέν ἐστιν ἄνδρα ἀγαθὸν … χαλεπὸν ἀλαθέως".

Plato, *Protagoras* 343c7–344a4

The very beginning of the ode would seem to be crazy, if, when wanting to say that it is difficult for a man to become good, he inserted *men*. This insertion would appear to make no sense,[37] unless someone were to suppose that Simonides is speaking in dispute with the saying of Pittacus: when Pittacus says that 'it is difficult to be good', Simonides disagrees and says 'No, but to become a good man is *men* in truth difficult, Pittacus' – not truly good, for he does not mention truth in this connection, as though indeed there were some people who were truly good and others who were good, but not truly so – for this would be silly and not in the manner of Simonides. Rather, we must take 'truly' as a transposition (*huperbaton*) in the poem, and assume (ὑπειπόντα) Pittacus' saying in some such way as this, as if we were to imagine Pittacus himself speaking and Simonides answering: Pittacus says, 'Gentlemen, it is difficult to be good', and Simonides answers, 'Pit-

---

36 Cf. also Anon. Seg. 85 Dilts-Kennedy.
37 The meaning is here much disputed (cf. Denyer on 343d1–2).

tacus, you do not speak the truth: not to be but to become *men* a good man ... is truly difficult'.

Socrates seems to argue that the μέν, now made — if it was not before — *solitarium*, implies that something must have preceded;[38] for Socrates that of course is Pittacus' saying to which Simonides responds. This passage is the only instance in Plato of ὑπεῖπον: LSJ understand this example as 'suggest an explanation, hint, give a clue', which cannot be right, but LSJ s.v. 2 'say by way of preface, premise, suggest' seems closer to what is required here, and my 'assuming, prefacing it by' is a variation of this. Why this is important is that it is clear that, in line with his view of the *Tendenz* of the whole song, Socrates takes the opening of the song as an allusion to/expansion of Pittacus' saying, which is only explicitly quoted later; modern critics, however, have differed over whether Simonides' contemporary audience would inevitably hear Pittacus' saying behind the opening verses, before it was explicitly introduced, or whether this can only be a readjustment as the song proceeds or is heard for the second time. Be that as it may, Beresford, following Most, is clearly right that Socrates 'supplies a rich dialectal context for the opening of the song', but what is that context? According to Beresford:[39]

> [Socrates] claims that to understand the opening you have to imagine that Pittacus has just uttered his saying and that Simonides is answering it directly (343d1–6). He then says, again, that we have to assume that Simonides has "just mentioned" Pittacus' saying (ὑπειπόντα τὸ τοῦ Πιττακοῦ, 343e4). As if the opening lines were the second half of an exchange in which Pittacus' saying forms the first half (343e6) etc.

Leaving aside the question of whether ὑπειπόντα can bear the sense Beresford gives it, I think it is worth insisting that Socrates is not saying that there actually was an exchange, a face-to-face ἀγών if you like (as though — cf. Beresford's twice-used 'just' — Simonides lay in wait for Pittacus in his presence to repeat his *bon mot* and then responded in kind), but he is arguing that μέν evokes a piece of knowledge familiar to the audience *as if* (ὥσπερ 343d3, ὥσπερ ἂν εἰ 343e4) Simonides was responding to Pittacus. Particularly where Sages were concerned, the notion and imagery of contest and eristic exchange came naturally to any Greek (we have very many anecdotes precisely of such exchanges and repartee in which one poet or philosopher 'responds' to another), but Plato's Socrates is here rather struggling with such traditional forms to express a

---

38 Cf. Denyer on 343d1–2.
39 Beresford 2008, 249.

really quite sophisticated idea of how language refers in the abstract, *away from* particular performance contexts in the 'real world'. Wherever and whenever Simonides' poem is sung, Pittacus' saying is, according to Socrates, always activated for the audience, they will 'assume' it in their reception of the opening verses, regardless of where Simonides and Pittacus actually are. We have here a(nother) very important hermeneutic moment, one which looks forward in all kinds of ways to the history of modern debate about intertextuality, about how texts use and resonate with each other, and about the parameters of allusion. If that is the large (and much more interesting) picture, the narrow point is that Beresford (2008, 248–249) has not really demonstrated that when Socrates refers τοῦτο γέρας to Pittacus' saying (344c1–3), that is compatible with his (Beresford's) reconstruction, on the grounds (so Beresford) that, for Socrates, Pittacus' saying quite literally precedes the opening statement, in accordance with the idea of a face-to-face exchange.

3

In the final section of this paper I want to bring together, in a perhaps more accessible way than has been done before, those passages from the *corpus Theognideum* which seem close in thought to *PMG* 542 and which may, therefore, throw light upon it.[40] These passages will very likely be somewhat earlier than the Simonides, though perhaps not much earlier; if Simonides, *PMG* 542 has often been thought to be a sympotic performance, there can hardly be any doubt about the milieu of the *Theognidea*.

When Simonides says that no man can be πανάμωμος because, unlike gods, we are subject to the vicissitudes of fortune, he makes the labels κακός and ἀγαθός reflect social standing and power; we might make this plain by putting these words in vv. 17–18 in inverted commas to show that they are labels applied by society.[41] The standard, though not universal,[42] position in the Theognidean corpus, on the other hand, is that κακός and ἀγαθός are categories which are not dependent on status, wealth or power (cf., e.g., 315–318, 321–322, 430–431 ('no one has devised a way to make a fool wise and an *esthlos* out of a *kakos*'), 437–8 etc). The corpus in fact very strongly suggests that when Simoni-

---

40 Dickie 1978 has perhaps made the most fruitful use of elegy in considering Simonides' poem. González 2010 has a number of remarks about similarity of material between Simonides generally and the *corpus Theognideum*.
41 I am well aware that I am here being very dogmatic about a hotly disputed issue.
42 Cf., e.g., vv. 53–58.

des speaks of ἀμήχανος συμφορά overtaking someone (v. 16), he is above all thinking of poverty (cf. vv. 17–18), or we (and Scopas ?) should be.⁴³ At Theognis 383–399 poverty is the mother of ἀμηχανίη, which corrupts a man's moral sense and leads him into wicked action against his will (388, 391, cf. Simonides fr. 260.28 Poltera) by placing him κρατερῆς ὑπ' ἀνάγκης (387, cf. Simonides fr. 260.29–30 Poltera). The theme is recurrent in the collection:

> ἄνδρ' ἀγαθὸν πενίη πάντων δάμνησι μάλιστα,
> καὶ γήρως πολιοῦ, Κύρνε, καὶ ἠπιάλου·
> ἣν δὴ χρὴ φεύγοντα καὶ ἐς βαθυκήτεα πόντον
> ῥιπτεῖν καὶ πετρέων, Κύρνε, κατ' ἠλιβάτων.
> καὶ γὰρ ἀνὴρ πενίηι δεδμημένος οὔτε τι εἰπεῖν
> οὔθ' ἔρξαι δύναται, γλῶσσα δέ οἱ δέδεται.
>
> Theognis 173–178

Poverty, Cyrnus, overwhelms a man of worth more than anything else, including hoary age and fever. To escape from it, Cyrnus, you should throw yourself to the monsters of the sea or down from lofty cliffs. For in effect a man overwhelmed by poverty is powerless to say or accomplish anything, and his tongue is bound fast (trans. D.E. Gerber).

Unsurprisingly, the theme of change of 'good' for 'bad' when circumstances change (Simonides fr. 260.14–20 Poltera) is also found in Theognis:

> οὐδ' ὀμόσαι χρὴ τοῦθ', ὅτι 'μήποτε πρῆγμα τόδ' ἔσται'·
> θεοὶ γάρ τοι νεμεσῶσ', οἷσιν ἔπεστι τέλος·
> †καιπρῆξαι † μέντοι τι· καὶ ἐκ κακοῦ ἐσθλὸν ἔγεντο
> καὶ κακὸν ἐξ ἀγαθοῦ· καί τε πενιχρὸς ἀνήρ
> αἶψα μάλ' ἐπλούτησε, καὶ ὃς μάλα πολλὰ πέπαται
> ἐξαπίνης †ἀπὸ πάντ' οὖν† ὤλεσε νυκτὶ μιῆι·
> καὶ σώφρων ἥμαρτε, καὶ ἄφρονι πολλάκι δόξα
> ἕσπετο, καὶ τιμῆς καὶ κακὸς ὢν ἔλαχεν.
>
> Theognis 659–666

And you shouldn't swear 'this will never be', for the gods are resentful and the outcome depends on them. They act, what's more: good comes from bad and bad from good; a poor man suddenly gets very rich, and he who has acquired a great deal suddenly loses it all in one night: a sensible man errs, fame often accompanies the fool, and even a base man wins honour (trans. D.E. Gerber).

---

43 Commentators rightly compare συμφορά in Bacchylides 14.1–7, a poem with much in common with *PMG* 542 (Dickie 1978, 24–25).

Poverty is not of course the only ἀμήχανος συμφορά in archaic elegy (cf., e.g., Mimnermus fr. 2.11–16), but it is never far away.[44] Other themes of the 'Scopas-ode' too are reflected in sympotic elegy:

ἀλλ' ἄλλωι κακόν ἐστι, τὸ δ' ἀτρεκὲς ὄλβιος οὐδείς
ἀνθρώπων ὁπόσους ἠέλιος καθορᾶι.
ὃν δὲ θεοὶ τιμῶσιν, ὁ καὶ μωμεύμενος αἰνεῖ·
ἀνδρὸς δὲ σπουδὴ γίνεται οὐδεμία.

Theognis 167–170

One man is wretched this way, another that, and no one of all whom the sun looks down upon is truly fortunate. Even the fault-finder praises one whom the gods honour, whereas a man's zeal counts for nothing (trans. D.E. Gerber).

These four verses are usually read as discrete couplets, but they pick up several Simonidean themes (the impossibility of complete human happiness, the theme of μῶμος etc); so too, when Theognis notes (799) that 'no man on earth is free of *psogos*' or (1183–1184) that 'the rays of the shining sun do not look upon any man over whom blame (μῶμος) does not hang', we are certainly not far from either conventional wisdom or from Simonides.

It comes as no surprise, of course, that Simonides' lyrics (as indeed the lyrics of Pindar and Bacchylides) share important gnomic themes with archaic elegy, but there is at least one important issue of literary history lurking here which it might be worth trying to tease out. As it happens, Theognis is the subject of the Platonic episode which, though on a much smaller scale, comes closest in spirit to that of the Simonides-episode of the *Protagoras*.[45] In the *Meno*, Socrates adduces an alleged contradiction between Theognis 33–36 and 434–438 as part of a demonstration that no one is sure whether virtue is teachable (*Meno* 95c9–6a5).[46] It is not explicitly stated under what criterion Theognis is adduced, except that *qua* poet he presumably carries some cultural authority; Socrates' demonstration of uncertainty and contradiction ranges across prominent citizens (of both Athens and Thessaly), sophists and poets, here represent-

---

44 It is perhaps worth noting that the ἀμήχανος συμφορά of the 'Scopas-ode' looks rather different from the various passions which lead a man away from goodness in *PMG* 541 = Simonides fr. 256 Poltera, cf. Poltera 2008, 443; Donlan 1969 does not convince me otherwise. Bowra 1968, in seeking to strengthen the case for Bacchylides as the author of *PMG* 541, argued that the passions listed in that poem would come under the συμφορά of Bachylides 14 (cf. previous note), but that too I find unpersuasive.
45 It is at least curious that Theognis 35–6 are also cited at Xen. *Mem.* 1.2.20, along with the anonymous hexameter of *Protagoras* 344d8, cf. above p. 542.
46 Cf. Giuliano 1991, 124–125.

ed by Theognis. We are clearly not to press too hard on Socrates' poetic interpretation here, except as a manifestation of what was, for Plato, an important objection to granting the poets any philosophical seriousness.[47] Be that as it may, it is perhaps surprising that in the *Meno* Socrates is not made to call Theognis σοφός or something similar, and he is certainly not set up as a claimant to wisdom, as is Simonides in the *Protagoras*; the appeal to contradiction in his verses in fact almost looks like a brief and humorous footnote to a conversation which is really concerned with the attitudes of prominent citizens (καλοὶ κἀγαθοί) and sophists. There is in fact very little Theognis in Plato.[48]

Ought we to be surprised that there is no Theognis, nor indeed elegy of any kind, in the discussion of poetry in *Republic* 2–3? It is easy enough to think of good reasons for this — the non-mythical (as we would say) nature of the material, the fact that *mimesis* is of a very different kind in elegy, the fact that a fair proportion of the elegy we have actually preaches a form of upright morality (cf. Isocrates, *To Nicocles* 43 on Hesiod, Theognis and Phocylides as 'the best advisors for human life'), which would not easily fit Socrates' argument there. We might, however, wonder also whether sympotic elegy, performed by symposiasts themselves, rather than by 'professional' poets or actors or rhapsodes, and importantly devoted to confirming the ideologies of a closed group while dark forces raged outside, was 'felt' differently than the performances of individual poets, such as Simonides, even if such poetry was also 'sympotic', and than poetry which had a place at the heart of public life — Homer and tragedy, most of all — even when, as with Theognis and the Scopas-ode, they shared much material. Theognis carried less cultural authority, and hence less cultural threat, not just because he was less well known, but because the voice of elegy was 'felt' as a collective voice, and perhaps also as an aristocratic one: is it a coincidence that Theognis' most prominent appearance in Plato before the conservative characters of the *Laws* is in the context of καλοὶ κἀγαθοί in the *Meno*?

---

47 Cf. Halliwell 2000, 102–106.
48 At *Laws* 1.630a–c the Athenian names Theognis as a citizen of Sicilian Megara and contrasts a Theognidean couplet (vv. 77–78) with the poetry of Tyrtaeus; *Lysis* 212e cites Solon 23 W, which is closely related to Theognis 1255–1256, and at *Gorgias* 484a there may be an allusion to, or quotation of, Theognis 347–348. We would of course love to know more of 'Xenophon, περὶ Θεόγνιδος' (test. 5 Gerber, cf. Selle 2008, 58–62).

Appendix: Pindar and the 'Scopas-ode'

There is no clear evidence, though we should no doubt keep an open mind on the subject, that anyone in antiquity knew or read the 'Scopas-ode' except through the *Protagoras*. It may, however, be worth considering whether Pindar glanced at it in a famous passage:

ἁ Μοῖσα γὰρ οὐ φιλοκερδής
  πω τότ' ἦν οὐδ' ἐργάτις·
οὐδ' ἐπέρναντο γλυκεῖ-
  αι μελιφθόγγου ποτὶ Τερψιχόρας
ἀργυρωθεῖσαι πρόσωπα μαλθακόφωνοι ἀοιδαί.
νῦν δ' ἐφίητι <τὸ> τὠργείου φυλάξαι
ῥῆμ' ἀλαθείας < u - > ἄγχιστα βαῖνον,
'χρήματα χρήματ' ἀνήρ'
ὃς φᾶ κτεάνων θ' ἅμα λειφθεὶς καὶ φίλων.

Pindar, *Isthmian* 2.6–11[49]

For at that time the Muse was not yet greedy for gain nor up for hire, nor were sweet, soft-voiced songs with their faces silvered over being sold from the hand of honey-voiced Terpsichore. But now she bids us heed the Argive's adage, which comes ... closest to the truth: 'money, money makes the man', said he who lost his possessions and friends as well.

(trans. W.H. Race)

Callimachus (fr. 222 Pf) and the Pindaric scholia famously associate this passage with Simonides, by then of course the paradigm *par excellence* of the mercenary poet, though such biographical criticism seems now out of favour.[50] Like Pittacus' saying that 'it is hard to be good', however, the saying of 'the Argive', i.e. — so the scholia tell us — Aristodemus the Spartan, was taken into the proverb collections and obviously well known; Andron of Ephesus (probably fourth century BC) classed Aristodemus among the Seven Sages,[51] and the Peripatetics Dicaearchus and Hermippus both listed him as a potential 'Sage' (Diogenes Laertius 1.41–42). If Pindar here indeed had Simonides in mind, and — to extend speculation — not just Simonides in general, but the Scopas-ode in particular, then Pindar would be matching the saying of one Sage (Pittacus) with that of another (Aristodemus), and Aristodemus' saying would have a particular point

---

49 On this subject, see now Rawles 2018, 145–148, and on the opening of *Isthmian* 2 see Spelman 2018, 268–275.
50 Cf., e.g., Privitera *ad loc.*, Woodbury 1968, 529–530, Kurke 1991, ch. 10.
51 Cf. Busine 2002, 71–72. Fehling 1985, 32–33 argues that 'Andron' is simply a mistake for the better known Atthidographer Androtion.

when applied to Simonides. This can, of course, be no more than one faint possibility, if even that, but it is clear that Pindar here alludes to Alcaeus fr. 360, cited by the Pindaric scholia and Diogenes Laertius 1.31:

> ὡς γὰρ δή ποτ' Ἀριστόδα-
> μον φαῖσ' οὐκ ἀπάλαμνον ἐν Σπάρται λόγον
> εἴπην, χρήματ' ἄνηρ, πένι-
> χρος δ' οὐδ' εἷς πέλετ' ἔσλος οὐδὲ τίμιος.

Alcaeus fr. 360 Voigt

> For they say that Aristodemus once expressed it shrewdly at Sparta: 'Money is the man, and no poor man is good or honorable'.

(trans. D.A. Campbell)

An allusion to Alcaeus follows naturally upon the reference which opened the poem to earlier lyric poets who sang παιδεῖοι ὕμνοι; if Simonides fr. 260 Poltera really is involved here, then Pindar's allusion would be pitting not just Sage against Sage, but Simonides and Pittacus against Pittacus' most famous opponent, Alcaeus. We are still of course completely in the realm of speculation, but as Alcaeus praises an οὐκ ἀπάλαμνος λόγος about the conditions under which one can be ἐσθλός and τίμιος, the Scopas-ode is perhaps not so far away after all. Is it, moreover, just a coincidence that both Alcaeus fr. 360 and Simonides fr. 260 Poltera use the Homeric *hapax* ἀπάλαμνος?

Bibliography

Asper, M. 2006. '"Literatursoziologisches" zu den Sprüchen der Sieben Weisen', in: J. Althoff/ D. Zeller (eds.), *Die Worte der Sieben Weisen*, Darmstadt, 83–103

Babut, D. 1975. 'Simonide moraliste', *Revue des Études Grecques* 88, 20–62.

Baltussen, H. 2004. 'Plato Protagoras 340–48: commentary in the making', in: P. Adamson/H. Baltussen/M.W.F. Stone (eds.), *Philosophy, Science and Exegesis in Greek, Arabic and Latin Commentaries*, London I, 21–35.

Beresford, A. 2008. 'Nobody's perfect: a new text and interpretation of Simonides *PMG* 542', *Classical Philology* 103, 237–256.

Beresford, A. 2009. 'Erasing Simonides', *Apeiron* 42, 185–220.

Bowra, C.M. 1968. 'Simonides or Bacchylides?', *Hermes* 91, 257–267.

Brittain, C. 2017. '*Deinos* (wicked good) at interpretation (*Protagoras* 334–48)', in: V. Harte/R. Woolf (eds.), *Rereading Ancient Philosophy*, Cambridge, 32–59.

Busine, A. 2002. *Les sept sages de la Grèce antique*, Paris.

Coby, P. 1987. *Socrates and the Sophistic Enlightenment*, Toronto.

Dickie, M. 1978. 'The argument and form of Simonides 542 *PMG*', *Harvard Studies in Classical Philology* 82, 21–33.

Donlan, W. 1969. 'Simonides, fr. 4D and *P. Oxy.* 2432', *Transactions of the American Philological Association* 100, 71–95.
Fehling, D. 1985. *Die sieben Weisen und die frühgriechische Chronologie*, Bern.
Ferrari, G.R.F. 1989. 'Plato and poetry', in: G.A. Kennedy (ed.), *The Cambridge History of Literary Criticism*, Vol. I: *Classical Criticism*, Cambridge, 92–148.
Ford, A. 2010. 'Plato's two Hesiods', in: G.R. Boys-Stones/J.H. Haubold (eds.), *Plato and Hesiod*, Oxford, 133–154.
Ford, A. 2014. 'The function of criticism at the present time (432 BC): text, interpretation and meaning in Plato's *Protagoras*', *Poetica* 46.1–2: 17–39.
Ford. A. 2020. 'The wisdom of Simonides: σοφὸς καὶ θεῖος ἀνήρ', in: P. Agócs/L. Prauscello (eds.), *Simonides Lyricus*, Cambridge, 179–196.
Gibson, R. 2002. '"Cf. e.g.": a typology of "parallels" and the role of commentaries on Latin poetry', in: R.K. Gibson/C.K. Kraus (eds.), *The Classical Commentary: Histories, Practices, Theory*, Leiden, 331–357.
Giuliano, F.M. 1991. 'Esegesi letteraria in Platone: la discussione sul carme simonideo nel *Protagora*', *Studi classici e orientali* 41, 105–190.
González, J.M. 2010. 'Theokritos' *Idyll* 16. The Χάριτες and civic poetry', *Harvard Studies in Classical Philology* 105, 65–116.
Graziosi, B. 2010. 'Hesiod in classical Athens: rhapsodes, orators, and Platonic discourse', in: G.R. Boys-Stones/J.H. Haubold (eds.), *Plato and Hesiod*, Oxford, 110–132.
Halliwell, S. 2000. 'The subjection of muthos to logos: Plato's citations of the poets', *Classical Quarterly* 50, 94–112.
Henry, W.B. 1999. 'Simonides, PMG 542.1–3', *Classical Quarterly* 49, 621.
Hunter, R. 2008a. *On Coming After. Studies in Post-Classical Greek Literature and its Reception*, Berlin/New York.
Hunter, R. 2008b. 'Hesiod, Callimachus, and the invention of morality', in: G. Bastianini/A. Casanova (eds.), *Esiodo: cent'anni di papiri*, Florence, 153–164 [= Hunter 2008a, 559–571].
Hunter, R. 2012. *Plato and the Traditions of Ancient Literature: The silent stream*, Cambridge.
Hunter, R. 2014. *Hesiodic Voices*, Cambridge.
Hunter, R. 2017. 'A striking parallel?', in: *Albert's Anthology*, Cambridge MA, 91–92.
Hutchinson, G.O. 2001. *Greek Lyric Poetry*, Oxford.
Kurke, L. 1991. *The Traffic in Praise*, Ithaca NY.
Kurke, L. 2011. *Aesopic Conversations*, Princeton.
Ledbetter, G. 2003. *Poetics before Plato*, Princeton.
Lidov, J.B. 2010. 'Meter, colon, and rhythm: Simonides (*PMG* 542) and Pindar between archaic and classical', *Classical Philology* 105, 25–53.
Manuwald, B. 2010. 'Ist Simonides' Gedicht an Skopas (*PMG* 542) vollständig überliefert?', *Rheinisches Museum* 153, 1–24.
Mayhew, R. 2011. *Prodicus the Sophist*, Oxford.
Morgan, K.A. 2009. 'Philosophy at Delphi: Socrates, sages, and the circulation of wisdom', in: L. Athanassaki/R.P. Martin/J.F. Miller (eds.), *Apolline Politics and Poetics*, Athens, 549–568.
Most, G.W. 1994. 'Simonides' ode to Scopas in contexts', in: I.J.F. de Jong/J.P. Sullivan (eds.), *Modern Critical Theory and Classical Literature*, Leiden, 127–152.
Nünlist, R. 2009. *The Ancient Critic at Work*, Cambridge.
Poltera, O. 2008. *Simonides lyricus*, Basel.

Radermacher, L. 1951. *Artium scriptores*, Vienna.
Scodel, R. 1986. 'Literary interpretation in Plato's *Protagoras*', *Ancient Philosophy* 6, 25–37.
Selle, H. 2008. *Theognis und die Theognidea*, Berlin/New York.
Steiner, D. 2001. *Images in Mind*, Princeton.
Trapp, M. 1987. 'Protagoras and the great tradition', in: Michael Whitby/P. Hardie/Mary Whitby (eds.), *Homo Viator. Classical Essays for John Bramble*, Bristol, 41–48.
Wilamowitz-Moellendorff, U. von. 1913. *Sappho und Simonides*, Berlin.
Wolfsdorf, D. 2008. 'Hesiod, Prodicus, and the Socratics on work and pleasure', *Oxford Studies in Ancient Philosophy* 35, 1–18.
Woodbury, L. 1968. 'Pindar and the mercenary muse: *Isthm.* 2.1–13', *Transactions of the American Philological Association* 99, 527–542.

31 Serpents in the Soul: The 'Libyan Myth' of Dio Chrysostom

The 'Libyan Myth'

The *Fifth Oration* of Dio Chrysostom, the 'Libyan Myth', is an important document of ancient mythography, for it both tells a myth and also interprets it allegorically for us (both before, during and after the telling); it begins, moreover, with a brief general account of how myth can function educationally.[1] In the context of the current book, it has a particular importance, as it is a myth which uses maps (in a broad sense) as part of its meaning. The myth ('Once upon a time, long ago, it is said ...'. 5.5) tells of creatures that infested Libya, composite beasts made up of 'the most widely divergent elements, completely unexampled (ἄτοπον)' (5.6). Part hideous snake, part beautiful woman,[2] they had vicious talons (5.15) with which they would grab their victim so that the lower snaky part could kill and devour him; they moved at a speed which made escape impossible. Their favourite food was human flesh and they lured men to their death by showing them a glimpse of the body of the beautiful woman (we may here compare the Sirens).[3] A Libyan king succeeded in wiping out a good number of the beasts by setting fire to their lairs, but some survived to take vengeance; these were apparently finally destroyed by Heracles as part of his mission to cleanse the whole world of 'beasts and tyrants' (5.21), although the essay ends with a reported incident in which two young men seem to have been killed by one of these creatures long after Heracles' visit (5.24–27). Dio introduces this story as about human passions (ἐπιθυμίαι, 5.4), breaks off in the middle to repeat the message ('the passions are irrational and beastlike, they offer the prospect of pleasure and lead on the foolish by deceit and bewitchment, and then destroy them in the grimmest and most pitiable way' 5.16), and after Heracles' intervention he returns to put yet more detail on his interpretation:

I am grateful to Greta Hawes and to audiences at Bristol, Bryn Mawr, Harvard, Liverpool and Stanford for instructive criticism and discussion.

---

1 There is much of value in the discussion of *Oration* 5 in Gangloff 2006, 224–235; I have not recorded every place where our analyses are in agreement.
2 As such, as Leigh 2000, 105 n. 92 notes, the women may recall the Hesiodic Echidna (*Theogony* 295–305); it may be relevant in the present context that Echidna mated with Typhon.
3 Dio's snake-women may, in turn, have been one of the sources for Lucian's ensnaring vine-women in the *True Histories*, cf. Georgiadou/Larmour 1997.

τυχὸν οὖν ὁ μῦθος αἰνίττεται λέγων τοὺς πολλοὺς μὲν εἴ πού τις ἐπεχείρησε καθῆραι τὴν αὑτοῦ ψυχὴν ὥσπερ ἄβατον καὶ μεστόν τινα θηρίων χαλεπῶν τόπον, ἐξελὼν δὴ καὶ ἀπολέσας τι τῶν ἐπιθυμιῶν εἶδος, ἐλπίσαντας ἀπηλλάχθαι καὶ διαπεφευγέναι, οὐκ ἰσχυρῶς αὐτὸ δράσαντας, ὀλίγον ὕστερον ὑπὸ τῶν λειπομένων ἐπιθυμιῶν ἀπολέσθαι καὶ διαφθαρῆναι. Ἡρακλέα δὲ τὸν Διὸς καὶ Ἀλκμήνης ἐπεξελθεῖν καὶ ἀποφῆναι καθαρὰν καὶ ἥμερον τὴν αὑτοῦ διάνοιαν· καὶ τοῦτο αὐτῷ βούλεσθαι δηλοῦν τῆς γῆς τὴν ἡμέρωσιν.

Dio Chrysostom 5.22–23

Perhaps the myth is hinting that when one of the many tries to clear out his soul, as though it was an unpassable region full of dangerous beasts, by removing and destroying the desires, but does not do this thoroughly, he is not long afterwards destroyed and corrupted by the remaining desires. Heracles, however, the son of Zeus and Alcmene, succeeded in making his mind pure and tame; this is what the civilizing of the earth means.

That men's souls are like a 'pathless/inhospitable region full of dangerous beasts' makes explicit the importance of the Libyan setting of the myth, and takes us back to the introduction to the essay which contains a relatively lengthy description of the grimly impassable Syrtis, one of the beasts' favourite hunting-grounds (though they by no means restricted themselves to that area), and a very familiar part of the Libyan landscape in ancient literature and imagination.[4] The Syrtis too is a 'pathless/inhospitable region full of dangerous beasts'; once caught in its shoals it is all but impossible to find a way out (5.8–11).

Dio and Plato

Dio's myth, which may be largely his own creation, has a thick Platonic texture; two passages are particularly important. The first is the famous passage of the *Phaedrus* (229c1–30a6) in which Socrates rejects mythic 'rationalisation' as a waste of time, a passage which considers the possibility of 'probable' explanations for mixed creatures such as Hippocentaurs and Chimaeras; the coincidence between Dio's παντελῶς ἄτοπον, 'completely unexampled', monster and Socrates' refusal to 'rationalise' ἀτοπίαι τερατολόγων τινῶν φύσεων (229e1), 'weird and fantastic forms', can hardly be pressed, because of the familiarity of such language, but elsewhere there is no doubt that Dio is alluding to this pas-

---

4 Leigh 2000 is particularly important here; my remarks to some extent fill in the gaps of his survey. The area of the Great Syrtis was clearly never a very desirable location, even if 'in reality' it was not as grim as poets imagined it (cf. Strabo 17.3.20).

sage of the *Phaedrus*. The very beginning of the 'Libyan Myth' echoes Socrates' disparagement of mythical rationalisation,[5]

μῦθον Λιβυκὸν ἐκπονεῖν καὶ περὶ τὰ τοιαῦτα κατατρίβειν τὴν περὶ λόγους φιλοπονίαν οὐκ εὐτυχές κτλ.

Dio Chrysostom 5.1

To elaborate a Libyan myth and to exhaust one's literary industry on such matters is not a happy procedure…

ἐγὼ δέ, ὦ Φαῖδρε, ἄλλως μὲν τὰ τοιαῦτα χαρίεντα ἡγοῦμαι, λίαν δὲ δεινοῦ καὶ ἐπιπόνου καὶ οὐ πάνυ εὐτυχοῦς ἀνδρός κτλ.

Plato, *Phaedrus* 229d2-4

Phaedrus, I think that such explanations are, generally speaking, witty, but they belong to a clever man given to considerable labour, who is not altogether happy …

and he picks up this same passage of the *Phaedrus* when he breaks off 'decoding' the myth:

καὶ γάρ τοι καὶ τὸ λοιπὸν τοῦ μύθου ταύτῃ τρέπειν οὐ χαλεπὸν ἀνδρὶ ἀδολέσχῃ καὶ πλείω σχεδὸν ἢ ἔδει σχολὴν ἄγοντι.

Dio Chrysostom 5.18

Indeed, to turn the rest of the myth in this direction would not be difficult for a man who is a good talker and perhaps has more leisure at his disposal than is appropriate.

… αἷς εἴ τις ἀπιστῶν προσβιβᾷ κατὰ τὸ εἰκὸς ἕκαστον, ἅτε ἀγροίκῳ τινὶ σοφίᾳ χρώμενος, πολλῆς αὐτῷ σχολῆς δεήσει.

Plato, *Phaedrus* 229e3-4

If someone disbelieves these [compound creatures] and seeks to force each of them to conform with probability by using some rustic kind of wisdom, he will require a great deal of leisure.

---

5 Cf., e.g., Gangloff 2006, 228–230. The opening sentence of Dio 5 is in fact omitted by a significant part of the tradition and is thus held by von Arnim to be spurious, but the apt Platonic resonance is hard to explain away; this issue cannot of course be treated in isolation from the more general question of the structural integrity of *Oration* 5, cf. n. 26 below. Gangloff 2006, 229 suggests that Dio's opening comparison of productive allegorical readings to the ἐμπειρία τῶν γεωργῶν, 'experience of farmers', who fertilise barren plants through grafting, picks up and plays with Socrates' rejection of the ἀγροῖκος σοφία, 'rustic wisdom', of the rationalisers in the *Phaedrus*.

The second important Platonic passage for Dio's myth is the extraordinary image of the tripartite soul-beast in Book 9 of the *Republic*, a passage which Dio reworks elsewhere in the *Orationes* and indeed combines with material from the *Phaedrus*.[6] The description of the irrational, appetitive part of the soul, 'a variegated (ποικίλον) and many-headed beast' (588c7–8), is very likely indebted to Typhon,[7] who is explicitly named by Socrates in the *Phaedrus*, and this passage, like that of the *Phaedrus*, also makes use of the distinction between θηρίον, here associated with the passionate part of the soul (588c7–8, 588e5), and ζῷον, here referring to the man whose frame contains the soul-beast (588e1).

The importance of the *Phaedrus* in this context is at least twofold. First, Socrates investigates whether he himself is 'a *beast* (θηρίον) more complex (πολυπλοκώτερον) and more inflated than Typhon' or 'an *animal* (ζῷον) which is gentler and simpler (ἡμερώτερόν τε καὶ ἁπλούστερον)' (230a3–5); Socrates' investigation is not explained further, but it seems very likely, both from the *Phaedrus* itself and from the passage of the *Republic* noted above, that we are to understand that Socrates is concerned (at least primarily) with the nature of his soul and, in particular, with the violent passions which may lodge there.[8] We might well be tempted to remember this passage when Dio tells us that Heracles succeeded in making his mind (διάνοια) 'pure and tame', καθαρὰ καὶ ἥμερος, by completely extirpating the destructive passions represented by the Libyan beasts, and that this was the meaning of the ἡμέρωσις, 'taming, civilising', of the earth which he was said to have performed;[9] in several contexts καθαρός, 'pure', and ἁπλοῦς, 'simple', are virtual synonyms and their opposite is ποικίλος, 'complicated, tricky'. Heracles in fact may be thought to be simultaneously both 'simple' (as the long-suffering paradigm of virtue) and 'complex' (as a 'beast' of violence and desires); to Heracles we shall return.

The second (related) way in which Socrates' dismissal of simple rationalization in the *Phaedrus* is important here is that Socrates' suggestion, through the figure of Typhon, of a different approach to myth, one which we might well describe as a form of allegorisation, is clearly very relevant to Dio 5. The verbal echoes of the *Phaedrus* in Dio 5 make the point that Dio's myth is, as it were, a

---

6 Cf. Hunter 2012, 81–84. The relevance of this passage of the *Republic* to Dio 5 is briefly noted by Said 2000, 173 and Gangloff 2006, 325.
7 Cf. Hunter 2012, 85; the discussion in Hunter 2012 allows me to keep the present discussion relatively brief.
8 Cf. Rowe 1986, 140–141.
9 The allegorisation of Heracles' labours as the conquest of various passions and diseases of the soul was of course familiar, cf. esp. Heraclitus, *Hom. Probl.* 33 (a Stoic allegory) and below p. 567 on Herodorus of Heraclea.

demonstration of the kind of mythic meaning which Socrates advocates in the *Phaedrus*;[10] Dio has understood what Socrates has been saying — there is absolutely nothing 'probable' about Dio's monsters, for the pursuit of 'probability' is both a waste of time (cf. *Phaedrus* 229e1, cited above) and misses the whole point about what the mythic imagination can do for us. We simply cannot say how closely Dio has followed the typical characteristics of 'Libyan myths',[11] but it is clear that his interpretation follows the lines which Socrates' words have suggested. What Dio claims to pursue is a way in which myths may bring us significant benefit (χρεία), and this will happen if myths are 'in some way dragged towards what is appropriate [or 'necessary'] and set alongside the real and true' (ἑλκόμενά πῃ πρὸς τὸ δέον καὶ παραβαλλόμενα τοῖς οὖσι καὶ ἀληθέσιν, 5.1).[12] Translation is here unusually difficult, but it may be suggested that Dio's expression is (again) a variation upon what Socrates rejects in the *Phaedrus*: Socrates describes the business of rationalising away composite mythical beasts as προσβιβάζειν κατὰ τὸ εἰκός, 'force to conform with probability', a difficult phrase[13] which Dio perhaps varied with τὸ δέον, 'the appropriate, the necessary', replacing τὸ εἰκός, 'the probable'; elsewhere we find βιάζεσθαι used of 'forced' allegorical interpretations,[14] and Dio's ἑλκόμενα, 'dragged', clearly has something of this flavour also. Dio's further suggestion that such myths were in

---

10 My account of the *Phaedrus* passage differs fundamentally from, say, that of Werner 2012, 27–43; much closer to my understanding of Typhon as a figure for whom Socrates sees a philosophical (and allegorical) usefulness is Brouwer 2014, 149–163.

11 Aelius Theon 73.2 Sp. lists Λιβυστικοί as one category of μῦθοι alongside Aesopic fables, fables of Sybaris etc., cf. Arist. *Rhet.* 2.1393a30–31, *RE* 6.1719–20; at 73.19 Sp. Theon names one 'Kybissos of Libya' as a μυθοποιός, whom we are presumably to understand as the figure to whom 'Libyan myths' were ascribed, cf. Babrius, *Prol.* 2, 5–6. Aeschylus fr. 139 R and Quintilian 5.11.20 suggest that these were animal fables, not unlike Aesopic fables, but Theon 73.6 Sp. cites a typical opening as 'A Libyan man ...', suggesting that they were not only animal fables. Dio's fable has obvious similarities with other tales of dangerous man-eating women, cf., e.g., Philostratus, *VA* 4.25, Lucian, *VH* 2.46.

12 Leigh's 'became a parable of the real and the true' (2000, 105) is perhaps more explicit and clearer than Dio's Greek. Dio's language finds a close parallel in Eustathius' description of how some of Homer's allegorical myths were not his own invention but were ἑλκόμενοι ... χρησίμως καὶ εἰς τὴν τούτου ποίησιν, 'imported ... usefully into his poetry also' (*Hom.* 1.39).

13 Yunis 2011 *ad loc.* translates 'he will bring each item into line with the probable', but does not expand on how that meaning is reached.

14 Cf., e.g., Plutarch, *How to study poetry* 19e, with Hunter/Russell 2011, 111. Dio's subsequent image of adding helpful morals to otherwise silly stories as like grafting fruit-bearing plants on to the wild and uncultivated has more than a little in common with Plutarch's images at the opening of *How to study poetry* of how to control the 'fruitless' and over-luxuriant excesses of poetry by pruning and by 'mixing in' philosophy, like water mixed with wine (15e–f).

fact originally composed as allegories uses a very familiar claim of ancient mythic and poetic interpretation; Plato was one, and perhaps the most important, writer who did indeed create myths for allegorical purposes.

Heracles in the desert

We have another extensive description in Greek of the Libyan desert of the imagination, namely the wanderings of the Argonauts in the fourth book of Apollonius' *Argonautica*.[15] Here too the emptiness of the Syrtis takes centre stage and is described at length (4.1235–1249), and here too Heracles is to be found, killing the snake which guarded the Golden Apples of the Hesperides and then disappearing into immortality. In Apollonius' Libya also, people die of snakebite (Mopsus, 4.1502–1536). Apollonius' Libya is, like the landscapes of *Odyssey* 9–12 which it explicitly replaces (cf. 4.1228–1235),[16] a land of the imagination, where the emptiness is filled with semi-magical or 'dream' encounters with female figures and with myth (Μουσάων... μῦθος, 4.1381), a land of traces (of Heracles, for example) and mirages, a land only to be captured through simile.[17] If it is a land of despair rather than desire, nevertheless some of the semi-magical figures may, like Dio's female monsters, come from within, just as the despair, like the desire, is what we would call a psychological state, one in keeping with the bleak nothingness of the landscape,[18] one induced perhaps by terror and fear of the unknown (4.1278–1287), and helped on by lack of nourishment (4.1295). Here is a landscape, a map if you like, actually created by myth. When we place our two Libyas side by side, we can find a significant amount of shared material taken in different interpretative directions, and some of that shared material shows how fluid the boundaries between kinds of mythic elaboration and interpretation may be. Consider Heracles. In Apollonius, as standardly, the Apples of the Hesperides appears to be the hero's last challenge, the accomplishment of which marks his achieving of immortality; henceforth, all searching for him

---

15 On this episode see now Griffiths 2012, with rich bibliography, Mori 2008, 16–18, and Hunter 2015.
16 For the Libyan adventures and the *Odyssey* cf., e.g., Dufner 1988, 189–195, Hunter 2008b, 122–125.
17 Cf. Vian 1981, 64, 191–192, Hunter 1993, 135–137; for the Apollonian Libya's likeness to the Underworld, cf. Hunter 1993, 29–32.
18 Many commentators have noted the remarkable sympathy of landscape and psychological mood in the Syrtis-episode, cf., e.g., Fusillo 1985, 291, 314 n. 7.

would be in vain (4.1481–2).[19] Dio lays stress upon the fact that Heracles, who managed eventually to rid his mind of all the disturbing passions (which does not seem to be the case with Apollonius' Heracles), was the son of Zeus (5.23) — how many ordinary mortals can achieve this 'pure and gentle' state? Or should we rather ask whether such absolute control of our passions is the nearest to divinity that mortals can achieve? The two texts, when put together, show us just why myth was such a productive mode for ancient literary discourse.

In the Libyan adventures, moreover, Apollonius has perhaps fashioned an alternative to both allegory and rationalisation. The dream-like mirages of the desert suggest reading myth (or at least some myths) as precisely dreams or mirages, which share the quality of both being real (people *do* dream and *do* see mirages), but also of being utterly insubstantial, of disappearing in an instant (cf. *Arg.* 4.1330, 1408–1409), so one can wonder whether they actually ever happened at all. Dreams are, moreover, not to be held accountable to standards of plausibility, let alone historicity, but operate to a different narrative logic, which many might want to call symbolic; this does not lessen their importance to us — quite the opposite in fact, and there is at least some analogy here with how we, as well as other, very different cultures, remember and use our own 'myths'. The Australian Aboriginal 'dreaming' (which is in essence very different from 'dreams') precisely maps the landscape — every rock, every tree — so that myths are the maps by which one navigates; the desert literally teems with signs, markers, and traces which offer direction and certainty. As one student of Aboriginal culture has described the 'spirit-beings' of the Dreaming:

> 'No place on the map has escaped their originatory gesture in the form of mythic explanation. These places have all been named, and they perpetuate an existence which is entirely otherworldly. Language has embraced their immutable forms and transformed these into a topography of prose and ritual. No place is silent in the wake of the passage of these spirit-beings at the time of the Dreaming. Every corner of the earth is blessed with its own story, its own narrative desire to enter the minds of men as a sequence of divine events'.[20]

Heracles, like the figures of the Dreaming, changed (or created) the landscape as he went, in his case taking the Apples and creating a spring. Unlike the figures of the Dreaming, however, he is now utterly beyond our reach, 'no searcher would ever come across him again' (4.1481–2), and in this the figures of the Dreaming are utterly different, because they are always there, always inside those who live the life and inside the land they created. In Apollonius' Libya,

---

19 Cf. *RE* 15.1245, Feeney 1986, 53, Hunter 1993, 29, citing earlier bibliography.
20 Cowan 1994, 18.

however, even Heracles' 'traces' are wiped out by blowing sand (4.1463–1464),[21] and this too would never happen — or be said to happen — in the Aboriginal desert.

Heracles in the Libyan desert had been allegorised long before Dio Chrysostom, as had so many of Heracles' adventures. In his voluminous work on Heracles, Herodorus of Heracleia (late fifth-early fourth century BC) had allegorised the Libyan episode, as we read in the following extract from a late compilation:

> They depict [Heracles] wearing a lionskin instead of a tunic and carrying a club and holding three apples. The story is that he gained the three apples when he had killed the snake with his club, that is when he had overcome the wicked and varied reasoning of bitter desire (τὸν πονηρὸν καὶ ποικίλον τῆς πικρᾶς ἐπιθυμίας λογισμόν)[22] with the club of philosophy, surrounding himself with his noble thoughts (γενναῖον φρόνημα) as with a lionskin. In this way he gained the three apples, that is three virtues: avoidance of anger, avoidance of greed for money, avoidance of the pursuit of pleasure. Through the club of his enduring soul and the skin of his reasoning, very bold and wise, he defeated the earthbound (γήϊνον) struggle of wretched desire, practising philosophy until death, as the very wise Herodorus recorded ...
>
> Herodorus of Heraclea fr. 14 Jacoby-Fowler[23]

This passage seems to look forward to Dio 5 in many ways,[24] but let me just pick on one detail. What Heracles overcame is 'the wicked and varied reasoning of bitter desire' (τὸν πονηρὸν καὶ ποικίλον (or τὸν πολυποικίλον) τῆς πικρᾶς ἐπιθυμίας λογισμόν), and the ποικιλία of desire may remind us of the (somewhat later?) Platonic Socrates wondering whether he is a 'beast more complex (πολυπλοκώτερον) ... than Typhon' (*Phaedrus* 230a4), where Typhon is chosen *inter alia* because of the changefulness and manifold combinations of the Hesiodic Typhon (*Theogony* 820–835).

---

21 For a rather differently nuanced account cf. Thalmann 2011, 87–88.
22 The tradition is divided between this reading and τὸν πολυποικίλον κτλ., cf. below p. 575.
23 For a full apparatus for the fragment see Fowler 2000 *ad loc*. How much of the fragment reports Herodorus accurately is open to some doubt (cf. Fowler 2013, 328), but it may nevertheless serve as illustrative of a wide tradition of interpretation.
24 Both Feeney 1986, 53 and Leigh 2000, 107 bring this passage into association with *Argonautica* 4.

Interpreting stories

The closing section of Dio 5 comes as something of a surprise.[25] Heracles has once and for all rid the world (and himself) of the beast-women, but then Dio apparently undertakes — the text is somewhat uncertain (see below) — to add a little bit more of the myth 'for the younger people' (νεώτεροι). He reports that 'they so firmly believe the story and consider it true, that they say that at some time later on one of this race appeared to Greek θεωροί (envoys) as they were travelling to the oracle of Ammon...' (5.24); the beast-woman succeeded in killing two of the young men, one of whom it also ate, whereas the body of the second was found 'rotting and decaying' (σαπρόν τε καὶ μυδῶντα) and the Libyan guides forbade anyone to touch the body, 'lest all would die'. This unexpected reappearance of the monstrous brood raises interesting questions of narrative technique and mythic interpretation.

Discussion of this final episode must begin from an interesting textual problem:

βούλεσθε οὖν βραχύ τι καὶ τοῖς νεωτέροις λόγων ἐπιχαρισώμεθα τοῦ μυθολογήματος;
Dio Chrysostom 5.24

Do you want me to add a little more myth-telling to please my younger audience?

The transmission is divided between τοῖς νεωτέροις λόγων and τῶν νεωτέρων λόγων; all recent editors have adopted the dative, together with von Arnim's deletion of λόγων. That Dio should now address 'the young(er)' suits the claimed indulgence of ἐπιχαρισώμεθα and the fact that it is the young who are, of course, most attached to μῦθοι; we may compare 4.74 where Diogenes tells Alexander 'the Libyan myth', 'as wet nurses console and comfort (χαριζόμεναι) children', and there too the point of the myth is to do with the state of Alexander's soul (4.75).[26] On the other hand, what Dio proceeds to narrate seems to be set in historical, rather than 'mythic', time; we are now in a world of 'Greek

---

25 For a striking expression of puzzlement cf. Anderson 2000, 156.
26 I here glide over the difficult problems of the structure of *Oration* 4 and the relationship between that speech and the Libyan myth, which has often been thought to have originally been part of (one version of) *Oration* 4, cf. von Arnim 1891, 382–392, 1898, 412–414, Moles 1983, 254, Swain 1996, 194. Photius (*Bibl.* 209 = 3.107 Henry) describes the Libyan oration as 'dependent' (ἐξημμένος) upon the kingship orations (1–4), but this may merely refer to the mention of the Libyan myth at 4.73–74.

θεωροί' and of a famous oracle,[27] not the πάλαι ποτέ of the main myth. The detail of the considerable escort of cavalry and archers which attended the *theoroi*, together with the 'ethnographic' detail of Libyan female dress and the practice of local women prostituting themselves to passing travellers,[28] all serve to fashion a quite different world from that of the earlier myth of Heracles and the snake-women. 'Something of more recent stories' would, therefore, make good sense in context. The reappearance of the creatures after their destruction by Heracles is hardly an insurmountable narrative weakness, and we do not have to fall back on the explanation that, just as the Libyan king's force was wiped out by those of the beasts who were not at home when he attacked them, so Heracles only destroyed those beasts who happened to be in the vicinity when he arrived. Rather, the logic of the allegory is that each of us has the beasts (or the potential for them) within us, and so Heracles' cleansing of the world could only ever apply to himself; the two young men who rush towards exposed female flesh in the final anecdote have clearly not rid themselves of all unhealthy passions. Nevertheless, such an explanation does not seem wholly to account for the marked difference between this closing episode and the rest of the essay.

Any distinction between mythic and historical time is not, of course, to be pressed very hard, but Dio seems in fact to have inscribed such a distinction in the text, and we may wonder whether that distinction is also relevant to the mode of interpretation appropriate to the different eras. The main body of the 'Libyan myth' is set in that ill-defined mythic past in which events cannot be verified, and so questions of historicity must inevitably give way before more productive modes of interpretation, such indeed as allegorisation. Stories from historical times, where multiple eye-witnesses were present and written records often survive, give both less and more room for interpretative freedom: less, because there is a 'real event' to be respected, even in outline, in any telling, and more, because the (paradoxical) uncertainty of event and interpretation which 'historicity' unleashes encourages explanatory excess; much of our thinking on these issues goes back, of course, to Thucydides' famous programmatic chapters.

---

27 Although the importance of the oracle of Ammon at Siwa, in the Libyan desert to the southeast of the Great Syrtis, declined somewhat in importance in imperial times (cf. Strabo 17.1.43, *RE* 1. 1859, Fakhry 1944, 45–46), it was certainly still functioning in Dio's time; *SGO* 08/01/01 records an oracle for Kyzikos in the time of Hadrian. Cf. further Rutherford 2013, 515 s.v. Ammon, and for the oracle more generally Fakhry 1944, Kuhlmann 1988. In the context of Dio 5, it is certainly noteworthy that the oracle plays an important role — or rather does not, as Cato refuses to consult it — in Lucan, *BC* 9.511–586, cf. Section 5 below.
28 Dio may here remember and vary Herodotus 4.189.1–2 on Libyan female dress.

In the current instance, the story of this later appearance of a specimen of the brood comes from those who believe firmly in the historicity of the story: to what extent, then, does such belief require constant re-affirmation? Or rather, are such 'reappearances' precisely the result of conviction, that is, do they arise from within us? The appearance of this single creature has in fact something of the mirage about it — 'They thought (δόξαι γὰρ αὐτοῖς κτλ.) ...' — and this is not the case for the earlier description of how the beasts hunt their human prey (5.14). This is not, of course, to be pushed too hard, but we might at least wonder whether some of the party of travellers knew the 'Libyan myth' and so were almost waiting for a mirage to happen; this is one way in which myths function in the present, and can indeed affect our perception of the present. At the very beginning of the myth we have been told that 'still to this day' Libya seems to produce 'all kinds of living forms, reptiles and other beasts' (5), and it would be hard not to let this information prey upon your mind as you travelled through the desert wastes. There is, moreover, the curious fact that the beast did not eat the second young man after killing him. We might interpret this as indeed a closural act: the creatures really have now gone for good, but left behind a visible trace of their power. On the other hand, such rotting of the flesh was precisely believed to be the real effect of the bite of a particular kind of deadly Libyan viper, and is described in very similar terms both in poetry and in writers of natural history; this is in fact the very effect which the snakebite has upon Mopsus in the *Argonautica* (4.1530–1531).[29] The rotting of the body of the nameless young man at the end of Dio's 'Libyan myth' thus leads us to ask questions similar to those raised by the first part of the final section. Was the young man in fact killed, not by one of the mythical monsters, but by a Libyan snake, and this gruesome death then gave rise to the belief in the reappearance of one of the mythic creatures? In other words, does Dio here invite us to 'rationalise', where the predominant mode has, rather, been allegorical? When the second young man was attacked, the creature 'put its snake part first' (προϊσχόμενον τὸν ὄφιν), and we might at least wonder whether anyone actually saw the female part. What state of mind leads us to create such images and/or what kind of knowledge of stories leads us to see them becoming real? If we keep such myths and images 'before our eyes' (5.17), what indeed are we likely to see as we

---

29 Cf. Hunter 2015 on vv. 1530–1531.

pass through life (let alone Libya)? How much more likely are you to see a ghost in a house that you are certain is haunted?[30]

It is through the suggestiveness of the juxtaposition of different narrative elements in the 'Libyan myth' that Dio has not merely taken on board the Platonic lesson, but goes beyond Plato in asking about the conditions under which such images and myths arise. The final section of the work raises in fact a number of possible 'rationalisations' of the myth, but of a quite different kind than those which Socrates dismisses in the *Phaedrus*, and different also from 'rationalisations' which were readily available. Herodotus argues that Greek images of Athena's aegis were copied from the dress of Libyan women, who drape goatskins over themselves with tassels 'which are not snakes but made of leather' (4.189, cf. Ap. Rhod. *Arg.* 4.1348–1349). It would certainly not have required much effort to explain a Libyan snake-woman myth as arising from the dress of Libyan women, as canonised by Herodotus, but Dio does not, I think, invite us down that route. Rather, Dio, like Apollonius before him, explores the source of our terrors and our imaginings, lost as we are in the trackless wastes of ordinary existence. If the psychology of this lesson differs in fact little, as Dio himself tells us (5.17), from the use of bogey monsters to induce children to behave as we wish them to, then this ought not to surprise: it is the unknown which always terrifies, and the Libya of the literary imagination maps the unknown for us in terrifying detail. The Platonic Socrates, however, understood, as did the Delphic oracle, that the worst ignorance is of oneself.

If further encouragement in this general direction were needed, then we might find it in the account in Diodorus Siculus of the march of Ophellas' army through the snake-infested Libyan Syrtis at the end of the fourth century BC (20.41.1–42.1). Diodorus (or his source) takes this opportunity to tell the local myth of Lamia, a queen who took revenge for the death of her own children by ordering the killing of all newborn children in her kingdom; in the most familiar version of the story (though Diodorus is not explicit about this), Lamia herself then ate the babies. In Diodorus' account, the only time that she did not exercise this savage authority was when she was drunk and did not care what was going on around her; as a result her subjects supposed that she could not see, and so put about the story (ἐμυθολόγησαν) that at such times she took her eyes out and put them into a container (for wine). Here clearly we have a rationalisation along familiar Palaephatan lines: a very ordinary story – a queen gets

---

[30] Leigh 2000, 106 suggests that Dio does not explain the final anecdote 'indicating that a very few such women still survive ... presumably because it is now up to [the young] to figure it out', but this hardly does justice to Dio's richly suggestive text.

drunk and her subjects take advantage of it — becomes, through a misunderstanding of linguistic expressions, an outlandish myth.[31] Diodorus tells the story because Ophellas' army pass by the cave in which Lamia was said to have been born, but motifs shared with Dio's 'Libyan myth' suggest that rationalisation was indeed at home in the 'Libyan' context, and Dio too may well have gestured towards this kind of interpretation.

Lucan's desert

There is one further Libyan 'adventure' of classical poetry which must be added here, namely the march of Cato and his men through the Libyan desert in Book 9 of Lucan's *Bellum ciuile*. This episode, most famous for its account of the plague of snakes which Cato's soldiers encounter and for the extraordinary deaths which are described with such apparent relish, is usually seen as a remarkable elaboration from the historical record and/or a Lucanian version of the tortured wanderings of Odysseus, but one of Lucan's epic starting-points was certainly the Argonauts' trip through the Libyan desert in *Argonautica* 4. The carrying of the *Argo* through the desert was the very stuff of myth:

> Μουσάων ὅδε μῦθος, ἐγὼ δ' ὑπακουὸς ἀείδω
> Πιερίδων, καὶ τήνδε πανατρεκὲς ἔκλυον ὀμφήν,
> ὑμέας, ὦ πέρι δὴ μέγα φέρτατοι υἷες ἀνάκτων,
> ᾗ βίῃ, ᾗ ἀρετῇ Λιβύης ἀνὰ θῖνας ἐρήμους
> νῆα μεταχρονίην ὅσα τ' ἔνδοθι νηὸς ἄγεσθε
> ἀνθεμένους ὤμοισι φέρειν δυοκαίδεκα πάντα
> ἤματ' ὁμοῦ νύκτας τε. δύην γε μὲν ἢ καὶ ὀιζύν
> τίς κ' ἐνέποι, τὴν κεῖνοι ἀνέπλησαν μογέοντες;
>
> Apollonius Rhodius, *Argonautica* 4.1381–1388

This tale is the Muses', I sing obedient to the daughters of Pieria. This report too I heard exactly: that you, much the greatest sons of gods, by your strength and by your prowess placed the ship and all that it contained aloft upon your shoulders, and carried it for twelve whole days and an equal number of nights through the desert sand-dunes of Libya. Who could tell of the suffering and wretchedness which was the fate of these men as they laboured?

Lucan turns history into myth, and at its centre stands not the ἀρετή (v. 1384) of the Argonauts, but the *uirtus* of a single leader, Cato; both expeditions are summoned *ad magnum uirtutis opus summosque labores*, 'to the great task of

---

31 For other rationalisations of Lamia cf. 'Heraclitus', *De incred.* 34, Hawes 2014, 115–116.

virtue and the greatest toils' (Lucan 9.381).³² Libya, always a land of paradox (a land where men carry ships rather than vice versa), becomes a veritable theatre of paradox in Lucan's poetry. The Syrtis, neither sea nor land (*in dubio pelagi terraeque*, 9.304), now almost stands outside nature itself (9.310–311). Nowhere are the paradoxes thicker than in the descriptions of death by snake poison, and this is much more than a matter of rhetorical wit. Snakes first came to this parched, barren land as a bloody fertilising rain (9.697–699, cf. *Arg.* 4.1513–1517), and when a body rots away as the result of the bite of a *seps* there is the flood of *letum fluens*, 'flowing death' (9.789), which is the only flood Libya ever sees: *natant* (770), *fluxere* (770), *liquitur* (772), *destillant* (772), *fluunt* (773), *manant* (780), *fluunt* (782), *stillasse* (783). The whole passage may be seen as a remarkably extended elaboration, an αὔξησις, of the death of the prophet Mopsus in the *Argonautica* (4.1522–1531),³³ and death from the *prester*, a death characterised by unstoppable swelling rather than melting, produces another corpse which, like the final victim of Dio 5, is not to be touched by man or beast (9.802–804).³⁴

Very many readers of Lucan have wanted to see the episode in the Libyan desert as an allegory of Stoic truth or virtue, though they have differed radically on how 'seriously' or 'comically' to take the passage. For Matthew Leigh, for example, 'the poet goes out of his way to invite an allegorical interpretation, but only one which shows the hopeless failure of Cato's moral instruction';³⁵ Leigh and others rightly catalogue our temptation to see the effects of the snakes, particularly the thirst-inducing *dipsas*, as evocative or representative of the disturbances caused by insatiable appetite and desire, which the virtuous man, whether a Heracles or a Cato, must overcome, and already Seneca had drawn a philosophical moral from Cato's endurance of extreme heat and suffering (*Epist.*

---

32 For Lucan's use of the *Argonautica* and Argonautic themes more generally cf. Murray 2011, where however the Libyan episode is not discussed. Griffiths 2012 emphasises the importance of ἀρετή in Apollonius' Libyan episode, but does not refer to Lucan.

33 An intermediate source is of course the 'flowing' death inflicted by Nicander's ἑρπηστῶν βασιλεύς, cf. *Theriaca* 403–404. The closest parallel in Lucan to the manner of Mopsus' death is not in fact the death of Sabellus from a *seps*, but rather the death of Laevus from a 'serpent of the Nile': *nulloque dolore / testatus morsus subdita caligine mortem / accipis et socias somno descendis ad umbras*, 'feeling no pain from the bite, you accept death as darkness steals over you, and you descend to the shadows which join with sleep' (9.816–818). Both deaths evoke the descent of 'the mist of death' in martial epic. On Lucan's debt to Nicander cf., e.g., Cazzaniga 1957.

34 Here again (cf. previous note), the direct source is Nicander's *Theriaca* (vv. 405–410).

35 Leigh 1997, 267. For a bibliography of Stoic readings cf., e.g., Leigh 1997, 265 n. 83, Bartsch 1997, 34, adding, e.g., Behr 2007, Skelenar 2003.

104.33, cf. *Epist.* 24.5–7). Here in fact the contrast between Heracles' crazed assuaging of his thirst in Apollonius' Libya (*Arg.* 4.1441–9), 'like a grazing beast', and Cato's paraded and more than human refusal of water in Lucan (9.388–403, 500–510, 591–593, 617–618 etc) is very striking.[36] As in Dio the snake-females stand for 'irrational and brutish desires' (Dio 5.16), such as 'luxury or money or sexual pleasure or reputation' (5.17), so in Lucan, to quote Leigh again, 'Lucan invites the reader to allegorize the burning thirst of Aulus as the *sitis* of appetite and cupidity, the "thirsty poison in his heart" (*sitiens in corde uenenum*)'.[37] Lucan's expostulation against those who seek (historical) truth from poets (9.359–360), in the very context of Heracles and the Apples of the Hesperides, is similarly often read as precisely inviting us to read allegorically. If, however, Dio 5 and other texts allow us to hypothesise an earlier tradition of such a moralising reading of the dangers of the Libyan desert (which in any case seems all but certain), Lucan exploits our knowledge of such traditions to challenge the very possibility of meaningful allegorical reading within a world as full of paradox and chance as the Libyan desert. Cato survives, and it is not unreasonable to see this as a result of his *uirtus*; those who perish in the most bizarrely theatrical manner are, however, not obviously punished for their appetites, but rather because they were in a place where no man should be (9.854–862).

Nevertheless, the temptation persists to set Lucan within the tradition descending from Plato which I have been pursuing, and other factors too strengthen that temptation. Lucan re-literalises Virgilian metaphors of passion in a way which almost forces us to wonder about what kind of reading strategy is demanded here; in particular, it is Dido's erotic suffering, expressed in images of fire or poison in the heart (*Aen.* 1.660, 688, 713, 4.1–2, 66–69, 101 etc.), a suffering which Dido 'drank in' (*Aen.* 1.749), of which we are most reminded. When the soldier Aulus is bitten by a *dipsas*, the evocation of the Virgilian heroine is all but explicit:

---

36 The fact that Nicander seems to have borrowed Apollonius' description of Heracles' wild drinking to describe the effects of the bite of a *dipsas* (*Ther.* 340–342) perhaps suggests an amusing gesture by Nicander towards a rationalising interpretation, just as I have suggested for the end of Dio 5, particularly as it immediately precedes the poet's telling of the myth of that snake. Leigh 2000, 106 rather speculates that this echo 'may suggest a previous symbolic interpretation of [the *dipsas*] of the sort apparent in Lucan and Lucian'.
37 Leigh 1997, 271–272. Leigh also (p. 273 n. 102) notes that the swelling effect of the bite of the *prester* is like the classic effects of anger, particularly as described by Seneca, and that Pollux 2.134 says that πρηστήρ is a word for the veins of the neck swollen by anger.

> ecce subit uirus tacitum, carpitque medullas
> ignis edax calidaque incendit uiscera tabe.
>
> Lucan, Bellum ciuile 9.741–742

> Behold! The poison rises unseen, and the devouring flame feeds on his marrow and sets his vitals on fire with a burning wasting.

In Lucan, we are now dealing with 'real' poison, 'real' thirst, and 'real' inner fire, but the recall of Dido's suffering suggests that such language always operates on more than one level. The snakes which teem in Lucan's Libyan desert are, as they are in Apollonius' *Argonautica*, the offspring of the snake-hair of the severed head of the Gorgon Medusa, but what strikes us most is their sheer variety and profusion, and the variety of the deaths they inflict, and here we may be tempted (again) to recall the ποικιλία of the desire which Heracles overcame in Herodorus' account (cf. above). In *Oration* 8, Dio's Diogenes, who had told Alexander 'the Libyan myth' in *Oration* 4, delivers a diatribe on the battle with pleasure (ἡδονή), here primarily depicted through the figure of the Homeric Circe. Pleasure (again) does not attack us ἁπλῶς, 'in a single way', but rather πάντα τρόπον, 'in every manner', 'seeking to destroy us through our sight and hearing, smell or taste or touch, in our food and our drink and in desire for sex, equally when we are awake and when we are asleep' (8.21). Moreover, Diogenes speaks of 'the various (ποικίλοι), deadly snakes and other crawling things which arise from pleasure, and which attend upon pleasure as they hang around her doors' (8.25), and pleasure gives men over to 'the most hateful and difficult labours (πόνοι)' (8.26). It comes as no surprise that Diogenes' model for his own resistance to pleasure is Heracles (8.27–28), and throughout this passage of Dio 8 we may well be reminded of Lucan's ninth book. Moreover, variety and change take us back (again) to Plato's Typhon, a complicated rather than a simple beast (*Phaedrus* 230a4–5), and, as we have seen (cf. above p. 563), the model for the image of the appetitive part of the soul in *Republic* 9; Hesiod's Typhon had a hundred snaky heads (*Theog.* 825) and the voice of every head changed constantly. We know that Plato had little time for ideas of metamorphosis and change, particularly where the divine was concerned, but I wonder — more specifically — whether Lucan's ποικιλία of serpents is one dramatisation, or rather perhaps deconstruction, of Plato's Typhon, here inviting us not towards rationalisation, but to a type of allegory which we have seen is only too common. The snakes and the changeability of the Hesiodic Typhon are thus reincarnated in the killing fields of Lucan's Libya, and it is the Platonic Socrates who has given the impetus to this. Whether or not the Stoic Cato is in fact another re-incarnation of the Platonic Socrates,[38] a man who famously could withstand both burning solar heat and freezing cold, a man who had freed his body from the passions and appetites which beset others, is a question at least worth asking.

Bibliography

Anderson, G. 2000. 'Some uses of story telling in Dio', in: S. Swain (ed.), *Dio Chrysostom: Politics, Letters, and Philosophy*, Oxford, 143–160.
Arnim, H. von. 1891. 'Entstehung und Anordnung der Schriftensammlung Dios von Prusa', *Hermes* 26, 366–407.
Arnim, H. von. 1898. *Leben und Werke des Dion von Prusa*, Berlin.
Bartsch, S. 1997. *Ideology in Cold Blood*, Cambridge MA.
Behr, F.D'A. 2007. *Feeling History. Lucan, Stoicism, and the Poetics of Passion*, Columbus OH.
Brouwer, R. 2014. *The Stoic Sage*, Cambridge.
Cazzaniga, I. 1957. 'L'episodio dei serpi libici in Lucano e la tradizione dei "Therika" nicandrei', *Acme* 10, 27–41.
Cowan, J. 1994. *Myths of the Dreaming*, Bridport.
Dufner, C.M. 1988. *The Odyssey in the Argonautica*, Diss. Princeton.
Fakhry, A. 1944. *Siwa Oasis: its history and antiquities*, Cairo.
Feeney, D. 1986. 'Following after Hercules, in Virgil and Apollonius', *Proceedings of the Virgil Society* 18, 47–85.
Fusillo, M. 1985. *Il tempo delle Argonautiche*, Rome.
Gangloff, A. 2006. *Dion Chrysostome et les mythes*, Grenoble.
Georgiadou, A./Larmour, D.H.J. 1997. 'Lucian's vine-women (*VH* 1, 6–9) and Dio's Libyan women (*Orat.* 5): variations on a theme', *Mnemosyne* 40, 205–209.
Griffiths, F.T. 2012. 'Claiming Libya: Peleus and the Ptolemies in Apollonius Rhodius' *Argonautica*', in: C. Cusset/N. Le Meur-Weissmann/F. Levin (eds.), *Mythe et pouvoir à l'époque hellénistique*, Leuven, 3–35.
Hawes, G. 2014. *Rationalising Myth in Antiquity*, Oxford.
Hunter, R. 1993. *The Argonautica of Apollonius: Literary Studies*, Cambridge.
Hunter, R. 2008a. *On Coming After*, Berlin/New York.
Hunter, R. 2008b. 'The poetics of narrative in the *Argonautica*', in: T. Papanghelis/A. Rengakos (eds.), *A Companion to Apollonius Rhodius*, Leiden, 2nd ed., 115–146 [= 2008a, 343–377].
Hunter, R. 2012. *Plato and the Traditions of Ancient Literature: the silent stream*, Cambridge.
Hunter, R. 2015. *Apollonius of Rhodes, Argonautica Book IV*, Cambridge.
Hunter, R./Russell, D. 2011. *Plutarch, How to Study Poetry*, Cambridge.
Kuhlmann, K.P. 1988. *Das Ammoneion: Archäologie, Geschichte und Kultpraxis des Orakels von Siwa*, Mainz.
Leigh, M. 1997. *Lucan: Spectacle and Engagement*, Oxford.

---

[38] On the Stoic use of the Socrates cf. Brouwer 2014, ch. 4, citing earlier bibliography.

Leigh, M. 2000. 'Lucan and the Libyan tale', *Journal of Roman Studies* 90, 95–109.
Moles, J. 1983. 'The date and purpose of the Fourth Kingship Oration of Dio Chrysostom', *Classical Antiquity* 2, 251–278.
Mori, A. 2008. *The Politics of Apollonius Rhodius' Argonautica*, Cambridge.
Murray, J. 2011. 'Shipwrecked "Argonauticas"', in: P. Asso (ed.), *Brill's Companion to Lucan*, Leiden, 57–79.
Rowe, C. 1986. *Plato: Phaedrus*, Warminster.
Rutherford, I. 2013. *State Pilgrims and Sacred Observers in Ancient Greece*, Cambridge.
Said, S. 2000. 'Dio's use of mythology', in: S. Swain (ed.), *Dio Chrysostom: Politics, Letters, and Philosophy*, Oxford, 161–186.
Skelenar, R. 2003. *The Taste for Nothingness*, Ann Arbor.
Swain, S. 1996. *Hellenism and Empire*, Oxford.
Thalmann, W.G. 2011. *Apollonius of Rhodes and the Spaces of Hellenism*, New York.
Vian, F. 1981. *Apollonios de Rhodes, Argonautiques, Chant IV*, Paris.
Werner, D.S. 2012. *Myth and Philosophy in Plato's Phaedrus*, New York.

32 'Palaephatus', Strabo and the Boundaries of Myth

One of the principal problems confronting anyone concerned with the ancient critical reception of Homer and/or the broader question of how the Greeks began to construct distinctions in what they heard and read between history, fiction, and myth, or indeed between science and non-science, is that it is very difficult to get back to a 'state of grace': most of our ancient texts in these areas seem already contaminated by sophistications of one kind or another. That, however, may well be the point: there may never have been such a pure state, at least in the historical period covered by our extant texts. Rather, therefore, than trying to distinguish between Archaic texts, which come from a world that still understood, indeed functioned through, poetry and myth, and postclassical texts which had lost their intellectual virginity and for whom all this was play, I want to begin *in mediis rebus* with a text that is relatively early (late fourth century BCE), but also — when viewed from another perspective — seems very late indeed. This is the extant Preface to the collection of mythical rationalizations that goes under the name of 'Palaephatus':[1]

τάδε περὶ τῶν ἀπίστων συγγέγραφα. ἀνθρώπων γὰρ οἱ μὲν εὐπειθέστεροι πείθονται πᾶσι τοῖς λεγομένοις, ὡς ἀνομίλητοι σοφίας καὶ ἐπιστήμης, οἱ δὲ πυκνότεροι τὴν φύσιν καὶ πολυπράγματοι ἀπιστοῦσι τὸ παράπαν μηδὲ γενέσθαι τι τούτων. ἐμοὶ δὲ δοκεῖ γενέσθαι πάντα τὰ λεγόμενα. οὐ γὰρ ὀνόματα μόνον ἐγένοντο, λόγος δὲ περὶ αὐτῶν οὐδεὶς ὑπῆρξεν· ἀλλὰ πρότερον ἐγένετο τὸ ἔργον, εἶθ' οὕτως ὁ λόγος ὁ περὶ αὐτῶν. ὅσα δὲ εἴδη καὶ μορφαί εἰσι λεγόμεναι καὶ γενόμεναι τότε, αἳ νῦν οὐκ εἰσί, τὰ τοιαῦτα οὐκ ἐγένοντο. εἰ γάρ <τί> ποτε καὶ ἄλλοτε ἐγένετο, καὶ νῦν τε γίνεται καὶ αὖθις ἔσται. ἀεὶ δὲ ἔγωγε ἐπαινῶ τοὺς συγγραφέας Μέλισσον καὶ Λαμίσκον τὸν Σάμιον ἐν ἀρχῇ λέγοντας 'ἔστιν ἃ ἐγένετο, καὶ νῦν ἔσται'. γενομένων δέ τινα οἱ ποιηταὶ καὶ λογογράφοι παρέτρεψαν εἰς τὸ ἀπιστότερον καὶ

A version of this essay was delivered as the Walsh Memorial lecture at the University of Chicago in March 2015; I have not sought to remove every vestige of oral presentation. I would like to express my very warm thanks to the Department of Classics at Chicago for the invitation and to the audience there for much stimulating discussion and criticism. This paper has also benefitted from the reactions of audiences at Princeton University and the University of Texas at Austin.

1 For the sake of simplicity I will henceforth omit the quotation marks around the name. For Palaephatus and the relevant bibliography, see esp. Hawes 2014a and 2014b; I have not thought it necessary to record every place where I agree with or differ from Hawes' helpful accounts. The translation of the Preface offered here is awkwardly literal, but that seems necessary in the circumstances.

θαυμασιώτερον, τοῦ θαυμάζειν ἕνεκα τοὺς ἀνθρώπους. ἐγὼ δὲ γινώσκω ὅτι οὐ δύναται τὰ τοιαῦτα εἶναι οἷα καὶ λέγεται· τοῦτο δὲ καὶ διείληφα, ὅτι, εἰ μὴ ἐγένετο, οὐκ ἂν ἐλέγετο. ἐπελθὼν δὲ καὶ πλείστας χώρας ἐπυνθανόμην τῶν πρεσβυτέρων ὡς ἀκούοιεν περὶ ἑκάστου αὐτῶν, συγγράφω δὲ ἃ ἐπυθόμην παρ' αὐτῶν. καὶ τὰ χωρία αὐτὸς εἶδον ὡς ἔστιν ἕκαστον ἔχον, καὶ γέγραφα ταῦτα οὐχ οἷα ἦν λεγόμενα, ἀλλ' αὐτὸς ἐπελθὼν καὶ ἱστορήσας.

'Palaephatus', *On incredible things*, Preface[2]

I have recorded these things concerning unbelievable matters. Some men are gullible and believe everything which is reported, as they have no familiarity with wisdom and knowledge, whereas others who are more subtle by nature and questioning completely disbelieve that any of these things ever happened. My view is that everything which is reported happened [in some form], for they were not merely names without any stories about them;[3] first came the fact and then the story about the facts. As for the shapes and forms which are reported and [allegedly] occurred then, and which do not exist now, these did not exist; for if <anything> ever existed in another time, it both exists now and will do so in the future. I have always approved the prose-writers Melissos and Lamiskos the Samian[4] who say, at the beginning of their work,[5] 'there are things which were and which will be again'. Poets and chroniclers have turned some of the things which have happened in the direction of the unbelievable and wonderful in order to amaze men. But I know that things are not possible such as they are reported, but I have also understood that, if they had not happened [in some form], there would not have been reports. I travelled to very many countries and made enquiries of the older people as to what they had heard about each of these things, and I record what I learned from them. I myself saw the condition of each place, and I have written these things not as they have been reported, but after myself going and making investigations.

Uncertainties of text and interpretation do not dampen the interest of the Preface, which has indeed often been regarded as much more interesting than the rationalizations that follow in the Palaephatan collection. The possibility, some would say very strong likelihood, that this text dates from peripatetic circles in the late fourth century, that is, at a crucial time for the development of collecting and thinking about the nature of myths and myth, merely adds to its inter-

---

2 Except for punctuation, this is the text given by Festa 1902 and Santoni 2000.
3 The text here is almost certainly corrupt; the translation and supplement are not intended to offer a solution to the textual problem.
4 τὸν Σάμιον is often regarded as an intrusive marginal gloss, originally referring to Melissus, who was from Samos. This is no doubt possible, but hardly certain, given the games with authority that Palaephatus is playing here; the only relevant Lamiskos of whom we know is a character from the circle of Archytas who was known to Plato (cf. *Epist.* 7.305b; Diog. Laert. 3.22). For the use Palaephatus makes of Eleatic 'Being', cf. Hawes 2014a, 44.
5 It is not certain that this is what the transmitted text means; corruption can (again) not be ruled out.

est.⁶ For all that Palaephatus' denial of the possibility of weird and hybrid forms seems to look forward to Lucretius' very similar and certainly serious denial (5.855–924; cf. 4.722–748), the most obvious thing about this text, one might think, is that it is a knowing bluff or rather po-faced joke, although this is not how it is normally regarded. Although some modern scholars have recognized that Palaephatus probably did not go on extensive research trips, the Preface is almost universally taken as a serious justification for the practice of myth rationalization, even by those who recognize that Palaephatus is adopting a pose.⁷ The reasons for this attitude probably lie deep within the nature of classics and classicists, but for the moment let us stay with the nature of this text itself.

Palaephatus' Preface is in places reminiscent of the tone, if not the arguments, of Lucian's *True Histories*, and the historiographical pose is in fact the single most prominent thread that runs through the rhetoric of this introduction.⁸ The opening τάδε περὶ τῶν ἀπίστων συγγέγραφα, with its witty tension between the historiographical verb and the subject matter ('things you can't believe'), uses a version of the same kind of paradoxical clash between style and subject that we find at the head of Seneca's *Apocolocyntosis*, *quid actum sit in caelo ... volo memoriae tradere*, another preface that plays with issues of belief in the unbelievable, the authority of sources, and a historiographical voice. If, however, the style, rather than the paradoxical subject, reminds us of Hecataeus' famous opening,⁹ it is in fact Herodotus whose presence, flagged by the closing ἱστορήσας, by the whole language of belief and the recording of reports, and by the self-representation of the writer as a traveling inquirer after truth,

---

6 Cf. Hawes 2014a, 227–238 (a full collection of the evidence), Trachsel 2005, 551–554. Theon *Prog.* 96 sp. refers to 'Palaephatus the Peripatetic', and the *Suda* π 70 makes Palaephatus a contemporary of Artaxerxes; the date of Athenion frag. 1 K-A, where a cook who explains how his art has been responsible for human progress is called 'a new Palaephatus', is unfortunately uncertain.

7 Whitmarsh 2013, 17–18 considers to what extent Palaephatus' rationalizations are laughable or ludic, but does not discuss the Preface; so too, Hawes 2014b, 126 observes that 'we might indeed wonder about how seriously we should actually take this text', but she too is there discussing the 'irredeemably banal' and repetitive mythic explanations, not the Preface.

8 On 'Palaephatus' and myth rationalization in the historians, cf., e.g., Nestle 1942, 131–152, Stern 1996, 10–16, 1999, 219–220, Santoni 2000, 19–21 (a good discussion of the introduction), 30–32. Hawes 2014a, 13 rightly notes that 'rationalistic interpretation has a natural affinity with *historia*'.

9 Cf. Santoni 2000, 19. Santoni also rightly cites Antiochus of Syracuse fr. 2 Jacoby, Ἀντίοχος Ξενοφάνεος τάδε συνέγραψε περὶ Ἰταλίας, ἐκ τῶν ἀρχαίων λόγων τὰ πιστότατα καὶ σαφέστατα; this is the kind of historiographical rhetoric that Palaephatus turns on its head.

hangs over this whole passage.[10] This is, however, a Herodotus mediated to us through the famous passage with which Thucydides concludes his account of how ignorant people can be of even relatively recent history:

οὕτως ἀταλαίπωρος τοῖς πολλοῖς ἡ ζήτησις τῆς ἀληθείας, καὶ ἐπὶ τὰ ἑτοῖμα μᾶλλον τρέπονται. ἐκ δὲ τῶν εἰρημένων τεκμηρίων ὅμως τοιαῦτα ἄν τις νομίζων μάλιστα ἃ διῆλθον οὐχ ἁμαρτάνοι, καὶ οὔτε ὡς ποιηταὶ ὑμνήκασι περὶ αὐτῶν ἐπὶ τὸ μεῖζον κοσμοῦντες μᾶλλον πιστεύων, οὔτε ὡς λογογράφοι ξυνέθεσαν ἐπὶ τὸ προσαγωγότερον τῇ ἀκροάσει ἢ ἀληθέστερον, ὄντα ἀνεξέλεγκτα καὶ τὰ πολλὰ ὑπὸ χρόνου αὐτῶν ἀπίστως ἐπὶ τὸ μυθῶδες ἐκνενικηκότα, ηὑρῆσθαι δὲ ἡγησάμενος ἐκ τῶν ἐπιφανεστάτων σημείων ὡς παλαιὰ εἶναι ἀποχρώντως.

Thuc. 1.20.3–21.1

So little trouble do people take to search out the truth, and so readily do they accept what first comes to hand. From the evidence I have presented, however, one would not go wrong in supposing that events were very much as I have set them out; and no one should prefer rather to believe the songs of the poets, who exaggerate things for artistic purposes, or the writings of the chroniclers, which are composed more to make good listening than to represent the truth, being impossible to check and having most of them won a place over time in the imaginary realm of fable. My findings, however, you can regard as derived from the clearest evidence available for material of this antiquity.

Trans. J. Mynott

Palaephatus repeats Thucydides' charge against the unreliability of 'poets and chroniclers' and the reasons for it (to make what is told more impressive, more effective as ἔκπληξις, to use the language of later criticism), but he does not accept that such things are ἀνεξέλεγκτα ('beyond investigation'). What matters, in fact, is what you are seeking to investigate, that is, what questions one might reasonably ask of mythic material. Much of the rich tradition of mythographical writing in the postclassical period may indeed be seen as a series of attempts to meet Thucydides' pessimistic claim, and this applies not just to texts that are normally thought of as 'mythographic'. In a famous passage that opens his *Life of Theseus*, Plutarch compares himself to 'researchers in geography' (ἐν ταῖς γεωγραφίαις ... οἱ ἱστορικοί) and historical time to a map where 'the parts which escape their [i.e., geographers'] knowledge' are put around the edge with labels which amount (as would say) to 'here be dragons'. The equivalent distinction for the historian is between periods of time 'that may be reached by probable

---

[10] Lucian offers a related parody of such inquiry when he notes that he made serious inquiries (ἀναζητοῦντος ... ἐμοῦ καὶ διαπυνθανομένου) of the locals who lived by the Eridanos about the myth of Phaethon and his sisters, though he happened to be in the vicinity by chance on another errand (*Electr.* 2).

reasoning and offer territory for history which stays close to real events' (τὸν ἐφικτὸν εἰκότι λόγῳ καὶ βάσιμον ἱστορίᾳ πραγμάτων ἐχομένη χρόνον) and those that are 'the stuff of marvel and tragedy, inhabited by poets and mythographers, where there can be no confidence or certainty' (τὰ ... τερατώδη καὶ τραγικὰ ποιηταὶ καὶ μυθογράφοι νέμονται, καὶ οὐκέτ' ἔχει πίστιν οὐδὲ σαφήνειαν). The Thucydidean heritage that gives primacy to the process of investigation, to the drawing of inference from evidence, the how rather than the what, if you will, is very clearly on show here.[11] Plutarch will not give up on the remote edges of time, but rather will do what he can to bring them under a familiar umbrella:

> εἴη μὲν οὖν ἡμῖν ἐκκαθαιρόμενον λόγῳ τὸ μυθῶδες ὑπακοῦσαι καὶ λαβεῖν ἱστορίας ὄψιν· ὅπου δ' ἂν αὐθαδῶς τοῦ πιθανοῦ περιφρονῇ καὶ μὴ δέχηται τὴν πρὸς τὸ εἰκὸς μεῖξιν, εὐγνωμόνων ἀκροατῶν δεησόμεθα καὶ πρᾴως τὴν ἀρχαιολογίαν προσδεχομένων.
>
> Plutarch, *Theseus* 1.3
>
> May I succeed in cleaning out[12] the mythical element and making it obedient to reason and giving it the appearance of history. Where, however, it wantonly scorns credibility and will not accept an admixture of the probable, I ask for an audience that is well-disposed and that receives this account of the distant past with indulgence.

Plutarch accepts that there are some *mythika* that are beyond the exercise of *logos*. Palaephatus was not so faint-hearted.

With a nod and a wink, Palaephatus sets out to show that even 'those things that have won their way to mythic status contrary to believability [ἀπίστως]' will yield before the march of σοφία and ἐπιστήμη. The mixed signals which Palaephatus gives out are perhaps part of the point. Thucydides had claimed that men uncritically (ἀβασανίστως) receive reports (ἀκοαί) about events in the past, 'even if they occurred in their own country' (1.20.1);[13] Palaephatus, having

---

11 Cf., e.g., Hawes 2014a, 150–151.
12 The image is perhaps that of a land cleared of beasts (by a Heracles, for example), i.e., a continuation of the 'map' image with which the work opens, rather than of the pruning of luxuriant vegetation, as Hawes 2014a, 151 translates, despite the interesting parallel at *How to study poetry* 15e–f.
13 Thucydides' rhetoric may find another echo in a similar context at 'Heraclitus' *Hom. Probl.* 3.2, where the author is dismissing those who take Homer's poetry at face value and therefore regard him as impious: ἀβασάνιστος αὐτοῖς ἡ τῆς ἀληθείας κρίσις ἔρριπται; cf. esp. Thuc. 1.20.3 (cited above), οὕτως ἀταλαίπωρος τοῖς πολλοῖς ἡ ζήτησις τῆς ἀληθείας. Thucydides would perhaps not have been amused to learn that his defense of the painstaking pursuit of 'historical truth' was repeatedly echoed in support of the proper understanding of, and hence the usefulness of, the mythical. More in the Thucydidean tradition is Philostratus *Heroicus* 7.10, where the Phoenician notes that when he was a child he believed the μῦθοι that his nurse told him,

distanced himself from the tall tales of the 'poets and chroniclers', now tells us that what he is writing is what, in response to his enquiries (πυνθάνεσθαι), the older people in any locality 'had heard' about their past. There is, admittedly, some unclarity here. The final sentence might be taken to be relevant merely to its immediate context, so that Palaephatus is simply here denying that he has 'uncritically' written down what he has been told in each place he visited, but it seems more natural to understand it as picking up the opening of the Preface in a kind of ring composition. Some people, thus, simply believe τὰ λεγόμενα and some deny their truth entirely, but Palaephatus positions himself between these two extremes, by stressing both the fact that the *legomena* preserve significant traces, an idea that is in fact crucial for Palaephatus' own *logos*,[14] and also the 'on the spot' research he has actually done; he has gone to do his own investigations, which consist in part of listening to the stories of old men, a practice familiar from such serious later researchers as Pausanias (cf. 6.24.9). It has been argued that such an appeal to oral sources for myth lends 'credibility' to the mythic analyses that follow,[15] but it seems more likely that the effect of Palaephatus' claim is just the opposite: Palaephatus knows that this claim will undermine any residual faith in his earnestness to which we may still be clinging. Commentators solemnly point out that asking even a very old man you might meet on a Colchian street about, for example, the Golden Fleece is unlikely (to say no more) to take you as far back as Palaephatus' rationalizations apparently go, but it should by now be clear that solemnity is perhaps not the right mood in which to approach this text.

Blanket skepticism, then, is in fact anti-intellectual (it resists the impulse to investigate and ask questions) and self-defeating. It would be easy to respond that this claim too is at best a ludic trope: we are all now (this probably being the late fourth century BCE) πεπαιδευμένοι *avant la lettre*, we know that myths as simple narrative material are being systematically collected and collated, the very idea of 'myth' is being interrogated, and Callimachus' *Aitia* is not so many years away. This is, it must be noted, no longer the 'there was once a time'

---

but when he became a young man (μειράκιον) 'I thought that these things should not be accepted ἀβασανίστως'; cf. Kim 2010, 184.
14 For a related, but very different, privileging of *logos* in a similar context of rhetorical self-advertisement we may compare Libanius' introduction to his *ekphrasis* of the Chimaera (Viii 518 Foerster): 'Unexpected/irrational [παράλογοι] forms emerged randomly [ἐκ τύχης] in the beginning, but having come into existence did not succeed in remaining; *logos* however preserved the forms which time concealed'. Here we should sense the distant echo of Empedoclean cosmogony.
15 Cf. Hawes 2014a, 45–47, 2014b, 1378.

world of the early poets; 'mythography', which has clear fifth-century roots but of which from some perspectives Palaephatus may be considered the first extant example,[16] changes everything. There is clearly truth in these objections, but Palaephatus' claimed approach to story-telling is in fact not all that different from that of a Hecataeus or even a Herodotus. From one perspective, Thucydidean strictures allowed the explicit written formulation of what was, and continued to be, inherent in Greek mythic narrative: Hesiod, and it may be argued Homer also, knew that 'mythic' discourse was different from other modes, not worse or better, but certainly different; we exaggerate that difference, or rather exaggerate its importance, because so much of our evidence comes from those who were precisely interested in collecting this particular mode of discourse (an Apollodorus, for example), but Thucydides' formulation in fact merely allowed people to say more clearly what they had always wanted to say.[17]

One of the most enduring features of the literary recording and elaboration (διασκευή) of myth (broadly conceived) in antiquity was its capacity for embracing, indeed appearing to invite, the ludic. Comic poets, for example, found little difficulty in writing plays on the 'Oedipus' theme, and the most significant mythological poems of antiquity, Callimachus' *Aitia* and Ovid's *Metamorphoses*, give a very prominent place to humor and irony of all kinds. Palaephatus has usually just been a footnote in this history, and yet he has more than a few notions in common with some of the most splendid examples of such literary elaboration. Consider, for example, the famous opening (rather than the Preface) of Apuleius' *Metamorphoses*. Lucius joins two other travelers on the road to Thessaly (land of wonders, a place where 'traces' of another order, buried elsewhere by change and progress, might well [be believed to] survive) and the first thing he hears is an imprecation against 'absurd and monstrous lies' (1.2); he asks to be allowed to listen in, 'as someone who, though not *curiosus* [we think perhaps of Palaephatus' πολυπράγματοι], wishes to know everything, or at least nearly everything' (1.2). To the complete skepticism of one of his fellow-travelers he feels compelled to oppose the fact that things that seem novel or difficult often

---

16 Cf., e.g., Trzaskoma 2013, xvii–xviii. The earliest occurrence of μυθογράφος/μυθογραφία seems to be in a pseudo-Aristotelian text of (probably) the late fourth century; cf. Fowler 2000a, 2000b, xxvii–xxviii, 2013b, xiv, unless the concluding tag of Palaephatus 26, ἀφ' οὗ οἱ μυθογράφοι τὸν μῦθον ἔπλασαν, is in fact earlier than that text. On the rise of a genre of mythography, cf. Fowler 2000b, xxvii–xxxvi, 2006, 2013a, 2013b, xiv–xv.

17 This is clearly not the place to revisit the whole *mythos-logos* debate, or even the emergence of mythography (see previous note) as something distinct from historiography, though of course these form crucial parts of the background to any consideration of Palaephatus; Fowler 2011 offers important guidance and a rich bibliography.

prove not to be so, *si paulo accuratius exploraris* (1.3); here the Thucydidean (and then Palaephatan) tradition of 'investigation' is to be put (paradoxically) to the defense of the marvelous. After Aristomenes has told his story of the death of Socrates, Lucius again defends what we might call 'an open mind' – *nihil impossibile arbitror*; there are many *mira et paene infecta* which happen, but which people simply do not believe when they are related (1.20). It is not just that Palaephatus shares with Apuleius' narrator an interest in εἴδη καὶ μορφαί, but that both sketch out the territory of response to myth in a shared language, even though one put to utterly different uses. What we might think of as Lucius' plea on behalf of gullibility is in fact a pointed reminder that the Thucydidean tradition can go too far; for his part, Palaephatus pleads for a middle way that seeks to go beyond simple skepticism in explaining how myth arises. The origin of the *legomena* has itself now become an appropriate object of research.

Apuleius' opening consideration of the credible and the impossible finds a close parallel in the (roughly contemporary?) Φιλοψευδεῖς ἢ ἀπιστῶν of Lucian, in which 'Tychiades' plays the role of the cynical skeptic confronted, as was Apuleius' skeptic, with πολλὰ τὰ ἄπιστα καὶ μυθώδη (5);[18] to the more credulous, however, his blanket skepticism is laughable (16). Tychiades knows, moreover, that he is in the minority:

> καίτοι τὰ μὲν τῶν ποιητῶν ἴσως μέτρια, τὸ δὲ καὶ πόλεις ἤδη καὶ ἔθνη ὅλα κοινῇ καὶ δημοσίᾳ ψεύδεσθαι πῶς οὐ γελοῖον; εἰ Κρῆτες μὲν τὸν Διὸς τάφον δεικνύντες οὐκ αἰσχύνονται, Ἀθηναῖοι δὲ τὸν Ἐριχθόνιον ἐκ τῆς γῆς ἀναδοθῆναί φασιν καὶ τοὺς πρώτους ἀνθρώπους ἐκ τῆς Ἀττικῆς ἀναφῦναι καθάπερ τὰ λάχανα, πολὺ σεμνότερον οὗτοί γε τῶν Θηβαίων, οἳ ἐξ ὄφεως ὀδόντων Σπαρτούς τινας ἀναβεβλαστηκέναι διηγοῦνται. ὃς δ' ἂν οὖν ταῦτα καταγέλαστα ὄντα μὴ οἴηται ἀληθῆ εἶναι, ἀλλ' ἐμφρόνως ἐξετάζων αὐτὰ Κοροίβου τινὸς ἢ Μαργίτου νομίζῃ τὸ πείθεσθαι ἢ Τριπτόλεμον ἐλάσαι διὰ τοῦ ἀέρος ἐπὶ δρακόντων ὑποπτέρων ἢ Πᾶνα ἥκειν ἐξ Ἀρκαδίας σύμμαχον εἰς Μαραθῶνα ἢ Ὠρείθυιαν ὑπὸ τοῦ Βορέου ἁρπασθῆναι, ἀσεβὴς οὗτός γε καὶ ἀνόητος αὐτοῖς ἔδοξεν οὕτω προδήλοις καὶ ἀληθέσι πράγμασιν ἀπιστῶν· εἰς τοσοῦτον ἐπικρατεῖ τὸ ψεῦδος.
>
> Lucian, *Philops.* 3

The stories of the poets are perhaps not so bad, but how can it not be laughable that cities and whole peoples tell lies in unison and in public? The Cretans feel no shame in exhibiting Zeus' tomb, the Athenians claim that Erichthonius rose up from the earth and that the first men sprang up from Attic soil like vegetables. Their story, however, is much more serious than that of the Thebans who relate that sown Men sprouted from a snake's teeth. If

---

18 Cf., e.g., Kim 2010, 200–201. It is perhaps noteworthy that Lucian's essay includes a narrative of 'magic gone wrong' (35–37), just as Lucius' failure to reverse his transformation is what sets the narrative of the *Metamorphoses* going. On the question of whether the title should be Φιλοψευδής or the now conventional Φιλοψευδεῖς, cf. Ogden 2007, 3.

anyone considers that these absurd stories are untrue, and through rational examination thinks that only a Koroibos or a Margites would believe that Triptolemus drove through the air with winged serpents or that Pan came from Arcadia to help at the battle of Marathon or that Oreithyia was snatched away by Boreas, they think that this man is an impious fool for refusing to believe such obviously true facts. So great is the sway of falsehood.

The final myth that Tychiades cites is also a source reference. Lucian is here reworking the famous passage of Plato's *Phaedrus* in which Plato seems to make Socrates reject myth rationalization (and perhaps Palaephatus' forerunners also):

ἐγὼ δέ, ὦ Φαῖδρε, ἄλλως μὲν τὰ τοιαῦτα χαρίεντα ἡγοῦμαι, λίαν δὲ δεινοῦ καὶ ἐπιπόνου καὶ οὐ πάνυ εὐτυχοῦς ἀνδρός, κατ' ἄλλο μὲν οὐδέν, ὅτι δ' αὐτῷ ἀνάγκη μετὰ τοῦτο τὸ τῶν Ἱπποκενταύρων εἶδος ἐπανορθοῦσθαι, καὶ αὖθις τὸ τῆς Χιμαίρας, καὶ ἐπιρρεῖ δὲ ὄχλος τοιούτων Γοργόνων καὶ Πηγάσων καὶ ἄλλων ἀμηχάνων πλήθη τε καὶ ἀτοπίαι τερατολόγων τινῶν φύσεων· αἷς εἴ τις ἀπιστῶν προσβιβᾷ κατὰ τὸ εἰκὸς ἕκαστον, ἅτε ἀγροίκῳ τινὶ σοφίᾳ χρώμενος, πολλῆς αὐτῷ σχολῆς δεήσει. ἐμοὶ δὲ πρὸς αὐτὰ οὐδαμῶς ἐστι σχολή· τὸ δὲ αἴτιον, ὦ φίλε, τούτου τόδε. οὐ δύναμαί πω κατὰ τὸ Δελφικὸν γράμμα γνῶναι ἐμαυτόν· γελοῖον δή μοι φαίνεται τοῦτο ἔτι ἀγνοοῦντα τὰ ἀλλότρια σκοπεῖν. ὅθεν δὴ χαίρειν ἐάσας ταῦτα, πειθόμενος δὲ τῷ νομιζομένῳ περὶ αὐτῶν, ὃ νυνδὴ ἔλεγον, σκοπῶ οὐ ταῦτα ἀλλ' ἐμαυτόν, εἴτε τι θηρίον ὂν τυγχάνω Τυφῶνος πολυπλοκώτερον καὶ μᾶλλον ἐπιτεθυμμένον, εἴτε ἡμερώτερόν τε καὶ ἁπλούστερον ζῷον, θείας τινὸς καὶ ἀτύφου μοίρας φύσει μετέχον.
Plato, *Phdr.* 229d2–230a6

But I, Phaedrus, think such [rationalizing] explanations are very pretty in general, but are the inventions of a very clever and laborious and not altogether enviable man, for no other reason than because after this he must explain the forms of the Centaurs, and then that of the Chimaera, and there presses in upon him a whole crowd of such creatures, Gorgons and Pegasuses, and multitudes of strange, inconceivable, portentous natures. If anyone disbelieves in these, and with a rustic sort of wisdom, undertakes to explain each in accordance with probability, he will need a great deal of leisure. But I have no leisure for them at all; and the reason, my friend, is this: I am not yet able, as the Delphic inscription has it, to know myself; so it seems to me ridiculous, when I do not yet know that, to investigate irrelevant things. And so I dismiss these matters and accepting the customary belief about them, as I was saying just now, I investigate not these things, but myself, to know whether I am a monster more complicated and more furious than Typhon or a gentler and simpler creature, to whom a divine and quiet lot is given by nature.

Whereas Socrates, for his own reasons, rejects simple ἀπιστία and notes that anyone who wished seriously to apply σοφία to some myths and outlandish mythic hybrids would be an unhappy and very busy man, Lucian's Tychiades presents such an exercise of rationality as ἐμφρόνως ἐξετάζων, but one that incurs a reputation for being 'impious and foolish'. For Tychiades the matter is one of 'truth' or 'falsehood', which also stand, for example, at the center of the discussion about fabulous myths in Philostratus' *Heroicus*; for the Platonic Socrates, however, there is another way forward, one that deals with more interesting monsters such as Typhon and which does not seek to reduce stories to the banally 'probable', one whose aim, moreover, is not the explanation of myth, but rather the employment of myth in the investigation of human psychology, rationality, and passion. We might as well call that way forward 'allegory',[19] and it is worth reminding ourselves that when perhaps some five centuries later 'Heraclitus', who also appeals to ἐπιστήμη (*Hom. Probl.* 6.2), notes that 'the ignorant' take as 'mythical inventions/fictions' what Homer spoke 'philosophically' (*Hom. Probl.* 3.2), he too in fact stands within the Platonic path, for all that he then vents his spite against the philosopher in the following chapter. 'Rationalization', particularly in its simpler forms, is itself a form of allegorization;[20] one thinks of the very opening of the *Iliad* – this is not Apollo shooting his arrows, this is a plague ('Heraclitus', *Hom. Probl.* 6.5).[21] It is in fact Plato who shows us how productive Palaephatus' rejection of 'blanket skepticism' could actually be.

Before leaving Palaephatus we may note that his (alleged) attempt to steer a middle way in the interpretation of myth is one of a number that survive from antiquity and beyond and that testify to the very vigor of the debate which the nature of Homeric poetry, in particular, provoked. No mode of interpretation was of course more fiercely contested than allegorical interpretation. When 'Heraclitus' begins his allegorizing treatise with the observation that 'if Homer used no allegory, all his poetry is impious' (*Hom. Probl.* 1.1), he makes clear that this was indeed a view that some held. Such ignorant people (cf. *Hom. Probl.* 3.2)[22] occupy the same structural role for 'Heraclitus' as do those 'who believe all the *legomena*' for Palaephatus; both groups know nothing of σοφία and/or φιλοσοφία. The debate is set out for us at rather fuller length in Eustathius' introduction to his commentary on the *Iliad* (*Hom.* 3.13–14), and here – as elsewhere – Eustathius will be drawing on earlier sources, as well as upon the fruits

---

19 Cf., e.g., Hunter 2012, 84–85. I therefore differ from those, such as Werner 2012, 27–43, who see Socrates in the *Phaedrus* as rejecting all philosophical utility in myth and forms of mythic interpretation; for an approach closer to mine, cf. Ferrari 1987, 11–12, Brouwer 2014, 149–163. This passage of the *Phaedrus* is also central to Dio's discussion of mythic interpretation in *Oration* 5; cf. Hunter 2017.
20 Cf., e.g., Hopman 2012, 181, with the bibliography cited there; Hawes 2014a, 28–36.
21 On 'rationalization' in 'Heraclitus', cf., e.g., Ramelli 2003, 45.
22 Russell and Konstan adopt Heyne's ἀμαθεῖς for the transmitted ἀμαθῶς at 3.2, but the reading does not of course affect the point being made.

of his own reflections and learning.²³ For Eustathius, the two extremes are represented by those who 'turn everything into allegory', even events and characters that are rooted in reality, what Eustathius terms τὰ ὁμολογουμένως ἱστορούμενα, 'so that the poet seems to speak to us in dreams'.²⁴ On the other side are those 'who have torn off Homer's wings and never allow him to soar aloft', by refusing to allow any allegorical interpretation; for these people, whose 'lawgiver' was Aristarchus,²⁵ myths are just that — myths. For Eustathius, the third way, and the way he will follow, is, like Palaephatus' middle way, the way of careful examination and discrimination, rather than the imposition of totalizing and undiscriminating systems; he will not be the last scholar to use such a rhetoric about the difference between his work and that of others, nor will he be the last whose practice is much less clear-cut, and much more of a compromise, than his proclaimed methodology.²⁶ Eustathius lines himself up alongside οἱ ἀκριβέστεροι, who take the trouble to investigate the material properly: that which is historical is accepted as it is, but with myths, they first consider their origin, nature, and plausibility and then the nature of the truth that lies within them, which must be revealed through allegorical interpretation, θεραπεία — whether that be φυσικῶς ('pertaining to the nature of the world') or κατὰ ἦθος ('ethical', 'moralizing') or ἱστορικῶς. This last method refers to the fact that many myths contain a central core of reality, an event or events that really did happen, but that reality has been distorted by mythical material to make it more marvelous (τοῦ δὲ μύθου τὸ ἀληθὲς ἐκβιαζομένου πρὸς τὸ τερατωδέστερον) and

---

23 On Eustathius' allegorizing sources, cf. Van der Valk 1971–1987, 1, cxi–ii, 2, lxxvi–ii; Reinhardt 1910, 36–58. Browning 1992, 143 helpfully discusses Eustathius on allegory.
24 Cesaretti 1991, 241 n. 13 suggests that Eustathius here recalls Dio's criticisms of Homer at 11.129; Eustathius certainly knew the *Trojan Oration*, cf. *Hom*. 460.6–7. As for Eustathius' target, Cesaretti 1991, 231 suggests allegorists such as Metrodorus of Lampsacus from the fifth century BCE (cf. Hunter 2012, 92, citing earlier bibliography); it is tempting, however, to think that Eustathius is thinking of allegorists nearer in time than Metrodorus.
25 Eustathius is of course referring to Aristarchus' famous view (D-scholium on *Il*. 5.385; cf. *Hom*. 40.28–34, 561.29–30) that 'what is said by the poet should be accepted mythically, in accordance with poetic licence, and readers should not busy themselves [περιεργαζομένους] with anything beyond what the poet said'; for differing assessments of what Aristarchus actually meant by this, cf., e.g., Porter 1992, 70–74, Nünlist 2009, 180–181. Eustathius' description of his own work — περιεργάσεταί που [τοὺς μύθους] ἀκολούθως τοῖς παλαιοῖς — may indeed scornfully pick up Aristarchus' verb.
26 For a helpful survey, cf. Cesaretti 1991, 222–274.

must therefore be recovered by the interpreter.[27] Here Eustathius, like Palaephatus before him, is the heir of Thucydides,[28] as well also of Strabo, a text that he knew very well indeed. The appeal to ἀκρίβεια, coupled with the necessity for close investigation, may itself descend (at an unknown number of removes) from the same programmatic chapters of Thucydides: at 1.22.2 the historian claims his account of what actually happened in the war was not based on that of any chance source, but on careful examination and weighing of the evidence (ὅσον δυνατὸν ἀκριβείᾳ περὶ ἑκάστου ἐπεξελθών).

Palaephatus had introduced his collection by noting that a readiness to believe all the stories that one is told was a sign of being unacquainted with σοφία and ἐπιστήμη; if, as we have seen, he also notes the dangers of being 'too clever', he nevertheless flags up "science" (to use a loose approximation to σοφία καὶ ἐπιστήμη) as a sphere of both activity and discourse which stands in opposition to that of myth. This is not of course the place for anything like a full account of the history of these oppositions – the *'mythos-logos debate'* – but Palaephatus does invite us to consider something of the various ways in which Hellenistic and later scholars sought to make sense of the stories with which they were confronted. For Palaephatus, stories are distorted traces of real events – they do not arise *ex nihilo* – and as such we might naturally be tempted to associate Palaephatus with the first book of Strabo's *Geography*, which discusses Homer and Homer's geography in the light of Eratosthenes' criticisms that (1) poetry was concerned with entertainment, not instruction and (2) the accuracy of Homer's geography made no contribution to his skill as a poet anyway. Strabo takes a view of poetic historicity not entirely unlike Palaephatus.[29] For Strabo, too, legends, even apparently outlandish ones, are not 'inventions [πλάσματα] of poets and prose-writers' but rather 'traces [ἴχνια] of people and events of the real past' (1.2.14). For Strabo it is almost axiomatic that Homer would not simply create from nothing; I say 'almost axiomatic', because, although Strabo does in fact just assert this (to him self-evident) truth, proof, which we at least would label circumstantial, exists for him in Homer's whole character and that of his poetry. As for the former, the opening paragraphs of book 1 precisely depict Homer as a man of, in Palaephatus' phrase, σοφία καὶ

---

[27] Eustathius makes very similar points at the head of the *Odyssey*-commentary, where the purpose of τὸ τερατεύεσθαι is the creation of ἡδονή and ἔκπληξις for the audience (*Hom.* 1379.13–14).

[28] According to van der Valk 1971–1987, 1, ci, Thucydides is only cited directly on a couple of occasions by Eustathius (395.34–35, 795.37).

[29] Cf. Kim 2010, 71–77. On Strabo's attitude to 'myth', cf. also Patterson 2013.

ἐπιστήμη, a φιλόσοφος in fact, and also a πολυπράγματος in the best sense of that term; Apuleius' Lucius, we recall, 'wished to know everything, or at least nearly everything', whereas Strabo's Homer 'took pains [ἐσπούδασεν] to know as many πράξεις as possible and to hand them down to those who came after him' (1.1.2). It is easy enough here to see that Strabo's Homer is, in part, fashioned from the poet's own Odysseus, the man who 'knew the cities and minds of many [rather than 'very many'] men' and who did indeed record these for posterity, and in part on Strabo's own sense of himself as a serious man of education in a culture where the βίος πολιτικός was indeed at the center of the interests of the real or imagined audience. Like Palaephatus, at least in his self-presentation, Strabo too was a great traveler (2.5.11) and enquirer, standing in a line of descent that goes back to Odysseus and Homer himself.[30]

We have seen that Palaephatus placed himself in the Herodotean tradition of the traveling enquirer, and it is of course familiar that Homer is regularly depicted in the *Lives* as a traveler, so it was not difficult to bring these two traditions together in making Homer a kind of proto-Herodotus (as Herodotus himself may to some extent have already done), and this is precisely what we see Strabo, who in fact appeals to the Homeric *Lives* (1.2.29), doing in the course of his rebuttal of Eratosthenes. For Strabo, prominent characteristics of Homer are τὸ φιλείδημον and τὸ φιλέκδημον (1.2.29), which may be seen as a transcription of the opening verses of the *Odyssey* into the language of scholarship. Strabo's Homer indeed will have traveled in Egypt, just like his successor. We must remember that when 'Longinus' famously describes Herodotus as Ὁμηρικώτατος (*Subl.* 13.3), the poet had in part long been fashioned in the image of the historian; Ὅμηρος Ἡροδοτικώτατος had just as good a claim to reality for part of the critical tradition. In introducing Homer as a man of consummate knowledge both of public life and of the geography of the whole world, Strabo notes:

οὐ γὰρ ἂν μέχρι τῶν ἐσχάτων αὐτῆς περάτων ἀφίκετο τῇ μνήμῃ κύκλῳ περιιών

Strabo 1.1.2

For [if this were not the case] he would never have reached as far as the furthest bounds of the inhabited world as he traveled around it in a circle in his description.

'Traveling' for an enquirer can take more than one form, and Strabo here (surely deliberately) runs the language of description and the language of traveling

---

30 For an excellent recent account (and bibliography) of Strabo's discussion of Homer, cf. Kim 2010, ch. 3. Patterson 2013, 219–221 calls attention to similarities between Strabo and Hecataeus.

together;[31] modern editors and translators differ as to whether τῇ μνήμῃ should be taken with ἀφίκετο (so, e.g., Radt, Aujac) or with περιιών (so, e.g., H. L. Jones in the Loeb), but it is rather the richly significant language that is to be noted. Poets, Homer above all, travel around the world and thus 'map' it for us. μνήμη itself need not be ambivalent, but a glance at *LSJ* will remind us that this word for 'memorial, record' also has a marked intellectual sense as 'memory', and Strabo's language here hovers between placing Homer as an actual traveler and the picture offered some two centuries later by Maximus of Tyre of a Homer whose soul, like that of Aristeas of Proconessus or of the philosopher as Socrates describes him in the *Theaetetus*, travels all over the world gathering information.[32]

If we turn from the poet to his poems, we may infer, so Strabo implies, from the fact that the vast bulk of what Homer describes is either factual or has a factual basis that this applies to the poems as a whole; moreover, as Homer's poetry is universally acknowledged as a suitable subject for philosophical investigation (a φιλοσόφημα), this could not be the case if it was simply invented *ex nihilo* (1.2.17). Whereas for Palaephatus myth arose as a kind of sideways leap into error arising from misunderstanding, a misunderstanding that fundamentally changed the nature of what was being described, for Strabo the mythical and the fantastic are rather additions that may to some extent distort but do not fundamentally alter the truths that remain visible below the accretions. Homer takes his ἀρχαί, his starting points, from ἱστορία (1.2.9). What does Strabo mean by the ἱστορία from which Homer took his starting points? According to Radt, it is 'die historische Überlieferung'; for Aujac, 'sa vaste information'; for Jones, simply 'history'. The remainder of the chapter and the following one on the Argonautic expedition (1.2.10), however, make plain that Strabo understands Homer to have drawn on his own knowledge (the verb εἰδέναι is repeatedly used) in building his mixture of the true and the false, and so the question becomes one of the source of that knowledge. Strabo's first set of examples perhaps poses more questions than it answers:

ἔλαβεν οὖν παρὰ τῆς ἱστορίας τὰς ἀρχάς, καὶ γὰρ τὸν Αἰόλον δυναστεῦσαί φασι τῶν περὶ τὴν Λιπάραν νήσων καὶ τῶν περὶ τὴν Αἴτνην καὶ Λεοντίνην Κύκλωπας καὶ Λαιστρυγόνας ἀξένους τινάς· διὸ καὶ τὰ περὶ τὸν πορθμὸν ἀπροσπέλαστα εἶναι τοῖς τότε καὶ τὴν Χάρυβδιν καὶ τὸ Σκύλλαιον ὑπὸ λῃστῶν κατέχεσθαι.

Strabo 1.2.9

---

31 The same language recurs, but at greater expansiveness and therefore with less complex resonance, at 1.1.10.
32 Max. Tyr. 26.1; cf. Hunter 2012, 52–54.

Homer took his starting points from *historia*. For they say[33] that Aeolus ruled over the islands around Lipari, and the inhospitable Cyclopes and Laistrygonians over the regions around Aetna and Leontini; the result was that the area around the strait was unapproachable for men of that time and Charybdis and the Skyllaion were the haunt of pirates.

Whereas we would be tempted to say that these 'historical facts', what Strabo elsewhere (e.g., 3.4.4) calls τὰ ἱστορούμενα, were in fact post-Homeric interpretations of Homeric geography, and in one case at least a rationalizing interpretation of Homeric myth (cf. Palaephatus 20 on Skylla as a Tyrrhenian pirate ship), Strabo seems to take these 'reports' as evidence for the historical core of Homer's account of Odysseus' wanderings, or perhaps even as themselves the source of Homer's knowledge: through ἱστορία, then, Homer learned things for which, though of course Strabo does not say this, Homer is himself the principal authority. Another way of putting this is to say that, in searching for the historical core upon which Homer has elaborated, Strabo seizes upon the results achieved by various post-Homeric traditions which had sought precisely to demythologize Homer and to find ways of accommodating him both to contemporary geography and to a sense of what is possible in nature; Strabo has done no more than accept, and make use of (in a rather eclectic way), the work of those who had gone before him. The very vagueness of ἱστορία and (probably) φασί masks Strabo's operation and casts back into an indeterminate past a popular knowledge which may, so we are led to believe, have been available to Homer himself.

In an important methodological statement Strabo considers the task of the critic:

ἔτι δὲ ἐπεὶ οὐ πάντα μυθεύουσιν, ἀλλὰ πλείω προσμυθεύουσι, καὶ μάλιστα Ὅμηρος, ὁ ζητῶν τί οἱ παλαιοὶ προσμυθεύουσιν οὐ ζητεῖ, εἰ τὰ προσμυθευόμενα ὑπῆρξεν ἢ ἔστιν, ἀλλὰ καὶ μᾶλλον οἷς προσμυθεύεται τόποις ἢ προσώποις, περὶ ἐκείνων ζητεῖ τἀληθές, οἷον τὴν Ὀδυσσέως πλάνην, εἰ γέγονε καὶ ποῦ.

(1.2.19)

Since the tellers of myth, and most of all Homer, do not tell myths in all they say, but for the most part add myth, the person who investigates what mythical element the ancients

---

33 Casaubon's φασί for the transmitted φησί seems hard to resist, for Homer manifestly does not 'say', e.g., that Aeolus ruled over the Lipari islands. Biraschi 2005, 78 sees here an example of Strabo failing to differentiate between what is explicitly in Homer and what is in the exegetical tradition about Homer, but — apart from other considerations — this does not suit the rhetoric of Strabo's chapter (cf. further Kim 2010, 69 n. 55). Jones retains φησί with ἱστορία as the subject, which is hard to believe.

added does not investigate whether the added mythical elements existed or exist, but rather investigates the truth concerning the places or the people to which the mythical elements were added; for example, whether the wanderings of Odysseus happened and where.

Strabo indeed finds proof of this 'additive theory' of myth, one not of course all that far in fact from what Thucydides had said about the activities of poets and logographers, not just in what Homer describes, but in the language in which he describes processes of artistic and verbal creation. In 1.2.9, in very quick succession, Homer's process of προσμυθεύειν is compared to Hephaestus' making of the shield of Achilles in *Iliad* 18, Athena's beautification of Odysseus in *Odyssey* 6 (which Homer had compared to another piece of skillful metalwork), and finally to Odysseus' false tale "like truth" to Penelope in *Odyssey* 19. This final example takes us, as is well known, not just sideways to what the Muses say to Hesiod at the opening of the *Theogony*, but also forward — via Plato[34] — to the development of what we might call a 'theory of fiction' in the Hellenistic and later periods. Basic to any such theory, ancient or modern, is a distinction between types of narrative; the most famous such ancient distinction was that between 'history', 'fictional narrative' or πλάσμα, and myth,[35] and Strabo's discussion should be seen as a contribution to emerging ideas of the fictional and the mythical.

Strabo returns repeatedly to these themes in the course of the *Geography*. When discussing the Iberian Peninsula, for example, Strabo considers the evidence that Homer, 'a man of many voices and much learning' (πολύφωνός τις ὢν καὶ πολυΐστωρ),[36] knew something of these areas (3.2.12–13). Thus, for example, 'one might conjecture' that Homer named Tartaros from Tartessos, of which he had heard something, 'adding also a myth, thus preserving the poetical element'. It was Homer's habit always 'to derive his myths from historical facts' (τοὺς μύθους ἀπό τινων ἱστοριῶν ἐνάγων), and this in fact accounts for the genesis of the two great poems:

> καὶ ἡ τοῦ Ὀδυσσέως δὲ στρατεία δοκεῖ μοι δεῦρο γενηθεῖσα καὶ ἱστορηθεῖσα ὑπ᾽ αὐτοῦ παραδοῦναι πρόφασιν, ὥστε τὴν Ὀδύσσειαν καθάπερ καὶ τὴν Ἰλιάδα ἀπὸ τῶν συμβάντων μεταγαγεῖν εἰς ποίησιν καὶ τὴν συνήθη τοῖς ποιηταῖς μυθοποιίαν.
>
> Strabo 3.2.13

---

34 Cf. esp. *Resp.* 2.382c10–d4, with the discussion of Gill 1993.
35 For discussion and bibliography, cf., e.g., Rispoli 1988.
36 The latter adjective is also apparently applied to Homer in a (probably Chian) inscription of Augustan date, cf. Jones 2015; Strabo uses it also of Callimachus (9.5.17).

I think that the expedition of Odysseus took place here and the fact that he had gathered information about it gave him an opportunity [πρόφασις]. The result was that, just as he had done with the *Iliad*, he transferred the *Odyssey* from events which had happened into poetry and the inventive myth which is customary for poets.

Strabo then goes on to detail the traces of the *nostoi* of the Greeks and the wanderings of the Trojans that exist in the West:

ἥ τε τοῦ Αἰνείου παραδέδοται πλάνη καὶ Ἀντήνορος καὶ ἡ τῶν Ἑνετῶν· ὡσαύτως καὶ ἡ Διομήδους τε καὶ Μενελάου καὶ ἄλλων πλειόνων. ὁ τοίνυν ποιητὴς τὰς τοσαύτας στρατείας ἐπὶ τὰ ἔσχατα τῆς Ἰβηρίας ἱστορηκώς, πυνθανόμενος δὲ καὶ πλοῦτον καὶ τὰς ἄλλας ἀρετὰς (οἱ γὰρ Φοίνικες ἐδήλουν τοῦτο) ἐνταῦθα τὸν τῶν εὐσεβῶν ἔπλασε χῶρον καὶ τὸ Ἠλύσιον πεδίον...

Strabo 3.2.13

The wanderings of Aeneas are transmitted, as are those of Antenor and the Henetoi, and also of Diomedes and Menelaus and Odysseus and many others. The poet, therefore, having gathered information about so many expeditions to the furthest parts of Iberia and having heard about the wealth and the other advantages [of the area] (for the Phoenicians were making this clear) fictionally placed the place of the blessed and the Elysian plain here...

What should be most striking here, as before, is Strabo's language of historical process, which both seems confidently to carry an argument forward, but is also extraordinarily vague and short on detail. Homer has Phoenician informants (μηνυταί, 3.2.14), but the actual nature of his ἱστορίαι, to say nothing of the process of transmission (παράδοσις) of 'historical information', is left entirely impressionistic. The vagueness works, of course, in Strabo's favor: we are so used, above all from Herodotus, to such language, and to the distinctions between history and myth, that Strabo appears to be describing the most natural process in the world, whereas in fact he is creating a historical and historicizing Homer before our eyes. The very audacity of the undertaking is too often overlooked in our understandable concern with Strabo's sources, a concern not infrequently reinforced by a sense that Strabo is not the intellectual equal of those sources.

Strabo's discussion of Homer is, in part, a contribution to emerging ideas of the fictional and the mythical, and it opens a window not merely onto ancient Homeric criticism, but also, as does Palaephatus' Preface, onto ancient attempts to delineate the boundaries of the mythical. In conclusion, however, it must be stressed that so many of these critical and interpretative issues were not merely sharpened in the discussion of Homer, but could be seen to have always been already there in Homer. One Homeric episode, in particular, raises these questions in a particularly sharp way.

Menelaus' account to Telemachus of his *nostos* in *Odyssey* 4 foreshadows Odysseus' account of his own return in various ways,[37] but does so, not just at greatly reduced length, but also in a 'lower', more realistic key. Not of course that there is anything strictly realistic about sea-goddesses, disguising oneself as a seal, and the metamorphoses of Proteus; indeed the figure of Proteus was subject to some of the most richly allegorical readings of any Homeric character. Nevertheless, whether we consider the geography of Menelaus' travels, which, whatever view one takes of them (cf. Strabo 1.2.31), stands in sharp contrast to those of Odysseus (cf. lines 83–85), or motifs such as that of the companions' hunger, for which the attempted cure is fishing rather than killing the Cattle of the Sun (lines 368–369), it is clear that Menelaus' *nostos* is (in many, though not all, respects) 'ordinary' in comparison to that of Odysseus; Menelaus, πολλὰ παθὼν καὶ πόλλ' ἐπαληθείς (4.81), is clearly in fact set up by Homer as an 'Odysseus-light'. When Menelaus is, like Odysseus, driven off course while rounding Cape Malea (3.287), he ends up in Egypt, where (so Nestor reports and Menelaus confirms) 'he traveled around collecting rich resources and gold' (3.301; cf. 4.81–91), a detail that reminds us perhaps of Odysseus' Cretan tales (cf. esp. *Od.* 14.285–286); Odysseus, on the other hand, was swept for nine days from Cape Malea to the land of the lotus-eaters. The reason for Menelaus being detained in Egypt, his failure to offer sufficient sacrifices to the gods before setting out (lines 351–352, 472–480), reads in fact very like the kind of post-factum explanation for problems that anyone could make in antiquity: no inference from trouble is more common in ancient texts than that some god or gods must have been offended, an inference that also suggests a cure. This is not of course (or not necessarily) to suggest that we are to suspect that the whole episode of Eidothea, the seals, and the metamorphoses of Proteus are to be understood as figments of Menelaus' imagination, dressing up a very ordinary explanation for lack of forward progress in exotic mythological clothing, especially of course as modern scholars have repeatedly speculated that Menelaus' adventures were, in an earlier version of the *Odyssey*, precisely Odysseus' adventures.[38] Be that as it

---

[37] Cf., e.g., de Jong 2001, 105–106; on some of the narrative problems raised by Menelaus' account, cf. Danek 1998, 113–120.

[38] For this argument and bibliography, cf. West 2005, 60–11; 2014, 117–118. The effect would be not unlike that produced if we take, as a number of scholars have suggested, the Cretan tales either as 'realistic fiction' (*vel sim.*) or as remnants of earlier versions of the *Odyssey*, now surpassed in their poetic extravagance (and artfulness) by Books 9–12; cf., e.g., Woodhouse

may, however, once Menelaus has made his sacrifice it is all (apparently) smooth sailing, but once Odysseus eventually gets home, he not only has the suitors to deal with, but he also has the famous journey carrying an oar to the ends of the earth to look forward to, an elaborate sacrifice to Poseidon, and then, when he gets home again, further sacrifices "to all the immortals in succession" (11.119–134). We might sense here, not just the way in which Homer arranges Menelaus' *nostos* to the greater glory of Odysseus (observe in particular Menelaus' total dependence upon Eidothea, whereas in the Cyclops adventure, for example, the bringing of the wine, the blinding, and the trick of the sheep are all the products of Odysseus' intelligence, 9.213–215, 316–8, 420–424), but the beginnings of a difference between what later critics would call *plasma* and *mythos*. If certain aspects of Menelaus' *nostos* do indeed recall the Cretan tales, then we will also be reminded that those tales, as 'false things like true...', occupy a very special place in the history of, and theorizing about, fictional narrative. Palaephatus and Strabo are important stages on a journey that began with Homer himself.

Bibliography

Biraschi, A.M. 2005. 'Strabo and Homer: A Chapter in Cultural history', in: D. Dueck/H. Lindsay/S. Pothercary (eds.), *Strabo's Cultural Geography*, Cambridge, 73–85.
Brouwer, R. 2014. *The Stoic Sage*, Cambridge.
Browning, R. 1992. 'The Byzantines and Homer', in: R. Lamberton/J. Keaney (eds.), *Homer's Ancient Readers*, Princeton NJ, 134–147.
Cesaretti, P. 1991. *Allegoristi di Omero a Bisanzio*, Milan.
Danek, G. 1998. *Epos und Zitat*, Vienna.
Ferrari, G.R.F. 1987. *Listening to the Cicadas*, Cambridge.
Festa, N. 1902. *Palaephati περὶ ἀπίστων, Heracliti qui fertur libellus περὶ ἀπίστων, Excerpta Vaticana (vulgo Anonymus De incredibilibus)*, Leipzig.
Fowler, R.L. 2000a. *Early Greek Mythography*, Vol. 1, Oxford.
Fowler, R.L. 2000b. '*P. Oxy.* 4458: Poseidonios', *ZPE* 132, 133–142.
Fowler, R.L. 2006. 'How to Tell a Myth: Genealogy, Mythology, Mythography', *Kernos* 19, 35–46.
Fowler, R.L. 2011. 'Mythos and Logos', *JHS* 131, 45–66.
Fowler, R.L. 2013a. *Early Greek Mythography*, Vol. 2, Oxford.
Fowler, R.L. 2013b. 'Herodotos and the early Mythographers: The Case of the Kabeiroi', in: S.M. Trzaskoma/S. Smith (eds.), *Writing Myth: Mythography in the Ancient World*, Leuven, 1–19.

1930, 132, Reece 1994. For Cretan traditions and the *Odyssey* more generally, cf. Martin n.d., Levaniouk 2012.

Gill, C. 1993. 'Plato on falsehood – Not fiction', in: C. Gill/T.P. Wiseman (eds.), *Lies and Fiction in the Ancient World*, Exeter, 38–87.
Hawes, G. 2014a. *Rationalising Myth in Antiquity*, Oxford.
Hawes, G. 2014b. 'Story Time at the Library: Palaephatus and the Emergence of Highly Literate Mythology', in: R. Scodel (ed.), *Between Orality and Literacy: Communication and Adaptation in Antiquity*, Leiden, 125–147.
Hopman, M.G. 2012. *Scylla: Myth, Metaphor, Paradox*, Cambridge.
Hunter, R. 2012. *Plato and the Traditions of Ancient Literature: The Silent Stream*, Cambridge.
Hunter, R. 2017. 'Serpents in the Soul: The "Libyan Myth" of Dio Chrysostom', in: G. Hawes (ed.), *Myths on the Map*, Oxford, 281–298 [= this volume 560–577].
Jones, C.P. 2015. 'The Earthquake of 26 BCE in Decrees of Mytilene and Chios', *Chiron* 45, 101–122.
Jong, I.J.F. de. 2001. *A Narratological Commentary on the "Odyssey"*, Cambridge.
Kim, L. 2010. *Homer between History and Fiction in Imperial Greek Literature*, Cambridge.
Levaniouk, O. 2012. 'οὐ χρώμεθα τοῖς ξενικοῖς ποιήμασιν: Questions about evolution and fluidity of the Odyssey', in: F. Montanari/A. Rengakos/C. Tsagalis (eds.), *Homeric Contexts*, Berlin, 269–409.
Ogden, D. 2007. *In Search of the Sorcerer's Apprentice: The Traditional Tales of Lucian's "Lover of Lies"*, Swansea.
Martin, RP. n.d. 'Cretan Homers: Tradition, Politics, Fieldwork', *Classics@ 3*. https://chs.harvard.edu/classics-an-online-journal
Nestle, W. 1942. *Vom Mythos zum Logos²*, Stuttgart.
Nünlist, R. 2009. *The Ancient Critic at Work*, Cambridge.
Patterson, L.E. 2013. 'Geographers as Mythographers: The Case of Strabo', in: S.M. Trzaskoma/S. Smith (eds.), *Writing Myth: Mythography in the Ancient World*, Leuven, 201–221.
Porter, J.I. 1992. 'Hermeneutic Lines and Circles: Aristarchus and Crates on the exegesis of Homer', in: R. Lamberton/J.J. Keaney, *Homer's Ancient Readers*, Princeton NJ, 67–114.
Ramelli, I. (ed.) 2003. *Anneo Cornuto: Compendio di teologia greca*, Milan.
Reece, S. 1994. 'The Cretan Odyssey: A Lie Truer than Truth', *AJP* 115, 157–173.
Reinhardt, K. 1910. *De Graecorum theologia capita duo*, Diss., Humboldt University of Berlin.
Rispoli, G. 1988. *Lo spazio del verisimile*, Naples.
Santoni, A. 2000. *Palefato: Storie incredibili*, Pisa.
Stern, J., trans., comm. 1996. *Palaephatus, ΠΕΡΙ ΑΠΙΣΤΩΝ: 'On Unbelievable Tales'*, Wauconda IL.
Trachsel, A. 2005. 'L'explication Mythologique de Palaiphatos: Une stratégie particulière', *Maia* 57, 543–556.
Trzaskoma, S.M. 2013. 'Introduction', in: S.M. Trzaskoma/S. Smith (eds.), *Writing Myth: Mythography in the Ancient World*, Leuven, xv–xxiv.
Trzaskoma, S.M./Smith, S. (eds.), *Writing Myth: Mythography in the Ancient World*, Leuven.
Van der Valk, M. 1971–1987. *Eustathii Archiepiscopi Thessalonicensis Commentarii ad Homeri Iliadem pertinentes ad fidem codicis Laurentiani*, Leiden.
Werner, D.S. 2012. *Myth and Philosophy in Plato's 'Phaedrus'*, New York.
West, M.L. 2005. 'Odyssey and Argonautica', *CQ* 55, 39–64.
West, M.L. 2014. *The Making of the 'Odyssey'*, Oxford.
Whitmarsh, T. 2013. *Beyond the Second Sophistic*, Berkeley/Los Angeles.
Woodhouse, W.J. 1930. *The Composition of Homer's 'Odyssey'*, Oxford.

33 The Rhetorical Criticism of Homer

Homer and Homeric Criticism

Homer's grip on Greek literate culture gave him a dominant role in education, scholarship and criticism of all kinds, and this predominance is reflected in the centrality of the Homeric texts to the growth of critical practice and terminology, particularly as we can trace these from Aristotle onwards. This chapter will be largely concerned with critical practices and ideas which flourished, and in some cases arose, in the Hellenistic period, but it is important always to bear in mind the classical, and in some cases, archaic roots of these phenomena. The modern study of 'ancient literary criticism' has always suffered from uncertainty as to what actually is being studied and where and how early the relevant material is first found. Does one start, for example, with Odysseus' praise of the Phaeacian bard Demodocus (*Od.* 8.487–491) and Alcinous' praise for the manner in which Odysseus himself tells his tale (*Od.* 11.363–368),[1] with Pindar's rich 'metatextual commentary' on his own and others' poetry,[2] with tragedy and satyr-play, where some of the richest reactions to Homer and the Homeric ethos are to be found, even though the explicit dramatisation of scenes from Homer is very uncommon in our surviving texts (Euripides' *Cyclops*, [Euripides] *Rhesos*),[3] with Attic Old Comedy – and, most notably, the *Frogs* of Aristophanes, or with Plato?[4] The concerns and critical practices of the *Frogs* were certainly influential for centuries, texts such as the famous discussion of an ode of Simonides in Plato's *Protagoras* and of the expertise of the rhapsode in the *Ion* foreshadow important concerns of Alexandrian scholarship,[5] and – above all – the criticisms (in both senses) of Homer in the *Republic* set an agenda for the discussion of poetry which was to last throughout antiquity.

Some histories of the ancient reception and criticism of Homer would choose in fact to begin with the *Odyssey*, a poem which is widely held to acknowledge and react to the *Iliad*, not only in the general spirit and values of the (almost certainly) later poem, but also in specific passages (such as the

---

[1] The bibliography on Homeric 'poetics' is of course daunting; Halliwell 2011, ch. 2 offers a thought-provoking guide through the maze.
[2] For foreshadowings in Pindar of later critical ideas cf., e.g., Richardson 1985.
[3] For the *Cyclops* as a 'reading' of Homer cf. Hunter 2009a, ch. 2.
[4] Ford 2002 is an excellent guide to these issues and their bibliography. For origins and beginnings of ancient scholarship see also Novokhatko 2015.
[5] On this aspect of the *Ion* cf. Hunter 2011 and 2012, 89–108.

Nekuia)⁶ and by the device of largely ignoring the ground covered by the more martial poem. It may indeed be argued that the *Odyssey* is the first 'post-classical text', if by that is meant a text which consciously exploits its sense of otherness and distance from (to put it simply) a more heroic past. The first four books of the poem show Telemachus growing up and learning about the past, searching, if you like, for 'the classical' before it was lost, and in that search, no less than in Odysseus' confrontation with the past in the *Nekuia*, the 'critical' spirit which explains that earlier world (and its poetry) is being formed before our eyes. As for Telemachus' father, Odysseus is πολύτροπος, the man 'of *many* turns'; however that epithet is to be interpreted (cf. further below), the repeated stress in the opening verses on multiplicity and hence complexity and change, 'the man of *many* turns wandered a very great deal … he saw the cities of *many* men … and suffered *many* griefs…', was to take its place within a long discourse in which the world gets ever more 'complex' and the past looks ever more 'simple'. When in the Platonic *Hippias Minor* (cf. below) Hippias contrasts a 'very straightforward' (ἁπλούστατος) Achilles with a 'very twisting' (πολυτροπώτατος) Odysseus (364c4–365b6), we are already on the way to what was to be an influential contrast between the ethical values of their respective poems.

The broad concerns of ancient discussions of Homer, and of literature more generally, may be roughly divided into the stylistic, the didactic (i.e. what did Homer know and what can we learn from him), the rhetorical and the ethical, though little weight is to be given to the boundaries between these four categories.⁷ Thus, for example, style was always regarded as an expression of *êthos* and very closely tied to rhetorical analysis, just as a principal aim of rhetorical analysis was establishing the *êthos* of the speaker; whether the subject be ethics or rhetoric, moreover, 'Homer as (our) teacher' was a theme never far away, and dominates one of the most important ancient texts about Homer to have survived, namely Strabo's defence of Homer's technical knowledge against Eratosthenes' claim that the only concern of poetry was ψυχαγωγία, not διδασκαλία (Strab. 1.2.3–8).⁸ As Aristophanes' *Frogs* shows very clearly, the idea that our behaviour is influenced by what we hear recited or read or see in the theatre took hold very early, and the language of 'teaching' covers both what, as we would say, the poet sets out to impart and also what we take away from our exposure to literary art, regardless of what the poet 'intended'; poets were to be

---

6 Cf. Usener 1990.
7 See Nünlist 2015.
8 For discussion and bibliography cf. Kim 2010, ch. 3.

held responsible for the effects they (and their characters) produced, an assumption which is central to Plato's censure of poetry in *Republic* 2–3 and 10.[9]

Much of the earliest critical discussion of which we know may be classed as broadly allegorical, in the sense that it seeks to uncover meanings in the text which are not patent from what the text appears to say 'on the surface'; the allegorical interpretations of an 'Orphic' cosmogonical poem in the 'Derveni papyrus' have greatly increased our knowledge of some (perhaps rather extreme) allegorical modes practised as early as the fifth century BC.[10] Allegorical readings (of various kinds) have indeed some claim to be the longest-lived of all ancient ways of reading Homer; in the Hellenistic period such readings are particularly associated with Crates of Mallos and the Pergamene school,[11] they flourished in the early empire (Cornutus,[12] 'Heraclitus', *Homeric Problems*), and dominated the later Platonist and neo-Platonist tradition of Homeric criticism.[13] As for their beginnings, a scholium on *Iliad* 20.67 which derives from Porphyry, notes that the Homeric Battle of the Gods was entirely 'inappropriate', ἀπρεπές, and that some explained this (away) by taking these scenes as allegories of how the world is made up of opposed natural forces, the wet and the dry, the hot and the cold and so forth, here called by the names of appropriate gods; the scholium also notes that states (διαθέσεις) are sometimes given the names of gods – φρόνησις is Athena, folly is Ares, desire Aphrodite, and so forth. This kind of defence (ἀπολογία) of Homer was, according to the scholium, 'very ancient' and started with the rhapsode Theagenes of Rhegium (late sixth century), 'who was the first to write about Homer'.[14] It seems likely enough that, by the end of the fifth century at least, complex moral and physical or cosmogonical interpretations of Homer circulated widely, though it is not always easy to identify their authors or to form a clear sense of the outlines of these interpretations.

The majority of our evidence for moralising and allegorical interpretations comes, of course, from the post-classical period, and only very rarely are we able to pick apart the various layers of interpretation which often survive in

---

9 Cf., e.g., Halliwell 2000.
10 For the 'Derveni papyrus' see Kouremenos/Parassoglou/Tsantsanoglou 2006, Bernabé 2007, 171–269; for orientation and bibliography on ancient allegorical interpretation cf. Buffière 1956, Richardson 1975, Lamberton 1986, Dawson 1992, Ford 2002, 67–89, Boys Stones 2003a, Struck 2004, Ramelli/Lucchetta 2004, Pontani 2005a, Naddaf 2009, Gutzwiller 2010, 354–359, Copeland/Struck 2010.
11 Cf., e.g., Porter 1992, Broggiato 2001; on the nature of Stoic 'allegorising' cf. Long 1992.
12 Cf. Most 1989.
13 Cf. esp. Lamberton 1986, 1992.
14 Theagenes fr. 2 D K, cf. MacPhail 2011, 240–243.

summary form in later texts, notably in the scholia. Nevertheless, it is also likely that some relatively simple kinds of interpretation persisted over centuries. The explanation of Athena as φρόνησις, for example, recurs persistently throughout antiquity, very often in connection with the φρόνιμος hero *par excellence*, Odysseus.[15] A particularly interesting manifestation of this concerns Odysseus indirectly, namely Homer's representation of the development of the hero's son Telemachus in the early books of the *Odyssey*; this example also neatly illustrates how ancient arguments and interpretations very often foreshadow modern readings.

In one of the extant *hypotheseis* to *Odyssey* 1 (*hypothesis* c Pontani) we read that Athena, in the guise of Mentes, advises Telemachus to visit Pylos and Sparta, and then, 'This business of Athena going to Ithaca to encourage Telemachus to make enquiries about his father hints at (αἰνίττεται) nothing but the fact that *phronêsis* is called Athena, and Telemachus, who is a child (παῖς) but then grows up and comes into wisdom (γνῶσις), is roused by Athena, that is by his own *phronêsis*, to make enquiries about his father'.[16] Heraclitus offers a much extended version of this interpretation:

> Right at the very beginning we find Athena despatched by Zeus to Telemachus – reasonably (εὐλόγως) so, since he is no longer extremely young and is coming into his twentieth year and the passage to manhood. Reasoning (λογισμός) about what was happening had come into him, and he realised that he should not put up any longer with the wantonness of the suitors which had lasted for four years. Homer has allegorised (ἠλληγόρησεν) this gathering power of reasoning in Telemachus as the appearance of Athena. She comes in the likeness of an old man, for Mentes is said to be an aged friend of Odysseus. Grey hair and age are the sacred harbours of our final years, a safe anchorage for men, and as the strength of the body wanes, so the force of the intellect (διάνοια) increases.
> Heraclitus, *Homeric Problems* 61

Heraclitus then pursues this interpretation in some detail. The maturing Telemachus considers where it would be best to enquire about his father and realises that the old and wise Nestor and Menelaus, who himself had recently returned 'from eight years wandering', were obvious sources of advice and information. Athena-Mentes' mild rebuke to Telemachus,

---

15 For some discussion and bibliography cf. Hunter 2014.
16 Almost identical is the scholium on 1.270a Pontani, except that there the object is getting rid of the suitors, rather than enquiring about Odysseus. For a full and illuminating study of ancient traditions about Telemachus' 'education' cf. Wissmann 2009.

οὐδέ τί σε χρή
νηπιάας ὀχέειν, ἐπεὶ οὐκέτι τηλίκος ἐσσί

Homer, *Odyssey* 1.296-297

you should not continue in childish ways, for you are no longer a child

becomes a kind of 'pull yourself together' reflection by Telemachus himself (63.1). So too, the claim that 'Reason, acting like a *paidagôgos* and a father, roused in him a readiness to undertake responsibility' (63.2) draws on Telemachus' own words to Athena-Mentes at 1.307 'you say these things with kindly intention, like a father advising his son...'

The textual facts with which this interpretation of Book 1 is grappling are familiar to any reader of the *Odyssey*; even if one does not agree that '[Telemachus] is the only Homeric character who develops in the course of the story',[17] it is plain that Book 1 dramatises the issue of growing up with very unusual insistence. As she leaves, Athena puts μένος καὶ θάρσος, 'spirit and courage', into Telemachus' spirit (vv. 320-321), and he returns to the suitors as an ἰσόθεος ἀνήρ, 'a godlike man' (v. 324). In his next speech he corrects his mother who has tried to stop Phemios from singing of the return of the Greeks, tells her to go back to her 'woman's work', and emphatically declares himself both an ἀνήρ ('a man') and the holder of κράτος ('power') in the house (vv. 358-9). Penelope obeys 'in amazement' (θαμβήσασα), just as the suitors are amazed (382) at the boldness of Telemachus' next speech to them; Telemachus' response to Eurymachus, who has asked for information about the stranger who has just visited, would do an Odysseus proud in its caution and economy with the truth (vv. 412-420).[18] When we first saw Telemachus he was deep in depressed thoughts as he wondered 'whether his father would ever return to scatter the suitors' (vv. 114-116); the book closes with Telemachus again deep in thought (427), but now it is about what *he* must do, and he spends the night 'thinking over in his heart the journey which Athena had marked out' (444).

The various different interpretative traditions which we glimpse through the surviving scholia show how thin is the line between some types of 'allegorical' reading[19] and the 'non allegorical': was Telemachus merely instructed by

---

17 De Jong 2001, 20; De Jong there gives helpful bibliography on the character of Telemachus.
18 The exegetical scholia on v. 413 rightly note Telemachus' strategy of 'keeping the suitors relaxed'.
19 I am aware that for the purposes of this discussion I have simply ignored some aspects of some 'allegorical' readings of Athena in *Odyssey* 1 which are less easily taken over. Thus, for example, the allegorising scholia on v. 96 explain that Athena's 'lovely sandals' denote the

Athena (cf., e.g., the scholia on 354) so that he becomes φρόνιμος, or is Athena actually herself φρόνησις? φρόνιμος is of course one of the standard scholiastic glosses for πεπνυμένος, the 'formulaic' epithet for Telemachus, which makes its first appearance (v. 213) in the poem immediately after Athena's first address to the young man, where it comes almost as confirmation of Athena's concluding assertion of how like Odysseus Telemachus is. Another sign of how such interpretative modes run together is the concern in the scholia, which seem in this case to go back to Porphyry, with why Athena sends Telemachus away from Ithaca at what looks like a moment fraught with danger and on a mission which is essentially fruitless; this ζήτημα has of course also much exercised modern scholars.[20] Porphyry's long discussion[21] adduces the fact that, brought up 'by a woman' on Ithaca and surrounded by hostile men, Telemachus could never have learned the appropriate skills or had the appropriate experiences to become like his father; he would therefore have either remained in this impossible situation or launched an inevitably doomed attack upon the suitors by himself. Enquiries about his father are therefore the πρόφασις of the trip, but the real σκοπός is 'education', παίδευσις, which involves learning about his father, and it is from this that Telemachus will acquire the κλέος which the Homeric Athena holds out for him (v. 95, cf. 13.422). Such an aim, as Porphyry points out, is 'appropriate to Athena', in part (we should infer) because Athena is associated with intelligence, education and μῆτις. Part at least of this reading of the Telemachy, which has of course considerable overlap with the standard modern reading, will go a very long way back in antiquity;[22] it seems first to surface for us in Philodemus, *On the Good King according to Homer*, where, in a recently restored, if still broken, column, the philosopher precisely discusses Telemachus' journey:[23]

> ... to be one who has constantly lived among guests not living according to his will, since in addition it is necessary for him to be one who has neither seen nor heard of many

---

powerful effects in action of *phronêsis* and her spear its 'striking power' (τὸ πληκτικόν), 'for through his own reason the *phronimos* strikes the unruly'. There is, of course, a range of allegorical, as of non-allegorical, views and gradations of detail within any one such reading.
20 Cf., e.g., West 1988, 53–55.
21 Scholia to 1.94 and 1.284. Some of the earlier history of Porphyry's arguments may be visible at Philodemus, *On the Good King according to Homer* col. xxxiii Dorandi if, as (e.g.) Asmis 1991, 38 suggests, καὶ ἀθέατον ἀνάγκη καὶ ἀνιστόρητον εἶναι πολλῶν καὶ παρρησίας ἄπειρον ἰσηγόρου πολλάκις ἐξεπαίδευσεν refers not to Odysseus, but to Telemachus.
22 Herter, *RE* V/A 351 suggested that it might have figured in Antisthenes' 'Athena or Concerning Telemachus'.
23 Cf. Fish 2002, 193–194, with discussion in Fish 1999; 2002, 213–215, and 2004 113–114.

things and has had no experience of free speech with equals (παρρησίας ἄπειρον ἰσηγόρου), and for the most part even uneducated, for which reason ... the poet ... brings Telemachus to Pylos and Sparta where he was to have dealings with such great men, for he was certainly not going to achieve anything (more) concerning his father, who was by then already on Ithaca...

Philodemus, *On the Good King according to Homer* col. 23, trans. J. Fish

Just as Odysseus learned on his travels, so did his son.

Finally, we may note that the 'allegorical' conception of Athena as φρόνησις or σύνεσις or νοῦς is capacious enough to embrace both Achilles' inner struggle in *Iliad* 1, where violence and restraint compete in a moment of extraordinary passion,[24] and the more gradual intellectual and moral assertiveness which develops in Telemachus in Book 1, as Athena tells him to 'give thought' (φράζεσθαι) to the future (v. 295); the interventions of Athena in *Iliad* 1 and *Odyssey* 1 are in fact exemplary for their respective poems — the poem of violence and passion, and the poem of caution and forethought, of biding one's time and seizing the opportunity.

The standard language in which to describe allegorical interpretations is 'finding the ὑπόνοιαι'[25] or allegations that the poet 'hints at' (αἰνίττεσθαι) particular meanings. At *Republic* 2.378d6-7 Plato makes Socrates observe that blasphemous episodes in Homer must not be part of education, whether composed with or without ὑπόνοιαι, because the young cannot recognise a ὑπόνοια and are therefore affected by 'the literal truth' of what they read. The motives for such readings will have been various. In part they will indeed have been designed to save Homer from apparently disgraceful representations, such as the adultery of Ares and Aphrodite in Demodocus' second song in *Odyssey* 8 (cf. Xenophan. frr. 11–12 D K), and in part they may have been an attempt to reserve true understanding of the great poet to a particular élite, as Homer's status as universal pan-Hellenic poet grew, and in part they may have arisen from a desire to demonstrate that one's own views of how the world worked had Homeric authority; we can hardly doubt that the element of 'display' (ἐπίδειξις), of showing off one's cleverness, also played its part. The extraordinary continuity of the tradition is well seen in the fact that the Battle of the Gods, the subject of Porphyry's note on the history of allegorical interpretation (cf. above), is the one passage of Homer which 'Longinus', one of the most perceptive ancient critics of Homer to have survived, also claims must be interpreted allegorically, 'be-

---

24 Cf. Hunter 2012, 60–67.
25 Plutarch (*Mor.* 19e) notes that ὑπόνοιαι was the old term for 'what are now called ἀλληγορίαι'.

cause it is completely blasphemous (ἄθεα) and does not preserve propriety (τὸ πρέπον)' (*Subl.* 9.7).

One text which may, with all proper caution, be used to catch some of the flavour of the classical discussion of Homer is Plato's *Hippias Minor*. Here Socrates engages with the great sophist just after the latter has given a public ἐπίδειξις on the subject of Homer. Socrates asks him what may well have been a very frequently asked question — one asked of or by schoolboys, perhaps: 'Which of Achilles and Odysseus do you consider the better man and in what respect?' (364b4–5). Hippias replies that Homer made Achilles best (ἄριστος), Nestor wisest (σοφώτατος) and Odysseus 'most πολύτροπος', and he explains that πολύτροπος means 'lying, false' (ψευδής), which is everywhere the characteristic of Odysseus; Achilles' famous words to Odysseus at *Iliad* 9.308–314 ('Hateful to me as the gates of Hades is the man who conceals one thing in his heart and says another…') are adduced to demonstrate that Achilles is indeed ἀληθής τε καὶ ἁπλοῦς, 'truthful and straightforward', whereas Odysseus is πολύτροπός τε καὶ ψευδής (365a–b). In the subsequent questioning, Socrates has little trouble in demonstrating that Achilles in Book 9 contradicts himself, in other words 'lies', by saying that he will sail home but never making the slightest attempt to do so; Hippias' attempted distinction between 'deliberate' and 'unwilling' falsehood does not survive Socrates' onslaught for very long. Certain aspects of this (very amusing) exchange may be highlighted in the present context. We know that πολύτροπος in the opening verse of the *Odyssey* had indeed attracted considerable discussion; the scholia preserve a long notice from Antisthenes in which the word is understood to characterise Odysseus as the master of τρόποι, i.e. of all manner of speech appropriate to different circumstances and interlocutors. Secondly, the terms in which the scholia adduce Antisthenes' discussion are almost identical to those of the *Hippias Minor*, including an allusion to the same verses of *Iliad* 9, so that we can trace both a relationship between Plato and Antisthenes and the striking continuity of the critical tradition over several centuries.[26] Moreover, the scholia frame their citation of Antisthenes as a 'problem' (ἀπορία or ζήτημα) and its 'solution' (λύσις): we would expect πολύτροπος to be a term of approbation, as it is applied to the hero in the opening verse of his poem, but its 'natural' meaning seems rather disparaging, and this is the 'difficulty' which Antisthenes solved. So too, the other problem to which Socrates points in the *Hippias Minor*, namely an apparent inconsistency in what Achilles says and does in Book 9, is exactly the kind of 'difficulty' to which sub-

---

[26] For the bibliography and interpretation of the scholium cf. Luzzatto 1996, Pontani's notes in Pontani 2007, 7–9, and Montiglio 2011, 20–47.

sequent critics turned their minds, and we know that Achilles' contradictory assertions in Book 9 were indeed the subject of scholarly head scratching and 'solutions'.²⁷ The present case will have played its part in a lively ancient discussion, descending at least from Aristotle, about Achilles' inconsistent (ἀνώμαλος) character.²⁸

The Homeric texts remained in fact throughout antiquity an irresistible impulse towards display and paradox. Unsurprisingly, it is precisely Odysseus ὁ πολύτροπος who is often at the centre of such display, for it was this character more than any other which prompted rhetorical and philosophical elaboration.²⁹ From one perspective, for example, Plutarch's essay *That animals have reason*, often referred to as *Gryllus* after one of the characters, may be seen as standing in this line descending from the Platonic *Hippias Minor*. This work is cast as a dialogue between Odysseus, Circe and a Greek whom Circe has transformed into a pig, *Gryllus* 'Grunter';³⁰ the pig demonstrates to Odysseus that animals are actually more virtuous and live happier lives than men. The dialogue is perhaps to be imagined as taking place immediately after Circe has told Odysseus about his voyage home and warned him of the consequences of interfering with the cattle of the Sun (12.137–141); 'I think I understand and will remember these things, Circe, but I would gladly hear from you…', begins Plutarch's Odysseus, in one of what might have been a not uncommon ancient game of writing new and often unusual 'scenes' for the *Odyssey*.³¹ Odysseus' request is to know whether there are any Greeks among the metamorphosed animals under Circe's

---

27 Cf. Erbse's note on schol. 9.682–683, citing Porphyry.
28 Cf. Nünlist 2009a, 250 with n. 42.
29 Cf. Montiglio 2011.
30 Odysseus and his crew were, therefore, not Circe's first Greek visitors – another blow to Odysseus' list of achievements. A different view, adopted e.g. by Kidd in Waterfield/Kidd 1992, 375 and Indelli 1995, is that Gryllus was in fact one of Odysseus' companions; this would necessitate a setting in the tenth, rather than the twelfth, book. Much might seem to hang on the clearly disturbed text at 985e where the word ἑταίρους or ἑτέρους is transmitted (Hubert adopts von Wilamowitz's deletion of the word), but this alternative view seems to make nonsense of the opening exchanges with Circe and certainly destroys any close link with the Odyssean narrative; so too Circe's comment at 986a that if the animals win the argument, Odysseus will be shown 'to have determined badly concerning himself and his friends' seems to support the view taken here. At 989e Gryllus claims to have once seen Odysseus on Crete; the expression certainly does not suggest that he was actually one of Odysseus' companions (so, rightly, e.g. Russell 1993, 337), and in any case Gryllus here turns Odysseus' Cretan tale (!) to Penelope (*Od.* 19.221ff.) back against the hero himself. There is a useful account of the philosophical background of Plutarch's essay by Ziegler in *RE* XXI 1951, 739–743.
31 One thinks of the letter which Ovid's Penelope writes to Odysseus (*Her.* 1).

control so that, with Circe's permission, he can restore them to human shape from the 'pitiable and dishonourable existence' they now lead and take them back to Greece; this, says, Odysseus would bring him καλὴ φιλοτιμία with the Greeks. Circe's response is very sharp:

οὗτος ὁ ἀνὴρ οὐχ αὐτῶι μόνον οὐδὲ τοῖς ἑταίροις, ἀλλὰ τοῖς μηδὲν προσήκουσιν οἴεται δεῖν ὑπ' ἀβελτερίας συμφορὰν γενέσθαι τὴν αὐτοῦ φιλοτιμίαν.

Plutarch, *Gryllus* 985d

This man thinks that his desire for glory (φιλοτιμία) should, through his stupidity, prove a disaster not just for himself and his companions, but for complete strangers.

Circe here produces a re-writing of the opening of the *Odyssey*, which is very much not to Odysseus' credit. 'This man', the famous ἀνήρ, will be the undoing not just of himself and his ἑταῖροι (contrast *Od.* 1.5), but of many other Greeks as well; his companions will not perish 'by their own reckless foolishness' (*Od.* 1.6),[32] as in Homer, but through Odysseus' stupidity and desire for glory, a force which drives him to pursue 'an empty form of goodness and a phantom in place of the truth' (986a). Such a reading takes its initial impetus from Odysseus's assertion of his own κλέος at *Odyssey* 9.19–20, but behind it lies (again) a long tradition of interpretation and re-writing.[33]

Like πολύτροπος, φιλοτιμία may have positive or negative connotations, and (again) these differences may then bring differences of narrative with them. φιλοτιμία, as the principal motivating force of Odysseus 'most φιλότιμος of men' (986b), seems, for example, to have played a significant role in Euripides' *Philoctetes*, as this can be reconstructed from Dio 52 and 59.[34] Odysseus seems to have begun the prologue of that play by expressing his worries that his reputation for cleverness may be undeserved, given the trouble he voluntarily gives himself; that fear in fact comes true in the *Gryllus* when, in his opening remarks, Gryllus observes that Odysseus' reputation for cleverness and surpassing wisdom will all have been for nothing (μάτην), if he will not accept improvement, just because he has not given the matter proper thought (986c–d). The Euripidean Odysseus then proceeded to explain that good leaders such as himself are driven by φιλοτιμία and the desire for δόξα and κλέος to undertake very difficult

---

[32] Among the scholiastic glosses for ἀτασθαλίαι are ἄνοιαι (D schol. on *Iliad* 4.409) and μωρίαι (D schol. on *Od.* 1.7); Circe's ἀβελτερία is a variant of this.
[33] For Odysseus' φιλοτιμία in the scholastic tradition cf. the scholia on *Odyssey* 5.401 (a remarkable text) and 9.229.
[34] Cf. frr. 787–789 Kannicht, Stanford 1954, 115–116.

tasks; when Odysseus stated that 'nothing is as keen for acclamation (γαῦρος) as a man' (fr. 788.1 Kannicht), it is hard not to remember Gryllus' criticisms of human folly. So too, the thesis that the life of a pig, a life of "all good things" (986d), including 'deep, soft mud' (989e), is much to be preferred to the life of a man, particularly an Odysseus, overturns the very rich mainstream tradition of interpretation of the Circe-scene and of the *Odyssey* as a whole. This is particularly true of the insistent argument that pigs and animals generally are not victim to the lustful desires of the flesh, unlike human beings, whereas the normal interpretative view (cf., e.g., Hor. *Epist.* 1.2.24–26) is that men are precisely turned into pigs by their slothful lusts and the pursuit of pleasure. The *Gryllus* is of course full of witty reworkings of the *Odyssey* and its critical tradition:[35] throughout antiquity, the critical interpretation and creative mimesis of the Homeric text travelled hand-in-hand.

The tradition of critical 'problems' and their 'solutions' which was illustrated above from Plato's *Hippias Minor* is one of the longest lived ancient critical practices:[36] we can see it already in full (if satirical) swing in Aristophanes' *Frogs*,[37] significant excerpts from Aristotle's *Homeric Problems* are preserved (and cf. also *Poet.* ch. 25), and the tradition is very much alive and well in Alexandrian scholarship and, as we have seen, in the Homeric scholia.[38] This critical framework allowed scholars to appeal, *inter alia*, to change over time in cultural practice, to both diachronic change and synchronic difference, for example between dialects or in language usage more generally, and to the need to pay close attention to shifting contexts, particularly rhetorical contexts, in the course of a long poem. Aristotle is the crucial figure in establishing that poetry had its own standards of 'correctness' (ὀρθότης), and that what matters is not

---

[35] No full account is possible here. At 986f Gryllus tells Odysseus that he once heard him describing the land of the Cyclopes to Circe in the terms which Odysseus in fact had used in his narration to the Phaeacians (9.108–111); we are presumably to understand that the conversation took place during the year's stay with Circe (10.467–468), but the apparent misrepresentation of the *Odyssey* serves at least two purposes. Plutarch is shown to be as wittily concerned as Homer with the 'How do you know?' question which can always be posed to a narrator (cf. *Od.* 12.389–390), and there is a suggestion that the braggart Odysseus used to bore Circe (presumably in bed) with the same tales which he told the Phaeacians (and subsequently Penelope) and which she of course knew already anyway (cf. 10.457–459). For recent views of the literary form of the *Gryllus* cf. Fernández Delgado 2000 and Herchenroeder 2008.
[36] See Novokhatko 2015, Dubischar 2015, and Nünlist 2015.
[37] Cf. Hunter 2009a, 21–25.
[38] Cf. Pfeiffer 1968, 69–71, Nünlist 2009a, 11–12, Slater 1982. Some of Slater's conclusions need modification in view of Blank/Dyck 1984, but the continued importance of 'problem solving' criticism is not in doubt.

the existence of factual errors or inconsistencies *per se*, but rather the quality and nature of those phenomena;[39] such a realisation focused attention again on the need for scholarly judgement as shown in decision making, *krisis* in both its senses. The challenge to Socrates which Plato puts in Protagoras' mouth was to foreshadow the principal thrust of Alexandrian criticism:

> I consider, Socrates, that the greatest part of *paideia* for a man is to be clever about verses (περὶ ἐπῶν δεινόν);[40] this means to be able to understand (συνιέναι) what the poets say and what has been composed well (ὀρθῶς) and what not, and to know how to make distinctions and, when questioned, to give an account.
>
> Plato, *Protagoras* 338e6–339a3

Protagoras' test to see whether Socrates fits the bill then precisely concerns an alleged inconsistency in a poem of Simonides. According to Aristotle in the *Poetics*, there are five standard grounds for identifying a problem requiring a solution: that something is impossible, or irrational, or harmful, or contradictory, or contrary to artistic correctness (1461b23–24). These categories recur constantly in the critical traditions which came after Aristotle, but their roots are deep and early.

The history and characteristics of textual and interpretative 'scholarship', given perhaps their most authoritative expression in Rudolf Pfeiffer's *History of Classical Scholarship* of 1968, are relatively well understood (as are the many areas of doubt and uncertainty) and offer a reasonably clearly defined area of study.[41] 'Literary criticism', under any definition, plays a major role in such scholarship, and it is the scholia to Homer which offer probably our richest sources for this.[42] Any attempt, however, to separate 'readings' and 'interpretations' of Homer from the history of reworkings of Homer within Greek literature is bound to tie itself in unnecessary definitional knots, as well as almost inevitably presenting a misleading view of the pervasive ancient engagement with the epic texts.[43] The matter is particularly acute when we reach the rich prose literature of the Second Sophistic, in which revisions of Homer are a very major presence, and into which a now long tradition of Homeric scholarship is ab-

---

39 Cf., e.g., Hunter, 2012, 100–103.
40 The pointed ambivalence of this phrase is marked by Socrates' later observation of the multivalency of δεινός (341a7–b5). I have discussed some features of this passage of the *Protagoras* in Hunter 2011, 36, and for a fuller account and bibliography of the discussion of Simonides' poem cf. Hunter 2020.
41 Recent contributions include Matthaios/Montanari/Rengakos 2011, Montanari/Pagani 2011.
42 Cf. Richardson 1980, Schmidt 2002, Nünlist 2009a and 2015.
43 For a sketch of some approaches to Homeric reception in Greek literature cf. Hunter 2004.

sorbed and re-used in new, often epideictic and/or paradoxical contexts.⁴⁴ In the discussion which follows I focus (largely) on explicit indications, in scholia and in rhetorical and critical treatises, of how Homer should be understood, rather than the implicit interpretations which Homeric reworkings in creative literature, at both macro-and micro-level, bring with them. The forms of expression in which reflection upon the epic heritage was couched were, however, as varied as approaches to the texts themselves, and even the limited case-study which follows can make no claim to do other than scratch the surface.

Homer and Rhetorical Criticism

Rhetorical criticism, that is the study of the strategies of both language and substance which lead to the effective presentation of arguments and characters, played a very prominent, perhaps indeed the dominant, role in the ancient criticism of literature; 'literary criticism', as we might understand it, fell — at least in post-classical antiquity — within the province of *rhētorikē*.⁴⁵ The basis of much of the educational system, once the earliest preliminary studies were completed, was the study of how speakers in the past, above all in epic, drama and oratory, achieved particular aims, and how those achievements could be replicated in the present;⁴⁶ as with so much of ancient educated culture, the seeds (and in some cases the full flowering) of virtually all rhetorical forms was to be found — or so it was believed — in Homer.⁴⁷ The rhetorical turn was, as has often been observed, also an important reason why, on the whole, ancient critics seem less concerned with the meaning and interpretation of whole works than with the study of parts, often detached from the context, a feature of ancient criticism which has often puzzled their modern successors.

---

44 I borrow the term 'revisions' from Zeitlin 2001. For guidance to the Homeric presence in the Second Sophistic cf. Kindstrand 1973, Zeitlin 2001, Hunter 2009b, Kim 2010, Porter 2011.
45 Cf., e.g., Classen 1994, Nünlist 2009a, 6.
46 For the connection between literary criticism and rhetoric see also Nünlist 2015.
47 Valuable guidance on the place of rhetoric in ancient education in Morgan 1998, Chapter 6. For Homer as the font of rhetorical forms and teaching cf. above all Quintilian's encomium at 10.1.46–51, and see also [Plutarch], *De Homero* 172 (with Hillgruber *ad loc.*), Radermacher 1951, 6–9; Karp 1977 is an attempt to reconstruct a rhetorical 'system' from the Homeric texts. Among lost works may be mentioned the 'On the rhetorical figures found in Homer' and the 'On rhetoric in Homer' of the second century AD grammarian Telephos of Pergamon (cf. *RE* V/A. 369–371).

From the Hellenistic period on, an elaborate systematisation of rhetoric and rhetorical education was developed, about which we are relatively well informed from a large corpus of surviving rhetorical treatises and handbooks. At the heart of this system lies the study of the texts of the past, what we would call 'classical literature', and it is within the parameters of this system that the foundations of a set of critical rules, amounting to no less than a body of ancient 'literary theory', were established. If Aristotle's *Rhetoric* represents a sophisticated level of intellectual analysis never really reached again, the subsequent tradition is also at pains to explain the need for system and agreed modes of analysis. Thus, for example, a treatise of perhaps the late second or third century AD, wrongly ascribed to Dionysius of Halicarnassus and entitled 'On the examination of *logoi*' (i.e. literary works in general, though the focus of the treatise is on declamation),[48] begins by noting that positive and negative judgements about *logoi* are usually offered without any system or 'knowledge', with the result that there is no uniformity of judgement about particular works; in a claim that can appear extraordinarily modern, the author observes that we tend to be swayed by the reputation of those making the critical judgements, rather than by the judgements themselves or by our own judgement. Therefore, what is required, according to the author, are agreed standards of composition and criteria of judgement with regard to the four principal areas of character, thought, art and diction (II 374.7–375.9 U R). Where, however, ancient students and their teachers principally differed from their modern counterparts, though having important aims in common with, say, English classical education of the nineteenth century, was that the former were not, in the first place, concerned with classical literature 'for its own sake', but for what it offered to their own development as speakers, writers and theorists of speech: 'reading nourishes speech' had long been the watchword (Ael. Theon 61.30–31 Sp.). Study must be turned into daily practice, and very frequently it was the Homeric poems which provided the material through which teachers displayed their skills and students learned to spread their wings.

The works of Libanius of Antioch (fourth century AD) offer some of the most instructive examples of this 'Homeric' material;[49] Homeric characters make their famous speeches all over again, but in different words (e.g., Achilles' reply to Odysseus' embassy, Libanius 5.303–360 Foerster), or write speeches to which

---

[48] The treatise is pp. 374.7–387.14 of Vol. II of the edition of Dionysius of Halicarnassus by Usener and Radermacher; for discussion of this treatise cf. Russell 1979.
[49] Most of the relevant texts are found in vols. 5 and 8 of Foerster's Teubner edition of Libanius; cf. further Webb 2010.

Homer, the 'common ancestor of Greek wisdom' as Libanius calls him (8.144.6–7), merely alluded. During the *teichoskopia* in *Iliad* 3, for example, the Trojan Antenor recalls the embassy of Menelaos and Odysseus to Troy to negotiate Helen's return:

> ἀλλ' ὅτε δὴ Τρώεσσιν ἐν ἀγρομένοισιν ἔμιχθεν,
> στάντων μὲν Μενέλαος ὑπείρεχεν εὐρέας ὤμους,   210
> ἄμφω δ' ἑζομένω, γεραρώτερος ἦεν Ὀδυσσεύς·
> ἀλλ' ὅτε δὴ μύθους καὶ μήδεα πᾶσιν ὕφαινον,
> ἤτοι μὲν Μενέλαος ἐπιτροχάδην ἀγόρευεν,
> παῦρα μέν, ἀλλὰ μάλα λιγέως, ἐπεὶ οὐ πολύμυθος
> οὐδ' ἀφαμαρτοεπής· ἦ καὶ γένει ὕστερος ἦεν.   215
> ἀλλ' ὅτε δὴ πολύμητις ἀναΐξειεν Ὀδυσσεύς
> στάσκεν, ὑπαὶ δὲ ἴδεσκε κατὰ χθονὸς ὄμματα πήξας,
> σκῆπτρον δ' οὔτ' ὀπίσω οὔτε προπρηνὲς ἐνώμα,
> ἀλλ' ἀστεμφὲς ἔχεσκεν ἀΐδρεϊ φωτὶ ἐοικώς·
> φαίης κε ζάκοτόν τέ τιν' ἔμμεναι ἄφρονά τ' αὔτως.   220
> ἀλλ' ὅτε δὴ ὄπα τε μεγάλην ἐκ στήθεος εἵη
> καὶ ἔπεα νιφάδεσσιν ἐοικότα χειμερίῃσιν,
> οὐκ ἂν ἔπειτ' Ὀδυσῆΐ γ' ἐρίσσειε βροτὸς ἄλλος·
> οὐ τότε γ' ὧδ' Ὀδυσῆος ἀγασσάμεθ' εἶδος ἰδόντες.

Homer, Iliad 3.209–224

When they mingled with the assembled Trojans, Menelaos with his broad shoulders rose above him as they stood, but when they were sitting, Odysseus was the more distinguished. When they were weaving their words and devices to all assembled, Menelaos indeed spoke fluently; his words were few, but very clearly spoken, since he is not a man of many words nor a rambler, and also younger by birth. When Odysseus of many guiles leaped up, he stood looking down with his eyes fixed on the ground, and he moved his staff neither back nor forwards, but he held it unmoving and seemed like an ignorant man. You would have said that he was sullen and merely a fool. When, however, he sent forth his great voice from his chest and words flowed like snowflakes in winter, then no other mortal could compete with Odysseus, and then we were not so struck by his appearance.

This passage was to become perhaps the most important foundational passage for the later analysis of different styles of speaking and writing;[50] Libanius takes off explicitly from this passage to write the speeches which Menelaos and Odysseus were supposed to have delivered on this occasion (5.199–221, 228–286

---

50 The only other claimant to such an honour is *Il.* 1.247–249 (Nestor); the scholia on *Il.* 3.212 match Menelaos–Odysseus–Nestor with Lysias–Demosthenes–Isocrates as the prime representatives of the three styles. For further discussion and bibliography cf. Hillgruber 1999, 370–372.

Foerster). For Libanius, this is a chance to show the different techniques of compression and extension of the same material (5.200.3–7 Foerster), and the result is that the speech of Menelaos, 'not a man of many words', takes twenty-two pages in Foerster's edition, and Odysseus' fifty-eight. Such exercises were a real test of the powers of εὕρεσις (*inuentio*) for the orator, as there was no Homeric text from which to work, and Libanius is not slow to point out to his pupils just how successful he has been (5.228.5 Foerster).[51] A related but different challenge was the exercise of seeking to affirm (κατασκευή) or disprove (ἀνασκευή) the events of which poets, most notably Homer, had told. Perhaps the most famous exercise of this kind, though it is in fact much more than that, is Dio Chrysostom's *Trojan Oration* (11), in which Dio sets out reasons for wholesale rejection, not just of Homer's account of the Trojan War, but for much of the generally received story of Paris and Helen.[52] A very powerful weapon in such arguments was the appeal to 'probability' (εἰκός), and so it is that the first in our collection of Libanian ἀνασκευαί is 'That it is not probable (εἰκός) that Chryses went to the Greek ships' (8.123–128 Foerster), and that one of the κατασκευαί is 'That the story of Achilles' anger is probable' (8.143–150 Foerster); this latter speech contains much which functions as a rebuttal of the ἀνασκευή about Chryses.[53] One of the things which is most striking about these exercises is the psychological depth and the level of calculation ascribed to Homeric characters; this may be the fruit of rhetorical invention, but it is also very instructive about how poetical texts were read and the sort of 'characters' that one expected to find there. In many ways, Libanius' modes of argument foreshadow some modern debates about 'character' in literature, notably in Greek drama, and what sort of intelligibility and motivation we are to ascribe to poetic characters. Thus, for example, we learn that Agamemnon would not have opposed the wishes of

---

51 Despite this, Russell 1983, 110 claims that the speeches of the Libanian Menelaos and Odysseus are 'not at all clearly differentiated'; Libanius 'seems ... to have been content to give a very general impression'.
52 Cf. Hunter 2009b, Kim 2010, Chap. 4, Minon 2012 (esp. pp. xli–xlvi on the links to rhetorical exercises).
53 Libanius' two exercises have more than a little in common with the εὕρεσις on show in Dio's account of Chryseis' own motivation and calculations in *Oration* 61, cf. Drules 1998, 77–79, Kim 2008, 617–620. That the opening scene of the *Iliad* should figure so prominently in rhetorical texts is hardly surprising, given that this was probably the most familiar piece of Homer, one known to every schoolboy. Kim 2010, 613–617 rightly associates the reading practice which 'fills in the gaps' in Homer's account of his characters' psychology and motivation with the grammarians' interpretative principle of κατὰ τὸ σιωπώμενον, although that is usually used to explain apparent problems and omissions in Homer's presentation of 'facts', rather than of motivation.

the majority, as Homer (*Il.* 1.22–25) says he did, because he knew that the security of his rule depended upon the goodwill of those under him (8.126–127), whereas on the other side it can be said both that Agamemnon acted as a careful commander by throwing a potential Trojan spy out of the Greek camp (8.146.6–9) and that the nature of Chryses' subsequent prayer (*Il.* 1.37–142) makes perfect sense:

> Chryses knew that he would cause Agamemnon the greatest distress if he destroyed his position, caused his power to crumble and put an end to his rule. For it is not the same for a man to meet once and for all with disaster as to remain alive and in despair; the dead have no sensation of anything, whereas the man who lives in pain is truly punished. Moreover, Chryses also knew that if Agamemnon died and the war ended, then his daughter would go off with the Greeks, whereas if the Greek army was oppressed by plague and was being destroyed, there would be an enquiry into this misfortune, the reason would emerge, and he would recover his child.
>
> Libanius, *Progymnasmata* 8.147.9–148.1 Foerster

Libanius here elaborates on one of the 'solutions' offered in the exegetical scholia on v. 42 to the 'problem' of 'why Chryses curses the Greeks who urged (*Il.* 1.22–23) that his daughter should be returned to him and not rather (just) Agamemnon': 'If Agamemnon died, the cause of the plague would remain uninvestigated, and if the Greeks sailed back to their country, Chryseis would not be given back to him'.[54] It would be easy to dismiss such 'filling in the story' as simply fertile display, without any real connection to, or warrant in, the Homeric text, and yet the persistent questioning of action and motivation reveals a kind of 'close reading' and active supplementation which has not always been applied to ancient texts in more recent times, and, more importantly, which the opening books of the *Iliad* (at least) might be thought to invite. It was just such close reading and pondering on motivation which contributed significantly to the development, precisely in rhetorical schools, of what we label *plasma* or fiction and which distinguished itself from *mythos*, where such chains of both physical and psychological plausibility no longer held; that is why, perhaps (or perhaps not), μῦθος so often required the sideways interpretative move of alle-

---

54 Cf. also 'Heracl.', *Quaest. Hom.* 6.3–4, where it is claimed that the view that Apollo killed the Greeks who had in fact urged respect for Chryses and spared Agamemnon is the result of spiteful malice, Eust., *Il.* 37.6–10. The other reasons given by the exegetical scholia are also predominantly 'psychological': 'Because the Greeks had given Chryseis to Agamemnon after sacking Thebes [*Il.* 1.366–369], because Agamemnon himself is included in the Danaans, and because Chryses, being a barbarian, regards all Greeks as enemies'.

gorisation, to match that similiarly sideways narrative jump, well captured by the term παράδοξον, which so often travels with the idea of μῦθος.

The treatise of Aelius Theon of (probably) the early imperial period,[55] one of the principal witnesses for the 'preliminary exercises' (*progymnasmata*) which, as we have seen in Libanius, prepared students for the formal study of rhetoric, offers a further helpful guide to the mindset which determined the rhetorical approach. One kind of exercise which attracts particular notice in the current context is 'paraphrase', the exercise of rewriting passages from classical texts 'in your own words'. Theon points out that, just as the same event or material affects us in more than one way, so any φαντασία which presents itself to our minds can be expressed in a variety of linguistic modes, i.e.as questions, prayers etc., according to the system of variations which pupils of the rhetorical schools followed. He evidences this claim by citing the fact that all classical writers, poets and prose writers alike, 'made excellent use of paraphrase, by refashioning both their own work and that of each other' (62.23–25 Sp.), and he then cites passages in which first Archilochus and then Demosthenes and Aeschines might be thought to have paraphrased Homer, a passage where Theopompus has paraphrased Thucydides, and several examples where one Attic orator has used the words of a predecessor; finally he observes that 'Demosthenes often paraphrases himself, not only by transferring what he has said in another speech to elsewhere, but also by clearly saying the same thing myriad times (μυριάκις) in the one speech, although the audience do not notice because of the variety of expression' (63.29–64.4 Sp.). The theory of paraphrase, at the heart of which lies a distinction between what we say and how we say it, the distinction expressed elsewhere as that between διάνοια and λέξις, is one first step along the road to a theory of what modern scholars would call allusion, echo, even intertextuality, and that step is framed within rhetorical education.

Theon is entirely typical in seeing the same rhetorical system governing the writing of the ancients as is practised in his own day; the teacher of rhetoric must first 'collect excellent examples of each exercise (γύμνασμα) from ancient writings and instruct his pupils to learn them off by heart' (65.30–66.2 Sp.). Thus the ancients supply the material for the rhetorical system, not merely the προγυμνάσματα, but are also themselves the principal examples of, and hence authorities for, that system. In particular, as has already been noted, the foundations of all rhetoric and rhetorical analysis were to be found in Homer. Rhetorical criticism of, and illustration from, Homer shares with an approach to

---

55 For discussion of the author and date of the treatise cf. Patillon/Bolognesi 1997, vii–xvi; Heath 2002–2003 proposes a radical re-dating to the fifth century AD.

literature through 'problems' and their 'solutions' an assumption that the characters of literature have a familiar psychological depth which allows us to draw in our analysis of their strategies upon motivations and calculations not made explicit in the text;[56] when confronted by apparent anomalies, the best interpretative strategy will usually be to give these characters the benefit of the doubt. Working together with this fundamental assumption is the overriding importance assigned to the notion of appropriateness (τὸ πρέπον) and to the shifting demands imposed by the particularities of any situation (ὁ καιρός). Both are neatly seen together in an observation of Theon, in the context of the rhetorical exercise of προσωποποιία:

> We praise Homer because he gave appropriate (οἰκεῖοι) words to each of the characters he introduces, and we criticise Euripides because his Hecuba philosophises when the situation does not require it (παρὰ καιρόν).
>
> Aelius Theon, *Progymnasmata* 60.28–31 Sp.

This analytical framework gave ancient critics a powerful tool for the analysis of the speeches, and of the motives behind the speeches, in (particularly) epic and drama. 'Rhetorical criticism' is fundamentally the examination of why the characters of literature act and speak as they do; it is not limited merely to the formal analysis of speeches into their constituent parts. For a specific, though not necessarily typical, example let us consider Agamemnon's famous 'testing' of the troops in *Iliad* 2.

Zeus honours his promise to Thetis by sending a dream to Agamemnon which (deceptively) leads him to think that the time for the capture of Troy is at hand; Agamemnon calls a council of the Greek leaders,[57] tells them of his dream and then concludes:

> ἀλλ' ἄγετ', αἴ κέν πως θωρήξομεν υἷας Ἀχαιῶν.
> πρῶτα δ' ἐγὼν ἔπεσιν πειρήσομαι, ἣ θέμις ἐστίν,
> καὶ φεύγειν σὺν νηυσὶ πολυκλήϊσι κελεύσω·
> ὑμεῖς δ' ἄλλοθεν ἄλλος ἐρητύειν ἐπέεσσιν.
>
> Homer, *Iliad* 2.72–75

> But come, let us see whether we can arm the sons of the Achaeans. I shall first test them with words, as is appropriate (*themis*), and I shall urge them to retreat in their many-benched ships; you however must use words to restrain them, each in your various positions.

---

56 On 'problems' as a critical form cf. above, and Nünlist 2015.
57 Dio 56.10 praises Agamemnon for wisely consulting the Greek elders before following the advice of the dream.

After a rather curiously inconsequential speech from Nestor, which Aristarchus athetised and which does not even mention Agamemnon's proposal of a test,[58] the Greek army is assembled and Agamemnon urges departure, as there is now no chance of the mission being successful (for his arguments, see below); the army (and perhaps also all the leaders except Odysseus) rush for the ships,[59] as Agamemnon indeed seems to have expected (cf. v. 75 above),[60] and that would indeed have been the end of the expedition, had not Hera dispatched Athena to intervene, which she does by stirring Odysseus to action. This sequence of events was much discussed in antiquity, and has attracted a very large modern bibliography;[61] the most cursory glimpse at that bibliography will, however, show just how many 'modern' arguments are essentially refinements of what was already said in antiquity.

Why does Agamemnon 'test' the troops, or — to put it in language that we have found in Libanius — was Agamemnon's test 'probable' (εἰκός)? Aristotle discussed the matter in his *Homeric Problems*, and Porphyry's report of his discussion, even if it does not all go back to Aristotle, is worth citing at some length, as much ancient and modern discussion may in fact be traced back to it:

> The army was worn out from the plague and unmotivated because of the length of time [of the war]; Achilles and his forces had withdrawn; Agamemnon himself, when taking Briseis away in the assembly, had said in order to frighten the others: 'anyone else should shrink from the idea of speaking on equal terms or placing themselves on an equal footing with me' (*Il.* 1.186–187); there had been disturbance at Achilles' withdrawal. In these cir-

---

58 The various reasons for the athetesis given in the scholia on 2.76 do not necessarily (all) go back to Aristarchus (cf., however, Lührs 1992, 260–261), though all are instructive about ancient criticism: the poet should not have said that Agamemnon sat down after his speech, because he did not stand to deliver it; Nestor has really nothing to say (οὐδὲν περισσόν); it was silly to have Nestor say that they would only have believed such a dream from 'the best of the Achaeans', because the powerful do not dream any differently from the rest of us, and (finally), if the verses are deleted, then ποιμένι λαῶν in v. 85 will refer to Agamemnon, as it should do, rather than to Nestor. Nestor's speech has recently been discussed by Nünlist 2012d; the kinds of argument that Nünlist adduces to explain the speech are in fact interestingly reminiscent of the kinds of 'rhetorical' explanation that we find in the scholia and in Libanius (cf. above). Schofield 1986, 29 calls Nestor's observation about the dream not being a deception because of who dreamt it 'ingenious as well as tactful'.
59 The apparent unclarity about the actions and knowledge of the commanders who had heard Agamemnon's speech has long been highlighted by those seeking to reconstruct the creation of the text; cf., most recently, West 2011, 103–105 (notes on vv. 73–75, 192–197).
60 The bT-scholia try to get around this interpretation of v. 75, but it seems inevitable.
61 Cf. McGlew 1989, Latacz 2003, 29–30, 41, Cook 2003; helpful guidance to older discussions in Katzung 1960.

> cumstances, it was reasonable for Agamemnon not immediately to exhort them to go out [against the Trojans], but to think that he should test their mood. If without a test he had ordered men in this condition to make war and some men had opposed him, the whole expedition would have been ruined and everyone would have rebelled ... Therefore the test was necessary, together with his instruction to the leaders to oppose him...
>
> Aristotle fr. 366 Gigon = 142 Rose[62]

That Agamemnon did not really have any option but to test whether the war-weary men were ready to go out against the Trojans is the conclusion of most ancient discussion of the matter; the test, together with the precaution of telling his colleagues how they are to act, is not, therefore, a sign of Agamemnon's weakness and mistaken leadership, but rather of his strategic good sense (cf. also Eust., *Il.* 173.24–33). In seeking to understand the text we must consider the position which the character finds himself in and think out how he might best handle that, even if these calculations are not made explicit in the text; here modern critics of the *peira* have followed the ancient.[63]

Much ancient discussion of Agamemnon's subsequent speech to the troops, like much modern criticism, is focused upon the fact that a good part of what he says seems designed to lead the troops to stay, rather than to go home, which is the professed purpose of the speech. Later rhetoricians took very great interest in this speech, for it seemed to be overtly arguing for an outcome which the speaker did not in fact want.[64] The treatise *On the method of forcefulness*, which is transmitted with the Hermogenean corpus, thus makes Agamemnon's speech the Homeric paradigm of 'accomplishing something by arguing the opposite". In this figure the speaker will use arguments which are 'easily refuted and contradictory and can be turned around':

> Homer did this. Agamemnon is testing the Greek army and wants them to remain, while saying that they should not remain but should flee. Through his whole speech he says things which are easy to refute and turn around, thus giving openings to his opponents, and at the end he says contradictory things. For to say 'The timbers of the ships have rotted and the ropes are loose' (2.135) is very obviously opposed to 'Let us flee'. How could

---

[62] Much of this has found its way into the scholia on *Iliad* 2.73; cf. also Dio 2.22, where, however, Alexander (Aristotle's pupil) misrepresents the events in *Iliad* 2, by omitting Agamemnon's *peira* speech entirely.
[63] This was the basis of the discussion in Kullmann 1955, who saw the *peira* as a motif dependent upon a situation of the Greek army known to the audience from the *Kypria*. For a more recent attempt to explain the origin both of the *peira* and of the opening of Book 9 (see below) cf. West 2011, 100–105, 214–215.
[64] Cf. further Hillgruber 1999, 357–359.

they flee without ships? This is the argument of someone who wants to prevent them from sailing away, not an argument for doing what he is saying.

Hermogenes 437.14–438.4 Rabe

Pseudo-Hermogenes' example is perhaps not the strongest which could have been chosen, but it may serve to remind us of how ancient critics tended carefully to think through the implications of what the poet and his characters said; as we have already seen, 'close reading' was at the heart of the rhetorical interpretation of texts. The rhetorical *technê* ascribed to Dionysius of Halicarnassus offers a more extended analysis of Agamemnon's speeches along the same lines (II 327.19–330.25 U-R),[65] and modern commentators have added further examples of arguments which seem to cut both ways, but [Dionysius] also argues that the army's reaction to the speech, which could be (and no doubt had been) argued to show how mistaken Agamemnon was, is in fact also part of his strategy: in this way Agamemnon draws the hostile but concealed feelings of the army out into the open, where they can be controlled by Odysseus and Nestor (II 328.13–25 U-R). Less radically, perhaps, Eustathius argues that Agamemnon's excellent stratagem is not to be judged by its near-disastrous outcome; 'events' can overturn even the best-laid plans (Eust., *Il.* 185.38–186.10). Moreover, for [Dionysius], Agamemnon's greatest rhetorical achievement — and one from which we should learn — is the manner in which he conceals his stratagem, for it will be no use at all if one's opponents perceive what one is up to (II 329.19–24 U-R). This Agamemnon does by the emotional beginning of his speech (*Il.* 2.110–118); by criticising Zeus in this way, he suggests that his speech is prompted by grief rather than by a cunning stratagem (II 330.15–24).

Much ancient rhetorical training of course would have shown that the implicit argument that 'emotion is a guarantee of sincerity' was a very unsafe assumption in oratory. Nevertheless, in his 'testing' speech in reply to optimistic words from the steersman Tiphys in Book 2 of Apollonius' *Argonautica*, which clearly reflects not just the Homeric *peira* but also scholarly discussion of that episode, Jason also begins in a distraught and highly emotional way which would seem likely to assure anyone that it was grief, not design, which prompted his words:

---

[65] Cf. Russell 2001a, 160–163. Dentice di Accadia 2010b is a recent and helpful attempt to take the arguments of [Dionysius] seriously; the present chapter was drafted before the appearance of that article, and I have not signalled the various places where our two accounts agree or differ. Dentice di Accadia 2010a is now the standard edition of the treatises, and cf. also Schöpsdau 1975, Hillgruber 1999, 357–359, Heath 2003.

αὐτὰρ ὁ τόνγε
μειλιχίοις ἐπέεσσι παραβλήδην προσέειπεν·
Τῖφυ, τίη μοι ταῦτα παρηγορέεις ἀχέοντι;
ἤμβροτον, ἀασάμην τε κακὴν καὶ ἀμήχανον ἄτην·
χρῆν γὰρ ἐφιεμένοιο καταντικρὺ Πελίαο
αὐτίκ' ἀνήνασθαι τόνδε στόλον, εἰ καὶ ἔμελλον   625
νηλειῶς μελεϊστὶ κεδαιόμενος θανέεσθαι.
νῦν δὲ περισσὸν δεῖμα καὶ ἀτλήτους μελεδῶνας
ἄγκειμαι, στυγέων μὲν ἁλὸς κρυόεντα κέλευθα
νηὶ διαπλώειν, στυγέων δ' ὅτ' ἐπ' ἠπείροιο
βαίνωμεν, πάντηι γὰρ ἀνάρσιοι ἄνδρες ἔασιν.   630
αἰεὶ δὲ στονόεσσαν ἐπ' ἤματι νύκτα φυλάσσω,
ἐξότε τὸ πρώτιστον ἐμὴν χάριν ἠγερέθεσθε,
φραζόμενος τὰ ἕκαστα. σὺ δ' εὐμαρέως ἀγορεύεις,
οἶον ἑῆς ψυχῆς ἀλέγων ὕπερ· αὐτὰρ ἔγωγε
εἶο μὲν οὐδ' ἠβαιὸν ἀτύζομαι, ἀμφὶ δὲ τοῖο   635
καὶ τοῦ ὁμῶς καὶ σεῖο καὶ ἄλλων δείδι' ἑταίρων,
εἰ μὴ ἐς Ἑλλάδα γαῖαν ἀπήμονας ὔμμε κομίσσω.
ὣς φάτ', ἀριστήων πειρώμενος· οἱ δ' ὁμάδησαν
θαρσαλέοις ἐπέεσσιν.

Apollonius, Argonautica 2.620–639

But Jason answered him in return with soft words: 'Tiphys, why do you offer me these consolations in my grief? I have erred; my wretched folly offers no remedy. When Pelias gave me his instructions, I should have immediately refused this expedition outright, even if it meant a cruel death, torn apart limb from limb. As it is I am in constant terror and my burdens are unendurable; I loathe sailing in our ship over the chill paths of the sea, and I loathe our stops on dry land, for all around are our enemies. Ever since you first assembled for my sake, I have endured a ceaseless round of painful nights and days, for I must give thought to every detail. You can speak lightly, as your worries are only for yourself. I have no anxiety at all for myself, but I must fear for this man and that, for you no less than for all our other companions, that I shall be unable to bring you back unharmed to Greece'. So he spoke, testing the heroes, and they all shouted words of encouragement.

Jason's speech too has divided modern critics, particularly over its purpose (if it is not simply an anguished retort to Tiphys' optimism) and over whether or not his attitudes are here in any way feigned;[66] unlike Agamemnon, whose opening appeal to *atê* Jason echoes, Jason does not apparently have a specific plan in mind (he does not propose that they now turn around), though the two choices facing the crew are obviously, as in Homer, pressing forward or abandoning the

---

[66] Fränkel 1968, 214–221, arguing that πειρώμενος in 2.638 means 'seeking to provoke', not 'testing', has been an influential discussion; further observations and bibliography in Hunter 1993, 20–22.

expedition. Like Agamemnon, Jason focuses on his own situation and, like the Agamemnon of the later rhetoricians, some of his arguments would be very easy to refute; the rebuke to Tiphys of vv. 633–634 had in fact already been shown to be false by the narrative of Tiphys' role in the passage through the Clashing Rocks (2.581–585), and it is patently absurd to charge the steersman with concern only for himself. Over Jason's speech in fact hovers the ubiquitous ancient parallel between the ruler and the steersman, each responsible for the safety of the 'vessel' under his command and the people in it;[67] Tiphys, no less than Jason, could claim that it is his duty to bring the Argonauts safe back to Greece. From the perspective of ancient rhetorical criticism (best attested for us, of course, in texts considerably later than the *Argonautica*), Jason's speech would indeed be understood as a clear example where the speaker 'says one thing and conceals another in his heart', as Achilles rebuked Odysseus and Agamemnon for so doing (*Il.* 9.313), in verses which were indeed to become associated with λόγοι ἐσχηματισμένοι.[68] Whether or not we receive Jason's speech as unprepared and unguided as his crew does depends importantly upon the disputed meaning of the introductory μειλιχίοις ἐπέεσσι παραβλήδην (2.621), but two observations are relevant here. Apollonius has sought to make the effect of his *peira* more dramatic than Homer's by omitting any clear indication of what Jason is actually up to, so that, whatever the meaning of 2.621, the external audience is placed more in the position of the audience in the text than is the case in Homer, where we have been very explicitly warned about Agamemnon's real intentions; secondly, we may perhaps use this passage of the *Argonautica* to trace ancient discussion and rhetorical analysis of Agamemnon's speech in the *Iliad* back to a much earlier date than that of the scholia and the rhetorical texts I have been considering.

The scholia on Agamemnon's *peira* largely follow the interpretative patterns already outlined: Agamemnon knows that the men are weary and depressed at Achilles' withdrawal and that his standing with them is fragile (Schol.AbT 2.73). A close engagement with the text again lies at the heart of interpretation: Agamemnon calls the troops ἥρωες Δαναοί because such praise works against any desire for flight (Schol. bT 2.110b); he says φεύγωμεν (v. 140), when he might have said στείχωμεν, so that the dishonourable word will have a

---

[67] Particularly striking when set against Jason's speech is Dio 3.62–67 in which the good ruler is first compared to the steersman battling a storm while all the other passengers are idle and then to a general on campaign who must look after every soldier, whereas each ordinary soldier only looks after himself.
[68] Cf. Philostratus, fr. 542 Wright on Polemo.

negative effect,[69] and so forth. A further argument in the same scholium about Agamemnon's implicit calculations may be expanded along the following lines: Agamemnon's stratagem will help recover some of his standing, because the ordinary troops do not like generals who are recklessly 'gung-ho' about fighting, and so he has nothing to lose — if the men want to abandon the expedition, then the other leaders will dissuade them, and if not, then well and good, and no one will be any the wiser about the stratagem, but the men will know that he at least does not gamble recklessly with their lives. So too, the pseudo-Plutarchan treatise *On Homer*, which absorbs and reflects a great deal of the mainstream of ancient criticism, makes a rather similar point:

> Does not Agamemnon ... use rhetorical art, when he says to the mass the opposite of what he wants, so that he can test their spirit and not become hateful to them by forcing them to fight on his behalf? He himself speaks in a way which will please them (πρὸς χάριν), but one of those others with the power to persuade them will turn them back and make them stay, as this in truth is what the king wanted.
>
> [Plutarch], *On Homer* 2.166

Great men do not make 'mistakes'; one merely has to try to understand their stratagems. This portrait of a cunningly calculating Agamemnon, who prepares the ground for the hostility of the troops to be displaced on to other leaders rather than himself, is deeply rooted both in the analysis and debates of rhetorical education and in the agonistic realities of ancient political and oratorical struggle; modes of interpretation, then as now, unsurprisingly reflect the culture that gave rise to them.

The final part of Agamemnon's speech is particularly worthy of note:

> ἐννέα δὴ βεβάασι Διὸς μεγάλου ἐνιαυτοί,
> καὶ δὴ δοῦρα σέσηπε νεῶν, καὶ σπάρτα λέλυνται,
> αἳ δέ που ἡμέτεραί τ' ἄλοχοι καὶ νήπια τέκνα
> εἴατ' ἐνὶ μεγάροις ποτιδέγμεναι· ἄμμι δὲ ἔργον
> αὔτως ἀκράαντον, οὗ εἵνεκα δεῦρ' ἱκόμεσθα.
> ἀλλ' ἄγεθ', ὡς ἂν ἐγὼ εἴπω, πειθώμεθα πάντες·
> φεύγωμεν σὺν νηυσὶ φίλην ἐς πατρίδα γαῖαν,
> οὐ γὰρ ἔτι Τροίην αἱρήσομεν εὐρυάγυιαν.
>
> Homer, *Iliad* 2.134–141

---

[69] Some modern commentators (cf., e.g., the Basel-commentary on 1.173 and 2.74) observe that φεύγειν does not necessarily have a negative connotation; it may suggest 'withdraw from a position' rather than 'flee'. This may be true, but we must also recognise that, even in formulaic epic style, the same words can resonate differently with different audiences.

> Nine of great Zeus' years have gone past, and the timbers of the ships have rotted and the rigging hangs loose. Our wives and young children sit waiting for us at home, while the task which brought us here is utterly unaccomplished. Come, let all of us do as I say: let us retreat in our ships to our beloved native lands, for we shall never take Troy with its broad streets.

The influence of the rhetorical approach to literary speeches is very obvious in a scholium on the final verse of the speech, which reports that this verse was not transmitted in some copies because it 'removes the ambiguity'; although we do not, of course, have to accept that this was indeed the reason for the omission of the verse, the argument is instructive. For a rhetorical critic, Agamemnon here speaks too straightforwardly in a speech which depends upon ambiguity; this closing appeal to the troops contains no 'sub-text' which urges the opposite course of action than the one apparently being proposed, and a modern critic might add that φίλην ἐς πατρίδα γαῖαν in the previous verse carries a powerful emotional weight which is not offset by any other resonance. By contrast, the equally emotive reference to the men's wives and children is offset by the unfinished job which the army came to do (137–138), and the bT-scholium gloss the doubleness of ποτιδέγμεναι in v. 137: 'Therefore let us depart because our wives long for us (ποθούμενοι), or [we should not depart] because we have accomplished nothing to match their expectations (προσδοκία)'.[70] A modern critic might observe that the juxtaposition of an explicit reference to the decay of the ships over nine years to the 'waiting wives' carries with it the powerful implication that the wives too are not getting any younger. Some version of this reasoning may in fact be reflected in the A-scholium on vv. 136–137 which warns against punctuating after ἄλοχοι, because that would make the meaning ἀπρεπές; the point is presumably not merely the disrupted syntax which would result, but also the 'low' implication that the wives too, like the ships and the ropes, are 'rotting and loose'.[71] This clearly is not what Agamemnon wants to say, but the verses are indeed held together by the idea of the long passage of time — the children will be νήπια τέκνα no longer — and behind the scholiastic worry about punctuation lies a recognition of this resonance.

For many modern critics, the principal literary effect at work here is 'tragic irony': Agamemnon's (deceptive) claim to have been deceived by Zeus (vv. 111–114) is more true than he knows, and when Agamemnon repeats some of the

---

[70] Cf. also Eust., *Il.* 187.43–47.
[71] In later literature there are some graphic examples of ageing women compared to ships (cf. esp. Meleager, *AP* 5.204 (= *HE* 4298–4307)), and these Homeric verses may in fact have been influential in that sceptic tradition.

verses, though without the ones which might seem most ambiguous in their effect, in very different circumstances at the council (or assembly) which opens Book 9, the full force of that irony hits home.⁷² It is an obvious question why (as far as we know) ancient critics too did not elaborate such an approach to this passage. In fact, however, critical positions may indeed have embraced something very like this, and ancient critics seem in fact to have been divided as to whether or not Agamemnon's speech in Book 9 (vv. 17–28), which – after a different opening address (cf. further below) – repeats verbatim vv. 111–118 and vv. 139–141 from Book 2, was another 'test', parallel to that of Book 2, just as some at least seem to have entertained the idea that his third plea for withdrawal (14.75–81) was also a test (bT scholium *ad loc*). Pseudo-Dionysius appears to take for granted that the speech in Book 9 is such a test (II 325.14–16 U R), but the absence of vv. 23–25, which could be taken to suggest that Troy might still be taken, from Zenodotus' shortened version of the speech and the *athetêsis* of those verses by Aristarchus point to the other view; thus the A scholia on vv. 23–25 observe that '[Agamemnon] is not making a test, but he is speaking sincerely about withdrawal as Zeus has inflicted setbacks upon them', and the bT scholia consider it ὑπόψυχρον to hesitate on this subject when in Agamemnon's situation.⁷³ This second view is not an expression of 'tragic irony' as such, but it draws upon the same contrasts as that modern critical approach. In this difference of critical effort – seeking to account for the text as it confronts us or removing verses to produce the 'coherent' text we want – lies foreshadowed, of course, much of the history of Homeric criticism.

The bT scholia on v. 17 produce interesting reasons for believing that the speech of Book 9 is indeed another 'test':

> He now makes this second test of the Argive leaders (i.e. not of the whole army), because he fears lest the defeat and the rout inflicted by Zeus has destroyed even their resolve.

---

72 As representatives of this standard reading cf., e.g., Katzung 1960, 55, Reinhardt 1961, 113–114, Lohmann 1970, 217, Taplin 1992, 92; cf. also De Jong 2004, 190, who finds the scholiastic hesitations "curious" (284 n. 94). Hainsworth's note on 9.18–28, which expresses reservations about irony here, would offer excellent material for a study of the assumptions behind much modern (though now outdated?) Homeric criticism; cf. also Griffin on vv. 17–27, 'It is inept to argue that the repetition is in some way 'ironical': it is just a repetition…'. The very length of Hainsworth's note, however, suggests a worry that it is actually hard to keep at bay here what he sees as the dangerous tide of 'over-interpretation'. For some of the ways in which the opening scene of Book 9 foreshadows the exchanges with Achilles to come later in the book cf. Lynn George 1988, 83–84.

73 Cf. also Eust., *Il.* 732.68–733.2, where the contrast is between speaking ἐσχηματισμένως and speaking ἀληθῶς.

> That Agamemnon is testing in this council too is clear from the way in which he puts up with Diomedes' rebuke, when he did not put up with the speeches of Achilles who was a better man, and from the fact that Nestor, a man who understands the king's thought, praises Diomedes, though he had previously rebuked Achilles.
>
> bT-scholium on *Iliad* 9.17b

The comparison with *Iliad* 1 reflects a proper critical sense, much echoed (though not always with proper acknowledgement of ancient criticism) by modern scholars,[74] of how Book 9 acts as a kind of reprise of Book 1 and a reaffirmation of Achilles' withdrawal, here at another time of great crisis. In Book 1 Agamemnon is known to have spoken without any σχῆμα of concealment; whereas Achilles' speeches there simply made Agamemnon angrier and more determined, his (unrecorded) reaction, here taken for silent acquiescence, to Diomedes' speech in Book 9 professing enthusiasm for the fray shows that Diomedes' reaction, apparently the reverse of what Agamemnon was arguing for, was in fact just the reaction the king wanted. Agamemnon's speech was therefore a λόγος ἐσχηματισμένος, a 'figured speech'. As for Diomedes himself, the standard critical position was that, whereas in Book 4 he had not responded when rebuked by Agamemnon, he now feels free to attack because of the authority given to him by his great martial deeds described in the intervening books.[75] Ancient rhetorical critics start with the assumption that great men know what they are doing and rise above circumstances. For both ancient and modern critics, Agamemnon's apparent silence after Diomedes' speech speaks volumes (cf. further below), but what it says may differ according to critical idiom. Eustathius, for whom Agamemnon's speech in Book 9 is 'sincere', perhaps has in mind arguments such as that of the bT-scholiast on v. 17 (above) when he observes that 'the king puts up with the rebuke both because of the rule (θέμις) of

---

74 Cf., e.g., Lohmann 1970, 217–218.
75 Cf. bT Schol. on 4.402, 9.31, Plut. *Hom.* 2.168, Plut. *Mor.* 29b. For a different view cf. Dion. Hal. II 314.19–316.14 U R. Reeve 1972, 2–3 argues that vv. 32–39 belong to a later stage of the tradition than vv. 40–49. It is interesting to compare the ancient accounts of Diomedes' speech with a modern account of its rhetoric, namely Martin 1989, 24–25, and cf. also 125. Without reference to ancient views, Martin sees Diomedes' speech as that of a novice speaker who imitates, sometimes with inelegant repetition, phrases that he has heard in the mouths of others; he made no reply in Book 4 because 'he needs time to compose his reply' (contrast, however, Martin 1989, 71–72 on Diomedes' 'cunning silence'). Both the ancient scholiasts and Martin account for the difference between Book 4 and Book 9 in terms of Diomedes' development, but do so in rather different ways; on the other hand, there is more than a little in common between [Dionysius of Halicarnassus'] account of major Homeric speeches as λόγοι ἐσχηματισμένοι and Martin's account of Homeric 'flyting' in which the participants know the rules of the game. Cf. further Scodel 2008, 60–61.

the assembly [cf. v. 33] and because the rebuke is not false, but in this matter the hero speaks the truth...' (Eust., *Il.* 733.22).

After Agamemnon's first speech in *Iliad* 9 there is an awkward silence:[76]

ὣς ἔφαθ'· οἳ δ' ἄρα πάντες ἀκὴν ἐγένοντο σιωπῆι,
δὴν δ' ἄνεω ἦσαν τετιηότες υἷες Ἀχαιῶν.
ὀψὲ δὲ δὴ μετέειπε βοὴν ἀγαθὸς Διομήδης·

Homer, *Iliad* 9.29–31

So he spoke. They all remained silent and for a long time the sons of the Achaeans were quiet and downcast. At length Diomedes, powerful in the war-cry, addressed them...

The bT-scholium on v. 30 explains the silence as follows: 'They neither had good prospects if they remained nor did they think flight was something which would redound to their credit. Moreover, having seen the former test, they were suspicious about the speaker's intention. The poet himself seems to be uncertain whom he should put in opposition to Agamemnon's speech which was well done and showed concern for his men'.[77] The first reason given there for the silence will help explain τετιηότες, and the second interprets the length of the silence as uncertainty brought on by a recognition (nowhere made explicit in the text, of course) that they have heard these words before. Uncertainty in the audience as to how to react does not, of course, mean that the speech is another *peira*; it might, however, mean that the audience are (*inter alia*) using their recent experience to interpret what they hear. Should we too be in doubt? Most modern critics do not even mention the possibility that this speech might be a further test,[78] in part (I suppose) because this would go against the 'natural' sense of the text and, as Hainsworth (note on *Il.* 9.18–28) puts it, there is no "hint in the text" that Agamemnon is here less than sincere. Moreover, Homer — as ancient critics recognised (cf., e.g., Plut., *Quomodo adul.* 19a–e) — sometimes gave the audience a steer (to the credit or otherwise of the speaker) as to how a speech is to be interpreted before (and sometimes after) the speech is deliv-

---

[76] West 2011, 215 rightly notes that this pattern of silence after a speech which takes the plot in a new direction is itself 'typical'. This, however, is a particularly marked example: v. 30 occurs elsewhere in the corpus only as v. 695 of the same book, when vv. 29–31 are (pointedly) repeated as the reaction to Odysseus' report of the failure of the embassy to Achilles.
[77] Cf. also Eust., *Il.* 733.2: 'The others are silent, fearing lest this speech of the king also is a test of the Achaeans'.
[78] An exception is the discussion by Scodel 2008, 68–69.

ered.⁷⁹ Here there is no explicit 'steer', except that Agamemnon is very upset (v. 9) and weeps as he speaks (vv. 14–16); 'feigned' emotion as a guarantee of 'sincerity' was, as we have noted, seen in his *peira* speech of Book 1, but forced tears might be hard to believe, however often Attic comic poets saw this as a regular ploy of orators. It is noteworthy, however, that, to judge by the bT-scholia on v. 14, the view that the tears were part of Agamemnon's performance does indeed seem to have been held by some ancient readers.

The further scholiastic interpretation of the silence — it is also a marker of the poet's hesitation — seems in some ways remarkably modern: a textual gesture reflects upon the nature of the poem itself. If the scholia do not quite put it in these terms, it is clear that the whole thrust of their interpretation is built upon the many correspondences and reversals between the scenes of Book 2 and Book 9, and the silence, expressed in conventional 'formulaic' terms, is one of these; the first *peira* speech in Book 2 was greeted by frenzied activity and noise. Modern critics, with their focus on the text rather than the author (particularly where Homer is concerned), might see this silence more in terms of the uncertainty of *both* audiences, i.e. not just the Achaeans in the text, but also the audience, i.e. ourselves, outside the text, rather than as a marker of authorial uncertainty. How *should* we react to Agamemnon's speech? Is it in fact a straight choice between 'test' or 'no test'? The scholiastic view that the audience in the text thought it might be a test is far from obviously absurd, and modern discussion has too often run together the questions of Agamemnon's 'intention' and of how the speech is received. If we ask what more we know than the audience in the text knows, then the poet has stressed the grief of the ἄριστοι (v. 3) and the fact that Agamemnon is 'knocked over by great grief in his heart' (v. 9), but this amounts to little more than confirmation of the very visible manifestations of distress all around. Here at least there is little distance between the levels of knowledge of the two audiences, particularly if we take the view, held by many ancient (and some modern) readers,⁸⁰ that only the Greek leaders,

---

79 Cf. Edwards 1970, Hunter 1993, 141–142, Nünlist 2009a, 316–317, Hunter/Russell 2011, 106. The verbs which Plutarch uses are προδιαβάλλειν and προσυνιστάναι; the former is not used in the scholia, whereas the latter is commonly used of the poet 'introducing/paving the way' for a character or later narration, but is also found in the narrower sense in which Plutarch uses it (bT scholium to *Iliad* 1.247–248).

80 Ancient critics, unlike for the most part their modern successors (but see von Wilamowitz Moellendorff 1920, 33–34), were divided on whether the first gathering of Book 9 was of the leaders only (e.g. bT-scholia on 9.11, 17, D-scholia on 9.12) or of the whole army (cf., e.g., Plut. *Mor.* 29c). Aristotle discussed the problem posed by 9.17 if one held that the whole army was

young and old, are present to hear the second *peira* speech, not the entire army; given that, apart from the omission of verses, the only change from Book 2 to Book 9 is that Agamemnon now addresses ὦ φίλοι, Ἀργείων ἡγήτορες ἠδὲ μέδοντες rather than ὦ φίλοι, ἥρωες Δαναοί, θεράποντες Ἄρηος, the ancient views, which certainly take account of what are, by any criteria, mixed signals in the text, deserve our respect.[81] Should we too not be forced into puzzled silence by a repetition across a large body of intervening text which, by any standards, calls attention to itself?

Explicit silence in the text invites, indeed all but demands, interpretation. Irene de Jong notes that 'the addressees do not (nor, as a matter of fact, [does] Agamemnon himself) comment upon the repetitious character of [*Iliad* 9] 17–28. It is left to the [external audience] to detect the significance of the repetition, "the complete reversal of meaning"'.[82] For the scholiasts, as we have seen, silence *was* in fact an eloquent comment. Perhaps there is more. In a text from a later age, at least, modern critics would have no doubt but that Diomedes' ἦ θέμις ἐστίν (v. 33) is a sarcastic allusion back to the former occasion when Agamemnon was ἀφραδέων (v. 32) and had claimed — in what has become a famous problem of modern Homeric criticism — that his proposed testing of the troops was also ἦ θέμις ἐστίν (2.73).[83] Diomedes would be showing that he at least knew where he had heard Agamemnon's words before; moreover, his reference to the availability of 'very many' ships to take Agamemnon home (9.43–44) could be a pointed reversal of Agamemnon's (misleading) lament about the state of the ships in the first *peira* speech (2.135). Some moderns might even be tempted to associate Diomedes' reference to how Zeus has honoured Agamemnon 'with the sceptre' (9.38) with the poet's famous account of Agamemnon's

---

present and explained (fr. 382 Gigon) that 'the ordinary soldiers are entitled to listen, but the leaders can also act'.

81 The matter certainly deserves more discussion than it receives in Hainsworth's note on v. 17; Lohmann 1970, 216 merely observes that the 'stolz und kriegerisch' address of Book 2 is 'characteristically altered', without asking what the address in Book 9 actually means; Griffin's note on v. 17 acknowledges that that verse 'suggests that Agamemnon is talking to the chiefs', but can only conclude that there is "a lack of exact focus on the facts"; West 2011, 214 sees in this unclarity ('11 and 17 suggest a meeting of leaders ... the present gathering, however, soon appears as an assembly of the whole army [30, 50]') another argument for his view that the opening of Book 9 was composed before, and was the model for, the parallel scene in Book 2. De Jong 2004, 190 mistakenly makes 2.110 identical to 9.17, thus blurring the question of addressee.

82 De Jong 2004, 190.

83 So Martin 1989, 24; the standard commentaries are silent. Why the ancient scholiasts apparently did not note the repetition is also a question worth asking.

sceptre immediately before the first *peira* speech (2.100–108); Diomedes did not, of course, 'hear' that description, though he will have seen Agamemnon leaning on the sceptre as he delivered the *peira* (cf. 2.109).

Ancient rhetorical criticism, then, picks away to open up the significance of the correspondences and differences between the analogous scenes in Books 2 and 9, whereas modern criticism has, on the whole, sought to close interpretation down, to seek *the* explanation (and textual history) of these really very remarkable scenes; that difference is a fact of intellectual and scholarly history which is worth pondering.

Bibliography

Asmis, E. 1991. 'Philodemus' poetic theory and *On the Good King according to Homer*', *ClAnt* 10, 1–45.

Bernabé, A. (ed.) 2007. *Poetae epici Graeci. Testimonia et fragmenta 2, 3, Musaeus, Linus, Epimenides, Papyrus Derveni, Indices*, Berlin/New York.

Blank, D.L./Dyck, A.R. 1984. 'Aristophanes of Byzantium and problem-solving in the Museum: notes on a recent reassessment', *ZPE* 56, 17–24.

Boys-Stones, G.R. (ed.) 2003. *Metaphor, allegory, and the classical tradition: ancient thought and modern revisions*, Oxford/New York.

Broggiato, M. (ed.) 2001. *Cratete di Mallo. I frammenti, ed., introd. e note*, La Spezia.

Buffière, F. 1956. *Les mythes d'Homère et la pensée grecque*, Paris.

Classen, C.J. 1994. 'Rhetorik und Literarkritik', in: F. Montanari (ed.), *La philologie grecque à l'époque hellénistique et romaine*, Vandœuvres/Genève, 307–360.

Cook, E.F. 2003. 'Agamemnon's test of the army in *Iliad* Book 2 and the function of Homeric *akhos*', *AJPh* 124, 165–98.

Copeland, R./Struck, P.T. 2010. *The Cambridge Companion to Allegory*, Cambridge.

Dawson, D. 1992. *Allegorical Readers and Cultural Revision in Ancient Alexandria*, Berkeley.

Dentice, di Accadia S. 2010. 'La 'prova' di Agamennone. Una strategia retorica vincente', *RhM* 153, 225–246.

Drules, P.-A. 1998. 'Dion de Pruse lecteur d'Homère', *Gaia* 3, 59–79.

Dubischar, M. 2015. 'Typology of Philological Writings', in: F. Montanari/S. Matthaios/A. Rengakos (eds.), *Brill's Companion to Ancient Greek Scholarship*, Leiden, 545–599.

Fish, J. 1999. 'Philodemus on the education of the Good Prince: PHerc. 1507, col. 23', in: G. Abbamonte/A. Rescigno/R. Rossi (eds.), *Satura. Collectanea philologica Italo Gallo ab amicis discipulisque dicata*, Naples, 71–77.

Fish, J. 2002. 'Philodemus' *On the Good King according to Homer*: columns 21–31', *CErc* 32, 187–232.

Fish, J. 2004. 'Anger, Philodemus' *Good King*, and the Helen episode of the *Aeneid*: a new proof of authenticity from Herculaneum', in: D. Armstrong/J. Fish/P.A. Johnston/M.B. Skinner (eds.), *Vergil, Philodemus, and the Augustans*, Austin, 111–138.

Ford, A.L. 2002. *The Origins of Criticism: Literary Culture and Poetic Theory in Classical Greece*, Princeton.

Fränkel, H. 1968. *Noten zu den Argonautika des Apollonios*, Munich.
Gutzwiller, K.J. 2010. 'Literary Criticism', in: J.J. Clauss/M. Cuypers (eds.), *A Companion to Hellenistic Literature*, Chicester/Malden, 337–365.
Halliwell, S. 2000. 'The subjection of muthos to logos: Plato's citations of the poets', *CQ* 50, 94–112.
Halliwell, S. 2011. *Between Ecstasy and Truth: Interpretations of Greek Poetics from Homer to Longinus*, Oxford.
Heath, M. 2002–2003. 'Theon and the history of progymnasmata', *GRBS* 43, 129–160.
Heath, M. 2003. 'Pseudo-Dionysius *Art of Rhetoric* 8–11: figured speech, declamation, and criticism', *AJPh* 124, 81–105.
Hillgruber, M. 1994–1999. *Die pseudoplutarchische Schrift De Homero*, 2 vols., Stuttgart/Leipzig.
Hunter, R. 1993. *The Argonautica of Apollonius. Literary Studies*, Cambridge.
Hunter, R. 2009. 'The *Trojan Oration* of Dio Chrysostom and ancient Homeric interpretation', in: J. Grethlein/A. Rengakos (eds.), *Narratology and Interpretation*, Berlin/New York, 43–61 [= 2009b], [= this volume 487–505].
Hunter, R. 2009. *Critical Moments in Classical Literature: Studies in the Ancient View of Literature and its Uses*, Cambridge [= 2009a].
Hunter, R. 2011. Plato's *Ion* and the origins of scholarship', in: S. Matthaios/F. Montanari/A. Rengakos (eds.), *Ancient Scholarship and Grammar: Archetypes, Concepts and Contexts*, Berlin/New York, 27–40, [= this volume 506–520].
Hunter, R. 2012. *Plato and the Traditions of Ancient Literature: The Silent Stream*, Cambridge.
Hunter, R. 2014. 'Horace's other *Ars Poetica*: *Epistles* 1.2 and ancient Homeric criticism', *MD* 72, 127–151, [= this volume 376–398].
Hunter, R. 2020. '"Clever about verses?" Plato and the "Scopas Ode" (*PMG* 542 = 260 Poltera)', in: P. Agócs/L. Prauscello (eds.), *Simonides Lyricus*, Cambridge, 197–216, [= this volume 537–559].
Hunter, R./Russell, D. 2011. *Plutarch, How to Study Poetry (De audiendis poetis)*, Cambridge.
Karp, A.J. 1977. 'Homeric origins of ancient rhetoric', *Arethusa* 10, 237–258.
Katzung, P.G. 1960. *Die Diapeira in der Iliashandlung*, Diss. Frankfurt.
Kim, L. 2008. 'Dio of Prusa, Or. 61, Chryseis, or reading Homeric silence', *CQ* 58, 601–621.
Kim, L. 2010. *Homer between History and Fiction in Imperial Greek Literature*, Cambridge.
Kouremenos, T./Parássoglou, G.M./Tsantsanoglou, K. (eds.) 2006. *The Derveni Papyrus*, Florence.
Kullmann, W. 1955. 'Die Probe des Achaierheeres in der *Ilias*', *MH* 12, 253–273.
Lamberton, R. 1986. *Homer the Theologian*, Berkeley.
Latacz, J. 2003. *Homers Ilias, Gesamtkommentar*, Band II.2, Munich/Leipzig.
Lohmann, D. 1970. *Die Komposition der Reden in der Ilias*, Berlin.
Long, A.A. 1992. 'Stoic Readings of Homer', in: R. Lamberton/J.J. Keaney (eds.), *Homer's Ancient Readers: The Hermeneutics of Greek Epic's Earliest Exegetes*, Princeton, 41–66.
Lührs, D. 1992. *Untersuchungen zu den Athetesen Aristarchs in der Ilias und zu ihrer Behandlung im Corpus der exegetischen Scholien*, Hildesheim/Zürich/New York.
Luzzatto, M.T. 1996. 'Dialettica o retorica? La polytropia di Odisseo da Antistene a Porfirio', *Elenchos* 17, 275–357.
Lynn-George, M. 1988. *Epos. Word, Narrative and the Iliad*, Atlantic Highlands.
MacPhail, J.A. Jr. 2011. *Porphyry's 'Homeric Questions' on the Iliad. Texte und Kommentare* vol. 36, Berlin/New York.

Martin, R.P. 1989. *The Language of Heroes*, Ithaca.
Matthaios, S./Montanari, F./Rengakos, A. (eds.) 2011. *Ancient Scholarship and Grammar: Archetypes, Concepts and Contexts*, Berlin/New York.
McGlew, J.F. 1989. 'Royal power and the Achaean assembly at *Iliad* 2.84–393', *ClAnt* 8, 283–295.
Minon, S. et al. 2012. *Dion de Pruse, Ilion n'a pas été prise. Discours "troyen" 11*, Paris.
Montanari, F./Pagani, L. (eds.) 2011. *From Scholars to Scholia: Chapters in the History of Ancient Greek Scholarship*, Trends in Classics Supplementary Volumes 9, Berlin/New York.
Montiglio, S. 2011. *From Villain to Hero. Odysseus in Ancient Thought*, Ann Arbor.
Naddaf, G. 2009. 'Allegory and the origins of philosophy', in: W. Wians (ed.), *Logos and Muthos*, Albany, 99–131.
Novokhatko, A. 2015. 'Greek Scholarship from its Beginnings to Alexandria', in: F. Montanari/S. Matthaios/A. Rengakos (eds.), *Brill's Companion to Ancient Greek Scholarship*, Leiden, 3–59.
Nünlist, R. 2009. *The Ancient Critic at Work: Terms and Concepts of Literary Criticism in Greek Scholia*, Cambridge.
Nünlist, R. 2012. 'A Chapter in the History of Linguistics: Aristarchus' Interest in Language Development', *RhM* 155, 152–165.
Nünlist, R. 2015. 'Poetics and Literary Criticism in the Framework of Ancient Greek Scholarship', in: F. Montanari/S. Matthaios/A. Rengakos (eds.), *Brill's Companion to Ancient Greek Scholarship*, Leiden, 706–755.
Patillon, M./Bolognesi, G. 1997. *Aelius Théon, Progymnasmata*, Paris.
Pfeiffer, R. 1968. *History of Classical Scholarship from the Beginnings to the End of the Hellenistic Age*, Oxford.
Pontani, F. 2005. *Eraclito. Questioni omeriche sulle allegorie di Omero in merito agli dèi*, Pisa.
Porter, J.I. 1992. 'Hermeneutic Lines and Circles: Aristarchus and Crates on the Exegesis of Homer', in: R. Lamberton/J.J. Keaney (eds.), *Homer's Ancient Readers: The Hermeneutics of Greek Epic's Earliest Exegetes*, Princeton, 67–114.
Porter, J.I. 2011. 'Making and unmaking: the Achaean wall and the limits of fictionality in Homeric criticism', *TAPhA* 14, 1–36.
Radermacher, L. 1951. *Artium Scriptores: Reste der voraristotelischen Rhetorik*, Wien.
Ramelli, I./Lucchetta, G.A. 2004. *Allegoria. I, L'età classica, introd. e cura di R. Radice*, Milano.
Richardson, N.J. 1975. 'Homeric Professors in the Age of the Sophists', *PCPhS* 21, 65–81.
Richardson, N.J. 1980. 'Literary criticism in the exegetical scholia to the *Iliad*: a sketch', *CQ* 30, 265–287.
Richardson, N.J. 1985. 'Pindar and later literary criticism in antiquity', *Papers of the Liverpool Latin Seminar* 5, 383–401.
Russell, D.A. 1979. 'Classicizing rhetoric and criticism: the pseudo-Dionysian Exetasis and Mistakes in Declamation', in: H. Flashar (ed.), *Le classicisme à Rome aux Iers siècles avant et après J.-C.*, Vandœuvres/Genève, 113–130.
Scodel, R. 2008. *Epic Facework: Self-Presentation and Social Interaction in Homer*, Swansea.
Slater, W.J. 1982. 'Aristophanes of Byzantium and problem-solving in the Museum', *CQ* 32, 336–349.
Stanford, W.B. 1954. *The Ulysses Theme*, Oxford.
Struck, P.T. 2004. *Birth of the Symbol: Ancient Readers at the Limits of Their Texts*, Princeton.
Taplin, O. 1992. *Homeric Soundings*, Oxford.
Usener, K. 1990. *Beobachtungen zum Verhältnis der Odyssee zur Ilias*, Tübingen.

Waterfield, R./Kidd, I. 1992, *Plutarch, Essays*, London.
Webb, R. 2010. 'Between poetry and rhetoric: Libanios' use of Homeric subjects in his progymnasmata', *QUCC* 95, 131–52.
West, M.L. 1988. 'The Rise of the Greek Epic', *JHS* 108, 51–172.
West, S.R. 'The Papyri of Herodotus', in: D. Obbink/R. Rutherford (eds.), *Culture in Pieces. Essays on Ancient Texts in Honour of Peter Parsons*, Oxford, 69–83, Pl. 7.
Wilamowitz-Moellendorff, U. von. 1920. *Die Ilias und Homer*, Berlin.
Wissmann, J. 2009. 'Athena's "unreasonable advice": the education of Telemachus in ancient interpretations of Homer', *GRBS* 49, 413–452.
Zeitlin, F.I. 2001. 'Visions and revisions of Homer', in: S. Goldhill (ed.), *Being Greek under Rome*, Cambridge, 195–266.

34 The *Hippias Minor* and the Traditions of Homeric Criticism

Homer plays an important role in the discussion in the *Hippias Minor* of voluntary and involuntary action and their relation to knowledge and goodness. Unlike the *Ion*, to which it bears in some ways a striking resemblance, and not merely in the manifestly parodic presentation of the eponymous figures of the two dialogues,[1] poetry and performance are not the principal subjects of the *Hippias Minor*. However, this dialogue arguably sheds as much or even more light on the Homeric criticism of the late fifth and early fourth centuries as does the *Ion*, and — again like the *Ion* — it looks forward to, and significantly influenced, the rich tradition of Hellenistic and later Homeric criticism, for which our best witnesses are the Homeric scholia.[2] In this paper, I want both to consider how Plato[3] presents Socrates' treatment of Achilles and Odysseus in the *Hippias Minor* and also to make the case more strongly than it has been made before that this dialogue was an important influence on the later critical tradition.[4] I hope also to highlight some of the important and still pressing critical questions that this dialogue's treatment of Homer brings to the fore, even when they are not formulated explicitly here by Plato.

When the dialogue opens, Hippias has just delivered an ἐπίδειξις on poetry (363c1–3), including περὶ Ὁμήρου (cf. 363b1, c2–3).[5] Eudikos is encouraging

---

1 Cf., e.g., Kahn 1996, 100–4; particularly striking are the respective claims of the eponymous figures to superiority, cf. *Ion* 530c7–d7 ~ *Hipp. Min.* 364a7–9.
2 For this aspect of the *Hipp. Min.* cf. esp. Giuliano 1995; for the *Ion* Hunter 2011 and 2012, 89–108.
3 Throughout this paper I assume without discussion that the *Hippias Minor* is indeed the work of Plato; for bibliography on this question cf. Pinjuh 2014, 35–9.
4 This paper makes no claim to contribute to the 'philosophical' issues of the dialogue; thus, for example, I translate ψευδής etc. as 'liar' etc., without regard to the important questions of capability v. disposition and so forth. Helpful guidance and bibliography for the philosophical issues of the dialogue can be found in Blondell 2002, 128–64 and Pinjuh 2014.
5 Although 363c1–3 suggests that Hippias' performance had been a wide-ranging one, we are very likely intended to understand that this ἐπίδειξις was Hippias' 'Trojan Oration', cf. below, n. 18. *Pace* Pinjuh 2014, 99, καὶ γάρ at 363b1 need not imply that Hippias had discussed the question which Socrates is subsequently to pose to him, although 364c1–4 may in fact carry that implication: note the use of the imperfect tense in Socrates' questions there to Hippias. Blondell 2002, 132 n. 110 similarly suggests that καὶ γάρ implies that Hippias too shares Apemantos' view; this is unnecessary (cf. Denniston 1954, 109), though the dialogue will make clear that Hippias would have sympathy with Apemantos' view of Achilles and Odysseus, if not

Socrates to react to Hippias' performance by either 'joining in the praise' (a possibility that shows how little Eudikos knows of Socrates) or by proving him wrong (ἐλέγχειν), and Socrates tells him that one thing he would like to ask Hippias derives from an opinion that he had heard expressed by Eudikos' own father, Apemantos:

> καὶ γὰρ τοῦ σοῦ πατρὸς Ἀπημάντου ἤκουον ὅτι ἡ Ἰλιὰς κάλλιον εἴη ποίημα τῷ Ὁμήρῳ ἢ ἡ Ὀδύσσεια, τοσούτῳ δὲ κάλλιον, ὅσῳ ἀμείνων Ἀχιλλεὺς Ὀδυσσέως εἴη· ἑκάτερον γὰρ τούτων τὸ μὲν εἰς Ὀδυσσέα ἔφη πεποιῆσθαι, τὸ δ' εἰς Ἀχιλλέα. περὶ ἐκείνου οὖν ἡδέως ἄν, εἰ βουλομένῳ ἐστὶν Ἱππίᾳ, ἀναπυθοίμην ὅπως αὐτῷ δοκεῖ περὶ τοῖν ἀνδροῖν τούτοιν, πότερον ἀμείνω φησὶν εἶναι...
>
> Plato, *Hippias Minor* 363b1–c1

> I used to hear your father Apemantos [saying][6] that Homer's *Iliad* was a finer poem than the *Odyssey*, and that it was as much finer as Achilles was better than Odysseus; for of these two poems, so he said, one had been composed about Odysseus and the other about Achilles.[7] If Hippias is willing, this is what I would like to ask him: which of these two men does he say is the better...

How banal is Apemantos' view intended to sound? Is it simply the late fifth-century *communis opinio*, at least as Plato reconstructs it?[8] We might think that such a *synkrisis* leading to the establishment of a hierarchy of value came naturally to agonistic Greek gentlemen, particularly when the Homeric poems themselves and the literature which they influenced gave such prominence to comparisons between individual characters;[9] nevertheless, the translation of what turns out to be a moralising or ethical judgement about the central characters of the poems into a judgement about the value of the respective poems is, however unsurprising it may now seem to us, deceptively significant.[10] It would be a

---

necessarily with his opinion about their respective poems. For the περὶ Ὁμήρου tradition more generally cf. Hunter 2012, 91–2.

6 Some critics assume that Socrates here refers to a written work by the otherwise obscure Apemantos, cf., e.g., Luzzatto 1996, 29; this view is not, of course, ruled out by ἤκουον, but a reference to informal conversation seems to me more likely. A third alternative would be that Socrates heard a 'lecture' by Apemantos (cf. Pinjuh 2014, 98 n. 227).

7 As Giuliano 1995, 32 notes, this apparently inconsequential observation seems to look forward to the later ζήτημα, preserved for us by the exegetical scholia on *Il.* 1.1, as to why the *Iliad* was not entitled the 'Achilleid', despite *Odyssey* being the title of Homer's other poem.

8 So, e.g., Giuliano 1995, 20, 31. Wilamowitz 1920, 136 describes the question of 'which is better' as 'rather childish' and the inference which follows about the relative merit of the poems as 'still more childish'.

9 Cf. Giuliano 1995, 32–34, adducing *Il.* 2.761–769 and other passages.

10 Pinjuh 2014, 99–101 studies the inter-relations of the various senses of καλός and ἀγαθός.

familiar move for the Platonic Socrates to begin his discussion from a piece of very commonplace wisdom, which he can then proceed to deconstruct, but — as again with the *Ion* — we should sense here a long history of ancient criticism beginning to unfold. In the *Ion* also, one of the things at issue was the καλόν in poetry, what makes a poem καλῶς πεποιημένον and who is to judge this; in that dialogue the criterion which was made to bear the principal weight was that of the accuracy of the information provided in the poem. In the *Hippias Minor*, however, moral judgements about the characters are to carry that weight, but both dialogues lead forward to a style of criticism in which the καλόν of poetry indeed subsumes judgements about such things as the accuracy of what is described and the moral value of the characters, and also looks to other, what we might loosely call 'aesthetic', criteria. Moralising always remained at the very heart of mainstream criticism, and it could hardly be otherwise, given the very close links between 'literary criticism', education and rhetoric. Characters who were morally questionable, let alone morally worthless, were always to prove a bit awkward to handle. Aristotle found no place in tragedy for the μοχθηροί (*Poetics* 1452b36–3a4), and he condemned the Menelaos of Euripides' *Orestes* as showing 'unnecessary πονηρία of character' (1454a29); as is well known, Aristophanes of Byzantium elaborated this into a view that all the characters of that play except Pylades were φαῦλοι — the play was χείριστον τοῖς ἤθεσι — although the play itself was a great success (*Hypoth.* 43–4 Diggle).[11]

One detail of expression which is connected to this link between the moral goodness of characters and critical judgements about the works in which they appear is the oscillation between Socrates' original question as to 'which (of Achilles and Odysseus) is better' (cf. 363b7c1, 364b4) and Hippias' answer in terms of characteristics 'made by Homer' (364c5); Socrates then adopts Hippias' mode in referring to his initial question at 370d7–e1 (and cf. 364e5–6). However inconsequential this may seem, the difference between 'Achilles is better than Odysseus' and 'Homer has made Achilles better than Odysseus' is, from the perspective of the history of criticism, potentially very significant, particularly when it is placed, as it is in the *Hippias Minor*, within the overall context of a question as to which of their respective poems is 'better'. If we translate ποιεῖν as 'represent', then we can see how easy is the slippage between 'represent a character as better' and 'represent a character better'; the predicative adjective fuses eventually into a quality of the representation rather than of the character, and this was clearly a significant development towards a 'literary' or 'aesthetic' mode of criticism. This is not Plato's concern in the *Hippias Minor*, but the part

---

11 See Fantuzzi 2014.

that this dialogue played in opening up potentially powerful critical questions certainly deserves more attention than it normally receives.

Another Platonic passage which Apemantos' view should call to mind is Protagoras' famous view of the 'most important part of education', expressed at the head of the discussion of Simonides' poem for Scopas:

> ἡγοῦμαι, ἔφη, ὦ Σώκρατες, ἐγὼ ἀνδρὶ παιδείας μέγιστον μέρος εἶναι περὶ ἐπῶν δεινὸν εἶναι· ἔστιν δὲ τοῦτο τὰ ὑπὸ τῶν ποιητῶν λεγόμενα οἷόν τ' εἶναι συνιέναι ἅ τε ὀρθῶς πεποίηται καὶ ἃ μή, καὶ ἐπίστασθαι διελεῖν τε καὶ ἐρωτώμενον λόγον δοῦναι.
>
> Plato, *Protagoras* 338e7–339a2

> Socrates, I consider that the most important part of a man's education is to be clever about verses. That means being able to understand in what the poets say what is correctly composed and what is not, and knowing how to distinguish them and give an account when asked.

The Platonic Hippias will indeed claim to be περὶ ἐπῶν δεινός and to be able to 'make distinctions'; Socrates asks Hippias 'How did you distinguish between (διέκρινες) Achilles and Odysseus?' (364c2), and he later claims that he had thought that it was 'difficult to judge (δύσκριτον) which of the two was better concerning lying and truth-telling and the rest of virtue' (370e23). Protagoras' discussion of Simonides' ode is to draw attention to an alleged inconsistency in the poem, an inconsistency which, so Protagoras claims, would deprive it of the soubriquet of being καλῶς (or ὀρθῶς) πεποιημένον (339b7–10); the *epideixis* by Socrates which follows in that dialogue is (in part) an attempt to remove the charge of inconsistency. In the *Hippias Minor* also, conversation will turn to an alleged inconsistency in Achilles' words and deeds in *Iliad* 9. In this dialogue, it will be Socrates who insists on the inconsistency, though not (at any rate, not explicitly) in order to 'downgrade' Homer, but rather simply to refute Hippias' view of the relative merits of Achilles and Odysseus; Hippias, for his part, admits the inconsistency, but seeks to explain it. The recurrent pattern running through the *Protagoras* and the *Hippias Minor* may be thought to point to a Platonic recreation of a genuine moment (or moments) in the history of criticism; it is, for example, easy enough to imagine a setting (and/or an origin) both for such 'comparative' criticism and for allegations of 'inconsistency' in sympotic discussion, and we shall see that Hippias' answer to Socrates' initial question may lend some weight to that suspicion.

Finally, we may wonder to what extent the view ascribed to Apemantos is reflected elsewhere in the literature of the late fifth century. It is, for example, a stand-by of modern criticism of Sophocles' *Philoctetes* that Odysseus is somehow 'sophistic' and that the confrontation of Achilles and Odysseus in *Iliad* 9 forms a particularly important part of the background to Sophocles' play. The *Hippias Minor* can serve to remind us that behind the tragedy lies not only Homer, but also contemporary and earlier discussion of the Homeric poems. When Odysseus (v. 119) holds out to Neoptolemus the possibility of winning a reputation as both σοφός and ἀγαθός, i.e. both an Odyssean and an Achillean reputation, it is hard not to think of the kind of debates which we see reflected in the Platonic dialogue. When, moreover, Neoptolemus tells Odysseus that he would 'rather act nobly and fail than win an ignoble victory' (vv. 94-95), the Sophoclean scholia (on v. 94) gloss this distinction as one between 'telling the truth' and 'lying' (ψευδολογία), and observe that 'Sophocles brings [Neoptolemus] on speaking his father's speech, 'Hateful to me like the gates of Hades ...'. As is very well recognised, the opening scene between Odysseus and Neoptolemus replays in various ways the exchange of speeches between Odysseus and Achilles in *Iliad* 9; the scholiast certainly did not need the *Hippias Minor* to remind him of Achilles' famous opening words, but we may well suspect that those words came as readily to the minds of some of Sophocles' audience as they did to that of the scholiast, and the *Hippias Minor* may thus shed suggestive light on aspects of the reception of Homer at the end of the fifth century. Sophocles' play was not an 'unmediated' creative response to Homer and the cyclic poems, but rather one which reflected contemporary discussion of early epic, and itself was a contribution to an ongoing and vibrant debate. Drama is in fact some of our best evidence for such critical debates, however difficult this evidence is to use at the level of detail.

When Socrates gets his chance to question Hippias, he asks him 'Which (of Achilles and Odysseus) do you say is better (ἀμείνων) and in what respect (κατὰ τί)?' (364b4-5) and (a potentially different question) 'How did you distinguish them?' (364c2). Hippias' answer has perhaps become stale with familiarity, but its oddness is important:

> φημὶ γὰρ Ὅμηρον πεποιηκέναι ἄριστον μὲν ἄνδρα Ἀχιλλέα τῶν εἰς Τροίαν ἀφικομένων, σοφώτατον δὲ Νέστορα, πολυτροπώτατον δὲ Ὀδυσσέα.
>
> Plato, *Hippias Minor* 364c4-7
>
> I say that Homer made Achilles the best man of those who went to Troy, Nestor the wisest and Odysseus the most *polytropos*.

In ascribing ἄριστος to Achilles, Hippias might be thought to be picking up Socrates' question as to which of the two was ἀμείνων, but the manner of the answer, in which three, not two, heroes are ascribed superlative qualities, suggests that Hippias rather is referring to Achilles' unchallenged supremacy in battle — he is 'best of the Achaeans' — whereas it is others who take the prize in other qualities. The form of Hippias' answer may be seen as a version of the familiar sympotic 'What is best?' question or of the kind of popular 'priamel' of which we find 'literary' instances in, for example, Sappho fr. 16 Voigt and at the head of Pindar's *First Olympian*. An elegiac couplet which turns up in various forms in archaic and classical literature (cf. Soph. fr. 356 R) offers one of the clearest instances of the pattern:

κάλλιστον τὸ δικαιότατον· λῷστον δ' ὑγιαίνειν·
πρᾶγμα δὲ τερπνότατον, τοῦ τις ἐρᾷ, τὸ τυχεῖν.

Theognis 255–256

What is most just is fairest; best is to be healthy; the sweetest thing is to get what you desire.

Despite the familiarity of its form, however, there is something remarkable in Hippias' answer which is rarely acknowledged. It would be easy enough to imagine a fifth-century discussion as to which of Homer's heroes was 'best' or 'wisest', as the quality being judged (prowess in battle, wisdom) was shared among more than one hero, although Achilles was always likely to be ἄριστος, provided that word was interpreted as Homer was normally understood to have used it, for Homer himself appeared to have cast his vote for that hero (cf. esp. *Il.* 2.768–769). The crown for σοφία, particularly as exhibited in rhetoric,[12] might, however, well have been disputed between Nestor and Odysseus, and there is some late evidence that a way was discovered to accommodate the claims of both; here again it is not difficult to see the *Hippias Minor* as a stimulus to the critical tradition. In his commentary on the proem of the *Odyssey*, Eustathius notes that in the *Iliad* Odysseus was not yet 'wiser' (σοφώτερος) than Nestor, but his great wanderings after the war brought him huge ἐμπειρία, 'experience', which allowed him to surpass even Nestor (*Hom.* 1381.61–1382.2, cf. also 240.17–18); this interpretation is connected with a view that νόον ἔγνω in *Od.* 1.3 does not (or not only) mean '[Odysseus] learned the minds [of many men]' but rather '[Odysseus] gathered intelligence', i.e. became himself more intelligent as a result of his wanderings.[13] The opening of the *Odyssey* clearly

---

12 For Nestor and Odysseus as Homer's principal rhetoricians cf. esp. Pl. *Phdr.* 261b-c; a contrast between these two 'orators' was to have a very long critical history, cf. the following note.

13 Cf. the scholia on 1.3 f–h Pontani. The *Hippias Minor* also played a role in the rich tradition of rhetorical discussion about the competing speeches of Odysseus and Nestor in Book 2 of the *Iliad*; Agamemnon seems to award the palm for speaking to Nestor (2.370–374), and the critical tradition worked overtime to justify and/or nuance that decision.

produced ancient responses along the lines of 'travel broadens the mind'; a scholion on v. 3 explains that Homer added νόον ἔγνω because 'there are foolish people who visit many cities and lands and never learn anything' (Schol. 1.3 g Pontani). How far back such criticism goes we cannot of course say, but the idea that Odysseus' wisdom developed through his adventures certainly set in early in the critical tradition, and of course many modern critics have argued that such a development is already discernible in the *Odyssey* itself, as Odysseus seeks not to repeat the nearly terminal 'mistakes' of the Cyclops-episode.

If, however, one might reasonably debate about 'Who was the wisest of the Greeks?', the same could hardly be said of 'Who was the most πολύτροπος?'. This epithet occurs only twice in the Homeric corpus (*Od.* 1.1, 10.330), on both occasions with reference to the Odysseus of the *Odyssey*; that it is applied to Odysseus in the opening verse of that poem makes it, of course, almost his signature epithet. The question 'Which of the heroes was most *polytropos*?' would, on the face of it, be to anyone but the Platonic Socrates a non-question.[14] One can just about imagine a sophistic *epideixis* demonstrating that a hero other than Odysseus was the most πολύτροπος, because although this epithet is only applied by Homer to Odysseus, it actually refers to a quality shared by more than one hero; if indeed we can imagine this, however, it is primarily because that is what Socrates in fact offers us in the *Hippias Minor*.[15] It is presumably important that no one in the *Hippias Minor* makes the (to us obvious) point that Homer applies the epithet only to Odysseus, and that fact was hardly unavailable or unknown in the fifth and fourth centuries BC; certainly, one does not need the *TLG* to discover it. When Socrates claims that he had absolutely no idea what Hippias meant by saying that Homer made Odysseus 'most *polytropos*', his words presumably gesture to a debate about the term,[16] but they leave us no wiser as to why Plato made Hippias answer in this way.

One common (and attractive) answer to this problem is that Plato here preserves a genuine fragment of Hippias' Homeric criticism; Diels–Kranz offer it a place as illustrative of Hippias' *Lehre* (86 A10), and the manner of Hippias' response to Socrates, 'I am willing to go through for you even more clearly than I did then what I say both about these men and others' (364c3–4), suggests that we are to imagine that Hippias' *epideixis* was a frequently heard performance

---

14 Cf., e.g., Blondell 2002, 135.
15 That Socrates' Homeric 'performance' in the *Hippias Minor* amounts to an *epideixis* περὶ Ὁμήρου is another feature shared with the *Ion* where, despite Ion's best efforts, it is Socrates who delivers such a lecture about poetry.
16 Cf. further below.

(note the present tense of λέγω at 364c4). So too, it is regularly argued that the discussion which follows, which highlights Hippias' negative view of πολυτροπία, shadows the real Hippias' discussion of Odysseus, to a greater or lesser degree.[17] Not incompatible with the view that we have here a 'fragment' of Hippias would be the observation that Hippias thus not only denies to Odysseus the acclaim of being σοφώτατος, but also avoids the obviousness of a simple *synkrisis* between bravery and wisdom, with the central figure of each poem assigned to one category; such a simple distinction would have foreshadowed the interpretation of the quarrel between Odysseus and Achilles, reported in Demodocus' song at *Od.* 8.75–77, as a dispute over the relative merits of ἀνδρεία and σύνεσις or φρόνησις (cf. scholia on vv. 75, 77), an interpretation which may well in fact go back to the fifth century at least (we think again of Sophocles' *Philoctetes*). So obvious a gambit is, however, not worthy of a Hippias in his epideictic pomp, a figure who, moreover, clearly sets himself up as 'the Nestor for this generation'.[18] The smart paradox (as Hippias sees it) in his answer, a paradox which Socrates' exclamatory βαβαί in part acknowledges (364c7), is that he finds a hero other than Odysseus who is σοφώτατος and is thus able to assign another (very surprising) superlative to the Ithacan hero.

In seeking to unravel this question further, we enter the very murky waters of the relationship between the *Hippias Minor*, the known views of the 'real' Hippias, and the discussion of πολύτροπος by Antisthenes, which is partially preserved for us by Porphyry in his note on the opening verse of the *Odyssey*. The problems surrounding this fascinating text cannot be dealt with here at any length,[19] but they can also not simply be ignored. The relevant part of the scholion reads as follows in Pontani's text:[20]

---

17 A variant of this view is that the answer of the Platonic Hippias goes back to a representation of Hippias by Antisthenes, cf. further below.
18 Lampert 2002, 238, cf. Blondell 2002, 134 on Nestor as 'ancestor and paradigm' for sophists such as Hippias. Hippias wrote a 'Trojan Oration' in which Nestor advised Neoptolemus on how a young man could achieve renown (*Hipp. Mai.* 286a5–b4, Hippias, 86 A2, 9 D-K); this was, very likely, the very *epideixis* to which Socrates had just listened as the *Hippias Minor* opens (cf. *Hipp. Mai.* 286b5–6). Socrates' ironic praise of Hippias at *Hipp. Mai.* 281c2–3 is perhaps intended to echo Hippias' own claims in the 'Trojan Oration'. Brancacci 2004 suggests that Hippias' plea to Socrates and Protagoras at *Prt.* 337e2–338b2 is modelled on that of Nestor to Achilles and Agamemnon at *Il.* 1.274–279; the idea is attractive, particularly in view of Hippias' obvious interest in the figure of Nestor.
19 Cf. Pfeiffer 1968, 37, and esp. Giuliano 1995 and Luzzatto 1996, both of whom supply rich bibliography; further bibliography may be traced also through Montiglio 2011, 21–24. The text bristles with problems, both textual and interpretative, but many do not affect the limited scope of the present discussion. Richardson 1975, 77–81 offers a general survey of Antisthenes

οὐκ ἐπαινεῖν φησιν Ἀντισθένης Ὅμηρον τὸν Ὀδυσσέα μᾶλλον ἢ ψέγειν, λέγοντα αὐτὸν πολύτροπον. οὔκουν τὸν Ἀχιλλέα καὶ τὸν Αἴαντα πολυτρόπους πεποιηκέναι, ἀλλ' ἁπλοῦς καὶ γεννάδας· οὐδὲ τὸν Νέστορα τὸν σοφόν οὐ μὰ Δία δόλιον καὶ παλίμβολον τὸ ἦθος, ἀλλ' ἁπλῶς τῷ Ἀγαμέμνονι συνόντα καὶ τοῖς ἄλλοις ἅπασι καὶ εἰς τὸ στρατόπεδον εἴ τι ἀγαθὸν εἶχε συμβουλεύοντα καὶ οὐκ ἀποκρυπτόμενον. καὶ τοσοῦτον ἀπεῖχε τοῦτον τοιοῦτον τρόπον ἀποδέχεσθαι ὁ Ἀχιλλεύς, ὡς ἐχθρὸν ἡγεῖσθαι ὁμοίως τῷ θανάτῳ ἐκεῖνον,
ὅς χ' ἕτερον μὲν κεύθῃ ἐνὶ φρεσίν, ἄλλο δὲ εἴπῃ (Il. 9.313)
λύων οὖν ὁ Ἀντισθένης φησί· τί οὖν; ἆρα γε πονηρὸς ὁ Ὀδυσσεύς ὅτι πολύτροπος ἐρρέθη; καὶ μήν, διότι σοφός, οὕτως αὐτὸν προσείρηκεν μήποτε οὖν τρόπος τὸ μέν τι σημαίνει τὸ ἦθος, τὸ δέ τι σημαίνει τὴν τοῦ λόγου χρῆσιν· εὔτροπος γὰρ ἀνὴρ ὁ τὸ ἦθος ἔχων εἰς τὸ εὖ τετραμμένον. τρόποι δὲ λόγου †αἴτιοι αἴ† πλάσεις· καὶ χρῆται τῷ τρόπῳ καὶ ἐπὶ φωνῆς καὶ ἐπὶ μελῶν ἐξαλλαγῆς, ὡς ἐπὶ τῆς ἀηδόνος·
ἥ τε θαμὰ τρωπῶσα χέει πολυηχέα φωνήν (Od. 19.521)
εἰ δὲ οἱ σοφοὶ δεινοί εἰσι διαλέγεσθαι, ἐπίστανται καὶ τὸ αὐτὸ νόημα κατὰ πολλοὺς τρόπους λέγειν· ἐπιστάμενοι δὲ πολλοὺς τρόπους λόγων περὶ τοῦ αὐτοῦ, πολύτροποι ἂν εἶεν. εἰ δὲ οἱ σοφοί, καὶ ἀγαθοί εἰσι. διὰ τοῦτό φησι τὸν Ὀδυσσέα Ὅμηρος σοφὸν ὄντα πολύτροπον εἶναι, ὅτι δὴ τοῖς ἀνθρώποις ἠπίστατο πολλοῖς τρόποις συνεῖναι.

Schol. Hom. Od. 1.1l. Pontani = Antisthenes fr. 51 Caizzi

Antisthenes says that Homer does not praise Odysseus so much as blame him, in calling him *polytropos*.[21] He did not make Achilles and Ajax *polytropoi*, but straightforward and noble; nor, by Zeus, was the wise Nestor devious and unstable in his character, but he dealt straightforwardly with Agamemnon and everyone else, and if he had any good advice for the army he gave it and did not conceal it. So far was Achilles from accepting such a character that he considered as hateful as death any man 'who concealed one thing in his heart and said another' [Il. 9.313]. Antisthenes' solution was as follows. What then? Was Odysseus a bad man because he was called *polytropos*? Rather, he called him this because he was wise. Is it not the case that *tropos* may mean 'character', but also means 'the use of words'? A man who is *eutropos* has a character which is turned towards the good, but the *tropoi* of words are...And [Homer] uses *tropos* both for the voice and for the exchange of songs, as of the nightingale, 'who frequently rings the changes as she pours out her richly varied voice' [Od. 19.521]. If the wise are clever at dialogue, they know also how to express the same thought in many *tropoi*; as they know many *tropoi* of words about the same thing, they would be *polytropoi*. If they are wise, they are also good. For this reason

---

as a Homeric critic, but his view of the discussion of πολύτροπος has been superseded. One aspect of the matter which has not yet received the attention it deserves is that Dio Chrys. 71.2-3 juxtaposes a reworking of *Hipp. Min.* 368b-d to a description of Odysseus which seems all but certainly indebted to Antisthenes' discussion of πολύτροπος, cf. Fornaro in Nesselrath 2009, 144. That passage of Dio is, admittedly, an intertextual patchwork: ἀπαρχὰς τῆς σοφίας in 71.2 seems to go back to Plato, *Prt.* 343b1, which is more fully reworked in 72.12.

20 I accept the now standard view that the last part of the scholion, beginning with a reference to Pythagoras, has nothing to do with Antisthenes. For other English translations of the scholion cf. Kahn 1996, 122-123, Montiglio 2011, 21-22.
21 On the difficulties that this sentence has caused cf. Luzzatto 1996, 306-308.

> Homer says that Odysseus, who is wise, is *polytropos*, because he knows how to converse with men in many *tropoi*.

The obvious contradiction between the two claims in the scholion about what Antisthenes said is most easily explained by the fact that the negative view of πολύτροπος with which the text opens was indeed expressed in a work of Antisthenes, but it is not a view to which Antisthenes himself subscribed. This has often led to the view that this work was very likely a dialogue, and the suggestion (or assumption) has, moreover, often been made that this will have been a dialogue between Hippias, who expressed the negative view with which the text begins, and Socrates. I am very sceptical of at least the second half of this account, and Maria Luzzatto rightly, I think, remains non-committal about the nature of Antisthenes' text; Porphyry offers the familiar shape of a Homeric 'problem' and its 'solution', but we cannot assume that this is how Antisthenes presented it – his work, perhaps the περὶ Ὀδυσσείας, might have been an essay, not a dialogue. Be that as it may, the *Hippias Minor* certainly lends colour to the suggestion that the negative view of πολύτροπος expressed in Antisthenes' work was there associated with Hippias; the features shared between the two texts, including the quotation of the opening of Achilles' speech to Odysseus in *Iliad* 9, are certainly very striking. Scholars have sought arguments as to whether Plato is responding to Antisthenes, or vice versa, or whether both are responding independently to Hippias, or indeed whether the truth lies in some combination of these possibilities; the problem has both a specific interest for the history of Socratic discussion, and also a broader methodological importance for the study of fourth-century philosophical texts in general, but neither can properly be pursued here.

Antisthenes' account of πολύτροπος turns on a semantic analysis of the kind in which we know he was very interested. τρόπος has, in this analysis, two meanings, and in πολύτροπος Homer is alleged to use the noun in its linguistic sense of 'form of speech, speech-usage'; the evidence for this claim is apparently found in the use of τρωπάω of the nightingale and its voice in one verse of the *Odyssey*. There is no other evidence to support this alleged usage of Homer, and so we might at least wonder in passing what was the tone of Antisthenes' defence of Odysseus. Modern readers are very quick to see Socrates' treatment of Achilles in the *Hippias Minor* as unserious or even as a parody of Homeric criticism,[22] but we might think that Antisthenes' argument, as far as the scholion of

---

[22] Cf. below, pp. 650, 653. I suspect that we may be able to see the influence of Antisthenes' discussion in the famous riddling epigram of Philitas about the alder-tree (fr. 10 Powell = 25

Porphyry allows us to reconstruct it, has at least as good a claim to have been 'playful', in whatever sense we wish to interpret that. That Antisthenes seems to have represented Odysseus as a master of Socratic-style dialectic must increase our sense that this *epideixis*, like so many sophistic performances, was leavened with a generous dose of the humorously paradoxical. We may perhaps compare the claim of the Platonic Protagoras that Orpheus, Homer, Hesiod and so forth were all sophists *avant la lettre* (*Prt.* 316d–e). As for what might have been Antisthenes' discussion of the other meaning of τρόπος, namely ἦθος, 'character', we can reconstruct little of this, but — as critics have noted — Eustathius' observation (*Hom.* 1381.41) that Homer never uses τρόπος in this sense, and so πολύτροπος could not mean 'having an unstable/changeable character', may eventually go back to a fuller version of Antisthenes' text; certainly, Porphyry's citation is in turn an important source for Eustathius' discussion.

One further aspect of Porphyry's summary of Antisthenes is important in the present context. Although the negative view of πολύτροπος, whether that was expressed in the character of Hippias or by Antisthenes himself before he demolished it, contrasts Odysseus with Achilles and Ajax and cites Achilles' speech from *Iliad* 9, it is hard to believe that Antisthenes' defence of Odysseus and of the positive meaning of πολύτροπος was not rooted in the *Odyssey*, rather than in the *Iliad*. As Socrates' initial citation of Apemantos' view in the *Hippias Minor* shows, a contrast between Achilles and Odysseus must (almost inevitably) be a contrast between the central figure of the *Iliad* and the central figure of the Odyssey; it is, after all, the Odysseus of the *Odyssey* whom Homer called πολύτροπος. Hippias' mistake (or one of them) was to ground his argument in Book 9 of the *Iliad*, despite how Socrates introduced the subject; Hippias does observe that 'Homer made Odysseus [a liar] in many places both in the *Iliad* and in the *Odyssey*' (365c1–2), but in making no distinction between the character in the two poems, he not only shows himself (again) a not particularly sophisticated reader, but also plays into Socrates' hands. As we have already seen, later criticism at least was clear that Odysseus' character 'developed' between the two poems,[23] and it would not surprise to learn that such views were already familiar in the late fifth and fourth centuries. One might indeed think

---

Spanoudakis = 12 Sbardella). Cerri 2005 has persuasively connected this poem with Odysseus and, if this is correct, the final verse μύθων παντοίων οἶμον ἐπιστάμενος may evoke πολύτροπος, as explained by Antisthenes, just as (so Cerri) πολλὰ μογήυας in v. 3 evokes πολύτλας and similar epithets.

23 Cf. above, pp. 638–639.

that Hippias' confusion in the *Hippias Minor* either must be read against the existence of such a critical view or itself was one of the stimuli to this later view.

When Socrates asks Hippias for clarification of his view, the question is again phrased not as we might have expected: 'Was not Achilles represented as *polytropos* by Homer?' (364e5–6). Hippias' answer had in fact not excluded the possibility that Achilles had been so represented, as Hippias had been dealing in superlatives; our inference from what follows may be that Socrates phrased his question in this way because he did not (yet) understand how Hippias was using the term, for it is only after Hippias' fuller response that he claims to begin to see that, for Hippias, πολύτροπος is a synonym of ψευδής (365b7–8, cited below). The technique of slow revelation suggests, as indeed we would have known from elsewhere, that the actual meaning of πολύτροπος was anything but undisputed. Hippias' response is that the Homeric Achilles was 'not at all' πολύτροπος, but rather 'very straightforward and most truthful' (ἁπλούστατος καὶ ἀληθέστατος), and in support of this he cites, as apparently also did Antisthenes, the opening of Achilles' great speech to Odysseus in *Iliad* 9:

διογενὲς Λαερτιάδη, πολυμήχαν' Ὀδυσσεῦ,
χρὴ μὲν δὴ τὸν μῦθον ἀπηλεγέως ἀποειπεῖν,
ὥσπερ δὴ κρανέω τε καὶ ὡς τελέεσθαι ὀίω·   310
ἐχθρὸς γάρ μοι κεῖνος ὁμῶς Ἀΐδαο πύλῃσιν,   312
ὅς χ' ἕτερον μὲν κεύθῃ ἐνὶ φρεσίν, ἄλλο δὲ εἴπῃ.
αὐτὰρ ἐγὼν ἐρέω, ὡς καὶ τετελεσμένον ἔσται.

Homer, *Iliad* 9.308–314

ἐν τούτοις δηλοῖ τοῖς ἔπεσιν τὸν τρόπον ἑκατέρου τοῦ ἀνδρός, ὡς ὁ μὲν Ἀχιλλεὺς εἴη ἀληθής τε καὶ ἁπλοῦς, ὁ δὲ Ὀδυσσεὺς πολύτροπός τε καὶ ψευδής· ποιεῖ γὰρ τὸν Ἀχιλλέα εἰς τὸν Ὀδυσσέα λέγοντα ταῦτα τὰ ἔπη.

Plato, *Hippias Minor* 365a1–b6[24]

'Son of Laertes, god-born, Odysseus of the many plans, I must speak out straightforwardly as I judge it and think will come about. As hateful to me as the gates of Hades is that man who conceals one thing in his heart and speaks another. But I will tell you how it will be.' In these verses he reveals the character of each man: Achilles is truthful and straightforward, Odysseus *polytropos* and a liar, for he represents Achilles speaking these verses to Odysseus.

Here the later critical tradition was to follow where Hippias, at least the Platonic one, had led,[25] and it is worth pausing a moment to note the conclusions which

---

24 The omission of v. 311 is most naturally explained by the fact that it would not contribute to Hippias' argument.

were later drawn from these verses. The exegetical scholia on vv. 307–309 claim that they represent Achilles as φιλότιμος, ἁπλοῦς, φιλαλήθης, βαρύθυμος, εἴρων, and the scholia on v. 309 note that his speech is, as we might say, a rhetoric-free zone: περιπλοκὰς οὐκ οἶδε λόγων. His speech is marked by 'unelaborated free-speaking' (ἀκόσμητος παρρησία). The contrast, of course, as in Hippias' account, is with Odysseus. περιπλοκὰς οὐκ οἶδε λόγων (of Achilles) all but explicitly denies that one of the most familiar ancient interpretations of πολύτροπος was applicable to Achilles, whereas the whole thrust of the exegetical scholia to Odysseus' speech had been towards working out its strategies, why he speaks as he does and what implicit, 'concealed' meanings lie behind his words (cf. e.g. scholia on 226, 252, 259–260); with Achilles, however, it is changes of style which are foregrounded, for there is no doubt (for the scholia) about what he is actually saying. As for Hippias' understanding of πολύτροπος as synonymous with ψευδής, it is a reasonable conclusion that something very like this was mooted (only to be rejected) by Antisthenes, but there is in fact no other evidence to suggest that such an interpretation was generally familiar before, or indeed widespread thereafter, although πολύτροπος, 'cunning', might at any time carry a negative resonance.[26] It is Antisthenes and Plato who established that interpretation within the tradition.

The description of Achilles in the scholia on vv. 307–309 as εἴρων is of some interest also in this connection. The Homeric scholia and other critics regularly see the trope of εἰρωνεία in Homeric speeches,[27] and in those of Achilles no less than any others, including his speech to Odysseus in Book 9 (cf. scholia on vv. 348, 359, 399). Outside Aristotle, εἰρωνεία is not necessarily incompatible with a commitment to truth-telling,[28] but in the binary system of oppositions between Achilles and Odysseus which the scholia have inherited and which they elabo-

---

25 Cf. Giuliano 1995, 50–52. Modern scholars have been much exercised by whether, despite the generalising form of vv. 312–313, Achilles in fact has Agamemnon or Odysseus in mind in these verses, cf. Heiden 2002, 432–433, citing earlier bibliography; the Platonic *Hippias* has no doubt that the reference is to Odysseus, and again the later scholiastic tradition was to follow suit, cf. the T-scholia on vv. 312–313 with Erbse's note.
26 Cf. the passages collected by Montiglio 2011, 162–163.
27 Cf. van der Valk's edition of Eustathius, vol. II p. lx n. 6; Nünlist 2009, 212–213 on 'rhetorical irony'; Nünlist however perhaps underplays the range of effects which the scholia identify by this term.
28 Eustathius' note on this speech of Achilles tracks that of the exegetical scholia very closely, but he omits εἴρων from the list of adjectives which describe Achilles (*Hom.* 751.24); this may be because of the negative associations that the term could carry: Eustathius would not wish his pupils to find such negative characteristics in Achilles.

rate, it is hard not to see the suggestion that, if Achilles is εἴρων, then Odysseus must be ἀλαζών; even in the Aristotelian system, although the mean between ἀλαζονεία and εἰρωνεία is the condition (ἕξις) of being truthful, it is in fact the *alazon* who 'takes delight in ψεῦδος' (*EN* 4.1127b9–11), who is truly the opposite of the truthful man, 'for [the *alazon*] is worse [than the *eiron*]' (*EN* 4.1127b31–32). The scholia attribute ἀλαζονεία to a number of Homeric characters and speeches, including in fact to one verse (v. 401) of Achilles' speech to Odysseus in *Iliad* 9, but it is for the scholia a particular characteristic of Hector and the Trojans, often labelled as ἀλαζονεία βαρβαρική.[29] Although we ought not place too much weight upon the fact, it is certainly noteworthy in this connection that the principal term used in the *Hippias Minor* to denote 'deceivers', such as (in the common view) Odysseus, against whom Achilles' speech is directed, is indeed ἀλαζών (cf. 369e4, 371d2), and it is precisely in this quality that Socrates, with shocking paradox, claims Achilles surpassed Odysseus (371a2–7). It would of course not be sensible to claim that the *Hippias Minor* lies at the root of a distinction between Achilles and Odysseus as εἴρων and ἀλαζών: too much of what Odysseus says in the *Odyssey*, notably in Books 9–12, was (or could be taken as) such obvious ἀλαζονεία that the idea must have been a commonplace.[30] Rather, we might think of such a commonplace coming together with an opposition between Odysseus and Achilles, an opposition centred upon their confrontation in *Iliad* 9, and itself engendering, perhaps under the influence of Aristotle, the idea that Achilles was εἴρων. The process was presumably messy and unsystematic, but it is hard to doubt (I think) that the *Hippias Minor* played some part in this critical development also, particularly as Odysseus' speech to Achilles is not, as Socrates is going to make very clear, ἀλαζονικός, certainly by Odysseus' standards elsewhere. As is well known, binary oppositions tend to multiply, even where they do not all equally fit the case.

The embassy to Achilles in *Iliad* 9 was a very famous text for later rhetoricians and declaimers,[31] and Achilles' opening words are very often cited or evoked. A history of that reception would in fact deserve its own essay, and the

---

29 Cf., e.g., the scholia on *Iliad* 8.182, 515, 10.417, 12.441, 16.833.
30 In discussing Menelaos' account of his travels in *Odyssey* 4, Strabo observes that 'everyone who recounts his own wanderings is an ἀλαζών' (1.2.23), and it is indeed hard in that context not to remember Odysseus; in recalling Strabo's *bon mot*, Eustathius applies it to both Menelaos and Odysseus (*Hom.* 1381.59).
31 It is the first passage mentioned by Quintilian (*Inst. orat.* 10.1.47) in his list of Iliadic passages which are of particular interest to the would-be orator.

Hippias Minor would play a major part in any such history,[32] but let me point to only one further aspect of Hippias' quotation which looks forward to the later critical tradition. 'In these verses', says Hippias, 'he reveals each man's character (τρόπος) …' (365b5–6); Hippias twice in this passage makes clear that the verses are spoken by Achilles, but the subject of δηλοῖ, 'he reveals', must be Homer. Nothing of course is more familiar in ancient quotation-practice than the ascription of the views of a character in a narrative or drama to the poet himself, and the present case is normally dismissed in this way.[33] This may, however, be to let Hippias off too lightly. An Aristotle certainly would have known that although these verses tell us much about Achilles, we should judge Odysseus from his own words, not from those of others; when Aristotle says (*Poetics* 1450b7–10) that 'character (ἦθος) reveals (δηλοῖ) the nature of moral choice (προαίρεσις)', he might almost have been thinking of this same opening to Achilles' speech in *Iliad* 9. Socrates' refusal to take Achilles' self-presentation at face value, without also examining his actions (which also, of course, are revelatory of προαίρεσις (*Poetics* 1454a17–18)), might then be thought to be a simple critical step forward, but it is one whose repercussions are still with us. We might also recall that, in later Homeric criticism at least, many apparent 'problems' in the Homeric text were solved by appealing to the fact that they arise from what a character, not the poet himself, says; this is the so-called λύσις ἐκ τοῦ προσώπου. Something like this can be identified as early as Aristotle (frr. 146, 163 Rose = 370, 387 Gigon),[34] but familiarity with the general principle might again be much earlier, and in the present context it is of some interest that Lucia Prauscello has identified such a case, and one associated with Antisthenes, in Plato's *Laws*.[35] Here again, then, is another simple critical principle of which the Platonic Hippias is ignorant.

When Socrates picks up the Homeric thread at 369a8, he has apparently established that the true and the false man must be the same, not different, but Hippias is not convinced and wants to restart the debate about Achilles and Odysseus; as several critics have recognised, the argument with Socrates as to whose opinion will prevail is set up by Hippias as a kind of internal reflection of the debate as to which of Achilles and Odysseus is 'better':

---

[32] The *Hippias Minor* has, for example, a role in the later connection between Achilles' words and rhetorical teaching about 'figured speeches', cf., e.g., Philostratus, *VS* 542.
[33] Cf., e.g., Pinjuh 2014, 111, 113. Eustathius also ascribes the thought of *Il.* 9.312–13 to 'the poet' and in the context of the poet's rejection of a negative form of πολυτροπία (*Hom.* 1381.39).
[34] For bibliography and discussion cf. Nünlist 2009, 116–119.
[35] Prauscello 2017.

εἰ δὲ βούλει, σὺ αὖ ἀντιπαράβαλλε λόγον παρὰ λόγον, ὡς ὁ ἕτερος ἀμείνων ἐστί· καὶ μᾶλλον εἴσονται οὗτοι ὁπότερος ἄμεινον λέγει.

Plato, *Hippias Minor* 369c6-8

If you like, oppose argument to argument, showing that the other one is better. These people will then know more clearly which man speaks better.

Ancient criticism was indeed a very competitive, agonistic business. In Hippias' mind, so we are to understand, it is also clear that he himself is the Achilles; at the beginning of the dialogue he had presented himself as 'never having met anyone better (κρείττων) than himself' in the business of ἀγωνίζεσθαι at Olympia (364a6–8),[36] and now he portrays Socrates as an Odysseus:

ὦ Σώκρατες, ἀεὶ σύ τινας τοιούτους πλέκεις λόγους, καὶ ἀπολαμβάνων ὃ ἂν ᾖ δυσχερέστατον τοῦ λόγου, τούτου ἔχῃ κατὰ σμικρὸν ἐφαπτόμενος, καὶ οὐχ ὅλῳ ἀγωνίζῃ τῷ πράγματι περὶ ὅτου ἂν ὁ λόγος ᾖ·

Plato, *Hippias Minor* 369b7–c2[37]

Socrates, you are always weaving arguments like this, and you pick out the most difficult part of the argument and you stick to it, examining it in detail, and you never deal with the whole subject of the discussion.

Socrates turns this pattern also on its head when he subsequently accuses Hippias of himself playing the role (μιμεῖσθαι) of Odysseus (370e10–11). That Hippias shows both Achillean and Odyssean traits might be seen as an ironic dramatisation of Socrates' argument that the true and the false person are one and the same.[38]

---

36 Hippias' 'contest' with Socrates is therefore Olympic as well as Homeric; cf., e.g., Lampert 2002, 234.
37 Rather similar is Hippias' complaint about Socrates' methods of argumentation at *Hipp. Mai.* 301b2–5. The idea of Socrates as an Odysseus has often been brought into connection with the end of our dialogue (376c), where the Homeric discussion all but otherwise disappears. There Socrates uses the image of 'wandering' for the state of *aporia* into which the apparently inevitable, but obviously (at the very least) counter-intuitive, conclusions of the *logos* have led him, cf., e.g., Blondell 2002, 159. Whereas Odysseus was able to end his wanderings when he 'reached' (*Od.* 11.122) people who did not know the sea, Socrates and other ἰδιῶται will never cease from wandering, even after 'reaching' the σοφοί, for the σοφοί themselves are no less wanderers. For another view of Socratic πολυτροπία in the *Hippias Minor* cf. Montiglio 2011, 42.
38 Later, an association between Odysseus and Hippias became familiar (cf., e.g., Dio Chrys. 71. 2–3) and may of course have been promoted by Hippias himself.

Socrates proceeds to identify inconsistency, and hence 'falsehood', in Achilles' speech.[39] The hero said, as he had already said to Agamemnon (*Il.* 1.169–171), that he would return home 'tomorrow', but there is no sign that he ever made the slightest move towards doing so (*Il.* 9.357–63). Odysseus, on the other hand, tells no lies in the verses which Hippias had quoted, by which Socrates presumably means all of Odysseus' speech to Achilles in Book 9.[40] Modern criticism has made much of Odysseus' 'economical' report to Achilles of what Agamemnon had said,[41] although (interestingly) it is not clear that anyone in antiquity ever did; the scholia on v. 392 do link Achilles' use of the term βασιλεύτερος to Agamemnon's use at v. 160, but that is not the same as accusing Odysseus of deliberate misrepresentation. Hippias makes no attempt to deny the facts as Socrates stated them, but rather seeks to explain them away; here, as we have seen, the discussion takes the familiar (later) form of a Homeric 'problem' and its 'solution'.[42] Hippias' defence of Achilles appeals to a distinction between voluntary and involuntary falsehood, something which any follower of the Platonic Socrates will recognise as very likely to lead to dialectical disaster:

> οὐ γὰρ καλῶς σκοπεῖς, ὦ Σώκρατες. ἃ μὲν γὰρ ὁ Ἀχιλλεὺς ψεύδεται, οὐκ ἐξ ἐπιβουλῆς φαίνεται ψευδόμενος ἀλλ' ἄκων, διὰ τὴν συμφορὰν τὴν τοῦ στρατοπέδου ἀναγκασθεὶς καταμεῖναι καὶ βοηθῆσαι· ἃ δὲ ὁ Ὀδυσσεύς, ἑκών τε καὶ ἐξ ἐπιβουλῆς.
> Plato, *Hippias Minor* 370e5–9

> You do not look at this in the right way, Socrates. When Achilles lies, he obviously does this not by design, but unwillingly, as he is compelled by the terrible situation of the army to remain and offer assistance; when Odysseus lies, he does it willingly and by design.

When Socrates returns to the attack by noting that Achilles says something different yet again to Ajax, namely that he will not fight until the Trojan advance reaches his very own camp (9.650–655), Hippias can explain that as well:

> ἀλλὰ καὶ αὐτὰ ταῦτα ὑπὸ εὐνοίας ἀναπεισθεὶς πρὸς τὸν Αἴαντα ἄλλα εἶπεν ἢ πρὸς τὸν Ὀδυσσέα· ὁ δὲ Ὀδυσσεὺς ἅ τε ἀληθῆ λέγει, ἐπιβουλεύσας ἀεὶ λέγει, καὶ ὅσα ψεύδεται, ὡσαύτως.
> εὐνοίας F: εὐηθείας TWf
> Plato, *Hippias Minor* 371d8–e3

---

[39] There are, of course, much deeper philosophical issues about 'speaking (un)truth' to which this section of the dialogue points, but I here leave them out of account.
[40] Socrates' οὐδαμοῦ at 369e5 perhaps resonates with Hippias' πολλαχοῦ at 365c2.
[41] Cf., e.g., Lynn-George 1988, 118–122, Elmer 2015, 168, citing earlier bibliography.
[42] The truth or otherwise of Odysseus' report back to the Greek commanders at the end of Book 9 was certainly later discussed as a ζήτημα, cf. below, pp. 654–655.

> Here too Achilles was led by goodwill towards Ajax to say different things than he said to Odysseus; Odysseus, on the other hand, always speaks by design, both when he tells the truth and when he lies.

Hippias' explanations have received a favourable reception in modern criticism, from Wilamowitz on.[43] In her study of the debate about the term πολύτροπος, Maria Luzzatto described Hippias' account as 'from Homer's point of view undoubtedly correct',[44] and in her important discussion of the *Hippias Minor* Ruby Blondell describes Hippias' views as 'perfectly plausible', whereas Socrates' treatment of the Homeric scene is 'farcical', 'absurd' and 'ludicrous';[45] Charles Kahn too describes Socrates' account as 'a deliberately misleading account of Achilles' character, supported by a deep knowledge of the Homeric text ... [a] distorted picture of Achilles',[46] and suggests that the whole dialogue may be seen 'as a kind of *reductio* of the moralizing or 'allegorical' interpretation of Homer'. There may, again, be something to be said on the other side.

Before turning to Hippias' account itself, however, we may consider (again) the versions offered by the extant scholia, which themselves of course may (and probably do) show the influence of the *Hippias Minor*.[47] The exegetical scholia on v. 309c note the variations in Achilles' statements: he tells Odysseus that he will go away, Phoenix that he will stay, but not fight, which is in fact a not very accurate account of *Il*. 9.618–619, and Ajax that he will fight when 'necessity' makes him do so. In the context of explaining Achilles' adverb ἀπηλεγέως in v. 309, the scholia also note that 'those who wish to cause pain remove any optimistic hopes', and it may be thought that this applies particularly to the answer to Odysseus. The scholia on vv. 651–2 tell a similar, though rather more nuanced, story:[48]

> He says to Odysseus that he will sail away (for he was still terribly inflamed by anger), to Phoenix, when he is already growing calmer (πραϋνόμενος), that he will give thought to staying, and to Ajax he says, from a sense of αἰδώς, that he will come to their aid when the

---

43 See Wilamowitz 1920, 138.
44 Luzzatto 1996, 296.
45 Blondell 2002, 145–146; Blondell does, however, see a serious philosophic purpose here and also has useful remarks on the Socratic criticism of literary discussion based on selective quotation. Lampert 2002, 245 describes Socrates' Homeric exegesis as 'indefensible'.
46 Kahn 1996, 124. Schmiel 1983/4, on the other hand, is prepared to take Socrates' charges seriously.
47 My account here is inevitably close to the important discussion in Giuliano 1995, 50–52.
48 Cf., e.g., Pinjuh 2014, 186. [Plut.] *De Hom.* 2.169 also tells a similar story, though with rather different emphases.

enemy are near at hand; he does not want to make his return to the fighting appear to the Greeks either impossible or imminent, to make clear the magnitude of what he has suffered.

bT-scholia on Homer, *Iliad* 9.651–652

Whether or not this account of Achilles' behaviour is plausible, it does have the merit of at least taking account of the important interchange with Phoenix, which Hippias and Socrates both ignore in the *Hippias Minor*. Whether Plato expects us to notice the omission from Socrates' account of Phoenix's speech and of Achilles' non-committal response to him (vv. 618–619) may be thought uncertain; if the omission is deliberate, then it is tempting to see such an omission as a trap for Hippias, who proves not sharp enough to pick up the point, although some later critics obviously did.[49]

Hippias explains the fact that Achilles did remain at Troy from the fact that 'he was compelled by the disaster which befell the army to remain and come to their aid' (370e7–8). As we have seen, the scholia on 309c also appeal to 'necessity', but very differently so: on this view, Achilles tells Ajax that he will fight when he has to. The theme of 'constraint' upon Achilles appears elsewhere in the scholia, but I think we are at least entitled to ask how 'plausible' Hippias' account at 370e7–8 (cited above) actually is. We might take βοηθῆσαι to refer to Achilles allowing Patroclus to go out to fight in his own armour, but I doubt that many will be convinced that this is what Hippias means; at its best, his is a very loose paraphrase of what happens in the poem, and one of which no sophist, let alone a modern critic, should be proud. It is, of course, fair to point out that many ancient plot summaries may seem to us quite far removed from 'what actually happens', but Hippias' account in 370e is anything but a 'close reading'. As for Achilles' reply to Ajax, Hippias (371e1) ascribes this to εὐήθεια or εὔνοια, depending on the reading adopted,[50] whereas the scholia put it down to αἰδώς, as the A-scholia on vv. 618–619 also explain Achilles' concession to Phoenix. This latter motive is easy enough to understand: Ajax's words, like Phoenix's much longer speech before him, have stung Achilles' sense of how he is perceived by his colleagues — he acknowledges that Ajax's words are κατὰ θυμόν to him (v. 645) — and how it is expected that he should react to the supplicatory embassy which has now come to him; this precisely falls in the realm

---

[49] Cf. Lampert 2002, 245. Giuliano 1995, 51 n. 104 also notices the omission of Phoenix from the *Hippias Minor*, but asks rather different questions about it.
[50] Cf. further below.

of αἰδώς (note also αἴδεσσαι in v. 640).⁵¹ It is this too which inhibits the hero from simply leaving his colleagues to their fate and/or from refusing to meet Hector's challenge when his own fate and that of his beloved Myrmidons are at stake; he will, however, exact a very high price for the damage which has been done to his honour. It obviously makes a difference, as the scholia recognise, that he is speaking to Phoenix and to Ajax, not to Agamemnon, but we may well doubt whether either εὐήθεια or εὔνοια is a particularly good explanation for saying to Ajax that he will rejoin the fighting once Hector reaches the Myrmidon camp, 'after killing Argives and setting fire to the ships', a verse missing from Porphyry's quotation of the passage; at the very least, Ajax must have had mixed feelings about Achilles' professed intentions. Once again, it may be objected that I am in danger of demanding from Hippias the kind of 'close reading' and interpretation which we ourselves take for granted, and the absence of which is (notoriously) one of the things which often seems most puzzling about ancient discussions of literature. Whatever view one takes, however, it is I think clear that Hippias' brief explanation hardly does any kind of justice to the Homeric text.

As for the choice between εὐήθεια and εὔνοια, Giuliano has argued strongly in favour of the first alternative, which is that of the principal branch of the tradition, in the sense of '(possession of) good ἦθος' (cf. *Rep.* 3.400d11–e4), as ἦθος is always a central part of ancient discussions of Achilles; we might note that [Plutarch] precisely observes that Achilles' answer to each of the three ambassadors reveals his ἦθος γενναῖον ἅμα καὶ ἁπλοῦν (*De Hom.* 2.169),⁵² and it might be argued that εὐηθείας offers a better contrast to ἐπιβουλεύσας (371e3) than would εὐνοίας. Giuliano further notes that the alternative reading might have arisen because, as time passed, the pejorative sense of εὐήθεια had come to dominate.⁵³ On the other hand, we might be reminded of the link which Thucydides draws between τὸ γενναῖον, which Achilles certainly possesses, and τὸ εὔηθες (3.83.1), and it is at least curious that when Achilles observes to Odys-

---

51 Cf. also the bT-scholia on v. 642, and Cairns 1993, 92–95 and Gill 1996, 1937 (neither of whom, however, refers to the scholia).
52 This passage of [Plutarch] also reminds us of the irony of Socrates' πάνυ γενναίως at *Hipp. Min.* 370d5.
53 Giuliano 1995, 55, cf. also Luzzatto 1996, 320, Pinjuh 2014, 197–198, Culverhouse 2015, and εὐηθείας is also read by Vancamp 1996, 121. Giuliano 1995, 51 also seeks to make Hippias' explanation of εὐήθεια amount to much the same thing as the scholiastic explanation of αἰδώς; that seems to me mistaken. That εὐνοίας is preserved only in F is, of itself, no argument against this reading; on the nature and value of F cf. Dodds 1959, 41–47 and Vancamp 1996, 31–33. The account of this passage in Gaudin 1981, 149 seems to me without value.

seus that he will not allow Agamemnon to deceive him a second time (*Il.* 9.375-6), the AbT-scholia observe that it is a mark of εὐήθεια to be deceived once by a φίλος, but of μωρία to let it happen twice. Moreover, εὔνοια (towards Ajax) would be an explanation which minimised Achilles' 'deceitfulness', thus bringing him closer to an action which could be described as ἄκων, and would also acknowledge Ajax as a brave (and ἁπλοῦς)[54] hero in the Achillean mould; in other words, it explains specifically why it is Ajax to whom these words were spoken, and thus gestures towards the very long tradition of myth, art and literature linking these two heroes, not least with regard to the award of Achilles' arms after his death. The reading εὐνοίας thus seems to give Hippias a rather stronger rhetorical point against Socrates, if not necessarily a better reading of Homer.

If it is indeed the case that Hippias' defence of the 'inconsistency' in his and Achilles' position is not a very strong one, we might reflect that it could have been worse, when we remember how Ion 'defends' his position in the dialogue named after him. Socrates, of course, is not particularly interested in the interpretation of *Iliad* 9 for its own sake: the fact that Odysseus appears to tell the truth here but be a notorious liar elsewhere becomes one manifestation of the apparent paradox that the truth-teller and the liar are one and the same, together with the further problems to which that conclusion leads. For the Platonic Socrates, the Homeric text is a useful jumping-off point, not an end in itself. Plato, however, also pushes us towards a more far-reaching view, and one which still presses us urgently today, about the characters of literature. What kinds of questions are we to ask of what they say? How are we to move from what is said in epic or drama to the ethical situations which we ourselves face? By 'defamiliarising' Achilles for us, by showing us a πολύτροπος Achilles, Socrates, who is certainly in this dialogue a 'closer reader' than is Hippias, makes us confront the comfortable (and comforting) assumptions into which criticism of classic (and classical) texts too easily sinks. Socrates may not be particularly interested in proceeding much further down that path, but we can hardly shun the trail towards which he beckons us. Moreover, if we were to substitute ἀνώμαλος for πολύτροπος, the *Hippias Minor* would take us very close to a prominent ancient view of Achilles' character. Apparently in connection with Achilles' behaviour towards Priam in *Iliad* 24, Aristotle declared that Achilles' character was 'changeable, unstable', ἀνώμαλον,[55] and certainly his changes of

---

54 Cf., e.g., scholia on *Il.* 9.622, 17.720.
55 Fr. 168 R = 391 Gigon, cf. Eustathius, *Hom.* 783.18 (with Van der Valk's note), 1359.17–22, 1365.55–58, 1366.1, Richardson 1980, 273. On this aspect of Achilles cf., e.g., Else 1957, 462–463.

mood in that climactic episode might well deserve such a label, however psychologically true modern readers might find this extraordinary portrait of emotional fragility.

Ancient scholars, like their modern descendants, were also much interested in the question of why, when the ambassadors report back at the end of *Iliad* 9, Odysseus only reports the straightforward refusal which Achilles gave to him, without mentioning the rather more hopeful responses to Phoenix and Ajax.[56] The exegetical scholia on vv. 682–683 ascribe various motives, honourable as well as disreputable, to Odysseus, but in his extended discussion of the matter Eustathius adds (*inter alia*) that one reason for Ajax's own silence might have been his knowledge of the fact that Achilles had made different promises to each of the three ambassadors; as a result of this, Ajax does not think that one should pay any attention to Achilles, given that hero's 'inconsistency' (παλιμβολία).[57] Whether or not such an observation had ancient forerunners we cannot say,[58] but it is very hard here not to be reminded of the *Hippias Minor*, where Achilles' πολυτροπία consists precisely in the different responses he gave to Odysseus and Ajax. So too, Porphyry reports that one of the Homeric 'problems' discussed at the Museum in Alexandria was why Odysseus' report back to the Greeks omitted what Achilles had said to Ajax, thereby not reporting 'the truth'.[59] The solution offered was that Odysseus did indeed give a true report of what Achilles had said to him, but by saying that Achilles only 'threatened' (v. 682) to sail away on the following morning, Odysseus in fact takes account of the different answers which Phoenix and Ajax had received and which he had heard. Here again, then, is a debate in which Odysseus' truthfulness is championed and Achilles' changefulness, whether that be ἀνώμαλον or πολύτροπον, hangs heavy in the background.

The *Hippias Minor*, then, may well lie, at an unknown number of removes, behind more than one important strand of the ancient discussion of *Iliad* 9. More importantly perhaps, we will again be reminded that Socrates' account of

---

56 Cf. Hainsworth's note on *Il.* 9.682–683 and Griffin on 9.676ff. The helpful account of the matter in Scodel 1989 is in fact very close to the ancient discussions and to that of Eustathius; of particular interest is her stress on how often Achilles changes his mind, from Book 1 on, a characteristic which, so she argues, the ambassadors in Book 9 might see as a mark of Achilles' 'inherent unreliability'.
57 *Hom.* 783.17–19, cf. 1359.19 on Achilles' παλίμβολον ἦθος; on the choice here and elsewhere between παλιμβουλία and παλιμβολία cf. van der Valk *ad loc.*
58 Diomedes' conclusion that the only thing which will influence Achilles is that hero's θυμός (*Il.* 9.702–703) might also have played some role in the subsequent critical tradition.
59 Cf. MacPhail 2011, 156–159, and the D-scholia on v. 679.

Achilles and Odysseus in that book pointed the way towards a reading which was certainly not dismissed out of hand, as it too often is today, by various communities of readers at particular times in the past. With our own philosophical and moral concerns, we may want to insist, like Hippias, that Achilles may be 'inconsistent', but that does not make him a 'liar' or indeed even πολύτροπος; that, however, is a different matter from seeking fairly to assess the claims of the *Hippias Minor* and the critical tradition which seems to have been influenced by it.

I have been largely concerned in this essay with critical traditions which are most visible to us from the Homeric scholia, but it may be that we can in fact trace the influence of the *Hippias Minor* at a much earlier date and in a very significant place. The meeting of Odysseus and Achilles in *Iliad* 9, and in particular Hippias' account of the opening of Achilles' speech, might well be seen with hindsight not merely as a confrontation of two very different characters (in both senses), but also as a marker of the difference between the two poems of which they are the principal focus; the same, of course, might be true for their subsequent meeting in the Underworld in *Odyssey* 11, but that is not something to be pursued here. Certainly, it would not be difficult to show that the *Iliad* is in many senses ἁπλοῦς, whereas the *Odyssey* is both complex and πολύτροπος.[60] One reason, of course, that it would not be difficult is that Aristotle has already shown the way. For Aristotle, the *Iliad* is ἁπλοῦν καὶ παθητικόν, whereas the *Odyssey* is πεπλεγμένον καὶ ἠθική (*Poetics* 1459b14–16).[61] When Aristotle describes the well-constructed tragic plot (ὁ καλῶς ἔχων μῦθος) as 'single' and as involving a 'change from good fortune to bad fortune, not because of any wickedness, but because of a great *hamartia* on the part of a character such as I have stated [i.e. someone of high reputation and prosperity] or a character who is better rather than worse' (1453a12–16), it is hard not to think of the *Iliad*, if only because Aristotle proceeds to award second prize to a plot which is explicitly like the *Odyssey* (1453a32), and if Homer comes second, then only Homer can also come first.

---

[60] This holds good, I think, despite the ancient view (cf. the scholia on *Odyssey* 1.1c and d Pontani) that Homer devised the Telemachy in order to add ποικιλία to his poem, or as the scholion on 1.1c puts it, ἵνα μὴ μονότροπος ᾖ τῆς ποιήσεως ὁ τρόπος, an observation which almost invites us to remember πολύτροπος. There is of course an important distinction between the πεπλεγμένον and the ποικίλον. Eustathius expands on how Homer fills out the brief and simple narrative which forms the story of the *Odyssey* (*Hom.* 1379.41–44), cf. Pontani 2000, 28; Eustathius ascribes to the *Odyssey* a 'depth of thought amidst surface simplicity (ἁπλότης)'.
[61] For how this distinction may play out in the area of language use cf., e.g., Elmer 2015.

The essence of the πεπλεγμένον lies in περιπέτεια καὶ ἀναγνώρισις (*Poetics* 1455b33), and the *Odyssey* in fact is 'recognition all the way through' (1459b15); recognition itself is defined as 'a change from ignorance to knowledge, [leading to] either friendship or hostility' (1452a29–30). There is much that could be (and has been) said about both the power and the limits of Aristotle's distinctions, but his categorisation of the *Odyssey* clearly gives the greatest weight to 'recognitions' of personal identity, which are central to Odysseus' poem. There is, moreover, another way in which the *Odyssey* cannot be ἁπλοῦς for Aristotle, namely that its structure (σύστασις) is double, διπλῆ, because 'the better and worse characters end up in opposite ways' (*Poetics* 1453a31–33); we are probably entitled to draw the inference that I just have, namely that the *Iliad* is, in this respect also, ἁπλοῦς (cf. also 1453a12), though we are here entering some of the thorniest problems of the *Poetics*. Nevertheless, a link between the discussion of the characters of Achilles and Odysseus in the *Hippias Minor* and Aristotle's classification of narrative and plot structures seems not implausible.

Aristotle's view of the two Homeric poems, at least in the relevant parts of the *Poetics*, seems to follow, almost as an afterthought, from his developed views about tragedy. Nevertheless, epic may well have played a role in the development of those views, both of the 'simple' and the 'complex' and of *pathos* and *ethos*, given the stark nature of some of the differences between the *Iliad* and the *Odyssey*. *Pathos* and *ethos* would require extended discussion, but for what it is worth Aristotle at one point defines πάθος as πρᾶξις φθαρτικὴ ἢ ὀδυνηρά (1452b11), and he exemplifies such an action by 'deaths in full view, great agonies and woundings and such things'; he is writing of tragedy, but it is hard not to think of the opening of the *Iliad*, with the griefs and deaths caused by the μῆνις of Achilles; as for the *Odyssey*, there too we have 'many griefs suffered on the sea', but before that we are promised a poem about an ἀνὴρ πολύτροπος, a poem (in other words) of ἦθος. This is, however, a man whom we do not really get to see until Book 5, whereas in the *Iliad* the μῆνις and its consequences burst upon us almost immediately. The poem of outburst and confrontation is set against the poem of brooding and biding one's time, of plotting and deception. The point is familiar enough to need no further labouring.[62] Aristotle needed nothing other than the poems themselves to see how their plot structures differed and to formulate a distinction between them in terms of 'the simple' and 'the complex' (or 'entwined'), but we know that he knew the *Hippias Minor* (we would have assumed this anyway)[63] and it does not seem utterly implausible

---

62 For how this distinction may play out in the area of language use cf., e.g., Elmer 2015.
63 Cf. Arist. *Metaph.* 4.1025a6.

that the distinctions made in that dialogue about Achilles and Odysseus have had some influence on the arguments, or the formulation of the arguments, about plot structures in the *Poetics*. In other words, although epic follows in the *Poetics* on the coat-tails of tragedy, epic, mediated in part through the *Hippias Minor*, might have nudged Aristotle down the path he followed.

Bibliography

Blondell, R. 2002. *The play of character in Plato's dialogues*, Cambridge.
Brancacci, A. 2004. 'Il *logos* di Ippia: Plat. *Protag.* 337c–338b', in: G. Casertano (ed.), *Il Protagora di Platone: struttura e problematiche*. Volume I, Naples, 390–401.
Cairns, D.L. 1993. *Aidos: the psychology of honour and shame in ancient Greek literature*, Oxford.
Cerri, G. 2005. 'L'ontano di Filita: soluzione di un enigma e ricostruzione di un percorso critico', *Quaderni Urbinati di Cultura Classica* 80, 133–139.
Culverhouse, Z. 2015. Review of Pinjuh (2014), *Bryn Mawr Classical Review* 2015.08.08.
Denniston, J.D. 1954. *The Greek particles*, 2nd ed., Oxford.
Elmer, D. 2015. 'The "narrow road" and the ethics of language use in the *Iliad* and the *Odyssey*', *Ramus* 44, 155–183.
Else, G.F. 1957. *Aristotle's Poetics: the argument*, Cambridge MA.
Fantuzzi, M. 2014. 'Tragic smiles: when tragedy gets too comic for Aristotle and later Hellenistic readers', in: R. Hunter/A. Rengakos/E. Sistakou (eds.), *Hellenistic Studies at a Crossroads*, Berlin, 215–233.
Gaudin, C. 1981. 'Εὐήθεια: la théorie platonicienne de l'innocence' *Revue Philosophique* 171, 145–168.
Gill, C. 1984. 'The *ethos/pathos* distinction in rhetorical and literary criticism', *Classical Quarterly* 34, 149–166.
Gill, C. 1996. *Personality in Greek epic, tragedy, and philosophy*, Oxford.
Giuliano, F.M. 1995. 'L'Odisseo di Platone: uno ζήτημα omerico nell' *Ippia Minore*', in: G. Arrighetti (ed.), *Poesia greca*, Pisa, 9–57.
Heiden, B. 2002. 'Hidden thoughts, open speech: some reflections on discourse analysis in recent Homeric studies', in: F. Montanari (ed.), *Omero tremila anni dopo*, Rome, 431–444.
Hunter, R. 2011. 'Plato's *Ion* and the origins of scholarship', in: S. Matthaios/F. Montanari/A. Rengakos (eds.), *Ancient scholarship and grammar*, Berlin, 27–40 [= this volume 506–520].
Hunter, R. 2012. *Plato and the Traditions of Ancient Literature*, Cambridge.
Kahn, C.H. 1996. *Plato and the Socratic dialogue*, Cambridge.
Lampert, L. 2002. 'Socrates' defense of polytropic Odysseus: lying and wrong-doing in Plato's *Lesser Hippias*', *The Review of Politics* 64, 231–259.
Luzzatto, M.T. 1996. 'Dialettica o retorica? La *polytropia* di Odisseo da Antistene a Porfirio', *Elenchos* 17, 275–357.
Lynn-George, M. 1988. *Epos: word, narrative and the Iliad*, London.
MacPhail, J.A. 2011. *Porphyry's Homeric Questions on the Iliad*, Berlin.
Montiglio, S. 2011. *From hero to villain: Odysseus in ancient thought*, Ann Arbor.

Nesselrath, H.-G. (ed.) 2009. *Dion von Prusa: Der Philosoph und sein Bild*, Tübingen.
Nünlist, R. 2009. *The ancient critic at work*, Cambridge.
Pfeiffer, R. 1968. *History of Classical scholarship*, Oxford.
Pinjuh, J.-M. 2014. *Platons Hippias Minor*, Tübingen.
Pontani, F. 2000. 'Il proemio al *Commento all'Odissea* di Eustazio di Tessalonica', *Bollettino dei Classici* 21, 5–58.
Prauscello, L. 2017. 'Plato *Laws* 3.680b–c: Antisthenes, the Cyclopes and Homeric exegesis', *JHS* 137, 8–23.
Richardson, N.J. 1975. 'Homeric professors in the age of the Sophists', *Proceedings of the Cambridge Philological Society* 21, 65–81.
Richardson, N.J. 1980. 'Literary criticism in the exegetical scholia to the *Iliad*: a sketch', *Classical Quarterly* 30, 265–287.
Schmiel, R. 1983/4. 'Wily Achilles', *Classical Outlook* 61, 41–43.
Scodel, R. 1989. 'The word of Achilles', *Classical Philology* 84, 91–99.
Vancamp, B. 1996. *Platon, Hippias Maior, Hippias Minor*, Stuttgart.
Wilamowitz, U. von 1920. *Platon*, Volume i, 2nd ed., Berlin.

I am grateful to audiences in Cambridge and Munich for much stimulating discussion and to *CCJ*'s anonymous readers for further helpful advice.

35 Autobiography as Literary History: Dio Chrysostom, *On exile*

Dio of Prusa has a particular claim on the attention of those interested in Greek literary history and the writing of that history, in antiquity (and beyond); some of his orations and essays may be thought to fit comfortably into 'literary history' as commonly understood,[1] but many others suggest, with varying degrees of insistence, that Dio's own (real or alleged) experiences exemplify important patterns of literary and cultural history. In this essay I will be concerned with one striking example of such a mode, but I begin with Dio's intellectual context, for it is the literature and philosophy of the past which are at the heart of Dio's sense of his place in history.

From an early date, the only serious struggle for both territory and definition in which rhetoric, we might almost say 'literature', has been engaged is with philosophy, or perhaps one should rather say 'with φιλοσοφία'.[2] It was Plato who first drew the battle-lines between rhetoric and philosophy, and these lines, however they shifted back and forth over the centuries, always maintained a recognisably Platonic shape. It is in the period of (roughly) the first two and a half centuries AD, a period which we, following Philostratus, call the Second Sophistic, that these battle-lines become increasingly blurred.[3] In his account of the great sophists of the period, which is one of our most remarkable ancient texts of (*inter alia*) literary history, Philostratus famously begins by labelling 'the ancient sophistic', that is the sophistic of what we call the classical period, 'philosophising rhetoric' (ῥητορικὴ φιλοσοφοῦσα), because it discussed the same subjects as did the philosophers; whereas, however, philosophers proceeded dialectically through question-and-answer, sophists — and this distinction itself of course goes back to Plato — made proper speeches and claimed a knowledge for themselves which philosophers refused to claim.

Philostratus treats Dio as one of those philosophers whose fluency (εὔροια) earned them the name of 'sophist', though this is not in fact what they were. The

---

[1] *Oration* 52 on the *Philoctetes* — plays of the three classical tragedians is perhaps the most obvious example here, cf. Hunter 2009, 39–48.
[2] This, of course, in no way depends upon any particular interpretation of, or value assigned to, the Platonic Socrates' notorious claim of 'an ancient quarrel' between poetry and philosophy (*Republic* 10.607b6).
[3] There is of course a large bibliography on the interface of rhetoric and philosophy in the first two centuries of the Roman empire; for some initial orientation cf., e.g., Stanton 1973, Anderson 1989, 118–123.

category might seem to us a rather mixed bag — Eudoxus and Carneades, for example, are not usually placed in this company — and what is at stake is as much the definition of 'sophist' as of 'philosopher', but the two major figures of the Second Sophistic whom Philostratus groups together here are Dio and Favorinus. Dio is, then, a figure around whom questions of definition and category cluster; Philostratus indeed (*VS* 486) begins his account of Dio by admitting that he does not know what label to stick on him, though there are elements of both Demosthenes and Plato in the mix. Some two hundred years after Philostratus, Synesius of Cyrene begins his discussion of ideas in Dio from Philostratus' dichotomy, while taking pleasure in pointing out inconsistencies in Philostratus' account (*Dio* 1.9–10); Synesius sees Dio as a sophist who became a philosopher (*Dio* 1.4), a view for which Dio himself is explicitly Synesius' source, and the principal reference is presumably to *Oration* 13, 'On exile', that oration which will be the most important exhibit to be discussed in the current paper. From Dio's own account of his life, Synesius builds a very clear distinction between the sophistic/rhetorical works which preceded exile and the philosophical works which followed it, a distinction which seems to him to make sense of the otherwise very opposed attitudes towards philosophers apparently revealed in the corpus of speeches he knew (much larger than we possess today). As is well known, modern scholarship has done much to undermine the foundations of this simple two-part structure, but — as is equally well-known — literary history is a strange nursling which long since grew out of a need for historicity, or indeed for a historical narrative, but which finds it very difficult to abandon the sense of security that the historical blanket brings.

Several of Dio's most famous speeches may in part be seen as contributions to a kind of literary history which is concerned not only with the boundaries between rhetoric, poetry and philosophy, but also with the cultural accommodations that time has wrought.[4] *Oration* 7, the 'Euboikos', for example, in part dramatizes the claims of what we might call a philosophically-informed rhetoric not just to a voice in public policy and morality, but also the manner in which such a rhetoric should take the place of, or at least stand alongside, poetry, most notably — though not exclusively — the poetry of Homer, in its traditional role as public educator. So too, *Oration* 36, the 'Borysthenitikos', tells the story of Dio's visit to the now somewhat 'barbarised' city of Borysthenes (or Olbia) on the north coast of the Black Sea, where (so Dio claims) all the citizens were obsessed with Homer and celebrated cults of Achilles; for them, knowledge of Homer and imitation of Homeric characters are potent marks of their Greekness.

---

4 The subject requires much fuller discussion than can be pursued here.

Dio's account of his visit demonstrates (*inter alia*), however, that this clinging to Homer is in fact an impediment to real cultural and intellectual progress, which requires the arrival of an outsider such as Dio, who brings with him both political philosophy and a 'Zoroastrian' cosmic myth in which Hellenisation itself is made to confront its own 'foreign' heritage. These orations displace Homer from the centre, but they also trace the history of that displacement, and in both Dio is concerned, of course, also to stake a claim for the importance of his own voice within a new cultural order.

Oration 13, 'In Athens, concerning exile',[5] has reached us in an all but certainly incomplete form, and — like many of Dio's orations — probably carries traces of having been put together from more than one version, but what survives offers an account of how Dio's exile led directly to the development of philosophical interests and the emergence of Dio as a public preacher in a philosophical mode. The early part of Dio's narration moves from the moment of Dio's (real or alleged) exile, to the reflections to which that led on the subject of whether or not exile really was a terrible thing or just seemed so to some but not to others, and then his consultation of the Delphic oracle in an attempt to settle the matter. The oracle advised him, in Dio's own report (or paraphrase), to 'do the very thing on which I am engaged (ἐν ᾧ εἰμι) with all zeal as being an honourable and advantageous activity, until, he said, you come to the furthest part of the earth' (13.9).[6] Just as the consultation of the Delphic oracle very obviously

---

5 The title is often understood as 'concerning his [i.e. Dio's] exile', but this would usually need to be made explicit, and the opening sections, which are often determinative for a title, do indeed concern the state of the exile in general. Moreover, this is only one of several works from the first and second centuries on the subject of exile (cf. Verrengia 1999, 86–87, Whitmarsh 2001a), and Dio's description of the reflections to which his banishment led make clear that this will be a work of general significance: 'I gave thought to whether the matter of exile was a difficult misfortune, as the majority think, or whether all such things are another example [of the fact that some bear things easily and others less so] ...' (13.2). We might be tempted to see a movement through the speech from a version of a περὶ φυγῆς to something much more individual, cf. Moles 2005, 114.

6 On this scene cf. the fuller discussion at Hunter 2012, 121–123. Whereas Socrates in the *Phaedo* makes explicit how he understood the dream which told him to 'make *mousike* and work', Dio is less explicit as to the meaning of the instruction 'to do [the thing] on which I am', except that it appears to involve extensive travel. Whether the form of Dio's report of the oracle is intended to raise our doubts both about what question Dio asked and what exact answer he received seems uncertain. The matter over which he had been pondering was not 'exile/banishment/wandering or not' (that was fixed), but rather on whether or not such banishment was an opportunity to be welcomed or a terrible thing. Perhaps then, the emphasis in the god's riddling response is upon πάσῃ προθυμίᾳ, 'with all enthusiasm', and the response amounts, as Dio understands it, to advice to 'be positive' about the 'situation' in which Dio

fashions Dio as a Socrates (one of his most familiar *personae*), and quite specifically the Socrates of Plato's *Apology*,[7] so the god's instructions make Dio think (unsurprisingly) of Odysseus, to whom his thoughts had already turned in the opening general reflections on exile, for Odysseus became a wanderer again even after he had regained his home and family. In the Underworld, Teiresias had famously told Odysseus that, after killing the suitors, he should pick up an oar and travel until he reached men who have no knowledge of the sea or nautical matters and do not use salt in their food (*Od.* 11.119–125). The god, as reported by Dio, is much less specific to Dio, and it is perhaps open to Dio's audience to imagine that Dio did indeed eventually reach the 'last place on earth' (perhaps Olbia, or Scythia, or the land of the Getae? cf. 36.1).[8]

As a result of the god's response, Dio dressed himself in 'lowly clothing' and became a wanderer. Those who saw him called him 'wanderer/tramp' or 'beggar', though some called him 'philosopher'; there is here a tone of ironic amusement, as indeed had already crept into the previous chapter when Dio reasons that if Odysseus was happy to resume his wanderings on the advice of Teiresias, 'a man who was dead', then he could hardly fail to do the same when a god urged him to do so. Dio's development into a philosopher does indeed have its funny side.[9] The literature of the Second Sophistic is full of examples of jokes about the unkempt appearance of philosophers, as well as scorn for those who think that a beard and general lack of concern with appearance is enough to make one a philosopher;[10] Dio here is putting a new spin on familiar material. Epictetus, for example, reports how Euphrates tried to hide the fact that he was a philosopher and this proved 'advantageous' (ὠφέλιμον) to his way of life, for what is important is what one does, not the label one carries (4.8.17–20); so too, Socrates himself is said to have been so little recognized from his appearance as

---

found himself, as that situation offered splendid opportunities. Dio is thus both like and unlike Socrates, because exile is something new for the former, whereas philosophy was not for the latter.

7 Cf., e.g., Döring 1979, 85–86. Particularly close to the *Apology* is Dio's reflection that the god could not lie, cf. Pl. *Apol.* 21b6. On Dio's adoption of various personae in this account cf. Moles 1978, 96–99; Whitmarsh 2001a, 285–294 offers an excellent analysis of the tone and style of these opening chapters.

8 Moles 2005, 125–127 argues that we are to understand, as Dio eventually did, that the god was in fact commanding Dio to preach morality to the Romans, which is what he shows himself doing in the last extant part of *Or.* 13; Uden 2015, 60 adopts this interpretation without discussion. Moles 2005 is much the fullest treatment of *Or.* 13, and should be consulted both for many aspects of the speech on which I do not touch and for a comprehensive bibliography.

9 On the concern with a philosopher's appearance at this period cf., e.g., Castelli 2005.

10 Cf., e.g., Fornaro 2009.

a 'philosopher' that people would ask him to introduce them to philosophers (4.8.22–23, *Encheiridion* 46). In Dio's case, however, the fact that the label 'philosopher' stuck to him proved a blessing, as perhaps the god had predicted: people came to ask him questions about 'what seemed [to him] good or bad', a circumstance which 'compelled' him to give thought to such matters and, indeed, to make public speeches 'about men's duties (τὰ προσήκοντα) and what he thought would benefit them' (13.12–13). The implication, then, is that, without exile and without being 'mistaken' for a philosopher, Dio would not have given thought to these matters. As was a common view for Odysseus also, it was wandering which brought σοφία. It hardly needs saying that we are here in the realm of rhetorical self-fashioning, not of authentic 'history'. Dio has emplotted and narrated his own personal and intellectual history, from Roman-imposed exile to teacher of the Romans. John Moles describes *Oration* 13 as 'a wholly disingenuous account of [Dio's] philosophical career',[11] and Tim Whitmarsh rephrases this a little more kindly as 'a self-constructed aetiology for Dio's reputation as a brave and outspoken purveyor of Greek ideals in the face of Roman authority'.[12] Both views make it much more interesting to the literary historian than it would be, were it a 'true account' of Dio's intellectual development.

When Dio was first exiled, his thoughts naturally turned to the wanderer *par excellence*, Odysseus. Although Dio is soon to be encouraged by a memory of Odysseus to follow the advice of the Delphic oracle, he here makes clear, by placing the most famous 'exile', Odysseus, at the very head of his ruminations on the subject of exile that, in this oration at least, Odysseus is not in fact going to be his (principal) model. Dio wonders whether exile affects people differently, and he compares the situation to that of a mode of divination:[13]

---

[11] Moles 1978, 96; the influence of Moles's early account is very visible in, e.g., Bowie 1985, in which *Or.* 13 is 'dramatic posturing, intended to ... distract the reader's attention from [Dio's] treachery to philosophy in his youth'.
[12] Whitmarsh 2001a, 290.
[13] The final sentence (at least) is somewhat problematic, and this seems to be the only example in Dio of ἐκεῖ μὲν ... ἐνταῦθα δέ functioning as a correlative pair; the former presumably refers to the case of the women who use stones in divination, described in 13.2. As transmitted, ἐλαφρύνοντος describes the action of τὸ δαιμόνιον in both divination and human misfortunes, and although this elliptical mode of expression would not be impossible, it seems likely that a second participle is needed, e.g. ἐλαφρύνοντος <ἢ αὔξοντος> τὸ βάρος; Reiske suggested ἐλαφρύνοντος <ἢ βαρύνοντος> τὸ βάρος. χρωμένου has its familiar, rather vague sense of 'being affected', cf. Verrengia 1999, 128–129: the weight of the burden of exile depends upon the strength and intelligence of the person affected, and δύναμιν καὶ γνώμην lead naturally into the exemplum of Odysseus. κατὰ τὴν τοῦ πράγματος διαφοράν picks up τοῦ πράγματος in 13.2.

ἐκεῖναι γὰρ βῶλόν τινα ἢ λίθον αἴρουσαι σκοποῦσιν ἐν τούτῳ περὶ τοῦ πράγματος οὗ πυνθάνονται. καὶ δὴ ταῖς μὲν αὐτῶν φασι γίγνεσθαι κοῦφον, ταῖς δὲ βαρύν, ὡς μηδὲ κινῆσαι δύνασθαι ῥᾳδίως. μὴ ἄρα καὶ τὸ φεύγειν καὶ τὸ πένεσθαι καὶ γῆρας δὴ καὶ νόσος καὶ πάντα τὰ τοιαῦτα τοῖς μὲν βαρέα φαίνεται καὶ χαλεπά, τοῖς δ' ἐλαφρά τε καὶ εὔκολα· ἐκεῖ μὲν ἴσως κατὰ τὴν τοῦ πράγματος διαφορὰν ἐλαφρύνοντος τοῦ δαιμονίου τὸ βάρος, ἐνταῦθα δὲ οἶμαι πρὸς τὴν τοῦ χρωμένου δύναμιν καὶ γνώμην.

Dio 13.3

These women [engaged in divination] pick up a clod of earth or a stone and seek in it an answer to the matter about which they are enquiring. People say that some of them find what they pick up light, and others so heavy that it cannot easily be moved. Might not then [I thought] exile and poverty and old age and illness and all such things appear to some heavy and grievous, and to others light and easy? In one case perhaps [i.e. divination] the divinity lightens the weight in accordance with the importance of the matter, but in the case of exile it depends upon the strength and intelligence of the person affected.

Dio is here presenting, or recalling, himself in a pre-philosophic state, one in which he does not yet have any fixed, 'philosophical' view of exile, a matter which in fact he turns over to the Delphic god. The language in which Dio introduces his ruminations evokes Stoic discussions of 'indifferents', by linking 'exile' to other alleged misfortunes such as poverty, old age and illness;[14] Dio's evocation of Stoic thought, however, entirely avoids 'technical' language, while nevertheless clearly gesturing towards a specific moral theme. The ruminations prompted by Dio's exile are thus themselves the first of what turns out to be a series of aetiologies or origins for his coming to philosophy; unexpected events in our lives can lead to reflection which sets us on the path to philosophy. In Dio's case, the form in which that reflection was set already foreshadowed the turn his philosophy was ultimately to take: essentially, Dio was a Stoic before he was one.

When Dio comes to report the kinds of things he used to say when called upon to speak on the good for man, he begins with a general denunciation of the follies of mankind (including himself) who 'are in confusion (κυκώμενοι) and swept around in the same place and for virtually the same objects, money and reputation and certain bodily pleasures',[15] but entirely neglect how to rid themselves of ignorance and disturbance (ταραχή) and thus live a more reasonable and better life. Dio says that when he ran out of things to say (ὑπ' ἀπορίας) he would turn to 'an ancient speech, delivered by a certain Socrates':[16]

---

14 On this familiar aspect of Stoic ethics see Long/Sedley 1987, I 354–359.
15 There is a very similar passage at Arrian, *Discourses of Epictetus* 4.8.27, if κυκωμένων (Schweighaeuser, Reiske) is there accepted for the transmitted κοιμωμένων.
16 For other aspects of this passage cf. Hunter 2012, 19.

ταῦτα καὶ τὰ τοιαῦτα τούς τε ἄλλους ἅπαντας καὶ μάλιστα καὶ πρῶτον ἐμαυτὸν καταμεμφόμενος ἐνίοτε ὑπὸ ἀπορίας ἀνῆγον[17] ἐπί τινα λόγον ἀρχαῖον, λεγόμενον ὑπό τινος Σωκράτους, ὃν οὐδέποτε ἐκεῖνος ἐπαύσατο λέγων, πανταχοῦ τε καὶ πρὸς ἅπαντας βοῶν καὶ διατεινόμενος ἐν ταῖς παλαίστραις καὶ ἐν τῷ Λυκείῳ καὶ ἐπὶ τῶν δικαστηρίων[18] καὶ κατ' ἀγοράν, ὥσπερ ἀπὸ μηχανῆς θεός, ὥς ἔφη τις. οὐ μέντοι προσεποιούμην ἐμὸν εἶναι τὸν λόγον, ἀλλ' οὗπερ ἦν, καὶ ἠξίουν, ἂν ἄρα μὴ δύνωμαι ἀπομνημονεῦσαι ἀκριβῶς ἁπάντων τῶν ῥημάτων μηδὲ ὅλης τῆς διανοίας, ἀλλὰ πλέον ἢ ἔλαττον εἴπω τι, συγγνώμην ἔχειν, μηδὲ ὅτι ταῦτα λέγω ἃ τυγχάνει πολλοῖς ἔτεσι πρότερον εἰρημένα, διὰ τοῦτο ἧττον προσέχειν τὸν νοῦν. ἴσως γὰρ ἄν, ἔφην, οὕτως μάλιστα ὠφεληθείητε. οὐ γὰρ δή γε εἰκός ἐστι τοὺς παλαιοὺς λόγους ὥσπερ φάρμακα διαπνεύσαντας ἀπολωλεκέναι τὴν δύναμιν.

Dio 13.14–15

While I was making these and similar reproaches of everyone else but especially and first of all of myself, I sometimes retreated, out of incapacity, to an ancient speech which used to be delivered by a certain Socrates; he never stopped making it, but would shout and declaim[19] it everywhere and to everyone, in the wrestling-schools and in the Lyceum and the law-courts and in the agora, like a god on the machine, as someone said. I did not pretend that the speech was mine, but identified the source, and I asked them, if I was unable to remember all the phrases in detail or the thought in its entirety, and should say too much or too little, to pardon me and not to pay less attention because I was saying things which had been said many years before.[20] 'Perhaps', I used to say, 'you will in fact in this way derive the greatest benefit. For it is not likely that the words of antiquity have evaporated like potions and lost their power.'

'A certain Socrates' strikes a remarkable note, particularly if the speech was indeed addressed to Athenians, for whom Socrates' fate was one event of their

---

17 On this reading cf. Verrengia 1999, 145–146.
18 Cobet's ἐργαστηρίων (Cobet 1878, 63–64) for the transmitted δικαστηρίων has been universally adopted, but caution at least is required. ἐργαστήριον occurs nowhere in Plato or Xen. Mem., and neither writer makes Socrates frequent 'workshops', although, as Cobet notes, later writers did; Cobet also points to Isocrates, Areop. 15, where ἐργαστηρίων of the best manuscript has been corrupted to δικαστηρίων. As far as we know, neither the real nor the literary Socrates regularly 'declaimed' in law courts, but these are certainly a place where Athenians gathered; if the transmitted text is correct, Dio may have been thinking not just of the Apology, which is certainly much in his mind here, as elsewhere in Or. 13 (cf. 17c8–9 ἐν ἀγορᾷ ἐπὶ τῶν τραπεζῶν, with δικαστήριον immediately below), but also of the opening of the Euthyphro where the Lykeion and the court at the 'King's Stoa' are mentioned together.
19 The sense of διατεινόμενος may be disputed; Slings 1999, 94 regards it as 'a misunderstanding' of the disputed ὑμνοῖς at Clitophon 407a8, but that does not strike me as very probable, despite the fact that ἐπιτιμῶν from the same passage of the Clitophon seems to be picked up at 13.16.
20 Dio's request for indulgence (συγγνώμη) and for his audience's attention (προσέχειν τὸν νοῦν) is very likely another reflection of Plato's Apology, cf. 17d4–18a5, also as part of the preface to the speech proper.

classical past over which a veil might be discreetly drawn.²¹ The tone is (again) very difficult to catch. Is the suggestion that, at the time he is allegedly recalling, Dio was such a philosophical beginner that he did not even know who Socrates was?²² Perhaps, but we may also wonder whether the indefinite pronoun does not (also) alert us to the fact that the Socrates we are about to meet is not necessarily the one with whom we are most familiar.²³ In Plato's *Apology*, Socrates tells the jurors that in Aristophanes' *Clouds* they all saw 'a certain Socrates' talking and behaving in ways that they know he does not (19c3); Socrates there distances himself from a representation which he claims has nothing to do with him. If, as seems not improbable, Dio here has this Platonic passage in mind, then he will be borrowing Socrates' technique to stress that he himself has nothing to do with the speech he borrowed and reportedly delivered. Be that as it may, it is standardly (and rightly) pointed out that the description of Socrates' persistence in chapter 14 looks to the philosopher's declaration in Plato's *Apology* in response to the notion that the Athenians might set him free on condition that he abandons philosophy:

> Gentlemen of Athens, I am grateful and very fond of you, but I will obey the god rather than you, and as long as I breathe and have the strength, I shall never cease philosophising and exhorting you and remonstrating with each of you whom I happen to come across. I will make my usual speech: 'Good sir, you belong to Athens, the city which is the greatest in, and enjoys the greatest reputation for, wisdom and strength; are you not ashamed to concern yourself with getting as much money as possible, and reputation and honour, while having no concern nor care for intelligence and truth and making your soul as fine as it can be? If one of you disputes this and says that he is concerned, I shall not let him go nor shall I go away, but I shall question and examine and test him, and if he does not seem to me to possess virtue, but claims to do so, I shall reprove him because he sets the smallest store on the things of greatest value, and a higher value on what is of little value.'
> Plato, *Apology* 29d2–30a2

If Dio's Athenian hearers also heard the allusion, then the memory should (once again) have been painful for them. What is certain is that this passage and its

---

21 Trapp 2013, 40 n. 33 suspects that the title 'In Athens' is 'a misapprehension, based on the depiction of Socrates within the speech'; Moles 2005, however, argues strongly for delivery in Athens. At the opening of *Oration* 3, which has some notable similarities with *Or.* 13 (cf. further below), Dio addresses Trajan and introduces Socrates 'whom you know by repute lived many years ago'; once again the tone is hard to catch.
22 Cf., e.g., Döring 1979, 90, Whitmarsh 2001b, 163. Emendation to remove the puzzle has also been attempted: Weil deleted Σωκράτους and Verrengia tentatively suggests τοῦ Σωκράτους.
23 This is, of course, true of the 'Socrates' conjured up by Clitophon in the *Clitophon*, which is soon to assume considerable importance.

continuation in Plato's *Apology* became central to the idea of Socrates as a protreptic voice, and it is that voice which is to prove crucial for the second half of Dio 13. The description of Socrates 'shouting and declaiming' all over the public spaces of Athens certainly does not sound like 'our' Socrates; even less so does the claim which follows almost immediately that 'whenever [Socrates] saw a number of people gathered in the same place, he would reprove and upbraid them, shouting out very boldly and without dissimulation' (13.16).[24] It may be that Dio's Socrates is deliberately presented here as more like a 'cynic preacher' than the Platonic portrait, in part as a kind of 'updating' of the model, who now begins to resemble some of its more recent descendants, including of course Dio himself.[25] The other obvious explanation is that Dio has here elaborated upon Clitophon's description of Socrates, which introduces the speech from which Dio is (apparently) about to quote; although the *Clitophon* is normally now regarded as not an authentic dialogue of Plato, there is no evidence that it was ever so regarded in antiquity:

ἐγὼ γάρ, ὦ Σώκρατες, σοὶ συγγιγνόμενος πολλάκις ἐξεπληττόμην ἀκούων, καί μοι ἐδόκεις παρὰ τοὺς ἄλλους ἀνθρώπους κάλλιστα λέγειν, ὁπότε ἐπιτιμῶν τοῖς ἀνθρώποις ὥσπερ ἐπὶ μηχανῆς τραγικῆς θεὸς +ὕμνοις+ λέγων 'Ποῖ φέρεσθε, ὤνθρωποι; κτλ.'

[Plato], *Clitophon* 407a5–b1

Socrates, I have often been amazed when I listen to you, and I think that you speak better than anyone else, when you reprove men, like a god on the tragic machine, with your speech: 'Where are you heading, gentleman?...'

Dio had used the phrase 'like a god on the machine' to describe Socrates' speechifying in chap. 14 (quoted above) and there acknowledged it as a quotation (ὡς ἔφη τις); given that in both the *Clitophon* and Dio 13.14 the phrase is used in the same unexpected sense,[26] it is very hard to believe that Dio has here any other source than the *Clitophon* in mind.[27]

---

24 Cf. Slings 1999, 45–46. Bryan 2012, 17 sees some analogy in Xenophon's representation of Socratic speeches at *Mem.* 1.5.1 and 1.7.1, and Dio's Socrates does indeed have a strong Xenophontic flavor (cf. further below), but the two passages of the *Memorabilia* are in both substance and tone quite unlike the situation described in Dio 13.
25 This is the view of, e.g., Moles 2005.
26 Cf. Slings 1999, 89 n. 166, 95; the expected sense would be a reference to a sudden 'miraculous' solution of a problem. I cannot agree with Slings that, in the *Clitophon*, the phrase is 'a highly functional element of ridicule', as I do not share his apparent view that Clitophon's introductory speech at 407a is ironic or sarcastic. Fornaro 2009, 173 associates the phrase in *Or.* 13 with the 'theatricality' of contemporary philosophy.
27 Dio in fact uses parenthetical ὡς ἔφη τις without further specification in four other places (1.13, 5.4, 12.38, 20.3), and with the apparent exception of 20.3 the reference is always to Plato.

In chapter 14 Dio says that he had recourse to Socrates' 'ancient *logos*'; ὑπὸ ἀπορίας, which in context must imply 'when I could not think of anything else to say [on the subject of human folly]'. The phrase thus suggests rhetorical *copia* (and its lack), rather than any philosophical ἀπορία, though that familiar philosophical expression perhaps allows us to sense some of the cultural and intellectual history written into this speech; Dio's ἀπορία is not that puzzlement about himself which set Socrates on the path to philosophy,[28] but rather the need to have something to say. The difference from, rather than similarity to, Socrates is marked in another way also. In Plato's *Apology*, which, as we have seen, is very much in Dio's mind here, Socrates states that it was not ἀπορία λόγων which led to his condemnation:

> Perhaps, gentlemen of Athens, you think that I have been convicted because of a shortage of such words (ἀπορίᾳ λόγων ... τοιούτων) as would have persuaded you, if I had thought that I should do and say anything in order to be acquitted. Far from it. I have been convicted through a shortage, not however of words, but of boldness and shamelessness and not wanting to say to you the kinds of things which you would have found most pleasant to hear...
>
> Plato, *Apology* 38d2–8

What Socrates does have, and what Dio — left to his own resources (πόροι) — conspicuously lacks, at least in what remains of Or. 13, are philosophical *logoi* exhorting men to care of their souls.[29] Why Dio presents himself in this apparently unflattering way is a question to which I shall return.[30]

When Dio was first taken for a philosopher and asked to speak on human morality, his first recourse, as we have seen, was to commonplaces on the folly of the pursuit of wealth, reputation and pleasure, at the expense of efforts to eliminate ignorance and confusion which hold out the prospect of a truly better life (13.13). We are all swept along in the daily whirlpool and make no effort to drag ourselves out. Both the sweeping generalisations about 'all men' and the nature of the commonplaces themselves recall nothing so much as the opening of Horace's first satire:

---

28 Cf. Aristotle fr. 709 Gigon: the starting-point for Socrates' ἀπορία καὶ ζήτησις was the Delphic maxim 'Know yourself'.
29 At 71.1 Dio says that some people claim that the philosopher should never 'run short of such words (ἀπορεῖν λόγους) as will delight those he is with'.
30 Cf. below pp. 675–680.

> qui fit, Maecenas, ut nemo, quam sibi sortem
> seu ratio dederit seu fors obiecerit, illa
> contentus uiuat, laudet diuersa sequentes?
>
> Horace, *Satires* 1.1.1–3

> How does it come about, Maecenas, that no one lives content with the lot that reason has given him or chance put in his way, but rather praises those whose pursuits are different?

The parallel is of course not exact: Horace moves from universal human discontent with one's lot to an attack on avarice, whereas Dio's target is the folly of human pursuits in general, but the ethical arena of both seems very close, though Horace will go on to deny any alignment with a specifically Stoic 'diatribe'.[31] Moreover, when Dio turns immediately afterwards to quoting a speech of 'Socrates', it is, as in Horace, the pursuit of money which is foregrounded (13.16 ~ [Plato], *Clitophon* 407b2–5). So too, both Horace and Dio virtually admit the banality of their complaints, cf. v. 13 *cetera de genere hoc — adeo sunt multa* and Dio's description of his observations as ταῦτα καὶ τὰ τοιαῦτα (13.14). Dio expressly includes himself among the objects of his attack (13.14), whereas Horace leaves us to understand, at least initially, that 'no one' means 'no one, except Maecenas and Horace', thus opening the door to some very awkward questions about his own position.[32] What is most important, however, in the current context is that *Satires* 1.1 does not merely establish the style of the *Satires*, but also presents the poet's formation as a philosopher. The opening question to Maecenas is, as it were, also the question which led Horace to the kind of reflections that eventually found their way into the *Satires*. In Emily Gowers' words, 'How did Horace come to be the product of his ethical education, not a paragon but still awaiting construction, trailing an inchoate body of inherited lore from which to construct the means to speak to a great man?'.[33] Both the opening poem of Horace's *Satires* and Dio 13 present 'first philosophy' as a recourse to familiar commonplaces, the borrowing of others' voices, if you will, until a distinctive voice is found. When that point is actually reached in Horace's *Satires* is a question which may be left to others to pursue, but the process in Dio 13 at least is represented as a rather slow one; the loss of what may have been a substantial part of *Oration* 13 precludes us from knowing whether Dio ever repre-

---

31 Cf. Gowers 2012, 84–85 on Crispinus.
32 Cf. in general Gowers 2012, 58–62, citing earlier bibliography. Gowers 2012, 63 notes that *nemo* is modified somewhat by *raro* in v. 117; cf. Dio's initial πάντες ἄφρονες, ὡς ἔπος εἰπεῖν.
33 Gowers 2012, 59. It is striking that Gowers 2012, 58 describes *Sat.* 1.1 as 'a poem in which the speaker launches himself as an accidental philosopher', a description which would perfectly fit the Dio of *Or.* 13.

sented himself (in this oration) as having found such a voice. It is tempting, however, to think that the 'Kingship Orations' are in part the dramatization of that mature voice.

The borrowing of voices in Dio 13 moves to a different level with the introduction of the speech 'of a certain Socrates'. We may perhaps recall the Platonic Alcibiades' description of the effect of Socrates' words, 'when someone hears [Socrates] or someone else speaking [Socrates'] words, even if the speaker is a very poor one' (Plato, Symp. 215d3–4); what Alcibiades is referring to (Plato himself?) is something of a puzzle,[34] but Dio certainly gives us an example of the situation which Alcibiades had evoked, and Dio's inability faithfully to reproduce Socrates' words marks him, potentially at least, as — in the words of the Platonic Alcibiades — πάνυ φαῦλος, 'a very poor speaker'. As we have seen, the Clitophon has (all but certainly) already been cited in 13.14 (above pp. 667–668),[35] and the opening of Dio's borrowed speech (13.16 and the beginning of 13.17) offers a close quotation/paraphrase of the beginning of a protreptic speech which, in the Clitophon, the eponymous character says that he often heard from Socrates.[36] The two speeches then part company, though both continue to deal with the inadequacy of 'classical' education to produce good and just men and well managed cities; Dio elaborates the topic at much greater length than does [Plato], and he includes Socrates' alleged response to a defence based on the fact that it was that very classical education which allowed

---

34 Dio 13 reminds us that the Clitophon offers another example of 'someone else speaking Socrates' words', and it may be that, in the Symposium, Plato is indeed alluding to a wider tradition of Socratic literature. The case for seeing an evocation of the Symposium in Dio 13 is, I think, a little strengthened by the fact that Alcibiades says that everyone who hears Socrates or someone speaking his words ἐκπεπληγμένοι ἐσμὲν καὶ κατεχόμεσθα (215d5), and Clitophon notes a similar effect of Socrates' protreptic, ἐξεπληττόμην (407a6); the language is again commonplace, but the author of the Clitophon may himself be remembering the Symposium, and Dio has, then, recognized the relationship between the passages. Slings 1999, 271, in accordance with his general reading of the speech, regards the tone of the verb in the Clitophon as 'ironical', but I cannot agree.
35 It may be worth suggesting that, although the language is entirely ordinary, the opening of 13.13, οὐδεὶς οὐδὲν ὧν ἔδει πράττειν, anticipates 13.16 and is thus also influenced by the opening of the protreptic speech of the Clitophon (407b2–3).
36 The reference to the pursuit of money at the opening of the 'Socratic' speech is in fact verbally closer to Pl. Apol. 29d8–9 than to Clitophon 407b2–3. Dio may just be paraphrasing from memory, perhaps under the (unconscious) influence of the Apology which has just been at the forefront of his mind, or he may be running the two works together, perhaps not just because of their similarity, but to make a point about their connection. On the relationship between the Apology and the Clitophon more generally cf. Slings 1999, 103–105.

the Athenians twice to defeat the Persians (13.23-6).³⁷ After the conclusion of Socrates' speech, Dio reiterates that the whole was indeed Socrates' and that this is virtually what Dio himself repeated to his questioners, even though it was 'ancient/old-fashioned' (ἀρχαῖα).

The pattern whereby textual imitation, including particularly marked forms such as parody, begins with close verbal tracking of the model and then, having established the relationship, goes its own way is a familiar one, but modern scholarship has tended to fall into two camps in considering the origin of the first Socratic speech in Dio 13. Some have regarded it as an elaborate αὔξησις of the protreptic speech of the *Clitophon*; after an almost literal repetition of the opening section, Dio then builds his own variations on the themes of the original.³⁸ If some version of this view is correct, the speech itself would mimic one view of the education of a philosopher: from the simple learning and then repetition of the great texts of the past, one moves slowly towards finding a distinctive voice. This pattern still holds good, however, though with a rather different structure, if the whole speech is indeed ἀρχαῖον, that is a Socratic text from the classical period which — but for the opening of the *Clitophon* — has not reached us through any other route of transmission, and this indeed has now become the majority view, which takes its principal impetus from von Arnim's discussion.³⁹ An influential version of this view has it that the speech cited in Dio 13 is in fact by Antisthenes, and probably from one of his protreptic Socratic works;⁴⁰

---

37 Slings 1999, 96 appears to take Socrates' words at 13.24 about the Persians regarding nudity and spitting in public (cf. Xen. *Cyr.* 1.2.16) as 'the most shameful things' (αἴσχιστον) as serious praise. Rather, Socrates sarcastically cites these taboos as signs of how little the Persians actually knew about what really matters.

38 Cf. esp. Wegehaupt 1896, 56–64; further bibliography in Döring 1979, 86 n. 20, Moles 2005, 115. Uden 2015, 61–62 discusses Dio 13 as 'a copy of a copy', as the Socratic speech of the *Clitophon* was already a (poor) imitation of the real thing. Jones 1978, 47 (and cf. 195 n. 25) observes that the speech 'seems evidently made up by Dio', and he compares the speeches which Dio puts in the mouth of Diogenes; none of those speeches has, however, the insistent 'authenticity apparatus' of *Or.* 13, though cf. further below on *Or.* 3. Jones also raises the possibility that such pretence was appropriate to exile when it was 'unwise to speak too freely'. Cf. further below p. 679 on Dio's 'figured speech'.

39 Cf. von Arnim 1898, 256–260.

40 Giannantoni 1990, 4.350–353 offers a useful survey of the debate and the bibliography. Giannantoni 1990 in fact prints the relevant part of Dio 13 among the fragments of Antisthenes (2.222–225). Slings 1999, 94–96 rejects the suggestion that the speech comes from Antisthenes, largely on the grounds that verbal echoes of the *Clitophon* are not restricted to the speech of Socrates. It must, however, be admitted that the other suggested echoes are not very strong, with the exception of the 'god on the machine' (above p. 667). The apparently clear debt of the Clitophon to Plato's *Apology* (n. 36 above) may be thought to favour a 'Platonic', rather than an

there seems no very good reason to doubt that Antisthenes was an important model in many of Dio's works more generally. On this view, the protreptic speech of the *Clitophon* itself echoes the same work of Antisthenes. If this view, or something like it, is correct, then Dio has incorporated wholesale part of a protreptic speech placed by Antisthenes in Socrates' mouth, and has done so perhaps under the influence of the pseudo-Platonic *Clitophon*, whose author is assumed to have operated in a rather similar way. Precedent for such a technique was readily at hand in the Lysianic speech of the *Phaedrus* (and perhaps elsewhere also in the Platonic corpus).[41] An even more potent classical model for Dio would have been Prodicus' famous protreptic *epideixis* on the education of Heracles which the Xenophontic Socrates recites to Aristippus at *Mem.* 2.1.21–33. Socrates there makes plain that this is a speech which Prodicus has delivered many times and that Socrates' recall of it is not to be taken to be a verbatim quotation (cf. ὡδέ πως λέγω, ὅσα ἐγὼ μέμνημαι (2.1.21), οὕτω πως διώκει Πρόδικος τὴν ὑπ' Ἀρετῆς Ἡρακλέους παίδευσιν (2.1.34), particularly as Prodicus 'elaborated the thoughts in even grander phrases' (2.1.34).[42] Both the subject matter (παίδευσις, 2.1.34) and the importance of Xenophon as a model for Dio (cf. esp. 18.14–17) make the idea of influence from this authorizing model attractive; in the rhetorical culture of the Second Sophistic, such authorizing influence does not require specific verbal allusions.

Nevertheless, doubts must remain as to whether the 'Socratic' speech of *Or.* 13 is really to be traced back in its entirety to Antisthenes. Comparison with the *Third Kingship Oration* may be instructive here. That speech opens with a story about Socrates which looks like a version of the exchange between Socrates and Polus at Plato, *Gorgias* 470d–e concerning the happiness of the Great King of Persia; if so, Dio's paraphrase is anything but exact, though the story is recognizably the same one.[43] After the opening anecdote, Dio then addresses Trajan in his own voice on the subject of flattery; the final part of this section (26–28) is a further anecdote about Socrates, this time in conversation with Hippias. The source of this second anecdote is very clearly Xen. *Mem.* 4.4.5–6, which is close-

---

Antisthenic, origin for Socrates' speech in the *Clitophon*, but more complicated scenarios may also be devised.
41 Cf. further below. Protagoras' great speech in the *Protagoras* is perhaps another example, or one that could easily be taken to be such.
42 How closely Xenophon does in fact stick to the Prodican original is, of course, a matter of considerable scholarly debate, cf. Mayhew 2011, 203–204.
43 In Plato, the clear implication is, as is made explicit in Dio, that Socrates has never met the King, but Socrates' concern there is with how the King 'stands with regard to education and justice', and there is no explicit reference to the King's διάνοια or his ψυχή.

ly followed through chap. 26 and the first part of 27, but then Socrates' reference to the behaviour of liars brings the anecdote to a different conclusion and Dio returns to his own case. In Xenophon, the conversation continues its own way well beyond the point at which Dio stopped. In ch. 29 Dio resumes his discussion with the observation that he will 'attempt to say what Socrates thought about these matters', and he then apparently takes us back to the beginning of the speech: 'After his answer about happiness, the person who had put that question enquired of Socrates as follows ...'. What follows (30–41) has some loose connection with the discussion of the *Gorgias*, but there is no obvious direct indebtedness as Socrates and his interlocutor pursue questions of power and virtue; in chap. 42 Dio concludes by noting that 'this was the sort of thing Socrates was accustomed to say (εἰώθει λέγειν), as he persistently incited men to virtue in seeking to make better both rulers and private individuals'. As in *Or.* 13, Dio may in *Or.* 3 be thinking of Socrates in Plato's *Apology*; in *Apol.* 29d (cf. above) Socrates declares that he will never stop saying at every opportunity 'the things I always say' (λέγων οἷάπερ εἴωθα). Be that as it may, what *Or.* 3 shows is how Dio can slide from evocation of a specific classical text into what is claimed to be habitual 'Socratic' material; this experimentation with a Socratic and a 'post-Socratic' voice seems strikingly similar to one view of what is happening in *Or.* 13. The similarity may be thought to be strengthened by the fact that, for the rest of *Or.* 3, Dio proceeds to address Trajan again in his own voice.

One further similarity of Dio 13 to the *Clitophon* deserves brief attention, though it hardly carries decisive force. In Dio, Socrates' answer to the objection raised in chapter 23 that the Athenian victories over the Persians were gained by men educated in the traditional way begins in reported speech (ἔλεγεν ὅτι κτλ.), but soon slips again into direct speech, as is indeed common with reports introduced by ὅτι. Dio then summarises in chapter 26, 'In this way then he used to make clear that they were not receiving any useful education', before moving in chapter 27 to more of Socrates' arguments, now reported in the clearly indirect form of the accusative and infinitive, and then in chapter 28 to a further summary of Socrates' overall argument and the reasons for it. One effect of this syntactic variety and the use of the imperfect tense in Dio 13 is to increase the sense that these were Socrates' habitual arguments, repeated at every opportunity in Athens, and as such Dio's disclaimer of verbatim reportage (13.15) is both strengthened and justified; as is well known, the use of indirect, or 'transposed', speech emphasises the mediating role of a reporter. In the *Clitophon*, Clitophon's direct report of Socrates' habitual speech ends at 407e2, and is then followed (after an expression of Clitophon's admiration) by further citation of Socratic arguments, but now in the indirect form of the accusative and infinitive.⁴⁴ Like both Dio and Horace (cf. above p. 669), Clitophon then makes clear that the arguments which he has just cited are, as it were, *exempli gratia* — there were many similar such things that he could have cited (τούτοις δὴ τοῖς λόγοις καὶ ἑτέροις τοιούτοις παμπόλλοις καὶ παγκάλως λεγομένοις κτλ., 408b5–7).

Both [Plato] and Dio 13, then, move from direct to indirect speech to capture something of the frequency of Socrates' protreptic speeches and the wealth of argument which he brought to bear, as he sought to turn his hearers to a proper philosophical care of themselves. If indeed Dio wants us to remember the *Clitophon* here, there is of course at least one obvious question which follows. The *Clitophon* subsequently turns into an attack on Socrates, because, so Clitophon alleges, his splendid protreptic speeches lead nowhere: Socrates makes fine speeches about justice, but simply does not give people any idea what justice is, thus in fact doing a disservice to those who have been won over by the protreptic speeches (410e7–8, the close of the dialogue). If we were certain of the origin of the Socratic speeches in Dio 13, and also of how the speech actually ended, then the intertextual question of how we use or erase the memory of the *Clitophon* while reading Dio 13 would become very urgent indeed.⁴⁵ As it is, we must suspend judgement, while, however, noting that any use of the *Clitophon* in later Socratic texts will raise similar issues of voicing and possible irony.

One further aspect of Dio 13 which may be relevant to the question of the origin of the included 'Socratic' speech is the fact that Dio's Socrates is in part a very Xenophontic Socrates. Although protreptic is apparently at the heart of Plato, *Apology* 29d cited above,⁴⁶ and we have seen a number of 'fragments' of the *Apology* littered through the oration, protreptic in its simplest forms is particularly a characteristic of the Xenophontic character. The close of the *Memorabilia* sums up Socrates' mission as 'testing others, demonstrating error to those who went wrong and exhorting (προτρέψασθαι) them to virtue and excellence (καλοκἀγαθία)' (4.8.11), and the theme of the pursuit of καλοκἀγαθία is

---

44 For other aspects of the use of indirect speech in the *Clitophon* cf. Bryan 2012, 9–10.
45 Moles 2005, 119 explains the difficulty away: 'the Socrates parodied in the *Cleitophon* was very like the Socrates championed by the Cynics and by Antisthenes'.
46 In 13.28 Dio seems to say that Socrates did not usually exhort people explicitly 'to do philosophy' (φιλοσοφεῖν), but rather to seek to be 'good men' (cf. further below). Slings 1999, 96 observes that both verb and noun are absent from the *Clitophon*, but it is worth noting that the terms become rather insistent in the relevant passage of the *Apology* (cf. 28e5, 29c9, d5), all with reference to Socrates' own life. It may well be true that the Platonic and Xenophontic Socrates does not constantly urge people 'to be philosophers', but rather to be concerned with the state of their souls etc.; nevertheless, the nest of occurrences of the terms in the *Apology* was perhaps the trigger for Dio's observation in ch. 28.

insistent through both the *Memorabilia* and the *Symposium*. Not only does Xenophon close the *Memorabilia* with this theme, but his opening summary of the 'human things' (τὰ ἀνθρώπινα) which concerned Socrates concludes that they were 'things, knowledge of which he thought made men excellent (καλοὺς κἀγαθούς), whereas those ignorant of them might justly be called slavish' (1.1.16). Dio's Socrates might well be reworking this sentence when, in his denunciation of contemporary education, he declares (in the final utterance which is quoted directly) that the uneducated (ἀμαθεῖς) are 'not those who do not know how to weave or make shoes, nor those who do not know how to dance, but those who are ignorant of the things knowledge of which makes a man excellent (καλὸν καὶ ἀγαθόν)' (13.27). For Dio's Socrates, in fact, τὸ φιλοσοφεῖν is nothing other than the striving to be καλὸς καὶ ἀγαθός (13.28), and here we feel the Xenophontic heritage very strongly.[47] Xenophon's Socrates, with his commitment to familiar communal values and the shared political life of the city, is after all a much better model for Dio (and others like him) than is the much more 'difficult' and idiosyncratic Platonic character.

Whatever the history of the first 'Socratic' speech in *Or.* 13, we must still ask why Dio represents himself as, not merely borrowing Socrates' words, but making it plain to his audiences that this is what he is doing (13.14–15). John Moles sees here a 'defensive assertion' in the face of (true) accusations of 'playing a Socratic role without acknowledging that he was doing so',[48] and there may of course be some truth in such a historicising view; this does not, however, seem an entirely adequate explanation for Dio's very striking mimetic technique. What Dio's apparent 'transparency' dramatizes in fact is that, when speaking εἰς τὸ κοινόν (13.12), he does not pretend to be able to improvise from his own rhetorical resources, unlike so many sophists of his age.[49] Philostratus famously regards improvisation as a hallmark, perhaps indeed *the* hallmark, of the oratory of the 'Second Sophistic', and we might well think that the culture of improvisational performance is, *inter alia*, a reaction to the existence of a fixed body of 'classical' texts which not only provide material for *mimesis*, but also act to inhibit particular forms of innovation. The matter, including its important foreshadowing in Phaedrus' desire 'to practise performing' (μελετᾶν) with a speech

---

47 Slings 1999, 96 sees rather Stoic influence in the notion that philosophy is living the life of a καλὸς καὶ ἀγαθός; this seems to me unnecessary.
48 Moles 1978, 98.
49 Dio has, also of course self-servingly, some harsh things to say about improvisational rhetoric in 33.4–5.

of Lysias at the opening of Plato's *Phaedrus*,[50] requires discussion at much greater length, but in *Or.* 13 Dio represents himself as explicitly removing his public performances from this culture of improvisation. No self-respecting 'sophist' would admit to ἀπορία λόγων, as Dio does. The reason may be that Dio is here establishing himself as something quite other, namely a φιλόσοφος, and his attempt to do so opens for us vistas of both rhetorical and philosophical history. As in the 'Euboikos' Dio both reworks Homer but also seeks in some ways to replace Homer with his own brand of moralizing oration and/or essay,[51] so in *Oration* 13 Dio establishes a model of public, philosophical performance which is quite different from that which there is good reason to believe was a dominant model of his time, and of which, of course, Dio himself was one of the great masters.

Dio 13 thus opens a window into a wider world of public performance which is central to any consideration of the Greek literary and cultural history of the Roman empire. The history of the great 'performers' of the Second Sophistic has often been written, but we must always remember how this culture itself was replaying debates of the classical period. Our best witness here is the early fourth century work of Alcidamas '*On those who write written speeches* or *On the sophists*' which argues, with particular reference to the law courts, for the primacy of improvised speeches over the reading out or memorization of pre-prepared speeches. For Alcidamas the real skill lies in the ability to improvise (Alcidamas, *On those who write written speeches* 1.3–4):

> First, then, one would look down on writing because [the skill] is easy to acquire, simple, and accessible to any kind of nature. As for successful improvisational speaking on any subject and the ability swiftly to deploy a rich armoury (εὐπορία) of thoughts and words and accurately to follow the critical moment (καιρός) in events and the desires of one's fellow-men and to make the appropriate speech, this is not a matter for every nature or each and every form of education. To write over a long period of time, to make corrections at leisure, to gather the writings of past sophists and to collect their thoughts from many sources into the one place, to imitate what was well and successfully said, to make some corrections on the advice of the unskilled (ἰδιῶται), and to revise and rewrite other things after many times reflecting upon them oneself, this is easy even for those who have not been educated.

This εὐπορία is precisely what failed Dio in his early days as a philosopher and for what the great figures who fill the pages of Philostratus are admired; ἀπορία is, according to Alcidamas, the state of those who spend their time writing speeches and are then suddenly called upon to improvise (cf. 8, 15, 21). For Al-

---

50 Cf. Hunter 2012, 18–19.
51 Cf. above p. 660.

cidamas, writing speeches involves lengthy consideration of the 'writings of past sophists', and in a later passage he elaborates upon this in connection with those who claim to be philosophers:

> It is a terrible thing if a man who lays claim to philosophy and undertakes to educate others can make a display of his wisdom if he has a tablet or a book, but if he is without them, is no better than the uneducated, and can produce a speech if he is given time, but when confronted with immediate speaking on a subject set before him falls more silent than ordinary people, and professes skill in words (λόγοι), but obviously has within him no capacity at all for speaking. Practising writing produces the greatest helplessness (ἀπορία) in speaking.
>
> Alcidamas, *On those who write written speeches* 1.15

Here too the theme of 'reliance upon the book' resonates deeply in the literary (and often satirical) presentation of philosophers in the Second Sophistic,[52] but we may also remember Dio falling back at need on the words of Socrates, no doubt preserved in a book, when questioned about serious matters. Despite the differences in situation, Dio presents himself almost as an example of Alcidamas' 'worse case', not of course to reveal himself as a confused incompetent, but rather because he wants to put forward a very different intellectual model. There is much more to be said about the idea of improvisation, and the persistent tension through Greek culture over centuries between the 'scripted' and the 'unscripted', but suffice it for the present to note that Dio allows us to see rather more clearly why Philostratus chose to shape his image of the 'Second Sophistic' in the way that he did.

After rehearsing his Socratic arguments, Dio moves to the situation in which he found himself in Rome (presumably, then, after his exile).[53] Very conscious that his habitual 'Socratic' speech is ἀρχαῖον and that he may be laughed at for his ἀρχαιότης and ἀμαθία (13.29), he reports the arguments he went over with himself: perhaps the Romans will not in fact laugh, or if they do he will tell them that he is using the words of the wisest of all the Greeks,[54] and he then proceeds to report, first in indirect (13.31–33) and then direct speech (13.34–36), what he used to say at Rome. He tells us that these were public addresses to great crowds, because at Rome it was not possible to meet people 'in twos and threes in wrestling-schools and public walks'; here there seems to be, not just

---

52 One thinks particularly of the opening of Lucian's *Hermotimus*, cf. Hunter 2012, 1–4.
53 Cf. Verrengia 1999, 78–85, Moles 2005, 124–125.
54 Kaibel's σοφώτατον for the transmitted σοφόν in ch. 30 is very attractive.

an alleged difference between Rome and Athens,[55] but a further specific allusion to the habitual settings of Socrates' conversations, as reported by Plato and Xenophon. Whereas Dio had previously presented Socrates, somewhat surprisingly, as a street-preacher not unlike a Dio himself (cf. above p. 665 n. 18; p. 667), he now puts further distance between himself and the 'classical' Socrates. Moreover, the status of the speech (or summary of speeches) which he proceeds to report is ambiguous, though the fact that the end is all but certainly lost enjoins caution in drawing any conclusions. Dio has said that, if the Romans laugh at his speech, he will tell them, with another allusion to Plato's *Apology*, that these were the words of the wisest of the Greeks. At one level, the difference from how Dio introduced his performances in the Greek world is indeed a marker of difference between Greek and Roman culture, but there seems also to be a qualitative difference in the two 'Socratic' speeches themselves.

It is perhaps unclear whether we are to understand that the 'Roman' speech could also be presented to its audiences, including the audience reading *Oration* 13, as 'Socratic', i.e. as something that Socrates himself originally said, or whether we are now rather listening to words for which Dio himself claims responsibility, though obviously built upon a Socratic foundation, just as Dio's own self-representation is clearly modelled upon that of the classical Socrates. Certainly, Dio ascribes the sentiments of the speech to himself ('I said ... I said ...' etc.), and he presents this second speech as an 'imitation' (μιμούμενος, 13.29), rather than as an attempt to 'remember' as accurately as he could (13.15). Chapters 31–32 in fact rewrite Dio's earlier reported speech (esp. chap. 16) and are even closer than that earlier speech to the protreptic of Plato's *Apology* (esp. 29d–e). Such rewriting (and re-speaking) 'in new words' is the technique which is at the very heart of *mimesis*, and it may be that we are indeed to see here a progression in Dio from repetition to properly mimetic composition, a progression which itself mimics the standard progression of elite education and, so it might also be thought, tracks a large swathe of the literary, rhetorical and indeed philosophical history of post-classical antiquity. Whether we are also to see here a dramatization of the move of Greek literature and culture to Rome, with Roman culture still rooted in, and imitative of, the Greek past, but now speaking with a different voice in a quite different political setting, must remain open, though the temptation to do so is surely a strong one.

In the 'Roman' speech, the subject is again the need for proper education, but Dio now stresses the need to acquire 'real' teachers, 'regardless of whether

---

[55] Cf. Trapp 2013, 39–40, who sets this within the context of a 'status difference between Greek and Roman receptiveness to philosophical culture'.

they be Greeks or Romans, a Scythian or an Indian', someone in fact to heal 'the sicknesses of the soul' (13.32). Once they find such a man, they must welcome him with open arms: Socrates and Dio are the first two names Dio wants us to think of, though not necessarily in that order. Dio has offered his Greek (and probably Athenian) audience two protreptic speeches which he claims he delivered to other audiences. One, a speech which Socrates used to deliver in Athens to their 'classical' forebears, and one which Dio himself delivered in Rome to Romans; in other words, neither speech is addressed to Dio's audience directly, and yet of course both in fact are, and both contain lessons which contemporary Greeks would do well to take to heart. Socrates speaks to the Athenians of Dio's own day, just as classical Athens offers a warning paradigm to imperial Rome.[56] As well, then, as the differences in how the two speeches are introduced, Dio's indirectness, itself a kind of 'figured' speech used with rhetorical knowingness,[57] both establishes clear distinctions between the two speeches and yet also draws them together; like Bakis and the Sibyl (13.36), Dio speaks — if not in riddles — then at least less than straightforwardly.[58] The structure of the intellectual history which Dio has created urges us to compare the two speeches which we have been offered.

The ἀρχαῖον first speech is characterized by a stress on the purposelessness of education in wrestling, poetry (including Homer) and music for deliberation about the public good; the folly of current education and the accumulation of wealth is illustrated from the great, 'mythological' figures of tragedy, and the Persian Wars become a flashpoint in debate between Socrates and those who would take a different view of current education. Though this speech supposedly derives from some five hundred years before Dio used it on his travels, we recognize many of the uses of exempla drawn from the classical past which are

---

56 Cf., e.g., Jazdzewska 2015, 262. Moles 2005, 128–131 offers a subtle account of how Dio both exploits and elides differences between Greeks and Romans.
57 Rhetorical accounts of 'figured speech' (λόγος ἐσχηματισμένος) see the use of 'substitute audiences', whereby words addressed to one audience are really intended for another, as one such 'figured' mode and associate this with the need for τὸ ἀσφαλές, cf. [Dion. Hal.] II 336.11–15 U-R. The acknowledgement of an unnamed 'source' for particular views can be a form of σχηματισμός, and the standard example is Eur. fr. 484 K from *Melanippe the Wise*, κοὐκ ἐμὸς ὁ μῦθος, ἀλλ' ἐμῆς μητρὸς πάρα κτλ., where Euripides was held to be alluding to Anaxagoras, cf. [Dion. Hal.] II 308.23–309.18, 345.9–346.9 U-R. The case is somewhat different, and the form of words very common, but it is noteworthy that Dio alludes to this turn of phrase at 13.15 in the introduction to the 'Socratic' speech.
58 For 'Bakis and the Sibyl' cf. Dio 35.2, Pfeiffer on Call. fr. 195.31; the Callimachean use is close to that of Dio 13.36, as there it follows a riddling metaphor, though one rather more extended than Dio's brief ship-simile.

standard in the Greek rhetoric of the Roman empire, not least in the works of Dio himself;[59] this ἀρχαιότης is thus in some ways also surprisingly familiar. Dio's second speech delivered at Rome — at least as much of it as survives — avoids such commonplaces in its attack upon τρυφή and πλεονεξία; Homer is now not (ludicrously) a guide to how to run a modern city, but rather a source of striking ethical similes: the great accumulation of possessions will ignite 'hybris and wanton behaviour', as certainly as the winds which Achilles invoked in Iliad 23 set alight Patroclus' pyre, piled high as it was with oil, fat and luxury goods (13.36–7).

There is, then, an arc of cultural history which may be tracked from the first speech to the second, and here too Dio's own experiences are the vehicle through which the pattern of that history is displayed. Dio's account of his exile thus offers a window not just into a very particular moment of Greek cultural and literary history, and one to which engagement with the classical past was central, but it also shows us how biography or autobiography, which uses evocations of "classical" texts to make a coherent cultural narrative out of the movement from past to present, is itself a form of literary history or, at the very least, has an immanent sense of such history at its very core.

Bibliography

Anderson, G. 1989. 'The *pepaideumenos* in action. Sophists and their outlook in the early empire', in: W. Haase (ed.), *Aufstieg und Niedergang der römischen Welt*, Berlin, II 33.1 79–208.

Bowie, E. 1985. 'Dio of Prusa', in: P. Easterling/B.M.W. Knox (eds.), *The Cambridge History of Classical Literature*, Cambridge, I, 669–672.

Bryan, J. 2012. 'Pseudo-dialogue in Plato's *Clitophon*', *Cambridge Classical Journal* 58, 1–22.

Castelli, C. 2005. 'Ritratti di sofisti. Fisiognomica ed ethos nelle *Vitae sophistarum* di Filostrato', in: E. Amato/J. Schamp (eds.), *ΗΘΟΠΟΙΙΑ. La représentation de caractères entre fiction scolaire et réalité vivante à l'époque impériale et tardive*, Salerno, 1–10.

Cobet, C.G. 1878. *Collectanea Critica quibus continentur observationes criticae in scriptores Graecos*, Leiden.

Döring, K. 1979. *Exemplum Socratis*, Wiesbaden.

---

[59] An instructive example here is *Or.* 17, 'On 'desire for more' (περὶ πλεονεξίας); exempla from tragic myth, the Persian Wars and Herodotean history (the tyrant Polycrates) there follow hard on each other's heels (chs. 13–16). Dio there calls explicit attention to the fact that he has drawn his *paradeigmata* 'both from the very ancient and those later and from both poetry and other sources of story' (ch. 15).

Fornaro, S. 2009. 'Wahre und falsche Philosophen in Dions Werk und Zeit', in: H.-G. Nesselrath (ed.), *Dion von Prusa. Der Philosoph und sein Bild*, Tübingen, 163–182.
Giannantoni, G. 1990. *Socratis et Socraticorum Reliquiae*, Naples.
Gowers, E. 2012. *Horace. Satires Book 1*, Cambridge.
Hunter, R. 2009. *Critical Moments in Classical Literature. Studies in the Ancient View of Literature and its Uses*, Cambridge.
Hunter, R. 2012. *Plato and the Traditions of Ancient Literature. The Silent Stream*, Cambridge.
Jazdzewska, K. 2015. 'Do not follow the Athenians! The example of Athens in Dio Chrysostom's Orations', *Classical Philology* 110 (3), 252–268.
Jones, C.P. 1978. *The Roman World of Dio Chrysostom*, Cambridge MA.
Long, A.A./Sedley, D.N. 1987. *The Hellenistic Philosophers. Volume 1, Translations of the Principal Sources with Philosophical Commentary*, Cambridge.
Mayhew, T. 2011. *Prodicus the Sophist. Texts, Translations, and Commentary*, Oxford.
Moles, J.L. 1978. 'The career and conversion of Dio Chrysostom', *Journal of Hellenic Studies* 98, 79–100.
Moles, J.L. 2005. 'The thirteenth oration of Dio Chrysostom: complexity and simplicity, rhetoric and moralism, literature and life' *Journal of Hellenic Studies* 125, 112–138.
Slings, R. 1999. *Plato. Clitophon*, Cambridge.
Stanton, G.R. 1973. 'Sophists and philosophers. Problems of classification', *American Journal of Philology* 94(4), 350–364.
Trapp, M. 2013. 'Philosophia between Greek and Roman culture: naturalized immigrant or eternal stranger?', in: F. Mestre/P. Gómez (eds.), *Three Centuries of Greek Culture under the Roman Empire*, Barcelona, 29–48.
Uden, J. 2015. *The Invisible Satirist. Juvenal and Second-century Rome*, Oxford.
Verrengia, V. 1999. *Dione di Prusa. In Atene, sull'esilio (or. XIII)*, Naples.
von Arnim, H. 1898. *Leben und Werke des Dio von Prusa*, Berlin.
Wegehaupt, J.M.E. 1896. *De Dione Chrysostomo Xenophontis sectatore*, Göttingen.
Whitmarsh, T. 2001a. 'Greece is the World': exile and identity in the Second Sophistic', in: S. Goldhill (ed.), *Being Greek under Rome. Cultural Identity, the Second Sophistic and the Development of Empire*, Oxford, 269–305.
Whitmarsh, T. 2001b. *Greek Literature and the Roman Empire. The Politics of Imitation*, Oxford.

36 Eustathian Moments: Reading Eustathius' Commentaries

Eustathius' commentaries (παρεκβολαί) on the *Iliad* and the *Odyssey* were declared by Paul Maas to be 'the most important grammatical achievement of the Middle Ages',[1] but for most modern classicists, even many 'Homerists', Eustathius remains little more than a name. There are a number of reasons for this, not least the fact that the *Odyssey* commentary must be consulted, whether online or in book-form, in an edition of 1825–6, and even in the case of the *Iliad*, where we are lucky enough to have the edition of Marchinus van der Valk in four bulky volumes (1971–1987), one of the most extraordinary achievements of modern philology, Eustathius does not make things easy for modern readers. A very common structure in the commentaries is for 'general' discussions of a passage or episode to be followed by more detailed, often line-by-line, observations, but Eustathius also regularly goes back on himself to take a second (or third) look, refers to discussions elsewhere in the voluminous commentaries, or picks up a discussion after what looks to modern eyes like a long digression; reading Eustathius on Homer requires practice and patience, and – even then – one can often be left unsure whether Eustathius' last word on a subject has actually been found. Moreover, Eustathius fills out his discussions with a great deal of illustrative matter drawn from classical and later literature, and much of this would not pass modern tests of 'relevance'; page after page can seem filled with a miscellany which might appear to a modern classicist as more 'stream of consciousness' than commentary directed to the illumination of Homer.

Some of the material presented here formed part of an opening lecture delivered at the conference on Eustathius in Thessaloniki in February 2015; I am very grateful to Rebecca Lämmle, Filippomaria Pontani, and a seminar audience at Venice International University for much helpful criticism of earlier versions. I am very conscious that I know far less about Byzantine culture and history than anyone who undertakes to write on this subject should know, but I hope that my essay, and this volume, will encourage other classicists to take the plunge; there is a great deal to do. Van der Valk's edition of the commentary on the *Iliad* (1971–1987) is cited throughout by author name and volume number; references to the commentaries use the traditional continuous numeration found in the editions of Stallbaum (*Odyssey*) and van der Valk (*Iliad*).

1 Maas 1973, 512. The best brief modern introduction to the commentaries is perhaps Pontani 2005, 170–178, and cf. also Pontani 2015, 385–393.

Beyond the sheer difficulty, a deeper reason for the relative neglect of Eustathius arises perhaps from the nature of much of what he writes. Eustathius clearly had access to collections of scholia on Homer very much like those we ourselves possess,[2] and much of the commentary repeats (often verbatim) and elaborates ancient and Byzantine views which are available to us elsewhere; this has led to the charge, the danger of which Eustathius himself acknowledged (*in Il.* 3.3–7), that he is simply an unoriginal compiler, who is not worth the time even of classicists interested in the ancient interpretation of Homer, for anything which is valuable in the *Commentaries* can be sought in, and is owed to, his sources.[3] It is easy enough to point out that such a perspective is remarkably parochial, for this modern search for 'das Eustathische in Eustathius', for his 'original' contribution to the commentaries, is to treat him merely as a source for our own interest in ancient and Byzantine Homeric criticism, and entirely to neglect the context and purpose of the παρεκβολαί. As well as Paul Maas, however, Eustathius can in fact muster some pretty heavyweight voices in his defence,[4] none more heavy perhaps than Wilamowitz, who stressed what Eustathius himself had contributed from his own learning and declared that some Byzantinist should write a proper monograph about him,[5] a wish which (I believe) remains to this day unfulfilled. Be that as it may, what should matter to us is the study of the παρεκβολαί as an extraordinary moment of Homeric reception, and one poised, as we shall see, between ancient exegesis and a much more modern way of reading Homer.

Eustathius' commentaries were based upon the teaching in rhetoric and classical literature that he gave in Constantinople over several decades before he moved to become Metropolitan of Thessaloniki (c. 1178); the commentaries show signs of gestation and revision over a significant period, and it is also

---

2 Cf. van der Valk I lix–lxiv, Erbse 1950, 1–22, Pagani 2017.
3 Notably damning is Wilson 1983, 198, who also (204) cites Voltaire's 'Le secret d'ennuyer est de tout dire'; the same essentially damning view of Eustathius' Homer-commentaries appears at Reynolds-Wilson 1974, 62 (= 2013, 70–71, where, however, an acknowledgement of Eustathius' 'high level of scholarly ability' has been added). This essay will only be concerned with identifying Eustathius' 'sources' when that can help in understanding Eustathius' own methods. On the issue see also Pontani 2017.
4 There is a helpful bibliographical guide in Kambylis 1991, 1 n. 1. The attitude that classicists too often take to Byzantine culture is rightly castigated by, e.g., Alpers 1988, 348–349, and some reviews of Wilson 1983 took a similarly corrective line, cf., e.g., Speck 1986, Dyck 1986a. There is a nice appreciation of the commentaries in Browning 1992.
5 Wilamowitz 1920, 22, cf. Erbse 1950, 7, Browning 1995, 85–6. It is remarkable that exactly the same wish is expressed by Browning 1995, 90, but without reference to Wilamowitz.

clear that he continued to add material after moving west, perhaps under the influence of access to different books.[6] We must, moreover, assume more than one audience for the commentaries. On the one hand, there will be Eustathius' students, and it is to the young that the commentaries are explicitly addressed: for them, broadly speaking, what matters is what their teacher has to say and how they can learn from him, not where his learning and material come from. There will, however, also have been Eustathius' fellow teachers and contemporary (and rival) πεπαιδευμένοι; the important element of learned display and self-fashioning on show in the commentaries may be thought primarily aimed at them, and it is perhaps not idle to recall that a particular style of modern commentary on classical texts also places a high value on the display of the commentator's learning. Moreover, claims that Eustathius seeks to conceal his sources and his debt to earlier writers and compilers can be overstated; the seriousness of the charge has certainly been exaggerated. Whether he cites his sources or not, the material in the commentaries is aimed at the benefit and education of his audience, and accurate 'footnoting', as we might call it, unsurprisingly takes second place to that. So too, Eustathius often cites a classical author as though that author is, at that moment, in his hands or the front of his mind, whereas in fact we can establish that the citation is mediated through an anthologising source; this may be in part an *epideixis* of learning, the attempt to appear more learned than was in reality the case,[7] but it is hardly just empty show. When such citational practices are seen within a didactic context, let alone within the contemporary circumstances governing the consultation and quotation of earlier literature, the seriousness of the charge might be thought to be greatly diminished. It is obviously more impressive and memorable for students if a point is illustrated, for example, from Aristotle than from 'Aristotle reported by Strabo' or from Thucydides rather than from 'Thucydides as cited by the lexicon of Stephanus'. The fact that Eustathius does not behave entirely as a modern classical commentator might does not seem a very grave charge; what, after all, would be gained from the more 'accurate' mode of quotation? The task of establishing Eustathius' exact sources is, of course, very important for the study of Byzantine reading, scholarship and the availability of books, and Eustathius' methods can certainly lead to confusion and error, but his is a view of

---

6 The most important case here is that of the citations from Athenaeus, cf. van der Valk, I xvi–ii; on the period of composition of the commentaries cf. also van der Valk, I cxxxvii–ix. For examples of added material cf. below 703–704, 710 n. 67, 715, 718, 719, 736.
7 So, e.g., van der Valk, I xlviii.

Greek tradition which is synoptic, cumulative and all-embracing, and that in itself is a very important lesson about Byzantine learning and teaching.

If a great deal, perhaps the majority, of Eustathius' work does indeed have roots in earlier critical traditions, often preserved for us by the Homeric scholia, much also extends or elaborates that inherited material in such a way that the attempt clearly to delineate 'das Eustathische' can become both fraught with difficulty and methodologically problematic. Let me offer just one example. Among the most famous similes of the *Iliad* is 22.199-201 in which Achilles' pursuit of Hector is compared to a similar pursuit in a dream:

> ὡς δ' ἐν ὀνείρωι οὐ δύναται φεύγοντα διώκειν·
> οὔτ' ἄρ' ὃ τὸν δύναται ὑποφεύγειν οὔθ' ὃ διώκειν·
> ὣς ὃ τὸν οὐ δύνατο μάρψαι ποσίν, οὐδ' ὃς ἀλύξαι.
>
> Homer, *Iliad* 22.199-201

> As in a dream [one man] cannot catch [another] trying to escape; neither can the one get away, nor the other catch; so [Achilles] could not catch [Hector] in running, nor Hector get away.

Aristarchus had excised these verses, and the scholia allege against them that they are weak in both language and thought, inconsistent with what is said elsewhere (notably the horse simile of 22.162-166), and diminish Achilles' renown for speed; the whole pursuit was in fact the subject of an intense critical discussion in antiquity, as it seemed beyond comprehension to some critics that Achilles could not catch Hector. The exegetical scholia point out that the resort to φαντασία (i.e. a dream) rather than reality is a very good way to represent τὸ ἄπρακτον, the 'lack of success', on both sides, that is in both escaping and pursuing. The strikingly compressed expression of the verses, something to which Aristarchus may have taken exception, had also been commented upon and explained long before Eustathius. Eustathius clearly starts from similar lore in noting that to illustrate the fact that both run equally fast, almost a kind of standstill (each with a relative speed of zero, as we might say), Homer uses a simile from φαντασία, rather than from truth (*in Il.* 1266.2-3). Moreover, the remarkably compressed and speedy (τροχαστική) expression of the simile, with its monosyllabic pronouns and a complex ἀπὸ κοινοῦ syntax which unites the pursuer and the escaper within the same verbal forms, functions as an analogy to what is actually being described; the brevity is a way of expressing the vigorous swiftness of the (in)action (τὸ γοργόν) as vigorously as possible (γοργότατα,[8] 1266.4–13). Far from being worthy of *athetesis*, these verses are another *tour de force* by Homer.[9] What is on show here, whether or not we wish to accept (all or some of) the analysis, is a 'close reading', and one very attentive to the text as something to be performed, a reading which can in fact seem, from one perspective, very modern indeed. Not, however, that modern Anglophone commentators have much time for Eustathius' account. Leaf, Richardson and de Jong do not even mention Eustathius' discussion, although Richardson is certainly in the Byzantine's wake in noting that '[T]he repetitions are surely deliberate, suggesting constant, frustrated effort'.

Unsurprisingly, rhetorical teaching plays a prominent role in the commentaries on Homer, as it always had in the long tradition of Homeric criticism.[10] Eustathius places help for 'the prose-writer and the young man wishing to achieve well-timed citations (παραπλοκαί) in rhetoric' at the top of the list of his target audience (*in Il.* 2.28). The spirit of the teacher, which is never far from the surface in Eustathius, can, for example, offer appropriate praise for, and describe the rhetorical category (τὸ ἐγκωμιαστικὸν εἶδος) and style (γλυκύτης) of, Odysseus' famous speech of praise to Nausicaa in *Odyssey* 6.149-185 (cf. *in Od.* 1556.61, 1557.12–20); here both Homer and his character Odysseus show their consummate rhetorical skill in the grasp of the *kairos*, a relationship between poet and character which is sharply pointed by the fact that Homer makes Odysseus use the same comparison of Nausicaa to Artemis which he himself had put in the narrative immediately before. Eustathius' pupils will be expected to admire and imitate such attention to the *kairos* in their own encomiastic productions, for which Byzantium offered almost limitless opportunities.

So too, Eustathius can precisely visualise the speech which Antenor says Odysseus made when he and Menelaus came on an embassy to Troy and his words fell 'like snowflakes in winter' (*in Il.* 408.3–4).[11] We may smile as we see

---

[8] On Eustathius' fondness for this stylistic classification, which he owes to the Hermogenean tradition, cf. van der Valk, I xciii.

[9] Eustathius' method here of discerning a relation between a particular verbal style and the meaning conveyed was not, of course, unique to him, cf., e.g., schol. bT *Il.* 1.530c, schol. *Od.* 3.461a, Nünlist 2009, 215–217.

[10] Cf., e.g., Lindberg 1977, van der Valk, I xcii–iii; II, li–lxx, Nünlist 2012; for the influence of Hermogenes in other writings of Eustathius cf. also Stone 2001. On the importance of rhetoric in Byzantine high culture more generally cf., e.g., Papaioannou 2013.

[11] Eustathius will have had many predecessors here; Libanius' versions of the speeches of Menelaus and Odysseus are preserved, 5.199–221, 228–286 Foerster, cf. Hunter 2015, 687–689. When Eustathius says that Odysseus is likely to have proceeded through the use of a κοινὸς τόπος, the point seems to be that the case was one of 'admitted wrong-doing' (cf., e.g., Nico-

the teacher in Eustathius award prizes: Nestor is 'Homer's orator', with a skill which comes from his very long experience ('for experience is the mother of intelligence'), and Odysseus takes second prize after him (*in Il.* 96.42), though when the ambassadors in Book 9 must reply to Achilles, Odysseus leaps in first, 'reckoning, as seems likely, that he would either persuade Achilles and carry off first prize for persuasion, or — if he could not persuade him — that he would subsequently knock down the tower of Achilles' anger through the speeches of those close to him, Phoenix and Ajax, as it were by a second and a third siege-engine' (*in Il.* 749.26–28). This last example is particularly interesting, and not just for the striking military image which Eustathius uses (and presumably used in his teaching — siege-engines were something very real to twelfth-century Byzantines). The question of why Odysseus responded first to Achilles seems to have been much discussed in antiquity.[12] The exegetical scholia note that we are not to put this down to any unhealthy sense of rivalry (βασκανία) from Odysseus, but rather he draws Achilles' hostility on to himself and away from the others, and perhaps he also realized that if Achilles' friends spoke first and failed, then there was absolutely no hope of success (cf. schol. D and bT *Il.* 9.223). Eustathius shares some of this analysis, but his Odysseus is also an ambitious pupil who wants to shine; no doubt Eustathius had seen a few such tiresome creatures. Moreover, it is the teacher who deserves as much attention as the pupil. Achilles, for whom in Eustathius' view Homer had a very soft spot,[13] was particularly fortunate in having had Phoenix and Cheiron as his teachers in rhetoric (*in Il.* 7 61.8, 1362.40–42), and when in *Iliad* 24 Achilles consoles Priam with the story of Zeus's two jars,[14] Eustathius goes out of his way to point out that he either owes this inventiveness to his teachers or that in fact he took the idea from his teachers; no doubt, too, Eustathius had seen more than one of his pupils parade as his own jewels borrowed from the teacher's lessons (*in Il.* 1362. 40–42).

Eustathius' Homer, who filled out 'the narrow path' of the main story of the *Odyssey* with 'torrential rivers of rhetoric' (*in Od.* 1379. 47–48), has in fact more than a little of the Eustathius about him. The famous 'epitome' of *Odyssey* 9–12

---

laus, III 470.18–19 Sp.) — no-one could deny that Paris had stolen Helen — and so Odysseus could use the *topoi* that one used to attack such a wrongdoer, without wasting his time demonstrating that wrong had actually been committed.

12 The embassy to Achilles was a centerpiece of Homeric rhetoric and its study in antiquity, cf., e.g., Aelius Aristides, *Or.* 16 Keil (an address to Achilles); Plut., *De Homero* 2.169–170; Libanius, *Decl.* 5 (5.303–360 Foerster, Achilles' reply to Odysseus).
13 Cf. below pp. 701 702.
14 Cf. below pp. 717–719.

which Homer narrates that Odysseus offered to Penelope in bed at *Od.* 23.310–343 and which Aristarchus athetised is actually Homer (and Odysseus) showing us that he knows how to deliver the same material with different narrative orderings, as the order of the epitome follows the order of the events (*in Od.* 1949.15–22); whereas Homer was renowned for the complexity of his narrative ordering, he can, when the *kairos* demands it, narrate also κατὰ φύσιν or κατὰ τάξιν, i.e. in simple, chronological sequence.[15] Homer in fact would have excelled in the Byzantine rhetorical curriculum.

A related lesson may be drawn from one of the most famous interpretative cruces in the Homeric poems. After the battlefield meeting of Glaukos and Diomedes in *Iliad* 6, Diomedes suggests an exchange of armour so that they will know not to fight against each other in future, and they dismount and make their pledges to each other. What follows is one of Homer's great surprises:

ἔνθ' αὖτε Γλαύκωι Κρονίδης φρένας ἐξέλετο Ζεύς,
ὃς πρὸς Τυδεΐδην Διομήδεα τεύχε' ἄμειβεν   235
χρύσεα χαλκείων, ἑκατόμβοι' ἐννεαβοίων.

Homer, *Iliad* 6.234–236

Then did Zeus, son of Kronos, take away Glaukos' wits: he exchanged armour with Diomedes, son of Tydeus, gold for bronze, a hundred oxen's worth for nine.

These famous verses were the subject of almost as many explanations in antiquity as they have been in modern times,[16] and Eustathius' discussion (*in Il.* 638.40–54) naturally draws upon the critical heritage.[17] What is important for him – and here it will not be unfair to hear the moralising teacher at work – is that Glaukos imitates the generosity and nobility of his ancestors in giving Diomedes a gift far more valuable than he himself received, and (on a more practical note) he adds that bronze offered no less security on the battlefield than did gold, implicitly thereby rejecting a charge against Glaukos of neglecting his

---

15 On these ideas cf. Hunter 2009b, 53–54. The rhetorical labelling of the passage is already found in the scholia *ad loc.*, but, as often, Eustathius elaborates on the earlier critical tradition in ways which illustrate the particular focuses of his commentary. Eustathius' observation about narrative ordering is all but repeated by de Jong 2001, 563, though without any reference to Eustathius.
16 For discussion and bibliography cf. Stoevesandt on vv. 234–236, Graziosi/Haubold 2010, 38–40.
17 Cf. the schol. (b) T *Il.*6.234a.

personal safety in stripping off his armour.[18] More striking, perhaps, to a modern student of Homer will be Eustathius' explanation of v. 234, an explanation which he explicitly takes over from Porphyry:[19] ἐξέλετο does not mean 'took away', but rather ἐξαιρέτους ἐποίησεν, i.e. 'made exceptional', so that Zeus in fact is doing honour to Glaukos, not making him look foolish.[20] Eustathius thereby produces a consistent (and didactic) reading of the Homeric passage, even if one which seems to us impossible. Eustathius is well aware that on the two other occasions on which this or similar phrases appear (*Iliad* 9.377, 19.137, both of Agamemnon) the meaning must be 'Zeus took away the wits', but this merely shows the poet's considerable τέχνη in being able to use the same words to express two quite opposite meanings (*in Il.* 757.11), a skill which we may well imagine Eustathius' pupils were encouraged to practise. Here again, then, Homer is both our teacher and also 'one of us'.

Homer nourishes us, just as do Eustathius' commentaries, but the images of hospitality and nourishment with which the commentaries are filled are neither just ornamental nor indeed just biblical and moralising. Rather, the language of criticism draws on, and mingles with, the language of the texts with which it works. In describing the nourishment which Homer offers, Eustathius observes that no serious student in antiquity, whether of philosophy or rhetoric, ever 'came to Homer's tent without receiving hospitality, but all lodged with him', some to stay for the rest of their lives, others just to fulfill a particular need and to take 'something useful' from him for their own discourses (*in Il.* 1.11–16). Hospitality is a key, perhaps in fact one of *the* key Homeric themes, and scenes of hospitality become in Hellenistic and imperial literature (*inter alia*) a setting for inter-generic experimentation or, indeed, for confrontations with the past and the literature of the past. Eustathius' image, however, evokes some of the great scenes of the *Iliad*, notably the embassies to Achilles by the Greeks in Book 9 and by Priam in Book 24. Those moments of unforgettable narrative power become our own, and our predecessors', experience of reading and listening to Homer, who — it is suggested — has crafted these scenes as models for the educational and consolatory experience of listening to epic. Priam becomes

---

[18] For a view of the passage which is not far removed from this, and which may well have stimulated Eustathius, cf. Aristotle fr. 379 Gigon (= 155 R), cited by Porphyry.

[19] Porphyry in fact (cf. MacPhail 2011, 114–116) ascribes this view to 'certain critics' and does not, *pace* Eustathius, himself explicitly approve it.

[20] Tzetzes offers a similar explanation (*alleg. Il.* 6.65–66 = Goldwyn/Kokkini 2015, 166): 'Fate extolled (ἐδόξασε) the mind of Glaukos, for the sake of friendship to exchange gold for bronze'.

one model for the audience of poetry, and Eustathius' complex image figures Homer as Achilles, dispensing his wisdom to all who will be bothered to listen.

The commentary form in fact lends itself readily to images of food and nourishment. In the Preface to his commentary on the geographical poem of Dionysius Periegetes, which he addressed to John Doukas,[21] Eustathius produces an elaborate image of how, by commenting selectively only on things which would prove 'useful' to those who were to imitate Dionysius whether in prose or verse, he has produced a full 'mixing-bowl of wisdom, free of all grapeskins and rough grapestones' (in Dion. Per. 204.110–121 Müller). He then somewhat changes the image so that what he offers John is 'like the marrow of wisdom, with all the bones of poetic harshness banished', and this he sets before John as Cheiron is said to have reared Achilles on animal marrow; classical poetry and myth was a currency of discourse among this educated Byzantine elite, rather indeed as it had been for the elite of the Second Sophistic. So too were images drawn from the realms of food and drink, and here again – as indeed with Homer's rhetoric – the watchwords are συμμετρία and τὸ εὔκαιρον (in Dion. Per. 205.1–2, cf. 206.25). Eustathius continues to John: 'I have blended anything which was tasty (νόστιμον) in Dionysius' poem into a dish of friendship … brightening it up with exotic sauces, so that there is nothing mean about our hospitality.' The image almost becomes a kind of theory of commentary. Whatever is said must be relevant to what the author has said, for to go beyond that would be nothing but φιλοτιμία κενὴ καὶ φαύλη δοξοσοφία, 'empty showing-off and a vain pretence of learning'. Eustathius proclaims that he will stick closely to Dionysius' text, 'changing some things around to explain them as when paraphrasing, but explicating other passages in Dionysius' own words; if something needs to be added, I will add that, and so I will, as it were, with appropriate measure (συμμέτρως) put a little weight on the slender narrative and gently increase the size of this little text' (in Dion. Per. 205.10–16).[22] Commentary here becomes a form of nutritional science. A poem with its commentary is always going to be fatter, have – to use the modern euphemism – a fuller figure, than a poem on its own, but what matters is the measure of that difference. No commentary should be simply calorific junk food, although too often modern classicists (in particular) have approached Eustathius' commentaries as though that indeed is what they are.

---

21 Cf. Kazhdan/Franklin 1984, 139.
22 This imagery can, of course, be traced at least as far back as the Aristophanic Euripides, cf. *Frogs* 939–944. Eustathius picks up the 'weight' metaphor shortly afterwards at *in Dion. Per.* 205.36–39.

In the introduction to the commentary on Dionysius, Eustathius then elaborates further on how he sees his role as a commentator. What Eustathius writes there cannot, of course, simply be taken as reflecting also upon the commentaries on Homer, as it is clear that Eustathius was very conscious that the nature of his commentary had to fit not only the utility of those who read the *Periegesis* and the purposes for which they read it, but also the nature of Dionysius' poem itself, a poem which he characterizes by τὸ λεπτὸν τῆς ἱστορίας, 'the slenderness of the narration', and τὸ μικρὸν ὑποκείμενον 'this little text' (*in Dion. Per.* 205.14–15). These are not descriptions that anyone, let alone Eustathius, would apply to Homer:

> Dionysius is an excellent and sweet poet, lively (γοργός) in expression, full of narrative of every kind, one who saw the cities of many men and, with his eyes and the teaching of the Muses, knew their minds.[23] This commentary of mine works with these qualities of Dionysius towards the things which a student of literature (ἀκροατὴς φιλόλογος) wishes to know. If Dionysius sometimes addresses well advanced students in a summary way, then this commentary serves as a reminder by expatiating on what is necessary (τὰ καίρια) for the sake of beginners who are less sophisticated. If, on the other hand, Dionysius elsewhere speaks to beginners, then the present work speaks at greater length for those who enjoy learning. It does not fill in gaps as though what Dionysius has said is incomplete, but rather it expands at greater length on his own topics, as is appropriate for a prose work. ... It also removes much of the labour:[24] the things which a student might wish to learn from somewhere else, he can now acquire here in this commentary, without effort, at least to a reasonable degree (πρὸς τὸ μέτριον) and as is necessary for the subject in hand. Dionysius was concerned to produce a general description of the earth and a review of its peoples; he was not very concerned in every case to set down where or among whom names arose or the characteristics of places and peoples. I have preserved the general limits which Dionysius set himself. In doing this, I do not correct the periegete, nor do I fill in

---

[23] Eustathius here combines a citation of *Odyssey* 1.3 (cf. also *in Dion. Per.* 215.3) with an echo of Dionysius' own boast that he is transported over the world, not physically, but by the 'mind of the Muses' (*Perieg.* 715, alluded to in the Introduction at *in Dion. Per.* 211.11–12, 214.23), cf. Hunter 2004, 228–229. Eustathius recognizes too the Hesiodic frame (*Op.* 646–662) for the disavowal of knowledge based on personal experience, cf. *in Dion. Per.* 343.17–42. Eustathius' claim that Dionysius 'saw the cities of many men with his eye' may simply misrepresent (cf. *Perieg.* 707 οὐ μὲν ἰδὼν κτλ.), or it may rather be a way of establishing Dionysius as an Odysseus, as Dionysius himself does (though with the significant difference that he did not 'wander'). Dionysius and his readers both see with 'the mind's eye', cf. *in Dion. Per.* 210.26, in a virtuoso passage about the transport of both poet and reader. For Dionysius putting the reader in the same position as himself cf. *in Dion. Per.* 343.32–36.

[24] For this motif cf. also, e.g., *in Dion. Per.* 207.20–25, 210.24; it is tempting to think that its use here picks up the motif of 'ease' with which Dionysius, like other didactic poets before him, plays, cf. Hunter 2004, 223–224, Lightfoot 2014, 419–420.

what has been unnecessarily omitted, as I noted above, but I follow my audience's wishes in softening what is imposed by the metrical nature of the narration.

Eustathius, *Commentary on Dionysius Periegetes*, 205.22–206.11 Müller

Eustathius is thus very conscious of Dionysius' limited aims and of the limited scope of his 'small little body of poetry' (τὸ μικρὸν τῆς ποιήσεως τοῦτο σωμάτιον), a smallness more than compensated by its rich poetic beauties (*in Dion. Per.* 216.27–30). The constant forward movement of the *periegesis*, a movement driven by names and catalogues, clearly lent itself to a very different type of commentary, and one with a much more clearly delimited scope, than did the Homeric poems. Not every verse demands commentary, and the problem of 'lemmatisation', the 'what to discuss' question, almost solves itself. Homer is different in almost every way. The epic was all-encompassing, in a way which, as Eustathius' words make clear, Dionysius deliberately avoided, and in a way which demanded a different type of commentary.

The Homer-commentaries reflect Eustathius' sensitivity not merely to genre but also to the particular place Homer held in the Byzantine view of the classical past and in Byzantine education. Their cumulative nature, the sense that they are never finished, that one is always thinking and re-thinking what one wants to say about Homer, reflect this. Eustathius sees his role as a commentator as not limited to the elucidation of the Homeric text, as we might understand that in a strict sense; nor, however, is he simply accumulating 'facts' in a spirit of 'the more the merrier'. The commentaries bear impressive witness to the power of Homer's poetry to generate multiple interpretations, once the 'literal' meaning has been established, but they also aim at the broader 'literate education' of their readers, and in the fulfillment of that aim Homeric poetry can be a jumping-off point, as well as the end to which everything moves. Eustathius' readers and pupils were indeed communities which embraced multiple readings and which sought and found openness, rather than closure, in classical texts (which did not of course mean that there were not 'right' and 'wrong' readings); to this extent, they remain very different from most modern readers of Homer, even from those who actively seek interpretative openness. The fact that Eustathius and those around him read Homer as Christians and therefore, despite all their admiration for the pagan epic, were always dealing with a text to which they could not be ideologically committed, strengthened the drive towards multiple interpretation. There is, in Eustathius, an interpretative generosity and capaciousness which — to generalise sweepingly — is utterly different, for example, from systematising neo-Platonic interpretations of Homer.²⁵

In praise of Eustathius

In one sense the aim of ancient and indeed Byzantine teaching was to produce pupils who resembled (without of course surpassing) the teacher, and we are lucky that the funerary lament (μονῳδία) for Eustathius by someone who was his pupil survives. This is Michael Choniates who was Metropolitan of Athens at the end of the twelfth century (AD 1182–1204) and whose niche in the world of classicists is secured by the fact that he seems to have known (and possessed?) and quoted from the *Hecale* and perhaps also the *Aitia* of Callimachus;²⁶ we do not know of anyone after Michael of whom the same can be said. Michael's lament²⁷ for Eustathius will strike anyone unfamiliar with Byzantine rhetoric as emotionally over-heated (to say no more), but near the beginning of the speech Michael himself self-consciously poses the dilemma of whether speechless grief, 'resembling those turned to trees and stones in myths', or the full outburst of lamentation is the appropriate response; this overt concern with the καιρός (284.27 Lampros) does not merely remind us that these works are 'performative' in the sense that there is always a sense of the judging audience, but that, for the classically trained, an important part of that judgement, and hence of the display of the speech, is a 'generic' one where what matters is indeed what is appropriate. In the introduction to his eyewitness history of the Norman capture of Thessaloniki in 1185, Eustathius himself discusses what style of narrative is appropriate, on the one hand, to historians describing events in which they were not involved and, on the other, to those describing events in which they took part and with which they are therefore closely involved.²⁸ Here too it is questions of καιρός and τὸ σύμμετρον which dominate; as a teacher of rhetoric, Eustathius was heir, not merely to *progymnasmata* on the capture of cities,²⁹ but

---

25 Lamberton 1986 remains indispensible here.
26 Cf. Wilson 1983, 205, Hollis 1990, 38–40, Pontani 2011, 114–117, Harder 2012, 1.71–72. For an outline of Michael's life cf. Kolovou 1999, 9–23, and for his period in Athens cf. Kaldellis 2007, 318–334, with the bibliography cited there.
27 Cf. Lampros 1879, 283–306; I cite the speech by Lampros' page and line numbers. On Byzantine *monodiai* in general cf. Hunger 1978, I 132–145.
28 Preface, 2–4 Melville Jones.
29 For the importance of *progymnasmata* in Byzantine rhetorical education cf. Hunger 1978, I 92–120.

also to a long classical tradition of discussions of appropriateness in historiography. For both Eustathius and Michael, questions of rhetorical appropriateness were not merely, as we might say, a 'literary' matter, but were central to how one's life and character are revealed to others.

Michael's funeral oration portrays Thessaloniki mourning for its 'fair bridegroom, lovely shepherd, wise teacher, the saviour of the city, the bulwark and unbending pillar, as Pindar put it [*Ol.* 2.82]' (285.25-28 Lampros); it is as if the city has been sacked all over again (286.2-3), a trope also used by another friend of Eustathius, Euthymios Malakes, in his μονῳδία for Eustathius, delivered shortly after the Bishop's death (*PG* 136.7 57 Migne). It is, however, Constantinople whose loss is even greater, for it was there where Eustathius had himself been educated and where he then shared his wisdom unstintingly with his pupils (286.14-22). Michael's rhetoric is, as we would expect, everywhere adorned with echoes of classical literature: the reference to Eustathius as a κοινὸν πρυτανεῖον λόγου καὶ σοφίας πανδεχὴς ἑστία, 'common meeting-hall for literary culture (*logos*) and a hearth of wisdom, open to all' 286.20-21), for example, suggests through evocation of Plato (*Protagoras* 337d) and Athenaeus (5.187d-e) that Eustathius himself was the modern embodiment of, or perhaps replacement for, classical Athens as the centre of Greek learning. Michael, who recognises and values the discursive and digressive nature of Eustathius' lectures and commentaries (287.22-288.2 Lampros), praises his teacher for having initiated young men into the 'mysteries' of literature, rhetoric, metre and mythical allegory (288.17- 289.4); in no time at all, Eustathius 'the hierophant' guided young men from the outside of the shrine to the innermost secrets of learning (288.21-25).

It is of course Homer who is at the centre of Michael's representation, both because Homer was central to Eustathius and because Michael is displaying the fruits of Eustathius' learning and teaching. Eustathius is indeed almost a second Homer, claimed — like Homer — by more than one continent (294.9-21). Homer of course also afforded the best images to describe the power of Eustathius' oratory and teaching; his *logoi* were like Homer's lotus-plant: once you started listening, you would forget to go home (290.10). As in the *Odyssey* itself, the Lotus-eaters and the Sirens are variants upon the same theme: 'Eustathius' Sirens' (τῶν Εὐσταθίου Σειρήνων) put all other rhetorical graces in the shade (289.12-13). The compliment is indeed a commonplace: in Euthymios' version (*PG* 136.7 60 Migne), no educated person would put wax in their ears to avoid listening to Eustathius' enchanting words, and once heard the only remaining wish was to die surrounded by that sweetness, as indeed the Homeric Sirens had caused the death of so many:

ἤθελον δὲ τῇ ἀκροάσει καὶ ἐπαποθανεῖν, καὶ αὐτῇ συναποθανεῖν τῇ γλυκύτητι.
Euthymios Malakes, *PG* 136.7 60 Migne

They wanted to die in response to what they had heard and surrounded by that sweetness.

Euthymios here alludes, not just to Homer, but also to a famous passage of Plato's *Symposium* in which Phaedrus claims that the gods honoured Achilles exceedingly because he chose to avenge his lover Patroclus, not only 'by dying for him, but also in addition to him', ὑπεραποθανεῖν ἀλλὰ καὶ ἐπαποθανεῖν (180a1). Euthymios thus evokes, in Eustathius' honour, not just the Sirens of the *Odyssey*, but also the central hero of the *Iliad*, and the echo of Plato acknowledges the depth of Eustathius' classical learning.

However commonplace the comparison of poets and orators to Sirens may be, it is tempting to see in the phrase τῶν Εὐσταθίου Σειρήνων an allusion to the opening words of Eustathius' commentary on the *Iliad*, τῶν Ὁμήρου Σειρήνων; Eustathius begins the *Iliad* commentary with a variation on the very familiar 'allegorising' of the Sirens as the charms of literature more generally.[30] Whether or not Michael is indeed specifically evoking these opening words may be left open, but there can be little doubt, I think, that he has in mind Eustathius' extended discussion of the allegory of the Sirens in the commentary on the *Odyssey* (*in Od.* 1706.23–1711.10).[31] Eustathius is there heir to a very long tradition of allegorising on why the philosopher Odysseus, but not his companions, can listen to the alluring song of the Sirens, but of particular interest is Eustathius' account of 'what song the Sirens sang?'. The answer, broadly put, is 'literature' or, as Eustathius puts it:

...stories, old tales, histories, collections of myths, both philosophical and other; a philosopher too will, when appropriate (ἐν καιρῷ), give ear to these. From some he will take sensible pleasure, from others he will take what is useful (τὸ χρήσιμον), and he will mix what is excellent (καλόν) in these sources into his own writings and will himself become, as it were, a marvellous Siren (θεσπεσία Σειρήν).
Eustathius, *Commentary on the Odyssey* 1708.39–43

The traditional idea that one reads 'classical literature' in order to nourish one's own writings and speeches shows Eustathius as very much within the tradition

---

[30] Cf. Hunter/Russell 2011, 79–80, citing earlier literature. Kaldellis 2007, 314–315 discusses the possible ironies of Eustathius' appeal to the Sirens.
[31] Wedner 1994, 155–165 offers an accurate account of Eustathius' treatment of the Sirens, but does not discuss the matters raised here.

of rhetorical teaching,[32] but the striking idea that one can in this way become a Siren oneself clearly stuck in Michael's mind. In Eustathius' idealising vision, then, the Sirens, if listened to in the right way, become model teachers who can reproduce themselves in their pupils, and Michael identifies Eustathius himself as the very embodiment of that vision. For Eustathius, as the opening of the *Iliad* commentary has already shown us (and cf. further below), there was one special 'Siren' above all others, and that of course was Homer himself. For Eustathius (and not for Eustathius alone), Homer uses the song of the Sirens to advertise the pleasures of his own poetry and of poetry more generally (*in Od.* 1709.1–18). What is it that the Sirens, or any individual Siren, most notably Homer himself, offers? 'Pleasure and knowledge' is the Homeric answer (*Od.* 12.188), and Eustathius stresses that this is indeed what Homer offers us. Michael's implication, and perhaps also already Eustathius', if — as seems likely — there is a degree of 'self-reference' in his description of how to use the literature of the past in one's own work to become a 'Siren', is that this is also exactly what his pupils and audiences took from Eustathius. Elsewhere in the oration, Michael is very explicit about what was to be gained from listening to his teacher's lectures.

Eustathius' account of Odysseus and the Sirens does not stop with the pleasure and knowledge to be gained, for there is also the question of what role 'listening to the Sirens' should play in the life of an educated man engaged in public activity, a πολιτικὸς φιλόσοφος, as Eustathius puts it (*in Od.* 1709.18). The answer is that such a man cannot spend all his time listening to the Sirens, for he has to move on to practical activity in the world. The Sirens, in fact, represent 'theory' or, to put it another way, learning or education (μάθησις); as even an Odysseus knows that learning never stops, so 'I learn as I grow old' (1709.26) comes very readily to Eustathius' pen, and therefore Odysseus wants to hear the Sirens, but he knows that he must also get away from θεωρία into πρᾶξις, for the 'complete philosopher' is put together out of both (1709.23–30). 'Theory' has a very proper and necessary place (ἐν χρῷ, 1709.22), but there is more to a full life than that. Eustathius is here heir to a very long tradition, going back at least to Plato and Aristotle, of argument about the relative merits of the life of activity and the life of philosophical speculation,[33] but it is difficult not to wonder about Eustathius himself, particularly if we take into account his later life in Thessaloniki. He was a man whose life did indeed 'mix action with

---

32 Cf. Hunter 2009a, ch. 4 on Dionysius of Halicarnassus.
33 Key texts here include Plato's *Gorgias* and Aristotle, *EN* 10. On this topic in Eustathius, see also Pizzone 2017.

theory' (1709.21), a man who had reservations (to say no more) about those monks who devoted themselves to ascetic contemplation removed from the world of action. How deep a chord might the Sirens-image have struck in twelfth-century Constantinople (or even Thessaloniki)? In using Eustathius' commentaries to describe his life, or rather allowing the one to seep into the other, Michael may indeed have (again) merely been following Eustathius' own lead. We may bring another famous Odyssean figure into the picture here.[34] Both explicitly in the *Odyssey*-commentary (*in Od.* 1618.31–32) and by clear allusion in his theological writing (*Opusc.* 148.38–48 Tafel), Eustathius compares ascetics and hermit monks to the Cyclopes of the Odyssey, 'who, trusting in the immortal gods, neither plant crops with their hands nor do they plough, but everything grows unsown and unploughed ... they have neither meeting-places where counsel is offered nor laws, but they dwell on the peaks of lofty mountains and in hollow caves, and each man administers law over his children and wife, and they take no thought for each other' (*Odyssey* 9.107–115). Eustathius here seems to take over the ancient view, found as early as Antisthenes, if not before, that the inconsistency between this description of the Cyclopes and the blasphemous savagery of the Cyclops is to be explained by the fact that Polyphemos is a one-off: all the other Cyclopes are indeed god-fearing, and when Polyphemos says they are not, he is simply lying (*in Od.* 1617.61–1618.1). In the related passage in Eustathius' encomium of St Philotheus,[35] the tone is perhaps more humorously dismissive (hermits 'cram themselves into caves ... and slip into holes in the ground' in their attempts to avoid the life of community, τὸ πολιτικὸν καὶ σύμβιον), but Eustathius then proceeds to acknowledge that the hermits' solitary struggle for virtue, a struggle seen only by God, is indeed a noble and praiseworthy one. Greater, however, was St Philotheus' open struggle in 'the theatre of life' where so many obstacles stand in the way, but where there are also thousands of spectators to see the struggle and — and this is what is most important — be stimulated to imitate the struggle in God's service which they witness. It is not hard to see Philotheus here not just as a model for Eustathius, but also as (here at least) a representative for him and for his view of the public role and responsibilities of a priest. For Eustathius, Homeric allusion is never far away from that role.

---

[34] For what follows cf. Kazhdan/Franklin 1984, 151–153; on some of Eustathius' problems with the monks and lay people of Thessaloniki cf. Magdalino 1996.
[35] *Opusc.* p. 148.38–48 Tafel. This passage also seems to rework Hesiod's famous verses on the path towards ἀρετή (*Op.* 286–92).

Just as, for Eustathius, Homer was a place where one could receive board and nourishment for as long as one wished (*in Il.* 1.11–16, cf. above 689), so for Michael Eustathius was an 'unlocked garden of wisdom, a rich field ... and a gushing spring of *logoi*' (286.22–24 Lampros) where no one need go hungry or thirsty.³⁶ According to Euthymios, the stream of Eustathius' words watered the city, surpassing even the cataracts of the Nile; now, however, after the master's death, those who drank so eagerly are dry and burning with thirst (*PG* 136.7 57 Migne). Using an elaborate version of the same *topos* as Michael, Euthymios describes Eustathios himself as a new paradise open to all, where many came and plucked the fruit of his virtue and teaching, filling themselves to their heart's content (*PG* 136.7 60 Migne). Even the figure of the Cyclops makes an unexpected appearance here also: for Michael, Eustathius' lectures dripped honey and were like 'distillations (ἀπορρῶγες) of nectar' (287.9 Lampros), a phrase which Michael has taken from the Cyclops' description of the very strong wine which Odysseus has offered him, 'a distillation of ambrosia and nectar'; whereas, however, Odysseus' wine befuddled the Cyclops and eventually left him unconscious, Eustathius' lectures entered his pupils' souls, there to remain forever.³⁷ Once again, Michael's praise activates a memory of the teaching which it celebrates: Eustathius wrote a long note on the relevant Homeric phrase and, in particular, on the metaphorical uses of ἀπορρώξ (*in Od.* 1633.39–58).

It should of course be no surprise that food and drink are almost as obsessively interesting in Byzantine society as in classical times, and just as rich a source of critical imagery. It is certainly no surprise that they recur insistently in Eustathius' account of the capture of Thessaloniki in 1185, for a city under siege is a city where food and drink assume an even greater significance than ever. At one point Eustathius offers a marvellous account of how the invaders had no appreciation for the properly aged local wine, which was not sweet enough for their barbarian tastes, and so it was just wasted and poured out (§136, 148 Melville Jones). Instead, virtually unfermented new wine which 'seethed and bubbled' was swilled down with a gay abandon which, to Eustathius' delight, was often enough to prove fatal, particularly as the barbarians combined it with gorging themselves on the flesh of pigs and cattle and on the local 'excellent garlic'. Eustathius himself has some marvellous food descriptions,³⁸ and he can

---

36 For the classical roots of the image cf., e.g., Philostratus, *Heroicus* 4.11.
37 Michael in fact says that Eustathius' teaching was 'burned into' his pupils (287.11 Lampros), but I wonder whether the burning of the Cyclops' eye plays some (? unconscious) role here; the metaphor comes from encaustic techniques in art.
38 Cf., e.g., Kolovou 2006, 63–68.

reach for a high level of poeticism: thus, for example, he describes a *coq au vin* washed in wine, 'as Homer says the sun is washed in Ocean' (*Epist.* 5 Kolovou). Eustathius was certainly no ascetic: in several places in Eustathius' letters in fact one is strongly reminded of Petronius' *Satyrica*.

When Michael comes to describe the throng who sought Eustathius out, it is of course Homer to whom he again turns:

> Whenever I watched his pupils coming and going, I was reminded of the Homeric simile. As hordes (ἔθνη) of bees come out from a hollow rock, so every day did countless swarms (σμήνη) of students flit to and from Eustathius' hive like bunches of grapes (βοτρυδόν).
> Michael Choniates, *Funeral Oration for Eustathius* 289.21–28 Lampros

Bees have a very long history as a *comparandum* for students and their teachers,[39] but Michael's evocation of *Iliad* 2.87–90, the comparison of the Greek army rushing to assembly like swarming bees, is not chosen at random:

> ἠΰτε ἔθνεα εἶσι μελισσάων ἀδινάων
> πέτρης ἐκ γλαφυρῆς αἰεὶ νέον ἐρχομενάων,
> βοτρυδὸν δὲ πέτονται ἐπ' ἄνθεσιν εἰαρινοῖσιν·
> αἱ μέν τ' ἔνθα ἅλις πεποτήαται, αἱ δέ τε ἔνθα·   90
> ὣς τῶν ἔθνεα πολλὰ νεῶν ἄπο καὶ κλισιάων
> ἠϊόνος προπάροιθε βαθείης ἐστιχόωντο
> ἰλαδὸν εἰς ἀγορήν·
> Homer, *Iliad* 2.87–93

> As hordes of dense bees come out in an ever-ending stream from a hollow rock, and like bunches of grapes fly to the spring flowers, some this way in great numbers and some that, so did the many hordes [of Greeks] proceed in troops from the ships and huts along the deep shore to the place of assembly.

This is the first extended simile in the *Iliad*, as Eustathius notes in his commentary (*in Il.* 179.28), and Eustathius had prefaced his detailed commentary upon it with one of the fullest and most important surviving discussions of the technique of Homeric similes (*in Il.* 176.23–178.1). Moreover, one of Eustathius' letters (3 Kolovou), accompanying a gift of shining grapes of the kind called in contemporary speech κουκούβαι ('owls'), is almost an extended riff on the analogy between grapes and bees which this Homeric simile inaugurates: if Homer can say that bees fly βοτρυδόν, then Eustathius can say that his grapes are piled up μελισσηδόν, and so forth. In his discussion of the Homeric passage, Eu-

---

39 Cf., e.g., Hunter/Russell 2011, 16, 183, citing earlier literature.

stathius draws heavily upon ancient criticism,[40] but a leitmotif is that the extended simile is for Homer a technique for τὸ διδάσκειν, by which is meant not just making the narrative vivid and lively by drawing upon images from the everyday, but also teaching the audience about the world around them.

Michael clearly remembers Eustathius' own 'teaching' through his evocation of the Homeric simile and of Eustathius' discussion. One aspect of this discussion was Eustathius' insistence that the point of the comparison is the similarity between the movement of 'swarms' of bees and 'swarms' of men; this is not one of the, in Eustathius' view, rare Homeric examples where every aspect of the tenor matches every aspect of the vehicle. After all, the bees are coming out from one location and then dispersing in various directions, whereas the Greeks are coming together in one place, having been previously scattered among their own camps and ships. Michael's image of students both 'alighting on' and 'flying off' from the one place, which is 'the hive of Eustathius', an image which deliberately omits the destination for which the bees are headed, draws vehicle and tenor closer together, very likely under the influence of Eustathius' discussion. Moreover, Homer had used ἔθνεα of both the bees and the Greeks, and this had drawn the attention of both the scholiasts and then of Eustathius; the latter explains at some length that the proper term for bees is not ἔθνος, but σμῆνος (in Il. 178.10–19). Michael picks up this strand of criticism by referring to the φιλολόγων σμήνη μυρία who thronged Eustathius' 'hive', thus varying Homer's seepage from vehicle to tenor, again under the influence of Eustathius' teaching; the verbal wit is reinforced by using βοτρυδόν of these 'swarms' of students, whereas in Homer this adverb had been applied to the bees, with ἰλαδόν describing the parallel movement of the Greek soldiers.[41]

If Eustathius was an embodiment of Homer, his power of words also evoked the central figures of Homer's two poems. Like Achilles, Michael's Eustathius 'sang of heroic deeds', ἄειδε κλέα (in Il. 291.8, cf. Iliad 9.189), but Homer's 'heroes' (ἀνδρῶν) are replaced by βασιλέων μεγαλουργῶν καὶ ὑψιθρόνων πατριαρχῶν, 'powerful kings and high-throned patriarchs', who after all were indeed the contemporary equivalent of Homer's elite. Eustathius had in fact noted that, in contrast to Paris' lascivious lyre-playing (Iliad 3.54), the poetry of both Achilles and Homer was praiseworthy, 'for Homer's poetry too sings of the glorious deeds of men' (in Il. 381.4–5); in his discussion of the famous passage in which

---

[40] For relevant bibliography cf. Hunter 2006, 83 n. 8.
[41] Michael here perhaps also remembers Eustathius' observation that 'some ancient' reversed Homer's usage by writing of a 'swarm of grapes' (σμῆνος βοτρύων), in Il. 179.33–34; van der Valk, I cix conjectures that this is from a lost work of Himerius.

the ambassadors find Achilles entertaining himself with poetry in *Iliad* 9, Eustathius observes that Achilles makes those of whom he sung ἀοίδιμοι, 'just as the poet had made him' (*in Il.* 745.52). Michael's Homeric allusion in ἄειδε κλέα thus in fact reincarnates Eustathius as both Achilles and Homer. For Eustathius Homer was φιλαχιλλεύς, 'fond of Achilles',[42] and the poet's attachment to Achilles is a leitmotif of the commentary on the *Iliad*, the last words of which record that while the dead Hector deserved pity, this was not how Homer saw it, because that was not how Homer's *philos* Achilles saw it.[43] Eustathius' devotion to and writing about Homer has now made him as dear to the poet as Achilles himself was. In introducing Achilles' account to Priam of Zeus's jars in *Iliad* 24,[44] Eustathius notes that the poet wanted to show 'his beloved Achilles' as also eloquent (λόγιος), which was only reasonable given the quality of his teachers in rhetoric, Cheiron, Peleus, and Phoenix, and Achilles' speech of consolation is analysed by rhetorical criteria (*in Il.* 1362.39–48);[45] it is perhaps not altogether fanciful to imagine that Eustathius himself sometimes daydreamed about what it would be like to teach rhetoric to an Achilles — a star pupil, if ever there was one and, as a 'kingly young man devoted to the Muses', the very model of a young member of the Byzantine élite. Eustathius' commentary insistently impresses upon his pupils what a good teacher can do for you.

Eustathius' fondness for Achilles, which matches Homer's own, may shape interpretation, as we have seen in Eustathius' view of the very end of the poem (above and n. 43). In the discussion of *Iliad* 23.187, where Homer reports that Aphrodite protected Hector's corpse with ambrosial oil, 'so that he should not disfigure him as he dragged him [around the walls]', the subject of the verb is obviously Achilles, who has been at the centre of our thoughts for some time and whose preparations at Patroclus' pyre have just been described; Achilles is not, however, named explicitly, and grammarians and teachers obviously felt

---

42 This compound is not apparently applied to Homer in the extant scholia. On this topic see also van den Berg 2017.
43 At *in Il.* 1362.59 Eustathius calls Achilles, in the context of his consolatory speech to Priam (cf. below pp. 717–719), 'the dear comrade of the poet, who was both brave and eloquent'. Eustathius' view of the end of the *Iliad* is an outlier among ancient and scholiastic interpretations; he notes the speed and brevity with which Homer brings the poem to a conclusion, but focuses not, as seems to have been traditional, on how Homer saved material for the *Odyssey* (see on this also Nünlist 2017), but rather on the absence of details of the actual burial rites and on the absence of funeral games. He then closes with the remark about Achilles which is cited above.
44 Cf. below pp. 717–719.
45 Note especially πίστιν τεχνικῶς τῷ λόγῳ πορίζων κτλ. at *in Il.* 1362.46.

some difficulty. The D-scholia explain that the reference is to Achilles, and Eustathius is in touch with this same grammatical lore (cf. *in Il.* 1294.13 ὁ Ἀχιλλεὺς δηλαδή); the paraphrase in the exegetical b-scholia also names the hero, as though this was necessary for full understanding. Eustathius, however, goes on to note that, because the action of dragging Hector was κακόν (cf. *Il.* 23.176–177 and further below), Homer has, at the price of unclarity, suppressed the name of 'his dear Achilles', thus forcing us to bring it over ἀπὸ κοινοῦ from its last appearance eighteen verses previously. By contrast, notes Eustathius, when Homer describes the funeral procession for Patroclus (23.134–140), 'which was a praiseworthy thing', he names Achilles three times in six verses (*in Il.* 1294.50–59). Homer thus controls every detail of his poem, and when something catches our attention, like a slight grammatical unclarity, we should ponder what that might mean; no aspect of the poem, however apparently trivial, is without purpose.[46]

The fondness of the poet and commentator for Achilles does not, however, put the hero beyond criticism. Achilles' funeral for Patroclus and his maltreatment of Hector's body, for example, belong to ἱστορία, to 'what happened', and what matters therefore is how Homer chose to present these events. If in the passage just considered Homer is claimed to have done what he could to play down Achilles' responsibility for a 'bad' action, neither Homer nor Eustathius can deny the action itself. Homer had famously called Achilles' treatment of Hector ἀεικέα ἔργα (*Il.* 22.395, cf. 23.24), and Eustathius could draw on a rich critical tradition in seeking to explain the adjective, just as the phrase has become a focus for modern discussion of the narratorial voice in Homer.[47] Eustathius (*in Il.* 1276.1–4) is clear that Homer condemns the dragging of Hector's body, both from the fact that in *Il.* 22.395 he calls the Trojan δῖος and from the fact that the things which were done to him were ἀεικέα, that is, in Eustathius' view, ἀπρεπῆ, 'not fitting' [for Hector], one of the rival interpretations of ἀεικέα which Eustathius inherited from the grammatical tradition (cf. schol. b *Il.* 22.395a2).[48] There are thus limits to Homer's, and Eustathius', fondness for Achilles.

---

46 This critical principle of οὐδὲν μάτην, i.e. the poet included (or excluded) nothing without a purpose, was part of Eustathius' broad debt to the ancient critical tradition, cf., e.g., Dio Chrys. 2.40,48, schol. bT *Il.* 11.58 and 12.292–293 etc.
47 Cf., e.g., Hunter/Russell 2011, 108, de Jong on *Il.* 22.395.
48 In the second instance of ἀεικέα ἔργα in this context, *Il.* 23.24, where the reference is less obvious than it is in Book 22, Eustathius notes that Achilles was 'overcome by anger' (*in Il.* 1285.30).

Even worse than the dragging of Hector's body was, of course, Achilles' human sacrifice at Patroclus' tomb:

δώδεκα δὲ Τρώων μεγαθύμων υἱέας ἐσθλοὺς
χαλκῶι δηϊόων· κακὰ δὲ φρεσὶ μήδετο ἔργα.

Homer, *Iliad* 23.175–176

[And he threw on the pyre] twelve noble sons of great-hearted Trojans, killing them with bronze; in his heart he devised grim deeds.

Homer's comment on the action seems unequivocal, even if some modern commentators have read the second half of v. 176 as devoid of criticism of Achilles. The exegetical scholia refer to Achilles' natural ὠμότης, and also note that Patroclus' death 'has made [Achilles] more savage' (πλέον ἠγρίωσεν). Eustathius makes three points about this brief passage (*in Il.* 1294.18–23). First, we have to understand ἐνέβαλλε πυρῆι, 'threw into the fire', from vv. 172 and 174, as what Achilles actually did to the young men: Homer shrank from explicitness here, and this silence (formally an ἔλλειψις) must be judged appropriate (καιρία). Unlike the case of *Il.* 23.187 considered above, modern readers might judge Eustathius at least over-sensitive here: there is no real risk of unclarity, and the syntax would seem to make Achilles' action with regard to the young Trojans explicit. Nevertheless, the hero's actions are very carefully described in vv. 168–177, and expressions for 'threw in the fire' occur three times in a brief space; such a pattern suggests to Eustathius that the 'omission' in vv. 175–176 is deliberate and prompts him to ask 'why?'. These should still be the instincts of a modern commentator, however much they are rooted in the analyses of ancient grammarians. Secondly, the language in which the young Trojans are described, μεγαθύμων υἱέας ἐσθλούς, dignifies them (ἀποσεμνύνας), and, finally, Homer explicitly calls Achilles' action κακόν. In a subsequent addition to the commentary, Eustathius goes further:

[Achilles' action] was beastlike (θηριώδης) and truly barbarian, if one reflects upon the fact that we are told that it was the custom of Gauls to sacrifice the prisoners, whenever they enjoy some success in wars. That custom, however, had some rationale, as it was an offering to the divine, like a sacrifice, whereas Achilles' action is of a completely different kind.

Eustathius, *Commentary on the Iliad* 1294.22–24

Eustathius here extends the traditional criticism of Achilles — 'beastlike and truly barbarian' is an intensification of the scholiastic charge of ὠμότης and ἀγριότης against Achilles — but his use of the case of the Gauls as a *comparandum* for Achilles' action also has an interest beyond that.⁴⁹ Aristotle seems to have explained Achilles' dragging of Hector's body around Patroclus' tomb from the fact that such actions were still in his day a Thessalian funeral practice (fr. 389 Gigon = 166 Rose); such appeal to 'other' customs was of course a standard way of dealing with literary 'problems'. Eustathius is heir to such a tradition, but here uses the existence of this custom among 'barbarians' as evidence for the abhorrent nature of Achilles' action; Aristotle's Thessalians were at least Greeks, whereas Gauls are entirely beyond the pale. If anything, the comparative method here complicates the difficulty of the text, rather than providing a 'solution'.

For Michael Choniates, as we have seen, Eustathius was an Odysseus, as well as an Achilles. No figure comes of course more readily to mind in any rhetorical context than Odysseus,⁵⁰ but Michael uses this figure in a perhaps surprising way at one crucial point of his eulogy. Eustathius' death was a falling asleep:

> [Sleep] escorted you through the Gates of Dreams to death or, to put it more fittingly, conveyed you as if from your stay here in a foreign land to your homeland over there, just as in poetry a heroic wise man of much wandering is conveyed while sleeping from a foreign island to the island which bore him.
>
> Michael Choniates, *Funeral Oration for Eustathius* 302.6–11 Lampros

The allusion to Odysseus being transported by the Phaeacians from Scherie to Ithaca could hardly be clearer:

> ὡς ἡ ῥίμφα θέουσα θαλάσσης κύματ' ἔταμνεν
> ἄνδρα φέρουσα θεοῖσ' ἐναλίγκια μήδε' ἔχοντα,
> ὃς πρὶν μὲν μάλα πολλὰ πάθ' ἄλγεα ὃν κατὰ θυμόν,
> ἀνδρῶν τε πτολέμους ἀλεγεινά τε κύματα πείρων·   90
> δὴ τότε γ' ἀτρέμας εὗδε, λελασμένος ὅσσ' ἐπεπόνθει.
>
> Homer, *Odyssey* 13.88–92

---

⁴⁹ Eustathius draws his example of the Gauls from Athenaeus 4.160e where the custom is cited in a quotation of verse by Sopater (fr. 6 K-A); Eustathius, however, seems to have known Athenaeus only in a version of the Epitome (cf. van der Valk I, lxxxiv–v, Hunter 1983, 32), and in the Epitome the Gaulish custom is cited but the poetic context concealed. On Eustathius and the customs of other populations see Cullhed 2017.
⁵⁰ For some aspects of the use of the figure of Odysseus in Comnenian literature cf. the bibliography in Pontani 2015, 392 n. 473.

So did [the Phaeacian ship] cut through the waves of the sea in its swift course, bearing a man whose counsels were like the gods'. In the past he had suffered very many griefs in his heart, as he passed through the wars of men and the grievous waves; but at that time he slept quietly, forgetful of all that he had suffered.

Eustathius has gone home: Heaven is where he really belongs (not much later Michael describes the Gates of Heaven opening to receive him [303.23–24]). The Homeric allusion, as so often, is not mere idle display: like Odysseus, Eustathius too was a man 'whose plans were like those of God[s], who before had suffered very many griefs in his heart' but now was asleep, 'forgetting all that he had suffered'. Why the Phaeacians did not wake Odysseus up was a famous Homeric 'problem' which Eustathius had of course discussed (*in Od.* 1733.1–23);[51] once again, then, Michael offers us a truly Homeric Eustathius.

Eustathius and allegory

As what mattered to Eustathius in the commentary on Dionysius Periegetes was 'the useful' (cf. above), so too in the commentaries on Homer. In the Preface to the *Iliad*-commentary (*in Il.* 2.17–47), Eustathius stresses his wish that the commentary be χρήσιμον for young men who are still learning and who wish to understand Homer in order to use that understanding for the benefit of their own rhetoric; we have already seen such a model of 'benefit' in Eustathius' use of the image of the Sirens, and there is certainly something in common between how Eustathius wants us to read Homer and how we are to read his commentaries. A particular problem, however, is posed by myth and the question of allegory, for allegorising is a crucial weapon in making poetic myth 'useful' in an educational context. Eustathius notes that Homer is not to be criticized for being 'full of myths', because his myths are not there to make us laugh, but rather 'they are shadows or screens (παραπετάσματα) for noble thoughts', some of which Homer himself created, whereas others which were pre-existing have been transferred (ἑλκόμενοι) to serve a useful purpose in his poetry; both kinds of myth are to be interpreted allegorically (*in Il.* 1.35–40). Eustathius' language here is reminiscent of the interpretative language of the neo-Platonists, notably Proclus, for whom the surface meaning and language of the poems are indeed a set of 'screens' which those who properly understand will remove in their reading to reveal the allegorised truth which they conceal, a truth which will howev-

---

51 For discussion and further bibliography cf. Hunter 2009a, 199–201, Hunter/Russell 2011, 155.

er always remain invisible to the uninitiated and the vulgar.⁵² Thus, for example, Proclus notes, in regard to poetry about the gods, that these surface features of the text, which apparently assimilate divine society and behaviour to our own, are rather 'appropriate screens (παραπετάσματα) for ideas about the gods, which are transferred (ἑλκόμενα) from events which came after the gods to the gods themselves' (*in Plat. Remp.* 1.66.7–9 Kroll).⁵³ Myths seek to conceal the truth 'by screens which can be seen' (παραπετάσματα φαινόμενα, 1.73.15–16 Kroll, cf. 1.74.18–20), a phrase which draws on the distinction fundamental to any allegorising interpretation, namely that between what the text 'appears' to say and what it 'really' means. Both Proclus and Eustathius are, of course, concerned with the useful teaching which lies concealed behind the 'screens', but Eustathius sees Homer's aim, not entirely unlike his own, as much more strictly introductory and educational: 'because they are attractive to the many, Homer wove myths into his poetry with the intention that the outward appearance (τὸ προφαινόμενον) would lure and bewitch those who shunned the subtleties of philosophy so that he might catch them, as they say, "in the nets"; once he had given them a taste of the sweetness which lies in truth, he would release them to go their own way and search for that sweetness elsewhere' (*in Il.* 2.1–4). Homer's aim in fact was precisely in line with how the educational tradition had used him for centuries, namely as an introduction to the higher studies of philosophy; this is, for example, the principal perspective from which Plutarch presents poetry in *How the young man should study poetry*.⁵⁴

In Plato's *Republic* (2.378d-e), Socrates, speaking of some of the most notorious acts of violence by Homer's gods against each other, notes that such passages cannot be accepted into the ideal city, 'whether they have been composed with or without underlying meanings (ὑπόνοιαι)', because the young are unable to discern what is and is not such an underlying meaning. Almost immediately before, Socrates had outlawed stories such as Ouranos' castration by his son in Hesiod's *Theogony* 'even if they are true' (2.377e–378a); if, however, they must be told, it should only be to a very small group, and in secret after appropriate sacrifices. From these two passages Proclus developed the view that Socrates/Plato held that there were two kinds of myth, each appropriate to a different audience at different stages of intellectual development:

---

52 Cf., e.g., Festugière 1970, 62–63, Sheppard 1980, 16–17, Lamberton 1986, 185.
53 Both the language and the thought go much further back than Proclus, cf., e.g., the opening sections of Dio Chrysostom 5, 'the Libyan myth' on which cf. Hunter 2017.
54 Cf. esp. Plutarch's programmatic statement at *aud. poet.* 15f–16a.

One kind of myth is educational (παιδευτικόν), the other initiatory (τελεστικόν); one contributes to ethical virtue, the other to our union (συναφή) with the divine; one can benefit the majority of us, the other is appropriate for very few;[55] one is common and familiar to men, the other secret and inappropriate to those who do not strive to be completely situated in the divine; one corresponds to the condition of the souls of the young, the other scarcely reveals itself after sacrifices and mystical training.

Proclus, *On the Republic* 1.81.13–21 Kroll

In accordance with the purpose of the *Commentaries*, Eustathius gives pride of place to the first, educational myths; these are what his readers will find χρήσιμα. The distinction which he proceeds to draw concerns the kind of interpretation to be applied to the Homeric text, and he sets his discussion (*in Il.* 3.13–34) within the history of previous interpretation.[56] For Eustathius, the two extremes are represented by those who 'turn everything into allegory', even events and characters which are rooted in reality, what Eustathius terms τὰ ὁμολογουμένως ἱστορούμενα, 'so that the poet seems to speak to us in dreams'.[57] On the other side are those 'who have torn off Homer's wings and never allow him to soar aloft', by refusing to allow any allegorical interpretation; for these people, whose 'lawgiver' was Aristarchus,[58] myths are just that — myths. For Eustathius the third way, and the way he will follow, is the way of careful examination and discrimination, rather than the imposition of totalising and undiscriminating systems; he will not be the last scholar to use such a rhetoric about the difference between his work and that of others, nor will he be the

---

55 Proclus' word ἐλαχίστοις picks up *Resp.* 2.378a6.
56 What follows re-uses some material from Hunter 2016, which should be consulted for the background to Eustathius' discussion. Eustathius is heir to a very long tradition, not just of allegorizing itself, but of classifications of types of allegory, and Eustathius' division was not the only one current in late antiquity and Byzantium — cf., e.g., scholia on *Odyssey* 1.8h,1.26j Pontani etc.
57 Cesaretti 1991, 241 n. 13 suggests that Eustathius here recalls Dio's criticisms of Homer at 11.129; Eustathius certainly knew the *Trojan Oration*, cf. *in Il.* 460.10–12. As for Eustathius' target, Cesaretti 1991, 231 suggests allegorists such as Metrodorus of Lampsacus from the fifth century BC (cf. Hunter 2012a, 92, citing earlier bibliography); it is tempting, however, to think that Eustathius is thinking of allegorists nearer in time to himself than Metrodorus.
58 Eustathius is of course referring to Aristarchus' famous view (schol. D *Il.* 5.385, cf. *in Il.* 40.28–34, 561.29–30) that 'what is said by the poet should be accepted mythically, in accordance with poetic licence, and readers should not busy themselves (περιεργαζομένους) with anything beyond what the poet said'; for differing assessments of what Aristarchus actually meant by this cf., e.g., Porter 1992, 70–74, Nünlist 2009, 180–181; 2011. Eustathius' description of his own work — περιεργάσεταί που [τοὺς μύθους] ἀκολούθως τοῖς παλαιοῖς — may indeed scornfully pick up Aristarchus' verb.

last whose practice is much less clearcut, and much more of a compromise, than his proclaimed methodology.⁵⁹ Eustathius lines himself up alongside οἱ ἀκριβέστεροι, who take the trouble to investigate the material properly: that which is historical is accepted as it is, but with myths, such readers first consider their origin, nature and plausibility and then the nature of the truth which lies within them, which must be revealed through allegorical interpretation, or — in the evocative language which Eustathius inherited — θεραπεία, whether that be φυσικῶς ('pertaining to the nature of the world') or κατὰ ἦθος ('ethical', 'moralising') or ἱστορικῶς, by which last method Eustathius means that many myths contain a central core of reality, an event or events which really did happen, but that reality has been distorted by mythical material to make it more marvellous (τοῦ δὲ μύθου τὸ ἀληθὲς ἐκβιαζομένου πρὸς τὸ τερατωδέστερον) and must therefore be recovered by the interpreter.⁶⁰

Eustathius' *Commentaries* contain allegories from right across the board, from the simplest and most familiar to what can seem the most remarkably *recherché*, although Eustathius does not of course necessarily endorse every theory or interpretation to which he offers space, and it is not rare for a modern reader to feel that mutually incompatible reading strategies have simply been juxtaposed. Often, as for example in his ample commentary on the song of Demodocus about the adultery of Ares and Aphrodite (*in Od.* 1597.42–1598.9), Eustathius offers a list of competing allegories as part of making his commentary 'useful', though in the case of Demodocus' song it is clear that Eustathius in fact endorses a simple *a fortiori* moral didacticism which demonstrates that 'even among those above us (οἱ κρείττονες) wicked deeds do not prosper' (cf. *Od.* 8.329).⁶¹ Often, of course, it will be the relative didactic weight which determines to which allegories Eustathius gives space: when Athena tells Zeus that Odysseus 'longing to see even the smoke rising from his own land, desires to die' (*Od.* 1.58–59), Eustathius notes an allegorical interpretation by which Homer chooses to dwell on smoke, which like philosophy mounts up to the sky, because philosophical knowledge at first seems murky, whereas the full revelation (i.e. the fire which causes the smoke) is brilliant and bright. If you cannot attain that full and final revelation, then the murky first beginnings are much

---

59 For a helpful survey cf. Cesaretti 1991, 222–274.
60 Eustathius makes very similar points at the head of the *Odyssey*-commentary, where the purpose of τὸ τερατεύεσθαι is the creation of ἡδονή and ἔκπληξις for the audience (*in Od.* 1379.13–14). On the ἀκριβέστεροι see Pagani 2017; on the general issue, see van den Berg 2017.
61 On the use of this verse as a 'moral' for the story of Ares and Aphrodite cf. Hunter/Russell 2011, 108, Hunter 2012b, 96.

better than nothing, just as even if you cannot stuff yourself with honey, a little taste is something to be desired (*in Od.* 1391.46–48); Eustathius' pupils and colleagues will not have needed to have the lesson made any plainer.

As an illustration of very familiar and relatively simple allegorising, we may take the case of Athena as φρόνησις or σύνεσις; this is one of Eustathius' most common allegorical strategies, and it was one which had a very long history, stretching back in fact to the beginnings of allegorical interpretation itself.[62] The account, for example, of Nausicaa's reaction to the appearance of the naked Odysseus, when all her maidservants flee, gestures to this interpretation, even though that is not made explicit:[63]

οἴη δ' Ἀλκινόου θυγάτηρ μένε· τῆι γὰρ Ἀθήνη
θάρσος ἐνὶ φρεσὶ θῆκε καὶ ἐκ δέος εἵλετο γυίων.
στῆ δ' ἄντα σχομένη·

Homer, *Odyssey* 6.139–141a

Alcinous' daughter alone remained, for Athene put courage into her heart and removed fear from her limbs. She stood still facing him.

Nausicaa alone remained and did nothing ignoble (ἀγεννές) because of her good sense (σύνεσις). For this reason the poet says that Athena put courage into her heart and took fear from her limbs … [Nausicaa] reckoned sensibly (φρονίμως) that there is nothing frightening on the island … and so there is nothing to fear in the man who has appeared. This also demonstrates Homer's skill in the arrangement of his narrative (δεινότης διὰ τὸ εὐπλαστότερον). If the king's daughter had fled, Homer's fiction (πλάσις) would have become bathetic (κακόζηλον) and succeeding events would not have been plausible.

Eustathius, *Commentary on the Odyssey* 1555.28–31

So too, in *Iliad* 2, when Odysseus rises to address the army after having quashed Thersites' short lived impudence, Athena stands beside him in the guise of a herald to command silence so that everyone in the audience could hear what he has to say and 'take note of his advice' (*Iliad* 2.279–282). For Eustathius, Athena here (as so often) represents Odysseus' good sense (σύνεσις): the Greeks fall silent because they want to hear what Odysseus has to say, as they know of that

---

[62] Cf., e.g., Democritus, 68 B2 D-K; *LfgrE* I 210–211; for further discussion and bibliography on this allegory cf. Hunter 2012a, 60–67; 2014b, 34–35.

[63] So too, Eustathius observes that it is appropriate that it is Athena who is responsible for making Odysseus larger and more handsome to look upon, 'because it was his *phronesis* which made him admired and seem more impressive' (*in Il.* 258.1); van der Valk *ad loc.* suggests that Eustathius has misremembered that it is Laertes who is transformed at *Od.* 24.368–370, but cf. *Od.* 6.229–235, 18.69–70.

quality of good sense and intelligence (*in Il.* 220.14–17). That expectation itself obviated the need for a herald, but Homer necessarily represents this sequence of events with the typical 'divine machinery' of epic.[64] Again, when in *Odyssey* 13 Athena shows Odysseus the landmarks of Ithaca to prove to him that he has finally reached home and scatters the mist which had prevented him from seeing clearly, this is really the workings of φρόνησις: Odysseus knows that the Phaeacians have not cheated him, and Athena's words represent an internal process of reflection and dawning memory, by which he recognizes long familiar landmarks one by one; the mist which Athena scatters is the 'mist of forgetfulness' (*in Od.* 17 43.35–39), and many modern readers of Homer would attest, I think, to the continuing power of such a critical account.

In the tradition of Homeric criticism, this allegory of Athena assumed particular importance with regard to *Odyssey* 1, where Athena's advice, given in the guise of Mentes, to Telemachus to go in search of information about his father was standardly interpreted as the stirrings of φρόνησις within the maturing young hero.[65] This simple allegory was also often found in conjunction with the allegorizing of Athena's father, Zeus, as νοῦς, as φρόνησις is a product of the mind, and indeed its 'natural', desired state. Eustathius notes that, even if Zeus/the mind is darkened by anger or desire and turns away from the light of Athena/*phronesis*,[66] this will never last long (*in Il.* 717. 43–44). The allegory also comes prominently into play at two crucial moments of the poem involving Achilles. Athena's appearance to Achilles in *Iliad* 1 when he is choosing between drawing his sword on Agamemnon or checking this angry impulse is naturally seen as Achilles coming to his senses, as ἀγχίνοια and φρόνησις now take over (*in Il.* 81.28–82.22).[67] Secondly, in considering (*in Il.* 1267.6–25) the scene in *Iliad* 22 in which Athena tells Achilles to stop pursuing Hector around

---

64 Eustathius' explanation must also be set within the context of a rich critical tradition about the speeches of Odysseus and Nestor in *Iliad* 2; in that tradition Odysseus is indeed the 'people's choice'.
65 Cf. *Hypothesis* c Pontani and the scholia to *Odyssey* 1.44c, 270a etc.
66 Eustathius is fond of the epithet φωσφόρος for Athena, cf. van der Valk I 704; this is not, I believe, attested before Eustathius, though it is obviously connected with the goddess' association with the moon, for which cf. *LfgrE* I 211.
67 On the allegorising tradition of this scene cf. Hunter 2012a, 60–7 Hera's role in sending Athena is interpreted either in connection with Agamemnon's royal status or, in a later addition to the commentary, through the familiar equation of Hera with ἀήρ: 'Understanding, which is Athena, is sent because the afterthought arising from change of mind comes upon him in obscurity (ἀερίαν) and darkly and, as it were, unseen and unexpected' (*in Il.* 81.43–44). For Eustathius' further assimilation of Athena's intervention to Socrates' δαιμόνιον (*in Il.* 82.9–11) cf. Max. Tyr. 8.5–6, Hunter 2012a, 63 n. 71.

the Trojan walls as she will deceive him into standing to face Achilles (vv. 214–215), Eustathius begins by noting that, although Homer might seem to downplay Achilles' prowess by giving Athena all the credit for his victory, this is not in fact problematic, for us or for Homer; for Eustathius 'the facts' (ἡ ἱστορία) are clear: 'Hector was brave, but was overthrown by Achilles who was bravest'.[68] The distinction between ἱστορία and the elaborations and 'allegories' of poetry and myth, to which (for Eustathius) Athena obviously belongs, is fundamental to Eustathius' procedure as a commentator (though not of course just his alone), and it is to poetry that Eustathius next moves:

> In its typical fashion, poetry prefers to set out events in ways surpassing the normal (τερατωδέστερον), rather than to set them out as they happened (ἀληθῶς) but in a less exalted way (ταπεινότερον). Here he prefers to show Achilles as dear to the gods than as just brave; many other people are brave, but it is rare to be so loved by the gods ... This passage is also educative, if the divine cares about men to this extent.
> Eustathius, *Commentary on the Iliad* 1267.10–17

If the last observation in this passage is very clearly owed to Eustathius' Christian perspective, then what follows is a remarkable rationalising account of Achilles' thought-processes: the whole scene seems to hint (ὑπεμφαίνειν) that intelligence (φρόνησις) has come to Achilles' aid. Realising that both he and Hector were tired, Achilles stopped for a break, which caused Hector, as a result of his own (deceptive) reasoning, also to cease from running away and to stand to face Achilles. One has a choice in fact, notes Eustathius: either we simply understand that Achilles had a rest-break, after which he was too strong for Hector, or that, in addition, Hector gained new courage to face Achilles; either way φρόνησις/Athena was responsible, destroying Hector and bringing glory to Achilles (*in Il.* 1267.18–24).

Even if with such a well-established allegory as Athena ~ φρόνησις, however, the commentator and reader must exercise judgement; 'allegorical' reading is not simply a matter of 'global change', so that wherever Athena is named, one can substitute φρόνησις. Part of the depth of Homeric poetry precisely arises from the interpretative demands it makes upon readers. In *Iliad* 5, for example, Athena encourages Diomedes to fear no one, not even Ares, in combat and takes her place beside him in his chariot by dislodging his comrade Sthenelos:

---

[68] On Eustathius' fondness for Achilles, and his belief that Homer was similarly fond, cf. above pp. 701–702.

ὣς φαμένη Σθένελον μὲν ἀφ' ἵππων ὦσε χαμᾶζε,
χειρὶ πάλιν ἐρύσασ', ὃ δ' ἄρ' ἐμμαπέως ἀπόρουσεν·
ἣ δ' ἐς δίφρον ἔβαινε παραὶ Διομήδεα δῖον
ἐμμεμαυῖα θεά· μέγα δ' ἔβραχε φήγινος ἄξων
βριθοσύνηι· δεινὴν γὰρ ἄγεν θεὸν ἄνδρά τ' ἄριστον.

Homer, *Iliad* 5.835–839

So saying, she pulled Sthenelos back with her hand and pushed him out of the chariot to the ground; he quickly leapt clear. With great eagerness the goddess then mounted the chariot alongside the noble Diomedes; the axle made of oak creaked loudly under the weight, for it bore a dread goddess and the best of men.

Eustathius here weighs up the options:

Note that this passage is entirely unallegorical (ἀναλληγόρητον) and an excellent example of poetic marvellousness (ποιητικὴ τερατεία). It is not possible to understand as factual (νοεῖν ἱστορικῶς) that Sthenelos stepped down from the chariot through some inner thought (κατά τινα σύνεσιν) so that Diomedes would himself be both rider and charioteer, unless such a myth is to be read to mean that Diomedes so cleverly (δεξιώτατα) controlled the whole business of fighting in the chariot that the charioteer Sthenelos is not even to be reckoned into the deeds.

Eustathius, *Commentary on the Iliad* 612.36–41

Eustathius thus works through the possible ways in which this passage could be read with the common allegorisations of Athena as 'forethought' (σύνεσις etc.) or 'skill' (δεξιότης); one he rejects outright and another he offers without apparent confidence. He may have been strengthened in his view that this scene is not to be read allegorically by the following verses (athetised by Aristarchus) in which the chariot groans beneath the weight of the great hero and the dread goddess; intellectual qualities such as σύνεσις tend to be imagined as 'light' rather than heavy. It is, however, typical of Eustathius' methods that he then proceeds to address this question, but in a way which does not sit particularly comfortably with his earlier discussion. He notes that the question of how Athena could weigh so much had been raised, as she should be 'weightless', and he cites a neo-Platonic solution to the problem: the intelligible (τὸ νοητόν) is indeed weightless, but when it takes on perceptible form, then it appears to have weight. Rather, however, than trying to combine Eustathius' views on, first, Athena's removal of Sthenelos and, second, the groaning chariot into one single 'coherent' view, we should note that here Eustathius, like the ancient commentators, moves from single problem to single problem, even when they appear close together in the text and might well be thought to be related.

The *Commentaries* contain some remarkable examples of 'physical allegory', such as an extended discussion (*in Il.* 150.40–152.25) of Hephaestus bringing an end to the quarrel of Zeus and Hera at the end of *Iliad* 1 as 'heat' bringing about a reconciliation between 'dry' and 'wet'. The sources of many of these allegories are unknown, though modern scholars are fond of evoking the name of Demo, a female Homeric critic of perhaps the fifth century AD who is indeed cited on more than one occasion by Eustathius.[69] Let me consider here a relatively straightforward physical allegory from *Iliad* 23. In that book Achilles prays to Boreas and Zephyros to come to fire the pyre on which lies the body of Patroclus, surrounded by dead animals and the bodies of twelve young Trojans:

ἔνθ' αὖτ' ἄλλ' ἐνόησε ποδάρκης δῖος Ἀχιλλεύς·
στὰς ἀπάνευθε πυρῆς δοιοῖς ἠρᾶτ' ἀνέμοισι
Βορρῆι καὶ Ζεφύρωι, καὶ ὑπίσχετο ἱερὰ καλά·   195
πολλὰ δὲ καὶ σπένδων χρυσέωι δέπαϊ λιτάνευεν
ἐλθέμεν, ὄφρα τάχιστα πυρὶ φλεγεθοίατο νεκροί,
ὕλη τε σεύαιτο καήμεναι. ὦκα δὲ Ἶρις
ἀράων ἀΐουσα μετάγγελος ἦλθ' ἀνέμοισιν.
οἳ μὲν ἄρα Ζεφύροιο δυσαέος ἀθρόοι ἔνδον   200
εἰλαπίνην δαίνυντο· θέουσα δὲ Ἶρις ἐπέστη
βηλῶι ἔπι λιθέωι. τοὶ δ' ὡς ἴδον ὀφθαλμοῖσι
πάντες ἀνήϊξαν, κάλεόν τέ μιν εἰς ἓ ἕκαστος.

Homer, *Iliad* 23.193–203

> The swift-footed noble Achilles had a different thought. He stood away from the pyre and prayed to the two winds, Boreas and Zephyros, and he promised them fine sacrifices. Pouring many libations from a golden cup, he begged them to come, so that the corpses could be consumed by fire as soon as possible, and the wood would quickly catch alight. Iris heard the prayers and quickly went as a messenger to the winds. They were all together feasting in the dwelling of the stormy Zephyros. Iris arrived at a run and stood on the stone threshold; when they laid eyes on her, they all leapt up, and each of them called her to himself.

The swiftness of Iris's response is marked by her sudden intrusion, mid-verse, into the narrative, prompting Eustathius to draw his students' attention to Homeric technique (καὶ ὅρα τὸ κατὰ τὴν Ἶριν, *in Il.* 1295.65); he points out that either Achilles prayed also to her, but Homer did not mention this (the principle of κατὰ τὸ σιωπώμενον),[70] or else it was simply Iris's job (which, standardly in epic, it was) to report such things to the winds. What follows, however, offers apparently a clear and explicit two-part explanation: first, ἡ ἀλληγορία, and then ὁ μῦθος. The allegory here is a physical one. Iris is the rainbow, and rain-

---

69 On Demo cf. Pontani 2005, 87–88, citing earlier bibliography.
70 Cf. Nünlist 2009, ch. 6.

bows are signs not just of rain and war, but also sometimes of winds;[71] when the winds leap up at her arrival, this indicates that the appearance of the rainbow has stirred the winds to blow. They all leap up, because rainbows can rouse winds from all directions; Iris herself, however, departs quickly because rainbows do not linger long, and she heads off to Ocean because rainbows are associated with moisture and appear in fact through raindrops (*in Il.* 1296.1–6). As usual, scholarly interest has been focused on Eustathius' sources, but what is striking here is both the didactic clarity and completeness of Eustathius' exposition and the typical independence of the allegorical interpretation from the narrative which calls it forth. Behind such physical allegories stands (again) the idea of the poet as teacher, and an interpreter, such as Eustathius, here stands in for, almost ventriloquises, the poet's teaching. The closer that teaching is to our own (and to Eustathius' students') experience, the greater the poet's authority; this authority, established through what is now seen to be an accurate account of the physical world, carries over into the non-allegorical narrative: the poet who accurately reports the physical world can also teach us about the moral and ethical world.

After the allegory, the μῦθος,[72] that is simply the narrative of the poem as the poet tells it. Here Eustathius is perhaps uncharacteristically brief: 'Each of the winds calls Iris [to himself] as they are in love with her (ἐρῶντας)' (*in Il.* 1296.17–18). Eustathius knew, as did the scholiasts, that poets after Homer had created a romantic relationship between Iris and Zephyros (in Alcaeus fr. 327 V they were the parents of Eros),[73] but here the Homeric text clearly invited a rather more ribald reading. A beautiful woman entering a male feast can mean one of only a few things, and it was easy enough to see each of the winds suddenly competing for her sexual favours, like symposiasts squabbling over a flute girl; the exegetical T-scholium in fact makes the tentative suggestion that the winds' erotic excitement can be explained by the fact that they were a bit tipsy (ἀκροθώρακες). Iris, however, makes her excuses and beats a hasty retreat. One strand of ancient interpretation certainly took this view; the schol. bT *Il.* 23.206a observe that Iris tells a lie in order to escape these pestering men (οἱ ἐνοχλοῦντες, the standard verb for 'sexual harrassment'). Of this, there is not a

---

[71] For an association of the two cf., e.g., Anaxagoras fr. 19 D-K, Empedocles fr. 50 D-K (cited by Tzetzes in the *Allegories of the Iliad*, Goldwyn/Kokkini 2015, 274), West on Hes. *Theog.* 266.
[72] Eustathius in fact returns to physical allegory concerning the winds after dealing with the μῦθος (*in Il.* 1296.10–12), but not to Iris' relationship to the winds.
[73] Plutarch himself offers an elaborate, Platonising allegory of this fragment at *Amatorius* 765 df, cf. Hunter 2012a, 195–197. For the later attestations of this version cf. Page 1955, 271 n. 7.

word in Eustathius, and it is not, I think, unreasonable to infer that he here averts his students' eyes from a type of male behaviour that he certainly would not want them to imitate. Rather, he follows another line, familiar also from the scholia (schol. bT *Il.* 23.206b), that the gods really have withdrawn from Troy, now that the course of action concerning Achilles and Hector has been decided (*in Il.* 1296.24–25). As always, however, Eustathius is alive to how one part of the poem corresponds to another. So here, he recalls how, at the onset of the μῆνις, Thetis reported to Achilles at *Il.* 1.423–424 that all the gods had gone off to the Ethiopians; Eustathius' point is not that we have what we would call a simple ring-composition, but rather that the two instances of divine feasting with the Ethiopians are quite different, and 'this is a sign of Homer's skill as he avoids, as far as possible, sameness in his writing' (*in Il.* 1296.25).

Eustathius turns his attention elsewhere also to Iris, and comparison with his discussion of *Iliad* 23 may prove instructive. In *Iliad* 5 Iris, again entering the narrative without introduction, leads Aphrodite away from the battle after she has been wounded by Diomedes. The bT-scholia on *Il.* 5.353 observe that Iris' role here is because 'she serves all the gods in common or is ἐρωτική [i.e. and therefore associated with Aphrodite]'. Eustathius follows this tradition, but seeks to explain it in terms (again) of the physical allegory: because of the rainbow's beautiful colours it has 'something of Aphrodite' (τι ἐπαφρόδιτον) about it, and it is therefore closely connected to Aphrodite (*in Il.* 555.31–33). He then turns to Iris' speed, another characteristic which is always foregrounded in poetry. From the allegorical point of view, this (again) is to be understood from the fact that rainbows appear and disappear very quickly (555.36), but when looked at μυθικῶς, i.e. as poetry depicts the anthropomorphic Iris, she has wings to indicate her speed, as also does Hermes, who is, like her, a messenger, and 'speed is the virtue of the messenger'. Eustathius also notes here, as he does elsewhere (cf. below), that Iris and Hermes share an etymology from εἴρειν, interpreted as 'to tell, announce'.[74] In a subsequent addition to his text Eustathius notes that he has already observed that Iris appears in two forms, one anthropomorphic (σωματοειδής) and the other 'the sign in the sky'; as an example of the former manifestation he cites *Iliad* 3.121, where Iris (again without explicit narrative causation) comes as a messenger to Helen, having taken the shape of Laodike, 'the most beautiful of Priam's daughters', in order to make Helen come to watch the duel between Paris and Menelaos.

---

[74] The etymology is not, of course, original to Eustathius, cf., e.g., Plat. *Crat.* 408b, *Etym. Magnum* 475.38–40 Gaisf.

The exegetical bT-scholia on *Il.* 3.121 note that Iris must have been sent by Zeus to Helen and they offer two reasons for the choice of Iris: 'a woman can persuade another woman', and secondly — the explanation we have found elsewhere — Iris is an ἐρωτική goddess and 'is always present with Aphrodite'. This second explanation presumably not only assumes the very close relationship between Helen and Aphrodite, but also the fact that after having spoken to Helen, Iris is said to throw 'sweet desire' into Helen's heart to see her former husband. Eustathius' note on the passage (*in Il.* 391.21–34) is, once again, arranged into ἀλληγορία and μῦθος, although this time it is the latter which comes first. Under this heading, Eustathius places the now familiar (to us) wings, denoting speed, and the etymology of her name. The physical allegory is of course of the rainbow, and here Eustathius notes that the etymology from εἴρειν, 'to tell, announce', is appropriate here too, because rainbows 'announce in the midst of the rain that something is to happen'; for this reason 'she is said to be the messenger of Zeus, that is of the air'. It may, however, not be obvious to us what a rainbow might have to do with Helen being drawn to the walls of Troy, particularly as — as Eustathius in his note on *Il.* 5.353 implicitly acknowledges — Iris here takes on a very human shape to address Helen.[75] Here therefore Eustathius calls on 'the more common treatment (θεραπεία) of the myth', namely that Iris represents φήμη, 'report, rumour', a kind of allegorising (though that is not the word which Eustathius uses) for which the etymology from εἴρειν is also appropriate.[76] It is rumour about the duel, here transmitted by Laodike, which brings Helen out on to the walls, just as when at *Il.* 2.786–806 Iris tells Priam of the mustering of huge Greek forces, that too is the operation of φήμη. Here we might well think that we are very close to epic modes familiar from elsewhere, most notably Virgil's *Aeneid*. Virgil's famous picture of malicious *Fama* may in fact suggest at first, not just Homeric Eris, but also the rainbow, in a gesture to the linkage between Iris and φήμη which Eustathius attests:[77]

> Fama, malum qua non aliud uelocius ullum:
> mobilitate uiget uirisque adquirit eundo,   175

---

[75] Such considerations do not, however, deter Tzetzes for whom Iris' likening of herself to Laodike does indeed mean that she became a rainbow, 'from which Helen realized what was going to happen, as if someone had given her a full and clear account' (*alleg. Il.* 3.82–87 = Goldwyn/Kokkini 2015, 136).
[76] φήμη is one of the meanings of Iris found at *Etym. Magnum* 475.45 Gaisf.
[77] On *Fama* cf. above all Hardie 2012 (where, however, there does not seem to be any mention of Iris and the rainbow).

parua metu primo, mox sese attollit in auras
ingrediturque solo et caput inter nubila condit.

Virgil, *Aeneid* 4.174–177

Rumour, the quickest of all evils: movement gives her strength, and she increases in force as she proceeds. Small at first through fear, soon she raises herself to the sky and treads the earth with her head hidden in the clouds.

In the *Commentaries* the allegorical and the non-allegorical in fact constantly bleed into each other, as Eustathius jumps backwards and forwards through his material, repeating here, reworking there. Another excellent illustration of this is the discussion of one passage of the *Iliad* which is itself at least quasi-allegorical, namely Achilles' famous account to Priam of the human condition:

ὣς γὰρ ἐπεκλώσαντο θεοὶ δειλοῖσι βροτοῖσιν,   525
ζώειν ἀχνυμένοις· αὐτοὶ δέ τ' ἀκηδέες εἰσίν.
δοιοὶ γάρ τε πίθοι κατακείαται ἐν Διὸς οὔδει
δώρων οἷα δίδωσι, κακῶν, ἕτερος δὲ ἑάων·
ὧι μέν κ' ἀμμείξας δώηι Ζεὺς τερπικέραυνος,
ἄλλοτε μέν τε κακῶι ὅ γε κύρεται, ἄλλοτε δ' ἐσθλῶι·   530
ὧι δέ κε τῶν λυγρῶν δώηι, λωβητὸν ἔθηκε,
καί ἑ κακὴ βούβρωστις ἐπὶ χθόνα δῖαν ἐλαύνει,
φοιτᾶι δ' οὔτε θεοῖσι τετιμένος οὔτε βροτοῖσιν.

Homer, *Iliad* 24.525–533

This is the fate which the gods have allotted to wretched mortals, that they should live in grief; they themselves are free from cares. Two jars stand on Zeus's floor containing the gifts he gives: [one contains] bad things, the other good things. The man to whom Zeus who delights in thunder gives a mixture sometimes meets with ill and at other times with good. However, the man to whom he gives [only] grim things is brought to ruin, and evil hunger drives him over the holy earth, and he wanders honoured by neither gods nor men.

Achilles then proceeds to apply this lesson both to his own father, Peleus, and to Priam himself; both had been very prosperous, but now they live out a wretched old age which has brought them nothing but pain. Since at least the time of Pindar (cf. *Pyth.* 3.80–82), these verses and their sentiment were echoed, discussed and sometimes rejected, as by the Platonic Socrates (*Resp.* 2.379d) who banned them from the ideal state on the grounds that they make the god responsible for κακά. Much has been written about the consolatory effect of Achilles' image, a point already made in the scholia and repeated by Eustathius (*in Il.* 1362.57), who was of course very conscious of the 'rhetorical genre' of the speech, but Eustathius' discussion of the image offers a particularly interesting example of the cumulative way in which some parts of his commentary unfold and of how what is by any standards a remarkable Homeric passage has prompted commentary which pays particular attention to the power of Achilles' fable to generate multiple interpretations, once the 'literal' meaning has been established.

The exegetical scholia on *Il.* 24.526 note that when Achilles says that the gods are ἀκηδέες, 'without cares', he must be talking about the truly divine, τὸ φύσει θεῖον, for the gods of poetry, particularly of course those of Homer, certainly feel grief and other human emotions; that Homer's gods are ἀνθρωποπαθεῖς is a commonplace of ancient and Eustathian commentary. The scholia also quote Epicurus to the effect that 'the immortal and indestructible neither feels trouble nor provides it to others; therefore it has nothing to do with anger or grief' (*Kyr. Dox.* 1).[78] The scholia on the following verses about the jars cite Plato's condemnation of them in the *Republic*, but explain that Achilles has invented the jars in order to console Priam. Eustathius helpfully puts these notices about Epicurus and Plato together as 'what the philosophers say' (*in Il.* 1363.8), to be opposed to the poetic view of gods with human emotions which include an unwillingness to allow those beneath them to enjoy equal happiness, a view expressed with allusion to a passage of Herodotus (7.10ε).[79] Eustathius then proceeds to explain the mixture of good and bad that Homer sets out as the model for human life, illustrating this from Demodocus in the *Odyssey* 'to whom the Muse gave good and bad' (*Od.* 8.63); human beings are unable to get unmixed good things from the one jar that contains them, but may get unmixed bad. In a subsequent addition to the commentary, Eustathius illustrated the inevitability of mixed fortune by two characters (including Ptolemy Philadelphus) drawn from the pages of Athenaeus.[80]

Having explained, as it were, the 'literal' meaning of Achilles' jars,[81] that human life necessarily involves misfortune, Eustathius now turns to various

---

78 Text and interpretation of this saying are very disputed.
79 Van der Valk notes that Eustathius 'pretends' ('simulat') that he has taken the observations direct from Plato and Epicurus, rather than from scholia; whether or not this is correct, such a perspective entirely ignores the utilitarian purpose of teaching for which the commentaries are written, cf. above 684.
80 Eustathius seems to have made much greater use of Athenaeus when adding to the commentary in Thessaloniki than he did in Constantinople, cf. van der Valk, I xvi–xvii; it is natural to connect such differences to the availability of books.
81 I pass over an intervening note in which Eustathius contrasts the Homeric passage with the Hesiodic jar which Pandora opened; Eustathius will have known that the scholiastic tradition made the Homeric passage Hesiod's 'source' (schol. A and T *Il.*24.527–528a–b, cf. Hunter 2014a, 244), but that is not his interest here.

forms of allegorical interpretation; as often, the shift is marked by ἰστέον δέ, 'Observe, moreover ...' (*in Il.* 1363.27). The most common way of deflecting Plato's charge against the verses was to explain that Zeus here stands for 'fate', but Eustathius notes that 'Zeus' could here stand for νοῦς, 'mind, intention', a very common allegorical equation.[82] Not just Zeus's mind, but human intention and will can cause both good and evil, and so the two jars may represent different 'states of mind'. If so, Eustathius continues, then human beings may indeed receive any of the three possible options – unmixed good, unmixed bad, and a mixture of good and bad. The first is 'complete blessedness' (ἄκρα μακαριότης) and the second 'wretchedness in the soul' (ἀθλιότης ψυχική), both of which are presumably to be understood in Christian terms: pagan texts, particularly great texts such as Homer, teach eternal messages, which for Eustathius and his pupils must be understood in Christian terms. The third option utilizes the fundamental division for any priest between the religious or spiritual realm and that of 'ordinary' life, for the category of 'the mixed' refers in this scheme to our day-to-day life (κατάστασις πολιτική), in which we all must indeed accept human limits to good fortune.

Eustathius' Christianising interpretation is testimony to the extraordinarily productive power of Achilles' image, which – as is often pointed out – is in many ways closer to folktale and fable than to 'high poetry'. Eustathius too feels something of this 'strangeness' about the image, for he draws attention to the spherical shape of jars which associates them with the heavens above; by choosing πίθοι, Homer has been concerned, in Eustathius' account, to lend τὸ σεμνόν to an image for which more vulgar equivalents could easily have been found (the gifts of the gods could have been made to 'lie on the floor or be kept in boxes or pits'). Eustathius also notes that πίθοι are common in mythic tales; he cites (again) the story from *Iliad* 5 of Ares bound and chained and the leaky jars of the Danaids. In a subsequent addition to the commentary, Eustathius collects some appearances of πίθοι in proverbs and takes the chance to offer an allegorical (συμβολικῶς) interpretation of Hesiod's gnomic advice on how best to use a πίθος (*Op.* 368–369). The discussion of the jars then closes with an account of the difficult syntax of the verses, made all the more necessary by the fact that, as Eustathius observes, some thought that Homer indicated that Zeus had in fact three jars, two of bad things and one of good. Eustathius appeals to Homeric usage in ruling that there were only two jars, though he will admit that Homer has been guilty of unclarity; the syntactical discussion is, as often, indebted to the same grammatical tradition which has fed into the scholia.

---

82 Cf., e.g., *LfgrE* I 210, above 36.

The Achaean wall

At the opening of *Iliad* 12 the narrator foretells the complete obliteration by Poseidon and Apollo after the fall of Troy of the Achaean fortification which had been constructed at the end of Book 7; the interpretative problems concerning this narrative sequence remain of great interest to modern students of the *Iliad*, and offer a very interesting test-case for Eustathius' use of the critical heritage and for the focuses of his commentary.[83] I will here follow his discussions sequentially (though with some omissions), in order to confront the text as his students and readers may have done; some of the problems which modern scholars find in the conception and role of the wall will, therefore, here find little discussion, because Eustathius did not in fact discuss them, but this itself will, I hope, carry its own instructive value.

The making of a defensive wall and ditch to protect the Greek ships and encampment is first suggested by Nestor at *Il.* 7.325–344, and the Greeks carry out Nestor's instructions almost to the letter at 7.433–441.[84] The scene then switches to Olympus where the gods are watching the Greeks at work. Poseidon complains to Zeus that the successful building of this wall, although the Greeks had offered no sacrifices to the gods, will lead to a decline in concern with the gods and also to the eclipse of the walls of Troy which he and Apollo had built:

Ζεῦ πάτερ, ἦ ῥά τίς ἐστι βροτῶν ἐπ' ἀπείρονα γαῖαν
ὅς τις ἔτ' ἀθανάτοισι νόον καὶ μῆτιν ἐνίψει;
οὐχ ὁράᾳς ὅ τε δὴ αὖτε κάρη κομόωντες Ἀχαιοὶ
τεῖχος ἐτειχίσσαντο νεῶν ὕπερ, ἀμφὶ δὲ τάφρον
ἤλασαν, οὐδὲ θεοῖσι δόσαν κλειτὰς ἑκατόμβας;   450

---

[83] Cf. Porter 2011, which has been an important stimulus to the present discussion. Some of Porter's arguments have elements in common with Ford 1992, 147–157, though Ford rather sees the wall as (in part) an image for the composition of the *Iliad* itself: 'I conceive of the episode of the wall, for all its ancient elements, as formulated along with the plan to construct a monumental text of the *Iliad* of the sort we now have' (151); some of the concerns of Ford and Porter are picked up by Bassi 2014. Scodel 1982 stresses that the obliteration of the wall by flood marks a complete break between the time of the heroes and the time of Homer and his audience, and West 1995 associates the destruction of the wall with the Assyrian destruction of Babylon in 689–688 BC. Cf. further Grethlein 2008, 32–35.

[84] Eustathius (*in Il.* 689.54–55) notes that the σκόλοπες of v. 441 were not in fact mentioned by Nestor and, with a properly didactic eye, he points out how, quoting (but not spelling the quotation out) Eur. *Hipp*. 436, this shows that 'second thoughts are wiser'. Clearly, though Homer does not say so explicitly, the Greeks gave further thought, beyond Nestor's speech, to what kind of fortifications were needed; on this exegetical principle of κατὰ τὸ σιωπώμενον cf. Nünlist 2009, ch. 6.

τοῦ δ' ἤτοι κλέος ἔσται ὅσον τ' ἐπικίδναται ἠώς,
τοῦ δ' ἐπιλήσονται, τὸ ἐγὼ καὶ Φοῖβος Ἀπόλλων
ἥρωι Λαομέδοντι πολίσσαμεν ἀθλήσαντε.

Homer, *Iliad* 7.446–453

Father Zeus, is there any mortal on the boundless earth who will in the future reveal his intention and plan to the immortals? Do you not see that now the long-haired Achaeans have built a wall in defence of the ships and dug a ditch along it and have not offered splendid hecatombs to the gods? The fame of this wall will stretch as far as dawn is scattered, but they will forget the wall which I and Phoebus Apollo laboured to build for the hero Laomedon.

Zeus, however, will have none of this, but grants that once the Achaeans have left, the wall may be utterly destroyed:

'ὦ πόποι ἐννοσίγαι' εὐρυσθενές, οἷον ἔειπες. 455
ἄλλός κέν τις τοῦτο θεῶν δείσειε νόημα,
ὃς σέο πολλὸν ἀφαυρότερος χεῖράς τεμένος τε·
σὸν δ' ἤτοι κλέος ἔσται ὅσον τ' ἐπικίδναται ἠώς.
ἄγρει μὰν ὅτ' ἂν αὖτε κάρη κομόωντες Ἀχαιοὶ
οἴχωνται σὺν νηυσὶ φίλην ἐς πατρίδα γαῖαν, 460
τεῖχος ἀναρρήξας τὸ μὲν εἰς ἅλα πᾶν καταχεῦαι,
αὖτις δ' ἠιόνα μεγάλην ψαμάθοισι καλύψαι,
ὥς κέν τοι μέγα τεῖχος ἀμαλδύνηται Ἀχαιῶν.'
ὣς οἳ μὲν τοιαῦτα πρὸς ἀλλήλους ἀγόρευον,
δύσετο δ' ἠέλιος, τετέλεστο δὲ ἔργον Ἀχαιῶν. 465

Homer, *Iliad* 7.455–465

'Shame, Earthshaker of mighty strength, for what you have said! Some other god might fear this scheme, one much weaker than you in might and strength. Your fame will stretch as far as dawn is scattered! Come then: when the long-haired Achaeans return in their ships to their own dear land, then break down the wall and pour it all into the sea and cover over the whole shore again with sand, so that the Achaeans' great wall will be nothing.' Thus they spoke to each other; the sun set and the Achaeans' task was completed.

Since the Achaeans finished the task as the sun set, the building of the wall had taken them one long day. At the opening of Book 12, the poet reports how Poseidon and Apollo did indeed obliterate all trace of the wall after 'the city of Priam had been sacked in the tenth year'. The passage naturally attracted critical attention as one of the very few places where the poet explicitly refers to Trojan events that lie outside the scope of his poem and, in particular, to the fall of Troy. Eustathius himself links this to the familiar critical notion (cf. esp. the scholia on *Iliad* 1.1a–b), going back at least to Aristotle, that although Homer severely limited the time-frame of the events of the *Iliad*, his technique allowed him to embrace events outside that frame:

> Observe that, just as in the previous book Homer had, in full accordance with his technique (εὐμεθόδως), inserted some of what happened before the Trojan war, such as the raising of the army and associated events,[85] so here, through the trope of 'foreshadowing' (προαναφώνησις), he vividly (γοργῶς) and briefly sets out the end of the war and some of the events after that ... This is his normal practice, so that, even if the opening he laid down for the *Iliad* was the wrath of Achilles, nevertheless we would not fail to hear about some of the major events outside that, namely what happened before the wrath and after it.
>
> Eustathius, *Commentary on the Iliad* 889.38–43

Before turning in detail to the Olympian conversation in Book 7, Eustathius discusses the Greek wall:

> Observe that the ancients (οἱ παλαιοί) took the view that this Greek wall was a fiction (πλάσμα) of Homer. It did not, they say, happen in truth, but the poet invented (ἐπλάσατο) the wall-building beside the ships and what happened there; he was not relating an event which happened but setting forth one as though it had happened (οὐχ ἱστορῶν πρᾶγμα γενόμενον ἀλλ' ὡς γενόμενον ἐκτιθέμενος), nor was he speaking the truth, but rather supposing what might have happened (τὰ εἰκότα δὲ ὑποτιθέμενος). His purpose in doing this was later on to be able to exercise (ἐγγυμνάσῃ) his rhetorical skill in [the depiction of] sieges (τειχομαχίαι) and the dangers associated with them, which was for various reasons not possible with Troy itself, but particularly because of Achilles' wrath; without Achilles, the Trojans could not be hemmed in their city and endure a siege, because the will of Zeus which had been announced before [*Iliad* 1.5] had to be brought to fulfillment. The poet invented (ἐπλάσατο) the construction of towers at the ships very convincingly (οὐκ ἀπιθάνως) thanks to the rich variety and abundance of his writing (διὰ πάνυ πολλὴν ποικιλίαν καὶ εὐπορίαν γραφῆς).
>
> Eustathius, *Commentary on the Iliad* 689.56–63

In drawing attention to the fictionality of the wall, as something which 'might have happened' rather than as something which did, and to the fact that this is an opinion which he has inherited from 'ancient' scholarship, Eustathius uses what would have been to him and his pupils a very familiar classification of narrative material into the 'true', the 'as if true (fictional)' and the 'fantastic/ mythical'. In the repetitive fullness with which he notes the difference between what is true and merely probable, it is perhaps not fanciful to hear the careful, didactic voice of the teacher, making sure that his pupils understand. What matters to Eustathius, moreover, is the opportunity that this poetic fiction gives him to highlight Homer's rhetorical virtues, and the way the note is constructed

---

85 The reference is to Nestor's account at *Il.* 11.769–790.

makes it impossible to identify where the views of 'the ancients' end and Eustathius takes over. Homer wanted to exercise (or practise) the rhetorical description of a τειχομαχία, a 'battle involving walls',[86] a term which need not be synonymous with 'siege', but which easily slips into such a meaning, as suits Eustathius' didactic purposes. Eustathius' use of ἐγγυμνάζειν points clearly to rhetorical exercises or *progymnasmata*. Aelius Theon cites the siege of Plataea in Book 3 of Thucydides as a model for the exercise of *ekphrasis* (118.25–26 Sp.= p. 67 Patillon-Bolognesi), and *ekphraseis* of a πεζομαχία and a ναυμαχία are preserved under the name of Libanius (8.460–464, 489–490 Foerster).[87] For any Byzantine of the twelfth century, however, sieges were not simply a subject for school-exercises, but a familiar and awful reality; long before the siege of Thessaloniki in 1185, which he describes so vividly in his history of the Norman sacking, Eustathius will have known all about the κίνδυνοι associated with such events (*in Il.* 689.59). There is, of course, as in fact Eustathius' own introduction to his account of the siege of Thessaloniki makes clear, no gulf between the description of 'real' events and a concern with rhetorical convention and appropriateness, such as he ascribes to Homer here. It was indeed that very concern and the extraordinary riches of his poetic talent which made Homer's account 'utterly convincing'.[88]

If, for Eustathius, the Achaean wall can be explained through rhetorical need, the reason why that rhetorical need could not be fulfilled through a siege of Troy must be explained somewhat differently. It would, of course, be very easy for us to say that the whole design of the *Iliad* excludes a siege of Troy, which might ultimately have led to its fall, and Eustathius' explanation is not in fact far removed from that consideration of the whole sweep of the poem. A siege, he explains, is incompatible with Achilles' wrath and hence withdrawal from fighting, because only Achilles could make the Trojans stay within their walls, and this too does not fit with the 'plan of Zeus', here clearly understood as the promise to Thetis to grant success to the Trojans until the Greeks recompense her son's outraged honour (*Iliad* 1.508–510).[89] Whatever one might think of this explanation, what is notable is the way Eustathius places his discussion

---

[86] This explanation also survives, though less clearly expressed, in the schol. T *Il.* 12.3–35. Plato, *Ion* 539b2 shows that τειχομαχία was a title given to all or part of what we call *Iliad* 12.
[87] Cf. also Aphthonius *prog.* 12.2. p. 148 Patillon.
[88] Eustathius frequently refers to the ποικίλον element of Homeric poetry (cf. van der Valk, II lvi–ii), but it is noteworthy that Aphthonius stresses the need in *ekphrasis* to use different σχήματα in order to lend τὸ ποικίλον to the description (12.3 Patillon).
[89] At *in Il.* 20.21 Eustathius notes this explanation as one of several current for the Διὸς βουλή of *Iliad* 1.5.

of the building of the wall within a wider view of the narrative. The difference that Achilles made is, of course, a recurrent motif of ancient discussion of the design of the poem. The exegetical scholia on the opening verse note, as one explanation of why Homer began in what was to be the last year of the war, that the Trojans did not come out to fight while Achilles was actively engaged on the Greek side, and so there was actually little action to describe, and this is an explanation which Eustathius too offers (*in Il.* 7.6–14). Eustathius thus places the making of the wall within a view of the economy of the poem as a whole; with such a view, ancient and modern worries about why the Greeks only got around to building a defensive wall in the tenth year of the war fade into insignificance. So too, van der Valk (I 493) suggests that the Christian Eustathius deliberately ignored an explanation which is found in the exegetical scholia to *Iliad* 12.3–35, namely that Homer could not stage operations at the walls of Troy because they had been built by (pagan) gods; to focus on this, however, is to fail to appreciate how Eustathius has in fact thought through Homer's overall strategy.[90]

Having explained why Homer has introduced the wall, Eustathius then turns to the Olympian conversation which guaranteed the wall's eventual destruction. Here Homer's purpose was to prevent anyone proving that he had invented the wall by pointing to the complete absence of any traces 'of such a famous piece of wall-building' (*in Il.* 689.68).[91] Poseidon's anger and jealousy (φθόνος) and his rousing of Zeus against the Greek failure to sacrifice will lead to the complete obliteration of the wall and hence to an explanation of why no single trace of it survives. The instruments of that obliteration will naturally be 'earthquake and flood waters, which are in the control of Poseidon together with Apollo' (*in Il.* 690.4–5).[92] Homer can therefore (though Eustathius does not, for once, use a culinary metaphor) 'have his cake and eat it': he can both have a 'most brilliant τειχομαχία at this invented wall' and also 'avoid being convicted of lying', for, and now Eustathius cites Aristotle (fr. 162 R = 402 Gigon, which Eustathius presumably took from Strabo 13.1.36), 'the poet who devised the wall also obliterated it'.[93]

Two points of note may be mentioned here. We know from the scholia that Zenodotus, Aristophanes of Byzantium and Aristarchus all concurred in the *athetesis* of *Iliad* 7.443–464, i.e. the Olympian conversation, on the grounds, as

---

[90] Porter 2011, 13–14 discusses the relevant scholium.
[91] This motive is expressed more briefly in the exegetical schol. T *Il.* 7.445 and 12.3–35.
[92] On Apollo's role cf. below pp. 730–732.
[93] Cf. also Strabo 2.3.6, citing Posidonius, and the schol. T *Il.* 7.443–464c.

represented by the surviving schol. A *Il.* 7.443–464a, that it was an unhappy anticipation of what is said in Book 12. Eustathius presumably knew of this *athetesis*, but (as often in such cases)[94] he does not mention it, perhaps because to do so would weaken the force of what he is teaching, namely that Homer is operating to a well-devised scheme in which each part plays its role. He will, moreover, pick up and elaborate the themes of divine anger and jealousy and of Poseidon as a god of earthquake in his subsequent discussion; here (*in Il.* 689.63–690.8) they are merely briefly adumbrated, because it is Homer's purpose in creating the divine conversation, not the nature of Homer's gods, which for the present moment is where Eustathius' attention is directed. Secondly, Eustathius' otherwise unusual emphasis on the obliteration of the fictional wall reflects a long tradition, visible not just in the scholia, of critical interest in this poetic construction;[95] Eustathius' discussion, however, is directed towards the whole sequence as an illustration of Homeric poetic technique. That Eustathius is less interested in the notion of fiction than in how this particular fiction functions within the Homeric text is hardly surprising, but the holistic view of the text which he here takes is in fact one which ancient (and Byzantine) commentators are often accused of lacking.

It is the entirely fictional nature of the wall which also accounts, in Eustathius' explanation, for why Homer has it built in a single day (v. 465) and says so little about the building. Eustathius now moves to a consideration of this matter before going back to the individual details of the speeches of Poseidon and Zeus, because this hangs together with the previous discussion of Homer's strategy. That the wall was finished so quickly is not improbable given the large numbers of Greeks available (*in Il.* 690.9, 18), and Homer says so little about the construction – no architects, no builders, nothing about where the wood and other material came from etc. etc. – so as not to waste words in a great rigmarole about something which was a simple invention;[96] to do so would have thrown suspicion 'on his whole poem' and would have created disbelief 'also about what really happened' (690.16). Eustathius draws attention to Homer's elaborate description of the fetching of the wood for Patroclus' pyre (*Iliad* 23.109–126) as an example of how Homer could describe building operations if he wanted to; Patroclus' 'little pyre' (ὀλίγη πυρά) was the object of 'many words' (πολὺς λόγος) and an elaborately detailed description from

---

[94] For a further example cf. below pp. 733–734.
[95] Cf. Dio Chrys. 11.75–6, Philostr. *Her.* 7–8.
[96] Van der Valk, II 494 notes here a typical Byzantine interest in the proper construction of walls.

Homer,[97] whereas nothing comparable accompanies the building of the wall. In his discussion of the differences between Patroclus' pyre and the Achaean wall, modern critics might perhaps say that Eustathius anticipates the idea that 'effects of the real' lend plausibility to fiction, were it not for the fact that, for Eustathius, Patroclus' pyre is not fictional. On the other hand, Homer has made entirely plausible (πιθανόν) the fact that the wall was so completely swept away, as it had been built in a day as an improvised structure on sand (*in Il.* 690.18–19); Eustathius here operates very close to a form of 'rationalising', but he has his eye principally on how well Homer has handled the whole fiction of the wall and its destruction.

One aspect of the whole episode which for Eustathius obviously belongs to μῦθος, rather than to the 'as if true', are the Olympian gods. Eustathius now turns briefly to them, juxtaposing their mythical status to the πιθανότης of Homer's handling of the wall. At one level it is important for Eustathius' students to remember that 'nothing happens without God' (*in Il.* 690.20), but these are Homeric gods and, as was very familiar in ancient criticism, Homer makes his gods act ἀνθρωπίνως, 'like human beings', and ἐμπαθῶς, 'with human emotions' (690.21, 26).[98] The idea is perhaps most familiar to us from 'Longinus', *On the Sublime* 9.7. So here Eustathius elaborates on a point he has briefly mentioned before, namely Poseidon's emotions. The god acts from φθόνος, a notorious characteristic of 'the Greek gods', and φιλοτιμία, and he acts against the Greeks, even though they are his φίλοι; he also stirs Zeus to anger against an 'impiety deserving of punishment'. Eustathius thus assimilates a scene which, as we have seen, aroused considerable critical discussion, to the ordinary patterns of Homeric poetry. When Poseidon merely mentions the wall and the ditch (7.449), rather than repeating the detail of vv. 440–441, Eustathius sees here too very 'human' emotions: 'Observe that in his anger Poseidon did not speak at length about the fortification. He said nothing about the towers and the stakes or even about the nature of the ditch, but it is as though the very mention of the fortification upset him' (*in Il.* 690.47–48).[99]

---

[97] Eustathius does not want us to remember that here Homer refers to the μέγα ἠρίον for Patroclus and Achilles at *Il.* 23.126.
[98] Cf. van der Valk II 107; Eustathius commonly comments on the fact that Homer's gods are ἀνθρωποπαθεῖς, cf., e.g., in *Il.* 1363.10, 1597.50 and the following note.
[99] The exegetical T-scholium on *Il.* 7.445 note that Apollo does not speak at all in the exchange whereas 'Poseidon, being a pro-Greek god [or 'though he is a pro-Greek god'] seems to accuse the Greeks ἀπαθῶς'. The adverb is difficult to understand, and Cobet suggested ἀμαθῶς; Porter suggests that the term implies that Poseidon is 'acting inconsistently, as though he lacked all feeling for the Greeks whom he otherwise favors' (Porter 2011, 16). This interpretation

Eustathius returns to the fictionality of the wall when he considers Poseidon's claim that 'the fame (κλέος) of [the Greek wall] will stretch as far as the dawn light scatters', whereas the wall which he and Apollo built will be forgotten (*Iliad* 7.451–453):

> The ancients said that poets also had to be prophets, and this is how Homer appears both elsewhere and here when, trusting in the power of his own eloquence (λογιότης), he has Poseidon say that 'the fame' of the wall he has invented 'will stretch as far as the dawn light scatters', that is over the whole earth beneath the sun, as far obviously as his own poetry is distributed. The expression is hyperbolic, for 'as far as the dawn light scatters' embraces both the inhabited and the uninhabited world; the sun's brightness spreads over deserted lands also. This could however be understood differently, with reference, not to space, but to time. In imitation of Homer, Euripides says 'gratitude lasts a long time' (*Hecuba* 320), and so here it could be understood that the fame of the wall will be eternal and everlasting, for as long as the light of day shines. This is clear from the fact that Poseidon says that 'they will forget' our wall, thus opposing forgetfulness to long memory ... Observe also that here the poet puts his own invented (πλαστόν) wall on a par with the historical and real wall of Troy. Only the fame of both of them lives on, while in reality neither is visible, but the Homeric one is now the more renowned. Because of the poet's eloquence, this wall exists in some way, having come from nothing, whereas the real Troy has in the sweep of time passed from real existence into nothing and disappeared.
> Eustathius, *Commentary on the Iliad* 690.54–64

James Porter has rightly drawn attention to the remarkable nature of Eustathius' reflection on how Homer's poetic fiction now has an 'existence', in contrast to the 'real' wall of Troy.[100] There is indeed much one could say about τὸ μὴ ὄν and the idea of fiction, just as there is much to be said about the very long tradition of contrasting the permanence of poetic 'monuments' with the inevitable decay of their physical counterparts,[101] but from Eustathius' point of view it is indeed the lasting power of Homer's poetry which is proved here. If one looked back

---

might be supported by the scholium on v. 450 which notes that the lesson there is that, though Poseidon is friendly to the Greeks, he grants no pardon when they do not reverence the gods. Eustathius' discussion perhaps suggests another solution. Might Poseidon speak not ἀπαθῶς, but rather ἐμπαθῶς? I once also toyed with ἀνθρωποπαθῶς: for the adverb cf. Hermogenes 391.18 Rabe, and the exegetical scholia regularly use the adjective of Homer's gods (schol. (b) T *Il.* 4.2a, 5.563, 13.521a, 14.168a, 176b), and cf. Eust. *in Il.* 563.44.
100 Porter 2011, 17–20; 2016, 370–371. Taplin 1992, 140 observes, 'The reason why we, the audience, know about the wall, despite its total obliteration, is that it is preserved in poetry ... The poet prompts the thought that it is significant that the gods have not obliterated the *Iliad*'; Taplin makes no reference to Eustathius. See also van den Berg 2017.
101 Important moments in that tradition include Pindar, *Pyth.* 6.5–14, Simonides, *PMG* 531 and Horace, *Odes* 3.30.

from twelfth-century Constantinople (or Thessaloniki) at the classical past, there were physical 'ruins' and 'survivals' or 'traces' everywhere, though Troy was not alone in having utterly disappeared. More potent than any such physical, archaeological remains, particularly for a teacher, priest and scholar like Eustathius, was the immanent power of the book of classical poetry that one could hold in one's hand: this really did have an existence, whereas the physical world of Troy had utterly disappeared. Homer was, as we might be tempted to say, Eustathius' contemporary. It is indeed the sweep of time, ἡ τοῦ χρόνου φορά, and Homer's power to survive it, which Homer's wall has impressed (once again) upon Eustathius' consciousness. We may here catch something genuinely Byzantine.

Here again we can point to the kind of earlier critical tradition upon which Eustathius was drawing. A bT-scholium on *Iliad* 7.451(a) reads as follows (in Erbse's text):

τοῦ δ' ἤτοι κλέος ἔσται, ⟨ὅσην τ' ἐπικίδναται ἠώς⟩: ἴσως διὰ τὴν ποίησιν αὐτοῦ· διὰ γὰρ ταύτην τὸ τεῖχος ἀοίδιμόν ἐστιν, οὐ δομηθὲν τοῖς Ἕλλησιν, ἀλλ' Ὁμήρῳ γενόμενον ἕνεκεν τῆς ἐπ' αὐτῷ μάχης.

'the fame of [the Greek wall] will stretch (as far as the dawn light scatters)': perhaps because of his poetry, for it is because of this that the wall is celebrated, not built by the Greeks, but created by Homer because of the battle over it.

The scholium is lacunose, and the reference to Homer in αὐτοῦ comes in rather suddenly, but the meaning can hardly be doubted, and is confirmed — in as much as such things ever can be — by the passage of Eustathius we are considering.[102] The scholiast, like modern scholars, found Poseidon's prophecy[103] puzzling (hence ἴσως, 'perhaps') and wondered whether the reference was to Homer's poetry. No such uncertainty for Eustathius — far from it. From his perspective, Homer's prophecy of the fame of his poetry and of everything in it (such as the Achaean wall) has more than come true.

In the passage cited above Eustathius offers a second possible interpretation, to which he obviously feels drawn: Poseidon does not say that the fame of the Greek wall 'will stretch as far as the dawn light scatters', but rather 'for as long as the dawn scatters its light', i.e. forever,[104] and he sees support for this

---

[102] Porter 2011, 21 seems to interpret διὰ τὴν ποίησιν αὐτοῦ, at least at the first level of reading, as 'owing to the making of [the wall]', but that cannot, I think, be correct.
[103] Eustathius too saw Poseidon as a tool of Homeric prophecy, *in Il.* 690.52–54.
[104] Whether the textual variation in v. 451 between ὅσον and ὅσην (Aristarchus), of which Eustathius might have known, played any role in alerting him to the possibility of alternate

interpretation in Poseidon's following verse: '[men] will forget' the wall built by Poseidon and Apollo. 'Forgetting' is a function of time, rather than space. 'Haud recte' is van der Valk's laconic comment on this second interpretation, which is, however, hardly a foolish one: κλέος is habitually associated with time — κλέος ἄφθιτον does not die, but escapes the 'forgetting' of death and is forever, just as, Eustathius notes, is the fame of the Greek wall. It would be very pointed indeed for Poseidon, an immortal, to prophesy that the Achaean wall will be 'immortal', whereas the divinely made one will 'perish' and be forgotten.

Space and time may, of course, co-exist in such contexts, but it is time which predominates in Greek thinking, particularly in the context of poetic survival. We may think of Theognis' prophecy of Kyrnos' fame (Theognis 237–254): from one point of view, Kyrnos, like the Achaean wall, is a poetic construct and construction, who owes his very existence, present and future, to the poet; he will not 'lose his *kleos*, even after death' but he will be celebrated 'as long as there is earth and sun' (Theognis 245, 252, cf. *in Il.* 690.59).[105] A Hellenistic inscription in fact declares that the *kleos* of Homer's poetry will last 'while night and the sun revolve' (*SGO* 06/02/18, vv. 7–8). We may say that time and space do indeed already co-exist implicitly in the words which Homer gives to Poseidon, and that Eustathius is drawing a false division in opposing two interpretations which in fact work poetically together; if, however, it was the grammarian and teacher in Eustathius which made him express the matter in terms of alternative interpretations, 'space' vs 'time', it was his deep sympathy with how traditional concepts were expressed which brings him to make this distinction and to draw out the implications of Poseidon's concern with 'forgetting' in ways which go well beyond anything that modern commentary has to offer.

When Eustathius picks up the story of the wall in his commentary on Book 12, he begins first with the theme of the wall as Homer's πλάσμα (*in Il.* 888.52–54), and then with its destruction by Poseidon and Apollo. Here one detail seems to stand out as surprising:

> Together with the foundations, Homer also removed the possibility that he could later be found out [i.e. be shown to have invented the wall] and he brought the wall down through the agency of Poseidon and Apollo, that is through earthquake, as was reasonable (εἰκός), and inundation; the first of these is under the control of Poseidon, the 'earth-shaker'

---

interpretations cannot move beyond speculation. In his famous translation, Richard Lattimore indeed took the text to mean 'as long as dawn light is scattered', but to what extent this was a 'deliberate misinterpretation' I do not know.

105 Another telling example is the famous epigram on Midas' tomb to which Simonides responded (*PMG* 581), cf. Yunis on Pl. *Phdr.* 264d4–7.

(σεισίχθων) and the one 'who makes the earth quake' (ἐννοσίγαιος), and the second is controlled by the sun which gathers the clouds (νεφεληγερέτης).

Eustathius, *Commentary on the Iliad* 888.53–57

Eustathius assumed readers who knew that the gods who destroyed the fictional wall are themselves to be understood as poetic allegories for natural phenomena: the wall was utterly destroyed by seismic movements and floods, which Homer typically ('mythically') presents as gods. Poseidon's seismic role is expected,[106] and it is Zeus who, as also expected, sends torrential rain (*Iliad* 12.25–26, cf. *in Il.* 889.1,26). Apollo's role seems to be that of Poseidon's helper, and Homer makes him bring all the local rivers together in an overpowering torrent (*Iliad* 12.24, cf. *in Il.* 889.26). The purpose of the note cited above is to explain the simple allegory by means of stock epithets of the gods concerned; νεφεληγερέτης, 'cloud-gatherer' can only be Zeus, but the sun makes a completely unexpected appearance with that epithet, and the sun certainly has nothing to do with the alleged destruction of the wall.[107] Eustathius repeats the explanation a few pages later, and here again there seems to be some confusion:

> The earth-shaker is obviously responsible for the earthquake ... and Zeus, as has been explained, the sun, for the inundation, as he sent down rain not just once but continuously through Zeus's air and brought the mouths of the rivers together in flood.
>
> Eustathius, *Commentary on the Iliad* 890.38–40

In this latter passage there is no mention of Apollo and his Homeric task of turning the mouths of the rivers seems rather to be ascribed to Zeus. In contrast to this apparent confusion in Eustathius' explanations, Tzetzes identifies Apollo here as time, 'which is completed through the movement of the sun' (*alleg. Il.* 12.8–9, 18),[108] and a role for time might well seem at least true to the resonance of this extraordinary Homeric passage.

Homer seems to describe two separate cosmic phenomena which led to the obliteration of the Achaean ramparts: Apollo brought the rivers together and unleashed their combined force at the wall (*Il.* 12.24–25), whereas 'Zeus' rained

---

106 The history of the 'rationalisation' of 'Poseidon' as referring to earthquakes goes back at least to Herodotus 7.129.4, where however de-mythologising is only at a half-way point: *if* you think that Poseidon causes earthquakes, then it is reasonable to say of the effects of earthquakes that they are the works of Poseidon.
107 In other contexts, of course, particularly neo-Platonic ones, Zeus could be interpreted as the sun, cf., e.g., *in Il.* 987.33.
108 Cf. Goldwyn-Kokkini 2015, 232. Apollo as the sun is Tzetzes' standard interpretation of the Homeric god.

continuously (12.25–26); Eustathius' paraphrase (in *Il.* 889.26–9) makes plain this division of labour. Poseidon is imagined to have directed operations (*Il.* 12.28) and to have used the water to sweep away the Greek foundations and then covered over all the erstwhile traces with sand (12.27–33). Given that in Book 7 Zeus had given Poseidon permission to destroy the wall, once the war was over, and that at 12.17–18 the destruction is said to have been the plan of 'Poseidon and Apollo', it would have been easy enough for any ancient reader to understand the reference to Zeus in 12.25 as an allegorical *façon de parler*, with the 'real gods' involved being Poseidon and Apollo, acting out of protective jealousy for their own Trojan wall. On the other hand, the manner of the destruction strongly suggests the work just of Poseidon, the powerful god of earthquake and water. For an ancient reader attuned to allegorical interpretation, Apollo's presence is an awkward one,[109] for Apollo's principal cosmic manifestation, the sun, has no role to play in the destruction, unless we were to imagine a rather different version in which, after the wall had been swept away, the action of the sun dried up the waters leaving what is now to be seen at the site: sand with no trace left of the wall (cf. 12.30–32 on Poseidon's 'repair work').

In Pseudo-Heraclitus' *Homeric Problems* the destruction of the wall is indeed entirely the work of the allegorised Poseidon (*qu. Hom.* 38), and we may recall how in Book 7 Apollo had been silent as Poseidon remonstrated with Zeus over the Greek fortifications; in discussing that passage, Eustathius had noted that Poseidon was responsible for earthquake and inundation 'together with Apollo' (*in Il.* 690.5), and the awkwardness of Apollo's role here is again very plain to see. What then we perhaps have in the references to the sun in Eustathius' discussion of the opening of Book 12 are remnants of an attempt, in which, as we have seen, Tzetzes succeeded, to find a role for an allegorised Apollo in the destruction, but an attempt which failed before the clear indications of the text. We may even be able to trace the origin (or one of the origins) of such an attempt. In discussing the epithet 'holy' for Troy in the second verse of the *Odyssey*, Eustathius first notes the standard ancient explanation, namely that the city was founded by Poseidon and Apollo, and then he catalogues a couple of 'rationalisations' of this story. One of these is that any form of building requires 'Poseidon' (i.e. water or moisture) and 'Apollo' (i.e. the heat of the sun) to dry out the building-works, and that this entirely general explanation was applied in particular to the building of Troy (*in Od.* 1382.50–53). As at the

---

109 That at *Il.* 21.446–449 Poseidon — in a speech to Apollo — claims all the credit for the building of the Trojan walls certainly does not lessen the oddity of Apollo's role in Book 12.

building, so at the destruction: a place is found for both gods, even at the expense of some awkwardness.

Finally, it is worth noting that when in Book 15 Apollo breaches the wall as easily 'as a child knocks over a sandcastle' (*Il.* 15.361–366), a simile for which Eustathius expresses the greatest admiration, both the scholia and Eustathius are concerned with the question of how the god could do this so easily, when it later took Apollo and Poseidon nine days (*Il.* 12.25) to obliterate the wall entirely.[110] Eustathius' answer (*in Il.* 1019.58–61) is that in Book 15 we are dealing with 'the Apollo of myth', i.e. the Homeric Olympian, whereas in Book 12 Apollo and Poseidon are 'not the gods of myth',[111] but are allegorical figures. What is most interesting here is not so much welcome confirmation for the above interpretation of the discussion of Book 12, but rather the capacious modes of explanation which allowed Byzantine readers a complete picture of Homeric technique and which assumed a Homer working with principles of consistency familiar to them.

Love and sex

It is a commonplace of modern criticism of the *Iliad* that the scenes in Book 3 in which Aphrodite compels Helen to visit Paris after his duel with Menelaus and make love with him and in Book 14 in which Hera 'deceives' Zeus by arousing him to sleep with her, thus being distracted from what is happening in the battlefield, may be mutually explicative. Paris and Zeus, after all, share verses in which they express their arousal. The similarity between the scenes was certainly not lost on Eustathius, and it is of some interest to see how a Byzantine handles such material. As with the discussion of the Achaean wall of Books 7 and 12, I shall (as far as possible) follow Eustathius' discussion sequentially.

Eustathius certainly does not dissent from the standard view of the scholia that the scenes in Book 3 depict Paris as an outrageously dissolute individual, plunged helplessly in τρυφή and ἀκολασία (cf., e.g., *in Il.* 428.14–16). Aphrodite's seductive description to Helen of Paris catches his attention particularly:

---

[110] Critics were also of course bothered by the fact that the gods took nine days to destroy what the Greeks had built in a day, cf. schol. T *Il.* 12.25, with Porphyry's note cited by Erbse *ad loc.*, Eustathius, *in Il.* 890.34–40.
[111] For Tzetzes, however, the allegories continue: the Achaean ditch had been weakened by rain, and 'the sun made it collapse like a dry loaf of bread' (*alleg. Il.* 15.140–141 = Goldwyn-Kokkini 2015, 278).

δεῦρ' ἴθ', Ἀλέξανδρός σε καλεῖ οἶκόνδε νέεσθαι·
κεῖνος ὅ γ' ἐν θαλάμωι καὶ δινωτοῖσι λέχεσσιν,
κάλλεΐ τε στίλβων καὶ εἵμασιν· οὐδέ κε φαίης
ἀνδρὶ μαχεσσάμενον τόν γ' ἐλθεῖν, ἀλλὰ χορόνδε
ἔρχεσθ', ἠὲ χοροῖο νέον λήγοντα καθίζειν.

Homer, *Iliad* 3.390-394

Come here – Paris is calling you to return to your dwelling. He is there in the bedroom on the intricately carved bed, gleaming with beauty and fine clothing. You would not think that he had returned from a duel with a man, but that he was going to a dance or was resting after a recent dance.

When Eustathius notes that this description would suit 'a bridegroom or some other man of *truphe*' (*in Il.* 428.10), it is tempting to think that he has caught some of the sense, as also has modern criticism, that this scene does not just evoke the first time Aphrodite 'led' Helen to Paris' bed, but is also a kind of 'wedding' in which the bride is transferred to the groom's house.[112] Be that as it may, it is a mark of how Eustathius thinks through the implications of the text that he works out the basis of Aphrodite's comparison of Paris to a dancer:

He mocks the luxurious Paris, who is not pained like someone who has been beaten, but loves like a dancer, having sweated (ἐνιδρώσας) for a very brief time in the fighting as a dancer in the dance.

Eustathius, *Commentary on the Iliad* 428.15-16

This might seem to us wrong-headed, as Aphrodite's comparison refers merely to Paris' appearance and dress (as Eustathius [*in Il.* 428.30] goes on to point out, we are to understand that Aphrodite not only saved Paris from the battlefield, but also beautified him), but Eustathius typically sets the comparison within a holistic reading of the scene as one which mocks Paris; it is not so much (despite Priam's abuse of his remaining sons at *Il.* 24.261) that being a χορευτής is disreputable, as it is transient – Paris is (to put it briefly) a dilettante in warfare. The reference to sweat perhaps picks up a possible implication of Aphrodite's στίλβων, 'gleaming'.[113]

---

112 On Homer's technique of 'replaying' incidents beyond the temporal scope of his poem cf. above pp. 723-724.
113 Cf. Theocritus 2.79, where the reference is presumably to the use of oil after exercise. Through ἐνιδρώσας Eustathius perhaps recalls Xen. *Symp.* 2.18, the only occurrence of this compound verb in the literature of the classical period, where (the notoriously ugly) Socrates uses it precisely in the context of dancing.

Helen's recognition that the old woman standing in front of her was in fact Aphrodite was a famous moment for the ancient critics:

ὣς φάτο· τῆι δ' ἄρα θυμὸν ἐνὶ στήθεσσιν ὄρινεν·
καί ῥ' ὡς οὖν ἐνόησε θεᾶς περικαλλέα δειρὴν
στήθεά θ' ἱμερόεντα καὶ ὄμματα μαρμαίροντα,
θάμβησέν τ' ἄρ' ἔπειτα, ἔπος τ' ἔφατ' ἔκ τ' ὀνόμαζε·

Homer, *Iliad* 3.395–398

So [Aphrodite] spoke and stirred the spirit in Helen's chest. When she saw the goddess' beautiful neck and lovely breasts and sparkling eyes, then she was amazed and addressed her as follows...

Two issues dominated ancient criticism: How could Helen recognise the disguised goddess?, Why does Helen speak to the god as she proceeds to do? Aristarchus in fact athetised all of 396–418, thus removing the angry exchange between god and mortal altogether; his reasons for doing so seem to have been various, but the improbability of the verses describing the god's lovely body (396–397) and the inappropriateness of the exchange of insults seem to have loomed large (cf. schol. A *Il.* 3.395). The presence of the allegedly intrusive verses was ascribed to someone who took θυμὸν ... ὄρινεν in v. 395 to mean 'stirred her anger', rather than 'stirred (i.e. aroused) her spirit/desire'. Those who did not accept these arguments noted that, as the exegetical scholia on v. 397 'lovely breasts' put it, 'there is nothing odd in the goddess appearing naked: she came to be recognised by Helen, but conceals herself from the Trojan women'. In other words, the goddess at this moment grants Helen special vision which she denies to everyone else. Modern critics too would be inclined to note that there is (at least) a special relationship between Helen and Aphrodite, whether or not they subscribe to some version of the view that Aphrodite is 'a projection of personal emotions' (Kirk on vv. 396–398); this scene has always been one of the strongest cases for those who wish to see the interventions of the Homeric gods as, at least in part, a way of describing internal psychological processes and drives. As is his habit, Eustathius does not even mention the Aristarchan athetesis; after all, the scene is a morally didactic one: it shows us Helen strongly, and indeed angrily, resisting Aphrodite's 'pimping' (μαστροπεία), a harsh word which Eustathius repeats with pointed effect.[114] Eustathius also does not waste words over how Helen could recognize the disguised god, and whereas

---

[114] Cf. *in Il.* 429.8, 24. The idea itself, but not the word, is already in the scholia, cf. προαγωγόν in the schol. bT *Il.* 3.383a.

the exegetical scholia accept that vv. 396–397 mean that Helen at least saw part of the female body which is normally concealed, for Eustathius 'beautiful neck and lovely breasts and sparkling eyes' are 'simply praise of a beautiful woman' (*in Il.* 428.33); we perhaps here catch a glimpse of Byzantine court society peeping through the commentary. What, however, Eustathius particularly draws our attention to is how this 'simple praise' of beauty is itself 'beautified' (κεκαλλώπισται) in vv. 396–397 by the use of three *parisa*, or noun-adjective phrases of equal length; the rhetorician and stylist in Eustathius is never far away. Thus he also notes that Helen's angry words to Aphrodite (vv. 406–411) come out in short, choppy phrases, a familiar effect of anger (*in Il.* 430.24).

When Helen sarcastically accuses Aphrodite of trying to deceive her and suggests that the god will pass her on to one φίλος after another, just as she gave her to Paris (vv. 399–404), Eustathius suggests that Helen here 'praises herself as being famous and worthy of being loved (ἀξιέραστον)', as Aphrodite would certainly not behave like this if Helen was not a gift worth having (*in Il.* 429.23–24, cf. 429.19). The observation is again driven by a concern with the rhetorical effect of what every character says, with the strategies of speaking; when Nausicaa offers Odysseus the imaginary speech of the jealous Phaeacians about the handsome stranger at her side (*Od.* 6.275–285), another passage which Aristarchus athetised as being inappropriate to the character speaking, Eustathius not only expresses his admiration for the 'wondrous technique' by which Nausicaa declares her love as though someone else was speaking, but — as with Helen in Book 3 — he similarly notes that the princess here subtly suggests to Odysseus that she is ἀξιέραστος, given the number of Phaeacian admirers which she has (*in Od.* 1563.49). The only other occurrence of the term in the *Commentaries* is at *in Il.* 989.26 where the famous catalogue of Zeus's conquests which he recites to Hera as a prelude to their love-making, a passage once again athetised by Aristarchus (as well as Aristophanes before him), is understood as part of Zeus showing himself ἀξιέραστος; if he has had so many lovers, then there must be something worth having there! The strategy of explanation in all three cases is similar. In each of the three cases a plurality (or potential plurality) of lovers or admirers is implicitly a mode of self-praise; in Book 3, however, Helen is not speaking to a man whom she wishes to impress, but to Aphrodite, and Eustathius' interpretation of her words might have been influenced by his reading of the other scenes, in particular perhaps by Zeus's words in Book 14; as we have already seen, Eustathius recognised the scene in Book 14 as very close in some respects to the analogous scene in Book 3.

Central to the critical engagement with this scene was the outrageous behaviour of Paris: a man who has just been beaten in a duel by the husband whose wife he stole can think only of sex. Why does Homer portray him as so degraded?[115] The man is, as Eustathius puts it, simply μαχλότατος (*in Il*. 431.20). In a later addition to the commentary, Eustathius suggests that Paris' ἐρωμανία is perhaps (ἴσως) to be explained by the effect of the *kestos* which Aphrodite wears and which plays such an important part in the 'deception of Zeus' in Book 14 (*in Il*. 431.24–29); the *kestos* is not mentioned in Book 3, but how else to explain Paris' extraordinary desire? Other than Zeus in Book 14, the other parallel which springs to Eustathius' mind is Herodotus' Candaules, whose obsessive *eros* for his own wife brought him to a nasty end. Eustathius uses exactly the same parallel in his discussion of Zeus's desire in Book 14, and there he elaborates upon ancient semantic discussions[116] to make clear why *eros* is not what a man should feel for his wife:

> A man might be said to love (φιλεῖν) his own wife and cherish (ἀγαπᾶν) her and be of one mind (ὁμονοητικῶς ἔχειν) with her,[117] but not *eran* her. Eros refers to things which are not in our power or control, as it is an excess of desire for things which we do not really have. Herodotus indeed reports that Candaules felt *eros* for his own wife, but this brought him the bad end we all know about. Zeus too will get nothing good from the *eros* he feels for Hera, as he did once in the beginning, but he will lose the chance to watch what is happening.
>
> Eustathius, *Commentary on the Iliad* 988.30–33

It is tempting to think that it was consideration of Book 14 which led Eustathius to his second thoughts on Paris' behaviour in Book 3. Be that as it may, the parallels which Eustathius draws, with Zeus and Hera and Candaules and his wife, confirm that Eustathius stands in the critical tradition which viewed Paris and Helen, in this scene at least, as a 'married couple', however unusual an example of the institution. Nowhere is this more striking than in the critical attitude to the verses which close the scene:

> ἦ ῥα, καὶ ἄρχε λέχοσδε κιών· ἅμα δ' εἵπετ' ἄκοιτις.
> τὼ μὲν ἄρ' ἐν τρητοῖσι κατηύνασθεν λεχέεσσιν...
>
> Homer, *Iliad* 3.446–447
>
> So he spoke, and led the way to the bed; his wife followed after him. Those two lay on the worked bed...

---

115 For some discussion and bibliography cf. Hunter 2009a, 21, Hunter/Russell 2011, 105.
116 Cf. van der Valk's note *ad loc*.
117 When, however, Odysseus famously wishes ὁμοφροσύνη, 'like-mindedness', for Nausicaa and her future husband (*Od*. 6.180–185), Eustathius wryly comments that this is actually rarely found in married couples, most of whom spend all their lives squabbling (*in Od*. 1558.26).

For Eustathius these verses describe 'chaste marital relations' (*in Il.* 434.9); however strongly one might wish to stress Helen 's σωφροσύνη in this scene, I think that most modern critics would take a rather different view. The exegetical scholia compare the 'going to bed' of Zeus and Hera at the end of Book 1, while also noting that Paris and Helen are not a 'standard' married couple:

Ζεὺς δὲ πρὸς ὃν λέχος ἤϊ' Ὀλύμπιος ἀστεροπητής,
ἔνθα πάρος κοιμᾶθ' ὅτε μιν γλυκὺς ὕπνος ἱκάνοι·
ἔνθα καθηῦδ' ἀναβάς, παρὰ δὲ χρυσόθρονος Ἥρη.

Homer, *Iliad* 1.609–611

Then Zeus, the Olympian who sends lightning, went to the bed where previously he slept whenever sweet sleep took him. He climbed in and slept, and beside him was Hera of the golden throne.

In that scene also the husband and wife have squabbled immediately before (though Hephaestus has tried to calm things down), and there too the exegetical scholia draw a moralising lesson, which one might think anything but appropriate: 'The poet is teaching [us] that a husband and wife should share the same bed, so that her absence will not pain him' (schol. bT *Il.* 1.611b).[118]

Eustathius is alive not merely to the variety of tones in Helen's short address to Paris (like a good rhetorician she is πολυειδής, *in Il.* 431.30), but he also envisages the scene in his mind's eye and helps his students to see it. Thus Paris looks at Helen ἀσέμνως, when really he should cover his head in shame (*in Il.* 431.20), and Helen's gesture of v. 427, ὄσσε πάλιν κλίνασα, which the exegetical scholia see as a further mark of her σωφροσύνη, is acknowledged as an open gesture of multiple possible implications, and here (as so often) Eustathius has set the pattern for modern commentary.[119] On the one hand the gesture is almost flirtatious (*in Il.* 431.31), but she also seeks to avoid his gaze, because she knows that the eyes are the source of *eros* (a very familiar piece of ancient erotic lore)[120] and she does not want to feel the desire which he himself feels (432.5), and Eustathius makes the point by drawing a verbal link between ὁρᾶν and ἐρᾶν, though he does not (quite) imply that Helen herself knew of the etymological

---

118 It would be typical of a scholiast to view things from the male perspective, and the note gives due attention to the ordering of the Homeric text, but I have wondered whether we should not read αὐτήν, i.e. 'so that the husband does not pain his wife by his absence'.
119 Cf., e.g., Kirk's n. on v. 427. In Tzetzes' account, Helen is unable to resist Paris' beauty, despite her inner struggle (πολλὰ ζυγομαχήσασαν πρὸς ἑαυτήν), because Paris was born under the sign of Aphrodite (*alleg. Il.* 3.163–171 = Goldwyn/Kokkini 2015, 142).
120 Cf., e.g., Calame 1999, 19–23.

link. For good measure he adds a quotation about desire and the eyes from Euripides (*Hippolytus* 525–526) and cites 'some later rhetorician' for the idea that *eros* flows (ῥέειν) from the eyes.[121]

Paris describes his desire by recalling the very first occasion on which he and Helen made love:

> οὐ γάρ πώ ποτέ μ' ὧδέ γ' ἔρως φρένας ἀμφεκάλυψεν,
> οὐδ' ὅτε σε πρῶτον Λακεδαίμονος ἐξ ἐρατεινῆς
> ἔπλεον ἁρπάξας ἐν ποντοπόροισι νέεσσιν,
> νήσωι δ' ἐν κραναῆι ἐμίγην φιλότητι καὶ εὐνῆι,   445
> ὥς σεο νῦν ἔραμαι καί με γλυκὺς ἵμερος αἱρεῖ.
>
> Homer, *Iliad* 3.442–446

> Never before has desire so covered my mind, not even when I first took you from lovely Lacedaemon and sailed away with my seafaring ships and made love to you on a rocky island, as now I feel desire for you and sweet longing lifts me.

Eustathius' analysis of Paris' language is a good illustration both of his habit of accumulating various interpretations, in a manner which was to prove very influential on the later commentary tradition, and of his persistent attempt to see Homeric language and imagery as hanging together in a large-scale and meaningful picture:

> ἀμφεκάλυψεν ['covered over'] is either taken from the likeness to a cloud, as *eros* darkens the sun which is the soul, or is a metaphor from nets which, when they are spread out, cover what has been caught,[122] or is simply taken over from whatever conceals what is covered or makes it disappear … αἱρεῖ ['takes hold of'] is from the language of hunting, and so it follows on from ἀμφεκάλυψεν, so that he is saying '*eros* has covered me in his nets and has caught me, but it is a sweet catching'.
>
> Eustathius, *Commentary on the Iliad* 433.11–12

At *Il.* 14.294 the poet uses similar language of the effect which the sight of Hera has upon Zeus, and there (*in Il.* 987.29–33) Eustathius repeats the explanation that ἀμφεκάλυψεν is a metaphor from hunting-nets, but he also notes that one could take it as a metaphor from clouds (Zeus's mind is, after all, the sun in some allegorical interpretations of the cosmos), and — perhaps most surprising of all to us — he draws a link between the two explanations by seeking to connect this occurrence of ἀμφεκάλυψεν with Zeus's subsequent promise to Hera that she need not worry about anyone seeing them, because 'I shall conceal

---

121 At Plato, *Cratylus* 420a9–b4 the link between ἔρως and ῥοή is explicit.
122 This explanation is also found in the schol. bT *Il.* 3.442.

(ἀμφικαλύψω) us in a golden cloud' (v. 343), and by the fact that the word νεφέλη denotes a particular kind of hunting-net, a fact which Eustathius illustrates from Aristophanes, *Birds* 194.[123] Here it is (again) tempting to believe that at least his knowledge of, if not his commentary on, the passage in Book 14 has fed back into the commentary on the analogous scene in Book 3, where the interpretation of ἀμφεκάλυψεν as a metaphor from clouds seems to come in very unexpectedly; if this is correct, it may be thought to have implications for Eustathius' habits of working.

Eustathius' discussion of the 'Deception of Zeus' in *Iliad* 14 naturally records allegorical readings of the joining of Zeus and Hera (*in Il.* 986.60–987.6), but what is perhaps of most interest, as it has also been to modern scholars, is the famous passage in which Zeus catalogues his past conquests as a way of expressing to Hera the strength of his present desire. Eustathius begins by noting that, within a context which is both erotic and 'unrelievedly mythical', i.e. stories about Homer's invented gods, Homer weaves in very brief διηγήματα of a similar kind (*in Il.* 988.25–26); in other words, Homer's technique here is, as we might say, a generically conscious one: the catalogue of erotic narratives, very briefly alluded to, reinforce the generic sense, 'myth', of the framing narrative. Eustathius will shortly return to the importance of the idea of 'myth' for this scene,[124] but he also subsequently points out that such a catalogue of brief allusions to stories has a didactic function in making the hearer πολυμαθής (*in Il.* 988.63). Here, as so often, Eustathius casts Homer's ideal audience in his own image.

In Eustathius' view Zeus is, as we have already noted, trying to make himself ἀξιέραστος to Hera by this display of his amorous past, but he is also speaking, 'already deprived of his *nous*' (*in Il.* 988.28), under the sway of the *kestos* which Hera is wearing and which makes him feel ἔρως ἄτοπος for his own wife (cf. above p. 736).[125] This disturbance of his intelligence, the taking away of his πυκιναὶ φρένες as Homer puts it (*Il.* 14.294), makes him 'pride himself on things he should not, artlessly and rather simply' (ἀφελῶς καὶ ἁπλούστερον, *in Il.* 988.29); as van der Valk notes, Eustathius here has in mind rhetorical discussions of ἀφέλεια as a characteristic of style (cf. Hermogenes, *Id.* 322–329 Rabe), and Eustathius' analysis suggests that Zeus is here behaving not unlike, for example, one of Theocritus' rustics, such as the Cyclops telling Galatea about all the wonderful delights of his cave. It might well be thought that this interpreta-

---

123 Cf. Dunbar *ad loc.* and Harder on Call. fr. 75.37 Pf.
124 Cf. below p. 740.
125 Cf. the schol. bT *Il.* 14.315b.

tion is not in fact very far off the mark. It is indeed the style and the manner of expression of the passage to which Eustathius wishes us to pay attention. The poet has, for example, 'beautified this erotic passage with the attractive (εὐειδής) figure of negation',[126] and Eustathius notes that the poet gives Zeus the negative οὐ nine times in his catalogue of past conquests; whereas Zeus dwells on this 'conspicuous figure' and also on the repeated reference to the fact that his unions bore fruit, he uses the word 'I desired' (ἠρασάμην) 'very sparingly',[127] only once in fact (v. 317), whereas it must be understood seven times with the individual items in the catalogue.[128] Zeus 'is ashamed of the word ἐρᾶν and does not wish to dwell upon it' (*in Il.* 988.39); the whole catalogue is in fact an excellent example (988.40) of how Homer can emphasise or suppress details in accordance with rhetorical need.

Eustathius then proceeds to a lengthy demonstration of how Zeus's catalogue illustrates Homer's stylistic *poikilia*:[129] to put it simply, Homer takes our minds off the sex by holding our attention on his style and manner of expression. The variation operates at every level of the catalogue: Zeus lists more mortal women than goddesses; he names the children of the mortals, but not of the immortals; the goddesses are given epithets, but the mortals — except for Danae — not, whereas the children of the mortals are given epithets, except for Minos; one mother and one child are followed by one mother and two children, then two mothers in one verse, each of whom had one child, then two mothers in two verses, and so on (*in Il.* 988.41–56). Ancient critics had also been interested in why Zeus says θεᾶς ἔρος οὐδὲ γυναικός, but then catalogues his mortal conquests first. One explanation (cf. schol. T *Il.* 14.315c) offered was that ἔρως for one's own kind (e.g. a god for a god) was less fierce than for someone of a different kind (e.g. a god for a mortal); Eustathius explicitly ascribes this view to

---

126 On the σχῆμα κατὰ ἄρσιν, which may amount to what we would consider little more than repeated anaphora of οὐ, cf., e.g., Hermogenes 293.16–25 R; Anon. περὶ σχημάτων III 129–30 Spengel.
127 This seems to be the meaning of πτωχικῶς at 988.39, i.e. it is a synonym of ἐλλιπῶς immediately following at *in Il.* 988.40; van der Valk suggests rather the meaning 'furtively'. πτωχικῶς also resonates against the illustration of the richness of stylistic *poikilia* which follows.
128 The grammatical observation is also found in the schol. A *Il.* 14.317a.
129 Erbse's note on the scholium to v. 317 transcribes the whole Eustathian passage, which he thinks contains material from scholia which have not survived; Janko's note on vv. 313–328 refers to Eustathius' 'fine analysis' and offers a summary of that analysis. Eustathius returns to the favourite theme of Homeric *poikilia* at *in Il.* 990.32, in the context of the variety of ways in which Hera can allude to Zeus's desire for sex, without being too explicit about the physical act.

'the ancients' (*in Il.* 988.59), but he adds that familiar evidence supports the point: 'for many men who are seized by desire prefer slave-girls to women of good family' (988.61). As so often, it would be very nice to know what (or whom) precisely he has in mind. It may of course (rightly) be objected that a man's desire for a slave-girl does not represent the same disparity of nature as that of a god for a mortal, which the schol. T *Il.* 14.315c describes as a desire for something παρὰ φύσιν, but we may either simply forgive Eustathius for a not particularly apt analogy of hierarchies, or we may wonder just how revealing that analogy is of how slaves were regarded in Eustathius' world.

The final verses of the scene are a famous example of almost cinematic metaphor and distraction:

ἦ ῥα, καὶ ἀγκὰς ἔμαρπτε Κρόνου πάις ἣν παράκοιτιν·
τοῖσι δ' ὑπὸ χθὼν δῖα φύεν νεοθηλέα ποίην,
λωτόν θ' ἑρσήεντα ἰδὲ κρόκον ἠδ' ὑάκινθον
πυκνὸν καὶ μαλακόν, ὃς ἀπὸ χθονὸς ὑψόσ' ἔεργεν.
τῶι ἔνι λεξάσθην, ἐπὶ δὲ νεφέλην ἕσσαντο   350
καλὴν χρυσείην· στιλπναὶ δ' ἀπέπιπτον ἔερσαι.

Homer, *Iliad* 14.346–351

So he spoke, and the son of Kronos took his wife in his arms. Beneath them the earth sent forth fresh grass, and dewy clover and crocus and hyacinth thick and soft to form a high barrier between them and the ground. There they lay and a lovely golden cloud enveloped them, as sparkling dew dripped around.

A standard critical approach to these verses is outlined by the exegetical scholia on vv. 347–351:

As he has to describe a vulgar matter, the poet has turned his verses in another direction, namely to the flowers which grow up from the earth and to the cloud; in this way he has stopped us wondering (πολυπραγμονεῖν) about what happens next.[130]

Eustathius duly offers a version of this explanation (cf. *in Il.* 991.9–10),[131] but he typically also adopts a stylistic approach to the moral problem raised by the

---

130 On the idea of πολυπραγμονεῖν here cf. Hunter 2009c, 60–61.
131 Eustathius also (*in Il.* 991.19) repeats the critical observation (schol. bT *Il.* 14.347) that Homer did not include roses among the flowers which the earth sent up because it would not be very nice to sleep on their thorns (!); the implication is that roses would have been expected in such an erotic context. He adds however that perhaps it was also not the season for roses, because roses do not bloom at the same time as crocus and hyacinth. Eustathius' interest in flowers and gardening is familiar from his letters and other texts, but it is hard here not to

verses. Thus v. 346 is harsh in its verbal expression 'so that the passage should not be entirely pleasant and smooth', and Homer also gets the matter over with very quickly (*in Il.* 990.52, cf. 991.30). In the end, however, Eustathius has (in his second thoughts) to admit that 'though neither 'love-making' (φιλότητι) nor 'took up in his arms' (ἀγκὰς ἔμαρπτεν) are very decent (σεμνόν), nevertheless the poet had no other way to express this passage more decently, however hard he tried to express it appropriately' (991.39).

Eustathius and Koraes

In 1804 Adamantios Koraes published in Paris a two-volume edition with ample commentary of one of the last great works of pagan Greek literature, the *Aithiopika* of Heliodorus.[132] In the long prefatory epistle to his edition, Koraes surveys the history of the Greek novel in antiquity, and then follows this with a scathing attack on what we now call the Byzantine novel; much of Koraes' scorn is of course reserved for the utterly artificial language (as he sees it) of such fiction. When he comes to Heliodorus himself, Koraes naturally draws attention to the very Homeric narrative structure of the *Aithiopika* and to Heliodorus' marvellous depiction of character, which is indeed worthy of being mentioned in the same breath as Homer's. He then turns to the nature of his own commentary, and in particular to its very full coverage of linguistic matters, particularly as regards the relation between ancient Greek and 'this new language which we speak today'. Here Koraes says that his model for the commentary was the 'wise and useful bishop' Eustathius. For Koraes, it was truly remarkable that, at a time of cultural and linguistic decay and political enslavement, when the despised Byzantine novel was being produced and 'other barbarous writings saw the light of day, which are fit only to be buried beneath the earth for all time', Eustathius interpreted the first and greatest poet of Greek wisdom, 'from whom all waters ... flow', citing *Iliad* 21.196–197, which — as Koraes well knew, though he does not let on — Eustathius himself had quoted at the head of his *Iliad*-commentary (*in Il.* 1.9). No one can doubt the services which Eustathius had performed for the Greek people; he was truly φιλογενής, as in the scholiastic

---

remember the Cyclops' words to Galatea at Theocritus 11.58–59. Here one might think that Eustathius' didacticism is somewhat misplaced.

132 On Koraes' edition of the *Aithiopika* cf. Tabaki 2010, 161–167; there is an Italian translation of the prefatory epistle in Rotolo 1965.

tradition Homer himself was φιλέλλην, though here again Koraes does not make his 'learned' allusion explicit.

Koraes' expansive and self-confessedly digressive prefatory epistle (cf. τὰς μακράς μου παρεκβάσεις, p. να′ top) becomes indeed itself an exercise in Eustathian *mimesis*; we may recall Michael Choniates' praise (287.22–288.2 Lampros) for how Eustathius's lectures were filled (and filled out) with παρεκβάσεις which gave the student a complete picture, going far beyond merely explaining the text in hand, and how these 'digressions' were anything but 'inappropriate excursuses' (ἔξωροι παραδρομαί).[133] Here again, there is a direct line of descent from the Homeric text itself. Just as ancient criticism never tired of pointing to the *poikilia* of the texture of the Homeric poems, which always kept the audience refreshed and attentive through variations of scene-type and emotional level, so Eustathius advertises the variety and careful structure of the *Commentaries* which 'are not stretched out in a single text and body of unbroken continuity, which would weary the reader with the lack of breaks' (*in Il.* 2.43–44); rather, 'anyone proceeding on his way through [the *Iliad* commentary], will find many places, as it were, to stop and rest' (2.46).

Koraes then proceeds to discuss why Eustathius was not in a position to deal diachronically (as we would say) with the Greek language and in particular with the correction (διόρθωσις) of the 'common language', as extensively as Koraes has done in his commentaries:

> By 'correction' of the language I mean not only the changing of various barbarous words and structures, but also the preservation of many others which all who have not carefully investigated the nature of the language try to remove from the language as barbarisms. In Eustathius' time such correction was not possible. The time when things are collapsing is not the time for rebuilding.[134] The sensible house-owner laments from afar the inevitable destruction of his house; when the ruins have fallen and the dust has scattered, then he approaches and gathers what he can from the ruins in order to build a new house. At long last the desperately desired time for rebuilding has arrived, and day by day the Greek people are enriched by new Eustathiuses and freed from the horrors of [the language of Byzantine novels].

There follows Koraes' favourite subject of the reform of how the Greek language is currently taught and what should replace that;[135] there is more here than just

---

133 Cf. Browning 1995, 85. Not all moderns have agreed with Michael's assessment, of course.
134 Earthquakes were, of course, not unfamiliar to Koraes; the present passage perhaps evokes the state in which he found Smyrna and his own family-house on his return in 1779, cf. Kitromilidis 2010b, 5.
135 Cf. esp. Mackridge 2010.

the fact (remarkable enough in itself) that Eustathius has been adopted into, become indeed a standard-bearer for, Koraes' project for the rebirth of the Greek people and the Greek language, to become almost an Enlightenment figure *avant la lettre*. Koraes is here, in fact, at his most Eustathian, both generally in the close connections he draws between language and morals, and also more specifically. He draws, he tells us, on his experiences with non-Greeks in declaring that once one 'has drunk to the full the cup of this sorceress which is the language of the Greeks' then one is no more a slave to the mere pleasures of the body; the beauty of the Greek language is in fact more entrancing than the Trojan elders found the beauty of Helen (νβ′–νγ).[136] The allusion, of course, is to the Homeric Circe whose bewitching and metamorphosis of Odysseus' men had been allegorised, many centuries before Eustathius, as the enslavement to bodily pleasure which the sight of beautiful women can produce in the unwary. Odysseus, however, was protected by the μῶλυ which Hermes had given him, and in the allegorical interpretation which Eustathius had accepted (*in Od.* 1658.26–30), Hermes was understood as λόγος with μῶλυ as παιδεία, 'education'.[137] The root of μῶλυ, Homer tells us, is black, and this means, in Eustathius words, that 'for those starting out on education, the end (τέλος) is obscure and hard to see' — the first steps are anything but 'sweet', but the flower is white because the end of education truly is 'bright and gleaming, and sweet and nourishing'.

Koraes — perhaps under the influence of other ancient allegories, such as the explanations for the drug which Helen placed in the drink of Menelaos and Telemachus — has re-mixed Circe's potion, so to speak, so that it is now λόγος which entrances, Greek λόγος to be precise, and which protects the young from the lusts of the body. Koraes does not conceal that learning Greek properly is difficult, but 'the reward for the labours is inexpressible pleasure (ἡδονή)' (p. νγ′); here again it is impossible not to be reminded of Eustathius' account of the 'sweet' (ἡδύ) rewards of education as represented by the μῶλυ which protected Odysseus. Both Eustathius and Koraes address themselves to young men, νέοι, and their aim is to help by offering τὸ χρήσιμον (cf. *in Il.* 2.21); Koraes has, he

---

136 Cf. Mackridge 2010, 132.
137 This allegory is of a very common kind; we may compare Dio Chrys. 16.10 where the magic potion that Jason received from Medea for protection against the fire-breathing bulls and the dragon was in fact received from φρόνησις, with Μήδεια implicitly connected with μῆτις and μήδομαι. Dio says that we should follow this example and 'show contempt to all (such) things, for otherwise everything will be fire for us and everything sleepless dragons'. In most extant versions of the story, Medea's ointment only protected Jason from the bulls, the dragon being overcome with different magic.

tells his addressee, no aim other than offering 'common benefit to the Greek nation' (νε'). Eustathius remains above all an educator and a didactic model. Koraes indeed once planned a new six-volume edition of Eustathius' Homeric commentaries, but for various reasons (including, of course, money) it never came to pass.[138] When Greece recovers, Koraes proclaimed, it should raise statues of Eustathius, an honour which – as far as I am aware – remains unbestowed, though Athens has done the right thing by Koraes himself;[139] there he sits outside the University building on Panepistimiou, an elderly man slightly bowed forward like a kindly and didactic uncle, as though carrying the whole of Greek tradition on his shoulders. The now somewhat worn inscription declares that the statue was erected so that young men should have a model to emulate; Eustathius would have deserved no less.

Homer and Heliodorus, Eustathius and Koraes. The temptation to play with the parallelisms and differences is almost irresistible. Heliodorus was well known and influential in the eleventh and twelfth centuries,[140] and seems also to have been subject to allegorical critical practices ultimately derived from Homeric criticism.[141] Although Eustathius cites Heliodorus only rarely in the *Iliad* commentary we may, I think, assume that he knew the novel, and its 'Homeric' qualities, well.[142] Homer and Heliodorus frame classical antiquity, in one influential (and, who knows?, possibly even correct) view; Eustathius and Koraes were both strikingly interested in the history of the Greek language and how it was spoken in their own day, even if the Bishop lacked Koraes' reforming zeal.[143] Homer's poems were the ideological charter which had founded Greek identity and which was at the heart of how its living sense was handed on from generation to generation; Heliodorus' *Aithiopika* has 'identity', both Greek and other, at its very centre, and is clearly constructed not just as a rewriting of

---

138 Cf. Paschalis 2010, 113–116.
139 Cf. Kitromilidis 2010b, 27.
140 Cf. Gärtner 1969, Agapitos 1998.
141 On 'Philip the Philosopher's' famous allegorisation of the *Aithiopika* cf. Hunter 2005.
142 Van der Valk, I cvii lists two instances (*in Il.* 55.32–34, 160.15–16), both in the commentary on *Iliad* 1; we should perhaps add *in Il.* 159.25 (also on *Iliad* 1) where ἡμέρα διαγελᾷ looks like a borrowing from the very opening of Heliodorus' novel. A principal witness for Byzantine appreciation of Heliodorus' 'Homeric' qualities is Michael Psellus' comparison of Heliodorus and Achilles Tatius from the previous century, cf. Dyck 1986b; Psellus' account of how Heliodorus 'gives the reader breaks through variety and novel diction and episodes and turns of every kind' (61–62 Dyck) assimilates him closely to a familiar scholiastic view of the Homeric poems.
143 For Eustathius' interest in the development of Greek and the contemporary vernacular cf., e.g., Koukoules 1950, Hedberg 1946, Hunger 1978, II 64.

Homer, but as a monument to be set alongside the epic poems. The capacious inclusiveness of Heliodorus' narrative and Eustathius' *Commentaries* allows both to be seen (with hindsight) as innovative repositories of tradition and also as pointing forward to new literary and scholarly forms which would come to dominate their respective worlds. Even more important perhaps is the fact that Eustathius and Koraes both use Homer and Heliodorus respectively as leaping-off points for the promulgation of a larger educational and moral agenda. Homer was never just another text, or even simply just the best text: he was always much more than that.

Bibliography

Agapitos, P. 1998. 'Narrative, rhetoric, and 'drama' rediscovered: scholars and poets in Byzantium interpret Heliodorus', in: R. Hunter (ed.), *Studies in Heliodorus*, Cambridge, 125–156.
Alpers, K. 1988. 'Klassische Philologie in Byzanz', *Classical Philology* 83, 342–360.
Bassi, K. 2014. 'Homer's Achaean wall and the hypothetical past', in: V. Wohl (ed.), *Probabilities, Hypotheticals, and Counterfactuals in Ancient Greek Thought*, Cambridge, 122–141.
Browning, R. 1992. 'The Byzantines and Homer', in: R. Lamberton/J.J. Keaney (eds.), *Homer's Ancient Readers*, Princeton, 134–147.
Browning, R. 1995. 'Eustathios of Thessalonike revisited', *Bulletin of the Institute of Classical Studies* 40, 83–90.
Calame, C. 1999. *The Poetics of Eros in Ancient Greece*, Princeton.
Cullhed, E. 2017. 'Achaeans on Crusade', in: F. Pontani, V. Katsaros and V. Sarris (eds.), *Reading Eustathios of Thessalonike*, Berlin, 285–297.
Cesaretti, P. 1991. *Allegoristi di Omero a Bisanzio: ricerche ermeneutiche (XI–XII secolo)*, Milan.
de Jong, I. 2001. *A Narratological Commentary on the Odyssey*, Cambridge.
Dyck, A. 1986a. 'Review of Wilson 1983', *Speculum* 61, 484–486.
Dyck, A. 1986b. *Michael Psellus. The Essays on Euripides and George of Pisidia and on Heliodorus and Achilles Tatius*, Vienna.
Erbse, H. 1950. *Untersuchungen zu den attizistischen Lexika*, Berlin.
Festugière, A.J. 1970. *Proclus, Commentaire sur la République*, Paris.
Ford, A. 1992. *Homer. The Poetry of the Past*, Ithaca NY.
Gärtner, H. 1969. 'Charikleia in Byzanz' *Antike und Abendland* 15, 47–69.
Goldwyn, A.J./Kokkini, D. 2015. *Allegories of the Iliad, John Tzetzes*, Cambridge MA.
Graziosi, B./Haubold, J. 2010. *Homer, Iliad Book VI*, Cambridge.
Grethlein, J. 2008. 'Memory and Material Objects in the *Iliad* and the *Odyssey*', *Journal of Hellenic Studies* 128, 27–51.
Harder, A. 2012. *Callimachus Aetia*, Oxford.
Hardie, P. 2012. *Rumour and Renown. Representations of Fama in Western Literature*, Cambridge.
Hedberg, T. 1946. 'Das Interesse des Eustathios für die Verhältnisse und die Sprache seiner eigenen Zeit', *Eranos* 44, 208–218.
Hollis, A.S. 1990. *Callimachus Hecale*, Oxford.

Hunger, H. 1978. *Die hochsprachliche profane Literatur der Byzantiner*, Munich.
Hunter, R. 1983. *Eubulus, The Fragments*, Cambridge.
Hunter, R. 2004. 'The *Periegesis* of Dionysius and the traditions of Hellenistic poetry', *Revue des Études Anciennes* 106, 217–231 [= Hunter 2008, 718–734].
Hunter, R. 2005. '"Philip the Philosopher" on the *Aithiopika* of Heliodorus', in: S.J. Harrison et al. (eds.), *Metaphor in the Ancient Novel*, Groningen, 123–138 [= Hunter 2008, 829–844].
Hunter, R. 2006. *The Shadow of Callimachus*, Cambridge.
Hunter, R. 2008. *On Coming After. Studies in Post-Classical Greek Literature and its Reception*, Berlin/New York.
Hunter, R. 2009a. *Critical Moments in Classical Literature*, Cambridge.
Hunter, R. 2009b. 'The *Trojan Oration* of Dio Chrysostom and ancient Homeric criticism', in: J. Grethlein/A. Rengakos (eds.), *Narratology and Interpretation*, Berlin/New York, 43–61 [= this volume 487–505].
Hunter, R. 2009c. 'The curious incident …: *polypragmosyne* and the ancient novel', in: M. Paschalis/S. Panayotakis/G. Schmeling (eds.), *Readers and Writers in the Ancient Novel*, Groningen, 51–63 [= Hunter 2008, 884–896].
Hunter, R. 2012a. *Plato and the Traditions of Ancient Literature. The Silent Stream*, Cambridge.
Hunter, R. 2012b. 'The songs of Demodocus: compression and extension in Greek narrative poetry', in: M. Baumbach/S. Bär (eds.), *Brill's Companion to Greek and Latin Epyllion and its Reception*, Leiden, 83–109 [= this volume 18–45].
Hunter, R. 2014a. *Hesiodic Voices*, Cambridge.
Hunter, R. 2014b. 'Horace's other *Ars poetica*: *Epistles* 1.2 and ancient Homeric criticism', *Materiali e Discussioni per l'analisi dei testi classici* 72, 19–41 [= this volume 376–398].
Hunter, R. 2015. 'The rhetorical criticism of Homer', in: F. Montanari/S. Matthaios/A. Rengakos (eds.), *Brill's Companion to Ancient Greek Scholarship*, II, Leiden, 673–705 [= this volume 598–632].
Hunter, R. 2016. '"Palaephatus", Strabo and the boundaries of myth', *Classical Philology* 111, 245–261 [= this volume 578–597].
Hunter, R. 2017. 'Serpents in the soul: the 'Libyan Myth' of Dio Chrysostom', in: G. Hawes (ed.), *Myths on the Map*, Oxford [= this volume 560–577].
Hunter, R./Russell, D.A. 2011. *Plutarch, How to Study Poetry (De audiendis poetis)*, Cambridge.
Kaldellis, A. 2007. *Hellenism in Byzantium*, Cambridge.
Kambylis, A. 1991. *Eustathios über Pindars Epinikiendichtung*, Hamburg.
Kazhdan, A./Franklin, S. 1984. *Studies on Byzantine Literature of the Eleventh and Twelfth Centuries*, Cambridge/Paris.
Kitromilidis, P.M. (ed.) 2010a. *Adamantios Korais and the European Enlightenment*, Oxford.
Kitromilidis, P.M. 2010b. 'Itineraries in the world of the Enlightenment: Adamantios Korais from Smyrna via Montpellier to Paris', in: Id., *Adamantios Korais and the European Enlightenment*, Oxford, 1–33.
Kolovou, F. 1999. *Μιχαὴλ Χωνιάτης. Συμβολὴ στὴ μελέτη τοῦ βίου καὶ τοῦ ἔργου του. Τὸ Corpus τῶν ἐπιστολῶν*, Athens.
Kolovou, F. 2006. *Die Briefe des Eustathios von Thessalonike*, Munich/Leipzig.
Koraes, A. 1804. *Ἡλιοδώρου Αἰθιοπικῶν βιβλία δέκα*, Paris.
Koukoules, P. 1950. *Θεσσαλονίκης Εὐσταθίου τὰ Λαογραφικά*, Athens.
Lamberton, R. 1986. *Homer the Theologian*, Berkeley.
Lampros, S. 1879. *Μιχαὴλ Ἀκομινάτου τοῦ Χωνιάτου τὰ σωζόμενα* I, Athens.
Lightfoot, J. 2014. *Dionysius Periegetes, Description of the Known World*, Oxford.

Lindberg, G. 1977. *Studies in Hermogenes and Eustathios*, Lund.
Maas, P. 1973. *Kleine Schriften*, Munich.
Mackridge, P. 2010. 'Korais and the Greek language question', in: P.M. Kitromilidis (ed.), *Adamantios Korais and the European Enlightenment*, Oxford, 127–149.
MacPhail, J.A. 2011. *Porphyry's Homeric Questions on the Iliad*, Berlin/New York.
Magdalino, P. 1996. 'Eustathios and Thessalonica', in: C.N. Constantinides et al. (eds.), ΦΙΛΕΛΛΗΝ. *Studies in honour of Robert Browning*, Venice, 225–238.
Melville Jones, J.R. 1988. *Eustathios of Thessaloniki. The Capture of Thessaloniki*, Canberra.
Nünlist, R. 2009. *The Ancient Critic at Work*, Cambridge.
Nünlist, R. 2011. 'Aristarchus and allegorical interpretation', in: S. Matthaios/F. Montanari/A. Rengakos (eds.), *Ancient Scholarship and Grammar*, Berlin/New York, 105–117.
Nünlist, R. 2012. 'Homer as a blueprint for speechwriters: Eustathius' commentaries and rhetoric', *Greek, Roman, and Byzantine Studies* 52, 493–509.
Nünlist, R. 2017. 'Was Eustathius Afraid of the Blank Page?' in: F. Pontani/V. Katsaros/V. Sarris (eds.), *Reading Eustathios of Thessalonike*, Berlin, 149–166.
Pagani, L. 2017. 'Eustathius' Use of Ancient Scholarship in his Commentary on the *Iliad*: Some Remarks', in: F. Pontani/V. Katsaros/V. Sarris (eds.), *Reading Eustathios of Thessalonike*, Berlin, 79–110.
Page, D.L. 1955. *Sappho and Alcaeus*, Oxford.
Papaioannou, S. 2013. *Michael Psellos. Rhetoric and Authorship in Byzantium*, Cambridge.
Paschalis, M. 2010. 'The history and ideological background of Korais' *Iliad* project', in: P.M. Kitromilidis (ed.), *Adamantios Korais and the European Enlightenment*, Oxford, 109–124.
Pizzone, A. 'History has no End: Originality and Human Progress in Eustathios' Second Oration for Michael III *o tou Anchialou*', in: F. Pontani/V. Katsaros/V. Sarris (eds.), *Reading Eustathios of Thessalonike*, Berlin, 331–355.
Pontani, F. 2000. 'Il proemio al *Commento all' Odissea* di Eustazio di Tessalonica', *Bollettino dei Classici* s. III 21, 5–58.
Pontani, F. 2005. *Sguardi su Ulisse*, Rome.
Pontani, F. 2011. 'Callimachus cited', in: B. Acosta-Hughes/L. Lehnus/S. Stephens (eds.), *Brill's Companion to Callimachus*, Leiden, 93–117.
Pontani, F. 2015. 'Scholarship in the Byzantine empire', in: F. Montanari/S. Matthaios/A. Rengakos (eds.), *Brill's Companion* to *Ancient Greek Scholarship*, I, Leiden, 297–455.
Pontani, F. 2017. '"Captain of Homer's guard": the reception of Eustathius in modern Europe', in: F. Pontani, V. Katsaros and V. Sarris (eds.), *Reading Eustathios of Thessalonike*, Berlin, 199–226.
Porter, J.I. 1992. 'Hermeneutic lines and circles: Aristarchus and Crates on the exegesis of Homer', in: R. Lamberton/J.J. Keaney (eds.), *Homer's Ancient Readers*, Princeton, 67–114.
Porter, J.I. 2011. 'Making and unmaking: the Achaean wall and the limits of fictionality in Homeric criticism', *Transactions of the American Philological Association* 141, 1–36.
Reynolds, L.D./Wilson, N. 1974. *Scribes and Scholars*, 2nd ed., Oxford.
Reynolds, L.D./Wilson, N. 2013. *Scribes and Scholars*, 4th ed., Oxford.
Rotolo, V. 1965. *A. Koraìs e la questione della lingua in Grecia*, Palermo.
Scodel, R. 1982. 'The Achaean wall and the myth of destruction', *Harvard Studies in Classical Philology* 86, 33–50.
Sheppard, A.D.R. 1980. *Studies on the 5th and 6th Essays of Proclus' Commentary on the Republic*, Göttingen.
Speck, P. 1986. 'A more charitable view', *Klio* 68, 615–625.

Stone, A.F. 2001. 'On Hermogenes's Features of Style and other factors affecting style in the Panegyrics of Eustathios of Thessaloniki', *Rhetorica* 19, 307–339.
Tabaki, A. 2010. 'Adamance Coray comme critique littéraire et philologue' in: P.M. Kitromilidis (ed.), *Adamantios Korais and the European Enlightenment*, Oxford, 151–183.
Tafel, T.L.F. (ed.) 1832. *Eustathii Metropolitae Thessalonicensis Opuscula*, Frankfurt.
Taplin, O. 1992. *Homeric Soundings*, Oxford.
Van den Berg, B. 2017. 'Eustathios on Homer's Narrative Art: the Homeric Gods and the Plot of the *Iliad*', in: F. Pontani/V. Katsaros/V. Sarris (eds.), *Reading Eustathios of Thessalonike*, Berlin, 129–148.
Wedner, S. 1994. *Tradition und Wandel im allegorischen Verständnis des Sirenenmythos*, Frankfurt.
West, M.L. 1995. 'The date of the *Iliad*', *Museum Helveticum* 52, 203–219 [= *Hellenica* I (Oxford 2011) 188–208].
Wilamowitz-Moellendorff, U. von 1920. *Die Ilias und Homer*, Berlin.
Wilson, N.G. 1983. *Scholars of Byzantium*, London.

37 Dionysius of Halicarnassus and the Idea of the Critic

Histories of the idea of the 'critic', the man who 'judges' literature, have often been written, but it is worth beginning from the fact that in recent years the familiar story has become more complicated and perhaps more interesting. In particular, the decipherment of carbonized papyrus rolls from Herculaneum has taught us more and more about the κριτικοί of the Hellenistic period who preceded Dionysius, and we now have a slightly clearer, though still desperately fragmentary, view of the background to Dionysius' intellectual context in Augustan Rome;[1] rather, however, than offering another survey of 'where we are now',[2] I wish in this chapter to take one sounding in Dionysius' own practice to try to tease out some of the assumptions which underlie his critical practice. Dionysius' concern both with the overarching conceptions of classical literature and with how those conceptions play themselves out at the micro-level of language makes him a figure of the greatest importance in the history of what we think we are doing in studying literature and how the ancients perceived that task.

In his treatise *On Thucydides*, with which I will here largely be concerned, Dionysius marks a structural break in the essay by recapitulating its purpose to his addressee, Quintus Aelius Tubero:[3]

> [I shall discuss the matter] under broad headings and by subjects, offering examples of narration and rhetorical speeches and setting out the reasons for his successes and failures in both subject-matter and expression. I request again of you and of all other scholars (φιλόλογοι) who will read my account to take note of my intention in choosing (προῄρημαι) this subject, namely to set forth all the features of his style which require comment, in the hope of being of assistance to those who wish to imitate this writer.
>
> *Thuc.* 25.1–2[4]

This is the very lightly revised text of the closing lecture given to the Leiden conference; I have not sought to eliminate all marks of oral performance or to disguise the fact that it was expressly aimed at a 'wider' audience than most of the papers at the conference. I am indebted to Casper de Jonge for much helpful criticism.

---

1 On the κριτικοί, see Hunter/de Jonge 2019, and Viidebaum 2019 and de Jonge 2019.
2 For a brief account of Dionysius and contemporary criticism, cf. Hunter/de Jonge 2019.
3 On Quintus Aelius Tubero, see Wiater 2019, 74 with further references. Quintus Aelius Tubero was one of the sources of Dionysius' *Roman Antiquities*: see Oakley 2019, 154.
4 Translations are my own.

There is much here which is typical of Dionysius and his criticism — the appeal to a like-minded audience, the emphasis on the intention or purpose, the προαίρεσις, of a writer, ancient or modern (cf. *Orat. Vett.* 4.2, *Ant. Rom.* 1.1.2, 3.6), to say nothing of the language of success and failure, are hallmarks of how Dionysius approaches his critical task. The wording in fact takes us back to the very beginning of the treatise. In looking at the work of the ancients, there are, so Dionysius tells us through a description of his largely lost work *On Imitation*,[5] two broad areas to consider:

> In the essays I published on the subject of imitation, Quintus Aelius Tubero, I examined those poets and prose-writers whom I considered to be most illustrious, and I briefly indicated the virtues of each in both subject-matter and style; I also indicated where failures caused each most to fall short of his own standards, whether because his purpose (ἡ προαίρεσις) did not foresee every issue down to the finest detail or because his powers (ἡ δύναμις) were not up to the task throughout. My purpose was that those who undertake (οἱ προαιρούμενοι) to write and speak well should have excellent and tested standards (κανόνες) to employ in each of their own exercises; they should not imitate everything which they find in these writers, but rather take over their virtues and guard against their failings.
>
> *Thuc.* 1.1–2

The sentences pose more than one specific difficulty of interpretation, but the overall sense is clear: προαίρεσις, what a writer plans to do, what — as we might say — his project is, and δύναμις, how he actually carried it out, are the two concerns of the critic,[6] and it is around those two poles that Dionysius' analysis will hinge. As he says of Thucydides:

> When his purpose and his powers come together, the nature of his success is perfect, more than human; but when his powers fall short and the intensity (ὁ τόνος) is not maintained throughout, then his language becomes obscure because of the speed of his narration and this brings with it other unattractive blemishes.
>
> *Thuc.* 24.12

There are blemishes (κῆρες) on the Thucydidean body which are not pretty to look at, and we might remember Dionysius' comparison in *On Imitation* of a perfect work to that of a perfectly beautiful woman,[7] with no *menda* ('stain') anywhere in sight, as Ovid might have said (cf. *Am.* 1.5.18). Be that as it may, the language of προαίρεσις and δύναμις is not of course unique to Dionysius, but

---

5 On this work see Battisti 1997, Hunter 2009, ch. 4, Wiater 2011a, 78–83.
6 For a collection of passages involving this dichotomy, cf. Aujac 1991, 145.
7 *On Imitation*, Epitome 1.4, cf. Hunter 2009, ch. 4.

repetition makes it very particularly his; προαίρεσις, in particular, is a word with a strong resonance of ethical theorizing — the choices we make reveal moral character — and this is very relevant here also, not just because of the traditionally intimate link between ethical and rhetorical criticism,[8] but also because Thucydides' choices of what to write and what to write about are to reveal much about him, not all of it very pretty. The dichotomy of προαίρεσις and δύναμις is in fact part of Dionysius' rhetoric of being a critic — writers and orators can go wrong in any number of ways, and the ability to group successes and failures under different heads is one of the ways in which the critic establishes his authority. Modern critics used occasionally to compare Horace's *Ars Poetica*, and they were surely correct to do so:

> sumite materiam uestris, qui scribitis, aequam
> uiribus et uersate diu, quid ferre recusent,
> quid ualeant umeri. cui lecta potenter erit res,
> nec facundia deseret hunc nec lucidus ordo.
>
> Hor. *Ars* P. 38–41

> You who write should choose a subject equal to your strength, and consider for a long time what your shoulders cannot carry and what they can. The writer whose choice of subject is in accordance with his powers,[9] will not find himself abandoned either by the flow of words or by clarity of order.

As usual, Horace has expressed 'textbook ideas' in a strikingly novel and concrete fashion: he plays with the physical sense of *materia*, 'wood, the trunk of a tree' (cf. *OLD* s.v. 2, Greek ὕλη) to conjure a picture of the would-be poet struggling to test just how much his shoulders can actually carry.[10] Horace too, like Dionysius, claims to be giving practical instruction for young people who themselves want to write creatively: 'criticism' is in antiquity rooted in education and instruction, rather than, for example, in what we tend to think of as 'scholarship'.[11] There would, in fact, be much to be said by way of comparison between Horace and Dionysius, contemporaries working in the same city,[12] but in this case it is the difference within similarity which attracts attention. Horace plays with contemporary critical ideas through image and metaphor, whereas — as we

---

8 Cf., e.g., Russell 1981, 11.
9 The meaning is disputed, cf. Brink 1971 *ad loc.*
10 We may compare 'Ps-Scymnus', *Periodos* 36–42 — the 'bundle of wood' image taken from Apollodorus of Athens.
11 Cf., e.g., Russell 1981, 11.
12 Cf. Hunter 2009, 124–127, de Jonge 2019, 242–266.

shall see — some of Dionysius' most interesting effects come through allusion and literary reminiscence, where the critic practises what he preaches. This is not, I think, the result of the difference between the Greek rhetorician and the Latin poet — we might, after all, have expected the techniques to be reversed — but rather of the fact that, whereas Dionysius is so immersed in 'classical' literature that he clothes his own essays in the language of that past, Horace creates a fresh critical discourse which is neither technical nor trite and which allows him to keep a distance, both didactic and ironical, from the poetic forms he discusses.

If we go back to the opening of the *On Thucydides*, we will find three different layers of προαίρεσις: that of the classical writers themselves, that (*Thuc.* 1.2) of the modern students who wish to write and orate in imitation of the ancient pattern, and finally the προαίρεσις (*Thuc.* 1.3) of Dionysius, the teacher and critic, himself. This verbal repetition is one small marker of something both very obvious and also very important: the modern student has in fact two guides along the way of his rhetorical and political career — the great classics themselves, and the contemporary critic's distillation of the virtues and failings of those classics; students are to approach the literature of the past in ways approved by teachers such as Dionysius — only the properly trained can really appreciate the emotional power of that literature. The pedagogical situation ought to make those of us who teach in universities smile with recognition. In another way, however, Dionysius' role as critic and teacher is very different from anything practised today. Let us go back to *On Thucydides* 25.2.

Dionysius tells us that his aim (σκοπός) is to give help (ὠφέλεια) to people who wish to imitate 'the man'. In the context (and cf. σκοπεῖν in Dionysius' text immediately before) it seems very hard not to sense here an echo of Thucydides' own most famous programmatic claim, one which Dionysius knew well, one which he evokes in other works (most notably, of course, in the opening sections of the *Roman Antiquities*)[13] and one which has in fact been explicitly cited earlier in the treatise (*Thuc.* 7.3):

καὶ ἐς μὲν ἀκρόασιν ἴσως τὸ μὴ μυθῶδες αὐτῶν ἀτερπέστερον φανεῖται· ὅσοι δὲ βουλήσονται τῶν τε γενομένων τὸ σαφὲς σκοπεῖν καὶ τῶν μελλόντων ποτὲ αὖθις κατὰ τὸ ἀνθρώπινον τοιούτων καὶ παραπλησίων ἔσεσθαι, ὠφέλιμα κρίνειν αὐτὰ ἀρκούντως ἕξει. κτῆμά τε ἐς αἰεὶ μᾶλλον ἢ ἀγώνισμα ἐς τὸ παραχρῆμα ἀκούειν ξύγκειται.

Thuc. 1 22.4[14]

---

13 Cf. esp. *Ant. Rom.* 1.1.2: see Oakley 2019, 130, 141–142.
14 On the significance of this passage to Dionysius' *Roman Antiquities*, see Oakley 2019, 141–142.

> The absence of the mythical will perhaps make my work less appealing when heard. But it will be sufficient for me if all who wish to receive a clear account of what happened and of what is likely at some future time to happen again in this and similar ways should judge this work useful. It has been written to be a possession for all time, rather than a display-piece for immediate hearing.

The echo points in a number of important directions, as well as affirming the structural parallelism of author and critic.[15] The implications of Thucydides' statement have been endlessly discussed, but Dionysius will certainly have understood him to be expressing the hope that his readers, 'those who wish to receive a clear account', judge his work useful, particularly given the likelihood of similar events occurring again in the future. 'Repetition' is built into Thucydides' intellectual structure here, as it is also in Dionysius: 'imitation', which is a particular form of 'repetition' and one sanctioned by Isocrates, to whom Dionysius owes so much of his conception of both classical culture and historiography in particular,[16] is thus not just a classicizing exercise, but is in fact *the* classical practice, whether that be the affairs of states or the composition of creative literature, as, for example, Longinus' account in *On the Sublime* of all the great classical authors who were 'very Homeric' most famously sets forth (*Subl.* 13.4).

To return. Part in fact of where Thucydides went wrong, according to Dionysius elsewhere (*Pomp.* 3.6), was precisely that his pursuit of novelty led him to choose a disastrous subject, unlike Herodotus who was willing to do battle with his predecessors, as indeed Dionysius' students are being urged to do, and unlike Dionysius himself was to do, as he repeatedly stresses in the proem of the *Roman Antiquities* (1.1.2, 2.1); to put it very crudely indeed, Herodotus followed Dionysius' advice, whereas Thucydides did not.[17] The parallelism of the two sentences which I am pursuing, however, shows us that Thucydides did in fact understand crucial Dionysian principles — just not enough of them, as it turned out, unfortunately.

---

15 Weaire 2005 is an important study of Dionysius' appropriation of a Thucydidean voice. See also de Jonge 2017.

16 Cf. Isoc. *Paneg.* 7–10, with the remarks of Wiater 2011a, 146–147. There is, incidentally, much more to be done on Dionysius' creative imitation of Isocrates, which is one of the most powerful strains in his writing. The famous dedicatory opening of Dionysius' great work *On Composition*, for example, offers a virtuoso blend of Homer and Thucydides within a frame borrowed from the dedicatory opening of Isocrates' homily *To Demonicus* (cf. Hunter 2009, 123–124), and such cases could no doubt easily be multiplied.

17 Cf. Wiater 2011a, 2011b.

Dionysius returned to Thucydides' programmatic statement in the conclusion and summary of his work. Here he pleads once more that one must make distinctions within the *Histories* and separate those parts which are useful for modern imitators and students from those whose idiosyncrasy rules them out of court:

> Let me draw things together. There is no sense in considering equally worthy of imitation those passages of the historian which lack clarity (τὰ μὴ σαφῶς εἰρημένα) and those which combine clarity with his other virtues. We must admit that the more perfect is better than the less perfect and the clear than the unclear. Why on earth, then, do some of us praise the whole of the historian's language, being forced to claim that Thucydides wrote this for his contemporaries, to whom it was familiar and well known, whereas he gave no thought to us who would come after, while others throw out the whole of Thucydides' style as useless in court-rooms and public assemblies. Why do we not agree that the narrative part of it (τὸ διηγηματικὸν μέρος) is, with a few exceptions, marvellously well done and adapted for all kinds of uses, whereas the oratorical part (τὸ δημηγορικόν) is not all suitable for imitation, though it contains material which all men can easily understand, even if not all are capable of such composition.
>
> *Thuc.* 55.3–4

Thucydides claimed that the style of the *Histories* was determined by the needs of present and future readers: is it then likely, asks Dionysius, that he gave no thought (no λόγος) to 'us' who would come after? 'We' are, of course, those for whom Dionysius is writing, students of rhetoric who wish to imitate and use the historian in the composition of πολιτικοὶ λόγοι; whether or not Thucydides ever in his worst nightmares imagined the rise of such a group, we can hardly say, but Dionysius' argument grows from a structure within Thucydides' own expression and offers a reading of Thucydides' claims which itself claims to be self-evident. Only, in other words, by accepting Dionysius' analysis of Thucydides, which involves the identification of success and failure within Thucydides' history, can one be true to the meaning which Thucydides himself gave to his work: what critic could be truer to his subject than that? We know from Cicero that Dionysius is certainly not original in rejecting Thucydides' more elaborate stylistic turns within the speeches as material that the modern orator should not (or could not) imitate (cf. Cic. *Brut.* 287–288, *Orat.* 30–32),[18] but to enlist Thucydides himself in support of the argument is a remarkable feat. When Dionysius ends the work with a close echo of what Thucydides reported Nicias to have written to the Athenians, we will therefore see more than just a final flourish:

---

18 Cf. de Jonge 2008, 214–216.

τούτων ἡδίω μὲν εἶχόν σοι περὶ Θουκυδίδου γράφειν, ὦ βέλτιστε Κόιντε Αἴλιε Τουβέρων, οὐ μὴν ἀληθέστερα.

Thuc. 55.5[19]

I could, my dear Quintus Aelius Tubero, have written you something about Thucydides which was more pleasant (ἡδίω), but it would not have been more true.

τούτων ἐγὼ ἡδίω μὲν ἂν εἶχον ὑμῖν ἕτερα ἐπιστέλλειν, οὐ μέντοι χρησιμώτερά γε, εἰ δεῖ σαφῶς εἰδότας τὰ ἐνθάδε βουλεύσασθαι. καὶ ἅμα τὰς φύσεις ἐπιστάμενος ὑμῶν, βουλομένων μὲν τὰ ἥδιστα ἀκούειν, αἰτιωμένων δὲ ὕστερον, ἤν τι ὑμῖν ἀπ' αὐτῶν μὴ ὁμοῖον ἐκβῇ, ἀσφαλέστερον ἡγησάμην τὸ ἀληθὲς δηλῶσαι.

I could have sent you different, more pleasant news, but certainly not more useful, if you are to have clear knowledge of the situation here when you make your plans. I also was conscious of your nature: you want to hear the most pleasant news, but afterwards you find fault, if anything does not turn out in accordance with your expectations; as a result of this, I thought it safer to tell you the truth.

Thuc. 7.14.4

Not only is the critic's voice now blended with that of the subject of his work, but through this echo Dionysius calls our attention to the fact that Nicias' hard words in fact reprise the themes of 1.22.4 — pleasure on one side, truth ('clear knowledge') and usefulness on the other;[20] just as Dionysius here alludes to Thucydides 7.14.4 and through that passage to 1.22.4, so in 7.14.1 the Thucydidean Nicias had 'alluded to', and thus confirmed the truth of, the historian's words at 1.22.4. Dionysius and Thucydides can indeed speak with one voice.

In 1.22.4 Thucydides expresses the hope that a particular section of his audience will 'judge' (κρίνειν) his work helpful. Dionysius does not use the verb at *Thuc.* 25.2 (above pp. 750–751), but it is obviously implicit in his renewed appeal to his audience. Here again we are taken back to the prologue of the work: in *Thuc.* 2.4 Dionysius notes that the work's addressee and τῶν ἄλλων φιλολόγων ἕκαστος, 'all other men of learning', will judge whether his words are 'true and appropriate to himself'. If the critic's job is to pass κρίσις about classical texts (award prizes in the various categories of style, in fact, cf., e.g., *Isoc.* 11.1–5), then the critic too will be judged. As is well known, the language of judging, of accusation and defence, is everywhere scattered throughout Dionysius' critical works; nit-picking criticism can be συκοφαντεῖν (*Thuc.* 2.2), and one's oppo-

---

19 Aujac 1991, 125 suggests ἡδίω μὲν <ἂν> εἶχόν σοι, presumably in part to bring this even more closely in line with the Thucydidean model.
20 Cf. also Weaire 2005, 255–256 and de Jonge 2017, who, however, associate the final sentence of the work only with Thuc. 1.22.4.

nents — as, most famously, Callimachus' were — are, unlike Dionysius himself (*Thuc.* 2.3, 34.5), driven by envy and malice (4.1). The critic is, quite literally, on trial for his life,[21] and — as was normal in trials of the classical period — it is the defendant's life which must be laid bare by his defence. So it is that Dionysius tells us that he has only once before 'in his whole life' brought an accusation against anyone (κατηγορῶ τινος, *Thuc.* 2.3), and that was 'on behalf of πολιτικὴ φιλοσοφία', in other words in defence of everything 'we' hold dear, and he did this to ward off unjust attacks against her.[22] If Dionysius cannot, unlike Socrates in Plato's *Apology*, legitimately claim that he has never had anything to do with 'courtrooms' before, he can at least disclaim any experience of malicious or carping criticism (in both senses) (*Thuc.* 2.3), and also call 'witnesses' (*Thuc.* 3.3) to the fact that what he has been doing, and will do in the current treatise also, is entirely within the best traditions of classical practice. The witnesses he calls are Aristotle and Plato: their disinterested concern with truth, one which naturally leads them to be in part critical of their predecessors, is the same as Dionysius' (*Thuc.* 3.3–4). If we are tempted here to observe that elsewhere Dionysius has very harsh words for Plato's 'envious' attacks on his predecessors and, particularly, on Homer, we should recall the overriding importance to Dionysius, as to Isocrates, of the ideas of τὸ πρέπον and καιρός, of choosing the appropriate arguments to fit the rhetorical circumstances: these ideas apply as much to works of criticism as they do to the great works of the past on which criticism is practised. Dionysius is on trial and his arguments are indeed appropriate to the situation.

The forensic world of classical Athens, no less than the political and rhetorical arenas of contemporary Rome, is thus a crucial part of the living context in which the Augustan critic — both judge and judged — plies his trade; it is indeed central to the classicizing ideals which Dionysius promulgates that the Athenian and Roman situations form a continuum embodying similar ethical and rhetorical values. This context, however, has no room for the faint-hearted. If some of Dionysius' opponents — not, of course, Quintus Aelius Tubero and the rest of 'the jury' to whom Dionysius addresses himself (*Thuc.* 2.1) — will criticize his τόλμα (2.2), Dionysius' only concern, as it has been throughout his career, is the truth:

---

[21] Cf. Pavano 1958, 14.
[22] It is normally thought that this refers to a lost treatise against the Epicureans, cf., e.g., Bonner 1939, 11–12 and Hunter/de Jonge 2019, 2.

τούτους οὖν ἐπὶ πάντων ἐγὼ τῶν ἐμαυτοῦ θεωρημάτων κανόνας ὑποτιθέμενος οὔτε πρότερον ὤκνησα τὰ δοκοῦντά μοι φέρειν ἐς μέσον οὔτε νῦν ἀποτρέψομαι.

Thuc. 35.1[23]

I have adopted these principles in all my investigations and I have never in the past shrunk from placing my views in the public domain and I will not hold back now.

Dionysius will not be silenced from placing his views ἐς μέσον, 'into the public arena', just as (elsewhere) he will speak freely, μετὰ παρρησίας (Dem. 23.1), thus enjoying the same freedom as a citizen of classical Athens.[24] There is something Periclean about his (alleged) fearless consistency (cf. Thuc. 2.61.2), or perhaps rather something Demosthenic. The formulation οὐκ ἀποτρέψομαι is found only here in Dionysius, but turns up three times in a single speech of Demosthenes and twice in the 'prologues' transmitted with the Demosthenic corpus, which Dionysius might well have accepted as genuine.[25] Demosthenes was not just, for Dionysius, the greatest classical orator and rhetorician,[26] but he was also a famous figure who said what needed to be said, even when it was deeply unpopular.

The same is not true for Dionysius' opponents, who play to the masses (Thuc. 4.1, cf. 2.3) with, as far as Dionysius' somewhat elliptical phrasing allows us to judge, the spiteful (ἐπίφθονον) charge that Dionysius is neither the historian Thucydides was nor the orator that Lysias, Demosthenes and the others were:

There is one further matter in which I must offer a defence: it is a charge motivated by envy (ἐπίφθονον ... κατηγόρημα) and one which wins the approval of the many, but is easily rebutted as unsound.[27] If my powers (ἡ δύναμις) fall short of those of Thucydides and the other historians, I have not also lost the right to examine them. Those who do not have the same artistic skills as Apelles and Zeuxis and Protogenes and the other famous painters are not prohibited from passing judgement on them, and the same is true for craftsmen who fall short of Pheidias and Polycleitus and Myron. I pass over the fact that the layman (ὁ ἰδιώτης) is no less competent a critic of many things than the expert (ὁ τεχνίτης), the

---

23 The text at the beginning of the passage is uncertain, but the sense is clear.
24 Discussed by Wiater 2011a, 319–320.
25 Cf. Dem. 24.2.1, 104.3, 200.2, Dem. (?) Exord. 23.1, 32.3; the last passage, 'I shall not turn away from saying what I think', is particularly close to Dionysius.
26 See Yunis 2019, 84.
27 The translation in Aujac 1991, 48 suggests that she understands Dionysius to be saying that he is being charged with jealousy, not that the charge is motivated by spite; that does not seem to me the natural way to read the text. Pavano 1958 and Usher 1974 adopt the view that I have followed here.

things indeed which are apprehended by irrational perception (δι' αἰσθήσεως ἀλόγου) and by the emotions, and that every art aims at such criteria and takes its beginning from them.

Thuc. 4.1–3

At issue is the relation between being a critic and being a practitioner of the art of which you are a critic, a subject famously discussed by T.S. Eliot in his 1923 essay on 'The Function of Criticism', not (incidentally) the only point of contact between that essay and the works of Dionysius: when Eliot observes that 'comparison and analysis...are the chief tools of the critic', any reader of the *Letter to Pompeius* can almost hear Dionysius nodding in vigorous agreement.

Dionysius' answer to the charge falls at first glance into two related parts. One does not need to be a Rembrandt or a Vermeer to be an art critic, so why should you need to be a Thucydides to write critically about historiography? At one level this might seem in fact a rather silly charge to throw at Dionysius, however it is to be understood; Aristophanes' *Frogs* had indeed dramatized the idea that Aeschylus and Euripides were 'experts' (τεχνῖται) in the criticism of tragedy, but the critical tradition had long been in the hands of those with little claim to be themselves makers of creative art. In Dionysius' case, however, the charge might have pricked a nerve. We have already seen how Dionysius has suggested that what he is doing is an activity parallel to that of the classical writers, that he is in fact in part ventriloquising Thucydides, but it would not have been hard simply to point out that that is not really so. Moreover, Dionysius, like his addressee, was himself a writer of history. Whatever the chronological relationship between his rhetorical works and the final form of the *Roman Antiquities*, the first part of which was apparently published in 8/7 BC (cf. *Ant. Rom.* 1.7.2), it would (again) not have been difficult, particularly for Thucydides' many fans (of whom more anon), to point out that Dionysius' δύναμις as a historian fell very well short of the historian he chose to criticize.

The second part of Dionysius' defence against the charge, a defence introduced with the *praeteritio* of a past master, is that the layman (ἰδιώτης) is as good a judge as the expert (τεχνίτης) when it comes to works of art which are to be apprehended by 'irrational perception' (αἴσθησις ἄλογος) and the emotions, and that these are in fact the target of 'every art'. The text here is problematic, but the distinction between two kinds of critic, the layman and the expert, is a fundamental part of Dionysius' criticism throughout the rhetorical works;[28] both are able to judge literature by the 'irrational criterion', the criterion of which one

---

28 Cf., e.g., Damon 1991, 45–49.

cannot give an 'account' (cf., e.g., *Dem.* 24.11), though the αἴσθησις of the expert may have been honed and trained through long habituation — Longinus famously describes ἡ τῶν λόγων κρίσις as the 'final product (ἐπιγέννημα) of much experience' (*Subl.* 6.1) — and it is the expert who will be able to add a technical, critical λόγος on top of the αἴσθησις.[29] One of Dionysius' clearest and best known statements of principle occurs in the *Lysias*:

> Teachers of music advise those who wish accurately to listen to musical harmonies, so that they should not miss even the smallest difference in the scale, to train their hearing and to seek no more accurate criterion than this. I too would urge those who read Lysias and wish to understand the charm (χάρις) of his writing to do the same:[30] over a long period of time and with long practice and the use of irrational feeling they must train their irrational perception.
>
> *Lys.* 11.3–4

The analogy which Dionysius, very typically, uses is music, but we might be tempted rather to think of wine-tasting, another act of connoisseurship practised among consenting adults, and one which depends upon an 'irrational' talent honed by long years of both practice and 'theory'; Cicero in fact uses such an analogy of rhetorical style (*Brut.* 287–288). Why, however, does Dionysius introduce this matter of the αἴσθησις ἄλογος at *On Thucydides* 4.3? In his commentary on the *On Thucydides*, Giuseppe Pavano suggests that Dionysius' critics had been demanding *ingenium* from the critic as well as *ars*, and Dionysius' appeal to the universal αἴσθησις ἄλογος is one answer to that challenge.[31] Dionysius would of course normally regard himself as a τεχνίτης, so there is a kind of *a fortiori* argument: 'if an ἰδιώτης can judge such matters, then how much more right has a τεχνίτης such as myself'. Coming, however, immediately after a roll call of the greatest painters and sculptors of the Greek past, it is very hard not to feel that τεχνίτης also evokes the sense 'artist', and this shift, effected through a semantic glide in an important word, is not in fact untypical of Dionysius' criticism. The conventional dichotomy between 'layman' and 'expert', so familiar to Dionysius' audience, and Dionysius' favourite theme of 'irrational perception' are here reinforced, and in fact shown to be correct, by the manifest example — so manifest it requires no discussion — of art criticism. I shall return presently to Dionysius' reliance on appeals to what everyone knows.

---

29 On the αἴσθησις ἄλογος, cf., e.g., Schenkeveld 1975, 1988, Porter 2006, Viidebaum 2019 and Yunis 2019, 100, 116–120.
30 On Lysias' χάρις, cf. Viidebaum 2019.
31 Pavano 1958, 16–17.

I have been talking freely about Dionysius' 'opponents', and it is well known that if ancient critics (like some modern scholars) did not have opponents, they tended to invent them; the agonistic context of criticism, just one more part of the 'trial' in which Dionysius is involved, was fundamental from the earliest period — we might think of competing sophists or competing sophistic interpretations (cf. Plato, *Protagoras*) or the rhapsode Ion's pride in his superiority to other interpreters of Homer (Plato, *Ion* 530c9-d3).[32] Callimachus, for example, begins his most famous and influential poem with a 'Reply' to his own malicious and envious (as he would have us believe) critics, and ancient scholars at least thought they could identify these 'Telchines'.[33] Some at least of Dionysius' targets, if not his opponents, recur later in the treatise when, in the context of Thucydides' speeches, he turns his attention to Thucydides' fan club, 'those who admire him beyond what is reasonable/moderate (τὸ μέτριον), as though he differed in no way from those who are divinely inspired' (*Thuc.* 34.3). That Thucydides did have such a fan club of admirers and imitators in Rome we know from other sources (cf. Cic. *Orat.* 30-2) — Dionysius' addressee Tubero appears to have been among them — and this should not surprise:[34] the style of the speeches is so idiosyncratic that the claim to appreciate them and then to be able to imitate them would have been an irresistible way for some to establish intellectual and cultural credentials which set them apart from others; it is easy enough to think of modern parallels for such fashionable trends in the worlds of music, art and scholarship. It is, as always, τὸ μέτριον, the happy 'nothing in excess' middle way, which for Dionysius is to be imitated, for πολιτικοὶ λόγοι have, after all, a practical aim and a real audience. Those parts of Thucydides which are to be imitated (*Thuc.* 27.3) are those where ordinary people will find nothing outlandishly difficult and hard-to-follow to put them off, and the educated specialist will not be able to exercise his μῶμος, 'fault-finding', on anything which is common, trite and unpolished. Dionysius, like Demosthenes in rather more serious times, will not allow his audience to sleepwalk to disaster. The fans, however, like infatuated lovers, will hear nothing at all against anything their darling ever wrote, in fact he is the epitome of all beauty and all the virtues; like lovers, they are slaves to the beloved (*Thuc.* 34.5), their critical judgement in a stupour (Thuc. 34.6), whereas Dionysius and his ilk are incorruptible:

---

32 Cf. Hunter 2012, 91.
33 Cf. the 'Florentine scholium', Callim. fr. 1b Harder.
34 Cf., e.g., Weaire 2005, Canfora 2006, de Jonge 2008, 214–215; 2011; 2017.

Those who preserve an attitude which is uncorrupted (ἀδέκαστος) and employ correct standards in the examination of literature, whether they have the gift of some natural power of judgement or have built up strong criteria of judgement through instruction, neither praise everything equally nor find fault with everything, but they offer appropriate acknowledgement to what is successful, and withhold praise from passages in which mistakes are made.

Thuc. 34.7

Dionysius is here quite close to Plutarch who compares an unwillingness to find any fault with the figures of Homeric poetry, which amounts (again) to an 'enslavement of the judgement', to those who imitate Plato's stoop or Aristotle's lisp (*Mor.* 26b); for Plutarch, too, it is rather a matter always of judging what is appropriate, πρέπον, for this is what the critic does, and when something falls short the critic (or student) must not hesitate to say so. The critic is not a worshipper at a shrine, even if σέβας, religious awe, is due to the great figures of the past (cf. *Pomp.* 1.1); Homer for one had long since been regarded as divine (θεῖος) and accorded cult. Where Plutarch is concerned with the moral behaviour and utterances of the characters of classical literature, Dionysius is concerned with style as a reflection of ethical προαίρεσις — the manner of your life and the manner of your writing are not to be separated (cf. *Orat. Vett.* 4.2), and here he will distribute both praise and blame as indeed appropriate (*Thuc.* 1.1, 34.7) and without fear or favour. Here in fact is another way in which Thucydides failed to live up to Dionysian principles: Thucydides went through Athens' mistakes and defeats in great detail, but 'when things went according to plan, he either did not mention them at all or did so as though under compulsion' (*Pomp.* 3.15).

The critic, then, has clear and strong principles of criticism, κριτήρια: we are most certainly not in a postmodern free-for-all in which subjective diversity is to be celebrated (cf. *Thuc.* 34.6). Authority derives not just from the use of appropriate κριτήρια, but also from the (real or alleged) tradition in which the critic is working. Dionysius is always anxious to stress that his critical views and practice fall within familiar parameters and have authoritative models (cf. above on *Thuc.* 3.3–5). One aspect of this is his frequent recourse to what we call rhetorical questions of the 'Who would not agree...?' or 'Who is so ignorant as not to realize...?' kind with which his work is littered;[35] the rightness of the crit-

---

[35] Cf., e.g., Wiater 2011a, 285–286. Such a rhetoric was already commonplace with the *logographoi* of the classical period, according to Arist. *Rh.* 3.1408a33–36, and was successful because 'the listener agrees out of shame not to know what everyone else knows'; Aristotle is

ic's views is a matter of shared human sensibility — 'it is impossible to hold another view', he says on one occasion (*Dem.* 13.2) — a sensibility shared not just by like-minded εἰδότες ('connoisseurs'):

> There is no one who does not agree, on the basis of his own experience and what he has heard, that Lysias is the most persuasive of all orators.
>
> *Lys.* 10.2

We need critics not to startle us with their brilliance, people — as Dionysius puts it elsewhere — 'who judge matters with an eye to their own reputations rather than to the truth' (*Dem.* 23.6),[36] and, as Dionysius' successors, modern scholars must count themselves fortunate that no such literary critics exist on either side of the Atlantic today. What we need is, unsurprisingly, what Dionysius has on offer: a critic who will set forth the emotions he feels when reading the great figures of the past, emotions which, he assures us, are 'common to everyone and not unique to him' (*Dem.* 21.4), a critic, in other words, who is able to articulate a set of shared values and responses. T.S. Eliot (again), at least, would recognize the discourse. Dionysius, moreover, has no wish to appear 'to make novel and paradoxical claims', παράδοξα καινοτομεῖν πράγματα (*Thuc.* 2.2): the text and construction are unfortunately uncertain, but this phrase has a strongly negative flavour in Greek, much more so than the 'lone pioneer breaking new and unexpected ground' of the standard English translation.[37] If, on the other hand, κοιναὶ δόξαι, 'common opinions' (*Thuc.* 2.2), are wrong, they need to be corrected, and this — after all — has happened throughout history. When Dionysius comes in the *Letter to Pompeius* to defend the criticism (κατηγορία) of Plato to be found in his treatise on Demosthenes, he assures his addressee that he has done nothing 'new or paradoxical or contrary to universal belief' (*Pomp.* 1.2). Dionysius is able to produce a roll call of names to show that he was 'neither alone nor the first' (*Pomp.* 1.15) to criticize (in a negative sense) Plato; the list is a very heterogeneous one, but the key point is that these figures are alleged (with greater and lesser degrees of truth) to have been engaged in the business 'not of making fun [of Plato] out of spite or quarrelsomeness but of searching for the truth'.[38] That Plato is 'a great man of nearly divine nature'

---

sometimes thought to have Isocrates, in particular, in mind, but this is certainly not a necessary inference.
36 Cf. Wiater 2011a, 339. Aujac mistakenly translates δόξας here as 'l'opinion'.
37 Usher 1974, 465.
38 Both Usher 1974 and Aujac 1991 understand κωμῳδοῦντες to refer to what Plato's critics actually did do, but this seems to ignore the careful balance of the sentence, and Dionysius

(*Pomp.* 2.2) should not, then, protect his style from the relentless pursuit of critical truth, and it never has.[39]

Dionysius' self-defence in the *Letter to Pompeius* sheds considerable light on one conception of the critic's task. He first distinguishes what he claims to have done from the business of ἔπαινος, 'praise', in which it is virtues, ἀρεταί, rather than τὰ ἀτυχήματα, 'failures', which should take precedence (*Pomp.* 1.3); this is the generic principle, the καθεστηκότες νόμοι, which govern what he almost immediately afterwards calls 'encomium' (*Pomp.* 1.4). This was not, so we are told, what Dionysius was doing: he in fact was trying to establish relative claims among great figures by the comparative method. Rather than considering (again) just how disingenuous this defence may be, let us rather concentrate on the language of criticism. Of particular importance to Dionysius will have been (as always) Isocrates (note, in particular, the 'generic' concerns — the difference between defence and encomium — with which Isocrates' *Helen* opens), but from the very earliest days critical practice had been indissolubly linked to praise and blame; this may be traced back to the emergence of criticism from the internal self-reflection of poetry itself — some poets, most notably Homer himself, were engaged in the business of celebration (κοσμεῖν), whereas for others the task was blame (ψόγος), and critical practice followed suit. 'Praise and blame' are another way in which the public language of oratory and rhetoric provides the context for what the Dionysian critic does: the figures of the past are held up to a 'public' examination, and the natural mode of such examination, if indeed its crucial importance is to be acknowledged, is encomium or attack.[40]

As, however, Aristotle knew very well, the two practices of praise and blame attract people of different moral characters and are revelatory of the difference. Hence Dionysius is always at pains, whether he is discussing the figures of the past or his own critical practice, to examine the διάθεσις, 'attitude', with which views are expressed. Thus, for example, Plato's manifold virtues are spoiled by the spirit of τὸ φιλότιμον, 'competitiveness, desire for praise', which was engrained in his nature (*Pomp.* 1.12), a spirit most on show in his envy of Homer; Longinus, however, shows us how precisely the opposite, positive 'spin' could be put on this same eristic relationship — one can wish to compete for glory

---

does not want any suggestion here that he too is involved in κωμῳδεῖν; it is unclear how Fornaro 1997, 115–116 construes the sentence.

[39] I am not convinced by Fornaro 1997, 156 that we should see irony in this description of Plato.

[40] For some relevant passages on 'praise' and 'blame' in oratory and rhetoric, cf. Lausberg 1960, 55.

with the great figures of the past, and it was very much to Plato's credit that he did so (*Subl.* 13.4). As for Dionysius himself, it is (again) 'truth' which is his constant watchword (*Pomp.* 1.6), and it is a pity that it was not Plato's (*Pomp.* 1.14). Truth is, however, not simple, and Dionysius' flexible conception of it deserves a moment's notice.

In chapter 45 of the *On Thucydides* Dionysius criticizes the historian for giving Pericles such a defiant speech in book 2 when the Athenians turned against him, a speech which could only have made the Athenians angrier, rather than a pleading speech of apology:

> It would be amazing, if Pericles, the greatest orator of the time, did not know what anyone of average intelligence knew, namely that those who unsparingly praise their own virtues are always burdensome to the audience, but especially in trials before a law-court or assembly; here the risk they face is not loss of honour but punishment (μὴ περὶ τιμῶν...ἀλλὰ περὶ τιμωριῶν). In such circumstances, they are not only burdensome to others, but the cause of misfortune to themselves, as they attract popular malice (φθόνος). Where the judges and the prosecutors are the same, one needs endless tears and appeals for pity to achieve the good will of your hearers.
> *Thuc.* 45.3

Aspasia perhaps saw Pericles in floods of tears, but the Athenian assembly never did. Dionysius finishes his analysis of this particular Thucydidean misjudgement as follows:

> As I said at the beginning, the historian is expressing his own opinion about Pericles' virtue and he has said these things inappropriately (παρὰ τόπον). Certainly, he should have expressed whatever view he wanted about the man, but he should have given him humble words and ones capable of assuaging anger when he was on trial; this would have been appropriate (πρέπον) for a historian who wished to imitate the truth.
> *Thuc.* 45.6

In her edition Aujac suggests that there is an allusion here to Thucydides' own famously problematic account of his procedure with regard to speeches:[41]

> καὶ ὅσα μὲν λόγῳ εἶπον ἕκαστοι ἢ μέλλοντες πολεμήσειν ἢ ἐν αὐτῷ ἤδη ὄντες, χαλεπὸν τὴν ἀκρίβειαν αὐτὴν τῶν λεχθέντων διαμνημονεῦσαι ἦν ἐμοί τε ὧν αὐτὸς ἤκουσα καὶ τοῖς ἄλλοθέν ποθεν ἐμοὶ ἀπαγγέλλουσιν· ὡς δ' ἂν ἐδόκουν ἐμοὶ ἕκαστοι περὶ τῶν αἰεὶ παρόντων τὰ δέοντα μάλιστ' εἰπεῖν, ἐχομένῳ ὅτι ἐγγύτατα τῆς ξυμπάσης γνώμης τῶν ἀληθῶς λεχθέντων, οὕτως εἴρηται.
> *Thuc.* 1 22.1

---

41 Aujac 1991, 111 n. 1.

> As to what was said by all parties, either in the run-up to the war or when they were actually engaged in it, it has been difficult to recall the exact wording of what was said, both for me with regard to speeches I myself heard and those who have supplied me with reports from elsewhere. Therefore, I have recorded what seemed to me it was most appropriate for anyone to say in the situation prevailing at any time, while remaining as close as possible to the general import of what was in truth said.[42]

Two related points of interest arise, whether or not we accept that Dionysius is indeed alluding to this passage of Thucydides. One is whether Dionysius understood (or chose to interpret) Thucydides' τὰ δέοντα, 'what the case demanded', itself of course an expression redolent of rhetorical theorizing, as τὰ πρέποντα, 'what was appropriate', for Dionysus the most potent determinant of what was to be said. Whether or not we believe that there is a fundamental contradiction at the heart of Thucydides' programme for his speeches,[43] we can nevertheless see how the Thucydidean expression differs from the Dionysian πρέπον, but it is also clear how one could take them as essentially synonymous, and how Dionysius might well have done so.[44] Secondly, Dionysius might be saying that an orator such as Pericles will certainly have followed the rules of rhetoric as known to Dionysius,[45] and so this is the kind of speech which Thucydides should have given him. This may be another example of what Stanley Bonner called Dionysius' 'singular lack of mental elasticity',[46] but it is also much more interesting than that. What is clear is that 'imitation' is Dionysius' business, not Thucydides' (the historian, alas, was not one of Dionysius' pupils), and 'truth' may not be the Thucydidean 'what was truly said', that is, a matter of historical record, but rather the 'truth' imposed by a way of looking at the world, a way governed by rules determining how to behave and speak in particular situations, a rhetorical 'truth' in other words about τὸ πρέπον, just as appeals to 'life' in literary critical situations ('O Menander and life...') are not pleas for documentary realism.[47] There is of course a connection between the two forms of 'truth', and a more intimate one than our own preconceptions might allow us to accept: a rhetorical view of what the world is like is indeed just that — a view of what the world is like — and is not necessarily consciously partial or selective.

---

42 My translation of this tormented passage has, of course, a very limited purpose.
43 Helpful summary of the arguments and some of the bibliography in Hornblower 1987, 45–66, adding Schütrumpf 2011.
44 Dionysius' discussion of 2.60.5 immediately before (*Thuc.* 45.1–2) is not, I think, decisive against this view.
45 Cf. Pavano 1958 *ad loc.*
46 Bonner 1939, 72.
47 Cf. further Halliwell 2002, 292–295, Hunter 2014, 373–379.

We may compare, while acknowledging the important differences, the links which Dionysius creates in the opening of the *Roman Antiquities* between historical 'truth', 'the origin of φρόνησις and σοφία' (*Ant. Rom.* 1.1.2), and the choice of grand, uplifting themes which will benefit readers (1.1.2, 3.6).[48] In a rhetorically informed world, whether that issues in rhetorical criticism or historiography, truth is never neutral, it must always serve proper and important ends.

When Dionysius says that 'someone whose aim is truth and who wants to be an imitator of nature (τὴν ἀλήθειαν... τις ἐπιτηδεύων καὶ φύσεως μιμητὴς γίνεσθαι βουλόμενος) would not go wrong if he followed the model of Lysias' composition, for one which is truer (ἀληθεστέραν) than this cannot be found' (*Lys.* 8.7), it is again not a view of what a defendant 'really said' which is at issue. Dionysius is of course under no illusion that the truth of Lysias' style is a reproduction of 'the way people spoke'; perhaps to us, paradoxically, it is in fact rather 'truer' than that.[49] For Dionysius, Lysias is ποιητὴς κράτιστος λόγων who has discovered his own kind of ἁρμονία in prose, which is as different as one may be from ordinary conversation (*Lys.* 3.8); Lysias is however also a ποιητής who avoids any suspicion of the ποιητικόν (*Lys.* 14.1).[50]

My comparison to the rich ancient tradition about how comedy, and above all Menander, 'imitated life' is not chosen at random. As one looks through ancient discussions of Menander, it is hard not to be reminded of Dionysius' *Lysias* and of his *On Lysias*. The surviving epitome of Dionysius' praise of Menander in *On Imitation* praises the purity and clarity of comic diction in general and of Menander's mastery of τὸ πραγματικόν in particular (Menander T87 K-A). We may perhaps fill this out a little from Quintilian's discussion, as the general closeness of Quintilian to Dionysius in these famous chapters is a commonplace: for Quintilian, Menander *omnem uitae imaginem expressit*, 'represented a total image of life' (*Inst.* 10.1.69), and his plays were thus a particularly important model for the budding orator, both because of their rhetorical *copia et eloquendi facultas* and because of the way in which the speeches were suited to a very wide range of characters. The three leitmotifs of ancient criticism of Menander are in fact the purity of his language, his portrayal of character and his *charites*, and this group of virtues makes it hard indeed not to think of Dionysius' *Lysias*; the Menander of the extant epitome of Plutarch's *Comparison of Aristophanes and Menander*, for example, is very close to Dionysius' *Lysias*.[51]

---

48 Cf. Oakley 2019, 130, 138–139.
49 On Dionysius' presentation of Lysias, cf. esp. Viidebaum 2019.
50 Cf. de Jonge 2008, 253–256.
51 On this work, cf. Hunter 2009, 78–89. On χάρις Viidebaum 2019.

However unusual much of Dionysius' extant criticism may seem to us, therefore, he can be seen, at least in part, to be operating with ethical and rhetorical categories and distinctions which were fundamental to ancient criticism of all kinds. It is indeed perhaps the fusion of traditional categories with a distinctive brand of classicizing aestheticism which is the most striking aspect of Dionysius' criticism. Dionysius was heir to more than one critical stream, and the debates which are on show in his treatises offer a remarkable view of a particular moment and a particular place — Augustan Rome — in the history both of criticism and of the idea of the critic.

Bibliography

Aujac, G. 1991. *Denys d'Halicarnasse: Opuscules rhétoriques*, vol. 4, Paris.
Battisti, D.G. 1997. *Dionigi di Alicarnasso: Sull'imitazione*, Pisa.
Bonner, S.F. 1939. *The Literary Treatises of Dionysius of Halicarnassus. A Study in the Development of Critical Method*, Cambridge.
Brink, C.O. 1971. *Horace on Poetry. The 'Ars Poetica'*, Cambridge.
Canfora, L. 2006. 'Thucydides in Rome and Late Antiquity', in: A. Rengakos/A. Tsakmakis (eds.), *Brill's Companion to Thucydides*, Leiden, 721–753.
Damon, C. 1991. 'Aesthetic Response and Technical Analysis in the Rhetorical Writings of Dionysius of Halicarnassus', *Museum Helveticum* 48, 33–58.
de Jonge, C.C. 2008. *Between Grammar and Rhetoric. Dionysius of Halicarnassus on Language, Linguistics and Literature*, Leiden.
de Jonge, C.C. 2019. 'Dionysius and Horace: Composition in Augustan Rome', in: R. Hunter/C. de Jonge (eds.), *Dionysius of Halicarnassus and Augustan Rome: Rhetoric, Criticism and Historiography*, Cambridge, 242–266.
Fornaro, S. 1997. *Dionisio di Alicarnasso: Epistola a Pompeo Gemino. Introduzione e commento*, Stuttgart.
Halliwell, S. 2002. *The Aesthetics of Mimesis: Ancient Texts and Modern Problems*, Princeton.
Hunter, R. 2009. *Critical Moments in Classical Literature. Studies in the Ancient View of Literature and Its Uses*, Cambridge.
Hunter, R. 2012. *Plato and the Traditions of Ancient Literature: The Silent Stream*, Cambridge.
Hunter, R./de Jonge, C. (eds.) 2019. 'Introduction', in: R. Hunter/C. de Jonge (eds.), *Dionysius of Halicarnassus and Augustan Rome: Rhetoric, Criticism and Historiography*, Cambridge, 1–33.
Lausberg, H. 1960. *Handbuch der literarischen Rhetorik*, Munich.
Pavano, G. 1958. *Dionisio d'Alicarnasso: Saggio su Tucidide*, Palermo.
Porter, J.I. 2006. 'Introduction: What Is "Classical" about Classical Antiquity?', in: J.I. Porter (ed.), *Classical Pasts. The Classical Traditions of Greece and Rome*, Princeton, 1–65.
Russell, D.A. 1981. *Criticism in Antiquity*, London.
Schenkeveld, D.M. 1975. 'Theories of Evaluation in the Rhetorical Treatises of Dionysius of Halicarnassus', *Museum Philologum Londiniense* 1, 93–107.

Schenkeveld, D.M. 1988. '*Iudicia vulgi*: Cicero, *De oratore* 3.195ff. and *Brutus* 183ff', *Rhetorica* 6, 291–305.
Schütrumpf, E. 2011. '"As I thought that the speakers most likely might have spoken". Thucydides *Hist.* 1.22.1 on composing speeches', *Philologus* 155, 229–256.
Usher, S. 1974. *Dionysius of Halicarnassus: The Critical Essays in Two Volumes*, Vol. 1, Cambridge.
Viidebaum, L. 2019. 'Dionysius and Lysias' Charm', in: R. Hunter/C. de Jonge (eds.), *Dionysius of Halicarnassus and Augustan Rome: Rhetoric, Criticism and Historiography*, Cambridge, 106–124.
Weaire, G. 2005. 'Dionysius of Halicarnassus' Professional Situation and the *De Thucydide*', *Phoenix* 59, 246–266.
Wiater, N. 2011a. *The Ideology of Classicism. Language, History, and Identity in Dionysius of Halicarnassus*, Berlin.
Wiater, N. 2011b. 'Writing Roman History – Shaping Greek Identity: The Ideology of Historiography in Dionysius of Halicarnassus', in: T.A. Schmitz/N. Wiater (eds.), *The Struggle for Identity. Greeks and their Past in the First Century BCE*, Stuttgart, 61–91.
Wiater, N. 2014. *Dionysius von Halikarnass: Römische Frühgeschichte Band 1: Bücher 1 bis 3*, Stuttgart.
Yunis, H. 2019. 'Dionysius' Demosthenes and Augustan Atticism', in: R. Hunter/C. de Jonge (eds.), *Dionysius of Halicarnassus and Augustan Rome: Rhetoric, Criticism and Historiography*, Cambridge, 83–105.

38 Dio Chrysostom and the Citation of Tragedy

'Dramatic fragments' are usually taken to refer to passages from lost plays, both those preserved on papyri and other ancient artefacts, as well as those preserved in quotation by other ancient (normally prose) writers.[1] An important tool, however, for the interpretation of those dramatic fragments is the other kind of 'dramatic fragment', namely quotations of surviving plays in later authors. With such quotations we have a control which allows us to see what quoting authors (and/or the scribes of their manuscripts) have done with the verses they are citing, and the knowledge gained can then be applied, as far as speculation allows, to extant citations from lost plays. There is a huge field of study here, and there has been much important recent work on the citational habits of writers such as Plutarch and Athenaeus. In this paper I consider two cases of citations of surviving Euripidean plays in Dio Chrysostom to see what (familiar) lessons may be drawn.

Dio is a particularly instructive source in this context because he sometimes explicitly discusses the rationale for citation. My first example is, however, something of 'a cheat' — as there is no actual citation in the text that survives to us. In the *Euboean Oration*, Dio discusses and demonstrates that the poor are in fact better hosts than the rich, and he explains that one draws on the wisdom of the poets as a kind of shorthand access to widely held beliefs:

ἆρ' οὖν οὐ σφόδρα ἄξιον ἄγασθαι τοῦ πλούτου κατὰ τὸν ποιητὴν καὶ τῷ ὄντι ζηλωτὸν ὑπολαβεῖν, ὅ φησιν αὐτοῦ μέγιστον εἶναι ἀγαθόν, τὸ δοῦναι ξένοις, καὶ ἐάν ποτέ τινες ἔλθωσι τρυφῶντες ἐπὶ τὴν οἰκίαν, μὴ ἀδύνατον γενέσθαι παρασχεῖν κατάλυσιν καὶ προθεῖναι ξένια, οἷς ἂν ἐκεῖνοι μάλιστα ἥδοιντο; λέγομεν δὲ ταῦτα μεμνημένοι τῶν ποιητῶν, οὐκ ἄλλως ἀντιπαρεξάγοντες ἐκείνοις οὐδὲ τῆς δόξης ζηλοτυποῦντες ἣν ἀπὸ τῶν ποιημάτων ἐκτήσαντο ἐπὶ σοφίᾳ, οὐ τούτων ἕνεκα φιλοτιμούμενοι ἐξελέγχειν αὐτούς, ἀλλὰ παρ' ἐκείνοις μάλιστα εὑρήσειν ἡγούμενοι τὴν τῶν πολλῶν διάνοιαν περί τε πλούτου καὶ τῶν ἄλλων ἃ θαυμάζουσι, καὶ τί μέγιστον οἴονταί σφισι γενέσθαι ἂν ἀφ' ἑκάστου τῶν τοιούτων. δῆλον γὰρ ὅτι μὴ συμφωνοῦντος αὐτοῖς τοῦ ποιήματος μηδὲ τὴν αὐτὴν γνώμην ἔχοντος οὐκ ἂν οὕτω σφόδρα ἐφίλουν οὐδὲ ἐπῄνουν ὡς σοφούς τε καὶ ἀγαθοὺς †γενέσθαι† καὶ τἀληθῆ λέγοντας. ἐπεὶ οὖν οὐκ ἔστιν ἕκαστον ἀπολαμβάνοντα ἐλέγχειν τοῦ πλήθους, οὐδ' ἀνερωτᾶν ἅπαντας ἐν μέρει, Τί γὰρ σύ, ὦ ἄνθρωπε, δέδοικας τὴν πενίαν οὕτως πάνυ τὸν δὲ πλοῦτον ὑπερτιμᾷς, τί δ' αὖ σὺ ἐλπίζεις κερδανεῖν μέγιστον ἂν τύχῃς πλουτήσας ἢ νὴ Δία ἔμπορος γενόμενος ἢ καὶ βασιλεύσας; ἀμήχανον γὰρ δὴ τὸ τοιοῦτον καὶ οὐδαμῶς ἀνυ-

---

[1] An important exception to my 'normally prose' assertion are those interpolated verses in extant tragedy which may be 'fragments' of lost plays; in this area, however, certainty is a very rare commodity. For the preservation of other kinds of verse 'fragments' within verse texts cf., e.g., the quotations from Apollodorus in the prologue of [Scymnus], *Periodos* 24–44.

στόν. οὕτως οὖν ἐπὶ τοὺς προφήτας αὐτῶν καὶ συνηγόρους, τοὺς ποιητάς, ἐξ ἀνάγκης ἴμεν, ὡς ἐκεῖ φανερὰς καὶ μέτροις κατακεκλεισμένας εὑρήσοντες τὰς τῶν πολλῶν δόξας· καὶ δῆτα οὐ πάνυ μοι δοκοῦμεν ἀποτυγχάνειν. τοῦτο δὲ σύνηθες δήπου καὶ τοῖς σοφωτέροις, ὃ νῦν ἡμεῖς ποιοῦμεν· ἐπεὶ καὶ αὐτοῖς τούτοις τοῖς ἔπεσιν ἀντείρηκε τῶν πάνυ φιλοσόφων τις, ὃν οὐδείς, ἐμοὶ δοκεῖν, φαίη ἄν ποτε φιλονεικοῦντα τούτοις τε ἀντειρηκέναι καὶ τοῖς ὑπὸ Σοφοκλέους εἰς τὸν πλοῦτον εἰρημένοις, ἐκείνοις μὲν ἐπ' ὀλίγον, τοῖς δὲ τοῦ Σοφοκλέους ἐπὶ πλέον, οὐ μήν, ὥσπερ νῦν ἡμεῖς, διὰ μακρῶν, ἅτε οὐ παραχρῆμα κατὰ πολλὴν ἐξουσίαν διεξιών, ἀλλ' ἐν βίβλοις γράφων.

Dio Chrys. 7.97–102

Is it not, then, most unfitting to admire wealth as the poet does and regard it as really worth seeking? He says that its greatest good lies in giving to guests and, when any who are used to luxury come to one's house, being in a position to offer them lodging and set such tokens of hospitality before them as would please them most. And in advancing these views we cite the poets, not to gainsay them idly nor because we are envious for their reputation for wisdom that they have won by their poems; no, it is not for these reasons we covet the honour of showing them to be wrong, but because we think that it is in them especially that we shall find the thought and feeling of men generally, just what the many think about wealth and the other objects of their admiration, and what they consider would be the greatest good derived from each of them. For it is evident that men would not love the poets so passionately nor extol them as wise and good and exponents of the truth if the poetry did not echo their own sentiments nor express their own views. Since, then, it is not possible to take each member of the multitude aside and show him his error or to cross-question everybody in turn by saying, 'How is it, sir, that you fear poverty so exceedingly and exalt riches so highly?' and again, 'What great profit do you expect to win if you happen to have amassed wealth or, let us say, to have turned merchant or even become a king?' Such a procedure would involve infinite trouble and is altogether impracticable. Therefore, because we must, let us go to their prophets and spokesmen, the poets, with the conviction that we shall find among them the beliefs of the many clearly put and enshrined in verse; and in truth I do not think that we fall very far short of our object in so doing. And our present procedure, I believe, is the usual one even with men wiser than myself. Indeed, one very great philosopher has expressly contradicted the sentiments contained in these same lines of Euripides, and he is a man whom I think no one would ever accuse of contradicting them and Sophocles' words about wealth in any spirit of captiousness. He objects briefly in the former instance but in more detail in the case of Sophocles, and yet not at great length as we are now doing, since he was not discussing the question *ex tempore* with an orator's full privilege but was writing in a book.

Translation by J.W. Cohoon

There is much that one could say about how Dio here uses (and inverts) the persona of Socrates from Plato's *Apology*,[2] but my concern here is with citational practice. This part of the speech is evidently a lecture based on a reading of a passage from Euripides' *Electra*, which was clearly well known to the anthologi-

---

2 Cf. Hunter 2018, 27–28.

cal and moralising tradition, namely the old peasant's meditation on the power of wealth:

ἐν τοῖς τοιούτοις δ' ἡνίκ' ἂν γνώμη πέσῃ,
σκοπῶ τὰ χρήμαθ' ὡς ἔχει μέγα σθένος
ξένοις τε δοῦναι σῶμά τ' ἐς νόσους πεσὸν
δαπάναισι σῶσαι· τῆς δ' ἐφ' ἡμέραν βορᾶς
ἐς σμικρὸν ἥκει· πᾶς γὰρ ἐμπλησθεὶς ἀνὴρ   430
ὁ πλούσιός τε χὠ πένης ἴσον φέρει.

Eur. *El.* 426–431

When my thought lights on matters like these,[3] I observe that while money has great power and allows you to give gifts to your guests and to keep your body alive when it has fallen into disease, it makes little difference to daily sustenance. When his belly is full, everyone, rich man and poor alike, holds an equal amount.

(Translation by D. Kovacs)

These verses are nowhere cited in our extant text of the *Euboikos*, but scholars have postulated that they may have been quoted in a lost opening of the essay or have dropped out somewhere along the way.[4] Commentators first (and rightly) detect their presence in chapter 82:

ἅπαντα δὴ τοῦτον τὸν λόγον διῆλθον οὐκ ἄλλως οὐδ' ὡς τάχ' ἂν δόξαιμί τισιν, ἀδολεσχεῖν βουλόμενος, ἀλλ' οὕπερ ἐξ ἀρχῆς ὑπεθέμην βίου καὶ τῆς τῶν πενήτων διαγωγῆς παράδειγμα ἐκτιθείς, ὃ αὐτὸς ἠπιστάμην, τῷ βουλομένῳ θεάσασθαι λόγων τε καὶ ἔργων καὶ κοινωνιῶν τῶν πρὸς ἀλλήλους, εἴ τι τῶν πλουσίων ἐλαττοῦνται διὰ τὴν πενίαν πρὸς τὸ ζῆν εὐσχημόνως καὶ κατὰ φύσιν ἢ τῷ παντὶ πλέον ἔχουσιν. καὶ δῆτα καὶ τὸ τοῦ Εὐριπίδου σκοπῶν, εἰ κατ' ἀλήθειαν ἀπόρως αὐτοῖς ἔχει τὰ πρὸς τοὺς ξένους, ὡς μήτε ὑποδέξασθαί ποτε δύνασθαι μήτε ἐπαρκέσαι δεομένῳ τινί, οὐδαμῇ τοιοῦτον εὑρίσκω τὸ τῆς ξενίας, ἀλλὰ καὶ πῦρ ἐναύοντας προθυμότερον τῶν πλουσίων καὶ ὁδῶν ἀπροφασίστους ἡγεμόνας·

Dio Chrys. 7.81–82

Now I have not told this long story idly or, as some might perhaps infer, with the desire to spin a yarn, but to present an illustration of the manner of life that I adopted at the beginning and of the life of the poor — an illustration drawn from my own experience for anyone who wishes to consider whether in words and deeds and in social intercourse the poor are at a disadvantage in comparison with the rich on account of their poverty, or in every way have the advantage. And really, when I consider Euripides' words and ask myself whether as a matter of fact the entertainment of strangers is so difficult for them that they can never welcome or succour anyone in need, I find this by no means to be true of their

---

3 The meaning of this verse is disputed.
4 Moles 1995, 179 n. 15 suggests that they dropped out from chapter 82 (on which see further below).

hospitality. They light a fire more promptly than the rich and guide one on the way without reluctance...

Translation by J.W. Cohoon

Opinions may differ as to whether this passage implies a yet earlier quotation of, or reference to, the Euripidean verses, but Dio's τὸ τοῦ Εὐριπίδου σκοπῶν is a remarkable example of what we might call meta-quotation. Whereas Euripides' peasant 'observes' (σκοπῶ) the power of wealth, Dio 'looks at' Euripides' verses on the same subject: general reflection on the way of the world is now for Dio a two-stage process, of which the first is the choice of appropriate classical texts to guide that reflection. There could hardly be a better microcosmic representation of the place of classical literature in the cultural mindset of educated Greeks under the Roman empire.

Dio's paraphrase in 7.82 of Eur. *El.* 426–431 is not a close one. We have the reference to ξένοι, but the ability to help someone else (or indeed yourself) who has fallen sick is replaced by the more general ἐπαρκέσαι δεομένωι τινί, 'bring help to someone in need', another traditional duty which wealth imposes upon those lucky enough to possess it.[5] ὑποδέξασθαι is too obvious a word in the circumstances to wish to tie it to the tragic text Dio has in mind, but I note (for what it is worth) that in vv. 404–405 Electra upbraids her husband:

ΗΛ. ὦ τλῆμον, εἰδὼς δωμάτων χρείαν σέθεν
τί τούσδ' ἐδέξω μείζονας σαυτοῦ ξένους;
Αυ. τί δ'; εἴπερ εἰσὶν ὡς δοκοῦσιν εὐγενεῖς,
οὐκ ἔν τε μικροῖς ἔν τε μὴ στέρξουσ' ὁμῶς;

Eur. *El.* 404–407

Electra. Fool, knowing the poverty of your house, why did you receive these men as guests who are grander than you?

Farmer. What do you mean? If they are as they seem well-born, will they not be content equally in straitened circumstances and in not?

In chapter 97, on the other hand, the reference to the verses from the *Electra* is unmistakable. We might, however, note in passing that if the verses of the *Electra* had not survived, then we can be sure that more than one nineteenth-century scholar would have tried to turn Dio's paraphrase into a 'fragment' in trimeters from a lost play. They might have got close, but it would not have been close enough, because Dio's paraphrase in chapter 97 is (again) a mixture of

---

5 Cf., e.g., Men. *Sam.* 15–16, with Sommerstein's note.

'quotation' and invention. τὸ δοῦναι ξένοις is indeed close to *El.* 428, but the peasant says nothing about τρυφῶντες, 'men used to luxury', coming to one's house. The motif is common enough (we will think of Menander's *Dyskolos*) and in part arises from the autobiographical narrative which Dio tells in the first part of the speech (cf. further below), but in fact what we have in chapter 97 is a trace derived from earlier parts of this scene in Euripides' play. When the peasant first catches sight of Orestes and Pylades his words imply that they do not look like country-people (vv. 341–344), and the exchange between Electra and her husband in vv. 404–407 (cited above) makes this very clear. In other words, Dio's paraphrase of the verses stretches out beyond the particular passage he is 'citing' (as we would say), but we would never know that if the *Electra* had not in fact survived. Even more strikingly, παρασχεῖν κατάλυσιν, 'to offer them lodging', picks up Orestes' δεξώμεθ' οἴκων καταλύσεις, 'let us accept lodging in the house', in v. 393 and προθεῖναι ξένια οἷς ἂν ἐκεῖνοι μάλιστα ἥδοιντο, 'set such tokens of hospitality before them as would please them most', picks up Electra's words in her instructions to her husband to fetch the old shepherd who will lead to the recognition:

κέλευε δ' ταὐτὸν τόνδ' ἐς δόμους ἀφιγμένον†
ἐλθεῖν ξένιά τ' ἐς δαῖτα πορσῦναί τινα.
ἡσθήσεταί τοι καὶ προσεύξεται θεοῖς,
ζῶντ' εἰσακούσας παῖδ' ὃν ἐκσῴζει ποτέ.

Eur. *El.* 413–416

[Go to his house][6] and tell him to come and bring some guest provisions for a feast. He will surely be overjoyed and offer prayers to the gods when he hears that the child he once rescued is alive.

Translation by D. Kovacs

The paraphrase in chapter 97 thus brings together 'fragments' scattered throughout a whole scene, not just the particular verses which were well known to the anthological tradition. This lesson is hardly new, but it is important and bears repetition, particularly for those who believe that the prose-writers of the Second Sophistic worked largely (or indeed entirely) from anthologies of passages (the forebears of Stobaeus) and not from texts of, or their knowledge of, whole plays.

Although Dio draws on very many classical texts in the *Euboean Oration*, it would not be unfair to consider the *Odyssey* and Euripides' *Electra* as the prin-

---

6 The text of v. 413 is uncertain.

cipal 'sources' for the part of the speech (chaps. 1–102) concerned with rural, rather than urban life. In focusing on the hospitality which the poor can and cannot offer, Dio is presumably reflecting a long tradition of critical and moralising discourse; for what it is worth, a fragmentary hypothesis to the *Electra*, which survives on a papyrus of the third century AD (P.Oxy. 420), also singles out this theme of hospitality with respect both to the farmer and to the gifts which the old family-retainer brings at vv. 494–500. Dio's narrative of his hospitable welcome by Euboean rustics can be seen to be shaped, not just by the return of the disguised Odysseus to Eumaeus' hut, but also by the return of the disguised Orestes to Electra's rustic dwelling in Euripides' tragedy, whether or not Dio had explicitly referred to those scenes in a lost opening to the *Euboean Oration*. This link between the 'rural' experiences of Odysseus and Orestes is a variation on the exploitation of Odysseus' return by (particularly) Sophocles and Euripides in their dramatization of Orestes' return in their respective *Electra* tragedies, which in its turn draws on, and varies, the persistent analogy in the *Odyssey* between the story of Odysseus, Telemachus and Penelope and that of Agamemnon, Orestes and Clytemnestra. More specifically, we may wonder whether the critical tradition had already traced a line of descent from Odysseus' reception at the hut of Eumaeus to Orestes' reception by Electra's poor rustic husband in Euripides' play; Dio's narrative and subsequent moralising reflections could then be seen as a kind of 'window allusion' written very large, in which one text which is thought to reflect an earlier text is combined with it to form a new 'combinatory' rewriting.

My second example is another famous passage of Euripides well known to the ethical tradition, namely Jocasta's plea to Eteocles in the *Phoenissae* on the subject of φιλοτιμία:

τί τῆς κακίστης δαιμόνων ἐφίεσαι
Φιλοτιμίας, παῖ; μὴ σύ γ'· ἄδικος ἡ θεός·
πολλοὺς δ' ἐς οἴκους καὶ πόλεις εὐδαίμονας
ἐσῆλθε κἀξῆλθ' ἐπ' ὀλέθρῳ τῶν χρωμένων·
ἐφ' ᾗ σὺ μαίνῃ. κεῖνο κάλλιον, τέκνον,   535
Ἰσότητα τιμᾶν, ἣ φίλους ἀεὶ φίλοις
πόλεις τε πόλεσι συμμάχους τε συμμάχοις
συνδεῖ· τὸ γὰρ ἴσον νόμιμον ἀνθρώποις ἔφυ,
τῷ πλέονι δ' αἰεὶ πολέμιον καθίσταται
τοὔλασσον ἐχθρᾶς θ' ἡμέρας κατάρχεται.

Eur. *Phoen.* 531–540

Why do you strive for Ambition for power, the basest of divinities, my son? Do not do so: she is an unjust goddess! Often she goes in and out of prosperous cities and houses and ruins those who have dealings with her! Yet for her you have lost your senses. Far finer, my son, to honour Equality, which binds friends to friends, cities to cities, and allies to allies. For Equality, men find, conduces to lawfulness, whereas the lesser is always hostile to the greater and making war against it.

Translation by D. Kovacs, adapted

Dio cites these verses in *Oration* 17, which our manuscripts label περὶ πλεονεξίας:

καὶ μὴν ὅ γε Εὐριπίδης, οὐδενὸς ἧττον ἔνδοξος ὢν τῶν ποιητῶν, τὴν Ἰοκάστην εἰσάγει λέγουσαν πρὸς τὸν Ἐτεοκλέα, παρακαλοῦσαν αὐτὸν ἀποστῆναι τοῦ πλεονεκτεῖν τὸν ἀδελφόν, οὕτω πως·

τί τῆς κακίστης δαιμόνων ἐφίεσαι
Πλεονεξίας, παῖ; μὴ σύ γ'. ἄδικος ἡ θεός.
πολλοὺς δ' ἐς οἴκους καὶ πόλεις εὐδαίμονας
εἰσῆλθε <κἀξῆλθ'> ἐπ' ὀλέθρῳ τῶν χρωμένων·
ἐφ' ᾗ σὺ μαίνῃ. τοῦτο κάλλιστον βροτοῖς,
Ἰσότητα τιμᾶν καὶ φίλους εἶναι φίλοις
πόλεις τε πόλεσι συμμάχους τε συμμάχοις
συνδεῖν· τὸ γὰρ ἴσον νόμιμον ἀνθρώποις ἔφυ,
τῷ πλέονι δ' ἀεὶ πολέμιον καθίσταται
τοὔλασσον, ἐχθρᾶς θ' ἡμέρας κατάρχεται.

παρεθέμην δὲ ἑξῆς τὰ ἰαμβεῖα. τὸ γὰρ τοῖς καλῶς εἰρημένοις αὐτοῖς χρῆσθαι νοῦν ἔχοντός ἐστιν. ἐν δὴ τούτοις ἅπαντα ἔνεστι τὰ συμβαίνοντα ἐκ τῆς πλεονεξίας, ὅτι μήτε ἰδίᾳ μήτε κοινῇ συμφέρει, τοὐναντίον δὲ καὶ τὴν τῶν οἴκων εὐδαιμονίαν καὶ τὴν τῶν πόλεων ἀνατρέπει καὶ διαφθείρει· καὶ πάλιν ὡς νόμος ἀνθρώποις τιμᾶν τὸ ἴσον, καὶ τοῦτο μὲν κοινὴν φιλίαν καὶ πᾶσιν εἰρήνην πρὸς ἀλλήλους ποιεῖ, τὰς δὲ διαφορὰς καὶ τὰς ἐμφύλους ἔριδας καὶ τοὺς ἔξω πολέμους κατ' οὐδὲν ἕτερον συμβαίνοντας ἢ διὰ τὴν τοῦ πλείονος ἐπιθυμίαν, ἐξ ὧν ἕκαστος καὶ τῶν ἱκανῶν ἀποστερεῖται. καίτοι τί τοῦ ζῆν ἀναγκαιότερόν ἐστιν, ἢ τί τούτου περὶ πλείονος ποιοῦνται πάντες; ἀλλ' ὅμως καὶ τοῦτο ἀπολλύουσι χρημάτων, οἱ δὲ καὶ τὰς πατρίδας τὰς αὑτῶν ἀναστάτους ἐποίησαν. μετὰ ταῦτα τοίνυν ὁ αὐτὸς ποιητὴς οὔ φησιν ἐν τοῖς θείοις εἶναι πλεονεξίαν· διὰ τοῦτο ἄφθαρτα καὶ ἀγήρῳ μένειν αὐτά, τὴν προσήκουσαν ἓν ἕκαστον ἑαυτῷ τάξιν φυλάττοντα, τήν τε νύκτα καὶ τὴν ἡμέραν καὶ τὰς ὥρας. εἰ γὰρ μὴ τοῦτον εἶχε τὸν τρόπον, οὐκ ἂν αὐτῶν οὐδὲν δύνασθαι διαμένειν. ὅταν οὖν καὶ τοῖς θείοις ἡ πλεονεξία φθορὰν ἐπιφέρῃ, τί χρὴ νομίζειν τἀνθρώπεια πάσχειν ἀπὸ ταύτης τῆς νόσου; καλῶς δὲ μέμνηται καὶ μέτρων καὶ σταθμῶν, ὡς ὑπὲρ τοῦ δικαίου καὶ τοῦ πλεονεκτεῖν μηδένα μηδενὸς τούτων εὑρημένων.

Dio Chrys. 17.8–11

And further too, Euripides also, a poet second to none other in reputation, brings Iocasta on the stage addressing Eteocles and urging him to refrain from trying to overreach his brother, in some such words as these:

Euripides, *Phoen.* 531–540

I have cited the iambic verses in full sequence; a sensible man will use what has been excellently said in that form. In this passage, then, are enumerated all the consequences of greed: that it is of advantage neither to the individual nor to the state; but that, on the contrary, it overthrows and destroys the prosperity of families and of states as well; and, in the second place, that the law of men requires us to honour equality, and that this establishes a common bond of friendship and peace for all toward one another, whereas quarrels, internal strife, and foreign wars are due to nothing else than the desire for more, with the result that each side is deprived even of a sufficiency. For what is more necessary than life, or what do all men hold as of more importance than this? But nevertheless men will destroy even that for money, and some too have caused even their own fatherlands to be laid waste. The same poet then goes on to say that there is no greed among the divine beings, wherefore they remain indestructible and ageless, each single one keeping its own proper position night and day and through all the seasons. For, the poet adds, if they were not so ordered, none of them would be able to survive. When, therefore, greed would bring destruction even to the divine beings, what disastrous effect must we believe this malady causes to human kind? And he aptly mentions measures and weights as having been invented to secure justice and to prevent any man from over-reaching another.

Translation by J.W. Cohoon, adapted

Here, then, we have first citation and then paraphrase, first of the cited verses themselves and then (rather more loosely) of the verses which follow the cited passage. The methodology is familiar, but what is of particular importance here is that we can for once be as confident as due caution allows that Dio only cited vv. 531–40 before he reverted to paraphrase. It is a very familiar problem of the study of embedded citations that our manuscripts may preserve less of the citation than the citing author originally offered, whether because scribes get bored or on a kind of 'part for whole' principle. Here, however, Dio marks the shift from paraphrase of the cited verses to paraphrase of the uncited by μετὰ ταῦτα τοίνυν ὁ αὐτὸς ποιητής..., 'the same poet then goes on to say ...'. The shift serves a purpose, of course: in this way Dio keeps control of his own essay — he does not let Euripides take it over completely. Balance between citation and paraphrase was important: Chrysippus was famously criticized for essentially abandoning his essays to citations.[7]

The most striking thing about Dio's citation is, of course, the replacement of personified Φιλοτιμία by (presumably personified) Πλεονεξία; this textual change is unique in the rich indirect tradition of these verses. In his note on v. 532 Donald Mastronarde calls Dio's citation of this passage 'extraordinarily unreliable' and also notes that πλεονεξία 'is the more obvious word here and intruded for that reason'. Of these three claims, the first is a matter of judgement, the second demonstrably true and the third demonstrably untrue. Πλεο-

---

7 Cf. Hunter/Russell 2011, 12.

νεξίας has replaced Φιλοτιμίας because that is the subject of Dio's essay, as (for example) chapter 6 of the oration makes very clear, whatever credit we wish to give to the title transmitted in our manuscripts. How painless the switch in terms was, however, is made plain both by the evidence which Mastronarde adduces for the virtual synonymity of πλεονεξία and φιλοτιμία in its negative sense and by the emphasis on the acquisition of τὸ πλέον throughout Jocasta's speech (cf. vv. 539, 552–553). The speech moves backwards and forwards between claims about desire for tyranny and claims about desire for greater possessions, so that the two are virtually equated, as indeed they are to some extent in Greek thought; the triad of πλέον — ἴσον — ἔλασσον structures Jocasta's plea. Dio seems also to acknowledge his own textual shift later in the speech: πλέον ἄλλος ἄλλου φιλοτιμούμεθα (17.20).

It would, I think, be very difficult to deny that Πλεονεξίας is what Dio actually 'cited', but whether we should ascribe the switch to a knowing act of rewriting or a faulty memory or something in-between is rather harder to say. Whether or not Dio had predecessors in this textual change we also cannot say, though the circumstantial evidence suggests not. Things happen, of course. When, for example, in Dio's citation of *Orestes* 2 at 4.82 the unmetrical συμφορὰν δαιμόνιον has replaced συμφορὰν θεήλατον, I think that most readers would blame the scribes of Dio's manuscripts, not Dio himself, whereas when (6.55) he cites *Orestes* 6 with κεφαλῆς rather than κορυφῆς, we might feel greater hesitation; the phenomenon is very familiar from, for example, the citations of Homer and other poets which we find in the manuscripts of Plato. What makes the present case of great interest is that Dio again comments upon his own citational practice:

> παρεθέμην δὲ ἑξῆς τὰ ἰαμβεῖα. τὸ γὰρ τοῖς καλῶς εἰρημένοις αὐτοῖς χρῆσθαι νοῦν ἔχοντός ἐστιν.
>
> Dio Chrys. 17.10

> I have cited the iambic verses in full sequence; a sensible man will use what has been excellently said in that form.

How unusual Dio wants us to consider such a generous practice is unclear, but this is a precious (and underappreciated) testimony to what might seem normal in antiquity. In the circumstances, particularly if we remember Mastronarde's characterization of this citation, Dio's claim might seem either charmingly disingenuous or simply deceitful. We must be careful here, however, and I do not think that we can take the introductory οὕτω πως as necessarily preparing us for the fact that this will not be a verbatim quotation. Dio's claim apparently is that he has not, by selectivity, i.e. presumably by omitting verses, misrepresented Euripides, and we have already seen that the change from Φιλοτιμίας to Πλεονεξίας has indeed not essentially changed the meaning of the passage. Whether this claim can, however, shed light on the mental (and scriptural) process by which Πλεονεξίας entered his text, i.e. does it help us with how knowingly deliberate a change it was, must remain doubtful. It is also, I think, not clear that any of the other differences between the vulgate text of Euripides and the transmitted citation in Dio change the significance of the verses in any important way. What is of some interest, however, is that, although the change of Φιλοτιμίας to Πλεονεξίας is of a very common kind, namely the substitution of a more common synonym, we have seen good reason for thinking that on this occasion it did not 'intrude' (to use Mastronarde's verb) in an entirely normal way, whereas some of the other changes in Dio's citation are also of very familiar kinds and may have happened in very familiar ways, whether before or after Dio.

Of these other changes the most interesting, and the one with perhaps the greatest ramifications for the study of dramatic fragments more generally, is the substitution in v. 535 of τοῦτο κάλλιστον βροτοῖς for κεῖνο κάλλιον, τέκνον. The removal from cited passages of references which would anchor the verses in a particular dramatic context is a very familiar phenomenon, but what stands out here is that, in introducing the passage, Dio goes out of his way precisely to give us that particular dramatic context. Does this suggest that Dio is using a text already influenced by the anthological tradition, or is Dio's strategy to combine a very specific scene-setting, thus anchoring his quotation to the didactic authority of a well known passage of a very well known play,[8] with a statement of the widest general significance, τοῦτο κάλλιστον βροτοῖς, one which falls into a very familiar kind of ancient *gnōmē*, namely what is κάλλιστον for mankind? These are questions with obvious implications for anyone interested in the quotation of dramatic fragments, and they are not made less interesting by another quotation of part of this passage. In *On exile* Favorinus, who may well have known Dio's essay (cf. Philostr. *VS* 490),[9] takes a leaf out of Jocasta's book to taunt those who are stupidly proud of the offices they hold and the lineage of their family:

πρὸς δὲ τοὺς ἐπὶ τοῖς τοιούτοις φυσωμένους εἴποι τις ἂν ἅπερ ἡ μήτηρ πρὸς τὸν Πολυνείκην λέγει νουθετοῦσα·

τί τῆς κακίστης δαιμόνων ἐφίεσαι,

---

[8] Cf., e.g., Whitmarsh 2001, 137.
[9] Cf., e.g., Cribiore 2001.

Φιλοτιμίας, παῖ; μὴ σύ γ'· ἄδικος ἡ θεός·
πολλοὺς δ' ἐς οἴκους καὶ πόλεις εὐδαίμονας
ε[ἰσ]ῆλθε ἐπ' ὀλέθρῳ τῶν χρωμένων·
ἐφ' ᾗ [σὺ] μαίνῃ.

ἐγὼ δὲ ταῦτα τῇ Ἰοκάστῃ προσ[......· τ]ί δὲ κομπάζεις, ὦ δύστη[νε, καὶ ἐπ]ὶ σαυτῷ φρονεῖς μέγα;

Favorinus, *On exile* 20.3-4

To those puffed up by such trappings, one might speak Jocasta's words of reproach to Polyneices: 'Why, my son, do you pursue the vilest of divinities, Ambition? Do not! That goddess is unjust: she visits many wealthy houses and cities, with ruinous results for those who cultivate her. She is the one whom you are craving madly'. I would supplement the words of Jocasta as follows: Why are you boasting, you wretched man, and why do you exalt in your station?

Translation by T. Whitmarsh, adapted[10]

Favorinus then proceeds to pour scorn on the pursuit of high position in a passage which may, but need not, be seen as a free-wheeling expansion of Jocasta's verses on the same theme (vv. 549–554). Our papyrus text of Favorinus, essentially reproduced above, shares with the manuscripts of Dio the omission of <κἀξῆλθ'> in v. 534; this is an easy scribal error which could happen twice independently, but even so it gives pause for thought. Of modern editors, Adelmo Barigazzi at least thought that the second verb had been (deliberately) omitted in the anthological tradition 'for greater clarity' and that both Dio and Favorinus took over from that tradition and kept a metrically deficient verse;[11] others have thought that the omission might be due to Dio and/or Favorinus themselves.[12] To what extent both the anthological tradition and moralisers such as Dio and Favorinus were prepared to tolerate metrically deficient trimeters is another question of obvious broader interest in the context of the study of dramatic fragments.

Favorinus, like Dio also, gives an explicit dramatic context for the passage he cites, but he does not name the poet and he claims that the verses are ad-

---

10 Cf. Whitmarsh 2001, 317
11 Barigazzi 1966, 477. Favorinus seems to cite the second half of Eur. *Ph.* 536 (ἢ φίλους ἀεὶ φίλοις) as καὶ φίλους αἰεὶ φίλους, whereas Dio's manuscripts offer καὶ φίλους εἶναι φίλοις; the phrase appears to have become proverbial (cf. Barigazzi 1966, 470), and both Dio and Favorinus offer versions appropriate to their own contexts, but the small difference might at least make us pause before accepting that both were drawing on an identical anthological tradition.
12 Cf. Tepedino Guerra 2007, 190, who also however acknowledges the possibility of simple scribal error.

dressed to Polyneices, rather than to Eteocles, though Eteocles is in fact explicitly named as the addressee in v. 529, immediately before the cited passage. Again, however, we must not here leap to hasty conclusions. The mistake of the name, which there is no reason to ascribe to the scribe of the papyrus rather than to Favorinus himself, cannot of itself prove that Favorinus is here using an anthological text which started from v. 531 only, though that is indeed (as Dio too shows) the 'natural' place to start; the preceding verses themselves entered the anthologising tradition and they have a rich indirect tradition,[13] but it is essentially a separate one from vv. 531–540. What this mistake does show, I think (and again this is hardly a revolutionary thought), particularly when added to the omission of <κἀξῆλθ'>, is that our tendency to think in terms of citing from anthologies or citing from fuller texts of plays is too simple a dichotomy. It is not just that there are more than two possibilities, but rather that the various possibilities themselves are not necessarily distinct. Whereas Dio's citational practice in one section of the *Euboean Oration* suggested that he was using (written or remembered) 'texts' of a significant section of a play, the example from the *Phoenissae* offers much more mixed signals. We also tend to think too simply in terms of yet another dichotomy, namely that between citation and paraphrase: again, things may not be so clearcut. How and when does one bleed into the other is yet another important question in the study of dramatic fragments?[14]

One further matter thickens the plot of this 'fragment' of Euripides' *Phoenissae* yet further. In a chapter περὶ ἀδικίας Stobaeus (3.10.3) cites a passage which he ascribes to Menander:

πλεονεξία μέγιστον ἀνθρώποις κακόν·
οἱ γὰρ θέλοντες προσλαβεῖν τὰ τῶν πέλας
ἀποτυγχάνουσι πολλάκις νικώμενοι,
τὰ δ' ἴδια προστιθέασι τοῖς ἀλλοτρίοις.

Men. fr. 722 K–A

Desire for more is the greatest ill for mankind. Often those who wish to secure their neighbours' possessions are beaten and fail, and add their own possessions to those that others hold.

---

13 Cf. further below.
14 For some related considerations cf. Hunter 2010.

Both Kaibel and Kassel-Austin doubt the ascription to Menander on linguistic grounds, but more important in the present context is that Meineke recognized that Dio seems to be paraphrasing this passage in chap. 7 of *Oration* 17:

> ἡ πλεονεξία δὲ μέγιστον <μέν> ἐστιν αὐτῷ τινι κακόν· λυπεῖ δὲ καὶ τοὺς πέλας.
>
> Dio Chrys. 17.7
>
> Desire for more is the greatest ill for each man [who has it], but it also damages his neighbours.

It is hard, I think, to doubt that Meineke's intuition was correct: the two passages are close enough verbally (note, particularly, πέλας) to assuage, if not entirely eradicate, doubt. In these circumstances it is intriguing that the status of the comic fragment should be uncertain, but we may also wonder whether the paths of this fragment and of the passage from the *Phoenissae* crossed at some point in the long history of the anthological tradition; we will presently see such a phenomenon with regard to a fragment of Sophocles and a passage of the *Phoenissae*. The fragment of (?) Menander is quoted by Stobaeus as an example of ἀδικία and Jocasta indeed proclaims Φιλοτιμία to be an 'unjust goddess', just as Dio's Jocasta labels Πλεονεξία.

Finally, we may note that Jocasta's plea to Eteocles, the subsequent history of which we have been tracing, is itself introduced by verses which point to what she is about to say as just the kind of wise moralizing which was almost bound to be anthologized:

> ὦ τέκνον, οὐχ ἅπαντα τῷ γήρᾳ κακά,
> Ἐτεόκλεες, πρόσεστιν· ἀλλ' ἡμπειρία
> ἔχει τι λέξαι τῶν νέων σοφώτερον.
>
> Eur. *Phoen.* 528–530
>
> My child, not every feature of old age, Eteocles, is bad. Experience can express a wiser thought than the young can muster.

This sense that she is about to say something which has long been proved true is strengthened by the fact that these introductory verses themselves reflect familiar proverbial wisdom suitable to very many different contexts.[15] Euripides lived in a world in which poets were cited precisely for their gnomic wisdom and where the practice of textual anthologising was all but certainly already underway; cases such as *Phoen.* 528–530 show how poets themselves invited

---

15 Cf. Mastronarde on vv. 528–529.

and expected the anthological practices which we tend rather to associate with later ages.[16] We shall see another such case presently.

To close this brief paper, I turn to what is certainly a fragment of a lost play, Sophocles, *Aleadai* fr. 88 Radt:

τὰ χρήματ' ἀνθρώποισιν εὑρίσκει φίλους,
αὖθις δὲ τιμάς, εἶτα τῆς ὑπερτάτης
τυραννίδος θεοῖσιν ἀγχίστην ἕδραν.
ἔπειτα δ' οὐδεὶς ἐχθρὸς οὔτε φύεται
πρὸς χρήμαθ' οἵ τε φύντες ἀρνοῦνται στυγεῖν.   5
δεινὸς γὰρ ἕρπειν πλοῦτος ἔς τε τἄβατα
καὶ †πρὸς τὰ βατά†, χὠπόθεν πένης ἀνὴρ
οὐδ' ἐντυχὼν δύναιτ' ἂν ὧν ἐρᾷ τυχεῖν.
καὶ γὰρ δυσειδὲς σῶμα καὶ †δυσώνυμον†
γλώσσῃ σοφὸν τίθησιν εὔμορφόν τ' ἰδεῖν.   10
μόνῳ δὲ χαίρειν κἂν νόσων ξυνουσίᾳ
πάρεστιν αὐτῷ κἀπικρύπτεσθαι κακά.

Soph. fr. 88 Radt

It is money that finds friends for men, and also honours, and finally the throne sublime of royalty, nearest to the gods. And no one is an enemy to money, or if they are, men deny their hatred of it. For wealth has a strange power to get to places sacred and profane [text uncertain], and to places from which a poor man, even if he effects an entry, could not get what he desires. For wealth makes an ugly person beautiful to look on and a man of bad name [text uncertain] eloquent in speech; and wealth alone can enjoy pleasure even in sickness and can conceal its miseries.

Translation by H. Lloyd-Jones, adapted

The reason I single out this (textually very difficult) passage[17] is because it seems all but certain that these are the verses which Dio pairs with the citation from Euripides' *Electra* in chapter 102 of the *Euboean Oration* (cited earlier). The philosopher to whom Dio there refers appears to be Cleanthes (cf. *SVF* I 562), part of whose treatment of the Euripidean verses seems to survive in Plutarch's *How the Young Man Should Study Poetry* 33c. The fragment is quoted in full with the poet's name and play-title by Stobaeus 4.31.27; vv. 6–10 are cited by Plutarch (*Mor.* 21b), without poet or play-title, but in a context that strongly suggests that they are by Sophocles;[18] v. 1 is also cited separately by Stobaeus

---

16 Cf. further below; Wright 2016 is a valuable study of these developments.
17 My discussion of this text will not touch on the most difficult textual cruces within it, and for this reason I have not provided a proper apparatus.
18 Cf. Hunter/Russell 2011, 119.

(4.31.103) and, in discussing how money wins you 'friends', particularly if you are childless, Plutarch cites the following passage as from Euripides:

τὸ δ' ὑπὸ τοῦ Εὐριπίδου λεγόμενον,

τὰ χρήματ' ἀνθρώποισιν εὑρίσκειν φίλους
δύναμίν τε πλείστην τῶν ἐν ἀνθρώποις ἔχειν,

οὐχ ἁπλῶς ἀληθές, ἀλλ' ἐπὶ τῶν ἀτέκνων· τούτους οἱ πλούσιοι δειπνίζουσιν, οἱ ἡγεμόνες θεραπεύουσιν, οἱ ῥήτορες μόνοις τούτοις προῖκα συνηγοροῦσιν.

Plut. *De amore prolis* 497b–c

As for Euripides' saying that 'Money (allows) men to gain friends and to have the greatest influence on human affairs', this is not just simply true but particularly of the childless. The rich give them dinners, leaders court them, to them alone do lawyers give their services for free.

The passage of Euripides that Plutarch has in mind is *Phoenissae* 439–440:

πάλαι μὲν οὖν ὑμνηθέν, ἀλλ' ὅμως ἐρῶ·
τὰ χρήματ' ἀνθρώποισι τιμιώτατα
δύναμίν τε πλείστην τῶν ἐν ἀνθρώποις ἔχει

Eur. *Phoen.* 438–440

This has been very familiar for a long time, but I shall say it nevertheless: it is money to which men give most honour and which offers them the greatest influence on human affairs.

It is usually said that Plutarch (or his source) has here erroneously substituted a version of the very similar v. 1 of Sophocles fr. 88 Radt for *Phoen.* 440; this is presumably, at some level, correct, but the 'mistake' may be rather more interesting than that. First, it is worth noting that Polyneices marks his γνώμη as a piece of proverbial wisdom (v. 438). When Strabo (9.2.40) cites vv. 439–440, without name of poet or title of play, he introduces the verses as ὁ κοινὸς λόγος, which may be (but of course does not have to be) a memory of v. 438. That it is in fact such a memory is perhaps suggested by the fact that, in his collection of ἔπαινος πλούτου, Stobaeus (4.31.2) includes v. 438 with his citation of vv. 439–440; it looks, then, as though the introductory verse travelled with the γνώμη. James Diggle, though not Donald Mastronarde, accepts the modern deletion of vv. 438–442 from Euripides' text, but the subject which the verses raise most urgently is (again) that of poets writing verses, if not designed to be anthologised, then at least in the knowledge that such things happened. Matthew Wright has recently well set out the kinds of questions which need to be asked.[19] The history of poetic anthologies has been fruitfully studied,[20] but we should accept that the anthological habit (or perhaps 'mindset') probably much predated the early fourth century, which seems to have been the key period in this development. Early elegy, where we find gnomic verses designed to be used and re-used on many successive occasions, will have been very important in developing that 'mindset'.

Plutarch's two changes from the Euripidean vulgate, namely infinitives for finite verbs and τὰ χρήματ' ἀνθρώποισιν εὑρίσκειν φίλους for τὰ χρήματ' ἀνθρώποισι τιμιώτατα, are both appropriate to the context in which he cites the verses. This may simply be a case of an accidental or wilful change, but, again, something more interesting may also be going on. Although the text is uncertain, it is clear that in Soph. fr. 88 Radt, the speaking character makes a link between wealth and τυραννίς, and this latter has a famously significant role in the same scene of the *Phoenissae* which we have been considering: in v. 506 Eteocles describes τυραννίς as τὴν θεῶν μεγίστην, just as the Sophoclean character refers to τῆς ὑπερτάτης/τυραννίδος.[21] Less striking perhaps, but at least worthy of note, is the correspondence between τιμάς in Sophocles fr. 88.2 and τιμιώτατα in Euripides. What seems to be going on here, though this can of course be no more than a suspicion, is that Sophocles fr. 88 Radt travelled with Euripides, *Phoenissae* 438–440 in some anthological and moralising traditions and that there was what amounted to a process of cross-fertilisation. From the point of view of someone interested in the text of Euripides, this may amount to textual corruption, but for those interested in what happens to passages of drama in citational traditions, that is not the best way to look at it. Rather, we might think of a kind of 'mix and match' in which elements from such 'fellow travellers' can be taken over and swapped at need (and with very varying levels of consciousness). Much about these processes must remain vague and only dimly perceived, but this whole set of phenomena suggests an attitude to texts and their meaning which is very different from our continuing pursuit of 'the original text'. It is no surprise that dramatic fragments have very much to teach us about ancient reading practices and the interpretation of texts.

---

19 Wright 2016.
20 Cf. Hunter/Russell 2011, 15–26, citing earlier bibliography.
21 θεοῖσιν in v. 3 of the Sophoclean fragment, as cited above, is however Conington's emendation for the transmitted ἄκουσιν or τ' ἄγουσιν.

Bibliography

Barigazzi, A. 1966. *Favorino di Arelate, Opere*, Florence.
Cribiore, R. 2001. 'The grammarian's choice: the popularity of Euripides' *Phoenissae* in Hellenistic and Roman education', in: Y.L. Too (ed.), *Education in Greek and Roman Antiquity*, Leiden, 241–259.
Hunter, R. 2010. 'Rhythmical language and poetic citation in Greek narrative texts', in: G. Bastianini/A. Casanova (eds.), *I papiri del romanzo antico*, Florence, 223–245 [= this volume 462–484].
Hunter, R. 2018. *The Measure of Homer*, Cambridge.
Hunter, R./Russell, D. 2011. *Plutarch, How to Study Poetry*, Cambridge.
Moles, J. 1995. 'Dio Chrysostom, Greece, and Rome', in: D. Innes/H. Hine/C. Pelling (eds.), *Ethics and Rhetoric*, Oxford, 177–192.
Tepedino Guerra, A. 2007. *L'esilio (Pap. Vat. Gr, 11 verso), Favorino di Arelate*, Rome.
Whitmarsh, T. 2001. *Greek Literature and the Roman Empire*, Oxford.
Wright, M. 2016. 'Euripidean tragedy and quotation culture: the case of Stheneboea F661', *AJPh* 137, 601–623.

39 Some Problems in the 'Deception of Zeus'

In this paper I consider two sets of scholia on the Iliadic 'Deception of Zeus' which raise important, if familiar, questions about Zenodotus, Aristarchus and the grammatical tradition and about the composition and structure of our corpus of scholia. It is hoped that the issues which these scholia raise have a significance beyond the specific passages discussed.

Zeus wakes up

I begin with Zeus' speech to Hera near the beginning of *Iliad* 15, after he wakes up and realises that she has tricked him:

ἀλλ' εἰ δή ῥ' ἐτεόν γε καὶ ἀτρεκέως ἀγορεύεις,	
ἔρχεο νῦν μετὰ φῦλα θεῶν, καὶ δεῦρο κάλεσσον	
Ἶρίν τ' ἐλθέμεναι καὶ Ἀπόλλωνα κλυτότοξον,	55
ὄφρ' ἣ μὲν μετὰ λαὸν Ἀχαιῶν χαλκοχιτώνων	
ἔλθῃ, καὶ εἴπῃσι Ποσειδάωνι ἄνακτι	
παυσάμενον πολέμοιο τὰ ἃ πρὸς δώμαθ' ἱκέσθαι,	
Ἕκτορα δ' ὀτρύνῃσι μάχην ἐς Φοῖβος Ἀπόλλων,	
αὖτις δ' ἐμπνεύσῃσι μένος, λελάθῃ δ' ὀδυνάων	60
αἵ νῦν μιν τείρουσι κατὰ φρένας, αὐτὰρ Ἀχαιοὺς	
αὖτις ἀποστρέψῃσιν ἀνάλκιδα φύζαν ἐνόρσας,	
φεύγοντες δ' ἐν νηυσὶ πολυκληΐσι πέσωσι	
Πηλεΐδεω Ἀχιλῆος· ὃ δ' ἀνστήσει ὃν ἑταῖρον	
Πάτροκλον· τὸν δὲ κτενεῖ ἔγχεϊ φαίδιμος Ἕκτωρ	65
Ἰλίου προπάροιθε πολέας ὀλέσαντ' αἰζηοὺς	
τοὺς ἄλλους, μετὰ δ' υἱὸν ἐμὸν Σαρπηδόνα δῖον.	
τοῦ δὲ χολωσάμενος κτενεῖ Ἕκτορα δῖος Ἀχιλλεύς.	
ἐκ τοῦ δ' ἄν τοι ἔπειτα παλίωξιν παρὰ νηῶν	
αἰὲν ἐγὼ τεύχοιμι διαμπερὲς εἰς ὅ κ' Ἀχαιοὶ	70
Ἴλιον αἰπὺ ἕλοιεν Ἀθηναίης διὰ βουλάς.	
τὸ πρὶν δ' οὔτ' ἄρ' ἐγὼ παύω χόλον οὔτέ τιν' ἄλλον	
ἀθανάτων Δαναοῖσιν ἀμυνέμεν ἐνθάδ' ἐάσω,	
πρίν γε τὸ Πηλείδαο τελευτηθῆναι ἐέλδωρ,	
ὥς οἱ ὑπέστην πρῶτον, ἐμῷ δ' ἐπένευσα κάρητι,	75

I am very grateful to participants in the Oxford conference in July 2018 and to an anonymous OUP reader for much helpful criticism, and to Adrian Kelly for valuable editorial advice.

ἤματι τῷ ὅτ' ἐμεῖο θεὰ Θέτις ἥψατο γούνων,
λισσομένη τιμῆσαι Ἀχιλλῆα πτολίπορθον.

Il. 15.53-77

'But if you speak straight and truly, go now to the company of the gods, and summon Iris to come and Apollo of the silver bow, that she may then go to the army of the bronze-girded Achaeans and tell lord Poseidon to cease from war and return to his own house; Phoebus Apollo is to urge Hector to battle and again breathe strength into him, so that he forget the pains which are now wearing down his mind. By raising spiritless panic he should turn the Achaeans back, and they will flee back and fall among the ships of Achilles, son of Peleus. He will rouse up his comrade Patroclus, and in front of Troy glorious Hector will with his spear kill him who has destroyed so many splendid heroes, including my son noble Sarpedon. In anger for this, godlike Achilles will kill Hector, and after that I would fashion a continuous pursuit from the ships until the Achaeans capture steep Troy through the plans of Athena. Until then my anger does not cease and I shall not allow any other of the immortals to aid the Danaans until the desire of the son of Peleus has been fulfilled. So did I undertake for him in the beginning, and confirmed it with a nod of my head, on that day when the divine Thetis touched my knees, begging me to grant honour to Achilles, sacker of cities.'

Aristophanes of Byzantium and Aristarchus athetised vv. 56–77, and our scholia offer a rich selection of charges against and defences of those verses. I begin with three related issues arising from the A-scholium on *Il.* 15.56a:

... ἀθετοῦνται στίχοι εἴκοσι δύο, ὅτι οὐκ ἀναγκαίως παλιλλογεῖται περὶ τῶν ἑξῆς ἐπεισαχθησομένων καὶ κατὰ τὴν σύνθεσίν εἰσιν εὐτελεῖς.

Σ A *Il.* 15.56a *Ariston.*

Twenty-two verses are athetised because without necessity he recapitulates about the events which will follow subsequently and because the verses are banal in composition.

The appeal to ἀνάγκη, 'necessity', raises the question of how this criterion operates in ancient discussions of athetesis and of poetic form more generally, what the origins of an appeal to 'necessity' are, and whether and how it is linked to the poetic 'necessity' (τὸ ἀναγκαῖον, χρή *etc.*) to which poets and their characters themselves can appeal, as for example with Odysseus' trip to the Underworld.[1] Although Socrates' appeal to ἀνάγκη and ἀνάγκη λογογραφική in Plato's *Phaedrus* (264b3-8) was very influential and often echoed in subsequent criticism, it is hard not to believe that peripatetic ideas, most familiar to us, if not actually descending from, Aristotle's *Poetics*, were the principal influence upon

---

1 I have briefly discussed this and other cases in Hunter 2018b, 463–465.

the development of this critical principle.² Aristotle uses the idea of necessity in various ways throughout the treatise, as for example in his discussion of the pattern of 'beginning-middle-end' (1450b25–31) or when acknowledging that some irrationalities and wickedness may be 'necessary' in drama (1461b19). The present case is somewhat different from any of these Aristotelian situations, and the idea that Zeus' lengthy account, which includes both 'repetition' and foreshadowing ('prolepsis'), is 'unnecessary' will in part be driven by the critical sense, which sits comfortably enough with an acknowledgement of repetition as a fundamental element of Homeric style, that Homer does not waste words.³ Nevertheless, the idea that the μῦθος must constantly move forward and must not be 'unnecessarily' delayed, particularly by such detailed anticipation of what will subsequently be at the centre of the narrative, may be seen as a 'softer' version of Aristotelian 'necessity'. Critical 'necessity' may, however, differ significantly from poetic conceptions of the idea and, although the genealogy of such critical ideas will be neither simple nor uniform, it is not unreasonable to associate the critical perspective with a powerful (and powerfully limiting) conception of what is appropriate in literature, what — in other words — makes good literature, in this case epic; we know of no more powerful such conception from antiquity than Aristotle's.⁴ The idea that verses are 'necessary' occurs regularly in the scholia as a defence against proposed athetesis, and it is standardly connected with the need for the audience (and the characters in the poem) to be informed about what is conveyed in the suspect verses; but such 'necessity' is itself always a matter for judgement, and this too is where the post-Aristotelian critical tradition inevitably took a broader and less philosophically informed view of 'necessity' than did Aristotle himself.

The use of παλιλλογεῖσθαι in the A-scholium on v. 56 (Σ A Il. 15.56a *Ariston.*), which is also used in the A-scholium on Il. 1.365 (Σ A Il. 1.365a *Ariston.*) in reporting the athetesis of Achilles' lengthy recapitulation, and the two 'parallels' offered in Σ T Il. 15.64c *ex. (Did.?)* might suggest a certain confusion (or, perhaps, overlapping) among ancient grammarians between 'recapitulation' and 'foreshadowing', between ἀνακεφαλαίωσις and προανακεφαλαίωσις; Eustathius (*Comm. Il.* iii.701) points out that Zeus' speech both 'repeats' his promise to

---

2 On the relations between Aristotelian principles and Alexandrian criticism in general cf. esp. Schironi 2009, citing earlier bibliography.
3 Cf., e.g., Nünlist 2009, 40, 46.
4 This is not, of course, also to seek to trace the very origin of such ideas to Aristotle; important parts of the critical debate in Aristophanes' *Frogs* are driven by a sense of what poets should and should not do; cf. vv. 1030, 1053 (which anticipates in some respects the 'unnecessary' wickedness of character of Menelaos in Eur. *Or.*, according to Arist. *Poet.* 1454a29), 1058.

Thetis in Book 1 and foreshadows future events. Whereas for Eustathius this is a demonstration of Homer's mastery, for Aristarchus this prolixity offends against the presupposition that Homer does not waste words. Both the exegetical scholia on *Il.* 1.366 and Eustathius, himself of course a master rhetorician (*Comm. Il.* i.186), defend the recapitulation in Book 1 as a rhetorical lesson to us from Homer, but no such defence is offered by the scholia here.

Secondly, the A-scholium on *Il.* 15.56 (Σ A *Il.* 15.56a *Ariston.*) appeals to the εὐτέλεια of the athetised verses, a very common charge which may be unqualified (as, e.g., in Σ A *Il.* 24.6–9a¹ *Ariston.*) or be specified as referring (as here and, e.g., at Σ A *Il.* 10.497a *Ariston.* and Σ A *Il.* 11.767 a¹ *Ariston.*) to σύνθεσις or (as, e.g., at Σ A *Il.* 3.395 *Ariston.*) to διάνοια or (as, e.g., at Σ A *Il.* 8.164–166a *Ariston.* and Σ A *Il.* 11.130a *Ariston.*) to κατασκευή or to a combination of these.[5] The accusation is levelled at verses which are felt to be 'jejune' in a manner in which Homer would not compose, especially verses in which commonness or vulgarity of subject-matter and/or vocabulary is not felt to be elevated by any stylistic features worthy of Homeric epic.[6] This was something about which critics could disagree. Aristarchus, for example, athetised *Iliad* 24.476 (Priam's arrival at the tent of Achilles, 24.475b–476):

νέον δ' ἀπέληγεν ἐδωδῆς
ἔσθων καὶ πίνων· ἔτι καὶ παρέκειτο τράπεζα.

Achilles had recently ceased from his meal, both eating and drinking; the table still lay beside him.

The grounds for the athetesis seem to have been that the verse offended against Homeric custom (tables were not removed once eating had finished), but the exegetical T-scholium (Σ T *Il.* 24.476b *ex.*) also reports the charge of εὐτέλεια, which must refer to the banality of the phrase 'eating and drinking' and to the ordinariness of a 'dining-table'; the scholiast, however, adduces in defence other expressions from both Homeric poems which refer to very ordinary things and actions which do not seem in way stylistically elevated, and he cites the grammarian, Seleukos of Alexandria, as describing all such phrases as examples of ἔμμετρος λαλιά, 'ordinary speech in metre'. A similar case may be *Odyssey* 5.94–95 (Hermes' visit to Calypso):

---

5 Cf., e.g., Schironi 2009, 299–302, 2018, 436–437, 470, 570.
6 Cf. further Nünlist 2009, 296, Hunter 2018a, 182–183.

αὐτὰρ ὁ πῖνε καὶ ἦσθε διάκτορος Ἀργεϊφόντης.
αὐτὰρ ἐπεὶ δείπνησε καὶ ἤραρε θυμὸν ἐδωδῆι [...].

And Hermes the messenger then drank and ate. When he had dined and satisfied his heart with food [...].

A scholium on this passage (Σ HP¹ *Od.* 5.94a *Ariston.?*) categorises the verses as εὐτελεῖς 'in both style and thought'; unfortunately, it is unclear to which verses the remark was intended to apply and whether or not these verses had actually been athetised.[7] Another illuminating case is *Odyssey* 4.511 in Proteus' telling of Ajax's death at sea:

ὣς ὁ μὲν ἔνθ' ἀπόλωλεν, ἐπεὶ πίεν ἁλμυρὸν ὕδωρ.

So he perished there, when he drank bitter water.

The scholia *ad loc.* (Σ HP¹ *Od.* 4.511a *Did.?*) report:

ἐν οὐδεμιᾷ ἐφέρετο. καὶ λίαν γάρ ἐστιν εὐτελής. θαυμάσαιμεν δ' ἂν πῶς παρέλαθε τὸν Ἀρίσταρχον ὀβελίσαι αὐτόν.

This verse was transmitted in no copy, and it is also very jejune. We might wonder why Aristarchus failed to obelise it.

The meaning of the first observation has been much discussed,[8] and the (probably not ironic) comment about Aristarchus is an interesting footnote in the history of the grammatical tradition, but the charge of εὐτέλεια also deserves attention. 'When he drank salt water' does indeed refer to something so banal and obvious that it might well have been thought beneath Homer's dignity, but Eustathius (*Comm. Od.* i.178) thought that the 'cheapness' of the verses resided in the fact that Proteus seemed to be punning on ἁλμυρόν: the water was naturally 'bitter' because it was salt-water, but also 'bitter' to the drinker because it marked his death. Proteus should here not have been joking; εὐτέλεια is, thus, like virtually every stylistic judgement about Homer, also linked to notions of καιρός and πρέπον. It was, for example, very probably reasons of 'propriety'

---

[7] As v. 96 could not have followed v. 93, Aristarchus will not have athetised just vv. 94–95. Many editors, including von der Mühll and West, follow Eustathius (*Comm. Od.* i.202) in taking the scholium to refer to the first two verses of Hermes' response (vv. 97–98) and to imply an athetesis of those verses, cf. Pontani's apparatus *ad loc.*
[8] Cf. Apthorp 1980, 51–52. Many modern editors omit the verse on the strength of the scholiastic comment, and yet the verse is transmitted in all our witnesses to the text.

that led grammarians to remark unfavourably on the narrator's famous comment on Odysseus' reaction to Penelope's speech to the suitors:

ὣς φάτο, γήθησεν δὲ πολύτλας δῖος Ὀδυσσεύς,
οὕνεκα τῶν μὲν δῶρα παρέλκετο, θέλγε δὲ θυμὸν
μειλιχίοισ' ἐπέεσσι, νόος δέ οἱ ἄλλα μενοίνα.

Od. 18.281–283

Thus she spoke, and godlike much-enduring Odysseus rejoiced, because she was soliciting gifts from them and enchanting their hearts with soft words, but her mind had other intentions.

The scholia report that v. 282 is εὐτελές, and for that reason Aristophanes of Byzantium marked it with a critical sign (the *keraunion*); whether or not this indicated athetesis is uncertain.[9] Penelope's apparent greed, as she urged the suitors to bring her gifts, was likely thought to be below the dignity of epic and of Penelope. However familiar such behaviour might be in everyday life, it did not fit the elevated picture which epic offered, and was therefore labelled 'cheap'.

One final example, and one on a scale more comparable to the case of Zeus' speech in *Iliad* 15, is Aristarchus' athetesis of Andromache's description of what awaits Astyanax now that Hector is dead (*Il.* 22.487–499); as with Aristarchus' large-scale atheteses, the verses could be removed with very little syntactic or other disruption.[10] The charges against these verses reported in the A-scholia are that they are ἀδιάθετοι, 'not arranged', because it is improbable that Astyanax would be reduced to begging while the Trojan royal family continues and (a closely related observation) the verses contain nothing which is particular to Astyanax, but they would fit any orphan (Σ A *Il.* 22.487a *Ariston.*). The exegetical scholia add that the verses are εὐτελεῖς 'in style' and inappropriate (τῷ καιρῷ ἀνάρμοστοι), as they make Andromache inordinately long-winded; modern readers of Homer may not sympathise with the defence to the latter charge which the scholia also report: 'Women normally prattle on (φλυαρεῖν) when they are grieving and particularly when they are rousing emotion for [the death of] their children' (Σ bT *Il.* 22.487b *ex.*). Here the charge of εὐτέλεια was (again) very likely driven by the very 'ordinariness' of the scene described — a wretched

---

9 Cf. West 2017, 24.
10 Cf. Hunter 2018a, 159. West 2001, 265–266 offers a complex account of the genesis of the passage.

fatherless child maltreated and needing his mother — and by some of the 'ordinary' vocabulary for clothing and a drinking-cup.

In this case again, the charge of εὐτέλεια does not stand alone, but is added to a particular charge against the contextual inappropriateness of the verses. The grounds for the accusation of εὐτέλεια seem clear enough, whereas in the case of Zeus' speech at the start of *Iliad* 15, where εὐτέλεια is just one of several accusations, there is room for doubt about the nature of the 'cheapness', although the very rapid foreshadowing of unelaborated events — little more in fact than a list of names and verbs — was presumably central to that charge. Although, as we have seen, there are cases where εὐτέλεια is the only charge against verses which we know to have been athetised, there are practically no clear examples in Erbse's edition of the *Iliad*-scholia where an argument from εὐτέλεια, whether simple or qualified, stands alone as the reason for athetesis.[11] This itself points us to difficult, if familiar, questions about the abbreviation of our texts of the scholia, but also, just as interesting, the processes by which Alexandrian grammarians went about their business. Was it, at least in some cases, εὐτέλεια, of whatever kind, which first attracted their attention to particular passages or rather something else, for example apparent contextual inappropriateness, which they then found confirmed by the alleged εὐτέλεια? It is, after all, a familiar modern experience that editors discover alleged stylistic weakness in passages (or indeed whole poems) that they suspect on other grounds.[12] The broad range of the charge of εὐτέλεια also perhaps suggests that it could be (and was) levelled in a somewhat vague manner, which is not to say that any particular instance will not be specific and pointed.

A relatively high number of the extant charges of εὐτέλεια are answered head on by the exegetical scholia; this too might suggest that the charge was an impressionistic one. A case of particular interest is the nameless scholar who splutters in a bT-scholium about those (Aristophanes and Aristarchus) who, for multiple reasons including εὐτέλεια, had atheised the description of Achilles' nocturnal memories of Patroclus at *Iliad* 24.6–9:[13]

οἱ δὲ ἀθετοῦντες τοὺς στίχους πῶς οὐκ ἐμβρόντητοι, ῥηματίων κακοσχόλως ἐχόμενοι καὶ τοιούτων ἐπῶν κατηγοροῦντες […].

Σ bT *Il.* 24.6–9b

---

11 Debatable cases include Σ A *Il.* 10.497a *Ariston.* and Σ A *Il.* 22.199–201a *Ariston.* (cf. Hunter 2017, 12–13).
12 Cf. Hunter 2002.
13 On the ancient interpretation of this passage cf., e.g., Fantuzzi 2012, 211–215; on the athetesis cf. also Schironi 2018, 166–167.

> How stupid are those who athetise these verses, mischievously grabbing on to small words and accusing verses such as these [...].

This is the only occurrence of κακοσχόλως in the Homeric scholia and it is tempting to see it not just as 'frivolously, flippantly', as often understood, but as a claim that the athetisers are abusing their position — they are, in other words, not good 'scholiasts'. Grammarians, no less than epigrammatists,[14] need to stake out their territory by attacking others. Be that as it may, the scholia on *Iliad* 24.6–9 are an excellent illustration of how a passage which raises doubts on one score (in this case, the nature of Achilles' πόθος for Patroclus) will soon attract linguistic and stylistic objections as well.

Finally, to return to the A-scholium on *Il.* 15.56a, we may note that, only at the end of a long list of charges, is Aristarchus named:

> ἐν δὲ τῷ 'Λισσομένη τιμῆσαι' [i.e. v. 77] φησὶν ὁ Ἀρίσταρχος ὅτι οὐδαμῇ τὸν Ἀχιλλέα 'πτολίπορθον' εἴρηκεν, ἀλλὰ 'ποδάρκη' καὶ 'ποδώκη'.
>
> Σ A *Il.* 15.56a Ariston.

> With regard to v. 77, Aristarchus says that [Homer] nowhere called Achilles 'sacker of cities', but 'strong of foot' and 'swift of foot'.

What inferences, if any, can we draw from the fact that this is the only argument among many explicitly ascribed to Aristarchus? What, if anything, does this imply for the other arguments? Moreover, the scholium is here likely to be in error of some kind, for πτολίπορθος is found of Achilles in three other places in the *Iliad*; Aristarchus clearly discussed these instances, but his views on why this epithet is particularly associated with Odysseus rather than Achilles (cf. Σ DE²JR²⁸ *Od.* 1.2h¹, with Pontani's note) must remain unclear.[15] At every turn, then, we are confronted with questions as to how and by whom our corpus of scholia was formed; only rarely can give confident answers.

The A-scholium on *Iliad* 15.64b (Didyman) and the T-scholium on 64c (perhaps ultimately Didyman) turn our attention to Zenodotus:

---

14 It is tempting to wonder whether the author of the T-scholium on *Il.* 24.6–9 shared a chronology with the well known attacks on pedantic grammarians by Antiphanes, *AP* 11.322 (= IX Gow-Page) and Philip, *AP* 11.321 (= LX Gow-Page). For a recent study of these poems cf. Cairns 2016, ch. 6.

15 Cf. further Σ A *Il.* 2.278a Ariston., Erbse's note on Σ A *Il.* 15.56a Ariston., Schironi 2018, 634–635. In the *Iliad* πτολίπορθος is used four times of Achilles, twice of Odysseus, and four times of other figures (including divine figures). In the *Odyssey* πτολίπορθος (six times) and πτολιπόρθιος (twice) are used only of Odysseus; Odysseus' boast to the Cyclops at *Od.* 9.504 suggests that he sees it as something of a 'signature' epithet.

64b (*Did.*) [...] Ζηνόδοτος δὲ ἀπὸ τοῦ Πηλεΐδεω Ἀχιλῆος [*i.e.* v. 64] ἕως τοῦ 'Λισσομένη τιμῆσαι' [*i.e.* v. 77] οὐδ' ὅλως ἔγραφεν. **A**
64c (*ex. (Did.?)*) [...] Ζηνόδοτος ἐνθένδε ἕως τοῦ 'Λισσομένη' [*i.e.* v. 77] οὐδὲ ἔγραφεν· ἐοίκασι γὰρ Εὐριπιδείῳ προλόγῳ ταῦτα. ἐναγώνιος δέ ἐστιν ὁ ποιητὴς καί, ἐὰν ἄρα, σπέρμα μόνον τιθείς, 'κακοῦ δ' ἄρα οἱ πέλεν ἀρχή' (*Il.* 11.604). τάχα δὲ ὁ ταῦτα ποιήσας καὶ τὸ 'ᾠχόμεθ' ἐς Θήβην' (*Il.* 1.366) καὶ τὸ 'ἤρξατο δ' ὡς πρῶτον Κίκονας δάμασ'' (*Od.* 23.310) <ἐποίησεν>. **T**

64b (*Did.*) [...] Zenodotus did not write any of vv. 64–77. **A**
64c (*ex. (Did.?)*) [...] Zenodotus did not write vv. 64–77, for they resemble a Euripidean prologue. The poet prefers dramatic action and, if [he does make foreshadowings], he only plants a seed, [such as] 'that was the beginning of disaster for him' (*Il.* 11.604). Perhaps the person who composed these verses also [composed] Achilles' recapitulation in *Iliad* 1 and Odysseus' recapitulation in *Odyssey* 23. **T**

There are here at least two important Zenodotean questions: what is meant by the note that Zenodotus 'did not write' vv. 64–77 and, secondly, does the reason given in Σ T *Il.* 15.64c *ex. (Did.?)* for that 'omission' go back in whole or part to Zenodotus himself.[16] The battle-lines here are very familiar. As is well known, the terminology with which the scholia report absences or 'omissions' in Zenodotus' text is variable and overlapping. Nevertheless, it is hardly in doubt that grammarians recognised both atheteses and 'omissions', though there is still room for disagreement about the difference between the two. Fierce debate still surrounds the 'omissions'. Does this report mean that, in the Zenodotean text (or texts) which Aristarchus could consult, those verses were simply absent, or were they still present but marked in some way for deletion?[17] If the former, *i.e.* the verses were physically absent, does that mean that Zenodotus had actually removed them, presumably by creating his own text without them, or did he simply take over and 'mark up' a pre-existing text in which those verses were not there.[18] As for his reasons for 'not writing' the verses, here there is more than one question. What was known or believed about Zenodotus' reasons for his textual decisions? Did he in fact leave some explanations in writing, whether in the margin of his text or elsewhere? Was there a persistent and, at least partly, accurate memory of his oral teaching, perhaps committed to writing by a pupil at some stage? Or are all the reasons which our scholia ascribe to him simply

---

16 At the Oxford conference René Nünlist suggested that οὐδὲ ἔγραφεν in Σ T *Il.* 15.64c *ex. (Did.?)* might indicate that the note about Zenodotus had originally been preceded by another note, e.g., about the Aristarchan athetesis.
17 Cf., e.g., Montanari 1998, 5–9, Montanari 2015 (with bibliography). For a recent restatement of the view that the verses really were 'not there' cf. Rengakos 2012.
18 Cf. West 2001, 33–44.

guesswork by later scholars?¹⁹ In the present case (as in others), a decision on the second question will have consequences for the first. If it was believed that Zenodotus had explained his decision not 'to write' the verses, then he will not just have been marking up an eccentric rhapsodic copy, but exercising editorial judgement, as indeed most modern scholars suppose.

The explanation, or set of explanations, attached to the claim concerning Zenodotus in Σ T *Il.* 15.64c *ex. (Did.?)* is of considerable interest. The comparison of Zeus' prolepsis of future events and his expression of continuing χόλος to a Euripidean prologue is a good example of the sense of literary history in ancient grammatical arguments which we too often underestimate.²⁰ Euripidean prologues do indeed foreshadow (sometimes vaguely or even misleadingly) what is to come,²¹ even though what struck the ancients more forcibly about Euripides' prologues was their detailed narrative of the past, the προπεπραγμένα of the play, rather than their foreshadowing (cf. Ar. *Frogs* 946–947, Eur. T 191–193 Kannicht).²² We may, however, wonder whether the comparison also draws on a critical sense that such Euripidean prologues come relatively late in the history of tragedy and, as such, they may be compared to the non-Homeric sensibility of whoever composed (presumably after Homer) the lengthy recapitulations in *Iliad* 1 and *Odyssey* 23; the apparent suggestion that all three epic passages are the work of one composer shows a willingness to think about the nature of the non-Homeric, not just the Homeric. The standard grammatical position is that Homer prefers to keep the audience in suspense rather than to tell them everything in advance;²³ ἐναγώνιος can, however, also carry the sense of Homer's preference for (what we would call) the dramatic, for action over lengthy narrative (which 'Longinus' famously saw as characteristic of the *Iliad* rather than the *Odyssey*), and the two senses can — as here — slide into each other.

In his discussion of Achilles' recapitulation in Book 1, Eustathius also offers a very interesting and somewhat idiosyncratic view of the relationship between Homer and Euripides in this matter. After citing a version of the familiar doctrine that Homer begins *in mediis rebus* but then finds ways to refer to events

---

19 Cf. Bolling 1925, 153.
20 Nickau 1977, 247 seems to accept that the comparison to a Euripidean prologue may well come from Zenodotus, even if nothing else in the scholia does.
21 Cf. Nickau 1977, 249.
22 The striking similarity between those verses of *Frogs* and Arist. *Rhet.* 3.1415a19 (= Eur. T 191 Kannicht), καὶ οἱ τραγικοὶ δηλοῦσι περὶ <οὗ> τὸ δρᾶμα, κἂν μὴ εὐθὺς ὥσπερ Εὐρίπιδης κτλ., is worth noting, cf. Meijering 1987, 198. There is a valuable collection of scholiastic material on Euripides' prologues in Meijering 1987, 190–198.
23 Cf., e.g., Meijering 1987, 204–205, 287 n. 212, Nünlist 2009, 142.

from 'before' his poem as well as foreshadowing events beyond it, Eustathius notes that later poets imitated this Homeric technique and 'most of all Euripides, who also begins in the middle of the stories he dramatizes (ἐκ τοῦ μέσου τῶν δραματικῶν ἀρχόμενος ὑποθέσεων), and then brings in past events and very skillfully interweaves (παρενείρει) what will happen in the future, either in the form of guesses based on what is probable or of oracular predictions [...] so that the viewer and listener are not unaware of any part of the previous story or the plot' (*Comm. Il.* i.12). It seems likely enough that, whether or not this account is original to him,[24] Eustathius is referring both to the prologues and to the *dei ex machina* who often make predictions at the end of the play, and as such he may be seen as, in this respect at least, the heir of Zenodotus (or whoever lies behind the comparison made in the scholium to *Il.* 15.64c). The analogy may seem to us very forced, but it is a reminder of the remarkable critical schemata to which a belief in Homer as the fount of all literary practice gives rise.

Zenodotus' text, whatever its origin, leaves intact Zeus' detailed account to Hera of what he is going to tell Iris and Apollo to do, while omitting the more detailed foreshadowing of vv. 64–71 and Zeus' reaffirmation of his promise to Thetis. Homeric practice would have led us to expect him to give some indication of why he wants her to summon the two gods,[25] but it was presumably felt that Zeus had no need to be this expansive to his wife, and Aristarchus may well have felt the same. Moreover, if our texts moved seamlessly from v. 63 to v. 78, I do not think anyone would have felt that we were missing something. Martin West rightly stressed that v. 72 'logically' connects with v. 63, not with v. 71, but we might also ask what *need* there was for Zeus to recall to Hera the meeting with Thetis in Book 1, which had so upset her (unless, of course, this is a part of the husband's calculated retribution). We are, in other words, back with the question of poetic necessity. Modern critics (usefully summarised by Janko 1992, 228–229) note that Hera is now reconciled to Zeus' plan because she learns that his support for the Trojans is merely temporary and not final, but again we might think that the poem does not 'require' that explanation. We might also recall that Zeus' promise to Thetis in Book 1 is entirely open-ended: he promises to bestow τιμή upon Achilles and to grant the Trojans the upper hand (κράτος) until the Greeks show honour to Achilles (1.505–510). Hera shortly afterwards had voiced her suspicions that her husband had promised to Thetis to 'destroy many by the ships of the Achaeans' (1.559), but that is *not* in fact what Zeus had promised. As often, then, the text which Zenodotus championed is not obvious-

---

24 Van der Valk *ad loc.* leaves the matter open.
25 Cf. West 2001, 230.

ly deficient; our problem, as was also to some extent the ancient problem, is to determine what *would* constitute a 'deficient' text.

Why Lemnos?

In *Iliad* 14 Hera requires the help of Sleep in her plan to trick Zeus and, after having got what she wanted from Aphrodite, she travels from Olympus to Lemnos, 'city of godlike Thoas', where she finds Sleep (ἔνθ' Ὕπνῳ ξύμβλητο, v. 231). Why was Sleep on Lemnos, and did Hera know that he was? The D-scholia and the exegetical bT-scholia on this verse offer a number of possible answers to both questions:

231a¹ (*ex.* | *Did.* (?)) ἔνθ' Ὕπνῳ ξύμβλητο: φίλοινοι γὰρ ὡς ἀπόγονοι Θόαντος τοῦ Διονύσου. καὶ Εὔνεως οἶνον πέμπει, καὶ Ὀδυσσεὺς ἀπὸ Θρᾳκῶν τὸν οἶνον δέχεται, καὶ οἱ σὺν Ῥήσῳ κοιμώμενοι ἀνῃρέθησαν καὶ οἱ Λήμνιοι ὑπὸ τῶν γυναικῶν. καὶ οἱ Ἀχαιοὶ ἐν Λήμνῳ πίνουσι 'κρητῆρας ἐπιστεφέας οἴνοιο'. ἢ διὰ †πασιθέαν τὴν γυναῖκα Ἡφαίστου πάρεστιν αὐτὸς λιπαρῶν τυχεῖν τῆς ἀδελφῆς (τὸ δὲ χαλκεῖον Ἡφαίστου ἐν Λήμνῳ). οἱ δὲ ὅτι Φιλοκτήτης ἐδεῖτο αὐτοῦ εἶναι ἐκεῖ διὰ τὰς ὀδύνας. οἱ δὲ ἐκ τύχης συντετυχηκέναι. | τινὲς δὲ <προσ>γράφουσιν 'ἐρχομένῳ κατὰ φῦλα βροτῶν ἐπ' ἀπείρονα γαῖαν'. T
231a² (*ex.*) πολυοίνων ὄντων καὶ φιλοίνων τῶν Λημνίων εἰκότως ἐκεῖσε διατρίβει ὁ Ὕπνος· καὶ γὰρ πολὺν ἔχουσιν οἶνον ὥστε καὶ τοῖς Ἕλλησι χορηγεῖν· καὶ γὰρ καὶ οἱ Λήμνιοι παῖδες Αἰγύπτου ὑπὸ τῶν γυναικῶν διὰ τὴν πολλὴν ἀναιροῦνται ἀκρασίαν. b(BCE³) εἴωθε δὲ ὁ Ὕπνος ἐπὶ πάντας καὶ μᾶλλον ἐπὶ τοὺς μεθύσους ἐνδιατρίβειν. b(BCE³E⁴)
231b (*ex.*) <ἔνθ' Ὕπνῳ ξύμβλητο:> οὐκ οἶδεν Ὕπνου οἶκον, ὡς Ποσειδῶνος ἐν Αἰγαῖς, ἐπεὶ τρίτῳ βήματι ἐκεῖ ἂν εὕρετο ἡ θεός. T

231a¹ (*ex.* | *Did.* (?)) [The Lemnians] are wine-lovers since they are descendants of Thoas the son of Dionysos. Euneos sends wine [from there] (*Il.* 8.467–469) and Odysseus receives wine from the Thracians (cf. *Od.* 9.196–211). Rhesus' men were killed while they slept (cf. *Il.* 10.470–497) and the men of Lemnos by their wives, and the Greeks on Lemnos drink 'mixing-bowls full with wine' (*Il.* 8.232). Or Sleep is there because of [Charis], Hephaestus' wife: he is very keen to get her sister Pasithea (Hephaestus' forge is on Lemnos).[26] Some say that Philoctetes asked Sleep to be there because of his sufferings, and others that she met him by chance. | And certain people add the verse '[met Sleep] as he was going among the tribes of mortals over the boundless earth' (= *Il.* 14.231a). T
231a² (*ex.*) As the Lemnians have a rich supply of wine and are wine-lovers, it is reasonable that Sleep spends time there. They have so much wine in fact that they can supply it to the Greeks. And the Lemnian children of Aigyptos are killed by their wives because of their very wanton behaviour. b(BCE³) Sleep visits everyone but particularly those who are drunk. b(BCE³E⁴)

---

[26] The text of the T-scholia in this sentence has suffered corruption, but the sense can easily be restored from the D-scholia.

231b (*ex.*) Homer does not know of Sleep's house, as [he knows] of Poseidon's at Aigai, as [otherwise] the goddess would have reached it with her third step. **T**

διὰ ποίαν δὲ αἰτίαν ἐν τῇ Λήμνῳ μάλιστα ὁ Ὕπνος διατρίβει; ῥητέον ὅτι Λήμνου μὲν ἦν δεσπότης Ἥφαιστος, γυνὴ δὲ τούτου Χάρις. Πασιθέας δὲ τῆς Χάριτος ἀδελφῆς ἐρωτικῶς ἔχων ὁ Ὕπνος ἐκεῖ διέτριβεν· ταύτην δὲ αὐτῷ ἐπαγγέλλεται γυναῖκα δώσειν ἡ Ἥρα. δύναται δὲ καὶ φυσικώτερον λυθῆναι, ὅτι οἰνοφόρος ἡ Λῆμνος, καθὼς λέγει 'νῆες δ' ἐκ Λήμνοιο παρέστασαν, οἶνον ἄγουσαι'· τοῖς δὲ πολυποτοῦσι μάλιστα ὁ ὕπνος παρέπεται.

Σ D *Il.* 14.230

For what reason did Sleep spend most time on Lemnos? Our answer must be that Hephaistos was the master of Lemnos, and his wife was Charis. Sleep spent time there because he was in love with Charis' sister, Pasithea; this is the lady whom Hera promises to give him as wife. [The problem] can also be given an answer from nature: Lemnos was rich in wine, as shown by *Iliad* 7.467, 'ships from Lemnos were present bearing wine'. Sleep most of all attends those who drink a lot.

The reasons offered for the meeting on Lemnos are: (i) that the Lemnians are fond of wine, which their island produces in abundance, and it is natural to find Sleep in a place where there are heavy wine-drinkers; (ii) Sleep is wooing Hephaestus' sister-in-law, and Lemnos is the site of Hephaestus' forge; (iii) Sleep has come in answer to a request by Philoctetes for relief from his sufferings; (iv) it was simple chance that he was on Lemnos. Another approach, which sits comfortably with the explanation from chance, was that Sleep was going on his regular travels when Hera met him, and an extra-verse was in fact added to the text to make that plain.

The details of the Homeric text invited, indeed required, explanation, and 'Why Lemnos?' was just such an unexplained detail; after all, Homer very rarely did anything without a purpose (οὐδὲν μάτην).[27] Although the nature of our scholia makes conclusions about the full textual structures which lie behind them difficult, the order of the reasons offered for the meeting on Lemnos is suggestive. The starting-point is the immediate context, *i.e.* Homer has himself indicated the answer with the reference to Thoas: the son of Dionysos indicates that this is the area in which the explanation lies. This is then confirmed by the role which Lemnos plays elsewhere in Homer: the island is connected with Hephaestus (cf. *Il.* 1.593, and it is where the god goes when he has set his trap for Ares and Aphrodite in *Odyssey* 8), with wine consumption and export, and it is where the Greeks exposed Philoctetes (*Il.* 2.721–724). Preference is given to the 'Dionysiac' explanation because this is the one apparently indicated by Homer

---

[27] Cf. Hunter 2018a, 132, citing earlier bibliography.

himself. What is the tone of such an explanation? Eustathius at least thought it rather witty (ἀστείως, *Comm. Il.* iii.625), and — given its nature — we might indeed be tempted to seek a 'sympotic' context, or even origin, for it. From the fact that Sleep does not return to Lemnos after his mission is completed, some interpreters at least concluded that he did not live there, and, moreover, Sleep is of course not restricted by place (see Σ b *Il.* 14.361a² *ex.*, cf. Eust. *Comm. Il.* iii.625);[28] this perhaps increases the possibility that the Dionysiac explanation has indeed something of the ludic and/or epideictic about it.

The exegetical T-scholium to *Il.* 14.231 seems to imply that both Rhesus' men and the Lemnian husbands were killed when they lay in a wine-induced slumber; Erbse, however, notes that he knows of no other ancient evidence which gives wine a role in the Lemnian story, and at *Il.* 10.471 Rhesus' Thracians are said to be exhausted from κάματος, not drunk. We may therefore be dealing with an ancient equivalent of the much-maligned notes in modern commentaries which list numerous passages introduced by 'cf.' which, upon closer inspection, are all in one or way or another problematic; in other words, we have here a trace of someone (perhaps again in a witty, sympotic context) bolstering a weak argument (or simply making a mistake?) by trying to bring wine into every familiar story about Lemnos and the Thracian mainland opposite. Alternatively, the process of compression has caused the scholium to appear misleading: Rhesus' men and the Lemnian husbands were adduced to illustrate a connection between sleep, not drunken sleep, and Lemnos/Thrace, but the placing of these examples inside the discussion of Lemnian wine has, not unnaturally, led to a false interpretation. Eustathius may be our earliest witness to such a misreading, if misreading it is, for in adducing the example of the Lemnian husbands (he does not mention Rhesus' men) he adds that they were 'stuffed full of wine, as seems likely (ὡς εἰκός)' (*Comm. Il.* iii.625); the addition and the qualification shows that he too had to draw inferences from an ambiguous text.

The citation in the exegetical T-scholium on *Il.* 14.231 of *Il.* 8.232 suggests in any case a rather fuller critical discussion of the wider passage than survives today:

αἰδώς, Ἀργεῖοι, κάκ' ἐλέγχεα, εἶδος ἀγητοί.
πῆ ἔβαν εὐχωλαί, ὅτε δὴ φάμεν εἶναι ἄριστοι,
ἃς ὁπότ' ἐν Λήμνῳ κενεαυχέες ἠγοράασθε,   230
ἔσθοντες κρέα πολλὰ βοῶν ὀρθοκραιράων,

---

[28] Wöhrle 1995, 13 claims that we learn from *Iliad* 14 that Sleep has a 'Wohnsitz' on Lemnos, but he says nothing about the difficulties, and the ancient discussion, of such a view.

πίνοντες κρητῆρας ἐπιστεφέας οἴνοιο,
Τρώων ἄνθ' ἑκατόν τε διηκοσίων τε ἕκαστος
στήσεσθ' ἐν πολέμῳ; νῦν δ' οὐδ' ἑνὸς ἄξιοί εἰμεν
Ἕκτορος, ὅς τάχα νῆας ἐνιπρήσει πυρὶ κηλέῳ.

Il. 8.228–235

Shame, you Argives, disgraceful wretches, admirable only in looks! Where are those claims that we were the best, made when you were boasting emptily on Lemnos, as you ate large amounts of the meat of straight-horned cattle and drank bowls full to the brim with wine? Each of you said that you would stand in warfare against one hundred Trojans, or two hundred, but now we are no match for one man, Hector, who will soon set blazing fire to the ships.

Agamemnon here reproaches the Greeks with the empty boasts they once made on Lemnos, apparently while drinking 'mixing-bowls full with wine', a claim so improbable that it presumably gave rise to the variant στήσαντες for πίνοντες (v. 232) which occurs in the indirect tradition and is modelled on a Homeric formula. Aristarchus athetised v. 231, apparently because it is wine-drinking, not meat-eating, which causes empty boasting (Σ A *Il.* 8.231a *Ariston.*; cf. Ath. 2.39d–e), and the exegetical scholia solemnly make Homer the πρῶτος εὑρέτης of armies which drink too much (Σ bT *Il.* 8.231–232 *ex.*). There was, then, a grammatical tradition that the empty boasts of 8.230–234 were caused by excessive drinking and the scholia on 14.231 reflect that tradition also, as part of the body of evidence for a link between Lemnos and heavy drinking. As for the Lemnian husbands killed by their angry wives, it is perhaps possible that the reference in the b-scholia to their πολλὴ ... ἀκρασία represents a confusion about their drinking a great deal of unmixed (ἄκρατος) wine.[29]

The two other explanations offered by the scholia similarly grow out of the Homeric text itself, for marriage to the Grace Pasithea, 'for whom I long every day', is precisely the reward which Sleep demands of Hera (*Il.* 14.275–276), and as Hephaestus' wife in the *Iliad* is Charis ('Grace'), a family connection and an explanation why Sleep was hanging around Lemnos was not difficult to make.[30] Here again, however, we may wonder about tone and origin. Homer's image of a lovesick Sleep not only made him an easy target for Hera's plans, but also invit-

---

29 ἀκρασία was presumably intended to refer to the men's 'lust' for slave-girls, as in its two other appearances in the exegetical scholia (Σ bT *Il.* 3.383a *ex.*, Σ bT *Il.* 9.128a *ex.*). The apparent confusion in the same scholium between the Lemnian men and the Danaids, the children of Aigyptos, presumably goes back to a mistake caused by the similarity of the stories.
30 The exegetical scholia on vv. 275–277 offer an interesting discussion of the links between sleep and χάρις.

ed the free play of wit: lovers traditionally cannot sleep, so it would hardly surprise if someone in antiquity had joked about Sleep being 'sleepless on Lemnos', but lovers certainly also hang around in the vicinity of the beloved (διέτριβεν is the verb used by the D-scholia), and so it was entirely natural to suggest that that was what Sleep was doing on Lemnos.

The case of Philoctetes is rather different. In the Catalogue of Book 2 Homer describes his terrible suffering on Lemnos and also his imminent return:

ἔνθ' ὅ γε κεῖτ' ἀχέων· τάχα δὲ μνήσεσθαι ἔμελλον
Ἀργεῖοι παρὰ νηυσὶ Φιλοκτήταο ἄνακτος.

Il. 2.724–725

There he lay in pain, but the Argives beside the ships were soon to remember lord Philoctetes.

Philoctetes' story might well have occurred to any critic going through the role of Lemnos in Homer and in Greek literature and myth more generally, but Zenodotus had athetised vv. 724–725 of this passage, and grammarians were well acquainted with the question of whether or not Philoctetes in epic was fetched from Lemnos back to Troy (cf. Σ A *Il.* 2.724 *Ariston.*); any collection of Lemnian stories was almost bound to include him. Nevertheless, it is hard to believe that somewhere behind the claim that Philoctetes asked Sleep to come 'on account of his pains' (διὰ τὰς ὀδύνας) does not lie the famous invocation of Sleep as the reliever of pain ("Ὕπν' ὀδύνας ἀδαής, Ὕπνε δ' ἀλγέων) sung by the chorus in Sophocles' *Philoctetes* (vv. 827–832), as the hero lies sleeping in front of them.[31] Who first connected the Homeric meeting of Hera and Sleep with Philoctetes we cannot know, but it is not unlikely that the critical association between Philoctetes and *Iliad* 14 took shape within a wider ancient acknowledgement of the thick Homeric texture of Sophocles' play; it may in fact be that a grammarian's suggestion that Sophocles 'derived' his song to Sleep from the role of Sleep in *Iliad* 14 has then fed back into the Homeric critical tradition. Did Sophocles himself in fact exploit a pre-existing link between Sleep and Lemnos? If so, is the famous invocation of the *Philoctetes* an element (*inter alia*) of 'local colour'?

Finally, there is 'chance', *i.e.* Sleep just happened to be on Lemnos. There are two broad versions of such an interpretation, one 'weaker' than the other. Perhaps there was no special reason why Sleep happened at that moment to be on Lemnos – this is just where he was on his 'rounds' – but that does not mean that Hera did not know that she could find him there. The stronger version is

---

31 ὕπνος also features twice in Neoptolemus' short speech to the chorus before their song.

that 'Hera [...] meets Sleep at Lemnos [...] apparently by luck [...] Sleep had no special business on Lemnos, which is merely a convenient spot on Hera's route [from Olympus to Mt Ida]'.³² Such an 'unlikely coincidence' (Janko 1992 on v. 225–279), however, seems to run against the pattern of the text, as Hera's plan involves making Zeus 'desire' to make love to her and then putting him to post-coital sleep (vv. 163–165). She does what she can by making herself look as desirable as possible, but then leaves nothing to chance by enlisting Aphrodite's aid; sleep is a familiar aftermath to love-making, but it can never be guaranteed, and so, in order to leave nothing to 'chance', Hera deliberately seeks out Sleep, who is as responsible for sleep as Aphrodite is for desire. The strong version of the 'chance' explanation seems therefore unlikely, and would, I think, have done so to most ancient critics, despite the fact that some clearly argued for it, though in what context and with what tone we will probably never know.

Grammarians were well aware that Homer did not use the word τύχη,³³ but this does not mean that 'chance' is absent. As the exegetical scholia on *Il.* 20.127 put it, 'Homer does not know [the word] τύχη, but he does know its consequences' (Σ bT *Il.* 20.127 *ex.*). The scholia regularly draw lessons from Homer about the operation of τύχη; on the lot-drawing of *Il.* 3.325 the exegetical scholia comment that Homer shows us that the gifts of fortune are purposeless (κενά) for those who do not deserve them (in this case Paris), as part of a regular scholiastic contrast between τύχη and ἀρετή (Σ bT *Il.* 3.325a *ex.*). Grammarians also find τύχη at work in the poems themselves, though — by most reckonings — not very often, particularly if we limit the search to the poet's own narrative. Generals can suffer bad luck (Σ bT *Il.* 10.3–4 *ex.*), just as people get killed in war or shipwreck by mischance (Σ bT *Il.* 13.411 *ex.*, Σ DH *Od.* 1.9g1 *Porph.*, ll. 34–36) and so on. Nevertheless, grammarians on the whole saw a purposeful avoidance by Homer of the operation of chance: 'Homer normally describes the results of τύχη as arising from a cause (αἰτία)'.³⁴ The two cases from the *Odyssey* which fall under this scholiastic 'rule' are in fact interesting examples of how modern readers and ancient grammarians view some matters differently and some in similar ways. At *Od.* 9.154–155 (cf. further below) Odysseus claims that the Nymphs put mountain-goats in the Greeks' path, 'so that my comrades might

---

32 Janko 1992 on vv. 225–279 and 231. For a much more complicated explanation of Sleep's presence on Lemnos, which has some overlaps with ancient interpretations, cf. West 2011, 292–293.
33 Cf. Σ T *Il.* 4.106b *ex.*, Σ T *Il.* 11.684a *ex.*, Σ bT *Il.* 20.127 *ex.*, Richardson 1974, 289, Hunter 1995, 25–27.
34 Σ bT *Il.* 22.328–329a¹ *ex.*, cf. the scholia *Od.* 9.154, 12.427, Nünlist 2009, 32.

eat'. To ascribe a successful hunt to divine action seems entirely natural; luck is of course involved in hunting, but so is the favour of countryside divinities. We have no reason to doubt that Homer 'meant' here exactly what he had his character say: the Nymphs *were* involved. When, however, Odysseus ascribes the loss of his ship to Zeus who struck it with his thunderbolt (*Od.* 7.249–250), the scholia on v. 249 draw an interesting distinction (Σ HP¹T *Od.* 7.249a¹ *ex.*):

> τὸ μὲν ναυαγῆσαι ἀνθρωπίνης τύχης, τὸ δὲ περισωθῆναι τῆς ἀπὸ τῶν θεῶν εὐνοίας σημεῖον. τῷ ἀποτελέσματι οὖν θαρρῶν τὸ ἐκ τῆς τύχης συμβεβηκὸς εἰς τοὺς θεοὺς ἀναφέρει, εἰς ἔλεον ἐπισπώμενος τοὺς Φαίακας.

> To suffer shipwreck is a matter of human chance, but to be saved after shipwreck is a sign of the gods' goodwill. Odysseus takes confidence in what has happened to him and ascribes what happened by chance to the gods, in order to make the Phaeacians pity him.

Here too any Greek might well ascribe a destructive storm at sea to Zeus, as well as survival of such a storm to the goodwill of the gods; Zeus is not just a 'façon de parler' in such situations. The scholia however betray a later, by no means necessarily Christian, perspective in which 'chance' really does have a role to play in every step of our lives (cf. Horace, *Odes* 2.13). It is hardly surprising if Odysseus, given the tale of woe which he has for the Phaeacians, sees 'evil purpose' (cf. ὄφρα) behind a shift of winds that takes him back to Scylla and Charybdis (*Od.* 12.426–428).

A notorious case comes in the scholia on the spear-thrust which is to prove fatal to Hector:

> [...] οὐδ' ἄρ' ἀπ' ἀσφάραγον μελίη τάμε χαλκοβάρεια,
> ὄφρά τί μιν προτιείποι ἀμειβόμενος ἐπέεσσιν.
>
> *Il.* 22.328–329

> [...] but the ashen spear, heavy with bronze, did not slice the windpipe, so that Hector might respond to him with words.

328–329a1 [...] ἴσως ἐκκλίναντος αὐτοῦ πλαγία γέγονεν ἡ τομή. εἴωθε δὲ τὰ ἐκ τύχης ὡς ἐξ αἰτίας λέγειν· 'ἦλθε δ' ἐπὶ νότος ὦκα, / ὄφρ' ἔτι τὴν ὀλοὴν <ἀναμετρήσαιμι Χάρυβδιν>' (*Od.* 12.427–428), 'ὦρσαν <δὲ> Νύμφαι <αἶγας ὀρεσκῴους>, ἵνα δειπνήσειαν ἑταῖροι' (*Od.* 9.154–155). οἰκονομικὸν δὲ καὶ τοῦτο, ἵνα καὶ ἀποθνήσκων μὴ ἀπροσφώνητος εἴη. ἔστι δὲ πρόληψις ὁ τρόπος. **T**
328–329a2 [...] ἴσως δὲ ἐκκλίναντος αὐτοῦ πλαγία γέγονεν ἡ πληγὴ καὶ οὐ διεκόπη ὅλος. **b**(BCE³E⁴) καὶ τοῦτο δέ, ἵνα καὶ ἀποθνήσκων μὴ ἀπροσφώνητος ᾖ. εἴωθε δὲ τὰ ἐκ τύχης ὡς ἐξ αἰτίας λέγειν. **b**(BE³E⁴)
329 [...] ἀθετεῖται, ὅτι γελοῖος, εἰ ἡ μελία ἐπετήδευσεν μὴ ἀποτεμεῖν τὸν ἀσφάραγον, ἵνα προσφωνήσῃ τὸν Ἀχιλλέα. ἀπολογούμενοι δέ φασιν ὅτι τὸ ἐκ τύχης συμβεβηκὸς αἰτιατικῶς ἐξενήνοχεν [...]. **A**

328–329a1 (*ex.*) [...] Perhaps as he ducked, the blow was a glancing one. [Homer] normally ascribes causes to what happens by chance, as with 'the south wind rose quickly, so that again I must pass by Charybdis' (*Od.* 12.427–428) and 'the Nymphs stirred up mountain-goats, so that my companions might eat' (*Od.* 9.154–155). This is also important for the plot, so that he should not die without speaking; the trope is prolepsis. **T**
328–329a2 (*ex.*) [...] Perhaps as he ducked, the blow was a glancing one and did not cut right through. **b**(BCE³E⁴) The point of this is so that he should not die without speaking. [Homer] normally ascribes causes to what happens by chance. **b** (BE³E⁴)
329 (*Ariston.*) The verse is athetised, because the idea that the spear should purposefully not cut the windpipe so that Hector might address Achilles is laughable. In defence they say Homer gives causes for what has happened by chance [...]. **A**

Aristarchus' athetesis of v. 329 on the apparent grounds that it is 'laughable' to ascribe motivation to a spear has its own interest, but in the present context it is the verse's defenders who have more to teach us. Eustathius repeats the defence offered by our scholia, but then goes on to see an instance here of the familiar technique, productive of rhetorical γλυκύτης, whereby Homer gives, as it were, life and motivation to objects. Moreover, 'it is as if Homer's Muse here admits that she has made the spear not cut the windpipe, so that the dying Hector can utter something before death' (*Comm. Il.* iv.624–625).³⁵ Irene de Jong takes a different tack; she sees 'a special use of ὄφρα, to express the natural consequences expected in the circumstances', as though we have here a result, rather than a final clause.³⁶ The case of Achilles' spear is, however, not in the speech of a character, but in the narrative of the poet, and the action which confirms the ὄφρα clause, namely Hector's dying words in vv. 338–343 and 356–360, do not follow immediately, but come after Achilles' intervening speech (vv. 330–336). In the circumstances, it is hard (as so often) not to feel sympathy for Eustathius. An extraordinary moment in the poem brings an extraordinary technique from the poet.

The scholia use the phrase κατ' ἐπιφοράν in connection with two Homeric choices, namely the details of the nails on Agamemnon's sword (cf. Σ A *Il.* 2.45 *Ariston.* and Σ A *Il.* 11.30 *Ariston.*) and why the 'Catalogue of Ships' begins with the Boeotian contingents (cf. Σ D *Il.* 2.494); it is clear from Σ b *Il.* 2.494–877 *ex.* that κατ' ἐπιφοράν must be synonymous with οὐκ ἔκ τινος παρατηρήσεως and

---

35 Cf. Wilamowitz 1920, 102, West 2011, 389 (though neither acknowledges Eustathius).
36 de Jong 2012, 141. Cf. Kühner-Gerth 1898–1904 II, 379–380. De Jong's parallels do not persuade: at *Od.* 9.13 Odysseus tells Alcinous that he has asked about the hero's sufferings, ὄφρ' ἔτι μᾶλλον ὀδυρόμενος στεναχίζω, where a final clause might be too pointed a rebuke, but which in other respects seems very different from the case of Achilles' spear; at *Il.* 2.359 the clause might well be final, and the same seems true for *Od.* 1.302 and 11.94.

mean something like 'on impulse, for no special reason'.[37] The question of the start of the 'Catalogue' is of particular interest, in part from the range of answers given to this 'problem', and in part because of what looks like an Aristarchan *bon mot* preserved in the D-scholia: 'Aristarchus said that Homer began the Catalogue with the Boeotians on impulse; if he had begun with another people, we would have been looking for the reason for that beginning'. This looks like not merely a claim that there was no particular reason to begin with the Boeotians,[38] but also a wry comment on the business of Homeric scholarship: grammarians, like Aristarchus himself, always want to explain something, even if there *is* no special explanation. We should not assume, on *a priori* grounds, that self-irony was a mode unknown to Aristarchus. The comment seems in fact to anticipate the famous scene of Lucian's *True Histories* in which the narrator questions Homer and, after learning that all the verses which Zenodotus and Aristarchus had athetised were in fact genuine, asks the poet a famous Homeric 'problem', namely why 'wrath' (μῆνις) is the first word of the *Iliad*; Homer responds that this opening came to him without any particular planning (μηδὲν ἐπιτηδεύσαντι *VH* 2.20).[39] The Lucianic Homer may thus echo Aristarchus himself. Both certainly have their eyes on the οὐδὲν μάτην principle (cf. above), and this is where we turn back to Hera's meeting with Sleep on Lemnos; Hera could not afford to 'miss' Sleep and therefore must have known where to find him.

With all due caution, therefore, we may see a move within the explanations listed in the scholium about Sleep on Lemnos from the one most rooted in the immediate Homeric context to that which, in the opinion of the critics, gives least credit to Homer; 'chance' brings up the rear in more ways than one.[40] Those critics who said it just happened 'by chance' may well have had larger critical fish to fry and more points to prove 'against' Homer than this one detail. If there was no particular reason for Lemnos, why should there be any particular reason for any such detail in the poems: when the skein of authorial planning starts to unravel, where need the critic stop?

---

37 Cf. Eustathius, *Comm. Il.* i.400, Nünlist 2009, 175 n. 7, Schironi 2018, 509.
38 So, e.g., Nünlist 2009, 182–183.
39 Cf. Hunter 2018a, 132.
40 Eustathius, by contrast, places this explanation first (*Comm. Il.* iii.625), and in a manner which suggests that this is his preferred explanation. On the critical diminution of chance as a plot factor in Homer cf. also Nünlist 2009, 32.

Bibliography

Apthorp, M.J. 1980. *The Manuscript Evidence for Interpolation in Homer*, Heidelberg.
Bolling, G.M. 1925. *The External Evidence for Interpolation in Homer*, Oxford.
Cairns, F. 2016. *Hellenistic Epigram. Contexts of Exploration*, Cambridge.
Fantuzzi, M. 2012. *Achilles in Love*, Oxford.
Hunter, R. 1995. 'The divine and human map of the *Argonautica*', *Syllecta Classica* 6, 13–27 [= Hunter 2008, 257–277].
Hunter, R. 2002. 'The sense of an author: Theocritus and [Theocritus]', in: R. Gibson/C. Kraus (eds.), *The Classical Commentary*, Leiden, 89–108 [= Hunter 2008, 384–404].
Hunter, R. 2008. *On Coming After. Studies in Post-Classical Greek Literature and its Reception*, Berlin/New York.
Hunter, R. 2017. 'Eustathian moments', in: F. Pontani/V. Katsaros/V. Sarris (eds.), *Reading Eustathios of Thessalonike*, Berlin, 9–75 [= this volume 682–749].
Hunter, R. 2018a. *The Measure of Homer*, Cambridge.
Hunter, R. 2018b. '*regius urget*: Hellenising thoughts on Latin intratextuality', in: S. Harrison/S. Frangoulidis/T.D. Papanghelis (eds.), *Intratextuality and Latin Literature*, Berlin, 451–469 [= this volume 411–430].
Janko, R. 1992. *The Iliad: a commentary, Volume IV: books 13–16*, Cambridge.
Meijering, R. 1987. *Literary and Rhetorical Theories in Greek Scholia*, Groningen.
Montanari, F. 1998. 'Zenodotus, Aristarchus and the *ekdosis* of Homer', in: G.W. Most (ed.), *Editing Texts, Texte edieren*, Göttingen, 1–21.
Nickau, K. 1977. *Untersuchungen zur textkritischen Methode des Zenodotos von Ephesos*, Berlin.
Nünlist, R. 2009. *The Ancient Critic at Work*, Cambridge.
Rengakos, A. 2012. 'Bemerkungen zum antiken Homertext', in: M. Meier-Brügger (ed.), *Homer, gedeutet durch ein großes Lexikon*, Berlin, 239–252.
Richardson, N.J. 1974. *The Homeric Hymn to Demeter*, Oxford.
Schironi, F. 2009. 'Theory into practice: Aristotelian principles in Aristarchean philology', *Classical Philology* 104, 279–316.
Schironi, F. 2018. *The Best of the Grammarians: Aristarchus of Samothrace on the Iliad*, Ann Arbor.
West, M.L. 2001. *Studies in the Text and Transmission of the Iliad*, Munich/Leipzig.
West, M.L. 2011. *The Making of the Iliad*, Oxford.
West, M.L. 2017. 'Aristophanes of Byzantium's text of Homer', *Classical Philology* 112, 20–44.
Wilamowitz, U. von. 1920. *Die Ilias und Homer*, 2nd ed., Berlin.
Wöhrle, G. 1995. *Hypnos, der Allbezwinger*, Stuttgart.

Part VII: **Miscellaneous**

40 The Letter of Aristeas

The so-called *Letter of Aristeas* (henceforth *Ar.*)[1] is not only one of the few surviving pieces of extended literary prose from Ptolemaic Alexandria, but its subject — the translation of the Hebrew sacred texts into Greek and, more generally, the interaction of Greek and Hebrew traditions and culture — places it very firmly at the centre of the 'creation of a Hellenistic world' and of how that world was imagined by those who actually lived in it.

In the form of a 'letter' addressed to one Philokrates, *Ar.* narrates the story of how, at the instigation of Demetrios of Phaleron, Ptolemy II Philadelphos brought to Alexandria the best scholars from Jerusalem to produce an authoritative Greek version of Hebrew scripture. Although debate still rages, it is now generally assumed that *Ar.* is the work of an Alexandrian Jew with good knowledge of the workings of the Ptolemaic administration and is to be dated to the second century BC; *Ar.* thus purports to offer an eyewitness account, by a Greek (rather than a Jewish) courtier, of something which happened at least a century and a half before the work was, as far as we can tell, actually written. It would, I think, be fair to say that *Ar.* does not enjoy a high reputation: Gunther Zuntz, who shed important light on *Ar.* in two seminal studies, denies the author even 'moderate imagination' and castigates the 'helplessness evidenced where [the author] had no substantial tradition to follow',[2] though Erich Gruen's stomach is strong enough for him to call it 'occasionally entertaining' and even to find something like humour lurking previously unnoticed.[3] In her recent

---

This chapter is here reproduced much as it was delivered in Edinburgh; footnotes, on what is a very thorny subject, have been kept to an absolute minimum. It will not need to be stressed that I am completely unqualified to enter the debate on most of the central issues concerning the Letter, particularly as they touch the history and practices of Hellenistic Judaism. My purpose in allowing this paper to go further than the oral presentation is rather to prompt classicists, particularly the large number currently working on Hellenistic and later prose narratives, to pay it more attention than they have hitherto.

---

1 There are accessible texts in Hadas 1951, Pelletier 1962, and Calabi 1995; English translations are available in Hadas 1951 and Shutt 1985. The fullest study is now Honigman 2003, but Calabi 1995 remains a valuable bibliographical resource, and cf. also Fraser 1972, II 972–973 and Birnbaum 2004, 131–138. Fraser 1972, I 696–703 offers a succinct introduction to the work and its problems (and see also ibid. II 970–972 on the date of the work). A case for believing in the essential historicity of the narrative of *Ar.* has been stated by Collins 2000.
2 Zuntz 1959, 110, 125 [= 1972, 127, 142].
3 Gruen 1998, 218–221.

study, Sylvie Honigman calls 'close to unreadable for modern readers' the account of how Philadelphos posed ethical and political questions to the Jewish scholars who had come to Alexandria to produce the text for the Royal Library.[4] Whether her explanation for this ('changes in literary taste') is sufficient is at least open to question. Why *Ar.* is not, for most people, an easy read could actually be an interesting question to which more attention might well be paid by those concerned with the history of literary form and reading practices. Scholarship on *Ar.* has, however, perhaps not unreasonably been more concerned with issues of readership and purpose, and of what we can actually learn from the work about the history of the Ptolemaic Library and of the Alexandrian Jewish community.

Whether or not *Ar.* is a 'real letter' is essentially a non-question, but the ethical and quasi-private turn of this essay to Philokrates is something to be considered in the context of the making of the Hellenistic world and the particular quality of the writing and ideas it produced. Philokrates is chosen as the addressee for a number of explicit reasons, but prominent among these are his virtuous 'love of learning' (1–2, cf. 322), his concern for his ψυχή (soul) (5), and the 'impulse towards the καλόν (noble)' (6) which he shares with 'Aristeas'. History, and reading history, are now directed towards individual improvement. The prologue of *Ar.* has often been connected with certain trends in Hellenistic historiography, and we may be reminded, in particular, of Polybius' distinctions between types of potential reader and of the reasons why one might read history; one can read for pleasure or one can be, like Philokrates, φιλομαθής (fond of learning).[5] Like Thucydides' *History*, the programmatic chapters of which *Ar.* seems to echo,[6] and indeed like Polybius' *Histories*, *Ar.* is written with τὸ χρήσιμον (the useful) and τὸ ὠφέλιμον (the beneficial) in mind, but it is now what is 'useful' for the improvement of the individual mind and soul which is important. The encomium of *paideia* with which the prologue concludes tells us much about the world which produced *Ar*, and it is a world which is neither exclusively Greek nor exclusively Jewish: 'neither the charm of gold nor any other of the embellishments prized by the vainglorious confers as great benefit as education and attention devoted to culture'.[7]

Whether or not anything remotely like the events of the 'Letter' did indeed happen under Philadelphos (or indeed under any Ptolemy) is a matter of per-

---

4 Honigman 2003, 18.
5 Cf. esp. Polybius 7.7.8; for discussion and bibliography cf. Hunter 1994, 1070–1071.
6 Cf. below, pp. 820–821.
7 This and all subsequent translations are taken from Hadas 1951, modified where appropriate.

haps fiercer debate now than for a long time. It is easy enough to point to elements of the narrative which seem 'unhistorical' — thus, for example, there were very good reasons to include both Demetrios of Phaleron and Philadelphos, the two figures most closely connected with the legends of the Library, in the story of the translation, although most scholars accept that Demetrios' scholarly activity in Alexandria did not outlive Ptolemy I Soter[8] — but the historicity of the basic structure of the story remains a thornier problem. The linguistic and other arguments in favour of the historicity of some translation of Hebrew books into Greek in the first half of the third century are not to be lightly dismissed, and it cannot at any rate be doubted that translations existed by the middle of the second century. So too, the old view that, regardless of when the Hebrew scriptures were first translated into Greek, *Ar.* misrepresents the procedure at least in presenting it as driven by the concerns of, and conducted according to (a rather garbled version of) the scholarly protocols of, the royal Library, seems now less secure than it was; the translation was in fact, so the argument went, the initiative of the Alexandrian Jewish community. Broad consensus does, however, seem to have been reached that the translation (or translations) were the work of Jews resident in, and using the koine of, Egypt, rather than scholars shipped in from Palestine. The question of the initiative for the translation may, however, serve as a reminder of how easy it was for writers to construct history in terms of royal policy (or, in the language of *Ar.* and Hellenistic administration, royal *prohairesis* or *prothesis*) rather than within the framework of more messy social constructs. The practices of ancient bureaucracy in which decisions were inscribed on stone or papyrus as the personal decisions of kings will have helped this way of thinking about how things happen; so perhaps too will the systems of judicial administration prevalent in Ptolemaic Egypt. There is an important question here about what kind of socio-political structure, what kind of *polis* in fact, *Ar.* creates and to what extent this has resonance, beyond the work's own narrow concerns, into the wider Hellenistic world. Finally, the presentation of the interaction of Ptolemy and his courtiers and of the king's personal interest in the details of the Library's holdings takes us in different ways back towards the world of Herodotus and forwards (on the now standard chronology) to the 'historical novel' of Chariton and others. Students of Greek fiction have certainly paid too little attention to *Ar.*

Ar. is an imaginative reconstruction of, *inter alia*, Alexandria and the exercise of Alexandrian power in its heyday; it is often noted that the observation in ch. 28, 'these kings used to administer all their business through decrees and

---

[8] Cf., e.g., Honigman 2003, 88–90. The opposite case is fundamental to Collins 2000.

with great precaution; nothing was done negligently or casually', not only apparently ruptures the fiction of the work but also almost suggests a nostalgia for a time now lost. We can perhaps see here something of the origins of the shaping of history which was to culminate in Strabo's Augustan myth of an Egypt which was well administered by the first three Ptolemies, but was then ruined by a succession of kings given to excessive τρυφή (luxury), only to be restored to its former well administered glory by Augustus who put an end to 'drunken violence against Egypt' (17.1.11). For Strabo, Alexandria is 'the greatest supermarket (*emporion*) in the world' (17.1.13), a place to which all the riches both of Egypt and the rest of the world flow; so too, the import of cultures is central to *Ar.*'s imagining of Alexandria, as perhaps of any such imagining.[9] Alexandria as *cosmopolis*, as both the centre of the trade routes which cross the world and as itself a whole *kosmos* within a *polis*, is fundamental to standard ancient descriptions of the city,[10] and is of course built into the city's foundation legends (cf. e.g., *Alexander Romance* 1.32). Dio Chrysostom's famously double-edged encomium of the Alexandrians makes them by implication the true mercantile heirs of Alexander who control 'the whole *oikoumenē*' — their trade reaches even to the Indian Sea and 'the most remote tribes' (as did Alexander's conquests); the world is now a *polis* writ large: '[Alexandria] is like the *agora* of a single city which gathers all men into the same space, shows them to each other, and — as far as possible — makes them members of the same race (ὁμοφύλους)' (Dio 32.36).[11] It is perhaps not too anachronistic to see something very like this rhetoric informing the emphasis in *Ar.* on the intellectual, moral, and religious 'kinship' of Greeks and Jews (even if Jewish culture always remains one step ahead).

In *Ar.* Demetrios is given the wherewithal 'to bring together (συναγαγεῖν), if possible, all the books in the world' (9); this is the intellectual heritage of Alexander, just as the city's trade represented his mercantile heritage. Demetrios is however represented, not unreasonably, as being particularly concerned with books (such as the Jewish holy books) which 'deserve' a place in the Library; intellectual collection can never be divorced from selection and judgement.[12] So too, the High Priest worries about the safe return of the Jewish scholars because he knew 'how the king in his love of excellence regarded it as a very great gain,

---

9 Selden 1998 is in part a stimulating discussion of this.
10 Achilles Tatius 5.1 is the most sustained display of these paradoxes.
11 For other aspects of this passage cf. Trapp 2004.
12 A similar phenomenon is the shifting distinction between the interest of the Library and its scholars in *all* Greek books and their particular interest in those authors who came eventually to form the lists of 'the included' (helpful summary in Easterling 1996).

wherever he heard of a man surpassing others in culture and intellect, to summon him to himself' (124); the High Priest had heard that the King believed that 'by having about himself just and prudent men he would have the greatest protection for his kingdom, for friends frankly advise what is best' (125). The gathering of (the best) books and the gathering of wise men are thus parts of the same project, in more ways than one. These elements of what we might call 'the Alexandrian myth', such as we have seen it in, say, Dio Chrysostom, are in fact familiar from the earliest days. Callimachus' *Aitia* which gestures both towards a potential claim to embody 'all the rituals and stories of the world' and which demonstrates the inevitability of selection, is the key text here, both in its overall shape and in particular episodes. We may note, on the one hand, Pollis the Athenian's transplantation of Athenian rituals to Alexandria (fr. 178 Pfeiffer = 89 Massimilla),[13] a passage in which Alexandria, where the scene is all but certainly set, is again imagined as a place where everyone and every culture sooner or later washes up and is then preserved. On the other hand, we have the poet's insistence (fr. 43 Pfeiffer = 50 Massimilla) that the Muses fill in a gap in his otherwise pretty comprehensive knowledge of the foundation stories of the cities of Sicily: συμπλήρωσις — the filling in of gaps — is also what drives Demetrios' activities in the Library (cf. *Ar.* 29). Much has been written recently about how the Ptolemies' claim to be the true heirs to Alexander, and to the Greek heritage more generally, was bolstered not merely by their possession of Alexander's body (cf. Strabo 17.1.8) but also by their equally displayed cultural patronage, most visible in the institutions of the Museum and Library;[14] the politics of Ptolemaic cultural activity are now firmly on the scholarly agenda. Moreover, Ptolemy and his Library were not to be restricted to Greek culture — they were, again like Alexander himself, both discerning and potentially omnivorous.

Much has been written in recent years — some, but by no means all, stimulated by Foucault — about the organization of knowledge in historical societies and hence about the library as an image of the state or *kosmos* (Umberto Eco's *The Name of the Rose* is the best-known popularisation of the idea); classification and categorisation are needed not just for library books, but for the successful management of whole states. As for the Ptolemaic Library, 'there is something imperialist in the treatment of the books themselves', as Andrew Erskine put it.[15] The possessions of the Library, no less than Alexander's body

---

[13] For discussion and bibliography on this passage cf. Fantuzzi/Hunter 2004, 76–83; add now Dettori 2004, Kaesser 2005.
[14] Cf., e.g., Erskine 1995, Too 1998, 115–126, Maehler 2004, Whitmarsh 2004, 122–130.
[15] Erskine 1995, 45.

and Pollis' Attic rituals, required 'preservation', or (in the words of *Ar.*) 'royal care', πρόνοια βασιλική (30). Philadelphos' concern for the repair of books 'which had fallen into disrepair' (29) perhaps suggests that already here the Library is an image, or microcosm, of the whole state, which flourishes under the king's benevolent eye. Aspects of the presentation of the monarchy in *Ar.* may indeed remind us of Theocritus' 'Encomium for Philadelphos': numbers and stock counts matter to Philadelphos (*Ar.* 10, cf. Theocritus 17.82–84);[16] those he watches over 'go about their business in quiet', as Theocritus puts it (17.97), and he not only keeps safe the stock he inherited, but also adds to it (Theocritus 17.104–105). Collection is, moreover, not necessarily an end in itself: what is collected is to be used for the greater glory of the gods (or of God) and of the people under Philadelphos' control (Theocritus 17.106–111). As for Ptolemaic scholarship, the hallmark Alexandrian search for authentic, original texts, whether on book-hunting expeditions or through the arts of textual criticism, which is here extended to the translation of the Hebrew scriptures, speaks to the centralisation of power; not for Ptolemaic scholars of Greek literature the minefield of allegorical interpretation which might allow the creation of meaning 'at the point of reception' and hence offer space to a multiplicity of authoritative voices. Although the modes of Jewish exegesis on display in *Ar.* are very different, here too the Jewish scholars produce an agreed translation, and there is a very strong sense that the 'reading and clarification of each passage' (ἡ ἀνάγνωσις καὶ ἡ ἑκάστου διασάφησις, 305) led also to agreed 'meaning'; translation and interpretation cannot be separated. Just as no further change of any kind is to be permitted in the text (chapters 310–311), so interpretation has (to some extent at least) been closed down, which is of course very far from what actually happened in the history of the reception and understanding of Jewish scripture.

Later traditions invented, or at least elaborated, a predecessor for Ptolemy in this rôle: Peisistratos and/or his sons are said to have arranged for the production of an authoritative text of Homer at Athens and for its regular performance at the Panathenaia, and the tyrant is said to have been the first to establish a 'public library' at Athens. The reliability or otherwise of these accounts is not at issue here.[17] If some at least of this is a retrojection from later ages – and the very late story that Peisistratos established a group of 72 *grammatikoi* to produce his text of Homer is almost certainly influenced by the narrative of

---

16 Cf. Hunter 2003, 158.
17 The testimonia are gathered by Platthy 1968, 97–108. For arguments on both sides cf. Allen 1913, Merkelbach 1952, Davison 1955, Pfeiffer 1968, 6–8, Canfora 1987, 185–186.

Ptolemy and the translation of the Pentateuch[18] — the parallelism may offer some comfort that we are not completely on the wrong track in these interpretations of representations of Ptolemaic cultural policy. Peisistratos is thus imagined to have tried to 'own' (the genuine) Homer, who notoriously belonged to no individual city, and to have placed his prize possession at the heart of the principal display of Athenian identity and power, the Panathenaia; so, in the Alexandrian myth, Ptolemy tried to own all of Greek culture, though inevitably Homer, and the quest for the authentic text of the epics, took pride of place.

At one level, Alexandria was consciously fashioned as 'the new Athens',[19] as in its turn Rome was to be fashioned as 'the new Alexandria'. How the Athenian paradigm of autochthony was transmuted in a city where still potent historical memory denied the possibility of autochthony cannot be pursued here, but the idea of Alexandria as 'the new Athens' already informs Callimachus' description of Pollis' displaced rituals (above p. 815), as it seems clearly implied in *Ar.* by the rôle of Demetrios of Phaleron and the use, not just of Aristotelian traditions, but apparently also of specific Aristotelian texts.[20] The importance of Athenian institutions as models for the Museum and Library is well recognised, but how self-consciously that paradigm was elaborated is less clear. Thucydides makes Pericles declare to the Athenians that 'because of the size of [our] city everything arrives here from the whole world, and we have no freer enjoyment of our own splendid products than of those of other men' (2.38.2). The parallel with the encomia of Alexandria which we considered earlier may just be a rhetoric shared by all imperial cities, but it may also be something more. It is the 'funeral speech' of the Thucydidean Pericles which we also remember when reading the claim of Andron of Alexandria (first century BC?), as reported by Athenaeus, that 'the Alexandrians were the people who had educated all the Greeks and the barbarians, when general education (ἐγκύκλιος παιδεία) was disappearing because of the continuous disturbances which occurred in the period of the successors of Alexander' (*FGrHist* 246 F1 = Athenaeus 4.184b–c); the words of the Thucydidean Pericles, 'In summary, I declare that our whole city is an education (παίδευσις) for Greece…' (2.41), had already been echoed more than once by Isocrates.[21] The text of Athenaeus perhaps leaves uncertain whether Andron and

---

18 The story would illustrate a kind of reverse of the pattern for which Honigman 2003 argues in the case of the Hebrew Bible. A rival account had Peisistratos gathering together four wise men for this task.
19 Cf. Hunter 2003, 37.
20 Cf. Honigman 2003, 23–24 on the description of Jerusalem and Aristotle, *Politics* Book 7.
21 On these texts cf., e.g., Pfeiffer 1968, 252–253, Whitmarsh 2001, 7–9.

others imagined two periods in which Alexandria saved the *paideia* of the world — one under the early Ptolemies and the other (paradoxically) dating from the reign of Ptolemy VIII, whose expulsions of intellectuals fostered the growth of *paideia* all over the rest of the Greek world — but the link between political peace and 'culture' (understood very broadly) which underlies this historical narrative is one which we recognise from early Ptolemaic rhetoric, such as (again) Theocritus' *Encomium of Ptolemy Philadelphos*, and one which was to be taken over by Octavian/Augustus.

The question of what sort of imaginative reconstruction *Ar.* represents can hardly be divorced from questions of readership. Broadly speaking, the debate has been a tussle between a Greek readership and a Jewish one.[22] For those who favour the former, the point of *Ar.* is to introduce Greeks to Jewish culture and wisdom, both of which had won the admiration of so cultured a monarch as Philadelphos. If, on the other hand, the readership is primarily Jewish, the point will be to make clear that the Greek Bible (or a particular version of it) carries the same authority as the Hebrew scriptures themselves and that those who read only it, and not the Hebrew original, will not be missing anything important. The story of the translation and its subsequent public promulgation seems, on the one hand, to have been modelled on the *Exodus* story of the origin of the Hebrew Law itself;[23] on the other hand, most scholars now also stress the influence of the paradigm of Alexandrian Greek scholarship, and particularly scholarship on Homer. In her recent study, Sylvie Honigman stresses that the authority of the Greek Bible is commended in *Ar.* in much the same way as Aristarchus' text of Homer seems to have become 'canonical' within a very short time; both the Hebrew scriptures and the text of Homer are now 'corrected' (διηκριβωμένα, cf. *Ar.* 31, 310) and hence authoritative. Whatever we may think of this account of the dissemination of the Aristarchan edition, on any showing *Ar.*'s narrative of the process of translation does seem to make (rather confused) use of the Alexandrian scholarly practice, which was not of course a universal practice, of the comparison of different texts in order to arrive at the best, most authentic version;[24] the existing Hebrew texts have not yet been submitted to such collation, or, in the courtly phrase of Demetrios, 'they have not received royal attention' (*Ar.* 30). Here we might be tempted to think that *Ar.* has more than one audience in mind; Greek or Jewish paradigms can be emphasised in

---

22 Gruen 1998, 221 considers the matter now clearly decided in favour of a Jewish readership: 'those Gentiles who happened to read the work would not have found it particularly edifying'.
23 Cf., e.g., Orlinsky 1989, 542–548.
24 Zuntz 1959 is fundamental here.

accordance with the needs of different audiences.[25] The peculiar mixture of stemmatics and collective discussion, which is represented by shutting the Jewish scholars up on an island to get on with their business, looks to more than one set of exegetical practices.[26]

Similar conclusions may be drawn from the long episode of the sympotic instruction of Ptolemy by the Jewish sages.[27] The political questions posed by the king put flesh on the idea of Ptolemy as god's representative and reflection here on earth, an idea which was (*inter alia*) very powerful in Ptolemaic ideology[28] and in Hellenistic kingship theory more generally; 'as God benefits (εὖ ἐργάζεται) all men, so you, in imitation of Him, benefit those under you' (281, cf. 190) is as clear a statement as one could wish. Some of what the sages advise the king hardly differs from, say, what Pindar advises Hieron or the terms in which Theocritus praises Ptolemy,[29] and no reader, Greek or Jewish, is going to find material for surprise here. Some bits of the sages' advice even sound like Greek gnomic wisdom; μὴ πολλῶν ὀρέγου, 'do not aim for [too] much' (211), τῶν ἀνεφίκτων μὴ ἐπεθύμει, 'do not desire the unreachable' (223). Philadelphos is, moreover, certainly depicted as *sympotikos*, if not in quite the same way as in other texts (cf. Theocritus 14.60–64); he is even depicted as a Plutarch before his time – concerned with the appropriate conduct of symposia (286). Be that as it may, the whole episode reveals a union of philosophical, religious and political power which works to confirm both Philadelphos and the sages in their respective, and inter-connected, spheres. Other ways of writing such a scene were certainly available. We may contrast Philostratus' later account, written at a time when history provided more than one model of a 'bad king', of a dinner of the Indian sages which was attended both by Apollonius of Tyana and by the local Indian king, who used to consult the sages on all matters.[30] Philostratus

---

[25] I am conscious that this observation is not too far from one modern view, particularly associated with scholars such as Ludwig Koenen, Susan Stephens, and Dan Selden, of how Egyptian motifs, or what are alleged to be such, resonate in Alexandrian Greek poetry.
[26] Honigman's claim (2003, 46–47) that this collective enterprise would rather have recalled the work of 'Alexandrian grammarians' seems at best doubtful; Greek scholars notoriously worked alone and notoriously quarrelled with each other.
[27] Cf. esp. Murray 1967.
[28] Cf. Hunter 2003, 94–95.
[29] With the stress on justice (193, 209, 212, 291 etc.) cf. *Pythian* 1.86; with the importance of benefactions and the proper use of wealth (205, 226) cf. *Pythian* 1.91; with the importance of truthfulness (206) cf. *Pythian* 1.87.
[30] It is perhaps noteworthy that Murray 1967, 347 n. 3 compared Alexander's interview with the gymnosophists to the sympotic narrative of *Ar*.

depicts the king as someone who does not know how to behave at symposia (he drinks too much. *Life of Apollonius* 3.30.1) and as someone who is too self-important to take advantage of the presence of such wise men; Philadelphos, by contrast, is the model of an enlightened king who constantly seeks self-improvement.

I have labelled *Ar.* an 'imaginative reconstruction', and that would seem to imply a view about how it was regarded by its first readers (whoever they were). The status of *Ar.*'s claims to truth has always been at the heart of modern argument about the nature of the work. Sylvie Honigman argues that *Ar.* does indeed present a 'true' account, but that we have to understand that truth, reasonably enough, within the conventions of Hellenistic historiography and rhetoric. For what it is worth, my impression is that there is a rather uneasy conjunction in Honigman's book between this perfectly proper emphasis on historiographical and rhetorical convention and the idea (owed to Oswyn Murray) of *Ar.* as a 'charter myth'. Be that as it may, what exactly is it that we are being asked to believe, and what is supposed to be the nature of that 'belief'? Is it just the basic story of a translation conducted by the best Jewish scholars in the time of Philadelphos? If it is true that *Ar.*'s first readers were 'highly educated Alexandrian Jews',[31] then we might be loath to accept that they will have regarded much of the work as 'historically true' in any meaningful sense. Much modern discussion seems to credit the readers of *Ar.* with very few critical reading skills, and appeals to repeated characteristics of 'Hellenistic (or Alexandrian) Jewish literature' only defer the problem;[32] readers understand 'conventions' as well as authors do. Appeals to 'plausibility' cut both ways (and Chariton might (again) be a key text for comparison here). The presentation of the dealings of Philadelphos and Demetrios is a brilliant evocation of how civil servants work — if you want something done you have to make the boss believe that it was his idea — but why should we, or anyone, give this narrative any more credit than Chariton's picture of the dealings of the Great King of Persia with his chief eunuch? Appeals to the practices of Hellenistic historiography do not allow us to evade the central question: what sort of a narrative is this? Here is where the recent outpouring of work on Greek and Latin narrative and fiction allows the hope of future progress in the case of *Ar.* also.

---

31 Honigman 2003, 29.
32 Cf. Johnson 2004, xii–xiii on how such texts 'persistently combine historical verisimilitude with patent fiction without betraying the least awareness of contradiction or absurdity'.

Ar. begins and closes with what look like allusions to Thucydides and Thucydidean ideals:[33] the matter is ἀξιόλογον, 'worthy of record' (cf. Thucydides 1.1.1) and the account will be σαφής (clear and true) and 'useful' (cf. Thucydides 1.22.3–4). It is hard not to think of Thucydides again when the author tells Philokrates that (almost paradoxically) he will get more 'pleasure' from *Ar.* than from the 'books of the *mythologoi* (322, cf. Thucydides 1.21.1, 1.22.3–4). That the Thucydidean allusions are not generally recognised may be attributed both to a sense that the author of *Ar.* had, in Oswyn Murray's words, 'little interest in classical Greek literature'.[34] and to the fact that Thucydidean ideals had long since become part of the fabric and common language of historiographical rhetoric and thus to some extent divorced from their origins; we may again think of Polybius. The claims to 'truth' which these Thucydidean allusions would seem to reinforce are nowhere stronger than in the passage which closes the account of the king's questioning of the wise men at a series of banquets:

> I suppose that everyone likely to get hold of this account will find it incredible. But to falsify concerning matters extant in writing is not what one should do; indeed, if I were to pass over any point, it would be an impiety in a subject of this sort. But I describe (διασαφοῦμεν) the event exactly as it happened (ὡς γέγονεν), solemnly acquitting myself of all error. Accordingly I endeavoured to procure particulars of what transpired from those persons who transcribe the proceedings (ἕκαστα τῶν γινομένων) at the king's audiences and in his banquets, so impressed was I with the power of [the sages'] discourse. For it is the custom, as you surely are aware, to record in writing everything said and done from the moment the king begins to give audience until he retires to bed — a good and useful practice. On the day following, before audiences commence, the actions taken and the remarks uttered on the previous day are read through and if any procedure is incorrectly recorded it receives rectification (διόρθωσις). As I have said, then, I obtained accurate information on all particulars from the archives, and have recorded it in writing because I know how you cherish useful learning.
>
> *Letter of Aristeas* 296–300

Here again we have a Thucydidean concern with offering a clear account of 'what actually happened', together with a Thucydidean painstakingness for finding this out; the language of detail, ἕκαστα τῶν γινομένων, picks up a language of historiography (and epic poetry) familiar from Aristotle onwards.[35] The appeal to written records offers a form of 'authorising fiction ('Beglaubigung-

---

33 Here, in particular, I have benefited from, but unwisely disregarded, the proper scepticism of the Edinburgh audience, particularly Robin Lane Fox.
34 Murray 1987, 22.
35 Cf. Hunter 2005, 159–162.

sapparat')', which however is ambiguous in its implications.³⁶ It is not, I hope, irreverent to be reminded of the scene between Peisetairos and the oracle-monger in Aristophanes' *Birds* (λαβὲ τὸ βιβλίον); 'if you don't believe me, go and consult the records' is a challenge which few readers are likely to take up. 'I know that what I have written will seem incredible' may be a device for emphasising the truth of the account,³⁷ an instance of protesting too much, or a rather cheeky piece of self-knowingness. It is perhaps helpful to remember Lucian's protestations in the *True Histories*, particularly in his account of life on the moon: 'I am reluctant to tell you about the eyes [of the moon-people], lest someone think that I am lying because the account seems incredible…anyone who does not believe that this is a true account, will realise that I am speaking the truth if ever he himself gets to the moon' (1.25–26).

What in fact places *Ar.* firmly in the mainstream of Greek Hellenistic prose is its knowing anxiety about genre; it is a work filled with 'effects of the real', one of which of course is the simple fact that it is structured as an address to a single individual, and the history of its reception shows just how convincing (and how distracting) those effects have been. Here, as much as anywhere, it is a Hellenistic creation, as it also calls into creation a Hellenistic world of the imagination.

Bibliography

Allen, T.W. 1913. 'Pisistratus and Homer', *CQ* 7, 33–51.
Birnhaum, E. 2004. 'Portrayals of the wise and virtuous in Alexandrian Jewish works; Jews' perception of themselves and others', in: W.V. Harris/G. Ruffini (eds.), *Ancient Alexandria between Egypt and Greece*, Leiden/Boston, 125–160.
Calabi, F. 1995. *Lettera di Aristea a Filocrate*, Milan.
Canfora, L. 1987. *The Vanished Library*, London.
Carleton Paget, J. 2004. 'Jews and Christians in ancient Alexandria from Ptolemies to Caracalla', in: A. Hirst/M. Silk (eds.), *Alexandria, Real and Imagined*, Aldershot, Hants, 143–166.
Collins, N.L. 2000. *The Library in Alexandria and the Bible in Greek*, Leiden.
Davison, J.A. 1955. 'Peisistratus and Homer', *TAPA* 86, 1–21.
Dettori, E. 2004. 'Appunti sul "Banchetto di Pollis" (Call. fr. 178 Pf.)', in: R. Pretagostini/E. Dettori (eds.), *La cultura ellenistica. L'opera letteraria e l'esegesi antica*, Rome, 33–63.
Easterling, E. 1996. 'Canon', in: S. Hornblower/A. Spawforth (eds.), *The Oxford Classical Dictionary*, 3rd ed., Oxford, 286.

---

36 I hope that it does not need saying that the historical reality of the courtly practice described in these chapters for the time of Philadelphos is not what is at issue here.
37 Cf. the phrases studied by Stinton 1976.

Erskine, A. 1995. 'Culture and power in Ptolemaic Egypt: The Museum and Library of Alexandria', *Greece & Rome* 42, 38–48.
Fantuzzi, M./Hunter, R.L. 2004. *Tradition and Innovation in Hellenistic Poetry*, Cambridge.
Fraser, P.M. 1972. *Ptolemaic Alexandria*, Oxford.
Gruen, E.S. 1998. *Heritage and Hellenism*, Berkeley.
Hadas, M. 1951. *Aristeas to Philocrates (Letter of Aristeas)*, New York.
Hirst, A./Silk, M. (eds.) 2004. *Alexandria, Real and Imagined*, Aldershot, Hants.
Honigman, S. 2003. *The Septuagint and Homeric Scholarship in Alexandria*, London.
Hunter, R.L. 1994. 'History and historicity in the romance of Chariton', in: W. Haase/H. Temporini (eds.), *Aufstieg und Niedergang der romischen Welt II* 34.2, Berlin/New York, 1055–1086 [Hunter 2008, 737–774].
Hunter, R.L. 2003. *Theocritus. Encomium of Ptolemy Philadelphus*, Berkeley.
Hunter, R.L. 2005. 'Generic consciousness in the Orphic *Argonautica*', in: M. Paschalis (ed.), *Roman and Greek Imperial Epic*, Rethymnon, 149–168 [= Hunter 2008, 681–699].
Hunter, R.L. 2008. *On Coming After. Studies in Post-Classical Greek literature and its reception*, Berlin/New York.
Johnson, S.R. 2004. *Historical Fictions and Hellenistic Jewish Identity*, Berkeley.
Kaesser, C. 2005. 'The poet and the "polis": the *Aetia* as didactic poem', in: M. Horster/C. Reitz (eds.), *Wissensvermittlung in dichterischer Gestalt*, Stuttgart, 95–114.
Maehler, H. 2004. 'Alexandria, the Mouseion, and cultural identity', in: A. Hirst/M. Silk (eds.), *Alexandria, Real and Imagined*, Aldershot, Hants, 95–114.
Merkelbach, R. 1952. 'Die pisistratische Redaktion der homerischen Gedichte', *Rheinisches Museum* 95, 23–37.
Murray, O. 1967. 'Aristeas and Ptolemaic Kingship', *Journal of Theological Studies* 18, 337–371.
Murray, O. 1987. 'The Letter of Aristeas', in: B. Virgilio (ed.), *Studi ellenistici*, II, Pisa, 15–29.
Orlinsky, H.M. 1989. 'The Septuagint and its Hebrew text', in: W.D. Davies/L. Finkelstein (eds.), *The Cambridge History of Judaism*, II, Cambridge, 534–562.
Pallatier, A. 1962. *Lettre d'Aristée à Philocrate*, Paris.
Pfeiffer, R. 1968. *History of Classical Scholarship*, Oxford.
Platthy, J. 1968. *Sources on the Earliest Greek Libraries*, Amsterdam.
Selden, D. 1998. 'Alibis', *Classical Antiquity* 17, 289–412.
Shutt, R.J.H. 1985. 'Letter of Aristeas', in: J.H. Charlesworth (ed.), *The Old Testament Pseudepigrapha*, Vol. 2, London 7–34.
Stinton, T.C.W. 1976. '"Si credere dignum est": some expressions in disbelief in Euripides and others', *PCPS* 22, 60–89 [= *Collected Papers on Greek Tragedy*, Oxford 1990, 236–264].
Too, Y.L. 1998. *The Idea of Ancient Literary Criticism*, Oxford.
Trapp, M.B. 2004. 'Images of Alexandria in the writings of the Second Sophistic', in: A. Hirst/M. Silk (eds.), *Alexandria, Real and Imagined*, Aldershot, Hants, 113–132.
Whitmarsh, T. 2001. *Greek Literature and the Roman Empire*, Oxford.
Whitmarsh, T. 2004. *Ancient Greek Literature*, Cambridge.
Zuntz, G. 1959. 'Aristeas studies II: Aristeas on the translation of the Torah', *Journal of Semitic Studies* 4, 109–126 [= *Opuscula Selecta* (Manchester 1972), 126–143].

41 Pulling Apollo Apart

(co-author Rebecca Laemmle)

Introduction

Despite much scholarly effort there is no modern consensus on the etymology of either Ἀπόλλων or Φοῖβος,[1] and in antiquity too no member of the Olympian pantheon seems to have offered so fertile a stimulus to the very different ancient practices of etymologising. Texts from all periods of classical antiquity bear eloquent witness to how the god's two principal names fed the etymologising impulse. In this paper we consider two particularly important moments of ancient etymologising about the god. The first is Socrates' account of the god's name in Plato's *Cratylus*, to which all subsequent ancient discussions of the matter are indebted; this text both has a special, foundational importance for the subject and also looks back to, and subsumes within itself, the rich tradition of etymological play in pre-Platonic poetry. The second text with which we shall be concerned is part of Plutarch's essay *The E at Delphi*, a later (Platonising) text which, like the *Cratylus*, gives full rein to the breadth of Apollo's spheres of activity, while also emphasising the essential and unchanging nature of the god. Our concern is what these texts can tell us, not just about the practice of ancient etymologising, but about how Apollo himself was imagined, what, in other words, both he and his name 'meant'.[2] As the choice of the Plutarchan text suggests, moreover, an important focus will be on μαντική, the Apolline art which will prove both close to and illustrative of the practices of ancient etymologising; if Apollo is not quite the 'god of etymology' as he is the 'god of prophecy', the analogy will prove not untrue to his significance for the ancient investigation of the meaning of words.

In the course of this paper we shall often have occasion to refer to 'explicit' etymology. By this we mean, as is in fact common usage, not merely the expla-

---

[1] The dictionaries of Frisk, Chantraine and Beekes all class the etymologies of both Ἀπόλλων and Φοῖβος as 'unerklärt', 'inconnue' etc. Burkert 1975 was a very influential intervention in the debate about the etymology of Ἀπόλλων, cf. Heubeck 1987, Nagy 2004. On the practice of etymology in antiquity cf. Sluiter 2015 and Most 2016, both with further bibliography. Sluiter 2015 is an important discussion of the etymologies of Apollo in the *Cratylus*, but her focus is different from ours.
[2] We are very conscious that the present discussion is the tip of an iceberg — Stoic etymologising of the god's name, for example, would occupy a long paper by itself.

nations of words found in the etymological lexica which survive from late antiquity and the Byzantine period, but also passages of classical texts in which an etymology is clearly marked or pointed out, standardly through one of a familiar set of adverbs (ὀρθῶς etc.) and/or linguistic markers (γάρ etc.) denoting causality.³ Although the nature of our evidence, with prose only coming into the picture in the fifth century, imposes caution, there is much which suggests a link between the growth of such 'explicit' etymologising and the linguistic and anthropological interests of some of the leading figures of the fifth-century sophistic movement. Such a link would fit nicely, for example, with the impression that, in what survives of Attic tragedy, 'explicit' etymologising is more common in Euripides than in Aeschylus or Sophocles.⁴ In the wake of these fifth-century developments, Plato's *Cratylus*, or rather the way in which it was read in antiquity, played a crucial role in establishing something like an equation between 'explicit' etymology and etymology *tout court*, an equation which still exerts a hold over modern discussions of ancient practice; we shall return to this at the end. That classical texts from Homer onwards, however, are also full of 'implicit' etymologising or 'etymological play' of a richness that defies systematic cataloguing is too well known to require demonstration, and it will become clear that this is no less true of the *Cratylus*, in which Socrates' 'explicit' etymologies are only one part of the extraordinary linguistic texture of the dialogue. What is most important in fact — as scholarship has indeed increasingly recognized — is not to fetishise the difference between 'explicit' and 'implicit' etymologising (of all kinds) in the interpretation of ancient texts; to do so misrepresents something important about the ancient etymological project.

Socrates' Apollo

The account of Apollo's name in the *Cratylus* (404c5–406a4)⁵ competes with the discussion (403a5–405b4) of Hades, where all of us are destined to dwell longest, for the honour of being the longest of Socrates' discussions of individual divine names. Apollo, however, certainly wins in terms of the number of etymologies offered: whereas Socrates discusses only two etymologies for Ἅιδης, an allegedly common one from ἀ-ιδ-, 'unseen', 'hidden from view', and the one

---

3 Cf., e.g., below on A. *Ag.* 1082.
4 For a particularly pointed 'Apolline' etymology in Euripides cf. *Phaethon* fr. 781.11–13 Kannicht (= 224–226 Diggle). On etymologising in Euripides more generally cf., e.g., Van Looy 1973, Segal 1982.
5 Cf. Sluiter 2015, 896–922.

Socrates adduces from εἰδέναι (404b3), he offers at least four (or five) explicit etymologies of Ἀπόλλων, corresponding to the god's four functions (δυνάμεις), in a discussion marked by a striking ring composition (404e1 ~ 405e4):[6]

ἰατρική	ἀπολούων and ἀπολύων
μαντική	ἁπλοῦν[7]
τοξική	ἀεὶ βάλλων
μουσική	ὁμοπολῶν

Beyond these explicit etymologies, the introductory section of the discussion, where Apollo is first brought in alongside Pherrephatta, twice clearly points to, but avoids spelling out the ill-omen of, another well-established etymology of Ἀπόλλων from ἀπόλλυμι or related forms; Socrates will again allude to (and reject) this etymological connection at the conclusion of his discussion of the name of Apollo (405e4). The very same words which evoke this dangerous etymology (πολλοὶ μὲν καὶ τοῦτο φοβοῦνται τὸ ὄνομα [sc. Φερρέφατταν] καὶ τὸν Ἀπόλλω, 404c5-6, and περὶ τὸν Ἀπόλλω ... πολλοὶ πεφόβηνται περὶ τὸ ὄνομα τοῦ θεοῦ, 404d8-e2) moreover hint at yet another, and again very common, etymological explanation of the god's name as ἀ-πολύς, 'not many/much'. πολλοὶ φοβοῦνται/ πεφόβηνται might in fact suggest Φοῖβος Ἀπόλλων, particularly to anyone familiar with a verse such as Homer, *Iliad* 17.118: θεσπέσιον γάρ σφιν φόβον ἔμβαλε Φοῖβος Ἀπόλλων, 'Phoebus Apollo cast indescribable fear into them'. How 'etymological' a hearer or reader do you have to be *not* to hear φόβον ἔμβαλε resonate against Φοῖβος Ἀπόλλων here?[8] One reader of Homer at least, and one with a very sharp eye for etymology, namely Eustathius, recognised παρήχησις between φόβος and Φοῖβος (note on *Il.* 17.118, *Hom.* 1098.9).[9] The etymology in the *Cratylus* of Ἀπόλλων as archer-god (< ἀεὶ βάλλων) suggests that the similarity between -πόλλων and βάλλων was easy enough to feel in

---

6 Cf. Sluiter 2015, 913.
7 Sedley 2003, 95 suggests that this etymology is itself double and that in τὸ ἀληθές τε καὶ τὸ ἁπλοῦν at 405c2 the first syllable of ἀληθές is also involved in the etymology. We are sympathetic to this view, although it is not confirmed in the summary at 406a2 and it was the etymology from ἁπλοῦν which was to be remembered by the subsequent tradition. Sluiter 2015, 914 adopts the traditional view. Cf. further below.
8 For Phoibos/Apollo and φόβος cf. also Hom. *Il.* 15.326-327, ὡς ἐφόβηθεν Ἀχαιοὶ ἀνάλκιδες· ἐν γὰρ Ἀπόλλων / ἧκε φόβον, Τρωσὶν δὲ καὶ Ἕκτορι κῦδος ὄπαζεν.
9 Rank 1951, 71–72 notes the sound-play between φόβος and Φοῖβος in this Homeric verse, but without reference to Eustathius or comment on -βαλε ~ -πόλλων. For another such paronomastic play of φόβος and Φοῖβος cf. A. *Pers.* 205–206 (within an account of a bird-omen).

antiquity.¹⁰ We will return at the end to what such examples can teach us about etymological readings.

The discussion of 'Apollo' in the *Cratylus*, then, pullulates with etymologies. This god is, of course, far from unique in the multiplicity of his etymologies and indeed, as David Sedley put it, 'the most highly vaunted etymologies [in the *Cratylus*] are ... those which identify two or more co-existent meanings in the same word'.¹¹ Nevertheless, it is important to note that no other name or word in the *Cratylus* is given the number of etymologies with which the name of Apollo is honoured. There may, however, seem to be a tension between the Platonic etymology of Ἀπόλλων in connection with μαντική as 'single' (ἁπλοῦν) and the multiplicity of etymologies, but that tension will in fact reveal something important about the god and about the field of language in which both prophecy and etymology move.

In considering the etymologising of Apollo in the *Cratylus*, it is indeed the field of language with which we must begin. Whereas Socrates asserts that the name of mantic Apollo proclaims his truthfulness, it is above all Hermes and his son Pan, who are associated with the mutability and potential deceptiveness of language:

ΣΩ. Καὶ τό γε τὸν Πᾶνα τοῦ Ἑρμοῦ εἶναι υἱὸν διφυῆ ἔχει τὸ εἰκός, ὦ ἑταῖρε.
EPM. Πῶς δή;
ΣΩ. Οἶσθα ὅτι ὁ λόγος τὸ πᾶν σημαίνει καὶ κυκλεῖ καὶ πολεῖ ἀεί, καὶ ἔστι διπλοῦς, ἀληθής τε καὶ ψευδής.
EPM. Πάνυ γε.
ΣΩ. Οὐκοῦν τὸ μὲν ἀληθὲς αὐτοῦ λεῖον καὶ θεῖον καὶ ἄνω οἰκοῦν ἐν τοῖς θεοῖς, τὸ δὲ ψεῦδος κάτω ἐν τοῖς πολλοῖς τῶν ἀνθρώπων καὶ τραχὺ καὶ τραγικόν· ἐνταῦθα γὰρ πλεῖστοι οἱ μῦθοί τε καὶ τὰ ψεύδη ἐστίν, περὶ τὸν τραγικὸν βίον.
EPM. Πάνυ γε.
ΣΩ. Ὀρθῶς ἄρ' ἂν ὁ πᾶν μηνύων καὶ ἀεὶ πολῶν Πὰν αἰπόλος εἴη, διφυὴς Ἑρμοῦ υἱός, τὰ μὲν ἄνωθεν λεῖος, τὰ δὲ κάτωθεν τραχὺς καὶ τραγοειδής. καὶ ἔστιν ἤτοι λόγος ἢ

---

10 That Φοῖβος is not apparently connected with φόβος in what survives of explicit ancient etymologising is not a strong argument against the clear resonances in Plato's text. There have, in fact, been modern attempts to derive Φοῖβος from φόβος, cf. Schmid 1923–1924, Kretschmer 1927, 199.

11 Sedley 2003, 36; cf. also Sluiter 2015, 912 on the 'simultaneously true' etymologies of Apollo's name in the *Cratylus*. The account of Socrates' discussion of Apollo's name in Trivigno 2012, 47–49 seems to suffer from a misunderstanding of the nature and purpose of ancient etymologising: he finds the etymologies 'particularly implausible' and suggests that their very number shows that Apollo is 'certainly not *simple* [emphasis original] but varied and complex'. For Trivigno 2012, 54 it is 'impossible' that 'all of these etymologies are jointly *correct*' [emphasis original], and we are offered no way of 'choosing amongst competing etymologies'.

λόγου ἀδελφὸς ὁ Πάν, εἴπερ Ἑρμοῦ υἱός ἐστιν· ἀδελφῷ δὲ ἐοικέναι ἀδελφὸν οὐδὲν θαυμαστόν.[12]

Soc. And it is indeed reasonable, my friend, that Pan is the double-natured son of Hermes?
Herm. How so?
Soc. You know that *logos* signifies everything and circulates and is forever on the move and it is double, both true and false.
Herm. Yes indeed.
Soc. So, the true part of it is smooth and divine and lives up there with the gods. The false part, however, lives down among the mass of men and is rough and *tragikon*; for here are the majority of myths and falsehoods, in the *tragikos* life.
Herm. Yes indeed.
Soc. So the one who bears witness to everything and is always on the move would correctly be 'Pan *aipolos* [goatherd]', the double-natured son of Hermes, in his upper parts smooth, but down below rough and in the form of a goat [*tragoeides*]. And Pan is either *logos* or the brother of *logos*, if he is the son of Hermes; it is nothing remarkable if brother should resemble brother.

Pan, it is claimed, is the son of Hermes ('he who created speech', 408b1), and as such he is either the brother of *logos* or *logos* itself. The statement that 'speech signifies everything' (ὁ λόγος τὸ πᾶν σημαίνει) seems to facilitate the identification of *logos* with Pan,[13] whose name also 'means everything', as is explicitly spelled out already in the (almost certainly 5th century) *Homeric Hymn to Pan*:[14]

...πάντες δ' ἄρα θυμὸν ἔτερφθεν
ἀθάνατοι, περίαλλα δ' ὁ Βάκχειος Διόνυσος·
Πᾶνα δέ μιν καλέεσκον, ὅτι φρένα πᾶσιν ἔτερψεν.[15]

...and all the immortals were delighted in their hearts, and most of all Bacchic Dionysus; and they called him Pan, because he delighted the hearts of all.

τραγικός, the epithet which Socrates particularly associates with Pan, is echoed later in the text in connection with the history of language, when Socrates observes that the first words have been buried under later interventions, which he subsumes under the term τραγῳδεῖν:

---

12 Pl. *Cra.* 408b6–d4.
13 The identification is perhaps also punningly confirmed by Hermogenes' repeated πάνυ γε, in response to claims about the near-identity of Πάν and *logos*. It is tempting to see in this effect also an allusion to Pan's erotic connection to Echo, but that is not certainly attested before Hellenistic poetry.
14 On the *Homeric Hymn to Pan* see Thomas 2011 (with 169–172 on the date).
15 h.Pan. 45–47.

ΣΩ. Ὦ μακάριε, οὐκ οἶσθ' ὅτι τὰ πρῶτα ὀνόματα τεθέντα κατακέχωσται ἤδη ὑπὸ τῶν βουλομένων τραγῳδεῖν αὐτά, περιτιθέντων γράμματα καὶ ἐξαιρούντων εὐστομίας ἕνεκα καὶ πανταχῇ στρεφόντων καὶ ὑπὸ καλλωπισμοῦ καὶ ὑπὸ χρόνου.[16]

Soc. My friend, do you not know that the words which were first given have long since been covered over by those who wished to *tragōidein* them; they add and subtract letters for the sake of euphony and distort the words in every way both to prettify them and through the passage of time.

Logos/Pan is constantly 'on the move' (πολεῖ ἀεί), and ἀεὶ πολῶν becomes the explanation of the second part of his full name, Pan Aipolos. Both Pan's name and his epithets change before our eyes: Pan evolves into Pan Aipolos, and τραγικός shifts between 'goatlike' and 'tragic'. In this persistent mobility Pan really does embody *logos*: words (λόγος) change over time — not only Heracliteans might say that they are in constant flux — and their true meaning is distorted, often beyond recognition, whether deliberately or simply through the 'natural' lapse of time.[17]

In the *Cratylus*, Logos/Pan's διπλοῦν nature casts him in opposition to Apollo, whose prophecy is ἁπλοῦν (405c2), as also does his lower, τραγικόν half, which is ψευδές; Pan's upper, divine half, however, which is emphatically ἀληθές,[18] shows, on the other hand, a marked overlap with the mantic and truthful Apollo. This is reflected in the tantalising explanation of his epithet αἰπόλος which combines two words which, in isolation, are also parts of Apollo's etymologies in the *Cratylus* (ἀεί from ἀεὶ βάλλων, πολῶν from ὁμο-πολῶν).[19] Here is a crucial way in which the mantic art and etymologising, as we see it in the *Cratylus*, overlap. Words change and/or may be used in shifting, ambiguous ways, but it is etymology which, it is claimed, reveals the settled truths that lie

---

16 Pl. *Cra.* 414c4–7.
17 It is noteworthy that three other etymologies in the *Cratylus* combine ἀεί and ῥεῖν – ἀήρ (410b2), ἀρετή (415d), αἰσχρόν (416b3–5) — in accordance with the Heraclitean theory discussed in the dialogue.
18 Cf. further below. Callimachus too seems to play with an opposition, both real and etymological, between Apollo and Pan in the *Hymn to Apollo* (vv. 9 and 110).
19 Similarly, the address to the sun at Timotheus, *PMG* 800 as τὸν ἀεὶ πόλον ... λαμπραῖς ἀκτῖσ' Ἥλιε βάλλων, seems to evoke Apollo's name through the juxtaposition of ἀεὶ πόλον, cf. Hunter 1986, 59. For the evidence for the identification of Apollo and the sun in classical texts cf. Pfeiffer on Call. fr. 302; Diggle 1970, 147. In the *Cratylus*, Socrates makes no explicit link between Apollo and Helios, in part apparently because he wishes to associate the principal heavenly bodies with flux and cosmic change (cf. Sedley 2003, 105–106), which are so notably absent from the Apolline etymologies. One of Socrates' etymologies for Ἅλιος / Ἥλιος is ἀεὶ εἰλεῖν and another is αἰολεῖν, which is glossed as ποικίλλειν (409a1–5).

behind language, truths impervious to the changes and distortions of time, just as the mantic art understands the past and the present and the future, even if the language in which it is expressed may be ambiguous and hard to comprehend. The apparent paradox which the Platonic Socrates parades is thus intended to provoke thought about the nature of the god. Apollo has no share in falsehood or constant movement and shifting; rather, as we shall see at greater length in Plutarch, the god is very often associated with an established and eternal (ἀεί) order, and one which resists both the multiplicity and the change which characterise Pan. Etymology, at least as it is on show in the *Cratylus* and the subsequent tradition which was so heavily indebted to Plato, explains settled verities which may be hidden behind the distortions which language undergoes: so too, Apollo himself is *always* healer, prophet, archer and musician.[20]

The association of Apollo with truth was long established; Pindar had declared of the god's all-knowing mind:

> ψευδέων δ' οὐχ ἅπτεται, κλέπτει τέ μιν
> οὐ θεὸς οὐ βροτὸς ἔργοις οὔτε βουλαῖς.[21]

[Apollo's mind] has nothing to do with falsehoods, and no god or immortal deceives him in actions or words.

Elsewhere, the Platonic Socrates too insists, though in more than one tone of commitment or irony, on the god's unswerving truthfulness (cf., e.g., Pl. *Ap.* 21b 6–7, *R.* 2.383a8–c5 on A. fr. 350 Radt). Socrates' nonchalant equation in the *Cratylus* ('they are the same thing') of τὸ ἀληθές and τὸ ἁπλοῦν (405c2–3),[22] bound together by τε καί to confirm the equation linguistically, is also knowingly disingenuous. Nevertheless, whatever Socrates' tone here, Plato may already be 'pythagorising', as he is clearly about to do with his discussion of μουσική:[23] at least subsequently, but presumably earlier as well, Apollo was associated by Pythagoreans with the number One (e.g. Plu. *Isis and Osiris* 381f, cf. 393c), and despite Plato's appeal to the Thessalian term Ἅπλουν for the god (*Cra.* 405c4), the etymology from ἁπλοῦν very likely implicitly reflects the ἀ + πολλ-

---

[20] These certainties are reflected, for example, in the pronouncements of the newborn god in the *Homeric Hymn to Apollo* (vv. 131–132) and in the *in utero* prophecy of the Callimachean god at *Hymn to Delos* (vv. 162–195).

[21] Pi. *P*.3.29–30. Pindar is here so emphatic in part because he is implicitly rejecting the Hesiodic story of how a raven informed Apollo of Coronis' betrayal: the scholia amusingly call the story of the raven 'complete nonsense' (τέλεον ... ληρώδης, II 70 Drachmann).

[22] Cf. Sluiter 2015, 914.

[23] Cf. Burkert 1962, 75–76.

etymology to which the beginning of the passage has already alluded. Given the importance of Apollo for Pythagoras, who himself bore a markedly Apolline name and who at least later was believed to have been interested in name-giving and perhaps also etymology,[24] there was no god for whom such 'pythagorising' etymology was more appropriate. μαντική and oracular utterance are indeed associated with Socrates' etymological operations in the dialogue itself (*Cra.* 396d–e, 411b4, 428c6–7),[25] and at the beginning even Cratylus' attempts at etymologising are referred to as μαντεία (384a5). Although these passages have given rise to much discussion of Plato's potential debt to the religious 'expert' Euthyphro, they are usually passed over as playful jests, which of course they in part are. The undeniable playfulness, however, should not stop us from asking what might lie behind the teasing. The presentation of, and attitudes to, μαντική and divination in the Platonic corpus are in fact very diverse,[26] but their association with etymology seems to have been no passing whim.

μαντική itself has a familiar place in the history of Greek etymology. In Euripides' *Bacchae*, Teiresias, an Apolline μάντις, but here speaking on behalf (and perhaps under the power) of Dionysus, associates the term with μανία, an association which modern etymology confirms:

μάντις δ' ὁ δαίμων ὅδε· τὸ γὰρ βακχεύσιμον
καὶ τὸ μανιῶδες μαντικὴν πολλὴν ἔχει·
ὅταν γὰρ ὁ θεὸς ἐς τὸ σῶμ' ἔλθῃ πολύς,
λέγειν τὸ μέλλον τοὺς μεμηνότας ποιεῖ.[27]

This god is also a seer (*mantis*), for the bacchic and the manic contain prophetic powers (*mantike*) in large measure. Whenever the god enters with force into someone's body, he causes those who have been maddened to tell the future.

In a famous passage of Socrates' 'palinode' in the *Phaedrus*, Socrates makes much of the link between μανία and μαντική, as he sets out the benefits which, through divine gift, μανία has brought to mankind, for μανία is not an evil 'pure and simple' (ἁπλοῦν, 244a5–6):

But it is worthwhile to adduce the point that among the ancients too those who gave things their names did not regard madness (μανία) as shameful or a matter for reproach; otherwise they would not have connected this very word with the finest of the sciences (ἡ

---

24 Cf. Cic. *Tusc.* 1.62, Ael. *VH* 4.17; further bibliography in Flinterman 2014, 346–347.
25 Cf., e.g., Morgan 2010, 69, Struck 2016, 48–49.
26 Cf., e.g., Morgan 2010, Struck 2016, ch. 1.
27 E. *Ba.* 298–301.

καλλιστὴ τέχνη), that by which the future is judged, and named it 'manic' (μανική). No, they gave it this very name thinking madness a fine thing, when it comes by divine dispensation: whereas people now crudely throw in the extra *t* and call it 'mantic' (μαντική). So too when the ancients gave a name to the investigation which saner men make of the future by means of birds and the other signs which they use, they call it 'oionoistic' (οἰονοϊστική), because its proponents in a rational way provide insight and information for human thinking; while the modern generation now call it 'oiōnistic' (οἰωνιστική), making it more high-sounding with the long *o*. So then the ancients testify to the fact that god-sent madness (μανία) is a finer thing than man-made sanity (σωφροσύνη), by the degree that mantic (μαντική) is a more perfect and more valuable thing than oiōnistic (οἰωνιστική), both when name is measured against name, and when effect is measured against effect.[28]

Opinions will differ as to how seriously we are to take all this,[29] and Socrates himself is subsequently to pour some cold water on it (*Phdr.* 264e–266b), but it was far from inevitable that μαντική, Apollo's καλλίστη τέχνη (*Phdr.* 244c1, cf. 265b3), should be explained through etymology and in connection with the ancient 'name-givers'. By resorting to etymology, did Socrates here choose a particularly appropriate mode of explanation, one which is — it should be noted — not used when he explains the other forms of beneficent madness (244d5–245a8)? Did Plato feel (not, perhaps, without a certain wry scorn) a special link between μαντική (and hence Apollo) and etymology, two 'arts' which claim to reveal truths about the world which are otherwise hidden from men? Like μαντική, etymology looks to the past (the name-givers) and to the present (in which the — often debated — significance of the names remains). As for the Apolline art *par excellence*, despite the fact that this passage of the *Phaedrus* lays stress upon both μαντική and οἰωνιστική as concerned with the future, in reality both were, like etymology, just as much directed both to the past (i.e. establishing the causes of something in the present) and the present itself;[30] the role of Calchas, who knows 'the present, the future and the past' (Hom. *Il* .1.70) is, as Plutarch was to make explicit (*The E at Delphi* 387b), a paradigmatic demonstration of this.

It is perhaps too rarely asked why in the *Phaedrus* Socrates gives this elaborate etymological *epideixis*. The explanation that it is a kind of extended foot-

---

28 Pl. *Phdr.* 244b6–d5 (trans. C. Rowe).
29 Cf., e.g., Sedley 2003, 33–34.
30 The distinction which Socrates makes between the 'crazed' but divinely inspired μαντική of, say, the Pythia and human οἰωνιστική is important in the context of Plato and the *Phaedrus*, but may be less so in assessing the cultural valuation of μαντική more generally; it sharpens for rhetorical purposes what was anything but a clear-cut distinction in the Greek practice and discourse of divination. For further discussion cf. Dillery 2005, Flower 2008, 84–90, Morgan 2010, 68.

note acknowledging that not all practices which are labelled μαντική have brought humans great benefits, but that is because the term μαντική is misapplied, seems true but too banal to explain the manner in which Socrates labours the point. Rather, we suggest that both kinds of prophetic art, divine μαντική and human οἰωνιστική, are etymologised here in part because of an important link, which is likely to have been felt well beyond discussion in the Academy, between etymologising and the mantic art, one which, as we have seen, is put on open display in the *Cratylus*. In etymologising the mantic art, then, as Socrates does in the *Phaedrus*, one is in fact (almost) practising it, and we will see presently a very similar example in Aeschylus' *Agamemnon*. It is tempting to go a little further and suggest that the two etymologies themselves illustrate the two forms of mantic practice which Socrates claims. If the derivation of μαντική from μανική was, as seems very likely, familiar both in Plato's day and already at the period in which the *Phaedrus* is set and was (paradoxically) regarded as anything but 'crazed', the explanation of οἰωνιστική is itself a good example of human οἴησις bringing νοῦν τε καὶ ἱστορίαν (244c8) and one which, quite literally, comes about δι' ὀρνίθων: Socrates looks at the birds, or (strictly speaking) the art of the birds (οἰωνιστική), and uses them to reconstruct the motivations of the name-givers of the past.

Both etymology and μαντική, when practised by experts, claim to allow us to understand the truth of things; as such, both practices might seem (though presumably not to Plato) also to resemble philosophy. Some later etymologists in fact rejected the link between μαντική and μανία in favour of a connection between μαντική and μῶ or μῶμαι, which was supposed to be synonymous with ζητεῖν (cf. *EM* 574.69–75); presumably the passage of the *Cratylus* which immediately follows the discussion of Apollo was crucial here:[31]

τὰς δὲ Μούσας τε καὶ ὅλως τὴν μουσικὴν ἀπὸ τοῦ μῶσθαι, ὡς ἔοικεν, καὶ τῆς ζητήσεώς τε καὶ φιλοσοφίας τὸ ὄνομα τοῦτο ἐπωνόμασεν.[32]

The Muses and music in general are, as it would seem, given this name from *mōsthai* and from searching and philosophy.[33]

We do not have to believe the Platonic Alcibiades that there is such a thing as ἡ φιλόσοφος μανία τε καὶ βακχεία (*Smp.* 218b3), but as philosophers, μάντεις and

---

31 Pl. *Phdr.* 244c–d is likely also to have contributed to these late definitions.
32 Pl. *Cra.* 406a2–5.
33 The unstated subject of the active ἐπωνόμασεν is, as standardly in the *Cratylus*, 'the name-giver'.

etymologists are all 'searching', it is easy enough to see how associations between them might arise and be exploited. For Plutarch, much later, the matter was clear:

> That the god is no less a philosopher than a prophet Ammonius seemed to all to postulate and prove correctly, with reference to this or to that one of his several titles; that he is *Pythios* for those that are beginning to learn and inquire (διαπυνθάνεσθαι); *Delios* and *Phanaios* for those to whom some part of the truth is becoming clear (δηλοῦται) and is being disclosed (ὑποφαίνεται); *Ismenios* for those who have knowledge (τοῖς ἔχουσι τὴν ἐπιστήμην); and *Leschenorios* when people have active enjoyment of conversation (διαλέγεσθαι) and philosophic intercourse with one another. 'Since', he went on to say, 'inquiry (τὸ ζητεῖν) is the beginning of philosophy, and wonder and uncertainty (τὸ θαυμάζειν καὶ ἀπορεῖν) the beginning of inquiry, it seems only natural that the greater part of what concerns the god should be concealed in riddles, and should call for some account of the wherefore and an explanation of its cause...'.[34]

Apollo himself uses etymology to reveal truths about himself and to encourage us towards intellectual investigation. Apollo is, then, exactly the god in and on whose name one would expect etymology to flourish.

It is this very close connection between Apollo and the decoding of meaning in language which gives a particularly bitter twist to one of the most famous (and earliest) etymologising passages of Greek tragedy, namely Cassandra's denunciation of Apollo in Aeschylus' *Agamemnon*:

ΚΑ.	ὀτοτοτοτοῖ ποποῖ δᾶ·	
	ὤπολλον ὤπολλον.	
ΧΟ.	τί ταῦτ' ἀνωτότυξας ἀμφὶ Λοξίου;	
	οὐ γὰρ τοιοῦτος ὥστε θρηνητοῦ τυχεῖν.	1075
ΚΑ.	ὀτοτοτοτοῖ ποποῖ δᾶ·	
	ὤπολλον ὤπολλον.	
ΧΟ.	ἥδ' αὖτε δυσφημοῦσα τὸν θεὸν καλεῖ,	
	οὐδὲν προσήκοντ' ἐν γόοις παραστατεῖν.	
ΚΑ.	ὤπολλον ὤπολλον,	
	ἀγυιᾶτ', ἀπόλλων ἐμός·	1081
	ἀπώλεσας γὰρ οὐ μόλις τὸ δεύτερον.	
ΧΟ.	χρήσειν ἔοικεν ἀμφὶ τῶν αὑτῆς κακῶν·	
	μένει τὸ θεῖον δουλίᾳ περ ἐν φρενί.	
ΚΑ.	ὤπολλον ὤπολλον,	
	ἀγυιᾶτ', ἀπόλλων ἐμός·	1086
	ἆ, ποῖ ποτ' ἤγαγες με; πρὸς ποίαν στέγην;	
ΧΟ.	πρὸς τὴν Ἀτρειδῶν· εἰ σὺ μὴ τόδ' ἐννοεῖς,	
	ἐγὼ λέγω σοι, καὶ τάδ' οὐκ ἐρεῖς ψύθη.[35]	

---

34 Plu. *The E at Delphi* 385b–c (trans. F.C. Babbitt, adapted).
35 A. *Ag.* 1072–1089 (text of D.L. Page).

Cass. Otototoi popoi daa! O Apollo o Apollo! *Ch.* Why have you raised this cry about Loxias? He is not such as to have anything to do with a mourner. *Cass.* Otototoi popoi daa! O Apollo o Apollo! *Ch.* Look, again she calls on the god in an ill-omened way; it is not appropriate for him to be present at lamentation. *Cass.* Apollo, Apollo, God of the street, my destroyer (*apollōn*), for you have easily destroyed (*apōlesas*) me for a second time. *Ch.* She seems about to prophesy concerning her own misfortunes; divine gifts remain even in the mind of a slave. *Cass.* Apollo, Apollo, God of the street, my destroyer (*apollōn*). Ah, where on earth have you brought me? To what kind of dwelling? *Ch.* To the house of the Atreidai. If you do not realise this, I am informing you, and you will not say this was untrue.

The divinely inspired Cassandra here moves from inarticulate speech, the mere repetition of syllables (ὀτοτοτοτοῖ πόποι δᾶ) which ὤπολλον ὤπολλον imitates (or to which it is assimilated), to a full meaning which emerges in explicit name etymology and explanation (ἀπώλεσας γάρ, 1082).[36] This transition is mirrored by the chorus, who move from a quandary expressed though the verb ἀνωτότυξας in v. 1074, which again echoes and intensifies the inarticulate cry, to the recognition that Cassandra is 'about to utter oracles' (χρήσειν ἔοικεν, 1083) under Apollo's influence. As an Apolline μάντις, Cassandra is merely 'doing her job' in etymologising or, as the chorus call it, 'uttering oracles' (χρήσειν) here. More importantly, the shift from a sequence of inarticulate syllables to meaningful language revealed in etymology tracks the role of Apollo in establishing a fixed order for both the past and the present which is uncovered through etymology.

Etymology, then, reveals the order, not just in the world but also in language (as a reflection of that world); it is itself a sign that language is both meaningful and settled. In many ancient ways of imagining cosmic history, it was not always so. Just as, in the Hesiodic account, the Olympian order replaced a violent disorder which proceeded, so too meaningful, settled language was never just a given. If we ask what, in the ancient imagination, came before Apollo and the name-givers whose work etymology seeks to recover, then various answers are possible, but one mytho-poetic answer was dramatised in the Hesiodic Typhoeus, a monster who, as is well recognised,[37] represents (*inter alia*) an inarticulate and disordered instability of sound and language (*Th.* 820–868). In the *Homeric Hymn to Apollo* Typhaon is the child of Hera who entrusts him for rearing to the Delphic serpent who is to be slain by Apollo (305–355, cf. further below). So too, in the famous opening of Pindar's *First Pythian Ode*,

---

36 γάρ is a very common etymological pointer, cf. Sluiter 2015, 914, discussing this same passage of the *Agamemnon*.
37 Cf., e.g., Too 2004, 18–50, Goslin 2010.

Typhos' fiery eruptions from below Mount Etna are opposed to Apollo's divine lyre-music and a permanent reminder of the disordered chaos to which the Apolline and Olympian order has put a harmonious end. Zeus and Apollo are responsible for that stability in language, but it is etymology which discloses it to us. Moreover, etymology can also reveal the history leading to that settled order; as such, etymology is very closely linked with aetiology. The story of Apollo's killing of the serpent is, as it were, sealed by a significant 'naming' (subsequently to be revealed by etymology), whether that be of Πυθώ from πύθειν (h.Ap. 363–374) or ἰὴ παιῆον from ἵει παῖ ἰόν (Call. Ap. 101–104). Examples could be multiplied, and there would be much to say about how this pattern intersects with the links between, for example, etymology and allegorising and etymology and the rationalisation of myth. What matters in the present context is that etymology and aetiology are both related manifestations of a way of thinking about cosmic order which was associated by the Greeks with Apollo more than with any other god. Apollo's island, Delos, also points to this truth. In the telling of the story of the island in Pindar and Callimachus, Asterie was a floating, movable island until Leto gave birth to Apollo there and the island became fixed and Δῆλος, 'clear' (Call. Del. 35–40), as it has remained, and remained as an example to us, ever since.

Immediately after the nest of Apolline etymologies in the *Cratylus* (covering the god himself, the Muses, Leto and Artemis), Hermogenes questions Socrates about Dionysus and Aphrodite:

> ΕΡΜ. Τί δὲ ὁ Διόνυσός τε καὶ ἡ Ἀφροδίτη; ΣΩ. Μεγάλα, ὦ παῖ Ἱππονίκου, ἐρωτᾷς. ἀλλὰ ἔστι γὰρ καὶ σπουδαίως εἰρημένος ὁ τρόπος τῶν ὀνομάτων τούτοις τοῖς θεοῖς καὶ παιδικῶς. τὸν μὲν οὖν σπουδαῖον ἄλλους τινὰς ἐρώτα, τὸν δὲ παιδικὸν οὐδὲν κωλύει διελθεῖν· φιλοπαίσμονες γὰρ καὶ οἱ θεοί. ὅ τε γὰρ Διόνυσος εἴη ἂν ὁ διδοὺς τὸν οἶνον Διδοίνυσος ἐν παιδιᾷ καλούμενος, οἶνος δ', ὅτι οἴεσθαι νοῦν ἔχειν ποιεῖ τῶν πινόντων τοὺς πολλοὺς οὐκ ἔχοντας, οἰόνους δικαιότατ' ἂν καλούμενος. περὶ δὲ Ἀφροδίτης οὐκ ἄξιον Ἡσιόδῳ ἀντιλέγειν, ἀλλὰ ξυγχωρεῖν ὅτι διὰ τὴν ἐκ τοῦ ἀφροῦ γένεσιν Ἀφροδίτη ἐκλήθη.[38]

> *Herm.* What of Dionysus and Aphrodite? *Soc.* O son of Hipponicus, you are asking about weighty matters. The names of these gods may be explained in both a serious and a playful manner. As for the serious one, you will have to ask others, but nothing prevents me giving you the playful account, as gods too like to play games. Dionysus, who gives wine (*didous ton onion*) might be called Didoinysos in jest, and wine (*oinos*), because it makes most drinkers think that they have good sense (*oiesthai noun*), when they do not, might very justly be called 'oionous'. As for Aphrodite, we should not contradict Hesiod, but should agree that she was called Aphrodite because of her birth from the foam (*aphros*).

---

38 Pl. *Cra.* 406b7–d2.

Socrates' apparent reticence about Dionysus is usually explained (if indeed it attracts much notice at all) with reference to the Mysteries: the 'serious' etymology for which Hermogenes will have to 'ask others' must have mystical significance.[39] In the present context, however, other questions arise. Does Plato actually reject the possibility of giving a 'serious' etymology of these gods? The case of Aphrodite is notably ambiguous: are we to understand that the Hesiodic etymology (cf. Hes. *Th.* 195–158) is the 'playful' one, or does the 'playful' ~ 'serious' distinction really apply only to Dionysus?[40] More broadly, we may want to ask how this distinction between 'serious' and 'playful' etymologies should affect our understanding of all the other etymologies which Socrates offers.[41] Does the fact that Dionysus seems to be, from an early date, associated with flux and change make him a difficult subject for etymologising? Is Dionysus in fact the exception which proves the rule or, rather, proves the value of the etymological enterprise? Plutarch's *The E at Delphi* will address these questions almost directly.

Plutarch, The E at Delphi

The E at Delphi is the report of a discussion of the meaning of the inscription of an E in the god's principal sanctuary.[42] The seven postulated explanations cover

---

[39] It is unclear whether the belief that Dionysus (and his name) was a latecomer to Greece (cf. Hdt. 2.49.1, 2.52.2, 2.145.1) has also contributed to Socrates' reticence; Herodotus reports that Melampous introduced both Dionysus' name and his rites to the Greeks, and this might put him in a rather different category, i.e. outside the activities of the ancient 'name-givers'. In the late fifth century, Stesimbrotus somewhere etymologised Dionysus' name as Διόνυξον, because when he was being born ἔνυξε τὸν Διὸς μηρόν with his horns (*FGrHist* 107 F13); it is a pity that we do not know the context.
[40] Diog. Apoll. A 24 D-K refers the ἀφρός in the god's name to male sperm, and this was to become a familiar etymology, cf., e.g., Corn. 24.3 (p. 45 Lang), *EM* 179.10–1. Any full discussion of this passage of the *Cratylus* might start from the fact that Dionysus and Aphrodite are frequently found together in Greek poetry and art (cf., e.g., Dodds ²1960 on E. *Ba.* 402–16) and that both gods themselves have a 'doubleness' which may, so Socrates hints, be reflected in etymology. If the παιδικόν etymology of Dionysus points to the pleasures of the symposium, rather than to the god's Mysteries and the terrors of Dionysiac cult, Aphrodite embodies both the erotic pleasures (and sufferings) of human beings and also something far grander and more cosmic; one thinks not just of the two Aphrodites of Pausanias' speech in the *Symposium*, but also of Aphrodite's role in Empedocles' cosmogony.
[41] Cf. Trivigno 2012, 49, though we cannot follow the inference which he draws.
[42] On this essay cf. esp. Moreschini 1997, Boulogne, Broze and Couloubaritsis 2006, Obsieger 2013, Thum 2013 (with very rich bibliography); Simonetti 2017, 119–177; there is a brief and

(*inter alia*) cultural and philosophical history, linguistics and mathematics. It is clear both that Ammonios' final Platonising disquisition has specially privileged status within the dialogue (cf. perhaps Diotima's speech in Plato's *Symposium*)[43] and that all of the explanations are in some sense in competition: the participants in the recalled discussion are searching for the 'real meaning' of the E, on the assumption that there is indeed a 'real meaning'. It is, however, also clear that the explanations sit comfortably alongside each other; one explanation may be more sophisticated than another, and some more easily dismissed (cf. 386a–b) and/or driven by personal motives (cf. 387f), but all respond, as the introduction to the essay makes clear (384f–385d), to the Apolline impulse to the search for knowledge and philosophical understanding. What matters for Plutarch in the end is not which explanation is 'true' in an absolute, historical sense, but rather the light they all, in different ways and through different intellectual approaches, shed upon the nature of the god in whose sanctuary the inscription stands and upon the history of that sanctuary.[44] As Elsa Giovanna Simonetti puts it, 'all the visions proposed by the characters ... must be considered *together*, since they *all* concur to create a complex, multifaceted and dynamic image of the god Apollo'.[45]

What is more, this accretive force at work in *The E at Delphi* is not only found elsewhere in Plutarch's philosophising essays, but, we suggest, also finds a clear analogy in ancient etymological practice, above all, of course, in the *Cratylus* which repeatedly offers multiple etymologies for one and the same name.

Etymology itself plays indeed a significant part in Plutarch's discussion of the meaning of the inscription and hence of the god himself. Plutarch explicitly cites the *Cratylus* once in *The E at Delphi* (391a–b, referring to *Cra.* 409a7–b8),[46]

---

accessible guide to the essay and its bibliography in Kindt 2016, 169–183, who is particularly concerned with how the attempts to find 'the real meaning' of the E are related to oracular discourse.
43 Cf., e.g., Babut 1992, 190, 194–202, Thum 2013, 4–6, 12–13, Simonetti 2017, 123, 162–166; this important structuring principle finds excellent analogies elsewhere in Plutarch, but by itself is insufficient for a full account of the treatise. On the relation between the views placed in Ammonios' mouth and those of Plutarch himself cf. also Whittaker 1969, Moreschini 1997, 12–33.
44 Cf. the remarks of Broze and Van Liefferinge in Boulogne, Broze and Couloubaritsis 2006, 80–81; they do not, however, consider the likeness to etymological practice.
45 Simonetti 2017, 129 (emphasis in the original).
46 At *The E at Delphi* 393c we are told by Ammonios, in the context of the standard explanation of Φοῖβος as 'pure and holy', that when their priests spend inauspicious days outside the temples on their own, the Thessalians call this practice φοιβονομεῖσθαι. The standard modern

but the importance of etymologising to, and the accretive force of, different 'rival' accounts of the god suggests that the influence of the *Cratylus* on Plutarch's essay is not limited to this one passing allusion. Some reactions to the suggested explanations of the E may in fact remind us of some modern views of the etymologies of the *Cratylus* and of ancient etymologising in general: 'Plutarch offers seven different explanations, all of which are fanciful and unsatisfactory, if not impossible'.[47] More importantly, the tension between competing claims to offer the 'true meaning' and expositions in support of those which offer access to cultural and philosophical 'truths', regardless of the historical validity of the exposition as an explanation for the E, can hardly fail to suggest the procedures of the *Cratylus*. It is that analogy to which we wish to draw attention.

Our principal interest is one of the best known passages of this work, for it is one of the few ancient texts which juxtapose Apollo and Dionysus in a way which seems to look ahead to the dichotomy which Nietzsche, above all, bequeathed to the modern world:[48]

> Now we hear the theologians affirming and reciting, sometimes in verse and sometimes in prose, that the god is deathless and eternal (ἄφθαρτος ... καὶ ἀίδιος) in his nature, but owing to some predestined design and reason, he undergoes transformations of his person, and at one time enkindles his nature into fire and makes it altogether like all else, and at another time he undergoes all sorts of changes in his form, his emotions and his powers, even as the universe does to-day; but he is called by the best known of his names. The more enlightened, however, concealing from the masses (κρυπτόμενοι ... τοὺς πολλούς) the transformation into fire, call him Apollo because of his solitary state (τῇ μονώσει), and Phoebus because of his purity and stainlessness (τῷ καθαρῷ καὶ ἀμιάντῳ). And as for his turning into winds and water, earth and stars, and into the generations of plants and animals, and his adoption of such guises, they speak in a riddling way of what he undergoes in his transformation as a tearing apart, as it were, and a dismemberment (διασπασμόν τινα καὶ διαμελισμόν). They give him the names of Dionysus, Zagreus, Nyctelius, and Isodaetes; they construct destructions and disappearances, followed by returns to life and regenerations – riddles and fabulous tales (αἰνίγματα καὶ μυθεύματα) quite in keeping with the aforesaid transformations. To this god they also sing the dithyrambic strains lad-

---

commentary (unsurprisingly) notes there is no other evidence for this word or practice, but it is perhaps more than a coincidence that Thessalians are involved, as they also were in the etymologies of Apollo in the *Cratylus* (405c).

47 Bates 1925, 240. For modern attempts to decode the E cf., e.g., Bates 1925, Berman and Losada 1975, Losada and Morgan 1984, Obsieger 2013, 9–16.

48 On this passage cf. Hunter 2011, 21–23, citing earlier bibliography, Thum 2013, 189–194, Simonetti 2017, 143–146.

en with emotion and with a transformation that includes a certain wandering and dispersion. Aeschylus, in fact, says (fr. 355 Radt)

μειξοβόαν πρέπει
διθύραμβον ὁμαρτεῖν
σύγκωμον Διονύσῳ

[Fitting it is that the dithyramb with its fitful notes should attend Dionysus in revel rout.]

But to Apollo they sing the paean, music regulated and chaste (τεταγμένην καὶ σώφρονα μοῦσαν). Apollo the artists represent in paintings and sculpture as ever ageless and young (ἀγήρων ... ἀεὶ καὶ νέον), but Dionysus they depict in many guises and forms (πολυειδῆ καὶ πολύμορφον); and they attribute to Apollo in general a uniformity, orderliness, and unadulterated seriousness (ὁμοιότητα καὶ τάξιν καὶ σπουδὴν ἄκρατον), but to Dionysus a variability combined with playfulness, wantonness, [seriousness], and frenzy (μεμιγμένην τινὰ παιδιᾷ καὶ ὕβρει [καὶ σπουδῇ][49] καὶ μανίᾳ ... ἀνωμαλίαν). They call upon him (*PMG* 1003)

εὔιον ὀρσιγύναικα
μαινομέναις Διόνυσον
ἀνθέοντα τιμαῖς

[Euoe Bacchus who incites womankind, Dionysus who delights 'mid his honours fraught with frenzy]

not inappositely apprehending the peculiar character of each transformation.[50]

The passage is replete with explicit and implicit etymologies of Apollo's name. The following is probably a partial list. (i) ἀίδιος (388f) looks to the god's connection with ἀεί, which we have already noted from the classical period; this etymology is then picked up by ἀγήρων ... ἀεὶ καὶ νέον at the end of the passage (389b). (ii) κρυπτόμενοι δὲ τοὺς πολλούς (388f) is a new spin on the familiar ἀ + πολλ-etymology: the true meaning of Apollo is 'not for the many' or 'away from the many',[51] which stands almost as a programmatic announcement of how some ancient philosophers and religious groupings used the 'mysteries' of etymology (cf. especially the famous allegorical etymologising of the Derveni papy-

---

49 *del.* Wilamowitz.
50 Plu. *The E at Delphi* 388e–389b (trans. F.C. Babbitt, adapted).
51 In the subsequent contrast between Apollo and Hades at *The E at Delphi* 394a, Plutarch contrasts Ἀπόλλων, 'not many', with Hades' name Πλούτων 'abundant', referring to the familiar idea that the dead are 'the many' or 'the more', cf., e.g., Ar. *Ec.* 1073, Call. *Epigr.* 4 Pf. For the etymology of Ἀπόλλων as 'not many/much' in the Pythagorean tradition cf. Whittaker 1969, 187.

rus). (iii) μόνωσις (388f) is standardly taken as another reference to the ἀ + πολλ-etymology. The inheritance of ἁπλοῦν from the *Cratylus* (cf. above §2) is, however, also felt here as elsewhere. In *Isis and Osiris* we are told (if we accept a very probable emendation) that the Pythagoreans called the number One (τὸ ἕν) 'Apollo' πλήθους ἀποφάσει καὶ δι' ἁπλότητα τῆς μονάδος, 'because of its rejection of plurality and the singleness of the monad' (381f), a phrase which gestures both to ἀ + πολλ- and to the etymology from ἁπλοῦν. *The E at Delphi* 393c is also very clear: Ἀπόλλων μὲν γὰρ οἷον ἀρνούμενος τὰ <u>πολλὰ</u> καὶ τὸ <u>πλῆθος</u> <u>ἀπο</u>φάσκων ἐστίν, Ἰήιος δ' ὡς εἷς καὶ μόνος κτλ.; here we have two complementary etymologies telling the same story.[52]

If Apollo is single, then *The E at Delphi* 388e–389b makes very plain that Dionysus is 'many' in every sense; πολυειδῆ καὶ πολύμορφον respond to the ἀ + πολλ-etymology of Apollo to point the difference. With Dionysus, ἀνωμαλία is the governing principle, both in myth and music. The repeated use of the prefix δια- in compounds, which spread from Dionysiac myth (διασπασμόν, διαμελισμόν) to Dionysiac music (διαφόρησιν), may at first seem to imply an etymology of the god's name, and yet the suggestion conveyed by δια- of scattering and dissolution seems to be cast in opposition to the directional, almost etymologising, force of ἀπο- at the head of the name of Ἀπόλλων.[53] What is clear, moreover, is that in this passage Apollo's unchanging significance is revealed in the etymologies of his two principal names,[54] whereas the significance of Dionysus is revealed in the very multiplicity of names and forms and the disordered mixture of his music. Even when the multiplicity of Apollo's titles too is recognised (as it is in *The E at Delphi*), their etymologies insist upon 'oneness' and 'unchangingness' (cf. *The E at Delphi* 393c). Purity in fact involves unchangingness and lack of mixture, for once change is introduced there is no longer purity; the etymologies of Apollo, Ieios and Phoibos work together in an Apolline harmony. The principal theme of Ammonios' final speech is indeed that Apollo as divine Being is 'eternal and uncreated and indestructible' and not subject to the changes which time brings (392e). This is not the same Apollo as the god of the *Cratylus*, but the line of intellectual descent is still visible.

---

52 Cf., e.g., Brout in Boulogne/Broze/Couloubaritsis 2006, 133. The etymology from ἁπλοῦν and Apollo's 'singleness' are central to Proclus' discussion of the god in his *Commentary* to Plato's *Cratylus* (pp. 96.12–102.9 Pasquali = Duvick 2007, 96–100).
53 We owe this suggestion to Cédric Scheidegger Laemmle.
54 Apollo has of course elsewhere very many names or titles, particularly in the context of his identification with the sun, all of which carry their own (sometimes multiple) etymological significance; Corn. 31 (pp. 65–70 Lang) and Macr. *Sat.* 1.17 are the two principal surviving discussions.

For Plutarch, Apollo is characterised by σπουδὴ ἄκρατος (389b), whereas Dionysus is characterised by an outrageous mixture[55] of which παιδιά certainly and σπουδή presumably (even with Wilamowitz's deletion)[56] are parts. Socrates' claim in the *Cratylus* that there is a serious and a playful etymology of Dionysus' name is precisely appropriate for Dionysus himself:[57] Socrates' distinction of two kinds of etymologies for the god tells us something very important about that god. Perhaps it is wine which — Socrates suggests — is the 'playful' manifestation of the god, whereas it is the mystic tearing apart, re-enacted in the ecstatic rites and ὠμοφαγία of Dionysiac cult and art, which represent the god in his 'serious' form; we might recall here the contrasts and similarities between Euripides' *Cyclops* and *Bacchae*, which both reveal the nature of the god, but in two very different modes. Moreover, in both Plato and Plutarch Dionysus remains resistant to etymologising,[58] and in Plutarch that is closely linked to his variety and instability: etymology can here reveal no truths about this god, because the only truth is changingness. It is, however, stable verities which etymology reveals.

Back to the Beginning...

As we have already noted, the influence of the *Cratylus* in both antiquity and modern scholarship has established something like an equation between etymology and 'explicit etymology', not merely through Socrates' demonstrations of etymology at work but also through the suggestion that the practice required specialist knowledge or gifts, like μαντική. As one of the consequences of this influence, it is also the *Cratylus*, or rather the way in which the *Cratylus* has been read, which has marked off etymologising in poetry, which is much more often 'implicit' than 'explicit', as an 'other' practice. From a historical point of view, this rightly recognises the background of the dialogue in explicit linguistic speculation; 'explicit' etymologising marks a particular, and particularly important, moment in the history of such speculation. Nevertheless, the distinction between the two modes is highly permeable, and the *Cratylus*, which is full of etymologies which are not explicitly pointed, is itself one of the prime wit-

---

55 The language of wine-mixing is of course evoked here.
56 Cf. above n. 49.
57 Cf. above § 2.
58 This of course is not to say that in other contexts the god's name could not be etymologised, cf., e.g., Macr. *Sat.* 1.18.12–13.

nesses of this. Part of the discussion of Pan which we have already considered is an excellent illustration:

> οὐκοῦν τὸ μὲν ἀληθὲς αὐτοῦ λεῖον καὶ θεῖον καὶ ἄνω οἰκοῦν ἐν τοῖς θεοῖς, τὸ δὲ ψεῦδος κάτω ἐν τοῖς πολλοῖς τῶν ἀνθρώπων καὶ τραχὺ καὶ τραγικόν.[59]
>
> So, the true part of it is smooth and divine and lives up there with the gods. The false part lives down among the mass of men and is rough and *tragikon*.

There is here a rather obvious play between τὸ ἀληθές and λεῖον καὶ θεῖον, but David Sedley calls this not an etymology but a 'quasi-etymological hint', 'because it does not constitute an actual etymology of ἀληθές to compete with the decoding of ἀλήθεια that will be offered later in the text (421b). Rather, it interprets two visual aspects of Pan as indirectly symbolising ἀληθές via its discrete vocal components'.[60] This example and Sedley's discussion show what is at stake in trying to make too firm a distinction between 'explicit' etymology and poetic and/or 'implicit' etymological play. What name would one give to the assonance of τραχύ and τραγικόν and the rhyme of λεῖον and θεῖον? Poetic stylisation or poetic etymologising, or both? The richly various forms of etymologising bleed into each other, as we have seen dramatised in Cassandra's anguish in the *Agamemnon*. Despite the familiarity of 'explicit' etymologising from Homer onwards and despite the almost inexhaustible variety of etymologising on display in the dialogue itself, it was the influence of the *Cratylus* which created a hierarchy of the 'explicit' and the 'implicit'.

One distinction which might be drawn between the two modes is that there will always be a residue (perhaps even a majority) of suggested cases of 'implicit' etymology where there will be room for disagreement as to the deliberateness of the effect. That etymological play has a significant role in Greek poetry of every period requires no elaborate demonstration, but it is equally uncontroversial that alleged cases are always matters for critical judgement, a fact which itself points to the peculiar purposes of ancient etymologising. What both the *Cratylus* and *The E at Delphi* illustrate is the cultural significance of these intellectual practices, regardless of one's view of how 'seriously' to take the Platonic dialogue, or indeed the Plutarchan explanations offered for the E at Delphi. Etymologising lays bare not merely structures of thought which pervade the world, but also the theological framework which keeps those structures in place.

---

[59] Pl. *Cra.* 408c5–6.
[60] Sedley 2003, 96.

To draw our discussion to a close, we want to go all the way back to Apollo's very entry into Greek literature:

> τίς τάρ σφωε θεῶν ἔριδι ξυνέηκε μάχεσθαι;
> Λητοῦς καὶ Διὸς υἱός· ὃ γὰρ βασιλῆϊ χολωθεὶς
> νοῦσον ἀνὰ στρατὸν ὦρσε κακήν, ὀλέκοντο δὲ λαοί,
> οὕνεκα τὸν Χρύσην ἠτίμασεν ἀρητῆρα
> Ἀτρεΐδης.[61]

Which of the gods brought the two of them together in strife? The son of Leto and Zeus. For in anger against the king he caused evil sickness through the army, and the soldiers perished, because the son of Atreus dishonoured the priest Chryses.

'The son of Leto and Zeus' may be a suitably epic circumlocution, but does it also avoid a name, the dangers of which are then revealed — or rather hinted at through etymology — by ὀλέκοντο δὲ λαοί? Is Ἀπόλλων already ὁ ἀπολλύων? Etymologising, like allegorising, can be dark and threatening, and Apollo's dread appearance in *Iliad* 1 was certainly much allegorised. Moreover, although medicine is, famously, the one of his four (later) arts which the baby god does not claim in his very first spoken words at *h.Ap.* 131–132, here at the opening of the *Iliad* he is already associated with disease (the healing god is also the bringer of plague, cf. Corn. 32.4 p. 65–66 Lang etc.) and destruction; in different ways, *Iliad* 1 certainly puts on display Apollo's three other arts — archery, prophecy and (at the end of the book, vv. 603–604) music.

If Apollo's first entry raises etymological queries, what of his action in response to Chryses' prayer?

> ὣς ἔφατ' εὐχόμενος, τοῦ δ' ἔκλυε Φοῖβος Ἀπόλλων,
> βῆ δὲ κατ' Οὐλύμποιο καρήνων χωόμενος κῆρ,
> τόξ' ὤμοισιν ἔχων ἀμφηρεφέα τε φαρέτρην·   45
> ἔκλαγξαν δ' ἄρ' ὀϊστοὶ ἐπ' ὤμων χωομένοιο,
> αὐτοῦ κινηθέντος· ὃ δ' ἤϊε νυκτὶ ἐοικώς.
> ἕζετ' ἔπειτ' ἀπάνευθε νεῶν, μετὰ δ' ἰὸν ἕηκε·
> δεινὴ δὲ κλαγγὴ γένετ' ἀργυρέοιο βιοῖο·
> οὐρῆας μὲν πρῶτον ἐπῴχετο καὶ κύνας ἀργούς,   50
> αὐτὰρ ἔπειτ' αὐτοῖσι βέλος ἐχεπευκὲς ἐφιεὶς
> βάλλ'· αἰεὶ δὲ πυραὶ νεκύων καίοντο θαμειαί.[62]

So Chryses spoke in prayer, and Phoebus Apollo heard him. Angry in his heart, he came down from the peaks of Olympus, with his bow and his hooded quiver slung around his

---

61 Hom. *Il.* 1.8–12. The textual difficulty in v. 11 does not affect the point we wish to make.
62 Hom. *Il.* 1.43–52.

shoulders. The arrows clanged on his shoulders as the angry god moved. He came like night. He then sat down away from the ships and launched an arrow; there was a terrible clanging from his silver bow. He aimed first at the mules and the swift dogs, and then he launched his piercing bolt at the men; pyres of the dead burned incessantly.

Βάλλ(ε) and αἰεί are separated by punctuation (as δέ shows), but can we be sure that the etymology for the archer-god's name which was to become so familiar from Plato and later texts (ἀεὶ βάλλων) does not already resonate here, or would be felt by Homeric audiences from a relatively early date?[63] More generally, these examples in the *Iliad* are excellent illustrations not just of the 'room for disagreement' to which we have already referred, but also of the (obvious) fact that 'implicit etymologising' demands the co-operation of the audience and that the nature of that co-operation is likely to change over time. Someone who knows the *Cratylus'* discussion of Apollo's name is bound to read *Iliad* 1.52 or 17.118 differently from someone who does not; (s)he will then have to decide how and if to use this knowledge in understanding Homer, but there will always be a choice to be made. Not entirely unlike etymologists, in fact, audiences of all kinds look for meaningful signs in texts and in collections (and collocations) of letters, and Apollo rarely disappoints.

Appendix: A Shot in the Dark

Apollo's response to Chryses' prayer at the start of the *Iliad* has no real parallel in other divine interventions in Homer, but certain elements of it appear again in Odysseus' famous, and famously problematic,[64] description of the εἴδωλον of Heracles in the Underworld:[65]

ἀμφὶ δέ μιν κλαγγὴ νεκύων ἦν οἰωνῶν ὥς,   605
πάντοσ' ἀτυζομένων· ὁ δ' ἐρεμνῇ νυκτὶ ἐοικώς,
γυμνὸν τόξον ἔχων καὶ ἐπὶ νευρῆφιν ὀϊστόν,
δεινὸν παπταίνων, αἰεὶ βαλέοντι ἐοικώς.[66]

About him the dead clamoured like birds as they scattered in all directions in panic, but he was like gloomy night, holding his bow at the ready with an arrow on the string, glaring around fiercely, looking like one who would shoot at any moment.

---

63 See further the *Appendix*.
64 For ancient discussion of some of the problems cf. Petzl 1969, 28–41.
65 Some of the parallels noted here are helpfully discussed by Karanika 2011, 12–13.
66 Hom. *Od.* 11.605–608.

The echoes of ἔκλαγξαν, κλαγγή (*Iliad*) ~ κλαγγή (*Odyssey*) and δεινή (*Iliad*) ~ δεινόν (*Odyssey*) would of themselves carry little significance, despite the fact that νεκύες, 'corpses', are central to both scenes, but αἰεὶ βαλέοντι ἐοικώς mirrors βάλλ'· αἰεὶ δε κτλ., and the two passages also share the only two occurrences in Homer of the verse-end νυκτὶ ἐοικώς. Whereas the fact that Apollo came 'like night' presumably refers not just to the speed with which he moved, but also suggests a frightening and mysterious power,[67] Heracles is most 'like gloomy night' in that the Underworld in which he stalks is itself of Stygian gloom; we may compare the only other occurrence of νυκτὶ ἐοικώς in early epic outside Homer:

ἐν λίκνῳ κατέκειτο μελαίνῃ νυκτὶ ἐοικώς
ἄντρῳ ἐν ἠερόεντι κατὰ ζόφον, οὐδέ κεν αὐτὸν
αἰετὸς ὀξὺ λάων ἐσκέψατο.[68]

He lay down in his cradle, like black night in the darkness of the gloomy cave; not even a sharp-sighted eagle would have seen him.

The baby god is essentially invisible in his gloomy cave; in blending into the darkness he is 'like black night', but there is nothing frightening about him, despite the mischief he is plotting.[69] The speaker of these verses is Apollo himself, Hermes' principal antagonist in the *Hymn*, and he uses a phrase which Homer had used of Apollo in the *Iliad*.[70] The poet of the *Hymn* thus almost provides a commentary on the Homeric phrase, which brings out another nuance of νυκτὶ ἐοικώς: the Greeks did not see the god who attacked them, for 'he sat far off from the ships' (*Il.* 1.48). Apollo's invisibility to the Greeks is then transferred to the baby hiding in his cradle in the depths of a gloomy cave.

The poet of the *Odyssey*-passage, however, presumably wished to suggest both the darkness surrounding the ghostly Heracles and the terror he inspired in the shades around him. The *eidolon* of Heracles cannot have been quite invisible, for Odysseus saw it (εἰσενόησα, 601), but more than one of the resonances carried by the phrase in *Iliad* 1 were taken over by the poet of the *Odyssey-*

---

67 Cf. Hunter 2018, 43–44.
68 *h.Merc.* 358–360.
69 Thomas 2020 on vv. 358–359 and 334–464 of the *Homeric Hymn to Hermes* argues that Apollo indeed wishes to cast Hermes as a threat; on the association of Hermes and night in the *Hymn* see also Thomas, *Introduction* § 44.3.
70 That the *Hymn* here echoes *Iliad* 1 has of course been suggested in the past, though scholars have differed as to the tone and purpose of the echo, cf. the notes of Gemoll 1886 ('unzweifelhafte Parodie'), Richardson 2010 and Vergados 2013 *ad loc.*

verses, in a passage whose import and syntax have puzzled readers since antiquity. The frightening Olympian archer and the frightening archer of the Underworld seem too alike to invoke coincidence or the fact that, in early epic, similar material will inevitably be described in similar or identical language. Rather, the conspicuous doubling within three verses of similes describing the *eidolon* of Heracles, both expressed with ἐοικώς at verse-end, suggests that the poet of these *Odyssey* verses had the opening of *Iliad* 1 in mind in composing the account of Heracles in the Underworld.

αἰεὶ βαλέοντι ἐοικώς, 'looking like someone who might shoot at any moment', may well, then, derive from βάλλ'· αἰεὶ δὲ πυραὶ κτλ. at *Il.* 1.52. If so, we will have at least one ancient testimony that βάλλ'· αἰεί in the *Iliad* might be felt to hang together, despite the punctuation which keeps them apart. But perhaps more crucially, the *Odyssey* may compare Heracles not to just anyone 'about to shoot at any moment' but to the one god who is truly ἀεὶ βάλλων – Apollon. Within the etymologising practices of antiquity, αἰεὶ βαλέοντι ἐοικώς reads like a gloss in which the *Odyssey* references and acknowledges the Iliadic pre-text.[71]

Bibliography

Babut, D. 1992. 'La composition des Dialogues pythiques de Plutarque et le problème de leur unité', *Journal des Savants* 2, 187–234.
Bates, W.N. 1925. 'The E of the Temple at Delphi', *AJA* 29, 239–246.
Berman, K./Losada, L.A. 1975. 'The Mysterious E at Delphi. A Solution', *ZPE* 17, 115–117.
Boardman, J. 1997. Pan. *LIMC* VIII Suppl. I: 923–941; II: 612–635.
Boardman, J. 2009. Pan. *LIMC* Supplementum I, 409; II, 197.
Boulogne, J./Broze, M./Couloubaritsis, L. (eds.) 2006. *Les Platonismes des premiers siècles de notre ère. Plutarque, L'E de Delphes*, Brussels.
Brommer, F. 1956. Pan. *RE* Suppl. 8, 949–1008.
Burkert, W. 1962. *Weisheit und Wissenschaft*, Nürnberg.
Burkert, W. 1975. 'Apellai und Apollon', *RhM* 118, 1–21 [= *Kleine Schriften*, Vol. 6, Göttingen 2011, 3–20].
Diggle, J. 1970. *Euripides, Phaethon*, Cambridge.

---

[71] We are very grateful to Cédric Scheidegger Laemmle, Constanze Guethenke and the participants of ETYGR 2018, 2nd International Conference on Etymological Theories and Practice in Greek (Nice, France) for much helpful discussion and criticism; we have also benefitted from the suggestions of the journal's two anonymous referees. Oliver Thomas very kindly gave us access to Thomas 2020 before its publication.

Dillery, J. 2005. 'Chresmologues and *Manteis*. Independent Diviners and the Problem of Authority', in: S.I. Johnston/P.T. Struck (eds.), *Mantikê. Studies in Ancient Divination*, Leiden, 167–231.
Dodds, E.R. 1960. *Euripides, Bacchae. Edited with Introduction and Commentary*, 2nd ed. Oxford.
Duvick, B. 2007. *Proclus, On Plato's Cratylus*, Ithaca NY.
Flacelière, R. 1974. *Plutarque, Œuvres morales, Vol. 6: Dialogues pythiques*, Paris.
Flinterman, J.-J. 2014. 'Pythagoreans in Rome and Asia Minor around the Turn of the Common Era', in: C.A. Huffman (ed.), *A History of Pythagoreanism*, Cambridge, 341–359.
Flower, M. 2008. *The Seer in Ancient Greece*, Berkeley CA.
Gemoll, A. 1886. *Die homerischen Hymnen*, Leipzig.
Goslin, O. 2010. 'Hesiod's Typhonomachy and the Ordering of Sound', *TAPhA* 140, 351–373.
Heubeck, A. 1987. 'Noch einmal zum Namen des Apollon', *Glotta* 65, 179–182.
Hordern, J.H. 2002. *The Fragments of Timotheus of Miletus*, Oxford.
Hunter, R. 1986. 'Apollo and the Argonauts', *MH* 43, 50–60 [= Hunter 2008, 29–41].
Hunter, R. 2008. *On Coming After. Studies in Post-Classical Greek Literature and its Reception*, Berlin/New York.
Hunter, R. 2011. 'Apollo and the *Ion* of Euripides. Nothing to Do with Nietzsche?', *Trends in Classics* 3, 18–37 [= this volume 84–102].
Hunter, R. 2018. *The Measure of Homer*, Cambridge.
Karanika, A. 2011. 'The End of the Nekyia. Odysseus, Heracles, and the Gorgon in the Underworld', *Arethusa* 44, 1–27.
Kindt, J. 2016. *Revisiting Delphi. Religion and Storytelling in Ancient Greece*, Cambridge.
Kretschmer, P. 1927. 'Literaturbericht für das Jahr 1924', *Glotta* 15, 161–201.
Losada, L.A./Morgan, K. 1984. 'The E at Delphi Again. Reply to A.T. Hodge.', *AJA* 88, 231–232.
Moreschini, C. 1997. *L'E di Delfi*, Naples.
Morgan, K. 2010. 'The Voice of Authority. Divination and Plato's *Phaedo*', *CQ* 60, 63–81.
Most, G.W. 2016. 'Allegoresis and Etymology', in: A. Grafton/G.W. Most (eds.), *Canonical Texts and Scholarly Practices*, Cambridge, 52–74.
Nagy, G. 2004. 'The Name of Apollo. Etymology and Essence', in: Id., *Homer's Text and Language*, Urbana/Chicago, 138–143.
Nightingale, A.W. 2003. 'Subtext and Subterfuge in Plato's Cratylus', in: A.N. Michelini (ed.), *Plato as Author. The Rhetoric of Philosophy*, Leiden, 223–240.
Obsieger, H. 2013. *Plutarch. De E apud Delphos. Über das Epsilon am Apolltempel in Delphi*, Stuttgart.
Petzl, G. 1969. *Antike Diskussionen über die beiden Nekyiai*, Meisenheim am Glan.
Pfeiffer, R. 1949. *Callimachus*, Vol. 1, Oxford.
Rank, L.P. 1951. *Etymologiseering en verwante verschijnselen bij Homerus*, Assen.
Richardson, N. 2010. *Three Homeric Hymns. To Apollo, Hermes, and Aphrodite*, Cambridge.
Schmid, W. 1923–4. 'Φοῖβος Ἀπόλλων', *Archiv für Religionswissenschaft* 22, 217–223.
Sedley, D. 2003. *Plato's Cratylus*, Cambridge.
Segal, C. 1982. 'Etymologies and Double Meanings in Euripides' Bacchae', *Glotta* 60, 81–93.
Simonetti, E.G. 2017. *A Perfect Medium? Oracular Divination in the Thought of Plutarch*, Leuven.
Sluiter, I. 2015. 'Ancient Etymology. A Tool for Thinking', in: F. Montanari/S. Matthaios/A. Rengakos (eds.), *Brill's Companion to Ancient Greek Scholarship*, Vol. 2, Leiden/Boston, 896–922.

Struck, P.T. 2016. *Divination and Human Nature*, Princeton NJ.
Thomas, O. 2011. 'The Homeric Hymn to Pan', in: A. Faulkner (ed.), *The Homeric Hymns. Interpretative Essays*, Oxford, 151–172.
Thomas, O. 2020. *The Homeric Hymn to Hermes*, Cambridge.
Thum, T. 2013. *Plutarchs Dialog De E apud Delphos*, Tübingen.
Too, Y.L. 2004. *The Idea of Ancient Literary Criticism*, Oxford.
Trivigno, F.V. 2012. 'Etymology and the Power of Names in Plato's Cratylus', *AncPhil* 32, 35–75.
Van Looy, H. 1973. 'Παρετυμολογεῖ ὁ Εὐριπίδης', in: AA.VV., *Zetesis, Album amicorum. Festschrift E. de Strycker*, Antwerp/Utrecht, 345–366.
Vergados, A. 2013. *The Homeric Hymn to Hermes. Introduction, Text and Commentary*, Berlin.
Whittaker, J. 1969. 'Ammonius on the Delphic E', *CQ* 19, 185–192.

42 The Poetics of Greek Inscriptions

Not all Greek verse inscriptions are anonymous, but the vast majority are.[1] This anonymity has not done them any favours in terms of the scholarly respect in which they are held. Anonymity still bothers us, in part because the name of the author is very often the principal frame through which ancient poetry is approached.[2] Fortunately, however, Greek verse inscriptions are slowly getting some of the attention they deserve. There are various reasons for this. One is simply the greater accessibility of the material, through editions such as Hansen's *Carmina epigraphica Graeca* (*CEG*) and Merkelbach and Stauber's *Steinepigramme aus dem griechischen Osten* (*SGO*). Another is the greater interest in inscribed poetry which has followed in the jetstream of the revolution in the scholarly study of what I will for the moment call, without further definition, 'literary epigrams'; this revolution has in part been fuelled by some very remarkable papyrus finds, which in their turn have generated a now very sizeable body of scholarship. The significant differences which have emerged between 'literary' epigrams and epigrams which survive only on stone — differences in verbal and metrical form, differences in technique and motif and differences in circulation and reception — have been a major gain for our understanding of aspects of Greek literary culture.

The current paper touches on some of the issues which arise, or should do so, repeatedly in the study of inscribed epigram, considers what kinds of questions it is legitimate to ask of such poetry, and offers some practical examples of a critical approach; the examples will be drawn entirely from funerary poetry, to provide the necessary thematic focus. A further preliminary observation is, however, necessary, if only because the matter will here not receive much further attention. A very high percentage of our inscribed epitaphs, particularly of the Hellenistic and imperial ages, cannot be dated with any approximation to precision, let alone precision itself. Chronology, like authorship, matters — antiquity is not a time-free zone — and its absence might seem to preclude the close attention to historical and social context which lies at the heart of modern

---

I am grateful to audiences in Cambridge, Dublin, Sydney and Warwick for much illuminating discussion and criticism.

---

1 For inscribed poems which name the author, cf. Santin 2009.
2 I have discussed various aspects of this, from a rather different point of view, in Hunter 2002; there is also much more to be said (on another occasion) about the positive advantages (as it were) which 'anonymity' brings to inscribed poetry.

critical approaches to Greek poetry. There is, of course, an undeniably strong continuity of theme and language across centuries in ancient epitaphic poetry, and some might even claim that chronology in fact matters far less in this field than in many; moreover, it is not merely the alleged 'sameness' of so much of this material which encourages the neglect of chronology. Many of the collections through which such material is accessed, most notably Werner Peek's *Griechische Vers-Inschriften* 1955, are not chronologically arranged,[3] and this has an effect, often imperceptible but inevitably deep and long-term, on how such poetry is imagined. Any attempted history of change over time is always going to be very lacunose, because of the state of the evidence and where it comes from, but sooner or later the attempt needs to be made.

One thing is very clear: the study of inscribed poetry is full of instructive surprises. We are, above all, continually reminded of what we do not know. CEG 475 is a probably early-fourth-century Attic epitaph for Nikomakhos of Lemnos:

Λήμνου ἀπ' ἠγαθέας κεύθει τάφος ἐνθάδε γαίας
   ἄνδρα φιλοπρόβατον· Νικόμαχος δ' ὄνομα.[4]

CEG 475

The tomb holds a sheep-loving man from the holy land of Lemnos; his name is Nikomakhos.

Who would have guessed that φιλοπρόβατος, a word otherwise attested only some 800 years later in Palladius, who uses it to describe Christ, the divine shepherd, and then again some 300 years after that in an imitation of Palladius, would turn up on an Attic grave monument of the early fourth century BC?[5] We may well agree with Christoph Clairmont 1970, 154–5, that 'it is clear that φιλοπρόβατος was not meaningless to those who erected the memorial', but that does not get us very far towards understanding its significance here. That is, moreover, not the only question to be asked. Who chose the epithet φιλοπρόβατος? — which is not necessarily the same question as 'who composed the distich?'. Was it Nikomakhos himself? The ancients very probably chose their own epitaphs and memorials as commonly as moderns do: Petronius' Trimal-

---

[3] This feature of *GVI* is severely criticised in Robert 1959.
[4] Here and elsewhere, for the sake of readability, I reproduce poems with some corrections of the original orthography. I have also indented all pentameters, regardless of their presentation on the original stones.
[5] Πρόβατος as a proper name is now apparently attested on a Theran inscription published in 1998 (Sigalas/Matthaiou 1992/98, 398); for such 'animal' names in general, cf. Wilhelm 1942, 141–145.

chio is fetchingly absurd for the nature of the funeral arrangements he makes, not because he makes his own.

We do not know who read inscribed poetry in antiquity and many have wondered whether anyone did; in a stimulating discussion, Peter Bing argued that, at least in the archaic and classical ages, very few people did, though this probably changed with the expanding reading culture of the Hellenistic age.[6] We can assume that poetry which survives on papyri or was transmitted successfully enough to be copied into manuscripts was written with an expectation of entering such a reading culture, but there is little such guarantee with inscribed poetry. This is not, of course, just a matter of literacy rates in antiquity, as the chances are that anyone who took the trouble to have, for example, a funerary poem composed for a tomb was at some level 'literate' (and we may again leave that undefined for now). This is a very big subject, and as my concern in this paper is largely with inscribed poetry of the Hellenistic and imperial ages, I will confine myself to a brief consideration of one very interesting poem which (*inter alia*) seems to play with this whole problem.

SGO 11/08/01 is a poem of (presumably) imperial date from north central Turkey:[7]

γράμματ' ἐπιστάμενος γνώσῃ τίνος οὗτος ὁ τύμβος.

σοὶ μὲν ἐγὼ γαῖαν πολλὴν ἐπέχευα θανούσῃ
σῆμα τόδ' ὑψώ[σα]ς, καλὴ Ἀκυλεῖνα πο[θεινή],
Φοῖβος σὸς γ[αμέτης], στήλην τ' ἔστησ[α υ – ×].
ἢν δέ με Μοῖρ' ὀλοὴ καθέλῃ θάνατός τε κραταιός,
τίς μοι ταῦτ' ἔρξει, τίνι δ' ὕστατα ῥήματα λέξω;
τίς δ' ἀδινὸν κλαύσας θρῆ[νόν τ' ἄδ]ων ὕμνον τε…

SGO 11/08/01

As/if you know your letters, you will realise whose tomb this is.

For you after death I piled up much earth, raising high this tomb, lovely and much missed Aquilina, I your husband Phoibos, and I set up this […] stele. But if destructive fate and overpowering death should overtake me, who will do this for me, to whom shall I utter my final words? Who will shed copious tears and [sing] a lament and hymn…

The 'advertisement' of the poem, a hexameter set off from the main text, varies a standard opening in which it is announced that the *stele* or the tomb will tell you who is buried there (cf. GVI 1617–1635); such an opening normally an-

---

6 Bing 2009, ch. 7. For some of the arguments on the other side, cf., e.g., Day 2010, 29–33.
7 For the circumstances of its discovery, cf. Anderson 1903, 22.

nounces a poem which identifies the deceased either in the third person or through a first-person address. Here we have rather a poem in which the grieving widower first addresses his dead wife, but then is led in his lamentation to a remarkable, if certainly not unparalleled, display of self-pitying abandonment and desolation. What we might call the 'Admetus-Alcestis' motif, a feature of a number of epitaphs for wives (cf. Hanink 2010, 27–28), is here prominent, but my concern is rather with the audience for the epitaph. The opening 'advertisement' — 'If/since you can read …' — prompts the question of what happens if you cannot read. Presumably, you will not know what you are missing, or will ask someone to read the *stele* to you, but the very fact that the poem calls attention to this matter is significant for the communal role which such inscribed records held; inscriptions could be both a cohesive force of social bonding, and a divisive tool for separating the educated from the uneducated. Two further questions (at least) arise. One is the connection, which I will not pursue here, between the technique of this poem and the many 'literary' epigrams which call attention to the act of reading or making out the letters on an inscription and, secondly, there is the question of carved representations ('pictures', if you like) on tombstones: might some of these at least have been there particularly (though not of course exclusively) for the benefit of the illiterate?

No single answer of course will do, but some of the issues are nicely illustrated by what in some respects is a very ordinary kind of inscribed poem from Rhodes (late first century BC or early first century AD):[8]

στήλη σοι λέξει τὸν ἐμὸν μόρον ἠδὲ χαρακτὰ
   γράμματα, πῶς τ' ἔθανον καὶ οὔνομα τῶν γονέων·
λύσας μὲν στήριγγαν ἁμάξης κάτθανα τλήμων,
   οἰνωθρῶν φόρτον βαρὺν ἐνεγκαμένης·
οὔνομά μοι Πλοῦτος, τριέτης μόλον Ἄιδος οὐδόν·
   Ἀντιοχὶς μήτηρ, ἣ τλήμονα μασθὸν ὑπέσχε,
καὶ γενέτης Πλοῦτος, ὅς μοι ἔτευξε τάφον.

GVI 1625

The *stele* will tell you of my fate, as will the engraved letters, how I died and the name of my parents. I died a wretched death when I undid the shaft of a wagon which was laden with a heavy load of vine-stakes. My name is Ploutos, I went to Hades' threshold at the age

---

8 Cf. Maiuri 1932, no. 30 with fig. 35, Vérilhac 1978–1982, 1.144–145; the current Covid-19 crisis has, unfortunately, meant that I have been unable to acquire an image of the *stele* for reproduction here. For a list of other poems in which the deceased allows the stone to speak for him or her, cf. Christian 2015, 187–188.

of three. My mother, who offered me her suffering breast, is Antiokhis, and my father is Ploutos; he built the tomb for me.

The representation on the *stele* divides the poem into two. Above the image of the parents and their small child, we have the story of the child's death and his name; this section of five verses ends with a hexameter, an ending which tells us, if we needed telling, that the poem is incomplete, that something is missing. That something, of course, is the identity of the child's parents, responsible for the monument, who are given pride of place by being identified in a couplet immediately below the representation. On the printed page it seems that the poem concludes with two hexameters followed by a pentameter, and such an 'irregular' pattern is in fact anything but uncommon;[9] as set out on the stone, however, we see that that probably misrepresents anyone's reading experience of the *stele*. The manner of the child's death, given in the brief narrative of verses 3–4, is hardly something that anyone could reasonably guess, and the picture will offer no help whatsoever (we will see a rather different case presently). What, then, were these pictures for, if indeed (as seems overwhelmingly likely) reference in the written text to the *stele* giving information is usually to the inscription, not to any picture that may be depicted on the *stele*? In the present case, there is the added issue that the depiction on the *stele* might seem to imply that the dead is the seated father, not the child lurking behind his mother; the image is of a very familiar kind, and we are perhaps dealing here with a 'standard', almost 'mass-produced' image, and/or with a reused *stele*. This common practice clearly complicates any attempt to formulate 'rules' for the interaction between text and image on funerary monuments of the later Hellenistic and imperial ages or to bring iconography into a general poetics of funerary verse.

As a kind of footnote, it is perhaps worth observing that *GVI* 1625 may shed light on one of Callimachus' most famous poems:

εἶπέ τις, Ἡράκλειτε, τεὸν μόρον, ἐς δέ με δάκρυ
 ἤγαγεν· ἐμνήσθην δ' ὁσσάκις ἀμφότεροι
ἥλιον ἐν λέσχῃ κατεδύσαμεν. ἀλλὰ σὺ μέν που,
 ξεῖν' Ἁλικαρνησεῦ, τετράπαλαι σποδιή,
αἱ δὲ τεαὶ ζώουσιν ἀηδόνες, ἧσιν ὁ πάντων
 ἁρπακτὴς Ἀΐδης οὐκ ἐπὶ χεῖρα βαλεῖ.

Epigr. 2 Pf. = *AP* 7.80

Someone, Heraclitus, told of your death and brought me to tears. I remembered how often the two of us sank the sun with our talking. You, my Halicarnassian friend, are I assume

---

9 Cf. Hunter 2019, 139, citing earlier bibliography.

ash four-ages old, but your nightingales live on; Hades, who snatches everything away, will not get his hands on those.

The poem reuses two of the most familiar of epitaphic motifs — the tears and memories of those left behind; countless tombs are inscribed with the name of the deceased, the name of the person who arranged the inscription and the purpose for which it was done, namely μνήμης χάριν. There is also a suggestive analogy between the opening verse of Callimachus' poem and the opening of *GVI* 1625, which might help with the strangeness of Callimachus' εἶπε ... τεὸν μόρον: the τις here takes the place of the funerary *stele* which is as absent as Heraclitus' body, but the whole Callimachean verse evokes the epitaphic convention. I once wondered whether we were to understand that the τις was in fact a 'passer-by' of Heraclitus' tomb who had carried the message of his death to the poet, as many tombs ask passers-by to do (cf. further below).[10]

The issue of the relation between gravestone images and the text of the poems which accompany those images is thematised throughout antiquity. Another funerary poem of Callimachus offers a commentary on the very process of recognition which is always involved:[11]

> Τιμονόη. τίς δ' ἐσσί; μὰ δαίμονας, οὔ σ' ἂν ἐπέγνων,
> εἰ μὴ Τιμοθέου πατρὸς ἐπῆν ὄνομα
> στήλῃ καὶ Μήθυμνα, τεὴ πόλις. ἦ μέγα φημί
> χῆρον ἀνιᾶσθαι σὸν πόσιν Εὐθυμένη.
>
> *Epigr.* 15 Pf. = *AP* 7.522

'Timonoe.' But who are you? By heavens, I would not have recognised you, if the *stele* did not have the name of your father, Timotheos, and Methymna, your home-city. I declare that your widowed husband Euthymenes is in great distress.

The poem is framed by the names of the dead woman and her husband. As we read the first verse, we come to see that 'Timonoe' is in fact spoken by the conventional 'passer-by' and it is the name he reads on the tombstone, presumably set apart (as it is, imitatively, in Callimachus' poem) from the rest of the (imagined) accompanying inscription. 'I would not have recognised you' plays with our knowledge of the apparently generic nature of so much funerary art; it is not so much that artists did not try to represent the dead, or not think that they were doing just that, but rather that both the medium and the conventions of sculp-

---

10 Cf. Bing 2009, 131 n. 31.
11 On this poem, cf. esp. Walsh 1991, 94–97, Fantuzzi/Hunter 2004, 318–320, together with the earlier literature which they cite.

ture in stone worked against anything that we would recognise as 'portraiture'. Here the thought processes of the speaker have turned for confirmation to the details of the stone and found there the name of the deceased's father and her home-city, thus confirming his fears; as he contemplates the *stele*, the grief of Euthymenes left behind comes home with full force, and the speaker's voice expresses the husband's grief, a motif found so often in epitaphic poetry. Here, however, we are (I think) to understand that the grief is not explicitly stated on the stone: the speaker's conviction shows that Euthymenes' imagined grief is in fact more certain and more painfully laid bare than the conventional, but insistently present, expressions of inscribed epitaphs can convey.

In some cases, of course, there can be no doubt that a particular image or set of images has been designed to accompany the text which appears with it; here I will consider briefly just three examples. The first is one of a considerable number of poems, both 'literary' and 'non-literary', in which the inscribed text comments on and/or explains the images on the stone; such poems have something in common with the decoding of riddles.[12] *SGO* 04/02/11 is a late Hellenistic poem from Lydian Sardis accompanying the depiction of a clearly significant woman:

κομψὰν καὶ χαρίεσσα πέτρος δείκνυσι. τίς ἐντί;
    Μουσῶν μανύει γράμματα· Μηνοφίλαν.
τεῦ δ' ἕνεκεν στάλᾳ γλυπτὸν κρίνον ἠδὲ καὶ ἄλφα,
    βύβλος καὶ τάλαρος, τοῖς δ' ἔπι καὶ στέφανος;
ἦ σοφίαν μὲν βίβλος, ὁ δ' αὖ περὶ κρατὶ φορηθείς
    ἀρχὰν μανύει, μουνογόναν δὲ τὸ ἕν,
εὐτάκτου δ' ἀρετᾶς τάλαρος μάνυμα, τὸ δ' ἄνθος
    τὰν ἀκμάν, δαίμων ἄντιν' ἐληΐσατο.
κούφα τοι κόνις ἀμφὶ πέλοι τοιῇδε θανούσῃ.
    αἴ, ἄγονοι δὲ γονεῖς, τοῖς ἔλιπες δάκρυα.

GVI 1881 = SGO 04/02/11[13]

The graceful stone shows a pretty woman: who is she? The Muses' letters tell you: Menophila. For what reason is there a lily and an alpha carved on the *stele*, a book and a basket, and above these a wreath also? The book bears witness to her wisdom, the wreath worn around her head her office, the 'one' [i.e. alpha, interpreted numerically] the fact that she was an only child, the basket is a witness of her decency and virtue, and the flower of the prime of her life which the death-spirit plundered away. May the dust be light

---

12 For this aspect of the poem, cf. Fantuzzi/Hunter 2004, 334–338.
13 The text of the final couplet poses difficult problems which do not, however, affect the limited point being made here. The poem and the *stele* are discussed also by Pircher 1979, 53–58, Prioux 2007, 286–290, Squire 2009, 161–165.

upon you, who died such a person. Alas! Your parents, to whom you left only tears, have no children any more.

Here the voice of the passer-by and that of the monument itself blend together; we may understand that the former's question, 'Who is she?', is answered when he sees the words inscribed above the image, 'The *demos* [in honour of] Menophila, the daughter of Hermagenes', but his further puzzlement about the images must be answered by the monument itself. As such, this inscribed poem operates with a complicated blending of voices, and it is tempting to associate this sophistication with the paraded association of the dead woman with books and written σοφία, an association which gives this monument a particular significance in the history of female learning in antiquity.

The opening verse poses an interesting problem of our approach to inscribed poetry in general. The first editor of the stele remarked that *nu* had been omitted at the end of χαρίεσσαν, and he translated accordingly: 'Comely and full of grace is she whom the stone displays' (Robinson 1923, 349); he apparently did not notice that the accusative would make the verse unmetrical, and there is no sign elsewhere that this poet would have allowed himself such a graphic (in both senses) license. The matter was (silently) corrected by Wilamowitz 1924, 10, in the following year, 'Schon der anmutige Stein zeigt eine elegante Frau', and (despite some rather odd equivocations)[14] this is the interpretation which holds the field;[15] the text of the poem indeed seems to allow of no alternative. The original editor himself seems subsequently to have adopted the revised interpretation (cf. Buckler/Robinson 1932, 109). What is clear, however, is that the editor's original instinct did not spring from nowhere. κομψός and χαρίεις are very frequently found together with reference to the same person or object, and χαρίεσσα would much more naturally refer to a woman than to a stone *stele*;[16] so too, καί remains somewhat awkward in the first verse, and we might perhaps have expected a definite article with πέτρος. Without overstating the case, everything — except metre — might have led us to expect 'pretty and graceful' to refer to the woman depicted on the *stele*. Whether or not this too

---

14 *SEG* IV 634 seems to suggest that the *nu* has in fact been wrongly added on the stone, but I can see no trace of this on the published photographs; Cumont 1942, 302 n. 1 and Pleket 1969, 15 seem to follow Robinson's original publication without comment on the metre.
15 So Squire 2009, 163: 'That she is refined even the graceful stone reveals.'
16 Funerary epigrams do, of course, regularly praise the monument on which they appear, and early inscriptions, for example, offer μνῆμα … χαρίεν, σᾶμ' … καλὸν κεχαρισμένον ἔργον and χαρίεν … τόδ' ἄγαλμα (*CEG* 42.2, 165.2, 205.2–3), but the much later inscription for Menophila seems a very different case.

was the poet's initial instinct, one subsequently overruled by metrical necessity, we cannot, of course, say, but at the very least χαρίεσσα might be thought still to colour the representation of Menophila, as well as the stone on which she is depicted. Here (as often) we may wonder about what, if any, 'principle of charity' should be operative in the interpretation of inscribed poetry.

Fig. 1: *IGUR* III 1326, from Marshall 1916: 215.

IGUR III 1326 is a poem and accompanying depictions from the lid of a sarcophagus found in Rome; the date is probably mid-late second century AD:

Μ. [Σεμπρώνιος Νεικοκράτης][17]
ἤμην ποτὲ μουσικὸς ἀνήρ
ποιητὴς καὶ κιθαριστής,
μάλιστα δὲ καὶ συνοδείτης·
πολλὰ βυθοῖσι καμών,
ὁδηπορίες δ' ἀτονήσας,
ἔνπορος εὐμόρφων γενόμην,
φίλοι, μετέπειτα γυναικῶν.
πνεῦμα λαβὼν δάνος οὐρανόθεν
τελέσας χρόνον αὖτ' ἀπέδωκα,
καὶ μετὰ τὸν θάνατον
Μοῦσαί μου τὸ σῶμα κρατοῦσιν.

IGUR III 1326[18]

M. [Sempronius Nicocrates]. Once I was a musical man, a poet and lyre-player, and above all a member of the Foundation of Artists. I struggled long on the ocean waves and was exhausted by journeys, but after that, my friends, I became a merchant in beautiful wom-

---

17 The name is preserved on early copies of the sarcophagus, which was subsequently damaged.
18 I have reproduced the text and spelling of the original; on the metre of this poem, cf. Vollgraff 1951, 377.

en. I received breath from heaven as a loan, and having completed my time, I have now given it back, and after death the Muses hold my body.

The editor of *IGUR* observes, apparently with some surprise, that Nicocrates advertises his second, more lucrative profession, namely selling 'beautiful women' (presumably slaves), *nullo pudore*: so much more fun, in fact, than being a kind of musical Odysseus, worn out with the constant travelling. Two questions, at least, arise. Why is φίλοι placed where it is in the poem, right in the middle of 'beautiful ... women'? Is it there to remind Nicocrates' friends precisely of how he supplied them with female company? Was Nicocrates' second career a more private service than the musical performances to mass audiences? Post-mortem male bonding is still male bonding; do we see the deceased here sharing a joke with his fellow party-animals? Secondly, there is the representation on the lid of the sarcophagus. In *IGUR* Moretti describes it as follows:

> To the left there is a tragic mask, then a seated poet with a box of books under his chair; his left hand is carrying a book and his right arm is leaning on a column, on which a standing Muse (Polymnia?) also leans. On the right there is again the poet and a Muse (Terpsichore?), depicted in virtually the same way, except that here we have a very large lyre in place of the column and beneath the poet's chair is another tragic mask, rather than a box of books. At the very edge is the image of a beardless youth who could be the dead man.

There is a very loud silence here. Where is the seller of beautiful women, or indeed the beautiful women themselves? Many explanations could be found, of course, and one might easily think of entirely banal and 'innocent' explanations, but the apparent disjunction between image and poem might also suggest a recognition of a difference between 'public' and 'private' communicative spaces. We might think that the act of inscription amounted to the 'publication', that is 'making public', of what was written in exactly the same way as the iconographic representation, but the address to Nicocrates' φίλοι and the nature of what he (or someone else) has chosen to represent gives pause: were in fact some parts of an inscribed *stele* more 'public' than others?

My final example is an even clearer case where image and poem belong together. The poem and relief, published in 1969, were found on the *Via Egnatia* at Edessa in Macedonia; they cannot be more precisely dated than to the second or third century AD.[19] I reproduce the text here from Cabanes 1995; the translation which follows must be regarded as very provisional:

---

[19] Much of the early discussion is helpfully summarised in Daux 1970, and cf. also *SEG* XXV 711, Cabanes 1995, 157–158.

Fig. 2: Inv. No. AKA 1674, Museum of Pella. By permission of the Ephorate of Antiquities, Pella.

χοῖρος ὁ πᾶσι φίλος τετράπους νέος ἐνθάδε κεῖμαι
Δαλματίης δάπεδον προλιπὼν δῶρον προσενεχθείς
καὶ Δυρράχιν δὲ ἐπάτησα Ἀπολλωνίαν τε ποθήσας
καὶ πᾶσαν γαίην διέβην ποσὶ μοῦνος ἄλιπτος.
νῦν δὲ τροχοῖο βίῃ τὸ φάος προλέλοιπα.
Ἠμαθίην δὲ ποθῶν κατιδεῖν φαλλοῖο δὲ ἅρμα
ἐνθάδε νῦν κεῖμαι τῷ θανάτῳ μηκέτ' ὀφειλόμενος.

CIGIME I 527 = *SEG* XXV 711

Pig, beloved of all, quadruped, a youngster, here I lie, having left behind the land of Dalmatia when offered as a gift. I trod upon Dyrrhachium and Apollonia as I had desired and on foot I crossed the whole land, alone never overtaken. But now I have left the light due to the violence of a wheel. I wanted to see Emathia and the phallus' chariot: I lie here now, no longer owed to death.

Here there seems to be a full narrative, both pictorial and verbal. At first blush, this seems to be an epitaph for a Dalmatian pig which, having perhaps been presented to a traveller (?), travelled south and picked up the *Via Egnatia*, the two western ends of which were Dyrrachium and Apollonia. The pig's destination was Emathia near Thessaloniki, but after crossing most of the Balkans the pig was crushed by a wheel in a road accident at Edessa. There are a number of textual and interpretative uncertainties,[20] but the bigger questions rightly dominated the intensive discussion of this poem which followed publication, even if some of the proffered answers probably never commanded much support: Is this is a real or fictive epitaph? Is it a poem for a pig or for a man (perhaps a slave) called Khoiros, who was either four-foot-tall or walked on all fours when a baby? No pig, we were told, could have travelled that distance 'alone', for men or beasts would certainly have killed and eaten it along the way; ὁ πᾶσι φίλος in verse 1 shows that this cannot have been a real pig because everyone knows that pigs are not faithful, devoted companions, a view which prompted indignant scholarly replies on behalf of pigs, even in the 1970s. As for the 'phallus' chariot' on which the pig had set his heart, this is taken to refer either to a (perhaps unsurprisingly) otherwise unattested place-name or to a local Dionysiac cult which the pig wished to view (and of which it may in fact have been part — as a sacrifice perhaps).[21] Unsurprisingly too, Jeanne and Louis Robert realised that there was some humour here, and they took μοῦνος ἄλιπτος together as a

---

[20] The meaning of προσενεχθείς in v. 2 is unclear: 'presented as a gift', 'offered to a god'? Several interpreters have accepted that the second δέ in v. 6 should be emended to τε.
[21] Chaniotis 2018, 394–395 suggests that the pig was 'probably trained to perform acrobatic tricks in festivals' and had travelled 'to attend a Dionysiac procession'.

gesture towards the language of athletic victories: the pig was crowned as 'never overtaken', as a victorious runner would be.[22]

The relief perhaps poses even more questions than the poem. There has been much discussion as to whether the front pig (or is it a dog?) is the same as the pig beneath the wheels, a before and after if you like, and is that rear pig already dead? Does the relief show in fact the fatal accident happening – the carriage going too fast downhill; notice that the mules – or are they donkeys? – are lower than the carriage and that the animals are braying with their ears set back, which is apparently a certain sign of anger among equids. What, moreover, is the gender of the wagon-driver, who may no longer have control of the wagon, and what is the object apparently transported on the wagon: a dead pig, or perhaps a mystic phallus, in which case are we being shown the very φαλλοῖο ἅρμα which the pig had wished to see? Or just some unremarkable supplies for the journey?

If the poem and the relief currently defy a full explanation, there are nevertheless aspects of the technique of the poem which deserve notice and which find wider resonance in the epitaphic tradition. The versification of the hexameters is reasonably correct within the normal standards of inscribed poetry of this date. The fifth verse, however, is a dactylic pentameter, that is, it is one metron short. Why? Such an occurrence is far from unique in our corpus of verse inscriptions, but is it fanciful to see a mimetic effect here? As life is cut short, so too is the verse that marks that death; both the verse and the pig's life come to a sudden, unexpected end. This may be seen as a further example of the larger issue of what kind of 'principle of charity' should be operating within the interpretation of inscribed poetry? Another such case is the last verse of the poem. What is striking here is that ἐνθάδε νῦν κεῖμαι τῷ θανάτῳ would be a perfect pentameter, were it three syllables longer; we expect a pentameter at the end – the pentameter is the rhythmical hallmark of an epitaph, that verse-length which marks the finality of death (cf. Hunter 2019, 140–141). Here it is only after θανάτῳ that we realise that this is not an 'ordinary' pentameter: death calls attention to itself, just as the gap on the stone before ἐνθάδε brings the hexameters to a close and introduces something new. ἐνθάδε νῦν κεῖμαι was certainly intended to sound like, indeed to be, the first half of a pentameter; μηκέτ' ὀφειλόμενος would be a perfect second half, although not for the particular beginning with which it is here paired. What is going on here? As it happens, we know that κεῖμαι τῷ θανάτῳ μηκέτ' ὀφειλόμενος existed as a funerary verse; from second-century-AD Athens there survives an epitaph for a musician:

---

[22] Robert/Robert 1970, 407. Chaniotis 2018, 394 translates ἄλιπτος as 'undefeated'.

ἐνθάδ' ὁ ταῖς Μούσαις ἀρέσας Πρεῖμός ποθ' ἁπάσαις
κεῖμαι τῷ θανάτῳ μηκέτ' ὀφειλόμενος.

GVI 370

Here I lie, Primus who once pleased all the Muses, no longer owed to death.

We can say, if we wish, that the incompetent poet of the Edessa inscription ran two different pentameters together, perhaps in part prompted by a desire to introduce a touch of ring composition through the repeated ἐνθάδε κεῖμαι, but we might also say that what mattered to him was the resonance, the ἦθος, of the pentameter, much more than 'getting it right' as a piece of verse-composition; what we have in effect is, as it were, two pentameters for the price of one. This poem thus raises important questions about the critical assumptions we bring to our reading of such poetry.

Another reason why inscribed epigrams have in the past not received the sustained attention they deserve is that literary scholars, particularly in the last decades, are drawn to what they regard as allusive, self-conscious poetry as moths to a flame. Inscribed poetry is thought to stand outside this web of allusivity, and so it does to some extent, but to *what* extent is the key question. This scholarly habit means in fact that inscribed poems which do seem to allude to other poems, whether 'literary' or not, have sometimes attracted more attention than others.[23] Allusion and evocation of Homer is, of course, a special case, for Homer's place in Greek education and culture meant that echoes of the *Iliad* and the *Odyssey* are found all over funerary epitaphs throughout antiquity and at almost every level of literacy.[24]

Issues of both a typical and a special kind are raised, for example, by a funerary epitaph of uncertain imperial date, perhaps the first half of the third century (cf. Laminger-Pascher 1992, 228), from Isauria in central Asia Minor:

---

23 Garulli 2012 is a major study; cf. also Bettenworth 2007.
24 Cf. Hunter 2018, 4–24 (with earlier bibliography).

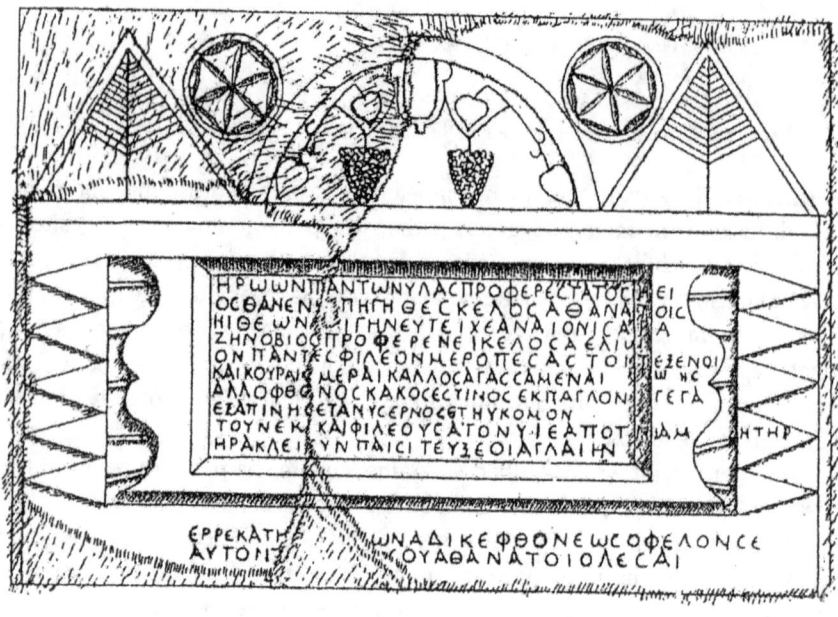

Fig. 3: *SGO* 14/13/05, from Ramsay 1906: 47.

ἡρώων πάντων Ὕλας προφερέστατος ἦεν
ὃς θάνεν ἐν πηγῇ θέσκελος ἀθανάτοις.
ἠϊθέων δ', οἳ γῆν εὐτειχέα ναῖον Ἴσαρα,
Ζηνόβιος πρόφερεν, εἴκελος Ἀελίῳ·
ὃν πάντες φίλεον μέροπες, ἀστοί τε ξένοι τε   5
καὶ κοῦραι θαλεραί, κάλλος ἀγασσάμεναι.
ἀλλ' ὁ Φθόνος κακός ἐστιν, ὃς ἔκπαγλον γεγαῶτα
ἐξαπίνης ἐτάνυσσ', ἔρνος ἅτ' ἠΰκομον.
τοὔνεκα καὶ φιλέουσα τὸν υἱέα πότνια μήτηρ
Ἡρακλεῒς σὺν παισὶν τεῦξέ οἱ ἀγλαΐην.   10
ἔρρε κατηφιόων, ἄδικε Φθόνε· ὡς ὄφελόν σε
αὐτὸν τ[έκνα τ]έ σου ἀθάνατοι ὀλέσαι.

GVI 1732 = *SGO* 14/13/05

Of all the heroes Hylas was the most outstanding, he who, like to the immortal gods, died in a spring. But of all the young men who lived in the land of Isara of the splendid walls Zenobios was outstanding, like to Helios. All people loved him, citizens and foreigners and blooming young girls who were struck by his beauty. But Malice is evil; it suddenly stretched him out when he had become marvellous, like a young tree with lovely foliage. Therefore his noble mother, Herakleis, who loved her son, together with her children constructed this splendour for him [i.e. the sarcophagus]. Off with you in shame, unjust Malice! May the immortals destroy you yourself and your children.[25]

The poem falls clearly into two halves, with the sudden intrusion of ἀλλά at the head of verse 7 marking the transition. Both halves are marked by a kind of ring-composition: the girls' admiration for Zenobios' beauty in verse 6 clearly brings back the opening image of Hylas, and Phthonos, 'Malice', frames the second half of the poem which considers Zenobios in death, no longer in the glorious life of the first half. Hylas seems to have been a favoured choice as mythico-poetical model for boys who died young, even if they did not drown, but the transference of female admiration from Hylas to his latter-day reflection is a striking effect of blurred temporal levels, one reinforced by the echoing effect of προφερέστατος (1) ~ πρόφερεν (4). That parallelism also governs the matching θέσκελος ἀθανάτοις (2) ~ εἴκελος Ἀελίῳ (4). The poet almost certainly took the Homeric θέσκελος to derive from θεοείκελος, which is a standard gloss on θέσκελος in the scholia and the late lexicographers; he presumably understood θέσκελος ἀθανάτοις to mean 'in the image of the gods', with θέσκελος differing from εἴκελος only by a reinforced sense of 'likeness to god'. The whole phrase will in fact have been an extended synonym for ἰσόθεος. Of particular importance in the development of this way of understanding the word may have been Achilles' account of Patroclus' ghost at *Iliad* 23.107, εἴκτο δὲ θέσκελον αὐτῷ (that is, to the 'living Patroclus'). The comparison of Zenobios to the sun may not merely contrast Zenobios' brilliance with the darkness of the death into which he is now plunged, and point to his superiority over all other young men as analogous to the supremacy of the sun in the sky, but may also evoke (again) the myth of Hylas. Although Hylas is normally described as disappearing in darkness, in Apollonius of Rhodes the nymph sees Hylas 'blushing red (ἐρευθόμενον) with beauty and sweet graces' in the moonlight (1.1229–1232) and in Theocritus Hylas falls into the 'black water' like a 'flaming shooting-star' (13.50 πυρσὸς ... ἀστήρ). The sun as the source of life brings out the essence of Zenobios' name, which may be understood as combining two words for 'life/to live' (ζῆν, βίος) and which stands in sad contrast to the fate that has befallen him.

The diction of the poem is markedly poetic. The obscure μέροπες is a source of comic amusement as early as the fourth century BC (Strato fr. 1.6–8 K-A); in

---

25 I have printed Wilhelm's supplement in the final verse, but unless we see a somewhat awkward adaptation of a standard curse formula, we will be bound to wonder who the 'children of Malice' are. Peek reads γ᾽ [ἀντὶ τό]σου. There is a temptation to look to the *envoi* of Callimachus' *Hymn to Apollo* as a model for the second half of the Isaurian poem, but that temptation should perhaps be resisted.

Homer it is always an epithet of 'men', but the use as a noun is early, though post-Homeric. εὐτειχέα, ἀγασσάμεναι, ἠΰκομον (in Homer only of people and gods), ἔκπαγλον and γεγαῶτα are also poetic 'fragments' far removed from ordinary discourse. In this context, the very frequent Homeric verse-end πότνια μήτηρ is not just a metrically convenient Homeric phrase, but continues the heroic stature of the dead. The poet has not only composed in a markedly high-style manner, but he has also echoed two specific passages of Homer to lend authority both to his poem and to the claims on Zenobios' behalf. The opening verse derives from Homer's description of the athletic games on Scherie, which contain the only Homeric example of the superlative προφερέστατος:

> οἱ δὲ παλαιμοσύνης ἀλεγεινῆς πειρήσαντο·
> τῇ δ' αὖτ' Εὐρύαλος ἀπεκαίνυτο πάντας ἀρίστους.
> ἅλματι δ' Ἀμφίαλος πάντων προφερέστατος ἦεν·
> δίσκῳ δ' αὖ πάντων πολὺ φέρτατος ἦεν Ἐλατρεύς,
> πὺξ δ' αὖ Λαοδάμας, ἀγαθὸς πάϊς Ἀλκινόοιο.
>
> *Od.* 8.126–130

Then they turned their hands to wrestling which brings pain, and here in turn Euryalus surpassed all the princes. And in leaping Amphialus was the most outstanding of all, and with the discus again by far the best of all was Elatreus, and again in boxing Laodamas, the excellent son of Alcinous.

These competitions between young men (8.110 νέοι πολλοί τε καὶ ἐσθλοί) are erased by the qualities of Hylas and Zenobios, who are counted as the finest *tout court* of the young men of the past and present, not merely the finest in a particular sport. Nevertheless, the echo of the Phaeacian games may also suggest some of the activities in which Zenobios (allegedly at least) displayed his supremacy and also perhaps the occasions on which he drew particularly admiring female glances.

Those commemorated in epitaphic verse are often described as 'shoots' (ἔρνη) of their parents, and the comparison of those who die too young to trees or saplings is well attested. *GVI* 1023 (Phrygia, first — second century AD) is spoken by a fourteen-year-old girl who 'grew up like a young tree and then became dust' (2 ἔρνος ὅπως ἀναβὰς ἔνθα κόνις γενόμην), and *GVI* 1555 (Messenia, second century AD) is a funerary poem for two boys (twins?) who died ἄμφω πρωθήβας, ἔρνεσιν εἰδομένους, 'both in first youth, like young trees' (v. 6).[26] Such comparisons, of course, have their origin in Homer. Twice in *Iliad* 18 Thetis describes Achilles as ἔξοχον ἡρώων, ὃ δ' ἀνέδραμεν ἔρνεϊ ἶσος, 'outstanding

---

[26] See further Hollis 2009, 196–197 on Call. *Hec.* fr. 48.7 Hollis.

among the heroes, and he shot up like a young tree' (*Il.* 18.56 = 437), and Eumaeus' lament for Telemachus, whom 'the gods nourished like a young tree (ἔρνεϊ ἶσον)' (*Od.* 14.175), might well be thought close to the lamentation for Zenobios, cut down before he reached his full potential. Zenobios was, however, 'stretched out', that is cut down, 'like a plant with lovely foliage', and the poet clearly has in mind the description (very much cited in antiquity) of the death of Euphorbus in *Iliad* 17:

αἵματί οἱ δεύοντο κόμαι Χαρίτεσσιν ὁμοῖαι
πλοχμοί θ', οἳ χρυσῷ τε καὶ ἀργύρῳ ἐσφήκωντο.
οἷον δὲ τρέφει ἔρνος ἀνὴρ ἐριθηλὲς ἐλαίης
χώρῳ ἐν οἰοπόλῳ, ὅθ' ἅλις ἀναβέβροχεν ὕδωρ,
καλὸν τηλεθάον, τὸ δέ τε πνοιαὶ δονέουσιν   55
παντοίων ἀνέμων, καί τε βρύει ἄνθεϊ λευκῷ,
ἐλθὼν δ' ἐξαπίνης ἄνεμος σὺν λαίλαπι πολλῇ
βόθρου τ' ἐξέστρεψε καὶ ἐξετάνυσσ' ἐπὶ γαίῃ·
τοῖον Πάνθου υἱόν, ἐϋμμελίην Εὔφορβον,
Ἀτρεΐδης Μενέλαος ἐπεὶ κτάνε τεύχε' ἐσύλα.   60

Il. 17.51–60

His hair, like that of the Graces, and his locks, which were plaited with gold and silver, were drenched in blood. As when a man nurtures a flourishing young olive tree in an isolated place, where water flows up in abundance — it grows splendid and flourishing, and the breaths of every wind shake it, and it is full of white flowers; but suddenly a wind with great gusts appears and uproots it from its trench and lays it stretched out on the earth. Such was the son of Panthous, Euphorbus of the splendid ash-spear, when Menelaus, son of Atreus, killed him and stripped him of his armour.

Verse 8 of the Isaurian poem both clearly echoes verses 57–8 of *Iliad* 17 (ἐξαπίνης ἐτάνυσσ') and also evokes, through ἔρνος ἅτ' ἠΰκομον, both the Homeric simile and Euphorbus' lovely hair. The exegetical scholia on this passage stress that the comparison of Euphorbus to an olive-tree emphasises the young man's youthful grace, because it is a tree 'which is shapely (εὐειδές) and preserves its beauty (κάλλος), as it is always flourishing';[27] the Isaurian poet has, we might say, found in Euphorbus the Homeric model for both Hylas and Zenobios. Whereas, however, Euphorbus was killed in battle by Menelaus and Hylas was taken by κοῦραι who did more than just 'wonder at his beauty', nothing is said about the manner of Zenobios' death (presumably from illness and otherwise unremarkable?), but the real cause of death is clear. Malice punished Zenobios

---

[27] Eust. *Il.* 1095.31–32 notes that this simile shows that Homer pitied Euphorbus 'more than any other fallen Trojan'.

for his beauty and moral grace (implied by the affection felt for him by 'all people'); however familiar the theme of Death as φθονερός (cf., e.g., Lattimore 1942, 147–149), Zenobios' virtues (1–6) leave no room for any other explanation.

Not the least remarkable feature of this poem is the decoration on the sarcophagus on which it is inscribed; the richness matches the poetic riches of the inscribed verses;[28] the mixture of local and imported 'high' elements might be thought to match the high style poem in honour of a 'local hero'. Verses 1–10 are inscribed (with some overrun at the ends of the line) on a recessed central panel of a familiar type; we cannot know the precise relationship between the decoration and the composition and inscription of the poem, but it is noteworthy that these verses, explicitly concerned with Zenobios, neatly fill the recessed area, without (as far as the published drawing allows one to judge) very much compression. The final couplet, which both follows on and, in the cursing of Phthonos, partly repeats what has preceded, may be read separately as a denunciation of Malice; as such it is in part detached from what has preceded, as indeed it is visually on the stone. It stands as a message to the world, as well as to Phthonos, and one which could be repeated from sarcophagus to sarcophagus.[29]

Before passing to an instance of allusion to a poem much closer in time than Homer, it is worth pausing to note that the Homeric phrases which we find everywhere in later epitaphic poetry may of course carry very different allusive weights. This is particularly the case for 'formulaic' phrases, where there is often much room for disagreement as to whether or not a specific passage of Homer is evoked. GVI 1632 is a hexameter epitaph of the second or third century AD for a doctor from ancient Tomi:

αἴ τις ἐμὰν μετὰ μοῖραν ἐμὸν βίον ἐξερεείνῃ
χὤτις ἔην τί τ' ἔρεξα, καὶ οὔνομα πατρίδος ἀμῆς,
μανύσει λίθος ἅδε καὶ ἐσσομένοισιν ἀκουήν·
πάτρα μοι πέλεται ματρόπτολις Εὐξείνοιο,
ἄστυ περικλήϊστον ἐϋμμελίαο Τομήτου·
οὔνομα δ' ἧς Κλάδαιος, τέχναν δ' ἐδάημεν ἄνακτος
Ἱπποκράτους θείοιο καὶ ἐσσομένοισιν ἀκουήν.

GVI 1632 = EG 537

---

28 The discussion of the sarcophagus in Ramsay 1904, 261–264 (repeated in Ramsay 1906, 46–50) is (amusingly) negative about the 'unintelligent' decoration.
29 The closest parallel seems to be the final couplet of GVI 1552 (late Hellenistic), which begins ἔρρε, Τύχη πανόδυρτε; that couplet, however, is firmly tied to the specific details of the poem.

If after my death someone should ask about my life and who I was and what I did and the name of my home-city, this stone will bear the news also to men of the future. My homeland is the mother-city of the Euxine, the famed city of Tometos of the splendid spear. Kladaios was my name, and I learned the art of the divine master Hippocrates, famed even to men of the future.

What little comment this poem has attracted has largely concerned what Kaibel refers to as the 'mira dialectorum confusio'; there are also textual uncertainties which do not, however, seriously affect interpretation.[30] There are relatively many elements of high/Homeric style (ἐξερεείνῃ, ἔρεξα, πέλεται, περικλήϊστον, ἐϋμμελίαο, θείοιο), and this, like the invocation of Hippocrates, will have suited the learned pretensions of a doctor; even the play on πάτρα ... ματρόπολις is part of the poetic texture of the whole. Most striking, however, is the repetition of καὶ ἐσσομένοισιν ἀκουήν in verses 3 and 7. καὶ ἐσσομένοισι occurs some ten times in Homer, most frequently in the verse-end καὶ ἐσσομένοισι πυθέσθαι, although twice as καὶ ἐσσομένοισιν ἀοιδήν (Od. 3.204, 8.580), which is close in structure to the repetition in the poem from Tomi. It is hardly surprising that the idea of the preservation of fame or report was picked up by the epitaphic tradition, but one Homeric instance stands out as potentially 'more equal' than others.[31] The first ghost whom Odysseus meets in the Nekuia of Odyssey 11 is that of the unburied Elpenor, who begs the hero to give him proper burial:

σῆμά τέ μοι χεῦαι πολιῆς ἐπὶ θινὶ θαλάσσης
ἀνδρὸς δυστήνοιο καὶ ἐσσομένοισι πυθέσθαι.

Od. 11.75–76

... and raise a marker for me, a wretched man, on the shore of the grey sea, for men of the future also to learn of me.

The Homeric prayer for a tomb has been fulfilled in the case of Kladaios, whose σῆμα now speaks to all men of future generations. The repetition of the phrase at the end of the poem is a kind of echoing effect which confirms the hopeful promise of καὶ ἐσσομένοισι: those as yet unborn *will* hear. Elpenor was an 'ordinary' man who died in 'ordinary' circumstances, and his self-pitying address to

---

30 The text printed above is that of GVI.
31 The Homeric phrase was by no means limited to epitaphic contexts. A poem celebrating the Attalid Sosicrates (third century BC) describes the Delian monument by Nikeratos in his honour as μνῆμα καὶ ἐσσομένοισιν ἀοίδιμον, which goes back to Helen's words at Il. 6.357–358; the transference of ἀοίδιμος from people to buildings and works of art occurs as early as Hymn. Hom. Ap. 298, cf. CEG 136.2. Bing/Bruss 2007, 11 suggest that ἀοίδιμον in the Delian poem predicts 'literary epigrams' about the monument.

Odysseus catches the horror of the idea of death; no wonder he appealed to the subsequent tradition as 'one of us'.

SGO 08/08/10 is an epitaph for a thirteen-year-old boy from Hadrianoi in Mysia; the date is uncertain, but Merkelbach and Stauber very tentatively classify it as 'late Hellenistic/early Empire':

"τίς τίνος;" ἦν εἴρῃ, Κλάδος οὔνομα· καὶ "τίς ὁ θρέψας;"
Μηνόφιλος· "θνῄσκω δ' ἐκ τίνος;" ἐκ πυρετοῦ·
"κἀπὸ πόσων ἐτέων;" τρισκαίδεκα· "ἆρα γ' ἄμουσος;"
οὐ τέλεον, Μούσαις δ' οὐ μέγα φιλάμενος,
ἔξοχα δ' Ἑρμείᾳ μεμελημένος· ἐν γὰρ ἀγῶσιν
πολλάκις αἰνητὸν στέμμα πάλας ἔλαχον·
Ἀπφία ἡ θάψασα δ' ἐμὴ τροφός, ἥ μοι ἔτευξεν
εἰκόνα καὶ τύμβῳ σῆμ' ἐπέθηκε τόδε.

SGO 08/08/10

If you ask 'Who are you and who is your father?', my name is Klados, and [if you ask] 'Who brought you up?', Menophilos. [If you ask] 'What was the cause of my death?', a fever. 'How old were you?', thirteen. 'Were you uneducated?'. Not entirely. I was not very dear to the Muses, but was a very special favourite of Hermes: in athletic contests I many times won the glorious wreath for wrestling. Apphia who buried me was my nurse, and she also had an image of me made and placed this marker on the tomb.

This seems to be a poem about a young 'jock', intellectually challenged but very good at martial arts; Hermes and the Muses, between whom he unevenly divided his attention, were the divinities who watched over the gymnasium.[32] In her very useful study of the epitaphs of children, Anne-Marie Vérilhac (1978–1982, 2.392) regards the poem as singularly unsuccessful because the deceased is made to acknowledge his 'lack of intellectual capabilities'; such honesty (though that is not the word Vérilhac uses) is 'tout à fait insolite'. Others may wish to detect some humour in the child's self-presentation. Be that as it may, it has long been recognised that this poem has a relationship with an epitaphic poem of Leonidas of Tarentum, which enjoyed a remarkable *Nachleben* (cf. Bettenworth 2007, 86–89, Garulli 2008, 642–648):

τίς τίνος εὖσα, γύναι, Παρίην ὑπὸ κίονα κεῖσαι;
"Πρηξὼ Καλλιτέλευς." καὶ ποδαπή; "Σαμίη."
τίς δέ σε καὶ κτερέϊξε; "Θεόκριτος, ᾧ με γονῆες

---

32 With v. 4, cf. Theocr. 11.6 (Nicias) ταῖς ἐννέα δὴ πεφιλημένον ἔξοχα Μοίσαις, and Call. *Aet.* fr. 1.2 (whatever the right reading). For a rather different reading of this poem, cf. Casey 2004, 75.

ἐξέδοσαν." θνῄσκεις δ' ἐκ τίνος; "ἐκ τοκετοῦ."
εὖσα πόσων ἐτέων; "δύο κεἴκοσιν." ἦ ῥά γ' ἄτεκνος;   5
"οὔκ, ἀλλὰ τριετῆ Καλλιτέλην ἔλιπον."
ζώοι σοι κεῖνός γε καὶ ἐς βαθὺ γῆρας ἵκοιτο.
"καὶ σοί, ξεῖνε, πόροι πάντα Τύχη τὰ καλά."

AP 7.163

Who are you and who is your father, lady, who lies under the Parian pillar? 'Prexo, daughter of Kalliteles.' Where were you from? 'Samos.' Who buried you? 'Theokritos, to whom my parents gave me.' What was the cause of your death? 'Childbirth.' How old were you? 'Twenty-two.' Were you childless? 'No, I left behind three year-old Kalliteles.' May he survive and reach a ripe old age. 'May Fortune also be very kind to you, stranger.'

The apparent replacement of ἄτεκνος by ἄμουσος may be thought particularly interesting in view of the frequent characterisation of intellectual and literary products as one's 'children' and the whole language of fertility which surrounded literary composition in antiquity. There is much too, however, that one would wish to know (for example) about the form in which the poet of *SGO* 08/08/10 knew Leonidas' poem and whether or not he expected any relationship between the two texts to be recognised; the study of inscribed poetry opens the door to very broad questions of the transmission of texts of all kinds (and at all periods) in antiquity. In the present case we might think that the opening τίς τίνος is so common that we can hardly expect any reader to be alert to any intertextual relationship after the first reading of those words. Leonidas' poem is a dialogue between a passer-by (to use the conventional designation for the anonymous interlocutor) and the deceased woman or (but the 'or' perhaps does not matter so much) her tombstone. As Valentina Garulli (2012, 127) acknowledges, however, the poem from Hadrianoi (once we accept Merkelbach's punctuation and articulation of verse 1) is not a real dialogue, but rather a monologue by the deceased (or his tombstone), in which the voice imagines the questions which the passer-by will pose: 'If you ask X, I will say Y; <If you ask> A, B; <If you ask> C, D', and so on and so forth. The form assumes and plays with our familiarity with epitaphic poems which are 'real dialogues'; it is an amusing effect that this thirteen-year-old knows the stuff of such exchanges so very well, despite his ἀμουσία.

One very interesting effect occurs in verse 2. In Leonidas' poem the passer-by asks 'What was the cause of your death?'; in the poem from Hadrianoi the boy/tombstone says '<if you ask> "What was the cause of my death?"'. Is this the result of a poet who could not quite keep control of the secondary formation of a dialogue reported by a single voice (as though the deceased suddenly slipped into a form of indirect speech), or is it rather a marker of the young man's self-obsession (which may be an unfair way to put it).³³ The matter is perhaps even more uncertain. In Leonidas' epigram, the direct question form is emphasised by the grammatically feminine forms used of and by the speaker and by the σε ... με, whereas in verse 1 of the inscribed poem we might wonder whether the full form would be "τίς τίνος <ἐγώ>;" ἦν εἴρηι ... καὶ "τίς <μ'> ὁ θρέψας;" or rather "τίς τίνος <σύ>;" ἦν εἴρηι ... καὶ "τίς <σ'> ὁ θρέψας;" In the absence of any other indication we would I think (silently) assume the latter, but verse 2 brings us up short. The creation of voice, what we have learned in literary texts to call *ēthopoiia*, is not the least attraction (and challenge) of our corpus of inscribed verse.

The kinds of problems and possibilities touched on in this chapter occur throughout our corpus of Greek verse inscriptions. We should not seek to minimise the differences between these poems and those which circulated solely in papyrus collections identified by author, but we should also do more to exploit a very rich resource for the study of Greek poetic language and imagery and for the circulation of texts in antiquity. No one should complain that there is nothing left to do.

Abbreviations

CEG   Hansen, P. *Carmina epigraphica graeca*, 2 vols, Berlin, 1983–1989.
CIGIME   Cabanes, P. et al. *Corpus des inscriptions grecques d'Illyrie méridionale et d'Epire*, Athens, 1995–.
EG   Kaibel, G. *Epigrammata graeca ex lapidibus conlecta*, Berlin, 1878.
GVI   Peek, W. *Griechische Vers-Inschriften*, Berlin, 1955.
IGUR   Moretti, L. *Inscriptiones graecae urbis Romae*, 4 vols., Rome, 1968–1990.
SEG   *Supplementum epigraphicum graecum*, Leiden, 1923–.
SGO   Merkelbach, R. and J. Stauber, *Steinepigramme aus dem griechischen Osten*, 5 vols., Stuttgart, 1998–2004.

---

33 Tueller 2016, 223–225 calls attention to the use of the present tense θνῄσκω, 'even when its intended time is clearly past', as almost entirely confined to inscribed epigram; he suggests that the usage increases vividness. Such an explanation would sit well with what I am suggesting for *SGO* 08/08/10.

Bibliography

Anderson, J.G.C. 1903. *A journey of exploration in Pontus*, Brussels.
Bettenworth, A. 2007. 'The mutual influence of inscribed and literary epigram', in: Bing/Bruss 2007, 69–93.
Bing, P. 2009. *The scroll and the marble*, Ann Arbor.
Bing, P./Bruss, J.S. (eds.) 2007. *Brill's companion to Hellenistic epigram down to Philip*, Leiden.
Buckler, W.H./Calder, W.M. (eds.) 1923. *Anatolian studies presented to Sir William Mitchell Ramsay*, Manchester.
Buckler, W.H./Robinson, D.M. 1932. *Sardis VII: Greek and Latin inscriptions*, part 1, Leiden.
Cabanes, P. 1995. *Corpus des inscriptions grecques d'Illyrie méridionale et d'Émpire*, vol. 1, Paris.
Casey, E. 2004. 'Binding speeches: giving voice to deadly thoughts in Greek epitaphs', in: I. Sluiter/R. Rosen (eds.), *Free speech in classical antiquity*, Leiden, 63–90.
Chaniotis, A. 2018. *Age of conquests: the Greek world from Alexander to Hadrian*, London.
Christian, T. 2015. *Gebildete Steine: zur Rezeption literarischer Techniken in den Versinschriften seit dem Hellenismus*, Göttingen.
Clairmont, C.W. 1970. *Gravestone and epigram*, Mainz.
Cumont, F. 1942. *Recherches sur le symbolisme funéraire des Romains*, Paris.
Daux, G. 1970. 'Epitaphe métrique d'un jeune porc, victim d'un accident', *BCH* 94, 609–618.
Day, J.W. 2010. *Archaic Greek epigram and dedication*, Cambridge.
Fantuzzi, M./Hunter, R. 2004. *Tradition and innovation in Hellenistic poetry*, Cambridge.
Garulli, V. 2008. 'L'*epigramma longum* nella tradizione epigrafica sepolcrale greca', in: A.M. Morelli (ed.), *Epigramma longum da Marziale alla tarda antichità*, Cassino, 623–662.
Garulli, V. 2012. *Byblos lainee: epigrafia, letteratura, epitafio*, Bologna.
Hanink, J. 2010. 'The epitaph for Atthis: a late Hellenistic poem on stone', *JHS* 130, 15–34.
Hollis, A.S. 2009. *Callimachus: Hecale*, 2nd ed., Oxford.
Hunter, R. 2002. 'The sense of an author: Theocritus and [Theocritus]', in: R. Gibson/C. Kraus (eds.), *The classical commentary*, Leiden, 89–108.
Hunter, R. 2018. *The measure of Homer*, Cambridge.
Hunter, R. 2019. 'Death of a child: grief beyond the literary?', in: M. Kanellou/I. Petrovic/C. Carey (eds.), *Greek epigram from the Hellenistic to the early Byzantine era*, Oxford, 137–153 [= this volume 267–285].
Laminger-Pascher, G. 1992. *Die kaiserzeitlichen Inschriften Lykaoniens I: Der Süden*, Vienna.
Lattimore, R. 1942. *Themes in Greek and Latin epitaphs*, Urbana.
Maiuri, A. 1932. *Clara Rhodos II*, Rhodes.
Marshall, F.H. 1916. *The collection of ancient Greek inscriptions in the British Museum*, vol. 4.2, Oxford.
Pircher, J. 1979. *Das Lob der Frau im vorchristlichen Grabepigramm der Griechen*, Innsbruck.
Pleket, H.W. 1969. *Epigraphica*, vol. 2, Leiden.
Prioux, E. 2007. *Regards alexandrins: histoire et théorie des arts dans l'épigramme hellénistique*, Leuven.
Ramsay, A.M. 1904. 'The early Christian art of Isaura Nova', *JHS* 24, 260–292.
Ramsay, A.M. 1906. 'Isaurian and East-Phrygian art in the third and fourth centuries after Christ', in: W.M. Ramsay (ed.), *Studies in the history and art of the Eastern provinces of the*

Roman Empire, London, 3–92.

Robert, J./Robert, L. 1970. 'Bulletin épigraphique', *REG* 83, 362–488.

Robert, L. 1959. Review of *GVI*, *Gnomon* 31, 1–30.

Robinson, D.M. 1923. 'Two new epitaphs from Sardis', in: Buckler/Calder 1923, 341–353.

Santin, E. 2009. *Autori di epigrammi sepolcrali greci su pietra: firme di poeti occasionali e professionisti*, Rome.

Sigalas, C./Matthaiou, A.P. 1992/98. 'Ἐπιγραφὲς Θήρας', *Horos* 10/12, 385–402.

Squire, M. 2009. *Image and text in Graeco-Roman antiquity*, Cambridge.

Tueller, M.A. 2016. 'Words for dying in sepulchral epigram', in: E. Sistakou/A. Rengakos (eds.), *Dialect, diction, and style in Greek literary and inscribed epigram*, Berlin, 215–233.

Vérilhac, A.-M. 1978–1982. *Παῖδες ἄωροι: poésie funéraire*, 2 vols., Athens.

Vollgraff, W. 1951. *Inhumation en terre sacrée dans l'antiquité grecque (à propos d'une inscription d'Argos)*, Paris.

Walsh, G.B. 1991. 'Callimachean passages: the rhetoric of epitaph in epigram', *Arethusa* 24, 77–105.

von Wilamowitz-Moellendorff, U. 1924. Review of Buckler and Calder 1923, *Litteris* 1, 3–15.

Wilhelm, A. 1942. *Attische Urkunden*, vol. 5, Vienna.

43 John Malalas and the Story of the Cyclops

One of the most remarkable ancient accounts of the story of Odysseus and the Cyclops is found in the fifth book of the *Chronographia* ('Universal History') of John Malalas, the sixth-century AD chronicler from Antioch, who worked both in his native city and subsequently in Constantinople. Not the least interest of Malalas' version (5.17–18, pp. 85–87 Thurn), parts of which are transmitted also in other mythographic traditions,[1] is that it apparently contains the last reference before the high Byzantine period to Euripides' *Cyclops*, the only fully extant Athenian satyr-play. Given the paucity of our knowledge about the history in later antiquity of the so-called 'alphabetical' plays of Euripides, to which grouping the *Cyclops* belongs, Malalas' narrative deserves particular attention from students of the fate of Euripides' dramatic corpus.

In Malalas' account of Odysseus' wanderings in Book 5 of his chronicle, the hero and his men land on Sicily, after losing nearly all his men in a war with the surprisingly (for those who know their Homer) military Lotus-eaters (5.16). Sicily is ruled by three powerful brothers called Kyklops, Antiphantes (or Antiphates) and Polyphemos, none of whom were well disposed towards strangers. On Sicily, Odysseus first encountered Antiphantes and his army of Laistrygonians who killed many of the Greek sailors. From there Odysseus fled to the part of the island ruled by Kyklops, who was 'large and hideous' (μέγας ... καὶ δυσειδής), but there too he lost many men in a battle; one of Odysseus' men was then disembowelled with a sword in full view of his comrades 'for having fought against Kyklops'. After this, Kyklops 'shut up all the survivors, wishing to kill them one by one (κατὰ μέρος)';[2] Odysseus, however, manages to escape through trickery and bribery, and when Kyklops discovers that they have got away 'in his fury he ordered rocks to be thrown into the sea, in case Odysseus had moored within his territory'. Odysseus, however, has successfully moved to the part of the island ruled by Polyphemos, where there is another nocturnal battle during which more of Odysseus' men are killed. What follows is an account of the hero's dealings with Polyphemos:[3]

> When morning came, Odysseus also offered Polyphemos guest-gifts and fell at his feet, saying that he had come from the troubles at Troy, forced off course by the waves (ἀπὸ

---

1 Cf. Cramer 1839, II 208–210, Dindorf 1855, I 4–5 and Alwine 2009.
2 The version at Dindorf 1855, I 4 has Odysseus 'himself shut up in a cave'.
3 Thurn supplements the manuscript of Malalas with additions (marked by ‹ ... ›) suggested by the other surviving versions, and I have followed him.

τῶν Τρωικῶν πόνων ἐλήλυθε πεπλανημένος ἀπὸ πολλῆς κυμάτων ἀνάγκης),[4] and he recounted to him all the catastrophes which had befallen him on the sea-voyage. Polyphemos was sympathetic <to his very many troubles> and pitied him and took in Odysseus and his men until it would be appropriate to sail. Polyphemos' daughter,[5] called Elpe, fell in love with a handsome man among Odysseus' comrades called Leion, and when a suitable wind blew they snatched her away <without Odysseus' knowledge> and sailed off from Sicily. <Polyphemus sent many of his own men after them and when they caught up with them they violently took Elpe away>. The most wise (σοφώτατος) Sisyphos of Cos has set these things out. For (γάρ) the wise Euripides set out a drama <in the poetic manner (ποιητικῶς)> about the Cyclops, in which he had three eyes, by which were indicated the three brothers, who were sympathetic to each other and looked out for each other's parts of the island and acted as allies and avengers for each other. [Euripides also said] that Odysseus made the Cyclops drunk (μεθύσας) with wine and was able to escape, because Odysseus made the same Cyclops drunk (ἐμέθυσε) on many possessions and gifts so that he would not devour (κατεσθίειν) his comrades, <that is, not waste them by slaughter (τουτέστι μὴ καταναλίσκειν σφαγαῖς) >. Moreover, he said that Odysseus took a fiery torch and blinded his one eye (τὸν ὀφθαλμὸν αὐτοῦ τὸν ἕνα), because he snatched away Elpe, the virginal only daughter (θυγατέρα) of his brother Polyphemos, who had been burned with the torch of love's fire; that means that, in taking away his daughter, he burned Polyphemos, one of the Cyclops' eyes. This interpretation is set out by the very wise Phidalios[6] of Corinth, who says that the wise Euripides changed (μετέφρασε) all these things in the poetic manner (ποιητικῶς) and did not agree with the very wise Homer in setting out the wanderings of Odysseus.

John Malalas, Chronographia 5.18 Thurn

This remarkable account of Odysseus' Sicilian adventures seems to be structured into two sections. The first, much longer one gives a sequential account of Odysseus' encounters with three brothers, Kyklops, Polyphemos and Antiphantes, who has been transported, with the Laistrygonians, to Sicily; the source for this account is apparently given as Sisyphos of Cos, a mythographer known only from Malalas, but who is generally thought to have borrowed extensively from Dictys of Crete (2nd–3rd cent. AD), another of Malalas' sources.[7] The three brothers seem to be a reflection of the fact that the three-cornered Sicily tended

---

4 Cf. below p. 881–882.
5 The version in Dindorf 1855, 4 has 'his only daughter' (θυγατέρα ἣν εἶχε μονογενῆ), which presumably reflects the Cyclops' single eye, cf. further below.
6 The transmission also offers Philadios and Pheidias, cf. D'Alfonso 2006, 19 n. 25.
7 For Sisyphos cf. *FGrHist* 50, Patzig 1903, Griffin 1907, 60–81, Cameron 2004, 149–150; there is no very good reason to regard Sisyphos and Phidalios as complete fictions, but caution is obviously necessary when dealing with material of this kind, cf. in general Cameron 2004: chapter 6. For a survey of Malalas' sources cf. Jeffreys 1990. I do not know why Thurn et al. 2009, 138 n. 168 think that Malalas' Sisyphos is Sisyphos of Pharsalos, the eponymous subject of the pseudo-Platonic *Sisyphos*.

to collect triads of all kinds,⁸ and the distinction between Kyklops and Polyphemos perhaps derives ultimately from observation of how the two 'names' are used in Homer and subsequent poetry. In the *Odyssey*, Odysseus always calls the monster '(the) Cyclops' until he has heard the other Cyclopes use the name 'Polyphemos' (cf. Schol. on *Od.* 9.403); both terms had first appeared at *Od.* 1.69–72, where Zeus reports Poseidon's continued anger about 'the Cyclops, whose eye [Odysseus] blinded, godlike Polyphemos, whose strength is the greatest of all the Cyclopes'. Κύκλωψ there might momentarily been understood as a name. In Euripides' *Cyclops*, Silenos twice uses the name Polyphemos (25, 91), but otherwise the monster is always '(the) Cyclops'.⁹

Some of the motifs of Malalas' account, e.g. the locking up of Odysseus' men, are recognizable as derived from Homeric elements of the story, in some cases presented in a rationalizing idiom. Thus, for example, the disembowelling of one of Odysseus' men 'before the eyes of Odysseus and all his comrades' seems to go back to the anguish of Odysseus and his men as the Cyclops for the first time grabs two of the sailors, smashes their brains out and devours them, 'entrails (ἔγκατα) and flesh and marrow-filled bones', while Odysseus and his men weep 'beholding dreadful (σχέτλια) deeds' (*Od.* 9.293–294). So too, the fact that Kyklops' slaves hurl rocks into the sea is clearly a toning down of how in Homer the Cyclops himself broke off and threw parts of a mountain at the departing ship. What is most striking about this narrative, however, is that nothing is said about the eyes of the brothers: the clear implication of the narrative is that they are two-eyed in the normal way. The story of Polyphemos' daughter leaving with Odysseus' men uses a very familiar motif of Greek narrative (we think of the opening of Herodotus' *Histories* or of Medea's elopement with the Argonauts), but may also be thought to rationalise the loss of Polyphemos' eye in the Homeric account as the snatching away of his κόρη, using a very familiar ambiguity in that word (cf. further below); Malalas, however, says nothing of this nor gives any indication that any of the brothers had only one eye.

The second, and much shorter part, of the account of Odysseus on Sicily is presented as a telling of the story of Euripides' *Cyclops* through a (rationalising) interpretation of it by Phidalios of Corinth, like Sisyphos known only from Malalas. The matter is complicated, however, by the γάρ which introduces Malalas' account from Phidalios of Euripides' play, immediately after the reference to Sisyphos, and which makes the nature of the link between the two accounts

---

8 The version found prefixed to a manuscript of the *Odyssey* (Dindorf 1855, I 4) seems indeed to link the three brothers to the fact that Sicily is three cornered (τρίγωνος).
9 Cf. further my note on Theocritus 11.72.

from Sisyphos and Phidalios to some extent uncertain. Nevertheless, certain patterns seem clear. In some respects, the Euripidean account may be seen as an attempt, however fanciful, to bring the traditional story into line with the version found in Sisyphos. Here, the cannibalism of the Cyclops, which is so prominent both in Homer and Euripides, is explicitly mentioned, but 'rationalised' away by Phidalios, if we accept the textual addition, by appeal to the familiar metaphorical use of κατεσθίειν to mean 'devour, waste (property)';[10] so too, Odysseus made the Cyclops (metaphorically) 'drunk' on gifts, rather than literally drunk on wine.[11] In this account it is indeed Kyklops who loses an eye, but still Polyphemos who loses a daughter, as Kyklops has three eyes, symbolising the three brothers. The Cyclops is very regularly depicted, particularly in Hellenistic and Roman art, as three-eyed, i.e. with a large central eye, as well as two 'normal' eyes,[12] though that artistic convention does not imply that, if the large central eye were blinded, the Cyclops could still see; in Malalas' account of Euripides' play, however, that possibility seems to be entertained. Unfortunately, we do not know who Servius has in mind when he notes (on Virg. *Aen.* 3.636) that '[some] say that Polyphemus had one eye, others two, others three',[13] but this reminds us that Phidalios/Malalas need not have drawn inspiration here directly from art.

In Euripides' play, the Cyclops is unequivocally single-eyed, and this in fact seems to be acknowledged by Phidalios/Malalas. The account begins with the Cyclops having three eyes, indicative of the three brothers (p. 87.81–82 Thurn), but he then explicitly loses 'his one eye' (p. 87.88 Thurn); the inconsistency between τὸν ὀφθαλμὸν αὐτοῦ τὸν ἕνα and ἕνα τῶν ὀφθαλμῶν τοῦ Κύκλωπος .... τὸν Πολύφημον (p. 87.90–91) cannot be explained away within this single narrative.[14] The inconsistency plainly arises from the attempt to juggle both a narrative in which the symbolism of the eye refers not to its owner, but to a brother or brother's daughter, and the famous story of the blinding of a one-eyed monster. The compressed version in Dindorf 1855, 4–5, however, does solve (or avoid) the problem, though Euripides is now not named, by changing the facts:

---

10 Cf. LSJ s.v. κατεσθίω 2.
11 Cf. LSJ s.v. μεθύσκω 1, μεθύω II 2.
12 Cf. *LIMC* s.v. Kyklops, Kyklopes VI 1, 157, D'Alfonso 2006, 21 n. 30.
13 Servius then dismisses these versions (*sed totum fabulosum est*) and replaces them with an allegorising reading of the placement of the Cyclops' single eye (he was *uir prudentissimus*, but Odysseus was even smarter).
14 The inconsistency is recognised by Hörling 1980, 151 n. 29.

Sisyphos of Cos has set these things out. For others have written in the poetic manner (ποιητικῶς) that the Cyclopes had three eyes, by which they indicated the three allied brothers, but Polyphemos one, which [Odysseus] blinded with fire, because, burned by love, he stole his daughter.

Here, then, is a rationalising version in which Polyphemos loses his one eye, i.e. his daughter, to a lovestruck Odysseus; it is just about possible to imagine such a reading, however apparently bizarre, based on an actual text of Euripides' play.

As for the three-eyed Cyclops, there is perhaps only one passage of Euripides' *Cyclops* which might in some way lie behind Phidalios/Malalas' narrative, namely Odysseus' foretelling of how he will blind the Cyclops' κόραι (plural):[15]

> κᾆθ' ὅταν κεκαυμένον
> ἴδω νιν, ἄρας θερμὸν ἐς μέσην βαλῶ
> Κύκλωπος ὄψιν ὄμμα τ' ἐκτήξω πυρί.
> ναυπηγίαν δ' ὡσεί τις ἁρμόζων ἀνὴρ   460
> διπλοῖν χαλινοῖν τρύπανον κωπηλατεῖ,
> οὕτω κυκλώσω δαλὸν ἐν φαεσφόρωι
> Κύκλωπος ὄψει καὶ συναυανῶ κόρας.

Euripides, *Cyclops* 457–463

And then when I see that [the stake] is heated, I shall lift it up and cast it blazing into the middle of the Cyclops' sight and melt his eye with fire. Just as a man who puts together the construction of a ship moves the drill like an oar by means of two straps, so I will rotate the torch in the light-bearing eyes of the Cyclops and wither his eyeball.

Homer of course does not use κούρη for the Cyclops' eye, and this may be an instance where subsequent elaborations detected a difference between Euripides and his model and exploited the ambiguity of κόρη to produce a rationalising version of the Homeric/Euripidean story and perhaps one in line with other romantic stories about Odysseus which were circulating, such as that ascribed by Malalas to Sisyphos of Cos.[16] In other words, the possibility remains that Sisyphos' story of Polyphemos' daughter's elopement with one of Odysseus' men originally had nothing to do with any version of the blinding; that possibility is only strengthened, if indeed the elopement happened 'without Odysseus' knowledge', as in the text preserved in Cramer 1839, 209 and restored by most

---

15 Cf. D'Alfonso 2006, 21–22.
16 Behind the Euripidean verses may also lie texts of the Sicilian Empedocles in which the ambiguity of κόρη is exploited (cf. D'Alfonso 2006, 22–23, Hunter/Laemmle 2020, 195), but it seems very unlikely that Empedocles has anything to do with the later rationalising tradition.

editors to Malalas. As for the version ascribed to Phidalios, we may here have a very interesting case where late sources explicitly point to differences between Homer and a later μίμησις of Homer (here Euripides' *Cyclops*) and ascribe to the mimetic text an allegorizing and/or rationalising intention not only absent from Homer, but in fact the means by which that later text marks itself as 'other' than the model. ποιητικῶς, 'in the poetic manner', often refers in Malalas (and elsewhere) to the fact that poets use allegory and other tropes to present stories in an 'other' way, which it is for the interpreter to decode. If something along those lines is happening here, then we have here a reflection of a well-developed sense of literary and critical history, which has not always been seen as characteristic of Malalas and some of his sources.

Nothing in Malalas' account of Euripides' play demands that Malalas or Phidalios necessarily had access to or direct knowledge of the text of Euripides' play or had seen it performed, though clearly some knowledge of at least the existence of the play must lie behind the account at an unknown number of removes. The only other reference to 'Phidalios of Corinth' in Malalas' chronicle may in fact be at least suggestive in this regard. Immediately after the account of Odysseus' adventures on Sicily, Malalas tells of his dealings with Circe. The main narrative concludes as follows: 'These things about Circe were set out by Sisyphos of Cos and Dictys of Crete, most wise men. The most wise Homer, however (δέ), described in the poetic manner (ποιητικῶς ἔφρασεν) how she metamorphosed …The wise Phidalios of Corinth, whom I have mentioned before, set out this poetic composition (τὴν ποιητικὴν ταύτην σύνταξιν) and interpreted it as follows …'; there follows an allegorising version, of a very familiar kind, in which metamorphosis into beasts in fact represents how men behave under the sway of erotic passion. At the conclusion of the entire Circe narrative, Malalas describes Phidalios' interpretation of Homer as σαφέστερον … καὶ ἀληθινώτερον, i.e. than Homer's own narrative (5.19, pp. 89.51–90.72 Thurn). The similarity of structure to the Sicilian narrative is clear: a main narrative ascribed to Sisyphos of Cos (together, in one case, with Dictys), followed by a 'poetic' version, followed by an allegorising/rationalising version ascribed to Phidalios of Corinth. This structural parallelism perhaps suggests that the (fantastic) account of Euripides' play came to Malalas together with Phidalios' interpretation; unfortunately, of course, Phidalios is no more than a name to us.

Malalas' account of Odysseus' Sicilian adventures thus proves disappointing for the history of the transmission of the *Cyclops*, especially since a later passage of Malalas (5.32–34 Thurn) offers both relatively accurate paraphrase and virtual quotation from the *Iphigenia in Tauris*, another 'alphabetical' play;[17] it is very clear that either Malalas or one of his principal sources had direct knowledge of that Euripidean play. As far as *Cyclops* is concerned, however, there remains one small but intriguing detail. In the account of Odysseus' adventures on Sicily which Malalas ascribes to Sisyphos of Cos, the hero falls at Polyphemus' feet and tells him that he had come from the troubles at Troy, forced off course by the waves (ἀπὸ τῶν Τρωικῶν πόνων ἐλήλυθε πεπλανημένος ἀπὸ πολλῆς κυμάτων ἀνάγκης).[18] Behind this lies Odysseus' first response to the Cyclops in the *Odyssey*:

ἡμεῖς τοι Τροίηθεν ἀποπλαγχθέντες Ἀχαιοὶ
παντοίοισ' ἀνέμοισιν ὑπὲρ μέγα λαῖτμα θαλάσσης,   260
οἴκαδε ἱέμενοι, ἄλλην ὁδὸν ἄλλα κέλευθα
ἤλθομεν· οὕτω που Ζεὺς ἤθελε μητίσασθαι.
λαοὶ δ' Ἀτρεΐδεω Ἀγαμέμνονος εὐχόμεθ' εἶναι,
τοῦ δὴ νῦν γε μέγιστον ὑπουράνιον κλέος ἐστί·
τόσσην γὰρ διέπερσε πόλιν καὶ ἀπώλεσε λαοὺς   265
πολλούς. ἡμεῖς δ' αὖτε κιχανόμενοι τὰ σὰ γοῦνα
ἱκόμεθ', εἴ τι πόροις ξεινήϊον ἠὲ καὶ ἄλλως
δοίης δωτίνην, ἥ τε ξείνων θέμις ἐστίν.

Homer, *Odyssey* 9.259–268

We are Achaeans who, on our return from Troy, have been driven by all manner of winds over the great surface of the sea; we are seeking to return home, but our journey and our routes have been quite different, as presumably Zeus has devised. We are proud to be from the army of Agamemnon, son of Atreus, whose fame under heaven now knows no equal; such a city did he sack and destroy many people. We however now come as suppliants to your knees, in the hope that you will provide a guest-gift or some other form of present, as is proper between hosts and guests.

There is, however, also what looks like a striking parallel in Euripides' play:

Σι. πόθεν Σικελίαν τήνδε ναυστολῶν πάρει;
Οδ. ἐξ Ἰλίου γε κἀπὸ Τρωϊκῶν πόνων.

Euripides, *Cyclops* 106–107

---

17 Cf. D'Alfonso 2006, 9–13. At one point during this account Malalas observes: 'This is set out in the poetic manner in a play by the very wise Euripides, of which these things are a small part' (5.33, p. 106.89–90 Thurn). The difference from how the *Cyclops* is introduced is small but apparently significant. On the *Nachleben* of the *IT* cf. Hall 2013, where, however, Malalas is not mentioned.

18 πόνων is the reading of Cramer 1839, 209 and is also, according to Thurn, suggested by the Slavic translation; the only manuscript of Malalas here offers τόπων.

Silenos. From where did you sail to reach Sicily here?
Odysseus. From Ilium and the troubles at Troy.

The expression 'the Trojan troubles' does not recur elsewhere in Malalas, if indeed it is correctly read in this place (5.19, p. 87.70–71 Thurn); Malalas otherwise refers to 'the Trojan war' (πόλεμος). 'The Trojan πόνοι' is, however, almost a signature phrase in Euripides' *Cyclops* (cf. 282, 347, 603, and also Soph. *Phil.* 247–248), and Odysseus refers to the war as a πόνος in his very first exchange with the Cyclops in Euripides' play (v. 282). This is very little to go one, but perhaps just enough to keep alive the suspicion that one at least of Malalas' sources had actually read the *Cyclops*.[19]

Bibliography

Alwine, A.T. 2009. 'The non-Homeric Cyclops in the Homeric Odyssey', *Greek, Roman and Byzantine Studies* 49, 319–333.
Cameron, A. 2004. *Greek Mythography in the Roman World*, Oxford.
Cramer, J.A. 1839. *Anecdota graeca e codd. manuscriptis Bibliothecae Regiae Parisiensis*, Oxford [repr. Hildesheim 1967].
D'Alfonso, F. 2006. *Euripide in Giovanni Malala*, Alessandria.
Dindorf, W. 1855. *Scholia Graeca in Homeri Odysseam ex codicibus aucta et emendata*, Oxford.
Griffin, N.E. 1907. *Dares and Dictys. An Introduction to the Study of Medieval Versions of the Story of Troy*, Baltimore.
Hall, E. 2013. *Adventures with Iphigenia in Tauris*, Oxford.
Hörling, E. 1980. *Mythos und Pistis. Zu Deutung heidnischer Mythen in der christlichen Weltchronik des Johannes Malalas*, Lund.
Hunter, R./Laemmle, R. 2020. *Euripides, Cyclops*, Cambridge.
Jeffreys, E. 1990. 'Malalas' sources', in: E. Jeffreys/B. Croke/R. Scott (eds.), *Studies in John Malalas*, Sydney, 167–216.
Patzig, E. 1903. 'Das Trojabuch des Sisyphos von Kos', *Byzantinische Zeitschrift* 12, 231–257.
Thurn, J. et al. 2009. *Johannes Malalas. Weltchronik*, Stuttgart.
Thurn, J. 2000. *Ioannis Malallae Chronographia*, Berlin/New York.

---

[19] It is a pleasure to contribute this very small Σικελικόν to a celebration of the work and teaching of Maria Cannatà Fera. I am very grateful to Rebecca Laemmle for encouraging my Malalan interests.

44 Homer in Origen, *Against Celsus*

As the greatest of poets and the poet who was seen as foundational for all of Greek intellectual and literary culture, Homer is never far away in the imaginative, rhetorical and ethical writings of the second and third centuries AD, that period which is often labelled 'the Second Sophistic'.[1] Writers of that period use classical literature, and above all Homer, as a kind of shared referential language, which can be used to mark similarity to and difference from the changed cultural world in which educated Greeks now found themselves. However shadowy a figure Celsus is for us, there can be no doubt that he too fits a familiar pattern of the second century AD, that of the Greek πεπαιδευμένος, 'educated/cultured man', equally at home in rhetoric as in (at least) the broad outlines of philosophical argument. His frequent recourse to citations from Homer must be seen within the remarkable prominence accorded to the poet in the literature, Christian as well as pagan, of this period,[2] and Origen's responses too can usually only be understood within the broader context of Homeric exegesis, with which both men were very familiar. In this paper I will try to set the use of Homer by both Celsus and Origen within that broader context; I hope that some sense of the contribution of poetic exegesis to the conduct of cultural debates in this period will emerge.

Celsus' primary aim was, of course, the demolition of Christian ideas and hence of those who followed those ideas, but his writing also allows us to see a concern with literary style typical of his age. Like other pagan critics after him, he apparently criticised the stylistic banality or 'cheapness' (εὐτέλεια) of the Christian scriptures (*CC* 6.2) and perhaps, to judge by Origen's response, contrasted this unfavourably with the beauty of the style of Plato, to whom Celsus

---

I am grateful to Simon Gathercole and James Carleton Paget for their invitation to contribute to this volume and for their guidance in areas where I am anything but expert; I am also much indebted to David Sedley for his advice. The paper has a deliberately narrow scope: many of the passages of *Against Celsus* in which Homer is cited lead into much wider philosophical and cultural questions about Celsus and Origen, but I must leave those to others better qualified than myself. I regret that Niehoff 2020 appeared too late to be taken into account.

---

1 The last few decades have seen an outpouring of scholarship on the use (and abuse) of Homer in this period; I list some relevant works at Hunter 2018, 24 n. 68.
2 The very frequent citations from Homer (as from other classical literature) in Athenagoras' apologetic *Legatio* (Schoedel 1972) are worth comparing in this regard; in ch. 21 Homer is the principal witness for the nature of the pagan gods, and arguments of this kind go back to Xenophanes and Plato.

owed both literary and philosophical allegiance.[3] For Origen, of course, what mattered rather was the beneficial message (ὠφέλεια) and the accessibility of the scriptures to those of every level of learning.[4] Celsus' scorn for the style of the scriptures was, however, not just one more bullet in the scatter-gun: it was intended precisely to appeal to other πεπαιδευμένοι, who knew instinctively that *how* you wrote, not just what you wrote, was crucial to your own self-presentation and to the perception which others had of you. If your style was persistently banal or 'cheap', so were you. Celsus' style, as far as it can be reconstructed, unsurprisingly shows off his easy familiarity with the standard texts of second century classicism and itself asks to be contrasted with the 'cheapness' of scriptural style.

In *CC* 4.23, for example, Origen reports a list of animal comparisons which Celsus used for the self-importance of the Jews and Christians:[5]

> νυκτερίδων ὁρμαθῷ ἢ μύρμηξιν ἐκ καλιᾶς προελθοῦσιν ἢ βατράχοις περὶ τέλμα συνεδρεύ-ουσιν ἢ σκώληξιν ἐν βορβόρου γωνίᾳ ἐκκλησιάζουσι καὶ πρὸς ἀλλήλους διαφερομένοις, τί-νες αὐτῶν εἶεν ἁμαρτωλότεροι κτλ.
>
> Origen, *Against Celsus* 4.23

> [He compared them all] to a cluster of bats or ants coming out of a nest, or frogs holding council round a marsh or worms assembling in some filthy corner, disagreeing with one another about which of them are the worse sinners.
>
> trans. Chadwick

In a manner typical of his age, Celsus here combines Homer with Plato:

> ὡς δ' ὅτε νυκτερίδες μυχῷ ἄντρου θεσπεσίοιο
> τρίζουσαι ποτέονται, ἐπεί κέ τις ἀποπέσῃσιν
> ὁρμαθοῦ ἐκ πέτρης, ἀνά τ' ἀλλήλῃσιν ἔχονται,
> ὣς αἱ τετριγυῖαι ἅμ' ἤϊσαν·
>
> Homer, *Odyssey* 24.6–9

> As when, in the depths of a mysterious cave, bats flit about squeaking and clinging to one another, when one of them falls down from the cluster on the rock, so did [the ghosts of the suitors] squeak as they proceeded.

And moreover, he said, [I am convinced that the world] is very large and that we who dwell from the Phasis to the Pillars of Heracles dwell in a small part of it around the sea,

---

[3] For ancient discussions of the style of Plato cf. Hunter 2012, ch. 4, citing earlier bibliography.
[4] Cf., e.g., Neuschäfer 1987, 258–262.
[5] On this passage cf. Andresen 1955, 226–228, Lona 2005, 234–236.

like ants or frogs around a marsh (περὶ τέλμα), and that many other peoples dwell elsewhere in many such areas.

Plato, Phaedo 109a9–b4

The Homeric passage, which describes the spirits of the dead suitors being led to the Underworld by Hermes, is of course derisory when applied to Celsus' opponents; these were verses which Plato (*Rep.* 3.387c) had included among citations which were not to be permitted in the ideal city because they gave a misleadingly frightening and corrosive impression of death. νυκτερίδων ὁρμαθῷ, 'to a cluster of bats', clearly signals the Homeric allusion which is gracefully worked into Celsus' own syntax, rather than simply being a verbatim quotation; Celsus' phrase also avoids the simple dative νυκτερίσι, which would give too monotonous a catalogue with what follows. As for the famous passage of the *Phaedo*, which Celsus cited verbatim elsewhere (*CC* 7.28), where it is again combined with a Homeric passage,[6] here Celsus has, as indeed the theory of literary *mimesis* recommended, sought to 'outdo' his model by treating the Platonic ants and frogs separately and giving the ants a more obviously appropriate location than a marsh.[7] The rising tricolon, marked by increasing length of the participles, greater variation of the prepositions than in Plato and elaboration of the third unit, where the 'worms' or 'larvae' have no antecedent in the Platonic model,[8] mocks the Jews and Christians by its stylistic polish, as well as by its absurd subject-matter. The frogs which 'hold council (or *synhedrion*)' and the worms which 'hold assembly' are suggestive of the world of Aesopic fable and it is this fantasy world of utterly insignificant creatures with delusions of grandeur to which Celsus dismisses the Jews and Christians.

Both Celsus and Origen were very clearly familiar, not just with the Homeric poems, but with the ways in which those poems were taught in the grammatical and educational traditions.[9] Some of the learning which Celsus parades is indeed of a rather elementary kind. Thus, for example, in *CC* 7.28 he adduces pagan parallels, or — as Celsus would have it — antecedents, for the Christian belief in a better world to come:

---

[6] Cf. further below.
[7] καλιή is a common term for a bird's nest and Call. *h.* 3.96 uses it of the 'lair' of a porcupine, but I know of no parallel for it used of an ant-hill or nesting-place for ants; Celsus is perhaps stretching the semantics of the word somewhat as he strives to vary the Platonic model.
[8] Elsewhere Celsus seems to have varied his own list, cf. *CC* 4.52 'the body of a bat or a worm (εὐλή) or a frog or a man'.
[9] The only recent consideration known to me of how Celsus and Origen employ Homer in their arguments is Villani 2012; cf. also Fédou 2003, Andresen 1955, 125–126. Cf. now Niehoff 2020.

Divinely inspired men of ancient times related that there is a happy life for fortunate souls. Some called it the Islands of the Blessed; others the Elysian Fields because they were there set free (ἀπὸ τῆς λύσεως) from the evils of the world. Thus Homer says:

ἀλλά σ' ἐς Ἠλύσιον πεδίον καὶ πείρατα γαίης
ἀθάνατοι πέμψουσι,
τῇ περ ῥηίστη βιοτή.

Origen, Against Celsus 7.28

'But immortals will send thee to the Elysian Fields and the ends of the earth ... where life is very easy.'

trans. Chadwick, adapted

These very frequently cited Homeric verses (*Odyssey* 4.563–564a, 565a)[10] are part of Menelaos' account to Telemachos of what he was told by Proteus when stranded on the island of Pharos. This is the only reference in the Homeric poems to Elysium, but the identification of Elysium and the 'Isles of the Blessed' was very familiar to both the poetical and the grammatical traditions, as also was the etymology of Elysium which Celsus here parades;[11] both are found in the extant scholia to these verses of the *Odyssey* and in the scholia to Hesiod's description of the Isles of the Blessed (cf. schol. 4.563b–e Pontani, schol. Hes. *WD* 171 Pertusi).[12] Of perhaps greater interest is the nature of Celsus' Homeric citation. As transmitted, the citation omits the second half of v. 564, ὅθι ξανθὸς Ῥαδάμανθυς, 'where is blond Rhadamanthys'. Poetic citations in prose texts are particularly prone to suffer damage, often curtailment, in transmission, and this should not be ruled out in the present case. There is, however, some reason to think that we are dealing with a deliberate omission by Celsus, for a specific reference to Rhadamanthys, sometimes the judge in the Underworld and sometimes the ruler of the Isles of the Blessed, might be thought to weaken the case for believing that the Christians have borrowed their ideas from Homer; what would Christians want with Rhadamanthys? If so, Celsus would be behaving (again) in an entirely typical way: citations were standardly (and silently) adapted to the rhetorical needs of the moment. That Origen does not comment on the omission need not be significant: he does not in fact deal with the Ho-

---

10 West's apparatus of citations is the simplest place to find these quotations.
11 Cf., e.g., West 1978 on Hes. *WD* 171, Hunter 2015 on Ap. Rhod. *Arg.* 4.811.
12 The Hesiodic scholium is in fact very close in wording to Celsus' text, but this is simply a sign that Celsus is here drawing on familiar grammatical lore. It is of some interest in the context of Celsus and Origen that Christian scholiasts sometimes identified Homer's description of Elysium or Hesiod's description of the Isles of the Blessed with Paradise, cf. Schol. *Od.* 4.563g Pontani, Schol. Hes. *WD* 171.

meric quotation at all, reserving his rebuttal rather for the particular weight which Celsus placed on Plato in this matter.

When necessary, of course, Origen could certainly pay attention to the detail of Celsus' Homeric citations. One of the most familiar Homeric tags in the context of constitutions and the organization of states was Odysseus' threatening words to ordinary soldiers as he put an end to the flight to the Greek ships in *Iliad* 2:[13]

> οὐκ ἀγαθὸν πολυκοιρανίη· εἷς κοίρανος ἔστω,
> εἷς βασιλεύς, ᾧ δῶκε Κρόνου πάϊς ἀγκυλομήτεω.
>
> Homer, *Iliad* 2.204–205

> Having many leaders is not a good thing. Let there be one leader, one king, to whom the son of Kronos of the crooked ways gave authority.

Celsus cited v. 205 (at least), which he apparently ascribed to 'a man of ancient times' rather than to Homer by name,[14] in warning Christians against setting up another 'king' in addition to the emperor (*CC* 8.68) and went on to warn them that imperial punishment was likely to follow; he may here have had in mind what Odysseus says immediately before the cited passage to any 'officer' of the Greeks whom he sees fleeing:

> ἐν βουλῇ δ' οὐ πάντες ἀκούσαμεν οἷον ἔειπε.
> μή τι χολωσάμενος ῥέξῃ κακὸν υἷας Ἀχαιῶν·
> θυμὸς δὲ μέγας ἐστὶ διοτρεφέων βασιλήων,
> τιμὴ δ' ἐκ Διός ἐστι, φιλεῖ δέ ἑ μητίετα Ζεύς.
>
> Homer, *Iliad* 2.194–197

> We did not all in council hear what he said;[15] there is a danger that he will get angry and do some harm to the sons of the Achaeans. Great is the anger of Zeus-nourished kings; their honour comes from Zeus, and Zeus the counsellor loves them.

---

13 Cf. West's apparatus of citations *ad loc.*; v. 204 was so familiar that it is cited by Hermogenes 9.15 Rabe as an example of a γνώμη. The quotation is very familiar in the Platonic tradition, and is also applied in the sphere of number: unity and the monad are good, plurality not, cf., e.g., Arist. *Met.* 11.1076a4, [Plut.] *Hom.* 2.145. Dio 1.11 uses the verse in the context of Trajan.
14 Such rhetoric will always be connected with Celsus' claim that the Jews and Christians do not preserve genuine remnants of the ancient wisdom which is found in other races, such as the Greeks and Egyptians, cf. Frede 1994, 5193–5196. On Celsus' use of this Homeric tag cf. also Lona 2005, 467–469.
15 From antiquity on, this has often been interpreted as a question, 'Did we not all …?'.

As these verses make clear and as the scholia on vv. 204–205 also emphasise, 'kingship' was standardly associated with Zeus, just as kings were often identified with (or identified themselves with) Zeus; ἐκ δὲ Διὸς βασιλῆες (Hes. *Theog.* 96) was one of the most familiar of all 'political' tags.[16] The Homeric scholia also make the point that the existence of Zeus himself and the organization of Olympus in Homer show that the gods themselves approved of monarchy. Here Origen of course must tread carefully, and his method is to accept that there should be 'one king', but to stress that this should be a king whose power is bestowed not by 'the son of Kronos of the crooked ways', but rather by a genuine God 'who manages all things and knows what he is doing in the matter of the institution of kings' (*CC* 8.68). What is beyond understanding is that one would allow a figure 'of crooked ways' and a very unpleasant mythology to have anything to do with the appointment of the king. Origen takes the pagan stress on the divine appointment of kings and accepts it: it is the nature of the divinity which has changed.

Origen of course, like other learned Christians, has a 'double', if not 'triple', view of Homer as the greatest of pagan poets, and thus both a great poet and the conveyor of material which no Christian could accept or find anything but ridiculous. The fame of Homer and the power of his verses could indeed be harnessed to preach an anti-Homeric, Christianising message. In *CC* 1.31, for example, in an account of the motivation of the disciples, Origen incorporates citations from the opening verses of *Iliad* 5, in which Athena inspires Diomedes, in order to set Christian belief against the mythical fantasies of the Greeks:

ἔνθ' αὖ Τυδεΐδῃ Διομήδεϊ Παλλὰς Ἀθήνη
δῶκε μένος καὶ θάρσος, ἵν' ἔκδηλος μετὰ πᾶσιν
Ἀργείοισι γένοιτο ἰδὲ κλέος ἐσθλὸν ἄροιτο·

Homer, Iliad 5.1–3

Then did Pallas Athena grant force and courage to the son of Tydeus, so that he might stand out amidst all the Argives and win great renown.

As the disciples of Jesus saw this and much more besides, which they probably learnt from Jesus in secret, and as they were also filled with a certain power, since it was not just a virgin imagined by a poet who gave them 'strength and courage' (μένος καὶ θάρσος) but the true understanding and wisdom of God (ἡ ἀληθῶς φρόνησις καὶ σοφία τοῦ θεοῦ), they

---

16 In Homer βασιλεύς may refer just to a leading figure or commander of a particular part of the army, one of 'the heroes', rather than a 'king' in the later sense; this semantic difference lies at the root of much ancient and modern discussion (and misunderstanding) of Homeric politics.

sought eagerly that they might 'become well-known among all men' (ἔκδηλοι μετὰ πᾶσιν), not only among 'the Argives', but even among all the Greeks and barbarians also, and that 'they might win great renown'.

Origen, *Against Celsus* 1.31 (trans. Chadwick, adapted)

The very ease with which Origen can incorporate the Homeric text while preaching a message which far outdoes it in both reach ('all Greeks and barbarians') and significance — the 'true intelligence and wisdom of God' set against 'some virgin from poetry' (i.e. Athena) — carries its own message of the superiority of Christian teaching to the Greek traditions it aims to surpass. Moreover, Origen here turns pagan exegesis back against itself. No moralizing or allegorizing reading of an Olympian deity in Homer was more common than that of Athena as 'wisdom', 'good sense' (φρόνησις or σοφία),[17] but here Origen appropriates that intellectual virtue for the Christian God: Athena was just 'some virgin imagined by a poet' (ποιητική τις παρθένος), and no clever pagan exegesis can withstand that force.

This 'double' view of Homer, which may produce what appear to be inconsistencies amounting almost to a kind of schizophrenia when it comes to the poet's virtues, can be amply illustrated from the *CC*, but I begin with a familiar passage in which Origen appears to adduce Homer's traditional virtues in a manner no different from the pagan grammatical tradition, but which proves curiously revealing of the limitations imposed upon him by his Christian training. In *CC* 7.36 Origen responds to a claim by Celsus in which the latter had imagined what Christians would say about the resurrection. For Origen the words ascribed to Christians by Celsus are simply things no Christian would say and therefore fall into the category of the 'inappropriate' (τὰ μὴ ἁρμόζοντα); what matters is that the content and style of what a character says should both fit that character and remain consistent throughout:

> The first point I have to make in reply to the words which he puts into our mouth, attributing to us statements purporting to be what we say in defence of the resurrection of the flesh, is that it is a virtue in a writer who puts words into the mouth of someone else to preserve consistency in the meaning and character (τὸ βούλημα καὶ τὸ ἦθος) of the person to whom the words are attributed; and it is a fault when anyone attributes to the mouth of the speaker words which are inappropriate (τὰ μὴ ἁρμόζοντα ... ῥήματα). Equally blameworthy are those who, in putting words into the mouth of a person, attribute philosophy which the author has learnt to barbarians and illiterate people or slaves, who have never heard philosophical arguments and have never given a proper account of them. It is unlikely that the person to whom the ideas are attributed would have known them. And, on

---

17 Cf., e.g., Hunter 2012, 60–67, citing earlier bibliography.

the other hand, those people are also blameworthy who attribute to persons assumed to be wise, and who have had knowledge of the things of God, statements such as are made by illiterate folk moved by vulgar passions, and assertions resulting from ignorance. This is the reason why Homer is admired by many. He keeps the characters of the heroes the same as they were when he started, such as that of Nestor, or Odysseus, or Diomedes, or Agamemnon, or Telemachus, or Penelope, or one of the others. But Euripides is mocked by Aristophanes for writing inappropriate verses (ἀκαιρορρήμων), because he often attributed to barbarian women or slave-girls words containing ideas which he had learnt from Anaxagoras or some other wise man.

Origen, Against Celsus 7.36 (trans. Chadwick, adapted)

Origen's views here on 'literary decorum' may be traced a long way back in Greek tradition, notably to the rhapsode Ion in Plato's dialogue named after him (*Ion* 540b) and to Aristotelian and peripatetic teachings about 'appropriateness' and 'consistency' of character (cf. Arist. *Poetics* 1454a22–37).[18] It was long ago pointed out[19] that Origen's formulation finds a very close parallel in Aelius Theon's account (? 1st century AD) of the value of the rhetorical exercise (γύμνασμα) of προσωποποιία (lit. 'character-creation'), which is precisely the context with which Origen frames his remarks:

> Because [the exercise is extremely useful], on the one hand we praise Homer because he has ascribed suitable words (οἰκείους λόγους) to each of the characters whom he brings on, but on the other hand we find fault with Euripides because his Hecuba philosophises inappropriately (παρὰ καιρόν).
>
> Aelius Theon, Progymnasmata 60.27–31 Spengel = p. 3 Patillon/Bolognesi

It may well be that Origen here wishes his debt to the pagan tradition to be clearly recognizable, for he makes clear that Celsus' claim is a worthless piece of writing, even by his own Greek/pagan standards. *CC* 7.36 is, we might suspect, a slightly repetitious elaboration (in rhetorical terms, an αὔξησις) of a passage such as that of Theon just cited; the rather miscellaneous list of major Homeric characters is intended to be rhetorically more powerful than a simple statement such as Theon's.[20] Theon's reference to the 'philosophising' of Euripides' Hecuba is, all but certainly,[21] to her notorious prayer in the *Trojan Women*:

---

[18] Cf. Neuschäfer 1987, 263–276, esp. 270.

[19] Cf. Chadwick 1953, 424 n. 3; I do not know whether Chadwick was the first to make the observation.

[20] It is tempting, however, to see some *ratio* behind Origen's list: Nestor and Odysseus are the two greatest 'orators' of the Homeric poems, Diomedes is a warrior not a talker, Agamemnon is notoriously a rather unsuccessful orator (though other judgements were familiar in antiquity, cf. Hunter 2015, 693–705), and Telemachus and Penelope, being a young man and a woman,

ὦ γῆς ὄχημα κἀπὶ γῆς ἔχων ἕδραν,
ὅστις ποτ' εἶ σύ, δυστόπαστος εἰδέναι,
Ζεύς, εἴτ' ἀνάγκη φύσεος εἴτε νοῦς βροτῶν,
προσηυξάμην σε· πάντα γὰρ δι' ἀψόφου
βαίνων κελεύθου κατὰ δίκην τὰ θνήτ' ἄγεις.

Euripides, *Trojan Women* 884–888

You that support the earth and have your seat upon it, whoever you may be, so hard for human conjecture to find out, Zeus, whether you are the necessity of nature or the mind of mortal men, I address you in prayer! For proceeding on a silent path you direct all mortal affairs toward justice!

trans. Kovacs

The scholia on v. 884 trace the origin of these verses to Anaxagoras, the Presocratic natural philosopher with whom Origen elsewhere links Euripides (*CC* 4.77), as was indeed common in the grammatical tradition;[22] it is clear that Origen here is in touch with the same critical streams as the scholia. Hecuba was indeed a 'barbarian woman', such as Origen exemplifies in Euripides. The desire for rhetorical elaboration is perhaps also seen here in ἀκαιρορρήμων, 'speaking inappropriately', which Origen applies to Euripides; this *hapax legomenon* looks like an elegant 'raising' of something more simple such as παρὰ καιρόν which we find in Theon. What really surprises in Origen's elaboration, however, is the reference to Aristophanes. There is no doubt, of course, that Aristophanes liked to poke fun at Euripides' alleged interest in contemporary science and philosophy — the opening scene of *Thesmophoriazousai* is as good an illustration of that as any other comic scene[23] — and 'inappropriateness' might well describe some of the charges brought against Euripidean plays in Aristophanes' *Frogs*,[24] but there is no obvious scene in the extant comedies to which Origen could here be referring.[25] My guess — and it can of course be no

---

were particular cases where 'appropriate' speech was necessary. The absence of Achilles from Origen's list may have no significance, but he was the Homeric character who was hardest to 'characterise' and whose speeches are also the most surprising.

21 Patillon/Bolognesi implausibly suggest that the reference is to verses spoken by the queen in Eur. *Hecuba*.
22 Cf. Eur. T 35–38 Kannicht, Chadwick on Origen, *CC* 4.77 (= Eur. T 37c Kannicht).
23 Cf. Clements 2014.
24 At *Frogs* 949–950 Euripides prides himself on the fact that characters of every type and social class spoke in his plays, 'women [or 'wives'], slaves, masters, young girls, old women'.
25 Editors at least as early as Koetschau identify the reference with *Acharnians* 393ff, which are rather different; there Euripides' servant is made to speak like his master, as the scholia on

more than a guess — is that a reference to criticism of Euripides, along the lines which we see in Theon, reminded Origen of Aristophanes' mockery of the tragedian and so he elaborated the reference in a way which was actually erroneous.[26] Aristophanes has (for once) nothing to do with the point of criticism of Euripides, and the reference to comic mockery may in fact be thought to weaken the rhetorical point which Origen wishes to make. If this speculation is at least on the right lines (and other scenarios could also be hypothesized), then we see Origen operating both within the familiar patterns of Greek criticism of Homer, but also far enough from them to produce distortions. How Homer is used in *CC* is both familiar and also distinctive, in part as the result of Origen's own hesitations about pagan critical traditions and in part because, for Christian interpretation of scripture and belief, far more than just rhetorical and critical judgement is at stake.

In *CC* 3.69 Origen replies to a statement by Celsus that 'it is very difficult to change [a man's] nature completely'. For Origen, it is, by contrast, easy for the divine *logos* to effect change even in a nature where vice has become embedded, provided that the human concerned entrusts himself entirely to God,

> With God (παρ' ᾧ ...) it is not true that
>
> ἐν δὲ ἰῇ τιμῇ ἠμὲν κακὸς ἠδὲ καὶ ἐσθλός·
>
> in equal honour are both bad and good
>
> *Iliad* 9.319
>
> nor do
>
> κάτθαν' ὁμῶς ὅ τ' ἀεργὸς ἀνὴρ ὅ τε πολλὰ ἐοργώς
>
> the idle man and he who has laboured much perish alike
>
> *Iliad* 9.320

And if for some it is very hard to change, we must say that the cause lies in their will, which refuses to accept the fact that the supreme God is to each man a righteous Judge of every past action done in this life.
          Origen, *Against Celsus* 3.69 (trans. Chadwick)

---

v. 369a observe. Kannicht (on Eur. T 151c) links Origen's comment to those Aristophanic scholia, but that does not seem helpful.

26 This is (I believe) the only reference to Aristophanes in Origen's extant works.

Achilles' famous response in *Iliad* 9 to Odysseus who has come to seek, through gifts and promises, to persuade him to return to the fighting against the Trojans is here cited apparently to construct Achilles' refusal to be persuaded, either by Odysseus or by Phoenix in the great speech which follows Achilles', as a pagan example of the man for whom change is 'very difficult', as it also was for Meleager in the parallel story which Phoenix tells. The grounds for Achilles' continuing anger and refusal to change (and thus submit himself to Agamemnon's leadership) are to be found in his perception that he receives no more τιμή than a coward, by which term he may be pointing to Agamemnon, and in the universal fact of death, whether one has laboured in battle or not.[27] How true it is that, for the Christian, the idle and the doer of deeds do not 'die equally' may be debated, and we may wonder whether the desire to find a pagan analogy to the Christian belief, an analogy which might (for all we know) have been suggested already by Celsus' text, has led Origen into what is at best a partial analogy. What the analogy does do is to create an opposition between Agamemnon, the Greek 'king' at Troy, and the heavenly King who is always a 'just judge' for everyone;[28] Achilles rejects Agamemnon's 'justice', but no one should reject the just allotment of God. In v. 318, immediately preceding the verses which Origen quotes, Homer had made Achilles already make much the same complaint:

ἴση μοῖρα μένοντι, καὶ εἰ μάλα τις πολεμίζοι.

Homer, *Iliad* 9.318

The share is the same, whether one remains idle or fights incessantly.

One grammarian at least, whose note is preserved in an exegetical scholium, explained that Achilles meant that this was the situation 'with you', i.e. in the Greek army (παρ' ὑμῖν), and Origen's claim may be shaped by such a reading, obvious though it is: 'with God' (παρ' ᾧ ...) the situation is quite different.

The creation of partial analogies seems almost inevitable, given Origen's rhetorical technique for finding pagan examples, above all in Homer, for biblical accounts which Celsus has criticized. In *CC* 2.76 Origen takes up the fact that the Jew whom Celsus used as a mouthpiece for Jewish objections to Jesus apparently criticized Jesus' apparent abusive threats and prophecies of doom ('Woe unto you ...'), which also amounted to an admission that he could not persuade those to whom he was speaking. Origen's retort first draws attention

---

27 Martin West follows some earlier editors in deleting 9.320 from the Homeric text, but there is no doubt that Origen read it in the place we do.
28 Cf. Villani 2012, 131.

to the very many similar things in the Old Testament and then points out that God and Jesus say such things, not as empty threats, but to convert their hearers (ὑπὲρ ἐπιστροφῆς). Origen's next argument again finds an apparent Homeric parallel:

> I will address a few remarks on this subject to Celsus, who professes to be a philosopher and also to know our beliefs: If, sir, Hermes says to Odysseus in Homer,
>
> > τίπτ' αὖτ' ὦ δύστηνε, δι' ἄκριας ἔρχεαι οἶος;
> >
> > Unhappy man, why are you going alone through the hills?
> >
> > *Od.* 10.281
>
> are you content to defend this by saying that the Homeric Hermes says such things to Odysseus with the intention of warning him (ὑπὲρ ἐπιστροφῆς)? For to flatter and compliment is the part of the Sirens, with whom there is
>
> > ἀμφ' ὀστεόφιν θίς
> >
> > a heap of bones all around
> >
> > *Od.* 12.45
>
> and who say,
>
> > δεῦρ' ἄγ' ἰών, πολύαιν' Ὀδυσεῦ, μέγα κῦδος Ἀχαιῶν
> >
> > Come hither, famous Odysseus, great glory of the Achaeans
> >
> > *Od.* 12.184
>
> On the other hand, if my prophets and Jesus himself with a view to the conversion of their hearers utter the word "Woe" and the abuse, as you regard it, is there in the use of such words no accommodation to the capacity of the hearers, and does he not apply such a warning to them as a healing medicine?
>
> Origen, *Against Celsus* 2.76 (trans. Chadwick)

Origen's argument is that Celsus and those like him find no problem when a Homeric god speaks harshly to a Homeric character, as Hermes does to Odysseus on his way to Circe's dwelling (*Od.* 10.281),[29] and yet will not accept similar patterns in the Bible. Moreover, just as Homer has in the Sirens (here evoked by *Od.* 12.45, 184) dangerously seductive creatures who, unlike Hermes, use only 'sweet words', so — we are to understand — the Christian will pay no heed to

---

29 Origen's text of *Od.* 10.281 differs at the beginning, as also does [Heraclitus]'s (cf. below), from the standard ancient text, but this does not seem significant in the current context.

temptations and encouragement along the path towards destruction.³⁰ Nevertheless, although Hermes forecasts destruction for Odysseus (vv. 284–285),³¹ we may think that the parallel between how he addresses Odysseus and how God and Jesus speak in the passages cited from Old and New Testaments is not really very close. More striking, however, than that apparent dissonance is Origen's claim that Hermes makes his speech to Odysseus ὑπὲρ ἐπιστροφῆς, just as God and the prophets speak in the Bible. Origen wants to make the two cases as parallel as possible, but how forced the parallelism is becomes clear in the embarrassment of translators: Chadwick and Borret agree that, with regard to the Bible, the phrase must mean 'for the purposes of conversion', but Chadwick makes Hermes speak to Odysseus 'with the intention of warning him', whereas Borret has 'pour le ramener au devoir'; of modern translations known to me, only Barthold keeps the absolute parallelism (Hermes' intention is 'Odysseus zur Umkehr bewegen').³² Hermes is certainly speaking to prevent Odysseus pursuing in ignorance a self-destructive course (Circe is, from one point of view, a 'Siren'), to make him 'think again', if you will, but no regular sense of ἐπιστροφή really fits the case. Origen seems to have allowed rhetorical effect to dictate the argument.

Here too, however, it is possible to see how Origen's use of Homer grows out of the critical tradition. Odysseus' encounter with Hermes in *Odyssey* 10 was a scene much discussed in the allegorising tradition, in which the associations between Hermes and *logos*, 'speech', and *logismos*, 'reason, rationality' were standard interpretative tools.³³ In the allegorising *Homeric Problems* of Pseudo-Heraclitus (perhaps early second century AD), the Hermes who confronts Odysseus is indeed the wiser second thoughts, or 'calculation', which come to Odysseus as he proceeds to Circe's house:

> At first Odysseus, carried away by anger and grief at what he has learned [about the fate of his comrades],³⁴ is in an uncontrolled and excited state. Little by little, however, these

---

30 On the 'sweet words' of the Sirens cf. Kaiser 1964, 127–131; for the role of the Sirens in Christian literature more generally cf. Hunter 2018, 217–219, citing earlier bibliography.
31 It is standard citational practice in antiquity, here and elsewhere followed by Origen, that a short quotation, as here often of the opening of a passage, evokes and brings into play the whole passage, not just the cited verses.
32 Fiedrowicz/Barthold 2011, II 504–505. Fiedrowicz's note attempts to justify the parallelism: 'Hermes wollte [Odysseus] zunächst abhalten weitergehen'. Hermes' opening words might certainly suggest that, but only to someone who does not know how the speech continues.
33 Fundamental for the subsequent tradition was Plato, *Cratylus* 407e5–408d5.
34 This description of Odysseus' emotional state is itself merely a critical inference; the Homeric Odysseus refers to neither anger nor grief, just the 'necessity' which is upon him (10.273).

passions fade, calculation of what is advantageous (τὸ μετὰ τοῦ συμφέροντος εὐλόγιστον) slips in ... This reasoning (ὁ λογισμός) came to Odysseus, replaced his uncontrolled anger, and reproached him for his pointless efforts:

> τίφθ' αὕτως, δύστηνε, δι' ἄκριας ἔρχεαι οἶος,
> χώρου ἄιδρις ἐών;
>
> Why thus, poor fool, do you travel alone through the hills, when you have no knowledge of the country?

Odysseus said this to himself, curbing his original impulse by reasoning which led to a change of mind (μετανοοῦντι λογισμῷ).

[Heraclitus], *Hom. Probl.* 73.2–3, 73.8–9

For a Christian such as Origen, it is in fact a small step from 'reasoning which led to a change of mind' to 'conversion', particularly as μετανοεῖν, the verb which [Heraclitus] applies to such *logismos*, is a standard Christian term for 'to repent'. Origen's choice of Homeric example and the interpretation he places upon it may thus be seen as a 'Christianising' of pagan critical traditions. Just as Odysseus was protected by 'Hermes', i.e. *logos/logismos*, so Christians are 'governed and guided by His *logos*', as Origen states in 2.76, immediately after his discussion of Odysseus and Hermes.

There is a further indication of Origen's debt here to the grammatical traditions of Homeric criticism. Origen describes Jesus' 'words of woe' as a παιώνιον φάρμακον, 'healing drug'. Behind him stand the same strands of the critical tradition which we have already exemplified from [Heraclitus]. The plant μῶλυ, which Hermes gives to Odysseus, a φάρμακον ἐσθλόν 'beneficent drug' (*Od.* 10.292), was standardly interpreted in the allegorical tradition as 'wisdom' or 'education', that virtue which enables the philosophical Odysseus to avoid the fate of his foolish comrades. [Heraclitus] puts the matter thus:

> Homer quite reasonably called wisdom (φρόνησις) μῶλυ, because it comes only (μόνους) to men or to a few with difficulty (μόλις). Its nature is that the root is black, 'but a flower like to milk' (*Od.* 10.304). The reason is that all good things of this type have beginnings which are steep and difficult, but if one struggles nobly and endures the initial labour, then in the light there is a sweet crop of benefits. Protected by reasoning of this kind, Odysseus overcame Circe's drugs.
>
> [Heraclitus], *Hom. Probl.* 73.10–13[35]

---

[35] Cf. further Kaiser 1964, 208–210. Eustathius, *Hom.* 1658.27–48 offers an extended allegorisation of μῶλυ.

Here, then, Origen has applied a technique from the Homeric critical tradition to a biblical situation; παιώνιος, which occurs nowhere else in Origen, is an almost explicit signal of what he is doing.³⁶ It is perhaps typical of Origen's eclectic rhetorical technique that his next argument is of a quite different sort. His response to the claim that Jesus was 'unable to persuade' is simply to throw the accusation back, by pointing out that this applies equally well to the Jewish prophets and to the Greeks:

> Moreover, is not his remark ludicrous that Jesus was unable to carry conviction? For it applies just as much not only to the Jew who has a lot of sayings like these in the prophets, but also the Greeks. Among the latter none of those who have made a great reputation for their wisdom has been able to carry conviction with those who conspired against him, or with his judges or accusers, so that they cease from evil and follow the path to virtue by philosophy.
>
> Origen, *Against Celsus* 2.76 (trans. Chadwick)

The evocation of Socrates is unmistakable: no charge should be brought against Jesus of which Socrates himself was guilty.³⁷

It is, of course, hardly surprising that Origen's use of Homer is steeped in the grammatical and critical traditions, many of which descend from his own Alexandria. Thus, for example, when he paraphrases (*CC* 7.6) the priest Chryses' appearance and prayer to Apollo at the beginning of the *Iliad* and interprets this scene within the context of his own daemonology, he sees Homer, here labelled 'best of poets', 'teaching (διδάσκων) what most of all persuades the daemons to do what the sacrificers want', and he also quotes an unnamed Pythagorean who also interpreted this scene 'didactically'. The point is a simple one, but a 'didactic' approach to this paradigmatic scene of prayer seems to have been familiar in the grammatical tradition, very probably before Origen. The exegetical scholia on *Il.* 1.43 note that Homer is here 'teaching how beneficial is purehearted prayer',³⁸ and this reading was to be greatly elaborated in the Homeric commentaries of Eustathius in the twelfth century who notes how Homer 'in order to educate us' (παιδευτικῶς) both gives the plague a moral, rather than a

---

36 Marcovich 2001, 147, following Borret, sees here an evocation of *Iliad* 5.401 = 900, τῷ δ' ἐπὶ Παιήων ὀδυνήφατα φάρμακα πάσσων. This is helpful as far as it goes, but it is the Odyssean critical tradition which explains Origen's rhetoric.

37 For the importance of Socrates to the apologetic tradition more generally cf. Frede 1999, 142–144.

38 It may be worth suggesting that εὐχὴ καθαρά perhaps contains a remnant also of an explanation of the name of Φοῖβος, which is explained (*inter alia*) as καθαρός, ἀμίαντος in the D-scholia.

purely physical cause, and shows us that 'no justified prayer remains unfulfilled' (*Hom.* 38.20–26).³⁹

The crucifixion and resurrection might seem to have posed the greatest difficulty for an apologist looking for Homeric analogies. Celsus (*CC* 1.66, 2.36) apparently mocked the Christian story of Jesus bleeding on the cross by observing that this blood was not 'ichor, such as flows in the blessed gods', a Homeric verse (*Il.* 5.340) describing the liquid which came from Aphrodite after she was wounded by Diomedes. Celsus may have chosen this very familiar Homeric passage⁴⁰ both because it describes the nature of the bodies and diet of 'gods' and because the comparison of Jesus to Aphrodite is obviously abusive; the soldier who poked Jesus' side with a spear (*John* 19.34–35, cited in *CC* 2.36) plays the role of Diomedes who wounded Aphrodite with a spear. For Celsus, the whole story of the crucifixion and resurrection was a δρᾶμα with its own improbable ending (καταστροφή, *CC* 2.55).⁴¹ The evidence for the resurrection, namely the pierced hands of the risen Christ, did not, according to Celsus, stand up to any scrutiny:⁴²

> Who saw this? A crazed woman (γυνὴ πάροιστρος), as you claim, and perhaps some other victim of the same sorcery (γοητεία), whether in a dream induced by a certain disposition of mind and in mistaken fancy hallucinating (φαντασιωθείς) in accordance with his own wishes — an experience which has happened to countless people — or, as is more likely, because he wished to amaze others by this absurd tale (τερατεία) and with these lies open the way for other imposters.
>
> Celsus cited in Origen, *Against Celsus* 2.55

The bulk of Origen's response to Celsus' attack on the idea of the resurrection does not concern us in the present context, but when in 2.61 he comes to the story of 'doubting Thomas' Origen once again has recourse to Homer:⁴³

---

39 Cf. Hunter 2018, 43.
40 The verse cited by Celsus is often associated with Alexander the Great.
41 Celsus appears to have drawn some comparison or contrast between the story of the passion of Christ and Euripides' *Bacchae*, cf. *CC* 2.34. Origen reverses Celsus' scorn by pointing out that those who condemned Jesus, namely the Jewish people, have indeed, like Pentheus, been torn apart and scattered over the earth. It is tempting to wonder whether the strange events which were said to have accompanied the death of Christ (e.g. *Matthew* 27.45, *Luke* 23.44–46) were not assimilated in some literature to the mysterious passing of Oedipus in Sophocles' *Oedipus at Colonus*.
42 Cf. Lona 2005, 162–163.
43 For Origen's treatment of Thomas more generally cf. Most 2005, 136–139.

On this account Thomas said: 'Unless I see, I will not believe', and even went on to say: 'Unless I thrust my hand into the print of the nails and touch his side, I will not believe.' This was said by Thomas because he thought that it was possible for the physical eyes to see the body of the soul in a form in every respect like its former shape,

> μέγεθός τε καὶ ὄμματα κάλ' ἐϊκυίης
> καὶ φωνὴν

> in stature and beautiful eyes and voice,

and often

> καὶ τοῖα περὶ χροῒ εἵματ' ἐχούσης

> having the same garments about the skin
> *Iliad* 23.66–67

But Jesus called Thomas to him and said: 'Reach hither your finger and see my hands; and reach hither your hand and put it into my side; and be not faithless but believing.'
Origen, *Against Celsus* 2.61 (trans. Chadwick)

The appearance in a dream of the dead Patroclus to Achilles in *Iliad* 23 is chosen, not just for its fame in antiquity[44] and because Thomas does believe in such appearances, though not in the 'physical resurrection' of which he has been told, but also (apparently) because Achilles does fit Celsus' claim, which Origen scornfully dismisses as Epicurean (2.60),[45] that such appearances come to those 'in a dream induced by a certain disposition of mind and in mistaken fancy hallucinating (φαντασιωθείς) in accordance with his own wishes'. When the ghost of Patroclus appears, Achilles has not eaten and is physically and emotionally exhausted (*Il.* 23.55–64), and Patroclus' appearance is certainly 'in accordance with [Achilles'] own wishes'. What Origen wants to make clear is that Jesus's appearance to the disciples after the resurrection was an entirely different matter from the Homeric dream.[46] Here again, however, we may detect the

---

44 On this scene cf. Gazis 2018, 47–76, though Gazis does not discuss how this scene was interpreted and reworked in antiquity.
45 Editors standardly (and rightly) cite Lucretius, *DRN* 1.132–135 and 4.37–45 on how we sometimes see the dead in our dreams.
46 Virgil's imitation of the Iliadic scene at *Aeneid* 2.269–279 brings it in fact closer to some aspects of the Bible story: when Hector appears to Aeneas in a dream he is as we last 'saw' him – filthy and covered in gore, with his feet pierced where Achilles had tied thongs to drag him behind the chariot. *quantum mutatus ab illo / Hectore* marks (*inter alia*) the difference from the Homeric scene.

influence of critical discussion of the Homeric text which preceded Origen (and Celsus). The scholia on *Il.* 23.66 inform us that Antisthenes, a sophist and polymath of the late fifth-early fourth century BC, used this passage of Homer as a demonstration of the fact that souls had the same shape as the bodies which surrounded them (ὁμοσχήμονας ... τὰς ψυχὰς τοῖς περιέχουσι σώμασι, fr. 57 Caizzi = fr. 193 Prince),[47] but that the Stoic Chrysippus claimed that, after separation from the body, souls became spherical in shape (σφαιροειδεῖς). It is not known whether Chrysippus also referred to the Iliadic passage in his discussion, but it is clear that the scene had entered discussion of what survives after death centuries before the advent of Christianity.

At the heart of Origen's claims is, of course, the pursuit of truth and the attempt to distinguish truth from μῦθος, and this truth may be 'historical truth' or it may be a deep-level truth which can only be revealed by various interpretative methods, most notably allegorizing. In an important chapter of Book 1, Origen sets out some of the difficulties confronting anyone who would investigate past realities:

> Before we begin the defence, we must say that an attempt to substantiate (κατασκευάζειν) almost any story as historical fact, even if it is true, and to produce complete certainty (καταληπτικὴν ... φαντασίαν) about it, is one of the most difficult tasks and in some cases is impossible. Suppose, for example, that someone says the Trojan war never happened, in particular because it is bound up (προσπεπλέχθαι) with the impossible story about a certain Achilles having had Thetis, a sea-goddess, as his mother, and Peleus, a man, as his father, or that Sarpedon was son of Zeus, or Ascalaphus and Ialmenus of Ares, or Aeneas of Aphrodite. How could we substantiate (κατασκευάζειν) this, especially as we are embarrassed by the fictitious stories which for some unknown reason are bound up with the opinion, which everyone believes, that there really was a war in Troy between the Greeks and the Trojans?[48] Suppose also that someone does not believe the story about Oedipus and Jocasta, and Eteocles and Polyneices, the sons of them both, because the half-maiden (μιξοπάρθενος) Sphinx has been mixed up with it (προσπεπλέχθαι). How could we prove the historicity of a story like this? So also in the case of the Epigoni, even if there is nothing incredible involved in the story, or in that of the return of the Heraclidae, or innumerable other instances. Anyone who reads the stories with a fair mind (εὐγνωμόνως), who wants to keep himself from being deceived by them, will decide what he will accept and what he will interpret allegorically (τροπολογήσει), searching out the meaning (τὸ βούλημα) of the authors who wrote such fictitious stories, and what he will disbelieve as having been written to gratify certain people. We have said this by way of introduction to

---

47 For discussion cf. Prince 2015, 664–666.
48 Editors here rightly refer to Dio Chrysostom 11, in which the rhetorician 'proves' that virtually nothing happened at Troy as Homer and other early epic report it; this speech may be seen (*inter alia*) as a rhetorical ἀνασκευή writ large, cf. Hunter 2009.

the whole question of the narrative about Jesus in the gospels, not in order to invite people with intelligence to mere irrational faith, but with a desire to show that readers need an open mind (εὐγνωμοσύνη) and considerable study, and, if I may say so, need to enter into the intention (τὸ βούλημα) of the writers to find out with what spiritual meaning each event was recorded.

Origen, Against Celsus 1.42 (trans. Chadwick, adapted)

Origen's language here is heavily indebted not just, as has long been recognized, to Stoic epistemology (καταλαηπτικὴ … φαντασία) but also to Greek rhetorical theory and practice: κατασκευάζειν is a standard verb for 'confirming' a story, and κατασκευή was the exercise in which the budding orator practised his skill at inventing arguments to 'confirm' stories from myth and poetry (often Homer);[49] this is just the situation which Origen conjures up here. The fact that, in our record of the past, mythical material was mixed up with, or used to embroider, 'truth', meant that the search for the latter was even more difficult and/or that confidence in 'the truth' could be undermined. The supposed 'half-maiden' Sphinx (Σφίγγα μιξοπάρθενόν τινα) can cast doubt on the whole Theban story.[50] Origen here echoes a considerable body of ancient discussion.[51] Of particular importance is Strabo's discussion of Homeric practice in Book 1 of the *Geography*. For Strabo, Homer added mythical material to give his true account broader appeal (1.2.9, 1.2.19); at the most general level, Strabo tells us that 'Homer ornamented (ἐκόσμησε) the Trojan war, which had really happened, with mythical stories', and Origen uses much the same example, though with a quite different spin. προσμυθεύειν, the verb that Strabo uses for the Homeric practice, refers to much the same activity as Origen designates in *CC* 1.42 by προσπλέκειν. The added myths can 'sweeten and ornament (ἡδύνων καὶ κοσμῶν)' what is said, just as Origen notes that it will be necessary to disbelieve stories invented to win χάρις with various people.

Origen insists that one has to make choices as to what will be accepted as 'true', what requires allegorical interpretation to reach the intention of the author, and what is to be rejected. Origen emphasizes the need for εὐγνωμοσύνη in our reading and in making such decisions; this seems to be not just good judgement, but something like, as Chadwick translates, 'an open mind'. Origen

---

49 Cf. Hunter 2015, 688–690.
50 μιξοπάρθενος is used of the sphinx at Eur. *Phoen.* 1023, and an echo of tragedy here reinforces the 'poetic', unbelievable nature of the creature; μιξοπάρθενος is as bizarre a formation as the Sphinx itself. The epithet occurs otherwise only of Echidna at Hdt. 4.9.1, in a very 'mythical' tale, and of Scylla at Lycophron, *Alex.* 669.
51 For what follows and for the matter as a whole cf. Hunter 2016, citing earlier discussions.

here seems to demand the same interpretative principle of charity or generosity when judging the truth of the gospel narrative, which he sees operative in the interpretation of pagan texts.[52] Here too Origen enters territory that had long been contested. Both Apuleius in the opening book of the *Metamorphoses* and Lucian in the *Lovers of Lies* had staged confrontations between those prepared 'to believe anything' and those whose instincts were always skeptical.[53] Apuleius' gullible Lucius, who considers nothing impossible (*Met.* 1.20), is a kind of parodic version of Origen's εὐγνώμων critic or, perhaps rather, a pagan version of the Christian of 'simple, unquestioning faith' (ψιλὴ πίστις καὶ ἄλογος). The important difference, however, is that, whereas the debates in Apuleius and Lucian concern simply the historicity of reported tales, Origen knows that there is more than one kind of 'truth' and, in both pagan and Christian texts, it is necessary to consider the intention (βούλημα) of the writers, just indeed as Strabo had been explicitly concerned with Homer's intentions. Where this matters most, of course, is where allegorical interpretation of some kind is required. In *CC* 4.38–39 Origen had quoted famous verses from Hesiod's *Works and Days* on the gods' fashioning of Pandora and the ills she let escape into the world from 'the jar' and also Diotima's myth of the birth of Eros from Plato's *Symposium* as examples from pagan literature of apparently laughable fictions which had been the object of deeply philosophical allegorizing by (in the latter case) those who sought Plato's 'intention' (βούλημα), an intention which he had concealed from 'the many' by clothing it in the form of a myth.[54] Origen demands the same availability of allegorising for, for example, stories from the Jewish Old Testament, a mode of interpretation which Celsus will not allow, although sympathizing with the 'more reasonable' (οἱ ἐπιεικέστεροι) of the Jews and Christians who wish to allegorise, out of embarrassment at the silliness of Bible stories (*CC* 4.38).[55]

Behind Origen stands a very rich classical tradition of allegorical criticism. The principal impulse to that tradition had (again) been the study of Homer, and in particular of the Homeric gods; a famous passage of Porphyry traced the allegorical reading of the Homeric gods back to Theagenes of Rhegium in the

---

[52] Cf. Lamberton 1986, 80–82.
[53] Cf. Hunter 2016, 250–251.
[54] Cf. Villani 2018, 115–116. For Origen's Platonism in *CC* more generally cf., e.g., Romaniuk 1961, Villani 2018.
[55] Cf., e.g., Pépin 1976, 447–448.

later sixth century BC.⁵⁶ Plato refers to this mode of defence when he makes Socrates ban particular poetic tales from the ideal city:

> Hera's fetterings by her son and the hurling out of heaven of Hephaestus by his father when he was trying to save his mother from a beating,⁵⁷ and the battles of the gods in Homer's verse are things that we must not admit (οὐ παραδεκτέον) into our city either wrought in allegory or without allegory (οὔτ' ἐν ὑπονοίαις πεποιημένας οὔτε ἄνευ ὑπονοιῶν). For the young are not able to distinguish what is and what is not allegory, but whatever opinions are taken into the mind at that age are wont to prove indelible and unalterable.
>
> Plato, *Republic* 2.378d2–e2 (trans. Shorey)

Origen echoes this passage of the *Republic* when he dismisses a particularly outlandish pagan fabrication:⁵⁸

> The traditions of the Greeks have concocted a legend about Athena, whom he puts with Helios, and, whether with or without some secret meaning (εἴτ' ἐν ὑπονοίαις εἴτε χωρὶς ὑπονοιῶν), assert that she was born armed from the head of Zeus. And they say that she was chased at that time by Hephaestus who desired to ruin her virginity. She escaped from him, but loved and brought up the seed resulting from his lust which fell to the earth, and called the child Erichthonios
>
> τόν ποτε (φασίν) Ἀθήνη
> θρέψε, Διὸς θυγάτηρ, τέκε δὲ ζείδωρος ἄρουρα.
>
> whom (they say) Athena the daughter of Zeus once brought up, an offspring of the grain-giving earth
>
> *Iliad* 2.547–548
>
> So we see that anyone who addresses worship to Athena, the daughter of Zeus, must accept (παρεκδεκτέον) many myths and fictitious stories which would not be accepted by anyone who avoids myths and seeks the truth.
>
> Origen, *Against Celsus* 8.66 (trans. Chadwick, adapted)

---

56 For a brief survey of the issues and some bibliographical guidance cf. Hunter 2018, 44–49.
57 Cf. below pp. 904–905.
58 As far as I know, this Platonic echo has not been pointed out before. This may also have been the passage in Origen's mind at *CC* 4.48, where he claims that Christians 'do not accept any myth which might harm the young even if it is to be understood allegorically', and *CC* 4.50 when he writes in general terms of Plato's dismissal of 'myths and poems' from the ideal city, rather than *Rep.* 2.379c–d to which the allusion is standardly referred; Origen may there, however, not have been thinking of any one passage of *Republic* 2.

The clear echoes of Plato (εἴτ' ἐν ὑπονοίαις εἴτε χωρὶς ὑπονοιῶν, παρεκδεκτέον) here reinforce the point that this story about Athena and Hephaestus is not just unbelievable, but is also as morally distorting as the myths which Plato dismisses. The citation of a familiar Homeric tag is, in essence, a variation on Plato's explicit naming of the poet: it is indeed poets such as Homer who are the purveyors of such absurd stories.

One of the most revealing of Celsus' allegorisations of Homer comes in a passage (*CC* 6.42) where, to judge from Origen's account, Celsus was arguing that the Christian conception of Satan is derived from misunderstandings of pagan myths and other riddling texts of writers such as Pherecydes and Heraclitus which required allegorical interpretation to reveal their inner depths; such understanding was of course beyond the Christians. Celsus cites two Homeric passages which had long been put together in the grammatical tradition,[59] although the story of Zeus hurling Hephaestus out of heaven had also been allegorized on its own, away from the other passage with which Celsus associates it.[60] Celsus introduces the passages with the identification of context which is necessary for their proper understanding:

> Οὕτω δ' ἀκούει καὶ Ὁμήρου, ὡς τὰ παραπλήσια τῷ Ἡρακλείτῳ καὶ Φερεκύδῃ καὶ τοῖς τὰ περὶ Τιτᾶνας καὶ Γίγαντας μυστήρια εἰσάγουσιν αἰνισσομένου ἐν τούτοις <τοῖς> τοῦ Ἡφαίστου πρὸς τὴν Ἥραν λόγοις, φάσκοντος·
>> ἤδη γάρ με καὶ ἄλλοτ' ἀλεξέμεναι μεμαῶτα
>> ῥῖψε ποδὸς τεταγὼν ἀπὸ βηλοῦ θεσπεσίοιο.
>>> Homer, *Iliad* 1.590–591
>
> καὶ τοῖς τοῦ Διὸς πρὸς τὴν Ἥραν οὕτως·
>> ἦ οὐ μέμνησ' ὅτε τ' ἐκρέμω ὑψόθεν, ἐκ δὲ ποδοῖιν
>> ἄκμονας ἧκα δύω, περὶ χερσὶ δὲ δεσμὸν ἴηλα
>> χρύσεον ἄρρηκτον; σὺ δ' ἐν αἰθέρι καὶ νεφέλῃσιν
>> ἐκρέμω· ἠλάστεον δὲ θεοὶ κατὰ μακρὸν Ὄλυμπον,
>> λῦσαι δ' οὐκ ἐδύναντο παρασταδόν· ὃν δὲ λάβοιμι,
>> ῥίπτασκον τεταγὼν ἀπὸ βηλοῦ, ὄφρ' ἂν ἵκοιτο
>> γῆν ὀλιγηπελέων·
>>> Homer, *Iliad* 15.18–24
>
>>> Celsus in Origen, *Against Celsus* 6.42

---

59 Cf. the A-scholia on *Iliad* 1.591.
60 Cf., e.g., 'Heraclitus', *Hom. Probl.* 26.3–16 (it is an allegory of the transmission of fire from the gods to men), 27 (Crates of Mallos understood it to be an allegory of Zeus' measuring of the universe, cf. Porter 1992, 95–100).

> Celsus also understands Homer in this sense, saying that he hints at the same truths as Heraclitus and Pherecydes and as those who teach the mysteries of the Titans and Giants, in these words which Hephaestus addresses to Hera: 'For once already when I intended to defend you, he took me by the foot and hurled me from the divine threshold'. And similarly in the words of Zeus to Hera: 'Do you not remember when you were hanging from on high, and I let two anvils hang from your two legs and threw golden and unbroken chains around your arms? And you were hanging in the aether and the clouds. And the gods protested throughout tall Olympus, but they could not set you free though standing by; whichever god I caught, I took him and threw him from the threshold until he came powerless to earth.' (trans. Chadwick, adapted)

If any passages of Homer cried out for allegorical interpretation, it was these, and the fact that the Platonic Socrates had explicitly banned the stories of 'Hera's bonds' and 'Hephaestus being thrown out by his father' in the passage which refers to the allegorisation of apparently impious passages (*Rep.* 2.378d2–4, cf. above) was in fact all but an invitation to allegorisation; the subsequent tradition had not disappointed. The standard allegorical interpretation saw in Hera's punishment, with considerable variation of detail, an allegory of the arrangement of the four elements in the coming together of the cosmos; the two anvils attached to the legs of Hera ('the air', ἀήρ ~ Ἥρα) were the earth and the sea.[61] According to Origen, Celsus' explanation was related to this standard allegory, but was also rather different:

> Commenting on the words of Homer [Celsus] says that the words (λόγοι) of Zeus to Hera are the words[62] of the god to matter and that the words to matter hint that from the first[63] it was in disorder (ἐξ ἀρχῆς αὐτὴν πλημμελῶς ἔχουσαν) and the god divided it in certain proportions (ἀναλογίαις), bound it together, and ordered it, and that he cast out all the daemons round it which were arrogant, inflicting on them the punishment of being sent down here to the earth. He maintains that Pherecydes (B5 Diels-Kranz = D13 Laks-Most) understood these words of Homer in this way, when he said: 'Beneath that land is the land of Tartarus, and it is guarded by the daughters of Boreas, the Harpies and Thyella ['Storm']; there Zeus casts out any of the gods if ever one becomes arrogant'.
> Origen, *Against Celsus* 6.42 (trans. Chadwick, adapted)

---

61 Cf. Cornutus 17, where, rather as in Celsus, Homer is said here to preserve 'a fragment of an ancient myth', 'Heraclitus', *Hom. Probl.* 40 (the fullest surviving account), [Plut.] *Hom.* 2.97, Buffière 1956, 115–117, Pépin 1976, 448–453, Ramelli 2003, 343–345, Pontani 2005, 209–210.
62 David Sedley points out to me that, for Celsus, the λόγοι of god towards matter, which are symbolised by the 'words' of Zeus to Hera, were probably 'ratios', cf. ἀναλογίαις τισί immediately below.
63 For Celsus' view of the notion of ἀρχή in the light of Plato, *Timaeus* 28b4–7 cf. *CC* 4.79.

This passage puts some of Celsus' own intellectual underpinnings on clear show. First, there is his own daemonology which sits comfortably within second-century Platonism, but which also allows a very direct association not just with these passages of Homer, but also with Hesiodic (*Theog.* 267, 868) and other texts, as here Pherecydes, about Zeus casting Hephaestus and other gods out of heaven; it is something of a *tour de force* to find here the model for the Christian view of Satan and the Antichrist. Secondly, the idea that Zeus and Hera respectively represent the divine, organizing force and matter clearly had good Stoic authority, though the details must remain unclear. In *CC* 4.48 Origen reports that Chrysippus (*SVF* II 1074) had interpreted a Samian painting depicting Hera fellating Zeus as 'matter receiving the generative principles of God (τοὺς σπερματικοὺς λόγους τοῦ θεοῦ) and containing them in itself for the ordering of the universe. For in the picture at Samos matter is Hera and God is Zeus' (trans. Chadwick, adapted).[64] Whatever the truth about this painting and Chrysippus' (humorous?) interpretation, there can be no doubt that Celsus has Stoic forebears in his interpretation of the Homeric passage. The key influence, however, presumably transmitted through an unknown number of intermediaries, is the cosmological account of the demiurge's creation in Plato's *Timaeus*, 'a speech concerning the All, how it was created or indeed was not created' (27c4–5).[65] Celsus' observation that 'from the first [matter] was in disorder' (ἐξ ἀρχῆς αὐτὴν πλημμελῶς ἔχουσαν) rewrites Plato's account in which everything visible 'was moving in disorder and without pattern' (κινούμενον πλημμελῶς καὶ ἀτάκτως, *Timaeus* 30a4–5) before the intervention of the demiurge; the adverb πλημμελῶς is here a signal to the model.[66] The Platonic version of creation from the four elements which follows deserves to be quoted at some length:

> Hence, in beginning to construct the body of the All, the god was making it of fire and earth. But it is not possible that two things alone should be conjoined without a third; or there must needs be some intermediary bond (δεσμόν) to connect the two. And the fairest of bonds (δεσμῶν) is that which most perfectly unites into one both itself and the things which it binds together; and to effect this in the fairest manner is the natural property of proportion (ἀναλογία) ... Thus it was that in the midst between fire and earth the god set water and air, and having bestowed upon them so far as possible a like ratio one towards another – air being to water as fire to air, and water being to earth as air to water, – he joined together and constructed a Heaven visible and tangible. For these reasons and out

---

64 Cf. also Diog. Laert. 7.187 (= *SVF* II 1071), Dio Chrys. 36.55–57, Pépin 1976, 454.
65 Cf. Andresen 1955, 142–145, Lona 2005, 359–360; for the importance of this passage more generally cf. Frede 1994, 5204–5205.
66 πλημμελής and related words are in fact Platonic favourites and may well have been felt as such.

of these materials, such in kind and four in number, the body of the Cosmos was harmonized by proportion (δι' ἀναλογίας ὁμολογῆσαν) and brought into existence. These conditions secured for it Amity, so that being united in identity with itself it became indissoluble by any agent other than him who had bound it together (ὑπὸ τοῦ ξυνδήσαντος).

Plato, Timaeus 31b–32c (trans. W.R.M. Lamb)

Like many Platonists after him, Celsus finds Homer and Plato in agreement, just speaking in rather different modes;[67] put differently we might say that Celsus has assimilated this passage of Plato to the Homeric allegorical tradition with which he was so familiar. The resulting analysis is both strange and familiar, as so much of later Homeric and Platonic exegesis can indeed appear. It was that almost counter-intuitive strangeness, as much as anything, which showed Origen where such analysis was most vulnerable.

Celsus' use of Homer and the Homeric critical tradition as rhetorical and argumentative tools is in fact of a familiar kind, and one which was to become even more familiar in the Platonising traditions of later antiquity. Origen was deeply knowledgeable about the critical frameworks in which Celsus and those like him had been brought up, and he used that knowledge in part to answer 'like with like', by showing that Celsus was condemned by the very rhetorical techniques which he himself had employed, and in part by moving debate to a higher plane, by insisting that what was at stake was far more important than could be served by the sophistications of traditional pagan criticism. From the perspective of ancient criticism, the *Against Celsus* is a remarkable treatise, which looks both back, not to just Celsus but to the whole tradition of pagan Homeric criticism, and forward to the increasing interweaving of Christian and pagan exegesis in later antiquity. From this limited perspective alone, it deserves greater attention than classicists have normally afforded it.

Bibliography

Andresen, C. 1955. *Logos und Nomos. Die Polemik des Kelsos wider das Christentum*, Berlin.
Buffière, F. 1956. *Les mythes d'Homère et la pensée grecque*, Paris.
Clements, A. 2014. *Aristophanes' Thesmophoriazusae. Philosophizing Theatre and the Politics of Perception in late fifth-century Athens*, Cambridge.
Fédou, M. 2003. 'La reference à Homère chez Clément d'Alexandrie et Origène', in: Perrone 2003, 377–383.
Fiedrowicz, M./Barthold, C. 2011. *Origenes, Contra Celsum/Gegen Celsus*, Freiburg.

---

67 The basic study here remains Lamberton 1986; cf. also Hunter 2012, ch. 2.

Frede, M. 1994. 'Celsus philosophus Platonicus' *Aufstieg und Niedergang der römischen Welt* II 36.7, Berlin/New York, 5183–5213.
Frede, M. 1999. 'Origen's treatise *Against Celsus*', in: M. Edwards/M. Goodman/S. Price (eds.), *Apologetics in the Roman Empire*, Oxford, 131–155.
Gazis, G. 2018. *Homer and the Poetics of Hades*, Oxford.
Hunter, R. 2009. 'The *Trojan Oration* of Dio Chrysostom and ancient Homeric criticism', in: J. Grethlein/A. Rengakos (eds.), *Narratology and Interpretation*, Berlin, 43–61, [= this volume 487–505].
Hunter, R. 2012. *Plato and the Traditions of Ancient Literature: the Silent Stream*, Cambridge.
Hunter, R. 2015a. 'The rhetorical criticism of Homer', in: F. Montanari/S. Matthaios/A. Rengakos (eds.), *Brill's Companion to Ancient Greek Scholarship*, Leiden, II 673–705, [= this volume 598–632].
Hunter, R. 2015b. *Apollonius of Rhodes, Argonautica Book IV*, Cambridge.
Hunter, R. 2016. "'Palaephatus', Strabo and the boundaries of myth', *Classical Philology* 111, 245–261 [= this volume 578–597].
Hunter, R. 2018. *The Measure of Homer*, Cambridge.
Kaiser, E. 1964. 'Odyssee-Szenen als Topoi', *Museum Helveticum* 21, 109–136, 197–224.
Lamberton, R. 1986. *Homer the Theologian*, Berkeley.
Lona, H.E. 2005. *Die 'Wahre Lehre' des Kelsos*, Freiburg.
Marcovich, M. 2001. *Origenes, Contra Celsum libri VIII*, Leiden.
Most, G.W. 2005. *Doubting Thomas*, Cambridge MA.
Neuschäfer, B. 1987. *Origenes als Philologe*, Basel.
Niehoff, M.R. 2020. 'Homer between Celsus, Origen and the Jews of Late Antique Palestina', in: J.J. Price/R. Zelnick-Abramovitz (eds.), *Text and Intertext in Greek Epic and Drama*, London, 187–209.
Pépin, J. 1976. *Mythe et allégorie*, Paris.
Perrone, L. (ed.) 2003. *Origeniana Octava. Origen and the Alexandrian Tradition*, Leuven.
Pontani, F. 2005. *Eraclito. Questioni omeriche sulle allegorie di Omero in merito agli dèi*, Pisa.
Porter, J.I. 1992. 'Hermeneutic lines and circles: Aristarchus and Crates on the exegesis of Homer', in: R. Lamberton/J.J. Keaney (eds.), *Homer's Ancient Readers*, Princeton, 67–114.
Prince, S. 2015. *Antisthenes of Athens: Texts, Translations, and Commentary*, Ann Arbor.
Ramelli, I. 2003. *Anneo Cornuto. Compendia di teologia greca*, Milan.
Romaniuk, K. 1961. 'Le Platon d'Origène. Les citations des *Lois*, du *Phédon*, du *Phèdre* et de la *République* dans *Contre Celse* d'Origène', *Aegyptus* 41, 44–73.
Schoedel, W.R. 1972. *Athenagoras, Legatio and De resurrectione*, Oxford.
Villani, A. 2012. 'Homer in the debate between Celsus and Origen', *Revue d'études augustiniennes et patristiques* 58, 113–139.
Villani, A. 2018. 'Platon und der Platonismus in Origenes' *Contra Celsum*', in: B. Bäbler/H.-G. Nesselrath (eds.), *Origenes der Christ und Origenes der Platoniker*, Tübingen, 109–127.
West, M.L. 1978. *Hesiod, Works and Days*, Oxford.

General Index

Academy, Athenian 257–9
Achilles 50, 204–9, 240, 386–7, 428, 605–6, 632–57, 687, 700–4, 710–11, 723–4, 794, 893, 899
Achilles Tatius 453, 458, 462
Adonis 319
Aeschines 471–3
Aeschylus 116–17, 119, 141, 143, 145, 515
Aesop, *Life* of 450, 462–7, 477–82
aetiology 184–90
Agamemnon 50, 387–8, 616–29, 893
Ajax 653, 654
Alcaeus 228, 349–50, 353
Alcibiades 3–17, 670
Alcidamas, *On the sophists* 396, 676–7
Alcman 216, 228
Alexandria 811–22
Alexis 119
allegory 69–71, 76–8, 81, 132–9, 377, 513, 560, 566–7, 569, 573–4, 587–8, 600, 601–4, 605, 695, 705–19, 730–1, 739, 744, 816, 880, 902–3, 904–7
Anaxagoras 376, 891
Antenor 383–4, 386, 387
Antigenidas, aulete 9
Antimachus 21–2, 286, 366
Antiphanes 119, 400
Antisthenes 61, 605, 640–5, 647, 671–2, 697, 900
Aphrodite 25–43, 186–90, 732–5, 736, 803, 836–7, 898
Apollo 8–11, 13, 30–1, 84–101, 168, 178, 308–9, 311, 730–2, 824–47
Apollodorus, *Library* 456
Apollonius Rhodius 565–7, 571
Apuleius 390–1, 450, 453, 458, 465, 590, 902
Aratus 75, 290–2
Archilochus 365–7, 534–5
Ares 25–43
Aristarchus 69, 289, 488, 517, 588, 617, 685, 688, 707, 724, 734–5, 788, 790–5, 801, 805, 806, 818
Aristeas, Letter of 811–22

Aristodemus, Spartan 556
Aristophanes 112, 113, 125, 399, 466, 526, 529–30, 531–2, 532–4, 891–2; *Acharnians* 103–6, 121; *Clouds* 117–19, 121; *Frogs* 84, 96, 104, 512, 599, 759; *Lysistrata* 119; *Peace* 217–18; *Wasps* 331
Aristophanes of Byzantium 69, 290, 522, 635, 724, 788, 793
Aristotle 15, 246, 252, 253, 261, 301–2, 334, 371, 394, 507, 518, 522, 549–50, 608, 611, 617–18, 645–6, 653, 704, 724, 757, 817, 821, 890; *Poetics* 54, 92–3, 105–8, 110, 123, 365, 404–5, 425–6, 488, 496, 497, 609, 635, 647, 655–6, 788–9
Artemis 181–2, 183, 186–8, 190
Asclepiades of Myrlea 288–94
Athena 8–14, 308, 601–4, 709–12, 889
aulos 8–12
Aulus Gellius 262

Bacchylides 76, 199, 510
Britomartis 179–86

Callimachus 27–8, 48, 74–6, 89, 91, 156–73, 175–90, 193, 259, 279, 286–304, 354, 368–9, 507, 584, 693, 761, 815, 836
Callinus 366
Candaules 736
Carey, Peter 455, 457–60
Carneades 297, 381
Cassandra 834–5
Cato 572–6
Catullus 316, 319, 321, 354, 408
Celsus 883–907
Chamaeleon 229, 352–3
Charition mime 120, 468–9
Chariton, *Callirhoe* 54–5, 451–3, 460, 470–7, 479, 813, 820
Chrysippus 380–1, 900, 906
Cicero 293–4; *Brutus* 258; *Pro Archia* 254
Circe 606–8, 744, 880

Clitomachus 296–7
Comedy 103–25, 521–35. See also Aristophanes, Menander
Comedy, Middle 96, 110
Comedy, New 92–6, 110. See also Menander
Comedy, Roman 108–12, 115, 123–5. See also Plautus, Terence
Cornutus 600
Crantor 380–1
Crates of Mallos 600
Cratinus 534
Crete 179–86
Cyclops 329–39, 697, 875–82

Delphi 86, 543
Demetrios of Phaleron 811, 813–14, 817
Demetrius, *On Style* 200, 218, 321, 357–8
Demo 713
Democritus 365, 507
Demodocus 18–43, 598, 708
Demosthenes 61, 471–3, 758, 761
Derveni Papyrus 80–1, 600, 840
Dictynna 179–86
Dictys of Crete 876, 880
Didyma 178
Didymus 261, 353–4
Dio Chrysosotom 388–9, 392, 506–7, 532–4, 659–80, 770–85; *Or.* 3 672–3; *Or.* 5 560–76; *Or.* 7 660, 676, 770–5; *Or.* 8 575; *Or.* 11 487–504, 613; *Or.* 12 161; *Or.* 13 661–80; *Or.* 18 261; *Or.* 33 533–4; *Or.* 36 660–1; *Or.* 57 385–6
Diodorus Cronus 297–300
Diodorus Siculus 183–4
Diomedes 625–6, 628–9
Dionysius of Halicarnassus 48, 61–2, 117, 203, 216, 218–19, 290, 350–1, 498, 611, 619, 624, 749–68
Dionysius Periegetes 690–2
Dionysius Thrax 289
Dionysus 85–9, 105–6, 170–2, 310, 799, 836–7, 839–42
Dioscorides 319–20
Diotima 3–4, 11, 902
Doukas, John 690

Douris of Samos 9, 14, 503
Dyrrachion see Epidamnus

Eliot, T.S. 759, 763
Elpenor 275, 869
Elysium 886
Empedocles 411–18
Enkelados 308–13
Epicharmus 223, 319, 331
Epictetus 662
Epicurus/Epicureanism 238–41, 296, 380
Epidamnus 431–44
Eratosthenes 259, 289, 310, 589
Erinna 320
etymology 824–47
Euhemerus 296
Eumaeus 343, 775
Eunapius 531–2
Euphorbus 867
Eupolis 114
Euripides 400, 479, 524–6, 796–7; *Antiope* 253–5; *Ba.* 86, 88–9, 93–4, 171, 842; *Cycl.* 331, 339, 842, 874, 877–82; *El.* 771–5; *Her.* 425–8; *Hipp.* 67–82; *Ion* 84–101; *IT* 881; *Medea* 116; *Orestes* 635; *Philoctetes* 607–8; *Rhesus* 116
Eustathius 30–3, 48, 62, 76, 330–1, 333, 497, 587, 619, 625–6, 638, 654, 682–746, 796–7, 800, 805, 897–8
Euthymios Malakes 694–5, 698

fables 482
Favorinus 660, 779–81

Galen 113–14
Gorgias, *Helen* 225–7, 500

Hades 825
Hecataeus 580
Hector 646, 702, 710–11
Hedylos 300
Helen 39, 220–32, 324, 716, 732–9
Heliodorus, *Aithiopika* 55–62, 460, 742–6
Hephaestus 6, 25–53, 712–13, 799, 904–5
Hera 39, 738–42, 797, 798–806, 905–6

Heracles 246–7, 425–8, 560–1, 563, 565–7, 569, 574–5
Heraclides Ponticus 228–9
Heraclitus 550, 904
'Heraclitus', *Hom. Probl.* 78, 132–3, 135, 587, 600, 731, 895–6
Hermes 30–1, 744, 827–9, 894–6
Hermesianax 365–7
Hermogenes 21, 214–16, 219–20, 330–1, 335–6, 470–1, 521–2, 531, 618–19
Herodorus of Heraclea 567
Herodotus 165, 168, 318, 399, 456, 490, 492–3, 495, 571, 580–1, 590, 594, 718, 736, 754, 813, 817
Hesiod 157–8, 160, 185, 212, 364, 538, 540, 584, 593, 837
Hippias 509, 639–40, 642–3, 672. See also Plato, *Hippias minor*
Hippolytus 67–82
Homer 18–43, 46–63, 92, 146–7, 157–8, 164, 185, 197, 202, 231, 275, 282, 325, 327–44, 365, 376–96, 426, 442–3, 445, 459, 487–504, 506–19, 578–96, 598–629, 632–57, 680, 682–746, 764, 775, 787–806, 817–18, 875–82, 883–907
Homeric Hymns 34–5, 157–9; *Aphrodite* 25–30; *Apollo* 176; *Demeter* 36, 275–81; *Dionysus* 18–19, 170–2
Horace 74, 134–5, 351, 363–5, 376–96, 411–18, 496–7, 512, 534, 669
Hylas 274, 277, 279, 865–6

interpolations, actors' 107, 112, 122
'Iolaos' papyrus 470
Iris 713–16
Isocrates 224–5, 364, 495, 549, 757, 764, 817
Istrus 168

Kelly, Ned 457–60
Koraes, Adamantios 742–6

Laertes 203, 343
Lamia 571–2
leeches 414–15
Lemnos 798–806
Lesches 501

Libanius 531–2, 611–14, 723
Library, Alexandrian 259, 811–12
Libya 560–76
Livius Andronicus 442
Longinus, *On the sublime* 261–2, 315, 590, 604, 726, 760, 764–5
Lucan 572–6
Lucian 532, *Philops.* 585–6, 902; *VH* 453, 580, 822
Lucilius 379–81, 417
Lucretius 417, 580
Lycurgus 112
Lysias 767

magic 41
Magna Graecia 440–1
Malalas, John 875–82
Marmor Parium 318
Marsyas 8–11, 13, 16
Maximus of Tyre 386–7, 389, 390, 591
McEwan, Ian 456
Menander 95, 112–13, 119–22, 124, 251–2, 275, 300, 401, 443, 477, 480, 521–32, 767
Menelaus 20, 595–6
metaphor 72–3
Metrodorus 508
Michael Choniates 693–705, 743
mime 42, 120–1, 209, 467–70, 529
Mimnermus 366, 368–72, 374
Moschus, *Europa* 20–1
Musaeus 365
Muse, Muses 33–5, 72, 229, 260
Museum, Alexandrian 259–60, 263–4, 815
myrtle 185

Narcissus 274
Nausicaa 230–1, 686, 709, 735
Nestor 383–8, 617, 638, 687
Nietzsche, Friedrich 84–5, 87–8, 91, 93, 96, 524
Niobe 428
Nossis 319

Odysseus 20, 22–5, 30, 46–63, 202–3, 360–1, 380, 388–92, 394, 396, 442–3,

459, 595–6, 599, 605–8, 632–57, 662–3, 687, 696, 704–5, 709–10, 875–82, 895–6
oracles 98–101
Orestes 775
Origen 883–907
Orpheus/Orphism 81, 365
Ovid 21, 31, 40–3, 184, 351–3, 368, 371, 584, 751

Palaephatus 571, 578–90
Palladius 851
Pan 827–9, 843
Pandora 902
pantomime See 'mime'
Paphos 27–8
Paris 39, 384, 386, 490–1, 732–8
Parmenides 421–3, 543
pathetic fallacy 330, 332, 338
Patroclus 725–6, 898–9
Peisistratos 816–17
Penelope 602
Persephone 275–6
Petronius, *Satyrica* 453, 458, 469
Pherecydes 904, 906
Phidalios of Corinth 877–80
Phidias 161, 166
Philemon 119
Philicus 179
Philitas 260, 368
Philo of Byzantium 163–6
Philoctetes 799, 802
Philodemus 199, 518, 603
Philostratus 586, 659–60, 675, 677, 819–20
Philotheus, St 697
Phocylides 364
Phrynichus, Atticist 114, 532
Phrynichus, tragedian 399
Phthonos, personified 865–8
Phylarchus 501
Pindar 70–1, 74–7, 160, 196–7, 201–2, 210–13, 308–9, 311, 510, 598, 717, 819, 830, 836
Pittacus 543, 550–2, 557
Plato 60, 93, 252–8, 260, 378, 382, 555, 561–5, 575, 598, 658, 719, 757, 763–5, 883–5, 902; *Apology* 242–3, 668, 673–4, 771; *Clitophon* 667, 670–4; *Cratylus* 824–45; *Gorgias* 4, 12–13, 16, 253–4, 672–3; *Hipp. Min.* 61, 599, 605–6, 632–57; *Ion* 72–4, 506–19, 632, 635, 890; *Phaedo* 243; *Phaedrus* 71–2, 144, 219–20, 223, 231, 256–8, 263, 376, 420, 422–3, 470, 528, 541, 676; *Protag.* 514, 536–57, 636; *Republic* 4; *Symp.* 3–17, 470; *Tht.* 254–6, 591; *Tim.* 906–7
Plautus 110–12, 115, 119, 121, 402–10; *Menaechmi* 431–44; *Most.* 443
Plutarch 87–8, 98–9, 302–4, 392–3, 526–7, 706, 762, 819; *E at Delphi* 824, 832, 834, 837–45; *Gryllus* 606–8; *Sympotic Questions* 527–31
[Plutarch], *On Homer* 652
Polybius 434, 501, 812
Polygnotus 501
Porphyry 603–4, 640, 643, 689
Poseidon 720–32
Pratinas 311–13
Proclus 72, 705–7
Prodicus 540, 672
Proetus, daughters of 359
Proteus 58–62, 595
Pronomos, aulete 9
Propertius 369–73
Protagoras 509–10. See also Plato, *Protagoras*
Ptolemy/Ptolemaic 176–81, 193, 232, 294, 298, 318, 344, 811–22
Pythagoras/Pythagoreanism 830–1

Quintilian 71, 135, 261, 525, 767

Reposianus 26–7, 36
Rhadamanthys 886
Rhesus 800
Rushdie, Salman 455

Samothrace 178
Sappho 52, 204, 227–8, 314–25, 349–62
satyr-play 123
Satyrus 524–5
[Scylax], *Periplous* 439, 441
[Scymnus], *Periodos* 437–8

Seneca 380, 573
Seneca, *Apocol.* 580
Seven Sages 538, 543–4, 556
Seven Wonders 163–4
Sextus Empiricus 287–9, 300
Silanion 318
similes 23, 37, 205–6, 699
Simonides 70, 76, 199, 210, 514–15, 536–57
Sinon 25
Sirens 694–6, 894
Sisyphos of Cos 876–9, 881
Sleep 798–806
Socrates See Plato, Xenophon
Sophocles *Philoctetes* 636–7, 640
Sophron 221–2, 319
Stesichorus 214–32, 319
Stesimbrotus 598
Stilpo 162–3
Stoics/Stoicism 301, 378–81, 575, 664, 901, 906
Strabo 183, 186–7, 290, 292, 489, 507, 518, 589–96, 599, 814, 901
symposia 3–17, 78, 151–4, 527–32, 555
Synesius 660
Syrianus 521–3
Syrtis See Libya

Teiresias 61
Telemachus 442, 601–4, 710
Terence 108–12, 115, 124, 401–2
Theagenes of Rhegium 600, 902–3
Theocritus 21, 193–213, 247, 318–20, 327–44, 548, 739; *Id.* 2 50–2, 221, 323–5, 358–9; *Id.* 7 340–1, 343; *Id.* 15 175–6, 319; *Id.* 16 193–213; *Id.* 17 816, 818–19; *Id.* 18 221–32; *Id.* 28 319–20
Theognis 364, 542, 552–5
Theon, Aelius 47, 376, 496–8, 615–16, 723, 890–1
Theophrastus 259–60
Thersites 6
Thucydides 48–50, 492–4, 497–8, 569, 581–5, 593, 652, 749–68, 821–2
Trimalchio 851–2
Triphiodorus 23, 25, 34, 35
Typhos 308–13, 563, 568, 575, 587, 835–6
Tyro 20–2
Tyrtaeus 367
Τύχη/τύχη 803–5

Varro 337
Vergil 21, 23, 25, 247, 327, 436, 574–5

White, Patrick 451–3
Wilde, Oscar 93

Xenophon 674–5; *Symp.* 3, 5–7, 14–15, 42, 252, 512, 517, 529
Xenophon of Ephesus 453, 460

Zenodotus 624, 724, 795–7
Zeus 39, 161–9, 710, 732, 735–6, 738–42, 787–806, 836, 888, 904–6

Index of Passages Discussed

Aeschines
Tim.
147   473

Aeschylus
Ag. 1072–89   834–5

Aesop, Life of
3   480–2
28   479–80
31–3   464
32   478–9
75–6   463–5

Alcaeus
Fragments (Voigt)
42   231–2
208   132–5
346   151–4
360   557

Anacreon
AP 7.226   144–50

Anacreontea
18   142–4

Apollonius of Rhodes
Arg.
2.620–639   619–21
3.284–90   321
3.962–5   321
4.16–19   322, 358 n.38
4.430–44   317
4.552–6   424
4.672–82   416–17
4.922–64   176–7
4.1381–8   572

Apuleius
Metamorphoses
1.3   584–5
10.22   467

Aristophanes
Acharnians
1–27   103–5
412–17   104, 399–400
Frogs
948–50   523
1482–99   255–6

Aristotle
Poetics
1456a25–31   106–8
1459a4–8   73

Asclepiades
AP 12.50   151–4

Aulus Gellius
NA
9.9.4–11   335–7

Callimachus (Pfeiffer)
Epigrams
2   316, 854–5
15   855–6
20   148–50
23   293–4
27   291
28   153
31   136–7
42   300–4
Hymn to Zeus
4–9   156–7
Hymn to Apollo
17–24   160, 177–8
105–13   74–5, 172–3
Hymn to Artemis
189–204   179–86
Hymn to Delos
137–47   310–11
316–324   159
Hymn to Athena
131–7   167

Fragments

1	262–3, 292–3, 307–13, 369
75	26 n.31
100	169
110	320
114	168
178	263
191	295–7
196	162–3
200	186–90
393	297–300
586	295–7

Callinus

fr. 1.1–4 West	372–3

Catullus

50	361–2
51	141, 355–8, 361–2
66.39	355

Chariton of Aphrodisias
Callirhoe

3.2.2	476–7
3.5.6	475–6
5.10.9	474
6.4.6	474–5
7.3.5	474
8.1.4	54–5

Cicero
Against Verres

2.4.127	318

De Natura Deorum

1.119	296

Demosthenes
On the false embassy

19.245	472

Dio Chrysostom

4.82	778
5.24	568
6.55	778
7.81–2	772–5
7.97–102	770–5, 783
11.24–5	497
11.26	502–3
11.28	499
11.29–30	500–1
11.38	493
11.49–50	490–1
11.64	491–2
13.3	664
13.9	661–2
13.14–15	664–70
13.27–8	675
17.8–11	775–82
18.6–7	525–6
32.11	114 n.23
32.36	814
33.10	533–4
55.9	378–9
55.12–13	381–2

Diodorus Siculus

20.41–2	571–2

Dionysius Calliphontis

88–90	188

Dionysius of Halicarnassus
Lysias

11.3–4	760

Thucydides

1.1–2	751–3
2.2	763
4.1–3	758–9
25.1–2	753–4
45	765
55.3–4	755–6

Empedocles
Fragments (D–K)

25	47 n.3
112	414–15

Ennius
Annales

14 Skutsch	442–3

Epigrams (anonymous)

FGE 444–9	238–9

Eustathius
Commentary on Dionysius Periegetes
205.22–206.11 Müller   691–2
For Eustathius' Homeric *Commentaries*
see entries under 'Homer' and General Index

Euripides
Andr.
1284–88	94–5

Ba.
298–301	831

Cyc.
52	339
457–63	879–80

Hipp.
73–87	67–82
380–7	249–50, 252
952–5	81
986–91	79–80

Her.
637–41	307–8
859	425
907–10	309
1314–21	427–8
1340–6	426–8

Ion
112–24	89–90
436–51	96–8
633–7	248–9
1346–7	98–9
1357–62	99 n.41
1501–15	94–5
1520–7	96
1619–22	90–1

Phoen.
438–40	784–5
528–30	782–30
531–40	775–82

Tro.
884–8	890–2

Favorinus
On Exile
20.3–4	779–81

Gorgias
Helen
1	226–7
5	226–7

Palamedes
4	46

Heliodorus
Aethiopica
1.8.6–7	55–7
2.21.3–5	55–7
2.22.3	57–8
2.22.5	58
2.24.4–5	58–9

Heraclitus
Hom. Probl.
61	601–2

Hermesianax
Fragments
fr. 7. 35–8 Powell	366–7

Herodotus
2.53	156–7
4.30.1	420–1
6.21.2	399

Hesiod
WD
311	541

Fragments (MW)
30	21 n.13

Homer
Iliad
1.1	53–4
1.8–12	844
1.37–42	158
1.43–52	844–7
1.46–7	158
1.590–1	904–6
1.609–11	737
2.72–5	616–22
2.87–93	699–700
2.110–41	618–23
2.134–41	622–3

2.136–7	623	22.328–9	804–5
3.121	715–16	22.395	702
3.191–202	333–4	22.437–61	280–1
3.209–24	612–13	22.487–99	792–3
3.390–4	733	23.107	865
3.395–9	734–5	23.175–6	703–4
3.399–404	735	23.187	701–2
3.427	737–8	23.193–203	713–15
3.442–6	738	23.206	714
3.446–7	736–7	24.6–9	793–4
5.340	898	24.475–6	790
5.835–9	711–12	24.525–33	717–19
6.58–9	500	*Odyssey*	
6.234–6	688–9	1.1	390, 640–3
6.311	167	1.3	639
7.350–3	384	1.58–9	708–9
7.443–65	720–32	1.69–72	877
7.451	728	4.351–92	20
8.228–35	800–1	4.277–9	454–5
9.17	624–5	4.511–12	791
9.17–28	623–6, 628	5.94–5	790–1
9.29–31	626–8	6.139–41	709
9.30	626	6.149–85	686
9.33	628	6.275–85	735
9.38	628–9	7.249–50	804
9.186–91	701	8.75–7	640
9.208–14	644–7	8.126–30	866
9.307–9	645, 650	8.266–366	25–43
9.313	621	8.269	371
9.321–7	209–10	8.499–520	22–5
9.651–2	650–1	9.2–11	245–6
12.1–33	720–32	9.154–5	803–4
14.231	798–806	9.444–5	333
14.294	738–9	9.447–60	329–39
14.312–28	739–41	10.273	424
14.346–51	741–2	10.304–6	896
15.53–77	787–98	10.487–93	424–5
15.56	790–1	11.235–59	20–2
15.361–6	732	11.482–91	204–6
15.18–24	904–6	11.605–8	845–6
16.7–10	207–8	14.175	867
17.51–60	867–8	16.205–6	202
17.118	826	17.197–214	340–4
20.67	600	18.281–3	792
21.257–64	205–6	23.310–43	688
22.59–65	282–3	24.6–9	884–5
22.199–201	488, 685–6		

Index of Passages Discussed — 919

Homeric Hymns
Homeric Hymn to Aphrodite
81–90	29–30
161–7	38–9

Homeric Hymn to Dionysus
1–4	170
1–16	18–19
53–9	171–2

Homeric Hymn to Hermes
358–60	846

Horace
Ars Poetica
1–13	411–18
38–41	752
73–82	364–7
148–52	63–4
304–18	393–5
453–76	411–18

Carmina
2.13.21–32	349–50

Epistles
1.2.1–16	377–88
1.2.17–22	388–92
1.6.65–6	368
2.2.99–101	369

Satires
1.1.1–3	668–9
1.1.23–5	6

Inscriptions
CEG
475	851

GVI
43	145
1331	279–70
1516	240–3
1595	277–8
1625	853–4
1632	868–70
1732	863–8
1881	856–8
2030	278–9

IGUR
III 1326	858–9

SEG
XXV 711	859–63

SGO
01/20/25	235–43
03/05/04	267–84
04/21/03	269–70
08/08/10	870–2
11/08/01	852–3
14/13/05	863–8

Isocrates
Panath.
18	508–9

Leonidas of Tarentum
AP 7.163	870–2
AP 7.198	237

Longinus
Subl.
10.3	356–7

Lucan
Bellum civile
9.741–2	574–5

Lucian
Dial. Gods 21
	38 n.71

Philops.
3	585–6

VH
1.4	456–7
2.17	242
2.20	497, 806

Onos
51	467

Lucretius
3.152–60	360–1

Macedonius
AP 5.235	139–43, 152

Meleager
AP 5.190	131–4

Menander
Fragments
fr. 722 K–A	781–2

Samia
13–22	251–2

Mimnermus
Fragments (West)
1	39–40, 368–72, 374
2	374

Origen
Against Celsus
1.31	888–9
1.42	900–2
2.55	898
2.61	898–9
2.76	893–7
3.69	892–3
4.23	884–5
4.38–9	902
6.42	904–7
7.6	897
7.28	885–7
7.36	889–92
8.66	903–4
8.68	887–8

Ovid
Amores
1.1.1–4	366–7
1.5.1–12	264–5
1.5.17–18	42–3
1.5.25	38
1.15	367–8
3.7.81–4	40–3

Heroides
15.1–4	351–2
15.31–6	352
15.91	351
15.133–4	352–3

Metamorphoses
4.185–9	31

Palaephatus
On incredible things
Preface	578–90

Papyri
P.Oxy. 413	468
P.Oxy. 4762	465–9

Parmenides
B8.42–9 D–K	421–2

Pausanias
9.19.6–7	187–8

Petronius
Sat.
108.13	476

Pindar
Isthm.
2.6–11	556–7
2.33–4	212

Nem.
3.76–9	70–1
7.17–24	200–2

Ol.
2.82–9	76–7
2.83–8	510–11

Fragments (Maehler)
123	140–1

Plato
Apol.
19c	666
29d–30b	13–14, 666–7
40c–1c	242

Clitophon
407a–b	667

Cratylus
404c–6a	825–37
406a	833–4
406b–d	836–7
408b–d	827–9, 843

Euthyd.
288b–c	60

Hipp. min.
363b–c	634–5
364c	637–40
365a–b	644–7
369b–c	648
370e	649–51

371d–e	649–53	Cas.	
Ion		5–20	110–12
530b–c	509–10	Capt.	
530c–d	507, 512–15	1029–34	404–5
530d	515–16	Menaechmi	
534a	72–3	7–12	402–3
539d–e	517–18	7–16	432–3
541e	59–60	72–6	432–3
Laws		227–8	434, 442
1.625a–c	419–20	234–8	436–41
Meno		247–8	437–8
95c–6a	554–5	263–4	435
Phaedo		Most.	
109a–b	884–5	1149–51	408–9
Phdr.		Poen.	
229c–30a	561–5, 586–7	1370–1	403
237a–b	215–16, 220	Trin.	
244b–d	831–3	705–7	406–7
245a	71–2		
264b–c	422	**Plutarch**	
Prot.		Alcibiades	
316d–e	643	2.4–6	7–14
338e–339a	609, 636	Gryllus	
339b	518	985d	607
Rep.		How to study Poetry	
2.378d–e	604, 706, 903–4	23d–e	383
9.588c	563	25b–c	392–3
10.606e–7a	516	On the education of children	
Symp.		6a–c	80
173c	262	On the love of offspring	
180a	695	497b–c	784–5
212b	3–4	On moral virtue	
215c–d	11	445d–6c	371–2
215d	670	On the restraint of anger	
215d–216a	11–12	455b–c	302–4
216a	13	The E at Delphi	
221d–a	15–16	381f	841
Tim.		388e–9b	87–8, 839–42
31b–2c	906–7	Theseus	
		1	581–2
Plautus			
Amph.		**[Plutarch]**	
50–63	405	On Homer	
88–96	405–6	2.166	622
861–8	409	Opinions of the Philosophers	
873–9	408–10	880d–f	294–7

Index of Passages Discussed

Porphyry
On Abstinence
3.3–4   454

Posidippus
Epigrams
50 A–B   148–50
122 A–B   314–18
AP 7.170 (131 A–B)   272–4, 283–4

Propertius
1.1.1–6   371–2
1.9.9–12   369–70
2.15.41–8   373

Quintilian
Institutio oratoria
10.1.63   349–50
10.1.66   116–17
10.1.69   525

Rhianus
AP 12.146   135–7

Sappho (Voigt)
fr. 1   351
fr. 31   141, 321–5, 353, 355–62
fr. 55   315–16
fr. 137   353

Scholia on Homer see under 'Homer'

Simonides
PMG 542   536–47

Sophocles
Philoctetes
119   637
827–32   802
1238   637
Fragments
fr. 88 Radt   783–5

Stesichorus (Finglass)
fr. 10   215
fr. 91a   226

frr. 172–4   217–19
fr. 277a   216
fr. 327   217

Strabo
1.2.19   592–3
3.2.13   593–4

Straton
fr. 1 K–A   119

Terence
Adel.
413–18   395–6
Andria
9–12   407–8
9–21   108–10
26   402
Eun.
30–41   109–10
232–64   110
Hec.
866–8   401–2

Theocritus
Id.
2.64–9   50–1
2.76–83   51–2
2.82   325, 359
2.88–91   322–3
2.100–3   323–4
2.106–10   323
2.140–1   51
3.1–5   334–7
4.32   343
7.75   223
7.93   344
11.19–24   319
11.72   319
12.1–2   140
14.31–42   206–10
16.1–4   194–5, 197
16.29–33   204–5
16.36–9   198–9
16.51–7   200–1
16.58–9   194
16.64–7   206–10

16.68–73	211–12	**Tibullus**	
16.75	212–13	1.1.55–8	373
16.90–7	198–9		
16.108–9	195–6	**Timon**	
18.7–8	228	fr. 30 Di Marco	258
18.16–18	223–5		
18.20	232	**Vergil**	
18.29–31	227	*Aen.*	
18.38–48	230–1	3.655–65	337–9
18.50–3	229	4.174–7	716–17
		Ecl.	
Theognis		1.19–25	344
167–70	554	6.48–51	359
237–54	729	9.23–5	336–7
289–92	77	*Georg.*	
667–82	137–8	4.315–18	34 n.61
679–82	78		
949–54	136	**Xenophon**	
1249–52	142	*Memorabilia*	
		1.2.20	542–3
Thucydides		1.2.56	541
1.20–1	581–2	2.1.21–33	672
1.22	589, 753–4, 756, 765–6	4.4.5–6	672–3
		Symposium	
1.97.2	418–19	2.22	15
2.38.2	817		
7.14.4	755–6		

www.ingramcontent.com/pod-product-compliance
Lightning Source LLC
Chambersburg PA
CBHW061701300426
44115CB00014B/2521